PENGUIN BOOKS

MEDIA LAW

Geoffrey Robertson Q.C. has argued many landmark media law cases in British and Commonwealth courts and in the European Court of Human Rights. He is Head of Doughty Street Chambers, a Recorder, Master of the Middle Temple and Appeal Judge for the UN Special Court for Sierra Leone. He has acted for many years as counsel to the *Wall Street Journal*, CNN, the *Far Eastern Economic Review* and other international publishers, and has represented many British newspapers and television companies. His books include *Freedom, The Individual and The Law*; *People Against The Press*; *Crimes Against Humanity: The Struggle for Global Justice*; *Geoffrey Robertson's Hypotheticals* and *Does Dracula Have AIDS*; a memoir, *The Justice Game*, was published in 1998. Mr Robertson has made many television and radio programmes, in Britain and Australia; his play *The Trials of Oz* received a BAFTA "Best Single Drama" nomination, and he was presented with the 1993 Freedom of Information Award. He is married to the author Kathy Lette: they live in London with their two young children.

Andrew Nicol Q.C. practises at Doughty Street Chambers. He has appeared in media cases in all levels of courts in the United Kingdom as well as advising clients in Hong Kong, Singapore, the United States and other jurisdictions. The Council of Europe has consulted him as an expert in media law and he has acted in Human Rights cases in Strasbourg. He is a Recorder of the Crown Court. He has worked and studied in the United States and Australia and taught law for 10 years at the London School of Economics. He has co-authored *Media Law and Human Rights* and *Subjects Citizens Aliens and Others* as well as an annual survey for the *Yearbook of Copyright and Media Law*. For three years he was the chair of the Immigration Law Practitioners' Association. He lives in London with his partner, Camilla Palmer, and their two sons.

AUSTRALIA
Law Book Co.
Sydney

CANADA AND USA
Carswell
Toronto

HONG KONG
Sweet & Maxwell Asia
NEW ZEALAND
Brookers
Wellington

SINGAPORE AND MALAYSIA
Sweet & Maxwell Asia
Singapore and Kuala Lumpur

Media Law

GEOFFREY ROBERTSON Q.C.

AND

ANDREW NICOL Q.C.

Fifth Edition

PENGUIN BOOKS

PENGUIN BOOKS

Published by the Penguin Group
Penguin Books Ltd, 80 Strand, London WC2R 0RL, England
Penguin Group (USA) Inc., 375 Hudson Street, New York, New York 10014, USA
Penguin Group (Canada), 90 Eglinton Avenue East, Suite 700, Toronto, Ontario, Canada M4P 2Y3
(a division of Pearson Penguin Canada Inc.)
Penguin Ireland, 25 St Stephen's Green, Dublin 2, Ireland (a division of Penguin Books Ltd)
Penguin Group (Australia), 250 Camberwell Road, Camberwell, Victoria 3124, Australia
(a division of Pearson Australia Group Pty Ltd)
Penguin Books India Pvt Ltd, 11 Community Centre, Panchsheel Park, New Delhi – 110 017, India
Penguin Group (NZ), 67 Apollo Drive, Rosedale, North Shore 0632, New Zealand
(a division of Pearson New Zealand Ltd)
Penguin Books (South Africa) (Pty) Ltd, 24 Sturdee Avenue, Rosebank, Johannesburg 2196, South Africa

Penguin Books Ltd, Registered Offices: 80 Strand, London WC2R 0RL, England

www.penguin.com

First published by Longman's Group UK Ltd 1984
Second edition published 1990
Third edition published by Penguin Books 1992
Fourth edition published by Sweet & Maxwell 2002
Published with additional changes by Penguin Books 2002
Fifth edition published by Sweet & Maxwell 2007
Published by Penguin Books 2008
1

Printed in England by Clays Ltd, St Ives plc

ISBN: 978–0–141–03021–0

M04415

ABOUT THE AUTHORS

Geoffrey Robertson Q.C. has argued many landmark media law cases in British and Commonwealth courts and in the European Court of Human Rights. He is Head of Doughty Street Chambers, a Recorder, Master of the Middle Temple, Visiting Professor at Queen Mary College, University of London and has served as a UN appeals judge for the Special Court for Sierra Leone. He has acted for many years as counsel to the *Wall Street Journal*, the *Far Eastern Economic Review* and other international publishers, and has represented many British newspapers and television companies. His books include *Freedom, The Individual and The Law; People Against The Press; Crimes against Humanity: The Struggle for Global Justice; Geoffrey Robertson's Hypotheticals* and *Does Dracula Have AIDS*. His memoir, *The Justice Game*, has sold over 100,000 copies and his latest work, *The Tyrannicide Brief*, tells how Cromwell's lawyers brought Charles I to trial. Mr Robertson has made many television and radio programmes, his play *The Trials of Oz* received a BAFTA "Best Single Drama" nomination.

Andrew Nicol Q.C. has acted in a large number of cases involving the media and freedom of expression, particularly those concerning reporting restrictions, contempt, privacy and confidence. He is a member of Doughty Street Chambers and a Master of Middle Temple. He sits as a Recorder and as a Deputy High Court Judge in the Administrative Court. He is the co-author of *Media Law and Human Rights* as well as a history of immigration and nationality law in the United Kingdom. He has been consulted as an expert on media law by the Council of Europe, the European Commission and other international bodies. He and his family live in London.

INTRODUCTION

"We define freedom of the press as that degree of freedom from restraint which is essential to enable proprietors, editors and journalists to advance the public interest by publishing the facts and opinions without which a democratic electorate cannot take responsible judgments."[1]

Freedom of speech is a portentous phrase: it has been a catch-cry of political dissidents; it has been the chant of the mob after the acquittal of courageous publishers; it has been a slogan for pornographers and racial vilifiers. In twenty-first century Britain, it gets protected commensurately with the public interest of the message that it conveys—a value divined, to some extent subjectively, by a relatively decent and liberal judiciary, at least when compared to its brethren when this book was first published almost a quarter century ago. Those judges (with the exception of Lord Scarman) did not think that free expression was any sort of right: they were knee-jerk suppressors of any information, however newsworthy, that might discomfort the security services or the government or the royal family or Mrs Mary Whitehouse. That judicial generation was, nevertheless, insouciant about invasions of privacy and rigorous in upholding the principle of open justice: after all, our courts had been open to all since the middle ages, and it was every Englishman's right to read about the sex lives of others in the Sunday tabloids. Values change, and the human rights revolution has made our current crop of judges over-sensitive to privacy claims and less than valiant in defence of the principles of open justice. The length of this book (the fifth edition being five times the size of the first) attests principally to the hyperactivity of parliament, in responding to advances in communications technology by creating more rules and more regulators to enforce them. The most important progress in recent years has been the recognition that information which is, quite literally, news*worthy*—in the sense that the public have a right to know it—should be communicated without let or hindrance. But at the same time there has been a greater aptitude, in both parliament or the courts, to censor what is regarded as "infotainment" —tabloid gossip and paparazzi photographs, interactive computer games and other mass-marketed electronic pleasures. We are still very far from accepting Milton's premise that "promiscuous reading is necessary to the constituting of human nature".

---

[1] Royal Commission on the Press, Final Report.

Nevertheless, it is a far cry from the atmosphere of the first edition, when *Time Out* journalists were threatened with 30 years in prison for exposing the existence of GCHQ; when the Labour government reneged on its promise of a Freedom of Information Act ("Only two of your constituents would be interested", sneered its Home Secretary); when whistle-blowers were routinely jailed; and citizens of Britain were stopped from reading a book—*Spycatcher*—published in every other country of the world. We had thought of calling the first edition *The Journalist's Toothbrush*, since journalists summoned to attend courts in those days were generally advised to bring a toothbrush in the possible event of an order to spend a night—or a few months—in the cells. Defending the media in this era was always difficult, because there were so few precedents that acknowledged the universality of the free speech principle. It was not part of the law of England.

It was, however, part of the history of England: the first freedom of the printing press, as the absolute Stuart monarchy tottered in 1641, helped to produce parliamentary sovereignty, judicial independence and comparative religious toleration. In that year, the abolition of the Star Chamber ended the torture that was officially inflicted on religious or political radicals, and the Levellers—polemical journalists opposing all abusers of power—courageously risked their lives in the cause both of arguing for democracy and criticising the prevailing authority. The next century saw John Wilkes in prison for obscenity and sedition and the printers of Tom Paine's *The Rights of Man* condemned to hard labour, followed in due course by the early post-Darwinian free-thinkers, damned for blasphemy. No book on media law should fail to celebrate these martyrs, whose continuing legacy is a recognition that the right of free speech is fundamental to democracy. However fashionable it may now be to treat Art.10 of the European Convention as the bedrock guarantee, the plain fact is that free speech is an English invention dating from the civil war, with martyrs who by their sufferings established this principle in our sentiments, if not in our law. The failure to entrench it there was the fault of the reactionary men in parliament and on the bench, who had no stomach for criticism and who allowed the law of libel and confidence and contempt to provide their class with exorbitant protection from it. They designed the criminal law so that it bears more harshly on editors and journalists than on burglars and rapists, through the creation of media offences that do not require proof of a guilty mind. In civil cases, they routinely suppressed the publication of important and newsworthy information on the ground that it is property that belongs in confidence to governments and corporations. They constructed a vast libel industry on the illogical presumption that defamatory allegations that lower a gentleman's reputation, whether deserved or not, are false, and hence the publisher has the burden of proving them true. They made Britain a country where it might be said that speech is free, but was often very expensive.

The Human Rights Act 1998, an election manifesto promise of the Blair government, provided what previous governments and generations of judges had never believed politic to entrench either in statute or common law, namely a guarantee of freedom of expression, i.e. a promise that "speech" would henceforth have a presumption made in its favour by any court invited to suppress it. This is the free speech principle, which assumes that liberty is best secured by a system that protects utterances irrespective of their merit, because in a free market of ideas and opinions the good will triumph over the bad. This is in no sense a "European" position—the Convention was drafted by British lawyers in 1953 as a talisman against the spread of Stalinism; it is a philosophy powerfully articulated by John Milton and repeated in an updated form by John Stuart Mill. The advent of Art.10 does not open a new era, so much as spell out, and provide a framework for, the operation in law of the principle that in a democracy, infringements on free speech can only be justified in cases of overriding necessity to prevent demonstrable harm to other citizens.

Welcome as the Human Rights Act has been in making better formal provision for free speech, both by Art.10 and by s.12 which gives Art.10 special importance, it must be said that the Convention has not been an unmixed blessing. Its most significant result has been to provide a formula for effectuating the free speech principle, i.e. by requiring the courts to make a presumption in its favour, defeasible only when "necessary" in response to a compelling social need to uphold a competing democratic value. In this respect, its beneficiaries have been serious newspapers, relieved from some libel claims over stories of genuine public interest, responsibly written and edited even though they turn out to be inaccurate and unprovable. But in other respects the Convention has shown its age, as a "lowest common denominator" statement of competing values. For example, in 1953 other European countries had less robust laws about hearings in open court and the "fair trial" provisions of Art.6 make a much weaker safeguard for open justice than English common law. So the enactment of the Convention has given the courts more excuses to sit in secret, especially to hear claims by defence lawyers where publicity would disturb children or would prejudice following trials. In consequence, the justice system is much less open and many terrorist trials are closed to contemporaneous reporting in case something be published that might have an impact on a jury in another case months or even years later. It is regrettable that many judges now proceed to "balance" their sense of fair trial against free press, with their professional instincts naturally favouring the former. This is not in fact the procedure laid down by Art.10 itself (which requires a presumption in favour of free speech which should only be overridden in cases of necessity by narrowly construed exceptions) but it is a process which has, regrettably, been adopted where one Article (i.e. Art.10) is said to be in conflict with another, e.g.

Art.6 (Fair Trial) or Art.8 (Privacy). In such cases, British judges have mistakenly reverted to the "balancing act" which they have always found congenial—it appears to have Libran objectivity but it permits their own prejudices to tip the scales. There is no doubt that the historical freedom to report the courts has been cut back by the adoption of the Convention.

Most dramatically, so has the right to invade privacy. This is not of itself a bad thing: as Art.8 puts it, "Everyone has the right to respect for his private and family life, his home and his correspondence". Everyone in the United Kingdom now enjoys that right, since the Human Rights Act came into force: before, personal information could only be protected indirectly and adventitiously, if it could be made the subject of an action for breach of confidence. Although the courts have recoiled from acceptance that there is now a privacy right that did not exist before, they have extrapolated from Art.8 a new civil action of "misuse of personal data" in circumstances where the claimant has "a reasonable expectation of privacy". This too is an acceptable development, so long as the information concerned is genuinely private (medical conditions, marital problems, child misbehaviour, etc.) in which case there would be a genuine need in democratic society to override Art.10 unless the public interest were overwhelming. The courts, however, have held that Art.10 must be "balanced" against Art.8, without presumptions either way. This "balance" will generally be in favour of privacy, sometimes at the expense of a newspaper vividly demonstrating dishonesty (e.g. the Naomi Campbell case) or preventing a partner from going public with his or her side of a tangled story. Some might find these results acceptable, although the cases so far have proved so unpredictable and subjective that publishers, especially biographers, have been left in a state of uncertainty. Much more egregious has been the error—first made by the European Court and now repeated by the Court of Appeal—of assuming that Art.8 contains a general "right to reputation". It does no such thing and the privacy it protects ought to be strictly related to personal and family matters, intimate letters and affairs of the hearth. The notion that it calls for a balance between a "right to reputation" and a "right to free speech" is a serious error which threatens to capsize Art.10, which in fact treats reputation as an exception.[2]

Confusion over the scope and effect of the Art.8 right to privacy had become the most acute problem for media law by 2007. The principle is clear enough: as Lord Hoffman explained in *Campbell*, "What human rights law has done is to identify private information as something worth protecting as an aspect of human autonomy and dignity."[3] So too is the jurisprudential method: the decision in

---

[2] The error of treating Art.8 as a general "right to reputation" is explained in the text: see para.2–012.

[3] See para.2–012.

Campbell stripped the action for breach of confidence of its requirement of a confidential relationship and it emerged as a fully fledged
right to restrain (or to sue for damages if unrestrained) publications
which make intrusions into the lives of claimants in situations where
they have a reasonable expectation of privacy. The vagueness and
subjectivity that attends such definitions can be placed in a satisfactory free speech perspective by making Art.8 privacy an Art.10(2)
exception to freedom of expression, i.e. when "necessary in a
democratic society. . . for the protection of the reputation or rights
of others". This solution would preclude the balancing act and allow
the free speech presumption full play. But the UK courts have
resolutely rejected it: they are wedded to the greater discretion that
an Art.8 versus Art.10 balances offers. So the solution for the
present must be for the press to live with that balance, but to insist
that the courts should narrowly and strictly interpret the Art.8 right,
which ought not to be a concept of privacy that encompasses
reputation, but one that simply protects the recognised intimacies of
personal and family life.

This approach has been diverted by a number of poorly reasoned
and badly expressed Strasbourg decisions, for example that Princess
Caroline of Morocco had a right to stop photographers from
snapping her in a public place because this in some unexplained way
hindered the development of her personality. "There is therefore a
zone of interaction of a person with others, even in a public context,
which may fall within the scope of private life", was the incoherent
verdict of the Strasbourg court. The court has a backlog of tens of
thousands of cases (mainly from Turkey and the former Soviet
Union states): its rushed seven judge decisions often lack intellectual
rigour and consistency, and even "grand chamber" decisions come
couched in Euro-prosaic generalities. It is regrettable that s.2 of the
Human Rights Act provides that Strasbourg decisions "*must* be
taken into account", because many are simply not worth the effort.
There is much to be said for the argument that the European
Convention has served its purpose of placing UK law within a
human rights framework: the next step should be a British bill of
rights, with firmer protection for freedom of speech and protection
for trial by jury (a subject unmentioned by the Convention),
entrenched in the written constitution promised by Gordon Brown.

In this present edition, we predict that it will take some years for
the courts to work out a satisfactory reconciliation between the free
speech right and individual privacy claims. One problem is in finding
appropriate test cases. Many potential claimants do not wish to give
true but embarrassing stories about them the publicity—it takes
unprepossessing people with the wealth and chutzpah of Naomi
Campbell to bring a case to court (Princess Diana, who wished to
create a privacy law by suing over surreptitiously taken gym photos,
quailed at the court door at the prospect of being cross-examined
about her own attitude to her husband's privacy and secretly paid the

defendant gym owner a vast sum of money to pretend he had lost the case). It may be that the British enjoy *schadenfreude* more than the Germans and outside the rarefied atmosphere of the higher judiciary we do not want to give up the pleasure taken in reading of the sex and drugs and family feuds that plague the lives of public figures. This is all part of the *chari-vari*, of the vanity fair that is London's celebrity life, covered by newspapers and magazines that are much more widely read (and much more entertainingly written) than their counterparts in France or Germany or Scandinavia. Judges will continue to wrestle with the demands of pop-stars and politicians who want only favourable publicity, and with the competing "public interest" humbug of newspapers which cater to the public love of gossip and entertainment. Their decisions will inevitably be subjective: the judge in the *Theakston* case solemnly held that a man who visited a brothel could have no reasonable expectation of privacy, although any judge who had actually visited a brothel might well take the opposite view. If there is any principle that can be extrapolated from the hard cases to date, it is that the courts, when they balance Arts 8 and 10, will come down on the side of human kindness. A claimant who moves the judge to pity at media-inflicted humiliation and distress is likely to recover: this is the only explanation for a decision that CCTV pictures of a man's public attempt at suicide could not be shown to illustrate the importance of the technology, or that the much harassed Princess Caroline could restrain photographs of her public shopping expeditions. The scenarios in this area are plentiful and the arguments for and against publication are endless: the decision in a close case will, we predict, turn on application of the judge's humanity rather than any application of legal principle.

This may not be a bad bargain for the time being, notwithstanding its infuriating lack of principled respect for free speech. Editors must ask why privacy is a value for which every human rights convention ever devised demands protection. That is because individuals do have a psychological need to preserve an intrusion-free zone for their personality and family and suffer anguish and stress when that zone is violated. Democratic societies must protect that zone, at least in the case of individuals who have done nothing wrong, as part of their facilitation of individual freedom, and must offer some legal support for the individual choice as to what aspects of intimate personal life the citizen is prepared to share with others. This freedom, in other words, springs from the same source as freedom of expression: a liberty that enhances individual life in a democratic community. Communist and fascist regimes are notorious for depriving all citizens of any right to privacy from the State, through an apparatus of informers and police spies, just as they are notorious for suppressing and censoring their critics. Democratic societies contrast most markedly by vouchsafing privacy rights, not only by curbing state powers of intrusion (although these powers tend to resurge in times of terrorism) but by providing a means of redress against violations by non-state actors—most notably by the media. The European Convention, drafted originally as a bulwark against the spread of Stalinism, thus guarantees by Art.8 a "right" to respect for private and family life, for home and correspondence. Beyond these narrow categories, which entitle citizens to live some part of their life behind a door marked "Do Not Disturb", the media is entitled under Art.10 to probe and publish without restraint. In order to effect this entitlement each state party has a duty to ensure that there is a legal power to deny the media entry to privacy zones that can be geographically defined: the cradle, the school and the hospital, the toilet, the bedroom and the grave.

The greatest victory for free speech since the last election came with the decision of the House of Lords in 2006 to provide a public interest defence in libel actions, by making *Reynolds* privilege a more workable exculpation for responsible editors. The worst feature historically of media law has always been its claimant bias in libel cases, which attracts wealthy forum shoppers from the US, Russia and Saudi Arabia anxious to put their media tormentors in the dock and to restore in London a reputation they cannot protect elsewhere. The case of *Reynolds* in 1998 saw the tentative creation of a defence for responsible journalism, but lower court judges, bred in the old law which required the media to prove the truth of any critical statement, were hostile. In the case of *Jameel v Wall Street Journal*, the trial judge and Court of Appeal rejected any such defence for a story of great international importance about the financing of terrorism that had no less than six sources, in Saudi Arabia and Washington, none of whom would come forward to stand it up. The House of Lords pointed out that this was exactly the kind of investigative journalism that deserved protection from libel action, and that protection would henceforth be available for investigative journalism into subjects of real public interest, if written and edited professionally and responsibly, even if they turned out to be wrong or if sources did not come forward to prove them true. This is a measurable advance for serious journalism, bringing its legal protection closer in the United Kingdom to the US position under the First Amendment where public figures may be defamed "absent of malice" (i.e. without recklessness towards the truth). Another recently recognised aspect of the public interest defence is "neutral reportage", the right to repeat defamations made in debate, so long as the reporter does not adopt them or accept them as true. If there is a public significance in the fact that the allegation has been made, e.g. because it has been made by a political figure or pressure group, the media will be entitled to repeat it. No longer will our media law allow a spectacle like that of Idi Amin's foreign minister, Princess Elizabeth of Toro, recovering heavy damages from every national newspaper which reported his crazed claim that he sacked her because she had been found having oral sex in a toilet at

Orly Airport. This was newsworthy—it showed Amin's slide into madness—and the media could not today be mulcted as they were in 1980 for reporting it unless they asserted the truth of the unsavoury allegation. In UK media law, this counts as progress.

One virtue of *Jameel v Dow Jones* is that it frees the media to engage in serious investigation of the shadowy world of terrorist crime, beyond beat-ups of police press releases. In the wake of 9/11 and 7/7, this must be the most important duty in a democratic society, and it is questionable whether the law permits it to be adequately carried out. Although in 2006 the Court of Appeal gave a spirited defence of the ability of juries to disregard media reports, too many terrorist trials have been veiled in secrecy by the device of "postponing" reporting until sentence or until associated trials are completed, which means that important trials are not reported at all, since stale news is no news. There has in consequence been little or no analysis of the defects in procedure which have contributed to the massive delays and cost-overruns in bringing terrorists to justice. (On the other hand, there have been many occasions following terrorist arrests where gullible reporters and sensation-seeking editors have been fed prejudicial nonsense by self-justifying policemen and self-promoting Home Secretaries). Although some provisions of the United Kingdom's rapidly expanding anti-terrorist law could theoretically impinge on journalists and threaten their sources, there has yet to be a test case: although, for example, the absurdly vague crime of "glorifying terrorism" might be applied to a sympathetic biography of Robespierre, it has thus far been confined to blood-curdling Islamist preachers, guilty in any event of the age-old crime of incitement to murder. The Blair government's only head-on collision with free speech was its squalid effort to pass a law against insulting religion, promised as a sop for Muslim electoral support: it was passed by lickspittle Labour M.P.s in the House of Commons, but returned from the more robust House of Lords with a built-in defence for free speech which effectively neuters it as a weapon against critics of the imams, scientologists and rabbis who clamoured for its passage.

The first edition of this book was critical of the six month prison sentence imposed on a young clerk in the MOD, Sarah Tisdall, for telling *The Guardian* when cruise missiles were coming to Greenham Common, and even more critical of the inept legal advice which persuaded the editor to hand over documents that identified her as his source. Thanks to Bill Goodwin, a courageous young journalist whose refusal to reveal his source, despite unanimous demands for the name from every level of the British judiciary, was upheld by Strasbourg, the media can stand up to government demands for source disclosure.[4] But M.P.s are apparently made of less stern stuff

---

[4] *Goodwin v UK* (1996) 22 E.H.R.R. 123.

and one of them squealed on his researcher who had obtained a secret document from an MOD official recording a conversation between Bush and Blair. The official and the researcher were arraigned at the Old Bailey for offences against the Official Secrets Act. The *Mirror* reported that the memo recorded the President threatening to bomb the Al Jazeera television station based in Qatar. The trial judge said that the *Mirror*'s story was inaccurate, but the evidence about the memo's true contents and the alleged damage which its disclosure would cause were taken in secret and covered by a reporting ban. The pair were found guilty: the official was jailed for six months and the researcher for three months. For some reason the media did not make much of their plight—the men for some reason adopted a low profile defence in which freedom of speech did not resonate, and declined to appeal: their case was not championed by opposition M.P.s or by human rights groups. Al Jazeera continues to press Downing Street for the memorandum under the Freedom of Information Act, to discover whether its reporters really were at risk from Presidential displeasure at their reporting.

This book has always argued—at times vehemently—against laws which threaten with prison any person professionally involved in the business of communication. So it comes as something of a shock for this fifth edition to urge the prosecution of those independent production companies and television executives who were exposed in 2007 as having for several years engaged in massive deception of the viewing public by gulling them into making premium rate calls (at up to £1.80 per time) to provide answers to quizzes that had already been "won". The scandal has besmirched some of the best loved broadcast programmes—*Blue Peter*, *Comic Relief*, *Richard and Judy*—and led to a collapse of trust in broadcasters generally and to the BBC in particular. OFCOM said that the broadcasters were "in denial" but this dozy regulator, which like ICSTIS (responsible for regulating premium rate phone lines) had failed to notice the fraud, opted for six-figure fines rather than for reporting culprits to the police. "Media regulation" in the United Kingdom has always been something of a confidence trick, designed to protect the "regulated" industry against the rigour of more heavy-handed statutory intervention, and although OFCOM and ICSTIS now promise more investigations and more fines, it is time for media practitioners to recognise that making profits by deceiving the public into parting with money is a serious criminal offence. The "why oh why" stories that have thus far emerged tend to blame the ignorance of Thatcher era broadcasting policy which encouraged greedy and competitive independent producers by requiring so many programmes to be outsourced to them, but this is no excuse for their criminal behaviour or for the way it was connived at or ignored. A new "clean up TV" campaign is required, with headquarters at Scotland Yard.

The only comfort for broadcasters was that the scandal was exposed by *Panorama*—one of the few effective contributions the television has recently made to investigative journalism. BBC news and current affairs has been badly damaged by fall-out from the Hutton Report, which condemned its flagship *Today* programme for alleging that the government had "sexed up" a dossier about the dangerousness of the weapons of mass destruction believed to be in the hands of Saddam Hussein. The allegation probably had some truth and probably did reflect the view of its source, Dr David Kelly, who committed suicide after being exposed through questioning by a parliamentary committee indirectly tipped-off by a BBC reporter. This conduct was worthy of censure, although Hutton was more concerned with condemning the BBC Board of Governors for standing up for its program makers against critical political assault. As a result of the Hutton report, the Board of Governors was prematurely abolished and replaced by something called the BBC Trust, although its trustees did not appear to know what to do as the premium line scandal and other examples of fakery in broadcast programmes erupted in 2001.

Lord Hutton had made the mistake of refusing an application from ITN to have his enquiry televised: his notion that the likes of Alastair Campbell, Geoff Hoon and Tony Blair could somehow be discomforted by the presence of cameras was risible. He later complained about the unfairly critical reception his report received in the media: it might have been more appreciated by the public had he allowed them to see the evidence for themselves. It is a sad reflection on the cravenness of the BBC that they did not support ITN's application to televise the inquiry: in other countries, television and radio routinely broadcast public inquiries, because that is how they become public. In Britain, despite a groundbreaking ruling that the Shipman inquiry could be televised, this remains the exception rather than the rule. As a result, tribunals investigating matters of such acute public interest as the "Arms to Iraq" affair and the Steven Lawrence and "Bloody Sunday" inquiries and doubtless the coronial inquiry into Diana's death, are only seen by the public in "dramatic reconstructions" in theatres and televisions, inevitably in a partial and edited form. The British public is denied the best evidence—the real thing—on which to make up its mind. It is a deflection on those who work in the communications industry that existing powers of judicial review have been invoked so infrequently as a means of challenging their exclusion from such tribunals, and from appellate courts. Compared with the legal activism of their counterparts in America, South Africa and even New Zealand who have taken every opportunity to extend their rights to televise public inquiries, UK broadcasting executives have singularly failed to use the courts to extend freedom to communication—a freedom that belongs to the viewers whose trust they betray by failing to extend it to the full.

There is one interesting point at which even the government admits that it has deliberately breached the Art.10 right to communicate information and ideas. Section 320 of the 2003 Communications

Act prohibits the broadcasting of any advertisement on a political subject or which promotes reform of the law, whether in Britain or abroad. This dragnet ban, unparalleled in any other country, prevents pressure groups like Amnesty or Greenpeace from promoting their causes, even if the cause (e.g. stopping Genocide in Darfur) happens to be government policy. This is such a blatant infringement of free speech that the government conceded as much when it refused to make the "Statement of Compatibility" between the Convention and the 2003 Act that is required for every new piece of legislation by s.19(1)(b) of the Human Rights Act—the first and only time it has shrunk from making such a declaration since the Human Rights Act was passed.

What is it about social or economic "advocacy advertising" that sends such a shiver through the British political classes that they unanimously determine to deny a freedom of broadcasting speech to pressure groups and NGOs, not merely during election periods but at any time? They are imbued with the anachronistic belief that television (and hence television advertising) is uniquely powerful, but in addition they have a fear (never admitted) that pressure groups might actually use such opportunities to exert pressure on the political process—a feature of democracy that they are not prepared to tolerate, because they are in power and do not want to be unduly disturbed by a public moved to emotional or even rational arguments that have been advanced on television. This blanket ban on political speech cannot be justified as necessary in democratic society, for the simple reason that political speech is the lifeblood of democratic society. But in British democracy, as the *ProLife Alliance* case showed by upholding the ban on a party political broadcast that opposed abortion (by showing the consequences), we do not want to be unduly disturbed, and the courts have thus far declined to find that s.320 is convention incompatible.

*   *   *

Journalism is not just a profession. It is the exercise by occupation of the right to free expression available to every citizen. That right, being available to all, cannot in principle be withdrawn from a few by any system of licensing or professional registration, but it can be restricted and confined by rules of law that apply to all who take or are afforded the opportunity to exercise the right by speaking or writing in public. There are, as the length of this book attests, a myriad of rules that impinge upon the right to present facts and opinions and pictures to the public: we have made an attempt to state and to analyse them as a comprehensive and inter-related body of doctrine, underpinned by the free speech principle.

Free speech is, in practice, what remains of speech after the law has had its say: in newspapers, it is what is left of the copy by the "night lawyer". At first blush, the array of media laws and regulations appears formidable—a minefield of criminal laws, civil laws and regulations. Newspapers and broadcasting organisations employ teams of lawyers to advise on stories that might otherwise court reprisals. Press lawyers are inevitably more repressive than press laws, because they will generally prefer to err on the safe side, where they cannot be proved wrong. The lawyer's advice provides a broad penumbra of restraint, confining the investigative journalist or broadcaster not merely to the letter of the law but to an outer rim bounded by the mere possibility of legal action. Since most laws pertaining to the media are of vague or elastic definition, the working test of "potential actionability" for critical comment is exceptionally wide. Journalists are often placed on the defensive: they are obliged to ask, not "What *should* I write?" but "What *can* I write that will get past the lawyers?" The lawyers' caution is understandable if they are instructed by proprietors who want to avoid the high legal costs of defending, even successfully, actions brought by the Government or by wealthy private claimants.

For all these obstacles, however, media law is not as oppressive as it may at first appear. When there is a genuine public interest in publishing, legal snares can usually be side-stepped. We have been anxious, in writing this book, to emphasise ways in which legal problems can be avoided in practice. Many laws that are restrictive in their letter are enforced in a liberal spirit, or simply not enforced at all. Editors and broadcasters will be familiar with the solicitor's "letter before action", threatening proceedings in the event that investigations unflattering to clients are published. Often such letters are bluff, and it is important to know how and when that legal bluff can be called. In addition, it must be remembered that the law can give as well as take away: quite apart from Freedom of Information legislation, there are many little-known publicity provisions that can be exploited by inquisitive reporters. Although the law creates duties, it also provides rights that assist those who know what to look for and where to find it. In the chapters on reporting significant areas of power and influence—the courts, central government, local government, Parliament and business—we have endeavoured to highlight sections of the law that help, rather than hinder, the investigative journalist. Our hope is that journalists and broadcasters and their lawyers will regard the book not merely as a manual for self-defence, but as a guide to a complicated armoury of legal weapons for battering down doors unnecessarily shut in their faces.

It is prudent to remember that the expression of facts and ideas and opinions, unlike the imagining of them in the individual thought process, never can be absolutely free. Words can do damage—by betraying a military position or by prejudicing a trial, or by inciting racial hatred. Even the Americans have come to agree that Congress can, despite the First Amendment, make laws stopping people from shouting "fire" in crowded theatres. It behoves all who wish journalists and broadcasters to enjoy "rights" to acknowledge that others have valid claims to legal protection as well—to lead a private life free from media harassment and embarrassment, to undergo a trial free from sensational prejudice, and to have false accusations corrected swiftly and with the same prominence as they are made. These "rights" have in the past been too poorly protected, as the blind Goddess of British justice raised her sword against investigative journalism while her other hand fondled the Sunday muckraker. Those who work in media will enjoy the freedom promised by the right to publish facts and opinions that are in the public interest, but as a *quid pro quo* they have had to forgo some of the comparative freedom they enjoyed to publish facts and opinions that are not.

The law is only one method of control over what is placed in the public arena. Communicators are restrained by other forces: by shared ethical assumptions, by non-legal rules that find favour with the Press Complaints Commission, by pressure from advertisers, by the political predilections of proprietors, and by the host of subjective considerations that go to make up "editorial discretion". Press monopolies inhibit those with different views from launching out on their own. The law is often invoked by editors, executives, or lawyers to support decisions to censor that are taken on other grounds, or instinctively: legal advice of this sort is usually convenient rather than correct. The decision to publish will involve a calculation of many risks—it is only when the apparition of a successful legal action tips the balance against publishing a story of genuine public interest that "freedom of expression" has been meaningfully curtailed by law. That happens often enough to be a matter for public concern. Whether it *should* happen as often as it does is open to doubt. If editors and programme makers and journalists were more aware of their legal rights, and more courageous in calling the lawyers' bluff, they might find that the law is not quite the ass it sometimes appears. Those journalists who have been prepared to fight for the principle that stories that advance the public interest should be published have usually been vindicated. At every stage, the media must insist upon their right to investigate and to publish such stories: if they are right in their identification of the public interest, they are unlikely to come to harm in the long run.

* * *

The one and only proposition which is both absolute and undeniable in media law is that thought is free, and hence communicating with oneself via messages and images in the brain-pan cannot, however subversive or obscene, be interdicted. But communicate that message to anyone else, whether in a bottle cast onto the waves or in an e-mail silently sliding from a computer on the other side of the world, and the thought, thus emitted, becomes subject to interception by a network of laws designed to jam or distort it in the interests of States or corporations or other persons or entities whom the thought disquietens. This book examines the interference network, as it is liable to affect communications from and to and within the United Kingdom. The standpoint adopted, as in earlier editions, is not so much that of the message (which may be false, or horrible, or both) but that of the messenger, the human being with an absolute right to think and hence (we infer) a presumptive right to put the information or opinion contained in that message into the public domain.

Any lawyer who aspires to defend free speech cases will find it instructive to listen to the most effective legal argument ever presented on behalf of the media: Professor Herbert Wechsler's tape-recorded plea in *New York Times v Sullivan*, which persuaded the Supreme Court that British libel law was incompatible with the free speech guarantee in the first amendment to the U.S. Constitution. He spoke of colonial history, of George III's use of criminal libel and sedition laws, of Madison and his address to the Virginia Congress—in short, of the free market-place of ideas that was an object of his country's struggle for independence and democracy. It is a measure of the conservatism of Britain's legislators and senior judges that they refuse to allow legal arguments even to be tape-recorded, but this advance and many others indicated in our text will only come about if media advocates are able to pepper their arguments with quotes from Voltaire and John Wilkes and Tom Paine and H.G. Wells, and with the spirit of those British editors and authors who have suffered imprisonment and even death in the struggle to establish the principle for which Art.10 stands. It is for this reason that the first chapter of *Media Law* offers a brief account of the history and philosophy behind the free speech guarantee, because this dimension should inform and imbue argument and decision-making whenever freedom of expression is at stake.

Despite the exponential growth of case law and statutes affecting the media in the decade before the first edition, there was no academic or professional acknowledgement that "media law" might exist as a subject worthy of separate and coherent study. Defamation was part of the law of torts, breach of confidence was anchored in equity, official secrecy and contempt derived from specific statutes whilst blasphemy and sedition were crimes at common law. There were no textbooks on media law: a few elementary primers had appeared for trainee journalists, and for lawyers there was one weighty tome on libel and another on copyright, but no serious treatment of the subject in its entirety. The wood—or at least the overgrown jungle—of laws affecting the media could not be seen for the different trees of tort and property and crime. The object of earlier editions was to bring these disparate strands together, and to suggest that they might be approached by way of the organising principle in Art.10. Now that seven years have passed since the Convention became law, that organising principle has been imposed and the limitations of Art.10 when balanced with Arts 6 and 8 have become apparent. But what is emerging, notwithstanding the limitations of the Convention, is a better appreciation of the constitutional role of the right to freedom of expression, as guarantor of the independence of a fourth estate.

When this book was first published, judges invariably regarded the media with suspicion, and sometimes with contempt: this is being replaced by a grudging, and in some cases genuine, respect for the role of the media in a free democratic society. Indeed, we have felt obliged to point out the many ways in which media executives fail to live up to the new judicial expectations: they fail to assert their rights by challenging film and television and video censorship rulings; they supinely accept decisions to exclude broadcasters from courts and (especially) tribunals; they meekly comply with "D" notices and actually belong to the committee which issues them; they enthusiastically play along with the Press Complaints Commission, although it operates both as a shackle on the press and a fraud on the public. Unless the media organisations with the wealth (and the duty) to challenge censorship decisions do so in the courts, the cosy accommodations they prefer to make with politicians and power-brokers will be perceived by those they represent—the viewing and reading public—as selling out on the principle of freedom of expression entrusted to their stewardship.

This is a book about the legal rights of journalists, broadcasters, authors, internet providers, editors, dramatists, film makers, photographers, pornographers, e-mailers, website owners, producers and others who publish news or views through the communications media. The introductory chapters describe the common law safeguards of open justice, jury trial and the rule against prior restraint, and go on to explain how Art.10 provides a procedural pillar for freedom of expression in twenty-first century Britain. The next section states the basic laws that apply to all publishing enterprises—libel, contempt, privacy and confidence, copyright and obscenity. There follows an examination of the laws applicable to particular areas of reporting: the ground rules that open or close the doors of the courts, Executive government, Parliament, local government and commercial enterprises. Freedom of information, which should be the "Open Sesame" of bureaucracy, is discussed by way of analysis of the new Act. Finally, there is an account of the practices and procedures of our alphabet soup of regulatory bodies—the British Board of Film and Video Classification (BBFC), the Press Complaints Commission (PCC), the Advertising Standards Authority (ASA) and the British Advertising Clearance Centre (BACC), and finally ICSTIS and OFCOM.

The views expressed in this book have been formed in the course of defending individual writers, editors and artists, and it is to them that we owe the greatest debt of thanks. We are grateful to Tabitha Akers-Douglas and Afua Hirsch for their work on the manuscript; to our colleague Guy Vassall-Adams for research assistance, in particular for the chapter on Broadcasting; to our other colleagues, Anthony Hudson, Lucy Moorman, Gavin Millar Q.C. and Keir

Starmer Q.C. for their stimulating ideas and suggestions. We also thank Amanda Gordon of Penguin, Greg Smith and Naomi Booth of Sweet and Maxwell and Andrew Turner and Fiona Mullen for preparing the index and list of cases. Kathy Lette and Camilla Palmer in this, as in a surprising number of previous editions, deserve the first of an ever growing number of footnotes.

Geoffrey Robertson
Andrew Nicol

Doughty Street Chambers

January, 2008

STOP PRESS

CHAPTER 2: THE HUMAN RIGHTS ACT

Article 10 "Balanced" against Article 8, para.2–020

The text criticises a number of cases where 7-Judge Eurocourts have wrongly considered that Article 8 protects reputation as well as private life. This heresy was adopted in *Pfeifer v Austria* (November 15, 2007) where reputation was said to form part of "personal identity and psychological integrity". It does not, of course— reputation is what others think of you, and not what you think of yourself. But the court ruled, damagingly for free speech, that the state had a duty to protect reputations against "excessive criticism" even on matters of public interest. By this erroneous route, the court (by 5–2) found in favour of a thin-skinned journalist who demanded retribution against honest criticism, that he had hounded one of his own victims who had subsequently committed suicide. The result reached by this incoherent application of Article 8 so as to truncate Article 10 free speech once it becomes "excessive" and upsets its victim (whether it is justified or in the public interest or not) demonstrates the extent Article 10 freedom would be limited when reputation is treated as a free-standing but right, instead of an Article 10(2) exception. This case is unsatisfactory as a precedent because the all important question of whether private life includes reputation was never answered: incompetently, the lawyers for Austria agreed with the Claimant that it did, and the court was never shown the historical material set out in the text of this paragraph.

CHAPTER 3: DEFAMATION

Fair comment: *Burstein v Associated Newspapers,* para.3–052

The Court of Appeal confirmed the force of the right of *honest* comment (mislabeled "fair comment") by striking out a claim by a composer miffed by a bad—and arguably unfair—review of his new opera. So long as the critic was not malicious, and had actually seen the opera and honestly hated it, she was entitled to write an exaggerated, unreasonable and prejudiced review. The judge had thought the composer was likely to lose but had decided to leave it to the jury: the appeal court sensibly decided that honest criticism should not be put to the cost and inconvenience of a trial.

Qualified Privilege, para.3–061

A litigant is entitled to discover from the other side any documents relevant to the claim, but the compulsory nature of the disclosure should make them unavailable for subsequent use in a libel action. In *MacBride v Body Shop* (July 10, 2007) an ex-employee who had sued the store for discrimination and had obtained an inter-office email in which she had been described by her manager as "a compulsive liar" was not permitted to bring a defamation action founded upon that libel. As an honest communication between managers with a common interest it was protected by qualified privilege, and in any event the public interest in supporting the compulsory disclosure process debarred the use of disclosed documents for purposes extraneous to the claim in which they had been produced.

Public Interest Defence, para.3–061

The first beneficiary of the *Jameel* decision was a book by BBC Crime Reporter Graham McLagan: *Bent Coppers: The Inside Story of Scotland Yard's Battle Against Police Corruption.* It had been denied a public interest defence by the trial judge to an action brought by a policeman who had resigned following internal disciplinary proceedings. But the Court of Appeal, following *Jameel*, said that the judge had erred by failing to give proper weight to McLagan's honesty, expertise and professional evaluation of his carefully researched material, condemning the reporter "with the benefit of hindsight and the sharp eye of a trained lawyer". The Police Federation, which had backed the Claimant, was ordered to pay the full costs of the trial: *Chairman v Orion Books* (2007) EWCA Civ 972.

It is noteworthy that *Reynolds/Jameel* public interest privilege has now been adopted by the Ontario Court of Appeal: *Cusson v Ottowa Citizen* (November 13, 2007) ONCA 771.

CHAPTER 4: OBSCENITY, BLASPHEMY AND RACE HATRED

Sex Shops, para.4–027

In *Belfast City Council v Miss Behavin' Ltd* [2007] UKHL 19 the House of Lords acknowledged that pornography is protected by the freedom of expression guarantee in Art.10, although in such cases the guarantee "operates at a very low level" (Lord Hoffman)[1] is a

---

[1] Para.16.

"right of modest value" (Lord Roger)[2] and is "engaged at a relatively low level" (Lord Neuberger)[3]. This grudging recognition that pornography is a form of protected speech settles a long and arid debate, and while it is self-evident that freedom to publish erotic images is "not the most important right of free expression in a democratic society"[4] it must be recognised that obscenity law has in the past been deployed to silence minority views and to jail political dissidents, from John Wilkes' *Essay on Woman* to the cases of *Oz* and *The Little Red Schoolbook*. Whilst accepting Baroness Hale's somewhat sniffy point that "there are far more important human rights in the world than the right to sell pornographic literature and images in the backstreets of Belfast", the misery inflicted by Northern Ireland's joyless religious bigots may to some extent be alleviated by the presence of sex shops as symbols of a less repressive society. She went on to say that "pornography comes well below celebrity gossip in the hierarchy of speech which deserves the protection of the law", although it may be doubted whether run of the mill erotica is truly as offensive as the behaviour of rumour-mongers and paparazzi hustlers who prey on so-called "celebrities". That the Law Lords are now prepared to allow publishers of sexually explicit material any kind of "right" may be progress of a sort (compare their automatic assumption in 1972 that pornography was both depraving and unlawful[5]) and the case of *Miss Behavin'* does demonstrate what may be termed the qualitative elastic of Art.10, which stretches further in the protection of publications the more they are recognised to be in the public interest.

This is the jurisprudential significance of a case, unremarkable on its facts, which turned on a City Council's decision under the Local Government Miscellaneous Provisions Act to ban all sex shops from a central city district with family shopping, church and civic institutions nearby. The House of Lords held that this result did not breach Art.10, even if the councillors had never heard of it: human rights claims, unlike judicial reviews, turn on the result of a decision rather than on the fairness of the procedures for making it. The decision itself was unexceptional, so long as sex shops were available in other parts of the city or at least in the province: a wider ban would clearly have been disproportionate, notwithstanding Lord Hoffman's unrealistic suggestion that deprived Irishmen could always slake their appetites for erotica by travelling to Soho.

Blasphemy, para.4–067

The prospect of any future blasphemy prosecution was rendered unlikely by the Divisional Court in *R v City of Westminster*

---

[2] Para.28.
[3] Para.83.
[4] Para.16.
[5] *DPP v Whyte* (1972) A.C.

Magistrates (December 5, 2007) when it refused permission for a Christian pressure group to charge the BBC for showing *Jerry Springer—The Opera*. The court emphasized that the crime can only be committed if the publication endangers society and in some way threatens the community. "This element will not be shown merely because some people of particular sensitivity are, because deeply offended, moved to protest. It will be established if, but only if, what is done or said is such as to induce a reasonable reaction involving civil strife, damage to the fabric of society or their equivalent." (Para 16) This element will be difficult if not impossible to prove: a reaction of this extremity could hardly be considered "reasonable". The court also pointed out that blasphemy required an attack "on Christianity or what Christians held sacred," and that this play, on the contrary, was an attack on Jerry Springer.

CHAPTER 5: PRIVACY AND CONFIDENCE

Photographs, para.5–008

The 18-month old son of the Harry Potter author, J.K. Rowling, was photographed with his parents in a public street in Edinburgh. The picture agency sold the image which was published in the Sunday Express. The child (through his parents) sued for infringement of privacy and under the Data Protection Act. The paper settled the claim, but the agency fought it and succeeded in having both claims struck out. The picture had been taken from a distance and there were was no element of harassment or distress. The threesome were doing nothing embarrassing or intimate or anything special at all: they were simply moving down the street. The Judge said that it was the equivalent to the example of given in the *Campbell* case of a famous person being photographed while popping out for a pint of milk: there was no reasonable expectation of privacy in those circumstances. He said,

> "the law does not allow the claimant's parents to carve out a press-free zone for their children in respect of absolutely everything they choose to do. Even after *Von Hannover*, there remains, I believe, an area of routine activity which when conducted in public places carries no guarantee of privacy".

The picture agency had not been registered with the Information Commissioner as required, but, while processing personal data in these circumstances was a criminal offence, it did not prevent the agency from relying on the media defence in s.32 of the Data Protection Act 1998 and, even if there had been a breach of any of the requirements of the Act, the claimant could not show that any distress had been caused as a result of that breach: *David Murray (by*

*is litigation friends Neil Murray and Joanne Murray) v Express
Newspapers Ltd and Big Pictures (UK) Ltd* [2007] EWHC 1908 (Ch.).

Previous publication and public interest, para.5–014

In *Long Beach Ltd and Denis Christel Sassou Nguessou v Global
Witness Ltd* [2007] EWHC 1980 (QB) the claimants unsuccessfully
sought injunctions to require Global Witness to take down from its
website copies of Mr Sassou Nguesso's credit card statements. He
was the son of the President of the Republic of Congo and also the
head of Cotrade, the marketing arm of the Congo's state-owned oil
company. Long Beach was his off-shore oil company. Many of the
Congo's debts had been bought by a "vulture company" called
Kensington. Kensington had obtained disclosure of documents in
Hong Kong litigation which showed the ownership of Long Beach,
the receipt by Long Beach of revenue from sales of Congolese oil
and the payment by Long Beach of Mr Sassou Nguesso's credit card
bills. These documents were referred to at a hearing of the Hong
Kong court that was open to the public. Thereafter, they were passed
to Global Witness which ahd been carrying them on their website for
some two weeks when the claimants asked for an injunction from the
English court. Although the Hong Kong court had ruled that the
documents remained confidential despite being used at the earlier
hearing, the English judge disagreed: if the English action went to
trial, the claimants were not likely to establish that the documents
had any confidentiality left. In any case, the posting of them on
Global Witness's website had led to extensive publication, and that
was a factor against granting an injunction. But the judge also relied
on the public interest in publication:

> "It is an obvious possible inference that [Mr. Sassou Nguesso]'s
> expenditure has been financed by secret personal profits made
> out of dealings in oil sold by Cotrade. The profits of Cotrade's
> oil sales should go to the people of the Congo, not to those who
> rule it or their families."

He rejected the claimant's arguments that Global Witness could
have made their point without publishing all of the credit card
statements. He accepted the argument that there was a public
interest in showing precisely what expenditure had been paid for by
the off-shore company, and that was disclosed by the statements.

Privacy, para.5–018

The case which brought about the demise of Lord Browne as group
chief executive of BP illustrates how the tests for a reasonable
expectation of privacy and the public interest can be interwoven.
Lord Browne's former gay lover, Jeff Chevalier, had sold his story to

the *Mail on Sunday* which approached the peer for comment. He
leapt into court for an injunction. Critically, he lied to his lawyers
about how he had first met Chevalier and they (unwittingly) relayed
his lie to the judge. Although the claimant corrected his evidence
and apologised shortly afterwards, the judges took a serious view of
his attempt to mislead the court. The Court of Appeal refused to
enjoin the newspaper from spelling out the details of the lie which
thereupon appeared on the front pages of the national press and as
the first item on television news. The Court also refused to prevent
the paper from publishing its allegations that Lord Browne had used
BP's resources to set up Chevalier in business. There could be no
reasonable expectation of privacy in relation to that information. In
principle, a reasonable expectation of privacy could exist in relation
to business information, but whether an expectation of privacy was
reasonable would depend on the nature of the information, the form
in which it was conveyed and the fact of a confidential relationship.
The Court also rejected the argument that information about the
company should be circulated only to BP's officers and shareholders,
given the company's size and importance: *Lord Browne of Madingley
v Associated Newspapers Ltd* [2007] EWCA Civ 295.

Breach of confidence, para.5–035

The battle between the Douglases and *Hello!* magazine ended with a
Douglas victory in the Court of Appeal, but *OK!* (which had lost its
breach of confidence claim there) pursued the matter to the House
of Lords. By 3:2 the House restored the trial judge's award of over
£1 million. "Follow the money" was Lord Hoffman's motto in his
principal speech for the majority. *OK!* had paid £1 million for the
benefit of an obligation of confidence on all those present at the
wedding in respect of any photograph of the wedding. The Douglases were in a position to arrange their wedding so as to impose an
obligation of confidence on all who attended. Of course, *OK!* were
paying only for information in the form of photographs, but that did
not matter if information in that form was commercially valuable to
the magazine. The minority (Lord Nicholls and Lord Walker)
objected to the continued protection of confidentiality once *OK!* had
published other photographs. *Hello!*'s photographs were not significantly different and did not show the couple in a bad light. But for
Lord Hoffman and the majority this did not matter. *OK!* had bought
exclusivity and were entitled to protect it. The *Hello!* photographs
had not entered the public domain even though *OK!*'s photographs,
which they resembled, had already been published. The photographs
may have been alike but their impact could hardly be described as
trivial when the photographer had been paid £125,000 for them and
the judge had assessed that their publication had cost *OK!* such a
large sum: *OBG Ltd v Allan; Douglas v Hello! Ltd.; Mainstream
Properties Ltd v Young* [2007] 2 W.L.R. 920 HL.

Source Disclosure, International, para.5–071

Media organisations which operate in repressive states collaborate
with the regime at their peril, as *Yahoo* discovered when it dis-
gracefully handed its email records to the Chinese Government to
enable it to identify and persecute dissidents. It was sued in the US
by the families of two journalists who had in consequence been jailed
for 10 years, and accused by US Senators of behaving as a "moral
pygmy". The public shaming forced it to apologise and to salve its
conscience by setting up a fund to provide legal aid and human-
itarian relief to others prosecuted for their online activities.

CHAPTER 6: COPYRIGHT

Trade marks, para.6–060

In the context of comparative advertising, an interim injunction will
not be granted unless the claimant is more likely to succeed at trial.
The Court of Appeal so decided in a spat between rival producers of
pills for dogs. The defendant's advert alleged that the claimant's
product had less of the principal active (and expensive) ingredient
than its label claimed. The claimant recognised that it would not
obtain an injunction on libel or malicious falsehood grounds:
Bonnard v Perryman would mean that, once the defendant said that
he intended to defend his publication as true, an injunction would be
refused. Instead it relied on its alternative claim of trade mark
infringement. The defendant would have a defence to such a claim if
its use of the claimant's mark was in accordance with "honest
practice in industrial and commercial matters". An honest and
reasonable belief in truth would not be enough, the Court said. If
the defendant later turned out to be wrong, it would have to
compensate the claimant. The defendant lost its argument that the
Bonnard rule should also apply to claims such as this. Where
property rights—in a trade mark or goodwill—were concerned, that
would not be fair to a claimant. However, it also rejected the
claimant's case that the old *American Cyanamid* test was appropriate: simply considering the "balance of convenience" between the
parties would ignore the fact that freedom of expression was also in
issue. The right test was in s.12(3) of the Human Rights Act and the
claimant had to show that it was likely to succeed at trial. The
claimant pointed out that the House of Lords in *Cream v Banerjee*
had added that this might put too heavy a burden on the claimant
where the prospective damage from publication was "particularly
grave". However, the Court of Appeal dismissed the idea that this
qualification applied to the case before it. What the claimant feared
was damage to the reputation of its goods but, said the Court, "if
damage to reputation were itself considered to be 'particularly grave'

then nearly all cases would fall into that class and s.12(3) would be rendered virtually pointless". In this case the Judge had thought that the *defendant* was more likely to succeed at trial. The claimant could not satisfy s.12(3) and an injunction was refused: *Boehringer Ingelheim Ltd v Vetplus Ltd* [2007] EWCA Civ 583.

CHAPTER 8: REPORTING THE COURTS

Public Access to the Courts, para.8–014

The *Cream Holdings* precedent of judicial discreetness in declining to describe confidential information in judgments was followed in *Lord Browne of Madingley v Associated Newspapers Ltd* [2007] EWCA Civ 295 (see above). However, it was distinguished by Stanley Burnton J. in *Long Beach Ltd v Global Witness* [2007] EWHC 1816 (QB) when he ruled that there was no need for the court to restrain itself from repeating information that the claimants were unlikely to be able to show was still confidential.

Family Division publicity injunctions, para.8–056

In *T v BBC* [2007] EWHC 1683 (QB) an injunction was granted to prevent the identification of a vulnerable young (adult) woman who had given up her daughter for adoption in a BBC documentary about her and the adoption process. The programme followed the decision-making process and showed painful scenes of the mother and daughter including their final meeting together. The judge decided that the mother was plainly unable to give informed consent either to the filming itself or to the broadcast of the programme. It then fell to the Court to strike the balance between her rights to privacy which were clearly engaged and those of the broadcaster. In this case it decided that T's "rights" under Art.8 ought to prevail.

Reporting Restrictions, para.8–072

Prior to the *Keogh and O'Connor* Official Secrets trial in 2007 the *Daily Mirror* had published what it claimed was the subject matter of the memo which led to the prosecution of the two men. The trial judge described the report as "inaccurate" (without being more specific). He ordered that any evidence about the memo's contents and the harm that it allegedly caused should be held *in camera*. He also imposed a reporting restriction order under s.11 of the Contempt of Court Act to prohibit publication of any report of the proceedings which did or "might" reveal what had taken place. The Court of Appeal ruled that a s.11 order could only prohibit publication of what *had* been said in secret and there was no warrant for extending the order to cover inaccurate speculation.

Nonetheless it warned the media that an article which purported (albeit wrongly) to describe what had been said in closed session might constitute an *attempt* to commit contempt. Since orders under s.11 can only relate to reports of proceedings, the court's order led to the surreal position that the *Mirror*'s story could be recycled, but not if it was said that this had led to the prosecution of the two men. During the trial, an exchange took place between Keogh and his counsel which the judge thought infringed his ruling that discussion of the contents of the memo should take place only in closed court. He imposed a restriction on the reporting of this exchange under s.4(2) of the 1981 Act. The Court of Appeal ruled that the Judge was wrong to believe that he could impose an indefinite restriction under this power. However, since the judge had ordered that information about the memo's contents should be withheld from the public, an indefinite ban on the reporting of this exchange could also be covered by the order under s.11: *Re Times Newspapers Ltd* [2007] EWCA Crim 1925.

Secrecy Orders, para.8–075

The Sultan of Brunei tried unsuccessfully to have his name air-brushed out of a public judgment. The Claimant in *Aziz v Aziz* [2007] EWCA Civ 712 was trying to recover $2 million and some audio tapes of a confidential nature. The Sultan was not a party to the law suit, but he was the claimant's former husband and it was impossible for the judges to explain their reasons (including reasons for committing a person for contempt of court) without referring to him. They had not mentioned (in the public versions of their judgments) any sensitive or embarrassing details, but the Sultan had argued that he should have complete anonymity because of his position as Head of State. The Court of Appeal rejected this argument. The "dignity" to which a Head of State was entitled extended to his personal capacity but was primarily concerned with his physical safety. The Court said, it was hard to envisage any situation in which speech, otherwise permitted under English law, could be prohibited on the grounds that it was an attack on the dignity of a foreign Head of State, who could, like everyone else, have a remedy in defamation if falsely vilified.

Television and the Courts, para.8–111

The Constitutional Court of South Africa has held in *South African Broadcasting Corp. Ltd v National Director of Public Prosecution*[6] that courts could permit television and radio broadcasts through their power to regulate their own process. The majority cautiously said

---

[6] 21 B.H.R.C. 533 (2007).

that televising the courts should only be allowed if there was no risk that it would inhibit the justice process, although this case is notable for the compelling argument of the three dissenting justices, who held that the open justice rule *required* the presence of cameras in the courts. Justice Albie Sachs pointed to the need to break out of the catch 22 in which "cameras are excluded from courts because judges and counsel are unfamiliar with them, and judges and counsel are unfamiliar with cameras because they are excluded".[7] He pointed out that:

> ". . . the ineluctable logic of living in an open and democratic society is that where major institutions of state are engaged in the public aspects of law making and law enforcement there should be the greatest degree of public involvement that can reasonably be achieved. Such facilitation should not be looked upon as an inconvenient intrusion by the public, or as a favour to be granted or withheld from the broadcasters. It involves fulfilment of an obligation. . . Press reports are important, but reach only a limited section of the public. By their nature they will be compressed. There is no logical reason why coverage should not be extended beyond the portals of the courtroom, or why such broader coverage should be restricted to the print media only. This is not a matter for case by case analysis to be conducted by the judges of how comfortable or otherwise they might feel in the presence of cameras and microphones. The starting-off point of the analysis must be that the public has a right to know what is going on in the courts, and that the courts have a duty to encourage public understanding of their processes. The baseline, accordingly, is determined by the fact that we live in a participatory democracy, and not by the principle of business as usual."

It is unclear, at least in UK law, whether television is entitled to broadcast trial exhibits, which often include video interviews, CCTV and mobile phone pictures and the like. These are sometimes made available to the media by police after a conviction, when the defendant is in no position to protest, but there is no settled practice and many exhibits are withheld for fear of privacy claims. The Supreme Court of New Zealand, in *Rogers v TVNZ* (November 16, 2007) has ruled that the broadcaster could show a police video of Rogers' confessing ("I cut her throat like a sheep") after he had been acquitted by a jury which had not been allowed to see the confession, ruled inadmissible because it had been taken in breach of his right to a lawyer prior to interview. The court vigorously pointed out that Rogers could have no "reasonable expectations of privacy"

---

[7] 21 B.H.R.C. 533 (2007), para.146

when he agreed to a video-taped police interview, and that the public interest in debating the trial process (another man had been wrongfully convicted of the same murder years before) would have entitled TVNZ to have access to the tape had it applied to search the court records in criminal cases. These considerations overrode both Rogers' claim to privacy and the dubious way in which TVNZ had acquired the tape, from a disappointed policeman. It is likely that this decision would be followed in the UK, since the Privy Council has held that the public interest in publishing information about unethical behaviour by public figures, collected by police in the course of an inquiry which did not result in a prosecution, outweighed the confidentiality of such material. It had been turned even to the media by police officers disgruntled at the refusal of the D.P.P. to prosecute government ministers for corruption (he claimed that the laws were antiquated), but the media had not paid for the documents nor encouraged their removal from police storage. In these circumstances the freedom of the media to expose political chicanery outweighed the confidentiality which usually attaches to law enforcement investigations: *Commissioner of Police v Bermuda Broadcasting Co Ltd* (January 23, 2008).

CHAPTER 9: REPORTING LESSER COURTS AND TRIBUNALS

Inquests, para.9–004

Unlike ordinary courts, inquests cannot decide criminal or civil responsibility for the deceased's death. However, where the Convention rights to freedom of expression (Art.10) and private life (Art.8) compete, the same general approach is taken as to whether reporting restrictions should be imposed. So, the guidance given by the House of Lords in *Re S (A Child) (Identification: Restrictions on Publication)* [2005] 1 A.C. 593 is likely to be followed. Thus in the case of *Re LM: Reporting Restrictions; Coroner's Inquest* [2007] EWHC 1902 (Fam) the High Court was faced with applications to impose reporting restrictions on the inquest into the death of a young girl where the High Court in care proceedings had already found that she had been unlawfully killed by her mother. The reason for the application was that the girl's sister (aged almost six) was in a very delicate psychological state. It was argued by this girl's guardian, her parents and the local authority that stringent reporting restrictions should be imposed to prevent her learning by accident of the circumstances of her sister's death. The media conceded that the surviving sister should not be named (and that there should be no mention of her existence) but they successfully resisted the proposal that the parents and deceased child should also be anonymous.

CHAPTER 11: REPORTING EXECUTIVE GOVERNMENT

The Official Secrets Act—Crown Servants, para.11–008

The Independent Police Complaint Commission's members and employees are also treated as Crown Servants for the purposes of the Official Secrets Act 1989: see The Official Secrets (Prescription) (Amendment) Order 2007 (SI 2007/248).

Damaging Disclosure, para.11–008

An important defence to allegations against a whistleblowing crown servant is that the disclosure he makes to a journalist cannot be proved to be "damaging", at least if there are honest and expert views to the contrary. In January 2008 the case under s.1(3) against Derek Pasquill, a middle-rank FCO official who leaked documents about dealings with Islamic extremists to *The Observer* in protest against the department's recent policy of appeasing them was dropped shortly before trial. It had been based on evidence from senior officials that the leak had seriously damaged UK interests abroad, but it turned out that other senior officials, in secret emails disclosed at the last moment, had thought that national security had not been threatened and were opposed to the prosecution. This case demonstrates the importance, in official secrets cases, of the defence persisting in demands for full disclosure.

Official Secrets Act—burden of proof, para.11–013

David Keogh was a civil servant in a Whitehall communications centre. In April 2004 he leaked a copy of a letter recording a conversation between Prime Minister Tony Blair and President Bush about Iraq. Keogh gave the memo to Leo O'Connor who was a political researcher for Anthony Clarke, a Labour M.P. Mr O'Connor in turn placed it with his employer's papers. When the M.P. discovered it, he contacted the police. Keogh was charged with offences under ss.2 and 3 of the Official Secrets Act 1989 and O'Connor with an offence under s.5. Before the trial got under way, the judge ruled that ss.2 and 3 put the burden of proof on Keogh of showing that he did not know or have reasonable cause to believe that disclosure would be harmful. The Court of Appeal rejected this argument. Article 6 of the ECHR requires the prosecution to carry the burden of proof unless there is good reason to depart from this principle exceptionally. In this case there was none. That meant that there would be no offence unless the prosecution proved that the discloser knew or could reasonably be expected to know that the disclosure would cause harm. The Court read down the 1989 Act so that the Keogh defence had to do no more than raise the issue of lack of knowledge. This issue did not arise, however, in connection with O'Connor's s.5 charge: it was quite clear from the legislation that the prosecution had the burden of showing that he had the necessary mental state: *R v Keogh* [2007] EWCA Crim 528. The pair were convicted at the end of their trial. Keogh was sentenced to six months' imprisonment. O'Connor received a three month prison sentence. Neither appealed

Human Rights Act, para.11–015

A disappointing, indeed disgraceful, decision which renders Article 10 of little use to the media in Official Secrets Act cases emerged from the Grand Chamber decision in *Stoll v Switzerland* (December 10, 2007). It ruled that the journalist had been rightly convicted and fined for publishing extracts from a leaked document in which the Swiss Ambassador had outlined his hard-line strategy for negotiating with Jewish organisations on behalf of Swiss banks with unclaimed deposits by Holocaust victims. This was a matter of world-wide public interest, and the dispatch (which had been widely circulated within the government) had a low level of confidentiality and no impact on national security. Yet the Grand Chamber majority endorsed the criminal conviction because publication "was capable of undermining the climate of discretion necessary to the successful conduct of diplomatic relations in general and of having negative repercussions on the negotiations being conducted by Switzerland in particular". (Para 136) In other words Article 10 is powerless to protect journalists who receive and publish leaked documents that upset diplomats involved in sensitive negotiations. As the 5-judge minority pointed out, "this reasoning renders meaningless the principle whereby any interference with the right of free expression must be properly justified". The majority of the Euro-Judges, many themselves appointed by the government diplomats, accepted the craven and unsustainable proposition that the criminal law could be used against journalists to save diplomats from embarrassment. Notably, the French and Slovenian governments intervened in the case to support the Swiss government claim that all diplomatic cables must be protected by law from media publication and analysis. This case provides further support for the criticism that the European court, as presently comprised, lacks the calibre and intellectual rigour to give Article 10 its full force and effect when government sensitivities are at stake. The House of Lords which dealt with similar issues very differently in *Jameel v Wall Street Journal*, is now a far superior tribunal for media law issues.

Terrorism, para.11–054

The Electronic Commerce Directive (Terrorism Act 2006) Regulations 2007 (SI 2007/1550) provides exceptions for certain offences under the TA 2006 for internet service providers who do no more than act as conduits, cache or host unlawful terrorism-related material. The hosting exception applies only if the ISP was unaware that the material included unlawful terrorism related material or, once it was aware, took expeditious steps to remove or block the material.

Sedition, para.11–062

The Divisional Court, in *R v Westminster Magistrates* (December 5, 2007) noted that the last sedition prosecution had been *R v Caunt* in 1947, which arose from racial vilification which is now covered by the Race Relations Act 1965. "It is difficult if not impossible to envisage circumstances today in which a prosecution for seditious libel would be appropriate" (Para 22).

Freedom of Information Act 2000, para.11–074

The decision of the Information Tribunal in *Sugar v Information Commissioner* was quashed by the Administrative Court.[8] The Information Commissioner had decided that the Balen Report was held by the BBC for the purposes of journalism (and so not amendable to an FOIA request). The judge ruled that this decision of the Commissioner could not be the subject of an appeal to the Tribunal. The Court also held that the Commissioner had acted lawfully in making his decision on the evidence available to him at the time. Mr Balen could make another request in the light of the further evidence that had emerged subsequently (and he had done so) but the Commissioner had yet to make a decision on that matter.

In *Ministry of Defence v Information Commissioner and Evans*[9] the Tribunal largely upheld a request by Rob Evans, a journalist with the *Guardian* for a copy of the staff directory of the Defence Export Services Organisation. The only redactions which the Tribunal required were the names of junior officials and the telephone numbers and email addresses of all employees.

Investigation by the Department of Trade and Industry, para.13–030

The DTI has been rebranded under the new name of Department for Business, Enterprise and Regulatory Reform.

---

[8] *BBC v Sugar* [2007] EWHC 905 (Admin). The Court of Appeal dismissed an appeal on January 25, 2008.
[9] July 20, 2007.

CHAPTER 14: MEDIA SELF-REGULATION

ICSTIS, para.14–053

When the premium phone-line scandal broke in 2007 ICSTIS at least had a report on the way, although since these malpractices had been going on since 2003 this regulator was hardly pro-active. It condemned a number of phone-in programmes, including the makers of *Richard and Judy* for defrauding hundreds of thousands of viewers who had paid £1 a time to take part in a quiz they could not win. The matter should have been reported to the police, but ICSTIS—a body financed by the premium rates lines—does not want any of its sponsors to go to jail. Only if they do go to jail, however, will dishonest behaviour be deterred in future. ICSTIS and OFCOM have announced that they are collaborating in a joint investigation into BBC and ITV programmes alleged to have deceived viewers.

CHAPTER 15: CENSORSHIP OF FILMS AND VIDEO

Videogames: from *Carmageddon* to *Manhunt II*, para.15–021

In Europe, only the United Kingdom, Germany and Ireland bother to regulate interactive video games, in which players pit their skill against cartoon adversaries with increasing bursts of fantasy violence and degrees of black humour that censors do not find amusing. After the hard-fought 1997 decision to approve *Carmageddon,* video games flourished, with their protagonists coming into closer focus as the technology improved and humanoids were presented as targets to be annihilated by guns or knives or nuclear bombs. Public concern was fanned by M.P.s and the tabloid press after teenage violence was blamed on an addiction to interactive games, and the Board commissioned research into the subject. Its paper *Video Games* concluded that "most gamers see eliminating enemies as another step in the game rather than something to be savoured for itself", and that interactive games were escapist entertainment: "the violence helps makes the play exhilaratingly out of reach of ordinary life. . . gamers seem not to loose awareness that they are playing a game and do not mistake the game for real life."[10] But, in 2007 the Board ignored its own research and banned *Manhunt II* because it was "a game wholly devoted to stalking and killing human characters in a modern urban environment." The Board was exercised about "the sheer lack of alternative pleasures on offer to the gamer"— which was none of its business—and complained that "the game play

---

[10] *Video Games*, BBFC 2006, para.27.

involves making use of a full range of weaponry, including "axes, a mace, a baseball bat, plastic bags, Uzi machine-guns, night sticks, an iron-maiden, an industrial compressor and toilet cistern lids". The game required the players to show some skill (e.g. an ability to disable an enemy with a toilet seat) and to respond rapidly in self-defence, but this point was too subtle for the BBFC. An appeal to the Video Appeals Committee was upheld in December by a majority of 4–3, on the basis that the game was fantasy entertainment in which the gamer was not consciously committing acts of violence but was simply eliminating obstacles in the path of progress through its stages. It was not likely to harm adults, and was entitled to an "18" certificate because there was no evidence that it might harm any children who played it. The Divisional Court subsequently ruled that "harm" included psychological as well as behavioural harm, and the phrase "any harm that may be caused" meant any harm that was likely, in the sense that it was a "real possibility". *R v VAC, ex parte Rockstar* (January 24, 2008).

CHAPTER 16: BROADCASTING LAW

Reality Images, para.16–032

Channel 4 was reprimanded, but not fined, by OFCOM over a pathetic spat on *Big Brother* where some brainless housemates insulted Shilpa Shetty as a "Paki". This caused demonstrations in the Indian sub-continent and a diplomatic incident, from which Ms Shetty emerged considerably richer in money and fame. OFCOM did not make clear why it was reprimanding the channel rather than the makers of the programme. The British public was certainly up-in-arms about the racism, for which the production company, Endemol, might have been censured, although it did expose the degree to which unthinking prejudice is a fact of life. So far as OFCOM is concerned, however, reality television cannot show too much reality.

Sanctions, para.16–061

The premium rate phone scandals that broke in 2007 saw OFCOM reach for its maximum fines, perhaps to cover its own failure to spot a scam that had been going on for several years. It hit Channel 5 with a £300,000 penalty for faking winners and misleading viewers of its "Brainteaser" programme, where production team members pretended to be the winners.[11] Undoubtedly Channel 5 had failed to supervise premium rate quizzes in the greed-driven hope that profit

---

[11] Owen Gibson, *Watchdog Hands out Record Fine to Channel 5*, *Guardian*, June 27, 2007.

from them would offset falling advertising revenue, although the independent production company was blamed for gulling the viewers. An investigation should have followed into whether any criminal offence of, for instance, obtaining money by deception, had been commited.

The worst offender was GMTV, co-owned by ITV and Disney, which over four years extracted some £35 million from viewers who had no hope of winning competitions with their answers, phoned in at a premium rate of £1.80 a call. Twenty-five million fruitless calls had been made to GMTV, which offered to compensate callers and offer them a chance to win a free competition. Its Managing Director did the decent thing and resigned, although once again there was no talk of a police enquiry into those responsible for the swindle. In July 2007, OFCOM announced that broadcasters were "in denial" and promised more investigators in conjunction with ICSTIS although the best way of jolting them out of denial would have been to investigate in conjunction with Scotland Yard.

The BBC, para.16–065

The new BBC Trust arrangements had their baptism of fire in 2007 when some improper practices were exposed, including dishonesty and fakery in a number of much-loved programmes such as *Blue Peter*; *Children in Need* and *Comic Relief* and the deceitful editing of a programme trailer which suggested that the Queen had stormed out of a photo-shoot with Annie Leibowitz. In such circumstances the BBC Board of Governors would have taken decisive and draconian action to restore public confidence in the Corporation, but the new BBC Trust did not seem to know what was expected of it. Its chairman, Sir Michael Lyons, wittered on helplessly that "there was no question of being asleep on the job here", when BBC managers had obviously been asleep on their job. In consequence, public confidence plummeted to such an extent that the BBC was regarded as no more reliable than commercial television, itself wracked by a premium-line phone scandal. The BBC Trust was unable to restore trust in a BBC which had abandoned Reithian standards in a quest for ratings. A public broadcaster is no place for premium rate phone-in competitions. The BBC had dangled vast amounts of public money before independent production companies which cut ethical corners in order to compete for contracts and to sell their programmes on the lucrative and less scrupulous international market. (The fake trailer of the miffed monarch had been prepared for overseas sales.)

The BBC was rocked by its first OFCOM fine, not so much because of its size (of £50,000) but because of its cause—the defrauding of hundreds of children who phoned in to a competition on *Blue Peter* which had already been "won" by a young girl passing by the studio who was prevailed upon to pretend to be the winner, after a "technical glitch" had prevented analysis of the phoned-in answers. OFCOM held that this was a breach of the Broadcasting Code rule that "competitions should be conducted fairly" and more seriously was a breach of the rule that "due care must be taken over the physical and emotional welfare and the dignity of people under 18 who take part or are involved in programmes". Making a youngster complicit in this public deception was unconscionable. Investigations continue into allegations of breaches of the Code by other BBC programmes in the "fake phone-in scandal". OFCOM fines on the BBC can never be more than symbolic, since they are paid from one public purse into another. What is required, to deter dishonesty or fakery, is a police investigation into whether offences of misrepresentation or obtaining money by deception have been committed. It has yet to be seen whether OFCOM has the gumption to allow the criminal law to be the ultimate regulator of honesty in broadcasting.

Television Directive, para.16–071

The long-awaited amended Television Directive (Directive 2007/65/ EC) was promulgated by the European Parliament on December 11, 2007. The most significant features are:

- Adoption of the "Country of Origin" rule for the legal regime governing all audio-visual media: "Only one member state should have jurisdiction over an audio-visual media provider" unless a broadcast is "wholly or mostly directed towards the territory of another member state" (e.g. by advertising or subscription revenues which originate there or by use of its language). Paras 27, 28, 32–33
- To facilitate both the application of the "country of origin" principle and to fix editorial responsibility, member states should ensure direct and easy access to data about media service providers established within their jurisdiction, although registration requirements should not amount to licensing.
- Freedom to receive information requires that those exercising exclusive television broadcasting rights to an event of high interest should grant others the right to use short extracts in news programmes on "fair, reasonable and non-discriminatory terms". (Para.39)
- States should introduce rules to protect "the physical, mental and moral development of minors" in all audio-visual communications such as PIN codes, filtering systems and labelling regimes. (45)
- The right of reply is an appropriate legal remedy for television broadcasting and could also be applied in the online environment. (53)

- Product placement is, in effect, a necessary evil. Viewers should be informed and there should be no placement of cigarette brands or prescription medicines. Product placement should be prohibited, as well as sponsorship, if the practice might influence the content of the news and current affairs programme so as to affect editorial independence. (62–63)

CONTENTS

CONTENTS

CHAPTER 1

FREEDOM OF EXPRESSION

"Think of what our nation stands for—
Books from Boots and country lanes,
Free speech, free passes, class distinction,
Democracy and proper drains."[1]

COMMON LAW BEGINNINGS

In John Betjeman's England, "free speech" washes like fluoride **1–001** through the suburban water supply, but as a cultural assumption rather than a constitutional right. When liberty exists as a state of mind, unprotected by enforceable legal rights, it gets limited in ways congenial to those in power—those whom George Orwell termed "the striped-trousered ones who rule" (judges and attorneys general and treasury counsel and their acolytes the treasury solicitors). It was Orwell who pointed out, in his introduction to *Animal Farm*, that "if liberty means anything at all, it means the right to tell people what they do not want to hear". (His left-wing publisher, Gollancz, promptly refused to publish this introduction, because they did not want to insult Stalin.) Today, freedom of expression remains a struggle to tell inconvenient truths, against the wishes not only of governments but of increasingly powerful trans-national corporations and public figures. It is also a struggle against powerful groups with interests vested in political correctness or, more often now, in religious fundamentalism. When rational argument fails to deter these censors, the law must allow speech its freedom. But in England, the common law made by judges and the statute law made by politicians has often failed in this task, even after being bolstered by the Human Rights Act's guarantee of freedom of expression. This chapter surveys the handful of "rights" that have emerged from English legal history to support free speech claims today and which resonate independently of Art.10 of the European Convention.

The legal position of free speech in the United Kingdom, a country without a written Constitution has been explained by the Law Lords:

---

[1] "In Westminster Abbey", *Collected Poems*, John Betjeman (John Murray).

> "'Free' in itself is vague and indeterminate. It must take its
> colour from the context. Compare, for instance, its use in free
> speech, free love, free dinner and free trade. Free speech does
> not mean free speech: it means speech hedged in by all the laws
> against defamation, blasphemy, sedition and so forth. It means
> freedom governed by law. . .".[1a]

Although the European Convention, incorporated into British law
on October 2, 2000 by the Human Rights Act (HRA), was promoted
by the spin-doctor's slogan "rights brought home", Art.10 (which
guarantees freedom of expression) never has been at home in
Britain. Although many other sections of the Convention, guarantee-
ing free trial and habeas corpus and due process, owe their
providence to English law, and (as we shall see) the "open justice"
principle and rule against prior restraint were first formulated here,
no generalised right of free expression, however common in rhetoric,
entrenched itself in law. Magna Carta was silent on the subject, as
might be expected in 1215, an age in which kings and barons reacted
to an insult by lopping off the offending tongue—or head. The first
statutory prohibition on speech came in 1275, and it set an
unpropitious tone for British law ever since: the crime of "*scandalum magnatum*" expressly protected "the great men of the realm"
from any statements that might arouse the people against them.
Since true statements were especially prone to arouse public unrest,
Lord Coke's famous maxim "the greater the truth the greater the
libel" accurately reflected a criminal libel law invented to deter
critics of the establishment. To this end it soon developed some
irrational presumptions which survive today—e.g. that defamatory
statements are false unless proved true, and cause damage without
any need for the claimant to prove loss.

In 1476 Caxton's printing press rolled at Westminster, and it was
not long before the King's judges in the Star Chamber devised ways
to outlaw subversive exponents of this new technology. Sedition and
blasphemy (in the age when the King ruled by divine right) were
punished ferociously by cutting off the ears: a second offence meant
the stumps of the ears were cut off as well, and the brand "SL" for
"seditious libeller" burned into the author's forehead. In order the
better to censor subversive or heretical literature, a licensing system
was established giving a printing monopoly to members of the
Stationers' Company, empowered by Royal Charter in 1557 to
imprison unlicensed printers and destroy their presses. The first *civil*
law restriction on free speech came as a result of the Star Chamber's
efforts to stop duelling (the traditional method of redressing damage
to reputation): it encouraged protagonists to sue each other for libel

---

[1a] *James v Commonwealth of Australia* [1936] A.C. 578 at 627.

instead, with the loser paying damages. Henry VIII proclaimed that no play could be performed without a licence from "the Master of the Revels", an officer of the Lord Chamberlain, whose control over British theatre in the interest of good politics and (later) good taste was to last until 1968.

These licensing systems admitted of no appeal, and were deployed **1–002** to stamp out the work of those who were, when caught, sometimes hung, drawn and quartered for treason, or else tortured and imprisoned by the Star Chamber—the King's executive court. The most vicious attack on free speech came in 1636, when Charles I moved against puritan preachers: the Star Chamber lopped off their ears, slit their noses and branded their foreheads. Thousands fled from this persecution to New England, the desire to speak freely from their pulpits lodged deep in their embryonic American souls, whilst in England the Puritans were inspired to take their revenge against absolutist monarchs.[2] In 1641 parliament abolished the Star Chamber and torture, as well as licensing: it went to war against the King with the support of newly liberated news sheets—the "Mercuries" which brought to both sides the news, highly slanted, of battles on the field and debates in Whitehall. This was the beginning of the strident and propagandistic, but undoubtedly popular, press. In 1643 Cromwell's dour allies the Presbyterians insisted that licensing should be reintroduced, with licensors selected from "the good and the wise"—lawyers, doctors, schoolmasters and ministers of religion—who solemnly ordered seditious and irreligious books to be burned by the public hangman. The reintroduction of licensing at least provoked the poet Milton to utter his immortal cry for freedom of expression, the *Aeropagitica*:

> "Promiscuous reading is necessary to the constituting of human nature. The attempt to keep out evil doctrine by licensing is like the exploit of that gallant man who thought to keep out the crows by shutting his park gate . . . Lords and Commons of England, consider what nation it is whereof ye are: a nation not slow and dull, but of a quick, ingenious and piercing spirit. It must not be shackled or restricted. Give me the liberty to know, to utter and to argue freely according to conscience, above all liberties."

In this great *cri de coeur*, John Milton fashioned a rationale for media freedom that was taken up, centuries later, by John Stuart Mill and then by the judges of the US Supreme Court and finally, in the twenty first century by certain English Law Lords. It is the concept of the "free market place of ideas", where falsehood and evil doctrine, however initially seductive and dangerous, will eventually be driven out by truth—indeed, freedom to utter falsity will serve the public good by provoking authoritative correction:

---

[2] See Geoffrey Robertson, *The Tyrannicide Brief* (Vintage, 2006).

"And though all the winds of doctrine were let loose to play upon the earth, so truth be in the field, we do injuriously, by licensing and prohibiting, to misdoubt her strength. Let her and Falsehood grapple; whoever knew Truth put to the worse, in a free and open encounter?"

Republican and then royalist governments alike turned a deaf ear: licensing was given statutory force after the restoration in 1660, and Milton's *Paradise Lost* was sent to the hangman for burning because it suggested that an eclipse of the sun "with sudden fear of change perplexes monarchs". But where the *Aeropagitica* failed, bureaucracy and corruption succeeded: the licensing system was abolished for the printed word in 1695 after incompetence, fraud and extortion destroyed the Stationers' Company. The "glorious revolution" was not at all glorious for Catholics, but it produced the Bill of Rights of 1689, Art.9 of which declares: "That the freedom of speech and debates or proceedings in Parliament ought not to be impeached or questioned in any court or place out of Parliament."

1–003   This is the one free speech right to be found in English constitutional law, but it belongs only to M.P.s and to peers, giving them absolute privilege against libel actions over allegations they make in the course of Parliamentary proceedings. It has proved a useful democratic right, when extended in the nineteenth century to the press and then to the broadcast media when they carry reports of Parliamentary debates. But it means little more than free speech for elected politicians and elevated party hacks who are reluctant to use it in the confines of Westminster other than in their party's interest. It is a right with which the people and the press have never been trusted.

The demise of licensing as a means of suppressing attacks on church or State did not much matter, since the criminal courts began to punish libels, whether critical of the church (blasphemy), the Government (sedition) or the great men of the realm (criminal libel). In the course of the eighteenth century a fourth crime was added, namely obscene libel, an offence against good manners and decency. From the outset the targets were more political than pornographic: the radical pamphleteer M.P. John Wilkes outwitted the Government over his popular polemics excoriating George III and his ministers, but in 1763 he privately circulated a parody on Pope, on the theme that: ". . . life can little more supply than just a few good fucks, and then we die". The new law of obscenity provided the excuse for silencing him. This "Essay on Women" was solemnly read to the House of Lords by Lord Sandwich, one of his political enemies, and when one peer protested as the first four-letter word was uttered under Parliamentary privilege, the others shouted "go on, go on". Wilkes was jailed and disqualified as an M.P., but the public re-elected him—three times—while he was in prison. They turned up to support his courtroom battles against the

Home Secretary, Lord Halifax, and the sinister blind Treasury Solicitor who ordered the raids on his offices and home under "general warrants" to close down his printing presses and to seize anything of interest (malicious pleasure was taken in seizing Wilkes' stock of condoms). Like many great historical figures, Wilkes owes his fame to a good lawyer—in his case, Chief Justice Richard Pratt, who in a landmark constitutional ruling, *Entick v Carrington*, struck down "general warrants" as beyond the power of government.[2a] It was in the course of this struggle that "freedom of the press" was first heard in the streets of London, shouted by crowds who exulted in, "Wilkes, Pratt, and freedom of the press".

Meanwhile, the Draconian use of sedition laws against aggrieved colonists in America provided one of the cues for revolution, ignited in January 1776 by Tom Paine, the former English customs official, whose incendiary pamphlet *Common Sense* explained, when all the talk was of appeasement with the Crown, why it would be necessary to fight for liberty. It was Paine who, in this hour of universal ferment, lent his drafting skills to Jefferson for the Declaration of Independence and then to Lafayette for the French constitution; he returned to London for six months in 1790 to write *The Rights of Man* at the Angel Inn, Islington. It became one of the most influential books ever written, and Paine's work was hailed throughout Europe and America. But in Britain, the Englishman who can claim to be the founding father of free speech was persecuted for sedition: he fled back to France, so the trials continued of booksellers who dared to stock his work. (His later book, *The Age of Reason*, would send dozens of free thinkers to prison for selling a blasphemous libel.) It was, however, in the chant of the mob outside the Old Bailey at the end of these late-eighteenth century sedition trials that the free speech principle was heard again in the land: there being no judge to celebrate, the shout was, "Paine and the Freedom of the Press".

By this time, of course, the principle had been embedded in the **1–004** First Amendment to the US Constitution by way of a reaction to oppressive use of the common law of sedition. Free speech entered the US Constitution because it was perceived as a defining quality of Republican government. As Madison argued in his Report to the General Assembly of Virginia in 1798, the former British Sedition Acts should now be made unconstitutional because the revolutionary new American Constitution would create a form of government under which "the people, not the government, possess the absolute sovereignty". This form of government was "altogether different" from the British model, under which the Crown was sovereign and the people were subjects. "Is it not natural and necessary, under such different circumstances", Madison asked, "that a different degree of

---

[2a] *Enlich v Carrington* (1765) 19 St.Tr. 1030.

freedom in the use of the press should be contemplated?" It was, in the following words of the First Amendment:

> "Congress shall make no law respecting an establishment of religion, or prohibiting the free exercise thereof; or abridging the freedom of speech or of the press; or the right of the people peacefully to assemble and to petition the government for a redress of grievances."

The French, too, had canonised free speech in Arts 9 and 10 of the 1789 Declaration on the Rights of Man and the Citizen:

> "No-one is to be disquieted because of his opinions . . . Free communication of ideas and opinions is one of the most precious of the rights of man."

This was a tribute to the influence of Voltaire ("I don't like what you say but will defend to my death your right to say it"; "I know many books which fatigue, but none which have done real evil") and to the iniquitous system of *lettres de cachet* (imprisonment without trial on royal command) visited upon critics of the *ancien régime*. The sudden removal of censorship in France had a most striking effect, releasing a "polemical incontinence that washed over the whole country" within two years.[3] But in due course Napoleon found it necessary to punish citizens for badmouthing the officials he had dispatched to run his European empire, which is why his "insult" laws found a way into the Code Napoleon (its 1871 version remains law in France today). Most European countries retain these regressive criminal laws, which threaten journalists with heavy fines and imprisonment for insults offered to the pettiest officials and policemen as well as to ministers and top civil servants. The European Court has thus far lacked the gumption to declare that they plainly contravene Art.10 (which they plainly do) but has at least struck down as "disproportionate" all cases where a conviction has been followed by a substantial fine or a prison sentence.

It was free speech as the precursor to revolution that Pitt feared most, and the decade before and after the turn of the nineteenth century was marked in Britain by the Government's increased use of the sedition laws. At first, convictions were assured by virtue of the rule that the jury could only decide whether the defendant had published the libel: it was for the judge to decide whether the words were seditious or not. Lord Erskine, the barrister who defended Paine, famously prevailed upon a jury to defy the rule and acquit the Dean of St Asaph of seditious libel for urging universal suffrage. The judge, however, overruled the jury and entered a conviction, which

---

[3] Simon Schama, *Citizens* (Penguin, 1989), p.521.

was upheld by the appeal court. Public anger at judicial defiance of the jury procured the passage in 1792 of Fox's Libel Act, which reserved the decision on whether words were libellous to the jury alone. From this point, media defendants had a fighting chance: there were famous scenes where the mob carried Erskine in triumph from the Old Bailey after he secured acquittals for publishers of *The Rights of Man*. The Government responded by packing juries with men of property and "guinea men" (this was the sum they received if they convicted). Nonetheless, it was the chant of the mob outside the Old Bailey and the struggle for Fox's Libel Act that produced the impression—subsequently hardening into an unwritten article of constitutional faith—that the jury is a true guarantor of free speech.

The common law never adopted a free speech principle, although by the nineteenth century it had fashioned three procedural devices which still offer some practical support to the liberty of the press. Britain had trial by jury, an "open justice" principle, and a rule against prior restraint. It is instructive at this point to examine the present operation of the three safeguards devised by the common law, so as to understand why it was necessary to supplement them with a free speech principle drawn from the evolving international law of human rights.

TRIAL BY JURY

No citizen can lose his or her liberty for longer than a year (the 1–005 maximum sentence magistrates and a judge may impose) without at least the opportunity of trial by a jury of 12 good men and women and true. Legal history has many examples of "jury nullification" of bad laws or the directions of bad judges, beginning in 1670 when an Old Bailey jury (despite being locked up for several days without food or water or even a chamber pot) refused to convict the Quakers Penn and Mead for sedition. The jury system has served ever since to temper justice with mercy to defendants in the criminal courts,[3a] but in the course of the nineteenth century it came to be accorded a special role in the protection of free speech: the jury's constitutional right to acquit, irrespective of the law or of the evidence, was touted as a better practical protection for free speech than any number of constitutional guarantees. This argument was formulated by Professor A.V. Dicey, writing in 1885:

> "Freedom of discussion, is, then, in England little else than the right to write or say anything which a jury, consisting of 12 shopkeepers, think it expedient should be said or written . . . Yet nothing has in reality contributed so much to free the press

---

[3a] Lord Devlin, *Trial by Jury*, the Hamlyn Lectures (1956, revised edn, Stevens 1966).

from any control. If a man may publish anything which 12 of his countrymen think is not blameable, it is impossible that the Crown or the Ministry should exert any stringent control over writings in the press . . . The times when persons in power wish to check the excesses of public writers are times at which a large body of opinion or sentiment is hostile to the executive. But under these circumstances it must, from the nature of things, be at least an even chance that the jury called upon to find a publisher guilty may sympathise with his language . . . as fair and laudable criticism of official errors. What is certain is that the practical freedom of the English press arose in great measure from the trial of 'press offences' by a jury."[4]

Dicey's argument was dubious even at the time when it was made. True it was that Fox's Libel Act had given juries a power to decide the merits of defamation cases, and so some sedition prosecutions brought by George III's unpopular ministers had been thrown out in the 1790s. But other cases had succeeded, including hundreds brought for blasphemous libel in the nineteenth century when booksellers were regularly jailed for stocking *The Age of Reason* and one exceedingly pious panel even convicted the publisher of Shelley's *Queen Mab*. Indeed, only one of the hundreds of blasphemy prosecutions in the nineteenth century failed, and that was because the Lord Chief Justice summed up for an acquittal. There was a similarly high success rate for obscenity prosecutions, especially in respect of the works of foreign writers like Zola and Flaubert. Jury verdicts for much of the twentieth century serve further to undermine Dicey's theory: the propertied classes privileged to sit on juries disapproved of radicals, and generally convicted in trials involving libel or official secrecy.

What did give Dicey's theory a new lease of life was the abolition of property and age qualifications for jurors in 1972: the modem jury now has more shoplifters than shopkeepers amongst its numbers. The first beneficiaries of the change were pornographers, who had always been convicted before 1972. Now, they were increasingly acquitted by a younger and more broadminded generation of jurors (after a run of obscenity acquittals at the Old Bailey, Rupert Murdoch felt safe to introduce "Page 3" nudes to *The Sun*). After the acquittal of *Inside Linda Lovelace* in 1977, the DPP decided to mount no further obscenity prosecutions in relation to the written word. In 1985 an Old Bailey jury gave the final push to the discredited s.2 of the Official Secrets Act by acquitting Clive Ponting, despite the fact that he was obviously guilty of breaching it by supplying a Labour M.P. with secret information which falsified government statements about the sinking of the *Belgrano*. There

---

[4] A.V. Dicey, *An Introduction to the Study of Law of the Constitution*, (10th edn, Macmillan), pp.246–251.

have been other recent examples of juries showing a bias in favour of the freedom to publish, irrespective of the letter of the law or the weight of evidence. In 1992 the pacifists Randle and Pottle were acquitted of helping atom bomb spy George Blake to escape, despite (or because of) the fact that they had written a book confessing their guilt, entitled *The Blake Escape, How we Freed George Blake—and Why*.[5] In recent years, juries have still shown tenderness to honest radicals, acquitting demonstrators who destroyed genetically modified crops and attacked nuclear submarines. So government law officers are reluctant today to put journalists and publishers in the dock of a criminal court, for fear that "the gang of twelve" will live up to its historic reputation and acquit. For all their determination to pursue David Shayler, an MI5 official who sold his work secrets to *The Mail on Sunday*, the law officers refused to contemplate a prosecution of that newspaper or its journalists who had interviewed him.

The role of trial by jury as a guarantor of free speech is limited in **1–006** practice to protecting the speech of defendants who are likeable. Unpopular artists, essaying themes which shock or disgust, remain targets for jury prejudice, like *Gay News* in 1977 (convicted for publishing a "blasphemous" poem imagining Christ as a homosexual) and artists convicted for exhibiting "foetal earrings". Moreover, any sympathy towards the press displayed by jurors at the Old Bailey is replaced by hostility as they walk up Fleet Street to the High Court, where they bring back libel verdicts against newspapers. Jurors who would never send a journalist to jail are happy to award heavy damages against his proprietor, even on behalf of the likes of Jeffrey Archer. His award of £500,000 in 1986 (for an editor's logical assumption that since he had paid £2,000 to a prostitute he must have had sex with her) was followed by £1 million to Elton John and a £1.5 million award against the historian Nicolai Tolstoy. Damages of this order severely chilled investigative journalism in Britain during that Conservative era of the 1980s and early 1990s. Eventually the European Court declared that such massive and unprecedented awards infringed the right to freedom of expression.[6] Now libel damages are unlikely to exceed £200,000, and are invariably outstripped by legal costs.

The practical refutation of Dicey's complacent proposition that trial by jury is the guarantor of free speech is the fact that juries are being progressively eliminated. They remain the tribunal for common law crimes that are rarely charged (seditious, blasphemous and criminal libel), for obscenity and official secrecy offences and certain terrorist and "incitement to disaffection" crimes. This is not a long list, because successive British governments have tried to avoid the

---

[5] Randle and Pottle, *The Blake Escape, How we Freed George Blake—and Why*? (Harrap).
[6] *Tolstoy Miloslavsky v United Kingdom* (1995) 20 E.H.R.R. 442.

embarrassment and inconvenience of jury trial where media freedom is involved. They have returned to the "licensing" approach of the Star Chamber by appointing censorship bodies for film, television, video and even computer games and by relying increasingly on civil rather than criminal law to injunct and restrain media publication on grounds of copyright or confidence or official secrecy. Three unattractive expedients used to bypass the jury are:

Obtaining interim injunctions

1–007 Claimants—especially the Government—try to prevail on judges to ban publication for the "interim" period before trial on grounds of confidence or copyright on national security. Suppressed information soon becomes stale, and the case is not worth the cost to the media defendant of fighting a trial a year or so later.

Creating media offences triable only in magistrates courts

1–008 Breaches of restrictions on court reporting, for example, which carry fines of up to £5,000, are not triable by jury. In such cases, district judges are much more likely to convict.

Prosecuting for contempt of court

1–009 Contempt carries a maximum penalty of two years and is not triable by a jury. Judges in contempt cases are judges in their own cause, and have convicted in many cases where juries would probably have acquitted—e.g. Granada Television for refusing to name its "mole" within British Steel; Harriet Harman for giving a journalist access to documents read out in open court; *The Independent* for publishing excerpts from *Spycatcher* at a time when the Government was trying to stop the British public from reading a book on open sale in other countries; the BBC (initially) for a "cash for peerages" revelation in 2007.

The increasing tendency of governments to avoid the right of jury trial by running to High Court judges or by creating "media offences" punishable only by judges or magistrates is disturbing. A blatant example came in 1981 when it was made a criminal contempt punishable with two years' imprisonment for journalists, after a trial was over, to interview jurors about their deliberations. The crime was necessary, said the lawyer-M.P.s who supported the legislation, to preserve the integrity of the jury system. This integrity was hardly preserved by stripping jurors of their right to free speech by a new criminal offence that itself carried no right to trial by jury.

Where a right to trial by jury exists, the Attorney-General should not side-step it by approaching the High Court for an injunction to stop the publication or for a declaration that the publication is unlawful:

The Voluntary Euthanasia Society published a booklet entitled *A Guide to Self-Deliverance*, which discussed the pros and cons of committing suicide and described in detail a number of efficacious methods for so doing. After evidence came to light that some members of the Society had committed suicide by following methods described in the booklet, the Attorney-General sought to dissuade the Society from further dissemination of the *Guide* by applying to the High Court for a declaration that its publication amounted to the crime of aiding and abetting suicide. But this offence carries the right to jury trial, and the judge declined to usurp the jury's role by declaring that future conduct by the Society would necessarily amount to an offence.[7]

The principle that judges in civil courts must not usurp the jury's **1–010** role of deciding a publisher's guilt or innocence is of some constitutional importance, although today it is limited to occasional trials of publishers of material alleged to be obscene or officially secret or provocative of racial hatred. The jury functions as a regular media law tribunal only in civil defamation actions, where either party has a right to demand jury trial "unless the court is of the opinion that the trial requires any prolonged examination of documents" and the involvement of a jury would be "inconvenient" when compared to the savings in time and costs if the trial were heard by a judge sitting alone.[8] Although the court even then retains a discretion to order jury trial, the modern reluctance to do so is demonstrated by the case of *Aitken v Preston*:

Jonathan Aitken was a cabinet minister when *The Guardian* and *World in Action* accused him of procuring women for Arab clients, illegal arms-dealing and lying about a junket to the Ritz in Paris. Some of the allegations involved extensive documentary evidence, but *The Guardian* demanded that the claimant's integrity—or lack of it—should be decided by a jury, given the public perception that a jury verdict was more credible than that of a judge. The Court of Appeal, however, reached a contrary conclusion: the claimant's political standing meant that the public interest would be better served by a reasoned judgment, which by setting out the basis for its conclusions, would settle the allegations more authoritatively than a jury's verdict encapsulated in an answer "yes" or "no" to the question of whether he had been defamed.[9]

The reasoning in *Aitken* must apply whether there are documents to examine or not: a detailed judgment is preferred—by judges—to a

---

[7] *Att-Gen v Able* [1984] 1 All E.R. 277; and see *Gouriet v Union of Post Office Workers* [1978] A.C. 435.

[8] Supreme Court Act 1981, s.69, and see *Safeways Stores v Albert Tate*, December 19, 2000, when the Court of Appeal held that s.69 at least guaranteed an option for jury trial which could not be overborne by Civil Procedure Rules which allowed summary judgment in defamation cases.

[9] *Aitken v Preston* [1997] E.M.L.R. 415.

monosyllabic jury verdict. Judges naturally think that they afford quicker, cheaper and cleverer justice than the pooled wisdom of 12 citizens selected at random, but editors (especially of newspapers like the *Guardian*, regularly sued by unprepossessing politicians) feel that a jury would give them a fairer hearing and be more robust about inferring corrupt conduct. (Some evidence for this is provided by the "cash for questions" case in 1999, when the jury preferred to credit the earthy accusations of Harrods boss Al Fayed over what it must have regarded as the slick dissemblings of ex-M.P. Neil Hamilton.) However, tabloid editors sued by celebrities worry that jurors are dazzled by actors and soap-stars, whose complaints would underwhelm judges who do not watch them on television. So on the one hand, the media which bear the burden of proving truth can have that unfair burden lightened by the fact that "a jury can do justice, whereas the judge, who has to follow the law, may not".[10] On the other, jury sympathy is readily attracted to claimants who sit with tear-jerking family members carefully positioned directly in front of the jury box throughout the trial.

Juries gave ludicrously high awards in the days before defamation damages were capped, culminating in a £600,000 award to the wife of serial killer Peter Sutcliffe which famously provoked *Private Eye* editor Ian Hislop to exclaim, "If that's justice, I'm a banana". This case prompted the Court of Appeal to abandon its non-interventionist approach to jury verdicts, which have now, with help from the European Convention, been brought under control; but the punitive behaviour of civil juries towards newspapers has helped to persuade many that "it may now be over-romantic to conceive of juries as champions of freedom of speech as in the days of Perm and Mead".[11] In 2001 the Court of Appeal, for the first time, overturned a star-struck jury verdict on the ground that it was irrational in failing to comprehend all the evidence of corruption against the claimant, Bruce Grobbelaar,[12] although the Law Lords showed more respect: instead of rejecting the verdict as perverse, they reinstated it but reduced the greedy goalkeeper's damages to a derisory £1. For all that logic demands a reasoned judgement, jury trial is lodged deep in British sentiment, as the Court of Appeal reluctantly acknowledged in 2007 when it directed that a jury must hear the inquest into the death of Diana.[13]

1–011　　　The *Aitken* principle that public interest is better served by a reasoned verdict is a logical development if society looks to the courtroom as a mechanism for extracting and declaring truth. In criminal cases juries are not truth-finders, but rather decide whether

---

[10] Lord Devlin, *Trial by Jury: the Hamlyn Lectures* (1956, rev. edn Stevens, 1966).

[11] Lord Cooke, *Reynolds v Times Newspapers Ltd* [2001] 2 A.C. 127 at 226.

[12] *Grobbelaar v News Group Newspapers Ltd* [2001] 2 All E.R. 437 (Court of Appeal).

[13] *Jean Paul v Deputy Coroner of the Queen's Household* [2007] EWHC 408 (Admin).

guilt has been proven "beyond reasonable doubt". Most of those they acquit are in fact guilty, but have not been proven guilty to that high standard. But if society requires a symbolic public endorsement then "the verdict of the jury" carries the most popular imprimatur. Judges, anyway, can be lacking in street-wisdom and "common sense" and are always constrained by the rules of evidence. The Court of Appeal became quite starry-eyed in *Aitken* about the virtues of a reasoned judgment, ignoring the many reasoned judgments which history has shown to be based on tainted evidence or poor logic or social bias or simple ignorance of the way of the world. A libel action, it must be remembered, is not a Royal Commission, or any sort of inquisitive proceeding in which the judge acts as investigator of truth: he or she remains an adjudicator between adversary parties, confined to the limited evidence they are capable of calling. The trial is less appropriate as a vehicle for discovering truth than as a process for declaring and enforcing "rights", with the judge's main task to strike an overall compromise between (in libel) the right of free speech and the right of reputation, with the latter accorded respect to the extent that it does no serious damage to the former.

THE OPEN JUSTICE PRINCIPLE

One of the few examples of a free speech "right" embedded in the **1–012** British common law is the principle that justice must not only be done but must be seen to be done, and hence, "Every court in the land is open to every subject of the King." This was given the force of a constitutional principle by the House of Lords in the case of *Scott v Scott* in 1913, which adopted Jeremy Bentham's rationale:

> "Publicity is the very soul of justice. It is the keenest spur to exertion and the surest of all guards against improbity. It keeps the judge himself, while trying, under trial . . .".[14]

What Bentham was rationalising and applauding in this passage was not so much a public right as a tradition: the English court hearing emerged from the Middle Ages looking (and sounding) like an ill-conducted public meeting. Publicity was needed in order to attract witnesses to the trial and to promote the deterrent effect of the punishment, as well as serving to keep judges up to the mark and improving the behaviour of lawyers. But the "open justice" principle can also be characterised as an aspect of free speech:

> "Whether or not judicial virtue needs such a spur, there is also another important interest involved in justice done openly,

---

[14] *Scott v Scott* [1913] A.C. 417, approving Bentham at 447.

namely that the evidence and argument should be publicly known, so that society may judge for itself the quality of justice administered in its name, and whether the law requires modification . . . the common law by its recognition of the principle of open justice ensures that the public administration of justice will be subject to public scrutiny. Such scrutiny serves no purpose unless it is accompanied by the rights of free speech, i.e. the right publicly to report, to discuss, to comment, to criticise, to impart and to receive ideas and information on the matters subjected to scrutiny. Justice is done in public so it may be discussed and criticised in public."[15]

Open justice has other important virtues. The prospect of publicity deters perjury: witnesses are more likely to tell the truth if they know that any lie they tell might be reported and provoke others to come forward to discredit them. Media reporting of court cases enhances public knowledge and appreciation of the workings of the law, and it assists the deterrent effect of heavy jail sentences in criminal cases. Above all, fidelity to the open justice principle keeps Britain free from the reproach that it permits "secret courts" of the kind that have been instruments of repression in so many other countries.

1–013   The case that comes closest to accepting the principle as a rule of law enforceable by journalists is *R. v Felixstowe Justices Ex p. Leigh*[16]:

David Leigh, an experienced reporter on *The Observer*, was writing an article about a controversial case that had been heard in Felixstowe Magistrates' Court. The clerk of the court refused to supply him with the names of the lay justices who had decided it, pursuant to a policy that was being adopted by an increasing number of magistrates' courts of declining to identify justices to the public or the press. Leigh, with the backing of his newspaper and the NUJ, brought an action against the justices in the High Court, which granted him a declaration that the policy of anonymity was "inimical to the proper administration of justice and an unwarranted and unlawful obstruction to the right to know who sits in judgment". The judgment endorsed the importance of the court reporter as "the watchdog of justice", and the vital significance of press comment and criticism of the behaviour of judges and magistrates. Although there was no specific statutory requirement that justices should be named, the court deduced such a requirement from the fundamental nature of the open justice principle.

The importance of *Leigh* is that the court was prepared to treat the open justice principle as a "right", namely as an enforceable rule of law that could be asserted by a journalist to strike down a discretionary policy, rather than merely as a desirable state of affairs that could none the less give way to judicial convenience. This is, in

---

[15] *Home Office v Harman* [1982] 1 All E.R. 532 at 546–7 *per* Lord Scarman.
[16] *R. v Felixstowe Justices Ex p. Leigh* [1987] 1 All E.R. 551.

effect, the distinction between a "right" enforceable by a citizen-journalist against the State, and a paternalistic system which promises free speech but when it comes to the crunch, always "balances" that value against private rights that judges think are important, like reputation and State claims to national security. Just how little value may be placed in the balance on the side of press freedom is demonstrated by the majority of law lords in *Home Office v Harman*, which held solicitor Harriet Harman in contempt for showing documents to David Leigh, though they had been read out in open court. This decision (overtly influenced by the fact that the documents were used to criticise the Government's prisons policy) is a typical pre-Convention balancing act, where free speech—in this case, informed criticism of government—is given little or no weight against property rights, government policy, and a procedural rule that documents disclosed by a party in a civil action should only be used for the purposes of that action. The majority judges were unable to recognise a wider purpose of informing the public about the issues in the action. Harriet Harman M.P. took her case to Strasbourg, where the British Government was forced to concede that the decision against her was a breach of Art.10 of the Convention. The Rules of the Supreme Court were in consequence changed to allow general use of documents once they had been read in open court—an ironic example of how the European Convention can still be necessary to enforce a principle that derives from, and should have been fundamental to, British domestic law.

Article 6 guarantees the right of everyone on trial, whether for a criminal offence or as party to a civil action, to "a fair and *public* hearing". However, it goes on in Euro-weasel mode:

> "Judgment shall be pronounced publicly but the press and public may be excluded from all or part of the trial in the interests of morals, public order, or national security in a democratic society, where the interests of juveniles or the protection of the private life of the parties so require, or to the extent strictly necessary in the opinion of the Court in special circumstances where publicity would prejudice the interests of justice."

These exceptions are actually *wider* than UK domestic law allows **1–014** under the "open justice" principle of *Scott v Scott*, which confines the common law and limits exceptions to those contained in statutes passed by Parliament (which in recent years, unfortunately, have become legion). British courts have refused, for example, to permit "secret trials" on grounds of morals or public order, or to uphold gagging orders imposed to protect the private lives of witnesses or parties. Because Art.6 of the Convention permits the press to be excluded from courts in order to protect "the private life of the parties", the Convention could not have been used to challenge successfully such diverse rulings as an order not to name a witness from a famous family lest publicity might interfere with her cure for heroin addiction[17]; an order not to publish the address of a former MP defendant lest his estranged wife should discover his whereabouts and harass him[18]; and an order that reporters should leave the court so that a distressed defendant could explain in privacy the matrimonial problems that drove her to drink before she drove her car.[19] In all these cases trial courts had been moved by personal plight to overlook the fundamental principle that trials must be open in every respect. That this great principle is firmer in British domestic law than in the European Convention gives rise to an important question; namely whether the incorporation of the Convention could operate to cut down any of the basic rights that are already enjoyed—in this case, a basic English right which was watered down by the Convention draftsmen to accommodate the less vigorous practice in other European jurisdictions? Section 11 of the Human Rights Act, headed "safeguard for existing human rights" provides:

"11. A person's reliance on a Convention right does not restrict—

(a) any other right or freedom conferred on him by or under any law having effect in any part of the United Kingdom . . . .".

Article 6 of the Convention is more restrictive than the historic principle which emerges from the common law as declared in *Scott v Scott*. Section 11 may therefore have to be invoked to *prevent* judges from knee-jerk applications of an Art.6 exception, on the basis that a much more generous right of court reporting had crystallised in English law by 1998 and cannot be cut back by the mealy-mouthed exceptions in Art.6. But s.11 may, despite the promise of its headnote, mean no more than that the media can rely on *Scott v Scott* as well as Art.10 when it demands the right to report a trial[20]: this would not, for example, prevent defendants in later but connected trials asking for a postponement of reporting to prevent prejudice to those subsequent trials. In such cases, the Art.10 right to report, even though bolstered by *Scott v Scott* and common law, may not prevail over the demands for a fair trial, the issue being decided by a balancing operation under Art.6 rather than the Art.10 presumption in favour of press freedom and/or the common law "open justice" principle.

---

[17] *R. v Central Criminal Court Ex p. Crook, The Times*, November 8, 1984.
[18] *R. v Evesham Justices Ex p. McDonagh* [1988] 1 All E.R. 371.
[19] *R. v Malvern Justices Ex p. Evans* [1988] 1 All E.R. 371.
[20] Section 11 parallels Art.53 of the Convention: "Nothing in this Convention shall be construed as limiting or derogating from any of the human rights and fundamental freedoms which may be ensured under the laws of any High Contracting Party or under any other agreement to which it is a party."

In this respect, the advent of the European Convention has **1–015** actually and actively **diminished** media freedom to report court proceedings. In the days of multiple trials for East End gangs run by the Krays of the Richardsons, judges never suppressed reporting of earlier trials: jurors were judicially assumed to be made of stern stuff and were able to put media prejudice out of their mind. Today, however, postponement orders are often granted to stop reporting of terrorist gang cases, for fear that juries in later trials may in some way be contaminated (although the Court of Appeal has reiterated its faith in the ability of juries to disregard press stories about other cases). The police, as well as the media, are frustrated because the public cannot hear the evidence of what provoked controversial arrests; the public interest is undeniably sacrificed to what may be a very remote possibility of prejudice. The present law reports are full of acronyms—*R. v A, B, C,* down to *X, Y, Z* and back again—a symbol of the deleterious effect of the European Convention. The House of Lords has said—wrongly, but unappealably—that an Art.6 "balancing act" should replace the more robust common law principles in all court reporting cases (although this may be confined to the reporting of all cases involving children).[21] The advent of the European Convention has, in this respect, to some extent undermined the media's traditional freedom to report the courts.

There are also an increasing number of statutory exceptions to the open justice principle. Some of these are reasonable. For example, rape victims are entitled to anonymity in order to mitigate their humiliation and to encourage other victims to come forward. In youth courts, juvenile offenders may not be identified; the testimony given at pre-trial criminal proceedings usually cannot be published until the trial is over, to avoid prejudicing the jury. But other restrictions are less justifiable; the least being the law which enables judges to prevent publication of derogatory allegations in mitigation speeches and the practice of permitting injunctions against Sunday newspapers to be granted by judges on the telephone on Saturday, without any recording of the call let alone any provision that transcripts of it should be publicly available. Other secretive practices have been discouraged by the recent civil procedure reforms, such as the routine exclusion of the media from in-chambers hearings relating to property in divorce cases, to bail applications in Crown Courts, and to some applications for injunctions in the Queen's Bench Division of the High Court. These breaches of the open justice principle are incompatible with the rule in *Scott v Scott* and must now face a presumption in favour of public hearings.[22]

---

[21] *Re S (a child) (Identification Restrictions on Publication)* [2004] UKHL 47.

[22] See CPR, r.39.2 and the Practice Direction under CPR, Pt 39, para.1, which followed a decision favouring open justice in civil cases by Lord Woolf: *Hodgson v Imperial Tobacco* [1998] 1 W.L.R. 1056.

That it remains important to remind courts—and especially tribunals—of the constitutional necessity of complying with this rule is exemplified by the recent case of *R. v London (North) Industrial Tribunal Ex p. Associated Newspapers*[23];

> Council tax payers and ratepayers in North London were interested in, and doubtless appalled by the expense of, claims of sex discrimination and victimisation brought against Camden Council and its chief executive by his deputy, the Council solicitor. After the case received embarrassing coverage in the local press, Camden's Q.C. persuaded the employment tribunal that it would be better for everyone if the public hearings were not reported at all, at least until after the judgment. Local newspapers (the *Camden New Journal* and the *Ham and High*) protested in vain by letter, but lacked the funds to challenge this improper gag. *The Mail on Sunday* did so by judicial review, whereupon the High Court, applying *Scott v Scott* and *Leigh v Felixstowe*, held that the Tribunal should not have made the order. Although it had a statutory power to restrict reporting of evidence which identified persons affected by allegations of sexual misconduct, the open justice principle required that this power should only apply to those involved in the incident. It could not possibly be used to hide the name of the Council or the Chief Executive. Public reporting of judicial proceedings was a "fundamental constitutional principle" said Mr Justice Keane: it was so firmly embedded in English law that only statutory inroads were permissible, and they must be interpreted as narrowly as possible.

1–016   The judge in this case accepted that the European Convention added nothing to the common law principle of open justice. So English case precedents remain more helpful than the Convention in the continual battle against magistrates and judges and members of tribunals who will always believe in their hearts that the press should report only their judgment at the end of a case, and not confuse the public by prior reporting of the evidence.

One interesting application of the open justice principle is that reporters are accorded special status as "representatives" or "watchdogs" of the public. They should be invited to come into court in circumstances where it is inconvenient for the public to be admitted. In *R. v Waterfield* the trial judge had cleared the court while the jury was shown allegedly obscene films, fearing that "gasps, giggling and comment" from the press bench and the public gallery might distract the jurors from their solemn duty. The Court of Appeal said that the press should have been allowed to remain:

> ". . . the public generally are interested in cases of this kind, and for not unworthy reasons. Concepts of sexual morality are

---

[23] *R. v London (North) Industrial Tribunal Ex p. Associated Newspapers* [1998] I.C.R. 1212.

changing. Whenever a jury in this class of case returns a verdict, whether of guilty or not guilty, intelligent readers of newspapers and weekly journals may want to know what kind of film was under consideration. Experience during the past decades has shown that every acquittal tends to lead to the greater exposure to public gaze of what previous generations thought seemly only in private, if seemly anywhere. Members of the public have to depend on the press for information on which to base their opinions; but if allegedly indecent films are always shown in closed courtrooms the press cannot give the public the information which it may want and which is necessary for the formation of public opinion . . . It follows, so it seems to us, that normally, when a film is being shown to a jury and the judge, in the exercise of his discretion, decides that it should be done in a closed courtroom or in a cinema, he should allow representatives of the press to be present. No harm can be done by doing so: some good may result."[24]

Parliament has given journalists the right to be present, even though the rest of the public is excluded, in the case of youth courts[25] and family proceedings in magistrates' courts.[26] Similarly, the public but not the press can be kept out of an adult court while a child or young person gives evidence in relation to a sex offence.[27]

The principle that the press may remain to represent the public **1–017** should be applied in every case where a judge decides to clear the public gallery, except where national security is demonstrably at stake. Judges have power to order any reporting to be postponed until the end of the trial, and should do so rather than take the more Draconian course of excluding the press. Secret hearings are wrong in principle and (with the alternative of postponement orders under the Contempt of Court Act 1981) are unnecessary in practice. Journalists should be fully conversant with their rights to appeal against any exclusion from the courtroom or any secrecy order made under the Contempt of Court Act. These rights are contained in s.159 of the Criminal Justice Act 1988 and the rules made thereunder, and are set out in detail in Ch.8.

The principle of open justice has its physical symbol—the press bench—in almost every courtroom. This piece of furniture has become something of a shibboleth: both the Magistrates' Association and the NUJ have said that it should be regarded as sacrosanct. This attitude may have the effect of blunting the critical edge of press coverage, by encouraging court reporters to perceive themselves as part and parcel of the court process, rather than as objective critics

[24] [1975] 2 All E.R. 40.
[25] Children and Young Persons Act 1933, s.47(2).
[26] Magistrates' Courts Act 1980, s.69(2).
[27] Children and Young Persons Act 1933, s.37(1).

of its workings. However, the press should jealously protect its right to sit centre-stage in the interests of audibility and accuracy. As the United States Supreme Court has put it, while media representatives enjoy the same right of access as the public, they are often provided with special seating and priority of entry so that they may report what people in attendance have seen and heard. This contributes to the public understanding of the rule of law and to comprehension of the functioning of the entire criminal justice system.[28]

1–018 The next step that the courts must take to develop the "open justice" principle in conformity with the realities of modern communication, is to permit their own proceedings to be televised. Research consistently demonstrates that the British public mainly receives news from television, not from newspapers. The essential justifications for "open justice"—that it protects against perjury, encourages witnesses to come forward and deters judicial misconduct—would be better served by television or radio coverage of courts. The evidence in any particular case does not merely comprise the words that are spoken, but the way in which they are spoken. (For this reason, appeal courts are reluctant to disturb the findings of trial judges who have "had the benefit of seeing witnesses"—i.e. of observing their demeanour and body language.) If the public, too, is to "see justice done", its watchdog in the twenty-first century will be the broadcaster as well as the newspaper journalist. The rule which requires all courts and tribunals to admit the reporter clutching pen and notebook should logically be extended to admit the reporter with a digital video camera—subject to protocols which prohibit pictures of vulnerable witnesses and jurors.

The Tribunals of Enquiry (Evidence) Act of 1921 contains no bar on photography—indeed, s.2(a) enjoins the widest publicity. In October 2001 the first full-blooded assertion of a broadcaster's right to televise proceedings (of the inquiry into mass-murdering doctor Harold Shipman) was made by CNN, drawing upon the terms of the 1921 Act, the open justice principle and Art.10. Janet Smith J. was reluctant to acknowledge that broadcasters had a "right" to televise public inquiries, but she permitted cameras to capture and transmit the testimony of witnesses who did not object.[29] Television coverage of Shipman began in May 2002, under protocols which required a 60-minute delay between recording and broadcasting, in case there was a sudden need for a judicial edit. This was a real breakthrough:

---

[28] *Richmond Newspapers Inc v Commonwealth of Virginia* (1980) 448 U.S. 555 at 587, and see *Re Andrew Dunn and the Morning Bulletin Ltd* (1932) St. R. Qd. 1 at 15 where the existence of a press bench was said to be a crown command sanctioned by custom and common sense: on this basis, any decision to remove or requisition it for an overflow of lawyers might be challengeable.

[29] *The Shipman Enquiry: Application by Cable News Network (CNN)*, October 25, 2002, *per* Dame Janet Smith.

the next step would be to create a presumption in favour of broadcasters by requiring reticent witnesses to show good reason why their testimony should not be televised.

The BBC application to broadcast evidence at the Lockerbie trial was turned down by the Scottish courts, for the good reason that some key non-compellable witnesses who lived abroad would not attend for fear of reprisals if visually identified.[30] In the absence of such reasons, there should be no objection. Scottish appeal courts, for example, generally permit their proceedings to be televised and thus allowed BBC coverage of the Lockerbie appeal, having ascertained that neither prosecution nor defence objected. In England, there is an inconvenient statutory bar erected in 1925—long before the advent of television—by s.41 of the Criminal Justice Act, passed to stop photography in courtrooms. It might be argued that "photograph" in this legislation refers to the flash photography which famously captured Dr Crippen in the Old Bailey dock, and not to unobtrusive and stationary digital cameras—an interpretation which s.3 of the Human Rights Act would assist, since this construction of the statute is more in keeping with the Art.10 right of the media freely to impart information. English judges were deeply antagonised by television coverage of the O.J. Simpson trial, notwithstanding that it served the public interest by exposing an incompetent judge and a lying policeman. It was chiefly objectionable because of the accompanying "expert" commentaries and lawyers' press conferences, which would never be permitted under UK contempt laws and professional ethics rules. Courts and tribunals cannot indefinitely resist the logic of extending the open justice principle to the broadcaster as well as to the print journalist.

The campaign for broadcasting public enquiries received an **1–019** unnecessary setback in 2003, when Lord Hutton allowed the television cameras to be trained on him whilst delivering his verdict into the death of government scientist Dr David Kelly, but not upon the witnesses whose evidence he had so controversially assessed. ITN had applied to broadcast the most important witnesses (not Kelly family members) but Hutton held that these seasoned political and television performers would face "additional strain" and "might well be inhibited from speaking frankly" if they were subjected to the terrifying prospect of having their evidence telecast, or even recorded for radio broadcast. This reasoning was self-evidently preposterous in relation to such witnesses as Tony Blair, Alastair Campbell, Geoff Hoon and senior BBC reporters and executives. So what is the real reason why judges shrink from allowing public enquiries to be truly public? Judges—in Lord Hutton's case, perhaps subconsciously—want to have the final, authoritative word: their report must stand as the revealed truth, because they have seen and

---

[30] See *In the Petition of the British Broadcasting Corporation: High Court of Judiciary*, *per* Lord Macfayden, March 7, 2000, CA, April 20, 2000.

heard the evidence at close hand and observed the demeanour at close quarters of those who give it. Their assessment must therefore be perceived as correct, and their decision definitive. But if everyone can, through television, see the evidence close up, and are thereby given the opportunity to judge for themselves, they might make up their own minds and come to a different conclusion—the very reason why there is such an overwhelming public interest in giving them that opportunity. After all, in Britain 65 per cent of the public regard television as their main source of news (16 per cent hear it on the radio first, but only 15 per cent say that they rely on newspapers). Moreover, television can tell the unvarnished truth—in a case as politically charged as the Kelly inquest, it was impossible for newspaper editors and journalists not to intrude their own political preconceptions by way of headlines and their selection for quotation from the day's transcript. In the end, it was Lord Hutton himself who suffered most from his refusal to let the public see for themselves—his report was derided by the privileged journalists who had also seen the evidence being given, and had interpreted it differently from the judge. Another loser was the BBC, whose management showed itself to be unworthy of public trust by its refusal to support ITN's application to televise the proceedings.[31]

Both Lord Hutton and Dame Janet Smith (in her *Shipman* decision) wrongly rejected arguments based on Art.10, on the grounds that evidence heard in a court or tribunal "belonged" to the presiding judge and Art.10 "does not bear upon the right of access to information that another holds but has not made accessible and does not wish to impart".[32] This is a misunderstanding: Art.10 may not give a right of access to private information held by an individual or organisation,[33] but the information generated by witnesses at a public enquiry, including their demeanour and the way they give their testimony, is nonetheless information which the public is entitled to receive "without interference by public authority"—the authority in question being the presiding judge, who is only entitled to prevent its dissemination if such censorship would serve an Art.10(2) exception. Lord Hutton's insistence that the decision should be left to an Art.6 "balancing act" is mistaken, because that

---

[31] See ruling by Lord Hutton, August 5, 2003.

[32] Hutton ruling, para.7.

[33] This notion emerges from a controversial euro court decision—*Leander v Switzerland* (1987) 9 E.H.R.R. 43—which requires reconsideration in light of *Claude Reyes v Chile*, a decision of the Inter-American Court of Human Rights on September 19, 2006. That international court held that environmental groups were entitled, under an Art.10-style freedom of information guarantee, to have access to state-held information, under a proper freedom of information process. The nearest which the Strasbourg Court has got to this position has been to find that in some limited circumstances Art.8's protection of private life may involve a positive obligation to make environmental information available to those immediately affected—see *Guerra v Italy* (1998) 26 E.H.R.R. 357.

Article, the "right to a fair trial", applies only to trials between parties and not to public enquiries. Correctly interpreted, Art.6 is engaged only where a fair trial requires the exclusion of the press and not where applications are made for television or radio coverage to complement what would otherwise be exclusive (and necessarily edited and possibly distorted) newspaper coverage. Hutton, like Lord Phillips in his earlier BSE enquiry, at least accepted that final submissions by counsel could be televised: the next step is to recognise that no public inquest or inquiry can be truly "public" unless the evidence, at least when given by officials and public figures, is made available for radio and TV broadcast.

THE RULE AGAINST PRIOR RESTRAINT

The British contribution to the philosophy of free speech might be **1–020** summed up in the Duke of Wellington's phrase "publish and be damned". The media is free to publish and be damned, so long as damnation comes after, and not before, the word gets out. Journalists cannot claim to be above the law, but what they can claim, in every country that takes free speech seriously, is a right to publish first, and take the risk of conviction afterwards. That liberty was rejected by parliament, over Milton's stirring protest, when it appointed 27 fit and proper persons—schoolmasters, lawyers, ministers of religion, doctors (the sort of people found nowadays in the regulatory bodies for broadcasting and video)—to censor public reading. They were obliged to reject any book that was "contrary to good life or good manners". (Their modern counterparts are obliged to reject any television programme that is offensive to public feeling, good taste or decency.) In 1660 the restored royalist regime instituted the office of "Surveyor of the Press", a witch-finder general who raided printers sympathetic to republicanism and had them prosecuted and often executed for treason and sedition. The public grew to hate the licensors and the system was abolished in 1694 after evidence of widespread corruption. The rule against prior restraint was given definitive shape by the venerated legal writer Blackstone:

> "The liberty of the press is indeed essential to the nature of a free state; but this consists in laying no previous restraints on publications, and not in freedom from censure for criminal matter when published. Every free man has an undoubted right to lay what sentiments he pleases before the public; to forbid this is to destroy the freedom of the press; but if he publishes what is improper, mischievous or illegal, he must take the consequences of his own temerity."[34]

---

[34] William Blackstone, *Commentaries on the laws of England* (1765, Book IV), pp.151–2.

It was this message that went out in the eighteenth century, and became enshrined in the First Amendment to the American Constitution. It was endorsed by the Supreme Court, in its historic *Pentagon Papers* decision. The United States Government learnt of the *New York Times'* plan to publish a set of confidential army research papers on the history of American involvement in Vietnam. It tried to injunct the newspaper, on the ground that the papers contained military and diplomatic secrets, the disclosure of which would substantially damage the national interest. The Supreme Court refused:

> "Any system of prior restraint on expression comes to this court bearing a heavy presumption against its constitutional validity. The only effective restraint upon executive policy and power in the areas of national defence and international affairs may be an enlightened citizenry—informed and critical public opinion which alone can here protect the values of democratic government. For without an informed and free press there cannot be an enlightened people."[35]

The justices accepted that publication of those documents would harm the national interest and might even make the newspaper guilty of a criminal offence. But it was entitled to publish and be damned. Only when the Government could prove that disclosure would cause "grave and irreparable injury to the public interest"—details, for example, of troop deployment in wartime or information that might trigger a nuclear war—was a court entitled to stop the presses.

1–021 The rule against prior restraint thus became, for the United States, a constitutional consequence of the First Amendment. In England it was no more than an application of the general common law maxim that everything is permitted except that which is expressly forbidden—or retrospectively forbidden by a verdict of guilt or award of damages. In libel actions the principle has held up well, and there is a plethora of precedents for the proposition that no injunction will be granted to stop the circulation of defamatory statements prior to trial if the media defendant declares on affidavit that it intends to justify the defamation as true or else to plead fair comment or privilege.[36] In 2005 the Court of Appeal emphatically endorsed the rule against prior restraint on libels in *Greene v Associated Newspapers*. Martha Greene, a Blair "crony", could not stop publication of a defamation even though it was based only on the unreliable word of convicted conman Peter Forster: there was a

---

[35] *New York Times v US* (1971) 403 U.S. 713 at 729.
[36] *Bonnard v Perryman* (1891) 2 Ch. 269 (justification); *Quartz Hill Consolidated Mining v Beal* (1882) 20 Ch. D. 501 (privilege); *Fraser v Evans* (1969) 1 Q.B. 349 (fair comment).

slim prospect that this time he might be telling the truth. The Court traced the continuing robustness of the rule to the traditional respect for the constitutional function of juries in libel actions, and to the "pragmatic grounds that until there has been disclosure of documents and cross-examination at the trial a court cannot safely proceed on the basis that what the defendants wish to say is not true. And if it is or might be true the court has no business to stop them saying it."[37]

The lack of any constitutional provision in the United Kingdom has meant that before the Human Rights Act came into force the rule against prior restraint became badly eroded in other areas of media law. Applications for injunctions, which impose prior restraint by stopping presses from rolling and film from running, are most commonly based on a complaint that the information about to be revealed has been obtained in breach of confidence. Where that information relates to national security, all that the Government has to show is that publication might cause *some* injury to the national interest—a test that would ensure that the British equivalent of the *Pentagon Papers* would never see the light of day.

This main exception to the rule against prior restraint, namely the interim injunction granted for an alleged breach of confidence, was (until the Human Rights Act) generally decided upon the "balance of convenience" test. All that the claimant needed to do to obtain a restraining order was to show a prima facie (i.e. arguable) case, and that the public interest in protecting the confidence was not, on the "balance of convenience", outweighed by some urgent public interest in publication. In cases involving alleged military secrets, the courts have virtually applied a presumption in favour of granting the injunction until trial on the basis that if the information is allowed into the public domain the Government will be unable to repair the damage. Although in every case the judge must balance the commercial or property rights of the claimant in controlling the information against the value of the defendant's right of free speech, for many judges brought up in a world that accords pre-eminent value to rights of property, this seemed like balancing hard cash against hot air.

This tendency reached extraordinary heights during the *Spycatcher* **1–022** litigation, when a majority of Law Lords at one point narrowly upheld an interim injunction on newspapers publishing details from a book that was on open sale throughout the rest of the world, numerous copies of which were circulating in Britain.[38] This decision was ludicrous: all confidentiality in the information had evaporated with overseas publication, and no additional damage to the national interest could possibly have been done by re-publication of the contents of the book in the British press. The majority judges

---

[37] *Greene v Associated Newspaper Ltd* [2005] 1 All E.R. 30 at 57.
[38] *Att-Gen v Guardian Newspapers Ltd* [1987] 3 All E.R. 316.

evinced patriotic hostility to an MI5 turncoat and his publishers, whose profits they said they were entitled to curtail (although it was their own newsworthy action in banning the book which continued to increase the world-wide sales). The House of Lords in two subsequent cases has retreated from the position it adopted in the original *Spycatcher* litigation, by making plain that the Government must prove some damage to the national interest and that no such damage can be established where the information has already been placed in the public domain by being published abroad.

The European Court of Human Rights in 1991 held that the continuing injunction on publishing *Spycatcher* in Britain long after it had become a best-seller in other countries was an infringement of the Art.10 guarantee of freedom of expression. A narrow majority of the judges was not persuaded, however, that Art.10 prohibited prior restraint in all circumstances, at least when governments were concerned to protect security information that had not yet seen the light of day. But it did acknowledge that:

> ". . . the dangers inherent in prior restraints are such that they call for the most careful scrutiny on the part of the Court. This is especially so as far as the press is concerned, for news is a perishable commodity and to delay its publication, even for a short period, may well deprive it of its value and interest."[39]

It follows that courts in Britain, in order to comply with the Convention, must accept "newsworthiness" as a public interest value that weighs heavily against the grant of an interim injunction sought against newspapers and broadcast organisations.

1–023   The most enduring damage done by the *Spycatcher* litigation to the rule against prior restraint was the emergence of a legal doctrine that once a secrecy injunction has been granted against one newspaper, every other section of the media becomes effectively bound by its terms, on pain of punishment for contempt.[40]

This doctrine that an injunction against one publication can effectively bind all who know of it can seriously undermine the rule against prior restraint. It means that a claimant (often, the Government) can obtain, at a secret High Court hearing, an injunction against one defendant (perhaps a journal whose financial position does not permit a legal contest) and thereafter try to enforce it against every media outlet in the country. Although the doctrine was created in the course of a panicked reaction by the courts to bogus claims of a national security peril asserted by the Thatcher Government, it has subsequently been exploited by private corporations wishing to keep their secrets under wraps. It requires newspapers which wish to publish stories about a matter some aspect of which is

---

[39] *The Observer and Guardian v United Kingdom* (1991) 14 E.H.R.R. 153 at 60.
[40] *Att-Gen v Times Newspapers Ltd* [1992] 1 A.C. 191, HL.

affected by an injunction against another publication, to apply to the court for guidance on whether their story trespasses upon the order already in existence—a procedure calculated in national security cases to give the Government the whip hand. This is because the Treasury Solicitor, acting for the security services, must be notified, and he can make life very expensive for publishers by opposing and appealing any relaxation. "We have a bottomless purse" was the very first threat made by the Treasury Solicitor's office to the managing director of Heinemann, to dissuade him from publishing *Spycatcher*. (When this failed, MI5 sent an emissary to Heinemann's owner, Paul Hamlyn, threatening that he would never get a peerage if he published—a threat that made him even keener to do so. His peerage was amongst the first announced by the new Labour Government.)

The erosion of the rule against prior restraint by judges granting "interim injunctions" to restrain alleged breaches of confidence and copyright has been the most noticeable example of the law's failure to develop a coherent and principled approach to media freedom. Since the passage of the Human Rights Act the courts have been inclined to allow newspaper editors more freedom to determine for themselves whether publication will breach an existing injunction, and have notably rejected the Government's contention that they must first submit their article to the Attorney-General for clearance.[41] The absurdity of the *Spycatcher* ban was the result of a dogged judicial insistence on viewing the memoirs of a former MI5 employee as the "property" of the Government, and conducting the litigation as if he had stolen the office furniture. What has been overlooked in Official Secrets Act cases is the constitutional basis of the rule against prior restraint: namely that it is improper for a judge to usurp a function that by tradition belongs to a jury, the ultimate arbiter in all criminal cases other than contempt. A breach of official secrecy is a crime, irrespective of whether it may also amount to a breach of confidentiality. A more principled decision upholding the rule in respect of publications the legitimacy of which the law entrusts to jury determination is the *Voluntary Euthanasia Society* case, where the Attorney General was refused an injunction against a publication the authors of which were entitled to have the legality of their actions decided at a trial before a jury. On this principle it has been authoritatively stated that no injunction should be granted by the civil courts to restrain the dissemination of allegedly obscene books, as such a step would pre-empt the ultimate decision of a jury.[42]

The rule against prior restraint will not always prevail over the **1–024** sanctity of contract, however, and individuals who voluntarily agree to give up freedom of speech in return for employment or payment

---

[41] *Att-Gen v Punch* [2001] E.M.L.R. 24.
[42] Viscount Dilhorne in *Gouriet v Union of Post Office Workers*, fn.7 above.

can be held to their bargain if necessary by the court granting injunctive relief against publication, unless their revelations are trivial or have been published elsewhere or are important to the public interest. In 1990 the Court of Appeal had no hesitation in injuncting a former royal servant from publishing anywhere in the world his memoirs of life with the Royal Family. It dismissed the notion that a defence to the breach might be mounted on the basis that the secrecy clause in his employment contract was void as contrary to public policy, because it would deny to foreigners their rights to receive information.[43] The British courts are traditionally over-protective of royal privacy, and in other cases, where the public interest in the information is genuine, claimants may be refused an injunction and left to their remedy (if any) in damages. Decided cases suggest that in practice judges are predisposed to permit Royals and the security service to gag disloyal employees, but are sceptical of the rights of other employers like Mohammed Al Fayed, whose attempts to enforce confidentiality clauses against disloyal employees have always been rejected.

The rule against prior restraint has been given some force in breach of confidence injunction cases by s.12 of the Human Rights Act, subs.(4) of which requires the court in civil actions to have *particular regard* to the importance of the Art.10 right to freedom of expression, to ensure that every opportunity is given to the would-be publisher to be present (unless there are "compelling reasons" why he should not be notified of the application) and to refuse to grant an injunction restraining publication prior to trial *"unless the court is satisfied that the applicant is likely to establish that publication should not be allowed"* (s.12(3)). This section was passed in response to anxious lobbying by media interests, afraid that incorporation of the Convention would herald the introduction of Art.8 privacy injunctions. At first the courts were inclined to neuter s.12(3) by treating the test of "likely" to succeed at trial as merely requiring the applicant to show a "real possibility" of success, which was all that the previous "balance of convenience" test required. But in *Cream Holdings Ltd v Banerjee* the House of Lords held that it imposes a higher hurdle for seekers of injunctions against the media: they must show (other than in cases where temporary injunctions are granted to allow the judge time to consider the case properly, or where the consequences of publication would be very serious—a threat to life, for example) that ultimate success is very much on the cards— "sufficiently favourable to justify (an injunction) in the circumstances of the case."[44] The Law Lords lifted an injunction imposed because

---

[43] *Att-Gen v Barker* [1990] 3 All E.R. 257.
[44] See, for example, the decision of Kerr L.J. in *Cambridge Nutrition Ltd v BBC* [1990] 3 All E.R. 523, CA, where a company marketing a controversial diet was refused an injunction to stop a BBC programme notwithstanding a claim that the makers were in breach of contract. See also *Cream Holdings Ltd v Banerjee* [2004] UKHL 44 at 22.

the appellant merely had a "real possibility" of success, against newspaper publication of an ex-employee's confidential information about illegal activities by an entertainment conglomerate: the newspaper intended to run a public interest defence which would reduce the company's chances of success. To achieve prior restraint in such cases, applicants will have to prove that they have a higher than 50:50 chance of succeeding at the trial. Thus Posh Spice and her husband David Beckham were unable to stop author Andrew Morton from publishing a biography of them which drew on confidential revelations from their bodyguard.

In deciding whether to grant an injunction, the court must overcome the s.12 presumption that free speech will not be restrained before trial of any action which seeks to suppress it. Exactly how much weight it is given will depend on the personal values of the judge and the interest value of the story. But however damaging to individuals may be the consequences of a publication, the right to free speech must prevail unless the individuals possess an established legal right that the publication would infringe:

> In the case of *Re X (A Minor)* the mother and stepfather of a sensitive 14-year-old girl sought to stop publication of a book that ascribed depraved and immoral behaviour to her deceased father. There was evidence that the book, if published, would almost certainly come to her attention, and would cause her serious psychological damage. The judge at first instance invoked the wardship powers of the court to protect the girl: he weighed her interests against that of the publishers, and concluded that the balance came down in favour of restraining publication, since the book could be rendered harmless by excising a few paragraphs. The Court of Appeal held that this was an incorrect approach. Even if there were no public interest in publication, the right to free speech could not in principle be subordinated to the welfare of an individual whose established legal rights were not infringed. The court had a duty to protect the liberty to publish, by ensuring that the existing ambit of restraints was not extended.[45]

The *Spycatcher* principle that prior restraint is impermissible in **1–025** respect of information which has already been placed in the public domain (even if it is the international and not the domestic domain) must apply despite the fact that the activity of the defendant has placed it there. That was the conclusion of the European Court in *Vereniging Weekblad BLUF! v The Netherlands*, where that Government had seized the print-run of a left-wing newspaper (*BLUF!*), which had reproduced an internal report from its secret service. The editors immediately reprinted and defiantly distributed several thousand copies to crowds on the streets of Amsterdam. Applying *Spycatcher*, the Court held that this action destroyed the confidentiality of the material, so the order to withdraw the edition

---

[45] *Re X (A Minor)* [1975] 1 All E.R. 697, CA.

could no longer be maintained as necessary in a democratic society. The Dutch Government's argument that this was tantamount to accepting that "crime pays" was rejected by pointing out that the editors could have been prosecuted for distributing State secrets: what was impermissible was to restrain such material at a point when it was no longer secret.[46] This approach is something of a cop-out: a technical way for the court to invalidate an act of censorship without deriding a Government which has behaved oppressively (the report obtained by *BLUF!* proved the Dutch secret service had targeted the anti-nuclear movement so there was a public interest justification for reproducing it). The Court always adopts a restrained approach in these politically delicate cases. A good example is Ireland's abortion obsessions, when clinics were banned from telling women about the availability of abortions in other countries. Instead of condemning the Irish judges for their bigotry, the Court decided that since the information could be found by opening a telephone book, the ban on clinics providing it was "disproportionate".[47] Where injunctions serve no religious or security purpose, the Court may venture to be more outspoken. When the Swiss courts, at the behest of the manufacturers of microwave ovens, misused an unfair competition law to stop a "nutty professor" from expounding his views about the dangers to human health from irradiated food, this violation was vigorously condemned as censorship of an opinion which was fully entitled to be heard in public debate.[48]

The rule against prior restraint, so comprehensively ignored by English courts during the *Spycatcher* debacle, was making a come-back, even before the arrival of s.12, at least in cases which do not concern royalty, national security or children. In refusing to stop the Advertising Standards Association from publishing an adjudication which was subject to judicial review, Mr Justice Laws spoke of freedom of expression as a "sinew" of the common law, with a "traditional" principle that "the courts will not prevent the publication of opinion or the dissemination of opinion save on pressing grounds".[49] In an important development of prisoners' rights, the Court of Appeal refused the Home Secretary an injunction to stop transmission of a television documentary which included an unapproved prison interview with serial killer Dennis Neilson. The Government's claim that this would distress his victims' relations cut no ice (they could always switch off) and there was a public interest in the programme, if only in showing why the remorseless Neilson should never be released. Although the way in which the

---

[46] *Vereniging Weekblad BLUF! v The Netherlands* (1995) 20 E.H.R.R. 189.
[47] *Open Door Counselling and Dublin Well Women Clinic v Ireland* (1993) 15 E.H.R.R. 244.
[48] *Hertel v Switzerland* (1998) 28 E.H.R.R. 534.
[49] *R. v Advertising Standards Authority Ltd Ex p. Vernons Organisation Ltd* [1992] 1 W.L.R. 1289 at 1293.

programme-makers had obtained the video of the interview was murky and probably unlawful, the Court declined to grant an injunction.[50] However, the Courts have been much more anxious about media impact on children, and the paternalistic judges in the family division often injunct programmes about juveniles, however great the public interest. The most extreme example, *Re Z*, (these cases are all reported under the acronym of "X" "Y" or "Z") related to an inspirational television programme about a child who overcame learning difficulties with the help of a revolutionary learning technique developed in Israel. The Court of Appeal stopped the programme from being broadcast until the girl turned 18, deciding for itself, contrary to the view of the girl's conscientious and caring mother, that publicity deriving from the fact that her estranged father was a prominent politician would not be in her best interests. Such is the paternalism built into the English common law (as into English common life) that courts may one day decide they have the power to stop Mrs Worthington from putting her daughter on the stage.

FREEDOM FROM GOVERNMENT INTERFERENCE

The fourth pillar of freedom of speech in Britain is the principle that **1–026** the Government has no direct control over the press. If ministers wish to stop a news story they must, like any other litigant, ask the court to grant an injunction. The Government does have advantages over other litigants, namely a bottomless purse to pay for litigation and a judiciary disposed to believe, at first blush, that its claims about danger to national security are true. This is a far cry from controlling the press, which has never been attempted in practice since the collapse of licensing at the close of the seventeenth century. The Government may exert pressure behind the scenes through the operation of the D-notice committee, but a D-notice has no legal force: it is merely "advice" to the media, drawn up by a joint committee of representatives of the press and the armed forces. It is not a crime to break a D-notice—many newspapers have done so without prosecution, and it is difficult to understand why they bother to collaborate with a system which relies on nudges and winks rather than legal rules.

In extreme circumstances the Government does acquire certain direct legal powers over radio and television. In the case of the BBC, these are contained in the Licence Agreement that forms part of the Corporation's charter. Clause 19 enables the Home Secretary, when in his opinion there is an emergency and it is "expedient" so to act, to send troops in to "take possession of the BBC in the name and on

---

[50] *Secretary of State for the Home Department v Central Broadcasting Ltd, The Times,* January 28, 1993.

behalf of Her Majesty". This clause was framed during the General Strike, when Winston Churchill and other members of the Government wanted to commandeer the Corporation. It has never been used for that purpose, although Sir Anthony Eden contemplated invoking it for government propaganda during the Suez crisis, and during the Falklands recapture it provided the legal basis for the Government's use of BBC transmitters on Ascension Island to beam propaganda broadcasts at Argentina.

A more dangerous power is contained in s.13(4) of the Licence Agreement, which gives the Home Secretary the right to prohibit the BBC from transmitting any item or programme, at any time. The power is not limited, like cl.19, to periods of emergency. The only safeguard against political censorship is that the BBC "may" (not "must") tell the public that it has received a s.13(4) order from the Home Secretary. This clause was invoked in 1972 by the Director-General, Lord Hill, when the Home Secretary Reginald Maudling threatened a s.13(4) order to stop transmission of a debate about Government actions in Ulster. Lord Hill called his bluff by threatening to make public the reason why the programme could not be shown. Of course, a less courageous Director-General could simply cancel the programme without revealing the existence of a Government order. A parallel power in s.10 of the 1990 Broadcasting Act entitles the Home Secretary to order the Independent Television Commission (ITC) to "refrain from broadcasting any matter or classes of matter" on commercial television. These powers were last invoked for the purpose of direct political censorship in 1988 when the BBC and the IBA (the predecessor of ITC) were ordered not to transmit any interviews with representatives of Sinn Fein, the Ulster Defence Association, the IRA or certain other extremist groups, or to broadcast any statement that incited support for such groups. The ban was a plain infringement on the right to receive and impart information: it prevented representatives of lawful political organisations (several Members of Parliament and dozens of local councillors) from stating their case on matters that had no connection with terrorism, and it denied to the public the opportunity to hear supporters of violent action being questioned and exposed (the Thatcher Government believed that terrorists survive by the "oxygen of publicity", but television confrontations generally demonstrate the moral unattractiveness of those who believe that the end justifies the means). The ban prohibited only the actual voices of IRA and UDA members and supporters, so broadcasters minimised its impact by the simple expedient of using actors with Irish accents whose voices were dubbed. In 1991 the House of Lords, in refusing to strike down the ban as "unreasonable", drew attention to its limited effect, which, in view of the dubbing option, they regarded more as an irritant than an infringement.[51]

---

[51] *R. v Secretary of State for Home Dept Ex p. Brind* [1991] 1 A.C. 696.

The 1988 broadcasting bans are the only examples of direct **1–027** political censorship. A more subtle form of political influence on the content of television programmes is provided by the Government's power of appointment to controlling bodies (the BBC trustees and Ofcom). All recent governments have appointed some BBC and ITC members for political reasons. The make-up of these bodies can be particularly important when governments exert pressure over a particular programme, as happened to the BBC in the case of BBC *Today* programme (which had broadcast an allegation that the government had "sexed up" an Iraqi dossier, and which became the focus of the Hutton inquiry into the suicide of David Kelly) and *Real Lives* (an examination of the IRA sympathiser in Belfast), and to the IBA in the case of *Death on the Rock* (a *This Week* programme about the SAS shooting of the three IRA members in Gibraltar). The *Real Lives* episode in 1985 severely damaged the BBC's reputation for independence when its Board of Governors cravenly banned the scheduled programme after Mrs Thatcher had condemned it, unseen, as likely to encourage support for terrorists. BBC journalists took strike action in protest, and the programme was eventually screened with a few face-saving deletions, but the episode called into question the Board of Governors' commitment to freedom of expression. The IBA was made of sterner stuff when the Foreign Secretary called for the banning of *Death on the Rock*. It supported Thames Television's decision to screen the programme, which gave viewers a much fuller appreciation of the shootings than had been possible from Government statements and Ministry of Defence briefings. An independent inquiry chaired by Lord Windlesham conclusively refuted the Government's allegations that the programme had been deliberately biased and had prejudiced the inquest in Gibraltar.[52] The importance of the programme was later demonstrated by the European Court ruling against the United Kingdom that the shootings of the suspects had violated their right to life.[53]

The *Hutton Inquiry*, 2003–4, was a government initiative which, as the government intended, did some damage to the BBC, many of whose journalists were believed to be slanting their reports unfavourably to the controversial decision to invade Iraq. Publication of the Hutton Report led to the resignation of the BBC Chairman and the Managing Director (Greg Dyke) and some loss of confidence in its news presentation. The Inquiry was into the death of Dr David Kelly, a government scientist who had been the source for the *Today* programme's allegation that Alastair Campbell had "sexed up" the dossier that was published about the danger of Iraq's supposed "weapons of mass destruction". Kelly's death was undoubtedly suicide, in a state of mind brought about in part by the

---

[52] *The Windlesham Rampton Report on Death on the Rock* (Faber, 1989).
[53] *McCann v United Kingdom* (1995) 21 E.H.R.R. 97.

unconscionable conduct of a BBC journalist in exposing him, albeit indirectly, as a source for the "sexing up" allegation. The Inquiry solemnly decided that there had been no "sexing up", although it has since become even more obvious that the dossier had been irresponsibly exaggerated in several respects—whether by the Iraqi source or by his MI6 handlers in an effort to give the government the propaganda boost that it wanted—although Hutton was curiously uninterested in examining this question. Instead, his inquiry became an inquisition into BBC news standards, conducted by a Law Lord with little experience of free speech issues or media law. His criticisms of the BBC were in some respects misplaced: the exercise would have been more credibly conducted by a judge with some background in media law, sitting with editors as assessors: it would then have been respected by the industry. The media, which has few effective means of examining its own ethics, cannot complain if the government does so, and indeed a House of Commons Select Committee has taken evidence from many editors and journalists in the course of its consideration of the need for a privacy law or a more proactive PCC. The *Hutton Inquiry* demonstrates that the government retains a power to intimidate the BBC by putting it on trial before an unsympathetic tribunal of inquiry: this does not amount to censorship, but can nonetheless have a chilling effect on the freedom to criticise the government.

The best antidote to censorship is publicity. Reporters and producers have a public duty to speak out if their vision of truth is suppressed by Government appointees. When the IBA banned a programme about RUC brutality, the producers protested by making a copy available to the BBC, which had no hesitation in showing it as part of a news feature about the IBA decision. Most censorship decisions appear faintly ridiculous in the light of day. None more than the BBC's heavy-handed interference with *Willie—the Legion Hall Bombing*, a play by Caryl Churchill. The prologue criticised Ulster non-jury courts in a manner that BBC executives found unacceptable. So they rewrote and re-recorded the text. In protest, both Ms Churchill and her director succeeded in having their names removed from the credits by threatening legal action. Then they held a press conference to release their original text, which most newspapers juxtaposed with the sanitised version prepared by the Corporation in major news stories on the day of transmission. This ensured the play—and its intended message—a very much wider audience than it would otherwise have obtained.

1–028   The theatre has been free from political censorship since 1967, when the Lord Chamberlain's power to license stage plays was abolished. The cinema, however, is subject to the British Board of Film and Video Classification (BBFC), a private body, which nonetheless exercises considerable influence over the way the law is enforced. It is financed by the film and video industries, and will grant certificates only to movies that it considers are within the limits of public acceptability. In practice, the Director of Public Prosecutions does not prosecute films with BBFC certificates for cinema showing, so distributors prepared to pay the certification fee and to carry out the "cuts" insisted upon by the Board are in effect guaranteed freedom from police harassment. This arrangement secures a quiet legal life for the film industry in general, although it is resented by some film makers who are obliged to tailor their product to BBFC standards in order to secure distribution outlets. The Video Recording Act gives the BBFC statutory recognition as the body charged with licensing films for sale or rent on video cassettes and DVDs. In relation to videos, the BBFC has become a fully-fledged State censorship board, charged by law with determining whether material on video is "suitable for viewing in the home" and with determining whether particular cassettes can be sold or hired to children. Its decisions are enforced by police and by trading standards officers, and heavy fines and even prison sentences can be imposed for non-compliance with its directives.

Many of the criminal laws that affect the media—official secrets and prevention of terrorism, and most of the laws relating to contempt, reporting restrictions and obscenity—cannot be invoked in the criminal courts by anyone except the Attorney General or the Director of Public Prosecutions (who works under the Attorney's superintendence). Likewise, the Attorney alone may enforce the ITC's statutory duties in cases where no individual can show that a breach will involve a personal injury. In all these cases the Attorney General is not *bound* to take legal action, even if the law has clearly been broken. He has a *discretion*—to prosecute or not to prosecute—depending on his view of the public interest. In exercising his discretion he is entitled to take into account any consideration of public policy that bears on the issue—and the public policy in favour of free speech is important in deciding whether to launch official secrets or contempt or obscenity prosecutions. Under the policy guidelines drawn up for the Crown Prosecution Service which is a "public body" bound by the Human Rights Act, all such decisions to prosecute must comply with Art.10.

The Attorney General, despite his political role and supporter of **1–029** an advisor to the government, is meant to wear an apolitical hat in his *parens patriae* role as guardian of the public interest in deciding whether to prosecute for, or to seek an injunction against, contempts of court by the media. He is the official charged with acting to prevent unfair trials, through publication of material prejudicial to a defendant or destructive of a prosecution. Since any court persuaded to grant him a pre-publication injunction would break the rule against prior restraints, it can do so only when the potential publication would pose "a substantial risk of serious prejudice" to the trial of someone who has already been arrested. The Attorney's power to bring such proceedings came under justifiable criticism in 2007 when he sought to restrain the BBC and then the *Guardian* from publishing details of a Downing Street memo which could, so the police claimed, prejudice their "cash for peerages" inquiry.

> A Scotland Yard squad had for a year been attempting to pin a charge on the Prime Minister's chief fundraiser Michael Levy over allegations that peerages were offered as a reward for large contributions to Labour Party coffers. The police had consistently leaked details of their inquiry to the press, which reported it avidly. The BBC got hold of an inter-office memo written by Ruth Turner, a Downing Street official, which urged that the Prime Minister be told that Levy was asking her to present a version of events that did not accord with her memory. The Att-Gen asked the court for an injunction. Levy had been arrested for questioning some weeks previously, so the jurisdiction to grant the injunction technically existed, but publication of the document would obviously not pose a substantial (or any) risk of prejudicing seriously (or at all) a criminal trial which might never eventuate and which if it did—several years hence—would not meaningfully damage Levy, who would then have the opportunity to cross-examine Turner. Yet the judge—Wilkie J.—wrongly granted an injunction against the BBC for reasons he did not explain by the time the *Guardian*, two days later, got hold of another aspect of the same story and came before another judge—Swift J.—with a better understanding of the law of contempt. She refused the Att-Gen's claim for an injunction, which was made at night after the delivery vans had already left with the first edition of the newspaper (the government's lawyer suggested that they should be recalled by telephoning the mobiles of the drivers—a foolish suggestion, since the government had made it a crime for drivers to answer their mobile phones). Since the *Guardian* was allowed to publish its story, the BBC succeeded a few days later in having its injunction lifted and, a few days after that, the Court of Appeal[54] lifted the ban on publishing Wilkie J.'s judgment.

It is said that prior restraint for contempt is not a case of government interference because the Attorney General, although a member of the government, does not act as such when he brings the action. This pretence is difficult for the public to swallow, especially in a case as politically charged as the "cash for peerages" inquiry. The reality is that when the police came to him demanding a gag on the BBC, Lord Goldsmith had no alternative but to take the action: although he would be damned if he did (by media critics and eventually by the courts) he would be more damned if he did not because he would be accused of acting for party political reasons in refusing to assist a police investigation into his own party. An independent, non-political Attorney General would have shown these bumbling policemen the door—it should have been obvious that publication of the Turner letter would not run any risk of seriously damaging any trial.

There have been cases where the Attorney General has refused to act even after judges have called for prosecution. Sometimes his

---

[54] *Att-Gen v BBC* March 12, 2007, CA.

decisions are made on grounds of convenience: after most news-papers in Britain committed contempt of court over the arrest of "Yorkshire Ripper" Peter Sutcliffe, the Attorney General decided against prosecuting on the ground that he would have to put dozens of editors in the dock.[55] On other occasions the public interest of an "illegal" revelation has tipped the balance against invoking legal discipline against the journalist who revealed it. For example, it is usually contempt to publish a story that causes the discharge of a jury mid-trial. This consequence was caused by London Weekend Television when commentator Christopher Hitchens revealed that a juror in an official secrets case was a former member of the SAS, and by the *Guardian* when it published details of information discovered by police when they "vetted" a jury that was trying some anarchists.[56] In both cases the trial judges complained to the Attorney General, who decided that prosecution would not be in the public interest. No doubt the decision was heavily influenced by the fact that both stories were correct and had revealed controversial practices in the administration of justice.

There is a danger in placing over-much reliance on the Attorney General's discretion. He is, after all, a member of the Government, as well as the leader of the legal profession. In deciding "public policy", he will obviously be influenced by the outlook of the political party of which he is a member and by the values of the profession that he leads. These influences will not always incline him to the view that revelation of particular legal or political material is necessarily in the public interest. There is another danger. The decision to publish often hinges on the question: "Will the Attorney prosecute if we do?" There is a natural temptation to seek an answer from the horse's mouth, so to speak, by submitting the controversial material to the Attorney General for an indication of his attitude. This has been done by the BBC (which is notoriously craven in legal matters) and by several newspapers. It comes perilously close to making the Attorney General, in effect, a political censor, an official to whom the media can go, cap in hand, with the question "Please sir, may we publish this?" The danger, of course, is that if his answer is "no", the material will then not be published. This would be a pity if the Attorney General were bluffing, and the prospect of scaring off awkward media revelations will always provide a great temptation for attorneys-general to bluff.

Trial by jury, the openness of courts, the rule against prior restraint and the absence of laws permitting direct government interference have ensured that the British media enjoy a relative freedom from censorship, by comparison with many other countries. But the fact that media freedom was, until October 2000 when the Human Rights Act came into force, protected by unwritten convention rather than by a bill of rights meant that there was no external

---

[55] *Press Conduct in the Sutcliffe Case*, Press Council Booklet No.7 (1983), pp.50–2.
[56] David Leigh, *The Frontiers of Secrecy*, (Junction Books, 1980), Ch.4.

brake upon Parliament or the courts moving to restrict it in particular ways, as the mood of times or the exigencies of the cold war or the scale of IRA activities might permit. Britain was famously a country where "everything is permitted, which is not specifically prohibited", but the specific prohibitions became more numerous, without having to justify themselves against the overriding principle of public interest required by Art.10. Strasbourg court decisions became of increasing importance in the two decades following the *Sunday Times v United Kingdom* thalidomide case in 1979 and judges sometimes pronounced their satisfaction that the media law of England was compatible with Art.10 of the Convention, but in this they were frequently mistaken—as European Court decisions were prone to point out. The Human Rights Act deserves separate treatment: Art.10 has been a necessary step towards a constitutional right to freedom of expression, although there are signs that Art.8 (privacy) and Art.6 (fair trial) are being permitted to dilute some of the United Kingdom's open justice traditions described in this chapter.

CHAPTER 2

THE HUMAN RIGHTS ACT

THE INTERNATIONAL HUMAN RIGHTS MOVEMENT

Safeguards for free speech offered by common law were inadequate **2–001**
to protect public-interest journalism from attack for discomfiting the
government or the judiciary or wealthy private litigants. It lacked any
organising principle, of the kind which had come to shield the
American media through the First Amendment. This gap was
eventually filled by a free speech formulation taken from human
rights treaties to which English writers and lawyers had made a
significant contribution.

The law of international human rights did not take any meaningful
shape until the Nuremberg trial after the Second World War.
Previously, it had been assumed that international law could only
affect states and not individuals, and since it did not permit
intervention in the *internal* affairs of states, governments could gag
and oppress their citizens as they pleased. In Britain, the government
became more relaxed about the press as the nineteenth century
progressed and the danger of republican revolution passed. But in
the colonies—the far-flung British Empire—there remained an
imperial perception that laws were needed to prevent the natives
becoming restless. This was bluntly admitted in 1899 by the English
Law Lords who sat, as the court of final appeal for the colonies, in
the judicial committee of the Privy Council. Oppressive press laws
like "scandalising the court" served imperialistic (indeed, racist)
purposes:

> "Committals for contempt of court by scandalising the court
> itself have become obsolete in this country. Courts are satisfied
> to leave to public opinion attacks or comments derogatory or
> scandalous to them. But it must be considered that in small
> colonies, consisting principally of coloured populations, the
> enforcement in proper cases of committal for contempt of court
> for attacks on the court may be absolutely necessary to preserve
> in such a community the dignity and respect for the court."[1]

---

[1] *McLeod v St Aubyn* [1889] A.C. 549 at 561.

The imperial ambitions of major powers like Britain and France, and what seemed to be an endemic racism in America (manifested in its "Jim Crow" laws) stifled any political support for international human rights between the wars: the subject was never mentioned at the League of Nations and was never seriously advanced by any major thinker or statesman of the period.[2] Its revival began at the instigation and inspiration of British writer H.G. Wells, who led a campaign urging the adoption by "Parliamentary peoples" of a Declaration of Rights, which he prepared with the help of Viscount Sankey, a former Labour Lord Chancellor, and writers like J.B. Priestly and A.A. Milne (who would motor up from Pooh corner to help with the draft). In 1940 Penguin books published *H.G. Wells on the Rights of Man*. It was translated into 30 languages and syndicated in newspapers throughout the world, and inspired US President Franklin D. Roosevelt to make his "four freedoms" speech in 1941: an appeal for a post-war world based on four elemental freedoms, the first of which was freedom of speech. In the work of H.G. Wells and his colleagues we can locate the seeds of Art.19 of the Universal Declaration and Art.10 of the European Convention. In a modest English way he eschewed the messianic preambles of the revolutionary French and American declarations and declared that "man" (including woman) was entitled to:

> ". . . easy access to information upon all matters of common knowledge throughout his life, in the course of which he would enjoy the utmost freedom of discussion . . . A man is subject to the free criticism of his fellows, although he shall have adequate protection from any lying or misrepresentation that may injure him. All administrative records about a man shall be open to his personal and private inspection. There shall be no secret dossiers in any administrative department. All dossiers shall be accessible to the man concerned and subject to verification and correction".[3]

2–002   Here, for the first time since the eighteenth century revolutions, was an attempt by English writers to re-invent the human rights idea, in a homely and literate way. Their spirit—the spirit in which judges should now apply Art.10 and the Freedom of Information Act—is tolerant and fundamentally anti-bureaucratic. Government must have no secrets from its citizens, and courts must never restrain matters appropriate for discussion. There must be privacy for family homes, but no 30–year rules, covering up advice to Ministers, no secret dossiers except for ongoing police investigations. The vision which is central to the *right* to receive and to impart information is

---

[2] See G. Robertson, *Crimes Against Humanity—the Struggle for Global Justice*, 3rd edn, (Penguin, 2006), Ch.1.
[3] *H.G. Wells on the Rights of Man* (Penguin, 1940).

that we will get along better if access is easy and unrestricted, and that any attempt by government or by powerful groups to restrain that access must be viewed with the greatest suspicion.

This was the modern intellectual authority for Art.19 of the Universal Declaration of Human Rights, adopted by the UN in 1948. By this time, there was no doubt about the fundamental importance of free speech: Nazi ideology had gone without serious challenge in Germany in the 1930s because of Hitler's book burnings, and the Gestapo's arrests of opponents and their publishers. So Art.19 of the Universal Declaration provided that:

> "Everyone has the right to freedom of opinion and expression; this right includes freedom to hold opinions without interference and to seek, receive and impart information and ideas through any media and regardless of frontiers."

Article 19 is not absolute: Art.12 gives everyone the right to legal protection against "arbitrary interference with privacy" and against "attacks upon his honour and reputation", and reconciliation of the two Articles pivots upon the Art.29(2) rule that any freedom may be limited by laws if they are passed solely for the purposes of securing respect for the rights of others according to the just requirements of "the general welfare in a democratic society". (H.G. Wells had put it more pithily: "citizens should have adequate protection from lying, or misrepresentation which injures").

The Soviet Union and its puppets abstained from the vote in favour of the Universal Declaration in 1948, and the Berlin airlift and the millions confined in Stalin's gulag emphasised how much of a threat communism might become to the advancement of human rights. One response made by the nations of Western Europe was to draw up a European Convention on Human Rights, as a regional equivalent of the Universal Declaration, to provide a roll call of those rights under threat in the East. It borrowed almost word for word from Art.19 to construct Art.10(1):

> "Everyone has the right to freedom of expression. This right shall include freedom to hold opinions and to receive and impart information and ideas without interference by public authority and regardless of frontiers."

Instead of leaving exceptions to a vague sweeping-up provision at the end, the Convention sets them out in Art.10(2): **2–003**

> "The exercise of these freedoms, since it carries with it duties and responsibilities, may be subject to such formalities, conditions, restrictions or penalties as are prescribed by law and are necessary in a democratic society, in the interests of national security, territorial integrity or public safety, for the prevention

of disorder or crime, for the protection of health or morals, for the protection of the reputation or the rights of others, for preventing the disclosure of information received in confidence, or for maintaining the authority and impartiality of the judiciary".

The European Convention on Human Rights has now been ratified by all Member States of the Council of Europe. It was produced to establish a legal (alongside a military) bulwark against both the resurgence of fascism and the encroachment of communism—the latter prospect, when drafting began in 1949, serving as a special spur to entrench free speech and privacy rights of the very kind that Stalin was extinguishing in the east. The draftsman of the final text was a retired lawyer from the Home Office. Britain was the first country to ratify the Convention, which came into force in 1953—although for the next 20 years hardly anyone noticed. This was because it was not until 1966 that Britain permitted its individuals to petition the Court in Strasbourg: until then, the only complainants could be states, and they rarely took each other to court. The first successful individual complaint against the United Kingdom was not until 1975: it was brought by a prisoner whose correspondence was routinely read and censored by the prison governor.[4] In 1979 the European Court found the United Kingdom guilty of the first Art.10 violation of the rights of the media, committed by the House of Lords decision that *The Sunday Times* could not publish an account of the thalidomide tragedy, lest it affect civil damages claims which had long been stalled in the courts.[5] Thereafter, rulings against Britain were frequently delivered, although they had no direct impact on domestic law because the Convention was only a treaty, signed by Government, which could not become "law" unless and until its provisions were adopted by Parliament. This was finally done by the Human Rights Act 1998, which came into force on October 2, 2000.

From that date onwards, the Convention has operated as part of the United Kingdom's domestic law, introduced by a statute (the Human Rights Act 1998) which by s.12 gives Art.10 especial prominence. So Art.10 is now a constitutional right to the extent that freedom of expression can be asserted in all courts against all public authorities (although it cannot prevail over the clear words of a statute, which can only be changed by Parliament). No constitutional right can have meaning without some sense of the historical anvil on which it was forged. Article 10 may have entered UK law with the deceptive slogan of a "right brought home"; the plain historical truth is that free speech as a right never has had a home in Britain. It must be recognised as Tom Paine's right, for which dozens of his

---

[4] *Golder v UK* (1975) 1 E.H.R.R. 524.
[5] *Sunday Times v UK* (1979) 2 E.H.R.R. 245.

booksellers and his fellow free-thinkers, Williams and Carlisle and Bradlaugh, fought and were sentenced to hard labour by brutal judges, in prisons pervaded by filth and disease. It will be the sincerest tribute our courts can pay their memory if the common law under which they were persecuted—criminal libel, blasphemy and sedition—are declared incompatible with the new right to freedom of expression. A faltering first step in this direction was taken by the House of Lords in *Rusbridger and Toynbee v Att-Gen* where *Guardian* editor Alan Rusbridger and journalist Polly Toynbee invited the court to declare the 1848 Treason Felony Act which made the advocacy of republicanism a crime, and had been passed in that year of revolutions in order to have radical Irish newspaper editors transported to Botany Bay, incompatible with the Convention. It had not been deployed for over a century and the law lords made clear that its use against advocates of non-violent change was inconceivable today: it could not possibly survive Art.10 challenge. Having thus given the *Guardian* the result it wanted, the court somewhat illogically deterred applicants in respect of other obnoxious laws: the *Guardian* had not been at risk from the Attorney General's coy refusal to confirm that he would not prosecute, and it was not the court's job to keep the statute book up to date.[6] In future, editors will have to wait until they are actually threatened with prosecution for criminal or seditious or blasphemous libel before they can obtain a declaration that such laws are now incompatible with Art.10.

The advent of Art.10 in British law by way of the Human Rights **2–004** Act 1998 has not been an unmixed blessing. The importation of its jurisprudence has certainly created a presumption in favour of free speech and has encouraged judges to develop a public interest defence to defamation, for example, and to limit Art.10(2) exceptions like national security interests to situations where they can be proved to have overriding importance. But problems have arisen where other guaranteed rights—notably to Fair Trial (Art.6), Privacy (Art.8) and Respect for Religion (Art.9)—clash with the claims of journalists and artists to explain court proceedings, probe the private lives of public figures or treat sacred objects in ways that adherents consider blasphemous. The courts in Strasbourg, as well as in Britain, are in such situations adopting "balancing acts" between competing values and the balance sometimes does not come down acceptably in favour of media freedom. The correct approach must always be to strip the competing right to its core—in privacy cases, for example, to focus on the right to protect intimate personal details and the integrity of home and family against unauthorised direct invasion—and to ask whether it is engaged by a potential publication before embarking upon any balancing exercise that might interfere with media freedom. This is akin to the approach

---

[6] *Rusbridger v Att-Gen* [2003] UKHL 38.

adopted in *Re S*, where the House of Lords rejected a young child's claim that his privacy required that his mother, on trial for murder, should have her name suppressed in order to prevent his own identification.[7] Such bold claims are easy to reject: less so the issue of whether the media could authoritatively expose Naomi Campbell's lies that she did not take drugs by publishing photographs of her leaving a meeting of Narcotics Anonymous. On this issue the Law Lords divided 3:2 against the press (and the swing vote lost the *Daily Mirror* a fortune in legal costs). The European Convention, therefore, does not necessarily shine sunlight on "grey areas" of media law: Art.8, in particular, is bringing dark thunder clouds into what were, hitherto, common law patches of blue skies.

ARTICLE 10: THE CORE PRINCIPLES

2–005 The European Court of Human Rights has delivered many judgments declaring national laws or court decisions to be infringements of Art.10. Over the years it has crystallised its freedom of expression case law into a number of basic principles, the first formulated in a 1976 complaint from Great Britain over the suppression of *The Little Red Schoolbook* on the pretext of obscenity. The book gave robust advice to teenagers about sex and suggested that they might consider going on strike against poor teaching: a London judge ordered copies to be destroyed because it was "subversive of authority". This decision appears even more ridiculous today than it did at the time, and although the Eurocourt wrongly declined to uphold the complaint by Richard Handyside (the book's publisher), at least it articulated the first core principle of Art.10:

> **1. Freedom of expression constitutes one of the essential foundations of a democratic society and one of the basic conditions for its progress and for each individual's self-fulfilment. It is applicable not only to "information" or "ideas" that are favourably received or regarded as inoffensive or as a matter of indifference, but also to those that offend, shock or disturb. Such are the demands of pluralism, tolerance and broad-mindedness without which there is no "democratic society".[8]**

This principle echoes Voltaire: we may not like what you say, but liberal society defends to its death your right to say it. This embodies an assumption that free speech is necessary to the personality of the citizen, to the continuing health of democracy and to social progress:

---

[7] In *Re S* (a child identification: restrictions on publication) [2004] UKHL 47.
[8] *Handyside v UK* (1976) E.H.R.R. 737 at 48–49. For a recent formulation of the core principles see *Bladet Tromso v Norway* (1999) 29 E.H.R.R. 125.

these are the important goals which demand tolerance from governments.

The sentiments behind Art.10(1) are nonetheless subject to the many exceptions contained in Art.10(2), which avowedly protects:

(a) the public interest (national security, territorial integrity, public safety, prevention of disorder or crime, protection of health and morals);

(b) competing individual rights (such as a citizen's right to reputation and to keep private information confidential);

(c) the authority and impartiality of judges.

When do these exceptions override freedom of speech? Only **2–006** when they can rebut the presumption Art.10(1) erects in its favour:

2. This freedom is subject to exceptions, however these must be strictly construed and the need for any restrictions must be established convincingly.[9]

The first core principle would be meaningless if exceptions as broad as those in Art.10(2) could automatically defeat it. For that reason core principle 2 is all-important: the State defending the restriction bears the burden of proving its necessity in democratic society, i.e. not only that an Art.10(2) ground convincingly exists, but that it generates a "pressing social need" for the restriction in question. Article 10 should not be seen as requiring an equal "balance" between, on the one hand, the value of freedom of expression and on the other, the value of national security, crime prevention, etc. It does not decide a competition between free speech and the values listed in Art.10(2); the latter are simply "a number of exceptions which must be strictly interpreted".[10] There is an important, and unresolved, question of whether "the rights of others"—an Art.10(2) exception—can be treated in this way when the "right" derives from another free standing Convention Article, such as Fair Trial (Art.6), Privacy (Art.8) or Respect for Religious Belief (Art.9). Since free speech is fundamental to democracy, the approach of principle 2 should be adopted whenever the case essentially concerns the media's "watchdog" function, or an artist or writer's exploration of ideas. However, British judges love "balancing acts" (because the balance can always be brought down on the side they prefer) and they tend to adopt balancing exercises in many cases where they should apply a presumption in favour of free speech unless its override by an Art.10(2) exception is imperative.

3. Any infringement of free speech must be "prescribed by law". That means that the restriction must be clear, certain and

---

[9] *Observer and Guardian v UK* (1992) 14 E.H.R.R. 153 at 55 (The *"Spycatcher"* case).

[10] *Sunday Times v UK* (1979) 2 E.H.R.R. 245 at 271.

predictable. Law, to be "prescribed", must be adequately accessible and formulated with sufficient precision to enable citizens to regulate their conduct.

A judge who exercised some common-law power in an entirely novel way would be in breach of the Convention, even if he claimed to act "in the interests" of one of the excepted values. It has to be said, however, that the Court has been loathe to apply this rule, even in such obvious cases as the vague UK law of blasphemy. However, in a decision which will have important consequences for dragnet English crimes penalising conduct deemed contrary to public morals, the Court declared that the free-speech rights of fox-hunt protesters were wrongly infringed when they were bound over to keep the peace by not in future behaving *"contra bonos mores"*—a Latin phrase translated as "engaging in conduct which is wrong rather than right in the judgment of the majority of fellow citizens". This was insufficiently precise to amount to a legal rule at all: it did not define or describe the proscribed conduct, but merely referred to majority opinion which might characterise it as "wrong".[11] Thanks to Art.10 the will of the people is not, as such, the supreme law, or any law at all. A particular restriction will fail the test if it is not referable to any identifiable law: a patient detained in an Austrian psychiatric hospital whose request for access to radio and television was rejected out of hand succeeded at Strasbourg because the State had passed no law permitting or imposing such restrictions.[12] Although a proviso to Art.10 permits States to licence television and radio stations, they must do so by enacting a law which prescribes reasonable guidelines for applications. The Privy Council used European Court authorities on core principle 3 to invalidate the radio licensing system in Antigua, which gave unfettered discretion to the Government which it had used to grant licences only to the Prime Minister's family.[13]

4. Any infringement must be "necessary in a democratic society", and "necessary", although not synonymous with "indispensable", means more than "useful", "reasonable" or "desirable". It implies the existence of a "pressing social need".

2–007   This is the rule upon which most Art.10 cases eventually turn. Social needs found "pressing" usually relate to ensuring fair trial or defeat of terrorism or protecting the public from racial violence, but

---

[11] *Hashman and Harrup v UK* (2000) 30 E.H.R.R. 241 at 31–39. See also *Silver v UK* (1983) 5 E.H.R.R. 347 which emphasises that Government circulars purporting to restrict free speech cannot be "law" unless authorised by or under statute, or common law or European Union legislation.

[12] *Herczegfalvy v Austria* (1993) 15 E.H.R.R. 437; *Silver v UK* (1983) 5 E.H.R.R. 347.

[13] *Observer Publications Ltd v Matthews and Att-Gen of Antigua* (2001) 10 B.H.R.C. 252.

even these important needs are not overriding: they must be urgent, and the restriction must rationally serve to advance them. The *Spycatcher* decision, for example, rejected the UK Government's argument that it was "necessary" to punish MI5 turncoat Peter Wright by banning his book in Britain: given its massive sales throughout the world the ban was ineffective and "a futile measure cannot be a necessary one". This is an important ruling for cases where confidential information gets posted on the internet: the law cannot be asked to put genies back into bottles.

> **5. Even when the social need is pressing, the particular infringement, looking at the context and content of the banned communication, must be "proportionate to the legitimate aims pursued" and the Government bears the burden of passing the proportionality test by adducing sufficient reasons for the interference. In assessing whether the restriction is proportionate, the court will take into account such factors as the fairness of the proceedings, the procedural guarantees afforded, and the nature and severity of the penalties imposed.**[14]

The "proportionality test" is important, and novel in English law. It means that even when media restrictions have been imposed by a Government acting in good faith, in pursuance of a legitimate aim to advance a value contained in an Art.10(2) exception, the European Court will strike it down if, in all the circumstances of the case, the restriction was ineffectual to advance the aim, or irrelevant to it, or insufficiently justified (such as the ban on *Spycatcher* in the United Kingdom, which could not rationally support the interests of national security once the book was published elsewhere). The Convention cannot be used to complain of laws in the abstract, however Draconian their effect. There must be a "victim" who has suffered a real "violation" (see Art.34): if the law in question has a legitimate aim and responds to a pressing social need, a particular application or aspect of it may nonetheless be so disproportionate as to breach the convention. Thus in *Tolstoy v United Kingdom* the Court held that although the law of civil libel might in general terms respond to a social need to protect reputation from untruths, the lack at that time of proper judicial control over damages (leading, in that case, to a £1.5 million award) lacked all proportion and constituted a breach of the Convention. Similarly, in the *Mclibel* case, the damages of £60,000 were disproportionate because the penniless defendants had not been given legal aid and because an oddity of British libel law—the presumption of damage—meant that McDonald's did not have to prove that it had suffered any loss.[15] In

---

[14] See for a recent statement *Kwiecien v Poland* (Application Number 51744/99) Judgment January 9, 2007, court presided over by Sir Nicolas Bratza.
[15] *Steele & Morris v UK* (2005) Application Number 68416/01, para.95.

essence, the proportionality test requires the court to satisfy itself that the measures designed to meet the legislative object are rationally connected to it and that the means used to interfere with free speech were no more than is necessary to accomplish that objective.[16] On this basis the courts can strike down excessive damages in defamation and insure that journalists are not sent to prison for over-exuberant reporting.

6. It follows from principle 1 that the news media plays an essential watchdog role in a democratic society, and (subject to rights of confidence and reputation) it has a duty to impart information and ideas on matters of public interest. From this duty it follows that:

(a) **reporters have a correlative right to protect sources of information;**

(b) **since news is a perishable commodity and its publication urgent**

  (i) **there must be latitude allowed to journalists in their method of presentation—for error or exaggeration or even provocation**

  (ii) **even a short enforced delay in news dissemination engages Article 10 protection;**

(c) **the scope for criticism of politicians and power-wielders and persons whose conduct is of public importance is wider than that for private individuals: the need for open discussion of politics may prevail over the protection of reputation, because politicians unlike private individuals knowingly lay themselves open to close scrutiny of their words and deeds.**

Under this principle the Court has begun to develop a jurisprudence tailored to the particular needs of the news media. The right to protect sources, established by the *Goodwin* case, is the most notable example, but there are others which show how the Court is becoming educated in the way that the press actually has to function in order to get the news out. Its most important contribution has been the concept of news*worthiness*: that the public is entitled to receive information of topical interest as soon as practicable, notwithstanding inevitable errors or exaggerations, so long as these are corrected in due course. This approach has assisted the development by the Law Lords, in *Reynolds v Times Newspapers* and *Jameel v Wall Street Journal*, of the concept of journalistic responsibility as a standard for defending defamation actions.

In recent cases, particularly those decided by chambers presided over by the respected English judge Sir Nicolas Bratza, the court has

---

[16] See the decision of the Privy Council in *De Freitas v Permanent Secretary of Ministry of Agriculture* [1999] 1 A.C. 69 at 80, glossed in *Huang v Secretary of State for the Home Department* [2007] UKHL 11 at [19] with a reminder that the Courts must take account of the need to balance the interests of society with those of the individuals and groups.

deployed the news*worthiness* test to strike down penalties imposed on newspapers and journalists in European countries, especially resulting from Napoleonic criminal libel laws prohibiting "insult" to public officials. It has been particularly astute to protect comment and opinion, however provocative, refusing to accept for example that describing a Russian General as behaving "shamelessly and unscrupulously" could give rise to a penalty:

> "The requirement to prove the truth of a value judgement is impossible to fulfil and infringes freedom of opinion itself, which is a fundamental part of the rights secured by Article 10."[17]

Similarly in 2006 it struck down a penalty on a Moldavian journalist who had mocked a traffic policeman, describing him as behaving "like a madman". The government had argued that a policeman was a public servant and thus enjoyed a higher level of protection from undue criticism and scrutiny but the court said that on the contrary this fact made him a subject of closer scrutiny and his power over civilians meant that the watchdog role of the press was more important. It was significant that the criticism was expressed in moderate language and in good faith. Although the court did not have the gumption to say in terms that Napoleonic "insult" laws that put public servants on pedestals were now obsolete, or that criminal penalties against the media for defamation are always wrong, the case does show how the court seeks to deter the use of those penalties in relation to moderate attacks on wielders of state power.[18] Even when the newspaper is punished only by having to make a contribution to a local charity and paying court costs and issuing a retraction, the court will find such penalties disproportionate when imposed in relation to accusations about local political corruption, especially if this takes the form of satirical comment on local politicians.[19]

The court has been willing to take into account human rights **2–008** criticisms of certain states to show that press freedom is under pressure because of government interference. In *Ukrainian Media Group v Ukraine*[20] the court noted Amnesty and Human Rights Watch reports to this effect as a background for condemning the state over a newspaper's conviction for defamation for describing an important politician as "a scarecrow" and a "loudspeaker of the president". It noted that there were over 6,000 cases against

---

[17] *Grinberg v Russia*, Application Number 23472/03, decision October 21, 2005, para.30.
[18] *Savitchi v Moldova* (Application number 11039/02) final judgment January 11, 2006, chambers presided over by Sir Nicolas Bratza.
[19] *Sokolowski v Poland* (Application number 75955/01) final judgment June 29, 2005, Sir Nicolas Bratza.
[20] Application number 72713/01, final judgment October 12, 2005.

Ukrainian newspapers currently pending to "protect the honour" of public figures and that in the previous year over 1,000 such cases had been successful, thus making the state one in which press freedom was frozen. "The court observes that the publications contained criticism of the two politicians in strong, polemical, sarcastic language. No doubt the plaintiffs were offended thereby and may even have been shocked. However, in choosing their profession, they laid themselves open to robust criticism and scrutiny; such is the burden which must be accepted by politicians in a democratic society."[21]

The European Court under these principles has been astute to protect serious or quality journalism. Even when a Swedish newspaper published allegations it could not verify, accusing an individual of responsibility for murdering the prime minister, the Euro court confirmed that the public interest of the story was such that it was exculpated from defamation. The journalists had acted in good faith and in accordance with the ethics of journalism and in this case they could reasonably regard their sources as reliable. They had made sufficient professional efforts to authenticate their story.[22] This case, in 2006, parallels the approach of the House of Lords in the same year to a public interest defence to defamation: *Jameel v Wall Street Journal* afforded protection for serious investigative journalism. Interestingly, the European Court seems to be advancing a little further than British judges in its preparedness to excuse exaggeration and exuberance in the popular press. In 2006 a Chamber presided over by Judge Bratza struck down an Austrian court decision that a tabloid was guilty of defaming the mistress of a crooked politician, by describing the couple as "Bonnie & Clyde" when they ran off to Brazil.[23] The humourless Austrian judges had overlooked the fact that the article was entertaining and the mistress had undoubtedly assisted the politician to escape. They had also condemned the newspaper for publishing a photograph of the mistress, on the basis that this was "not of any informative value". The Euro court pointed out that the coverage had been entertaining and ironic—the first time that entertainment value has been judicially recognised as a public good. In the same year Judge Bratza's chambers struck down the conviction of a Polish journalist who had attacked the "turtle speed" of the judiciary in relation to a case involving a local mayor. The latter sued and the journalist was convicted of defamation and ordered to pay money to a charity and court costs. The court pointed out that although the penalty was relatively light the finding meant that the applicant had a criminal record and had been put on probation:

"His conviction amounted to a kind of censorship which was likely to discourage him from making criticisms of that kind in

---

[21] 72713/01, para.67.

[22] *White v Sweden*, September 19, 2006.

[23] *Wirtschafts-Trend (Number 3) v Austria* (Application number 66298/01) judgment March 13, 2006.

future. It was liable to hamper the press in the performance of its task of purveyor of information and public watchdog."[24]

Tabloid-style polemical attacks on individuals, at least where there is some basis for them, will be upheld: to describe a homophobic judge as conducting a court "in the tradition of medieval witch trials" and as delivering judgements full of "venomous hate" should not have resulted in convictions for a newspaper and journalist: they were "public watchdogs" and although their bark was shrill it was not without cause.[25]

7. Free elections and freedom of expression, particularly freedom of political debate, together form the bedrock of any democratic system. The two rights are inter-related and operate to reinforce each other. For this reason, it is particularly important in the period preceeding an election that opinions and information of all kinds are permitted to circulate freely. This principle applies equally to national and local elections.

This principle was notably applied by the court in *Bowman v UK* to condemn a section of the Representation of the People Act which had unnecessarily limited the amount that pressure groups could expend on supporting candidates at elections. It was applied by a Bratza court in 2007 in favour of a citizen who, during a local election in Poland, was ordered to apologise to a candidate and pay damages after being found guilty of a defamatory attack on the candidate's record. Legal provisions that enable expeditious examination of election-related disputes could not be used to curb free speech at election time, a period when it was particularly important that opinions of all kinds should circulate freely.[26] This decision has importance for UK election law, which provides fast-track injunctions against libels without satisfactory protection for defendants.

8. States enjoy a certain margin of appreciation in assessing the need for an interference with freedom of expression, but the extent of the margin will be strictly supervised by the Court which must decide whether the State has discharged the burden of proving the necessity principle (3 above). The national "margin of appreciation" is circumscribed by the interest of democratic society in ensuring and maintaining a free press.[27]

This principle only applies to decisions of the European Court of **2–009** Human Rights, and has no relevance to national courts which are tasked with applying the Convention. The "margin of appreciation"

---

[24] *Dabrowski v Poland* (Application number 18235/02) December 19, 2006.
[25] *Kobenter v Austria* (Application number 60899/00) judgment February 2, 2007.
[26] *Kwieschien v Poland* (Application number 51744/99) judgment January 9, 2007.
[27] *Worm v Austria* (1997) 25 E.H.R.R. 454.

is the latitude which an international court allows to nation states to bend human rights rules in the supposed interests of its own cultural values and traditions. Decisions that turn on the "margin of appreciation" are to that extent cop-outs, and the Strasbourg court has been particularly prone to cop-out on questions of morality. A pronounced Catholic bias in the appointed judges has led to several poorly reasoned rulings that censorship of anti-Catholic plays and films are within State margins, although it is pleasing to note that in 2006 the Euro court condemned the French courts for treating as defamatory an attack on the Catholic church over the support it gave to Nazis during the occupation. The French government defended this indefensible decision on the basis that the article offended its large Catholic community, but the court on this occasion refused to take the "margin of appreciation" way out: when it came to discussing the causes of crimes against humanity "restrictions on freedom of expression were to be strictly construed".[28] *Handyside* itself is an example of using the "margin of appreciation" doctrine to avoid a principled but potentially unpopular decision to condemn the ban on *The Little Red Schoolbook*, and the Court has similarly fudged decisions on blasphemy laws in Austria and in the United Kingdom by holding that they are within these States' "margin of appreciation". The important point to remember, however, is that these decisions do not mean that the blasphemy law is consistent with the Convention, but merely that any inconsistency is tolerable at an international level. The British courts, newly empowered by the Human Rights Act, could and should declare the law to be incompatible with Convention rights.

Confusingly, at an early stage of convention interpretation, UK judges appropriated the concept of the "margin of appreciation" when declining to strike down decisions of administrators entitled to some respect. This deference to officials is now more fashionably termed "latitude"—giving public authorities a "discretionary area of judgement" so they can make policy choices without undue interference from the courts. More recently, judges talk vaguely of subjecting such decisions to "more (or less) intensity of scrutiny" with freedom of expression decisions requiring scrutiny that is particularly "intense", albeit not so intense that the court can substitute its own decision on the merits. It is difficult not to see such linguistic wriggling as an attempt to avoid the application of Convention standards to officials and establishment bodies that are

---

[28] *Giniewski v France* (Application number 64016/00). Judgement April 31, 2006. See also *Clein v Slovakia* (Application number 72208/01) January 31, 2007, where a Bratza court struck down a finding of libel against a film critic who had condemned a Catholic bishop for his call to ban *The People v Larry Flint*. Although 70 per cent of the country was Catholic and the attack had come at Easter, the bishop had put himself forward as a censor and could not complain about being satirised.

presumed to be in touch with popular feeling although in reality are just in awe of government policy. The notion of "intensive review" may be little more than a judicial narrowing of eyes and a longer attention span in a particular case: it means that regulators will not themselves be regulated by the courts when they make censorship decisions. The House of Lords permitted the BBC to ban a "ProLife party" political election broadcast because it was entitled to some latitude in deciding what was offensive; the Court of Appeal approach, which had struck the ban down as an affront to free speech at election time, is to be preferred as a full-blooded assertion of a fundamental right.[29]

APPLYING THE CORE PRINCIPLES

Public Figures

The core principles of Art.10 have been supplemented by consistent **2–010** applications of them in familiar contexts or to familiar subjects. The free speech infringements most commonly struck down have been punishments for criticising governments and politicians. Here the principle is that democracy requires two kinds of latitude in communications relating to those who wield political power:

(a) comparatively greater freedom to publish information about them; and

(b) a very extensive freedom to comment upon their performances.

The leading case involved the Austrian journalist Peter Lingens, who had been convicted and fined under a criminal libel law for accusing the Chancellor, Bruno Kriesky, of "the basest opportunism" and "immorality" for seeking a political alliance with a party led by a former Nazi. This was plainly disproportionate: the Court declared that:

"Freedom of political debate is at the very core of the concept of a democratic society which prevails throughout the Convention. The limits of acceptable criticism are accordingly wider as

---

[29] *R. (ProLife Alliance) v BBC* [2003] 2 All E.R. 977, reversing the Court of Appeal decision (2002) 2 All E.R. 756. Lord Hoffman at para.80 curiously attached importance to the fact that the two BBC executives who made the decision were women (unlike, presumably, the male judges on the Court of Appeal) and would therefore be more likely to know whether the foetal images would be offensive to large number of viewers, especially to women who had gone through abortions. This is illogical: was Mrs Whitehouse (who wanted to ban everything concerning sex, but was in favour of pictures of abortions and executions) a better judge of "offensiveness", because she was a woman?

regards a politician as such than as regards a private individual. Unlike the latter, the former inevitably and knowingly lays himself open to close scrutiny of his every word and deed by both journalists and the public at large, and he must consequently display a greater degree of tolerance."[30]

While Art.10(2) allows politicians some privacy, when acting in an official capacity their reputations may be sullied in the interests of open discussion of political issues. This will certainly be the case in respect of value-judgments and opinions, offered in good faith, and not susceptible of proof or disproof. The lesson of *Lingens* is that comment on politicians must be free, even if factual statements about them can be made subject to defamation laws. In a subsequent case, a provocative attack on the neo-Nazi politician, Jorg Haider, was protected from a private prosecution brought by this hypocrite (who repeatedly complains to the court when his own freedom to criticise opponents is curbed). The Court emphasised that the "greater degree of tolerance" which *Lingens* enjoined politicians to display was the case "especially when he himself makes public statements that are susceptible of criticism".[31] By requiring the journalist to prove his opinion (as distinct from the facts on which it was based) the Austrian criminal libel law was a clear infringement of free speech. It remains an infringement, and Austria is a black spot where freedom of speech is concerned. That country was condemned again in 2006 for a libel finding against the magazine *Profil* for criticising Haider[32] but in 2007 a weak seven judge court upheld a forfeiture order on an Austrian newspaper which had made an attack on Haider in his role as regional governor of Corinthia, but had made an error of fact in so doing. The decision was by four votes to three, the Cypriot, Russian and Azerbaijani judges being joined by the Austrian judge whose casting vote was cast in favour of Austria (a clear case where the court majority decision was affected by its unacceptable practice of sitting with a judge from the defending state). This undistinguished majority concluded that because the newspaper had made a mistake of fact rather than of opinion, the forfeiture order could be upheld. The minority judges pointed out that the newspaper's error

"could easily have been rectified if Haider had requested it to publish a counter-statement. We are not convinced that the immediate recourse to the Media Act and civil proceedings against the journalists constituted a proportionate response. On the contrary, alternative methods for resolving disputes, such as

---

[30] *Lingens v Austria* (1986) 8 E.H.R.R. 407 at 42.
[31] *Oberschlick v Austria* (1991) 19 E.H.R.R. 389 at 59.
[32] *Wirtschafts-Trend v Austria* (Application number 58547/22) final judgment January 27, 2006.

> publication of a counter-statement, should be favoured at least
> as a first step in such a case."

This is a much more sensible way of dealing with errors of fact which
newspapers can subsequently correct.[33]

Factual statements (as opposed to comments) were considered in **2–011**
Castells v Spain, where an opposition politician had been convicted
of "insulting the Government" by accusing it in some detail of
supporting right-wing death squads in its Basque region. Castells had
sought to prove the truth of his allegations, but his evidence was
rejected as irrelevant: the crime was committed simply by insulting
the authorities in a manner which would contribute to public
disorder. The European Court emphasised the importance of free
speech for politicians, and the duty of the press to impart information and ideas, and ruled that "the limits of permissible criticism are
wider with regard to the Government than in relation to a private
citizen or even a politician".[34] The failure of Spanish law to admit
truth as a defence meant that this application of its sedition law was
beyond the needs of a democracy, even one torn by civil strife.

The European Court may articulate fine principles, but its appli
cation of them can, as in all courts, be influenced by political
pressures and prejudices. *Castells* was decided at a time when
Basque terrorism had receded, and after evidence had emerged that
supported Castells' allegations of Government complicity. For an
example of judicial cowardice in the face of the *Castells* principle,
compare the decision in *Zana v Turkey*, when 12 of the court's 20
judges upheld the conviction of a local politician who, whilst held in
a military prison, told journalists that he supported the PKK (but
was "not in favour of massacres"). For this statement, the prisoner
received an extra 12 months' imprisonment. In an unprincipled
judgment, the Eurocourt majority mouthed the core principles yet
found that the publication (for which Zana, as a prisoner, was not
responsible) might "exacerbate an explosive situation" and the
punishment was therefore "necessary in a democratic society". The
eight-judge minority correctly pointed out that since Art.10 applies
to ideas that offend or shock,

> "the mere fact that in his statement the applicant indicated
> support for a political organisation whose aims and means the
> Government rejects and combats cannot, therefore, be a suffi-
> cient reason for prosecuting and sentencing him".[35]

In less stressful times and countries, the Court has insisted that "a
person opposed to official ideas and positions must be able to find a

---

[33] *Standard Verlagsges ellschaft v Austria (Number 2)* (Application number 37464/02)
judgment February 22, 2007.
[34] *Castells v Spain* (1992) 14 E.H.R.R. 445 at 477, para.46.
[35] *Zana v Turkey* (1999) 27 E.H.R.R. 667 at 701 (partly dissenting opinion).

place in the political arena", and has followed *Castells* in according special protection to the views of the people's representatives, even if they only represent peoples at the European Parliament.[36] It condemned France for expelling from Polynesia a "green" German MEP for holding anti-nuclear demonstrations: free speech is permitted if it merely makes the natives restless, but not if it will persuade them to revolt.

Criticising the Judiciary

2–012 The importance of European Court decisions for English courts applying the Human Rights Act lies in the principles extrapolated from Art.10, rather than in the application of those principles to specific cases, which often turns on the "margin of appreciation" and can be internally inconsistent, especially when the decision is taken by an ordinary chamber of seven judges (rather than in a "grand chamber" of 17 or so). Inconsistency is particularly apparent in respect of rulings about the right of journalists to criticise the courts, which is subject to an Art.10(2) exception "for maintaining the authority and impartiality of the judiciary". The correct approach is to limit the free speech right by reference to the Art.6 right to a fair trial, so that attacks on defendants or on judges that are calculated to prejudice a particular trial are impermissible while the trial continues but not otherwise, subject of course to the redress offered by the law of civil libel (and judges, like anyone else, must be entitled to sue in order to redress false statements about themselves). This was the Court's approach in *De Haes v Belgium*, where it condemned the Belgian courts for awarding compensation to judges who had been severely (and to some extent unfairly) criticised in a series of magazine articles for having extreme right-wing sympathies and for extending them to favour a litigant with similar views. "Journalistic freedom" the Court said memorably "also covers possible recourse to a degree of exaggeration, or even provocation".[37] While not approving the polemical and aggressive tone of the articles, the Court was mindful of the fact that Art.10 protects not only information but the form in which it is conveyed.

This marked a welcome refusal to follow a previous case, *Prager and Oberschlick v Austria*, where a narrow majority (the vote was five to four) contrived to find that a criminal libel conviction for a justifiable critique of the Austrian judiciary ("Danger! Harsh Judges!") did not violate the Convention. The majority held that the article "undermined public confidence in the integrity of the judiciary as a whole"—ignoring the media's right in a democracy to question the integrity of judges as well as politicians.[38] It also made

---

[36] *Piermont v France* (1995) 20 E.H.R.R. 301.
[37] *De Haes and Gijsels v Belgium* (1998) 25 E.H.R.R. 1 at 55, para.46.
[38] *Prager and Oberschlick v Austria* (1996) 21 E.H.R.R. 1 at 20, para.36.

use of the *canard* that judges "are subject to a duty of discretion that precludes them from replying"—which is nonsense, since they can reply from their privileged position on the bench, or by suing for civil libel, or (in the United Kingdom) by having the Lord Chancellor's department put out a corrective statement. As the minority judgment points out, it was the deployment of criminal sanctions (the private prosecution was launched by one of the criticised judges) that is disproportionate—judges are public figures who enjoy public privileges, and "must in return accept exposure to unrestricted criticism where it is made in good faith".[39]

Restrictions on free speech are acceptable if they merely postpone publication of opinions on guilt or innocence until after a criminal trial conducted before jurors or lay judges: this is the premise of UK contempt law, which satisfies the Convention now that it only bites on publications that create a substantial risk that a trial will be seriously prejudiced.[40] But whenever judges deal with critics of the courts they sit as judges in their own cause and European judges are no less biased than national judges when it comes to approving punishment of those who criticise fellow judges. A blatant example is the Eurocourt decision in *Barfod v Denmark*, where a prosecution and fine for some perfectly temperate and substantially true remarks about the unfitness of local government employees to decide cases involving their own employer was upheld by the European Court, which said that the Danish court on which they set would be lowered in public esteem.[41] What lowered it in public esteem, of course, was not the article, but a fact to which the article drew attention, namely that the judges had put themselves in a position where bias was reasonably perceived.

These cases arise from continental laws derived from the *Code* 2–013 *Napoleon*, which penalised "insults" to public servants and officials. There are a number of unsatisfactory cases where European judges have shown a lingering attachment to the obnoxious idea that criminal law should protect public servants and policemen from verbal abuse. This is another area where the English tradition is more robust, and where English judges should use Art.10 in a more creative and liberal fashion than their Strasbourg colleagues, who in one case actually said that "civil servants must enjoy public confidence in conditions free of undue perturbation"—sentiments with

---

[39] *ibid* at 22, dissenting opinion of Judge Pettiti.
[40] This is the real justification for the decision in *Worm v Austria* (1998) 25 E.H.R.R. 454, which related to an article which argued that the defendant was guilty whilst he was being tried. Some of the language used by the Court majority on that occasion (its reference to "the spectacle of pseudo-trials in the media" having "nefarious consequences" for acceptance of courts as places of trial) was over the top.
[41] *Barfod v Denmark* (1989) 13 E.H.R.R. 478.

which Sir Humphrey Appleby would entirely agree.[42] English law, fortunately, has few parallels, other than in disciplinary rules for the armed services and prison inmates. There is a valuable ruling in *Grigoriades v Greece* where the Court judged that a conscript sentenced to three months in prison for writing a letter to senior officers condemning the Greek army as "a criminal and terrorist apparatus" had been wrongly prosecuted:

> "Article 10 does not stop at the gates of army barracks. It applies to military personnel as to all other persons and permits soldiers to express opinions, even directed against the army as an institution, so long as the manner and scope of their expression does not amount to a serious threat to discipline".[43]

Since soldiers have a correlative right to receive information, the ruling in *Grigoriades* may sound the death knell of the English offence of incitement to disaffection, or at least to the way it was used in the 1970s against pacifists who leafleted army bases urging conscientious objection to service in Northern Ireland.

The Newsworthiness Standard

2–014 There are a number of European Court judgments which have had a beneficial effect on the way English courts approach problems of media law, because they accept as a starting-point that the dissemination of news and opinion is a value to be protected so far as possible, and they teach that some protection must be extended to methods of news-gathering which get results, however unattractive or unfair or corner-cutting they may seem in the cold light of the courtroom. *Goodwin v United Kingdom* is a prime example of the Court endorsing a journalistic ethic—source protection—at odds with English judicial sensibilities. Another such case is *Jersild v Denmark*, which actually warns:

> "It is not for this Court, *nor for the national courts for that matter*, to substitute their own views for those of the press as to what technique of reporting should be adopted by journalists . . . Article 10 protects not only the substance of the ideas and information expressed, but also the form in which they are conveyed."[44]

This approach enabled the Court to condemn the conviction under Denmark's draconian race-hate laws of a television journalist

---

[42] *Janowski v Poland* (1999) 29 E.H.R.R. 705, para.33. Compare these pathetic comments by a grand chamber with the vigorous dissent of the English judge, Sir Nicholas Bratza, and with the different view of an earlier and better court in *Thorgeirson v Iceland* (fn.29 below).

[43] *Grigoriades v Greece* (1997) 27 E.H.R.R. 464 at 482, para.45.

[44] *Jersild v Denmark* (1995) 19 E.H.R.R. 1, at 26, para.31.

and editor for producing a news programme which looked at the rise of racism amongst young unemployed in Copenhagen. Not surprisingly, the professional judgment of the broadcasters was that the programme would have little impact unless racists were featured under their Ku Klux Klan banners and in their own neanderthal voices ("Niggers are not human beings, man, they are animals . . . so are foreign workers . . . we jump on their cars and throw white paint in their faces . . . people should be allowed to keep slaves, man"). These extremists were convicted for insulting a racial group (no Art.10 protection for *them* in Europe)[45] and the broadcasters were fined for abetting them. The Court ruled this a violation, since the broadcasters had no racist purpose themselves and had relied on their professional judgment that the item as transmitted had genuine news value. The Court pointed out that news reporting based on interviews, even with criminals, was an important technique used by journalists to serve their "public watchdog" role, and to convict them of criminal offences (even with small fines) would seriously hamper the media in producing public interest stories. *Jersild* is valuable, both to dissuade courts from imposing criminal convictions on journalists acting professionally and in drawing attention to the importance of protecting the methods of investigative journalism as well as its fruits.

Another seminal decision is *Thorgeir Thorgeirson v Iceland* where the applicant, an author, was convicted of "insulting civil servants" (in this case, policemen) by accusing them of brutality, the insults being contained in an "open letter" to the Minister of Justice urging a public inquiry. The Iceland Government argued that Art.10's latitude towards criticism of politicians, established by *Lingens* and *Castells*, did not apply to employed public servants, but on this occasion the Court observed that "there is no warrant for distinguishing between political discussion and discussion of other matters of public concern."[46] The airing of allegations of brutal policing, although second-hand and unprovable, were nonetheless matters of public concern appropriately mentioned in the course of a call for an independent inquiry to verify or refute them. It was therefore unreasonable to require the allegations to be proved true as a condition of avoiding a criminal conviction and a fine which even if small would still deter serious investigative journalism. This approach influenced the House of Lords when in 1998 it decided to extend a public interest privilege to articles which report serious

---

[45] The European Commission (which until 1998 would "filter" cases for the Court) always rejected complaints by racists about their hate-speech convictions on the ground that their Art.10 rights were trumped by Art.17 (which provides that nothing in the Convention implies "any right to engage in any activity . . . aimed at the destruction of any of the rights and freedoms set forth herein . . .". See *Glimmerveen v Netherlands* (1979) 18 D.R. 187, and comments in Ch.4.

[46] *Thorgeirson v Iceland* (1992) 14 E.H.R.R. 843 at 865, para.64.

allegations as part of a call for an inquiry, so long as journalists act reasonably and without malice.

2–015   In these cases, the Eurocourt was trying to deter the use of Napoleonic "insult" crimes against journalists and broadcasters who act according to professional conscience. Notwithstanding the fact that the usual punishment is a small fine, the court has repeatedly stressed the "seriousness of a criminal conviction . . . having regard to the existence of other means of intervention and rebuttal, particularly through civil remedies".[47] This should deter English prosecutors from charging journalists with crimes like official secrecy, sedition and contempt or even deploying criminal charges of an inconsequential nature which may have been committed incidentally in pursuing the story. Such a tactic will be more difficult after the *Fressoz and Roire* case:

> The applicants were the editor and a journalist from *Le Canard enchaîné*, the French equivalent of *Private Eye*. During a bitter strike over workers' wages at a major French car factory, the applicants got hold of its chairman's income tax return, showing how he had received massive pay increases at a time when he was denying any extra pay to his workers. It was an offence to publish tax assessments, and the applicants were convicted after doing so to illustrate and confirm their story about the chairman's pay rises. This information could lawfully have been obtained from other public sources, and in these circumstances the Court decided the conviction could not be justified:
>
> > "Article 10 protects journalists' rights to divulge information on issues of general interest provided they are acting in good faith and on an accurate factual basis and provide 'reliable and precise' information in accordance with the ethics of journalism."
>
> Since the purpose of the unlawful publication was not to damage the chairman but to contribute to a debate of public moment about remuneration in the car industry, the conviction was unreasonable and disproportionate. France was ordered to pay the applicants' legal costs and to reimburse them the sum of compensation (10,000 francs) they had been ordered to pay to the greedy executive.[48]

Fressoz and Roire is a significant case where the Eurocourt in grand chamber has (as in *Goodwin*, below) invalidated an application of otherwise unobjectionable domestic law because it is deployed against journalists who have acted in accordance with professional ethics. There was nothing objectionable about the French statute prohibiting publication of tax assessments—it was an elemental privacy protection for taxpayers, justifying prosecution of any tax officials who might leak such documents. The journalists had plainly

---

[47] *Lehideux and Isorni v France* (1998) 5 B.H.R.C. 540 at para.53. Even a token fine (for attempting to rehabilitate the Nazi collaborator, Marshal Pétáin) was held to be disproportionate, because of the stigma of criminal conviction.
[48] *Fressoz and Roire v France* 5 B.H.R.C. 654, para.54.

broken the law, although they had done so not with malice towards the taxpayer, but in order to verify for readers a story of public importance. The implication from the European Court judgment is that journalists who commit minor offences incidentally and in the course of developing or confirming important information should always be able to invoke a "public interest" defence. In other words, British statutory or common law crimes which do not have such defences (they are termed "strict liability offences") should not be levelled against journalists who have acted in conformity with their own professional codes.

The decision in *Fressoz and Roire* turned on a new core principle (our ninth) first developed in 1996 in *Goodwin v United Kingdom* (below), namely:

9. the safeguard offered by Article 10 to journalists in relation to reporting on articles of general interest is subject to the proviso that they are acting in good faith in order to provide accurate and reliable information in accordance with the ethics of journalism.

If this proviso is satisfied, then the journalist is entitled to defeat a claim under Art.10(2), no matter how clearly made out. Thus the French journalists were able to resist application of a criminal law they had undoubtedly broken, and Mr Goodwin was entitled to commit contempt by disobeying a court order to name his source. Another application of core principle 8, which has significance for English libel practice, is *Bergens Tidende v Norway*:

> The applicant, a Norwegian daily newspaper, had been ordered to pay very heavy damages to a cosmetic surgeon whose professional career and business were ruined by articles in which several of his clients detailed their unsuccessful operations. They spoke out after the surgeon had been favourably profiled in the same newspaper, and their accounts recited failures that had happened and their honest, if emotional, feelings. Although in reality the surgeon was not incompetent, as the article implied, because he had conducted thousands of successful cosmetic operations. The bad publicity had clearly damaged the surgeon's right to professional reputation, but this was not sufficient to override the freedom of the press to impart information on matters of legitimate public concern, where the newspaper had reported accurately and ethically on an important controversy relating to public health.[49]

The importance of this case is that the Court made a broad-brush **2–016** public interest judgment, namely that newspapers should not be penalised in damages for reporting the ordeals of women with leaky implants who had suffered damage while under the care of otherwise

---

[49] *Bergens Tidende v Norway* (2001) 31 E.H.R.R. 430.

competent plastic surgeons. British libel courts would have treated this case on a much more artificial footing, as turning on whether the "ordinary reader" would take the allegations to mean that the surgeon was incompetent. If so (and this was an impression which many readers would have gathered) then the newspaper would have lost, since it could not "justify" (i.e. prove true) this meaning. If the Human Rights Act is to have effect on libel pleadings, this narrow concentration on the meaning of words should be replaced by a broader test of whether the publication of them genuinely served the public interest, irrespective of damage to individual reputation. This was the approach taken by the Strasbourg court in another case involving a Norwegian newspaper held to have defamed seal-hunters by accusing them of unlawfully "flaying alive" their quarry. They had not been offered a right of reply, but since the allegations were based on an official report and the newspaper had given voice to all sides in its long-running balanced coverage of a controversial issue, the damage to reputation was a relevant but insufficient reason "to outweigh the vital public interest in ensuring an informed public debate over a matter of local and national as well as international interest".[50] This is a valuable example of the proportionality test protecting public interest journalism conducted in good faith, despite a failure to check facts and the presence of some error and exaggeration.

The European Court is currently using this test to permit the repetition of defamatory allegations made by others, without requiring the media to prove truth, if this is in the interests of important public discussions. The 2005 case of *Selisto v Finland* provides one such example where the defamatory statement was based on a police investigation record and repeated in good faith to highlight the dangers of drunken surgeons at public hospitals. The court held:

> "In the court's opinion no general duty to verify the veracity of statements contained in such documents can be imposed on reporters and other members of the media, who must be free to report on events based on information gathered from official sources. If this were not the case the efficacy of Article 10 of the Convention would to a large degree be lost."[51]

Similarly in *Thoma v Luxembourg*,[52] it was held that defamatory allegations published in a newspaper about a government official could be used as the basis for a radio discussion without requiring the participants in that discussion to deny or even distance themselves from the allegations.

The fact that the victim of the defamatory statement is not a public figure will not matter (as it does in the United States) if the

---

[50] *Bladet Tromsø v Norway* (1999) 29 E.H.R.R. 125 at para.73.
[51] [2005] E.M.L.R. 8, p.178 at para.60.
[52] [2003] 36 E.H.R.R. 21.

subject matter of the article is of genuine public interest. When a local newspaper published a list of names of those whom the municipal council believed had breached residence requirements, it included the name of a private individual who had, in fact, been removed from the list. The court held that Art.10 had been violated by an award of damages because the newspaper had acted fairly, firstly by obtaining and publishing his comment that his inclusion on the list "must be a misunderstanding" and then by publishing a correction in due course when it realised that its information had been out of date. Although the claimant was not a public or political figure, the newspaper served the public interest by treating local residency requirements as important: "Whether or not a publication concerns an issue of public concern should depend on a broader assessment of the subject matter and the context of publication". This is an important case, decided in March 2007, which shows that contrary to the rule of English defamation law, editorial responsibility must be judged by post-publication conduct, such as a willingness to publish a clarification, correction or apology. Here, the court attached particular significance to the fact that the newspaper had investigated where it had gone wrong and published a follow-up article based on an interview with the Chief Executive of the municipal council who had confirmed that the resident's name had been removed from the list and explained why the residency requirement did not apply to his property. This all served to put the record straight and to reduce any damage that the error had caused.[53]

Some problems with Euro-jurisprudence

It is important not to be starry eyed about the European Convention **2–017** and the Strasbourg courts charged with implementing it. As the Human Rights Act takes hold, British judges are requiring less Euro-correction: *Mclibel* was the last occasion where the Strasbourg court found a serious violation of Art.10 by the United Kingdom. At the same time, the Strasbourg court has been a victim of its own success: it must now deal with complaints against governments in 46 countries, many of them new entrants with legal systems still throwing off the oppressive shackles of communism. The result has been a flood of applications—by 2007 there were 89,887 of them pending before the court, 20 per cent against Russia, 12 per cent against Romania and 10 per cent against Turkey. It only manages to cope by accepting complaints about the worst abuses of state power, and these rarely emanate from the UK. The time when Britain was the worst offender—in the early years of the Thatcher government—is long gone. In 2006, when the court handed down 1,560 judgments,

---

[53] *Tønsbergs Blad v Norway* (Application Number 510/04) judgment March 1, 2007.

most concerned countries like Turkey (334), Slovenia (190) and the Ukraine (120).

The court is divided into four chambers of seven judges, applying the principles that the full court laid down in its earlier and more leisurely days. When there is need to consider a new principle of general importance or a new interpretation of a Convention right, the case may be referred to a "Grand Chamber" of 17 judges. The judgments are delivered in either English or French (depending on which of these two languages the applicant has chosen for the proceedings). Sometimes the judgments are translated into the other language but pressure of work means that there can be serious delays even for those judgments which are not translated. The judgments are written in a stilted and uninspiring Euro prose, and the quality of the judges, one appointed by each state, is variable. Judgments emerging from the chamber presided over by the respected English administrative lawyer Sir Nicolas Bratza will carry more weight in UK courts. The unacceptable practice in every case of including in the bench a judge from the state against which the complaint is brought reduces the value of 4:3 decisions in which that judge has provided a biased casting vote in favour of his own state. Although Sir Nicolas has been scrupulous in condemning the UK government (for which he once acted) whenever appropriate, it must be said that judges from some other states regard themselves as protectors of the government that appointed them, to the extent, sometimes, that they provide a lone dissent from a decision criticising it. These features serve to reduce the authority of many Strasbourg decisions.

A court comprising continental jurists will inevitably display some difference in emphasis over shared values, and the differences can be very evident in moral issues. While British courts have been reluctant to punish forms of "hate speech" that must be tolerated in the US under the First Amendment, unless it incites violence or causes demonstrable distress, the Euro-court has withdrawn Art.10 protection from racist speech on the Art.17 ground that this is aimed at destroying other rights (to life and non-discrimination) guaranteed by the Convention.[54] Hence David Irving's three-year jail sentence in Austria for holocaust denial would be improbable in the United Kingdom: British judges would have struck it down as a disproportionate infringement of Art.10, although in Strasbourg it would in all probability be upheld by judges from states with a national memory of Nazi occupation. On the other hand, the peculiar British obsession with pornography is not shared in Europe: the ideologically vapid hardcore found on TV channels throughout the continent has been solemnly classified by Strasbourg as "expression", at least of

---

[54] See *Lehideux v France* [1998] 5 B.H.R.C. 548. "The justification of pro-Nazi policy could not be allowed to enjoy the protection afforded by Article 10"—para.53.

ideas and fantasies, which adults have a right to receive.[55] An English judge would find it uncomfortable to accept this approach.

These differences reflect not so much incompatible moral values **2–018** as a difference in emphasis in respect to shared moral values. The Euro-court has always shrugged them off, with an excuse formulated in 1974 in its *Handyside* decision:

> "It is not possible to find in the domestic law of the various Contracting States a uniform European conception of morals. The view taken by their respective laws of the requirements of morals varies from time to time and from place to place, especially in our era which is characterised by a rapid and far-reaching evolution of opinions on the subject."[56]

Thirty years on, opinions should have evolved sufficiently to deplore the *Otto Preminger* case decision[57] in which the court upheld the seizure and destruction of a copy of a film screened in a private cinema because of the Austrian state's "responsibility to ensure the peaceful enjoyment of the right guaranteed under Art.9 to the holders of those beliefs and doctrines."[58] This was a bigoted and mistaken decision, protecting extremist Catholic sensibilities from the very *thought* that a film mocking Catholicism was being screened to willing adults at a private cinema club. There was no issue of public offence and obviously no question of interference with Catholic worship—which is the value actually protected by Art.9.[59] The court wrongly claimed that there was a conflict between Art.9 and Art.10 which should be resolved by a "balancing exercise" in which States had a margin of appreciation to bring national law down on either side. This approach caricatured the real issue, which had nothing to do with Art.9's right to hold and manifest religious beliefs, but should have been dealt with entirely under Art.10. The question was whether the "rights of others", ie of local Catholics annoyed at the thought that citizens might enjoy a film mocking the Pope, were entitled to override the right of adults (whether Catholic or not) to enjoy a film of recognised artistic and satirical merit. The answer should have been in the negative, because the free speech presumption erected by Art.10(1) could not be overridden in democratic society simply by the sensitivities and sentiments of a particular religious group, however numerous.

Regrettably, the *Otto Preminger* decision has not been overruled, and it still perverts the court's case law and contributes to the court's

---

[55] *Hoare v UK* [1997] HER LR 678.

[56] *Handyside v United Kingdom* [1979–80] 1 E.H.R.R. 737 at 48.

[57] *Otto Preminger* [1995] 19 E.H.R.R. 34.

[58] *Otto Preminger*, para.57.

[59] Art.9 reads: "Everyone has the right to freedom of thought, conscience and religion; this right includes freedom to change its religion or belief and freedom, either alone or in community with others and in public or private, to manifest his religion or belief, in worship, teaching, practice and observance."

main free speech failing, namely its refusal to protect works of literary and artistic merit. It influenced a disgraceful decision in 2005, *IA v Turkey*, in which the court divided 4:3 against condemning the blasphemy conviction of the publisher of a novel for a passage pointing out that Mohammed would ". . . break his fast through sexual intercourse, after dinner and before prayer . . . God's messenger did not forbid sexual relations with a dead person or a live animal".[60] The government relied upon *Otto Preminger* and argued that criticism of Islam could not be acceptable in a country where the majority were Muslims: the Turkish courts had weighed the conflicting interests of Art.9 and Art.10 and had come down in favour of the right of Muslims to respect for their religion.[61] This is plainly wrong: Article 9 does not protect "respect" for religion, only the right to hold and manifest a faith and to worship according to it. There was in consequence no balancing exercise to be done. These four erring judges were from Georgia, San Marino(!), Hungary and, of course, the casting vote of the biased Turkish judge—yet another example of how the court's own unfair practice of insisting (without asking the consent of the parties) that a state-appointed judge must always sit in the seven judge courts is capable of producing unprincipled decisions. The three judges in the minority—from France, Portugal and Czechoslovakia—correctly pointed out how absurd it was to take insulting statements in isolation "as the basis for condemning an entire book and imposing criminal sanctions on its publisher. Moreover, nobody is ever obliged to buy or read a novel." The minority judgment said in terms that the time had come to revisit *Otto Preminger* and its case law "which in our view seems to place too much emphasis on conformism or uniformity of the court and to reflect an overcautious and timid conception of the freedom of the press." Amen.

Article 10 "balanced" against Article 8?

2–019   An even worse problem with Euro-jurisprudence is the current confusion it has caused in the British courts over the so-called "balance" between Art.8 and Art.10. *Otto Preminger* and *IB v Turkey* were cases where a competing right (i.e. Art.9) was not, on proper analysis, engaged at all—nobody was stopping Muslims or Catholics from believing or worshiping, and so there was in reality no conflict. But there may, in a select number of cases, especially concerning paparazzi photographs, be a genuine clash between Art.10 and the Art.8 principle that, "Everyone has the right to respect for his private and family life, his home and his correspondence", which imposes a positive obligation on the State to take action to stop private bodies (such as the media) from indefensible violations.

---

[60] *IA v Turkey* (Application number 42571/98) judgment September 15, 2005.
[61] *IA*, para.27.

The occasions for such a clash will be limited, thanks to an important and deliberate decision taken back in 1951 when debating, drafting and approving Art.8. It was then suggested that as in other respects, this Article of the Convention should follow its equivalent in the Universal Declaration of Human Rights (1948), Art.12 of which reads:

> "No one shall be subjected to arbitrary interference with his privacy, family, home or correspondence, nor to attacks upon his honour and reputation."

It was decided to omit "the right to honour and reputation" from the scope of the European Convention's privacy Article because "honour" was too amorphous (and Napoleonic) a concept, whilst reputation was not a free-standing right that needed to be "balanced" against Art.10's right to free speech, but rather a subsidiary right best placed in Art.10(2), where a restriction may be justified as necessary "for the protection of the reputation or rights of others". Thus in the Convention system reputation can only triumph over free speech where its protection is necessary to respond to a pressing social need in democratic society (the Art.10 test). There can be no "balancing act" between reputation and free speech, because Art.8 simply does not protect reputation. It operates to protect from trespass, from lawless police searches and bugging operations: where the media is concerned, it can stop the publication of intimate personal details or stolen or intrusive photographs or details from lost or stolen diaries and letters. It can also protect against intimate personal revelations by servants or personal assistants who are contracted to confidentiality. Such publications may indirectly affect reputation, of course, but that cannot be the basis of the claim.[62]

This much is clear, although not always to the overworked judges **2–020** and their registrars churning out decisions in Strasbourg. In recent years, "reputation" was carelessly and illegitimately added to the protection afforded by Art.8 in a number of judgments, which refer to it as a right safeguarded under that Article. "Reputation" cannot be elevated to an ECHR right of equal standing with Art.10, for the simple reason that it is not a Convention right; it is only a Convention exception (in Art.10(2) where it is to be narrowly construed). The value of public interest journalism which does not pry into home or family or private correspondence cannot be outweighed by any claim to balance a "right" to reputation. The cases where this impermissible slight of hand took place were, interestingly, from France, which has always unduly protected privacy, particularly of old politicians and older Nazis. In *Radio France v France* a radio news item had distorted a newspaper revelation that

---

[62] See Professor Velu in Robertson, *Privacy and Human Rights* (1973), pp.15–18.

a public servant (a local police chief) had collaborated with the
Nazis: he had not, as it reported, supervised the loading of Jews on
an extermination train headed for Auschwitz, but he had forcefully
stopped a demonstration at the railway station aimed at protesting
against the deportations. Many would find the moral distinction
elusive, but the French courts (hypersensitive about the nation's
collaboration with the Nazis) found it defamatory, and the Euro-
court did not intervene. It carelessly indicated that reputation was
"an element" of Art.8. This was taken up more brazenly in *Chauvy v
France*, another war crime collaboration dispute over whether a
husband and wife, long celebrated as resistance heroes, had actually
betrayed Jean Moulin to the Gestapo. This was a straight forward
defamation in which the publishers could not justify their reliance of
the malicious accusations of Klaus Barbie, and Strasbourg should
simply have rejected the complaint. But in doing so, the court
suggested that "in this type of case" it had to check whether Art.10
was in fair balance with a right to reputation "a right which is
protected by Art.8 of the Convention as part of the right to respect
for family life".[63] Given the historical background and clear words of
Art.8, this is plainly wrong, and the *Chauvy* aberration does not
appear in the court statements of fundamental principles in *Steel and
Morris v United Kingdom*[64] nor in other recent cases where it has laid
down general principles,[65] but is becoming a common refrain in
claimants' arguments in UK courts.

Naomi Campbell shows that Art.8 may engage with Art.10 and
require a balance, but only in cases where the claimant had a
reasonable expectation of privacy for home, family, and
correspondence—aspects of "human autonomy and dignity". There
is no general right to privacy under Art.8 of equal force to the right
of free expression in Art.10, outside cases like *Campbell*, which
concern media invasion of personal or family space. And even in
such cases, where there is a high public interest served by the privacy
infringement, the European Court has been prepared to adopt an
Art.10 presumption in favour of free speech rather than a balancing
exercise between Art.8 and Art.10. In the unusual case of *Radio
Twist v Slovakia*,[66] a court presided over by Judge Bratza held that
state radio was entitled to broadcast unlawfully bugged conversations
between the Deputy Prime Minster and the Minister of Justice, at

---

[63] *Shauby v France*, para.70. This paragraph contains no footnote or other reference
to authority and overlooks the deliberate omission of "honour and reputation"
from Art.8. It may be that the court thought that "this type of case"—Mr and Mrs
Aubrac, decorated war heroes, were being accused after 60 years—involved an
invasion of their family privacy. But the paragraph is misleading and without
authority, although it was picked up by a grand chamber decision in December
2004—*Campana v Romania* (33348/86 of December 17, 2004).

[64] The *McLibel* case—Feburary 2005, para.87.

[65] e.g. *Stoll v Switzerland*—para.43 or *Selisto v Finland*—para.46.

[66] Application number 62202/00, judgment December 19, 2006.

the time the state broadcaster itself was subject to a disputed political take-over. Even though the tape recording of the telephone conversation was illegal, the public importance of the subject matter meant that it could not be characterised as private and journalistic ethics were irrelevant: this was a conversation between two high-ranking officials engaged in a power struggle over control of the state media. The broadcasters' conviction for defamation of the Minister of Justice was a clear violation of Art.10.

Another topical problem with Euro-jurisprudence is the occasional unprincipled statement that emerges without warning from Grand Chambers, lacking in precedent and without the benefit of proper argument from media interests. The worst example, which has caused great confusion and led to a great deal of self censorship by UK publishers, is the decision in *Von Hannover* where the judges took it into their heads to protect that over-indulged tax haven royal, Princess Caroline of Monaco, from being photographed in public places. This particular decision might have been justified on the grounds that like anyone else she needed protection against a paparazzi campaign of harassment, but the court unwisely went much wider:

> "Furthermore, private life, in the court's view, includes a person's physical and psychological integrity; the guarantee afforded by Article 8 of the Convention is primarily intended to ensure the development, without outside interference, of the personality of each individual in his relations with other human beings . . . There is therefore a zone of interaction of a person with others, even in a public context, which may fall within the scope of private life."[67]

This psychobabble provides no comprehensible basis for restrictions on freedom to communicate information which is obvious, or at least available to all those who have eyes to see. Article 8 was not, as it happens, intended to assist personality development, and it is difficult to fathom what is meant by "a zone of interaction of a person with others, even in a public context". British courts should have ignored this stumbling Euro prose and concentrated on the *Naomi Campbell*, which shoe-horned the jurisprudence of Arts 8 and 10 into a tort of breach of confidence (where there is a pre-existing relationship of confidence) and proclaimed a separate tort of misuse of private information—i.e. information unlawfully and surreptitiously obtained or purloined, which the publisher knows he cannot use. In such limited circumstances, an Art.8 v Art.10 balancing exercise will be appropriate, so long as public interest can always tip the scales. Otherwise, the vague generalities of *Von Hannover* should

2–021

---

[67] *Von Hannover*, para.50.

be shunned: there is no tort of invasion of privacy and Article 8 support for "physical and psychological integrity" should be strictly confined to intimate personal details—such as the medical treatment that the *Naomi Campbell* majority ruled should not have been revealed. That European judges sometimes do go on unprincipled and unprecedented frolics is shown by their reasoning in *Chauvy* and *Von Hannover*: it is important for UK judges to remember that s.2 of the Human Rights Act (1998), which says that Euro-court decisions "must be taken into account" does not mean that they must always be followed.[68]

It should finally be noted that Strasbourg's Art.10 jurisprudence is seriously defective insofar as it has to date refused to interpret the freedom of expression guarantee to require public or media access to information held in state archives or by public bodies which do not want to divulge it, however great the public interest. This approach is based on an old case—*Leander v Switzerland*[69]—which should be reversed in the interests of transparency and freedom of information. The Inter-America court has put Strasbourg to shame by its decision in *Marcel Claude Reyes v Chile*, where it held that a similar freedom of expression guarantee,

> "which specifically established the rights to 'seek' and 'receive' information, protects the right of all persons to request access to information held by the state, with the exceptions permitted by the restrictions regime of the Convention . . ."

In a democratic society it is indispensable that state authorities are governed by the principle of *maximum disclosure*, which establishes the presumption that all information should be accessible, subject to a restricted system of exceptions.[70] Overruling *Leander* is a matter of some importance, not only for countries like Spain, Italy and Greece which do not have proper FOI laws, but for cases in the United Kingdom outside FOI legislation where the government claims that Art.10 is not engaged by its refusal to provide media access.

ARTICLE 10: SOME UNITED KINGDOM DECISIONS

2–022 A number of cases from Britain have proved seminal in developing the core principles of Art.10, and they deserve special study because of the impact they have had on extending press freedom. The

---

[68] This reflection was curiously absent from the extensive survey of Euro-law and UK law on privacy in the case of *Ash v McKennit*, Court of Appeal decision December 14, 2006. Although the case itself turned on good old fashioned breach of confidence—Ash was a malicious personal assistant to a self-effacing Canadian folk singer, and set up a vanity publishing outfit to circulate a book full of confidential information she had gleaned about the singer's health and personal life.

[69] 1987 A116.

[70] *Reyes v Chile*, Inter-American Court of Human Rights, judgment September 19, 2006, paras 77 and 92.

potential of the Convention was first demonstrated by the *Sunday Times* case:

> *The Sunday Times* proposed to publish an article about the marketing of thalidomide, a pregnancy drug that had caused birth deformities, despite the existence of long-running legal actions for negligence between parents and the drug manufacturers which might eventually come to trial. English courts ruled that the article could not be published, because it "prejudged" issues in litigation, and was therefore a contempt of court. The newspaper and its journalists applied to the European Court, claiming that the ban was an infringement of their right to freedom of expression. The British Government argued that the contempt law, as applied in this case, was necessary to uphold both "the authority of the judiciary" and the legal rights of the drug manufacturers. The Court held for the *Sunday Times*. It said that the thalidomide disaster was a matter of public concern, and the mere fact that litigation was in progress did not alter the right and, indeed, responsibility of the mass media to impart information of public interest. The public had a right to be properly informed, which could be denied them only if the article unarguably presented a threat to judicial authority. In the circumstances, the article was moderate in tone and presented both sides of the case; it would not have prejudiced a trial (before a judge sitting without a jury) or added much to the growing moral pressure on the manufacturers to settle the claim. It followed that the interference by the English courts did not correspond to a social need sufficiently pressing to outweigh the public interest in freedom of expression. It was both out of proportion to any social need to protect the impartiality of the courts and the rights of litigants, and it was not a restriction necessary in a democratic society to uphold these values.[71]

The *Sunday Times* decision meant that because of its treaty obligations, the British Government was obliged to change the law on contempt of court. This it did by the 1981 Contempt of Court Act: no longer would investigative stories be stopped merely because they might "prejudice" litigation at some future time. This historic case marked the first impact of the Convention on English common law. There were more to come, although not all of them went to the Court for judgment. There was a filter—a European Commission of Human Rights—which excluded hopeless cases. If it decided that a case was likely to succeed however, it would offer "friendly settlement" so that the Government might put its law in order to avoid a court hearing. An historic case where the United Kingdom agreed to legislate to give the media specific legal rights is *Hodgson and Channel 4 v United Kingdom*[72]:

> Until 1989 newspapers and television stations had no right to challenge a gag order imposed by a judge at a criminal trial. Journalists had no

---

[71] *The Sunday Times v UK* (1979) 2 E.H.R.R. 245.
[72] *Hodgson and Others v UK and Channel 4 v UK*, Decision on admissibility, March 9, 1987, 51 D.R. 136.

standing to apply to the trial judge to lift the order, and there was no avenue open for them to appeal to any other court. This situation was in blatant breach of Art.13 of the European Convention, which requires that anyone whose rights (e.g. to freedom of expression) are violated should have an "effective remedy". Channel 4 had no remedy at all when the judge at the controversial Official Secrets trial of Clive Ponting issued an order banning the television station from using actors to read each evening from the day's transcripts. So both Channel 4 and Godfrey Hodgson (the programme's presenter) filed a complaint with the European Commission at Strasbourg, which upheld the complaint under Art.13. The UK Government accepted this ruling, and negotiated a "friendly settlement" with the complainants, which took the form of drafting a new law (now s.159 of the Criminal Justice Act 1988), giving the media a special right to appeal to the Court of Appeal against gag orders or decisions to exclude the press and public from any part of a trial.

The *Hodgson* case shows how individual journalists can use the Convention to enhance the rights of the media generally. The initiative originally came from an Old Bailey reporter, Tim Crook, who challenged a secrecy order in the Divisional Court, in a case that established that the media had no effective remedy under English law. (It is a strict prerequisite of a complaint to Strasbourg that any possible domestic remedy should first be exhausted.) He then filed his application with the European Commission, which was favourably settled by the British Government after the ruling in *Hodgson*. Both Crook and NUJ officials, along with Hodgson and Channel 4's lawyers, participated in the settlement negotiations which led to the drafting of s.159.

2–023 The European Court next struck a blow against national security, ruling that the use of pre-publication injunctions to stop *Spycatcher* from being published in England was an infringement of Art.10.[73] This decision hardly came as a surprise, although in this case the Court emphasised that the media had a duty to impart information (principle 6, above) and that the public had a correlative right to receive it: "Were it otherwise, the press would be unable to play its vital role of *public watchdog*". The Court uttered the warning about prior restraint discussed in Ch.1. After *Spycatcher* had been published outside Britain, the Government could only justify the ban on the basis that this would reduce sales and thus "punish" the author by loss of royalties thereby perhaps deterring other spies motivated to write memoirs for money. This, the Court decided, was a "relevant" but not "sufficient" reason for the ban: it could not prevail against the duty of the press to purvey information (already available overseas) on a matter of legitimate public concern.[74]

---

[73] *Observer and Guardian v UK*, 14 E.H.JR.R. 153 at 191, paras 59–60.
[74] *Observer* at paras 68–69.

Prime Minister Margaret Thatcher had been determined to punish Peter Wright and his publishers, no matter what damage she did to free speech or to the security service itself. Regrettably, many British judges of that time upheld the Government's bogus claim of national security. Their behaviour might be explained by the absence of any presumption in favour of free speech in the common law, in which they had been brought up, and which always gave precedence to rights of property. In similar vein, England's highest judiciary, *en masse*, could not understand how a journalist's promise to protect his source could prevail over a corporation's right to protect its profits: what came as a shock to the judges and as a boon to working journalists was the 1996 decision in *Goodwin v United Kingdom*, which extended Art.10 protection to journalistic sources:

> Trainee journalist Bill Goodwin had been fined (he could have been imprisoned) for contempt by refusing to disclose the identity of the source who leaked to him confidential information which showed that an aggressive private company's financial position was not as sound as it publicly pretended. Goodwin worked for *The Engineer* magazine, and had been tipped off with details from the company's still-secret business plan: when he rang the company to confirm them, it responded by rushing to court to obtain an injunction against any publication and an order for him to name his source. The company complained that public exposure of its refinancing problems might cost hundreds of jobs. The defendant denied that the source, who had provided him with reliable information before, was criminal or malicious, but this did not stop the British courts from inferring (wrongly) that the source had been involved in stealing a copy of the business plan or else must have been a high executive deserving exposure and punishment for corporate disloyalty. All judges at all stages in Britain held the journalist in contempt, but the European Court overruled them:

> > "Protection of journalistic sources is one of the basic conditions for press freedom . . . Without such protection, sources may be deterred from assisting the press in informing the public on matters of public interest. As a result the vital public watchdog role of the press may be undermined and the ability of the press to provide accurate and reliable information may be adversely affected . . . such a measure cannot be compatible with Article 10 of the Convention unless it is justified by an overriding requirement in the public interest."[75]

That the contempt finding was "necessary in a democratic society" **2–024** had to be proved ("convincingly established") by the United Kingdom in terms of a "pressing social need": criminalisation of the journalist had to be a proportionate response to the aim of

---

[75] *Goodwin v UK* (1996) 22 E.H.R.R. 123 at 143, para.39.

protecting corporate confidentiality. The Court decided that since the company was protected by the injunction against publication, it could not go further and demand the unmasking of the source in order to retrieve its document or sue for compensation or dismiss for disloyalty. Its obvious private interest in such reprisals was insufficient to displace the *public* interest in source protection. The punishment of the journalist was disproportionate to the aim of protecting corporate privacy, because this would have the consequence of "drying up" news sources.

In 1998 the United Kingdom suffered another unexpected defeat, when Art.10 was used to challenge an election statute—s.75 of the Representation of the People Act (1983)—which then prohibited pressure groups from spending more than £5 during the election period in promoting or opposing the election of a particular candidate. The £5 limit was a disproportionate restriction, unnecessarily severe in light of the legitimate aim of the legislation, namely of securing an equal playing field for all candidates. Decided in 1998, *Bowman v United Kingdom* was the first human rights claim opposed (and lost) by the new Labour Government.

> Mrs Bowman was secretary of an anti-abortion group which leafleted voters in various constituencies with a factual account of the views and voting records on abortion of all local candidates. She was prosecuted under s.75 for incurring more than £5 expenditure, in one particular constituency, after a complaint on behalf of Alice Mahon M.P., the pro-choice Labour candidate. Other pressure groups had been threatened with prosecution at these elections for promoting discussion of candidate positions on controversial issues (Charter 88 was warned that it could not spend more than £5 to hire a hall in which local candidates would be quizzed about their support for a bill of rights). The Euro-court held that a ban on the distribution of factual information about particular candidates at election time was disproportionate to the s.75 object of securing an equal playing field for individual candidates, because it had the effect of precluding third party campaigns in local constituencies. It derided the UK argument that Mrs Bowman could disseminate the information by standing for Parliament herself or by owning newspapers (which are exempted from s.75): she had no effective channel to communicate the facts other than by leaflets. A law which limited her expenditure to a futile £5 was unnecessary and disproportionate.[76]

Bowman, like *Goodwin* is an impressive example of the Court spelling out of Art.10 a free speech implication that had never previously been noticed. In both cases the test of "proportionality" is applied, to emphasise an implication drawn from the free speech

---

[76] *Bowman v UK* (1998) 26 E.H.R.R. 1 at paras 41–7. The law was in consequence amended by the Political Parties Elections and Referendums Act 2000, but only to permit expenditure of £500.

guarantee—that it entails source protection, or that it becomes especially precious during elections. In Bowman, the Court could give Art.10 particular force because it served to further another Convention objective, in this case the right to free elections "under conditions which will ensure the free expression of the opinion of the people in the choice of the legislature".[77] Where a complainant can demonstrate that an act of censorship had damaged, in its course, not only freedom of expression but another Convention right, the case for striking it down is particularly strong.

Given the pressure of business from countries where state abuses **2–025** of power are rife, it has become more difficult to have infringements on media freedom in the United Kingdom accepted as severe enough to engage the attention of Strasbourg, let alone a "Grand Chamber" of that court. One recent exception was the *McLibel* case, involving the longest trial in English history, in which a US multinational won £60,000 damages against two penniless protestors, despite the fact that it could not show any damage. In 2005 a Chamber held that the United Kingdom had, by permitting these *Goliath v David* proceedings, violated Art.6—the lengthy and complex trial had been unfair because the defendants had been denied legal representation. It was also found to have violated Art.10, because the award of damages was disproportionate given the modest means of the defendants and the fact that it could not establish that a single "Happy Meal" had been foregone as a result of any would-be customer reading their defamatory leaflets. This case—*Steel and Morris v UK*[78]—is an important authority because it confirms that there is a clear public interest in open debate about commercial practices: large corporations must, like politicians and other public figures, put up with a degree of uninhibited examination and discussion:

> "Large public companies inevitably and knowingly lay themselves open to close scrutiny of their acts and, as in the case of the businessmen and women who manage them, the limits of acceptable criticism are wider in the case of such companies."[79]

THE HUMAN RIGHTS ACT 1998

The European Convention was cemented into English constitutional **2–026** law by the new Labour Government in 1998. There was very little opposition to the measure: the slogan "rights brought home" emphasised that it would no longer be necessary to go off on a seven-year trek to Strasbourg to obtain relief which would now be

---

[77] See First Protocol to the ECHR, Art.3.
[78] [2005] 41 E.H.R.R. 22.
[79] *Steel*, para.94.

available instantly in the High Court. A handful of Tory cynics complained about the extra powers it would give to an untrustworthy judiciary (this had previously been a concern of Labour's left wing, which fell silent in the early flush of enthusiasm for Blairite manifesto reforms). Since previous governments had rejected demands for a Bill of Rights on the basis that it would undermine "Parliamentary sovereignty"—the right of a Government backed by a parliamentary majority to pass any law it liked, however absurd or inhumane, and to require the judiciary loyally to implement it—most interest in the Human Rights Act focused not on the Convention (which is imported into law as a Schedule to the Act) but on the new powers and procedures to implement it.

"This Bill will increase individual rights in the United Kingdom" announced the Prime Minister in his introduction to the 1997 White Paper (*Rights Brought Home*) which preceded the Human Rights Act. Its preamble declares it: "An Act to give *further* effect to rights and freedoms guaranteed under the European Convention . . ." [our italics].

"Further" is an important word, signalling that this is not legislation which preserves the *status quo*: rights like free speech are to be enhanced as a result of the legislation. The point is made again, although ineffectively, in s.11: the Convention should not be used so as to *restrict* a freedom enjoyed before its enactment. The really significant aspect of the Human Rights Act, however, is that it provides legal power for the media to go on the attack.

2–027   Section 6 makes it unlawful for a "public authority" (that phrase includes courts and tribunals) to act in a way which is incompatible with Art.10, unless such action is required by a statute passed by Parliament (i.e. by "primary legislation"). Where "secondary legislation"—rules made by government under powers given by primary legislation—is concerned, this must be construed so far as possible in conformity with the Convention, or else declared ultra vires unless the incompatibility is expressly required by primary legislation. In all other cases—i.e. where common not statute law is concerned ("common law" like libel and breach of confidence is law made by judges over the centuries), or where a judge is exercising a discretion (including cases where a statute gives that discretion) Art.10 is in the driving seat: the court must give it full force and credit. It is not sufficient for public authorities merely to "take account" of Art.10 or to "have regard" to it: they must not act in any way incompatibly with it.

"Public authorities" which are bound to act in accordance with the freedom of expression guarantee include not only courts and tribunals, but government departments, local authorities, police and prison officials and "any person certain of whose functions are functions of a public nature". This clearly includes statutory media regulators like Ofcom and certain private bodies which have acquired statutory functions, like the Advertising Standards Authority and the British Board of Film and Video Classification together with its Video Appeals Committee. It probably includes the Press Complaints Commission, which although it has no statutory under-pinning serves a public function and was established as an alternative to government regulation.[80] Newspapers of course are themselves private bodies. So are Channel 5 and the various cable and satellite broadcasters, although the ITC which regulates them is a public authority for the purposes of the Act. The BBC is set up under a Royal Charter and has undertaken regulatory duties parallel to those of the ITC: there is no reason why it should not be similarly bound. It has been challenged on judicial review—notably over its allocation of election broadcasts[81]—and in this and other respects it will be obliged by law to uphold Art.10 (and Art.8, which guarantees the right to privacy). Channel 4, as a statutory corporation with statutory duties, is likely to be similarly affected.

By s.7 of the Human Rights Act any victim whose free speech might have been infringed or is threatened with infringement may, within a year, bring a specific action against the infringing authority in the High Court, or else rely on Art.10 in legal proceedings brought on other grounds. There is only one catch: the claimant must be a "victim", i.e. a person directly affected by a violation, real or prospective. The Human Rights Act on this "victim test" incorp-orates Art.34 of the European Convention, under which journalists, publishers and printers have all been held "victims" of criminal and civil laws which affect publications. Since Art.10 protects the right to *receive* as well as to impart information and ideas, it may be possible for readers and viewers with a genuine interest in access to sup-pressed material to bring legal proceedings to quash a ban. On this basis, the European Court permitted Irish women of childbearing age to complain about a ban on the publication of information about overseas abortion facilities.[82] There is some uncertainty in Conven-tion jurisprudence about when victimhood is "potential" enough to permit action: Mrs Bowman was permitted to challenge the ban on election campaigning by her pressure group even though she had been acquitted—the fact that she had been prosecuted several times before made a future prosecution a real possibility.[83] The "victim-hood" test is an unnecessary and irritating technicality which will serve to protect some offensive laws and practices: many judges, led by Lord Woolf, protested about its adoption but to no avail—the

---

[80] The PCC, although a voluntary body, performs public duties and hence is arguably capable of being judicially reviewed: *R. v Press Complaints Commission, Ex p. Stewart Brady* [1997] E.M.L.R. 185 and see Lewis, *Judicial Remedies in Public Law* (2nd edn) para.2–069. The Government indicated its view that the PCC was a "public authority" for the purposes of the HRA: *Hansard* 314 H.C. Debs (6th series) col. 414.

[81] *R. v BBC Ex p. Referendum Party* [1997] C.O.D. 459. The Divisional Court declined to make a ruling on the BBC's liability to judicial review.

[82] *Open Door and Dublin Well Women Clinic v Ireland* (1992) 15 E.H.R.R. 244.

[83] *Bowman v UK* (1998) 26 E.H.R.R. 1.

Government wanted to avoid test cases brought by interest groups.[84] It is, however, unacceptable that rules and decisions which infringe human rights should persist because interest groups which could fund the litigation to strike them down are denied the standing to do so. Newspapers are handicapped in bringing test cases against obnoxious legislation: the *Guardian* also wanted to challenge the Act of Settlement 1701, which provides that the Crown should descend only to Protestants and to men ahead of women, but its editor, a male and a commoner, could not claim to be a victim. (The Princess Royal declined the newspaper's offer to fund her challenge to the line of succession.)

2–028   The *Guardian* did, however, achieve some relaxation in the "victim" test when it sought a declaration that the 1848 Treason Felony Act, which outlaws any advocacy of republicanism, had either to be interpreted, in conformity with Art.10, as incriminating only the advocacy of forcible overthrow of the monarch, or else must suffer a declaration of incompatibility. The law lords declared that the *Guardian* did not have to show that it was a victim of any actual prosecution in order to bring the case: a realistic possibility of prosecution would be sufficient, even if that threat was remote.[85] So long as the issue was not fact-sensitive (i.e. was a pure question of law) and there was a cogent public or individual interest which might be satisfied by a declaration, the court could act:

> "It may be a matter of constitutional importance. An historic anomaly in our political democracy could be examined by our courts. There is something to be said for the view that it ought not to be left to the court in Strasbourg to drag us to an obvious conclusion."[86]

In this case, however, the conclusion was all too obvious—the 1848 Act was "a relic of a bygone age" and any possibility of prosecution was unreal. The *Guardian* achieved its objective, although by a side wind: the courts were understandably concerned that they should not have to do parliament's job of updating legislation, but where archaic laws breach fundamental rights they should not hesitate to say so. The case would permit the media to take preventative action if threatened by the Attorney-General with prosecution for criminal or seditious libel or blasphemy or under some statute that is plainly incompatible with freedom of expression.

In the case of statutes which on their face require an unacceptable infringement of free speech, the court has two options. First and

---

[84] See Lester and Pannick, *Human Rights Law and Practice*, p.38.
[85] It referred to *Norris v Ireland* [1988] 13 EH RR, paras 32–4, where an Irish homosexual was held a "victim" for the purpose of complaining to Strasbourg, although "a risk of prosecution was minimal".
[86] *Rusbridger v Att-Gen* [2003] 3 All E.R. 784 at 794, para.24, *per* Lord Steyn.

foremost, it is given a brand new power of statutory interpretation—really, of statutory re-interpretation. Under s.3(1):

> "So far as it is possible to do so, primary legislation and subordinate legislation must be read and given effect in a way which is compatible with the Convention rights."

This is an imaginative way of reconciling the new judicial power to protect basic rights with the age-old constitutional principle that Parliament must retain sovereignty. If it is *possible* to give statutory language an interpretation which accords with the Convention, that interpretation must prevail. This is not a power to be underrated. When a barrister says that your case is "arguable", that decodes as meaning he will be happy to accept a fee for the pleasure of making an argument which is likely to fail. But s.3 turns that which is merely arguable into an argument which should succeed, if it is the only plausible argument which can make a statute conform to the Convention. In so far as language permits, the court must choose a construction of statutory words which most effectuates free speech—there will be a presumption in favour of the meaning which least restricts the media, even if it is a strained interpretation of the legislative language compared with other meanings which more honestly reflect Parliament's intention to ignore or limit human rights. Section 3 has a radical impact which means that "well-entrenched ideas may have to be put aside, sacred cows culled".[87]

If it is simply not possible to fashion the statutory language into a meaning consistent with Art.10, then the High Court may issue a "declaration of incompatibility". This will, in cases which the Government deems "compelling", provide the Minister with the power immediately to amend the law by an Order in Council. But "compelling" is a difficult test to satisfy, and this emergency power is unlikely to be used. Nonetheless, a "declaration of incompatibility" provides a real impetus to amend the law in due course, if only because it will be a clear signal for the European Court of Human Rights (which retains its supervisory role) to find Britain in breach of the Convention if no remedial action is taken. The courts insist, however, that such declarations must be a last resort: judges should strive to turn or twist legislative language "so far as it is possible" under s.3 of the Act to achieve an interpretation that is Convention-compliant. There must be no deference to what parliament meant in the original legislation, because what parliament meant by passing the Human Rights Act was that all its previous laws should be interpreted by the courts so as to comply with the Convention.[88]

As to the meaning of Art.10, there are three basic guides:

---

[87] *R. v Lambert* [2001] 3 All E.R. 577, HL *per* Lord Slynn at para.6. See also *R. v A* [2001] 3 All E.R. 1, HL, especially Lord Steyn at paras 32–46.
[88] *Ghaidan v Godin-Mendoza* [2004] 2 A.C. 557.

(i) the language of the Article itself, with its structure long established in Convention law;

(ii) s.2 of the Human Rights Act, which says that British courts *must* take into account Strasbourg case-law;

(iii) s.12 of the Human Rights Act, which gives "particular importance" to Art.10 in certain circumstances.

(i) Article 10 itself

2–029 We all have the right to freedom of expression, to hold opinions and to receive and impart information and ideas without interference, subject to such restrictions as are prescribed by law and are necessary in a democratic society in the interests of national security, prevention of crime, protection of morals, protection of the reputation and rights of others, preventing disclosure of confidential information or maintaining the authority of the judiciary.

The first trap for unwary judges is to think this is no more than a statement of the good old British balancing act, the "free speech does not mean free speech" approach in *James v Commonwealth*. But what the European Court has said, in its *Sunday Times v United Kingdom* judgment of 1979, is that Art.10 is *not* a balance between free speech and other values of equal weight. Article 10(2) should be looked upon as containing "a number of exceptions which must be strictly construed and narrowly interpreted and convincingly established". Once the Court is satisfied that there has been an infringement, the burden shifts to the Government or to the party seeking to justify the breach to prove that the infringing law is a clearly defined restriction which legitimately serves an Art.10(2) value and its application is necessary—not expedient—to serve a pressing social need in a democratic society, and is a reasonably proportionate response to that need. In short, the Act writes into British law, for the first time, a presumption in favour of free speech, putting the burden on the censor to justify, as a matter both of necessity and of logic, the restriction imposed.

(ii) European case law: the "core principles"

2–030 Section 2 of the Act says that the court must take into account any opinions of the European Court and even of the now defunct European Commission. This section is valuable, up to a point, because it gives authority to the "core principles" which Strasbourg has developed for Art.10. Equally, s.2 will provide precedent in English law for decisions like *Goodwin*, spelling out a right to protect journalistic sources from the general Art.10 guarantee, and *Bowman* with its insistence that the free marketplace of ideas is more, not less, important at election time.

But there are dangers in applying Strasbourg decisions, because many of them turn not on an application of principle but on what is called the "margin of appreciation"—a doctrine which accords some latitude to Member States in adapting the principles to their own culture and conditions. It is really no more than a self-denying ordinance developed by international courts for situations (especially in respect of laws relating to morals) where they are nervous about imposing their judgment over that of the domestic authorities. What English courts must appreciate is that they have *no* margin of appreciation: they sit *on* the margin, and Strasbourg decisions which apply this doctrine provide no precedent. The case of *Wingrove v United Kingdom*, for example, which rejected the complaint of a film-maker refused a certificate for *Visions of Ecstasy* because of blasphemy, provides no authority at all for an English court to reject a Human Rights Act challenge to the blasphemy law, because *Wingrove* was a decision taken by reference to the United Kingdom's "margin of appreciation", and the European Court said—in terms that our domestic courts are in touch with "vital forces" in this country, and it is for them to decide how or whether to protect religion.[89] So *Wingrove* should not inhibit British judges from giving Tom Paine at last his due by abolishing this oppressive and discriminatory relic of the common law.

It is important to note that s.2 says that Strasbourg cases must be "taken into account" (not followed slavishly and used as a precedent) and only "so far as it is relevant to the proceedings". This is just as well, because although the "core principles" of Art.10 are reasonably stated, some Eurocourt decisions—especially those emanating from seven-judge chambers—are unimpressive and a few have actually been retrogressive. It was a mistake for s.2 to require that attention be paid to all decisions of the now-defunct European Commission (originally, a filter for the Court) because some of them are short and poorly argued, especially decisions in the 1990s wrongly declaring inadmissible a flood of cases with which the court could not cope, and some in the 1970s before Art.10 principles were fully developed.

The application of Convention rights entails a measuring of what **2–031** has been done to an alleged victim against the relevant rule in the Convention, as elaborated in the "core principles" stated in Strasbourg case law. Sometimes, of course, the violation will be blatant, e.g. when an act of censorship directly infringes Art.10 and has no excuse (or "legitimate aim") that can relate to the exceptions in Art.10(2). More often, however, the decision is reached by applying what is termed the doctrine of *proportionality*—a legal approach that is new to English courts, but which has been introduced into their decision-making by the Human Rights Act. Firstly, the act which is subject of the complaint must be recognised as an infringement of the freedom of expression guarantee. Then, the

---

[89] *Wingrove v UK* (1996) 24 E.H.R.R. 1.

Court must inquire whether the rule authorising the infringement
was sufficiently clear to be "prescribed by law" and had a "legitimate
aim", i.e. an objective which corresponds to one of the exceptions set
out in Art.10(2). (If it has no "legitimate aim" then the Court need
go no further—it is a violation, pure and simple.) Then comes the
final question of whether the restriction is "necessary in a democratic society", i.e. whether it answers to a pressing social need.

This can often be resolved by applying the proportionality test—is
the infringement "proportionate" to the legitimate aim it pursues, or
does it go further than is necessary in a democratic society to achieve
that purpose—e.g. a "blanket" ban where a narrower ban would
suffice, or a restriction which discriminates between rich and poor,
or a punishment which is over-severe or not necessary at all because
a civil remedy would serve the same purpose. In judicial review
proceedings, English courts will declare unlawful an administrative
decision which is irrational, in that it bears little logical relationship
to the purpose it is meant to serve, but the proportionality test
permits a much broader review. The purpose must be "legitimate"
(in the sense that it genuinely reflects an Art.10(2) exception) and
the measures in pursuance of it must be fair and calculated sensibly
to achieve that purpose, and go no further than is necessary in a
democracy to protect the excepted value. Proportionality, in other
words, is a test of reasonableness which goes beyond the English test
of rationality (English judges refer to their rationality test, confusingly, as *Wednesbury* reasonableness"[90])—and it is a "reasonableness" constituted by avoiding any infringement of a bedrock
democratic right deemed basic to social progress and individual self-
fulfilment.[91] The "proportionality" test for reviewing administrative
decisions, imported into English law by the HRA, is transforming
the "*Wednesbury* unreasonableness" standard into a test of "reasonableness" *simpliciter*.[92]

(iii) Section 12—Freedom of expression

2–032 The passage of the Human Rights Act through Parliament was
marked by a display of a very English hypocrisy: the two institutions
which preach loudest about human rights—the church of England
and the press of England—both wanted to be exempted from it. The
church because it wanted to keep on discriminating against women
and the press because it wanted to continue to invade privacy.
Although God was given only a minor dispensation, Rupert Murdoch and his local vicar, Lord Wakeham (Chairman of the Press

---

[90] This phrase stems from the name of the case in which the irrationality test was
first adopted—*Associated Provincial Picture Houses v Wednesbury Corp* [1948] K.B.
223.
[91] See *Lingens v Austria* (1986) 8 E.H.R.R. 407 at 418–9, paras 41–2.
[92] This is the logical result of the House of Lords decision in *R. v Secretary of State
for Home Department Ex p. Daly* [2001] UKHL 26.

Complaints Commission), managed to persuade the Government to insert a novel provision to entrench "freedom of expression". Section 12 of the Human Rights Act provides that a court must have particular regard to the importance of the right to freedom of expression in actions against the media. It applies only to civil proceedings—although it is difficult to accept that freedom of expression can be particularly important in the High Court and important, but not particularly important, down at the Old Bailey. It applies not only when legal proceedings relate to "material which appears to the court to be journalistic" (which is fair enough) but to material "which the respondent *claims* to be journalistic" (where the *Sunday Sport* is concerned, the difference may be crucial). In such cases the court is enjoined by s.12(4)(b) to have particular regard to the public interest in publication or alternatively to "any relevant privacy code" which includes the PCC Code of Conduct). The section reads as follows:

> "1. This Section applies if a court (which includes a tribunal) is considering whether to grant any relief which, if granted, might affect the exercise of the Convention right to freedom of expression . . .
>
> 3. No such relief is to be granted so as to restrain publication before trial unless the court is satisfied that the applicant is likely to establish that publication should not be allowed.
>
> 4. The Court must have particular regard to the Convention right to freedom of expression and, where the proceedings relate to material which the respondent claims, or which appears to the Court, to be journalistic, literary or artistic material (or to conduct connected with such material), to—
>
> (a) the extent to which—
>
> (i) the material has, or is about to, become available to the public; or
> (ii) it is, or would be, in the public interest for the material to be published;
>
> (b) any relevant privacy code. . ."

The object of the media proprietors who lobbied for s.12 was to discourage the courts from using Art.8 to develop a privacy law. It is doubtful whether s.12 does this effectively, but it has a capacity to rise above its unprepossessing origins and to put Art.10 in lights by giving its presumption in favour of free speech a special force and states in terms that the public interest in publication is to be brought into particular consideration. It places obstacles in the path of that bane of Sunday newspaper life, the Saturday afternoon interim injunction. This can no longer be granted on the "balance of convenience" principle: the court must henceforth be satisfied that the claimant is likely to win—a test which is closer to that for libel injunctions (which are rarely granted). Moreover, the judge must pay particular regard not only to the freedom of expression right *and* to the public interest, but also "to the extent to which the material has, or is about to, become available to the public". So that's goodbye to *Spycatcher*, where the book was already on sale to every public except the British, and to cases where the information suppressed as "confidential" could have been gathered from press clippings. It means that courts should rarely if ever grant injunctions to suppress material which has "escaped" on the internet.

This requirement that the Court must take into account "the extent to which the material is about to become available" reflects the impossibility of containing newsworthy information, once it has escaped its gatekeeper, and signals the end of injunctions like that granted in 1999 against the *Sunday Telegraph* to stop premature publication of the Stephen Lawrence Report. This has been the consequence of the new Bill of Rights in South Africa, which has had a markedly liberalising effect on media law. In *Government of South Africa v Sunday Times* the facts were almost identical to the Lawrence Report case: the South African Government tried to injunct premature publication of a report into corruption by invoking a statutory regulation that prohibited publication of such reports until presented to the President. The court struck down the regulation as contrary to the freedom of expression guarantee, and held that no injunction could be granted in the absence of the clearest proof of serious harm.[93]

2–033   Section 12(3) makes new provision for pre-trial injunctions, by providing that no such relief (i.e. that might affect the right to freedom of expression) is to be granted "unless the court is satisfied that the applicant is likely to establish that publication should not be allowed". This makes clear that courts cannot simply apply the "balance of convenience test": in 2004 the House of Lords in *Cream Holdings v Banerjee* decided that however convenient it would be for an injunction to stop publication until trial—a year or so in the future—s.12(3) required the would-be injunctor to prove that such success was more likely than not, or likely enough to make an injunction inappropriate.[94] Difficult as it may be in the rushed circumstances in which applications are often heard and with the evidence then only in an incomplete state, the court will have to determine the likelihood of the claimant succeeding at trial. The onus is on the claimant who will have to demolish any realistic defences which might be advanced at trial.

Section 12 serves to entrench the right of free speech in newsworthy cases. But what about cases where the news is unworthy—of no public interest, obtained by outrageous invasion of privacy? The original point of s.12 was to give the media a special privilege so it

---

[93] *Government of the Republic of South Africa v Sunday Times Newspaper* (1995) 1 L.R.C. 168.
[94] *Cream Holdings v Banerjee* [2005] 1 A.C. 253.

could ward off privacy claims and injunctions. But this may backfire, because s.12(4)(b) requires the court to "pay particular regard to any relevant privacy code". It does not say "pay particular regard to the existence of an alternative remedy offered by the Press Complaints Commission (PCC) or the Broadcasting Standards Commission (BSC)". It says "pay particular regard to the relevant *code*". So: the very first thing the judge must ask in any civil action is "bring me the code". And, as the Home Secretary pointed out:

> "The fact that a newspaper complied with the terms of the code operated by the PCC—or conversely that it has breached the code—is one of the factors the courts should take into account in considering whether to grant relief".[95]

The news media, should in one respect gain from Art.8. It requires respect for private and family life, home and correspondence, and erects the barrier test of "necessity" to limit intrusions by State and public authorities. Strasbourg jurisprudence establishes that it protects a person's office or other place of work,[96] so it will in consequence benefit journalists who are faced with police searches or other intrusions by State agents. Although UK law requires police to go through a special procedure before they can seize journalistic material, in practice they encounter little difficulty from judges who are generally anxious to let them have, for example, unpublished photographs or untransmitted video footage of violent demonstrations. The Convention criteria of "proportionality" should inject a new rigour into judicial scrutiny of police applications.

A NEW LEGAL LANDSCAPE

The Human Rights Act has had important implications for every 2–034 area of media law and it will be some years before its impact can be finally assessed. British judges acquired some experience in giving force to constitutional protections for freedom of expression by dint of their service on the Privy Council, which still hears final appeals from a number of Commonwealth countries whose constitutions embody human rights guarantees. As early as 1967, for example, they struck down a Maltese law prohibiting civil servants from bringing into their place of work any newspaper that had been condemned by the Catholic Church.[97] In 1990 they stopped the prosecution of the Antiguan journalist, Tim Hector, who faced imprisonment for publishing "a false statement . . . likely to undermine public confidence in the conduct of public affairs". This law

---

[95] *Hansard*, July 2, 1998, 315 H.C. (6th Series) col. 538–9.
[96] *Niemetz v Germany* (1992) 16 E.H.R.R. 97.
[97] *Olivier v Buttigieg* [1967] 1 A.C. 115.

could not be justified as a necessary interference with free speech in a democratic society: since the very purpose of criticising officials was to undermine public confidence in their stewardship, the law was by its own definition a cloak for political censorship. The law was not saved by the requirement that the statement should be false: freedom of speech, the Privy Council correctly held, would be gravely impeded if would-be critics had to verify all their facts before they could speak without fear of criminal charges.[98]

A Convention-based approach to the free speech right is exemplified by another case from Antigua, *de Freitas v Permanent Secretary of Ministry of Agriculture*[99]:

> A Royal Commission in Antigua exposed the corruption which riddled that country's Government and tainted in particular the Minister of Agriculture, who declined to resign or pay back the bribes he had accepted. A civil servant in his department was observed at a peaceful demonstration against Government corruption: he was suspended and disciplined under a law which prevented public servants from expressing opinions on matters of political controversy. The Privy Council ruled that this blanket restraint was disproportionate to the legitimate objective of securing neutrality in the bureaucracy and could not reasonably be justified in a democratic society: it followed that his rights under the Constitutional guarantee of free speech had been infringed. The question was whether the challenged provision arbitrarily or excessively violated the enjoyment of a guaranteed right, to be decided by application of a tripartite test for proportionality, namely whether:
>
> (1) the legislative object is sufficiently important to justify limiting a fundamental right;
> (2) the measures designed to meet the legislative objective are rationally connected to it; and
> (3) the means used to impair the right or freedom are no more than is necessary to accomplish the objective.

It is a measure of the international reach of human rights jurisprudence that this tripartite test for disproportionality comes into English law via an Antiguan appeal to the Privy Council which adopted it from a decision of the Chief Justice of Zimbabwe who picked it up from decisions of South African and Canadian judges who had in turn drawn on the "proportionality" jurisprudence of the European Court of Human Rights. Despite (in fact, because of) this pedigree, the formula is unsatisfactory, with its plodding language and lawyerly "on the one hand but then on the other" qualifications. The Privy Council decision only came alive when it moved into the top gear of the First Amendment, citing with approval Justice Brennan's full-blooded condemnation of blanket bans on the expression of opinion:

---

[98] *Hector v Att-Gen of Antigua and Barbuda* [1990] 2 A.C. 312.
[99] *Ellroy de Freitas v Permanent Secretary of Ministry of Agriculture, Fisheries Lands and Housing* [1999] A.C. 69.

"The objectionable quality of vagueness and overbreadth (depends) upon the danger of tolerating, in the area of First Amendment freedoms, the existence of a penal statute susceptible of sweeping and improper application . . . These freedoms are delicate and vulnerable, as well as supremely precious in our society. The threat of sanctions may deter their exercise almost as potently as the actual application of sanctions . . . Because First Amendment freedoms need breathing space to survive, government may regulate in the area only with narrow specificity."[100]

Even in the "phoney war" period before the Human Rights Act took full effect, it had a major impact. The first recorded beneficiary was an Algerian refugee, Fateh Rechachi, who had been charged under s.16B of the Prevention of Terrorism Act with possessing information "likely to be of use to terrorists"—including guerrilla warfare books available from major bookstores. In 1999 he challenged the DPP's decision to prosecute him as irrational, on the basis that the DPP had an obligation to respect the Act and not prosecute in contravention of it, even though it was not yet in force. The Chief Justice, ruling on the Human Rights Act for the very first time, declared s.16B a "blatant contravention" of the Convention because it reversed the presumption of innocence (the defendant had to prove "reasonable excuse" for his possession of freely available literature once police suspected him of helping terrorists). This breached Art.6 (right to a fair trial) and violated Art.10 as well. The case against Rechachi was dropped.[101] This was an astonishing result, given the penchant of British judges to uphold anti-terrorist legislation, but there were more shocks in store, especially the opinion of the Law Lords in the case of *R v Home Secretary Ex p. Simms*[102]:

A prison rule prohibited prisoners from being interviewed by journalists. It was upheld by the Court of Appeal on the basis that conviction deprived persons of free speech rights, and that the rule served a legitimate aim in preventing publications which might distress victims or their relatives. The House of Lords, however, held that free speech rights could only be infringed so far as was necessary for prison discipline, not to prevent media investigations of miscarriages of justice. The Court accepted that the media had been of crucial importance in spotlighting wrongful convictions, and had a legitimate role in correcting errors in the functioning of the criminal justice

---

[100] *National Association for the Advancement of Colored People v Button* (1963) 371 U.S. 415, 432–33.

[101] Unlike the associated case against *Kebilene* which proceeded to the House of Lords, where it was held that the Divisional Court should not have reviewed the DPP's decision until the HRA came into force. See [2000] 2 A.C. 326.

[102] [2000] 2 A.C. 115.

system. Applying the proportionality approach of the European Convention, the Court struck down the rule in its blanket form as *ultra vires*, in that it unnecessarily curtailed both the prisoners' right to free expression and damaged "the safety valve of effective investigative journalism".

2–035   The force of Art.10 as entrenched by s.12 of the Human Rights Act was demonstrated in the landmark libel case of *Reynolds v Times Newspapers*.[103] The Human Rights Act helped the *Reynolds* court to fashion a new public interest privilege for news reporting and investigative journalism, so long as it is published without malice after reasonable checks for accuracy and with elemental fairness to the victim (e.g. by publishing his explanation or at least inviting his comments). In *Reynolds*, Lord Steyn describes the Human Rights Act as a "new legal landscape"—freedom of expression has become a constitutional right, a rule which exists in the highest legal order. Exceptions must be justified as necessary in a democracy:

> "In other words, freedom of expression is the rule and regulation of speech is the exception requiring justification . . . if it is underpinned by a pressing social need."

In redressing the traditional English imbalance which has historically favoured reputation over free speech, the judges produced in 1999 a solution which had been specifically rejected by an official committee in 1975 (the Faulks Committee on Defamation) when human rights law was unappreciated and (for most lawyers) non-existent. They did so by applying the "core principles" of Art.10, as explained in cases like *Goodwin* and *Lingens* and *Castells*, with assistance from decisions in other Commonwealth jurisdictions, whilst bearing in mind the imminent operation of the Human Rights Act with its s.12 requirement "to have particular regard to the importance of the right to freedom of expression". Interestingly, when it became apparent by 2006 that *Reynolds* was not working, the House of Lords in *Jameel v Wall Street Journal* recast its approach more favourably to the media but without the need to make much reference to Convention cases. This is some indication that the Human Rights Act has by now served its purpose: law lords, at least, are prepared to develop the "freedom of expression" principle as if it were ingrained in the common law.

The sea change wrought in media law by the Human Rights Act was apparent in the first House of Lords decision after it came into operation on October 2, 2000. In *McCartan Turkington Breen v Times Newspapers*,[104] a firm of Irish solicitors who had acted for a soldier (Mr Clegg) convicted of murder was defamed in a press

---

[103] [1999] 3 W.L.R. 1010.
[104] [2001] 2 A.C. 277.

release issued by a support group, extracts from which were published in *The Times*. Whether the newspaper could claim qualified privilege for a report of a "public meeting" depended on how that phrase—originating in a nineteenth century statute—should be construed. The lower courts had no doubt that it did not cover either a small gathering to which reporters were invited, or a press release which had not been read at the gathering. The House of Lords, however, insisted that the Victorian-era statutory language should be given a meaning consistent with modern society and "the crucial importance of press freedom" as the means by which public debates are now conducted. In order to permit informed participation by citizens in public life, the press served as "the eyes and ears of the public to whom they report"— not only by reporting protest meetings, but by attending press conferences (unknown in Victorian days) and reproducing press statements. The old legislation according a privilege in aid of reporting could therefore be extended to modern conditions, on the principle that "the path of safety lies in the opportunity to discuss freely supposed grievances and proposed remedies".[105]

That the Law Lords turned for guidance in their first post-Human Rights Act media law decision to a principle formulated by the notable American jurist Louis Brandeis (whose free speech utterances includes the classic "sunlight is said to be the best of disinfectants") is a hopeful sign that the developed law of the First Amendment will be used to enhance British media freedom, as well as the more cautious (and more Europrosaic) core principles of the European Court of Human Rights. This underlines the failure of the English common law, lacking any constitutional basis, to offer satisfactory intellectual principles by which free speech clashes with other values can be resolved. It also affords a pleasing irony, in that the philosophy behind US decisions has been heavily influenced by English writers like Tom Paine and John Stuart Mill, prophets who may now at last be honoured in their own country. The "free market place of ideas" which underpins US media law thinking derives from Mill's argument in *On Liberty* that any censorship of opinion is counterproductive, because it is only by "collision of adverse opinion" that truth will out. This was harnessed to the all-powerful American belief in competition to produce the theory, famously articulated by Justice Holmes in 1919, that "the best test of truth is the power of thought to get itself accepted in the competition of the market". Market distortions being what they later became in the United States, this was not altogether satisfactory and European jurisprudence reverts to a more classic Millian formulation, referring to "the demands of pluralism, tolerance and broadmindedness without which there is no democratic society". Courts in both

---

[105] Brandeis J., *Whitney v California* (1927) 274 U.S. 357 at 375–6.

countries have additionally recognised that free speech is a necessary condition of the individual soul—as Justice Thurgood Marshal put it in the self-exploring sixties, "Freedom of expression serves not only the needs of the polity but also those of the human spirit—a spirit that demands self-expression". The poet Milton put it rather better in the *Aeropagitica*, three centuries previously.

2–036   At any event, these portentous propositions are now a part of English law, thanks to s.12 of the Human Rights Act and Art.10. Lord Steyn promulgated them in his speech in *Simms*, striking down a prison rule that prohibited a convict from complaining to journalists that he had suffered a miscarriage of justice:

> "Freedom of expression is, of course, intrinsically important: it is valued for its own sake. But it is well recognised that it is also instrumentally important. It serves a number of broad objectives. First, it promotes the self-fulfilment of individuals in society. Secondly, in the famous words of Holmes J. (echoing John Stuart Mill), "the best test of truth is the power of the thought to get itself accepted in the competition of the market": *Abrams v US* (1919) 250 U.S. 616 at 630 *per* Holmes J., dissenting. Thirdly, freedom of speech is the lifeblood of democracy. The free flow of information and ideas informs political debate. It is a safety valve: people are more ready to accept decisions that go against them if they can in principle seek to influence them. It acts as a brake on the abuse of power by public officials. It facilitates the exposure of errors in the governance and administration of justice of the country."

These, then, are the human rights rationales for freedom of expression, finally incorporated into English law at the turn of the twenty-first century. When line-drawing exercises are called for in the courts, it will henceforth be necessary for the would-be censor to prove that public harm is real rather than speculative. In a reversal of a long-standing common law approach to street demonstrations (which permitted them to be banned if hypothetical bystanders would be outraged) the High Court in 1999 ruled that a tiresome bible-basher should not have been moved on by police from her makeshift pulpit on the steps of Wakefield cathedral. Justice Stephen Sedley remarked:

> "Free speech includes not only the inoffensive but the irritating, the contentious, the eccentric, the heretical, the unwelcome and the provocative provided it does not tend to provoke violence. Freedom only to speak inoffensively is not worth having. What Speakers Corner (where the law applies as fully as anywhere else) demonstrates is the tolerance which is both extended by the law to opinion of every kind and expected by the law in the conduct of those who disagree, even strongly, with what they

hear. From the condemnation of Socrates to the persecution of modern writers and journalists, our world has seen too many examples of state control of unofficial ideas. A central purpose of the European Convention on Human Rights has been to set close limits to any such assumed power . . ."[106]

---

[106] *Redmond-Bate v DPP* (1997) 7 B.H.R.C. 375.

CHAPTER 3

DEFAMATION

"We need more such serious journalism in this country and our defamation laws should encourage rather than discourage it."[1]

INTRODUCTION

London is the libel capital of the world. American journalists dub it **3–001** "a town named Sue" since its claimant-friendly environment attracts litigants unable or unwilling to take their chances under American or European defamation laws which afford better protection for media defendants.[2] The Russian oligarch Boris Berezovsky, defamed by *Forbes* (an American business magazine), chose to sue in London rather than America (where his prospect of success, thanks to the First Amendment, would have been minimal) although the dispute was between foreigners and had no connection with Britain.[3] Arab billionaires, too, choose to sue the American media—especially the *Wall Street Journal*—in London rather than in New York or in Brussels (where its European edition is based) and English law is the preferred option of international public figures because it has traditionally tilted the balance against freedom of speech, with the practical consequence that foreign publishers fearful of attracting an English libel action cut passages critical of wealthy and powerful public figures, or else do not publish here at all (the fate of Kitty Kelley's US best-seller alleging scandals in the monarchy, *The Royals*). Even Daniel Moynihan's celebrated aphorism about his friend Henry Kissinger ("Henry doesn't lie because it's in his

---

[1] Baroness Hale *Jameel (Mohammed) v Wall Street Journal Europe Sprl* [2006] UKHL 44, para.150.

[2] The classic study is *Gatley on Libel and Slander* (10th edn, Milmo & Rogers, 1998). A helpful and streetwise text is David Price, *Defamation: Law Procedure and Practice* (3rd edn, Sweet & Maxwell, 2005). The definitive account of increasingly important American law is by Judge Robert Sack, *Sack on Defamation*, 3rd edn, (Practising Law Institute, 1999). An enjoyable and insightful romp through famous libel trials is provided by David Hooper, *Reputations Under Fire* (Little, Brown and Co, 2000).

[3] *Berezovsky v Michaels* [2000] 1 W.L.R. 1004, HL.

interests. He lies because it's in his nature.") was solemnly edited out of books on American politics before they were published here. That Britain should have become a no-go area for information freely published elsewhere in the world poses a serious question: in the global village created by instantaneous electronic communication, does it make any sense for people to have different reputations in different parts of town?

Law must reconcile the right to free speech with the right to reputation. Since American law gives a great deal of protection to defamatory words published in good faith about public figures, and English law gives little, it would seem to follow that speech is accorded more respect in the United States. Ironically, the contrary is true: in Britain we have an almost supernatural belief in the power of words to wound and destroy. Any mildly critical reference to a prominent person brings forth a pompously threatening solicitor's letter, but in America defamatory words scattered on the raging sea of communication are usually ignored. (For all the apparent permissiveness of the First Amendment, those who write for American publication suffer the schoolmarmish omnipresence of the "fact checker"—a spur to professionalism unknown to the British journalist.) Those who believe the English law of libel is an exquisite flower to be preserved in full bloom fail to notice that it has produced a society where it is hard to keep a bad man down: see the crooked careers of Conrad Black (whose journalists had their snouts so deep in his trough they failed to notice the illegality under their noses) and Robert Maxwell (never exposed by the British press, partly because he owned 30 per cent of it but mainly because the other 70 per cent was intimidated by his libel writs). But the sad fact is that mainstream media interests do not much care about improving the right to report what powerful people do in their business, so long as they can tell readers what they do in bed.

There is nothing objectionable in the principle that a person's reputation should be protected from falsehoods: problems arise because the practices and procedures of the libel law can also work to prevent the exposure of wrongdoing. Cases that come to trial are merely the tip of an iceberg that deep-freezes large chunks of interesting news and comment. In news rooms, libel is the greatest inhibition upon freedom of speech. The task for the journalist and broadcaster is to understand it sufficiently to call the bluff of those who seek to suppress important truths. That the bluff succeeds more often that it should may be the fault of the unconscionably heavy legal costs that can attend even a successful defence, or the business caution of libel insurers who increasingly influence how, or whether, libel writs should be resisted. But journalists who are well versed in legal defences have more latitude than is commonly thought. When the destination is important, the writer's craft can often be steered around the libel minefield. As Lord Devlin pointed out,

"A man who wants to talk at large about smoke may have to pick his words very carefully if he wants to exclude the suggestion that there is also a fire: but it can be done."[4]

The presence of smoke can be reported much more readily now, **3–002** thanks to the incorporation of Art.10 of the European Convention on Human Rights, provided some careful checks are made to ensure that it is not bellowing from a smoke machine. That much was established by the 1999 landmark case of *Reynolds v Times Newspapers*, in which the judiciary, despairing of legislative reform by self-interested politicians, cautiously created a public interest defence, the first feature on the "new legal landscape" vouchsafed by the 1998 Human Rights Act. The decision proved to be overcautious, however, and in 2006 the defence had to be restated and strengthened by the law lords in *Jameel v Wall Street Journal* to provide a full-blooded justification for responsible journalism on subjects of public interest. To appreciate the way in which libel law may undergo further transformation, the past—that other country—must briefly be revisited.

HISTORY

Defamation began in the eleventh century, before the invention of **3–003** printing, as a creation of the ecclesiastical courts, which would set the village Murdoch in the stocks for disobeying the injunction of Leviticus: "Thou shall not go up and down as a tale bearer among the people". Slander initially was a criminal offence: the first statute came in 1275, creating the offence of "*scandalum magnatum*" expressly to protect "the great men of the realm" against discomfiture from stories which might rouse the people against them. It was the threat to civil order which was the gravamen of the criminal offence, hence Lord Chief Justice Coke's famous maxim, "The greater the truth the greater the libel"—the populace would be more likely to revolt if allegations against the aristocracy were real rather than imagined. As Coke himself explained, with homely seventeenth century sexism, "a woman would not grieve to have been told of her red nose if she had not one indeed". The Star Chamber enforced the libel laws with monumental ferocity—William Prynne had his ears cut off for criticising the immorality of courtiers; when he repeated his accusations in a *News of the World* style polemic aimed at the Queen and entitled *Women Actresses—Notorious Whores* they cut off the stumps of his ears, and branded his forehead with the letters "SL" for "seditious libeller". But this penal jurisdiction was always exercised on the basis of an apprehended threat to peace.

The Star Chamber permitted civil action for libel when it banned duelling, the traditional method of redressing damage to reputation.

---

[4] *Lewis v Daily Telegraph* [1964] A.C. 234 at 285.

As a result the courts became inundated with libel actions brought
by insulted nobles. There was plenty of raw material in early
common law to fashion a rule supportive of free speech over
reputation, although it was never expressed in broad principle,
always in pettifogging points of pleading. By the end of the
eighteenth century Erskine's stand against judicial control of the jury
had produced Fox's Libel Act (establishing the right of juries rather
than judges to decide whether words were defamatory) and the
claimant bore the burden of proving that the words were false, had
been published or spoken maliciously, and had caused real damage.
But in the nineteenth and twentieth century, the common law was
re-fashioned to serve the British class system from the perspective of
that extraordinary institution, the Victorian club. The idea that large
sums of money must be awarded to compensate people for words
which "tend to lower them in the estimation of right-thinking
members of society" directly derives from an age when social,
political and legal life was lived in gentlemen's clubs in Pall Mall, an
age when escutcheons could be blotted and society scandals resolved
by writs for slander. Libel damages came in this period to call for a
metaphysical evaluation of dignity, the idea being that they should
show the world a person's real value, rather than being used to
punish the publisher for error. Libel was a method for deciding
whether the claimant really was a gentleman (one leading case
involved allegations of cheating at cards, another of shooting foxes—
just not done, old chap, to *shoot* a fox: a gentleman hunts it down
with dogs). Public men had a social obligation to clear their names
from calumny (an obligation that did for Oscar Wilde): the judges
helped these upper-class claimants by creating "presumptions" that
any slur on their character must be false, published maliciously and
would do their reputations serious damage in "right-minded
society". These presumptions had the effect of reversing the burden
of proof, so that accusers (notably the emerging popular press) made
accusations at their peril.

Thus developed a law heavily weighted towards reputation over
free speech. Assertions of fact had to be proved by those who made
them, with no public interest defence, unless made on an occasion of
privilege, such as a debate in Parliament or by sworn evidence in
court. There were a limited number of occasions where social
intercourse amongst the upper classes demanded at least a qualified
privilege for defamation—notably to write critical references about
servants and tradesmen—but judges were always reluctant to extend
this indulgence to the media in respect of reporting to the public at
large. As recently as 1983, the Court of Appeal in *Blackshaw v Lord*
said that the only defamatory allegation the media might be privileged to report (and then only if it was believed true) would concern
an emergency such as the planting of bombs or the poisoning of
supermarket food.[5] Damages in this period were often awarded for

---

[5] *Blackshaw v Lord* [1983] 2 All E.R. 311 at 327.

statements subsequently proved true. Thus John Profumo, when Minister for War, collected libel damages for the suggestion that he was dallying with prostitute Christine Keeler, a few weeks before he admitted the truth in Parliament. Liberace won a fortune when the *Daily Mirror* insinuated he might be homosexual, which indeed he was. There were a large number of cases, and an untold number of settlements, where justifiable journalism was punished by heavy damages—hence the chill factor that inhibited the British press from proper reporting of enveloping scandals such as the sale of arms to Iraq and the collapse of Lloyd's of London. The common law of libel was condemned by the European Court of Human Rights because of the uncontrolled jury discretion to award massive damages,[6] and American courts refused (for the first time since the Boston Tea Party), to enforce British judgments—on the grounds that English libel law was "antipathetic to the First Amendment".[7] In America, defamation actions cannot succeed unless the media are proved at fault: the claimant must show that the allegations were false and published with a reckless or negligent disregard for the truth. What US courts found repugnant about UK law was how it placed the burden of proving truth on the defendant, and held him liable to pay damages for statements he honestly believed to be true and had published without negligence.

Evenutually, and spurred on by the Human Rights Act, judges **3–004** have recently found some way out of this impasse by developing the doctrine of qualified privilege—that mid-nineteenth century creation to allow masters to slander their servants. It was, Baron Parke had ruled in *Toogood v Spyring*,[8] for "the common convenience of society" that masters should communicate honestly with each other about the shortcomings of their workers, and this "common convenience" was later extended to allow newspapers to publish the results of professional disciplinary hearings, foreign court actions and the like. But the Appeal judges in *Blackshaw* pointed out that the media only enjoyed the privilege if they could prove they had a *duty* to publish, and it could not envisage the media having a *duty*, except in an emergency, to publish defamatory allegations which turned out to be untrue. But this narrow, formalistic concept of "duty" was rejected by the High Court of Australia and the Court of Appeal of New Zealand in cases brought in both countries by a former Prime Minister of New Zealand, David Lange.[9] It was, they ruled, for the common convenience of citizens of modern society that reasonably researched allegations should be published about

---

[6] *Tolstoy Miloslavsky v UK* (1995) 20 E.H.R.R. 442.

[7] *Bachan v India Abroad Publications*, 585 N.Y.S 2d 661 (1992); *Telnikoff v Matusevitch* 702A 2d 230 (Md. 1997).

[8] *Toogood v Spyring* (1834) 1 C.M.&R. 181.

[9] See *Lange v Atkinson No.1* [1998] 3 N.Z.L.R. 424 and *No.2* [2000] N.Z.L.R. 385 and *Lange v ABC* (1997) 189 C.L.R. 520.

powerful public figures, which would be "privileged" from libel actions even if they subsequently turned out to be untrue. This antipodean breakthrough was gratefully, if not wholly, accepted by the English courts (looking over their shoulder at the imminent arrival of the European Convention) in the cases of *Reynolds*[10] and *Gaddafi*,[11] to fashion a new public interest defence for investigative journalism. If the research is careful, the treatment fair, and the defamatory statements of fact honestly believed to be true, the media have a new public interest defence, although it came at first with a catch—a heavy duty on the publisher to prove that its editor and journalists acted fairly and reasonably and in reliance on apparently authoritative sources.

In the first seven years of its availability, a *Reynolds* defence succeeded only twice and on atypical facts. It proved a snare and an illusion—a snare because it lured editors and journalists into the witness box where they were accused of falling at one or more of the ten hurdles that *Reynolds* had erected for "responsible" journalism, and an illusion because it was usually rejected by trial judges brought up to believe that a "privilege" could only be claimed when there was a moral or legal *duty* to publish—and news stories, however newsworthy, rarely had this morally imperative quality other than in the *Blackshaw* examples of a terrorism or a food-contamination emergency. It took the crucial case of *Jameel v Wall Street Journal* for the House of Lords to reinvent *Reynolds* as a true public interest defence, shorn of its origins in common law privilege and pivoting upon the seriousness of the story and the quality of the journalism which produced it. Henceforth, many articles that are news*worthy*— in the sense that they are genuinely regarded by professional editors as significantly informing or advancing public debate—will be defensible if the defamation is relevant to their message, is believed true at the time of publication, and the story has been competently researched and fairly presented. There are limits to *Jameel*: it was a case involving the Wall Street Journal, a "gravely serious" newspaper (as Lady Hale commented, "some might find it seriously dull") and "not a newspaper with an interest in publishing any sensational information however inaccurate (or even in some cases, invented)".[12] If Sedley in *Jameel* is not to be a defence confined to "seriously dull" newspapers, and therefore denied to tabloids and to television "info-tainment" programmes through which most of the public receive their news, the courts will have to make allowances for populist presentation, so long as it does not plumb the depths of character assassination visited upon Grobbelaar and George Galloway, by newspapers which threw away their public interest shield by indulging in sensationalism and fiction.

---

[10] *Reynolds v Times Newspapers Ltd* [2001] 2 A.C. 127.
[11] *Gaddafi v Telegraph Group Ltd* [2000] E.M.L.R. 431.
[12] See *Jameel*, para.150.

Jameel is the most important case yet in the movement which is making freedom of expression a constitutional right, closer to that enjoyed by the US media under the first amendment. It does not provide an immunity for retailing falsities about public figures: as Lord Hoffman put it, "The question in each case is whether the defendant behaved fairly and responsibly in gathering and publishing the information".[13] If the information is of public importance, then the fact that it contains relevant but defamatory allegations against prominent people will not permit them to recover libel damages:

> A few months after 9/11, at a time when serious doubts were being expressed about the willingness of Saudi Arabia to co-operate with the US war on terrorist financing, the WSJE published a story that the Saudis were in fact co-operating to a hitherto unrecognised extent. They were, under a secret agreement, monitoring some of their leading businessmen, at the request of US agencies. The article actually named some of these businessmen, to show that they were in fact prominent and respectable. Mohammed Jameel, a billionaire Saudi car dealer whose family owned Hartwell Motors in Oxford, sued because the story defamed him by suggesting he was, at least in CIA eyes, a terrorist suspect. The judge and the Court of Appeal flatly rejected *Reynolds* privilege on many grounds, the main being that "naming names" was irresponsible journalism—the paper should have hidden Jameel behind the phrase "a prominent Saudi business identity". When the case reached the House of Lords, however, the judges showed a more realistic appreciation of the realities of newsgathering and news reporting. They ruled that the newspaper had been entitled to level serious allegations against individuals, in this case to report the CIA suspicions, so long as they "made a real contribution to the public interest elements in the article".[14] Judges with "leisure and hindsight" should not second guess editorial decisions made in busy newsrooms. Although the judges in the lower courts had said that Mr Jameel should not have been named, Lord Hoffman disagreed:

> > "The inclusion of the names of large and respectable Saudi business was an important part of the story. It showed that co-operation with the US treasury's request was not confined to a few companies on the fringe of Saudi society but extended to companies which were by any test within the heartland of the Saudi business world. To convey this message, inclusion of the names was necessary. Generalisation such as 'prominent Saudi companies' which can mean anything or nothing, would not have served the same purpose."[15]

The true significance of *Jameel*, a case with other important **3–005** features which will be discussed later, is that it makes the public interest defence turn, once public interest is established, upon the responsibility shown in making editorial judgments, rather than upon

---

[13] *Jameel*, para.54.
[14] Lord Hoffman, para.41.
[15] *Jameel*, para.52.

a judicial view of whether that judgment was correct. Editorial judgments cannot be second guessed and decided with the benefit of hindsight when the defamatory facts published turn out to be false. "Weight should ordinarily be given to the professional judgement of an editor or journalist in the absence of some indication that it was made in a casual, cavalier, slip-shod or careless manner."[16] Although the law lords did not expressly consider that they were creating any sort of absolute immunity for serious journalism, the fact that they decided for themselves that the defence was made out (without bothering to direct a re-trial) indicates that serious investigative journalism should be presumed to qualify for the defence unless the claimant can demonstrate irresponsibility. Lord Bingham did not need much evidence, beyond the article itself, to say "It might be thought that this was the sort of neutral, investigative journalism which *Reynolds* privilege exists to protect."[17] Lord Hoffman stated, "This case, in my opinion, illustrates the circumstances in which the defence should be available."[18] While Baroness Hale said: "If ever there was a story which met the test it must be this one."[19] It is a measure of the uncertainty and caution generated by the *Reynolds* case itself that four experienced judges in the trial and appeal courts had not discerned such an obvious quality in the story.

The importance of *Jameel*, for media law generally as well as for the law of defamation, (the most commonly applied of the free speech restrictions) is that it moves them towards a "fault" standard applicable in other torts. The writer and publisher on subjects of public interest will henceforth only be liable if he has acted negligently—by putting defamations believed to be true in the public domain without making reasonable checks. Negligence is an acceptable basis for tort liability, although adopting it as a standard requires public figures to put up with the publication of stories about them that they know to be false but which it may not be possible immediately to refute. The next challenge will be for courts to find a way of ensuring that false statements for which recovery of damages in libel is barred by *Jameel* can be nonetheless authoritatively corrected—by stretching the "journalistic responsibility" standard of *Jameel* to include editors' responsibility to set the record straight by a prominent correction as soon as the falsity is apprehended. In other words, if *Jameel* does presage a full-blooded defence for statements that serve the public interest at the time they are published but which subsequently turn out to be untrue, a precondition for asserting that defence should be that the falsity when established has been publicly and prominently admitted by the media defendant. The other major challenge for the courts in

---

[16] *Jameel*, Lord Bingham, p.33.
[17] *Jameel*, Lord Bingham, para.35.
[18] *Jameel*, Lord Hoffman, para.47.
[19] *Jameel*, Baroness Hale, para.148.

respect of defamation law will be less intellectual but far more practical: how to cut through the complexities of libel pleading and procedure and the daunting and mounting cost of defamation proceedings.

COSTS AND COMPLEXITIES

In Britain in the year 2007, a contested fortnight's defamation trial— **3–006** including all the applications which would proceed it—could easily cost each side over £1 million, and the loser would have to pay 75 per cent of the winner's costs, on top of damages which might amount to six figures. This level of legal fees deters all but wealthy claimants (or those, like police officers, who are backed by unions or associations). The main alternative to legal action is an approach to the Press Complaints Commission (PCC) which takes on the role of a poor person's libel court. But a ruling from this press-funded, toothless body cannot compare with a verdict after a trial by judge and jury: it comes with no award of damages, or even compensation for job loss or medical bills occasioned by the publication of falsehoods. (For the inadequacies of the PCC, see Ch.14.) The lack of legal aid for libel defendants amounts to a serious failure in the practical protection of free speech: individuals may be bankrupted, and small magazines sent into liquidation as the result of libel defeats. In 1999 *Living Marxism* was forced to close after an unnecessarily high libel award of £350,000 plus costs. There is a sense that this area of law really is the preserve of the rich: one official committee reported that any extension of legal aid would bring "over the fence" disputes to court (the poor being assumed to quarrel in crowded tenements rather more often that the rich accuse one another of cheating at cards).[20] Libel may be a wholly unsatisfactory law, but the answer is to reform it and not to deny its benefits to disadvantaged sections of society.

The inequalities of English libel law received a condemnation from the European Court—and international derision—as a result of the *McLibel* fiasco. McDonald's, the fast-food multi-national, sued two penniless protestors for casting slurs on their burgers, in leaflets which would have lain abandoned in gutters and refuse bins had its oppressive legal action not put them on the websites of the world. After the longest trial in English legal history, which lasted for 313 court days and produced a transcript of 20,000 pages together with 40,000 pages of documentary evidence and 130 witnesses, the multi-national was awarded damages of £60,000, which of course the unemployed defendants (who had at least been employed in defending themselves, albeit free of charge) could not pay. The Court of Appeal hearing lasted 23 days, and the entire length of the proceedings, from issue of writ until refusal of leave to appeal by the House

---

[20] The Faulks Committee on Defamation, Cmnd, 5909 (1975).

of Lords, was 9½ years. The European Court found that the proceedings had violated Art.6 of the Convention, which requires the state to provide access to the courts and to guarantee "equality of arms" at trial, as well as Art.10. It ruled that large corporations must, like politicians and other public figures, put up with a degree of uninhibited examination and discussion which a private individual would not be required to suffer, and that campaign groups played an important role in stimulating this public discussion. The award of damages had violated Art.10 because it was disproportionate: the plaintiffs were large and powerful corporate entities but were not required to prove that they had suffered any financial loss.[21]

Libel should be straightforward, but the law and court procedures have grown extremely complex. As long ago as 1966 the Court of Appeal said that "lawyers should be ashamed that they have allowed the law of defamation to have become bogged down in such a mass of technicalities".[22] But the mass continued to expand. In 1989 the same court described libel proceedings as "an archaic saraband"— lawyers reached for their dictionaries to find this meant "a slow and stately Spanish dance in triple time".[23] The fault was not solely that of libel solicitors—those "Sue Grabbit & Runne" practitioners whose overblown phraseology is a running joke in *Private Eye*. Lawyers are trained to take every available point, and judges have left them too many available points to take by pettifogging rules requiring each side to plead the "meaning" it claims the words are capable of bearing. Instead of each trial focusing on whether the jury accepts the claimant's case for overriding the defendant's right of free expression—an approach the European Convention would seem to require—the court engages in textual exegesis to determine which "meanings" the judge thinks the words are reasonably capable of bearing, before the jury hear evidence limited to those meanings to decide whether the true "meaning" (they may derive their own) has been justified. These pre-trial skirmishings add enormously to the costs: senior solicitors and Q.C.s charge about £400 an hour, so a major contested case can run up costs that are five times more than any likely damages, now conventionally set at a £200,000 maximum. Libel verdicts are notoriously unpredictable and sometimes irrational. Defences that should serve to protect the media, such as fair comment and qualified privilege, are contingent upon findings of fact, sometimes by star-struck juries: if claimants have more lovable characters and more celebrity witnesses than media defendants, these fine defences may not work as well as textbooks suggest they should. When media defendants face costs of up to £1 million to defend an action, (including a risk of paying 75 per cent of the

---

[21] *Steele and Morris v UK* [2005] 41 E.H.R.R. 22 and see John Vidal *McLibel, Burger Culture on Trial* (Macmillan, 1997).

[22] *Boston v Bagshaw & Sons* [1966] 1 W.L.R. 1126.

[23] *Morrell v International Thompson Publishing Ltd* [1989] 3 All E.R. 733.

claimant's similar costs in the event that they lose), then free speech becomes too expensive: there is overwhelming pressure to sacrifice it by apologising and paying substantial damages, or by not publishing the criticism in the first place.

Parliament's most recent attempt at reform—the extension in 1999 of conditional fee arrangements (CFAs) to fund libel actions— has not proved a sensible way forward. It was intended to make up for the denial of legal aid in libel cases by helping poor people traduced by the media. Lawyers can take their case on a "no win, no fee" basis—the inducement being that if they did win, they pocket twice the normal fee. This added a new risk dimension to a tort that is little better than a game of chance: since legal fees are so much higher than damages awards, it means that media defendants can be mulcted in millions if they fight and lose against CFA lawyers greedy for their "success fee". Although the CFA regime has allowed some poor people to achieve redress, it has been exploited by wealthy litigants and their lawyers to double the defendant's costs. Naomi Campbell, for example, won £3,500 in damages for breach of her privacy, but her cost of fighting the case was £280,000, doubled by virtue of the "success fee" owed to her lawyers who were acting under a CFA. The House of Lords declined to rule that CFA-backed libel claims by the rich and famous were in breach Art.10, but they did express some disquiet and called for a "legislative solution", although thus far any solution has eluded the legislature. The best way forward would be to abolish CFAs and to permit legal aid for deserving cases—those who can prove to an expert committee that they have been seriously and falsely defamed by a media defendant which has refused to make an appropriate retraction. **3–007**

The Law Society has produced a pre-action "protocol" for defamation which it claims will save expense and ensure that cases are dealt with quickly and fairly.[24] A letter of claim must be "sent out at the earliest reasonable opportunity" to the offending media, identifying the facts which are inaccurate or the comment alleged to be insupportable, preferably explaining the defamatory meaning which the claimant alleges the words to bear. The media defendant should give reasons for rejecting the claim and indicate the meaning that it attributes to its offending words. Since "meaning" is now a highly technical pleading matter on which cases can be won or lost, barristers will often be brought in to settle the "Letter of Claim" and "Response", thus increasing legal costs from the outset. The protocol recommends an alternative means of dispute resolution, namely arbitration by "a lawyer experienced in the field of defamation". It does not occur to the Law Society that many disputes are best resolved for free—i.e. without any lawyers, by the victim telephoning the editor and obtaining a retraction.

---

[24] Pre-Action Protocol for Defamation (August, 2000), submitted under the Civil Procedure Rules. The Protocol has no legal status, but breaches of it could induce an adverse award of costs.

Each case that goes to trial is an elaborate gamble. How much should be paid into court, and when? If the defendant makes a payment into court, the claimant may seize it and call it quits. If the claimant presses on and wins, but is awarded no more in damages than the amount of the "payment in", the claimant must foot the entire legal bill incurred by both the sides since the day of the payment.[25] In one celebrated case, a colonel with a penchant for spanking unsuspecting women sued the *Sunday People* for exposing his activities: because it exaggerated the truth, but not much, he was awarded a derisory halfpenny. But the newspaper was saddled with the legal costs of the trial, which it could have avoided by "paying in" the lowest denomination coin of the realm before the trial began. The publishers of *Exodus* had greater foresight. When sued for libel by Dr Dering, an Auschwitz prison doctor criticised in the book, they "paid in" the derisory sum of £2 before the trial. Dr Dering declined this contemptible compensation, and risked crippling legal costs on a trial that he hoped would win him heavy damages. The jury awarded him the libel raspberry—a halfpenny—so he was forced to pay for the whole action. When *Coronation Street* actor Bill Roache sued the *Sun* for suggesting that everybody thought he was as boring in real life as the character he played, the newspaper had the foresight to "pay in" £50,000, which Roache thought too small a sum to compensate him for the libel. The case went to trial, and the jury (who are kept in the dark, in true game-show tradition, about "payments in") awarded him precisely £50,000, leaving him to pay his own legal costs, estimated at over £100,000.[26] In circumstances like these, the temple of law becomes a casino.

DEFAMATION DEFINED

The test

3–008 Whether a statement is *capable* of bearing a defamatory meaning is a question of law, to be decided by the judge. A defamatory meaning is one that, in the circumstances of publication, would be likely to make reasonable and respectable people think less of the claimant. The test is variously described as "lowering the claimant in the

---

[25] The claimant has 21 days to accept the "payment in", CPR, r.36.11. After that time the claimant may still accept the offer, but only with leave of the court, which should not be granted if the risks have changed (e.g. by a new plea of justification): *Proetta v Times Newspaper* [1991] 4 All E.R. 46. A claimant can make a "Part 36 offer" of the remedies he is prepared to accept. If the defendant rejects this offer and the claimant does better than it at trial, the court can award: (a) indemnity costs; and (b) interest on costs (CPR, r. 36.21). For a defendant, losing in these circumstances can be very expensive.

[26] *Roache v News Group Newspapers Ltd* [1998] E.M.L.R. 161, CA.

estimation of right-thinking people generally"; "injuring the claimant's reputation by exposing him to hatred, contempt or ridicule"
and "tending to make the claimant be shunned and avoided". It is all
a question of respect and reputation—not just of the claimant as a
human being, but as a worker; a public official, business executive,
professional or performer. To allege incompetence at playing the
tuba would not lower most people in the eyes of their fellow
citizens—unless they happened to be professional tubists. To say
that someone votes Conservative is not a libel—unless it be said of a
Labour M.P., and, in consequence, would be defamatory in its
implication of personal and political hypocrisy.

False statements not necessarily libelous

The law of libel will not correct all, or even most, false statements. It **3–009**
can be activated only when a false statement actually damages a
reputation. An assertion is not defamatory simply because it is
untrue—it must lower the victim in the eyes of right-thinking
citizens. However irksome it may be to have inaccuracies published
about one's life or behaviour—dates misstated, non-existent meetings described, and qualifications misattributed—there must be a
"sting" in the falsehood that reflects discredit in the eyes of society.
To publish falsely of an Irish priest that he informed on members of
the IRA is not defamatory: it may cause him to be executed by
terrorists, but,

> "the very circumstances which will make a person be regarded
> with disfavour by the criminal classes will raise his character in
> the estimation of right-thinking men. We can only regard the
> estimation in which a man is held by society generally."[27]

Context and contemporary standards

Whether statements are capable in law of being defamatory depends **3–010**
on the content and context of the whole article or programme, and
the impression it would convey to the average reader or viewer. It is
not helpful to lay down hard and fast rules: judges and juries place
themselves (without very much difficulty) in the position of "right-
thinking members of society", and ask themselves whether they think
the statement would injure the claimant's reputation. A statement
that the claimant has supplied information to the police about a
crime would not, as we have seen, be defamatory. Nor would a
suggestion that claimants are poor—unless they are in business and
the implication is that they are unable to pay their debts. The court
must bear contemporary social standards in mind. The values of

---

[27] *Mawe v Pigott* (1869) I.R. 4 CL 54. And see *Byrne v Deane* [1937] 1 K.B. 818.

judges in the deep south of the United States, who once held it defamatory to suggest that a white person has "coloured" blood, would not be shared in Britain. Not, one hopes, for the reason given in 1848 by the Chief Justice, who held that being black was "a great misfortune, but no crime".[28]

Clearly these decisions call for value judgments: in 1921 a judge held that reasonable citizens would not think less of a trade unionist if it were claimed that he had worked during a strike[29]: some juries might reach a different decision today. Ideas about immorality and what constitutes dishonourable conduct change over time, but the views of judges change more slowly than most. Would it still be defamatory to describe a heterosexual as "gay"? Damages of £18,000 (a massive sum in 1959) were awarded against the *Daily Mirror* for that very imputation about Liberace, but by today's standards an imputation of homosexuality would not of itself be defamatory, unless made of a married person (in 1999 Tom Cruise and Nicole Kidman collected damages from the *Sunday Express* for suggesting that their marriage was a sham). In 1934 the Court of Appeal somewhat emotionally rejected the argument that it did not lower Princess Yousoupoff in reputation to suggest that she had been raped by Rasputin[30]; by today's standards it could hardly be said that the innocent victim of a sex (or any other) crime would be diminished in the eyes of "right-thinking" members of the community. However, libel juries are not noted for progressive thinking. The *New York Times* mistakenly said that superstar chef Marco Pierre White had "bouts with drink and drugs" in his past, and argued that its error was not defamatory—it meant he had successfully rehabilitated himself and so could not lower him in the eyes of right- (i.e. liberal) minded gastronomes.[31] The jury, however, awarded him damages of £75,000 to assuage his feelings.

Appellate judges are frequently at odds over what is capable of amounting to a defamation. In one case they expended thousands of words of legal learning over Julie Burchill's suggestion that actor Stephen Berkoff was particularly ugly. Lord Justice Millett, dissenting from the majority finding that this imputation could indeed defame the thespian, concluded,

> "However difficult it may be, we must assume that Miss Julie Burchill might be taken seriously. The question then is: is it defamatory to say of a man that he is 'hideously ugly'? It is a common experience that ugly people have satisfactory social lives—Boris Karloff is not known to have been a recluse—and it is a popular belief for the truth of which I am unable to vouch that ugly men are particularly attractive to women."[32]

---

[28] *Hoare v Silverlock* (1848) 12 Q.B. 630 at 632, *per* Lord Denman C.J.
[29] *Mycroft v Sleight* (1921) 90 L.J.K.B. 883, *per* Mr Justice McCardie.
[30] *Yousoupoff v MGM Pictures Ltd* (1934) 50 T.L.R. 581.
[31] *Marco Pierre White v New York Times*, April 7, 2000 (unreported).
[32] *Berkoff v Burchill* [1996] 4 All E.R. 1008.

Article 10 should now protect Burchillian speech which is offensive, shocking and distasteful, because readers must be credited with the ability to discern when it is the writer, rather than her target, who deserves these adjectives.

The "ordinary reader" test

In deciding what words mean for the purpose of defamation, the **3–011** intention of the writer or speaker is largely irrelevant. The test is the effect on the ordinary reader, who is endowed for this purpose with considerable wisdom and knowledge of the way of the world. The literal meaning is not conclusive: the ordinary reader knows all about irony. To say of John Smith "His name is certainly not George Washington" is capable of being a statement defamatory of Smith: the ordinary reader knows that George Washington could never tell a lie, and is likely to infer that Smith is therefore untruthful (a decision that may overestimate the capacities of today's tabloid readers).[33] The ordinary reader is impressed by the tone and the manner of publication, and the words chosen to headline a story. In a popular paper the headline, "False profit return charge against Investment Society", suggests fraud and not an arguable error by accountants in attributing profit to capital rather than income.[34]

The courts accept that ordinary readers are not literal-minded simpletons. They are capable of divining the real thrust of a comment, and able to respond to a joke, even a joke in bad taste, in the spirit intended by the commentator. In this sense, the author's intention does play an indirect part in determining the meaning of the words in question, because that meaning should be decided by the ordinary reader's response to the question, "What on earth is the author getting at?"[35]

However, this sensible approach has been overlaid by a more complicated set of instructions from the Court of Appeal, as a result of a rule change that gave trial judges the power to strike out pleaded meanings they think the offending words are not reasonably capable of bearing. This change[36] was intended to reduce the length and expense of jury trials by excluding unreasonable meanings and the evidence called to support the truth of such meanings, but ironically it has worked, instead, to encourage more expensive interlocutory skirmishes about "meaning" and to deprive some defendants of the right to defend the meaning they really intended. The principles, which seek to exclude meanings that are "strained of forced or utterly unreasonable" are[37]:

---

[33] *Grubb v Bristol United Press Ltd* [1963] 1 Q.B. 309, *per* Holroyd Pearce L.J.

[34] *English & Scottish Co-operative Properties Mortgage & Investment Society Ltd* v *Odhams Press Ltd* [1940] 1 K.B. 440 at 452 *per* Slesser L.J.

[35] *Schild v Express Newspapers Ltd The Times*, October 5, 1982, CA.

[36] First effected in 1994 and now contained in CPR, Pt 53, PD 4.1.

[37] These tests are extrapolated from a number of recent cases, beginning with *Mapp v News Group* [1997] E.M.L.R. 397; *Gillick v BBC* [1996] E.M.L.R. 267; *Skuse v Granada TV* [1996] E.M.L.R. 278.

(1) The material bears the natural and ordinary meaning it would convey to the ordinary reasonable reader or viewer absorbing it on one occasion.

(2) Ordinary and reasonable readers and viewers are neither naïve nor unduly suspicious; although they can read between the lines in the light of their general knowledge they are nevertheless fair minded and not "avid for scandal".[38]

(3) The court should be wary of conducting an over-elaborate analysis of the words complained of, and equally of taking an over-literal approach to its task: the ordinary reader does not analyse an article like a lawyer poring over a contract.

(4) The court should test the meaning by reference to the standard of comprehension of the likely readers or viewers.

3–012   However serious a prime-time television programme like *World in Action*, it will be watched for entertainment by some viewers whose first impressions must be brought into account. On the other hand, an article in a legal or accounting magazine will be tested by its impact on lawyers or accountants. Thus the meaning of an article about Russian tycoon Boris Berezovsky in *Forbes*—an American business magazine—might be tested by its impact not on the law's traditional construct of reasonableness, "the man on the Clapham omnibus", but by the man or woman in business class on the transatlantic jumbo.[39]

How the minds of ordinary readers receive and interpret newspaper stories is an interesting question of psychology, but evidence from ordinary readers as to how they understood the article is never admitted. In law, the answer depends on assumptions by lawyers. What do ordinary readers think when their eyes catch the fact that someone is being investigated by the police?

In *Lewis v Daily Telegraph* the newspaper announced:

> "INQUIRY ON FIRM BY CITY POLICE. Officers of the City of London Fraud Squad are inquiring into the affair of Rubber Improvement Ltd. The investigation was requested after criticisms of the chairman's statement and the accounts by a shareholder at a recent company meeting. The chairman is Mr John Lewis, former Socialist M.P."

3–013 The inquiry subsequently exonerated Lewis and his company. They sued, claiming that the news story implied, to the ordinary reader, that they were involved in fraud. The newspaper argued that the ordinary reader, possessed of a fairer and less suspicious mind, would presume innocence. The House of Lords held that the statement was not capable of meaning that the claimants were guilty

---

[38] *Lewis v Daily Telegraph*, fn.3 above, *per* Lord Reid.
[39] *Berezovsky v Forbes Inc*, unreported, November 10, 2000 Eady J.

of fraud. "The ordinary man, not avid for scandal", would not infer guilt merely because an inquiry was under way.[40]

So suspects, innocent until proven guilty, may be described as "assisting police with their inquiries" and have no remedy in libel. Unless, of course, the story is written in a way that suggests that police have reason to suspect them. Much—very much, in financial terms—depends upon the care with which the story is written, as the same newspaper once again discovered in *Hayward v Thompson*.[41]

> During police investigations into Norman Scott's allegations that he had been the target of a conspiracy to murder in order to protect a former lover (Liberal leader Jeremy Thorpe M.P.), the *Daily Telegraph* obtained a scoop from a police source. It published:
>
> "TWO MORE IN SCOTT AFFAIR
>
> The names of two more people connected with the Norman Scott affair have been given to the police. One is a wealthy benefactor of the Liberal Party . . . Both men, police have been told, arranged for a leading Liberal supporter to be 'reimbursed' £5,000, the same amount Mr Andrew Newton alleges he was paid to murder Scott."
>
> Mr Jack Hayward, the wealthy benefactor, claimed that the article meant that he was guilty of participating in or condoning a murder plot. The newspaper, relying on the *Lewis* case, said that the words would mean to the ordinary reader no more than that an inquiry was under way, and that Hayward would be able to assist it. The jury awarded Hayward £50,000, and the Court of Appeal upheld the verdict because the article *was* capable of implying guilt. Its headline put the wealthy benefactor "in" the Scott affair, and the copy never got him out of it. "In" means "in", and that implication of involvement with a conspiracy was reinforced by the phrase "connected with" and the inverted commas around "reimbursed". These stylistic features of the story as published would give the ordinary reader the impression that Hayward was an accomplice in the plot.

The *Hayward* case underlines the importance of the way in which **3–014** the story is presented to the public. The art is to put across the important information without using a language or style that carries a defamatory implication. That art was demonstrated with conspicuously different talents by British editors and journalists in the aftermath of the revelation that Jeffrey Archer, best-selling novelist and deputy chairman of the Conservative party, had paid a prostitute £2,000 to leave the country. Newspapers that jumped to the conclusion that he had engaged in sex with the woman were sued for libel, but were unable to discharge the burden of proving a case that hinged upon the word of a prostitute against the word of the

[40] [1964] A.C. 234.
[41] *Hayward v Thompson* [1981] 3 All E.R. 450.

claimant and his "fragrant" wife (in his case helped by evidence which many years later turned out to have been fabricated). The *Star* was ordered to pay £500,000 damages after a trial that amassed an estimated £750,000 in legal costs. Newspapers that had confined themselves to reporting the facts, and left readers to draw their own conclusions, were not sued.

However, any such invitation to readers should not load the odds in favour of a particular conclusion by inflaming their suspicions. The author who is anxious to wound but fearful to strike too obviously will not escape. If the reader is invited to be suspicious and is nudged towards a defamatory explanation that the writer "did not care or did not dare to express in direct terms", the publication will be capable of carrying a defamatory imputation and a lesser meaning based on mere (or even reasonable) suspicion may be withdrawn from the jury.[42] The decision on meaning is for the trial judge, who must bear in mind that it is "an exercise in generosity not parsimony".[43] He should not rule out a defence meaning unless it is one that no reasonable reader would gather from the article. The Court of Appeal has pointed out that this is a high threshold of exclusion:

> "Ever since Fox's Libel Act 1792 the meaning of words in civil as well as criminal libel proceedings has been constitutionally a matter for the jury. The judge's function is no more and no less than to pre-empt perversity."[44]

These rulings are generally made before the trial of the action, and the Court of Appeal may well intervene if the judge has excluded a defence meaning which would otherwise not be put before the jury.[45]

Bane and antidote

3–015   Libel is for the most part common law, i.e. created and developed by judges. For many generations they regarded journalists as akin to waspish insects whose "sting" (i.e. the defamatory meaning) might be "drawn" if the allegation was watered down or dismissed in subsequent passages. Other judges regarded journalists more as vipers, hence the "bane and antidote" rule that defamatory words (the poison) could be "cured" by applying an "antidote"—i.e. emollient expressions later in the text. This rule (although not its pejorative language) remains valuable because it underlines the

---

[42] See *Jones v Skelton* [1963] 1 W.L.R. 1362 and now *Forbes v Berezorsky (No. 2)*, July 31, 2001, where the Court of Appeal found that the "entire thrust" of the publication pointed to actual guilt rather than reasonable suspicion of guilt.

[43] Sedley L.J. in *Berezovsky v Forbes Inc* [2001] E.M.L.R. 10.30, at 10.40.

[44] Simon Brown L.J., *Jameel v Wall Street Journal Europe* (Number 1) [2003] E.W.C.A. at para.14.

[45] See Hirst L.J. in *Geenty v Channel 4 Television* [1998] E.M.L.R. 524 at 532.

importance of context: a complainant cannot single out a passage which taken in isolation is defamatory if the context makes clear it is not. The rule offers some protection to tabloids which sell on sensational headlines, because of the (often false) assumption that "ordinary readers" read the entire article:

> "STREWTH! WHAT'S HAROLD UP TO WITH OUR MADGE?" This *News of the World* banner headline was accompanied by a photograph which appeared to show the actors who played Harold and Madge Bishop, a respectable married couple from *Neighbours*, naked and engaging in perverse sexual antics. Only by reading the small text of the article did it become clear that the actors' faces had been superimposed on pornographic pictures without their consent, so as to become "unwitting stars of a sordid computer game" whose makers were castigated in what Lord Bridge noted was "a tone of self-righteous indignation which contrasts oddly with the prominence given to the main photograph". But for all the newspaper's humbuggery, it was saved by the "bane and antidote" rule which required the whole publication to be taken together, on the assumption that a fair-minded reader of the complete text would not think less of the actors since they were clearly described as the victims of a hoax.[46]

The *Neighbours* case was an example of the antidote in the article curing completely the bane of the defamatory headline and picture, at least for "readers" of *News of the World* who bothered to read every line. Most "bane and antidote" cases are more finely balanced, and will be decided by a jury which may take a dim view of exaggerated headlines and similar tabloid ploys. The *Express on Sunday* failed to persuade the Court of Appeal that a hagiographic article about the then wedded bliss of Tom Cruise and Nicole Kidman completely cured another article on the next page which retailed defamatory rumours about them. Rather than face the wrath of a star-struck jury with arguments about "bane and antidote" the newspaper apologised and paid a large sum in damages—a year before the happy couple announced their divorce.[47]

Defamatory innuendo

The test of the ordinary reader is subject to qualification in the case **3–016** of statements that are not defamatory on their face, but that carry discreditable implications to those with special knowledge. To say that a man frequents a particular address has no defamatory meaning to ordinary readers—except to those who know that the address is a brothel. Here, libel is by *innuendo*, i.e. the statement is defamatory to those with knowledge of facts not stated in the article.

---

[46] *Charleston v News Group Newspapers Ltd* [1995] 2 A.C. 65 applying *Chalmers v Payne* (1835) 2 Cr. M. & R. 156.

[47] *Cruise v Express Newspapers* (1998) E.M.L.R. 780.

If it is said of a barrister that he has refused to appear for an unsavoury criminal, the ordinary reader may applaud, but his professional reputation is lowered amongst colleagues who understand the story to mean that he has betrayed his ethical duty to appear "on the taxi rank" for all who seek his services. Where the sting is not a matter of general knowledge, its defamatory capacity is judged by its impact upon ordinary readers who have such knowledge—if the claimant can first prove that such persons were amongst the actual readership.

Libel and slander distinguished

3–017 There are irritating, complicated and unnecessary distinctions in law between two types of defamation—libel and slander. Libel is a defamatory statement made in writing or—in the case of films and videotapes—at least in some permanent form. Slander is a defamatory statement made by word of mouth or by gesture. Claimants may sue for libel even though they have suffered no financial loss, but for slander (with certain exceptions) they must be able to prove actual damage and not mere injury to feelings. Historically, the distinction is explained by the view that writing was a premeditated and calculated act, which affected reputation much more drastically and permanently than off-the-cuff comments. With the advent of radio, television and satellite broadcasting, this reasoning is anachronistic, and Parliament has enacted that words spoken in theatres, and in broadcasts for general reception, shall be deemed libels and not slanders.[48] The same provision is made for words spoken on television programmes.[49] However, the distinction still remains in certain areas, notably criminal libel, *ex tempore* statements at public meetings and noises of disapproval. Dramatists or actors whose work is maliciously booed or hissed off the stage must sue their tormentors for slander rather than libel.

The importance of the distinction is that there can be no action for slander unless the claimant has suffered damage that can be calculated in monetary terms. Victims of verbal assaults who suffer hurt feelings, sleepless nights, physical illness, or ostracism by friends and neighbours cannot bring an action.[50] There are only five exceptions: accusations of a crime punishable by imprisonment; suggestions that the claimant carries a contagious disease; adverse reflections on a person's ability to carry out an office, business or profession; slanders on the reputation or credit of tradespeople; and words imputing unchastity or adultery to a woman or a girl.[51] Only in these five cases may the claimant sue for slander without having to prove financial loss.

---

[48] See Theatres Act 1968, s.4(1) and Defamation Act 1952, ss.1, 16(3).
[49] Broadcasting Act 1990, s.166.
[50] *Argent v Donigan* (1892) 8 T.L.R. 432; *Lynch v Knight* (1861) 9 H.L. Cas. 592.
[51] Slander of Women Act 1891.

Malicious falsehood

A statement may be entirely false and deeply upsetting to the person **3–018** about whom it is made. But unless it tends to lessen respect for that person, then as we have seen it will not be defamatory. The victim may have an action for *malicious falsehood*, however, if it can be proved that the untrue statement was made spitefully, dishonestly or recklessly, and that it has in fact caused financial loss.

> Stephane Grappelli, the renowned jazz violinist, employed English agents who booked him for certain concerts. Grappelli claimed they acted without reference to him, and the concerts had to be cancelled. The reason given by the agents was: "Stephane Grappelli is very seriously ill in Paris and is unlikely ever to tour again". This was an entirely false statement, obviously damaging to a thriving professional musician. However, the statement was not defamatory: to say that someone is seriously ill might excite pity, but not ridicule or disrespect. Grappelli had to be content with an action for malicious falsehood.[52]

The action for malicious falsehood is less favourable to claimants than defamation. They have no right to jury trial, and they have to prove that the words were false (in libel, the burden of proving the words are true is on the defendant), that the words were published maliciously and that they were likely to cause financial loss. Their damages, however, if they surmount these hurdles, may well be on a similar scale to those in defamation, since the Court of Appeal has held they can recover aggravated damages for injury to feelings caused by publication of the untruth.[53] If there is real doubt over whether a falsehood is defamatory, complainants may be well advised to shoulder this extra burden by suing for malicious false-hood rather than have their "meanings" struck out as non-defamatory. But there is nothing to stop a claimant choosing to bring a defamation claim as a malicious falsehood. The leading case on the subject is *Joyce v Sengupta*[54]:

> Love letters written to Princess Anne by Captain Lawrence were stolen from her rooms in Buckingham Palace and delivered to *The Sun* newspaper. The police were unable to finger the culprit, but they boasted to the *Daily Mail* that they could prove it was Linda Joyce, Anne's maid. When this nonsense was published, the poor but innocent Ms Joyce could not afford to sue for libel—instead, she obtained legal aid which was then available to bring an action for malicious falsehood (malicious falsehood claims, like libel claims, cannot now generally be funded on legal aid). The newspaper, outraged that a poor person should have found a means of fighting its

---

[52] *Grappelli v Derek Block Holdings Ltd* [1981] 2 All E.R. 272.
[53] *Khodaparast v Shad* [2000] E.M.L.R. 265.
[54] *Joyce v Sengupta* [1993] 1 All E.R. 897, CA.

calumnies, argued that her action was an "abuse of process", but the
Court of Appeal had no sympathy: the necessary quality of "malice"
could be inferred from the grossness of the falsehood and the cavalier
way it was published. The newspaper settled the action by paying
substantial damages to Ms Joyce.

Complainants may wish to proceed against defamers in malicious
falsehood or for some obscure common law tort like "conspiracy to
injure" in order more easily to obtain an interim injunction. This
"prior restraint" is virtually impossible to obtain in libel, but may be
more readily available on the "balance of convenience" test which
applies to the grant of injunctions in other cases. However, s.12 of
the Human Rights Act 1998 largely corrects the anomaly, and courts
should not, on principle, be prepared to give injunctions in malicious
falsehood cases against publishers who wish to defend the truth of
their statement or the privilege of the occasion on which it was
made. Even before the Human Rights Act, courts indicated that
freedom of speech would be a crucial factor in any balancing
exercise involved in granting pre-trial injunctions. In a conspiracy to
injure case, "the important questions are questions of public interest,
not of private rights". The public interest of free speech, in allowing
allegations of financial misconduct to come to the attention of
investors and regulatory authorities, defeated the claimant's claim
for an injunction before trial.[55]

WHO CAN SUE?

3–019 Any living individual, if made the identifiable subject of defamatory
attack, may take legal action. This includes infants (who sue "by
their litigation friend"), lunatics, bankrupts and foreigners. Animals
however, are fair game.

The question of who *can* sue is less important than the question of
who *will* sue. The enormous cost of contested libel actions means
that many claimants will need financial support from unions or
employers. Some organisations find that supporting libel actions on
behalf of their members is politically convenient because it assures
them a better or more polite press; the Police Federation is one
example. There is nothing to stop such organisations offering to pay
the costs of libel actions, and editors deciding to settle will bear in
mind the strength of the organisation behind the claimant. In recent
years the use of *public* funds for individual libel actions has been
heavily criticised, and it may well be an unlawful use of ratepayers'
or taxpayers' money to fund libel actions brought by ministers or
civil officials over attacks on their political or moral integrity. John
Major when Prime Minister sued *The New Statesman* and *Scallywag*

---

[55] *Femis-Bank (Anguilla) v Lazar* [1991] 2 All E.R. 865.

for publishing rumours that he was having an affair with a Downing Street caterer: he was careful to pay his own legal expenses. There is nothing to stop a private benefactor from bankrolling libel victims and Sir James Goldsmith for many years sponsored a fund to assist right wing litigants. However, under s.51 of the Supreme Court Act 1981 the benefactor may have to pay the newspaper's costs if the latter is successful.[56] The wealthy but gullible backers of Neil Hamilton's unsuccessful libel action against Mohammed Al Fayed found to their discomfort that the court had power to unmask them, and then to order a contribution to the defendant's costs (although the judge eventually forebore to do so on the somewhat over-generous grounds that they had acted out of charitable motives to help a poor man assert a claim against a rich opponent).

The dead

The dead cannot sue or be sued for libel. Indeed, if a claimant dies **3–020** on the day before the trial, the action dies as well. Neither the trustees of the estate nor the outraged relatives have any form of legal redress. This right to speak ill of the dead is justified in the interests of historians and biographers, and by the practical diffi-culties of subjecting deceased persons to cross-examination. In 1975 the Faulks Committee on libel expressed great concern about stories that added to the grief of a widow, and recommended that relatives should be allow to sue within five years of death (a cynical estimate, critics suggested, of the length of a widow's solicitude). There may be some unseemliness about assassinating characters still warm in their graves, but at least they cannot feel the slings and arrows of outrageous libels.

Companies

A company may sue for defamation, but only in respect of state- **3–021** ments that damage its business reputation. In legal theory a com-pany has no feelings capable of injury, although adverse reports may lower the value of its "goodwill" asset. Normally, individual officers or employees identified from the criticism will additionally have an action, which makes the chilling threat to sue from the corporation itself all the more unnecessary. Corporate abuse of the power to sue for defamation—most notoriously in the *McLibel* action brought to crush protests against the fast-food multinational—have led to calls that the right of corporations to sue for libel should be abolished. This reform has been implemented in Australia, where the right is limited to companies employing less than ten people.[57] The Euro-pean Court upheld the complaints against the United Kingdom for

---

[56] *Singh v The Observer Ltd* [1989] 1 All E.R. 751; [1989] 3 All E.R. 777, CA; *Hamilton v Al Fayed, The Times*, July 23, 2001.
[57] See, for example, s.9 New South Wales Defamation Act 2005 (certain corpora-tions do not have cause of action for defamation) and also s.6, New Zealand Defamation Act 1992.

permitting the *McLibel* saga on the basis of inequality of arms between the parties and the disproportionality of the damages awarded: it accepted that restrictions on criticisms of large corporations, like those on criticisms of powerful politicians, must be limited and subjected to the "closest scrutiny".[58] But it did not contest their right to sue for libel. That right should at least be contingent upon the ability to prove actual financial damage, but in *Jameel v Wall Street Journal* the House of Lords narrowly rejected this limitation, although Lord Bingham indicated that Art.10 would prevent excessive damages awards to corporations. The £10,000 awarded in that case was not excessive.[59]

Local authorities

3–022 In 1993 the House of Lords held that a local authority could not bring an action in defamation because there was a danger of elected bodies using such a power to stifle legitimate public criticism of their activities. This case—*Derbyshire County Council v Times Newspapers*—was an early landmark in fashioning English law to favour free speech. The House of Lords warned of the "chilling effect" of defamation if public bodies could sue their critics. It was of "the highest public importance" that "any governmental body should be open to public criticism". The Law Lords approved a vigorous pronouncement that it "would be a serious interference . . . if the wealth of the State, derived from the State's subjects, could be used to launch against those subjects actions for defamation because they have, falsely and unfairly it may be, criticised or condemned the management of the country".[60]

State corporations

3–023 The decision in *Derbyshire* means that nationalised industries and government-run corporations lack standing to sue for libel. In *British Coal Corporation v NUM* it was held that BCC, which was established by the Government and very much subject to ministerial control, was a "governmental" body and hence disabled from using defamation law to sue a miner's newspaper which had accused it of impropriety in managing pension funds.[61]

Political parties

3–024 A further extension of the rule in *Derbyshire* disentitles political parties to sue for libel. Even if they exercise no "governmental" power, the "free market-place of ideas" in a democracy requires all

---

[58] *Steele and Morris v UK* [2005] 41 E.H.R.R. 22 at para.94.
[59] *Jameel v Wall Street Journal* [2006] UKHL 44 at para.19.
[60] *Derbyshire County Council v Times Newspapers* [1993] A.C. 534 at 557–9, *per* Lord Keith.
[61] *British Coal Corp v National Union of Mineworkers*, unreported, June 28, 1996, French J.

parties—even newcomers like the Referendum Party—to be subject to uninhibited public criticism, especially when contesting elections.[62]

Trade unions

Trade unions and most unincorporated associations cannot sue for **3–025** libel. This was decided in 1979 by *EETPU v Times Newspapers*, which held that the capacity of trade unions to sue had been removed by s.2(1) of the Trade Union and Labour Relations Act 1974.[63] The practical significance of this change is mainly to reduce the damages by removing one possible claimant, rather than by removing the prospect of an action. Most criticisms of trade unions will reflect upon individual officers, who will usually be financially supported by their union in efforts to vindicate their own reputations.

Fugitives

It could not have been imagined that fugitives from justice would be **3–026** permitted to sue from their place of refuge, until that child rapist and talented film director, Roman Polanski, was permitted to have his day in court by video link, and persuaded the jury to award him £50,000 for a trivial slight in Vanity Fair. Polanski had buggered a 13 year old schoolgirl in California in 1978. He pleaded guilty but was given bail prior to sentence, whereupon he fled to France which immediately gave him sanctuary. He dared not venture to London to sue Vanity Fair in 2003, for fear that he would be extradited to the United States to serve his sentence. Since jurors do not give damages to claimants unless they turn up in some form, he applied to give evidence by video link from his Paris hotel. A bare majority of three soft-hearted law lords indulged him, on the basis that notwithstanding his crime he was entitled to access England's world-famous libel law. So the Oscar-winning director, fully made-up, directed his own performance, and wowed the jury. It awarded him £50,000 for damage to his reputation (since his reputation was presumably that of a dissolute paedophile, as well as a genius film-maker, this was some achievement) and costs reportedly amounting to £1.8 million. Polanski had pleaded guilty to a sodomical attack on a child he had drugged and traumatised: it took an English libel judge and jury to restore his reputation in the eyes of right-thinking people, over Vanity Fair gossip that he had once put his hand on the thigh of a woman who was not his wife. On this basis Osama bin Laden, should

---

[62] *Goldsmith v Bhoyrul* [1997] 4 All E.R. 268, *per* Buckley J.
[63] *EETPU v Times Newspapers* [1980] Q.B. 585. Although note that this decision, by a single judge, has not been tested and its reasoning has been questioned: Gatley, 9th edn., para.8.23. Even so, the rule in *Derbyshire* should apply by analogy, since there must be an important public interest in permitting uninhibited criticism of powerful representative bodies like trade unions.

he ever be given sanctuary in Iran, might sue for libel in London and apply to have his reputation restored by video link arranged by Al-Jazeera.[64]

Groups

3–027   There is, in defamation law, a certain safety in numbers. Defamatory comment may not be actionable if it refers to people by class rather than by name. Whether an individual member of the class can sue depends upon the size of the class and the nature of the comment: there must be something in the circumstances to make the ordinary reader feel that the claimant personally is the target of the criticism. To say "All barristers are thieves" does not entitle any one of 12,000 barristers to sue—the class is too large for the comment to single out individuals. But to say "All barristers in chambers at 10 Doughty Street are thieves" might be sufficiently specific to allow the individual barristers in those chambers to take action, at least if the context showed the allegation was a serious reference to each person and not an example of "the habit of making unfounded generalisations . . . ingrained in ill-educated or vulgar minds, . . . or intended to be facetious exaggeration".[65] In 1971, the small group of regular journalists at the Old Bailey received £150 damages each for the intolerable insult of being collectively described in the *Spectator* as "beer-sodden hacks". The question always is whether the defamation is of the class itself (in which case no action arises) or whether ordinary readers would believe that it reflected directly on the individual claimant. When the *News of the World* alleged that unnamed CID officers from Banbury police station had committed rape, that allegation reflected on each officer at Banbury because that CID office had only 12 members.[66] Had the allegation been less specific—had it referred only to "certain police officers in Oxfordshire", for example—the Banbury officers would not have been able to prove that what was published related to them.

Identification

3–028   The test, in every case, is whether reasonable people would understand the words to point to the claimant personally, and the journalist cannot escape simply by widening the net of suspects. The statement "Either A or B is the murderer" entitles *both* A and B to sue over a statement that carries the defamatory meaning that there is a substantial prospect that each is guilty. The distinction is not always easy to keep in mind:

> Lord Denning, once Britain's most experienced judge in defamation cases, published a book in which he criticised a jury in Bristol for

---

[64] *Polanski v Condé, Nast Publications Ltd* [2005] 1 W.L.R. 637.
[65] *Knupffer v London Express Newspapers* [1944] A.C. 116, *per* Lord Atkin.
[66] See *Riches v Newsgroup* [1986] 1 Q.B. 265.

acquitting black defendants who had been charged with rioting. Two members of the jury threatened to sue, because the comments (which were based upon gossip at Temple dinners) suggested they had been false to their oaths by acquitting black defendants because they (the jurors) were black. The publishers, Butterworths, withdrew and pulped all 10,000 copies of the book.

A writer will not necessarily escape by criticising "some" members of a class if other evidence serves to identify the claimant as a member of the criticised section. An article stating that "some Irish factory-owners" were cruel to employees enabled one particular owner to obtain damages, because other references in the article pointed to his factory. "If those who look on know well who is aimed at", the target may sue.[67] Where the knowledge depends upon special circumstances of which not everyone is aware, the claimant has to prove that the article was published to persons who were able to make the identifying connection.

In the Jack Hayward case, the *Daily Telegraph* argued that the claimant could not be identified from the description "a wealthy benefactor of the Liberal party". Unfortunately for the newspaper that party had very few wealthy benefactors and evidence was admitted to show that others immediately made the connection. His friends put two and two together, and so did the media, which besieged his home by telephone and helicopter. In a national newspaper with a wide circulation the inference was that some readers would know the special facts which identified him.[68]

The moral of these cases is that journalists cannot avoid liability for defamation merely by avoiding the naming of names. Any story that carries the imputation of discreditable conduct by somebody will be actionable by a claimant who can show that at least some readers would recognise him as the person being criticised, or that the facts in the story necessarily imply such an allegation against him. An allegation that drugs are being supplied as a "liquid cosh" to modify behaviour at a particular prison may point a sufficient finger at the medical officers working at that prison, even though they are not referred to by name. When a newspaper falsely alleged that Kerry Packer had "fixed" the result of a cricket match involving the West Indian team, its captain (Clive Lloyd) was entitled to damages even though he was not named in the article and had not been playing in the particular match. The "ordinary reader" would infer that "fixing" had involved the team as well as Packer, and that the captain of the team would have been party to the plot even though he had not played in the match.[69]

---

[67] *Le Farm v Malcomson* (1848) 1 H.L. Cas. 637.
[68] See *Hayward v Thompson,* fn.34 above.
[69] *Lloyd v David Syme & Co Ltd* [1986] A.C. 350.

Those unintentionally defamed

3–029 Where a journalist *intends* to refer to an unnamed individual, it is reasonable that the individual should have an action for libel if others have correctly identified him or her as the target, whatever literary device has been used as camouflage. Asterisks, blanks, initials and general descriptions will not avail if evidence proves that readers have solved the puzzle correctly. Much less satisfactory, however, is the harsh rule that holds a writer responsible for *unintentional* defamation, where readers have jumped to a conclusion that never was in the author's mind. This rule has been the bane of fiction writers, who must take special care to ensure that the more villainous characters in their plots cannot be mistaken for living persons. The leading case is *Hulton v Jones*:[70]

> In 1909 the *Sunday Chronicle* published a light-hearted sketch about a festival in Dieppe, dwelling upon the tendency of sober Englishmen to lead a "gay" life (in the 1909 sense of the word) when safely across the Channel. "Whist! There is Artemus Jones with a woman who is not his wife, who must be, you know—the other thing . . .". Whist! There were very heavy libel damages awarded to one Artemus Jones, a dour barrister practising on the Welsh circuit. Five of his friends thought the article referred to him—an identification made all the more far-fetched by the fact that the fictitious character was described as a Peckham Church Warden. The House of Lords upheld the award, ruling that the writers' intention was immaterial; what mattered was whether reasonable readers would think that the words used applied to the claimant.

Authors who employ fictional characters with realistic status or occupations should check available sources to ensure their characters could not be confused with persons of the same name and position. The entire print-run of one major novel had to be pulped because the author had chosen the actual name of a noble family to describe a fictional unsavoury aristocrat. A check with *Debretts* or *Who's Who* would have revealed the danger.

3–030 The rule that imposes liability for unintentional defamation has absurd results, such as the case where the wife of a race-horse owner pictured with a woman he had described to the photographer as his fiancée was allowed to recover damages on the basis that her neighbours would think that she was living in sin.[71] Equally unsatisfactory is the decision that Harold Newstead, a bachelor hairdresser living in Camberwell, was libelled by a perfectly accurate report that another Harold Newstead, also a Camberwell resident, had been gaoled for bigamy ("I kept them both till the police interferred").[72] The *Newstead* case is used to warn young journalists

---

[70] *Hulton v Jones* [1910] A.C. 20.
[71] *Cassidy v Daily Mirror* [1929] 2 K.B. 331.
[72] *Newstead v London Express* [1940] 1 K.B. 377.

of the importance, in court reporting, of giving occupations and addresses of defendants and witnesses, so that confusion can be avoided. Journalists should insist on receiving these details from the court clerk by citing the case of *R. v Evesham Justices Ex p. McDonagh*[73]:

> A former Tory M.P. was charged with driving without a tax disc. He begged the court not to disclose his home address lest his ex-wife discovered it and harassed him. The court allowed him to write the address on a piece of paper rather than state it publicly. The Divisional Court held that defendants' addresses must be given publicly in court. The well-established practice, which helped to avoid wrongful identification and risks of libel action, should not be departed from for the comfort of defendants.

The problems of "unintentional defamation" underline the general unsuitability of libel law as a method of correcting innocent mistakes. The wife and the bachelor in the above cases should have been entitled to insist that the confusion be cleared up by a published clarification, but they should not have been able to obtain an award of damages against a newspaper that was not at fault. This is a problem that a "legal right of reply"—requiring a correction without compensation—could resolve more effectively than the cumbersome "offer to make amends" procedure which still requires damages and costs. Cases like *Hulton v Jones*, should they recur, are clear candidates for the "proportionality" axe under the 1998 Human Rights Act, and the days of "unintentional defamation" may be numbered since both the House of Lords (in *Jameel*) and the European Court are requiring proof of the defendant's *fault* as a precondition for damages. The first blow against unintentional defamation was struck in 2001 when an actress was denied the right to sue the *Sunday Mirror* over a squalid advertisement for an internet porn site which featured a model who was her "spitting image". Although her friends and relatives had been horrified by the belief that she had taken to pornography, Morland J. refused to follow the *Newstead* and *Artemus Jones* cases on the basis that Art.10 now excluded strict liability for "look-alike" defamation.[74] At charity auctions today large amounts are bid by people clamouring to have their name immortalised by any character in the works of leading fiction writers: humourless prigs like Artemus Jones should only be allowed to sue where their names are used maliciously or negligently.

WHO CAN BE SUED?

As a general rule, everyone who can sue for libel can also be sued **3–031** for libel if responsible for a defamatory publication. There seems to be an exception in the case of trade unions, which cannot sue for

---

[73] [1988] 1 All E.R. 371. In criminal cases, witnesses need not be asked for their address unless this is material to the case: *Archbold* 2001, para.8–71(a).
[74] *Kerry O'Shea v MGN Ltd*, May 4, 2001.

libel (see above) but can nevertheless be made defendants as a result of the abolition of their immunity in tort by s.15 of the 1982 Employment Act. Unincorporated associations are not entities which can be sued, but their officials and employees may be liable. Editors and journalists employed on journals published by these organisations are therefore at great financial risk, and should ensure that their contracts of employment indemnify them against costs and damages that may accrue from libel actions, which are often brought by opponents of their employers' policies.

Every person who is responsible for a defamatory publication is a candidate for a claim: author, editor, informant, printer, proprietor and distributor. Complainants invariably sue the corporate body which publishes or broadcasts the libel, and usually join the editor and the journalist. It is clear that a larger-than-life proprietor who personally owns the publishing business is liable, even if the defamatory article is published without his knowledge, because he selects and controls his editors,[75] but equally clear that the directors of publishing companies can only be sued if they knew about or were personally involved in the defamatory publication.[76] Where does a figure like Rupert Murdoch stand, the moving spirit in a corporate publishing empire?

> In 1995 the *Sunday Times* devoted its front page to a ridiculous story about former Labour leader Michael Foot, under the banner heading "KGB: FOOT WAS OUR AGENT". The false insinuation was extracted from a book by a former KGB agent which the newspaper, to Murdoch's knowledge, had bought for serialisation. Foot sued in the most spectacular way, by taking out a writ for exemplary damages against Murdoch personally, described as the "moving spirit" of *Times Newspapers* who had "caused to be published" the offending words. Murdoch moved to strike out the action, on the basis that the editor had authorised the publication, while Foot maintained that he was liable because he had chosen a compliant editor schooled in sensationalist journalism. The issue of proprietorial responsibility went unresolved: the *Sunday Times* settled the case with a public apology and payment to Foot of substantial damages and costs.

Normally the corporate defendant will pay all the damages and costs, and claimants will not bother to sue proprietors personally. However, a media mogul whose publications attack his political enemies might well be made liable for exemplary damages, on the theory pioneered in the *Foot v Murdoch* litigation. British newspapers have been dominated by larger than life chief executives: their power over policy and news values means they influence the "news" which the newspaper itself makes by front page "splash"

---

[75] *R. v Gutch* (1829) M.&M. 432, (Tenterden C.J.).
[76] *Evans v Spritebrand Ltd* [1985] 1 W.L.R. 317.

stories.[77] There may be cases where the jury considers it necessary that a chief proprietor who has encouraged and profited from publication of reckless and circulation-seeking defamations should be "taught that tort does not pay" by an award of exemplary damages because "one man should not be allowed to sell another man's reputation for profit".[78]

Avoiding responsibility

Journalists whose bylines are on defamatory stories can exculpate **3–032** themselves by proving that the defamation was added to their copy without their consent (a common occurrence where the "sting" emanates from clumsy sub-editing). They should think carefully before allowing their reputation to be sacrificed by a "tactical apology" prepared by lawyers acting in the interests of their employers. An important case that casts helpful light on a journalist's rights in this situation is *UCATT v Brain*.[79]

> A trade union employed a journalist to edit its newspaper. He was subject to the direction of the General Secretary, who sometimes insisted on the publication of articles seen as politically important for the union. One such article, written by the General Secretary, was ordered to be printed and the editor had no option other than to deliver it to the printers. It libelled the claimant, who issued a writ against the editor. The union's lawyers decided to apologise, and the editor was directed to approve the apology, which was to be made in open court. The editor, fearing that this would reflect on his credit as a journalist, declined. He was sacked. The Court of Appeal upheld his claim for damages for wrongful dismissal. It pointed out that he had a good defence to the action, namely that he was not responsible for publication. The solicitors had a conflict of interests, and should have arranged for him to receive independent legal advice. The union acted wrongfully in dismissing him for insisting on his legal rights.

Employers have no right to bargain away journalists' reputations without their consent merely because some sacrifice of those reputations would be in the interests of management. Journalists should take independent advice before they agree to fall on their pens.

Writers and speakers cannot be held responsible unless they authorise, or at least foresee, the publication that causes complaint. Participants in a television programme, for example, who are told

---

[77] It has long been accepted that notwithstanding the fact that a national newspaper is published by a company, "chief proprietors" exert a determinative influence on its character and contents: see *Royal Commission on the Press* 1947–49, Ch.V. The argument for fixing a mogul with liability irrespective of knowledge draws support from the assumptions of s.57 of the Fair Trading Act 1973 and the Broad-casting Act's restrictions on media ownership.

[78] *Rookes v Barnard* [1964] A.C. 1129 at 1226, *per* Lord Devlin.

[79] *UCATT v Brain* [1981] I.C.R. 542.

that it is a "pilot" that will not be transmitted, cannot be held responsible for defamatory statements they have made if it is subsequently screened at prime time. If the defamatory material has been supplied "off the record" by a third party, a difficult question arises. The informant is responsible in law but the journalist, having promised confidentiality, will be under an ethical duty not to reveal the name of the informant. The claimant may want, even more than damages, to discover the identity of the source. In defamation cases journalists can usually keep the identity of informants a secret although they may find that their refusal to answer such questions is a ground for increasing the sum total of damages.[80] It may also, of course, be the reason why the action is lost in the first place, because evidence for the truth of the statement is unavailable from the person who originally made it.

3–033   Book publishers usually insist on contracts in which the author indemnifies them against defamation liability or warrants that the manuscript is libel-free. This practice reflects the superior bargaining power of the publisher in negotiating the agreement rather than a custom appropriate to the book trade, so where an indemnity clause is over-looked, the courts will not imply one into the contract by reference to custom and usage.[81] Freelancers who submit articles to newspapers and magazines cannot in consequence be made automatically liable for all the publisher's legal costs of defending a libel action, in the absence of express agreement. However, even in the absence of a contractual agreement the courts can apportion liability between defendants responsible for the same publications.[82] In practice most publishers will be insured against libel and may pay for the defence of the author under their policy, until such point as interests in the litigation begin to diverge—usually by the insurers wishing to settle and the author wishing to fight. Legal aid is in practice unavailable for libel defendants and some authors in this position confront the agonising choice between denouncing their own story or mortgaging their home to pay for the legal costs of defending it.

Statements in open court

3–034 A public apology defames the author of the article apologised for by suggesting that the author has written carelessly. An author who has not approved the apology is entitled to sue the person who has issued it.[83] Unapologetic authors cannot sue if the retraction is made through the procedure known as "a statement in open court". These statements are privileged and so too are any press reports of them.

---

[80] *Hayward v Thompson*, fn.34 above, *per* Lord Denning at 459.
[81] *Eastwood v Ryder, The Times*, July 31, 1990.
[82] Civil Liability (Contribution) Act 1978, s.1.
[83] *Tracy v Kemsley Newspapers, The Times*, April 9, 1954.

Authors may nevertheless disassociate themselves from the apology, or even approach the judge before whom the statement is to be made and ask him to refuse to sanction it because of the reflection that it would cast upon their reputations. However, courts are predisposed in favour of settlements, and are reluctant to prevent statements being made that dispose of libel actions, even when such statements imply criticisms of others:

> The historian Richard Barnet sued both Brian Crozier and the *Spectator* over the allegation that he was associated with KGB-influenced institutions. The magazine found that it could not justify the Crozier allegations and agreed to apologise, pay damages and make a statement in open court publicly retracting the libel. Crozier sought to delay the making of the statement on the ground that it defamed him and might prejudice the jury in Barnet's action against him, which would come on for trial some six months later. The Court of Appeal held that although "the court should be vigilant to see that the benefit of the procedure of making a statement in open court is not used to the unfair disadvantage of a third party", the public interest in allowing libel actions to be settled outweighed the damage that Crozier apprehended. Had the statement been plainly defamatory of Crozier, the court would have ordered the settlement to be postponed until after his trial, and may not have allowed it to be made at all under the cloak of absolute privilege.[84]

The statement in open court is a procedural device used in many libel settlements, often after the claimant has "taken out" money that has been paid into court by the defendant. It is valuable as a means of helping the claimant to restore his reputation (at least when the statement is reported) but it can be exploited to present a false picture under the pressure to avoid trial. Although judges must approve the statement before it is made, they normally make no inquiries and allow the parties to say whatever they have agreed. Under pressure to compromise a legal action which will cost hundreds of thousands of pounds to fight, defendants often "agree" to statements by which claimants whitewash their conduct or praise themselves in hagiographic terms. It follows that "statements in open court" are sometimes more akin to public relations announcements than to records of truth.

A nice point arises when a defendant, for commercial reasons, makes a payment into court which is less than can properly be described as "substantial" (in 2007, an adjective that should only be applied to damages exceeding £10,000). Is a claimant, on taking that money, entitled to make a privileged statement in open court declaring himself vindicated? The Court of Appeal has held that "it is wrong for complainants to assume that if they do take money out of court they are entitled as of right to be whitewashed by defendants . . .". The judge "should look at the relationship between the

---

[84] *Barnet v Crozier* [1987] 1 All E.R. 1041.

gravity of the allegations in the alleged libel and the amount of money which is paid into court".[85] This guidance was applied in 1992 to prevent an Italian prince from declaring himself vindicated by a payment of £1,000 lodged by the *Daily Mail* which it claimed to have made to avoid the costs of the trial rather than in acknowledgment of the falsity of its gossip.[86] When the *Wall Street Journal* "paid in" a fraction of the cost of a long trial it objected to the claimant's draft statement unless it was permitted to read a counter-statement emphasising that its allegations had not been fully withdrawn.[87] Popplewell J. overruled the objection, but jurisprudence on Art.6 of the European Convention ("each party must be afforded a reasonable opportunity to present his case . . . under conditions which do not place him at a substantial disadvantage vis-à-vis his opponent"[88]) supports the case for such a counter-statement in rare cases when the parties have agreed to a settlement, but disagree over what to say about it. The preferable alternative of course, is to say nothing. However keen judges are to facilitate settlements, they should not lend the courts imprimatur to one-sided statements unless the claimant has obtained substantial damages or else the wording is agreed by the defendant.

Foreign publications

3–035   Many journalists resident in Britain write for overseas publications. American law provides a special "public figure" defence: however inaccurate a speculation about the conduct of a person in the public eye, the journalists who make it will not be liable unless they have acted maliciously. The better view is that no action can be brought in Britain against the author of an article circulated only in America unless the article is also actionable under the law of the country where the publication took place.[89] It would follow that journalists writing for American publications have considerably more latitude in criticising public figures so long as their articles are not reprinted in Britain.

The claimant-friendliness of English libel law, most notoriously its requirement that the media bears the burden of proving truth,

---

[85] *Church of Scientology of California v North News Ltd* (1973) 117 SJ. 566.

[86] *Ruspoli v Dempster*, unreported, December 14, 1992, Alliot J.

[87] *Keen v Dow Jones Publishing Co (Europe) Inc.* Dow Jones was given leave to appeal by the Court of Appeal, but the point was not pursued.

[88] *Dondo Beheer BV v The Netherlands* (1993) 18 E.H.R.R. 213, at 229–30. Australian courts adopt a similar approach, and insist that judges ensure the accuracy and fairness of statements in open court: *Eyre v Nationwide News Pty Ltd* (1968) 13 F.L.R. 180.

[89] This "double actionability rule" is preserved for defamation claims by the Private International Law (Miscellaneous Provisions) Act 1995, s.13. But if the author is domiciled in the UK, he can be sued in respect of publications in other European countries which are parties to the Brussels and Lugano Conventions, incorporated into UK law by the Civil Jurisdiction and Judgments Acts 1982 and 1991.

attracts many wealthy foreign forum-shoppers in search of favourable verdicts that they would not obtain at home, or in the home countries of publishers whose newspapers and magazines have an international circulation. The rule which gives them the opportunity to sue a foreign publication with a minute circulation in the United Kingdom dates from 1849, when the Duke of Brunswick dispatched his manservant to a newspaper office to obtain a back issue of the paper in order to sue for a libel he had overlooked for 17 years.[90] This single publication was deemed sufficient to constitute the tort of libel, and from this anachronistic case springs the absurd but venerated rule that in this country a single publication—even if only in a library—will be an actionable tort. The rigour of this rule is mitigated by the requirement that foreign publishers may only be served out of the jurisdiction by leave of the court, which should only be granted in the case of torts which are appropriate for trial in London. Thus when a European "gentleman of no occupation" came to England in the hope of collecting libel winnings from continental newspapers, a few copies of which had been circulated here, carrying articles accusing him of fraud, he failed to establish that his case was "a proper one for service out of the jurisdiction"(i.e. for dragging the foreign publishers into English courts) because he had no real and substantial grievance connected with England: the claimant, the publishers and the alleged fraud were all located abroad.[91] This was an early application of the *forum non conveniens* doctrine, whereby an English court can refuse to accept a case that would be more suitably tried, for the interests of the parties and the ends of justice, by the courts of another country.[92]

This doctrine has prevented American public figures from suing American magazines in England to protect reputations earned in America. A Californian company and its chief executive were sent packing because they had only a minor operation in Britain and the US magazine they wished to sue sold only 1,200 copies here: it would have been obviously unfair to force the publishers to defend themselves under a law foreign to both parties and in respect of an article mainly about US operations.[93] A similar fate befell Texan oil man Oscar Wyatt (on whom the *Dallas* character J.R. Ewing was based): his plea that he was connected with England directly through the presence of corporate offices and carnally because his son was the first to commit adultery with the Duchess of York was insufficient to maintain an action against *Forbes* magazine.[94] These claimants had made their reputations in America, which was the appropriate place for them to sue US magazines. It is different,

---

[90] *Duke of Brunswick v Harmer* (1849) 14 Q.B. 185.
[91] *Kroch v Rossell* [1937] 1 All E.R. 725.
[92] *Spiliada Maritime Corp v Cansulex Ltd* [1987] A.C. 460.
[93] *Chadha & Osicom v Dow Jones & Co Inc* [1999] E.M.L.R. 724, CA.
[94] *Wyatt v Forbes*, unreported, December 2, 1997, Morland J.

however, when the claimant is English or has worked here for many years, and will (all things being equal) be permitted to proceed against a foreign publication with a small circulation in the United Kingdom, especially if it has damaged him in a local or ethnic community.[95]

3–036   The global reach of the mass media, not only through satellite broadcasting and internationally distributed papers but most significantly by the internet, invites the courts of every advanced country to treat defamation as one global tort (rather than a multiple wrong committed by every single publication and every internet hit) and to yield jurisdiction to the country whose courts are best placed to decide the truth of the allegation. Any such development will have to come by international treaty: the Brussels Convention, an exercise of rigid pan-Europeanism, permits actions to be brought *either* in the European Union State where the publisher is based (with damages for the Europe-wide distribution) *or* in any and every EEC state where publication occurs (with damages in each action limited to reputational injury within the particular location).[96] This permits forum-shopping within Europe. The Law Lords have resisted any global theory of defamation liability, on the ground that it is incompatible with the primitive *Duke of Brunswick* rule that every publication is a separate tort[97]:

> Boris Berezovsky, the controversial Russian oligarch, sued *Forbes* magazine for the damage done to his "English" reputation by allegations that he had made his billions through corruption, gangsterism and murder. *Forbes* sold only 1,900 copies in England but 800,000 in the United States. The trial judge ruled that Russia and the United States were both more appropriate places for trying the action, because Berezovsky had an entirely Russian reputation and the defendant magazine was based in the United States. The Court of Appeal was more struck by Beresovsky's connections in England (he had property and ex-wives in Chelsea and children at Oxbridge and commercial connections here) and by the fact that UK-based banks and businesses would look at him askance. The Law Lords divided 3:2 over the correctness of the trial judges' decision, the majority ruling that he had paid insufficient attention to publication in Britain as a factor in favour of jurisdiction, the minority saying that he was "entitled to decide that the English court should not be an international libel tribunal for a dispute between foreigners which had no connection with this country".[98]

Lord Hoffman's words of caution about English courts arrogating to themselves the role of libel globo-cop have appealed to lower

---

[95] *Schapira v Ahronson* [1999] E.M.L.R. 735, although note that the defendant Israeli newspaper had made the tactical mistake of accepting service in England (thus assuming the burden of proving that England was inappropriate) and a good deal of the evidence was located within this jurisdiction.

[96] *Shevill v Presse Alliance* [1995] 2 A.C. 18.

[97] *Berezovsky v Forbes* [2000] E.M.L.R. 643.

[98] *Berezovsky v Forbes* [2000] E.M.L.R. 643 at 666, *per* Lord Hoffman.

courts and been frequently applied, most strikingly in "the other Jameel case" where Mohammed Jameel's brother Yousef sued the *Wall Street Journal Online* over a story about "The golden chain", a document which appears to list the Saudi billionaires who funded Al Qaeda when it turned from attacking the Russians in Afghanistan to attacking Americans everywhere. The newspaper had not actually published the document, which included Jameel's name, but had placed it on its website, to which readers of the article were directed by a hyperlink. The claimant was given leave (unopposed) to serve the defendants in New York: they entered a defence which protested that the action was an abuse of process. They could prove that only five UK subscribers had accessed their "golden chain" website page and three of these were agents of the claimant. The court had no hesitation in applying the rule in *Kroch v Rossell* and throwing the case out: Yousef's UK reputation would not be affected by two Internet hits. In this case, for the first time, the court was sceptical of the *Duke of Brunswick* rule: it would not be applied so as to permit an action ever an insubstantial Internet tort. The court added, "We do not believe that the *Duke of Brunswick* could today have survived an application to strike out for abuse of process". The Duke had sent his servant to obtain from a newspaper office a copy which had libelled him 17 years before: he acquired a technical cause of action but to bring it today would be condemned as an abuse of process. This is a valuable limit on the *Duke of Brunswick* rule that each publication and every downloading amounts to a separate tort. Where the downloadings are few and far between, the court will halt an action because "the game will merely not have been worth the candle, it will not be worth the wick".[99]

The collision between the Victorian assumptions of common law **3–037** libel and the reality of modern Internet publication was explored— unperceptively—by the High Court of Australia in *Gutnick v Dow Jones*:

> Joe Gutnick lived in Melbourne and funded its football team, when he was not in America allegedly manipulating the stock market or in Israel supporting right wing politicians or in Tuvalu, a South Pacific island in which he had bought a large stake. *Barrons*, a US finance magazine, critically analysed the man's character and the character of his US stock promotions: it had no print circulation in Victoria but was eagerly downloaded by members of Gutnick's synagogue and football

---

[99] *Dow Jones & Co Inc v Yousef Jameel* [2005] EWCA at 56 and 69. The abuse of process doctrine can be used to halt libel actions which are either attempts by the claimant to sidestep other actions which he has lost, or are simply cases where he could not obtain more than nominal damages. *Yousef Jameel* demonstrates that an attempt to use English libel courts to clear his name in respect of publications which are mainly directed to America and other countries is not something that the courts will lend their resources for him to achieve, at least if there is no substantial interest in this country in letting him do so.

team from wsj.com, a website with servers located in New Jersey. In so doing, the readers would send their electronic messages through cyber space to New Jersey, where they pulled the web pages from the server and brought them into the jurisdiction of the Victoria Supreme Court. Hence, argued Dow Jones, publication had taken place and the tort had been committed in New Jersey, where Mr Gutnick was welcome to sue them because they were an indelibly American magazine, written by Americans for Americans, and were edited and insured in America where they would not have paid any attention to Joe Gutnick had he not been ramping his shares on American stock exchanges. But the argument that he should sue in New Jersey did not appeal to the parochial Victorian courts which jealously guarded its Victorian era libel laws (the judge deplored arguments based on freedom of expression) and applied the *Duke of Brunswick* rule that every downloading, anywhere in the world, constituted a separate tort. On this basis, an Internet libel could be the subject of legal action in 191 different nations, many with state libel jurisdictions as well, but with different civil and criminal laws against defamation and very different methods of redress. The Australian High Court recognised the problem and said that courts should ensure that defamation actions were brought in the claimant's main state of residence, with damages limited to compensation for injury suffered in that state. It nonetheless upheld the Duke of Brunswick multiple publication rule, as providing notional liability in tort wherever and whenever in the world a libellous statement was downloaded.[100]

Although *Yousel Jameel* requires English courts to turn away the most blatant internet forum shoppers, they will always be tempted to take jurisdiction under the *Duke of Brunswick* rule over foreign web libels which besmirch the reputation of English citizens. Thus a local TV presenter who alleged she had been groped by Arnold Schwarzenegger at the Dorchester was entitled to sue the "Governator" and his press spokespersons for accusing her—in *The Los Angeles Times* and on its website—of lying. Since the grope had taken place in London, the court did not hesitate to try the case in London, although it might more realistically have held that since the claimant made her allegation to the *LA Times* in an effort to stop the rapacious actor from becoming governor of California, that was the place where the truth would most appropriately be tried.[101] The Court of Appeal has permitted American boxing promoter Don King to sue a US attorney for defamation over anti-Semitic allegations made on a Californian website—an unhappy decision which

---

[100] *Dow Jones & Co Inc v Gutnick* [2002] 210 C.L.R. 575. The case has been distinguished in Canada, in relation to an Internet libel in the Washington Post, where the claimant had recently moved to Canada from the country where he was accused of misbehaviour as a UN official: *Bangoura v The Washington Post*, Court of Appeal for Ontario, September 16, 2005.

[101] *Anna Richardson v Arnold Schwarzenegger* [2004] EWCA 2422; [2004] All E.R. (D) 432.

followed the green light that *Berezovsky* gave to forum shoppers. It is difficult to understand why Americans who fall out with each other in America should be permitted to take up the time of the UK courts with their slanging matches, rather than resolve them under their own law. If English courts routinely exercise their exorbitant jurisdiction over foreigners responsible for Internet libels, then those defendants who have no assets in England will simply be advised to stay away from any trial, especially if they are American, since their courts do not enforce English libel judgments (see later).

The courts have failed to take on board that the web is revolutionary because it serves (like a massive home library) as a repository of vast amounts of information and knowledge, accessible according to the searcher's requirements and not subject to the wishes or initiative of the website owner. The server is passive, apolitical and non-judgemental, like a professional librarian: it automatically divulges the knowledge that is sought without discrimination. It is this facility to disseminate knowledge that makes the Internet so important as a tool for enhancing the fundamental right of freedom of expression. Making such knowledge vulnerable to the defamation laws of any country, from Afghanistan to Zimbabwe, irrespective of whether they comply with freedom of expression guarantees, is a hostage to fortune. The High Court in Gutnick claimed that, "In all except the most unusual of cases, identifying the person about whom the material is to be published will readily identify the defamation law to which that person may resort." This is false reassurance, because there is no rule that restricts plaintiffs from suing anywhere they wish. As a result of globalisation there are hundreds of thousands of international public figures with reputations and relationships in more than one country. These include businessmen, lawyers, bankers, accountants and financial operators of all kinds; diplomats, politicians, journalists, sporting figures, actors, soldiers, aid workers, NGO executives, mafia leaders, money launderers, crime bosses, etc. Many corporations have operations, subsidiaries, employees and agents in dozens of countries. The High Court decision in *Gutnick*, if applied throughout the commonwealth, would chill free speech because it gives this very wealthy class of protected plaintiffs an opportunity to select the forum in which they perceive they can most easily harass the author or journalist who publishes facts that they would rather have hidden or criticisms they cannot abide. Defamation actions in most countries are essentially litigation for wealthy plaintiffs, the very people whose conduct is deserving of closest scrutiny. If there is a cause to suspect that they are (for example) drug dealers, confidence tricksters, financiers of terrorism or persons engaged in any other form of trans-border criminality, it is important that investigative journalism should be under no unnecessary inhibition in exposing them. Such inhibition would be created if *Gutnick* were widely followed, allowing people of this class to choose the forum with the most plaintiff-friendly libel law, by virtue of a few internet hits in that country. Even in multi-national media organisations, stories likely to attract expensive libel actions will be censored, irrespective of whether they are believed to be true. This is much more the case for publishers of private websites, whose freedom of speech is chilled because they cannot afford to defend a libel action in any foreign country where they may have assets.

3–038   So what is the best, or least worst, solution? Defamation is the means by which the law strikes a balance between the individual right to reputation and the public right to communicate and receive information. In the context of global dissemination of information by a technology which has no clear or close comparison with any other, a publication rule which does not expose publishers to liability in multiple jurisdictions, but which nonetheless provides plaintiffs with access to a court which can compensate them for all damage suffered, would strike the most acceptable balance. That would mean a rule which locates the act of publication in the place where the article was substantially prepared for downloading (assuming such place to have effective defamation laws) rather than in any place where it is downloaded by computer users—unless the publisher has, by its conduct in that place, instigated the downloadings. Every media corporation has a "centre of operations" where journalistic material is edited and prepared for publication and where the publication is insured. Usually this will be the place where the article is written and uploaded as well. The most satisfactory rule would locate the act of Internet publication in the place where the article is substantially produced, rather than in any place where it happens to be downloaded by computer users, unless:

a) the place of uploading is merely adventitious or opportunistic;

b) the publisher or author has instigated the downloading (e.g. by advertising the article or his internet site) and thus has waived the rule's protection and provided the state in which the downloading occurred with a clear interest in assuming the power to adjudicate the claim.

This is the kind of rule that publishing organisations should attempt to include in an international treaty. It is unlikely to result from judicial decisions in the increasing number of jurisdictional disputes over internet torts in countries around the world. There is a natural tendency for courts to indulge their own residents who wish to play "at home" against foreign publishers. This may be the place where their reputation is most at stake, but to haul a foreign publisher into court there will usually deprive him of the protection of the law under which the publication was written and insured. An obvious compromise solution would be to entitle residents to sue in their own state, but to require the courts of that state to apply the law of the place of publication. This place would usually be the United States, host to most Internet web servers and, thanks to the First Amendment, host to most publications that are likely to be regarded as defamatory in states less open to free speech. It would not be a bad compromise: courts in unreformed jurisdictions like Victoria would thereby be exposed to the values of the First Amendment.

Time limits

Justice requires libel actions to be brought as soon as possible **3–039** following publication to provide speedy and effective redress for wronged claimants and for the sake of media defendants who wish to justify, since "memories fade . . . sources become untraceable . . . records are retained only for short periods". This was the rationale for a reduction in the standard three-year period in which personal injury claims must be brought, a reform achieved by the 1996 Defamation Act, which requires claimants to sue in libel and in malicious falsehood within one year of "the date on which the cause of action accrued", i.e. the date of the defendant's last publication of the defamatory matter.[102] This salutary provision, which gives complainants a deadline by which to put up or shut up, is undermined in two respects. The 1996 Act gives the court a broad discretion to permit proceedings after the time-limit expires, if this is "equitable". There is a danger that judges will interpret "equitability" as turning on whether the action can still be fairly tried, rather than on the need to penalise tardy claimants whose usual excuse is that the libel did not come to their attention for over a year (which usually means it could not have done them much damage).[103] The second catch, which makes the provision useless for publishers of books remaining in circulation or even newspapers which sell "back issues", is that the

---

[102] Defamation Act 1996, s.5(2) and 5(4) amending s.4A and s.32A of the Limitation Act 1980.

[103] The court is, however, required to examine the reasons for the delay: it was unimpressed by one solicitor's excuse that he missed the deadline because he had consulted an out-of-date textbook: *Hinlcs v Channel 4*, March 3, 2000, Morland J.

reform does not affect the *Duke of Brunswick* rule that every sale is a separate cause of action. By making the deadline run from the last sale of a single copy (by which a cause of action accrues) rather than from the first appearance of the work, authors and publishers remain at risk for as long as the book remains in circulation or an article remains available on a newspaper's website.

The first "catch" in the 1996 Defamation Act requirement that any writ must follow within 12 months of publication—namely that judges might use their "equitable" discretion to extend time for tardy and undeserving claimants—has been discouraged by the Court of Appeal.[104] The judges emphasised that defamation is different to other torts, and free speech considerations should protect publishers from being vexed by delayed defamation actions. Since damages to reputation must be repaired promptly if it is to be repaired at all, claimants who delay longer than 12 months cannot be expected to be indulged.

However, the second "catch" identified in the 1996 reform—the *Duke of Brunswick* "multiple publication" rule that every publication constitutes a new and separate cause of action—will operate to deny any relief to publishers whose words remain in circulation for more than a year or are accessible through the worldwide web. American judges extirpated the rule from their common law after World War Two, adopting the more realistic "single publication rule", which treats the primary communication—the original circulation of a book or newspaper, or broadcast of a television program or uploading on to a website—as one global tort, from the time of which the limitation period begins to run in respect of every subsequent communication of the offending words. English judges, made of much less stern stuff, have despaired of change, because of "how firmly entrenched the principle in the *Duke of Brunswick*'s case is in our law".[105] This horse-and-buggy rule survives to shackle the internet, although the Court of Appeal helpfully suggested that a timely hyperlink might protect a web publisher from libel action:

> "Where it is known that archive material is or may be defamatory, the attachment of an appropriate notice warning against treating it as the truth will normally remove any sting from the material."[106]

Innocent dissemination

3–040 Distributors or wholesalers of newspapers, books and magazines have a special defence of "innocent dissemination". Obviously they cannot be expected to vet all the publications they sell, and it would

---

[104] *Steedman v BBC* [2001] EWCA Civ 1534.

[105] *Loutchansky v Times Newspapers (No. 2)* [2002] 1 All E.R. 652 at 673.

[106] *Loutchansky v Times Newspapers (No. 2)* [2002] 1 All E.R. 652 at 676e, *per* Lord Phillips MR.

be grossly unfair to hold them responsible for libels of which they could have no knowledge. In such cases they will escape, unless they have been negligent and ought to have known that the publication was likely to contain libellous matter. The strictness of the defence has unfortunate consequences for some controversial publications: distributors are prone to equate political radicalism with a propensity to libel, and are thus provided with a ready-made legal excuse for a decision not to stock them.

A claimant determined to damage a journal that torments him can, at least if that journal has a poor track record in libel actions, sue the distributors and settle on terms that they will not stock the publication in the future. For most small newsagents the prospect of defending a major libel case is frightening, and when Sir James Goldsmith threatened *Private Eye*'s distributors in this fashion, many of them caved in. The magazine's loss of circulation was dramatic and Lord Denning held that Goldsmith's flurry of "frightening writs" was an abuse of legal process. His fellow judges, however, pointed out that Goldsmith had merely *used* the legal process according to his rights. Any threats to press freedom came, not from Goldsmith, but from the law that allowed him to sue distributors of libel-prone magazines. If the law threatened press freedom, it was for Parliament, not the courts, to change it.[107]

Two decades later, Parliament got around to making some minor amendments to the innocent dissemination defence—most significantly by extending its protection to printers and to broadcasters of "live" programmes such as radio talk-backs and television chat shows, where the station has no control over off-the-cuff defamations uttered by studio guests. These two steps forward in the 1996 Defamation Act are accompanied by one step backwards: the distributor must prove not only that he took reasonable care but that "he did not know, and had no reason to believe what he did caused or contributed to the publication of a defamatory statement".[108] The old common law defence of "innocent dissemination" exculpated a disseminator who knew the statement was prima facie defamatory but reasonably believed it would not be held libellous because it was true or privileged or honest comment. Under the Act (which by implication supersedes the common law defence) the disseminator is not: "innocent" if he has some reason to think merely that a statement in a publication he distributes is defamatory (i.e. lowering the repute) of somebody. The statute requires "reasonable care" and potential knowledge of defamations to be tested by reference to "the nature of the publication" and "the previous conduct or character of the author, editor or publisher". This means that large distributors like W.H. Smiths will still insist on indemnities before they stock *Private Eye* or any new publication with a name like *Scallywag*.

---

[107] *Goldsmith v Sperrings* [1977] 1 W.L.R. 478.
[108] Defamation Act 1996, s.1(1)(c).

THE RULE AGAINST PRIOR RESTRAINT

3-041   The courts will not stop publication of defamatory statements where
the person who wants to make them is prepared to defend them.
Threats by angry complainants and their solicitors to stop the presses
with eleventh-hour libel injunctions are largely bluff:

> "The court will not restrain the publication of an article, even
> though it is defamatory, when the defendant says he intends to
> justify it or to make it fair comment on a matter of public
> interest. The reason sometimes given is that the defences of
> justification and fair comment are for the jury, which is the
> constitutional tribunal, and not for the judge. But a better
> reason is the importance in the public interest that the truth
> should out . . . The right of free speech is one which it is for the
> public interest that individuals should possess, and, indeed, that
> they should exercise without impediment, so long as no wrongful
> act is done. There is no wrong done if it is true, or if it is fair
> comment on a matter of public interest. The court will not
> prejudice the issue by granting an injunction in advance of
> publication."[109]

If the claimant can prove immediately and convincingly that the
defendant is intending to publish palpable untruths, an injunction
might be granted in advance of the publication, so long as the
precise terms of the libel can be identified.[110] Otherwise, the rule
against prior restraint must prevail in libel actions. When an
injunction was granted to stop the circulation of information by a
shipping exchange accusing the claimant of fraud the Court of
Appeal lifted it as a matter of principle, even though a hearing on
the merits was set for the following day. "The only safe and correct
approach is not to allow an injunction to remain, even for a single
day, if it was clearly wrong for it to have been granted."[111]
The rule against prior restraint is secure in libel cases "because of
the value the court has placed on freedom of speech and freedom of
the press when balancing it against the reputation of a single
individual who, if wronged, can be compensated in damages".[112] The
rule has also been justified "because a judge must not usurp the
constitutional function of the jury unless he is satisfied that there is
no case to go to a jury. The rule is also partly founded on the

---

[109] *Fraser v Evans* [1969] Q.B. 349, *per* Lord Denning at 360. The rule derives from
the case of *Bonnard v Perryman* [1891] 2 Ch. 269.

[110] *British Data Management v Boxer Commercial Removals Plc* [1996] 3 All E.R.
707, CA.

[111] *Harakas v Baltic Mercantile and Shipping Exchange* [1982] 2 All E.R. 701 at 703,
per Kerr L.J.

[112] *Herbage v Pressdram Ltd* [1984] 2 All E.R. 769, *per* Griffiths L.J.

pragmatic grounds that until there has been disclosure of documents and cross-examination at the trial a court cannot safely proceed on the basis that what the defendants wish to say is not true. And if it is or might be true the court has no business to stop them saying it."[113] It applies whenever the defendant raises the defences of justification and fair comment, and will apply if the defence is to be qualified privilege unless the evidence of malice is so overwhelming that no reasonable jury would sustain the privilege. The Court of Appeal has even refused to injunct a magazine that had published an allegation it could not justify, where it might succeed at trial for other reasons:

> Soraya Kashoggi sought an injunction to withdraw *Woman's Own* from circulation when it published a statement that she was having an extramarital affair with a Head of State. The magazine could not prove the truth of this statement, which it had sourced to an MI5 report, but claimed to be able to justify the "sting" of the libel, namely that the claimant was a person given to extra-marital affairs, a number of which had been referred to in the article without attracting complaint. The Court of Appeal held that the rule against prior restraint would still operate, given that this defence might succeed at the trial. If it did not, the claimant would be adequately compensated by damages.[114]

One important practical benefit of this rule is that journalists can **3–042** (as they *must* to obtain qualified privilege) approach the subject of their investigation for a response to an article in draft without fear that they will receive a pre-publication injunction instead of a quote. However, one trap for unwary players can be sprung by a determined litigant who seeks an interim injunction at the outset of his action. If the defendant invokes the rule against prior restraint by his intention to justify the allegation, but the defence of justification is not proceeded with when the matter comes to trial, or it fails dismally at trial, his conduct in recklessly signalling a defence that does not materialise can inflate the damages. *Private Eye* fell into this trap when it beat off an interim injunction from Robert Maxwell by promising to prove at trial that he had financed Neil Kinnock's foreign travel in the hope of being awarded a peerage. Its defence of justification was withdrawn at the trial when its "highly placed sources" went to ground. It escaped being required to identify them, but its conduct in promising a plea of justification and persisting in such a plea until the last moment was punished by damages of £50,000. The jury found the libel itself to be worth only £5,000.[115]

The stringency of the rule against prior restraint in defamation encourages claimants to frame their actions as claims for breach of confidence, where injunctions were granted more readily on the

---

[113] *Greene v Associated Newspapers Ltd* [2005] 1 All E.R. 30 at 46, para.57 per Brooke L.J.

[114] *Kaskoggi v IPC Magazines Ltd* [1986] 3 All E.R. 577.

[115] See *Maxwell v Pressdram* [1987] 1 All E.R. 656.

"balance of convenience" test.[116] This tactic has been rendered less effective by s.12 of the Human Rights Act, with its requirement that particular attention be paid in such cases to freedom of expression and to the extent to which the material has already been published and/or is in the public interest. Under s.12, the "balance of convenience" test is replaced by the burden on the applicant to prove that he is likely to succeed at trial—a higher hurdle. In breach of confidence claims, the claimant must now satisfy the court that he will probably ("more likely than not") succeed at the trial before it will grant an injunction.[117] But in libel cases, the rule against prior restraint remains undiluted: the applicant can never obtain an injunction against the defendant's determination to defend, unless he can prove that the defamatory statement is false. This was re-emphasised by the Court of Appeal in 2005 in *Greene v Associated Newspapers Ltd*[118] where a close friend of the Blairs was unable to stop a proposed newspaper story, even though it was based on evidence supplied by fraudsman Peter Foster and therefore likely (although not certain) to be false. There can be no Ex parte injunctions (the tactic of a claimant going privately to a judge and obtaining an injunction to stop publication for a few days until the case can be argued by both parties) because now an applicant must take all practical steps to notify the publisher of the hearing (s.12(2)).

When the principle of free speech collides with the principle of fair trial, however, the former must give way. Courts may grant injunctions to stop defamatory publications that would prejudice pending criminal trials. This jurisdiction is not often used—the normal procedure is for the Attorney-General to bring proceedings for contempt once the trial has concluded. But in 1979 the Court of Appeal, at the behest of Mr Jeremy Thorpe, stopped the *Spectator* from publishing an election address by Auberon Waugh, "Dog-Lovers Candidate" for North Devon, on the grounds that it contained defamatory matter that would prejudice Thorpe's impending trial for conspiracy to murder his former lover, whose dog had been shot instead by a soft-hearted hit-man.[119] The Attorney General subsequently stopped the staging of a musical comedy about the fraudulent life of Robert Maxwell, lest it prejudice the fraud trial of his sons. Election law has a special provision (s.106 of the Representation of the People Act) which permits injunctions to stop a "false statement of fact in relation to the candidate's personal character or conduct" during the election period, although the burden of proving falsity falls on the candidate. The courts will

---

[116] Although the courts were willing to look at the real grievance—see *Service Corp International PCC v Channel 4* [1999] E.M.L.R. 83, Lightman J.

[117] *Cream Holdings Ltd v Banerjee* [2004] UKHL 44 at 22, *per* Lord Nicholls.

[118] [2005] 1 All E.R. 30.

[119] *Thorpe v Waugh* (unreported). See (1979) Court of Appeal Transcript No. 282.

require proof to a high standard, because elections are the very time democracy demands the utmost freedom of speech.[120]

DEFENCES GENERALLY

Burden of proof

Claimants must prove that the words of which they complain have a **3–043** defamatory meaning, that the words refer to them, and that the defendant was responsible for publishing them. Once these matters are established the burden shifts to the defendants. They must convince the jury that the words were true, or the comment was honest, or that publication of the report was "privileged" or otherwise in the public interest. The burden of proving these defences rests squarely on the media, although proof does not have to be "beyond reasonable doubt" but rather "on the balance of probabilities": 51 per cent proof will suffice, unless the accusation is of a criminal offence, when juries are told "the more serious the allegation, the more cogent the evidence required to prove it". A simple but far-reaching reform in libel law, which would enhance freedom of expression, would be to reverse this burden: to oblige the claimant to prove, on balance, the falsity or unfairness of the criticism. This modest proposal was rejected in 1975 by the Faulks Committee: "it tends to inculcate a spirit of caution in publishers of potentially actionable statements which we regard as salutary"[121] was its pompous response to a reform now clearly seen to be necessary to effectuate free speech as well as to bring libel law into line with other civil actions. A reversal of the burden of proof is essential if the purpose of Art.10 is to be achieved, namely to inculcate a salutary spirit of caution in wealthy public figures who wish to use the law to silence their critics.

There is mounting evidence that this unfair and anomalous rule causes jury confusion and can produce injustice. The rule stems, of course, from the absurd presumption that every defamation is false. Libel trials commence with this (often false) assumption that the claimant has a spotless character and then the media defendant bears the burden of disproving it, and by admissible evidence. This is impossible where witnesses have died or have been promised

---

[120] *Bowman v UK* (1998) 26 E.H.R.R. 1.
[121] Committee on Defamation, HMSO, 1975, Cmnd. 5909, para.141. Compare American libel law, where both public figure and private claimants bear the burden of proving that allegedly libellous statements are false: *Philadelphia Newspapers v Hepps* 475 U.S. 797 (1986). The public figure must further prove express malice, although a private claimant may recover against a negligent publisher: *Curtis Publishing Co v Butts* 388 U.S. 130 (1967). The reversal of the burden of proof is the main reason why American courts refuse to enforce English libel awards.

confidentiality, and difficult when the evidence comes (as in sleaze cases it often does) from criminals or low-life characters or even from investigative journalists (who can look fairly grubby in the witness box). Juries instinctively hesitate to find they have proved their allegations against glamorous film stars or experienced policemen or popular sportsmen. In 2001 the Court of Appeal for the first time took the extreme step of quashing a libel jury verdict on the grounds of perversity. It had awarded £85,000 to an obviously corrupt Bruce Grobbelaar after having been "skilfully deflected from the path of logic" by forensic tactics and then "left undecided about Grobbelaar's story"—a result fatal to the defendants on whom the burden of proof lay.[122] (On appeal, the House of Lords did not find the verdict utterly irrational, but reduced damages to a derisory £1.00.) Had Grobbelaar borne the legal onus of disproving the *Sun*'s allegations, he would not have won the unjust verdict and would in all probability not have had the effrontery to come to court in the first place. In every other civil action claimants must prove their case in order to win damages: why should libel be any different?

The meaning of "malice"

3–044 A number of important defences available to the media in libel cases can be defeated if the claimant proves that the publication was actuated by "malice". In ordinary language "malice" means "spite" or "ill-will". But in libel law it generally refers to dishonest or reckless writing or reporting—the publication of facts that are known or suspected to be false, or opinions that are not genuinely held. These qualities may exist without feelings of spite or revenge, so that malice in law has a wider meaning than colloquial usage suggests. On the other hand, the mere existence of personal antagonism between writer and claimant will not defeat a legitimate defence if the published criticism, however intemperate, is an honest opinion. For the careful and conscientious journalist or broadcaster, the legal meaning of "malice" provides vital protection for honest comment, the more so because the burden of proving that malice was the dominant motive shifts to the claimant. Such proof is necessary before a claimant can succeed against unfair and exaggerated criticism (the "fair comment" defence) or against false statements made on certain public occasions (which are protected by the defence of "qualified privilege").

The importance of the legal meaning of "malice" in the defence of free speech is emphasised by the House of Lords' decision in the case of *Horrocks v Lowe*[123]:

> Lowe was a Labour councillor who launched an intemperate attack on Horrocks, a Tory councillor whose companies had engaged in land

---

[122] *Grobbelaar v Newsgroup Newspapers Ltd* [2001] 2 All E.R. 437.
[123] [1975] A.C. 135 at 149.

dealings with the Tory-controlled local authority. "His attitude was either brinkmanship, megalomania or childish petulance. . . he has misled the Committee, the leader of his party, and his political and club colleagues", said Lowe of Horrocks at a council meeting. Speeches on such occasions, and reports of them, are protected by "qualified privilege"—a defence that will fail only if the claimant can show that the defendant was actuated by malice. In the ordinary sense of the word Lowe *was* malicious—his political antagonism had, the trial judge found, inflamed his mind into a state of "gross and unreasoning prejudice". Nonetheless, he genuinely believed that everything he said was true. On that basis the House of Lords held that he was not "malicious" in law.

A passage in Lord Diplock's speech is generally regarded as the classic exposition of the meaning of legal malice:

"What is required on the part of the defamer to entitle him to the protection of the privilege is positive belief in the truth of what he published . . . If he publishes untrue defamatory matter recklessly, without considering or caring whether it be true or not, he is in this, as in other branches of the law, treated as if he knew it to be false. But indifference to the truth of what he publishes is not to be equated with carelessness, impulsiveness or irrationality in arriving at a positive belief that it was true. The freedom of speech protected by the law of qualified privilege may be availed of by all sorts and conditions of men. In affording to them immunity from suit if they have acted in good faith in compliance with a legal or moral duty or in protection of a legitimate interest the law must take them as it finds them . . . In greater or less degree according to their temperaments, their training, their intelligence, they are swayed by prejudice, rely on intuition instead of reasoning, leap to conclusions on inadequate evidence and fail to recognise the cogency of material which might cast doubt on the validity of the conclusions they reach. But despite the imperfection of the mental process by which the belief is arrived at it may still be "honest', that is, a positive belief that the conclusions they have reached are true. The law demands no more."[124]

"Malice" is an imprecise term, and bears a different nuance in the **3–045** defence of fair comment than in qualified privilege. To defeat a fair comment plea the claimant must prove dishonesty or at least a reckless disregard for the truth—the defendant's *actual* malice (his spite or hatred of the claimant) will not negative the defence so long

---

[124] [1975] A.C. 135 at 149.

as he honestly believed in the opinions he expressed.[125] Qualified privilege, however, may be lost if the defendant misused the occasion of publication for an ulterior and vicious purpose, even though he believed at the time in the truth of allegations which have turned out to be false. This will rarely be the case with mainstream media reporting, although actual malice may sometimes poison the motives of informants. Newspapers will not normally be aware of improper motives lying behind otherwise defensible statements they report from spiteful informants: in such cases the better view is that they are not "infected" by the improper motivation of the accusers, unless either they ought to have known of it or the accuser was in their employ.[126]

Recklessness as to the truth or falsity of accusations may amount to malice, but carelessness does not, nor do impulsiveness or irrationality. Lack of care for the consequences of exuberant reporting is not malice and nor is mere inaccuracy or a failure to make inquiries or accidental or negligent misquotation.[127] The claimant must show that the defendant has turned a blind eye to truth in order to advance an ulterior object. An example is provided by one Parkinson, a Victorian clean-up campaigner, whose moral objection to "public dancing" led him to allege that a ballet at the Royal Aquarium had involved a Japanese female catching a butterfly "in the most indecent place you could possibly imagine". Confronted with evidence that the performer in question was neither Japanese nor female, and in any event was dressed in pantaloons, Parkinson confessed that he had difficulty observing the performance and that his object in making the allegation was to have the Aquarium's dancing licence revoked. His pursuit of moral ends did not justify his reckless disregard for truth, and his malice destroyed the privilege to which he would otherwise have been entitled[128]: "The law protects the freedom to express opinions, not vituperative make-believe".[129]

It is sometimes said that criticism of the claimant after the claim form has been issued, and a failure to apologise prior to trial, is evidence of malice. This approach is wrong in principle. Other critical statements made about a claimant are irrelevant unless they shed light on the defendant's state of mind at the time he or she wrote the article that gave rise to the action. It is not necessarily a sign of "malice" to refuse an apology, or to repeat the allegations prior to trial or to persist in them at trial;[130] this may be no more

---

[125] *Albert Cheng v Tse Wai Chun Paul*, Court of Final Appeal, Hong Kong, November 13, 2000, judgment by Lord Nicholls.

[126] *Egger v Viscount Chelmsford* [1965] 1 Q.B. 248.

[127] *Pinninger v John Fairfax* (1979) 53 A.L.J.R. 691, *per* Barwick C.J.; *Brooks v Muldoon* [1973] N.Z.L.R. 1.

[128] *Royal Aquarium v Parkinson* [1892] 1 Q.B. 431.

[129] *Albert Cheng v Tse Wai Chun Paul*, Court of Final Appeal, Hong Kong, November 13, 2000, *per* Lord Nicholls.

[130] See *Broadway Approvals Ltd v Odhams Press Ltd* [1965] 2 All E.R. 523.

than steadfastness in the cause (although if the allegations turn out to be false, such conduct will increase the damages).

TRUTH AS A DEFENCE

The defence of justification

Truth is a complete defence to any defamatory statement of fact, **3–046** whatever the motives for its publication and however much its revelation is unjustified or contrary to the public interest. The legal title of the defence is "justification", and it operates whenever the defendants can show, by admissible evidence, that their allegation is, on balance, substantially correct. The question of "substance" may be significant—it is not necessary to prove that every single fact stated in the criticism is accurate, so long as its "sting" (its defamatory impact) is substantially true. Minor errors, such as dates or times or places, will not be held against the journalist if the gist of the allegation is justified. Even mistakes that diminish reputation will not count if they pale into minor significance beside the truth of major charges. Section 5 of the 1952 Defamation Act provides that the defence of justification shall not founder by failure to prove every charge, "if the words not proved to be true do not materially injure the claimant's reputation, having regard to the truth of the remaining charges". So even where baseless charges do "materially injure" a claimant's reputation, accurate criticisms in the same article may amount to a "partial justification", which reduces the damages by reducing the value of the reputation. To say that a man is guilty of terrorism and drunken driving will be justifiable if he is a teetotal terrorist. It will, however, be gravely libellous if he is a drunken driver but not a terrorist. There are limits, of course, to the distance that truth will stretch. A generalised criticism cannot be justified if it is based on one isolated incident. A statement that a reporter is a "libellous journalist" implies some proven propensity to defame: it is not justified by the fact that the journalist was once in his or her career obliged to apologise.[131]

Facts should normally be allowed to speak for themselves: to spell out a conclusion may spell danger. For example, it may be a fact that a writer has used the work of others without permission. But to describe the writer as a "deliberate plagiarist" may overlook another, but unknown fact: that he or she was assured at the time of using the material that the originator's consent had been forthcoming. It follows that although the writer is a plagiarist, he is not a *deliberate* plagiarist. Libel lawyers are nervous of the word "lie" because it implies that a person said something that he or she *knew* was untrue. Since this is usually difficult to prove, they will often suggest

---

[131] *Wakeley v Cooke* (1849) 4 Exch. 511.

changing it to "misled", "misrepresented" or some other phrase that does not necessarily connote a dishonest state of mind.

The fact that a defamatory statement has been made or the fact that a defamatory rumour exists is no "justification" for publishing it. The "repetition rule" requires the "truth" in such cases to be the truth of the rumour, not the truth of the fact that it is circulating. As Lord Devlin has explained:

> ". . . you cannot escape liability for defamation by putting the libel behind a prefix such as 'I have been told that . . . ' or 'it is rumoured that . . . ', and then asserting that it was true that you had been told or that it was in fact being rumoured . . . For the purpose of the law of libel a hearsay statement is the same as a direct statement, and that is all there is to it."[132]

3–047   However, the context of the article may remove or reduce the rumour's impact on the claimant's reputation. Much will depend on the reaction of the reasonable reader. In most cases the publication of a rumour will give it currency and credit. But if the gist of the article is genuinely to demolish the rumour, or to demolish the credibility of its mongers rather than its victim, the article as a whole may not bear a defamatory meaning. There was a week in 1986 when Fleet Street and Westminster were convulsed with a rumour that Home Secretary Leon Brittan had been caught interfering sexually with a small boy; no newspaper dared to print what all "in the know" were discussing until *Private Eye* published the story with the explanation that it was utterly false and circulated to damage the Home Secretary by an anti-Semitic faction in MI5. This form of publication reproduced the rumour in order to kill it, and a relieved Home Secretary announced that he would be taking no proceedings against *Private Eye*.

The "repetition rule" does not apply in *Reynolds* privilege as public interest defences where the media has impartially reported an allegation made in public debate without adopting it as accurate. A rumour may be reported (with great care) if its existence (irrespective of its truth) has public significance. Its victim should be allowed to reply and renounce the allegation and the publisher must be scrupulous not to indicate expressly or impliedly that the allegation is true. In many spheres of public life justice should be seen to be done, and officials should be seen to be above reproach. So a paper might report that a community believed that certain police officers had been unnecessarily violent in arresting suspects. The report would need to include any denial by the police, but it might go on to comment that irrespective of whether the allegations were true or not, their existence undermined the confidence of the community in

---

[132] *Lewis v Daily Telegraph Ltd* [1964] A.C. 234 at 283.

the officers, who for this reason should be transferred. Justification may fail if the newspaper cannot prove that the police officers had behaved in a way which brought reasonable suspicion upon them,[133] but the defendant would in this situation have the comfort of falling back on the *Jameel* defence of public interest publication.

Practical problems

Further problems with the defence of justification arise from the law's procedures. Although truth is a defence, proving it in court may be impossible. There is the burden of proof—squarely on the defendant. There is the crippling legal cost of preparing a full-blooded counterattack. There is the difficulty of calling witnesses who may have died or gone abroad, or who may have been promised confidentiality. And then there is the risk of failure, which inflates the damages on the basis that the defendant is not merely a defamer, but a defamer who has persisted in the injury to the last. There is no doubt that difficulties of this sort mean that many true statements are not published, or if they are, soon become the subject of apologies rather than defences.

3-048

Other problems stem from the ambiguities of language and the complex rules of pleading. Claimants will plead the most exaggerated meanings that their counsel consider the words will conceivably bear in order to maximise the insult and humiliation (and hence the damages). The defence may well be able to prove the words true in some less defamatory meaning, but will fail unless that is the meaning the jury chooses to adopt as the "true" meaning. There will be legal pressure to settle the case: successful defendants do not recover all of their costs, and the simplest of libel actions will run up a six-figure sum in costs for each party prior to trial. Damages, at the end of the forensic day, rarely exceed the cost of the lawyers who have obtained them.

No one defamation action is the same as any other: general rules about pleading and meaning require adaptation to an infinite variety of contexts and linguistic usage. What has to be justified as "true" is not a set of words in their literal meaning, but the imputation they convey—and they may convey several. English law's approach insists on one defamatory "sting", but a long article or broadcast programme may carry a number of defamatory meanings, some true and

---

[133] Because the so-called "repetition rule" that publication of rumour and suspicion can only be justified if there are reasonable grounds (objectively judged) which stem from some conduct on the part of the claimant. See *Shah v Standard Bank* [1998] 4 All E.R. 155, CA, and *Stern v Piper* [1997] Q.B. 123, CA. The rigidity of this rule is difficult to square with recent European Court decisions, notably *Bladet Tromsø v Norway* (1999) 29 E.H.R.R. 125 and *Thoma v Luxembourg*, March 29, 2001 (Application No.38432/97) and the Court of Appeal in *Roberts v Gable* (2007) has confirmed that the rule relates only to defences of justification and does not apply in cases of neutral reportage, which is a species of public interest privilege.

others false. This invites a great deal of pre-trial tactical skirmishing: the claimant will only sue on the false imputations, but the defendant will seek to call evidence of other "stings" that can be proved. This will not be allowed if the meaning is separate or distinct from the meaning of which complaint is made,[134] but in most cases there will be an overlap, if not a hopeless entanglement, and the judge will have to resort to case management techniques and proportionality doctrine to limit the issues and the evidence. The parties are not entitled to turn the proceedings into a wide-ranging investigation akin to a public inquiry, but in principle "the action should be so structured that the defendant is not prevented from deploying his full essential defence and so that the claimant, if he wins, will obtain proper vindication upon a proper basis".[135] Recent provisions for: (a) exchange of witness statements; (b) disclosure of documents which might be relevant to advancing or undermining either party's case[136]; and (c) threats of adverse costs orders unless the parties make "timely admissions of fact" to reduce the need for live evidence,[137] all follow the "cards on the table" philosophy of the Woolf reforms, although last minute evidence which tends to prove truth is usually admitted to avoid the reproach that a verdict for the claimant was a "false vindication". This is as it should be: the very publicity attending libel proceedings sometimes produces evidence that claimants hoped had disappeared forever. Claimants like ex-minister Jonathan Aitken, the soap actress Gillian Taylforth and South African journalist Jani Allen were fatally tarnished by evidence which only turned up in the hands of their nemesis, the late George Carman Q.C., in the course of their cross-examinations at the trial.

3–049 Placing a defence of justification on the record is a serious step: the media defendant takes upon itself the task of proving that its allegations are true, thereby adding insult to the original injury. A failed plea will mean heavier damages and much heavier costs. Before the pleading is entered a defendant must not only believe the truth of his words but also have some evidence to support them, or reasonable grounds for thinking that the evidence will be available at the trial. "Reasonable grounds" must be more than a Micawberish hope that something will turn up, but defendants who have reason to believe that the truth will out—e.g. from documents which must be in the possession of the claimant—are entitled to put down a plea of justification so as to oblige their opponent to disclose them.[138]

On the other hand, the difficulties of proving justification should not be exaggerated. The adage that "truth will out" is assisted by the law. The defendant may rely on facts that emerge after publication—

---

[134] *Polly Peck v Trelford* [1986] Q.B. 1000 at p.1002.
[135] *McPhilemy v Times Newspapers Ltd* [1999] E.M.L.R. 751 at 771.
[136] See *Evans v Granada TV* [1996] E.M.L.R. 413.
[137] See *US Tobacco v BBC* [1998] E.M.L.R. 816.
[138] *McDonalds Corp v Steel* [1995] 3 All E.R. 615.

and in such cases the length of time before trial may be a positive boon. Most importantly, the defence may be helped by court rules relating to "discovery of documents". Claimants must make available to the defence all documents in their possession that are relevant to the matters in dispute—and sometimes there will be found, amongst office memoranda and other internal documents, material that goes to justify the original allegation. The order for discovery is often the point of no return for the claimant in a libel action: it is the stage at which some prefer to discontinue rather than to open their files. The most sensational collapse of a libel case in recent British history was that brought by Neil Hamilton M.P. and lobbyist Ian Greer against the *Guardian* for publishing Al Fayed's claim that they accepted his bribes. A few days before the trial began, documents that they and the cabinet office (on *subpoena*) were forced to disclose indicated that both men had skeletons in their cupboards. Their last-minute withdrawal triggered the "Tory sleaze" allegations which, a few months later, swept that party from power in the 1997 elections.[139]

Finally there is always the prospect of cross-examining the claimant. Libel claimants are virtually obliged to go in the witness box. One claimant who failed to take the stand was David Bookbinder, leader of Derbyshire County Council, who in 1991 sued Norman Tebbitt over the latter's criticisms of his political policies. The tactic proved disastrous: Bookbinder was savagely derided for his cowardice by defence counsel, and the jury found Tebbitt's criticisms to be fair comment. Once in the witness box, claimants may be cross-examined in detail about matters relevant to their claim and may have their reputation traduced.[140] Their answers may support the defence of justification—although rarely as dramatically as football manager Tommy Docherty, a libel claimant who collapsed so utterly under cross-examination that he was subsequently prosecuted for perjury. A sympathetic jury acquitted him after his counsel had luridly described the terrors and confusions for claimants of undergoing cross-examination in libel actions. Jonathan Aitken, an M.P. and former cabinet minister, was destroyed not by cross-examination but by last minute discovery of hotel and airline records which proved him not only a liar but a scoundrel who had expected his wife and 16–year-old daughter to tell lies in support of his claim. He was jailed for 18 months—a sentence which could have been heavier, so as to deter anyone else prepared to suppress the truth by perverting the course of justice. The four year sentence imposed on Jeffrey Archer, for fabricating evidence in support of his libel action, may also have a deterrent effect.

---

[139] See David Leigh and Ed Vulliamy, *Sleaze—The Corruption of Parliament* (Fourth Estate, 1997).

[140] But not, regrettably, by reference to specific acts of misconduct that fall outside the pleaded meanings: see the rule in *Scott v Sampson* (1881–82) L.R. 8 Q.B.D. 491.

Reporting old criminal convictions

3–050   There are special rules relating to publication of past criminal convictions. A conviction—or, for that matter, an acquittal—by a jury is no more than an expression of opinion by at least 10 out of 12 people about the defendant's guilt. One ingenious convict, Alfie Hinds, sued a police officer for stating in the *News of the World* that he had been guilty as charged. Hinds convinced the libel jury that he had been wrongfully convicted, so the newspaper's defence of justification failed.[141] Parliament, recognising the danger—perhaps more to respect for the law than to press freedom—changed the law, so that now the very fact of a conviction is deemed to be conclusive evidence of its correctness. The prosecution's evidence does not have to be presented to the court all over again.[142]

However, this rule—and indeed the basic rule that truth is a complete defence—is subject to one exception in relation to past convictions. It is socially desirable that offenders should be able to "live down" a criminal past, and the Rehabilitation of Offenders Act 1974 is designed to assist this process. The Act applies only to convictions that have resulted in a sentence of no more than 30 months' imprisonment, and which have been "spent"—i.e. a certain period of time has elapsed since the passing of sentence. The length of that period depends on the seriousness of the punishment: where there has been any period of imprisonment between six months and 30 months, the conviction becomes "spent" after 10 years have elapsed. Seven years is the rehabilitation period for prison sentences of six months or under; five years for all other sentences that fall short of imprisonment, save for an absolute discharge, which is "spent" (not that it should carry a blameworthy connotation in any event) after a bare six months. There are short rehabilitation periods for juvenile offenders and persons subject to court orders or disqualifications.

The provisions of the Act are complex, but they have little effect on media freedom. The press may publish details of "spent" convictions and, if sued, may successfully plead justification or fair comment, unless the claimant can show that the publication of this particular truth has been actuated by malice.[143] Since there can be no dishonesty involved in stating the truth, an overwhelming desire to injure the claimant rather than to inform the public must, and it rarely can, be proved (newspapers have routinely reported the "spent" convictions of National Front leaders for example). But journalists minded to look at court or police records should bear in mind that an official persuaded to show them a "spent" conviction is

---

[141] *Hinds v Sparks (No. 2), The Times*, October 20, 1964; see similarly *Goody v Odhams Press Ltd, Daily Telegraph*, June 22, 1967.

[142] Civil Evidence Act 1968, s.13(1).

[143] Rehabilitation of Offenders Act 1974, s.8.

liable to a fine, and if they make their persuasion more persuasive by a bribe or obtain access to the record dishonestly, they themselves are liable to imprisonment for up to six months.[144]

There is no inhibition on digging up an old acquittal. Nor does the **3–051** fact of an acquittal debar the media from alleging that the defendant was really guilty after all. The jury's verdict is "final" only so far as punishment by the criminal court is concerned. Naturally, such allegations will rarely be made, although the defence of "justification" does not require them to be proved to the high criminal standard, "beyond reasonable doubt". Where there is a strong evidence of guilt, defendants given the benefit of the doubt by a jury in a criminal trial will normally be reluctant to chance their luck a second time by bringing a libel action, although the rule that the media must prove guilt by cogent evidence encouraged the acquitted Bruce Grobbelaar to sue the newspaper which had provided the prosecution evidence. It is noticeable that *Rough Justice* type programmes and books invariably deal with wrongful convictions and never wrongful acquittals (which are much more common). In this respect libel law clearly exercises a "chilling effect" on the media, which are forced to cover up the extent to which dangerous criminals sometimes walk free as a result of police or prosecution mistakes. A notable exception was made in the case of the men acquitted of the murder of black teenager Stephen Lawrence: the *Daily Mail*, which trumpeted their guilt, presumably calculated that they had neither the money nor the courage to sue.

FAIR COMMENT

The defence of "fair comment" protects the honest expression of **3–052** opinion, no matter how unfair or exaggerated, on any matter of public interest. The question for the court is, whether the views could honestly have been held on facts known at the time. Whether the jury agree with it or not is irrelevant. "A critic is entitled to dip his pen in gall for the purpose of legitimate criticism: and no one need be mealy-mouthed in denouncing what he regards as twaddle, daub or discord."[145] This means, as the court effectively held in 2007, that artists and writers who offer their work for public performance are fair game for any honest criticism, however, misconceived, so long as it is not actuated by malice.[145a] The defence is called "fair comment"—a misnomer, because it in fact defends unfair comment, so long as that comment amounts to an opinion that an honest (but not necessarily fair-minded) person might express on a matter of

---

[144] 1974 Act, s.9.
[145] *Gardiner v John Fairfax & Sons* (1942) 42 S.R. (NSW) 171, at 174 *per* Jordan C.J.
[145a] *Burstein v Associated Press* (2007). The claim by a composer that an opera critic had criticised his work unfairly was struck out.

public interest, and that has in fact been expressed by a defendant who was not actuated by malice.

> "Every latitude must be given to opinion and to prejudice, and then an ordinary set of men with ordinary judgment must say [not whether they agree with it, but] whether any fair man would have made such a comment. . . Mere exaggeration, or even gross exaggeration, would not make the comment unfair. However wrong the opinion expressed may be in point of truth, or however prejudiced the writer, it may still be within the prescribed limit. The question which the jury must consider is this—would any fair man, however prejudiced he may be, however exaggerated or obstinate his views, have said that which this criticism has said."[146]

Distinction between fact and opinion

3–053 The fair comment defence relates only to *comment*—to statements of opinion and not to statements of fact. This is the most important, and most difficult, distinction in the entire law of libel. A defamatory statement of fact must be *justified* (i.e. proved true)—which is a much more onerous task than defending a defamatory comment on the basis that it was made honestly. The difficulty arises when facts and opinions are jumbled together in the same article or programme. A form of words may, in one context, be opinion (and therefore defensible as "fair comment") while in another context appear as a factual statement, consequently requiring proof of correctness. There is no hard-and-fast rule: once again, the test is that of ordinary readers. Would they, on reading or hearing the words complained of in context, say to themselves "that is an opinion" or "so that is the fact of the matter"? Unattributed assertions in news stories and headlines are likely to be received as factual, while criticism expressed in personalised columns is more likely to be regarded as opinion, especially when it appears to be an inference drawn by the columnist from facts to which reference has been made. Writers can help to characterise their criticisms as comment with phrases like "it seems to me", "in my judgment", "in other words", etc., although such devices will not always be conclusive. To say, without any supporting argument, "In my opinion Smith is a disgrace to human nature", is an assertion of fact. To say, "Smith murdered his father and therefore is a disgrace to human nature", makes the characterisation a comment upon a stated fact.

---

[146] *Merivale v Carson* (1887) 20 Q.B.D. 275, at 280 *per* Lord Esher. "Fairness" plays no part in the "fair comment" defence, which is open to the obstinate and prejudiced commentator, and whose views must be honest but not necessarily reasonable or fair: *Branson v Bower* [2001] E.H.L.R. 33.

Where a defamatory remark is made baldly, without reference to any fact from which the remark could be inferred, it is not likely to be defensible as comment, especially if it imputes dishonesty or dishonourable conduct. In deciding the scope of a fair comment plea and the degree of interpretative sophistication to bring to bear on the question of whether a passage is "comment" or "fact", the court should have regard to the constitutional importance of the fair comment defence as a protection for freedom of expression.[147]

The cause of freedom of expression was damaged, however, by the House of Lords in 1991 in *Telnikoff v Matusevitch*, a decision that ignores the realities of newspaper reading and places a burden on editors to identify fully the subjects commented upon in their "letters" page.[148]

> The claimant wrote an article for the *Daily Telegraph* attacking the BBC World Service for recruiting mainly members of the USSR's national minorities for its Russia service. The defendant wrote, and the *Telegraph* published, a "letter to the editor" in response, characterising the claimant's views, as expressed in this article, as racist and anti-Semitic. The claimant sued and the outcome hinged on whether the words used in the letter could be construed as *comment* (in which case the defendant succeeded) or *fact* (in which case the defendant lost, because they were untrue). This in turn hinged on whether the jury could construe the letter in isolation (when it was read literally, it appeared to be making statements of fact) or in the wider context of the original article (on which the letter was plainly intended as a comment). The House of Lords, reversing the Court of Appeal, held that the jury should be permitted to look at the letter only as published. This decision is wrong, because letters to the editor are generally written—and sensibly read—as comments upon articles and opinions previously expressed in the newspaper.

The law should encourage readers to exercise free speech by writing letters to newspapers, and encourage editors to publish, in the public interest, as many of these letters as possible. The rule in *Telnikoff* requires editors either to reject or censor a letter if its critical statements cannot be proved in court, or else to republish the criticised article again so that its naïvest readers will realise that the letter is stating its author's *opinion*. As the latter course will normally prove impractical, the *Telnikoff* decision shrinks the area of robust criticism permitted to "letters to the editor" pages by the fair comment defence and provides some legal excuse for oversensitive editors who censor or reject letters critical of the newspaper's own correspondents. In any event the *Telnikoff* rule pre-dated the Human Rights Act and is incompatible with European Court decisions which

---

[147] See *London Artists Ltd v Littler* [1969] 2 Q.B. 375; *Slim v The Daily Telegraph* [1968] 2 Q.B. 157; *Silkin v Beaverbrook Newspapers Ltd* [1985] 2 All E.R. 516.
[148] *Telnikoff v Matusevitch* [1991] 4 All E.R. 817.

stress that allegedly defamatory words in a newspaper should be considered in light of previous articles on the same subject.[149] An editorial decision to publish a letter commenting critically upon a previous contribution to public debate woule now have a *"Reynold privilege"* defence.

3–054   Some assistance in deciding whether offending words are fact or comment may be derived from the policy behind the distinction, that defamatory statements which clearly reflect the writer's subjective value judgment (e.g. as an inference from or comment upon other facts) should be easier to defend because they do less harm: readers will not take them as gospel truth, but will be more likely to think about the facts for themselves and make up their own minds. This assumes, of course, that the facts upon which the comment is made are true, or (as provided by s.6 of the Defamation Act) stated truly enough to sustain the fairness of the comment. The burden of establishing that words are comment rather than fact, and express an opinion which a geniune commentator may honestly hold, falls on the defendant. If these conditions are objectively established the defendant must succeed, unless the claimant can prove that he was actuated by legal malice, i.e. that he did not genuinely hold the view to be expressed. Although proof of actual malice (improper motives such as spite or a private grudge) will defeat a claim of qualified privilege, it should not be permitted to undermine the protection the law affords to honest comment. This right to express opinions cannot be denied to commentators who wish to injure their political or personal enemies or are motivated by unworthy desires for publicity or revenge. As Lord Nicholls has pointed out,

> "The presence of these motives . . . is not a reason for excluding the defence of fair comment . . . liberty to make such comments, genuinely held, on matters of public interest lies at the heart of the defence of fair comment . . . commentators of all shades of opinion are entitled to "have their own agenda". Politicians, social reformers, busybodies, those with political or other ambitions and those with none, all can grind their axes. The defence of fair comment envisages that everyone is at liberty to conduct social and political campaigns by expressing his own views . . . .".[150]

The opinion must have some factual basis

3–055 The defence of fair comment will not succeed if the comment is made without any factual basis. An opinion cannot be conjured out of thin air—it must be based on *something*. And that something

---

[149] See *Bladet Tromso v Norway* (1999) 29 E.H.R.R. 125 and *Bergens Tidende v Norway* (2001) 31 E.H.R.R. 430.

[150] *Albert Cheng v Tse Wai Chun Paul*, Hong Kong Court of Final Appeal, November 13, 2000, p.10 of transcript.

should either be accurately stated in the article or at least referred to with sufficient clarity to enable to reader to identify it. It is not necessary to set out all the evidence for the writer's opinion: a summary of it or a reference to where it can be found is sufficient. Even a passing reference is sufficient if readers will understand what is meant. The leading case is *Kemsley v Foot*[151]:

> Michael Foot once launched an attack in *Tribune* on what he termed "the foulest piece of journalism ever perpetrated in this country in many a long year", indicating a particular article in the *Evening Standard*. The editor of that paper and the writer could not sue for this honest, if exaggerated, appraisal of their work. However, Foot's article was titled "Lower than Kemsley"—a proprietor whose stable of newspapers did not include the *Evening Standard*. Did the headline amount to a statement of fact—i.e. that Lord Kemsley was a byword for publishing dishonest journalism—or an opinion about the quality of journalism in Kemsley newspapers? The House of Lords held that the readers of *Tribune* in the context of the copy would regard the headline as a comment on the quality of the Kemsley press, rather than as a factual statement about the character of the proprietor. There was sufficient reference to the factual basis of the comment—namely the mass-circulation Kemsley newspapers—to enable readers to judge for themselves whether the comment was reasonable.

Given the rule that a fair comment must state or refer to the facts upon which it is based, to what extent might the falsity of those facts destroy the defence? Clearly, the comment that "Smith is a disgrace to human nature" could not be defended if the stated fact, e.g. that Smith was a patricide, was false. Often comments will be inferences from a number of facts—some true, some partly true, and some not true at all. These difficulties have resolved themselves into the question: is the comment fair in the sense of being one that the commentator could honestly express on the strength of such of his facts as can be proved to be true? Take the case of the prudish Mr Parkinson, who attended the butterfly ballet. His opinion that it was grossly indecent was genuine to the extent that his inclination was to think every form of dance indecent. However, his stated grounds for that opinion were a figment of his imagination: his misdescriptions of the performance were so fundamental as to vitiate any factual basis for his criticism. The defence of honest comment would not have availed him. The defence protects the honest views of the crank and the eccentric, but not when they are based on dishonest statements of fact.

The rule will not apply to defeat comments that are based on facts that, although untrue, have been stated on occasions protected by privilege. Trenchant editorials are sometimes written on the strength

---

[151] *Kemsley v Foot* [1952] A.C. 345 at 356, and see *Hunt v Star Newspapers* (1908) 2 K.B. 309.

of statements made in court or Parliament. These will be protected
as fair comment, even if the "facts" subsequently prove
unfounded.[152] However, a publisher has this additional latitude only
if, at the same time, it carries a fair and accurate report of the court
or parliamentary proceedings (or other privileged occasion) on
which the comment is based. Thus *Time Out* was not entitled to rely,
in factual support of a fair comment defence of an attack on boxer-
turned-businessman George Walker, on a statement made by a
police officer at his Old Bailey trial 35 years previously linking him
to membership of a criminal gang. Privilege attached to such a
statement only in the context of a fair and accurate report of the
case itself—a hearing in 1956 when the future chairman of Brent
Walker was gaoled for two years for stealing a consignment of
women's underwear.[153]

Absence of malice

3–056 The fair comment defence is defeated by proof that the writer or
publisher was actuated by malice. Defendants are entitled to give
evidence of their honest state of mind, and to explain why their
dominant motive, irrespective of any dislike they may feel for the
claimant, was to comment on a matter of public interest. The courts
have repeatedly insisted that "irrationality, stupidity or obstinacy do
not constitute malice though in an extreme case they may be some
evidence of it."[154] Carelessness, i.e. a failure to make enquiries, is not
evidence of malice. A failure to apologise or to publish a retraction
will not normally be evidence of malice, but rather of consistency in
holding sincere views. But editors who refuse to retract damaging
comments after clear proof that they are wildly exaggerated may lay
themselves open to the inference from this conduct that they were
similarly reckless at the time of the original publication.

Hard-hitting criticism and savage satire can generally be successfully defended as honest comment. *News of the World* editor
Derek Jameson notably failed to prove that the writers of the BBC
satirical programme *Week Ending* were dishonest in portraying him
as stupid and lubricious: his record as editor of down-market
newspapers allowed them to describe his editorial policy as being
"all the nudes fit to print and all the news printed to fit". It would
have been a sad day for British satire had Jameson won this
presumptuous action. To prove that virulent criticisms are "malicious" it must be shown that they do not reflect the honest belief of
their writer. Charlotte Cornwall was described as "a middle-aged
star [who] can't sing, her bum is too big and she has the sort of stage

---

[152] *Mangena v Wright* [1909] 2 K.B. 958; *Greek v Odhams Press Ltd* [1958] 2 Q.B.
276; *London Artists Ltd v Littler*, fn.27 above.
[153] *Brent Walker Group Plc and George Walker v Time Out Ltd* [1991] 2 All E.R. 753.
[154] *Turner v MGM* [1950] 1 All E.R. 449 *per* Lord Porter at 463.

presence that jams lavatories . . . looks just as ugly *with* make-up."
The defendants knew that the actress was aged 34 and was of normal
weight and appearance: the article was written with malice because it
had heaped upon her insults that could not have reflected anyone's
honest opinion.

Public interest

The defence of fair comment may be sustained only if the comment **3–057**
is on a matter of public interest. This is an easy test to satisfy: the
only cases where it has failed have been criticisms of the private lives
of persons who are not public figures. The courts have held that the
public is legitimately interested, not merely in the conduct of public
officials and institutions, but of private companies whose activities
affect individual members of the public. The conduct of a professional person towards a client or an employer towards a worker are
also matters that may attract legitimate public interest. Anyone who
throws a hat into a public arena must be prepared to have it
mercilessly, though not maliciously, trampled upon.

Whose comment is it?

There is an important question about the application of the fair **3–058**
comment defence to comment by a third party that is published in a
newspaper. The editor may not agree with sentiments in a "letter to
the editor"; if sued for libel, does the editor lose the defence of fair
comment because it cannot be said that the opinion is honestly his?
It is clear that publishers may rely upon the defence of fair comment
to the same extent as the person whose comment it was, so if the
author of the letter is also sued, or is prepared to testify, the honesty
of his or her views will support the newspaper's defence. If the
author does not come forward, however, the expression of opinion
may still be defended as fair comment if it can be shown to satisfy
the test of whether a hypothetical commentator person could
honestly express the opinion on the proven facts.[155] This was the
second—and more satisfactory—decision of the House of Lords in
Telnikoff v Matusevitch, which rejected the claimant's contention that
the defendant, to succeed on a fair comment defence, has to prove
that the comment was the honest expression of his views. On the
contrary, the burden is on the claimant to prove that a comment is
objectively unfair in the sense that no man, however prejudiced and
obstinate, could have held the views expressed by the defendant.[156]

---

[155] The minority view in the Canadian case of *Cherneskey v Armadale Publishers*
(1978) 90 D.LR. (3d) 371 is to be preferred to the majority opinion: see *Telnikoff*
[1991] 4 All E.R. 817, HL above, and *Lyon v Daily Telegraph* [1943] 2 All E.R.
316.

[156] *Telnikoff v Matusevitch* [1991] 4 All E.R. 817, HL.

Satire and Mere Abuse

3–059 Many a true word may be spoken in jest, and many a false word too—as humourless libel judges are quick to point out. Juries, however, tend to see jokes. When the *Wall Street Journal* labelled Harrods "The Enron of Britain" after it had been taken in by a clumsy Al Fayed hoax, the store pompously sued it for sarcasm. The case was laughed out of court. Lord Steyn has pointed out that Art.10 extends to information and ideas "that offend, shock and disturb" and,

> "To curtail the right of a satirist to deploy ridicule to the extent and in the manner in which he chooses would be a far-reaching incursion on freedom of speech. There is no warranty in our legal history, modern principles of public law, convention principles or policy for such an approach."[157]

These high-minded principles may have been applied by the jury which threw out the case brought by former M.P. Rupert Allason, a serial litigant, against the BBC's *Have I Got News for You Christmas Book*, which joked that "Given Mr Allason's fondness for pursuing libel actions, there are excellent reasons for not referring to him as a conniving little shit." It may be the jury thought that these words amounted to "mere abuse", an insult category that is, somewhat illogically, regarded as non-libellous.

ABSOLUTE PRIVILEGE

3–060 Accurate reports of certain public occasions are "privileged"—which is to say that any defamatory statements arising from them cannot be made the subject of a successful libel action. Privilege is either "absolute"—a complete defence—or "qualified", i.e. lost only if the speaker or reporter is actuated by malice. Although it is unseemly that the law should protect the publication of malicious falsehoods, absolute privilege is justified on the practical ground that without it, persons with a public duty to speak out might be threatened with vexatious actions for slander and libel. The existence of "absolute privilege" for the professional utterances of M.P.s and judges and lawyers is a recognition (by M.P.s and judges and lawyers) of the law's potential for suppressing truth and silencing justifiable criticism. Protection is given to the malicious and the reckless as the price of protecting from the threat of vexatious litigation all who are under a powerful duty to state facts and opinions frankly.

Thus politicians may say whatever they choose in Parliament or at the proceedings of select committees (see Ch.10). Judges, lawyers

---

[157] *Grobbelaar v Newsgroup Newspapers* [2002] 4 All E.R. 732 at 747 (para.38).

and witnesses may not be held responsible for any statement uttered in court. The Ombudsman's reports are absolutely privileged, as are ministers of the Crown, officers of the armed forces and high-level government officials in their reports and conversations about matter of State. Reports of the Lord Chancellor, the Legal Services Ombudsman, Director General of Fair Trading, the Monopolies Commission and other quasi-judicial authorities attract similar protection.[158] In these cases the absolute privilege attaches only to the maker of the statement: when it is reported or broadcast, the organisation that does so is protected by a privilege that is qualified and not absolute.

The one occasion when written and broadcast reports of statements made by persons who possess absolute privilege are themselves absolutely privileged is when they concern proceedings in the courts. This important media privilege is now consolidated in s.14 of the 1996 Defamation Act, which ordains absolute protection for contemporaneous reports of proceedings heard in public in any court in the United Kingdom, or in regional or international courts such as the European Court of Human Rights in Strasbourg, the European Court of Justice in Luxembourg and the Hague Tribunal dealing with war crimes in former Yugoslavia and Rwanda. The reports must be fair and accurate and the requirement of contemporaneity means that absolute privilege is only attracted when they are published as "news"—whether on television or the internet or in the papers—as soon as the practicalities of the medium permits. When published later, e.g. in a book or other retrospective on the case, the privilege will be qualified rather than absolute.

QUALIFIED PRIVILEGE AND PUBLIC INTEREST

The common law has long recognised the importance of encouraging **3–061** statements made from a social or moral duty. It accords them a privilege from action for defamation, on the condition that they are made honestly. However unfounded the allegations made on a protected occasion may subsequently prove, they are privileged unless made with malice. Communications made out of social or moral duty—references between employers, for example, or allegations about criminal conduct made to the police—are made on privileged occasions. So, too, are communications made to further a common interest—a circular published to shareholders in a company, or to fellow members of a trade union, or an inter-office memorandum. A communication is protected if it is made to a person who has a duty to receive and act upon it: thus complaints to "higher authority" are privileged whenever the authority complained to is in a position to investigate or discipline or supervise. Journalists

---

[158] For a complete list see *Galtey*, Ch.13, para.13.46.

who observe what they regard as improper behaviour by judges or lawyers could provide information to the Lord Chancellor's Department without running any risk of a libel action.[159]

The defence of qualified privilege has been developed in accordance with social needs. The early cases were overly concerned to protect the gentry's right to communicate gossip about disloyal or dishonest servants. The growth of commerce saw protection extended to references given by bankers and employers, and to information shared among traders. Parliament then intervened to give special protection to press reports of statements made on significant public occasions. The most recent development has been at the hands of the judiciary, extending qualified privilege to protect media investigations of public scandals. and then, in *Jameel v Wall Street Journal*, finally shedding the archaic language of "privilege" to permit a public interest defence.

This important development had been emphatically resisted by English judges throughout the twentieth century. "Privilege" arose from an occasion, or a relationship, which necessarily required the freedom to pass on rumours or suspicions. Passing on suspicions to the police was commendable: publishing them to all the world was deplorable, to be punished by heavy damages if they could not be proved correct. This was the judicial mindset in the Court of Appeal in *Blackshaw v Lord* decided in 1983—the last major free-speech case in which nobody bothered to mention the European Convention.[160] "No privilege attaches yet to a statement on a matter of public interest believed by the publisher to be true and in relation to which he has exercised reasonable care", said this court, 15 years before it was decided that such a privilege did exist. What, apart from a new generation of judges, can explain the sea-change?

3–062 Academic criticism of defamation—the only "tort" (civil wrong) in which recovery of damages did not hinge on proving "fault"—played some part, as did the decision of the US courts to refuse to enforce English libel awards partly because the law lacked any "public interest" defence. More importantly, by the time the Human Rights Act was passed, it had become apparent from cases such as *Lingens v Austria* that Art.10 of the European Convention required some such defence, at least for criticisms of politicians and powerful government figures. Lingens, a seasoned political commentator, published attacks on Bruno Kreisky, the President of the Austrian Socialist Party, accusing him of "immorality" and "the basest opportunism" for contemplating a political alliance with ex-Nazis. Lingens was privately prosecuted by Kreisky, and convicted and fined for defamation. The court held that this was a breach of the Convention guarantee of free speech, because it would deter journalists from contributing to public discussions of issues affecting the life of the community:

---

[159] *Beach v Freeson* [1972] 1 Q.B. 14.
[160] *Blackshaw v Lord* [1983] 2 All E.R. 311.

"The limits of acceptable criticism are wider as regards a politician as such than as regards a private individual . . . the former inevitably and knowingly lays himself open to close scrutiny of his every word and deed by both journalists and the public at large, and he must consequently display a greater degree of tolerance."[161]

Under the Convention, libel claims count as a restriction on press freedom and must therefore respond to a "pressing social need" and be no wider in operation than is "necessary in a democratic society". Some better protection for free speech had been forged by judges in the highest courts of Australia and New Zealand, fashioning a public interest defence out of the common law clay of qualified privilege, permitting it to cling to any occasion on which the media took all reasonable care in publishing information believed to be true about government or political matters.[162] This did not offer as much protection as the First Amendment, under which all public figures (whether politicians or not) were fair game "absent of malice", but it marked a cautious development of the common law in that direction. "Development" of law is a euphemism: judges in this situation effectively act as legislators and lack the precision tools (not to mention the democratic legitimacy) which fashion an Act of Parliament. However, it was obvious that M.P.s had no interest or inclination to reform the libel laws (from which they draw considerable financial and political benefit): an attempt to include a public interest defence in the 1996 Defamation Act was overwhelmingly rejected. There was nothing for it but for the courts to drag the law of libel into line with Art.10, and an extension of "qualified privilege" to protect publication to the world of important information was the only avenue the common law offered.

The Public Interest Defence

The Court of Appeal extended qualified privilege as a defence for **3–063** investigative journalism by two decisions in 1998, *Reynolds v Times Newspapers* and *Gaddafi v Sunday Telegraph*. The case law was more authoritatively framed by the House of Lords following the *Reynolds* appeal, in 1999. These cases establish that the publication to a general audience of information which the public has a "right to know" may, notwithstanding that it later turns out to be false, be made on an occasion of privilege—a status lost only if the publisher is actuated by malice, legal (i.e. dishonesty or recklessness towards truth) or actual (e.g. spite or desire for personal profit). So long as it is not acting maliciously, a newspaper is entitled to put into the public domain information which has been reasonably checked and

---

[161] *Lingens v Austria* (1986) 8 E.H.R.R. 407 at 425.
[162] See *Lange v Australian Broadcasting Corp* (1997) 189 C.L.R. 520.

sourced, as part of a discussion of matters of serious public concern. Journalists will not lose the protection of the defence if they refuse to disclose their sources, or if they have acted in the heat of the news moment to put out what seems at the time to be an important and newsworthy story.

Ironically, the case which created the defence did not extend it to the newspaper defendant, because the claimant had been unfairly treated:

> Albert Reynolds, the Irish ex-premier, sued the *Sunday Times* for accusing him (in its English edition), of lying to Parliament and deceiving his coalition partner, but made no mention of the explanation he had given to the House for his conduct. Its Irish edition carried a longer and more balanced article making no such allegations. The House of Lords rejected the newspaper's argument that because Reynolds was a powerful political figure the occasion of publication was necessarily privileged, but its ground-breaking judgment held that privilege *could* attach to any communication, whether or not about politics, so long as it related to a matter of serious public interest, was credible and had been published with reasonable care and fairness in all the circumstances. The *Sunday Times* lost because it had behaved unreasonably, omitting Reynold's explanation and unfairly sensationalising allegations never made in its Irish edition.[163]

Reynolds privilege was intended as a liberalising development, offering a new and effective defence to high quality investigative journalism in circumstances where the defamatory story could not be justified (e.g. because sources, fearing reprisals, would not testify) or where an important story, believed true at the time of publication, subsequently turned out to be erroneous. But *Reynolds* proved a false dawn for media freedom. The law lords had made the mistake of trying to force a fundamental freedom into the unsuitable and archaic concept of a "privilege" with its requirement of a "duty" to publish and a correlative "interest" in receiving the information. In the hands of trial judges bred to believe that there could never be a "duty", other than in an emergency, to publish defamations to the world at large, and that readers could never have an "interest" in receiving information that turned out to be untrue, claims of *Reynolds* privilege (a question of law, and hence for the judge to decide) were usually rejected. Moreover, the architect of *Reynolds*, Lord Nichols, had well-intentionally listed ten indicia of "responsible journalism" that the courts might care to take into account: trial judges erected them as hurdles, at which every media stumble might be fatal to a defence with which they had little sympathy. Worse still, any assertion of *Reynolds* privilege opened newspaper editors and journalists to searching cross-examination in a way that put their sources at risk and added vastly to the costs of an unsuccessful trial.

---

[163] *Reynolds v Times Newspapers Ltd* [2001] 2 A.C. 127.

The Times spent a fortune vainly defending its public interest journalism in *Louchansky*; in *Ashcroft* the claimant (the treasurer of the conservative party) was able to deduce, from documents that had to be disclosed to make good the defence, the name of the newspaper's source in the US Drugs Enforcement Agency. Although the case settled before trial, the source was subsequently prosecuted in America for leaking to *The Times* and was jailed for two years. By 2006, *Reynolds* privilege was widely regarded by the media as a snare and an illusion.

This impression was confirmed by the fate of *The Wall Street Journal* at trial and in the Court of Appeal, in respect of a story which could hardly have been more serious or more professionally researched or, at the time it was published, more significant. It shed new light on a politically charged question in the months following 9/11, namely whether Saudi Arabia, where most of the hijackers and their funding came from, was really co-operating with US attempts to staunch terrorist financing. The *Journal* was fortunate in having an Arabic speaking reporter, James Dorsey, stationed in Saudi: by his own journalistic efforts through sources he had cultivated, he learned from a businessman that the government had secretly agreed with the US to monitor certain of its most respectable and prominent corporations. This information he was able to confirm with a Saudi banker and a high government official, and two diplomats at the US embassy. To all these sources he promised anonymity for obvious reasons: Saudi Arabia was a repressive society where those who embarrassed the government were tortured and jailed. The newspaper's Washington correspondent, Glen Simpson, then contacted his own long-standing source in the US treasury, who in the manner of Water Gate "deep throat", did not deny (and thereby, pursuant to the Washington ritual, "confirmed") the names in the story. Headlined "SAUDI OFFICIALS MONITOR CERTAIN BANK ACCOUNTS—*Focus is on Those with Potential Terrorist Ties*", it was published in the Wall Street Journal (Europe). It was significant evidence that Saudi Arabia really was co-operating with US intelligence, to the extent of monitoring the leading members of its own business commercial establishment, albeit doing so secretly in order to avoid local difficulties from a public hostile to US policy in the Middle East. One of the "names" was Mohammed Jameel, a billionaire car dealer and former president of the Saudi Chamber of Commerce. Dorsey had contacted his company for a comment on the day before publication, but *Jameel* had been abroad and uncontactable, hence "could not be reached for comment". He was apoplectic when he learned of the story and hired the well-known firm of Carter Ruck to sue in London for the serious defamation that he and his company were suspected of having terrorist ties. The jury, sensibly of the view that CIA suspicions were not worth much, awarded them £30,000 and £10,000 respectively, after a three week trial costing the parties about £2 million each.

3–064

On these facts the House of Lords thought the article was exactly the kind of investigative journalism that *Reynolds* privilege had been devised to protect. It is a measure of the confusion engendered by *Reynolds* itself that this thought had never struck the trial judge nor the Court of Appeal. The defence had been rejected out of hand by Eady J. a most experienced libel practitioner and judge, on the grounds of editorial irresponsibility: a) the story would have been the same, and non-defamatory, had the "names" not been named, but instead referred to as "prominent Saudi businessmen"; b) since the article "blew the cover" of a sensitive and clandestine US–Saudi monitoring agreement, its publication was actually contrary to the public interest; and c) in any event, the journalist had not "held" the story for a day or so until *Jameel* had the opportunity to provide a comment—one of the ten "factors" which Lord Nichols had enumerated in *Reynolds*. The Court of Appeal grudgingly conceded that: a) the "names" added some news value to the story, but upheld the judge's findings on: i) the story was contrary to the public interest because it exposed the secret agreement; and ii) it should not have been published until *Jameel*'s comment could have been incorporated. The law lords had no hesitation in saying that c) was of no account: obviously *Jameel* would not know that he was being monitored (if he was) and could make no meaningful comment other than to evince surprise, and besides, this *Reynolds* "factor" was no more than one of many considerations in play, and should not have been determinative. They were particularly scathing about b), and the notion that the media should be bound by secret inter-governmental agreements. As Lord Scott put it:

> ". . . it is no part of the duty of the press to co-operate with any government, let alone foreign governments, whether friendly or not, in order to keep from the public information of public interest the disclosure of which cannot be said to be damaging to national interests."[164]

There was a sub-plot to the case, which illustrated another unsatisfactory aspect of the *Reynolds* privilege defence. Whether a "privilege" exists is a matter of law and hence entirely for the judge to decide. The jury is only involved where there are disputed issues of fact. In *Jameel*, the jury was asked to decide whether Dorsey's original business source existed, and whether (on a balance of probabilities) his information had been confirmed by the Saudi banker, the government official and the two US diplomats who had all seen the monitoring list. The jury found that the business source did indeed exist—Dorsey, fortunately for the defence, had kept some scraps of paper on which he had noted the meeting. But the

---

[164] See *Jameel*, para.142.

judge instructed the jury that in deciding whether the other sources had confirmed the story, they had to assume that the story was false—an assumption required by the absurd legal presumption that all defamations are false unless proved true by the defence of justification, which in this case the newspaper had not pleaded because the sources would not come forward. Inevitably, the bewildered jury could not find that the four sources had "confirmed" the information which the jury had to assume was false, because (applying that assumption) all four sources, having seen the list, would "know" that *Jameel*'s name was not on it—even if it was! The Court of Appeal ruled that this was a misdirection and that the presumption of falsity should henceforth not be applied to a *Reynolds* privilege case: jurors deciding factual issues should be told to make their findings irrespective of whether the story was true or false. The House of Lords endorsed this rule, although regrettably it declined to consider whether the presumption of falsity should itself be abolished. The *Jameel* decision recasts *Reynolds* privilege as a full-blown public interest defence. It must proceed in three stages:

a) **The public interest of the material**: The news articles or 3–065 broadcasts must be read as a whole, without isolating the defamatory statement. It is for the judge, not the editor, to assess whether the material is of genuine public interest as distinct e.g. from the prurience or scandalous gossip that interests most members of the public (here, the article was "a serious contribution in measured tone to a subject of very considerable importance"). The old duty/interest test of common law privilege was dissolved into the simple proposition that "if the publication is in the public interest, the duty and interest are taken to exist". The judge has no power to require some super-added "moral" or "legal" or "social" duty to publish.[165]

b) **Inclusion of the defamatory statement**: Was it justifiable to include the defamation in the public interest story? Yes, if it makes a real contribution to the public interest element of this story (in *Jameel*, the defamation—i.e. the suspicion that attached to *Jameel* by virtue of identifying him as a CIA target—was obviously important to stand the story up and to emphasise that those being monitored were not fly-by-night or fringe businessmen, but scions of the Saudi commercial establishment). Importantly, on this question the court should refer to editorial judgement:

> "If the article as a whole is in the public interest, opinions may reasonably differ over which details are needed to convey the general message. The fact that the judge, with the advantage of

---

[165] See *Jameel*, Lord Hoffman, para.50.

leisure and hindsight, might have made a different editorial decision should not destroy the defence. That would make the publication of articles which are, *ex hypothesi*, in the public interest, too risky and would discourage investigative reporting."[166]

c) **Responsible journalism**: Were the steps taken to investigate and publish the article responsible and fair? "Responsible journalism is the point at which a fair balance is held between freedom of expression on matters of public concern and the reputations of individuals".[167] The court will look at journalistic ethics and the PCC code of practice. The *Reynolds* "laundry list" factors are relevant but by no means decisive and must not be treated as obstacles to maintaining the defence. The court should look at the steps taken to verify the story in a practical and flexible manner. (Here, the repressive regime in Saudi could not be contacted for public comment and made anonymity of sources essential. There had been no effective challenge to the paper's confirmation of the story in Washington. Although it might have been "better" to delay publication for 24 hours until Jameel could comment, that factor alone could not deprive the paper of its public interest defence.) Importantly, Jameel had never asked for a retraction and his lawyers had snubbed an offer to have a "letter to the editor" published. Lord Scott draws attention to this important aspect of editorial responsibility: "Jameel could have requested, or demanded publication of an extradition of the Wall Street Journal Europe, of a response but he never did so."[168] Settling for a "letter to the Editor" goes against the grain of English libel solicitors—it is a resolution that deprives them of fees. But the "letters to the editor" page of the WSJE is its second most popular page, and it is a far more effective way of quickly negativing a libel—and building a case to destroy any public interest defence if the defamation is published again. The publisher will be protected so long as his editor exercised professional judgement after his journalists have made reasonable and competent checks to ensure that the story is accurate, and he publishes it without exaggerated sensation.

3–066 The laundry list of 10 "pointers" will still be relevant, amongst all the circumstances of the case, although they must never again be treated as hurdles or hoops, over or through which journalists must jump. As described by Lord Nichols in *Reynolds*, they are as follows:

1. *The seriousness of the allegation. The more serious the charge, the more the public is misinformed and the individual*

---

[166] *Jameel*, Lord Hoffman, para.51.
[167] Lord Nicholls, *Bonnick v Morris* [2003] 1 A.C. 300 at 309.
[168] Para.141.

harassed. This (like most of the 10 factors) cuts both ways. An allegation which is not serious will not have genuine public interest.

2. *The nature of the information, and the extent to which the subject-matter is a matter of public concern*. The more serious the allegation, the more it will be a matter of legitimate *public* concern. However the concern need not be national or affect a large segment of the public: local newspapers may equally avail themselves of the defence, as in *GKR Karate v The Yorkshire Post*[169]:

> A karate club sued a local newspaper over a story accusing it of "ripping off" members. The defence of justification would take six weeks to try, but the qualified privilege defence could be decided at a three-day hearing. The trial judge directed that the issues of privilege and malice should be tried first, and the Court of Appeal agreed—since these largely depended upon the defendant's state of mind, which had to be determined at the time of publication, they could logically be separated from the complicated factual dispute over the truth of the allegations. In due course, the trial judge found that the "balancing exercise" mandated by *Reynolds* came down in favour of the existence of the privilege: the journalist had acted honestly and reported allegations made by an authoritative source; the local public needed to be warned quickly for its own protection against dishonest door-to-door canvassing, and the article was unsensational in tone. Although there were some admitted inaccuracies and "over-egging", these did not outweigh the public interest in the free flow of information or amount to malice.[170]

3. *The source of the information. Some informants have no direct knowledge of events. Some have their own axes to grind, or are being paid for their stories*. Journalists will be expected to have checked out their sources, and to satisfy the court (especially where they choose to keep them anonymous) that their information was not tainted by malice. Since many sources of perfectly accurate but confidential information do divulge it out of spite or ambition or personal animosity this fact will not of itself defeat the privilege, but will place a greater obligation on the journalist to verify the story by making other inquiries. Similarly, purchased information is not for that reason unreliable, although it does place the journalist on notice that sensations in the story may be related to the source's sensation of receiving a large sum of money for revealing it. In these circumstances of "cheque-

---

[169] *GKR Karate Ltd v Yorkshire Post Newspaper Ltd* [2000] 2 All E.R. 931.
[170] Reported as *GKR Karate (UK) Ltd v Yorkshire Post (No. 2)* [2000] E.M.L.R. 410 (Sir Oliver Popplewell).

book journalism" the courts will expect the newspaper to have some corroboration.

4. *The status of the information. The allegation may have already been the subject of an investigation which commands respect.* The "status" of the information refers here to the authority that can be attributed to its source: an allegation given credit by an internal inquiry, audit or police investigation clearly has an impact which would assist the argument that the public ought to know of it. Similarly, defamatory remarks made (to use examples given by the Court of Appeal in *Reynolds*) in a "government press release, or the report of a public company chairman or the speech of a university vice-chancellor" would derive "status" from the respect due to their source, although (as Lord Steyn pointed out in his speech in *Reynolds)* this ought not to depend upon the leak coming from within the "establishment".

5. *The steps taken to verify the information.* This factor assumes that *some steps* will be taken, and journalists must demonstrate that these were reasonable enough in the circumstances. The implication is that editors who publish without making any available effort to corroborate will fail to satisfy the standard of "responsible journalism".

6. *The urgency of the matter. News is often a perishable commodity.* This dimension, taken from European Court judgments, calls for a recognition that information which can be characterised as "news" or "newsworthy" should be put into circulation as soon as possible. Of course this does not excuse a failure to make basic checks or (when fairness requires) to attempt to contact the victim. However, Lord Nicholls urged judges to remember that "journalists act without the benefit of the clear light of hindsight. Matters which are obvious in retrospect may have been far from clear in the heat of the moment". Until *Jameel*, judges tended to devalue this factor: they could not understand why a news story cannot wait a few days.[171]

7. *Whether comment was sought from the claimant. He may have information others do not possess or have not disclosed. An approach to the claimant will not always be necessary.* This is a feature of fairness. The claimant cannot complain if he had made himself unavailable for comment or was genuinely uncontactable at the time (a fact which should feature in the story). An approach is unnecessary if an explanation is unlikely to be forthcoming or is already on the record or if prior contact is reasonably feared to put sources at risk or provoke an application to injunct publication. The weight of

---

[171] See *James Gilbert Ltd v MGN Ltd* [2000] E.M.L.R. 680.

this factor in favour of the defence will be much reduced if the opportunity provided for comment does not give the victim a reasonable chance to make a considered response— if, for example, he is "ambushed" or "door-stepped", although post-*Jameel* the failure to obtain comment will not be determinative, especially in the case of a daily newspaper which offers to publish a follow-up story or a letter to the editor.

8. *Whether the article contained the gist of the claimant's side of the story.* This is a further factor determining fairness. The defence will not of course fail if the claimant goes to ground or declines to vouch-safe any explanation, and it will be enhanced if the claimant's explanation has been published without adverse comment or obvious cynicism. The House of Lords attached over-much importance to this factor in its actual decision in *Reynolds* (see above).

9. *The tone of the article. A newspaper can raise queries or call for an investigation. It need not adopt allegations as statements of fact.* This factor marks an important advance in the protection of investigative journalism, to the extent that it will permit the publication of rumour and suspicion if the writer does not adopt them as true, but rather examines them fair-mindedly and explains why the public interest demands further inquiry. Conversely, a tone of sensationalism or exaggeration in presentation will undermine the defence—as where rumour is luridly paraded as fact, guilt is pre-judged, and the claimant is subjected to a campaign of vilification. It was for deploying these techniques that *The Sun* lost its public interest privilege in exposing the corrupt behaviour of Bruce Grobbelaar.

> *The Sun's* claim to privilege for its exposure of goalkeeper Grobbelaar's acceptance of bribes to lose matches was rejected because of the sensational and unfair way in which the story— of admitted public importance—was investigated and presented. The paper, which had used an *agent provocateur*, trumpeted Grobbelaar's guilt in emotive terms on its front pages in a sustained character assassination. It door-stepped his wife ("shameful secret has Deb in tears") and delighted in the prospect of his young children being taunted at school. It was as if the paper "had placed Mr Grobbelaar in the stocks, to be publicly mocked, abused and derided for the amusement of the populace". If the media choose to present their exposés in this way, they cannot claim any privilege: they must prove them true—a task which *The Sun* in fact achieved, but only on this appeal.

10. *The circumstances of the publication including the timing.* This is a "sweep up" heading that permits other considerations to come into play. The question of timing will rarely be

definitive, since "news is a perishable commodity" but media defendants which rush headlong into "scoops" will derive some comfort if readers include those citizens who need to be warned quickly in order to protect themselves—e.g. against purchasing toxic food or falling prey to ongoing confidence tricks.

Post-Publication Responsibility

3–067 One factor which should be of great importance but which was omitted from this "top 10" is whether subsequently the media defendant has promptly and prominently acknowledged falsehoods and errors in the original story, and has proffered a suitable apology. Any sensible law of defamation should encourage defendants to "set the record straight", and there is no conceptual difficulty in speaking of a privilege being "lost" or "enhanced" by the publisher's subsequent conduct. Regrettably, *Reynolds* privilege was held to exist (or not) once and for all, at the time of first publication. There is scope here for further development, because European human rights jurisprudence recognises that the balance between free speech and the right to reputation should be viewed realistically over a period of time rather than artificially confined to the moment of publication.

The Court of Appeal decision in *Loutchansky v Times Newspapers Ltd (No.1),*[172] which held that the media's entitlement to a qualified privilege defence had to be judged at the time of publication, turning a blind eye to all that might emerge through subsequent investigation, is artificial: it ignores the reality of reporting on a rolling news story, where facts for and against the plaintiff may emerge over a period of coverage, and it prevents the court from making an informed judgment on editorial responsibility which in the real world continues long after the original defamation is published.[173] For example, responsible editors who promptly publish corrections and apologies should, under a qualified privilege plea, have this conduct taken into account in their favour.

Neutral Reportage

3–068 The Court of Appeal has permitted "neutral reportage" to claim *Reynolds* privilege without the need to verify defamatory allegations.[174] The newspaper had reported a vicious spat between leaders of the Saudi dissident community in London, which included allegations ("your mother is a whore") that were doubtless of interest to

---

[172] *Loutchansky v Times Newspapers Ltd* [2001] 4 All E.R. 115.
[173] *Loutchansky v Times Newspapers Ltd* [2001] 4 All E.R. 115. This decision appears to deny the newspaper the right to introduce detailed evidence of matters known only in outline to its reporters at the time of publication. This is not the position in a fair comment plea: see *Kemsley v Foot* [1952] A.C. 345.
[174] *Al-Fagih v H H Saudi Research Marketing UK Ltd* [2002] E.M.L.R. 215.

the readership but that the paper, in publishing, had (understandably) in no way attempted to verify. The trial judge had denied them *Reynolds* privilege on account of this failure, but the Court of Appeal pointed out that their arm's length position was the very reason why they should have it: "It is the fact that the allegation of a particular nature has been made which is in this context important, and not necessarily its truth or falsity."

Qualified privilege may henceforth be bestowed upon the neutral reporting of attributed allegations which the newspaper has made no effort to verify; so long as it does not "adopt" the allegation by suggesting that it is true. Although the *Al-Fagih* imputations were made in the context of a political dispute, the principle should cover accurate reportage of all outbursts that are "newsworthy because of the fact that they are made rather than the fact that they are true. This mitigates the straitjacket of the "repetition rule" which ordinarily requires newspapers that report another's accusations to be in a position to prove it: so long as the report is careful to give an accusation no extra credence, the fact that it has been made will, if newsworthy, obtain protection (although the paper would be well advised to seek out, and to publish, the reply of the party under attack). The papers which paid massive damages to the former Ugandan Foreign Minister, Princess Elizabeth of Toro, as a result of reporting *verbatim* Idi Amin's crazed allegations about her sexual behaviour in an airport toilet (see para.138) would today be protected by the public interest defence: her right to reputation would now be trumped by the need for the British public to know, of a dictator its government had helped to power, that he was mad, bad and dangerous to know.

> It is better to regard "neutral reportage" as an example of the public interest defence, rather than as a separate head of qualified privilege. The anti-racist magazine *Searchlight* was protected when reporting (with some relish) an acrimonious dispute between two members of a racist organisation.[175] But these occurrences are rare and there is no reason why the press should not be entitled to report—without adopting—accusations that have been flung at public figures and which have a public interest significance. It is notable that Lord Bingham, in *Jameel*, referred to "neutral investigative journalism", exemplified by Dorsey's article, as the very kind of journalism that a public interest defence should protect, i.e. as reporting significant accusations without adopting or embellishing them.

Other Considerations

Jameel supports a defence for cautious and responsible investigative **3–069** journalism, and not for tabloid sensationalism. The factors that bear on responsible journalism are legion, and those advanced in any

---

[175] *Roberts v Gable* [2006] E.M.L.R. 23 (Cady J.) confirmed by the Court of Appeal.

particular case will relate to the nature of the story. It may be easy enough, for example, to comply with ethics and PCC codes in the United Kingdom, but journalists working in conflict zones or seeking to expose human rights violations in repressive regimes may put their sources—or themselves—at risk by obtaining comments from the regime before the story is published, and will frequently have to resort to subterfuge and inference. The journalist in *Jameel* was followed and intercepted and one of his "on the record" sources for a previous story had been tortured and jailed—in these circumstances, he could hardly be expected to keep detailed notes of his meetings with them. The court permitted the defence to call evidence about the difficulties of reporting in the closed and secretive Saudi society and also permitted evidence (from former CIA chief James Woolsey) about the rituals and the protocols of obtaining confirmation from "Deep Throats" within the Washington administration. It should not be forgotten that the long-running Watergate "scoop" began when Woodward and Bernstein gained illegal access to grand jury material, or that one of Britain's best "Insight" journalists, Nick Tomalin, defined a good reporter as one "possessed of rat-like cunning, a plausible matter and a little literary ability". *Reynolds* privilege was not much help to good investigative journalism because it was lost as trial judges turned up their noses at journalistic techniques and short cuts, and sat themselves in the chair of a hypothetically high minded editor. The virtue of *Jameel* is that it removes them from that chair, and gives them more of a "judicial review" function of deciding, not whether the journalistic conduct was right, but whether it was reasonable.

The most difficult issue, which *Reynolds* does not resolve, is how the defence will operate when defamatory allegations in the story are based on confidential sources, whose "status" and reliability may be asserted but cannot by definition be proved. The Court of Appeal considered this problem in *Gaddafi v Telegraph Group*.[176]

> The eldest son of Colonel Gaddafi, dictator of Libya, sued over a story alleging his involvement in attempts to breach economic sanctions imposed as a result of the Lockerbie bombing. *The Sunday Telegraph* was permitted to enter a defence of qualified privilege, and to plead that its sources included members of a "western government security agency", whose lives could be at risk if their identities were disclosed. The court upheld the right of journalists to protect the confidentiality of their source whilst maintaining a qualified privilege defence, so long as sufficient disclosure was provided to enable some evaluation of the status and reliability of their information.

Gadaffi is a valuable ruling for investigative journalists, whose process of deduction is often assisted by sources who would be

---

[176] *Gaddafi v Telegraph Group Ltd* [2000] E.M.L.R. 431.

exposed to danger or embarrassment if named, and to whom confidentiality must be promised as a condition of assistance. It enables defendants to claim the defence, on condition that they provide enough detail to have claims for source reliability tested under cross-examination. It may be difficult for the claimant to prove that unidentified sources are tainted with malice, but equally the journalist will be handicapped in the courtroom by his refusal to prove just how well-placed and authoritative a source may have been. As Lord Steyn commented in *Reynolds*: "If a newspaper stands on the rule protecting its sources, it may run the risk of what the judge and jury will make of the gap in the evidence".[177] That risk has been lessened by *Jameel*, which accepted that the journalist was entitled to rely on local Saudi sources whom he could not identify for fear or reprisals, and on US diplomats who had to remain nameless. However he faced lengthy cross-examination over the circumstances of their meetings and the veracity of their information, and the claimant was permitted to introduce a range of evidence that might cast doubt on whether his sources were forthcoming or even existed. Whenever a journalist relies on anonymous sources he will need to persuade the jury of their credibility, and this is no easy matter if they cannot be identified, especially if no notes or other evidence has been kept to verify the meetings.

Reply to an attack

The "right of reply" privilege is often overlooked, but its constitu- **3–070** tional significance for the protection of freedom of expression deserves to be recognised. It is based on the simple proposition of self-defence: if you are verbally attacked, you are entitled to strike back with some vehemence to defend your reputation. The media that carry your response share your privilege, so long as the publicity given to your condemnation of your attacker is reasonably commensurate with the publicity given to the original attack. The right of reply privilege was established by the House of Lords in the case of *Adam v Ward*[178]:

> The claimant, an officer but not a gentleman, used his position as an M.P. to make a vindictive attack upon a general in his former regiment. The defendant, Secretary to the Army Council, issued a statement in support of the general, which defamed the M.P. and was published in newspapers throughout the Empire. The Law Lords held that this publication was protected by qualified privilege: the Council had a duty to leap to the general's defence, and the privilege was not lost by the fact of world-wide publication, because "a man who makes a statement on the floor of the House of Commons makes it to all the

---

[177] *Reynolds* above, at 214.
[178] *Adam v Ward* [1917] A.C. 309.

world . . . it was only plain justice to the General that the ambit of contradiction should be spread so wide as, if possible, to meet the false accusation wherever it went."

The rule in *Adam v Ward* offers consolation to victims of attacks made under the "coward's cloak" of parliamentary privilege: they may reply in kind through newspapers, which will be liable for the defamatory content of their reply only if it is irrelevant to the subject-matter of the attack, or if it defames other persons who bear no responsibility for the attack. The right of reply privilege does not merely protect responses to criticisms made in Parliament, of course; it is a privilege of general application, arising from the legitimate interest of individuals in protecting their reputations, and it is shared by the media when it facilitates that interest.

Parliamentary and court reports

3–071 At common law, all fair and accurate reports of Parliament and the courts are protected by qualified privilege. This is a safety net for press coverage that falls outside statutory protection for absolute privilege—because, for example, it is not published as soon as practicable after the event. The application of this qualified privilege is considered in detail in Ch.8 and Ch.10.

Other public occasions

3–072 Section 15 of and Sch.1 to the Defamation Act 1996 bestow qualified privilege on reports of a range of "official" public occasions and events which have taken place anywhere in the world. The Schedule is in two parts. The first accords qualified privilege unconditionally; the second grants it subject to the condition that a reasonable right of reply must have been afforded to victims of its privileged defamations.

Part I privilege extends to fair and accurate reports of public proceedings in parliaments, courts, public inquiries, international organisations and conferences, and to publication of extracts from public registers, statements by judges or court officers, or material produced by governments or international organisations or conferences.

Part II privilege extends, subject to affording the victim a reasonable right of reply, to fair and accurate reports of, inter alia:

- findings or decisions of any organisation formed in the United Kingdom or in Member States of the European Union, and empowered by its constitution to exercise control over, or adjudicate on, matters relating to:

  (a) art, science, religion or learning;
  (b) any trade, business, industry or profession;

    (c) persons connected with games, sports or pastimes and
        who are contractually subject to the association;
    (d) the promotion of charity;

- proceedings at any lawful public meeting, (whether or not admission is restricted) that is called to discuss any matter of public concern;
- proceedings at a general meeting of a UK company, and any document circulated to members;
- proceedings of any meeting open to the public within the United Kingdom of:

    (a) a local authority or its committees;
    (b) justices of the peace acting in non-judicial capacities;
    (c) committees of inquiry appointed by Act of Parliament or by the Government;
    (d) local authority inquiries;
    (e) bodies constituted under Acts of Parliament;

- "any notice or other matter" issued for the information of the public by or on behalf of any government or legislature within the European Union, or by any international organisation or conference. This includes notices issued by any agency performing "governmental functions", which include police functions. This does not, however, cover information that has been leaked from such sources, nor does it include unauthorised and off-the-cuff comments made by junior officials. To be protected, the information must be issued or approved by some person in departmental authority. Journalistic speculation and inference about official statements are not protected by statutory privilege, although may qualify in some circumstances for privilege at common law.[179]

These Pt II privileges are "subject to explanation and contradic- **3–073** tion", which means that they will not apply where an editor or programme controller has refused the claimant's request to publish a reasonable statement in reply, or has done so in an inadequate manner. Claimants must supply their own set of words—a bare demand for retraction is insufficient to defeat the privilege.[180] So long as it is reasonable in "tone and length", it must be published with a prominence appropriate to the original report.

These privileges attach to reports of public statements and public documents. They do not extend to the contents of confidential or internal documents or to reports of evidence given in closed court. However, the current tendency—under the impetus of the 1998

---

[179] *Blackshaw v Lord* above at fn.38.
[180] *Khan v Ahmed* [1957] 2 Q.B. 149.

Human Rights Act—is to give these statutory definitions of privilege (many of which date from nineteenth-century statutes) a wide and contemporary meaning. The approach is exemplified by the first case to be decided after the Human Rights Act came into force, *McCartan Turkington Breen v Times Newspapers*.[181]

> The claimants were a firm of Northern Ireland solicitors who had represented Private Lee Clegg at the trial in which he had been convicted of murdering a terrorist suspect. A support group held a press conference at which defamatory allegations were made about his lawyers' competence both in statements and in a press release handed out to journalists. Part II of the Schedule grants statutory privilege to fair and accurate reports of "public meetings", and the House of Lords held that this phrase was apt to cover both a press conference and a press release. The object of the statutory privilege was to encourage the media to serve as a channel for public debate, and these days press conferences and press releases have largely superseded the "public meeting" as a means of communicating political ideas and protests about injustice. The court went out of its way to recognise "the cardinal importance of press freedom" and the reporter's role as a medium of communication: the public interest supported a wide reading of the statutory privilege.

Most of the reports protected by Schedule I statutory privilege would attract the public interest defence at common law. The advantage of bringing them within statutory protection is that there can be no doubt that they specifically apply, and do not require a showing of responsible journalism to succeed.

3–074 Statutory qualified privilege has been available since the late nineteenth century, but limited to newspaper reports of courts and meetings and organisations within the United Kingdom. The 1996 reforms amplified the privilege to cover reports of courts and governments worldwide, and not merely in newspapers. This will mean, of course, that reports of libellous and lying statements made by or on behalf of barbaric dictators and oppressive regimes will be protected, although as the Neill committee pointed out, "What renders such Governments unattractive may very well from time to time lead to their being of particular legitimate interest to the British public".[182] The reform will prevent any repetition of the absurd cases in 1980 when Princess Elizabeth of Toro, accomplice of the mass-murdering Idi Amin, collected large libel damages from all English national newspapers. They had reported, accurately, Amin's crazed accusation, when he fired her as his foreign minister, that she had been found having oral sex in a toilet at Orly airport. The fact that he was capable of making such a statement was important evidence

---

[181] [2001] 2 A.C. 277.
[182] Supreme Court Procedure Committee Report on Practice and Procedure in Defamation (1991) Ch.XII. 6.

of the nature of the beast (first backed by Britain and then President of the OAU) and it was for that reason important that newspapers report it. Such reports should now attract Pt II privilege under Sch.1, para.9(1)(b) (as a statement by a head of government): Princess Elizabeth would be legally entitled to have published a reasonable letter contradicting it, but not to damages. A fair report quoting her denial would be protected by the common law public interest defence developed in *Jameel*.

The 1996 Defamation Act provides that Sch.1 qualified privilege will be lost if reports are not fair and accurate, and that the privilege will not protect "matter which is not of public concern and the publication of which is not for the public benefit" (s.15(3)). This should be easy to satisfy, since the public meetings and events listed in Sch.1 are, almost by definition, of public concern. The leading case on the approach to these questions is *Tsikata v Newspaper Publishing Plc*.[183]

> *The Independent* published in 1992 an article about politics in Ghana, which made a passing reference to the fact that a judicial inquiry 10 years before had accused the claimant (head of the country's secret service) of masterminding the murder of three judges. The newspaper's report was true as far as it went, although it did not add that the evidence against the claimant had been insufficient to support a prosecution and some of it had been retracted. Tsikata argued that the passing reference was not a "report" of the judicial inquiry that had condemned him 10 years before, and the lapse of time meant that in any event the reference was not "fair and accurate". The Court of Appeal said that the Schedule should be construed so as to give effect to the clear intention of Parliament and not by the adoption of a narrow linguistic approach. Thus the short statement of the inquiry finding was protected, irrespective of its timing (the Schedule does not require reports to be contemporaneous) and notwithstanding the subsequent developments to which the paper had made no reference. This failure to present the full picture did not mean that the report, as presented, lacked public benefit. The privilege to report matters of record overseas relieves the media of the expense of having to conduct its own foreign inquiries: investigative journalism may be a virtue, but the law should not make it a necessity.

It is curious that the archaic "public benefit" requirement survives: the whole point of providing qualified privilege for the records and events listed in Sch.1 is that they relate to matters of public concern, and the public benefit question only serves to confuse the jury. Nonetheless, the Court of Appeal has held that this issue, like the issue of fairness and accuracy, is a question of fact that must be left to the jury rather than be decided by the judge, even in cases where there are "strong grounds" in favour of a factual finding (of fairness

---

[183] [1997] 1 All E.R. 655.

or public benefit) that would conclude the issue in the media's favour at the outset.[184]

OTHER DEFENCES

Consent

3–075 People can—and often do for large sums of money—agree to be defamed. Should they then turn around to bite the hand that takes down their volunteered confessions, they will fail. Consent to publication is a complete defence.[185] The consent must, however, relate to the actual libel published, and not merely to the grant of an interview in which the libellous subject was not specifically canvassed. The narrowness of the consent defence—turning upon consent to the actual libel, or to publication of the words substantially as they were used—can no longer be justified under freedom of expression principles. If libel turns into a fault-based tort, claimants whose own conduct is responsible for scurrilous rumours should be denied recovery. Anyone who is the author of their own misfortune—by failing to check their own publicity, or failing to nail a lie at the earliest opportunity—should be open to a defence of "voluntary assumption of risk" or at least a reduction in damages on grounds of contributory negligence. This is the case in American law, where it is a complete defence to show that the defamation would not have been published at all had the claimant not acted so as to induce a belief in its truth.[186] But in London the *New York Times* was not permitted to argue that claimant Marco Pierre White was responsible for its correspondent's error in misreading an ambiguous passage in his "autobiography" (because White had not written it himself and had failed to check it prior to publication under his name). Morland J. held that defamation remained a tort of strict liability, offering no scope for "contributory negligence" or for a

---

[184] *Kingshott v Associated Kent Newspapers Ltd* [1991] 2 All E.R. 99. The Court of Appeal insisted that the question of whether allegations about corruption of local councillors, made by a mayor at a planning inquiry, was a "matter of public concern" and had to be left to the jury: it was not so obvious that it could be decided by a judge! *Kingshott* may be overruled if the issue returns to the House of Lords: see the discussion in *Reynolds* (above) at 636–7; 646 and in *McCartan Turkington* (above) at 933.

[185] *Monson v Tussaud's Ltd* (1894) I Q.B. 671 (note the characterisation of the defence as "acquiescence" by Davey L.J.; *Moore v News of the World* [1972] 1 Q.B. 441 at 448 A–B, *per* Lord Denning.

[186] "It would be ironical and certainly inequitable for the plaintiff to profit here from his own misstatements. Further, it would be no less unfair to treat the publisher as even partially culpable for a false publication where he has reasonably relied upon the plaintiff's own sworn representations": *Friedman v Boston Broadcasters Inc*, 13 Media Law Reporter 1742 at 1744, and see *Sack on Defamation* (2nd edn) Ch.2, para.2.

"consent" defence which alleged the claimant was at fault.[187] But watch this space.

Offer of amends

Most libel actions are settled, before or after service of the claim, by negotiations between solicitors which can result in published corrections and apologies (sometimes in open court) and payment of an agreed sum in damages. The Neill Committee was anxious, however, to discourage unreasonable claimants who had defendants "over a barrel" as the result of an indefensible defamation, but who refused all settlement offers in order to harass the defendants or to insist they be dragged to trial. The 1996 Defamation Act gives media defendants an opportunity to bail out by making an "offer of amends", i.e. a written offer to publish a suitable correction and sufficient apology in a reasonable manner, together with such compensation and legal costs as may be agreed (or fixed by the court). If the claimant refuses the offer, the defendant may raise it as a statutory defence so long as he has made a proper offer and runs no other defence: to rebut it, the claimant must justify his refusal by proving the original defamation was published maliciously (in the sense that the defendant knew it was false or was recklessly indifferent to the truth—a difficult allegation to prove).[188] A failure to rebut this defence will mean the claimant gets nothing—he cannot at that point take the offer and run. Unfortunately, Parliament managed to turn a good idea into a complicated and uncertain statutory provision,[189] which has spawned more litigation than it has saved.[190] There is no cap on damages, as with summary disposal (see later, "Summary Disposal") although the claimant is deprived of the chance to appeal to a potentially over-generous jury. Judges have given defendants a discount—up to 50 per cent off the damages they would have awarded had liability been contested—for capitulating at an early stage with an offer of amends, which includes publication of a suitable correction and apology.[191]

A prompt correction and apology for an indefensible defamation serves two purposes besides setting the record straight. In many

3–076

---

[187] *White v New York Times*, unreported, April 2000.

[188] See *Milne v Express Newspapers Ltd* [2005] 1 All E.R. 1021.

[189] See Defamation Act 1996, ss.2–5. Even if the defendant relies on some other defence to contest liability, he can still plead the offer to mitigate damages: (s.5(5)).

[190] Although having admitted the libel, a defendant may nonetheless argue aggressively that it is not worth much, given the claimant's general sleaziness or bad character. Hence there have been many disputes about evidence admissibility—see *Abu v MGN* [2003] 2 All E.R. 864.

[191] Such a discount was upheld by the Court of Appeal in *Nail v Newsgroup Newspapers Ltd* [2005] 1 All E.R. 1040. Libel aficionados will enjoy Eady J.'s deadpan account of the newspaper's attempts to minimise the damage caused by its imputations of Mr Nail's sexual indiscretions: ("Location can sometimes be critical", pp.1046–7).

cases it satisfies the complainant—and, where it is accompanied by payment of costs, it will satisfy his lawyer as well. If the complainant is still determined to become a claimant, the fact that a prompt apology has been made can be relied upon by the defendant to reduce the amount of damages. It is obviously prudent, however, for the potential media defendant to seek a disclaimer of further legal action as a condition of publishing the apology. Once an apology is given, the defendant will be hard put to contest liability later.

DAMAGES

3–077 Those who throw sticks and stones that break bones can be better off in law than those who project hurtful words that leave no permanent mark. In 1987 libel damages of £500,000 were awarded to Jeffrey Archer against a newspaper that alleged he had sex with a prostitute, and Elton John set a short-lived record with his £1 million settlement against the *Sun*. In 1989, the wife of the "Yorkshire Ripper" was awarded £600,000 by a jury to compensate her for a trifling story in *Private Eye*. This last award was described by the Court of Appeal as a sum "so unreasonable as to be divorced from reality".[192] and it urged judges in future to give some help to juries about the real value of money. In the first case in which such guidance was received, the jury returned with a new British and Commonwealth record of £1.5 million, against an author who had attacked Lord Aldington as a "war criminal" over his role in the forcible repatriation of Cossacks. The judge had warned the jury not to award "Mickey Mouse money", by which he apparently intended to refer to a sum so large as to be unrealistic (such as £1.5 million). The jury may have understood the phrase to refer to small or trifling amounts, and followed his direction by awarding the sort of sum they imagined in the coffers of Scrooge McDuck. The prospect of massive awards of damages served as a real threat to freedom of expression in the Thatcher era—which may be why some of her unprepossessing associates escaped exposure. In any event the award was so disproportionate that the European Court had no difficulty declaring it a breach of Art.10.[193]

In 1991 the Court of Appeal was empowered (by s.8 of the Courts and Legal Services Act) to substitute its own award in place of excessive damages, without having to put the parties to the inconvenience of a new trial. This power has been used (with impetus from Art.10) to effect a wholesale reform in the way libel damages are calculated. The break with the past began in 1993, when a jury award of £250,000 to television presenter Esther Rantzen was declared disproportionate to any damage she had suffered (her successful

---

[192] *Sutcliffe v Pressdram Ltd* [1990] 1 All E.R. 269, CA.
[193] *Tolstoy Miloslavsky v UK* (1996) E.M.L.R. 152.

television career had continued) and was cut by more than half.[194] The freedom of expression guarantee meant, said the Court of Appeal, that henceforth libel awards should not be so large as to deter investigative journalism, and juries should be given judicial guidance on how to keep them in proportion. This guidance had to be provided in a more concrete shape after Elton John persuaded a star-struck jury to compensate him over-lavishly for an invented story about his bizarre eating habits. In future, juries would be told about the level of damages which judges currently award for the pain and suffering resulting from negligently caused personal injuries (ranging from £25,000 for loss of an eye to £130,000 for serious brain damage) because

> "it is in our view offensive to public opinion, and rightly so, that a defamation plaintiff should recover damages for injury to reputation greater, perhaps by a significant factor, than if that same plaintiff had been rendered a helpless cripple or a insensate vegetable".[195]

With these words, the court ushered to a close an era in which celebrity claimants regularly won damages far in excess of £200,000, a sum which must now be seen as the outside limit for the worst defamations. Trial judges cannot trample on the constitutional right of a jury to set whatever figure it chooses, but the certainty of Court of Appeal intervention if it aims too high permits them to direct a jury more robustly. Juries are given an appropriate "bracket" or range: an award below it would be "niggardly" and above it "extravagant". By this means, jury damages in defamation are now kept within acceptable limits, although if juries go somewhat outside the recommended bracket the Court of Appeal will be unlikely to interfere.[196] The current ceiling was set by Eady J. in *Lillie v Newcastle City Council*[197] when he awarded £200,000 each to kindergarten teachers accused by a local council enquiry of having sexually abused the children in their charge. The enquiry panel had misunderstood a court hearing (at which charges against the teachers had been dropped) and had recklessly presumed them guilty of serious accusations that the judge was satisfied were invented. Where lives have been destroyed by deliberate rather than reckless character assassination, however, Lord Hoffman has warned that damages may go higher in order to have a deterrent effect.[198]

---

[194] *Rantzen v Mirror Group Newspapers* [1993] 4 All E.R. 975.
[195] *John v MGM Ltd* [1996] 2 All E.R. 35 at 54, CA. Damages for negligently caused personal injuries have since increased—the top of the range is about £200,000 (*Heil v Rankin* [2000] 3 All E.R. 138, CA) and this may now be taken as the cap on libel damages in the absence of proved financial loss.
[196] *Kiam v MGN Ltd* [2002] 2 All E.R. 219.
[197] [2002] All E.R. (D) 465.
[198] *Gleaner Co Ltd v Abrahams* [2004] 1 A.C. 628.

Compensatory and aggravated damages

3–078 The basic award will comprise "compensatory damages", i.e. a sum
that will sufficiently redress the wrong by nullifying the pain caused
by the false accusation and at the same time emphasising the value
of the good name that has been temporarily besmirched. This basic
sum (influenced by the gravity of the libel—especially whether it has
challenged the claimant's "core attributes of personality" such as
integrity, honesty and loyalty) may be "aggravated" by the injury
which the defendant has added to the insult by refusing to publish a
timely correction or apology, or by defending the action in a spirit of
enmity.

Damage to reputation is a concept that has no equivalent in
money or money's worth. It is inflated by the feeling that it should be
large enough to "vindicate" claimants by showing the world that
their names deserve respect and to "console" them for being
exploited to boost the circulation of tabloid newspapers. A refusal to
correct or apologise for an obvious mistake will enlarge the damages,
as will the seriousness of the libel and the degree to which it is
repeated. By the same token, the promptness of the apology, the
honesty of the mistake, and pre-existing flaws in the claimant's
reputation are matters that will go to reduce the final sum. The
extent of circulation and the prominence given to defamatory
remarks are factors that should influence the award, and the
claimant may also recover damages for the repetition of the libel in
other publications that the defendant might reasonably have foreseen would follow from his own publication.[199] Inspector "Slipper of
the Yard" Slipper won £50,000 libel damages from the BBC over a
programme depicting his oafish blunders as he failed to bring great
train robber Ronny Biggs back from Rio. Many years later, and after
Slipper's death, the National Archives released files which showed
that the programme allegations had been absolutely true and
Slipper's incompetence had been fully recorded by British diplomats
in Brazil. This case, like so many other libel victories for claimants,
was a miscarriage of justice. Foreign Office diplomats sat by idly
while it happened.[200]

Loud mouth celebrities must be particularly careful. Victoria
"Posh Spice" Beckham had to pay heavy damages to a shop keeper
when she lost her temper and accused him, in front of customers, of
selling a fake autograph of her husband: she should have foreseen

---

[199] Thus the BBC could be compelled to compensate a claimant defamed in a
drama-documentary not merely in relation to the damage done to his or her
reputation amongst those viewers who watched the programme, but also in
relation to newspaper readers who had read the "sting" of the defamation in
reviews of the programme. See *Slipper v BBC* [1991] 1 All E.R. 165.

[200] "How Slipper of the Yard Bungled his Attempt to Collar Ronnie Biggs in Rio",
Guardian, October 3, 2005.

that her slander would hit the headlines—"Posh Goes Stropping".[201]
The claimant's feelings may be wounded if he or she is subjected to
aggressive cross-examination, especially if it is designed to support
what transpires to be an unsuccessful plea of justification, so this
forensic factor may be brought into account. On the other hand, the
jury can be asked to take the claimant's own conduct into account in
reducing the damages. If the claimant has been cleared of the
allegations after a publicised inquiry, or has obtained retractions and
damages from other publications, his or her wounds may be considered to have partially healed.[202]

One aspect of the law of libel damages that is particularly irksome
for the defendant is the rule in *Scott v Sampson* which limits
evidence to proving the claimant's "general bad reputation" but does
not permit proof of specific acts of misconduct unless the jury has
heard about these pursuant to a defence of justification which has
failed to prove the truth of the real defamatory imputation.[203] This is
a ridiculous rule that can put the jury in blinkers when it makes a
damages award. Defamation committees have recommended its
abolition, but on the two occasions when reform has been introduced in Parliament (as part of the 1952 and 1996 Defamation Bills)
it has been resisted by M.P.s concerned lest their libel damages be
reduced once juries are reminded of discreditable incidents in their
past. In 2000 the Court of Appeal decided that the rule could be
side-stepped in relation to a trial in which the amount of damages
was the only issue, but it continues to apply, illogically, in cases
where the defendant contests liability.[204] Revisiting this vexatious
decision in 2006, the Court of Appeal reaffirmed that in determining
damages under an offer to make amends, the court could receive
evidence of specific acts of misconduct if this was "directly relevant
background evidence". Fairness required that the newspaper defendant should be entitled to show that the man they had admitted to
falsely accusing of forcing his wife to have sex with men, could show
that his distress at this allegation must have been lessened by the fact
that he had pressurised her to have sex with women. It is difficult to
see why the courts should not junk these old rules and the endless
case law surrounding them, in favour of the simple principle that
justice requires the admission of any evidence that is relevant to the
ultimate decision.[205]

---

[201] *McManus v Beckham* [2002] 4 All E.R. 497.
[202] s.12 of the Defamation Act 1952 permits evidence to be given of other damages
recovered for the same or similar libels, so as to ensure the claimant is not in
effect compensated twice over.
[203] See *Scott v Sampson* (1882) 8 Q.B.D. 491; *Plato Films v Speidel* [1961] A.C. 1090
and *Pamplin v Express Newspapers* [1988] 1 W.L.R. 116.
[204] *Burstein v Times Newspapers Ltd*, December 20, 2000, CA.
[205] *Turner v Newsgroup Newspapers Ltd* [2006] 4 All E.R. 613.

Exemplary damages

3–079   Damages in libel cases are not meant to punish the press, but when a
publisher deliberately or recklessly sets out to defame another, with
the object of making a profit out of that defamation by increasing
circulation, the law permits "punitive" damages to be awarded. In
Cassell & Co v Broome[206]:

> The young David Irving (who 30 years later failed to clear his name of
> holocaust-denial) wrote a book about the fate of a wartime convoy,
> blaming it upon the negligence of a particular captain, Broome. Cassell
> & Co published the book. The jury awarded punitive damages of
> £40,000 against Irving, and a further £40,000 against Cassell. The
> House of Lords upheld the award as punishment for author and
> publisher, as there was evidence that both were reckless about the
> truth of the defamatory statements in the book, and indeed hoped that
> they would cause a sensation so that the book's sales would increase.

Punitive damages in libel cases are a legal anomaly. They amount
to a fine for misbehaviour, but have no upper limit. They are
generally awarded by juries, who have neither the power nor the
proficiency to impose a sentence in any other area of law. They do
not, like other fines, go into the public purse, but into the pocket of
victims who have already been compensated by the same jury for
damage to their reputation. They are, indeed, difficult to distinguish
from the "aggravated damages" to which a claimant is entitled by
virtue of the suffering caused by the newspaper's high-handed or
insulting conduct. They are not awarded in Scotland, and the Faulks
Committee (and the Court of Appeal in 1985) recommended their
abolition.[207] However, in the *Elton John* case, the Court of Appeal
preferred to set stricter limits to the circumstances in which punitive
damages could be awarded, and to their amount. Critically, what
must be proved by the claimant is that the defendant cynically
published for profit an allegation in the truth of which he had no
honest or genuine belief. Carelessness is not enough, nor is the
routine fact of commercial publication: the court must be sure of
reprehensible behaviour, constituted by a deliberate calculation that
more money would be made by putting out a story that could well be
false than by waiting to check out its veracity. Only when these
conditions are satisfied, and it is further plain that compensatory or
aggravated damages are insufficient to teach the defendant that tort
does not pay, will an additional punitive award be justified. An
irresponsible front page "splash" story about Elton John's behaviour
at a party (which a simple check would have established he did not
attend) was calculated to increase circulation and so qualified for

---

[206] *Cassell & Co v Broome* [1972] A.C. 1027.
[207] See *Riches v News Group Newspapers Ltd* [1986] Q.B. 256.

exemplary damages, but the jury went over the top by awarding
£275,000. The tabloid would be taught its lesson, the Court of
Appeal somewhat optimistically concluded, by a reduced fine of
£50,000.[208]

Nominal and Derisory Damages

Nominal damages are awarded when the tribunal is satisfied of libel, **3–080**
but because, for instance, the distress caused has been minimal or
the publication technical, a small award (no more than £100) is
appropriate. It is sometimes said that corporate libels should be
visited with nominal damages if no loss is likely to have been
suffered. In these days of case management, where the cost of
defending libel claims can be vast and the time taken elaborate,
courts are very reluctant to allow cases to proceed where only
nominal damages are in prospect. Such cases may be treated as an
abuse of process—a game not worth the wick, let alone the candle.[209]

Derisory damages—traditionally "the lowest coin in the realm"
(although in these inflated times, usually £1)—are awarded to
claimants who do not morally deserve to win (see the Auschwitz
doctor and the spanking colonel, earlier para.3–007). The most
recent example was the corrupt goal keeper Bruce Grobbelaar who
against all the evidence persuaded a jury to give him £85,000
(apparently because, although he had accepted a bribe to throw the
match, he had not played badly). The Court of Appeal robustly
condemned this decision as "perverse" and reversed it, but the
House of Lords, with greater respect for "the lamp that shows that
freedom lives" (albeit, in this case, not press freedom) found some
method in the jury's apparent madness. But it quashed their award
and replaced it with £1:

> "The claimant had in fact acted in a way in which no decent or
> honest footballer would act and which could, if not exposed or
> stamped on, undermine the integrity of the game. It would be an
> affront to justice if a court of law were to award substantial
> damages to a man shown to have acted in such a flagrant breach
> of his legal and moral obligations."[210]

Trial by jury

Section 69 of the Supreme Court Act 1981 entitles any party to a **3–081**
defamation action to require a trial by jury, "unless the court is of
the opinion that the trial requires any prolonged examination of
documents or accounts or any scientific or local investigations which

---

[208] *John v MGN Ltd* above, fn.63 at 59–64.
[209] Lord Phillips, *Yousfl Jameel.*
[210] *Grobbelaar v Newsgroup Newspapers Ltd* [2002] 4 All E.R. 732.

cannot conveniently be made by a jury." Even in these cases the court has a discretion to order jury trial, although it will apply a presumption in favour of trial by judge alone if satisfied that otherwise the trial would be so complicated, costly and lengthy that the administration of justice would be likely to suffer.[211] The Court of Appeal has in such cases refused a jury even though the allegation accuses the claimant of committing criminal offences, although where the trial affects national interests or the honour and integrity of national personalities it may decide otherwise.[212] This was the case in *Lord Rothermere v Bernard Levin & Times Newspapers*, where the defendants had published an attack ("Profit and dishonour in Fleet Street") on Rothermere's integrity in closing down a newspaper. Although the trial would involve a prolonged examination of financial documents, the Court of Appeal was moved by the personal plea of the editor of *The Times* that free speech issues should be decided by a jury.[213] That was in 1973: in 1997 the Court of Appeal took a very different view:

> Jonathan Aitken M.P. resigned as a cabinet minister to sue the *Guardian* over claims that he was unfit for public office. The case would involve prolonged examination of documents and as such was inconvenient for jurors, but the newspaper argued that discretion ought nonetheless to be exercised in favour of trial by jury because that was the most acceptable tribunal for deciding whether the conduct of an elected official had fallen below proper standards. The court rejected "public perception" as a lode-star, in favour of the interests of justice which would be better served "by a painstaking, dispassionate, impartial, orderly approach to deciding where truth lies". A general jury verdict was no substitute for a reasoned judicial decision on whether the claimant had misconducted himself.[214]

Aitken reflects a more general judicial disenchantment with the jury as a sensible tribunal for settling libel actions. Claimants are less inclined to opt for jury trial in the hope of obtaining outsize damages now that awards have been brought under tighter judicial control, although the value and attendant publicity of vindication by a jury rather than a judge alone still exerts attraction for celebrities. Media defendants prefer juries for tactical reasons in cases where claimants are unpopular or unpleasant or politically controversial: their hope is that jurors will take a more instinctive, broad-brush approach to allegations in respect to which nit-picking judges might require a stricter standard of proof. Where a case involves what might be perceived as a choice as to which party is the lesser of the two evils—

---

[211] *De L'Isle v Times Newspapers Ltd* [1988] 1 W.L.R. 49.

[212] *Goldsmith v Pressdram Ltd* [1988] 1 W.L.R. 64; *Beta Construction Ltd v Channel 4* [1990] 1 W.L.R. 1042.

[213] *Rothermere v Bernard Levin & Times Newspapers*, unreported (1973).

[214] *Aitken v Preston* [1997] E.M.L.R. 15.

Mr Neil Hamilton or Mr Mohammed Al Fayed, for example—judges would be well advised to leave the decision in the inscrutable lap of 12 good men and women and true.

Summary Disposal

The Defamation Act provides an alternative to expensive jury trial **3–082** by way of summary disposal of claims by a judge alone.[215] But this procedural benefit carries the downside for claimants that their maximum in damages is £10,000. The courts are still (if reluctantly) prepared to recognise that defendants have a qualified right to trial by jury, sufficient to exclude libel actions from the general rule permitting summary judgment,[216] so long as there is a material issue of fact in dispute between the parties.

CRIMINAL LIBEL

If a libel is extremely serious, to the extent that a court is prepared **3–083** to hold that it cannot be compensated by money and deserves to be punished as a crime, its publisher may be made the target of a prosecution. Criminal libel is an ancient offence that is now unlikely to be invoked against the media by prosecuting authorities: the Law Commission has recommended its abolition,[217] and one Law Lord has further pointed out that its scope conflicts with the European Convention on Human Rights.[218] There have been a few modern instances in which it has been invoked by private individuals as part of a vendetta against their journalist-tormentors. In 1977 Sir James Goldsmith was granted leave to prosecute the editor of *Private Eye*.[219] The following year a London magistrate, struck by the notion that there should not be one law for the rich unavailable to the poor, permitted a man named Gleaves to bring proceedings against the authors and publishers of a book entitled *Johnny Go Home*, based on a Yorkshire television documentary that had exposed his insalubrious hospitality to feckless youths. Neither case was an edifying example of law enforcement. Goldsmith was allowed to withdraw his prosecution after a settlement with *Private Eye* and an Old Bailey jury took little time to acquit the authors of *Johnny Go Home* after a two-week trial. These precedents do not hold out great

---

[215] Defamation Act 1996, ss.8–10.
[216] CPR, Pt 24 was held ultra vires for libel actions: *Safeway v Tate* [2001] 2 W.L.R. 1377 as explained by *Alexander v Arts Council of Wales* [2001] 4 All E.R. 205 at 217.
[217] The Law Commission, *Working Paper No. 84* HMSO, 1982. The US Supreme Court has declared laws that punish falsehoods unconstitutional, unless that require proof of express malice: *Garrison v Louisiana* 379 U.S. 64 (1964).
[218] *Gleaves v Deakin* [1980] A.C. 477 at 493, *per* Lord Diplock.
[219] See Richard Ingrams, *Goldenballs* (Deutsch, 1979).

hope for private prosecutors determined to teach their critics a lesson in the criminal courts.

The arcane offence of *scandalum magnatum* was created by a statute of 1275 designed to protect "the great men of the realm" against discomfiture from stories that might arouse the people against them.[220] The purpose of criminal libel was to prevent loss of confidence in government. It was, essentially, a public order offence, and since true stories were more likely to result in breaches of the peace, it spawned the aphorism "The greater the truth, the greater the libel."[221] Overtly political prosecutions were brought in its name, against the likes of John Wilkes, Tom Paine and the Dean of St Asaph. Most of its historical anomalies survive in the present offence. Truth is not a defence, unless the defendant can convince a jury that publication is for the public benefit.[222] The burden of proof lies on the defendant, who may be convicted even though he or she honestly believed, on reasonable grounds, that what was published was true and a matter of public interest. In certain circumstances the offence extends to defamation of the dead,[223] and may even be brought where the attack has been published about a class of persons rather than an individual.[224]

For all its theoretical scope, there are several safeguards. Leave must be obtained from a High Court judge before any prosecution can be brought in, at least against proprietors and editors, in relation to an article in a newspaper or periodical.[225] This safeguard of leave from a High Court judge may be side-stepped by prosecuting only the journalist who supplied the copy, and the incorrigible Mr Gleaves made repeated use of this loop-hole in the statutory language of s.8. Although the Divisional Court in *Gleaves v Insall* approved a literal reading of this archaic section (which omits to mention reporters and journalists) it did so without the benefit of s.3 of the Human Rights Act, which should now allow the section to be construed so as to include them, since this would be the only possible reading which could conform with Art.10. (There being no necessity nor any public benefit in prosecuting journalists rather than

---

[220] *Goldenballs* p.10, and see generally J. R. Spencer, *"Criminal Libel—Skeleton in the Cupboard"* [1977] Crim. L.R. 383.

[221] *De Libellis Famosis* (1606) 5 Co. Rep. 125 (a) and (b).

[222] In *R. v Perrymann, The Times*, January 19—February 9, 1892, a jury actually found that an editor's allegation that a solicitor was party to a serious corporate fraud was true, but it was not in the public interest that this truth should be published!

[223] See *Hilliard v Penfield Enterprises* [1990] I.R. 38, where the deceased's wife sought to prosecute the publishers of a magazine for alleging that her husband had been a member of the IRA. Justice Gannon refused leave, on the grounds that criminal defamation of the dead required a malevolent intention to injure surviving members of his family by the vilification of his memory.

[224] See G. Zellick, *Libelling the Dead* (1969), 119 N.L.J. 769, and (in relation to class libels) *R. v Williams* (1822) 5 B. and Ald. 595.

[225] Law of Libel Amendment Act 1888, s.8.

editors for a criminal offence which in its terms infringes freedom of expression.)[226] The judge must be satisfied that there is an exceptionally strong prima facie case, that the libel is extremely serious and that the public interest requires the institution of criminal proceedings. In deciding whether these tests are satisfied the judge must look not just at the prosecution's case, but must take into account the likelihood of the newspaper successfully raising a defence.[227] In one 1982 case Mr Justice Taylor refused to allow a man who had been described by the *Sunday People* as a violent and drunken bully to bring a prosecution for criminal libel. He heard evidence from the newspaper that undermined the applicant's evidence, and decided that there was not "a case so clear as to be beyond argument a case to answer". He further held that in any event the public interest did not require the institution of criminal proceedings.[228] These same tests should be satisfied before a magistrate commits anyone for trial in relation to a libel that has not appeared in a newspaper or periodical. There is no offence of "criminal slander", with the result that public speakers appear immune, at least in relation to off-the-cuff remarks.[229]

Criminal libel corresponds to no "pressing social need" of the sort **3–084** that the European Court insists should justify restraints on free expression, and its continuing existence is difficult to reconcile with the decision in *Lingens v Austria*.

There have been suggestions that it should be replaced by a new law of criminal defamation, which would make it an offence deliberately to publish a serious falsehood. The difficulties of definition and of trial procedure, however, make such suggestions impracticable.[230] Moreover, as the Privy Council pointed out in *Hector v. Att-Gen of Antigua and Barbuda*:

> "it would in my view by a grave impediment to the freedom of the press if those who print or distribute matter reflecting critically on the conduct of public authorities could only do so with impunity if they could first verify the accuracy of all statements of fact on which the criticism was based."[231]

The absurdity of taking the law of criminal defamation seriously was well illustrated in 1990, when the British Board of Film Classification

---

[226] The Divisional Court decision in *Gleaves v Insall* (1999) E.M.L.R. 779 was given before the Human Rights Act came into operation, and did not consider the argument for giving the 1888 Act a construction consistent with it.

[227] *Goldsmith v Pressdram Ltd* [1977] Q.B. 83.

[228] *Desmond v Thorne* [1982] 3 All E.R. 268.

[229] Defamation Act 1952, s.17(2) and see *Gatley on Libel*, para.1600. Words broadcast on television or radio, however, are deemed to be published in permanent form: Broadcasting Act 1990, s.16(1).

[230] See G. Robertson *The Law Commission on Criminal Libel* [1983] Public Law 208.

[231] [1990] 2 All E.R. 103 at 106.

sought to ban the Pakistani feature video *International Guerrillas* on the grounds that it amounted to a criminal libel on Mr Salman Rushdie, whom it depicted, in James Bond-style fantasy, as a sadistic terrorist. Mr Rushdie announced that if criminal libel proceedings were brought on his behalf, he would give evidence for the defence. The Video Appeals Committee decided that the prospect of a prosecution, let alone a conviction, was too far-fetched to justify the ban.[232]

CONCLUSION

3–085   A claimant once brought a defamation action over the allegation that he was a highwayman. The evidence at the trial proved that he *was* in fact a highwayman. The claimant was arrested in the courtroom, committed to prison and then executed. Few defamation actions end so satisfactorily for the defence. In 2007, however, a CFA-backed lilywhite litigant turned up to sue a tabloid for the serious accusation that she had pleasured Wayne Rooney in a massage parlour. The newspaper confronted her with a confession made to police that she was a prostitute. Her lawyers fled (having withdrawn the CFA) and she ran from the court in tears as the judge recommended that the DPP prosecute her for perjury. On the other hand, in 2006 a jury (by seven votes to four) awarded Scottish M.P. Tommy Sheridan £200,000 damages over reports that he had visited sex clubs, despite 19 witnesses who had seen him there *in flagrante* and minutes of a party meeting at which he had apparently confessed. Truth and fiction remain as difficult to disentangle in the courtroom as in the newsroom.

The media constantly complain about defamation law, with some justice in respect of the burden of proof, the escalation of legal costs and other defects pointed out in this chapter. The recent development of a public interest defence in *Jameel* has improved protection for professionally-conducted investigative journalism, but the media as a body and newspapers as an industry have shown scant interest in improving ethical standards. No civilised society can permit a privately owned press to run vendettas against individuals powerless to arrest the spread of falsehoods and innuendoes. In the United States the Supreme Court held in the great case of *The New York Times v Sullivan* that no libel action could succeed if the claimant was a public figure and the allegation was honestly and diligently made.[233] This ruling has freed the American media to probe Watergate and Irangate in a depth and a detail that could not be attempted in equivalent circumstances in Britain, where the merest hint of impropriety in public life calls forth a libel writ. But the

---

[232] Video Appeals Committee, Appeal No.0007, September 3, 1990.
[233] *The New York Times Co v Sullivan*, 401 U.S. 265 (1964).

public figure doctrine denies virtually any protection to persons who are prominent in public affairs, simply because of that fact. True, public figures voluntarily step into a fish-tank that entails close public scrutiny of their every move, and they ordinarily enjoy greater access to channels of communication that provide an opportunity to counter false statements. But that opportunity is circumscribed, none the less, and in a country where proprietors with powerful partisan views control 80 per cent of national newspapers, there is an understandable reluctance to give them a blank cheque to attack political enemies.

Two essential freedoms—the right to communicate and the right to reputation—must in some way be reconciled by law. British libel law has erred by inhibiting free speech and failing to provide a system for correcting factual errors that is speedy and available to all victims of press distortion. American libel law gives no protection at all to the reputation of people in the public eye. Some European countries have opted for a more acceptable solution in the form of right-to-reply legislation, which allows an "ombudsman" to direct newspapers to publish corrections and counter-statements from those who claim to have been misrepresented. What is required is a speedy and effective legal procedure that secures corrections and counter-statements while reserving damages for cases where claimants have suffered financial loss or been the victims of malice. There is no indication that government or Parliament will bring forth legislation to provide such far-reaching reforms, and the ability of judges to do so by common law development is limited, save for their ability to "cull sacred cows" by virtue of the Human Rights Act.[234]

When journalists receive libel writs, they will generally be well **3–086** advised to seek expert assistance, although there are times where a robust extra-legal response will be more effective:

The much celebrated correspondence in the matter of *Arkell v Pressdram* involved only two letters: the first, from the solicitors Goodman Derrick & Co, to the editor of *Private Eye*, ended with the familiar legal demand:

> "Mr Arkell's first concern is that there should be a full retraction at the earliest possible date in *Private Eye* and he will also want his costs paid. His attitude to damages will be governed by the nature of your reply."

To this the magazine responded:

---

[234] See Lord Slynn in *R. v Lambert* [2001] 3 All E.R. 577, HL. Although the power of re-interpretation in s.3 of the HRA applies only to statutes, courts themselves are public authorities and must apply the common law compatibly with the Convention, a duty which permits them to abrogate long-standing doctrines. See *Aston Cantlow v Wallbank* [2001] 3 All E.R. 393.

"We note that Mr Arkell's attitude to damages will be governed by the nature of our reply and would therefore be grateful if you could inform us what his attitude to damages would be, were he to learn that the nature of our reply is as follows: fuck off."

CHAPTER 4

OBSCENITY, BLASPHEMY AND RACE HATRED

"The constitutional protection accorded to the freedom of speech and of the press is not based on the naive belief that speech can do no harm but on the confidence that the benefits society reaps from the free flow and exchange of ideas outweigh the costs society endures by receiving reprehensible or dangerous ideas."[1]

CENSORSHIP: AN INTRODUCTION

Censorship of writing, drama and film on grounds of morality is **4–001** achieved by laws that apply two sets of standards. One prohibits "obscene" articles likely to deprave and corrupt readers and viewers, while the other allows authorities to act, in certain circumstances, against "indecent" material that merely embarrasses the sexual modesty of ordinary people. Obscenity, the more serious crime, is punished by the Obscene Publications Act 1959, either after a trial by judge or jury or by "forfeiture proceedings" under a law that authorises local justices to destroy obscene books and films discovered within their jurisdiction. Disseminators of "indecent" material that lacks the potency to corrupt are generally within the law so long as they do not dispatch it by post, fax or email, or scream it down the telephone, or seek to import it from overseas, or flaunt it openly in public places. Both "obscenity" and "indecency" are defined by reference to vague and elastic formulae, permitting forensic debates over morality that fit uneasily into the format of a criminal trial. These periodic moral flash-points provide scant control over the booming business of sexual delectation. Occasional forfeiture orders, based upon the same loose definitions, are subject to the inconsistent priorities and prejudices of constabularies in different parts of the country, and offer no effective deterrent.

The deep division in society over the proper limits of sexual permissiveness is mirrored by an inconsistent and ineffective censorship of publications that may offend or entertain, corrupt or

---

[1] *Hercey v Hustler Magazine* (1988) 485 U.S. 959.

enlighten, according to the taste and character of individual readers. The problem of drawing a legal line between moral outrage and personal freedom has become intractable at a time when one person's obscenity is another person's bedtime reading.

Bedtime viewing, however, is subject to more stringent controls. Reliance is placed on statutory duties, imposed as a condition of broadcasting licenses, to ensure that nothing is transmitted that is in bad taste (although much television output undoubtedly is) or is likely to prove offensive to public feeling. This means that four letter words and programs about sex and drugs which might disquieten children are consigned to times after the "watershed" of 21.00, when children are (unrealistically) assumed to be in bed. Television was subjected to the Obscene Publications Act in 1990, although it is difficult to imagine how obscene material could slip through these controls and no prosecution has yet been brought against broadcasters. Films screened in public cinemas are subject to the test of obscenity, although the film industry, in order to obtain additional insurance against prosecution, has voluntarily bound itself to comply with the censorship requirements of the British Board of Film Classification, a private body established and funded by the industry itself. The importance of the BBFC is enhanced by local licensing requirements which generally require that all films screened shall have been approved by the BBFC and by the law that shops selling videos, DVDs and computer games shall carry only those that have been granted an appropriate BBFC certificate. Licensed sex shops are also obliged to sell only videos and DVDs that have been certified by the Board. In this way a form of pre-censorship is imposed on '18' rated films and videos that is not inflicted upon books or magazines or theatres.

The obscenity and indecency laws, and the arrangements for film censorship, are generally directed against sexual explicitness. However, the tests applied are sufficiently broad to catch material that encourages the use of dangerous drugs or that advocates criminal violence. Distributors of horror movies on video cassettes have been convicted on the basis that explicitly violent scenes are likely to corrupt a significant proportion of home viewers. In this chapter the scope and general principles of laws relating to obscenity, indecency, blasphemy, conspiracy and incitement to racial hatred are examined in some detail. In Chs 15 and 16 the extent to which their principles are applied to television, film and video will be considered separately along with the statutory duties and censorship systems that work in these media to regulate the treatment of controversial subjects.

Article 10

4–002 The Human Rights Act imports a generalised guarantee of freedom "to receive and impart information and ideas" and the arid debate over whether pornography imparts either has been long settled: it certainly conveys information about how people can copulate and ideas about sexual pleasure even if (in many cases) the message may decode as approval of the degradation of women. The freedom is subject only to restrictions necessary in a democratic society "for the protection of health and morals" but the European Court has acknowledged that there is no Europe-wide consensus on morality and has in consequence given States a very wide "margin of appreciation" to censor in accordance with parochial concerns about sex and religion. Its case law is in consequence of little value, other than its seminal statement of principal first uttered in *Handyside v UK*, a 1973 complaint about a court order to destroy *The Little Red Schoolbook*, on grounds of obscenity:

> "Freedom of expression constitutes one of the essential foundations of a democratic society, one of the basic conditions for its progress and for the development of every man. Subject to para.2 of Art.10, it is applicable not only to information or ideas that are favourably received, or regarded as inoffensive, but also to those that offend, shock or disturb the state or any sector of the population. Such are the demands of that pluralism, tolerance and broadmindedness without which there is no democratic society."[2]

This celebrated and regularly repeated dictum is tarnished only by the actual decision in *Handyside*, when the court illogically refused to apply it to a handbook of rights for teenagers capable of thinking and reading for themselves, and which are now taken for granted. The decision that a forfeiture order made by an Old Bailey judge was within the United Kingdom's margin of appreciation signalled the Euro-court's inherent reluctance to protect ideas that offend intolerant and narrow-minded (but powerful) sectors of a national population, in this case the late Mrs Mary Whitehouse and the strait-laced English judiciary of the period. A similar reluctance to intervene to protect artworks that shock and disturb was apparent in *Muller v Switzerland*[3] (although that decision also turned on the fact that the exhibition was open to children) and the court has expressly permitted national authorities to ban for blasphemy works of cinematic and theatrical merit which offend religious susceptibilities.

It is notable that in these three cases—*Muller, Otto Preminger*[4] and *Wingrove*[5]—the commission (at that time a filter for the court, comprising for the most part better and more independent judges) correctly ruled that the censorship was an infringement of Art.10, but the judges on the court itself relied on the "margin of appreciation" cop-out to avoid upsetting moral sensitivities (particularly from

---

[2] (1976) 1 E.H.R.R. 737 at 49.
[3] (1991) 13 E.H.R.R. 212.
[4] (1994) 19 E.H.R.R. 34.
[5] (1997) 24 E.H.R.R. 1.

Roman Catholics). This cowardice is understandable: at a time when the court was taking uncomfortable stands on other civil liberties (to such an extent that the Thatcher government sent its Lord Chancellor to Strasbourg to warn that Britain might withdraw as the result of a decision condemning its shooting of IRA suspects in Gibraltar) a decision in favour of Wingrove's "blasphemous" film would have been inopportune. But it has meant that the court lacks any jurisprudence which stands up for the rights of artists and writers to shake a complacent public, to perform what Kafka described as their duty "to wield their pen like an ice-pick, to smash the frozen sea inside us". In media law, Art.10 has notably protected political speech, however hack the journalist, and has acceptably offered a much more limited protection to commercial speech. That it should quail when invited to protect art and literature is ironic, given that the European contribution to culture is so much more impressive than its contribution (England excepted) to democracy.

OBSCENITY

History

4–003   The history of obscenity provides a rich and comic tapestry on the futility of legal attempts to control sexual imagination.[6] The subject-matter of pornography was settled by 1650; writers in subsequent centuries added new words and novel settings, but discovered no fundamental variation on the finite methods of coupling. The scarlet woman, pornography's picaresque and picturesque prop, gained one dimension with the development of photography and another with the abolition of stage censorship, but the modern exploits of Linda Lovelace were old hat to Fanny Hill.

The central irony of the courtroom crusade—what might be termed "the *Spycatcher* effect"—is always present: seek to suppress a book by legal action because it tends to corrupt, and the publicity attendant upon its trial will spread that assumed corruption far more effectively than its quiet distribution. *Lady Chatterley's Lover* sold three million copies in the three months following its prosecution in 1961, a circulation that its modest literary merit could not justify. The last work of literature to be prosecuted for obscenity in a full-blooded Old Bailey trial was an undistinguished paperback entitled *Inside Linda Lovelace*. It had sold a few thousand copies in the years before the 1976 court case: within three weeks of its acquittal 600,000 copies were purchased by an avid public. That trial finally convinced the Director of Public Prosecutions (DPP) of the foolishness of using obscenity laws against books with any claim to literary or sociological merit.[7]

---

[6] See generally Geoffrey Robertson, *Obscenity* (Weidenfeld & Nicholson, 1979) and Alan Travis, *Bound and Gagged—A Secret History of Obscenity in Britain* (Profile Books, 2000).

[7] *Committee on Obscenity and Film Censorship* (The Williams Committee), HMSO, 1979, Cmnd 7772, Ch.4, para.2.

The courts first began to take obscenity seriously as a result of private prosecutions brought in the early nineteenth century by the Society for the Suppression of Vice, dubbed by Sydney Smith "a society for suppressing the vices of those whose incomes do not exceed £500 per annum".[8] A law against obscene libel was created by the judges, although Parliament gave some assistance in 1857 with an Obscene Publications Act, which permitted magistrates to destroy immoral books found within their jurisdiction. The Act did not, however, define obscenity. Lord Chief Justice Cockburn, in the 1868 case of *R. v Hicklin*, obliged with a formula that has influenced the subject ever since:

> "I think the test of obscenity is this, whether the tendency of the matter charged as obscenity is to deprave and corrupt those whose minds are open to such immoral influences, and into whose hands a publication of this sort may fall."[9]

Under this definition of obscene libel, almost any work dealing **4–004** with sexual passion could be successfully prosecuted. The *Hicklin* test focused upon the effect of the book on the most vulnerable members of society, whether or not they were likely to read it. One "purple passage" could consign a novel to condemnation, and there was no defence of literary merit. *The Well of Loneliness* was destroyed in 1928 at the hands of a magistrate who felt that a passage that implied that two women had been to bed ("And that night they were not divided") would induce "thought of a most impure character" and "glorify a horrible tendency".[10] The operation of the obscenity law depended to some extent upon the crusading zeal of current law officers. There was a brief respite in the 1930s, after a banned copy of *Ulysses* was found among the papers of a deceased Lord Chancellor. But in 1953 the authorities solemnly sought to destroy copies of *The Kinsey Report*, and in 1956 a number of respectable publishers were tried at the Old Bailey for "horrible tendencies" discovered in their current fiction lists. The Society of Authors set up a powerful lobby, which convinced a Parliamentary Committee that the common law of obscene libel should be replaced by a modern statute that afforded some protection to meritorious literature.[11] The Obscene Publications Act of 1959 was the result. The measure was described in its preamble as "an Act to amend the law relating to the publication of obscene matter; to provide for the protection of literature; and to strengthen the law concerning pornography".

The 1959 Obscene Publications Act emerged from a simplistic notion that sexual material could be divided into two classes,

---

[8] *Edinburgh Review*, XXVI, January 1809.
[9] (1868) L.R. 3 Q.B. 360 at 371.
[10] See Vera Brittain, *Radclyffe Hall—A Case of Obscenity* (Femina, 1968) pp.91–92.
[11] See Norman St John Stevas, *Obscenity and the Law* (Seeker & Warburg, 1956).

"literature" and "pornography", and the function of the new statutory definition of obscenity was to enable juries and magistrates to make the distinction between them. The tendency of a work to deprave or corrupt its readers was henceforth to be judged in the light of its total impact, rather than by the arousing potential of "purple passages". The readership to be considered was the actual or at least predictable reading public rather than the precocious 14–year-old schoolgirl into whose hands it might perchance fall—unless it were in fact aimed at or distributed to 14–year-old schoolgirls, by whose vulnerability to corruption it should then be judged. It was recognised that a work of literature might employ, to advance its serious purpose, a style that resembled, or had the same effect as, the pornographer's: here the jury was to be assisted to draw the line by experts who would offer judgments as to the degree of importance the article represented in its particular discipline. Works of art or literature might be obscene (i.e. depraving or corrupting) but their great significance might outweigh the harm they could do, and take them out of the prima facie criminal category established by s.1 of the Act.

In fact, the 1959 Act worked to secure almost total freedom in Britain for the written word. It took two decades and a number of celebrated trials for the revolutionary implications of the legislation to be fully appreciated and applied. The credit for securing this freedom belongs not so much to the legislators (many of whom later professed themselves appalled at developments) but to a few courageous publishers who risked jail by inviting juries to take a stand against censorship, and to the ineptitude and corruption of police enforcement. The first major test case—over D.H. Lawrence's *Lady Chatterley's Lover*—enabled the full force of the reformed law to be exploited on behalf of recognised literature. The book fell to be judged, not on the strength of its four-letter words or purple passages, but on its overall impact, as described by leading authorities on English literature. In 1968 the appeal proceedings over *Last Exit to Brooklyn* established the right of authors to explore depravity and corruption without encouraging it: writers were entitled to turn their readers' stomachs for the purpose of arousing concern or condemning the corruption explicitly described. The trials of the underground press in the early '70s discredited obscenity law in the eyes of a new generation of jurors, and acquittals of hard-core pornography soon followed. These came in the wake of apparently scientific evidence that pornography had a therapeutic rather than a harmful effect. Popular permissiveness was reflected in jury verdicts, and the repeal of obscenity laws in several European countries made it impossible for the authorities to police the incoming tide of eroticism. And if pornography did not corrupt its readers, it certainly corrupted many of those charged with enforcing the law against it. Public cynicism about obscenity control was confirmed when 12 members of Scotland Yard's "dirty squad" were jailed after conviction for involvement in what their judge described as "an evil conspiracy which turned the Obscene Publications Act into a vast protection racket".[12] After the acquittal of *Inside Linda Lovelace* in 1976, the authorities largely abandoned the attempt to prosecute books for which any claim of literary merit could be made. The Williams Committee, which reported on the obscenity laws in 1979, recommended that all restraints on the written word should be lifted—a position that they thought had already been achieved de facto.[13]

Since the Williams Report, the only books that have been **4–005** prosecuted have either glorified illegal activities, such as the taking of dangerous drugs, or have been hard-core pornography lacking any literary pretension or sociological interest. In the late 1980s the need for education about the dangers of transmitting the AIDS virus justified a degree of public explicitness that would have been unthinkable in previous decades, and eventually the BBFC was obliged by the courts to license hardcore video pornography for adult purchase (see Ch.15) and adult "top-shelf" magazines followed this lead. The forces of feminism were strange bed-fellows with Mrs Whitehouse in challenging public acceptance of erotica but in this enterprise they have notably failed (except in Canada) although there can be no guarantee against some future legal onslaught. In 2005, the Home Office issued a paper, *Consultation: On the Possession of Extreme Violent Pornography*, which presaged the advent of new laws against the "hundreds of Internet sites offering a wide range of material featuring the torture of (mostly female) victims. . .". It proposed a new law that would provide heavy jail sentences for "realistic depictions" of "serious violence in a sexual context" or "serious sexual violence" which if taken literally would apply to a good deal of Jacobean drama, not to mention modern films like *Straw Dogs* or *Looking for Mr Goodbar*. There are still occasional threats against meritorious art or literature. In 1998, provincial policemen threatened Random House for publishing a lavish book of Robert Mapplethorpe photographs (priced at £75), a copy of which they had discovered in a university library. In 2002, a posse of policemen descended on the Saatchi gallery, stoked up by tabloid claims that a picture of naked children on a beach amounted to child pornography. In both cases a Q.C.'s opinion was necessary to persuade the DPP to drop the proceedings. The latitude he allowed to respectable white publishers did not extend to black "rap" artists from the American urban ghetto, and the Island Records group *Niggaz With Attitude* suffered the first obscenity case brought in relation to a compact disc. It was solemnly played to elderly lay justices at Redbridge Magistrates' Court, who found it impossible to conclude that whatever it was that they were hearing could excite sexually.

---

[12] Barry Cox, John Shirley and Martin Short, *The Fall of Scotland Yard* (Penguin, 1977), p.158.
[13] Williams Committee, *Obscenity and Film Censorship*, fn.3 above.

The test of obscenity

4–006 The complete statutory definition of obscenity is contained in s.1 of the Obscene Publications Act:

> "For the purposes of this Act an article shall be deemed to be obscene if its effect or (where the article comprises two or more distinct items) the effect of any one of its items is, if taken as a whole, such as to tend to deprave and corrupt persons who are likely, in all the circumstances, to read, see or hear the matter contained or embodied in it."

In any trial the prosecution must prove beyond reasonable doubt that the material is obscene. Its task is complicated by the following interpretations of the statutory definition.

The tendency to deprave and corrupt

4–007 "Deprave" means "to make morally bad, to pervert, to debase or corrupt morally" and corrupt means "to render morally unsound or rotten, or destroy the moral purity or chastity of, to pervert or ruin a good quality, to debase, to defile".[14] The definition implies that the tendency must go much further than merely shocking or disgusting readers.[15] Thus "obscene", in law, has a very different, and very much stronger, meaning than it possesses in colloquial usage. The convictions of the editors of *Oz* magazine were quashed because their trial judge had suggested that "obscene" might include what is "repulsive, filthy, loathsome, indecent or lewd". To widen its legal meaning in this way was "a very substantial and serious misdirection."[16]

In *Knuller v DPP* the Law Lords considered that the word "corrupt" implied a powerful and corrosive effect, which went further than one suggested definition, "to lead morally astray". Lord Simon warned:

> "Corrupt is a strong word. The Book of Common Prayer, following the Gospel, has 'where rust and moth doth corrupt'. The words 'corrupt public morals' suggest conduct which a jury might find to be destructive of the very fabric of society."[17]

Lord Reid agreed:

> ". . . corrupt is a strong word and the jury ought to be reminded of that . . . The Obscene Publications Act appears to use the

---

[14] See C. H. Rolph, *The Trial of Lady Chatterley* (commem. edn, Penguin, 1990) pp.227–8. The present law is stated in detail in Robertson, fn.2 above, Ch.3.
[15] See *R. v Martin Secker & Warburg Ltd* [1954] 2 All E.R. 683.
[16] *R. v Anderson* [1971] 3 All E.R. 1152.
[17] [1973] A.C. 435 at 491.

words 'deprave' and 'corrupt' as synonymous, as I think they are. We may regret we live in a permissive society but I doubt whether even the most staunch defender of a better age would maintain that all or even most of those who have at one time or in one way or another been led astray morally have thereby become depraved or corrupt."[18]

These dicta in *Knuller* emphasise that the effect of publication must go beyond immoral suggestion or persuasion and constitute a serious menace.

"Obscenity" is a much narrower concept that "sexual explicitness". This important distinction was emphasised by the Divisional Court in the 1991 case of *Darbo v CPS* when it held that an Obscene Publications Act warrant authorising police to search for "material of a sexually explicit nature" was invalid, because material in this category was by no means necessarily "obscene" in the sense that it might be likely to deprave and corrupt consumers.[19] This is recognised by the BBFC guidelines on 18R certificates issued in 2000 after the *Makin' Whoopee* decision. The Chief Justice of South Australia has said in respect of ideologically vapid pornographic publications: "there is, to my mind, something ludicrous about the application of such portentous words as 'deprave' and 'corrupt' to these trivial and insipid productions."[20]

The aversion defence

One important corollary of the decision that obscene material must **4–008** have more serious effects than arousing feelings of revulsion is the doctrine that material that in fact shocks and disgusts may *not* be obscene, because its effect is to discourage readers from indulgence in the immorality so unseductively portrayed. Readers whose stomachs are turned will not partake of any food for thought. The argument, however paradoxical it sounds, has frequently found favour as a means of exculpating literature of merit:

> *Last Exit to Brooklyn* presented horrific pictures of homosexuality and drug-taking in New York. Defence counsel contended that its only effect on any but a minute lunatic fringe of readers would be horror, revulsion and pity. It made the readers share in the horror it described and thereby so disgusted, shocked and outraged them that instead of tending to encourage anyone to homosexuality, drug-taking or brutal violence, it would have precisely the reverse effect. The failure of the trial judge to put this defence before the jury in his summing up was the major ground for upsetting the conviction.[21]

---

[18] [1973] A.C. 435 at 456–7.
[19] *David John Darbo v DPP*, *The Times*, July 11, 1991, Divisional Court (Mann LJ. and Hidden I.), June 28, 1991.
[20] *Popow v Samuels* [1973] 4 S.A.S.R. 594, *per* Bray C.J.
[21] *R. v Calder & Boyars Ltd* [1969] 1 Q.B. 151.

The aversion argument was extracted from its literary context and elevated into a full-blown defence of crudity in the *Oz* case:

> "One of the arguments was that many of the illustrations in *Oz* were so grossly lewd and unpleasant that they would shock in the first instance and then would tend to repel. In other words, it was said that they had an aversive effect and that, far from tempting those who had not experienced the acts to take part in them, they would put off those who might be tempted so to conduct themselves . . .".[22]

4–009 The most valuable aspect of the aversion defence is its emphasis on the context and purpose of publication. Writing that sets out to seduce, to exhort and pressurise the reader to indulge in immorality, is to be distinguished from that which presents a balanced picture and does not overlook the pains that may attend new pleasures. For over a century prosecutors thought it sufficient to point to explicitness in the treatment of sex, on the assumption that exposure to such material would automatically arouse the libidinous desires associated with a state of depravity. Now they must consider the overall impact; books that present a fair account of corruption have a defence denied to glossy propaganda. In deciding whether material depraves and corrupts, the jury must lift its eyes from mere details and consider the tone and overall presentation. Does the material glamorise sex or does it "tell it like it is?".

In 1991 the aversion defence assisted Island Records to argue successfully that a record by rap musicians *Niggaz With Attitude* was not obscene. Despite the profusion of four-letter words and aggressively unpleasant imagery, it was inconceivable that anyone in their right mind—or even their wrong mind—would be sexually aroused by songs like "One Less Bitch" or "To Kill a Hooker". These songs were said to be "street journalism", reflecting the degradation and depravity of life among the drug gangs in the ghetto suburbs of Los Angeles. The magistrates agreed that the record was more likely to arouse distaste and fear than lust, and directed that the 30,000 records, cassettes and compact discs seized by Scotland Yard's Obscene Publications Squad should be released.[23]

The target audience

4–010 An article is only obscene if it is likely to corrupt "persons who are likely, having regard to all relevant circumstances, to read, see or hear the matter contained or embodied in it". Thus the Act adopts a

---

[22] *R. v Anderson* [1971] 3 All E.R. 1152 at 1160.
[23] See "Niggaz Court Win Marks Changing Attitude", the *Guardian*, November 8, 1991; and "NWA Cleared of Obscenity Charges", *Melody Maker*, November 16, 1991.

relative definition of obscenity—relative, that is, to the "likely" rather than the "conceivably possible" readership. This is further emphasised by s.2(6) of the Act, which provides that in any prosecution for publishing an obscene article "the question whether an article is obscene shall be determined without regard to any publication by another person, unless it could reasonably have been expected that the publication by the other person would follow from the publication by the person charged." Where the charge is possession for gain, the question whether the article is obscene is similar (although stated in different and confusing words by s.1(3)(b) of the 1964 Act): it .

> "shall be determined by reference to such publication for gain of the article as in the circumstances it may reasonably be inferred he had in contemplation and to any further publication that could reasonably be expected to follow from it, but not to any other publication".

In other words, the jury must consider the impact not only on intended customers but on those to whom the customers could reasonably be expected to show or pass on the material, but not its impact on other persons who might (but could not reasonably be expected or be likely to) gain access to it as a result of the defendant's original act of publication.[24]

These statutory provisions ensure that the publication in question is judged by its impact on its primary audience—those people who, the evidence suggests, would be likely to seek it out and to pay the asking-price to read it, or else be sufficiently interested to borrow it or attend a viewing. They reject the "most vulnerable person" standard of *Hicklin*, with its preoccupation with those members of society of the lowest level of intellectual or moral discernment. They also reject another standard employed frequently in the law, that of the "average" or "reasonable" man, and focus on "likely" readers and proven circumstances of publication. A work of literature is to be judged by its effect on serious-minded purchasers, a comic book by its effect on children, a sexually explicit magazine sold in an "adults only" bookstore by its effect on adult patrons of that particular shop. The House of Lords has confirmed that "in every case, the magistrates or the jury are called on to ascertain who are the likely readers and then to consider whether the article is likely to deprave and corrupt them."[25]

In *R. v Clayton & Halsey* the proprietors of a Soho bookshop were charged with selling obscene material to two experienced members of

---

Scotland Yard's Obscene Publications Squad. These officers conceded that pornography had ceased to arouse any feelings in them whatsoever. The prosecution argument that the pictures were "inherently obscene" and tended of their very nature to corrupt all viewers was rejected.[26]

4–011   Although judges sometimes loosely talk of material that is "inherently obscene" or "obscene per se", it is clear that this concept is irreconcilable with the legislative definition of obscenity.[27] The quality of obscenity inheres whenever the article would tend to corrupt its actual or potential audience; the degree of that corruption becomes relevant when it is necessary to balance it against the public interest, if a "public good defence" has been raised under s.4 of the Act.

The "target audience" test is a protection for providers of pornography on commercial Internet sites which are accessible only after passing an age-check and supplying a credit card. These barriers effectively exclude any reasonable inference that children will be able to reach and download the pornographic web pages. In *R. v Perrin*, a filthy and fool-hardy Frenchman, resident in England, uploaded from a US web server an openly accessible "trailer" advertising his subscription site, which catered for copraphiliacs—as the open web page advertisement graphically illustrated. The court made the not unreasonable assumption that children are now regular Internet-surfers and would be as likely as adults to come across the preview page (and would perhaps be more curious about toilet training). It was not necessary for the prosecution to call evidence that "vulnerable" viewers had downloaded the preview page— juvenile interest in "forbidden fruit" was a reasonable inference. The decision puts beyond doubt that material on readily accessible Internet sites, wherever located, must comply with UK obscenity law, although the interesting questions of what amounts to a "publication" on the Internet (discussed in the context of libel in *Gutnik*, see earlier, para.3–037) were not explored.[28]

The significant proportion test

4–012 The 1959 Act requires a tendency to deprave and corrupt "persons" likely in the circumstances to read or hear the offensive material. But how many persons must have their morals affected before the test is made out? The answer was given by the Court of Appeal in the *Last Exit to Brooklyn* case. The jury must be satisfied that a *significant proportion* of the likely readership would be guided along the path of corruption:

---

[26] *R. v Clayton & Halsey* [1962] 1 Q.B. 163.
[27] *Att-Gen's Reference No. 2 of 1975* [1976] 2 All E.R. 753.
[28] (2002) EWCA Crim 747.

"Clearly section 2 cannot mean all persons; nor can it mean any one person, for there are individuals who may be corrupted by almost anything. On the other hand, it is difficult to construe 'persons' as meaning the majority of persons or the average reader. This court is of the opinion that the jury should have been directed to consider whether the effect of the book was to tend to deprave and corrupt a significant proportion of those persons likely to read it. What is a significant proportion is a matter entirely for the jury to decide."[29]

The significant proportion test has been applied at obscenity trials ever since. It protects the defendant in that it prevents the jury from speculating on the possible effect of adult literature on a young person who may just happen to see it, although it does not put the prosecution to proof that a majority, or even a *substantial* number of readers would be adversely affected. This was emphasised by the House of Lords in *Whyte*'s case, where local justices had mistakenly interpreted "significant proportion" to mean "the great majority". Lord Cross accepted that the significant proportion test was the standard that the justices were required to apply, but stressed that "a significant proportion of a class means a part which is not numerically negligible but which may be much less than half."[30]

The dominant effect principle

In obscenity trials before the 1959 legislation it was unnecessary for **4–013** juries to consider the overall impact of the subject-matter on its likely readers. Prosecuting counsel could secure a conviction merely by drawing attention to isolated "purple passages" taken out of context. The Select Committee on the Obscene Publications Act had stressed the importance of considering the "dominant effect" of the whole work.[31]

This recommendation was duly embodied in the 1959 statute, which provided that,

"an article shall be deemed to be obscene if its effect or (where the article comprises two or more distinct items) the effect of any one of its items is, if taken as a whole, such as to tend to deprave and corrupt . . .".

In the *Lady Chatterley* case Mr Justice Byrne instructed his jury to consider the total effect of the work after reading it from cover to cover: "You will read this book just as though you had bought it at a bookstall and you were reading it in the ordinary way as a whole."[32]

---

[29] *R. v Calder & Boyars Ltd*, fn.18 above.
[30] *DPP v Whyte* [1972] 3 All E.R. 12 at 24, 25.
[31] *Report of the Select Committee on Obscene Publications*, 1958, para.18.
[32] Rolph, *Lady Chatterley*, p.39.

The effect of the dominant impact test is to enable the courts to take account of the psychological realities of reading and film viewing, in so far as the audience is affected by theme and style and message, so that isolated incidents of an offensive nature are placed in context. The injunction that an article must be "taken as a whole" will apply to books and plays: in the case of magazines, however, which are made up of separate articles, advertisements and photographs, the dominant effect principle has less force. In such cases the publication is considered on an "item-by-item" basis: the prosecution may argue that obscenity attaches only to one article or photograph, and that the other contents are irrelevant.[33] A suggestion by the Court of Appeal in 1999 that the "item-by-item" test could apply to films is misguided, unless (possibly) the film were to comprise separate segments shot by different directors on different themes.[34] The intention of Parliament was to ensure that the jury considered the "dominant effect" of any artistic work, and the question is whether the experience of watching it through from beginning to end will have a corrupting effect on likely viewers, the impact of a single scene being considered in the context of the whole film, and not in isolation.

The publisher's intentions

4–014   The Obscene Publications Act is an exception to the general rule that criminal offences require an intention to offend. It does not matter whether the purpose is to educate or edify, to corrupt or simply to make money. The *effect* of the work on a significant proportion of the likely audience is all that matters in deciding whether it is obscene under s.1. However, the publisher's intentions may be very important when a public good defence is raised under s.4 of the Act, namely that although the work is obscene, its publication is nonetheless justified in the public interest. In the *Lady Chatterley* case Mr Justice Byrne directed that,

> "as far as literary merit or other matters which can be considered under s.4 are concerned, I think one has to have regard to what the author was trying to do, what his message may have been, and what his general scope was."[35]

A limited defence is provided by the Obscene Publications Act for those defendants who act merely as innocent disseminators of obscene material. Section 2(5) of the 1959 Act reads:

> "A person shall not be convicted of an offence against this section (i.e. the offence of publishing obscene material) if he

---

[33] *R. v Anderson* [1971] 3 All E.R. 1152 at 1158.
[34] See *Criminal Law Review*, October 1999, p.670 commenting on the decision in *R. v Goring*, January 14, 1999, CA.
[35] Rolph, *Lady Chatterley*, pp.121–122.

proves that he had not examined the article in respect of which he is charged and had no reasonable cause to suspect that it was such that his publication of it would make him liable to be convicted of an offence against this section."

The onus of proof is placed on the defendant under this section. The defendant must show, on the balance of probabilities, both that he did not examine the article and that he entertained no suspicions about the nature of its contents. It is often possible to judge pornographic books by their covers and a bookseller would probably fail if he admitted to catching sight of a provocative cover picture or suggestive title. In *R. v Love* the Court of Appeal quashed the conviction of a director of a print company who had been absent at the time a printer order for obscene books was accepted, and who had no personal knowledge of the contents of those books.[36] He could not be convicted unless he had been given specific notice of the offensive material. If the accused can show that the material came to him in the normal course of business from a reputable supplier, he should have a defence. Cases on the liability of distributors for libels in newspapers emphasise the importance for this defence of establishing that the business—of printing, distributing or retailing—was carried on carefully and properly. The test is whether the unwitting distributor *ought* to have known that the material would offend.[37] Until recently, distributors would routinely cover themselves by insisting upon a "counsel's opinion" before carrying each edition of a "top-shelf" magazine, but now the prospect of an obscenity prosecution is so unlikely that the practice has been discontinued. In 2003, there were only 39 obscenity prosecutions in the United Kingdom, confined to hardcore fetishistic material. Good clean pornography was untroubled, other than by occasional forfeiture orders.

The contemporary standards test

Although the Act does not make reference to the current climate of **4–015** opinion about sexual explicitness, juries in obscenity trials are enjoined to keep in mind the current standards of ordinary decent people. They "must set the standards of what is acceptable, of what is for the public good in the age in which we live."[38] Logically, of course, they do no such thing: however much the material offends the standards of decent people, the entirely distinct and key issue is whether it causes harm by tending to corrupt some of its readers or viewers. Contemporary standards should only be relevant to the

---

[36] *R. v Love* (1955) 39 Cr. App. R. 30.
[37] *See Emmens v Pottle* (1885) 16 Q.B.D. 354; *Sun Life Assurance Co of Canada v W. H. Smith Ltd* (1934) 150 L.T. 211.
[38] *R. v Calder & Boyars*, fn.18 above, at 172 *per* Salmon L.J.

obscenity decision as a yardstick to judge the behaviour of consumers after exposure, and perhaps to support the familiar defence arguments that the items prosecuted "pale into insignificance" or are "a drop in the ocean" besides lurid sexuality oozing from the top shelf of newsagents, Channel 5, women's magazines and satellite television.[39] The collective experience of 12 arbitrarily chosen people is assumed to provide a degree of familiarity with popular reading trends, with what is deemed acceptable on television and at cinemas and on the internet and with the degree of explicitness that can be found in publications on sale at local newsagents. A publisher is not, however, permitted to argue that he should be acquitted because his publication is less obscene than others that are freely circulated.[40]

The 1959 Act does, however, provide for two situations in which comparisons are both permissible and highly relevant. Under s.2(5), it may be that a defendant has "no reasonable cause to suspect" the obscenity of a book that he has not personally examined because he knows that similar books have been acquitted, or are freely circulated. And under the public good defence it may be relevant to the jury's task of evaluating the merit of a particular book to compare it with other books of the same kind, and to hear expert evidence about the current climate of permissiveness in relation to this kind of literature. This exception was recognised by Mr Justice Byrne in the *Lady Chatterley* case when he permitted expert witnesses to compare the novel with other works by Lawrence and various twentieth-century writers, and to discuss the standards for describing sexual matters reflected in modern literature. At one point in the trial he agreed that:

> "other books may be considered, for two reasons, firstly, upon the question of the literary merit of a book which is the subject-matter of the indictment . . . [where] it is necessary to compare that book with other books upon the question of literary merit. Secondly . . . other books are relevant to the climate of literature."[41]

Where a public good defence is raised, juries may be asked to make comparisons in order to evaluate the real worth of the publication at stake, and they may be told by experts about the state of informed contemporary opinion on subjects dealt with in those publications.

---

[39] A robust example of the Court of Appeal applying liberal contemporary standards—albeit to reject a hypothetical attempt by a sex line operator to avoid payment of its advertising bill by arguing that its own explicit adverts were obscene (and hence the contract was unlawful), is found in Simon Brown L.J.'s judgment in *Armhouse Lee Ltd v Chappell*, *The Times*, August 7, 1996.

[40] *R. v Reiter* [1954] 2 Q.B. 16; *R. v Elliott* [1996] 1 Cr. App. R. 432, CA.

[41] Rolph, *Lady Chatterley*, p.127.

Prohibited acts

There are two separate charges that may be brought in respect of **4–016**
obscene publications. It is an offence to *publish* an obscene article
contrary to the Obscene Publications Act of 1959, and it is an
offence to *have an obscene article for publication for gain*, contrary to
the Obscene Publications Act of 1964. A charge under the 1959 Act
requires some *act* of publication, such as sale to a customer or giving
an obscene book to a friend. There must be some evidence
connecting the defendant with movement of the article into
another's hands.[42] Mere possession of an obscene book will not
satisfy the definition of publication in s.1(3)(b), which governs both
Acts:

> "For the purposes of this Act a person publishes an article who
> (a) distributes, circulates, sells, lets on hire, gives, or lends it, or
> who offers it for sale or for letting on hire; or (b) in the case of
> an article containing or embodying matter to be looked at or a
> record, shows, plays or projects it, or where the matter is data
> stored electronically, transmits that data."[43]

The Act relates to an "article" which is widely defined by s.1(2) to
mean,

> "any description of article containing or embodying matter to be
> read or looked at or both, any sound record, and any film or
> other record of a picture or pictures".

Obscene negatives were included in the definition in 1964, and
prints processed from them which are found in the defendant's
possession for gain can be the subject of prosecution, irrespective of
who may own the copyright.[44] The 1959 Obscene Publications Act
definition catches forms of communication which were unheard of in
1959: the Court of Appeal made this clear in 1980 when deciding
that video cassettes were within it because they were articles which
produced pictures and sounds.[45] This decision was relied upon in the
1997 case of *R. v Fellows* which held that a computer hard disk was
an "article" and that data stored in the disk was "published" for the
purpose of the Act (i.e. was "shown played or projected") to those
who gained access to a "child porn" internet archive by means of a
password.[46] Anything that "ordinary literate persons" in 1959 would

---

[42] *Att-Gen's Reference No. 2 of 1975*, fn.24 above.
[43] The references to data were added by Sch.9 to the Criminal Justice and Public
Order Act 1994 to cover electronic transmission of obscene material.
[44] *R. v Taylor* (1995) Cr. App. R. 131.
[45] *Att-Gen's Reference No. 5 of 1980* [1980] 3 All E.R. 816.
[46] *R. v Fellows* [1997] 1 Cr. App. R. 244, CA.

understand as communicating words or pictures was capable of being the subject of prosecution, however new the technology. This means that anything which titillates through ocular or aural reception is covered: the only "articles" excluded would be those which provide erotic experiences by smell or taste or movement (a chair which offered a sensual electronic massage would not be an "article" for the purposes of the Act).

4–017   An article is "published" when matter recorded on it is included in a television or sound programme, and there is a defence for producers and participants who are unaware that a programme they are involved with might include obscene material, or that their material might be published in a way that would attract liability. Any seizure of recordings by police, or any prosecution, requires the consent of the Director of Public Prosecutions.[47]

Those who participate in or promote obscene publications are entitled to acquittal if they intend their work to be "published" in a manner that falls outside the Act, e.g. because they genuinely believe that distribution will be confined to a select group immune from corruption or to those countries that do not have laws against obscene publications. A film producer, for example, who makes a "blue movie" in England and then takes the negative to Denmark for development and ensuing commercial distribution is unlikely to be held to have committed an offence under English law, unless he is aware of plans to re-import copies for sale in Britain. But the prosecution is not put to specific proof that obscene material is intended for publication in a manner that will infringe the Act, if such publication is a common-sense inference from the circumstances of production. In *R. v Salter and Barton* two actors were charged with aiding and abetting by performing in an obscene movie, but they denied any knowledge of the producer's purpose or his distribution plans. The Court of Appeal held that ignorance could not avail them, although positive belief in a limited publication would have provided a defence. They could also have avoided liability if, more than two years before the prosecution was brought, they had taken some step to disassociate themselves from the continuing distribution of the film.[48]

The question of whether production or possession of magazines or films that might be considered obscene if published on the home market is in breach of the law if they are destined for export abroad will depend upon their likely effect on readers and viewers in the country of distribution. The courts cannot apply British standards of morality in such cases: they must consider the standards prevailing in the country of export, and the class of persons in that country who are likely to obtain them. The House of Lords has accepted that in some cases of this kind the court will not have sufficient evidence to

---

[47] Broadcasting Act 1990, s.162 and Sch.15.
[48] *R. v Salter & Barton* [1976] Crim. L.R. 514.

form an opinion: since the burden of proof rests upon the prosecution, there should be an acquittal. The same result should be achieved if evidence is received that the material is acceptable under the laws of the country for which it is destined.[49]

It is an offence in England to design, advertise or sell passwords to an obscene internet website, even if it is located abroad: the offending scenes are "published" under s.1(3)(b) when downloaded to the desk-top computers of password holders.[50] On the *Sulier & Barton* principle it should not be an offence to store images on a website abroad, honestly believing that they would not be transmitted back to Britain.

The public good defence

Section 4 of the Act provides that the defendant to an obscenity **4–018** charge "shall not be convicted"—despite the fact that he has been found to have published an obscene article—if "publication of the article in question is justified as being for the public good . . .". The ground upon which the defence may be made out is that publication, in the case of books and magazines, is "in the interests of science, literature, art or learning, or of other objects of general concern". The ground for exculpating plays and films is somewhat narrower: they must be "in the interests of drama, opera, ballet or any other art, or of literature or learning".[51] Section 3(1) of the Theatres Act 1968, the counterpart of s.4, was drafted in more restricted terms because the inclusion of "science" and of "other objects of general concern" was thought irrelevant to the protection of quality theatre: plays that could not be justified by reference to dramatic "art" or to "learning" were unlikely to be redeemed by any other feature. Television and radio programmes have the widest possible defences: the Broadcasting Act of 1990 combines the grounds of public good available for both books and films (Sch.15, para.5(2)).

"In the interests of"

The exculpatory grounds set out in s.4(1) might have been expressed **4–019** in terms of "merit", but public good is not served by merit alone. An article may be "in the interests of" literature and learning without being either literary or learned. Section 4(1) looks to the advancement of cultural and intellectual values, and the expert opinion as to the "merits of an article" must be able to relate to the broader question of "the interests of" art and science. A publication of obscene primitive art may lack objective merit, but nonetheless may

---

[49] *Gold Star Publications Ltd v DPP* [1981] 2 All E.R. 257.
[50] *R. v Waddon*, April 6, 2000, CA.
[51] Law Commission, *Report on Conspiracy and Criminal Law Reform, No. 76*, HMSO, 1976, Ch.3, paras 69–76.

be defended on the grounds of its contribution to art history. (The DPP once considered a complaint about the ancient drainage ditch at Cerne Abbas, which forms the outline of a giant with a truly giant-size erection. In the interests of history, and the interests of the local tourist trade, he declined the request to allow grass to grow strategically over the offending area.)

The *Oz* editors contended that although their "Schoolkids Issue" had no particular literary or artistic brilliance, its publication was "in the interests of" literature and art because it gave creative young-sters the opportunity to display their potential talents in a national magazine. The end product was in the interests of sociology, not because of any profundity in its contents, but because sociologists were interested in the results of the experiment of giving school-children an uncensored forum to air their grievances.

"Science, literature, art or learning"

4–020 The jury must decide as an issue of fact whether and to what extent obscene material serves the interests of any of these "intellectual or aesthetic values". The Court of Appeal has construed "learning" to mean "the product of scholarship . . . something whose inherent excellence is gained by the work of a scholar".[52] It follows that a publication cannot be defended under s.4 because of its value as a teaching aid, since this would require assessment of its effect upon readers' minds. A sex education booklet is not defensible because it provides good sex education, but if research has gone into its compilation, then no matter how ineffectual or misguided as an instructional aid, it possesses some inherent worth as "a product of scholarship". This result is hardly rational, but it represents a logical extension of the quest for intrinsic merit.

"Learning" overlaps with "science", which is defined in most dictionaries as "knowledge acquired by study". A publication may possess scientific interest if it adds to the existing body of knowledge or if it presents known facts in a systematic way. Recent legislation defines "science" to include the social sciences and medical research, and works with serious psychiatric, psychological or sociological interest would qualify for a public good defence. Studies of human sexual behaviour might contribute to scientific knowledge and even pornographic fantasies, if genuine and collected for a serious sociological purpose, could legitimately be included.

"Literature" is widely defined as "any printed matter", and the courts have been prepared to give copyright protection to the most pedestrian writing.[53] In the context of s.4, however, experts would be required to find some excellence of style or presentation to redeem the assumed tendency to corrupt. Excellence of prose style is not the

---

[52] *Att-Gen's Reference No. 3 of 1977* [1978] 1 W.L.R. 1123.
[53] See cases referred to in Ch.6.

only criterion for literary judgments, however, and books may be defended on the strength of wit, suspense, clarity, bombast or research if these qualities distinguish them in a particular genre of literature or in a particular period of literary history. Similarly, "art" comprehends the application of skill to any aesthetic subject, and is not conventionally confined to the production of beautiful images.[54]

In both the *Oz* and *Nasty Tales* cases underground comics were accepted as "art" for the purpose of a s.4 defence. One expert, the painter Felix Topolski, reminded the court that "unexpected elements, when brought together, produce an act of creation . . . I think one should accept that any visual performance if executed in earnest, is a branch of artistic creation."[55] In 1975 the New Zealand courts held that drawings of toilet fittings were artistic works—a conclusion that the surrealist school would never have doubted.[56]

"Other objects of general concern"

In *DPP v Jordan* the House of Lords ruled that the psychiatric health **4–021** of the community allegedly served by "therapeutic" pornography was not an "object of general concern" for the purposes of s.4. Their Lordships, horrified at the very thought that the promotion of masturbation could ever be for the public good, gagged sexologists and psychiatrists, including Professor Hans Eysenck, Dr. Edward de Bono and Reverend Chad Varah (founder of the Samaritans) who had been persuading juries up and down the country that sexual expressiveness was good for them. They declined to elucidate the phrase, beyond affirming that it had a "mobile" meaning, which changed in content as society changes, and that:

- it referred to objects of general concern similar to those aesthetic and intellectual values specifically enumerated in s.4;
- it could not comprehend any object that was served by direct impact of publication on the mind of likely readers;
- it related to "inherent personal values of a less transient character assumed, optimistically perhaps, to be of general concern".[57]

There are many objects that survive these three tests. Among the "objects of general concern" advanced on behalf of *Lady Chatterley's Lover* were its ethical and Christian merits: "I suppose the section is

---

[54] *Hensher (George) Ltd v Restawhile Upholstery (Lancs) Ltd* [1976] A.C. 64. See generally P. H. Karlen, "What is Art? A Sketch for a Legal Definition", 94 L.Q.R. 383.

[55] Tony Palmer, *The Trials of Oz* (Blond & Briggs, 1971), pp.170–171.

[56] *P. S. Johnson and Associates Ltd v Bucko Enterprises* [1975] 1 N.Z.L.R. 311.

[57] *DPP v Jordan* [1977] A.C. 699 at 719, *per* Lord Wilberforce.

sufficiently elastic to say that such evidence is admissible" remarked the judge, as he permitted the Bishop of Woolwich to testify to the book's contribution to human relations and to Christian judgments and values.[58] Other witnesses testified to its educational and sociological merits, and the editor of *Harper's Bazaar* was called as an expert on "popular literature". In the *Last Exit to Brooklyn* case the Court of Appeal conceded that "sociological or ethical merit" might be canvassed.[59] Other objects of general concern that have been relied upon at obscenity trials include journalism, humour, politics, philosophy, history, education and entertainment.

Expert evidence

4–022   Where a s.4 defence is available, experts can be called to give evidence, and indeed it is difficult to imagine the defence carrying any credibility without them. Strictly speaking, the Act requires the jury to conclude that the article is obscene before they consider the public good evidence, although in reality the impression made by the experts is likely to influence the decision on the obscenity issue. Expert opinion on the *effect* of the article is strictly inadmissible, but the Jesuitical distinction drawn by the courts between the "effect" of literature (which must not be canvassed) and its merits is wholly artificial. Literature and art have merit precisely *because* of their impact on the mind and their capacity to arouse emotions. Experts called under s.4 will inevitably give evidence about the theme and moral purpose of the work, and this evidence will be relevant, as a matter of common sense if not of law, to the question of whether it depraves or corrupts.

In certain cases the courts have permitted experts to be called by the prosecution and the defence to assist the jury in relation to the obscenity question if the subject-matter of the work or its impact upon a restricted class of consumer is not likely to be within the experience of the ordinary person. When a book about the pleasures of cocaine was prosecuted for obscenity, scientific evidence was called to acquaint the jury with the property of the drug and its likely effects, so that they could decide (it being assumed they would not themselves have experienced cocaine) whether, if the book did encourage experimentation, the behaviour of the experimenters could be characterised as depraved and corrupt.[60] Similarly, when a company that had manufactured chewing gum cards for distribution to very young children was alleged to have depraved their minds with scenes of violence, child psychiatrists were called to give expert opinion as to the likely impact of the cards on the mind and behaviour of children in that age group.[61]

---

[58] Rolph, *Lady Chatterley*, p.73.
[59] *R. v Calder & Boyars*, fn.18 above, at 171.
[60] *R. v Skirving* [1985] 2 All E.R. 705.
[61] *DPP v A. & EC Chewing Gum Ltd* [1968] 1 Q.B. 159.

These precedents were taken further in the *Niggaz With Attitude* case. Dr Guy Culmberbatch, a former Home Office expert on the effects of pornography, had been commissioned by Island Records to carry out field research on the effects of listening to NWA albums, which he did, with the co-operation of large numbers of disc jockeys, school and university students and members of rap clubs. His study was helpful in identifying that they understood the lyrics in the context of American black experience, and not as any encouragement to antisocial behaviour in England. There is no reason in principle why this sort of evidence by social scientists should not be called by parties who are "showing cause" under s.3 as to why an article should not be destroyed, and are consequently not bound by the rules of evidence in criminal cases.

Prosecution practice

The enforcement of the obscenity laws is now directed largely at 4–023 "hard core pornography". This has no legal definition, although juries are often told that "pornography is like an elephant. You cannot define it, but you know it when you see it".[62] It has become more and more indistinct, however, with the influx of European and American hardcore DVDs and magazines, so that prosecutions (as distinct from forfeiture orders) are now mainly confined to pornography featuring children or violent or grotesque acts. There is an acceptance by the DPP that pictures of "normal" heterosexual or homosexual behaviour will no longer be convicted by juries. This marks a twenty first century change: DPP officials have always had their lines to draw, and since the *Oz* decision in 1972 they drew them consistently at the male groin: nudity was acceptable and even artistic, but to erect a penis was to provoke a prosecution. But after the BBFC was required by the courts to change its guidelines in 2000 so as to permit 18R videos showing actual sexual intercourse, the DPP became more relaxed about erections in the pages of "top-shelf" magazines, so long as orgasm was forever delayed. (For modern censors, it was a case of Emission Impossible.)[63] The decision which caused the 18R revolution, and thus had a direct effect on liberalising "top shelf" erotica, was that of Hooper J. in *R. v Video Appeals committee Ex p. BBFC*.[64]

There is still an official distaste for semen, the sight of which upsets the CPS and makes the film censors at the BBFC reach for their scissors to cut, rather than cut to, the climax.[65] This, like the

---

[62] Judicial likening of obscenity to the definition of an elephant appears to have begun in 1964 with Justice Potter Stewart in *Jacobellis v Ohio*, 378 U.S. 184 at 197.

[63] Decision of Hooper J. in *R. v Video Appeals Committee Ex p. BBFC* (2000) EMLR 850.

[64] [2000] E.M.L.R. 850.

[65] The French film, *The Pornographer* was only given an 18 certificate if the producers agreed to remove all traces of semen from the face of a woman after oral sex. See Fenwick and Philipson, *Media Freedom under the Human Rights Act* (OUP, 2006), p.436.

embargo on erections, is probably explicable in psychiatric terms as a hang-up of male censors. Other scenes in movies and magazines that are likely to provoke a prosecution include "fisting", copraphilia, necrophilia, bestiality and all acts of torture depicted in a sexual context. The DPP has not yet had the imagination or gumption to prosecute fanatical Islamist websites or "martyrdom videos" for obscenity, although they would precisely satisfy the definition of material that tends to deprave and corrupt by encouraging vulnerable people to kill themselves and others. Muslim clerics who preach hatred of homosexuals, and protestors who call for the killing of Salman Rushdie and the Danish cartoonists, should equally be prosecuted for using obscene and indecent language in public. There are many academics and other critics who claim that the Obscene Publications Act is unworkable, but the real problem is that it has been so often made to work against the wrong targets.

The House of Lords has held that the arousing of libidinous thoughts falls squarely within the mischief aimed at by the Act,[66] but common-or-garden pornography is usually made the subject of forfeiture proceedings in which no conviction is recorded and no punishment (other than the destruction of the goods) can be imposed. These "section 3" proceedings (so called because the forfeiture code is contained in s.3 of the Obscene Publications Act 1959) serve little purpose other than to waste the time of the police and the local magistrates' courts. An order for forfeiture made by justices in one district is of no use as a precedent in others. The publishers of "top shelf" magazines cheerfully accept occasional stock losses, usually without even bothering to intervene (which s.3 entitles them to do) to argue that their goods should not be destroyed.

The essential quality of pornography is its breach of social taboos, hence its frequent references to behaviour that most consumers would never wish to emulate in real life—incest, bestiality, necrophilia, coprophilia and so on. The real obscenity of bestiality pictures lies not in their effects on readers' minds, but in the circumstances surrounding their production. Procuring women for intercourse with animals would seem to be an indefensible case of human exploitation, which could be prosecuted and punished under the Sexual Offences Act. The Cinematograph Films (Animals) Act of 1937 may also be relevant: it prohibits the exhibition of films the making of which involves cruelty to animals. This obscure piece of legislation is faithfully applied by the BBFC, which has ordered cuts in a number of Walt Disney films and videos with scenes that may have involved infliction of cruelty on animals. It should not, however, suppress films that are commentaries on cruel sports. The distributors of bizarre strains of pictorial pornography depicting extreme

---

[66] *DPP v Whyte* [1972] 3 All E.R. 12.

sexual violence, simulated necrophilia and human excretory functions are almost invariably convicted. Juries, inclined to support
freedom for voyeurs, are less keen to promote freedom for ghouls.

Drugs

There is no indication in the debates that surrounded the Obscene   **4–024**
Publications Act that "obscenity" pertained to anything but matters
of sex. United States legislation and practice is so confined, but in
Britain the courts have interpreted the statutory definition of
"obscene" to encompass encouragements to take dangerous drugs
and to engage in violence.

The first case to push the notion of "obscenity" beyond the
bounds of sex arose from forfeiture proceedings in 1965 against
Cain's Book, a novel by Alex Trocchi that dealt with the life of a
New York heroin addict. In the ensuing Divisional Court case, it was
held that:

> "there was a real danger that those into whose hands the book
> came might be tempted at any rate to experiment with drugs and
> get the favourable sensations highlighted by the book".[67]

Cain's Book contained seductive descriptions of heroin consumption, but cannabis smoking cannot be classed as a "depraved and
corrupt" activity;

> The publishers of some 20 books about prohibited drugs—
> *Cooking with Cannabis*, *The Pleasures of Cocaine*, *How to Grow
> Marijuana Indoors under Lights* and the like—were acquitted
> after a four-week trial at the Old Bailey. The prosecution failed
> to convince the jury that taking or cultivating cannabis was a
> depraved activity, given the widespread use of the drug, or that
> books that provided factual information about both the pains
> and the pleasures of harder drugs would be likely to encourage
> readers to experiment. Subsequently, however, the publishers of
> a pamphlet entitled *Attention Coke Lovers* were convicted
> because it exuded enthusiasm for "freebasing"—a highly dan-
> gerous method of inhaling a chemically-enhanced concentration.
> The Court of Appeal upheld the trial judge's decision to permit
> scientific experts to be called to explain the effects of cocaine to
> enable the jury to come to a proper conclusion as to the effect of
> the drug.[68]

The distinction between, on the one hand, providing factual
information about drugs and, on the other, encouraging their use

---

[67] *Calder v Powell* [1965] 1 Q.B. 509 at p.515.
[68] *R. v Skirving* [1985] Q.B. 819.

can be difficult to draw. Any publication that deals with drug-taking would be well advised to emphasise both the physical dangers and the criminal penalties that attach to drug usage. The rule against "highlighting favourable sensations" has never been applied to novelists: the favourable descriptions of opium-taking in the *Count of Monte Cristo* and the apparently productive use of cocaine by Sherlock Holmes have not led to obscenity prosecutions.

Violence

4–025 Any material that combines violence with sexual explicitness is a candidate for prosecution. Yet there are many gradations between a friendly slap and a stake through the heart, and most "spanking" magazines escape indictment. "Video-nasties", however, that combine pornography with powerful scenes of rape and terror have been successfully prosecuted. More difficulty is experienced with the depiction of violence in non-sexual contexts. The Divisional Court in one case approved the prosecution of a manufacturer of childrens' swap cards depicting scenes of battle, on the theory that they were capable of depraving young minds by provoking emulation of the violence portrayed.[69] In the *Last Exit* case the Court of Appeal confirmed that the test of obscenity could encompass written advocacy of brutal violence.[70]

Horror publications

4–026 In one respect the obscenity formula has been specifically adapted to outlaw depictions of non-sexual violence that might prove harmful to children. In 1955 Parliament sought to prohibit the importation and sale of American "horror comics", which had been blamed by psychiatrists for causing an upsurge in juvenile delinquency. The Children and Young Persons (Harmful Publications) Act 1955 was designed, in the words of the Solicitor-General, to prevent "the state of mind that might be induced in certain types of children by provoking a kind of morbid brooding or ghoulishness or mental ill-health".[71] It prohibits the printing, publication or sale of:

> "any book, magazine or other like work which is of a kind likely to fall into the hands of children or young persons and consists wholly or mainly of stories told in pictures (with or without the addition of written matter), being stories portraying
>
> (a) the commission of crimes; or
> (b) acts of violence or cruelty; or

---

[69] *DPP v A & BC Chewing Gum Ltd* [1968] 1 Q.B. 159.
[70] *R. v Calder & Boyars Ltd* [1969] 1 Q.B. 151.
[71] *Hansard*, H.C. Debs [1955] Vol. 539, Col. 6063. And see Martin Barker, *A Haunt of Fears: The History of the British Horror Comics Campaign* (Pluto, 1984).

(c) incidents of a repulsive or horrible nature;

in such a way that the work as a whole would tend to corrupt a child or young person into whose hands it might fall."

Although the measure was perceived as urgent and important at the time it was passed, there have been no prosecutions. Criminal proceedings require the consent of the Attorney-General, although this safeguard does not apply to imported comics, which may be seized and forfeited at the instance of customs officials. Southampton magistrates ordered the release of *The Adventures of Conan the Barbarian* after evidence from a child psychiatrist that the Conan legend would be perceived as moral and even romantic by children inured to the adventures of *Starsky and Hutch*.

Sex shops

The Indecent Displays (Control) Act, 1981 and sections of the Local **4–027** Government (Miscellaneous Provisions) Act of 1982 apply to these "adult only" centres. Section 2 of the latter legislation gives local authorities power to insist that sex shops and cinemas within their jurisdiction be licensed. Although the grant of a licence does not confer an immunity from prosecution for obscenity in relation to material stocked in the shop, it has meant in practice that authorities proceed more cautiously by way of inspection, rather than by seizure. The new licensing system has reduced the outlets for sex magazines and videos, as local councils may decide how many (if any) licences to grant on the basis of the needs and character of the locality in question. A shop will require a licence if it occupies premises:

"used for a business which consists to a significant degree of selling, hiring, exchanging, lending, displaying or demonstrating:

(a) sex articles; or
(b) other things intended for use in connection with, or for the purpose of stimulating or encouraging—

(i) sexual activity; or
(ii) acts of force or restraint which are associated with sexual activity."

This section applies only to sex shops: it does not cover the premises used by publishers to prepare and edit magazines or videos that deal with sexual activity. Nor would it cover general newsagencies or bookshops that stock small amounts of "adult" material— although the concept of "sex articles" is widely defined to encompass books, magazines, videos, records and films dealing with sexual subjects. The Divisional Court has ruled that the "significant degree of business" test exempts ordinary newsagents and corner stores whose sales of such items form a part of their turnover.[72] There is no

---

[72] *Lambeth Borough Council v Grewal* (1995) 82 Cr. App. R. 301, QBD.

requirement that these items should be "indecent": if they deal with sexual behaviour and their sale is a significant part of the business of the establishment, the shopkeeper will require a local authority licence. It is an offence to operate a sex shop without a licence or to breach a licence condition.[73]

Unless they sell child porn or extreme magazines of the kind which might feature unsimulated violence or torture, sex shops are unlikely to be the subject of prosecution and even in that event could claim protection from Art.10 as a result of the decision in *Sherer v Switzerland*. The Commission condemned the conviction of a sex shop, open only to adults, which sold homosexual erotica. It ruled that "where no adult is confronted unintentionally or against his will with filmed matter, there must be particularly compelling reasons to justify an interference."

In 2007 the House of Lords confirmed, in *Belfast City Council v Miss Behavin' Ltd*, that hard porn vended in sex shops is protected by Art.10, although the right is engaged at a relatively low level.[74]

Child involvement

4–028 Undoubtedly the greatest concern over sexually explicit publications is the prospect of the involvement of young people, either as consumers or as models. This concern is reflected in the 1959 Act by its reference to the circumstances of the publication and the likely readership. The test of obscenity varies with the class of persons likely to read or see the publication. Instead of imposing censorship at the point of distribution, by making the actual sale of erotic material to children a crime, it must be established that the material on trial is *aimed* at impressionable young people. The case of the chewing gum cards illustrates how material that could be considered harmless if sold to adults by inclusion in cigarette cartons may be made the subject of obscenity proceedings if it is marketed in children's chewing gum packets.

No mercy can be expected in the courts for those who involve young persons, even with their consent, in modelling sessions for sexually explicit photographs. Section 1(1) of the Indecency with Children Act 1960 provides that:

> "any person who commits an act of gross indecency with or towards a child under the age of fourteen, or who incites a child under that age to commit such an act with him or another, shall be liable on conviction on indictment to imprisonment . . ."

This provision would cover most cases in which children were encouraged to pose for erotic pictures, although the requirement of

---

[73] The prosecution must first prove the defendant's intention to do so: *Westminster City Council v Croyolgrange Ltd* [1986] 2 All E.R. 353.

[74] *Belfast City Council v Miss Behavin' Ltd* [2007] UKHL 18. See *Stop Press* section.

some indecent action "with or towards" the child may arguably exclude photographic sessions in which an indivdual child poses provocatively without any physical contact with, or direction from, the photographer or procurer.[75] The prosecution must prove that the defendant did not believe the child to be 14 or over.[76]

The Protection of Children Act 1978

The gap in statutory protection for children of 14 and 15 was closed **4–029** in 1978 by the Protection of Children Act. Section 1 of the Act makes it an offence, punishable by up to 10 years in prison[77]:

> "(a) to take, or permit to be taken, or to make any indecent photo-graph or pseudo-photographs of a child (meaning in this Act under the age of 16); or
>
> (b) to distribute or show such indecent photographs or pseudo-photographs; or
>
> (c) to have in his possession such indecent photographs, with a view to their being distributed or shown by himself or others; or
>
> (d) to publish or cause to be published any advertisement likely to be understood as conveying that the advertiser distributes or shows such indecent photographs, or intends to do so."

A defendant "distributes" photographs within the meaning of this section if he merely shows them to another, without any desire for gain. "Indecent photographs" include films, film negatives and any form of video recording and "data which is stored on a computer disc or by other electronic means which is capable of conversion into a photograph". The advent of the internet is signalled by the awkward concept of the "pseudo-photograph" clumsily defined as "an image, whether made by computer graphics or otherwise howsoever, which appears to be a photograph". This phraseology forced the Court of Appeal to decide that a collage—a photograph of the head of a young girl sello-taped onto a photograph of a woman's body—was not within the section since it appeared to be (and was) two photos rather than one, although had it been photocopied then the image may have been within the Act.[78] Computer-generated images of different body parts may fall within s.7(8):

> "If the impression conveyed by a pseudo-photograph is that the person shown is a child, the pseudo-photograph shall be treated for all purposes of this Act as showing a child and so shall a pseudo-photograph where the predominant impression con-veyed is that the person shown is a child notwithstanding that some of the physical characteristics are those of an adult."

---

[75] *R. v Sutton* [1977] 1 W.L.R. 1086, at 1089.

[76] *B v DPP* [2000] 2 W.L.R. 452.

[77] Increased from an original maximum of three years by s.41 of the Criminal Justice and Court Services Act 2000.

[78] *Atkins v DPP* [2000] 1 W.L.R. 1427.

The offences must be construed to relate to real and human children: obscene images of Rupert Bear (hero of the *Oz* trial) or of Bart Simpson, Rugrats and other cartoon juveniles are not prohibited, other than by the law of copyright.

The 1978 Act is effectively deployed against those who use computers to deliver child pornography. Anyone who consciously downloads such an image from the internet "makes" a photograph for the purposes of s.1(1)(a) and will be guilty if he deliberately prints them out, even if the internet site where they were uplinked is abroad.[79] (Ageing popstar Gary Glitter pleaded guilty to this offence in 2000, and received a four-month sentence for material kept for personal use.) Providing a "password" to access such data is a form of "showing" it.[80] Even accessing a forbidden image on the Internet without downloading it can constitute an offence, on the ground that the image would be created within the computer's cache, so long as the defendant knows that the image would be automatically stored.[81] The cases demonstrate that the courts will ignore technical or legislative distinctions in order to effectuate Parliament's intent to punish every new way in which sexual images of children may be exploited. These decisions prima facie breach Art.8 of the European Convention, which guarantees respect for privacy, but the interference will probably be justified "for the protection of health or morals, or for the protection of the rights and freedoms of others".

4–030   There is no defence to s.1(a) other than that the photographs are not indecent; or, if indecent, do not depict persons under 16; or that the accused in any event played no part in their production. The prosecution does not even have to prove that the defendant knew the child was under 16, and so paediatric evidence as to the age of the child is neither required nor admissible.[82] Section 1(d) does not even require the photographs on offer to be themselves indecent— an advertiser is guilty if his wording is "likely to be understood as conveying" a willingness to sell or show nude pictures of children within the prohibited age group. If the charge is laid under s.1(b) or (c), however, the distributor or exhibitor is entitled to an acquittal if he can establish on the balance of probabilities:

- that he had a legitimate reason for distributing or showing the photographs or (as the case may be) having them in his possession; or
- that he had not himself seen the photographs and did not know nor had any cause to suspect them to be indecent.[83] The defendant must show that he had no reason to suspect

---

[79] *R. v Bowden* [2000] 2 W.L.R. 1083.
[80] *R. v Fellows* (1997) Cr. App. R. 244.
[81] *R. v Jason Smith* [2002] 1 Cr. App. R. 13.
[82] *R. v Land* [1998] 1 Cr. App. R. 301.
[83] The Protection of Children Act 1978, s.1(4).

the photographs were indecent, *not* that he had no cause to
expect they were indecent photographs of children.[84]

The test of indecency

The courts have been unable to provide a meaningful definition of **4–031**
"indecent", short of "offending against recognised standards of
propriety" or "shocking, disgusting and revolting ordinary people".
The leading authority in cases concerning photographs of children
involved the decision that *Boys are Boys Again*, a book comprising
122 photographs of naked boys, was an indecent import. Mr Justice
Bridge accepted that the publication was not obscene, and would not
infringe the current standards of decency if it depicted naked
children without sexual overtones. But he held that this publication,
although borderline, lacked innocence:

> ". . . the conclusion that I reach is that if the book is looked at
> as a whole . . . the very essence of the publication, the reason for
> publishing it, is to focus attention on the male genital organs. It
> is a series of photographs in the great majority of which the
> male genitals, sometimes in close-up, are the focal point of the
> picture . . . they aim to be interesting pictures of boys' penises
> . . .".[85]

This precedent, although unreported, has been of crucial importance in limiting the Protection of Children Act offence to pictures
with some element of lewdness or sexual provocation. It was read to
the House of Commons by the Minister of State for the Home
Office to underscore a promise that "indecency" would not be
interpreted loosely: "that is exactly how I would expect the issue
under the Bill to be decided", he said of Bridge J.'s approach, "I
think, frankly, that there is no danger that ordinary family snapshots,
or legitimate sex education material, would be caught by the terms
of the Bill".[86] So when newsreader Julia Somerville's "ordinary
family snapshots" of her children in the bath were processed by
Boots and delivered, in an unpleasant breach of her family privacy,
to the local police, no action (apart from leaking the story to the
press) was taken. The *Sun & Health* case ruling was revived in 2001:

> The Saatchi gallery opened a photographic exhibition "I am a Cam-
> era", which was attended (at the instigation of *News of the World*) by
> Scotland Yard's paedophile squad. They threatened that unless the

---

[84] *R. v Matrix* [1997] Crim. L.R. 901, CA.
[85] *Commissioners of Customs and Excise v Sun & Health Ltd*, March 29, 1973
(unreported) Royal Courts of Justice, transcript, pp.5 and 6.
[86] *R. v Graham-Kerr* (1989) 88 Cr. App. R. 302; *R. v Smethurst, The Times*, April 13,
2001, CA.

gallery removed certain photographs, they would seize them and prosecute the gallery. One picture showed a five-year-old boy urinating in the snow by the side of an alpine road, and the other showed him (with his sister) naked on a Caribbean beach. The latter was on the cover of an expensive book which had been published to coincide with the exhibition: its publisher was threatened with prosecution unless it was withdrawn from sale. The police claimed the pictures would be of interest to paedophiles, as undoubtedly they would. However, the DPP decided that no action could or should be taken: applying the *Sun and Health* test, they were not "indecent" because they had not been posed provocatively (the photographer, in fact, was the children's mother) and there was no element of lewdness or erotic detail in these "ordinary family snapshots". The DPP's decision was justified, shortly after it was made, by the Chief Justice's comments in *Smethurst* (see below). Other reasons given for not prosecuting included a concern that the exhibitor and the book publisher could raise a "legitimate reason" defence.[87]

The "legitimate reason" defence

4–032   In deciding whether the photograph is indecent the jury is not permitted to hear evidence about the defendant's motive for taking it. The only intention that is relevant is the deliberate intention to take a photograph: whether it is indecent depends solely upon whether the jury is satisfied that the resultant picture is a breach of recognised standards of propriety.[88] That decision, however, must at least be informed by the age of the child: this may play a part in the question of whether the picture is a breach of recognised standards of propriety. Thus a photograph of a topless female model in a provocative pose that may not be accounted indecent if the model is above the age of consent may be held to infringe the Act once the jury realises that the model is 14—much younger than she looks.[89] It is doubtful whether expert evidence would be admitted as to the artistic merit of the photograph, unless this were advanced as a "legitimate reason" for showing or distributing it. There could be no objection in principle to such a defence being raised to justify an exhibition of photographs of historical interest, or pictures included in a documentary about the evils of child pornography. Photographic evidence of the torture or maltreatment of children may be highly indecent, but should not be the subject matter of a prosecution under this section where the purpose of the exhibition is legitimately to arouse anger or compassion.

---

[87] Lord Harris of Greenwich, May 18, 1978, *Hansard* Vol. 392, No. 81, col. 563 and see the Minister's speech during the third reading debate: "the test of indecency already exists to separate photographs which are offensive from those which are innocent or which have been taken with a clinical rather than a prurient approach". *Hansard*, H.L., Vol. 394, No. 103, col. 334.

[88] See the *Guardian*, March 10, 2001, pp.3 and 16 and March 16, 2001, p.1.

[89] *R. v Owen* (1988) 86 Cr. App. R. 291.

The legitimate reason defence is new to the criminal law, but it has a potentially wide application. It should protect investigative journalists who acquire indecent photographs of children in order to expose a corruption racket, so long as they do not pay money to procure the taking of the photographs that would not have otherwise come into existence. What constitutes a "legitimate reason" is in every case a question of fact: the Court of Appeal conceded in 2000 that it would protect a genuine researcher, although "a measure of scepticism" would be appropriate towards academics who stock-pile such material.[90] The "legitimate reason" defence received an important acknowledgment by the CPS in 2001 when giving reasons for the refusal to prosecute the Saatchi gallery over its "I am a Camera" exhibition. The DPP accepted submissions made on behalf of the gallery that the artistic merit of the pictures provided a "legitimate reason" to exhibit them in a reputable art gallery and to publish them in an expensive (£42) art book recording the show. Expert evidence of artistic merit would clearly be relevant if a defendant wished to raise such a defence in court.

There is no logic at all in allowing a legitimate reason defence to a distributor or exhibitor, but not a taker, of photographs that are found to be indecent. The decision in *Graham-Kerr* that the circumstances of the photography and the motivation of the photographer are irrelevant means that a paediatrician who photographs children's genitalia for legitimate medical purposes has no defence to a prosecution. The "safeguard" is that a prosecution can be brought only by the DPP, but a bad law is never justified by the hope that it will be sensibly enforced. Doctors will not be prosecuted, but "artists" who pose children provocatively are at risk. Photographers have no defence if the jury finds their pictures indecent, unless they can establish that they took the picture by accident or that the child just happened to run in front of the camera. When the *Graham-Kerr* rule excluding *mens rea* was challenged as inconsistent with Arts 8 and 10 of the ECHR, the Court of Appeal agreed that,

"No one could possibly suggest that a family taking photographs of their own children (naked) in the ordinary way would be a situation where it would be appropriate to prosecute" but declined to reinterpret the legislation or declare it incompatible.[91] A strict liability offence was the only way to protect children from exploitation, although an "inappropriate prosecution",

(such as was threatened by Scotland Yard against the Saatchi gallery) might well be held to infringe Art.10 and/or be stayed as an abuse of process.

[90] *Atkins v DPP* [2000] 1 W.L.R. 1427.
[91] *R. v Smethurst, The Times*, April 13, 2001.

Films

4–033 Section 7(2) of the Act defines "indecent photograph" to include "an indecent photograph comprised in a film", while s.7(3) provides:

> "Photographs (including those comprised in film) shall, if they show children and are indecent, be treated for all purposes of this Act as indecent photographs of children."

This section has complicated the task of the British Board of Film Classification when faced with feature films that include child actors in immodest or disgusting scenes. Such scenes are deemed, by s.7(3), to constitute "indecent photographs of a child" even if the child is not participating in, or even aware of, the indecency. A plot that calls for a child to discover parents making love may be difficult to film or to distribute without contravention of the Act, and the artistic merit or overall purpose will not redeem an offending scene. One orgy scene from the film *Caligula* was cut by the BBFC because among the onlookers were women suckling babies. The newborn infants were sleeping in blissful ignorance of the catamite revels, but technically the scene contravened the Act, because it was indecent and it depicted persons under 16. The Hollywood vogue for casting child actors and actresses in major "adult" movies means such films may require cuts before distribution in the United Kingdom, although much will depend on the cinematic merit of the film. In 1999 the BBFC courageously gave *Lolita* an "18" certificate: its scenes of pubescent sexuality were played by an actress over 16 and were not indecent in any exploitative sense, being redeemed by the integrity of the film (and the acting of Jeremy Irons). In the same year the BBFC finally agreed to classify *The Exorcist* as fit for video release despite some bad language from the "possessed" child: films which became classics (*The Exorcist* was released in 1973) cannot forever be denied the seal of BBFC approval.

Advertisements

4–034 Section l(d) affects film and magazine titles, and requires careful vetting of advertising copy. Even if the product itself does not infringe the Act, "any advertisement likely to be understood as conveying that the advertiser distributes or shows such indecent photographs" may be prosecuted, without the benefit of a "legitimate reason" defence. Films with titles that evoke the thought of under-age sex will be difficult to publicise. In the week that the Act came into force, one West End cinema pointedly changed the name of its current offering from *Schoolgirls* to *18–Year-Old Schoolgirls*.

Possession

4–035 In 1988 Parliament created a new offence of *possessing* an indecent picture of a child (Criminal Justice Act, s.160). This is another example of the law relating to obscenity extending to material confined to the privacy of the home, without publication or possession for gain. Another unattractive feature of the offence was added in 2000: the maximum penalty was increased to five years' imprisonment and/or an unlimited fine.[92] The defendant at least is permitted to raise the legitimate reason defence or to maintain that although the photograph was in his possession he had not viewed it and had no reason to suspect its indecency. He is also entitled to an acquittal if he can prove that the photograph was sent to him unsolicited "and that he did not keep it for an unreasonable time". This places a duty upon unwary recipients of child pornography in the post either to destroy it or to hand it in at their local police station. This offence is a candidate for attack under the Human Rights Act, although it may be doubted whether British and European judges would follow the lead of the Constitutional Court of South Africa, which struck down a prohibition on merely possessing indecent matter as being incompatible with constitutional guarantees of free speech and personal privacy.[93] Nevertheless, it may be doubted whether the mere purchase and downloading for personal and private use of images from available websites (some of them constructed by the FBI for "sting" operations) can really justify a five year maximum prison sentence, even on the basis that the consumer, by soliciting the images, shares some vicarious responsibility for encouraging the exploitation of children. Prison sentences, at least for occasional downloadings, might be regarded as disproportionate: in such cases the worst punishment can be publicity consequent upon placement on the sex offender's register (a fate ironically suffered by Pete Townsend of *The Who*, who had alerted his generation to the danger through the character of "Uncle Ernie" in his 60s rock opera, *Tommy*). Over 7,000 otherwise law abiding British citizens have been caught through their credit card access of FBI "sting" websites and are in the process of being named and shamed by "Operation Ore". The use of such *agent provocateur* tactics raises an Art.8 issue and it is noteworthy (although the press has not noted it) that a number of persons arrested by this Operation have committed suicide prior to their trial.[94]

Procedures and penalties

The offence of obscenity on a conviction by a jury, carries a **4–036** maximum term of three years imprisonment and an unlimited fine.

Defendants may elect to be tried in magistrates' courts, where the penalty is reduced to a maximum of six months and/or a fine of

---

[92] s.41, Criminal Justice and Courts Service Act 2000.
[93] *Case v Minister of Security* (1997) 1 B.H.R.C. 541.
[94] The current sentencing approach is set out in *R v Oliver* (2003) 1 Cr.App.R. 28 and see A Gillespie, *Revisiting Bowden: Downloading Internet Images*, New Law Journal, June 3, 2005.

£5,000. Such an election is rarely made, because magistrates are prone to convict for this offence with little hesitation or regard for legal niceties. Juries, on the other hand, can be reluctant to convict in cases that do not involve children, violence or animals. Prosecuting authorities, mindful of the difficulties of jury trial, prefer to use the forfeiture procedure laid down by s.3 of the Obscene Publications Act, which entitles them to seize under warrant a stock of obscene material and have it destroyed at the nearest magistrates' court. Any person claiming an interest in the material may contest its forfeiture, but the procedure has little deterrent effect: the case is brought against the material, rather than its publishers, and has no criminal consequence whatsoever. Section 3 is often used by police and prosecuting authorities as a device for avoiding jury trial. If a publisher wished to contest a s.3 seizure before a jury (at the risk of a jail sentence if convicted) he can invoke a parliamentary assurance that this wish will be granted.[95]

It is open to question whether s.3 forfeiture orders conform with the European Convention on Human Rights. Although States are entitled to use obscenity laws to protect the morals of their citizens, penalties must be proportionate to the aim of restricting freedom of expression only to the extent that is strictly necessary in a democratic society. In *Handyside v UK* the European Court of Human Rights declined to find that s.3 was a breach of the Convention when it was used (with Handyside's consent) to test the lawfulness of circulating *The Little Red Schoolbook*, which gave controversial advice to schoolchildren about sex and drugs.[96] The decision might be otherwise if the forfeiture procedures were used to destroy original artwork. In 1988 the European Court upheld a Swiss decision that paintings held to be obscene when publicly exhibited should be deposited in a National Museum for safekeeping and limited viewing: the artist had been entitled to apply for their return, which he successfully did some years later. However, the court recognised a "special problem" in the confiscation of original artworks, and the implication from its decision is that a forfeiture order under s.3 requiring the destruction of such items would be an infringement of Art.10.[97]

4–037   The only two significant countries that jail first offenders for obscenity offences are Great Britain and the People's Republic of China. The Court of Appeal in 1982 bound itself to send all pornographers to prison, irrespective of their circumstances, with a good deal of huffing, puffing and bluffing:

"When news of this judgment reaches Soho, we think it is likely that there will be a considerable amount of stocktaking within

[95] Given by Sir Peter Rawlinson, the Solicitor-General, on July 7, 1964. See *Hansard*, col. 302, and Robertson, *Obscenity*, p.106.
[96] *Handyside v UK* [1976] E.H.R.R. 737.
[97] *Müller v Switzerland* (1988) 13 E.H.R.R. 212.

the next seventy-two hours, because if there is not, there is likely to be a depletion of the population of that area in the next few months."[98]

This overblown rhetoric has never been formally recanted,[99] although the principle that the court should pass the shortest possible sentence consistent with its public duty means that pornographers spend less time in prison.[100] Severe fines might be a more sensible alternative. Those involved in making or distributing child pornography can always expect a substantial prison sentence and anyone convicted of possessing or distributing or smuggling indecent pictures of children will be automatically placed on the sex offenders' register, and required to notify police of any changes of name or address. This is a punishment—registration will exclude them from jobs and include them in lists of potential suspects for other crimes—but it is one mandated by Parliament: the court has no discretion to make or to cancel such an order.[101]

The cinema and film censorship

Film censorship today operates on three different levels. The distributors of feature films may be prosecuted under the Obscene Publications Act if the Director of Public Prosecutions deems that audiences are likely to be "depraved and corrupted" by their offerings. Irrespective of the DPP's decision, district councils may refuse to license particular films for screening within their jurisdiction. Most councils rely upon the advice of the BBFC, which may insist upon cuts before certifying the films' fitness for the public screen or for certain age groups, or may refuse to issue any certificate at all. Councils may also limit the number of sex cinemas in their locality, or prohibit such cinemas altogether. Finally, customs authorities are empowered to refuse entry to any foreign film they choose to classify as "obscene". Neither theatre producers nor book publishers suffer institutional restrictions laid down by trade censors or local councillors, and the standards of acceptability imposed by these bodies are such that cinema censorship is more pervasive and more arbitrary than the limitations imposed upon many other forms of artistic expression. These standards are examined in Ch.15. The present discussion is concerned only with the application of the obscenity law to films and video-cassettes. It was not until 1977, after ingenious private prosecutors had belaboured film distributors with

4–038

---

[98] *Holloway* [1982] 4 Cr.App.R. (S) 128.

[99] Although the six month prison sentence for a first offence approved by the Chief Justice in *R. v Ibrahim* [1998] 1 Cr.App.R. (S) 157.

[100] A more realistic approach is evident from *Tunnicliffe & Greenwood* [1999] 2 Cr.App.R. (S) 88. See also *Lloyd & Ristic* February 3, 1992, CA.

[101] Sex Offenders Act 1997, s.1 and Sch.1.

the old common-law offence of holding indecent exhibitions, that the Obscene Publications Act was extended to cover the public screening of feature movies.[102] In 1979 the Court of Appeal extended the Act to video cassettes by interpreting its wide language to include a form of entertainment that had not been foreseen when the Act was passed.[103]

Limitations on prosecution

4–039 The Criminal Law Act 1977 abolishes the common law offences, including the conspiracies to corrupt public morals and to outrage public decency, in relation to cinemas.[104] The consent of the DPP is required for any prosecution of a feature film, denned as "a moving picture film of a width of not less than sixteen millimetres", and no order may be made to forfeit such a film unless it was seized pursuant to a warrant applied for by the DPP.[105] The Law Commission recommended these restrictions on proceedings to ensure that uniform standards applied throughout the country, and to discourage vexatious or frivolous prosecutions.[106]

Public good defence

4–040 The public good defence provided for films by s.53(6) of the Criminal Law Act is narrower than that which applies to books and magazines, omitting the grounds of "science" and "other objects of general concern" in favour of those objects enumerated in the Theatres Act, namely the interests of "drama, opera, ballet or any other art, or of literature or learning". The Law Commission noted that "films have themselves an archival and historical value as social records, as well as being used for industrial, educational, scientific and anthropological purposes", and assumed that these merits would be canvassed under the head of "learning".[107] Cameramen who film contemporary horrors are providing evidence that will be "in the interests of" present and future scholarship. Expert evidence is admissible, and if a certified film were prosecuted, representatives of the BBFC could expatiate on the merits of the work. Such testimony might, in any event, be acceptable as evidence of fact: the BBFC certificate, screened at the commencement, would comprise part of the "article" on trial, and the jury would be entitled to an explanation of what it meant. In cases brought against horror movies, film

---

[102] Criminal Law Act 1977, s.53.
[103] *Att-Gen's Reference No. 5 of 1980* [1980] 3 All E.R. 816.
[104] See Criminal Law Act 1977, s.53(3).
[105] Criminal Law Act 1977, s.53(2) and (5). The DPP's consent should be obtained before application for a summons: See *R. v Angel* (1968) 52 Cr.App.R. 280; *Price v Humphries* [1958] 2 Q.B. 353.
[106] Law Commission, *Report No. 76*, Pt III, para.78.
[107] Law Commission, *Report No. 76*, at paras 69–76.

critics have been permitted to testify to the merits of the film as cinematic art, its technical qualities, its dramatic effects, its message or moral, and its value as popular entertainment. Not always successfully: when *Guardian* film critic Derek Malcolm was called to explain the merits of a video nasty entitled *Nightmares in a Damaged Brain* he claimed that it was "very well executed". "So was the German invasion of Belgium", snapped the judge.

Television and radio

The 1990 Broadcasting Act applies the Obscene Publications Act to **4–041** television and radio in much the same way as it has been applied to feature films. The s.4 defence is available (in a wider formulation than that which applies to plays and films) and no prosecution may be brought or forfeiture ordered except by or with the consent of the DPP. The censorship constraints on broadcasting are dealt with in detail in Ch.16.

THEATRE CENSORSHIP

In 1737 Sir Robert Walpole, goaded beyond endurance by carica- **4–042** tures of himself in plays of Henry Fielding, introduced legislation empowering the Lord Chamberlain to close down theatres and imprison actors as "rogues or vagabonds" for uttering any unlicensed speech or gesture. Thereafter political satire was banned or heavily censored for "immorality", and as late as 1965 the Lord Chamberlain would not allow a stage version of Fielding's *Tom Jones* to be performed with bedroom scenes.[108] In 1843 a new Theatres Act was passed to consolidate the Lord Chamberlain's power to prohibit the performance of any stage play "whenever he shall be of opinion that it is fitting for the preservation of good manners, decorum or the public peace to do so".

The Lord Chamberlain's office remained eager to impose political, as well as moral, censorship, until its powers were abolished in 1968. Commercial managements accepted political discipline without demur but State-subsidised companies had no profits at stake, and the RSC launched an all-out attack after the Lord Chamberlain objected to one of its plays on the grounds that it was "beastly, anti-American, and left-wing". In 1966 the Joint Committee on Theatre Censorship commenced its deliberations. Dramatists, State theatre companies and drama critics overwhelmingly demanded the abolition of the Lord Chamberlain's powers, and convinced the Joint Committee that pre-censorship provided a service neither to playgoers nor to dramatic art.[109] Its recommendations were embodied in

---

[108] Richard Findlater, *Banned!—A Review of Theatrical Censorship in Britain* (Mac-Gibbon & Kee, 1967), p.175. See Nicholas de Jongh, *Politics Privacy and Perversions—The Censoring of the English Stage 1901–1968* (2000).

[109] *Report of the Joint Committee on Censorship of the Theatre* (HMSO, 1967) H.C. 255; H.C. 503.

the 1968 Theatres Act. The 1843 Act was repealed and the test of obscenity installed as the sole basis for theatre censorship.

> ". . . a performance of a play shall be deemed to be obscene if, taken as a whole, its effect is such as to tend to deprave and corrupt persons who are likely, having regard to all relevant circumstances, to attend it."

Decisions on the interpretation of s.1 of the Obscene Publications Act now apply with equal force to stage plays, with the exception of the "item-by-item" test: all performances, even of revues comprising separate sketches, will not infringe the law by reason only of one salacious scene, unless it is sufficiently dominant or memorable to colour the entire presentation. Obscenity is defined by reference to the circumstances of the staging and to its impact upon an audience more readily ascertainable than readership for books on general sale. A more stringent test would apply to West End theatres, trading from tourists and coach parties, than to "fringe" theatres or clubs with self-selecting patronage.

Plays defined

4–043 The Theatres Act applies to "plays", defined as:

> "(a) any dramatic piece, whether involving improvisation or not, which is given wholly or in party by one or more persons actually present and performing and in which the whole or a major proportion of what is done by the person or persons performing, whether by way of speech, singing or acting, involves the playing of a role; and
>
> (b) any ballet given wholly or in part by one or more persons actually present or performing, whether or not it falls within paragraph (a) of this definition."

Reference to "improvisation" includes ad libbing and extempore performances, although the requirement of role play excludes the stand-up comedian, unless the routine consists of playing different characters in a series of sketches. It would exclude some variety performances, although music-hall numbers usually require melodramatic characterisations that, arguably, involve the "playing of a role". "Ballet" is broadly defined in the *Oxford English Dictionary* as the "combined performance of professional dancers on the stage" and subs.(b) expressly excludes the requirement of role play. It may therefore be more embracing than the 1843 Act, which applied only to dancing that was set within some dramatic framework.

In *Wigan v Strange*, a case under the 1843 Act, the High Court held that whether a "ballet divertissement constituted an entertainment of the stage" was a finely balanced question of fact:

> "A great number of females, it seems, dressed in theatrical costume, descend upon a stage and perform a sort of warlike

dance: then comes a *danseuse* of a superior order, who performs a *pas seul*. If this had been all nobody would have called the performance a stage play. But the magistrate adds that the entrance of the *première danseuse* was preceded by something approaching to pantomimic action. The thing so described certainly approaches very nearly to a dramatic performance: and it is extremely difficult to tell where the line is to be drawn."[110]

The Law Commission has doubted whether displays of tribal **4–044** dancing could be classed as "ballet", and ballroom or discotheque performances, even by professional troupes of dancers, would fall outside the definition.[111]

The Act applies to every "public performance", defined to include any performance "which the public or any section thereof are permitted to attend, whether for payment or otherwise", and any performance held in a "public place" within the meaning of the Public Order Act 1936, namely:

"... any highway, public park or garden, any seat bench, and any public bridge, road, lane, footway, square, court, alley or passage, whether a throughfare or not; and includes any open space to which, for the time being, the public are permitted to have access, whether on payment or otherwise."[112]

This would cover street theatre, open-air drama and "end of the pier" shows. It would also include performances in restaurants,[113] public houses,[114] buses and railway carriages,[115] and possibly boats on public hire.[116] But the Act does not apply to any performance "given on a domestic occasion in a private dwelling" or to a performance "given solely or primarily" for the purposes of rehearsal, or for the making of a film, a television or radio broadcast, or a performance to be included in a programme service.[117] Whether the occasion was "domestic" or whether the performance was "primarily" for rehearsal or recording purposes are questions of fact for the jury. Public "previews" of a play prior to its opening night would not be characterised as exempted rehearsals if tickets were issued to the general public, albeit at a reduced rate. Similarly, out of town "try outs" could not be classed as "rehearsals", although they are

---

[110] *Wigan v Strange* (1865) L.R. 1 C.P. 175, *per* Erle C.J.
[111] Law Commission, *Report No. 76*, Pt III, para.93.
[112] Theatres Act 1968, s.18 and Public Order Act 1936, s.9.
[113] *R. v Hochlauser* (1964) 47 W.W.R. 350; *R. v Benson* (1928) 3 W.W.R. 605.
[114] *R. v Mayling* [1963] 1 All E.R. 687.
[115] *R. v Holmes* (1853) Dears. C.C. 207 at 209; *Langrish v Archer* (1882) 10 Q.B.D. 44.
[116] *DPP v Vivier* [1991] 4 All E.R. 18 sets out the test to be applied to determine whether an area is a public place.
[117] Theatres Act 1968, s.7.

designed to test audience reaction and frequently occasion script changes prior to the West End run. A performance staged primarily for the purposes of recording or filming or broadcasting is exempt from the operation of the Act, even where a large audience is invited to supply appropriate applause. Outrages to public decency that take place at rehearsals and filmed performances could still be prosecuted at common law.[118]

Local councils retain control over the front of house displays, which they require to remain within the realms of public decency, and they are entitled to withhold licences from theatres that do not comply with fire regulations or other health and safety requirements. They are not, however, permitted to impose any licence conditions relating to the content of plays performed in the theatre. In 1987 Westminster Council contemplated action against the Institute of Contemporary Arts for staging a theatrical performance that featured a "female Lenny Bruce", but had to accept that it could not use its licensing powers as a back door method of censorship. Enforcement of the ban in the 1899 Indecent Advertisements Act on "any written matter which is of an indecent or obscene nature" may depend on the place of exhibition. The Royal Court theatre in Sloane Square bill-boarded Mark Ravenhill's *Shopping and Fucking*, but the play transferred to Shaftesbury Avenue in a blaze of neon asterisks, as *Shopping and F******g*.

Public good defence

4–045 The Joint Committee recommended that "every effort should be made to see the trial takes place in circumstances that are likely to secure a proper evaluation of all the issues at stage including the artistic and literary questions involved."[119] A public good defence contained in s.3 admits expert evidence to justify stage performances that are "in the interests of drama, opera, ballet or any other art, or of literature or learning". The "merit" to which experts must testify is not of the play itself, but of "the giving of the performance in question", so that pedestrian writing may be redeemed by the excellence of acting, direction or choreography. Experts who have not witnessed the performance may nonetheless testify to its dramatic, literary or educative value by reference to the script, which under s.9 "shall be admissible as evidence of what was performed and of the manner in which the performance . . . was given".

Limits on police powers

4–046 Police have no power to close down the performance, or to seize programmes, scripts or items of stage property unless they feature writing or representations that contravene the Obscene Publications

---

[118] s.7(2), which exempts rehearsals, etc., from the provision of the Theatres Act, also removes from these occasions the protection of s.2(4), namely the restriction on proceedings at common law.
[119] *Report on Censorship*, para.50.

Act. Their power is limited solely to attendance, and is enforceable by warrant issued under s.15 by a justice who is given reasonable grounds to expect that the performance will infringe the Act.

Liability for prosecution

The Theatres Act applies to any person who, whether for gain or **4–047** not, "presented or directed" an obscene performance. In *R. v Brownson*, the defendants "presented" and "directed" by their actions in commissioning the script, engaging the cast, directing rehearsals, organising the performances, managing the premises and promoting the production.[120] Although rehearsals themselves fall outside the scope of the Act, a director will be liable for scenes prepared under his instruction after opening night, even though his association with the production may have ended. Section 18(2) provides that a person shall be taken to have directed a performance of a play given under his direction notwithstanding that he was not present during the performance. A director is not responsible, however, for obscenity introduced after his departure: the Act applies to "an obscene performance", and imposes liability only on those who have presented or directed *that* performance. Promoters, on the other hand, may be vicariously liable for obscenity inserted without their knowledge if the play is presented under their auspices. The wording of s.2(2) suggests strict liability, and in *Grade v DPP*, a case under the 1843 Act, it was held that a promoter "presented" a play with unlicensed dialogue, although the offending words had been inserted without his knowledge and without any negligence on his part.[121] Producers who act in a personal capacity are more vulnerable than those who operate through a corporate structure, in which case s.16 imposes liability only on those who act knowingly or negligently.

Actors will not be liable for any offence arising from participation in an obscene performance unless the obscenity arises from their own deviation from the script, whereupon they become the "director" of their own unrehearsed obscenity. Section 18(2) provides:

(a) a person shall not be treated as presenting a performance of a play by reason only of his taking part therein as a performer;

(b) a person taking part as a performer in a performance of a play directed by another person shall be treated as a person who directed the performance if without reasonable excuse he performs otherwise than in accordance with that person's direction . . .".

What constitutes "reasonable excuse" is a question of fact, and actors unable to control themselves in shows requiring simulated sex

[120] *R. v Brownson* [1971] Crim. L.R. 551.
[121] *Grade v Director of Public Prosecutions* [1942] 2 All E.R. 118.

acts might perhaps plead automatism or provocation. The actors' union, Equity, insists that theatre managements give written notice of any scenes of nudity or sexual simulation prior to the contract of engagement.

The Theatres Act makes no reference to the liability of dramatists. The Solicitor-General advised the Joint Committee that an obscene playscript would constitute an "article" within the meaning of s.1(2) of the Obscene Publications Act.[122] A dramatist "publishes" a playscript by giving it to a producer, but it does not become an "obscene article" unless it is likely to deprave the people who read it—i.e. members of the theatre company, and not the theatre audience, who do not see "the article" (i.e. the script itself) but the play, which is not an "article" and is not "published" to them by the dramatist. Prosecution under the Obscene Publications Act would therefore be unlikely to succeed, and an author cannot normally be said to "present or direct" a performance that is contrary to the Theatres Act. It follows that dramatists are liable only if their script calls for blatant obscenity or if they assist in some other way to mount a performance that is likely to deprave and corrupt.

Evidence

4–048 Section 10 empowers senior police officers to order the presenter or director of a play to produce a copy of the script on which the performance is based. "Script" is defined in s.9(2) as the text of any play, together with stage directions for its performance. This script becomes admissible as evidence both of what was performed and of the manner in which the performance was given, thereby ensuring that courts are not obliged to rely upon police recollections of dialogue and action. Neither the effect nor the merit of drama can be fully appreciated from textual study, but there is an evidential obstacle to restaging the performance for court proceedings. In *R. v Quinn and Bloom* the Court of Appeal rejected the film of a striptease performance taken three months after the date of the offence, because there was no guarantee that the reconstruction exactly mirrored the performance on the date charged in the indictment.[123] *Quinn*'s case was a disorderly-house charge, which carried no public good defence, and it may be that the rule would be relaxed in a Theatres Act prosecution if the defence of dramatic merit were invoked. Comparative evidence has been admitted under s.14 of the Obscene Publications Act,[124] and reconstructions of accidents for the benefit of the court are common in civil cases.[125] A

[122] *Report on Censorship*, p.54.
[123] *R. v Quinn & Bloom* [1962] 2 Q.B. 245.
[124] *R. v Penguin Books* [1961] Crim. L.R. 176; see Rolph, *Lady Chatterley*, p.127.
[125] See *Gould v Evans & Co* [1951] 2 T.L.R. 1189 and *Buckingham v Daily News* [1956] 2 Q.B. 534.

restaged performance might be inadmissible on the question of obscenity on the occasion charged, but it would be highly relevant to a jury's assessment of theatrical merit.

On-stage blasphemy

The Theatres Act precludes prosecution of plays for common law **4–049** indecency offences and blasphemous libel (s.2(iv)) and as early as 1970 the irreligious *Council of Love* (a later film version of which was the subject of the *Otto-Preminger* case in Strasbourg) was performed on the London stage. *Jerry Springer—The Opera*, a sacrilegious satire on the tawdry confessional TV program, played to delighted audiences at the National and enjoyed a West End transfer without the public protest which subsequently attended its BBC transmission. Whether the play could have been performed at all had Jerry Springer interviewed a Mohammed character treated in similar fashion to Jesus (who appeared in nappies to discuss his sexual problems) is another matter: for modern dramatists, "the elephant in the room" is the bomb in the theatre if their play outrages extremist religious sensibilities. Christians may be trained to turn the other cheek but, as the Danish cartoon protests demonstrated, Muslims can be organised to react violently to any form of art which satyrises their prophet. It is telling that no theatre company has dared to provoke them and a theatre or film version of *The Satanic Verses* is unlikely to find backers. The worst form of cultural vandalism so far has come from the Sikh community, some hundreds of whose members tried to storm a Birmingham theatre which was presenting *Behzti*, a work by a young woman dramatist about sexual abuse by Sikh temple elders. The audience had to be evacuated, the playwright went into hiding after death threats and (to the abiding concern of insurers) the theatre building was damaged. Perhaps the worst feature of the incident was that a foolish junior Home Office Minister (Fiona MacTaggart) claimed that these protests were all part of a proud British tradition of free speech.[126] The Divisional Court thought otherwise: it approved police action imposing ASBOs on protestors who had refused police directions to move from the theatre foyer, where they were intimidating and harassing a matinee audience.[127]

The *Romans in Britain* prosecution

In 1981 a private prosecution was brought against Michael Bog- **4–050** danov, a National Theatre director, charging that he had procured an act of gross indecency between two actors on the stage of the Olivier Theatre as part of a scene in the play *The Romans in Britain*,

---

[126] See *Index on Censorship*, Volume II, 2005, pp.112, 121.
[127] *R (Pritpal Singh) v Chief Constable of West Midland Police*, May 11, 2005.

contrary to s.13 of the Sexual Offences Act 1956. This was a bold attempt to sidestep provisions of the Theatres Act that require the Attorney-General's consent to any prosecution of a stage play, and to avoid the defences that would otherwise be available under that legislation, notably the strict test of obscenity and the public good defence. The prosecution, in the event, collapsed mid-trial for technical reasons (a not uncommon risk in private prosecutions) and reportedly left the prosecutrix with a large bill in legal costs. It did, however, occasion some concern in theatrical circles. The Theatres Act does not protect persons connected with a play from prosecution for actual criminal offences simply because they happen to be committed on stage. What it was intended to protect them against, with the possible and very narrow exception relating to s.13 of the Sexual Offences Act, is subjection to any form of legal censorship other than that provided for by the Theatres Act itself.

The *Report of the Joint Committee on Censorship of the Theatre* specifically recommended "that no criminal prosecution (whether under statute or common law) arising out of the performance of a play should take place without the order of the Attorney-General having been first obtained."[128] This was to secure "the prevention of frivolous prosecutions" and to ensure the "most important" principle that "there should be an absolutely uniform application of the law throughout the country". When the Bill received its second reading in the House of Commons, its proposer assured the House that,

"No prosecution may take place without the consent of the Attorney-General. We considered this necessary to prevent vexatious or frivolous prosecutions by outraged individuals or societies and to ensure uniformity of enforcement."[129]

In the course of the debate this passage was approved and adopted by the Government spokesman (the Secretary of State for Home Affairs), who noted that,

"It would be particularly oppressive if a prosecution were otherwise launched . . . Those concerned with the presentation of plays are entitled to the protection which the Attorney-General's consent gives."[130]

This position was maintained during the Bill's passage in the Lords, where the Government spokesman noted that the Attorney was obliged to read a play of which complaint had been made and to ask himself the question, "Is it in the public interest that there should be

---

[128] H.C. 355, H.C. 503, para.48.
[129] Mr C. R. Strauss, February 23, 1968, *Hansard*, Vol. 759, col. 830.
[130] Mr C. R. Strauss, February 23, 1968, *Hansard*, Vol. 759, col. 866.

a prosecution here?"[131] Section 8 of the Theatres Act duly provides that proceedings shall not be instituted "except by or with the consent of the Attorney-General."

When *The Romans in Britain* was first performed at the National Theatre there was considerable criticism and comment about a scene that called for a simulated homosexual rape, perpetrated by three Roman soldiers upon a young Druid priest. Mrs Mary Whitehouse, the "clean up" campaigner, asked the Attorney-General to prosecute under the Theatres Act: the DPP investigated, and reported that no prosecution would be likely to succeed. The Attorney refused his consent to allow a private prosecution to go forward, whereupon Mrs Whitehouse sent her solicitor to view the play, and he convinced a magistrate to issue a summons against Bogdanov under s.13 of the Sexual Offences Act. This section is directed at male persons who masturbate themselves or others in public toilets and parks. It punishes men who procure the commission of acts of gross indecency in public. The allegation against Michael Bogdanov was that he, being a male, "procured" a male actor playing the part of a Roman soldier to commit an act of gross indecency with another male, namely the actor playing the young Druid. The artificiality of the proceedings is demonstrated by the fact that had any of the participants been female, s.13 could not have been applicable.

The prosecutrix had discovered a loophole in the law, applicable **4–051** in a very limited way to plays directed by males that contain scenes calling for simulation of homosexual activity that a jury might find to be "grossly indecent". Although the intention of Parliament was to abolish all residual offences in relation to the staging of plays, the section of the Theatres Act designed to achieve this was not comprehensively drafted. It abolished common law conspiracy offences, obscene and blasphemous libel and the like, but it overlooked the existence of s.13.[132] It could be argued that the prosecution was so obviously artificial that it would be oppressive to allow it to proceed, or that the Theatres Act by implication excluded a prosecution under s.13 where the purpose of the proceedings was to effect an act of censorship of drama.[133] This interpretation now had added force by application of s.3 of the 1998 Human Rights Act, which requires statutes to be interpreted "so far as possible" to conform with free speech guarantees. These issues have yet to be resolved, and the collapse of *The Romans in Britain* prosecution makes that case an unsatisfactory precedent. The judge held that the

---

[131] Lord Stow Hill, House of Lords, June 20, 1968, *Hansard*, col. 964.
[132] See Theatres Act 1968, s.2(4).
[133] It is apparent from a review of the Joint Report and the debates that Parliament intended the Theatres Act to "cover the field" of possible criminal offences committed in respect of the performance of plays. Neither the Law Officers (at p.54 of the Joint Report) nor the Home Office (p.106) suggested that s.13 of the Sexual Offences Act could be an appropriate charge.

prosecution had presented prima facie evidence of a s.13 offence. Had the case continued, the defence would have argued that even if s.13 were applicable, no offence had been committed by staging the play, because there was no act of "procuration" by the director. The acts and dialogue that formed the basis of the charge took place by agreement between the author, the director, the actors and others. A person who does something from his or her own free will "and without any force or persuasion on the part of any other person cannot be said to have been procured".[134] At the committal proceedings Sir Peter Hall described how the scene was the result of a consensus between the parties involved and refuted the suggestion that the director had exerted any pressure or persuasion upon the actors.[135]

Section 13 offences are committed for purposes of sexual gratification in circumstances that admit of no argument or ambiguity. The sex scene in *The Romans in Britain* was simulated in circumstances, and with a purpose, that negated the allegation of indecency.[136] The prosecution evidence was that the act of gross indecency consisted in one male actor holding his penis in an erect position, advancing across the stage and placing the tip of the organ against the buttocks of the other actor. This was the testimony of Mrs Whitehouse's solicitor, who had been seated, appropriately enough, in the gods— some 70 yards from the stage. He admitted, under cross-examination, that he may have mistaken the tip of the penis for the actor's thumb adroitly rising from a fist clenched over his groin. Shortly afterwards the prosecution collapsed, relieving the jury from further consideration of a "thumbs up" defence, which might have provided a complete answer to the charge.

INDECENCY LAWS

4–052   The obscenity laws are designed to ban material that is likely to cause social harm. Indecency, on the other hand, is not concerned with "harm" in any demonstrable sense, but rather with the outrage to public susceptibilities occasioned by unlooked-for confrontations with unseemly displays.

Obscenity is punished because it promotes corruption, "indecency" because it is a public nuisance, an unnecessary affront to

---

[134] *R. v Christian* (1913) 78 J.P. 112.
[135] For an account of this case, see Geoffrey Robertson, *The Justice Game* (1998, Vintage), Ch.7.
[136] Even if the motive of sexual gratification is proven, the assault must be "accompanied with circumstances of indecency on the part of the defendant": *Beal v Kelley* [1951] 2 All E.R. 763. No act can be divorced from the circumstances in which it takes place. See *R. v George* [1956] Crim. L.R. 52; *Wiggins v Field* [1968] Crim. L.R. 503; 112 S.J. 656; *Abrahams v Cavey* [1968] 1 Q.B. 479, and *R. v Armstrong* (1885) 49 J.P. 745.

people's sense of propriety. For the most part, the indecency laws will not affect freedom of expression or art. They are generally confined to maintaining decorum in public places. However, the prohibitions on sending indecent material through the post may affect the distribution of books and magazines, and the ban on importation of indecent articles was continually used to stop controversial feature films from entering the country until the European Court intervened in 1986 (see p.160). The most important aspect of "indecency" as a test for censorship does not derive from the criminal law at all, but from the statutory duty imposed on broadcasting bodies to ensure that anything offensive to decency is not broadcast on commercial radio or television. The legal definition can become relevant for the purpose of contesting their rulings.

The test of indecency

"Indecency" has been defined by the courts as "something that offends the ordinary modesty of the average man . . . offending against recognised standards of propriety at the lower end of the scale".[137] In *Knuller v DPP*, Lord Reid added:

    4–053

> "Indecency is not confined to sexual indecency; indeed it is difficult to find any limit short of saying that it includes anything which an ordinary decent man or woman would find to be shocking, disgusting or revolting."[138]

However, the courts recognise that minimum standards of decency change over time, and that "public decency must be viewed as a whole"; and the jury should be "invited, where appropriate, to remember that they live in a plural society, with a tradition of tolerance towards minorities."[139] This consideration assumes importance in those cases where the allegedly offensive article is destined for a restricted group whose right to receive material of minority interest may overcome the adverse reaction of jurors who do not share the same proclivities.

"Indecency" is not an objective quality, discoverable by examination as if it were a metal or a drug. In some cases courts have been prepared to accept that the context of publication may blunt the offensiveness of particular words or phrases:

> *Wiggins v Field* arose from a public reading of Allan Ginsberg's poem "America", which included the line "Go fuck yourself with your atom bomb". The reader was charged with using "indecent language" in contravention of a local byelaw, but the Divisional Court said that the case ought never to have been brought:

---

[137] *R. v Stanley* [1965] 1 All E.R. 1035 at 1038.
[138] *Knuller v DPP* [1973] A.C. 435 at 458.
[139] *Knuller* at 495, *per* Lord Simon of Glaisdale.

"Whether a word or phrase was capable of being treated as indecent language depended on all the circumstances of the case, the occasion, when, how and in the course of what it was spoken and perhaps to a certain extent what the intention was."

It decided that in the work of a recognised poet, read without any intention of causing offence, the word "fuck" could not be characterised as "indecent".[140]

That this question may assume crucial importance is illustrated by *Att-Gen, ex rel. McWhirter v IBA*. The Independent Broadcasting Authority, required by statute to ensure so far as possible that television programmes do not include anything that "offends against good taste or decency", defended its decision to screen tasteless scenes in a programme about avant-garde film-maker Andy Warhol on the ground that the dominant effect of the film was not offensive. The Court of Appeal agreed that the film "taken as a whole" was not offensive: it depicted "indecent incidents", but "whether an incident is indecent must depend upon all the circumstances, including the context in which the alleged indecent matter occurs."[141]

4–054   The question is whether "ordinary decent people" would be horrified, not at the publication itself, but by all the circumstances of its exposure.[142] This approach is consonant with the purpose of indecency offences: "the mischief resides not so much in the book or picture *per se* as in the use to which it is put . . . what is in a real case a local public nuisance".[143]

There is no measure of agreement about the extent to which the notion of indecency in law pertains to matters other than sex. It is usually used to denote sexual immodesty, which would exclude some publications that fall within the narrower statutory definition of "obscene". On the other hand, descriptions of drug-taking or brutal violence might be perceived as breaches of recognised standards of propriety, along with the expression of extreme social, political or religious viewpoints. Violence coupled with eroticism, such as sado-masochism and flagellation, is clearly within the definitions. In 1992 Customs and Excise obtained a jury conviction in relation to importation of a video film of pit bull terriers fighting brutally to the death. The indecency, and indeed obscenity, of the film was doubtless found in its tendency to encourage the keeping and organisation of fights involving these dogs, which had been made illegal in the United Kingdom after recent tragic incidents.

The indecent article must infringe current community standards. A "community standard" is something that emerges from the

---

[140] *Wiggins v Field* (1968) 112 S.J. 656; [1968] Crim. L.R. 503. For a similar approach in relation to pictures displayed in an avant-garde gallery, see *In The Appeal of Marsh* (1973) 3 D.C.R. (N.S.W.) 115.

[141] [1973] Q.B. 629, especially at 659.

[142] *Crowe v Graham* (1968) 41 AJ.L.R. 402 *per* Windeyer J.

[143] *Galletly v Laird* (1953) S.C. (J.) 16 *per* Cooper L.J. at 26.

consensus reached in a jury deliberation: it is neither a fact capable of proof nor an idea that can be canvassed by experts. Where the question of indecency turns on the circumstances or meaning of a publication, however, some assistance may be provided. In some cases expert opinion has been introduced as testimony of fact, to explain the reputation of authors and artists and to provide general information about the work at issue. In 1977 customs officers seized a number of books about classic art edited by international experts, despite the fact that many of the original pictures had been displayed at public galleries in England. Art critics testified to the standing of the editors and the artists, and gave details of a recent exhibition of some of the offending works at the Victoria and Albert Museum. In the same year a professor of English literature traced for a court the etymology of the allegedly indecent word "bollocks", from the literal meaning of "testicles", which appeared in early editions of the Bible (the King James edition replaced it by "stones"), to its modern colloquial meaning of "rubbish" or "nonsense". The promoters of the record album *Never Mind the Bollocks, Here's the Sex Pistols* were cleared of displaying an indecent advertisement, thereby relieving them from changing the title to *Never Mind the Stones, Here's the Sex Pistols*.

Indecency offences

It is an offence to deal with indecent articles in the following 4–055 circumstances.

Using the post

Section 11 85 of the Postal Services Act 2000 prohibits the enclosure 4–056 in a postal packet of "any indecent or obscene print, painting, photograph, lithograph, engraving, cinematograph film, book, and written communication, or any indecent or obscene article whether similar to the above or not". The penalty is a fine of up to £5,000 in the magistrates' court, or up to 12 months' imprisonment as well as a fine if prosecuted at a Crown Court. The prohibition applies whether or not the posting is solicited, and there is no public good defence available. In practice, prosecutions are generally confined to cases where complaints are made about unsolicited mailings, or where packages containing erotic magazines have broken open in the course of mailing. The possibility of prosecution is an irritant to publishers with mail order business: some, to be on the safe side, deliver their goods by rail, where there is no equivalent prohibition, although a much higher theft rate.

Section 4 of the 1971 Unsolicited Goods and Services Act provides:

"A person shall be guilty of an offence if he sends or causes to be sent to another person any book, magazine or leaflet (or advertising material for any such publication) which he knows or ought reasonably to know is unsolicited and which describes or illustrates human sexual techniques."

There is some ambiguity in the meaning of "human sexual techniques". The clause originally proscribed "sexual techniques", the word "human" being added at the insistence of the Ministry of Agriculture to protect its flow of breeding information to farmers. There was another ambiguity—was it essential for the "book magazine or leaflet" *itself* to describe human sexual techniques, or did the words in parentheses make it an offence for a leaflet merely to advertise a book about such techniques? The Divisional Court opted for the latter interpretation in a case where the unsolicited letter announced the firm's catalogue of books dealing with human sexuality without actually describing or illustrating either the catalogue or the books listed in it. The court ruled:

"It is clearly within the mischief of this legislation that there should be a prohibition of advertising material of that kind, even though the advertising material does not of itself contain illustrations or descriptions of human sexual techniques."[144]

Public display

4–057 The Indecent Displays (Control) Act of 1981 makes it an offence to display indecent matter in, or so as to be visible from, any public place. A place is "public", for the purposes of the Act, if members of the public have access to it, although it loses this quality if persons under 18 are refused admission. It also loses its character as a public place if access is by payment in order to see the indecent display, or the place is a shop with a prominent exterior display of a notice in the following terms:

"WARNING. Persons passing beyond this notice will find material on display which they may consider indecent. No admittance to persons under 18 years of age."

The prohibition on the public display of indecency contained in this legislation does not apply to:

- television broadcasting or programme services;
- exhibitions inside art galleries and museums;
- exhibitions arranged by, or in premises occupied by, the Crown or local authorities;

---

[144] *DPP v Beate Uhse (UK) Ltd* [1974] Q.B. 158.

- performances of a play;
- films screened in licensed cinemas.

The Act provides severe penalties for infringement, but its provisions have been much less dramatic in controlling indecent displays than the licensing powers given to local councils in the Local Government (Miscellaneous Provisions) Act 1982. These powers enable local councils to prescribe conditions to regulate displays and advertising of licensed sex shops and sex cinemas, and to withdraw licences if the conditions (which invariably prohibit public display of indecent matter) are breached.

There are some surviving local bylaws and nineteenth-century police "town clauses" Acts that entitle magistrates to fine persons involved with indecent acts and articles in public places. They are usually invoked by vice squad officers who frequent public lavatories in the hope of catching masturbators, but may have a wider application. The courts have been inclined to interpret these offences narrowly, confining them to situations where the public at large is caused genuine offence, as distinct from prying and provocative policemen.[145-6]

Grossly offensive telecommunication

Section 127 of the Communications Act 2003 makes it an offence to **4–058** "send any message by telephone which is grossly offensive or of an indecent obscene or menacing character". The purpose of s.127 is not to protect people against unsought or gratuitous offence—that is covered by s.1 of the Malicious Communications Act 1988. It is, so the Law Lords decided in *DPP v Collins* (2006), to protect public services from being used "for the transmission of communications which contravene the basic standards of society". For that reason it caught an irate racist who called his M.P.'s constituency office to berate him about grants of asylum to "black bastards", "wogs" and "niggers". The magistrates had decided that this language was offensive, but not "grossly offensive": the judges, however, found it "beyond the pail of what was tolerable in our society". It mattered not that the M.P. and his white party workers who had fielded these calls found them sad rather than personally offensive: the intention required was to grossly offend those at whom the insult was directed rather than the persons who happened to pick up the phone. Judges in the administrative court, who had dismissed the prosecutor's appeal, had been prepared to allow more latitude to communications from electors to their M.P.s and had been reluctant to condemn racist intemperance in the course of a political discussion.[147] The law lords conceded the relevance of this context of

---

[145-6] See *Cheesman v DPP* [1991] 3 All E.R. 54.

[147] *DPP v Collins* (2005) 3 All E.R. 326.

democratic discourse but applied the yardstick of "reasonably enlightened, but not perfectionist contemporary standards". Inevitably, the contemporary standards that will be applied are those of the higher judiciary, and not of the magistracy or the wider society they are supposed to represent. If electors are only capable of expressing their opinions to M.P.s in offensive terminology, it might be thought more in keeping with democratic tradition that M.P.s should suffer these tirades rather than report their constituents to the police. Outside this special context, however, *Collins* sends a clear message to lower courts that they should not tolerate public expression of crude racist intolerance.[148]

Customs offences

4–059 Section 42 of the 1876 Customs Consolidation Act prohibits the importation into the United Kingdom of "indecent or obscene prints, paintings, photographs, books, cards, lithographic or other engravings, or any other indecent or obscene articles".

The test of "indecency" imposed a different standard for imported books and magazines to that which governs home-produced literature, and the result, if not the intention, was for many years to protect the British indecent publications industry from overseas competition. Imported publications that did not tend to deprave or corrupt and could not therefore be suppressed by internal controls, were destroyed at ports of entry if they shocked or disgusted customs officials—people who have more experience in financial than in moral evaluation. The prohibition was even applied to film transparencies and negatives, inoffensive enough on casual inspection until processing and projection made their indecency apparent.[149] The phrase "any other indecent . . . article" was not interpreted *ejusdem generis* with the preceding references to printed matter: it covered sex toys, statutes, chessmen, dildos, inflatable rubber women, penis-shaped plastic mouth-organs and any other objects that the wit or perversity of the human imagination could make for indecent use.

It was a life-size rubber German sex-doll that finally broke the customs barrier and secured the right to import from the EEC films and books that were "indecent" but not obscene. It became the unlikely subject-matter of the important decision of the Court of Justice of the European Communities in *Conegate Ltd v Customs and Excise Commissioners in 1986*[150]:

> A sex-shop chain was ordered to forfeit a consignment of rubber dolls imported from Germany that British courts regarded as "indecent"

---

[148] *DPP v Collins*, House of Lords, July 19, 2006.
[149] *Derrick v Commissioners of Customs and Excise* [1972] 1 All E.R. 993.
[150] [1987] Q.B. 254.

within the 1876 prohibition. On reference to the European Court, it was held that the prohibitions on "indecent" imports breached Art.30 of the Treaty of Rome, which prevents restrictions on trade between Member States. The restriction could not be justified on public morality grounds under Art.36, because the British Government had not legislated to prevent the manufacture or the marketing other than by post or public display of indecent material within Britain. Since the item could be lawfully made and sold in Britain, because it was not obscene, Britain could not discriminate against Common Market suppliers by applying import restrictions.

The consequence of the decision in *Conegate* has, for practical **4–060** purposes, been to amend the 1876 law by removing the prohibition on indecent articles. Although in strict law this applies only to importations from Common Market countries, the Commissioners of Customs and Excise have accepted that it is impossible in practice to make distinctions between the same goods on the basis of the country of origin of their shipment. As a result, it abandoned the prosecution of Gay's the Word, a bookshop catering to homosexuals, which had imported a wide range of "indecent" literature from the United States. (The customs' evaluation of "indecency" may be gathered from the fact that the books included works by Oscar Wilde, Jean Genet, Gore Vidal and Christopher Isherwood.) It follows that prosecutions of literature under customs regulations will henceforth be confined to consignments of hardcore pornography, a ban on which the Court of Justice of the European Communities has held to be justifiable under Art.36 on public morality grounds.[151] There may also be forfeiture proceedings brought in relation to "borderline" books, in respect of which the decision will hinge on whether the court regards them as likely to be the subject of conviction if prosecuted in Britain under s.1 of the Obscene Publications Act. The Court of Appeal has held that in considering a customs forfeiture claim the court need decide only whether the books "tend to deprave and corrupt" likely readers so as to fall foul of the obscenity definition in s.1 of the 1959 Act: if so, it may order forfeiture without considering whether they might be exculpated by a s.4 "public good" defence.[152] This decision is difficult to reconcile with the reasoning in *Conegate* and may now be incompatible with incorporated Art.10 of the ECHR. If an obscene book may be manufactured and marketed within Britain because of its literary merit, there can be no logical reason or pressing local need for preventing its importation from other countries on moral grounds.

Customs officers who intercept articles considered obscene may proceed either by seeking forfeiture without criminal consequence to the importer, or by charging the importer with one of a variety of

---

[151] *R. v Henn & Darby* [1980] A.C. 850 and see *Wright v Customs and Excise* [1999] 1 Cr.App.R. 69.
[152] *R. v Bow Street Magistrates Ex p. Noncyp Ltd* [1990] 1 Q.B. 123, CA.

"smuggling" offences in the Customs and Excise Management Act 1979. A criminal charge will be preferred only where there is evidence of a positive and dishonest intention to evade the prohibition, so that cases other than commercial importation of hard-core pornography will normally proceed to a civil forfeiture hearing, either before local justices or before a High Court judge.[153] Whenever goods are seized, the importer must be notified and has one month to apprise the Commissioners of his intention to dispute their claim for forfeiture, otherwise the goods will be destroyed. In disputed cases the Commissioners must institute proceedings, unless they decide on reflection that the seizure was over-zealous, in which case they are empowered to release the goods subject to "such conditions, if any, as they think proper".[154] Conditions can be imposed only if the article has been seized at point of entry: an importer whose goods have cleared customs and who has paid the appropriate duty cannot, in the absence of dishonesty, be subject to any restriction if customs officers think with hindsight that it was an obscene import. One rule that should not survive ECHR challenge is that the customs can seize and the courts can condemn anything "mixed, packed or found with" material liable to forfeiture. It has been held that the court is entitled to forfeit all books seized from a person's flat, even though only some were found indecent or obscene. Customs interceptions are mainly confined to hard-core pornography. The last attempt to prohibit a work of artistic merit— *My Trouble with Women* by celebrated American underground cartoonist Robert Crumb (creator of "Felix the Cat" and "Mr Natural")—ended ignominiously at Uxbridge 1996. The magistrates, after hearing evidence of Crumb's genius, ordered customs to release the stock and pay £6,000 legal costs to the importer.

THE COMMON LAW

Corrupting public morals

4–061   There are several arcane common law offences that can be revived "to guard the moral welfare of the State against attacks which may be more insidious because they are novel and unprepared for".[155] The charge of "conspiracy to corrupt public morals", for example, could be used against any writing or broadcasting (unlike the Obscene Publications Act, it can apply to television) that a jury might hold to be destructive of the moral fabric of society. In practice it is now rarely used, and confined to publications that carry advertisements seeking to procure illegal sexual liaisons. It was thus

---

[153] Customs and Excise Management Act 1979, s.139 and Sch.3.
[154] Customs Act 1978, s.152.
[155] *Shaw v DPP* [1962] A.C. 220 at 28.

employed in 1981 against organisers of the Paedophile Information Exchange (whose publications had carried advertisements from members that the defendants would facilitate the distribution of child pornography).

The crime has had a colourful history. It was devised in 1663, in a test case involving the poet Sir Charles Sedley, who ended a drunken party on his Covent Garden balcony by "pulling down his breeches and excrementalising on the crowd below". The king's judges decided that they, and not the lax church courts, should henceforth punish any act that was "against public morality" and fined Sedley, who left the court complaining that he was "the first man to pay for shitting".[156] It was revived in 1961 to prosecute the publisher of *The Ladies Directory*, a "who's who" of London prostitutes.[157] Its scope was reduced by the House of Lords in 1971:

> *IT (International Times)* was convicted for publishing a "Gentleman's Directory" among its classified advertisements. The prosecution evidence established that these advertisements were answered by homosexuals through a box-number service provided by the magazine. The advertisements were worded in a way that could, and apparently did, attract school-children. The House of Lords affirmed the newspaper's conviction, on the ground that these box-numbered advertisements set up an "apparatus of liaison" that would facilitate homosexual contact with under-age youths.[158]

The Law Lords restricted the future ambit of the offence in the following ways:

- The defendant must *intend* to corrupt public morals in the manner alleged in the indictment. The prosecution had to prove that the editors of *IT* inserted the advertisements with shared intention to debauch and corrupt the morals of their readers by encouraging them to indulge in homosexual conduct.[159] In this respect, at least, the conspiracy charge is more onerous for the prosecution than an obscenity offence, in which the defendant's intention is irrelevant.[160]

- The jury must be told that "corrupt" is a strong word. It implies a much more potent influence than merely "leading astray morally". The jury must keep current standards in mind,[161] and not be given "too gentle a paraphrase or explanation of the formula".[162] The words "corrupt public

---

[156] See Geoffrey Robertson, *Obscenity* (London, Wiedenfeld, 1979), p.21.

[157] Robertson, p.21.

[158] *Knuller*, fn.27 above.

[159] *Knuller* at 460.

[160] See *Shaw v DPP* [1962] A.C. 220 at 228, CA.

[161] *Knuller* at 457, *per* Lord Reid.

[162] *Knuller* at 460, *per* Lord Morris.

morals" suggest conduct which a jury might find to be destructive of the very fabric of society."[163]

- The essence of the offence was not the publication of a magazine, but the use of that publication to procure the advancement of conduct that the jury considered corrupt. The corruption in the *IT* case did not arise from obscenity, but from "the whole apparatus of liaison organised by the appellants".[164] The jury may have decided that the only objectionable advertisements were those that might attract under-age youths, as distinct from practising adult homosexuals, when published in a magazine bought by thousands of young persons.

- The charge does not invite "a general tangling with codes of morality".[165] The courts possess no residual power to create new offences. The conspiracy charge should be applied only to "reasonably analogous" new circumstances.[166]

- Homosexual contact advertising, or any other sort of encouragement to homosexuality, does not necessarily amount to a corruption of public morality. In every case it is for the jury to decide, on current moral standards, whether the conduct alleged amounts to public corruption.[167]

- Prosecutions for conspiracy should not be brought against publishers who would, if charged under the Obscene Publications Act, be entitled to raise a public good defence. An undertaking to this effect was given to Parliament by the Law Officers in 1964, and it should be honoured by the legal profession.[168]

Outraging public decency: art galleries

4–062 A similarly restrictive approach was placed on the allied offence of conspiracy to outrage public decency in the *IT* case. That applied only to circumstances in which an exhibition would outrage those who were invited to see it, and the court stressed that prosecution would be subject to the Law Officers' undertaking that conspiracy would not be charged in any way that might circumvent the public good defence in the Obscene Publications Act.[169] But the common law offence of outraging public decency was revised in 1989 to

---

[163] *Knuller* at 491, *per* Lord Simon.
[164] *Knuller* at 446 (*arguendo*), at 497, *per* Lord Kilbrandon.
[165] *Knuller* at 490, *per* Lord Simon.
[166] *Knuller* at 455, *per* Lord Reid.
[167] *Knuller* at 490, *per* Lord Simon.
[168] June 3, 1964, *Hansard*, Vol. 695, col. 1212. See *Knuller*, fn.27 above, at 459 *per* Lord Reid, at 466 *per* Lord Morris, at 480 *per* Lord Diplock, 494 *per* Lord Simon.
[169] *Knuller*, above, at 468, *per* Lord Morris and at 494, *per* Lord Simon.

punish an artist and the proprietor of an art gallery who exhibited a
surrealist work featuring earrings that had been fashioned from
human foetuses. This prosecution, *R. v Gibson*, was a breach at least
of the spirit of the Law Officers' undertaking, since there were a
number of distinguished artists and critics prepared to testify that
the work had artistic merit but this evidence was inadmissible on the
common law charge, which has no public good or artistic merit
defence.

> The defendants were charged with creating a public nuisance and
> outraging public decency by exhibiting the foetal earrings as part of a
> sculpture displayed within an art gallery open to the public. As the
> work of alleged art was not plainly visible from the public footpath
> outside the gallery, the public nuisance charge was dismissed. The
> Court of Appeal upheld the public indecency conviction, because the
> requirement of "publicity" for that offence had been satisfied by the
> general invitation to the public to enter the gallery and view the
> exhibits. The Crown did not have to prove that the artist and
> proprietor had intended to outrage decency: although the prosecution
> must prove intention when it charges common law conspiracies, this
> fundamental requirement of criminal law can be avoided simply by
> charging the substantive offence.[170]

Although the facts of this case were highly exceptional, it showed
how the protections for art and literature solemnly enacted by
Parliament in 1959 could be circumvented by the device of charging
an offence at common law. The exhibit, however distasteful, did
attempt to convey a moral message about the superficiality of a post-
modern society where women can treat their abortions as lightly as
they wear their earrings. The test of "outrage" is vague and
subjective, calling for a value judgment verdict, which will depend
not on any provable public standard or any deliberate intention to
outrage, but on the "gut reactions" of the jurors who happen to be
empanelled to try the case. The majority verdict procedure, which
allows a conviction despite two dissenters, further undermines the
protection for minority tastes and views—it is not surprising that in
the "foetal earrings" case, the *Oz* trial and the *Gay News* blasphemy
prosecution, conviction was by 10:2 majority. The dissenters represented a substantial minority of citizens who presumably wished
either to have access to the material or not to interfere with the
rights of those who did.

The drafters of the 1959 Obscene Publications Act sought to
exclude the Philistine presumptions of common law by providing in
s.2(4), that "a person publishing an article shall not be proceeded
against for an offence at common law consisting of the publication
of any matter contained or embodied in the article *where it is of the*

---

[170] *R. v Gibson* [1990] 2 Q.B. 619.

essence of the offence that the matter is obscene" [our italics]. But in *Gibson* the Court of Appeal decided that "obscene" in s.2(4) had its special statutory meaning ("tending to deprave and corrupt") and hence did not ban prosecution for a common law offence the essence of which was the lesser charge of "indecency" (i.e. arousing feelings of shock and disgust). There is an alternative construction which would give effect to Parliament's obvious intent, namely to give "obscene" in s.2(4) its natural and ordinary meaning, the essence of which includes indecency and the arousing of feelings of disgust. The Chief Justice accepted that this was a "possible" construction,[171] and since it is the *only* construction consistent with freedom of expression it may be required by application of s.3 of the Human Rights Act 1998.

4–063   The offence of "outraging public decency" is so vague that any novel prosecution may not be "prescribed by law" for purposes of Art.10. The Court of Appeal has persistently refused to define it, other than as conduct which fills the jury with extreme distaste, such as (in 1999) secretly video-taping women in a public lavatory.[172] Prosecutors only reach for this charge when they have no other shot in their locker. It was noteworthy that it was not the basis for the conviction of sculptor Anthony-Noel Kelly, who had used the body parts of mummified corpses, purloined from a teaching hospital, to add a death-like dimension to his exhibits (he was caught after a gallery patron recognised a late relative). Although there is no property in a corpse, Kelly was convicted as accomplice to the theft of body parts which had been worked on for preservation and teaching purposes.[173]

Art galleries were regular targets for overzealous policemen, until the much-publicised collapse in 1970 of the case against John Lennon and Yoko Ono's lithographic account of their honeymoon. In 1987 the Bank of England brought a misguided but hilarious prosecution against an artist, Boggs, who had dared to "reproduce" the currency of the realm on large canvases: his triumphant acquittal (in record time) by an Old Bailey jury offers practical assurance that laws against counterfeiting will never again vex mischievous artists.[174] In 1997 the DPP declined all demands to prosecute the Royal Academy of Arts over its controversial *Sensations* exhibition. A pot of paint, but not a summons, was thrown at its picture of Myra Hindley, iconess of evil. The Academy was sensibly sensitive about suggestive sculptures of children by Jake and Dinos Chapman: these it confined to a guarded room to which only over-18s were allowed entrance.

---

[171] [1990] 2 Q.B. 619.
[172] *R. v Choi* May 7, 1999, CA.
[173] *R. v Kelly* [1999] Q.B. 621.
[174] *R. v Boggs* (November 1987, Central Criminal Court). See G. Robertson, *The Justice Game*, Ch.12 ("Come Up and See my Boggs").

The most serious attack on art came in 2001, when Scotland Yard's paedophile squad threatened the Saatchi gallery with prosecution unless they removed some photographs of nude children from the "I am a Camera" exhibition. This was a thuggish attempt at censorship by threat rather than by law: the pictures lacked the element of lewdness or repulsion necessary for "indecency", and Saatchi had the courage (and connections) to call the police's bluff by arranging for the photographs to be published, in colour, in *The Guardian*. (The BBC had promised it would show them at 23.00 as part of a late-night debate on the case, but the Corporation is always cowardly in such matters and—like the *News of the World*—scrambled the children's genitals, achieving a genuinely perverse effect.) One week after the police threat the DPP announced that since no jury would be likely to convict and the gallery might in any event have a "legitimate reason" for the exhibition, no further action would be taken.

This problem of excluding the infinitely elastic common law is not **4–064** suffered by producers of feature films or television and radio programmes. By 1977 the inadequacy of s.2(4) had been recognised, and the law was amended by adding a new subs.4(A), which excluded, in relation to films, any prosecutions at common law where the essence of the offence was indecency or conspiracy or offensiveness or disgust or injury to morality. The same blanket formula was used in para.6 of Sch.15 to the 1990 Broadcasting Act to remove the threat of common law prosecution from the electronic media.

Living theatre, happenings, performance art, strip-tease, disco theque programmes, variety shows and the like may fall outside the definition of a "play" for the purpose of the Theatres Act, but organisers and managers of premises where the performance takes place may be prosecuted for the common law offence of "keeping a disorderly house". This offence, created by eighteenth-century judges to curb cock-fighting and bear-baiting, is now primarily used against over-excitable hen parties and stag nights. A disorderly house is simply a place of common resort that features performances that are obscene, grossly indecent or "calculated to injure the public interest so as to call for condemnation and punishment".[175] The programme should be considered as a whole and not condemned because of an isolated incident of indecency, and the jury should bear in mind the place and circumstances of the performance, and the nature of the audience, in deciding whether there has been an outrage to public decency. ("A film shown in one place—for example a church fête—might outrage public decency, whereas shown in another place it might not."[176]) The prosecution has to prove that the premises were "habitually" used for indecent performances, which probably means, in practice, more than twice. In 1991

---

[175] *R. v Quinn & Bloom* [1962] 2 Q.B. 245.
[176] *R. v Cinecentre Ltd* (Bush J.) Birmingham Crown Court, March 15, 1976. See generally Robertson, *Obscenity*, pp.223–9.

the landlord of the Wagon and Horses in Rochdale had his conviction quashed because the "exotic male dancers" who had excited beyond endurance a party of 70 women had done so only on one isolated occasion.[177]

BLASPHEMY

4–065 Indecent descriptions applied to sacred subjects may amount to the crime of blasphemy. The offence relates to outrageous comments about God, holy personages, or articles of the Anglican faith, and is constituted by vilification, ridicule or indecency. The intention of the publisher is irrelevant and the words must speak for themselves. Once publication has been proved, the only question remaining for the jury is "whether the dividing line . . . between moderate and reasoned criticism on the one hand and immoderate or offensive treatment of Christianity or sacred objects on the other, has been crossed".[178]

There has only been one prosecution for blasphemy since 1922, the controversial case of *Whitehouse v Lemon*[179]:

> *Gay News* published a poem about a homosexual's conversion to Christianity, which metaphorically attributed homosexual acts to Jesus Christ. Professor James Kirkup intended to celebrate the universality of God's love; in so doing he referred explicitly to acts of sodomy and fellatio. Leave was obtained for a private prosecution against both editor and publishing company for the offence of blasphemous libel, in that they "unlawfully and wickedly published or caused to be published a blasphemous libel concerning the Christian religion, namely an obscene poem and illustration vilifying Christ in his life and in his crucifixion". The jury convicted, by 10 votes to 2, and the House of Lords confirmed by 3:2 the trial judge's ruling that the publisher's intentions were irrelevant, and that there was no need for the prosecution to prove any risk of a breach of the peace.

This decision confirms that blasphemy is no longer a crime of disbelief or irreverence. Attacks upon Christianity, no matter how devastating, will not be blasphemous unless they are expressed in an outrageously indecent or scurrilous manner. Although no evidence may be called about literary merit, the jury may be invited to consider the dominant effect of the work. Moreover, evidence of the place and circumstances of publication would be relevant to the likelihood of public outrage,[180] and evidence as to the character of the readership would be admissible on the issue of whether resentment was likely to be aroused.[181]

---

[177] *Moores v DPP* [1991] 4 All E.R. 521.

[178] *R. v Lemon and Gay News Ltd* (1978) 67 Cr.App.R. 70 at 82.

[179] *Whitehouse v Lemon* (1978) 68 Cr.App.R. 381. For an account of the *Gay News* Trial, see Geoffrey Robertson, *The Justice Game* (Vintage), Ch.6.

[180] *R. v Boulter* (1908) 72 J.P. 188.

[181] Transcript of summing up in *R. v Lemon*, Central Criminal Court, July 11, 1977, p.15.

The prosecution must lead prima facie evidence that the accused **4–066** was responsible for the blasphemous publication. The defendants may exculpate themselves by proving that the decision to publish was made without their knowledge and without negligence. This defence is provided by s.7 of the Libel Act 1843, which places the onus on the defendant "to prove that such publication was made without his authority, consent or knowledge, and that the said publication did not arise from want of due care and caution on his part". Section 7 will normally protect newspaper proprietors who entrust questions of taste to editorial discretion, although it would also avail an editor who was absent at the time of publication or had delegated responsibility for content to the editors of particular sections or pages.[182] Newspaper prosecutions must be commenced by leave of a High Court judge under s.8 of the Law of Libel Amendment Act 1888.

In a report on the law of blasphemy in 1986 the Law Commission recognised three fundamental defects[183]:

- Its ambit is so wide that it is impossible to predict in advance whether a particular publication would constitute an offence.
- The sincerity of the publisher is irrelevant.
- Blasphemy protects only Anglican beliefs,[184] and the criminal law is not an appropriate vehicle for upholding sectional religious tenets.

Although some have suggested that the law should be extended to protect all religions, the Law Commission despaired of any definition that could draw workable distinctions between Baptists, Scientologists, Rastafarians, Anglicans and Moonies and distinctions would, in any event, now amount to discrimination contrary to Art.14 of the ECHR. The majority of the Commission concluded that a reformed law of blasphemy would serve no purpose necessary to modern society. The claims of public order, morality and the rights of individuals provide insufficient justification. Its conclusion is reinforced by the absence of prosecutions for blasphemy in England between 1922 and 1977 and ever since 1977; the withering away of the crime in Scotland (there are no recorded cases since the 1840s, and it is doubtful whether the offence any longer exists); and the demise of prosecutions in Northern Ireland, despite the sectarianism

---

[182] *R. v Holbrook (No. 1)* (1877) 3 Q.B.D. 60; *R. v Holbrook (No. 2)* (1878) 4 Q.B.D. 42.

[183] Law Commission, *Working Paper No. 79: Offences Against Religion and Public Worship*, 1981.

[184] The difficulties in defining "religion" are exemplified in the Australian High Court decision that Scientology qualifies: *Church of the New Faith v Commissioner for Pay-Roll Tax* (1983) 57 A.J.L.R. 785.

of that most tragic "plural society". Apparently, the scope of the
offence in Wales is uncertain, as a consequence of the disestablish-
ment of the Welsh Church in 1920.[185]

4–067   It is unlikely that the DPP would take action against publications
with any literary or artistic value. *Whitehouse v Lemon* was a private
prosecution brought without official support: its wisdom was much
doubted by many Anglicans.[186] No action was taken against the
feature film *Monty Python's Life of Brian*, which held sacred subjects
up to considerable, if clever, ridicule, although the working title,
Jesus Christ—Lust for Glory, may well have provoked action.
However, the very existence of a blasphemy law is calculated to
encourage some Christians to believe they can enforce a conventional presentation of sacred themes in the arts. Martin Scorsese's
film *The Last Temptation of Christ* led to demands (most notably
from the retired *Gay News* trial judge) that its distributors should be
prosecuted. While its presentation of Christ's humanity was challenging and unorthodox, the film lacked any element of vilification
or scurrility, and on this basis the BBFC classified it as appropriate
for screening to adults and the DPP declined to prosecute. It now
appears dignified, by comparison to the cheap-jack brutality of Mel
Gibson's *The Passion of Christ* which broke box-office records in
2004. The irrelevance of blasphemy law was brought home to
Christians by the BBC screening of *Jerry Springer, the Opera*, a
scurrilous satire in which Jesus, swaddled in a nappy, appears beside
Satan to boost the talk show ratings. No less than 55,000 complainants jammed the BBC switchboards for days afterwards but the calls
to prosecute fell on deaf DPP ears. No wealthy Christian organisation was prepared to take the risk of mounting a private prosecution.
This underlined the fact that a criminal law that holds a publisher
strictly liable for an artistic work liable to shock the Christian on the
Clapham omnibus is inappropriate to an age in which the creeds of
passengers to Clapham, if they have any, are many and various.

The fate of blasphemy under the Human Rights Act 1998 has yet
to be decided: the English courts may declare it incompatible with
Art.10 of the Convention. This issue was raised in Strasbourg after
the BBFC used the possibility of a blasphemy prosecution as an
excuse for refusing to certify *Visions of Ecstasy*—a 20–minute
experimental video about the erotic trances of St Theresa of Avila.
The judges of the European Commission on Human Rights decided
overwhelmingly (by 14:2) that this ban was a breach of Art.10:
although it might be necessary for States to curb *gratuitous* offence
to religious sensibilities, the BBFC ban was a disproportionate act of
prior restraint because there was no danger, if the video were given
an 18 certificate, of adults being unwillingly confronted with it:

> "The fact that certain Christians, who had heard of the existence
> of the video, might be outraged by the thought that such a film

---

[185] Geoffrey Robertson, *The Justice Game* (Vintage), Ch.6.
[186] Law Commission, *Working Paper No. 79*, p.32.

was on public sale and available to those who wished to see it, cannot amount to a sufficiently compelling reason to prohibit its lawful supply".[187]

This simple—and correct—approach was muddied, however, when the case came before a chamber of the Court less impressively constituted than the Commission. It decided, by 7:2, that the BBFC ban was within a state's "margin of appreciation" (always elastic in matters of religion and morality). Because there was no European consensus about blasphemy laws, the question of their compatibility with free speech should be decided by national courts: "State authorities are in principle in a better position than the international judge" to decide whether or to what extent their laws protecting religious feelings are "necessary in a democratic society".[188] *Wingrove* is not a Euro-precedent in favour of blasphemy law, but rather a direction that every country must decide for itself. The Court majority drew attention to "the high level of profanation" required in English law to constitute the crime, suggesting that this might justify it as means to protect "the rights of others" under Art.10(2). The Commission's answer, that Christians cannot claim a "right" to stop others privately viewing profanation at a level which does not breach obscenity law, is more persuasive. The European Court, over-influenced by Catholic judges, had already made an unsustainable decision when permitting Austria to ban a film of the controversial play *Council of Love*.[189] It erroneously suggested that the Art.9 right to peaceful worship should be balanced against Art.10, but there is no logical sense in which the showing of a film in a cinema could infringe the right of Catholics to go to church. The Euro judges, as in *Wingrove*, showed no comprehension of how the freedom of expression right serves most importantly to protect art and culture: the invocation of the desirability of "religious peace" in Austria ignores Schiller's warning that such a state may be "the peace of the grave". The decision has been widely criticised and could only be justified if given a public order rationale—i.e. that the film was to be screened in a predominantly Catholic town, where zealots might turn violent. Allowing religious thuggery to override the individual right to experience cinematic art is hardly consonant with the philosophy behind Art.10.

Although Strasbourg is inclined to duck difficult moral issues by **4–068** reference to the nation's "margin of appreciation", English judges sit within that margin and can apply Art.10 with more force. Given the

---

[187] *Wingrove v UK* (1996) 24 E.H.R.R. 1, para.60 (Commission).
[188] *Wingrove* para.58 (Court). Latest evidence about British democracy is that although 26 million of the 59 million population have been baptised in the Church of England, only 13.9 per cent of citizens are members of any church and a mere 2.34 per cent attend Anglican services.
[189] *Otto-Preminger Institute v Austria* (1995) 19 E.H.R.R. 34.

law commission's recommendation to abolish blasphemy, a call in 2003 by the House of Lords select committee on religious offences,[190] and the impossibility of extending it to all faiths and cults, it may well be that any future prosecution would be struck down as unworkable, discriminatory and a breach of the principle of legal certainty. The Irish Supreme Court came to that conclusion in 2000 when rejecting a private attempt to prosecute the *Sunday Independent* over a cartoon which satirised the priesthood and the Eucharist. The blasphemy law, it ruled, was so uncertain that the prosecution should not be allowed to go ahead.[191] This refreshing decision should be followed in the United Kingdom, where the government's refusal of calls to abolish the offence does not imply parliamentary support for its use—the blasphemy law has not, despite the publicity given to the *Gay News* case in 1977, been deployed since. The unfairness of a law that protects only Christian sensibilities was highlighted in 1989 by the outrage felt amongst the Muslim community by the publication of Salman Rushdie's celebrated novel *The Satanic Verses*. This grievance was legitimate only to the extent that Muslims could correctly claim that the blasphemy law in Britain discriminated against their religion. But had it been extended to cover all faiths, Rushdie could have been prosecuted without the right to a literary merit defence, and without even being given an opportunity to argue that he had no intention to blaspheme. He would have been at risk of conviction merely by proof that the book was likely to outrage and insult believers—which it most certainly did, although much of the "outrage" seems to have been orchestrated by Muslim activists rather than to have arisen as a spontaneous reaction to reading the work. To punish Rushdie in these circumstances would have been offensive to justice, but no more so than the punishment of the editor of *Gay News*. The Secretary of State for the Home Department responded to Muslim demands for the extension of the blasphemy laws in a considered statement of the Government's position. He stressed "how inappropriate our legal mechanisms are for dealing with matters of faith and individual belief", remarked that a prosecution of *The Satanic Verses* would be "damaging and divisive", and noted that "the Christian faith no longer relies on the law of blasphemy, preferring to recognise that the strength of their own belief is the best armour against mockers and blasphemers".[192] The Rushdie affair demonstrated the absurdity of blasphemy law, either as a protection for Christianity or (in an extended and reformed version) as a protection for all religious sensibilities. In 1990 the Archbishop of Canterbury declared in favour of abolishing the law altogether, and the Divisional Court seemed of much the same view after examining it

---

[190] HL paper 95–1, April 10, 2003.

[191] *Corway v Independent Newspapers (Ireland) Ltd* (2001), IRLM 426.

[192] Statement by John Patten, November 1989.

for five days at the behest of Muslims who sought to commit Rushdie and his publishers for trial at the Old Bailey.

> The Bow Street magistrate had refused to issue a summons in respect of *The Satanic Verses* on the grounds that the offence of blasphemy protected only the Christian religion. The High Court held that this decision was correct: the early precedents established that the crime was confined to attacks upon the Established Church, so that it appears that other Christian denominations are protected only in so far as their fundamental tenets coincide with those of the Church of England. The court accepted that this was a "gross anomaly", but the anomaly arose from the "chains of history", which could be unlocked only by Parliament. Even if the court had power to extend the law to other religions, however, it would refrain from doing so because of the "insuperable" problems in defining religion, in expecting juries to understand obscure theologies, and because of the danger of divisive and obscurantist prosecutions. The court accepted that "the existence of an extended law of blasphemy would encourage intolerance, divisiveness and unreasonable interference with freedom of expression", and "would be likely to do more harm than good."[193]

The European Commission rejected an application by the Muslims who had brought *The Satanic Verses* case, on the ground that the Convention gave no right to bring a private prosecution and hence they could not show that any Convention right was infringed when it was rejected.[194] This approach, which is correct, is difficult to reconcile with the Commission's earlier rejection of an application by *Gay News* against their private prosecution. The Commission accepted that the conviction would not be justified as preventing disorder or protecting morals, but rather in protecting Mrs Whitehouse's right not to have her religious feelings offended[195]—the very basis upon which the Muslims had sought to prosecute Salman Rushdie. The Divisional Court's approach—that the Art.9 guarantee of freedom to manifest religious beliefs does not entitle believers to prosecute those who criticise or even ridicule those beliefs, is to be preferred.

RACE HATRED

Freedom of expression entails the right to entertain ideas of any **4–069** kind, and to express them publicly. The mode or the manner of the expression, however, may properly be regulated in the interests of the freedom of others to go about their business in public without being gratuitously assaulted or defamed, and may properly be curtailed in order to avoid public disorder which may follow

---

[193] *R. v Bow Street Magistrates' Court, Ex p. Chaudhury* [1991] 1 All E.R. 306.
[194] *Chaudhury v UK* Application No. 17439/90, March 5, 1991.
[195] *Gay News v UK* (1983) 5 E.H.R.R. 123.

provocative dissemination of racist ideas. This was the basis of the first anti-incitement laws, passed in Britain in 1965, after several years of racial violence of the most serious kind, by a Labour Government whose commitment to freedom of speech was weakened after the infamous Smethwick by-election in which a Labour majority evaporated in the face of the slogan, "If you want a nigger for a neighbour, vote Labour". This law has been amended on several occasions—the 1986 Public Order Act being the last—in an effort to make convictions easier to obtain. Nevertheless, prosecutions, which can be brought only with the Attorney-General's consent, are comparatively infrequent.

Section 18 of the 1986 Act makes it an offence to use threatening, abusive or insulting words or behaviour with the intent of stirring up racial hatred or in circumstances where racial hatred is likely to be stirred up. Section 19 makes it an offence to publish threatening or abusive or insulting material either with an intention to provoke racial hatred or in circumstances where such hatred is likely to be stirred up by the publication. "Racial hatred" means hatred against a group defined by colour, race or national origin, thereby including Jews, Sikhs[196] and Romany gypsies, but excluding Zionists, Rastafarians[197] and "gypsies" or travellers in general.[198] The term "racial group" is not defined by reference to religion, which means that Muslims in general (whose mosques are targets of much of the race-hate in the United Kingdom) are unprotected. The better view is that ethnic or country-based Muslim sects (such as the Ahmadis from Pakistan) are entitled to protection, but the DPP does not agree and the courts have so far refused to put him right.[199]

Section 22 of the Public Order Act has been amended by s.164 f the 1990 Broadcasting Act so that the offence of inciting racial hatred may now be committed by the transmission of television or radio programmes. Those vulnerable to prosecution are the television company (including the BBC), the programme producer and the person who is recorded making the incitement. This undesirable change in the law makes it more hazardous to produce programmes about racism, because the offence may be committed irrespective of the producer's intention, if "having regard to all the circumstances racial hatred is likely to be stirred up". Must current affairs programme makers henceforth ensure that racists say nothing that might attract the audience, and are editorially depicted in an unflattering light? The fact that this is generally the case when racists are allowed to speak for themselves will be sufficient if the programme is professionally produced and examines a subject of public

---

[196] *Mandla v Dowell Lee* [1983] 1 All E.R. 1062.
[197] *Crown Suppliers v Dawkins* [1993] I.C.R. 517.
[198] *Commission for Racial Equality v Dutton* [1989] 1 All E.R. 306.
[199] See *R. v DPP Ex p. Merton B.C.* [1999] C.O.D. 161, HC, and [1999] C.O.D. 358, DC.

interest: a prosecution in these circumstances would breach Article 10. This was the decision of the European Court in the important case of *Jersild v Denmark*:

> Broadcasters were convicted of racial insult by producing a documentary on the growing phenomenon of ethnic hatred amongst young people in Copenhagen. The purpose of transmitting interviews with racists was not to promote their xenophobia but to expose and analyse a matter of great public concern. The Court rejected the Government's argument that the producers should have "counterbalanced" or refuted these racist views: Art.10 did not permit the State to impose an editorial line or to tell journalists how to perform their professional duty. Although the racist statements that were broadcast did not of themselves enjoy protection under Art.10 (the interviewees themselves were convicted) this protection was attracted when they were repeated in the context of a serious media investigation. "The punishment of a journalist for assisting in the dissemination of statements made by another person in an interview would seriously hamper the contribution of the press to discussion of matters of public interest", and was in these circumstances an indefensible violation of Art.10.[200]

The offence can be committed by the public performance of a play **4–070** (s.20) although a drama's propensity to stir up racial hatred is to be judged with regard to all the circumstances and "taking the performance as a whole". Racist abuse heaped on Shylock and Othello by Shakespearean characters is therefore defensible, and there have been no prosecutions of stage plays since the offence first appeared in the Theatres Act of 1968. However, the Royal Court Theatre's cancellation of the play *Perdition* in 1987 after pressure from Jewish interests shows that the question may not be of entirely academic interest. It is noteworthy that the Sikh leaders who condemned *Bezhdi* did not seek to have it prosecuted for stirring up racial hatred, despite their classification as a "race" for such purposes in *Mandla v Dowell Lee*.[201] Their problem may have been that the play's illustration of sexist misbehaviour by Sikh leaders within their temple was all too true. That made their endorsement of violent protest doubly unacceptable.

Further potential for inhibiting free speech is contained in the offence of possessing racially inflammatory material or recordings with a view to publication in circumstances where racial hatred is likely to be stirred up (s.23). Authors and television researchers who collect such material in order to condemn it will not be at risk, but it might be argued that uncritical displays of Nazi memorabilia or unvarnished publications of "Hitler diaries" and the like could revive old hatreds. The protection of books of genuine historic interest is provided, not by the words of the Act, but by the need to obtain the

---

[200] *Jersild v Denmark* (1995) 19 E.H.R.R. 1.
[201] (1983) 1 All E.R. 1062.

Attorney-General's consent to prosecution. It is unfortunate that Parliament did not make s.23 subject to a defence that the play or the publication or collection was in the interests of drama, literature, history or other subjects of general concern.

There are various defences to these charges, generally pivoting upon lack of awareness of the real nature of the speech or writing or lack of any reason to suspect that they would be delivered or disseminated in circumstances where racial hatred would be provoked. If an offence is committed on a television or radio broadcast, the programme contractor and the programme producer and director may be prosecuted as well as the person who has uttered the offensive words. In the case of plays, liability is limited to producers and directors, unless an actor commits the offence by an unscheduled departure from the script—in which case he is deemed to be the "director" of his own impromptu performance. Section 25 of the Public Order Act permits a court to order the forfeiture of any written material or recording that has been used to commit an offence. Section 26 precludes reports of parliamentary proceedings and court reports from becoming the subject-matter of a prosecution under the Act.

4–071   There is no doubt that the race hate laws have a potential for punishing the expression of genuine political statements, albeit couched in crude or insulting terminology. This can apply particularly to activists from oppressed minorities, whose rhetoric is designed to jolt what they perceive as white complacency. In Britain the law was used, at least in its first decade of operation, more effectively against Black Power leaders than against white racists. The first person to be gaoled for a race hatred offence was Michael X, convicted by a white jury in 1967 for some fairly routine black-consciousness rhetoric of the period.[202] Ironically, Michael X was standing in for Stokely Carmichael, an American black activist banned from entering Britain, who 30 years later was applauded by the Macpherson Report into the Stephen Lawrence murder for identifying the phenomenon of "institutional racism" which had become rife in the Metropolitan Police. Enforcement history of the offence demonstrates the danger of prosecuting racist ideas (because it gives them more publicity). When in 1991 the Dowager Lady Birdwood, an old and rabid racist, was convicted for distributing anti-Semitic propaganda, Judge Brian Capstick Q.C. wisely frustrated her desire to be made a martyr: he imposed a conditional discharge and ordered her to pay prosecution costs.

Systematic racist vilification—such as crude cartoons in National Front newspapers—has been punished by prison sentences.[203] The Stephen Lawrence inquiry recommended an extension of the law to

---

[202] *R. v Malik* [1968] 1 All E.R. 582.
[203] See *R. v Edwards* (1983) 5 Cr.App.R. (S.) 145; *R. v Morse & Tyndall* (1986) 8 Cr.App.R (S.) 369.

punish racist utterances in private homes and meetings, but this would almost certainly breach Art.8 of the ECHR.[204] It would almost certainly result in jury acquittals. That was clear from the much publicised verdict in 2006 on Nick Griffin, leader of the British National Party, who had been prosecuted for racist utterances made in a speech to supporters at a private meeting in a pub. He had been secretly filmed by *Panorama*, which broadcast the vilest excerpts in a documentary about the spread of racism. Griffin was able to show that these had been taken out of context, from what in any view was a political speech to the converted. It was a fool-hardy prosecution, positively contrary to the public interest: the acquittal served only to promote the ugly policies of the BNP. The US Supreme Court has struck down hate speech laws which pivot on causation of anger or resentment rather than the incitement of violence.[205]

The common law offence of seditious libel can be committed by "promoting ill-will and hostility between different classes of Her Majesty's subjects". In *R. v Caunt*[206] the editor of *The Morecambe and Heysham Visitor* faced this charge for suggesting that violence against British Jews might be the only way of stemming Zionists' terrorists' activities against British forces in Palestine. He was acquitted. The statutory offences have effectively superseded this aspect of sedition and in 1990 the Divisional Court held that an attempt to prosecute the author and publisher of *The Satanic Verses* for sedition was misconceived. The allegation that publication of the book was calculated to create hostility between Muslims and other classes of citizens was, even if true, insufficient to constitute the offence: there had to be proof of incitement to violence against the State.[207]

The court also rejected an attempt to prosecute the publisher, Penguin Books, under s.14 of the Public Order Act, for provoking unlawful violence by distributing the books to shops that later suffered bomb attacks. Even if the book's contents could be described as "threatening, abusive or insulting" for the purposes of s.4, that section required that the unlawful violence should be the direct and immediate result of the publication of the insulting words. The act of distributing a book to retail outlets cannot sensibly be regarded as the immediate and direct cause of unlawful violence to which the bookseller may later be subjected by terrorists or fanatics.[208]

---

[204] Report of an Inquiry by Sir William Macpherson (1999), Recommendation 39.

[205] *RAV v City of St Paul*, 563 U.S. 377 (1992).

[206] Wade (1948) 64 L.Q.R. 203. See also Caunt, *An Editor on Trial* (privately published, 1947).

[207] *R. v Bow Street Magistrates' Court Ex p. Chaudhury*, fn.76 above.

[208] *R. v Horseferry Road Justices Ex p. Sadatan* [9911] 1 All E.R. 342.

HATRED AGAINST PERSONS ON RELIGIOUS GROUNDS

4–072 The government, unprepared to abolish blasphemy laws which discriminate in favour of Christians, has nonetheless insisted that because "Muslims" do not collectively constitute a racial group, and suffer much abuse which targets in particular their mosques, there must be a new offence of religious vilification. This is ingenuous, to the extent that Muslims (like everyone else) can be protected from vilification and abuse under s.5 of the Public Order Act which penalises "threatening, abusive or insulting" speech or writing or any "visible representation" that might cause alarm or distress—an offence which can carry a heavier sentence if aggravated by religious or racial hatred. That s.5 is apt to criminalise expressions of religious hatred that do public harm was determined by the High Court in *DPP v Norwood*.[209] Norwood displayed in his apartment window a BNP poster depicting the Twin Towers burning as background to the message "Islam Out of Britain—Protect the British People". The High Court approved his conviction and Strasbourg rejected his complaint, on the basis that:

> "Such a general, vehement attack against a religious group linking the group as a whole with a grave act of terrorism, is incompatible with the values proclaimed and guaranteed by the Convention, notably tolerance, social peace and non-discrimination."[210]

Despite the ruling in *Norwood*, the government pressed on with specific legislation against inciting religious hatred. The difference with racial vilification, of course, is that race is a characteristic that cannot be changed and involves no human choice: racist criticisms are for that reason always unfair and inhumane. Religious affiliation is a matter of choice which must be open to criticism, whilst religions are wealthy and powerful and in some cases deserving of the strongest disapprobation and most scurrilous satire. The Labour government was anxious in 2004 to curry electoral favour with the country's 1.6 million Muslims whose leaders craved the new law, some expressing the hope that it would at last permit the prosecution of Salman Rushdie. The House of Lords, after initial opposition, at least forced amendments that will largely draw the teeth of the new crime which has been inserted in the Public Order Act 1986 as s.29. It provides an unnecessarily long maximum sentence of seven years for any person "*who uses threatening words or behaviour, or displays any written material which is threatening. . . if he intends thereby to stir up religious hatred.*"

---

[209] *Norwood v DPP* (2003), W.L. 21491815.
[210] *Norwood v UK* (2005), 40 E.H.R.R. SE11.

This offence may be committed in a "private place" so long as this is not within a dwelling place. "Religious hatred" is defined as *"hatred against a group of persons defined by reference to religious belief or lack of religious belief"*—so to avoid discrimination, the law protects atheists from having their non-beliefs ridiculed. The prosecution must prove a malevolent intention—to stir up religious hatred—which means much more than simply provoking discussion or anger at particular religious practices.

There are two important features of the new law—both deriving from amendments made by the House of Lords against the government's wish. It will only apply to words or images which are "threatening"—the s.5 adjectives "abusive, insulting" were omitted precisely because some religious doctrines and practices justify abuse and insult. The matter itself must have an intimidatory impact, irrespective of any malicious intent in the person who utters or displays it. This dimension is further provided for by an important and novel "free speech defence" in s.29(j):

Protection of freedom of expression

> "Nothing in this Part shall be read or given effect in a way which **4–073** prohibits or restricts discussion, criticism or expressions of antipathy, dislike, ridicule, insult or abuse of particular religions or the beliefs or practices of their adherents, or of any other belief system or the beliefs or practices of its adherents, or proselytising or urging adherents of a different religion or belief system to cease practising their religion or belief system."

This free speech defence was inserted after the controversial case of *Jerry Springer—the Opera* and will protect satirists together with polemicists, preachers and politicians, so long as their attacks focus on beliefs and practices rather than on frightening believers or practitioners. In the result, the new offence is inapt for prosecuting Norwood's poster or the Griffin political rant, although it would certainly be capable of deployment against mullahs who threaten Christians with death at the hands of suicide bombers. Declarations of holy war are not exercises in "discussion" or "criticism".

Even in such extreme cases, it may be doubted whether s.29 adds anything to the reach of the good old common law offence of incitement to murder. That was the charge which put Abu Hamza al El-Masri, the preacher of hate at Finsbury Park mosque, in prison for ten years in 2006 after an Old Bailey trial which no-one has yet criticised as an unnecessary infringement of free speech. Section 18 of the Public Order Act remains the appropriate means of dealing with less serious emanations of hatred, generally by rather than against religious zealots. Those protestors against the Danish cartoons of the prophet, whose placards call for death to unbelievers, were dealt with by magistrates under this provision. Religious worship is protected under Art.9 of the European Convention on Human Rights as qualified by Art.17, which disallows any interpretation which could imply for any person *"any right to engage in any activity or perform any act aimed at the destruction of any of the rights and freedoms set forth herein."*

This limitation must be born in mind by any religious group seeking to invoke the law against its critics. It was notably overlooked in 2006 by the Jewish board of deputies, when it complained to local government authorities about London mayor Ken Livingstone's refusal to apologise for likening an Evening Standard reporter, who was Jewish, to a concentration camp guard. Incredibly, the adjudication panel solemnly held that Livingstone was guilty of misconduct and suspended him for four weeks: Justice Collins quashed the decision, reminding the panel that any code of conduct must be read subject to Art.10. There was a heavy burden on it to justify infringements upon free speech.

> "It was important that any individual knew that he could say what he liked, provided it was not unlawful, unless there were clear and satisfactory reasons within Art.10(2) to render him liable to sanctions."[211]

The mayor and the newspaper (whose editor, sensibly, had not called for Livingstone's suspension) went back to abusing each other on more rational grounds.

---

[211] *Livingstone v Adjudication Panel for England* (2006) EWHC 2533 (Admin).

CHAPTER 5

PRIVACY AND CONFIDENCE

"It is regrettable that so much of media law should impinge upon public interest reporting, and so little of it worked to eradicate discreditable press practices. The blind Goddess of Justice seems to raise her sword against investigative journalism while her other hand fondles the Sunday muck-raker."[1]

"Until very recently, the law of defamation was weighted in favour of claimants and the law of privacy weighted against them. True but trivial intrusions into private life were safe. Reports of investigations by the newspaper into matters of public concern which could be construed as reflecting badly on public figures domestic or foreign were risky. (The House attempted to address the balance in favour of privacy in *Campbell*. . .)[2]"

INTRODUCTION

Why is privacy a value for which every human rights convention ever **5–001** devised demands protection? Individuals have a psychological need to preserve an intrusion-free zone for their personality and family and suffer anguish and stress when that zone is violated. Democratic societies must protect privacy as part of their facilitation of individual freedom, and offer some legal support for the individual choice as to what aspects of intimate personal life the citizen is prepared to share with others. This freedom, in other words, springs from the same source as freedom of expression: a liberty that enhances individual life in a democratic community.

Communist and fascist regimes are notorious for depriving all citizens of any right to privacy from the state, through an apparatus of informers and police spies, just as they are notorious for suppressing and censoring their critics. Democratic societies contrast most markedly by vouchsafing privacy rights, not only by curbing

---

[1] Preface to *Media Law*, Robertson & Nicol (1st edn, 1984).
[2] Lord Hoffman, *Jameel v Wall Street Journal Europe*, 2006.

state powers of intrusion (although these powers tend to resurge in times of terrorism) but by providing a means of redress against violations by non-state actors—most notably by the media. The European Convention, drafted originally as a bulwark against the spread of Stalinism, thus guarantees by Art.8 a "right" to respect for private and family life, for home and correspondence. Beyond these narrow categories, which entitle citizens to live some part of their life behind a door marked "Do Not Disturb", the media is entitled under Art.10 to probe and publish without restraint. In order to effect this entitlement, each state party has a duty to ensure that there is legal power to deny the media entry to privacy zones that can be geographically defined: the cradle, the school and the toilet, the bedroom, the hospital and the grave.

How, and to what extent, this is achieved in respect to media intrusion will depend very much on national preferences and values. The United States has a tort of privacy invasion, which (thanks to the overriding First Amendment and a consequent reference for the publication of "newsworthy" information) protects only against the grossest breaches, such as publication of personal health records. Many of its states have developed detailed protection against celebrity harassment, however, ever since the US Court of Appeal defined paparazzo as "a kind of annoying insect, roughly equivalent to the English gadfly" when ordering photographer Ronald Galella to stay more than 30 feet away from Jacqueline Onassis and her Kennedy's children and to refrain from causing them alarm. In 2005, two British paparazzi were jailed in California for jeopardizing the safety of film stars whom they chased on motorbikes. In France, on the other hand, privacy protection is absolute and admits of no public interest defence, whether it concerns photographs of Sarah Ferguson having her toes sucked by a lover on a public beach or the ten year cover up of President Mitterand's prostate cancer. In the latter case, indeed, a permanent injunction against the publication of a book about his struggle against this illness whilst in office, imposed after his death, was struck down by the European Court as an unnecessary infringement of Art.10 without any privacy justification.

5–002   In Britain, until the ground-breaking *Naomi Campbell* case in 2005, privacy could only be protected through other actions, principally an action for breach of confidence, which required the claimants to establish that they were owed some duty of confidentiality, arising out of a confidential or contractual relationship. This enabled employers to sue or injunct disloyal servants who wanted to spill the beans—Cherie Booth Q.C. injuncted newspapers from publishing details of her home life provided by a former nanny and Lady Mary Archer successfully sued a newspaper and her former PA over a story that she had travelled to New York for a face-lift (the story was true, of course, which is why it was an invasion of her privacy, although few would have credited it until she did sue—a factor which acts as a deterrent to many would-be claimants). There were some occasions where breach of confidence actions came close to a privacy claim—Sarah Cox, for example, obtained damages from the *Sunday People* after it had published pictures, secretly snapped by telephoto lens, of her honeymooning naked with her husband. But it was not until the decision of the House of Lords in *Campbell's* case that the action for breach of confidence was clearly stripped of its requirement of a confidential relationship and emerged as a fully-fledged right to restrain (or to sue for damages if unrestrained) publications based on media intrusions into the lives of claimants in situations where they had a reasonable expectation of privacy.

It is too early to assess the full consequences of the decision in *Campbell*. Academics hail it as having created a new privacy law, although there have been few signs of any consequential tabloid restraint in their daily diet of "kiss and sell" stories. This may be because most potential claimants do not wish to give true but embarrassing stories further publicity—it takes unprepossessing people with the wealth and chutzpah of Naomi Campbell to bring a case to court. (Princess Diana, who wished to create a privacy law by suing over surreptitiously taken gym photos, quailed at the court door at the prospect of being cross-examined about her own attitude to her husband's privacy and secretly paid the gym owner/defendant a vast sum of money to pretend he had lost the case.) It may be that the British enjoy *schadenfreude* more than the Germans and outside the rarefied atmosphere of the higher judiciary we do not want to give up the pleasure taken in reading of the sex and drugs and family feuds that plague the lives of public figures. This is all part of the Vanity Fair that is London celebrity life, covered by newspapers and magazines that are much more widely read (and much more entertainingly written) than their counterparts in France or Germany or Scandinavia. Judges will continue to wrestle with the demands of pop stars and politicians who want only favourable publicity, and with the "public interest" humbug of newspapers which cater to the public love of gossip and entertainment. Their decisions will inevitably be subjective: the judge in the *Theakston* case solemnly held that a man who visited a brothel could have no reasonable expectation of privacy, although any judge who had actually visited a brothel might well take the opposite view. If there is any principle that can be extrapolated from the hard cases to date it is that the court—whether domestic or at Strasbourg—will, where Arts 8 and 10 are in balance, consider human kindness. A claimant who moves the judge to pity is likely to recover: this is the only explanation for a decision that CCTV pictures of a man's public attempt at suicide could not be shown to illustrate the importance of the technology, or that the much harassed Princess Caroline could restrain photos of her public shopping expeditions. The scenarios in this area are plentiful and the arguments for and against publication are endless: the decision in a close case may turn on application of the judge's humanity rather than any application of legal principle.

"Privacy" remains a frustrating area of law for both journalists and lawyers.[3] There is no single "privacy" statute or even a single body of case law. Instead there are many statutes which deal with different aspects of privacy and a disparate body of case law relating to both privacy and confidentiality which is in a state of flux. This lack of coherent structure means that readers will look in vain for bright line rules to guide them in what can and cannot be published. Indeed, it is not just at the point of publication that these laws of privacy matter. The process of gathering information can itself cross legal boundaries and so this chapter will also consider topics such as data protection and harassment. Confidentiality and privacy are not always enemies of free expression: "confidential sources" are part of the stock in trade of all journalists and this chapter will consider the extent to which a moral obligation to protect a source's anonymity is recognised by the law.

5–003   The English common law has long been resistant to any single overarching claim for "invasion of privacy". Even now, that remains the case.[4] The nearest, until recently, to which the law came was the action for breach of confidence. The spring from which this still flows is the case of *Prince Albert v Strange*.[5] It is, in one sense, a familiar example of English judges bending over backwards to please the Royal Family, but in so doing they found a way of restraining the modern celebrity rip-off.

> Queen Victoria and her consort, Prince Albert, amused themselves and their close friends by making private etchings and drawings, which were kept under lock and key at Windsor Castle. Prince Albert sent the etchings to a shop for impressions to be made of them; a workman took surreptitious copies which the defendant reproduced in a catalogue and sought to exhibit. The judges, in order, to give Prince Albert the utmost redress, did not decide in his favour on the basis of copyright, or even of property, but rather upon the principle of protecting privacy and providing relief against "a sordid spying into the privacy of domestic life" (the court was moved by evidence that the Queen—so unamused in public—obtained pleasure from making the etchings in private and giving them to close friends: her happy pastime would be sullied if they were put on public display). The court injuncted both the catalogue and the exhibition, on the grounds that they invaded the right to privacy, in the sense of a right to control one's possessions and enjoy them precisely because they are not seen or available to others.

---

[3] For a more detailed study of the topic see Tugendhat and Christie *The Law of Privacy and the Media* (OUP) and its 2nd cumulative supplement (2006).

[4] See *Wainwright v Home Office* [2004] 2 A.C. 406 and in consequence, the European Court of Human Rights found that there had been a violation of Art.8 (right to respect for private life) and Art.13 (right to an effective remedy) *Wainwright v UK* Application No. 12350/04 judgment September 26, 2006.

[5] (1848) 2 De G & Sm. 652.

As developed, breach of confidence allowed the courts to intervene to stop the escape of information imparted in the course of a confidential relationship, when the information remained confidential and when it had been or was about to be imparted in breach of that confidence. Arguably, the claimant had also to show that the breach would cause him harm. The need to show that the information derived from a confidential relationship was a serious obstacle to many claims and the common law was slowly pushing outward the circumstances in which they could succeed. Thus, in the *Spycatcher* case Lord Goff said that a duty of confidence would arise:

"where an obviously confidential document is wafted by an electric fan out of a window into a crowded street, or where an obviously confidential document, such as a private diary, is dropped in a public place and then picked up by a passer by".[6]

Mr Justice Laws extrapolated further in a case in 1995 when he said,

"If someone with a telephoto lens were to take from a distance and with no authority a picture of another engaged in some private act, his subsequent disclosure of the photograph would, in my judgment, as surely amount to a breach of confidence as if he had found or stolen a letter or diary in which the act was recounted and proceeded to publish it. In such a case, the law would protect what might reasonably be called a right of privacy, although the name accorded to the cause of action would be breach of confidence. It is, of course, elementary that in all such cases, a defence based on the public interest would be available.[7]

However, the major impetus for change has come from the 5–004 European Convention on Human Rights. When the Human Rights Bill 1998 was going through Parliament, the media was rightly nervous that it would lead to a law of privacy. The Convention has indeed given the courts both the power to expand the circumstances in which a confidentiality of privacy claim can succeed and the organising principles on which to proceed. Article 10 of the Convention, of course, provides a guarantee of freedom of expression, but it is qualified and permits restrictions "necessary in a democratic society" for the protection of the rights of others. Article 8 says:

"(1) Everyone has the right to respect for his private and family life, his home and his correspondence.
(2) There shall be no interference by a public authority with the exercise of this right, except such as is in accordance with the law and is necessary in a democratic society in the interests of national

---

[6] *Att-Gen v Guardian Newspapers Ltd (No.2)* [1990] 1 A.C. 109 at 281.
[7] *Hellewell v Chief Constable of Deryshire* [1995] 1 W.L.R. 804 at 807.

security, public safety or the economic well being of the country, for the prevention of disorder or crime, for the protection of health or morals, or for the protection of the rights and freedoms of others."

In its direct and clearest application, this is a protection against interferences by the state or public authorities. In this sense, Art.8 was addressed to the government rather than the media. However, the European Court of Human Rights has developed a concept of "positive obligations"— in certain respects the State Parties to the Convention like the United Kingdom must take positive steps to see that the rights in the Convention are protected and, in some cases, protected against interferences by other individuals or organisations. By 1998 the Strasbourg Court was already hinting that there was such a "positive obligation" to provide protection against unwarranted media intrusion into private lives.[8] However, it was only in 2004 that the Court unequivocally, but controversially, reached this conclusion in the *Princess Caroline* case.[9]

The United Kingdom courts have come to the same conclusion about the effect of Art.8, but to achieve what the Convention requires they have had to shoe-horn the new obligations into the action for breach of confidence. Where privacy rights of individuals are concerned, there is not much left of the old elements of breach of confidence. The requirement of a relationship of confidence has been declared redundant. Instead there must be a "reasonable expectation of privacy". The extent to which the information is public is relevant but not definitive—Princess Caroline was photographed on a public street. There are no bright lines here either, but if publication would be in the public interest, that is a highly material reason for not interfering with freedom of expression.

5–005   There have been a few high profile "privacy" cases, but not the plethora which the media feared. This may be due to the very modest level of damages which the courts have been prepared to award and also to the reluctance of those whose privacy has been invaded to prolong the embarrassment by bringing the matter to court. A bigger concern for the media has been the increased prospect of an injunction to protect private information. It is anomalous that Blackstone's rule against prior restraint, soundly embedded in libel law, should be more precarious when the case comes within a different legal category. The courts argue that damages can compensate an unjustified libel, whereas a secret, once published, cannot be made confidential again. But the danger of injunctions covering up iniquitous behaviour is demonstrated by the fact that six months before Robert Maxwell's corporate villainy came

---

[8] See for instance *Earl Spencer v UK* App. Nos 28851/95 & 28852/95 (1998) 92 DR 56.

[9] *Princess Caroline von Hannover v Germany* (2005) 40 E.H.R.R. 1.

to light upon his death, he was able to obtain injunctions preventing the press from publishing any suggestion that his companies had indulged in 'dubious accounting devices' or had "sought to mislead . . . as to the value of the assets of the company". The media were even banned from reporting the fact that the order had been made. The impact of an "interim injunction" is in practice "permanent" rather than temporary. It amounts to an order suppressing any publication of the information until trial of the action, which may not take place for many months. By that time, the information may be stale news or have been overtaken by events. Thus media organisations that lose the argument at the interim stage rarely bother to renew it at trial—and in such cases "prior restraint" effectively means permanent restraint.

Although there is now greater scope for obtaining privacy injunctions, the Human Rights Act has made important changes to the procedure which must be followed and the test which must be satisfied before an injunction is granted (see below para.5–027).

The "old" law of breach of confidence cannot be confidently consigned to the dustbin of history. Article 8's protection for correspondence and property may be invoked by companies but only individuals can have private lives. State organisations and certain kinds of public authorities probably cannot rely on the Convention at all. It is still not clear to what extent the changes to the breach of confidence cause of action will be carried over or continued in their case.

Article 8 and privacy interests feature in other chapters of this book. For instance, some of the powers of the courts to restrict the publication of names or other information is justified on privacy grounds and in some cases the High Court can grant injunctions to protect the private lives of children or vulnerable adults (see Ch.8 on Reporting the Courts). Copyright has been used as an indirect means of restricting publication of works which the owner would prefer to keep private (see Ch.6 on Copyright) and long before the courts were wrestling with the impact of Art.8, broadcasters had to live with regulatory regimes which prevented undue interferences with privacy (see Ch.16 Broadcasting Law).

PROTECTION OF PRIVATE INFORMATION

"Reasonable expectation of privacy"

This is the key concept in a claim for protection of private **5–006** information as can be seen from three important cases. They involved a lying and petulant model, a minor Euro-royal and a pair of Hollywood luvvies.

> The super model, Naomi Campbell, had denied that she had ever used illegal drugs. This was a lie. The *Daily Mirror* published a story about

her addiction and the steps she was taking to deal with it, including attendance at a Narcotics Anonymous clinic. The story was accompanied by a photograph taken covertly of her on the clinic's doorstep. She accepted that the newspaper was entitled to correct the false image she had painted of herself, but said that it was wrong to refer to her attendance at the NA and to publish the photograph. By 3:2 the House of Lords upheld her claim. The judges were agreed on the principles but differed on their application to the facts. The Art.8 approach was to be adopted and so the first question was whether her right to private life was engaged at all. This was determined by asking whether the claimant had a reasonable expectation of privacy in relation to the matters in issue. If the claimant passed this hurdle, the next question was whether the privacy interests of the claimant should prevail over the publisher's freedom of expression. The minority considered that the reference to NA and the photographs in the story caused minimal additional intrusion into her private life beyond the matters of which she did not (and could not) complain. The majority on the other hand, thought that her attendance at the NA clinic was analogous to other forms of medical treatment whose privacy the law should be particularly ready to protect. The swing vote was cast by a judge who thought that the photograph was the key issue. On the other matters, he thought that the balance between the two Convention rights was about even, which would then have produced a result in favour of the newspaper, but, he said, the picture was a gross invasion of her privacy (even though taken in a public street) because it identified the clinic and showed her as she left. The majority (unlike the dissenters) were not convinced by the argument that these were details which lay within editorial discretion and the publisher's margin of discretion. The 3:2 division on the facts demonstrates how unsatisfactory it is to have judges second-guessing editors at the behest of massively wealthy "celebrities" who exploit media fame when it suits them.[10]

Shortly after the House of Lords gave its judgment in *Campbell*, the European Court of Human Rights delivered its important judgment in the *Princess Caroline* case.

Princess Caroline von Hannover was part of the royal family of Monaco and, while she sometimes represented Prince Ranier, she had no official state function. She was a fashionable celebrity and a popular target of the paparazzi. She sued and lost in the German courts over the publication of a number of photographs taken of her when she was shopping, skiing, horse-riding or on holiday. All but one pictured her while she was on public property. The German courts said that she was a public figure *"par excellence"* and had to tolerate her photograph being taken and published when she appeared in public, even if she was only on her own private business. Her complaint to the European Court of Human Rights was upheld. The Court said that the German court's reasoning did not do justice to Princess Caroline's right to a

---

[10] *Campbell v MGN Ltd* [2004] 2 A.C. 457.

private life. Even public figures were entitled to this and it extended beyond the family circle and included a social dimension or a zone of interaction even in a public context which was protected by Art.8. Vigilance in maintaining this right to personality was particularly important in an era when technological progress meant that intrusion and dissemination was ever easier. Critically important for the Court was its inability to find any public interest justification for the photographs. Princess Caroline was not like a politician who might have to accept a narrower zone of legitimate expectation of privacy. The pictures contributed nothing to the public debate of issues of general importance. The German courts' differentiation between being in and out of the public eye was too vague a test to be applied.[11]

While the European Court had given many hints of its willingness to find a positive obligation to protect individual privacy against media intrusion, this was an odd case to find a violation of Art.8 on the facts. German law did give protection against media intrusion. The German courts had allowed Princess Caroline to recover damages for the publication of photographs of her in spaces, where, though public, she had "sought seclusion" (at a corner table in a restaurant to hold hands with her boyfriend). It defined "seclusion" as a place,

"away from the public eye—where it was objectively clear to everyone that she wanted to be alone and where, confident of being away from prying eyes, they behaved in a given situation in a manner which they would not behave in a public place".

In other words, you are entitled to privacy when you wish to be private and choose or take steps to manifest that wish. It is difficult to see why this test is any more vague than the numerous restraints on freedom of expression which the Court has said provide a sufficiently predictable standard to be "prescribed by law" for the purposes of Art.10(2). The German court decision goes much further than any previous English case, although it is entirely consistent with *Campbell*. It would prevent publication of a great deal of material which is routinely run in the British tabloids, of celebrities holding hands in restaurants and disporting themselves in public but secluded parts of a beach. By the time the case reached the European Court, what was in dispute was the publication of perfectly harmless photographs of the Princess walking down the street, shopping, horse riding and playing tennis. The Court's decision that Art.8 required Germany to have a law which banned publication of these photographs as well was unjustified. One explanation might be that the Court pitied the Princess who,

"alleged that as soon as she left her house she was constantly hounded by paparazzi who followed her every daily movement,

---

[11] *Princess Caroline von Hannover v Germany* (2005) 40 E.H.R.R. 1.

be it crossing the road, fetching children from school, out walking, practising sport or going on holiday".

However, one judgment of the English Court of Appeal has already rejected the argument that *von Hannover* is to be explained as a response to press harassment.[12]

5–007 *Douglas v Hello* illustrates *par excellence* (to borrow a phrase) the rapid development of the law of privacy in the United Kingdom.

> The actors Michael Douglas and Catherine Zeta-Jones were married on a glitzy occasion in New York in front of some 350 guests. They had sold exclusive rights to publish photographs of the wedding to *OK!* Magazine. The happy couple were to choose which photographs could be published. Guests at the wedding were warned not to take their own photographs. Nonetheless, sneak pictures were sold to *Hello!* magazine. The Douglases and *OK!* discovered this and sought an injunction to stop publication. They were unsuccessful because the Court of Appeal said that, since the couple had traded for money by far the largest part of any right to confidence or (supposing it existed) their right to privacy, any remaining loss could be compensated in damages.[13]

Hello! published its photographs and four years later, the litigation was back in the Court of Appeal after a trial of the action. This time the Court emphasised that the Douglases had retained the right to vet which photographs of their wedding were published. Notwithstanding the number of guests, the wedding remained a private occasion and they retained a right of private information apart from the photographs which they authorised. Of course, guests who were at the wedding would be free to describe the event in their own words, but a picture was worth a thousand words and photographs had a voyeuristic character that went beyond a verbal description. The couple would have felt understandable distress at the publication of unauthorised photographs and this remained real notwithstanding their sale of rights to *OK!* In view of *Campbell* and *Princess Caroline* the Court of Appeal thought that they now had an unanswerable claim and, with hindsight, the Court had been wrong to refuse an injunction.[14]

Private and public

Photographs and sound recordings

5–008 Since the purpose of Art.8 and the developing law in England is to protect individuals against publication of private information, there obviously comes a point where protection is unjustified because the

---

[12] *McKennitt v Ash* (see below) at para.41.

[13] *Douglas v Hello! Magazine Ltd* [2001] 2 All E.R. 289 CA.

[14] *Douglas v Hello! Magazine (No.3)* [2006] QB 125 (an appeal to the House of Lords was decided in 2007)—see *Stop Press* section.

information is no longer private. The Human Rights Act 1998 s.12(4) specifically requires the court to have regard to the extent to which the material has, or is about to, become available to the public.

However, these last three cases illustrate the fuzziness of the line between public and private. The Douglases succeeded although their wedding took place before 350 guests, because (as the trial judge put it),

> "to the extent that the privacy consists of the inclusion of only those who were invited and the exclusion of all others, the wedding was as private as was possible consistent with it being a socially pleasant event."

Naomi Campbell succeeded even though she had been standing in a public street because the photograph was intended to make the association with her therapy at Narcotics Anonymous. Princess Caroline succeeded although she was photographed in public places simply going about her private business.

All of these cases recognise the particular sensitivity of photographs. In all three, the publication of photographs was restrained although a verbal description of what had taken place would not have been prevented. This is a continuation of earlier decisions both in Strasbourg and the United Kingdom.

> Geoffrey Peck was suffering from depression when late at night he took a knife, went into Brentford High Street and tried to commit suicide by cutting his wrists. The Council had installed CCTV and an alert operator saw what was happening and called the police, who intervened and summoned medical help. The Council was proud of this positive outcome and released both still photographs and short clips to demonstrate the usefulness of CCTV. These were published in the local papers and shown on TV. The European Court of Human Rights found that the release of photographs and footage without Peck's consent and without adequate assurances that his identity would be masked infringed his rights under Art.8. He was in a public street, but he was not participating in a public event and he was not a public figure. Although he was carrying a knife, he was not charged with any criminal offence. He might have expected to have been spotted by a casual passer-by (or even by the CCTV operator) but not to have the image of this particularly distressing event in his life published and broadcast to thousands of viewers.[15]

Perhaps the decision can be justified as an act of kindness towards **5–009** a man whose mental state was disturbed at the time and for whom it would be cruelty to have his unbalanced conduct portrayed again and again on television. The Court's own reasoning is not convincing. Peck behaved on a public street in a manner that was calculated

---

[15] *Peck v UK* (2003) 36 E.H.R.R. 41.

to attract attention. He *created* a public event. The idea that he would not have expected to have the image of this event broadcast in the future is surely beside the point: he conducted himself in a way that created news.

In a pre-*Campbell* decision the High Court similarly recognised the additional intrusiveness of photographs.

> Jamie Theakston, a "Top of the Pops" presenter visited a brothel. The prostitutes sold their story to the *Sunday People*. An injunction was refused in relation to the text of what they had to say: there had been no express promise of confidentiality and the relationship between prostitute and client was not inherently confidential. A brothel was not a place where there was a reasonable expectation of privacy. Theakston had placed aspects of his sex life in the public domain and courted publicity and there was an element of public interest given his portrayal of himself as a respectable enough person to present programmes to young people. However, the court did prohibit publication of photographs the prostitutes had taken of him. Photographs were particularly intrusive. There was a reasonable expectation that photographs would not be taken in a brothel. Theakston had not authorised any photographs to do with his sex life and there was no public interest in the photographs themselves.[16]

This mention that photographs are more intrusive than words has been applied to sound recordings so that a secretly recorded private conversation may have two aspects: publication of the information revealed in the conversation, and publication or broadcasting of the recordings themselves. If Art.10 and freedom of expression justifies use of the information, it will not necessarily also justify broadcasting the tape recordings themselves.[17]

> David Mellor, when minister in a government that touted "family values", was secretly recorded having an adulterous sexual relationship: the tape was bought by *The Sun* and made accessible to the public for 30p on its telephone line service, but was soon withdrawn after a threat of a privacy ruling by the regulator, ICSTIS. The story had been front page news and the transcript had been reproduced, but the public interest in exposing hypocrisy stopped short of subjecting Mellor to this penultimate degradation (as it stopped short of inflicting on Theakston the ultimate degradation, of being shown caught on camera *in flagrante*).

On the other hand, the UK courts have still resisted the notion that celebrities can injunct publication of unwanted photographs of them when they have been taken in public. Sir Elton John, for instance, was unsuccessful in his effort to stop the *Daily Mail* from publishing a photograph of him in baseball cap and tracksuit that

---

[16] *Theakston v MGN Ltd* [2002] E.M.L.R. 22.
[17] *D v L* [2004] EMLR 1.

had been snapped on the street outside his London home. The photograph said nothing about his health, personal relations or anything else that would engender a reasonable expectation of privacy. There had been no harassment by the photographer.[18]

Information known to a limited number of people

Information will not lose its private character only because it has **5–010** been shared with a limited number of people. The important issue is whether the information is not generally available and is not intended to be made generally available.[19] Thus, Prince Charles was entitled to a privacy claim in relation to a journal which he had written about his attendance at the 1997 ceremony for the handover of Hong Kong to China. The journal (entitled "The Great Chinese Takeaway") had been circulated to between 20 and 70 recipients, but it was not intended to be disseminated more widely. The copies had been marked "private and confidential" and, though the Prince had been writing his journal and distributing limited copies in a similar fashion for 30 years, there had been no prior leaks.[20]

Once the information has become generally available the position is different. It was the failure of the House of Lords to acknowledge this obvious point in the *Spycatcher* case which led the European Court of Human Rights to find that the media's right to freedom of expression had been violated once publication took place in the USA and over a million copies had been sold worldwide.[21] The European Court went further when it found a violation of Art.10 in the case of *Vereinging Weekblad Bluf! v Netherlands*[22] where a leaked Dutch intelligence document had been published by a newspaper and some 2,500 copies had been sold to the public before the authorities took steps to have further distribution banned. The Court said that by then it was too late. The information was no longer confidential and there was no necessity in a democratic society to impose a ban.

The *Vereinging Weekblad Bluf!* case illustrates another important point. The information in that case had become public because of the newspaper's own actions. This was also so in *Weber v Switzerland*.[23] In neither case was this fact sufficient to justify a restriction on the applicant's freedom of expression. This is a sensible outcome. However galling it may be for the person whose confidence or privacy has been violated to find that the breaker of confidence has

---

[18] *Sir Elton John v Associated Newspapers Ltd* [2006] EMLR 27 Eady J.

[19] *Douglas v Hello! Ltd (No.3)* above.

[20] *HRH Prince of Wales v Associated Newspapers Ltd* [2006] EWHC 522 (Ch.); [2007] 2 All E.R. 139 CA.

[21] *Observer and Guardian v UK* (1991) 14 E.H.R.R. 153.

[22] (1995) 20 E.H.R.R. 189.

[23] (1990) 12 E.H.R.R. 508.

benefited from his own wrong, it would make no sense to allow the rest of the world to discuss and disseminate the information but not him. Depending on national laws there may be civil or criminal consequences for the initial violation, but that is a different issue from whether further publications should be restrained.

5–011 If swift action is taken to institute proceedings, a degree of publication will not necessarily mean that an injunction is a violation of Art.10. When President Mitterand's doctor published a book giving an account of his patient's cancer and its treatment a few days after his death, his family took instant action. Some 40,000 copies of the book were sold before an interim injunction was granted the following day, but the Strasbourg Court said that this degree of publicity was not sufficient to make the interim injunction a violation of Art.10. The final injunction which was granted some nine months later was different. By then, the family's immediate grief at his death must have lessened and there had been yet further dissemination of the book through the internet. By that stage as well, the element of public interest in Mitterand's medical condition at a time when he was President of France could also claim a higher priority.[24]

In the United Kingdom, there is a reluctance to draw a sharp line between matters to do with personal privacy which are in the public domain and those which are not. A number of cases have commented that further publication may still be restrained on privacy grounds if its former publication was limited in some way, unless it is clear that there is no longer anything left to be protected.[25] The electoral register is also open to inspection but its use for direct marketing has been held to infringe the privacy rights of electors.[26] The High Court banned further publication of the new identities of Venables and Thompson, the killers of Jamie Bulger, even if limited disclosure of these took place on the internet or abroad[27]; and the posting of a judgment in a Children's Act case on a website did not mean that all restrictions on further publication should be removed. The court said "the extent of publication is a matter of degree".[28] On rare occasions the Family Division has granted injunctions in the High Court to protect privacy interests of children without the usual proviso for information already in the public domain.[29] In *Green Corns Ltd v Claverley Group Ltd*[30] an injunction was imposed to

---

[24] *Editions Plon v France* (2006) 42 E.H.R.R. 36.
[25] e.g. *Att-Gen v Guardian Newspapers (No.2)* [1990] 1 A.C. 109 at p.260; *R. v Broadcasting Complaints Commission Ex p. Granada* TV [1995] E.M.L.R. 16; *W.B. v H. Bauer Publishing* Ltd [2002] E.M.L.R. 145; *McKennitt v Ash* [2006] E.M.L.R. 10 at [81].
[26] *R. (Robertson) v Wakefield MDC* [2002] QB 1052; *R. (Robertson) v Secretary of State for the Home Department* [2003] EWHC 1760.
[27] *Venables and Thompson v News Group International* [2001] Fam 430.
[28] *Att-Gen v Pelling* [2005] EWHC 414 (Admin) at [36].
[29] See for instance *Re X and Y (Children)* [2004] Fam 607.
[30] [2005] EMLR 31.

prevent publication through the news media or other means of mass communication of the addresses or locations of homes occupied by troubled children in the care of the claimants. This order was made even though the immediate neighbours of the homes would know the addresses.

Once public, always public?

In general, the information genie cannot be squeezed back into the **5–012** bottle once it has become widely available. An injunction in these circumstances would serve no useful purpose. That said, privacy is an area of law which defies universal propositions.

In *Douglas v Hello! Magazine Ltd* the Court of Appeal gave the example of a film star photographed in the nude beside a private swimming pool. Even widespread publication of the photographs might not be sufficient to preclude her from obtaining an injunction to stop further publications if they would reasonably add to her embarrassment. This was an example of how the protection of private information might go further than would be warranted if the information had once been confidential but impersonal.

Criminal convictions take place in open court and are therefore in public. Consequently, a police officer who disclosed a journalist's previous convictions to his editor could not be liable for breach of confidence even though the officer had allegedly used the Police National computer to obtain the details.[31] Yet, even in relation to previous convictions, public authorities at least must take care. "Naming and Shaming" schemes have to be carefully thought through to avoid successful allegations of an infringement of the Art.8 rights of the offenders[32] and the disclosure of the identities of convicted paedophiles by the police can be particularly sensitive because of the risk of vigilante violence. This was so in one case where the danger arose from the linking of the men, their convictions and a particular caravan site at which they were staying.[33]

Authorised publication imminent

The Human Rights Act 1998 requires the courts to take account of **5–013** the extent to which the information has been *or is about to* become available to the public[34] but how much significance should be attached to imminent authorised publication remains controversial.

---

[31] *Elliott v Chief Constable of Wiltshire, The Times* December 5 1996, CA. The journalist was not necessarily without a remedy. If he could prove that the disclosure was malicious, made with intent to harm him for an improper purpose and that he suffered damage as a result, the officer could be sued for misfeasance in public office. Unauthorised disclosure by the Criminal Records Agency or by an authorised recipient of its certificates is an offence under the Police Act 1997 s.124.

[32] See *R. (Ellis) v Chief Constable of Essex* [2003] 2 F.L.R. 566 DC.

[33] *R. v Chief Constable of North Wales Ex p. Thorpe* [1999] QB 396 CA.

[34] Human Rights Act 1998, s.12(4)(a)(i).

In a decision before the Act, the Court of Appeal had suggested that the imminent authorised publication of Lady Thatcher's memoirs made it harder to assert that they remained confidential. The point was not fully resolved. A second (and possibly more influential) reason for refusing the injunction was that the claimants were forced to concede a public interest in the publication of Lady Thatcher's views on John Major who was Prime Minister at the time of the proceedings, and other members of his Cabinet, so far as they were inconsistent with her previously published opinions. Drafting an injunction in sufficiently clear and precise terms to permit the defendant to publish this news proved impossible.[35]

Injunctions have been granted in the past to prevent the publication of confidential information even though authorised disclosure was imminent[36] or where future public exploitation of the idea had been the purpose of confidential discussions.[37] The *Sunday Times* serialised Peter Wright's book *Spycatcher* a few days before the whole book was published in the United States. Although the enormous sales of the book which then followed justified lifting the injunction on "disclosure" of the Wright's information in the United Kingdom, the House of Lords found that the paper had engineered a profitable scoop and had to account to the Government for its increased profits.[38] In *Douglas v Hello! Magazine Ltd No.3*[39] the fact that authorised photographs were due to be published very soon was not a reason to prevent the publication of *unauthorised* photographs. The trial judge in that case had said that he doubted whether the Thatcher memoirs case remained authoritative after the Human Rights Act.[40]

Public interest

5–014   Since the courts are engaged in a balancing exercise between rights of privacy and freedom of expression any public interest in publication will be particularly important. Well before the Human Rights Act, public interest was clearly recognised as a defence to a breach of confidence claim. For instance, John McVicar defeated a confidence action by a former policeman who had expressly asked for the information he provided to the journalist to be treated as confidential. He told McVicar to turn off his tape machine. McVicar did so, but kept a second recorder running. His proposed publication of the allegations of corruption based on the conversation were

---

[35] *Times Newspapers Ltd v MGN Ltd* [1993] EMLR 443 CA. It was subsequently reported that MGN paid £35,000 plus interest to settle the case: *Media Lawyer*, September/October 1999, p.11.
[36] *Gilbert v Star Newspaper Co Ltd* (1894) 11 T.L.R. 4.
[37] *Fraser v Thames Television Ltd* [1983] 2 All E.R. 101.
[38] *Att-Gen v Guardian Newspapers Ltd (No.2)* (above).
[39] See above.
[40] *Douglas v Hello! Magazine Ltd (No.3)* [2003] 3 All E.R. 996 Ch at [224].

undoubtedly a breach of confidence, but the judge accepted that the evidence of corruption could be revealed in the public interest. He said,

"newspapers have many functions and practices, some more attractive than others, but one function was to provide a means whereby corruption might be exposed. That could rarely be done without informers and often breaches of confidence".[41]

Lord Denning had no hesitation in rejecting an application to restrain publication of information obtained by an undercover investigator of scientologists. The information had been given in confidence but "there is good ground for thinking that these courses contain such dangerous material that it is in the public interest that it should be made known".[42]

The Chancery courts, which originally gave birth to the breach of confidence claim, explained that equity would not restrain the disclosure of "iniquity", but the public interest defence broadened out so that it extended beyond proof of crime or fraud to "any misconduct of such a nature that it ought to in the public interest to be disclosed to others."[43] Hence the Court of Appeal held that the *Daily Express* was permitted to publish internal documents extracted from the manufacturer of the intoximeter that revealed doubts about the efficacy of a machine being used to obtain convictions for drink-driving offences. No "iniquity" attached to the claimant, but the possibility of wrongful convictions raised a matter of vital public interest.[44]

A further example of the "public interest" defence is where the information corrects a false image which the claimant has sought to project.

The public relations officer employed by singer Tom Jones sold his memoirs to a newspaper which began to publish them under the rubric "Tom Jones Superstud. More startling secrets of the Family." The Denning-era Court of Appeal refused an injunction because the article revealed hypocrisy. It said,

"If a group of this kind seek publicity which is to their advantage. . . they cannot complain if a servant or employee of theirs afterwards discloses the truth about them. If the image which they foster was not a true image, it is in the public interest that it should be corrected . . . it is a question of balancing the public interest in maintaining the confidence against the public interest in knowing the truth . . . The public should not be misled."[45]

---

[41] *Cork v McVicar*, The Times, October 31, 1995.
[42] *Hubbard v Vosper* [1972] 1 All E.R. 1023 CA.
[43] *Initial Services Ltd v Putterill* [1968] 1 QB 396.
[44] *Lion Laboratories Ltd v Evans* [1985] QB 526.
[45] *Woodward v Hutchins* [1977] 2 All E.R. 771 CA.

5–015   This decision reflects Lord Denning's fervent middle class morality, which regarded any form of non-monogamous heterosexual
relationship as quasi-criminal and any religion other than the
established church as suspect. His decisions have been a boon to the
media which has used them to justify any exposure of celebrity
sexual indiscretion, especially if presented with mock disapproval.
But a more tolerant attitude towards sex and religion among the
current judiciary weakens these Denning precedents set, like Denning, behind lace curtains circa 1930. If the subject matter concerns
intimate personal life, public interest justification for publishing will
need more than moral disapproval.

The courts have been fond of reminding the media that there is a
difference between matters which are of interest to the public and
those which are in the public interest.[46] The former may be
measured simply by increased sales or viewing figures or the
opinions of marketing executives while the later calls for some
objective assessment of how important the story is. The difficulty
with this approach is that it does presume the existence of some
objective standard of "public interest" whereas in any liberal
democracy there is a wide range of opinion as to what is important
or what counts as virtue in politicians or other public figures. It is
tendentious to object that newspapers are in it for the money: of
course, as commercial operations, they will be interested in the
impact which their stories will have on circulation, but commercial
advantage and fulfilment of a public interest can often go together.

Nonetheless when trying to decide which of two competing values
should prevail, the courts have recourse to the notion of "balance"
and there are times when the balance comes down against publication, especially where intimate personal details are concerned and
especially where the press has enticed the revelation by paying for it.

> A newspaper paid £100 to employees of a health authority for details
> of two doctors who had been identified as having AIDS. The paper
> published one story saying that there were doctors who were continu-
> ing to practice despite having the disease and that the Department of
> Health and Social Security wished to conceal the fact. A second article
> intended to name the doctors. The health authority obtained an
> interim injunction. At trial the judge found that the public interest in
> protecting the confidentiality of patients generally and AIDS patients
> in particular (because they might not otherwise identify themselves)
> outweighed the public interest in publication. The health authority had
> done no wrong and the injunction did not stop the debate about AIDS
> or whether doctors who had the disease should continue to practise.[47]

5–016   An unhelpful response to public interest claims before the pre-
Human Rights Act was for the courts to accept that the public
interest justified *some* disclosure, but not to public at large. Thus

---

[46] e.g. *British Steel Corp v Granada* [1981] A.C. 1096, 1168.
[47] *X v Y* [1988] 2 All E.R. 648.

telephone intercepts which might have shown a breach of horse racing regulations could perhaps justify disclosure to the Jockey Club which regulates the sport, but not in the pages of the *Daily Mirror*.[48] Lord Griffiths in *Spycatcher (No.2)* similarly said that a person who came across confidential information of misdeeds by the security service might be entitled to tell the proper authorities, but not to publish it to the world at large.[49] These propositions may be justified in some contexts, for instance, the doctor who tells the police of his alarm at the unco-operativeness of a mentally ill patient[50] but they need to be applied with caution and a recognition that the "proper authorities" are sometimes lazy, incompetent or more inclined to leave their own skeletons undisturbed. In the Lion Intoximeter case the court accepted that the *Express* was entitled to take the view that publication would put more pressure on the department than a discreet behind-the-doors approach. A campaign of public pressure on authority was "an essential function of a free press, and we would all be the worse off if the press was unduly inhibited in this field".[51]

Another example is *Stone v South East Coast Strategic Health Authority*[52]:

> An independent panel had inquired into the care, treatment and supervision that Michael Stone had received prior to committing two murders and one attempted murder. Stone tried to prevent publication of the full report on the ground that it disclosed sensitive personal and medical information about him. He argued that publication might discourage future patients from being candid with health professionals. The Court dismissed the application. There was a true public interest in knowing what had gone wrong. Where individuals or agencies who had been involved in Stone's treatment were (or were not) criticised, the public had a legitimate expectation to know the full reasons. It would not be sufficient to restrict publication to other health professionals. Besides, the whole affair arose out of Stone's criminal acts, the victims or their relatives supported publication and much was already in the public domain.

All of these public interest arguments have been given added weight by the ECHR and the Human Rights Act. The Strasbourg Court has consistently emphasised the particularly important watchdog role of the press in a democracy, especially where matters of public interest are concerned.[53] The Human Rights Act specifically requires the court to have regard to the extent to which it is or would be in the public interest for the material to be published.[54]

---

[48] *Francome v Mirror Group Newspapers Ltd* [1984] 1 W.L.R. 892.
[49] *Att-Gen v Guardian Newspapers (no.2)* [1990] 1 A.C. 109.
[50] *W v Egdell* [1990] Ch. 59.
[51] *Lion Laboratories Ltd v Evans* [1985] QB 526.
[52] [2006] EWHC 1668 (Admin).
[53] See among the many judgments to this effect *Observer and Guardian v UK* (1991) 14 E.H.R.R. 153.
[54] Human Rights Act 1998 s.12(4)(a)(ii).

5–017   Courts still look back to some of the pre-HRA case law and public interest considerations can arise where the claimant is seeking to prevent publication of private information or commercial or governmental information that was held in confidence. Public interest arguments have recently succeeded where the media have wanted to use such information to show inadequate regulation of racing,[55] financial irregularities by a Liverpool nightclub company[56] or the impact of a proposed public private partnership agreement on the infrastructure of the London Underground.[57] Interim injunctions have also been refused where the publication of private or confidential information corrected a false impression projected by the claimants.[58] Naomi Campbell, of course, did not and could not complain of the disclosure of information that she had taken drugs because the *Mirror* would have had an obvious defence of this kind. There are, though, stirrings of judicial unhappiness at the ready resort to Denning-era decisions such as *Woodward v Hutchins* in order to displace obligations of confidence or expectations of privacy.[59]

In *Cream Holdings Ltd v Banerjee* the defendants had argued that disclosure should have been confined to the police or other authorities by analogy with the Whistleblowers' legislation, the Public Interest Disclosure Act 1998.[60] The House of Lords rejected the argument and said that these provisions were intended to give additional protection to employees, not to cut down the circumstances where the public interest may justify publication to the world at large.[61]

The balance between privacy and freedom of expression

5–018 In *Re S*, a case concerned with whether reporting restrictions should be imposed on a murder trial in the interests of a child of the defendant, Lord Steyn summarised the interplay between Art.8's protection of privacy and Art.10's protection of freedom of speech. He said[62]:

> "First, neither article has precedence *as such* over the other. Secondly, where the values under the two articles are in conflict, an intense focus on the comparative importance of the specific rights being claimed in

---

[55] *Jockey Club v Buffham* [2003] QB 462.
[56] *Cream Holdings Ltd v Banerjee* [2005] 1 A.C. 253.
[57] *London Regional Transport v Mayor of London* [2003] E.M.L.R. 4 CA.
[58] *Beckham v News Group Newspapers* QBD April 24, 2005 and *Wallace v News Group Newspapers* QBD May 9, 2005.
[59] See *Campbell v Frisbee* [2002] ICR 141; *McKennitt v Ash* [2006] EMLR 10 Eady J. and *McKennitt v Ash* [2007] EMLR 4 CA [33]–[36].
[60] See para.5–072 and Stop Press.
[61] *Cream Holdings Ltd v Banerjee* at [24].
[62] *Re S (Identification: Restrictions on Publication)* [2005] 1 A.C. 593 at [17].

the individual case is necessary. Thirdly, the justifications for interfering with each right must be taken into account. Finally, the proportionality test must be applied to each. For convenience I will call this the ultimate balancing test."

As this passage shows, the facts of the individual case will be all-important. The Courts are also still feeling their way in relation to these two provisions of the Convention. It is therefore impossible to lay down any general rules.

Lord Steyn's first proposition that neither article has precedence over the other and his language of balance is discordant with the comment of the European Court of Human Rights in the *Sunday Times'* case[63] that Art.10 does *not* call for a balance between rights, but establishes a general right of freedom of expression to which there are limited exceptions and the burden is on those seeking to restrict freedom of expression to establish that the particular interference is necessary in a democratic society. In that case, the Court had in mind the provision in Art.10(2) which allows restrictions which are necessary for the protection of the rights of others, but the Court did not focus on the position where those rights were also guaranteed by the Convention. Article 8 has the same structure as Art.10. Once the Strasbourg Court decided in *Princess Caroline* that this included a positive obligation on the parties to the Convention to ensure that privacy was protected from press intrusion, it would seem that Lord Steyn's approach was one answer to what would have seemed an intractable conflict. An alternative answer would have been that the European Court's approach in the *Princess Caroline* case was wrong and inconsistent with Anglo-American notions of freedom of expression and flatly inconsistent with the principle that there is an absolute right to take photographs in public places.[64] A third, and perhaps the best, approach is to give Art.8 equal weight with freedom of expression claims under Art.10, but *only* in its narrowly defined areas of intimate personal data, family and private correspondence. It may not, on this view, protect princesses while they spend their princessly wealth in shopping and skiing.

Lord Steyn's second proposition, that it is necessary to focus on **5–019** the comparative importance of the specific rights being claimed in the individual case, highlights the obvious feature that the importance of both privacy and freedom of expression rights vary enormously. Freedom of expression is of particular importance where the publication will concern matters of political or public interest. But where this is not the case, the rights of publishers to speak (and their readers or viewers to be told) are not eliminated.[65] Privacy interests also vary hugely. Public figures (particularly those who court publicity or have themselves publicised aspects of their private lives)

---

[63] *Sunday Times v UK* (1979–80) 2 E.H.R.R. 245.
[64] *Sports and General Press Agency v Our Dogs Publishing Co* [1916] 2 K.B. 880.
[65] See for instance *A v B Plc* [2003] QB 195 CA.

must tolerate a greater degree of press intrusion, but even they can claim at some indeterminate point that their privacy takes precedence over freedom of expression, as the Naomi Campbell and Princess Caroline cases showed.

The Naomi Campbell case also illustrated the courts' recognition of the particular sensitivity to privacy claims in relation to medical matters. It was because the majority saw the Narcotics Anonymous clinic as the equivalent of medical treatment that they considered the model's Art.8 rights prevailed.

Although intimate matters relating to health and family will prima facie be regarded as private, the law relating to private information is not concerned with trivia. As Megarry J. once said, "equity ought not to be invoked to protect trivial tittle-tattle, however confidential"[66] and so, for instance, the law would be unlikely to give a remedy if the defendant proposed to publish that the claimant had suffered from a bout of flu or from some minor injury.[67] Where fitness is a factor in public performance, of course, there can be no expectation of privacy. The condition of sporting figures just before some important contest is a subject of endless speculation and report, as was the case with Wayne Rooney's toe prior to the 2006 World Cup.

5–020 More significantly, it must be shown that the claimant has a *reasonable* expectation of privacy. So, if the claimant has discussed in public the same topic he cannot reasonably expect protection against other public discussion of what would otherwise have been his private life.[68] But this principle has its limits.

In *McKennitt v Ash*[69] a former friend of the Canadian folk-singer, Loreena McKennitt, published a book about their lives together. On her web-site the folk singer had listed principles by which she tried to live her life but did not pretend that she had been faultless in achieving them. This did not mean that the author was free to describe how the singer had fallen short. Loreena McKennitt's fiancée had died in a boating accident. She had sponsored a charity on water safety and to a limited extent discussed her reaction to his death. This did not allow Ms Ash to publish lengthy and intimate accounts of the distress that her former friend had gone through. Ms McKennitt disputed many of the details in the book but it was too simplistic to say that a reasonable expectation of privacy could not arise in relation to false allegations. The protection of the law would be illusory if in relation to a long and garbled story a claimant was obliged to spell out which of the revelations was accepted as true. The author's claim to be recounting matters of public interest was treated with circumspection because her falling out with the singer had left her too emotionally involved to be

---

[66] *Coco v A.N. Clark (Engineers) Ltd* (1969) RPC 41.
[67] *A v B, C and D* [2005] EWHC 1651 (QB).
[68] *A v B, C and D.*
[69] [2006] E.M.L.R. 10 Eady J.; [2007] E.M.L.R. 4 CA.

able to judge with detachment what was objectively in the public interest. In any case, on the judge's findings, there was nothing of public interest to set against the singer's reasonable expectation that her former friend and business colleague would preserve her privacy and confidentiality.

In a later case, the Court said that where defendants or those opposing an injunction alleged that the Claimants no longer had a reasonable expectation of privacy because of their own actions it would be necessary to closely scrutinise each public revelation and how it had come about. Polite chit chat, for instance, was not the same as a voluntary release of private information for public consumption.[70]

Kiss and tell

Sexual activities may also qualify for a high degree of protection; **5–021** but the hypocrisy or false image which publication might expose will sometimes weigh heavily in the other side of the balance.

Where the source of information is the other partner in these activities, the conflict between one party's privacy and the other's right to speak is acute. Here again, there needs to be a close focus on facts. As Mr Justice Jacob said in a 1997 case when Michael Barrymore was granted an injunction to prevent *The Sun* from publishing further articles based on interviews with Barrymore's former lover[71]:

> "The fact is that when people kiss and later one of them tells, that second person is almost certainly breaking a confidential arrangement. It all depends on precisely what they do. If they merely indicate that there has been a relationship, that may not amount to a breach of confidence and that may well be the case here, because Mr Barrymore had already disclosed that he was homosexual, and merely to disclose that he had a particular partner would be to add nothing new. However, when one goes into detail (as in *The Sun* article), about what Mr Barrymore said about his relationship with his wife and so on, one has crossed the line into breach of confidence."

The courts have suggested that there is a difference between parties to marriage or (what had been) a stable relationship (where privacy interests are stronger) and more causal encounters.[72] More recently, the Court of Appeal has warned that the English courts

---

[70] *X and Y v Persons Unknown* (2007) HRLR 4.
[71] *Barrymore v News Group Newspapers Ltd* [1997] FSR 600.
[72] See for instance, *A v B Plc* (above) and *Theakston v MGN Ltd* [2002] EWHC 137 (QB).

seem to have taken a less generous view of the protection that the individual can reasonably expect in respect of his or her sexual activities than has the Strasbourg court.[73] Since the Human Rights Act requires the English courts to be guided by the Strasbourg decisions, this is a strong hint of the greater willingness to protect sexual privacy.

5–022   An interim injunction granted by Mr Justice Eady in 2006 illustrated how willingly the courts have responded to these hints[74]:

> The defendant's wife had had an adulterous affair with the claimant for some months. The defendant was angry when he discovered this and threatened to publicise the fact of the affair and some of its details. He sent abusive phone and email messages to the claimant. The court's decision to grant an injunction to stop the harassment could not be criticised, nor could the decision to stop publication of the details of the affair which came from his wife's private papers, but the wider injunction preventing publication of the fact of the affair went too far. The claimant did not appear to contest that the defendant was the "wronged party" in that his trust had been betrayed. The Judge accepted that he should be able to complain to his friends, lawyers, or medical professionals, but not to the world at large. Yet he would be betraying no confidence in doing so and it is difficult to see why his wife's lover should have been able to argue that he had a reasonable expectation that the defendant would have treated the arrangement as private. The claimant's wife's mental health was delicate and their children would have been upset by publicity. Yet the court should surely have placed less weight on these unfortunate consequences which would have flowed from the claimant's own decision to go ahead with the affair.

Threats to life or safety

5–023 In extreme cases, intrusion into a person's privacy may threaten their life or security. Thompson and Venables, the killers of Jamie Bulger, were granted injunctions to prevent publication of their new identities and appearances because of the very real threat of revenge attacks.[75] Similar injunctions were granted to protect the new identities of the child killer Mary Bell and of Maxine Carr, convicted of assisting Ian Huntley (the Soham murderer).[76] However, in 2006 the *News of the World* journalist, Mazher Mahmood, failed to

---

[73] *Douglas v Hello! Magazine (no.3)* above at [74].

[74] *CC v AB* [2006] EWHC 3083 (QB).

[75] *Thompson and Venables v News Group Newspapers Ltd* [2001] Fam 430. The *Manchester Evening News* was later found to have broken this injunction— *Venables and Thompson v News Group International, The Times* December 7, 2001.

[76] *X (a woman formerly known as Mary Bell) and Y v News Group Newspapers Ltd* [2003] EMLR 37; *Maxine Carr v News Group Newspapers Ltd* [2005] EWHC 971 (QB).

convince a judge that his life would be in danger from criminals he had helped to expose if his photograph was published on the website of George Galloway, the Respect M.P. The judge said that a person intending to harm the journalist would need to know his where-abouts and habits. By itself, the photograph would be no help. The judge thought that the real purpose of the application was to protect Mr Mahmood's earning capacity, but that was not an interest which the Convention protected.[77]

The Serious Organised Crime and Police Act 2005 ss.82–94 creates a statutory regime for protection measures (including new identities) when these are implemented to help vulnerable witnesses, informants, law enforcement officials or others involved with the criminal justice process. Disclosure of the new identities or other protection measures is an offence unless it is unlikely that anyone's safety would be endangered as a result.[78] The maximum penalty is two years imprisonment. This regime does not extend to criminal defendants, such as Thompson and Venables (unless, the defen-dant's vulnerability is because he is also an informant or witness for the prosecution), who will therefore in most cases still have to persuade a court that a tailor-made injunction is necessary to protect their lives.

Article 8: a right to share

The private life interests which Art.8 seeks to protect are bound up **5–024** with an individual's human identity and dignity. It is common for those interests to be juxtaposed against the Art.10 right of another person to speak or to publish. However, it is a mistake to see the two provisions as inevitably opposed. There can be occasions when publication will advance the individual's identity and dignity. Thus in one case Mr Justice Munby had to consider the situation of teenage children who wanted to tell their stories in the media in circum-stances frowned upon by their adult carers. The court said[79]:

> "Amongst the rights protected by Article 8, as it seems to me, is the right as a human being to share with others and—if one so wishes—the world at large —one's own story, the story of one's childhood, develop-ment and history. The personal autonomy protected by Article 8 embraces the right to decide who is within the 'inner circle', the right to decide whether that which is private should remain private or whether it should be shared with others".

In that case, the judge decided that the children did have capacity to take these decisions for themselves and therefore Art.8 as well as

---

[77] [2006] E.M.L.R. 26 and see *Media Lawyer* May 2006 p.7.
[78] Serious Organised Crime and Police Act 2005 ss.88 and 89.
[79] *Re Roddy (A Child) (Identification: Restrictions on Publication)* [2004] 2 F.L.R. 949.

Art.10 were in favour of allowing publication to proceed. Similarly, the same judge refused to enjoin a documentary to be broadcast by Channel 4 about Pamela, a young woman with dissociative identity disorder.[80] He concluded that the Official Solicitor was not likely to establish that Pamela lacked capacity to decide whether she wished her story to be told. Therefore, Art.8, as well as Art.10, required an injunction to be refused. The judge went on to say that even if Pamela had lacked capacity, he would have been obliged to take her wishes into account, although they would then have had to be weighed with the arguments of those responsible for her in deciding what was in her best interests.

It is, of course, necessary to consider the impact of publication on all concerned. It does not follow that because a person can reveal their own private life, they can also expose confidential information in respect of which others are entitled to protection unless they consent.[81]

Codes

5–025 The Human Rights Act also requires the courts to consider any relevant privacy code.[82] Notably, this would include the Press Complaints Commission Code[83] which is discussed in Ch.14. This statutory reference to the codes means that they no longer exclusively operate as a system of self-regulation. In its decision on the interim injunction application in *Douglas v Hello! Magazine* the Court of Appeal said that,

> "A newspaper which flouts clause 3 of the code [the clause expressly concerned with privacy] is likely in those circumstances to have its claim to an entitlement to freedom of expression trumped by Article 10(2) considerations of privacy."[84]

In considering whether Naomi Campbell had a reasonable expectation of privacy when standing in the street outside the NA clinic, the majority of the House of Lords was influenced by the PCC's Code which acknowledged that "private places" where photography was unacceptable were "private *or public* property where there is a reasonable expectation of privacy."[85] This change in the Code had been a panicked reaction to anti-paparazzi feeling after Diana's death and thus proved an "own goal" for the media. Although the

---

[80] *E (by her litigation friend the Official Solicitor) v Channel 4* [2005] E.M.L.R. 30.

[81] *McKennitt v Ash* [2006] E.M.L.R. 10 at [77] Eady J. [2007] E.M.L.R. 4 CA at [28]–[32].

[82] Human Rights Act 1998, s.12(4)(b).

[83] *http://www.pcc.org.uk/cop/practice.html.*

[84] *Douglas v Hello! Magazine Ltd* [2001] QB 967 CA at [94].

[85] At the time the PCC's Code referred to "long lens" photography, a qualification which has since been dropped.

courts are therefore required to take account of relevant provisions of the Codes, they have been discouraged from relying on individual decision of the PCC "which at best are no more than illustrative of how the Commission performs its different responsibilities".[86] Nor will the courts slavishly follow the terms of a code.

> In *Tillery Valley Foods v Channel Four Television*[87] the producers of chilled meals for, among others, several NHS hospitals tried to injunct a *Dispatches* programme which was based on many hours of covert filming. The programme was due to allege that workers coughed and sneezed over the food being processed, that standards of hygiene were poor and that the meals had a high level of e-coli bacteria. Tillery argued that the programme should not be broadcast until they had been given an opportunity to respond to these allegations. They relied on the Independent Television Commission's Code (which the regulator, Ofcom, was using until it adopted its own Code). This said that where allegations of wrongdoing or incompetence were made or an individual or organisation was criticised, those concerned should normally be offered an opportunity to take part or otherwise comment on the allegations. The judge, however, found that it was not likely that Tillery would show that there had been a breach of confidence. If there was, the broadcaster had a good public interest defence. As for the Code, this was a code of practice for the regulator (whose sanctions did not include prior restraint), not an embodiment of the law for the courts.

Editorial judgment

To some extent the courts recognise that editors and other media 5–026 organisations are entitled to professional judgment or an area of discretion in how stories are presented, for example, to give credibility to a claim which might otherwise be denied by the object of the story. As the European Court of Human Rights said in *Jersild v Denmark*,[88]

> "It is not for this Court, nor for national courts for that matter, to substitute their own views for those of the press as to what techniques of reporting should be adopted by journalists. In this context the Court recalls that Article 10 protects not only the substance of the ideas and information expressed, but also the form in which they are conveyed."

The same message was conveyed by the House of Lords in *Jameel*: judges must resist the temptation to be editors. It was a temptation that the majority in *Campbell*'s case could not resist.

---

[86] *A v B Plc* [2003] QB 195 CA at [11] (xv).
[87] [2004] EWHC 1075 (Ch), *The Times*, May 21, 2004.
[88] (1995) 19 E.H.R.R. 1 para.31.

Interim injunctions

5–027   Interim injunctions are rare in libel cases because of the rule that they should not be granted if the defendant says that he intends to defend the publication as true or fair comment or covered by privilege. It is very unusual for the court to conduct any detailed examination of the merits of such a prospective defence.

When the claimant alleges that a publication will involve private or confidential information, the attitude of the courts is very different and, because of the difference the courts should be alive to the possibility that the claimant has dressed up what is in reality a defamation action as a confidentiality or privacy claim.[89] Before the Human Rights Act, the prevailing approach (defamation cases apart) was to consider whether the Claimant had merely an arguable case and then to decide where the balance of convenience lay.[90] Usually this meant preserving the existing position until a trial could take place and this test inevitably favoured the imposition of an injunction. It was also common for these injunctions to be granted by a judge without notice to the defendant.

The Human Rights Act made two important procedural changes. The norm is now for the publisher to be given notice of an application to the court (although the notice will often be extremely short). The court should only consider a claimant's application in the absence of the defendant if satisfied that all reasonable steps were taken to notify the defendant or if there are compelling reason why the defendant should not be notified.[91]

5–028   The second change was to make it a condition of granting an interim injunction that the claimant was "likely" to succeed at trial. The House of Lords has said in most circumstances this will mean a claimant showing that it is probable (or more likely than not) that he will succeed at trial. However, the test is sufficiently flexible that in certain circumstances a lower standard will do—but the court should be exceedingly slow to depart from the usual standard. It might properly do so, for instance, if the consequences of disclosure would be particularly severe (such as personal violence to the claimant) or if a short-lived injunction was necessary in order for the court to give proper consideration to the injunction application.[92]

A claim for an interim injunction is, of course, dependent on the claimant having advance knowledge of the proposed publication. He must satisfy the court that a publication of the type which he wishes to restrain is likely to take place unless an injunction is granted. The publisher is not obliged to co-operate. As Lord Denning said,

---

[89] *Service Corp International Plc v Channel Four Television* [1999] E.M.L.R. 83; *Tillery Valley Foods v Channel Four Television* [2004] EWHC 1075 (Ch), *The Times*, May 21, 2004.

[90] *American Cyanamid Co v Ethicon* [1975] A.C. 396.

[91] Human Rights Act 1998, s.12(2).

[92] *Cream Holdings Ltd v Banerjee* [2005] 1 A.C. 253.

"I am very concerned that no-one should think that on a speculative basis you can go to the courts and call upon the publisher of printed material or television or radio material to come forward and tell the court exactly what it is proposed to do and invite the court to act as censor. That is not the function of the court."[93]

This in turn will sometimes cause publishers to be understandably reticent about approaching the object of their story. But prudence on this score has to be weighed against the greater risk of making mistakes if no opportunity to respond is given. And if the story is also defamatory, not giving the person concerned a chance to comment will reduce the prospect of a successful public interest defence based on *Jameel*.[94] It can also be advantageous to allay concerns if the person being investigated has an erroneous or exaggerated idea of what the story will cover. As Lord Denning went on to say in *Leary*:

"It is different, of course, if there is solid evidence as to what the content of the publication will be and that evidence leads the court to conclude that prima facie there will be a contempt of court. Then it would no doubt be right that the defendant should be invited, but not compelled, to tell the court what in fact he intends to publish, because of course if he does not and there is a prima facie case that there will be contempt he will find himself faced with an injunction. But that is not the same thing as setting the courts up as a censorship body to which people must submit material on pain of being prohibited from publishing it."

Leary concerned contempt of court, but the same principles apply where it is alleged that a private right will be infringed.[95]

Damages

Levels of damages for publication of private information have been **5–029** modest. Naomi Campbell received £2,500 plus a further £1,000 aggravated damages. Michael Douglas and Catherine Zeta-Jones were awarded £3,500 each for the distress arising from the publication of the unauthorised photographs of their wedding plus a further £7,000 between them for the cost and inconvenience of having to select hurriedly the photographs which they wished to be published in *OK!* no later than the publication of the unauthorised photographs in *Hello!* Lady Archer was awarded £2,500 for leaked

---

[93] *Leary v BBC*, unreported, September 29, 1989, CA quoted in *A v B, C, D* [2003] EWHC 1651 (QB) at [21].

[94] See para.3–063.

[95] *McKennitt v Ash* [2006] E.M.L.R. 10 at [40].

information from her former personal assistant that included reference to cosmetic surgery.[96] Loreena McKennitt was awarded £5,000 for the publication of a book by a former friend which had intruded on her privacy.[97]

While this level of damages has probably discouraged some claimants, the media need to bear in mind that publication of private information can bring other risks.

As we have seen, the test for an interim injunction is more favourable to claimants than in libel cases even though the Human Rights Act has raised the bar somewhat. The knowledge that post-publication damages will be low may make some judges look even more favourably on the claim for an injunction[98] although in principle this factor should not be very influential where freedom of expression is at stake.

5–030   A cynical calculation that compensatory damages will cost the publisher less than the profit to be made by extra sales is exactly the type of consideration which can lead to an award of exemplary damages. This is not an area which has been explored yet, but the law relating to publication of private information is still in active development.

Finally, as MGN found to their quite literal cost, the damages which they had to pay Naomi Campbell were only a small part of the financial burden of losing the case which she had brought against them. Her lawyers were acting on a conditional fee agreement and, once their success fee was taken into account, the final bill to MGN was over a million pounds. The House of Lords later rejected their argument that this constituted a disproportionate curb on their freedom of expression.[99] It said that conditional fees provided a system of "swings and roundabouts" where claimants' lawyers took the risk of cases which might be unsuccessful because of the increased fees in those cases where their clients did win. The Lords said that requiring losing defendants to pay their opponent's reasonable costs *and* a contribution to the funding of other litigants was proportionate and consistent with Art.10. Naomi Campbell was very wealthy and needed no assistance, but the House of Lords also said that it was not incumbent on Parliament to devise a conditional fee system which was accessible only to those who would not otherwise have been able to afford to pay for their law suits.

Who can sue?

5–031   Normally the person whose privacy has been, or is about to be, interfered with is the obvious claimant. The Official Solicitor can intervene where vulnerable children or adults are the centre of

[96] *Lady Archer v Williams* [2003] E.M.L.R. 38.
[97] *McKennitt v Ash* [2006] E.M.L.R. 10.
[98] *Douglas v Hello! Magazine Ltd* (above) at [259].
[99] *Campbell v MGN Ltd (No.2)* [2005] 1 W.L.R. 3394 HL.

attention and local authorities can take action in relation to children in their care. Other institutions with the care of vulnerable may have their own confidentiality or privacy interests to assert and some-times, pragmatically, publishers have not insisted on one of the people in their care being joined as a claimant.[100]

Article 8 rights may extend to business and professional corre-spondence[101] but it is doubtful whether in any wider sense an artificial person such as a company can have a "private life" to be protected.[102] Convention rights do not extend to organs of the state or public authorities to the extent that they are exercising public functions.[103]

In *Douglas v Hello! Magazine Ltd* the Court of Appeal concluded that confidential or private information which was only protected by the law of confidence was not a type of property which could be assigned or transferred. This was one of the reasons why *OK!* could not sustain its independent claim against *Hello!*.[104]

COMMERCIAL AND GOVERNMENTAL CONFIDENTIAL INFORMATION

The rapid and continuing growth of case law concerning private 5-032 information will not always be relevant. The older law concerning confidential information may still be invoked where, for instance, what is in issue is a governmental or commercial secret which is unrelated to the type of privacy interests that Art.8 is intended to protect. Even where the material is private, the former law of confidence may give overlapping protection.[105]

Part of the Douglases' claim had been for their labour and expense in editing the selection of photographs to be published in *OK!* This had to be done hastily because of the imminent publication of *Hello!*'s spoiler. Since this claim related to information which was due to be published it was of a different type to their complaint about the publication of the unauthorised photographs themselves. The Court of Appeal summarised the position in this way:

> "Where an individual (the owner) has at his disposal informa-tion which he has created or which is private or personal and to

---

[100] *Ashworth Hospital Authority v MGN Ltd* [2002] 1 W.L.R. 2033; *Green Corns Ltd v Claverley Group Ltd* [2005] EMLR 31.

[101] e.g. *Stes Colas Est v France*, App 37971/97, judgment April 16, 2002.

[102] See Lord Mustill in CA in *R v BSC Ex p.BBC* [2001] QB 885 and the discussion in the Australian High Court in *Australian Broadcasting Corporation v Lenah Game Meats Pty Ltd* (2001) 208 C.L.R. 199.

[103] The Human Rights Act 1998 s.7 allows only an actual or prospective "victim" of Convention violations to rely on these rights. A victim is someone who could make an application to the Strasbourg court and Art.34 of the European Convention requires an applicant to be "any person, *non-governmental* organisa-tion or group of individuals".

[104] *Douglas v Hello! Magazine Ltd (no.3)* (above) at [119].

[105] See *HRH Prince of Wales v Associated Newspapers Ltd* [2006] EWCA Civ 1776.

which he can properly deny access to third parties, and he reasonably intends to profit commercially by using or publishing that information, then a third party who is, or ought to be aware of these matters and who has knowingly obtained the information without authority, will be in breach of duty if he uses or publishes the information to the detriment of the owner."[106]

Duties of confidence can be created expressly by contract as with employees of the intelligence services like Peter Wright[107] or those engaged in commercial enterprises which wish to guard their trade secrets jealously.

Corruption

5–033 The first matter to be considered by a media organisation which is offered information from an employee is not the civil law of confidence but the criminal provisions of the Prevention of Corruption Act 1906. It is an offence to offer an incentive or reward to any employee for doing any act in relation to his principal's business. These laws against bribery and corruption may in some circumstances apply to payments to informers. The media are protected by the requirement that any payment must be proved to have been made corruptly—a jury would doubtless acquit if the payment was necessary to extract information that revealed a public scandal. Payments to ex-employees are not caught so long as they were not promised prior to resignation, and a genuine consultancy fee would not be legally objectionable.

> In 1987 *The Observer* was prosecuted at the Old Bailey for an offence under the Prevention of Corruption Act. It had paid £10,000 to an employee of the Ministry of Defence for documents and information revealing that millions of pounds of public money had been lost through mismanagement and failure to supervise defence contractors. The employee had been gaoled at an earlier trial for corruptly accepting a bribe from *The Observer*, but the newspaper was acquitted of offering the money corruptly. The newspaper's editor and senior journalists explained that they had been led to believe that the employee had resigned his office before they paid him for acting as a consultant. This case demonstrates the importance of bearing the Prevention of Corruption Act in mind before any payment is made to a source.

Commercial information

5–034 Employment and consultancy contracts generally have "secrecy" clauses in which employers and advisers undertake to kept to themselves information acquired in the course of the relationship.

---

[106] *Douglas v Hello! Magazine Ltd (No.3)* (above) at [118].
[107] The Privy Council rejected an argument that such a contract was vitiated by duress *R v HM AG for England and Wales* [2003] E.M.L.R. 24 PC. In the United Kingdom, such contractual obligations are reinforced by the Official Secrets Acts—see para.11–007.

Even without a specific clause, the courts will imply an undertaking that the information given in confidence to the employee will not be used to the employer's detriment.[108]

Even where there is no contract the circumstances may be such that the information is obviously intended to be kept confidential. Thus lawyers who receive their opponents' confidential papers because of an obvious mistake are under an obligation to return them and can be prevented from using the confidential information[109] and the same would probably apply to obviously confidential documents which had been dropped by mistake in a public place.[110]

A duty of confidence was imposed on a press photographer who booked into a hotel in whose grounds the band "Oasis" was preparing a photographic shoot of their new album. Because of the security arrangements it was seriously arguable that the photographer ought to have realised that the assembly of props and people for the cover picture was confidential.[111] Similarly, the makers of the film *Frankenstein* obtained an injunction to restrain photographs of the set, costumes or prosthesis used in the film. The photographs had been taken on the set despite security arrangements and notices prohibiting photography.[112]

In other situations, the duty of confidence may restrict the use of **5–035** information beyond a particular purpose. Thus the process of disclosure, whereby one party to litigation is obliged to produce to his opponent all documents in his possession that are relevant to the case, is protected by both contempt and breach of confidence. An advocate or litigant who discloses their opponents' discovered documents to the media may be punished for contempt and the media may be restrained from publishing their contents by a breach of confidence injunction. The *Sunday Times* obtained some of its information about the manufacture of thalidomide by purchasing documents disclosed by Distillers to an expert witness. Despite the obvious public interest in the matter, the court granted an injunction on the basis that there was a greater public interest in protecting the process of discovery.[113] Another example of the misuse of information obtained for a limited purpose concerned Myra Hindley's confessions to the Moors' murders 20 years after the events. They were incorporated into a book written by the investigating officer who was sued by his employers for breach of confidence. This was a

---

[108] *Faccenda Chicken v Fowler* [1987] Ch. 117 CA. Unwanted disclosure is sufficient where the information is private personal information, but detriment is needed where the claimant is a public body and probably also where the information is commercial.

[109] See e.g. *English and American Insurance Co Ltd v Herbert Smith* [1988] FSR 232.

[110] See *Att-Gen v Guardian Newspapers Ltd No.2* [1990] 1 A.C. 109 at 281 per Lord Goff.

[111] *Creation Records Ltd v News Group Newspapers Ltd* [1997] E.M.L.R. 444.

[112] *Shelley Films Ltd v Rex Features Ltd* [1994] E.M.L.R. 134.

[113] *Distillers Co (Biochemicals) Ltd v Times Newspapers Ltd* [1975] QB 613.

clear case of the use of confidential material for non-policing purposes, i.e. for private gain. It is different where a statement to the police or an interview is deployed in open court. Even if the judge reads the statement in private, its contents may enter the public domain.[114]

It is not only the original confidant who can be sued. Others (such as journalists) to whom the secrets are leaked will owe a similar duty of confidence as long as they knew or should have known that the information was originally intended to have a restricted circulation. However, in a busy newsroom, where tip-offs come orally, at second and third hand, claimants may be hard pressed to prove that their information was still impressed with confidentiality.

> A company which published a private newsletter to a handful of clients providing confidential information about the cocoa market sued Dow Jones for breaking its confidence (as well as its copyright) by reporting the substance of the newsletter. Its journalist had obtained this information by telephone from several newsletter subscribers, who volunteered the information in breach of their own agreement with the claimant to keep it secret. The journalist did not know of this confidentiality arrangement so neither she nor her employer could be affected by it.[115]

The court's first task will be to decide whether the information is indeed confidential. Once material has been published, and assuming that individual privacy issues do not arise, it will be difficult to justify any restriction on further dissemination of the material.[116]

5–036 Even if the information has remained confidential, the public interest may justify publication. As can be seen above, many of the cases concerning public interest have involved material which is not private or personal. If there are no privacy or other Convention rights to be balanced, the Court should start with a presumption in favour of freedom of expression particularly where the application is for a pre-publication injunction.[117] The public interest in disclosure can prevail even in the face of an express contractual confidentiality clause,[118] although it is possible that the existence of an express contractual obligation of confidence will aid the Claimant's case when it comes to striking the balance.[119]

The Court of Appeal said in the context of the publication of one of Prince Charles' private diaries by the *Mail on Sunday* that the

---

[114] *Bunn v BBC* [1998] 3 All E.R. 552 Lightman J.

[115] *PCR Ltd v Dow Jones Telerate Ltd* [1998] F.S.R. 170.

[116] *Douglas v Hello! Magazine Ltd (no.3)* (above) at [105].

[117] See *Observer and Guardian v UK* (1992) 14 E.H.R.R. 153.

[118] *London Regional Transport v Mayor of London* [2003] E.M.L.R. 4 at [46] CA.

[119] Contrast *London Regional Transport v Mayor of London* (above) which said that the existence of a contractual obligation of confidence added nothing with *HRH Prince of Wales v Associated Newspapers Ltd* [2006] EWCA Civ 1776 which said that it could be an extra factor in the claimant's favour. It endorsed *Campbell v Frisbee* [2002] I.C.R. 141 CA which articulated the same view.

issue was not simply whether the information was a matter of public interest but whether in all the circumstances it was in the public interest that the duty of confidence should be breached. It gave the example of a Budget speech leaked by a disloyal employee in advance of the speech being delivered to Parliament. The content of the draft would be a matter of public interest, but preserving the Chancellor's confidence would take priority.[120]

Government confidences

In 1975 the Attorney-General sidestepped the criminal law and 5–037 invoked the civil law of confidence to try to stop publication of Richard Crossman's memoirs. The Lord Chief Justice agreed that public secrets could be restrained by a court, but it had to be satisfied that any restriction was in the public interest. Cabinet discussions came within this category and could be protected, but not forever. It is not the case that "once a confidence, always a confidence". Stale secrets could not be protected and the Crossman memoirs were not injuncted because they related to meetings which had taken place at least 10 years prior to publication.[121] The principle has been repeated several times since: if the claimant is a state organisation it can only prevent publication on breach of confidence grounds if it can show that a ban would be in the public interest.[122]

The magnitude of this task was shown when the Australian High Court refused to accept that its Foreign Minister could stop the publication of diplomatic cables between the Australian Embassy in Djakarta and Canberra on grounds of breach of confidence when no security secrets were revealed and their potential for embarrassment was insufficient to warrant an injunction:

"It is unacceptable in our democratic society that there should be a restraint on the publication of information relating to government when the only vice of that information is that it enables the public to discuss, review and criticize government action. Accordingly, the court will determine the Government's claim to confidentiality by reference to the public interest. Unless the disclosure is likely to injure the public interest, it will not be protected. The court will not prevent the publication of information which merely throws light on the past workings of government, even if it be not public property, so long as it does

---

[120] *HRH Prince of Wales v Associated Newspapers Ltd* [2007] 2 All E.R. 139 CA [67]–[68].

[121] *Att-Gen v Jonathan Cape Ltd* [1976] QB 752. See Hugo Young, *The Crossman Affair* (Hamish Hamilton and Jonathan Cape, 1976).

[122] See *Att-Gen v Guardian Newspapers Ltd (No.2)* (above) and *Douglas v Hello! Magazine Ltd. (no.3)* above at [104].

not prejudice the community in other respects. Then disclosure will itself serve the public interest in keeping the community informed and in promoting discussion of public affairs. If, however, it appears that disclosure will be inimical to the public interest because national security, relations with foreign countries or the ordinary business of government will be prejudiced, disclosure will be restrained."[123]

The principle was the key to the media's ultimate success in the English litigation over *Spycatcher*:

> The *Guardian* and *Observer* published the main allegations in Peter Wright's book, *Spycatcher*, at the time when the book was the subject of confidentiality proceedings in Australia. On the eve of publication of the book in the United States, the *Sunday Times* began to serialise it. All were injuncted in England from publishing any further matter from the book until a trial could take place in this country. The injunction was upheld by the House of Lords. In the meantime, the book, having been published in the United States, became an international best-seller. The newspapers continued to defend their right to publish at the trial and in subsequent appeals. They successfully opposed the grant of a permanent injunction. The House of Lords accepted that Peter Wright, like other members and former members of the security services, was under a life-long duty to keep confidential any information he learnt in the course of his work. However, the Lords endorsed the view of the Australian High Court (quoted above). The Government, unlike private individuals and organisations, had to show that the public interest would be harmed by publication. Because of the widespread dissemination of the book's contents, the Attorney-General could not do that and the injunctions against all the newspapers came to an end. The *Guardian* and *Observer* articles had contained nothing damaging to the public interest and so they did not have to compensate the Government for the stories they had already published. But the *Sunday Times* had jumped the gun and its instalment had included material from *Spycatcher* that had not been published elsewhere previously. It did not help the paper that publication of the whole book in the USA followed days later: it had deliberately engineered a profitable scoop and had to account to the Government for the profits it made by the increase in its circulation.[124]

5–038   In 1991 the European Court of Human Rights unanimously ruled that the injunctions upheld by the English courts after *Spycatcher* had been published abroad were an infringement of Art.10. Widespread foreign publications had destroyed all claim to confidentiality and the Government's case had undergone a "curious metamorphosis". It had used the same language ("the interests of

---

[123] *Commonwealth of Australia v John Fairfax Ltd* (1981) 32 ALR 485. For similar sentiments of the US courts, see *N.Y. Times v US* 403 US 713 (1971).

[124] *Att-Gen v Guardian Newspapers Ltd (No.2)* (see above).

national security") to disguise its real objective, in the post-publication period, of protecting the security service from embarrassment in Britain and deterring its past and present members who might be minded to follow in Wright's footsteps. That was not a sufficient reason to bring into play the national security exception to Art.10's freedom of expression guarantee. The Court narrowly (by 14 votes to 10) held that the Government had been entitled to seek an injunction on national security grounds *prior* to publication abroad, because of the risk that the book might contain material damaging to the intelligence services.[125]

A parallel case to *Spycatcher* concerned disclosures by Anthony Cavendish, a former MI6 officer.

> Cavendish was refused authorisation to publish his memoirs, *Inside Intelligence*. He nonetheless had copies printed and distributed them as "Christmas cards" in 1987 to 279 friends. The English courts granted an interlocutory injunction to prevent *Times* Newspapers from publishing the Cavendish material. *The Scotsman* refused to undertake not to publish. The House of Lords held that although members of the security service were under a life-long duty of confidence, the Crown would be granted an injunction to prevent publication only if the public interest would be harmed. Prior publication was the most relevant circumstance. An interlocutory injunction was refused. Lord Templeman referred to the standard in Art.10 that restraints should only be imposed where necessary in a democratic society. He said that the courts would be guided by legislation as to what was necessary and not impose restraints that were more severe than Parliament had thought appropriate. The Official Secrets Act had not come into force at the time of this decision, but Lord Templeman was guided by its requirement that publication of matters relating to the security services by an "outsider" would only be punishable if harm resulted.[126]

This chapter has already included other examples of cases where the government has been unable to obtain an injunction because publication was in the public interest. In 2006 the European Court of Human Rights emphasised that it is not a sufficient reason for interfering with the media's freedom of expression that the information which they wish to publish was illegally obtained.

> A state-owned insurance company in Slovakia was undergoing a stormy and controversial privatisation. In the course of this a telephone conversation between a government minister and a senior official was illegally intercepted. The intercept which concerned the privatisation dispute was leaked to a radio station which broadcast it. The station played no part in the illegality and was not itself guilty of a criminal offence. However, it was successfully sued in the Slovakian

---

[125] *Observer and Guardian v UK* (1991) 14 E.H.R.R. 153.
[126] *Lord Advocate v Scotsman Publications Ltd* [198] 2 All E.R. 852 HL. After this decision, the English court accepted that its injunction should not continue.

courts for defamation and interference with the privacy of one of the participants. The European Court found that its right under Art.10 had been violated. The illegality of the source's actions was not a sufficient justification. The tape concerned a quintessential issue of public interest.[127]

An alternative remedy which is less intrusive on freedom of expression than an injunction is to require the defendant to hand over the profits of his breach of confidence. The US Supreme Court used the device of a "constructive trust" to compel a former agent to give up his royalties from a book which he wrote in breach of a contractual obligation of confidence.[128] The House of Lords reached the same result by a different route when it ordered the spy, George Blake, to account for the royalties due from the publishers of his book, *No Other Choice*, which had been published in breach of his undertaking to MI6 not to disclose any official information gained by him as a result of his employment. Damages for breach of contract are normally intended to put the aggrieved party in the position he would have been in if the contract had been performed, but exceptionally the court considered that they should in this case be assessed by reference to Blake's profit.[129]

CONFIDENTIAL IDEAS

5–039 Breach of confidence is also relevant to the media in preventing, or compensating for, the unfair exploitation of programme ideas and treatments. Normally, this form of piracy is combated by an action for breach of copyright. However, as we shall see, there can be no copyright in an idea, or even in an elaborated idea that is not reduced to material form and substantially copied. The planning stage for television programmes and plays will frequently involve luncheons and meetings at which ideas are discussed, and the law will in some circumstances impose obligations to honour the confidence of those who impart original ideas that have commercial value. In order for the claimant to succeed:

- the concept must be clearly identifiable, and have some significant element of originality not already in the realm of public knowledge. The originality may consist in a significant "twist" or "slant" to a well-known story;

---

[127] *Radio Twist v Slovakia* App. No. 62202/00 judgment December 19, 2006.
[128] *Snepp v US* 444 U.S. 507 (1980).
[129] *Att-Gen v Blake* [2000] 4 All E.R. 385 HL. Blake's complaint to the European Court of Human Rights later succeeded, but only on the basis that the litigation had taken an unreasonable amount of time to be concluded. He was awarded 5,000 euros for non-pecuniary loss: *Blake v UK* Application No. 68890/01 September 26, 2006.

- the concept must have been developed to the stage at which it has commercial potential and is capable of being realised as an actuality. A full synopsis is not necessary in cases in which a short statement, or oral elaboration, fulfil these criteria;
- the concept must have been given or expressed to the defendant in circumstances in which all parties recognise a moral obligation not to make further use of it without the consent of the communicator.

These principles were laid down in the case of *Fraser v Thames Television*.[130]

> Thames screened a fictional series called *Rock Follies*, about the experiences of a three-girl rock group. The idea had originated with the manager of an actual group called Rock Bottom, who proposed to Thames that they should produce a series based on the formation of the group and the subsequent experiences of its members. The concept was discussed at a series of meetings with Thames executives, producer and writer, at a time when the latter were seriously considering production using the Rock Bottom group. This arrangement fell through, but Thames, using the other performers, developed the concept into a successful series. *Rock Follies* was substantially based on the characters and actual experiences of the Rock Bottom girls and their manager, and a number of "twists" and "slants" in the final treatment were based on information imparted by them in the course of negotiations in which all parties were jointly concerned commercially in the possible use of the idea. These negotiations would be recognised, in the television profession, as covered by an ethical obligation of confidence. The concept was clearly original: although the mere idea of an all-female rock group may be hackneyed, the "slant" of focussing on the members as characters and professional actresses in their own right, and using the actual experiences of Rock Bottom, put sufficient flesh on the idea to justify its protection. The very fact that it was eventually turned into a much-acclaimed series was evidence of its commercial attractiveness and its ability to be realised in actuality. The claimants were awarded damages in the order of half a million pounds.

In deciding whether an idea was imparted in circumstances which imposed a duty of confidence, the court will take account of trade practice and the subjective perception of the parties, but neither can be conclusive of this essentially objective question, i.e. were the circumstances such that a duty of confidence was imposed?[131]

For all the difficulties that confidence and copyright may pose to **5-040** exposure journalism, there is another side to these laws, which protect the creator of original work from having it copied and

---

[130] *Fraser v Thames Television Ltd* [1984] Q.B. 44.
[131] *De Maudsley v Palumbo* [1996] E.M.L.R. 460.

exploited without authorisation. The internet, digital copying and the vast array of technology now available for mass reproduction and dissemination has made creative talent exceptionally vulnerable to piracy and media interests have devoted a great deal of their resources to protective measures against copyright theft. At the most serious level, this involves well-organised piracy, which can be combated only by severe application of the criminal law. But as an everyday problem for media organisations, the question of giving credit where credit is due can involve the most complicated and delicate considerations. Plots and themes and ideas can be lost over luncheons, borrowed subconsciously, and pass through the minds of a daisy-chain of progenitors. Unless questions of plagiarism are amicably resolved, they can involve authors and programme-makers in bitter and costly legal disputes. A BBC department was plunged into an unedifying quarrel over Desmond Wilcox and his book of *The Explorers* series. The rights of journalists became hopelessly entangled in the dispute over "The Ballsoff Memorandum"—a confidential note, mentioning sources by name, passed between a journalist and the editor of the *Observer*, leaked to and published by *Private Eye*.[132] The claimant, supported by the *Observer*'s editor, claimed that the magazine's action was a breach of copyright, which damaged the public interest by revealing journalistic sources; *Private Eye* argued that the public interest was served by revealing these sources and by showing the machinations behind the editorial policies of a major newspaper. The case was eventually decided upon a technicality, but it demonstrated, in the course of a long trial and a complicated judgment, how the "rights" claimed for journalists can be mutually confusing and contradictory when one part of the press seeks to investigate the confidential arrangements of another.

PRIVATE PHOTOGRAPHS

5–041 The Copyright Act 1988 took a small step towards privacy in domestic photographs. Before the 1988 Act a person who commissioned a photograph was the first owner of copyright in it. That rule has been changed and copyright now first belongs to the photographer. However, if the photograph has been commissioned for private and domestic purposes, the person commissioning it has the right not to have the photograph issued to the public, displayed in public or broadcast. This right is included in the generic description of "moral rights" in the Copyright Act (see para.6–064).[133] The right is

---

[132] *Beloff v Pressdram Ltd* [1973] 1 All E.R. 241.
[133] Copyright, Designs and Patents Act 1988, s.85. For discussion of the meaning of "commission" in the Copyright Act 1956, see *Apple Corp v Cooper* [1993] F.S.R. 286 although for some obscure reason the definition of "commission" in the 1998 Act (see s.263) does not expressly apply to the moral rights part of the 1988 Act. This moral right lasts as long as the copyright in the photograph (see s.86).

not infringed if the photograph is incidentally included in an artistic work, film or broadcast.[134] More importantly, the right is not infringed if the commissioner has consented to its use.[135] The consent does not have to be in writing, but it would be prudent to obtain a written consent in order to avoid later argument about whether it was given or not. The practical result of these changes is that, for example, a photograph, commissioned by a family of a daughter who is later murdered, will not be able to be used without the family's consent. Courts are more than willing to award punitive damages against photographers for the "flagrancy" of a breach of copyright in circumstances where they supply private photographs of suddenly newsworthy people to the press.[136]

In addition to these statutory rights, photographs which intrude into areas where a person would have a reasonable expectation of privacy may now be able to stop their publication in accordance with the principles in the *Campbell*, *Princess Caroline* and *Douglas* cases discussed above.

DATA PROTECTION

Data protection legislation was overhauled by the Data Protection 5–042 Act 1998 under pressure from a European Directive.[137] A major innovation is that the regime applies not only to data held on computers but also to manual filing systems if they are structured by reference to individuals or by reference to criteria relating to individuals in such a way that particular information relating to a particular individual is readily accessible. However, whether held in a computer or manual filing system, the data is only caught if it affects the subject's privacy in his personal, business or professional life and the data subject must be a focus of attention. It is not sufficient that a document was retrievable by reference to the person's name.[138]

A second important difference is that data held for journalistic purposes (whether in manual systems or computers) will be exempt from many of the major requirements of the new scheme. However, because the exemption is dependent on conditions which will not always be fulfilled, it remains necessary for journalists to have a working understanding of the new system.

"Data controllers" (people who determine the purposes for which personal data[139] are processed) must be registered with, or give

---

[134] Copyright, Designs and Patents Act 1988, s.85(2).

[135] Copyright, Designs and Patents Act 1988, s.87.

[136] *Williams v Settle* [1960] 1 W.L.R. 1072.

[137] Directive 95/46/EC.

[138] *Durant v Financial Services Authority* [2004] FSR 28. Whether documents are part of a manual filing system is decided at the time of the data subject's request— *Smith v Lloyds TSB Bank Plc* [2005] EWHC 246 (Ch.).

[139] "Personal data" is widely defined as "data which relate to a living individual who can be identified from those data or from those data and other information which is in the possession of, or is likely to come into the possession of, the data controller" (s.1(1)).

formal notification to, the Information Commissioner if they use automated systems or if given special notice by the Commissioner.[140] Journalists are *not* exempt from the requirement to register or give notification.

5–043 Data subjects are ordinarily entitled to be informed that data about them is being processed, to be given a description of the data, the purposes for which it is being processed and the people to whom the data may be disclosed. They are also entitled to a copy of the data (unless this would involve disproportionate effort) and to be told its source (unless the source is an individual who does not consent to disclosure and it is not reasonable to require disclosure in any case).[141] In many cases data subjects can insist that personal data in respect of them is not processed[142] and a court may order that data which is inaccurate (i.e. incorrect or misleading as to any matter of fact) is rectified, blocked, erased or destroyed.[143]

Data controllers must also abide by the data protection principles. These are, in brief:

- the data must be processed fairly[144] and lawfully and only for one of the prescribed purposes. For data concerning "sensitive" matters[145] there is a narrower group of permitted purposes;[146]
- it must be adequate, relevant and not excessive for the purpose;
- it must be accurate and where necessary, kept up-to-date;
- it must not be kept for longer than is necessary;
- it must be processed in accordance with the rights of data subjects;
- appropriate technical and organisational measures must be taken against unauthorised or unlawful processing and against accidental loss or destruction of or damage to the data;

---

[140] Data Protection Act 1998, s.16.

[141] Data Protection Act 1998, ss.7 and 8. For the national security exceptions see s.28 and *Baker v Secretary of State for Home Department*, October 1, 2001.

[142] Data Protection Act 1998, s.10.

[143] Data Protection Act 1998, s.14.

[144] The meaning of "fairness" in this context was considered in *Johnson v Medical Defence Union* [2007] EWCA Civ 262.

[145] Defined as meaning racial or ethnic origin, political opinions, religious or other beliefs, trade union membership, physical or mental health or condition, sexual life, commission or alleged commission of any offence, or criminal proceedings in relation to the data subject, Data Protection Act 1998, s.2.

[146] Data Protection Act 1998, Schs 2 and 3. The Data Protection (Processing of Sensitive Personal Data) Order 2000 SI 2000/417 includes a public interest test for publication of sensitive personal data, but it is limited to disclosures of unlawful acts, dishonesty, malpractice and other seriously improper conduct, unfitness or incompetence or mismanagement—in any of these cases whether actual or alleged.

- it must not be transferred out of the EEA unless the country to which it is taken or sent gives adequate protection for the rights of data subjects.[147]

The Commissioner (currently Richard Thomas) can serve an enforcement notice if he is satisfied that a data controller has contravened any of these principles.[148] An individual who suffers damage because a data controller has contravened any requirement of the Act is entitled to claim compensation.[149]

The special provisions for journalistic material give exemption **5–044** from: the data protection principles (except those concerning security of data); data subject access rights; the rights of data subjects to prevent data processing; the rights of data subjects to correct inaccuracies; and rights concerning automated decision-making.[150] However, these important exemptions are dependent on satisfying three conditions:

- the processing is undertaken with a view to the publication by any person of any journalistic, literary or artistic material (importantly, in *Campbell v MGN Ltd* the Court of Appeal held that a publisher could continue to fulfil this condition even after publication had taken place)[151]; and
- the data controller reasonably believes that, having regard in particular to the special importance of freedom of expression, publication would be in the public interest; and
- the data controller reasonably believes that, in all the circumstances, compliance with the provision in question is incompatible with the purposes of journalism.

The Court can take into account a relevant and designated Code of Practice for the purpose of deciding whether a belief that the publication would be in the public interest is a reasonable one. By this means the Codes of the Press Complaints Commission, Ofcom, the Independent Television Commission, the Radio Authority and the Producers Guidelines of the BBC (all of which have been designated)[152] may be given more significance.

The Commissioner is given powers to investigate whether data is being held for journalistic purposes or whether it is being processed with a view to the publication of any journalistic, literary or artistic material which has not previously been published by the data

---

[147] Data Protection Act 1998, Sch.1.
[148] The Information Commissioner's Office has a website at *www.ico.gov.uk.*
[149] Data Protection Act 1998, s.13.
[150] Data Protection Act 1998, s.32.
[151] [2003] QB 633 CA. The House of Lords did not consider the data protection claim separately.
[152] The Data Protection (Designated Codes of Practice) (No.2) Order 2000 (SI 2000/1864).

controller.[153] To assist him to reach such a decision, he can demand access to relevant information by serving a special information notice.[154] These powers in principle permit a government official, albeit in an independent office, to investigate journalists' files although as of 2007 no such attempt has been made. It is also troubling that the exceptions for legal professional privilege and the privilege against self-incrimination are far from adequate. Appeals lie to the Information Tribunal against the Commissioner's demands for information and also against his determinations or enforcement notices.[155] There is some further protection in that an enforcement notice in relation to data processed for journalistic purposes can only be served with the leave of the court, which must be satisfied that the contravention of the data protection principles is of substantial public importance.[156]

There are further dangers for the media in the new offences of unlawfully obtaining, disclosing or procuring the disclosure of personal data or information contained in it without the consent of the data controller. However, there is a defence that in the particular circumstances the act was justified as being in the public interest.[157] These offences can only be prosecuted by the Commissioner or the DPP. They are not imprisonable. Magistrates are limited to a £5,000 fine. Defendants who elect or are sent for jury trial face an unlimited fine if convicted.[158]

UNAUTHORISED TELEPHONE TAPPING AND COMPUTER MISUSE

Unauthorised telephone tapping

5–045   Unauthorised tapping of a message in the course of transmission by a public telecommunications system is an offence (see para.11–039). The same provision bans interception of mail in the course of transmission in a public postal service.[159] Before 2000 tapping was not unlawful if it took place before the message reached the public telecommunications system (for instance between a cordless telephone and the base unit), but the European Court of Human Rights found that this lack of regulation infringed Art.8[160] and RIPA 2000

---

[153] Data Protection Act 1998, s.45.
[154] Data Protection Act 1998, s.44.
[155] Data Protection Act 1998, s.60. decisions of the Information Tribunal (which hears cases under both DPA and FOIA) are at *www.informationtribunal.gov.uk.*
[156] Data Protection Act 1998, s.46.
[157] Data Protection Act 1998, s.55.
[158] Data Protection Act 1998, s.60.
[159] Regulation of Investigatory Powers Act 2000, s.1(1). For authorised tapping and interception see para.5–079.
[160] *Halford v UK* (1997) 24 E.H.R.R. 523.

now covers intentional and unlawful interception of a message in the course of transmission in a private telecommunication system.[161] The 2000 Act also gives a private right of action where there has been unlawful interception.[162] It is neither an offence nor actionable for one party to a telephone conversation to record the conversation even without the other person's consent or knowledge. Though, as Sir Ian Blair, the Metropolitan Police Commissioner, discovered in 2006 when it was revealed that he had secretly recorded conversations with (amongst others) the Attorney-General, it can cause anger in the party recorded and embarrassment for the recorder when this practice becomes known.

Computer Misuse

Imprisonment for up to six months (as well as a fine) can be imposed **5–046** for the separate offence of gaining unauthorised access to computer material.[163] This offence was aimed at computer hackers[164] and it is an essential ingredient for the offence that the access to data which was secured was unauthorised. Access is of four types: altering or erasing the program of data; copying or moving the data, using it, or outputting it,[165] but if the defendant was authorised to have the type of access in question, no offence is committed merely because access of that type was secured for an unauthorised purpose.[166]

In 1995 journalist John Arlidge was charged with computer misuse. The *Independent* had run a story about the insecurity of British Telecom computers, which BT hotly denied. One of its employees, a computer operator, contacted the newspaper and offered to prove that BT's denials were false, which he did by demonstrating to its reporter how easily he could obtain sensitive information through access on his computer at BT's premises. Both operator and journalist were prosecuted, but the case against the operator collapsed since he had been given a password and general authorisation to secure the access, albeit he did so for a purpose (showing BT to be liars) of which BT would not have approved. The

---

[161] Regulation of Investigatory Powers Act 2000, s.192. The private system must be linked up to a public system, but it is not necessary that the particular intercepted message made use of this connection. At least part of the apparatus for the system must be in the UK and this part must be used for making the connection to the public service: s.2(1).

[162] Powers Act 2000, s.1(3).

[163] Computer Misuse Act 1990, s.1. The maximum is due to be increased to two years imprisonment as a result of the Police and Justice Act 2006, s.35.

[164] See The Law Commission Report No. 186, *Computer Misuse* (HMSO 819, 1989).

[165] Computer Misuse Act 1990, s.17(2). It will also be a crime to do an unauthorised act with intent to impair or being reckless as to impairing the operation of a computer—Police and Justice Act 2006, s.36, amending Computer Misuse Act 1990, s.3.

[166] *DPP v Bignall* [1998] 1 Cr.App.R. 1, DC, but see comments in *R. v Bow Street Met. Stipendiary. Magistrate, Ex p. Govt of USA* [2000] 2 A.C. 216.

case against Arlidge was in consequence dropped, but had the operator's authority been restricted the prosecution would have had to prove that the reporter knew of that restriction. In addition, it may be doubted whether a reporter who stands by and watches while an operator voluntarily obtains unauthorised access can be said to "cause a computer to perform any function"—an ingredient of the offence. The Law Commission intended the s.1 offence to "exclude mere physical access, and mere scrutiny of data, without interaction with the operation of the computer". It emphasised that "electronic eavesdropping" is not an offence.[167]

HARASSMENT AND TRESPASS

Harassment

5-047   The Protection from Harassment Act 1997 provides broad powers against harassment. Intended to give relief against "stalking", its ambit is much wider. It prohibits a course of conduct[168] which amount to "harassment".[169] A limited company can be a perpetrator but not a victim of harassment.[170] "Harassment" includes alarming a person or causing distress.[171] The attentions or investigations of unwelcome reporters often cause distress. There is a defence if the alleged harasser shows that the course of conduct was pursued for the purpose of preventing or detecting crime.[172] Although the Secretary of State can issue a conclusive certificate that conduct was done on behalf of the Crown in relation to the prevention or detection of crime—see s.12—there is no reason why an investigative reporter in appropriate circumstances should not also be able to prove that he had the same purpose and was therefore entitled to the defence. It is also a defence—see s.1(3)(c)—for the alleged harasser to show that pursuit of the course of conduct was reasonable, so if a charge was brought against a journalist, the fact that he was acting in accordance with his professional code would be relevant to show reasonableness.

---

[167] Law Commission, *Computer Misuse* above, para.3.26 and for *R. v Arlidge*, see Paul Davies, "Computer Misuse", *New Law Journal*, December 1, 1995, p.1776.

[168] "Conduct" includes speech, 1997 Act s.7(2). To be a "course of conduct" there must, in the case of a single individual victim, be conduct on at least two occasions in relation to that person. Where there are two or more victims, there must be conduct on at least one occasion in relation to each person, 1997 Act s.7(3) as substituted by Serious Organised Crime and Police Act 2005, s.125.

[169] Protection from Harassment Act 1997, s.1.

[170] (Perpetrator) *Majrowski v Guy's and St. Thomas's NHS Trust* [2007] 1 A.C. 224. A victim has to be an individual and not a company *DPP v Dziurzynski* [2002] A.C.D. 88 QB and see the definition of a "person" in Protection from Harassment Act 1997 s.7(5) as added by Serious Organised Crime and Police Act 2005, s.125.

[171] Protection from Harassment Act 2005, s.7(2).

[172] Protection from Harassment 2005, s.1(3)(a).

Harassment in breach of the Act is a summary criminal offence with a maximum penalty of six months imprisonment.[173] In 2004 a jilted lover was sentenced to three months imprisonment after posting pictures of his ex-girlfriend making love to a website and distributing cards with the website's address at her 21st birthday party.[174]

These powers were increased by the Criminal Justice Act 2001 and again by the Serious Organised Crime and Police Act 2005. Although Parliament had the activities of animal rights activists particularly in mind, they are capable of being used against the media, especially where there is a scrum of reporters and film crew outside a person's house. Section 42 of the 2001 Act gives the police powers to give directions to stop harassment of a person in their home. The directions can be to go away and to stay away for up to three months. Section 42A of the 2001 Act[175] makes it an offence to act outside a person's home in a way which will cause harassment alarm or distress to a resident or neighbour and for the purpose of persuading a person to do something that he is not under an obligation to do or not do something which he is entitled or required to do. SOCA also added a new offence to the 1997 statute where the harassment is by two or more persons and is intended to persuade the victim either to do something which he is not obliged to do or not to do something which he is entitled to do.[176]

Harassment is an arrestable offence, so the police can apprehend **5–048** a person whom they have reasonable grounds to believe has committed it.[177] In addition, the victim can take civil proceedings.

The Sun reported that three police officers had been disciplined for making a racist remark about an asylum-seeker, after they had been exposed by a "black clerk". Ensuing readers' letters waxed furious at the clerk's "treachery" and a subsequent article oozed with indignation at her behaviour. The clerk in question, Ms Thomas, received hate mail at work and suffered distress and anxiety, so she sued for compensation under the Protection from Harassment Act. The Court of Appeal stressed that it was not enough that articles contained unreasonable opinions or even that they would foreseeably cause distress—"harassment" described conduct targeted at an individual which is calculated to cause alarm or distress and which is oppressive and unreasonable. The *Sun*'s articles, calculated to incite racial hatred of an individual, were capable of amounting to harassment.[178]

As well as damages (including damages for anxiety) the court can grant an injunction.

---

[173] Protection from Harassment Act 2005, s.2(2).
[174] *The Times*, October 26, 2004.
[175] Added by Serious Organised Crime and Police Act 2005, s.126.
[176] Protection from Harassment Act 1997, s.1(1A).
[177] 1997 Act, s.2.
[178] *Thomas v News Group Newspapers Ltd* [2002] E.M.L.R. 4 CA.

In *Howlett v Holding*[179] the defendant was avowedly seeking to put the claimant through "living hell" in retribution for her past opposition to his planning application. He claimed that she was dishonestly claiming invalidity benefit. Over 4–5 years the defendant had been flying banners from aircraft referring to the claimant in abusive and derogatory terms. The defendant had previously lost two libel actions brought by the claimant over similar allegations. The court recognised that it would be curtailing the defendant's freedom of expression but considered that this was well justified in view of his campaign of harassment. The injunction also prevented surveillance of the claimant by the defendant in his efforts to gather evidence against her.

If the victim believes that the harasser has engaged in conduct which is prohibited by the injunction, a court may attach a power of arrest to the injunction. If breach of the injunction is made out without reasonable excuse the maximum penalty is increased to five years imprisonment.[180] A novel feature of the Act is that on conviction of a harassment offence, the criminal court can make an order restraining the defendant from specified conduct for the purpose of protecting the victim from further harassment.[181] This might, for instance, include a prohibition on going within a specified distance of the victim's house. In this exceptional case the court imposed an order that the defendant not publish anything about the complainant or his fiancée whether true or not.[182] The defendant had waged a campaign against the two of them for more than a year in revenge for what she considered to have been a sexually transmitted disease that she had caught from the complainant. The order followed pleas of guilty to several charges of harassment, computer misuse and perverting the course of justice. The order lasted indefinitely but the court always has the power to vary or discharge an order.[183] Breach of the restraining order without reasonable excuse is a separate offence with a maximum penalty of five years imprisonment.[184]

Trespass

5–049 Trespass is one of the oldest common law actions. It allows a landowner (or, more accurately, the person with the right to possess the land) to claim compensation for an invasion of his right and an injunction to stop it happening in the future. It has proved a tool of very limited use in dealing with complaints of intrusion by the media.

---

[179] [2006] EWHC 41 (QB), *The Times*, February 8, 2006.
[180] Harassment Act 1997, s.3 and s.3A, allowing the court to grant an injunction where there is an actual or apprehended breach of s.1(1A).
[181] Harassment Act 1997, s.5.
[182] *R. v Debnath* [2006] 2 Cr.App.R.(S) 25.
[183] Protection from Harassment Act 1997, s.5(4).
[184] Harassment Act 1997, s.5(5).

Apart from the time that it takes to obtain an injunction, even without notice, it could only restrain entry on to the claimant's own land.[185] Where a defendant stands on public ground or in a place where he is permitted to be and spies through binoculars or a telephoto lens, no trespass takes place. In *Bernstein v Skyviews Ltd*[186] Lord Bernstein failed to obtain an injunction to stop aerial photography of his house and grounds. A flight several hundred feet up from his grounds did not interfere with his right to enjoy it. This is still a useful case for its comments on trespass, but its further comment that there was no general right to stop the taking of photographs now needs to be qualified by reference to the potential reach of Art.8. The Court in *Bernstein* thought that constant surveillance might amount to a nuisance. *Howlett v Holding* (above) shows that it may also lead to a harassment injunction.

Of course, there is no trespass in doing what a landowner permits;

> A cinema owner agreed to pay a percentage of each day's takings to the owners of the films that he rented. The film owners employed inspectors to visit cinemas and check attendances. The cinema owner alleged that the inspectors were trespassing, because they came with a secret purpose for which they had no permission. The court held there was no trespass. The inspectors did nothing they were not invited to do and their motives for being present were irrelevant.[187]

The case is important for journalists whose reports are often unwelcome to those they visit. However, its limits are also important. A journalist would not normally exceed his or her licence by observing, remembering and reporting, but it may be different if entry was obtained by subterfuge. A court might then find that the dishonest misrepresentation made the journalist a trespasser from the beginning.

A general invitation to the public to enter land would probably 5–050 not extend to the operation of a television camera. This is why film crews have to submit to the sometimes irksome business of obtaining consent to film from landowners.

Unless paid for, licences to come on to land can also be revoked. The landowner must allow a reasonable period for invited journalists to depart, but after this lapses, the former invitees become trespassers.

The police occasionally invite film crews to accompany them on raids of premises. The warrant or statutory power that entitles the police to enter private property would not extend to such "tag-along" journalists and in the absence of permission from the owner or tenant of the property they would plainly be trespassers. In one

---

[185] *Victoria Park Racing Co v Taylor* (1937) 58 CLR 479.
[186] [1978] QB 479.
[187] *Byrne v Kinematograph Renters Association* [1958] 2 All E.R. 579, 593.

case[188] the High Court accepted that it was in the public interest for police forces inform the media about their activities. However, those informative and explanatory briefings should, generally, take place after the relevant events had occurred. Save in exceptional circumstances, the court deplored a general practice by any police force of inviting the media to be present when investigative procedures were being undertaken.

5–051   Even where the behaviour of the media plainly amounts to a trespass, it is a separate question as to whether they should be enjoined from publishing their photographs or film—as the fruits of that wrongful act. The courts have often refused an injunction on the basis that damages will be an adequate remedy.[189] After the Human Rights Act, judges can only grant an injunction if it accords with Art.10. Covert filming which has a serious and important public interest point to make will not be enjoined simply because it was obtained by a trespassing journalist.

Trespass is not usually a crime although "aggravated trespass" is.[190] The Serious Organised Crime and Police Act 2005, s.128 allows the Secretary of State to designate sites which are owned by the Crown, the Queen in her private capacity or relevant to national security. A number of RAF and naval bases have been designated.[191] In 2007 the list was extended to cover many other government and Crown buildings.[192] Trespassing on designated sites is an offence as is trespassing on premises licensed as a nuclear site.[193] The maximum penalty is 51 weeks in prison.

PROTECTION OF SOURCES

5–052 It is a basic tenet of journalistic ethics that, in the words of the NUJ code of conduct, "A journalist shall protect confidential sources of information." But English judges have such an ingrained hostility to

---

[188] *R. v Marylebone Magistrates' Court Ex p. Amdrell Ltd (t/a 'Get Stufffed')*, *The Times*, September 17, 1998.

[189] See *Church of Scientology v Transmedia Productions Pty Ltd* (1987) Aust. Torts Reports 80–101; *Lincoln Hunt (Aust) Pty Ltd v Willersee* (1986) 4 NSWLR 457; *Encorp Pty Ltd v Australian Broadcasting Corp* [1988] Qd. R 169; *Bradley v Wingnut Films Ltd* [1994] E.M.L.R. 195.

[190] This refers to trespass on land in the open air which is and is intended to, intimidate, deter, obstruct or disrupt people carrying out lawful activities on the land: Criminal Justice and Public Order Act 1994, s.68.

[191] Serious Organised Crime and Police Act (Designated Sites) Order 2005 (SI 2005/3447).

[192] Serious Organised Crime and Police Act (Designated Sites under s.128) Order (SI 2007/930) which names as designated sites, Buckingham Palace, the Ministry of Defence Building in Whitehall, St. James Palace, Thames House (the headquarters of MI5) and parts of Chequers, Downing Street, GCHQ premises at Harp Hill, Hubble Road, Scarborough and Woodford. Parts of Highgrove, the Palace of Westminster, Portcullis House, Sandringham and Windsor Castle are also designated.

[193] Serious Organised Crime and Police Act 2005, s.128(1A) and (1B) as added by Terrorism Act 2006, s.12.

those who breach confidence—particularly corporate confidence—
that they have developed the common law to provide themselves
with power to order the unmasking of anyone involved in tortious
wrongdoing. This is reasonable enough when it identifies corrupt
employees who sell trade secrets to competitors; it is unreasonable
when it threatens journalists with prison unless they breach their
code of conduct and betray their news sources. Legislation (namely
s.10 of the Contempt of Court Act 1981) invites judges to balance
the interests of free speech against four interests which may favour
revelation of sources, but this "balancing act" is highly subjective.
Judges, mostly ignorant of the way the media works, may not
understand the value of news as such (irrespective of whether it
reveals iniquity) and the vital need to protect the sources for it,
however unprepossessing or traitorous. This need was recognised by
the European Court in *Goodwin v United Kingdom* in a famous
statement of principle[194]:

> "Protection of journalistic sources is one of the basic conditions
> for press freedom, as is reflected in the laws and professional
> codes of conduct in a number of Contracting States and is
> affirmed in several international instruments on journalistic
> freedoms. Without such protection, sources may be deterred
> from assisting the press in informing the public on matters of
> public interest. As a result the vital public watchdog role of the
> press may be undermined and the ability of the press to provide
> accurate and reliable information may be adversely affected.
> Having regard to the importance of the protection of journalistic
> sources for press freedom in a democratic society and the
> potentially chilling effect an order of source disclosure has on
> the exercise of that freedom, such a measure cannot be compat-
> ible with Article 10 of the Convention unless it is justified by an
> overriding requirement in the public interest."

Under s.2 of the Human Rights Act English courts must treat
Goodwin as a precedent. Since it goes against the judicial grain, it is
worth explaining why the European Court's statement of principle is
correct.

Journalists are persons who exercise by profession the right to
freedom of expression guaranteed to all by Art.10 of the Convention. They can claim no special privilege by virtue of this profession:
journalists are not above the law of their land. But it is through their
professional commitment that in real life most information and
many ideas—the "expression" to which Art.10 refers—gets imparted
to the public. For that reason, the journalist is described as a
"watchdog" for the public: a creature trained to react at unusual or

---

[194] *Goodwin v UK* (1996) 22 E.H.R.R. 123, para.39.

suspicious movements, or when from instinct it gathers that things are not entirely what they seem. The watchdog is suffered and indeed protected by Art.10, because of the public importance of what it *may* do, notwithstanding that it often acts precipitously or mistakenly, by barking at shadows or frightening law-abiding citizens.

Although the case law relating to Art.10 predominantly concerns the expression of offensive or unfashionable political opinions or ideas, most of the information which is received and imparted in democracies falls under the generic description of "news"—the facts that are read in newspapers or heard on radio or television or internet news bulletins. It is the work of journalists to gather that raw factual material, to call up further research, to check and compare and conduct interviews, and ultimately to present the factual material as information for the public. This involves a combination of skills—of research and analysis, comprehension of complicated subjects, and of writing and presentation. But that is not all. One essential skill of investigative journalism is the cultivation of sources of information. Unless the law affords real protection to the confidential relationship between the journalist and his cultivated source, both the quantity and quality of "news" will be diminished.

5–053   Some news simply happens: the plane crash and the ferry disaster are public events, reported at first, then analysed with the help of sources inside the airline or ferry company, or the airline or ferry manufacturer, or inside the regulatory agency whose failure contributed to the disaster. A good deal of news, in modern society, is announced: by the press release, the publicity brochure, the press conference or the public relations department. There are in Britain 3,200 people employed in public relations offices in Government departments and quangos, *feeding* news to journalists. There are many more—hundreds of thousands—employed in the same capacity by public and private companies. All these professional propagandists are concerned not only to announce news, but to put a "spin" upon it—a version most favourable to their employer. Sometimes, journalists can read between the lines of press handouts, and divine the real news which may not be so favourable to the employer. But mainly they are reliant upon the sources that they cultivate for information which does, or may have, news value.

The cultivation of sources is thus professionally essential for journalists. It is a basic tool of their trade, the means by which newsworthy information is extracted, other than from those paid to give it a particular spin. Were it not for "unofficial sources" obligingly talking "off the record" to journalists, there would simply be much less news in newspapers. There would be fewer facts and less information for discussion, for dispute and sometimes for retraction, in democratic society. That is the first reason why Art.10 protects, not just the right to impart information to the public, but the preceding right to cultivate and protect the news sources which provide much of that information in the first place. If sources, frightened of exposure and reprisal, decide not to talk, there will not only be less news, but the news which is published will be less reliable. It will not be checked for spin.

Sources, however carefully cultivated, are delicate blooms. They come in many varieties. Invariably, they have some reason for seeking anonymity. Sometimes, the position they hold makes it unseemly that they should be identified speaking to the press. Mostly, they have come by the knowledge that they think it right to impart because they are in some relationship which can be termed confidential—an employee, or a professional adviser, or a friend or relative. They apprehend that they will in some way suffer if their identity is discovered: maybe just hostility, more often reprisals in the form of loss of job or loss of trust. Almost always, they could be sued for breach of confidence by those on whom they inform. So most journalistic sources would decide not to impart information at all if there was any appreciable risk that their identity would subsequently be disclosed. That is why it is so vital to the values protected by Art.10 that the initial channel of communication, between source and journalist, should not be closed by the source's fear of being found out.

So the way the free press works—and it is an institution that has 5–054 developed its working practices over centuries—is that journalists cultivate sources by promising them confidentiality. That is a solemn promise, made in the service of greater public interest, and it binds the conscience of the individual journalist. He should be prepared to go to prison, or suffer any financial penalty, rather than have the name dragged from him. The promise is not, however, absolute, because no promise of confidentiality *can* be absolute. Grounded in morality, it may have to give way when morality dictates that it must. Such occasions will be rare, but can readily be hypothesised: when the promise has been elicited by a trick, or it turns out that the source has tried to involve the journalist in a serious criminal conspiracy, or when breach of the promise is necessary to save an innocent life or to enable the recovery of a snatched child, and so on. No future source would distrust a journalist who breached his promise in such a case.

The law is entitled to provide for these situations, precisely because they are situations where source revelation is not inimical to the value of freedom of expression. Since source protection is an essential element in securing that value, then domestic law is only entitled to withdraw that protection to serve a value so imperative that it is more important than freedom of expression. The journalist whose source genuinely imperils national security, or threatens innocent life or continues to commit serious crime, can be obliged by law to break a confidence he should never expect to keep. Orders made in such rare cases would not frighten off sources who are the mainstay of news and information: they would recognise the moral imperative of disclosure, and would realise it could never happen to them.

Regrettably, despite the decision in *Goodwin*, English courts may and sometimes do order disclosure outside these exceptional circumstances. Their power to do so depends on who is asking the question and why.

The police and other investigators

5–055 If the inquiries are being made by the police (for instance, in connection with leaked information), journalists are in the same position as anyone else: they are, in general, under no duty to provide answers. Although this may make the police investigation more difficult, the obdurate interviewee is *not* committing the offence of obstructing the police in the course of their duties.[195]

However, the police have an exceptional power to insist on answers to their questions concerning suspected breaches of s.1 of the Official Secrets Act 1911.[196] The Home Secretary is politically responsible for these powers and must normally give his prior approval. Parliament made clear by the Official Secrets Act 1939 that compulsory inquisitions can be used only for detecting grave breaches of national security and, sensibly, it was not extended to suspected breaches of the Official Secrets Act 1989. The limited duty to tell the police of information relating to terrorist activities is considered in Ch.11.

There is a growing parliamentary trend to give investigators the power to compel answers from their interviewees. Under the Financial Services and Markets Act 2000 inspectors can be appointed by the Financial Services Authority, the Secretary of State or (in some cases) the Treasury to investigate specific allegations of a broad variety of offences or regulatory requirements with which providers of financial services are supposed to comply.[197] In addition to questioning those immediately involved, inspectors can require third parties to attend before them, answer questions, otherwise provide such information as the investigators may require and/or produce relevant documents.[198] If a person fails to comply with an inspector's requirements, the inspector can certify the default to the court which, if satisfied that the person failed without reasonable cause to comply with the requirement, may deal with him as if he were in contempt.[199] The phrase "without reasonable cause" would allow a journalist who was asked to reveal a source to invoke s.10 of the Contempt of Court Act and Art.10 of the Convention. It would then

---

[195] Police Act 1996, s.89(2); *cf. Rice v Connolly* [1966] 2 Q.B. 414.
[196] The Official Secrets Act 1920, s.6.
[197] Financial Services and Markets Act 2000, ss.14, 15 and 168.
[198] 2000 Act, ss.16, 172 and 173.
[199] 2000 Act, ss.18 and 177(1).

be for the inspector in the first place and the court in the second to consider whether the conditions under which a journalist can be required to reveal a source were fulfilled. So much was establish in the case of Jeremy Warner.

> Warner, of the *Independent*, was summoned by inspectors who were investigating suspected leaks of price-sensitive information from the Department of Trade and the Monopolies and Mergers Commission (the predecessor of the Competition Commission). Two stories by Warner indicated that he had a source in these departments. Warner refused to identify him or her. There was no specific defence for journalists in the legislation but the House of Lords ruled that s.10 of the Contempt of Court Act 1981 should be applied by analogy. In Warner's case they found that the disclosure of his source was necessary for the "prevention of crime" and he could be required to answer. Warner persisted in his refusal and was fined £20,000.[200]

If a person knows that an investigation is, or is likely to be **5–056** conducted, he commits an offence if he destroys, falsifies, conceals or otherwise disposes of a document which he knows or suspects is or would be relevant to the investigation. The offence is punishable with six months' imprisonment and/or a fine up to the statutory maximum (currently £5,000) in the magistrates' court and up to two years' imprisonment in the Crown Court.[201]

Similar powers to compel attendance and answer questions are given to inspectors appointed to look into a company's affairs.[202] Broadly the same powers are given to the Director of the Serious Fraud Office[203] and to the Office of Fair Trading when investigating a suspected cartel offence.[204]

A much wider extension of the power to issue disclosure notices is conferred by the Serious Organised Crime and Police Act 2005. This allows the DPP, the Director of Revenue and Customs Prosecutions and the Lord Advocate to compel the production of documents or the answering of questions for the purpose of investigating a very wide range of offences.[205] Importantly for the media, these powers

---

[200] *In Re An Inquiry under the Company Securities (Insider Dealing) Act 1985* [1988] A.C. 660 and the *Independent* January 27, Ch.D. The 1985 Act has since been repealed and the 2000 Act is its legislative successor.
[201] Financial Services and Markets Act 2000, at s.177(3) and (5).
[202] Companies Act 1985 ss.434 and 436. This does not expressly give a "reasonable excuse" defence, but the court's power to punish silence as contempt is discretionary and ought not to be exercised where Contempt of Court Act 1981 s.10 or Art.10 would apply.
[203] Criminal Justice Act 1987 s.2. A magistrates' court can punish non-compliance with a fine on level 5 (currently £5,000) or a sentence of six months imprisonment, but, as with the Financial Services and Markets Act 2000, only if there is no reasonable excuse.
[204] Enterprise Act 2002 s.193. Again the offence of not complying with a disclosure requirement is dependent on there being no reasonable excuse: s.201(2).
[205] Serious Organised Crime and Police Act 2005 ss.60–63.

cannot be used to gather "excluded material".[206] As we shall see, this includes any journalistic material which is held in confidence.[207]

Claimants in libel actions

5–057 There is a well-settled rule of practice that a defendant in a defamation action will not be required to name the writer or informant of the words complained of *at the pre-trial stage*.[208] This means that a publisher cannot be required to name its source in answer to a request for further information unless (exceptionally) the court orders otherwise. Although this protection lasts only until trial, it remains important because so many libel actions are settled before then. At trial, publishers now have the protection of s.10 of the Contempt of Court Act 1981 and Art.10 of the Convention and are unlikely to be ordered to disclose a source. Although the identity of a source may be important in a public interest/*Jameel* privilege defence, the courts have applied *Goodwin* to preclude disclosure, although the defence may suffer in consequence.[209] The rule has been applied in contempt proceedings so that the courts will not insist that the editor or publisher disclose the name of its source or writer.[210]

Claimants do not normally have difficulty in identifying someone to sue for an alleged libel in a newspaper. Every newspaper should carry the name and address of its printer (who is currently liable for any libel it contains; see para.3–031).[211] If this obligation is broken, the claimant cannot compel people who had no connection with the libel to reveal the printer's name simply because they are aware of his identity.[212]

The courts

5–058 In what circumstances will a court compel journalists to disclose their sources? In the first place, the journalist must be amenable to the proceedings. Journalists may attend court voluntarily to defend or assert their rights, or to give evidence on behalf of others, or they may be forced by a witness summons to attend to give evidence.

Witness summonses: admissible evidence and materiality

5–059 No witness can be made to answer a question or produce documents unless they are relevant to an issue in dispute between the parties.

---

[206] 2005 Act, s.64(5).
[207] Police and Criminal Evidence Act 1984, s.11.
[208] *Hennessy v Wright* (1888) 21 Q.B.D. 509; *BSC v Granada Television*, fn.25 above; CPR r.53.3.
[209] See *Gaddafi v Daily Telegraph* [2000] E.M.L.R. 431; *Jameel v Wall Street Journal Europe SPRL* [2007] 1 A.C. 359.
[210] *Re Bahama Islands Reference* [1893] A.C. 138.
[211] Newspapers, Printers and Reading Rooms Repeal Act 1869, Sch.2.
[212] *Ricci v Chow* [1987] 3 All E.R. 534, CA.

ITN successfully resisted a summons from a claimant in a civil action to produce all its untransmitted film of a rock festival at Windsor which had lasted several days. The Court of Appeal held that this was too wide and oppressive since the court was concerned only with one small incident. A television company will be ordered to produce its "off-cuts" only if they are clearly important to help the court determine an issue.[213]

The common law imposes wide-ranging duties on prosecutors to disclose material which might possibly have a bearing on the case. These duties have been refined by legislation,[214] but they still place a heavy onus of discovery on prosecutors and on governmental agencies that are part of "the apparatus of prosecution" such as the police and forensic science services. This is fundamentally different from the obligations which can be imposed on a third party witness, who can only be required to produce documents or things likely to be material evidence. The documents must be admissible in evidence and witness summonses cannot be used for fishing expeditions to obtain documents or evidence which might or might not prove on examination to be admissible.[215] Consequently a journalist who wrote about a conversation between a colleague and a police source in connection with the arrest of Kevin Maxwell successfully applied to have his witness order set aside: the only evidence which the journalist could give was inadmissible hearsay (i.e. what his colleague told him) and the identity of the colleague, who might have been able to give first hand evidence, was not itself material to any issue in the case.

Witness summonses can be issued by both magistrates' and crown courts and in both cases there is a procedure for setting aside the order.[216] Where the documentary material is voluminous or particularly sensitive the trial judge may, in his discretion, permit the witness to appoint an independent competent counsel to review the documents for their materiality to the issues in the trial.[217] This device was used at an Old Bailey trial in 1996 when an investigative journalist objected to production of his research documents and records of interviews.

Changes to the procedure for witness' summonses in the Crown Court made in 1996[218] mean that applications for summonses will

---

[213] *Senior v Holdsworth Ex p. Independent Television News Ltd* [1976] Q.B. 23, CA.

[214] Criminal Procedure and Investigations Act 1996, Pt I.

[215] *R. v Derby Magistrates' Court Ex p. B* [1996] A.C. 487.

[216] Magistrates' Courts Act 1980, s.97(1) and Criminal Procedure (Attendance of Witnesses) Act 1965 ss.2–2E. In the magistrates' court the applicant for the summons must demonstrate that the witness is likely to be able to give material evidence, although this burden is reversed in the Crown Court: *R. v Reading J.J. Ex p. Berkshire County Council* [1996] 1 Cr.App.R. 239 DC.

[217] *R. v W(G); R. v (W)(E)* [1996] Crim.L.R. 904, CA, Crim. Div.

[218] Criminal Procedure and Investigations Act 1996, s.66.

normally be on notice to the prospective witness and objections can be taken at that stage. If the order is made despite the objection, it can require production of documents in advance of the trial, which is a result that could already be achieved in the civil courts.[219] Disobedience to a witness summons can result in the issue of an arrest warrant and up to three months imprisonment.[220] There are conflicting decisions as to whether the issue of a witness summons by the Crown Court can be challenged by judicial review.[221]

Claims for Discovery

5–060 A witness summons assumes that there is an ongoing case against an identified defendant and with issues that are more or less defined. However, many of the most important confrontations between the courts and journalists over their sources have concerned a different type of claims. These are brought by claimants who believe that they have suffered a wrong but do not know who was responsible. The law gives the courts a discretionary power to order a third party who has in some way become involved in the wrongdoing (whether innocently or not) to identify the perpetrator. The paradigm situation which generates these proceedings against the media is where a confidential document or information has been leaked to the press. The claimant will allege that this was a breach of confidence by the source and seek an order requiring the journalist or publisher to identify who that was. The claimant may intend to take civil proceedings against the source, or to dismiss him (if an employee) or possibly to encourage criminal proceedings to be brought. The claimant will often allege that the publisher itself acted in breach of confidence by publishing the leaked information, but it is not essential that the publisher is also a wrongdoer: it is sufficient if by their actions they have in some way become involved in the source's wrongdoing. These claims are called *Norwich Pharmacal* proceedings after the first modern case in which they were used.[222]

Journalists' privilege: Contempt of Court Act s.10

5–061 The common law did not give journalists (or priests, or doctors, or anyone except lawyers) an absolute right to preserve the confidentiality of their sources, but it did recognise that the judge had a discretion as to whether to force them to name their sources even where their identity was relevant to an issue in dispute.[223]

---

[219] Civil Procedure Rules, r.34.2.

[220] Criminal Procedure (Attendance of Witnesses) Act 1965, ss.3 and 4.

[221] *Ex p. Rees, The Times*, May 7, 1986 DC says that it cannot because of Supreme Court Act 1981 s.29(3). *R (TB) v Stafford Combined Court* [2006] EWHC 1645 (Admin) says (without referring to *Rees*) that it can.

[222] *Norwich Pharmacal Co v Commissioners of Customs and Excise* [1974] A.C. 133 HL. The nature of the jurisdiction in press cases was reviewed by the House of Lords in *Ashworth Hospital Authority v MGN Ltd* [2002] 1 W.L.R. 2033.

[223] *BSC v Granada Television*, fn.25 above.

PROTECTION OF SOURCES   323

Journalist Jack Lundin succeeded in showing that a trial of a police
sergeant for corruptly providing information to a gambling casino
about its rival customers would not be assisted by his disclosing the
name of his source for an expose of the whole affair that he had
written for *Private Eye*. The prosecution case was already in a shambles
and his evidence could not repair the damage. He was not guilty of
contempt in refusing to answer because this was not necessary in the
interests of justice.[224]

The common law position has now been strengthened by s.10 of the
Contempt of Court Act 1981:

> "No court may require a person to disclose, nor is any person
> guilty of contempt of court for refusing to disclose, the source of
> information contained in a publication for which he is respon-
> sible unless it is established to the satisfaction of the court that it
> is necessary in the interests of justice or national security or for
> the prevention of disorder or crime."

The pre-conditions for the protection in s.10 have been interpreted broadly. Thus they apply even if the court's order is not in
terms to require the source to be identified but rather the doing of
an act (typically the return of a leaked document) which may have
that result.[225] The section also applies even though it is not certain
that the effect of the order will be identification of the source: it is
enough if there is a reasonable chance that this will happen.[226] The
phrase "contained in a publication for which he is responsible"
requires further analysis.

> The claimant, an internet service provider, was the target of a
> sustained attack by a contributor to the defendants' internet discussion
> groups. When it complained about the defamatory postings, they were
> removed and eventually the defendants barred the contributor from
> access to their sites. However, the claimant wanted to sue the
> contributor for libel and brought proceedings against the defendants to
> force them to identify him. The defendants argued that they promised
> their contributors anonymity. Disclosure would also infringe the Data
> Protection Act and be contrary to the Contempt of Court Act, s.10.
> Robert Owen J. ruled (uncontroversially) that the Data Protection Act
> 1998, s.35 allowed disclosure in obedience to a court order and/or for
> the purpose of legal proceedings. But he also held that s.10 only
> applied where a person was "responsible" in a legal sense for a
> publication. This is doubtful since s.10 can be invoked where there has
> been no actual publication and where no question of the defendant's

---

[224] *Att-Gen v Lundin* (1982) 75 Cr.App.R. 90.
[225] *Secretary of State for Defence v Guardian Newspapers Ltd* [1985] A.C. 339, see below.
[226] *Secretary of State for Defence v Guardian Newspapers Ltd* [1985] A.C. 339, see below.

legal responsibility arises. The judge went on, in his decision to find a disclosure order necessary in the interests of justice because of the seriousness of the defamatory postings, their persistence and the potentially vast audience which they could reach. Although a controversial interpretation of the law, this was not, of course, a case where the order put an investigative journalist's sources at risk of identification.[227]

Section 10 establishes a presumption in favour of journalists who wish to protect their sources, but that presumption will be rebutted if the court concludes that revelation is necessary on one or more of the four stated grounds. "Necessary" is the key word in the section—it is not satisfied by proof that revelation is merely "convenient" or "expedient". The source's name must be "really needed" in the following situations.

In the interests of justice

5–062 This is the widest and most dangerous of the exceptions to the general principle enshrined in s.10. Regrettably, the House of Lords has chosen to interpret it in a way that inevitably permits subjective judicial value judgments on a journalist's conduct and the importance of his information, rather than by reference to principle. The question the court must ask in any case when an application is made for an order that a journalist name his source is whether the interests of justice in providing the name to the applicant "are of such preponderating importance in the individual case that the ban on disclosure imposed by the opening words of the section really needs to be overridden".[228]

This means that a journalist's ethical duty to protect his source will be overridden whenever the court, conducting a "balancing exercise", decides that the public interest in the applicant's right (generally to take legal action against the source to protect property in information) outweighs the journalist's qualified right to maintain the pledge of confidence to his source. Some of the factors to be placed in the balance have been described by Lord Bridge:

"One important factor will be the nature of the information obtained from the source. The greater the legitimate public interest in the information which the source has given to the publisher or intended publisher, the greater will be the importance of protecting the source. But another and perhaps more significant factor which will very much affect the importance of protecting the source will be the manner in which the information was itself obtained by the source. If it appears to the court

---

[227] *Totalise Plc v Motley Fool Ltd* [2001] E.M.L.R. 29.
[228] *X v Morgan Grampian Publishers Ltd* [1991] 1 A.C. 1, *per* Lord Oliver at 44.

that the information was obtained legitimately, this will enhance the importance of protecting the source. Conversely, if it appears that the information was obtained illegally, this will diminish the importance of protecting the source unless, of course, this factor is counterbalanced by a clear public interest in publication of the information, as in the classic case where the source has acted for the purpose of exposing iniquity."[229]

This approach emerged from a case in 1990 where a young journalist narrowly escaped prison after defying the courts by refusing to name his source.

Bill Goodwin, a journalist on *The Engineer* magazine, received information from a source that a leading private company in a much-publicised field was, contrary to its publicity, experiencing financial difficulties and urgently seeking to raise a large loan. When Goodwin telephoned the company to seek information and comment, the company responded by obtaining a breach-of-confidence injunction and by seeking disclosure of the name of his source. It produced evidence that convinced the courts that the information leaked to the journalist must have come from a stolen copy of a confidential corporate plan, and that the source may well have been in contact with the thief. It needed the source's name in order to obtain further injunctions and perhaps to trace the thief. The Court of Appeal ordered the journalist to place the name of his source in a sealed envelope and to hand it to the court to abide the outcome of final appeal to the House of Lords. The journalist refused to put his source in peril by this device and was found guilty of contempt. The House of Lords subsequently confirmed that "the interests of justice" outweighed the prima facie protection of s.10, because the source had been complicit in a grave breach of confidentiality, the information did not reveal "iniquity" and had no great public interest value, and the company might suffer severe damage unless it was able to identify the employee or consultant who was prepared to pass its secrets on to the press. The journalist was ultimately fined £5,000 for refusing to obey the court's order against which he lodged a complaint to Strasburg.

The House of Lords' decision illustrates how the judicial value **5–063** accorded to property rights tends to prevail over ethical claims by the journalists in balancing exercises that require a subjective appreciation of competing public interests. The case arose from a routine situation where a journalist received unpaid and unsolicited confidential information of a newsworthy nature, and behaved very

---

[229] *X v Morgan Grampian Publishers Ltd.* This approach would endorse the decision in *Handmade Films v Express Newspapers Plc* [1986] F.S.R. 463, where a newspaper was held to be protected by s.10 from disclosing to a film company the source from whom it obtained photographs of pop-star Madonna on a film set: no serious damage was threatening the claimant, and its loss could be compensated in monetary terms.

properly in checking it with the company prior to publication. The English courts were not prepared, however, to recognise any public interest in news-gathering that fell short of revelation of "iniquity", and were overimpressed by allegations of potential damage made by company officials in affidavits that had not been tested under cross-examination. The importance of the Strasbourg decision in *Goodwin v United Kingdom*,[230] which held that the approach of the English courts (exemplified by Lord Bridge's "balancing act") had led to a breach of the Convention, is that it recognises the crucial importance of news-gathering as such to freedom of expression, and so casts that mantle of Art.10 protection over sources—whether high-minded or malicious and whether revealing front page iniquity or run-of-the-mill facts worth only a passing mention on the inside page. The European Court was unimpressed by Lord Bridge's balancing act: it pointed out[231] that Art.10 jurisprudence would generally "tip the balance of competing interests in favour of the interest of demo-cratic society in securing a free press". Thus the claimant's various interests, in eliminating the threat in its midst, in staunching the leak, in unmasking a disloyal aide or obtaining damages did not, even cumulatively, "outweigh the vital public interest in the protec-tion of the applicant's source". That would need "an overriding requirement in the public interest" which could not be found in *Goodwin*'s case: the claimant was substantially protected against further disclosure of its business plan by the injunction.

In two subsequent cases the European Human Rights Court followed *Goodwin*. Both concerned journalists who had published articles which had led to investigations as to whether their sources had committed criminal offences by leaking documents or informa-tion. In both cases judges had authorised searches and seizures of the journalists' homes and offices. In both cases the Court was not persuaded that there had been a sufficiently compelling justification for overriding the confidentiality of the sources.[232] The Court found that Art.10 had been violated in both.

In these cases and in *Goodwin* it is likely that the journalists were only able to obtain information because their sources believed that they would remain anonymous. In *Nordisk v Denmark* a television reporter had acted covertly in joining a (lawful) association of paedophiles.

> The journalists' observations and secret filming did not depend at all on the co-operation of the members who were unaware of his true purpose. After the research was complete the production company contacted those who had been filmed and promised them con-fidentiality. However, one of the members was already being investi-gated by the Danish police who were able to identify him when the

---

[230] (1996) 22 E.H.R.R. 123.
[231] para.45.
[232] *Roemen and Schmit v Luxembourg* Application No. 51772/99 February 25, 2003; *Ernst v Belgium* Application No. 33400/96 July 15, 2003.

programme was broadcast and they obtained an order for untransmitted footage of this man to be handed over. The Strasbourg Court
agreed that such an order still engaged Art.10, but the position was
very different to *Goodwin*. The Court referred to Recommendation
R(2000) 7 on the right of Journalists not to disclose their sources of
information (adopted by the Council of Ministers of the Council of
Europe on March 8, 2000) to say that the covertly filmed members had
not provided information, even in the passive sense of consenting to
being filmed and they could not therefore be regarded as "sources" in
the traditional sense. Besides, the Danish authorities were striving to
discharge their own obligations to take reasonable measures to protect
children from potential violations of Art.3 of the Convention. There
was no arguable breach of the Convention.[233]

In one important case, *Gaddafi v Daily Telegraph*,[234] the Court of **5–064**
Appeal applied *Goodwin* directly to permit journalists to protect
their sources even when asserting that they were so reliable there
was a "qualified privilege" in communicating their information (see
para.3–069). However, a different Court of Appeal in *Camelot
Group Plc v Centaur Communications Ltd*,[235] while purporting to
follow *Goodwin*, in fact travestied it by ordering the return of
financial accounts which exposed the greed and hypocrisy of national
lottery directors and which had been leaked to *Marketing Week*. The
Court of Appeal reasoned that the public interest was not engaged
because the accounts would have been published in due course. This
ignores the importance of news, and its perishability (recognised in
Reynolds) and is irreconcilable with other European Court
decisions.[236]

Camelot is a pre-Human Rights Act authority which should not be
followed. As the Court of Appeal said in the first case *after* the Act
came into force, "the decisions of the European Court demonstrate
that the freedom of the press has in the past carried greater weight
in Strasbourg than it has in the courts of this country"[237] *Ashworth*
itself marks a valuable recognition, as a result of *Goodwin v United
Kingdom*, that the "chilling effect" of court orders requiring source
disclosure is not affected by the importance of the information or
the mercenary motives of the source. As Laws L.J. put it,

> "the true position is that it is always prima facie contrary to the
> public interest that press sources should be disclosed; and in any
> given case the debate which follows will be conducted upon the

---

[233] *Nordisk Film and TV A/S v Denmark* Application No. 40485/02 December 8,
2005.
[234] [2000] E.M.L.R. 431.
[235] [1998] 1 All E.R. 251, CA.
[236] Notably *Fressoz and Roire v France* (1999) 5 B.H.R.C. 654.
[237] *Ashworth Hospital Authority v MGN Ltd* [2001] 1 W.L.R. 515 CA at [101]. The
House of Lords specifically endorsed this passage *Ashworth Hospital Authority v
MGN Ltd* [2002] 1 W.L.R. 2033 HL at [66].

question whether there is an overriding public interest, amounting to a pressing social need, to which the need to keep press sources confidential should give way".[238]

The *Ashworth* case arose out of a hunger strike by the moors murderer Ian Brady who was a secure patient in Ashworth Hospital. Brady himself had publicised his forced feeding and medical treatment but more detailed records from the hospital were leaked to an intermediary who in turn helped the *Daily Mirror* to write an article on the affair. The Hospital brought a *Norwich Pharmacal* claim against the publishers to discover the identity of the original source or alternatively of the intermediary. The House of Lords upheld the order as compatible with s.10 because the Hospital had a strong need to detect leaks of its medical records. In their particular institution the care of patients was fraught with difficulty and danger which were increased by leaks. Brady himself would probably not have had a claim against the source because of his own actions in putting his treatment into the public domain, but this did not prevent the Hospital from legitimately pursuing its own concerns. The House of Lords endorsed *Goodwin v UK* although it is clear that its order to disclose was influenced by the strength of the hospital's claim to preserve patient confidentiality and by the assumption that the original source was corrupt.[239]

MGN did not know the original source but it did disclose that the intermediary was the investigative journalist, Robin Ackroyd. In due course the Hospital Authority sued him for an order that he identify the original source. It was sufficiently confident to ask for summary judgment in its favour, but this was refused by the Court of Appeal.[240] On the further evidence which Ackroyd produced, it thought the source might have had an arguable public interest defence to a breach of confidence claim or that Ackroyd might be able to show that the presumption in favour of preserving anonymity of his source had not been displaced. Importantly, the Court said that it would have to be an exceptional case for source disclosure to be ordered on an application for summary judgment. In most cases there would have to be a trial.

At the subsequent trial the judge refused to order Ackroyd to disclose his source. He found (contrary to the assumption in the *MGN* litigation) that the source had not been paid. Although the source did not have a public interest defence for his disclosure he had probably acted for public interest reasons. The cloud of suspicion was a factor which weighed less heavily six years on (and after about 1/3 of the staff at the Hospital had left) and, in any event, when so many people could have been the source, the negative effect of suspicion was less influential. The medical records in question were not of the highest sensitivity and Brady's own attitude towards

---

[238] *Ashworth* at [101].
[239] *Ashworth Hospital Authority v MGN Ltd* [2002] 1 W.L.R. 2033 HL.
[240] *Mersey Care NHS Trust v Ackroyd* [2003] E.M.L.R. 36.

their disclosure meant that he could have no complaint. Just as important was Ackroyd's reputation as an investigative journalist, truly fulfilling the watchdog role of the press.[241]

In other cases, claimants have failed to obtain disclosure of media **5–065** sources because their own leak inquiries were inadequate. When Elton John's barrister tore up the draft of his confidential advice to the singer and left it in his Chambers' waste-paper bin, it quickly found its way- pieced back together—to the *Daily Express*. Morland J., over-impressed by the legal professional privilege attaching to the document, ordered the newspaper to identify its source, but the Court of Appeal pointed out that the fault lay with the Chambers in failing to have a proper security system or to institute any internal inquiry. Lord Woolf said that no journalist should be ordered to breach a solemn professional obligation unless all other ways of ascertaining the source had been exhausted.[242]

However, in *Interbrew SA Ltd v Financial Times Ltd*[243] the claimants wanted to discover the source of a leaked (and altered) document which allegedly showed their plan to take over South African Breweries. The Court of Appeal accepted that reputable private investigators had conducted an adequate leak inquiry and accepted as well that the source's purpose was maleficent and calculated to do harm whether for profit or spite. It agreed that the claimant had an urgent need to prevent any repetition. Interbrew had alleged that the leaked document was forged: the Court thought that it had at least been leaked in order to affect the company's share price. It was on this basis, i.e. that the journalists had been hoodwinked into becoming the innocent agents of a stock scam, that the Court of Appeal ordered them to disclose their source. As usual in such interlocutory cases, the court's factual findings were made on one-sided affidavits: the journalists in question did not accept that their source was a fraudsman. Moreover, the Court of Appeal had not ordered them to disclose their source to a Fraud Squad inquiry, but to a bullish private company out for reprisals. Interestingly, when the *Guardian* refused to hand over the leaked document (from which the source's identity might have been deduced) Interbrew's lawyers charged to the High Court demanding seizure of the newspaper's assets. This provoked an outcry in Parliament and the press, which threatened to damage the company's trade (no doubt the prospect of Britain's journalists refusing to drink Stella Artois

---

[241] *Mersey Care NHS Trust v Ackroyd (No.2)* [2006] E.M.L.R. 12 (QB). The decision was upheld by the Court of Appeal [2007] EWCA Civ 101.

[242] *John v Express Newspapers Ltd* [2000] 3 All E.R. 257 CA. See also *Special Hospital Services Authority v Hyde* (1994) 20 B.M.L.R. 75. For examples of other cases where source disclosure was refused see *Saunders v Punch* [1998] 1 W.L.R. 986; *Essex C.C. v Mirror Group newspapers Ltd* [1996] 1 FLR 585; *Maastricht Referendum Campaign v Hounam* May 28, 1993, unreported Ch.D; *Chief Constable of Leicestershire v Garavelli* July 30, 1996, QBD.

[243] [2002] E.M.L.R. 24.

would have dented its profits) and the company abandoned its quest for the source.

On occasions disclosure of their sources will put journalists in physical danger. In those cases, not only Art.10, but Art.2 of the ECHR will also be relevant. There would have to be a very strong reason indeed for a court to expose a journalist to a real risk to his life by an order for source disclosure.[244] The practical difficulty may be in showing that the journalist's fears are objectively justified. Sometimes it is possible to give enough information for the police to carry out an assessment, but in others this cannot be done without itself risking disclosure of the source's identity. The Saville Inquiry itself did not press one journalist to disclose his IRA sources, accepting that there was an Art.2 risk. Controversially, the Inquiry did order other journalists to disclose military sources for their stories. Several refused but, although contempt proceedings were threatened (and in one case begun), the Inquiry decided not to pursue them.

In the interests of national security

5–066 Journalists who withhold disclosure on this ground can expect to go to prison for their contumely. The precedent was created when three were gaoled at the Vassall spy tribunal, and in 1985 the editor of the *Guardian* declined similar martyrdom by handing over the documents from which the identity of his unknown source—Sarah Tisdall—was deduced. Journalists who have a direct relationship with their source, to whom they have personally promised confidentiality, may feel they have no alternative but to take punishment, even if the name is demanded on grounds of national security. It was some belated consolation to the *Guardian* that when its appeal reached the House of Lords, the final ruling at least applied a more stringent test to the evidence that the Government must produce to overcome the presumption in favour of protecting sources:

> The *Guardian* published extracts from papers that concerned the deployment of Cruise missiles at Greenham Common and that had been sent to it anonymously. The Secretary of State for Defence demanded their return but the newspaper refused, saying that this might reveal their source. The House of Lords held that the value of the documents was negligible and since the purpose of the exercise was to enable the Ministry to deduce the source, the paper could invoke s.10. The section applied even though there was only a reasonable chance (rather than a certainty) that the paper's source would be

---

[244] See *R v Lord Saville Ex p. A* [1999] 4 All E.R. 860 CA and *R v Lord Saville Ex p. 28 Widgerry Soldiers* [2002] 1 W.L.R. 1249 CA where the Court of Appeal concluded that the Saville Inquiry had to allow soldier witnesses to remain anonymous.

revealed. The burden of proof lay with the Government to demonstrate that one of the exceptions applied. Although three of the five Law Lords were persuaded that national security required the leaker to be identified, all of them stressed that this conclusion could not be reached merely upon the Government's say-so. There had to be realistic evidence that national security was imperilled.[245]

The prevention of disorder

The higher courts have not as yet been asked to consider the **5–067** meaning of this exception. It is difficult to see how it could be relevant to evidence given at civil trials, although journalists summonsed to criminal courts as witnesses in cases arising from continuing and violent industrial action might be called upon to answer. This exception is probably unnecessary, since the serious "disorder" required to overcome the presumption would inevitably entail the commission of criminal offences.

The prevention of crime

This is a significant exception for all journalists who publish inves- **5–068** tigations into crime and corruption. The very impact of their work may result in police inquiries or official investigations, and their sources will be sought after to provide the leads. Jeremy Warner suffered in exactly this way (see para.5–055). The House of Lords ruled that the phrase "prevention of crime" in s.10 does not require the investigator to show that disclosure is necessary to forestall a particular crime: it was sufficient if disclosure would enable prosecution for an offence already committed, or would assist in the prevention of crime in the future. The court will, however, be less inclined to order disclosure under this head at the instance of a private claimant or a body that has suffered crime but has no public duty to investigate or prevent it. The Health Authority that successfully suppressed the story about doctors with AIDS failed on this basis to obtain an order for the newspaper to disclose the name of its employee who had corruptly and criminally sold its records: it had no public duty to prosecute claims, and the purpose of its action was predominantly to stop publication rather than to stop crime.[246]

It might be noted at this point that US law, generally more favourable to the American media thanks to the First Amendment, is comparatively unhelpful about source protection. The decision in *Branzburg v Hayes*[247] denies journalistic privilege and, although most US states have enacted "shield laws" similar to s.10 of the UK Contempt of Court Act, they do not apply to federal grand jury

---

[245] *Secretary of State for Defence v. Guardian Newspapers Ltd* [1985] A.C. 339.
[246] *X v Y* [1988] 2 All E.R. 648.
[247] 408 U.S. 665 (1972).

investigations. Thus in July 2006 Judith Miller, of the *New York Times*, went to jail for several months for refusing to disclose who in the Bush Administration tipped her off about the identity of a CIA agent in an effort to discredit the agent's husband who was perceived to be an 'enemy' of the White House. Miller had been an eager propagandist for the Iraq war and although she saw herself as a champion of press freedom, many thought that she had been a willing tool of a particularly nasty plot to discredit a Bush critic. Eventually the source (Lewis Libby, the Vice President's Chief of Staff) owned up and Miller was released. The episode marked an irony about press/political interdependence which is not confined to the Washington beltway. As Sedley L.J. noted in the *Interbrew* case,

> "It should not be forgotten that in this country, then as now, the principal source of unattributable leaks to the media—in the form of off the record briefings—and therefore the principal beneficiary of a rule protecting the secrecy of sources, was government itself."[248]

Practical considerations

5–069 Even when disclosure would be necessary in the interests of justice or for one of the other purposes set out in s.10, the judge still has a discretion not to press journalists to disclose their source. As Donovan L.J. has put it:

> "over and above [the requirements that the answer is necessary and admissible] there may be other considerations, impossible to define in advance, but arising out of the infinite variety of fact and circumstances which a court encounters which may lead a judge to conclude that more harm than good would result from compelling a disclosure or punishing a refusal to answer."[249]

One such consideration is the undesirability of ordering disclosure prior to trial. So far as the purpose of interlocutory orders is to preserve the status quo, in most cases this can be adequately protected by orders prohibiting or limiting the use of the leaked material. Ordering the disclosure of a source or the return of documents to the claimant at the pre-trial stage does more than this. Once the source's identity is made known, the situation cannot be reversed if at trial it transpires that the claimants are not entitled to the order or documents they seek.[250]

---

[248] [2002] E.M.L.R. 24 at [7].

[249] *Att-Gen v Mulholland* [1963] 1 All E.R. 767, 773 and see Lord Denning at 771. Since the qualifying conditions of the 1981 Act are stringent, it will be rare that this discretion is exercised in favour of the journalist.

[250] *Mersey Care NHS Trust v Ackroyd* [2003] E.M.L.R. 36; *Francome v Mirror Group Newspapers Ltd* [1984] 2 All E.R. 413, 415, 416; *Handmade Films (Productions) Ltd v Express Newspapers Plc* [1986] F.S.R. 463.

On an interim application there is also a danger of the court making erroneous assumptions about the nature of the source. This area of the law is littered with cases where claimants and judges have presumed that the source is a senior executive only to have that assumption later confounded. Granada's BSC mole, for instance, was not at the board level, but a worker in its waste disposal unit. The *Guardian*'s source for the Greenham Common memo was not a senior MOD civil servant, but a junior clerk. The journalists may not know the identity of their source (if, as in the *Guardian*'s case, the material was sent anonymously) or, if they do, may quite rightly, be concerned that any information which they provide as to who their source is or is not will also provide a vital clue which will allow the source to be identified by the claimant.

Leaked documents

A media defendant sued for the recovery of leaked documents may **5–070** be tempted to resist the claim on the principle that it cannot be obliged to provide information that might implicate itself in a crime. This would be an arguable defence if, for instance, the circumstances of its obtaining the document could make it an accessory to theft or the handling of stolen goods. Such a defence was raised by Granada when British Steel sued to discover the identity of the television company's informant, but the courts ruled that the risk of prosecution was remote. The defence is a two-edged sword, because to admit to participating in possible criminal behaviour undermines any public interest claim that might be made in the same proceedings. A further problem is s.72 of the Supreme Court Act 1981, which removes the privilege against self-incrimination in civil proceedings that concern "commercial information or other intellectual property", although it is doubtful whether Government policy documents, for example, would fall into this category. The privilege against self-incrimination may be of value to journalists who refuse to co-operate with Scotland Yard inquiries into breaches of the Official Secrets Act 1989 after leaks to them of Government documents. Section 72 of the Supreme Court Act, designed to facilitate civil proceedings against video pirates, should not be deployed as a devious method for probing journalistic sources.

In practice, of course, a newspaper would now be advised to destroy any documents that might incriminate a source as soon as it is aware that the owner is likely to demand their return. If this step is taken before legal proceedings have been formally initiated, it will not amount to contempt of court[251] and the owner would be left with only a civil claim of minimal damages for lost property. Granada

---

[251] But it is an offence under Theft Act 1968 s.20 dishonestly to destroy or deface *original* documents of or belonging to a Government Department or court of justice.

Television adopted the expedient of mutilating the British Steel documents to remove all identifying marks before returning them. The *Guardian*, however, in the Sarah Tisdall case, made the mistake of both admitting to possession of the document and acknowledging the presence on it of identifying marks in correspondence with Government solicitors before legal action was taken. It preserved the document, in over-optimistic reliance on s.10 of the Contempt of Court Act.

Source disclosure in International Criminal Courts

5–071 War correspondents are now vulnerable to be summonsed to testify in various international tribunals established to try those accused of crimes against humanity and other crimes recognised in international law. The International Criminal Court has commenced sitting in The Hague, where the International Criminal Tribunal for former Yugoslavia has been established for some years. There are further UN war crimes tribunals in Sierra Leone, in Arusha (the International Criminal Tribunal for Rwanda) and in Cambodia and East Timor. These courts apply international law and *Goodwin v UK* is accepted as part of that doctrine. This was established by the ICTY in the case of *Jonathan Randall*, a *Washington Post* reporter who had been summonsed to give evidence at the trial of a Serb politician whom he had once interviewed. The Appeal Chamber of the ICTY set aside the witness summons, ruling that journalists should only be compelled to testify in cases where their evidence was vital to guilt or innocence and the evidence could not be obtained in any other way. Even where journalists did testify, they should be able to protect their sources' identities on *Goodwin* principles.[252]

The Special Court for Sierra Leone has extended the *Goodwin* rule to protect journalists and researchers for human rights organisations, such as Amnesty International and Human Rights Watch. If they testify, they will not be required to disclose their sources of information. The court may reduce the weight to be given to the testimony as a result, but they cannot be obliged to put their informants in peril.[253]

Public Interest Disclosure Act 1998

5–072 Some protection for sources who are "whistleblowers" is given by the Public Interest Disclosure Act 1998. The scheme is bolted on to employment legislation[254] so that dismissal where an employee has

---

[252] *Prosecution v Brdjanin and Talic: appeal of Jonathan Randall* ICTY judgment of Appeal Chamber December 11, 2002.
[253] *Prosecutor against Brima* Case Number SCSL-2004–16–AR73, Judgement May 26, 2006 see further para.11–072.
[254] The 1998 Act inserted a number of new sections into the Employment Rights Act 1996.

made a "protected disclosure" is unfair and gives a right to all the remedies for unfair dismissal[255] although the usual maximum limits on compensation for unfair dismissal do not apply in these circumstances.[256] A worker who suffers other detriment because of a protected disclosure is also entitled to compensation.[257]

All of these remedies depend on the employee having made a "protected disclosure". So what kinds of disclosures are protected?

In the first place the disclosure must be a "qualifying disclosure", that is the worker must reasonably believe that it tends to show the commission of a criminal offence, failure to comply with a legal obligation, a miscarriage of justice, the health or safety of an individual is endangered, damage to the environment or concealment of any of the above. The matters can be in the past, present or future; in or outside the United Kingdom. However, it does not apply if the worker commits a criminal offence by making the disclosure.[258]

In the second place, the Act does not necessarily protect even **5–073** qualifying disclosures to the press. The worker must make the disclosure in good faith, reasonably believe the information to be true and not make the disclosure for purposes of personal gain. In addition, he must reasonably believe that he would be subjected to a detriment if he made the disclosure to his employer, or he has disclosed substantially the same information previously to his employer or to a prescribed regulator[259] or there is no regulator and the worker reasonably believes that evidence would be destroyed if he made disclosure to his employer. A further condition is that the disclosure must be reasonable in all the circumstances. The statute sets out some of the matters to be examined in deciding whether disclosure is reasonable. They include the identity of the person to whom the disclosure is made, the seriousness of the employer's actions and whether they are continuing or likely to occur in the future.[260]

These requirements can be curtailed and a disclosure will still be protected if the relevant failure is of an exceptionally serious nature and the worker is in good faith, reasonably believes it to be true, does not act for personal gain and the disclosure is reasonable in the circumstances.[261]

---

[255] Employment Rights Act 1996, s.103A.
[256] Employment Rights Act 1996, at s.127B and Public Interest Disclosure (Compensation) Regulations 1999, (SI 1999/1548).
[257] Employment Rights Act 1996, at ss.47B, 48(1A) and 49(6).
[258] Employment Rights Act, s.43B.
[259] The regulators are defined by The Public Interest Disclosure (Prescribed Persons) Order 1999 (SI 1999/1549) as amended by SI 2003/1993, SI 2004/3265 and SI 2005/2464.
[260] Employment Rights Act 1996, s.43G.
[261] Employment Rights Act 1996, s.43H.

Any attempt by employers to make employees contract out of their rights under these provisions is void.[262]

Although the Act does generally apply to Crown employees, it does not apply to police officers[263] nor does it apply to employment for the purposes of MI5, MI6 or GCHQ.[264]

POLICE POWERS OF SEARCH AND SEIZURE

5–074 Prior to 1984 the right of the police to search premises and seize evidence was a confusing jumble of common law powers and statutes passed to cater for specific situations. The Police and Criminal Evidence Act 1984 both rationalised and broadened these powers.[265] It created a three-fold division which is examined below. Parliament has given the same powers to certain other investigators, such as the members of staff designated by the Independent Police Complaints Commission to look into allegations of misconduct by the police.[266]

Excluded material

5–075 This includes "journalistic material", defined as "material acquired or created for the purposes of journalism". The holder need not be a professional journalist if the material was acquired or created for journalistic purposes. The term would cover an anonymous package of leaked material sent to a journalist since it includes material that is sent to a recipient for the purposes of journalism.[267] Importantly, journalistic material is only "excluded" if it is held in confidence. This means that most film, whether taken by broadcasting crews or still photographers, is not "excluded material". Generally, the police are not entitled to a search warrant for excluded material. Exceptionally, they may do so if some other statute authorises the grant of a warrant. They must then obtain an order from a circuit judge (rather than a magistrate or district judge who would normally consider police applications for warrants).[268] The Official Secrets Acts are examples of statutes that may allow such an order to be made (see para.11–033).

---

[262] Employment Rights Act 1996, at s.43J.

[263] Employment Rights Act 1996, at s.200.

[264] Employment Relations Act 1999, Sch.8, para.1.

[265] However, the 1984 Act only applies to England Wales. Thus it does not protect media organisations in Scotland: 1984 Act, s.120(1). Nor does it protect media organisations in England or Wales for whose premises a Scottish court has issued a search warrant: *R. v Manchester Stipendiary Magistrate, Ex p. Granada Television Ltd* [2000] 1 A.C. 300.

[266] Police Reform Act 2002 Sch.3 para.19.

[267] Police and Criminal Evidence Act 1984, s.13. If the material is not in the possession of someone who acquired or created it for journalistic purposes, it loses its status as "journalistic material".

[268] Police and Criminal Evidence Act 1984, Sch.1, para.3.

Special procedure material

This includes journalistic material that is not "excluded material".[269] **5–076**
The police must again apply to a circuit judge, but the conditions on
which an order will be made are more relaxed than for excluded
material. They must show that there are reasonable grounds for
believing[270] that a serious arrestable offence has been committed,
that the material is likely to be of substantial value (whether by itself
or together with other material) to the investigation, and that the
material is likely to be relevant evidence. Finally and most importantly, the police must show that the public interest requires an order
to be made, taking into account the benefit to the investigation of
the material and the circumstances in which the material is held.[271]
Several courts (including the House of Lords) have echoed the
comment:

> "The special procedure . . . is a serious inroad upon the liberty
> of the subject. The responsibility for ensuring that the procedure
> is not abused lies with circuit judges. It is of cardinal importance
> that circuit judges should be scrupulous in discharging that
> responsibility."[272]

Applications are made, after notice to the holder of the material,
to a circuit judge. Either in the notice or at the hearing the police
must describe in broad terms the offences being investigated.[273]
Initially, the application is made to a judge in chambers, but in
hearing applications against the press, judges have shown themselves
willing to adjourn the case into open court so that the public can
attend and the case can be reported (see para.8–020).
On many occasions the police have used these powers to obtain
orders requiring the press to hand over film and photographs of
demonstrations. The first concerned disorders in Bristol[274]; the
second an investigation by the Police Complaints Authority into
complaints about the police violence at a major demonstration at
Wapping during the Times Newspapers dispute.[275] In every case the

---

[269] Police and Criminal Evidence Act 1984, s.14.
[270] "Reasonable grounds for *believing*" is a tougher test than the usual requirement
for a search warrant that there are "reasonable grounds for *suspecting*"—see *R. v
Crown Court at Southwark, Ex p. Bowles* [1998] 2 All E.R. 193, 200.
[271] Sch.1, para.2.
[272] *R. v Maidstone Crown Court, Ex p. Waitt* [1988] Crim. L.R. 384 cited with
approval in *R. v Crown Court at Southwark, Ex p. Bowles* [1998] 2 All E.R. 193,
200, HL.
[273] *R. v Crown Court at Manchester, Ex p. Taylor* [1988] 2 All E.R. 769.
[274] *Chief Constable of Avon and Somerset v Bristol United Press*, the *Independent*,
November 4, 1986, application for leave to apply for judicial review refused; *R. v
Crown Court at Bristol, Ex p. Bristol Press Agency Ltd* [1987] Crim. L.R. 329.
[275] *Wyrko v Newspaper Publishing Plc*, the *Independent*, May 27, 1988.

photographers argued that their job would be made more dangerous if the crowds they were photographing knew that their pictures could become prosecution evidence. One press photographer had already been killed in the Brixton disorders after capturing a looter on film and a leaflet distributed at a demonstration in autumn 1994 against the Criminal Justice Act condemned "the pigs and their friends in the media". If the danger increased, so too would the likelihood that violent confrontations would not be covered by photographers. In consequence, the public would be less well informed and the police investigators would not even have the benefit of photographs that would otherwise have been taken and published. No court has accepted these arguments although occasionally they have refused because the police have not tried other methods before seeking a production order, or have failed to demonstrate that the photographs will be of evidential value.

5–077   The Divisional Court in 2000 gave a powerful endorsement to protecting the media by the Special Procedure.[276]

> The *Guardian* published the text of a letter from David Shayler, an ex-MI5 employee who was at that stage living in Paris and resisting extradition to the United Kingdom on charges under the Official Secrets Act (Shayler had made various allegations of misdeeds by MI5 including hatching a plot to assassinate Colonel Gadaffi. The *Observer* published an article commenting on a letter which Shayler had previously sent to the Home Secretary again in connection with the alleged plot). An Old Bailey judge ordered the newspapers to produce all files, documents and records relating to the articles. The Divisional Court largely set aside the orders. It stressed:
>
> • Even in national security cases applicants for orders must produce evidence. If the evidence was too sensitive to be disclosed, it should be heard by the judge in chambers without the respondent being present.
> • The judge had to reach his own decision on whether the access conditions were fulfilled. It was not sufficient for the judge to decide that the police officer's view that they were, was reasonable.
> • The factors mentioned in the access conditions—the benefit of the material to the investigation and the conditions under which the person held the material—set the parameters for the public interest test. However, a broader range of factors could be taken into account when the judge exercised the residual discretion. These might include the impact of the order on third parties, the police delay, and any disproportion between the potential benefit to the investigation and harm to the respondent or the impact of an order on freedom of expression or the effect which it might have of implicating the journalist in a criminal offence.

Bright's case is a welcome reminder to circuit judges that they must not automatically accede to police applications for production

---

[276] R. (*Bright*) v *Central Criminal Court* [2001] 1 W.L.R. 662.

orders against newspapers. Nonetheless, it is unlikely to deter them from ordering disclosure of untransmitted footage or unpublished photographs of riots and demonstrations. Judges have regularly paid tribute to the courage of photographers and camera crews who cover such events, but they have also regularly been sceptical as to whether production orders would appreciably increase the risk that they face. The European Commission rejected a complaint from the BBC that a court order to produce untransmitted film from the Broadwater Farm disorders infringed Art.10.[277]

Once a person has been served with a notice of application for an order under these provisions, concealment, destruction or alteration of the material can be treated as contempt of court.[278] Nothing limits what can be done with the material before a notice is served. Four freelance photographers who were at a violent anti-Murdoch demonstration at Wapping transferred their negatives to the International Federation of Journalists in Brussels and gave up all further rights to them before they were served with notices. Alliott J. subsequently ruled that this was not a contempt of court.

Other material

This may be seized subject only to the normal safeguards for search **5–078** warrants. These may be granted by a magistrate without any right on the part of the media to object and without the need to apply the public interest test for "special procedure" material. Once police are lawfully present on premises (whether under a magistrates' warrant or because of some other power) they are entitled to seize (but not to search for) any material that they have reason to believe has either been obtained in consequence of the commission of an offence or is evidence of an offence, and which it is necessary to seize in order to prevent it being concealed, lost, damaged, altered or destroyed. If the material is held on a computer that can be accessed from the premises, the police can demand a print-out. Under these powers the police cannot demand material that is covered by legal privilege, but they can seize "special procedure" or "excluded" material.[279] Further (complex) provisions are made by the Criminal Justice and Police Act to give the police additional powers of seizure including situations where material which is otherwise seizable is mixed with special procedure or excluded material. Broadly, judicial consideration of whether to allow the

---

[277] *BBC v UK* (1996) 21 E.H.R.R. CD 93.
[278] Police and Criminal Evidence Act 1984, Sch.1, para.11. This obligation required a telecommunications company to intercept and preserve copies of emails which the police wanted to inspect even though this would otherwise be an offence under the Regulation of Investigatory Powers Act 2000, s.1: *R (NTL Group Ltd) v Crown Court at Ipswich* [2003] Q.B. 131.
[279] Police and Criminal Evidence Act 1984, s.19.

police to examine and use the material then takes place after the seizure.[280]

The debates over the Police and Criminal Evidence Act raised the issue of principle as to whether journalists should claim special protection from the normal process of the law. Although such protection was initially sought by media organisations, many of their members subsequently changed their minds when it became apparent that the special treatment awarded them in the Act would necessarily involve the courts in defining "journalism" and in operating a special regime that would accord to practitioners favoured treatment by comparison with ordinary citizens. The special status offered by the Act infringes the principle that journalism is not a profession, but the exercise by occupation of the citizen's right to freedom of expression. In retrospect, the media organisations (such as the Guild of British Newspaper Editors) who supported the Government's offer of "special protection" for journalists fell into an obvious trap, and damaged their members' interests. Prior to the 1984 statute, police had not been granted access to untransmitted material at common law. But once a statutory route for obtaining that material came into existence, albeit with "special protections", the police naturally exploited it and courts naturally decided that the protection was not very special after all. Judges generally believe that investigation of crime must have a higher priority than journalistic principles, and the decisions in the Bristol, Wapping and anti-Hunting Bill demonstration cases were all decided by this judicial preference. Police applications for untransmitted material have become routine after every violent demonstration, and the media objections to production are routinely dismissed.

AUTHORISED BURGLARY AND BUGGING

5–079 Dramatic powers to enter and interfere with property and radio signals were provided by the Police Act 1997. The powers can be exercised if the action would be of substantial value in the prevention or detection of serious crime and its objective could not reasonably be achieved by other means.[281] "Serious crime" for this purpose means that it involves the use of violence, results in substantial financial gain or is conduct by a large number of people in pursuit of a common purpose, or if it is an offence for which a person over 21 with no previous convictions could reasonably be expected to be sentenced to a term of three years imprisonment or more.[282] If these conditions are fulfilled authorisation can be given by senior police officers but if they are unavailable specified deputies

[280] Criminal Justice and Police Act 2001, ss.50–70.
[281] Police Act 1997, s.93(2).
[282] Police Act 1997, s.93(4).

can act in their place. The Act creates a series of Commissioners (headed by a Chief Commissioner) who will all be judges of the High Court or above. A Commissioner must be given notice of the authorisation. Usually this will be after the event, but in certain cases, a Commissioner must give prior approval. These special cases include situations where the action is likely to result in any person acquiring knowledge of "confidential journalistic material"[283] which is defined[284] in essentially the same terms as confidential journalistic material which is "excluded" for the purposes of the Police and Criminal Evidence Act 1984 (see para.5–075). Other special cases include authorisation for intrusions onto property used as a dwelling or an office.[285] This protection can be dispensed with where the authorising police officer believes that the case is urgent.[286] A complaints system has been set up under the Regulation of Investigatory Powers Act 2000 by way of an appeal to the RIPA Tribunal.[287] This is modelled on the complaints systems under the Security Services legislation and which had not upheld a single complaint in its first decade of operation.

The end of the Cold War and the peace process in Northern Ireland released the Security Service for an expanded role in combating serious crime within the United Kingdom,[288] (although after September 11, their time has largely been taken up by counter-terrorism). The definition of serious crime is the same as for the Police Act 1997 and despite the government's repeated statements that it was directed at organised crime, the statutory definition is far wider. The greater reach of the security services means a potentially wider domestic target for their substantial powers.

The Regulation of Investigatory Powers Act 2000 greatly increased the powers of the police and the security and intelligence services to intercept communications, and to carry out "intrusive surveillance." In the case of the police and customs, authorisation for such activities has to be approved in advance by a "Surveillance Commissioner" (one of the Commissioners appointed for similar purposes under the Police Act). The security and intelligence services need only the Secretary of State's approval. There is no special procedure for intrusions which will interfere with journalistic material. Complaints (in the unlikely event that a potential complainant learns of the surveillance) can again be made to the RIPA Tribunal.

The vague terms in which these powers are cast, the lack of adequate safeguards and the unsatisfactory character of the means

---

[283] Police Act 1997, s.97(2)(b).
[284] Police Act 1997, s.100.
[285] Police Act 1997, s.97(2)(a).
[286] Police Act 1997, s.97(3).
[287] Regulation of Investigatory Powers Act 2000, s.65.
[288] Security Services Act 1996, s.1 adding s.1(4) to the Security Service Act 1989.

of redress means that there will inevitably be a challenge to their compatibility with Art.8 of the European Convention on Human Rights.

CHAPTER 6

COPYRIGHT

"The sweat of a man's brows, and the exudations of a man's brains, are as much a man's own property as the breeches upon his backside."[1]

"Everyone has the right to the protection of the moral and material interests resulting from any scientific, literary or artistic production of which he is the author."[2]

INTRODUCTION

The law against breach of copyright protects creative work that has **6-001** been reduced to material form from being used by others without permission. It is the most technical branch of the law dealt with in this book. Its essential purpose, shared with the law against breach of confidence, is to prevent the plagiarism or unfair exploitation of creative work. As such, it affords vital protection to writers, and is the basis of the measures taken by publishing and broadcasting organisations to combat piracy. But as a corollary to this purpose, it may inhibit the media's freedom to report and expose matters of public interest, where such reportage necessarily involves publication of documents written by or belonging to persons or organisations who wish to keep them private.

The battles fought to enhance rights of writers and artists to prevent exploitation of their work by different forms of copying are worthwhile when they result in payment or credit for originality, but not when they are used by executors to injunct creative reinterpretations or criticisms of the work of deceased authors or by governments or corporations to stop the revelation of their own incriminating internal documents. In these situations Art.10 should apply with full force, but English judges, brought up to believe in the

---

[1] Laurence Sterne, *Tristram Shandy*.
[2] Universal Declaration of Human Rights 1948, Art.27(2). The International Covenant on Economic, Social and Cultural Rights 1966 Art.15(1)(c) is in almost identical terms.

pre-eminence of property rights over human rights, have thus far failed to give Art.10 any force at all, despite the fact that the courts have found that copyright protection extends, for example, to works of utter banality and even reproductions and verbatim transcripts. The relevant Court of Appeal decisions, relating to pictures of Diana and Dodi the day before their death and a memo by the Lib Dem leader about a coalition with New Labour, are notable for their inability to understand how the newsworthiness of the material justified publication in the public interest. Both were early HRA decisions and await review by the House of Lords (shortly to be called the Supreme Court). There is no reason why the broad public interest defence it provided in 2006 for serious journalism in *Jameel v Wall Street Journal* should not also be available to copyright claims.

The other block on creativity has been the behaviour of family executors, now allowed 70 years after the deaths of the creative genius, to "protect" their work. The untalented relatives executing the estates of James Joyce, and Samuel Beckett have become notorious for refusing permissions for re-interpretation or criticism. It may be reasonable to permit great grandchildren to profit from the talent of their forebears, but to permit them (or executors purporting to represent their interests) to stultify and suppress original work is plainly a breach of Art.10.[3] Most occasions on which the media will wish to use copyright material do not pose problems, either because the originator is only too happy for his or her exudations to be publicised, or because arrangements have been made to pay a suitable royalty or licensing fee. Difficulties are encountered, however, when use of copyright material is made without formal acknowledgment, or in the context of an article or broadcast that makes use of private documents for the purpose of criticising those to whom copyright belongs. Even with the best will in the world, the egos of artists involved in the different stages of putting together a feature may provoke irreconcilable differences of opinion as to the due credit to be given in the final product. Untangling such disagreements is hard for several reasons. The law of copyright was revised in the Copyright, Designs and Patents Act 1988, but its reforms generally apply only to works created after the statute came into effect. The Copyright Act 1956 (which it replaced) will therefore be important for years to come. In some cases it will be necessary to consult even earlier (and now repealed) legislation. To add to the confusion the 1988 Act has itself been amended often (under the impetus of requirements from the European Union) by regulations. These include the changes made necessary by the Copyright Directive (2001/291/EC)[4] which have been incorporated

---

[3] *Sweeney v Macmillan Publishers Ltd* (2002) RPC 651: preventing publication of a reader-friendly edition of *Ulysses* and *Godot* 1993 155 RIDA 225, where a French court prevented the staging of "Waiting for Godot" with female actors at the behest of the author's executors.

[4] The EU directives have been codified in the Directive on Copyright and Certain Related Rights (Codified Version) Dir 2006/116/EC of December 12, 2006.

into UK law by the Copyright Amendment Regulations 2003.[5] The structure of the law is still highly complex and a book of this type can only be a guide to its most important aspects. Specialist textbooks[6] give more detailed guidance.

There are five basic questions in copyright law.

Does copyright exist in the source material?

The 1988 Act establishes the following categories of copyright: **6–002**

    (a) original literary, dramatic or musical works;
    (b) original artistic works;
    (c) sound recordings;
    (d) films;
    (e) broadcasts;
    (f) published editions.

The legal meanings of these categories are broader than their everyday use. Moreover, multiple copyrights can exist in a particular work. In the case, for instance, of a television documentary, there will be literary copyright in the script, dramatic copyright in the screenplay and musical copyright in any background music. The totality will be entitled to copyright as a film, and once aired will have a further copyright as a television broadcast.

Copyright begins from the time the work is made. There is no longer any need to register the work, and even the copyright symbol © is not necessary in the United Kingdom, although it is if the work is to be published in a country that is a member of only the Universal Copyright Convention (see para.6–021). Until the 1988 Act it was common for this effective monopoly to last a very long time, particularly in the case of unpublished literary, dramatic and musical works, which could, in theory, enjoy perpetual copyright. The scope for rights to be perpetual has been virtually abolished. A rare exception is *Peter Pan*, for whose exploitation the Great Ormond Street Hospital is still entitled to collect royalties, thanks to the will of J.M. Barrie and a special amendment to the 1988 Act. All other works (such as those that were published under the 1956 Act) have finite protection, and once this is over, the work can be reproduced in any fashion. The standard period of copyright is now 70 years from the author's death (although there is a shorter period for certain types of copyright.

Who owns the copyright?

Ownership will decide who has the right to license use of the **6–003** copyright and who has the power to take legal action against infringement. The Act lays down rules for determining who is the

---

[5] SI 2003/2501.

[6] e.g. Laddie, Prescott, Vitoria, *The Modern Law of Copyright and Designs* (3rd edn, Butterworths, London, 2000, 4th edn forthcoming); Garnett *Copinger and Skone James on Copyright* (15th edn, Sweet and Maxwell, London, 2004).

first owner: usually this is the author or maker of the work. It also envisages the transfer of rights to others and specifies certain formalities if these are to be effective. "Moral rights" created by the Act cannot be transferred except to the estate of the author or maker on their death. They can, however, be waived.

Does the proposed use of copyright material infringe the law?

6–004   Copyright gives the owner an exclusive right to use the work in specific ways. Infringement is the use of the work in one of these ways without the owner's consent. The possible means of infringement may differ according to the type of work, but each involves some element of copying, reproduction or performance. Ignorance of the owner's rights is no excuse, but it may diminish the amount of compensation that has to be paid. A secondary type of infringement is committed by those in the chain of distribution of infringing copies who know that the merchandise is pirated.

Is there a defence?

6–005   There is no infringement if the reproduction was permitted or licensed by the copyright owner. In addition, there is an important statutory defence of "fair dealing" with the work for the purpose of criticism, review or reporting current events. There are other defences, protecting court reports, old films and preparations made for broadcasting. In some cases enforcement of copyright may be contrary to the policy of the law. This public interest defence has been strengthened by the Human Rights Act.

Will the publication infringe some other right similar to copyright?

6–006   Although a publication has successfully steered clear of the shoals of copyright, it may still run into legal difficulties because of other similar rights. An author who manufactures quotes may not infringe copyright, but can be sued for damages for false attribution of authorship. Malicious falsehoods about a rival's goods can be costly. Performers have rights that are akin to copyright. The 1988 Act also brought English law into line with the Berne Convention on Copyright and introduced the concept of "moral rights" for authors and directors: (a) to be identified as such; and (b) not to have their work subjected to "derogatory treatment". Regulations in 1996 introduced a new "publication right" for those who publish previously unpublished works in which copyright has expired.[7] And artists now have a right to benefit in certain circumstances from the resale of their works.[8]

---

[7] Copyright and Related Rights Regulations 1996 (SI 1996/2967), Regs 16–17.
[8] Artists Resale Rights Regulations 2006 (SI 2006/346) implementing EU Directive of the European Parliament and Council 2001/84.

The civil claim of "passing off" will sometimes provide a remedy for claimants whose name or work or goodwill is misappropriated by others for commercial gain. Thus Dow Jones Inc was able to force Ladbrokes to disband "The Ladbrokes/Dow Jones Index", a gambling operation related to the rise and fall of the Dow Jones Index, which wrongly implied that Dow Jones had consented to or benefited from the operation. *The Mail on Sunday* was able to obtain an injunction, on grounds of passing-off, to stop an advertiser from arranging with distributors and newsagents to insert printed advertising leaflets in its colour supplement. The newspaper successfully argued that the public would assume that the advertisements had its approval and were under its control, and that the connection might damage its goodwill.[9]

EXISTENCE OF COPYRIGHT

Original literary, dramatic or musical works

This is the first classification of material that is subject to protec- **6–007** tion.[10] "Literary" work does not imply any particular quality of language.[11] The most turgid prose can be a literary work, as can programme schedules, letters, football fixture lists, opinion polls and even railway timetables if reproduced in detail. However, the work must be "recorded in writing or otherwise".[12] There can be no copyright in a literary idea, or suggestion for a story, though it may be imparted in circumstances that would be protected by the law of confidence (see para.5–039). Copyright can exist in a literary work only if it is recorded, but it need not be recorded in writing. Memoirs dictated on to a tape are protected even before the tape is transcribed. Similarly, a speaker delivering a lecture from prepared notes will have copyright in the speech. Conversely a spontaneous or extempore speaker will not have copyright, unless, that is, the speech is recorded with or without the permission of the speaker.[13]

This will mean that people interviewed by reporters have copyright in the words they utter if the journalist has taken an accurate note or recorded them. However, there is a defence to prevent this extension of literary copyright acting as a form of censorship (see para.5–059).

An "original" work for the purposes of the Act has been variously described as a work the creation of which has involved the expenditure of "skill, labour and judgment"; "selection, judgment and

---

[9] *Associated Newspapers Plc v Insert Media Ltd* [1991] 1 W.L.R. 571, CA.

[10] Copyright, Designs and Patents Act 1988, s.3.

[11] *University of London Press Ltd v University Tutorial Press Ltd* [1916] 2 Ch. 601 at 608.

[12] Copyright, Designs and Patents Act 1988, s.3(2). "Writing" includes "any form of notation or code. Whether by hand or otherwise and regardless of the method by which or medium in or on which it is recorded": s.178.

[13] Copyright, Designs and Patents Act 1988, s.3(3).

experience"; or "labour, skill and capital". These tests operate to exclude protection only where compilations are basic and commonplace. In consequence, protection has been afforded to mathematical tables that the compiler had worked out for himself, hire-purchase forms, broadcast programme schedules and even street directories. The 1988 Act unambiguously provides that a computer program can be a literary work with its own copyright protection.[14]

6–008   Special provision is also made for copyright in databases.[15] In addition to copyright protection, there is a "database right" which prevents the extraction or reutilisation of the whole or substantial part of the contents of the database.[16] But a "database" for these purposes means a body of information which has been assembled and (sometimes) checked or verified. It does not apply where the person assembling the data also gives the assemblage an official stamp of approval. That amounts to the creation of something new rather than the assembly of existing independent material.[17] Where the database right does exists it lasts for only 15 years from the making of the database, but if during that time it is made available to the public the 15 years runs from that release. However, it is a common feature of databases that they are updated periodically. If any substantial change is made to the contents of the database which would result in the database being considered to be a substantial new investment a new term of protection will begin to run.[18]

Copyright can also be acquired in compilations, translations, abridgments and anthologies. So, for instance, a list of Stock Exchange prices and a football pools coupon have copyright. The requirement is the same: the author's own contribution must have required a degree of skill and labour that led to the new work having some recognisably different quality to its source or sources. A person who translates a speech into a different language clearly transforms it sufficiently to satisfy this test. Copying the translation would then infringe the rights of both the original author and the translator. A slavish copy, that adds nothing, rearranges nothing or selects nothing would have no claim to be a literary work unless, possibly, the text of the original were inaccessible.

The skill and labour expended by a reporter or stenographer in taking down a speech in shorthand may be sufficient to attract copyright protection against other newspapers that "lift" a substantial part of the report. Thus in *Walter v Lane*,[19] a *Times* reporter was

---

[14] Copyright, Designs and Patents Act 1988, s.3(1)(b).

[15] See CDPA, s.3(1)(d), s.3A and other amendments to the Act made by Copyright and Rights in Databases Regulations (SI 1997/3032). The Regulations were prompted by the EU Directive on the Legal Protection of Databases Council Dir. 96/9/EC.

[16] Database Regulations, Reg.16.

[17] *British Horseracing Board v William Hill Organisation Ltd* [2005] RPC 35, CA

[18] Database Regulations Reg.17.

[19] [1900] A.C. 539.

entitled to damages when his version of a politician's public speech was copied word for word by a rival newspaper. This would not mean, of course, that no other paper could report the speech: another reporter present would have an equal right to file a separate account of it. Though both accounts might be identical, neither would be derived from the other and both would enjoy copyright. As each of these reporters would have copyright, both papers could prevent their less diligent rivals from copying their reports. (The politician in *Walter v Lane* would, since the 1988 Act, have copyright in his speech because of the act of the reporter in recording it, but the reporter's defence (see para.6–059) would mean that the politician could not prevent its appearance in the paper.) The term "originality" is also misleading. The work must require some skill and labour, but it need not also be novel. It is enough if the creator of the work can truthfully say "this is all my own work".[20]

Walter v Lane was endorsed in a case concerning music composed **6–009** by Lalande for the courts of Louis XIV and Louis XV.

> There were, of course, no contemporary recordings and such written notations were unplayable. However Dr Sawkins "combined scholarship and knowledge with a substantial amount of artistic inventiveness" and after some 300 hours on each piece produced performing scores. These were used by a choral and orchestral ensemble to perform the music which Hyperion recorded and sold. To Dr Sawkins' claim for copyright infringement they objected that the music they had performed was Lalande's and he had been dead for well over two centuries. However, the Court held that Dr Sawkins had invested very considerable skill and labour in producing his scores. It was immaterial that his objective had been to render as faithfully as possible the original work of Lalande. Dr Sawkins had a new musical copyright which the defendant had infringed.[21]

A "dramatic work" is a work with or without words or music which is capable of being performed before an audience and its action must also have a certain unity.[22] The concept is not limited to conventional plays, but the makers of a computer games programme that simulated various games of pool failed to establish that they had devised a "dramatic work". The game had a set of rules, but what would appear on the screen depended very largely on the player's input. The sequence of images would differ from one game to another and so there was no unity of action.[23]

False attribution of authorship

Copyright apart, journalists must exercise care in attributing quota- **6–010** tions or in ghosting articles for others. False attribution of remarks to which exception is taken can lead to a claim for damages.

---

[20] Whitford Committee, *Copyright Law 1977* HMSO, Cmnd. 6732, para.33.
[21] *Hyperion Records Ltd v Sawkins* [2005] 1 W.L.R. 3281, CA.
[22] *Norowzian v Arks* [2000] FSR 363, CA.
[23] *Nova Productions Ltd v Mazooma Games Ltd* [2006] EWHC 24 (Ch).

Dorothy Squires obtained £100 damages for false attribution of authorship in 1972 from the *News of the World*, whose reporter had inaccurately written up an interview concerning her marriage to Roger Moore. This sum was in addition to libel damages that were awarded in the same case. The paper was not excused because it was following an apparent Fleet Street custom of making up quotes for willing interviewees. The paper was liable if the "author" disliked "her" lines.[24]

Parody is an unreliable defence:

The *Evening Standard* published a weekly spoof, "Alan Clark's Diaries", satirising the right-wing opinions of the former cabinet minister and flamboyant libertine and diarist. Clark's name and photograph appeared at the head of column. So too did the name of the real author, Peter Bradshaw, but its impact was not enough, so the judge ruled, to disabuse the reader who skimmed the newspaper of the impression that the Diaries really had been written by Mr Clark. Much was obvious fantasy, incredible and wild exaggeration, but the judge thought that a substantial body of readers would be fooled into thinking that Clark was truly the author. Although a false attribution of authorship could be neutralised, the corrective had to be as bold, precise and compelling as the false statement so that it would prevent a substantial body of readers from being misled. The test is whether a substantial (or large) number of the paper's ordinary readers would be misled more than momentarily. Its application to the facts was highly questionable. The judge treated the *Evening Standard* as a publication which is skim-read by morons in a hurry to get home after a tiring day at the office. He seemed over-impressed by Clark (who had a Toad-like quality of inspiring affection) and lacked understanding of the art of parody: his ruling that the *Evening Standard* should have put Bradshaw's authorship in lights would have made the whole exercise heavy-handed and unfunny. The decision can only be justified on the grounds that the *Evening Standard* is the kind of paper in which readers would not expect to find a parody (or believe it was a parody when they saw it) and for this reason it has not lead to a change of practice in *Private Eye* and other magazines whose readers do expect parodies.[25]

The 1988 Act substantially enlarges the scope of false attribution, which it categorises as a matter of moral rights. It prohibits the false attribution of authorship of a literary, dramatic, musical or artistic

---

[24] *Moore v News of the World* [1972] 1 All E.R. 915. *Cf. Jenkins v Socialist Worker*, *The Times*, February 28, 1977. Similar care must be taken with quotes attributed to the dead. Their estates can claim damages for false attributions made up to 20 years after death: Copyright, Designs and Patents Act 1988, s.86(2).

[25] *Clark v Associated Newspapers Ltd* [1998] R.P.C. 261, Lightman J. The judge also held that the spoof had been "passed off" as the real thing. The *Standard* was injuncted from repeating anything similar and an inquiry as to damages was ordered.

work and falsely describing someone as the director of a film. It prohibits falsely representing a literary, dramatic or musical work as an adaptation of a person's work or a copy of an artistic work as having been copied by the artist. An altered artistic work must not knowingly be passed off as the original. The section now spells out in detail who is to be liable for these wrongs: in some (but not all) cases they are confined to those who knew or had reason to believe that the attribution was false; in certain cases the liability is limited to those who deal with the falsely described article in the course of business.[26]

News stories and programme formats

There is "no copyright in news itself, although there is copyright in **6–011** the form in which it is conveyed".[27] This means merely that a newspaper cannot obtain exclusive rights to cover an event by being first on the scene, or stop rivals from repeating facts of public importance that it is first to report.

The *Daily Express* sued *Today* newspaper for breach of copyright because, in time-honoured press tradition, *Today* had "copied", in its second edition, an "exclusive" *Express* story on prostitute-about-town Pamela Bordes. *Today* responded by suing Express Newspapers for breach of copyright when its own exclusive story—from a Royal relative it had paid to criticise the Royal Family—was pirated. The Vice-Chancellor, Sir Nicolas Browne Wilkinson, refused to find that there could be copyright in the substance of a news story, although there would have been a breach if a substantial part of the original reporter's words had been copied verbatim:

> "I would hesitate a long time before deciding that there is copyright in a news story which would be infringed by another newspaper picking up that story and reproducing the same story in different words. Such a conclusion would strike at the root of what I think is the practice of the national press, namely to search the columns of other papers to find stories which they have missed and then using the story so found in their own newspaper by rewriting it in their own words. If it were the law that such practice constituted breach of copyright, the consequences, as it seems to me, would be that a paper that obtained a scoop from a confidential source would obtain a monopoly on that piece of news. That would not be in the public interest as it would prevent the wider dissemination of the news to the public at large."[28]

---

[26] Copyright, Designs and Patents Act 1988, s.84. The prohibitions apply to *any* part of a protected work, not just substantial parts: see 1988 Act, s.89(2).

[27] *Springfield v Thame* (1903) 89 L.T. 242. Note that this case was decided before Parliament gave the press a "fair dealing" defence for reporting current events.

[28] *Express Newspapers Plc v News (UK) Ltd* [1990] 1 W.L.R. 1320.

What *is* protected by copyright, under the rubric of "form" or "mode of expression", is not merely language and paragraph arrangement, but *original work*, which in the case of a news article would include the skill, labour and judgment that had been expended upon research, "putting together" and presentation. The principle is that,

> "the plaintiff has a right to say that no one is to be permitted . . . to take a material and substantial part of his work, his argument, his illustrations, his authorities, for the purpose of making or improving a rival publication".

6–012 Journalists who find their stories "borrowed" in detail by other publications, without an agency agreement and without an appropriate attribution, may have a good cause of action. If what is pirated is merely the facts, retold in different words, then the courts will find that this is a custom engaged in by newspapers over a very long time, and impliedly consented to by all who work on them. But where the borrowing is substantial and verbatim, and reproduces quotations from third parties (who have a separate copyright), then the principle in *Walter v Steinkopf* is likely to be applied:

> Rudyard Kipling's news dispatches, printed in *The Times*, were regularly and substantially reproduced without that newspaper's consent in the *St James Evening Gazette*. Mr Justice North held that its copyright had been infringed:

> "In the present case what the defendants have had recourse to is not a mental operation involving thought and labour and producing some original results, but a mechanical operation with scissors and paste, without the slightest pretension to an original result of any kind; it is a mere production of 'copy' without trouble or cost . . . it is not immaterial to look at the number and character of the passages taken, in the whole; and also to bear in mind that it is not a mere casual trespass on the plaintiff's right, occurring now and again at long intervals, and not likely to be repeated; but deliberate, persistent abstraction of matter from the plaintiff's paper, which the defendants justify and insist on their right to continue. For the purposes of their own profit they desire to reap where they have not sown, and to take advantage of the labour and expenditure of the plaintiffs in procuring news for the purpose of saving labour and expense to themselves.

> It is said there is no copyright in news. But there is or may be copyright in the particular forms of language or modes of expression by which information is conveyed, and not the less so because the information may be with respect to the current events of the day . . ."[29]

The problem of deliberate borrowing in journalism will be considered further in relation to the requirement of "substantiality" and the defence of "fair dealing".

---

[29] *Walter v Steinkopf* [1892] 3 Ch. 489.

A similar issue is the extent to which a person who has expended **6–013** considerable skill and labour in carrying out research for his work can complain if a later author makes use of that labour for his own work. The point was illustrated in the high profile litigation over the *Da Vinci Code*:

> The authors of a book called *Holy Blood Holy Grail* argued that their book had been heavily used by Dan Brown, the author of the *Da Vinci Code*. They could not show any significant copying of the actual words of *HBHG* and they had to accept that Dan Brown was free to use the "facts", themes and ideas from their book. However, literary copyright will also extend to the way in which the facts, themes and ideas are presented. They argued that Brown had impermissibly taken these as well and copied the central theme or architecture of *HBHG*. They sued Random House, the publishers of *Da Vinci Code* and, coincidentally, publishers of *HBHG*. However, the judge concluded that *HBHG* did not have the central theme on which they relied and the claim failed. The courtroom was packed each day of the trial and the evidence of witnesses closely reported including that of one of the authors of *HBHG* who admitted that he might have phrased his witness statement more felicitiously. "Yes", said the cross examiner, "you could, for example, have told the truth." The idea of secret codes must have been infectious. The judge, Peter Smith J., italicised certain letters in his judgment. Strung together these formed a secret message. Dan Tench of Olswangs, cracked the code (which itself was mentioned in the *Da Vinci Code*) and found that it referred to the judge's hero, Admiral Fisher (who commissioned the Dreadnought battleships).[30]

Literary copyright will obviously exist in the scripts of television and radio programmes. In some cases they will also have protection as dramatic works. However, the badge or characteristic of other programmes may be less easy to define. Hughie Green discovered how difficult it was to prevent others using the same idea.

> Hughie Green had compered *Opportunity Knocks* in the United Kingdom for many years. He had devised the use of a "clapometer" to measure the audience's reaction to the different acts that appeared in his talent contest. Certain stock phrases, such as "For X . . . opportunity knocks", were used in most programmes, but the content of each programme changed each week and Hughie Green's own words were usually ad lib. New Zealand Television took the same idea and used similar techniques in a television programme with the same name. Hughie Green failed in his attempt to injunct them. The title was too trite to attract copyright. The clapometer and the other features of the programme's format were too nebulous to be described as a "dramatic work" and too imprecise to be protected as "literary copyright".[31]

---

[30] *Baigent v Random House Group Ltd* [2006] E.M.L.R. 16; upheld by CA [2007] EWCA Civ 247.
[31] *Green v Broadcasting Corp of New Zealand* [1989] R.P.C. 700.

6–014　　There is a lively current debate over the fairness of the *Opportunity Knocks* decision, and a lobby (enthusiastically supported by lawyers for the entertainment industry) for its reversal by legislation and for the creation of "format rights" that would entitle creators of ideas for game shows to stop others from copying these ideas. The makers of *Have I Got News for You*, popular for its rehearsed spontaneity, sued in Australia a local show, *Good News Week*, which was obviously based on their format. They lost—both were comedy programmes relying upon similar routines, but the jokes which were the essence of both programmes were completely different. Freedom of expression is better advanced by retaining the present copyright rule, which protects the way in which ideas are expressed, but not the ideas themselves.

Published editions

6–015　In addition to protecting the content of a literary, musical or dramatic work, the 1988 Act also gives copyright to its typographical arrangement (assuming that it has been published[32]). Originality is not required, but a straightforward reproduction of a previous published edition is not given a new copyright.[33] What is protected is the whole of the "edition". An edition is the product, generally between covers, which the publisher offers to the public. The idea of this copyright is to give protection to the skill and labour in the overall design of the edition. Applying this test the House of Lords decided that a practice by Marks and Spencer of circulating photocopies of interesting clippings from newspapers to its senior executives did not infringe the copyright of the newspapers in their published editions. Although the photocopies obviously copied the typeface and arrangement of the individual articles, they did not take all or even a substantial part of the overall design of the newspaper as a whole.[34]

Published edition copyright is a more restricted right than other copyrights in that it lasts for only 25 years from the end of the year of publication (by comparison with 70 years after the death of the author(s) for published literary works) but for that period, facsimile copies can be made only with the consent of the owner of this copyright as well as the owner of the literary or other work itself.

---

[32] Copyright, Designs and Patents Act 1988, ss.8 and 15.

[33] 1988 Act, s.8(2).

[34] *Newspaper Licensing Agency Ltd v Marks and Spencer Plc* [2003] 1 A.C. 551. The Court of Appeal [2000] 4 All E.R. 239 had decided that when a newspaper came in several sections or supplements, the "edition" was the composite whole. The House of Lords thought that separate and distinct parts might have their own copyright of this kind.

Artistic works

Copyright can subsist in the following original artistic works.[35]   **6–016**

    (a) irrespective of artistic quality: paintings, drawings, diagrams, maps, charts, plans, engravings, etchings, lithographs, woodcuts or similar works (collectively referred to as "graphic works"), photographs, sculptures or collages;

    (b) works of architecture, being either buildings or models for buildings;

    (c) works of artistic craftsmanship not falling within (a) or (b).

The first of these categories is likely to be most important for journalists—in particular, paintings, drawings and photographs. These words are given a wide definition. In one case a picture of a hand holding a pencil that was marking a cross next to the name of a favoured election candidate was said to be a sufficient drawing to have copyright.[36] Cartoon comic strips also have copyright under this head.[37]

"Photograph" means "a recording of light or other radiation on any medium on which an image is produced or from which an image may be any means be produced and which is not part of a film".[38] Films are excluded because they are separately protected. This apart, the definition is broad and would include, for instance, holograms and also the photographic "plates" that are used in photolithographic printing.

As with literary works, artistic works in the first category are **6–017** protected whatever their aesthetic value. Similarly, all "artistic works" are only protected if they are "original", in the sense that some skill and labour must have been involved in producing them. Buckingham Palace is a hackneyed subject for tourists' photographs but each picture enjoys copyright, as in each case the photographer will have chosen the distance and angle from which to take it. Similarly, a photocopy montage of clippings or headlines may have sufficient originality to have photographic copyright, but a photocopy of a page of someone else's work falls on the other side of the line: as an exact copy it lacks originality and no particular skill or labour has been required to produce it.[39]

    The band Oasis organised a photographic shoot at a country club hotel for the cover of their new album. A Rolls Royce was arranged so as to

---

[35] 1988 Act, s.4.

[36] *Kenrick & Co v Lawrence & Co* (1890) 25 Q.B.D. 99, decided under the Copyright (Works of Art) Act 1862.

[37] *King Features Syndicate Inc v O. & M. Kleeman Ltd* [1941] A.C. 417, HL.

[38] Copyright, Designs and Patents Act 1988, s.4(2).

[39] *Reject Shop Plc v Manners* [1995] F.S.R. 870.

appear to be rising out of the swimming pool. Members of the group were placed around the pool in different poses. A photographer from the *Sun* managed to book a room in the hotel, gained access to the shoot and took photographs of his own which were then published in the paper. Oasis' licensee failed to establish copyright in the scenes which had been photographed: the assembly was too ephemeral to qualify as a "collage" and had nothing in common with "sculpture". It was not an "artistic work". The claimants did, however, succeed in obtaining an interim injunction on breach of confidence grounds similar to that which led to the damages claim against the cunning photographer in *Douglas v Hello* (see *Stop Press* section).[40]

Sound recordings

6–018 This expression is widely defined as:

(a) as a recording of sounds from which the sounds may be reproduced; or
(b) as a recording of the whole or any part of a literary, dramatic or musical work from which sounds reproducing the work or any part may be reproduced;
(c) regardless of the medium on which the recording is made or the method by which the sounds are reproduced or produced.[41]

Consequently while this type of copyright is commonly used to protect recordings of music, it would include, for example, a tape recording of a conversation. There is no test of originality, but a copy of a previous sound recording does not acquire its own copyright.[42]

The sound track accompanying a film is to be treated as part of the film[43] but this does not affect any copyright subsisting in the film sound track as sound recording copyright.[44] Thus if an infringer copies the film plus the sound track only the owner of the film copyright can take action but if the infringer instead (or as well) copies the sound track on its own it is the owner of the sound recording copyright who is able to complain.

Films

6–019 "Films"[45] are again broadly defined as "a recording on any medium from which a moving image may by any means be produced". It is therefore irrelevant whether the film is shot on an ordinary camera

---

[40] *Creation Records Ltd v News Group Newspapers* [1997] E.M.L.R. 444, Lloyd J.
[41] Copyright, Designs and Patents Act 1988, s.5A(1).
[42] 1988 Act, s.5A(2).
[43] 1988 Act, s.5B(2).
[44] 1988 Act, s.5B(5).
[45] 1988 Act, s.5B.

or by using a magnetic videotape or captured by a digital camera. As with sound recordings, there is no requirement of originality, but again as with sound recordings, a mere copy of a previous film does not attract a fresh film copyright.[46] The recording of a computer program that produces abstract patterns when fed through a machine would also qualify as a "film". Dramatic works or sound recordings that are only embodied in a film can now enjoy a separate copyright, but a photograph that is part of a film does not have its own copyright.[47] This limitation is less appropriate to cartoon films. Each drawing made for the animation has a separate artistic copyright. This was clearly the case when animators like Walt Disney commissioned separate paintings for each frame. The huge costs of that method of production can now be cut by using a single drawing and washable inks. The picture can then be rephotographed for the following frame, by altering only the part that needs to "move". The picture in each state lasts only a few minutes and this impermanence creates a doubt as to whether each enjoys artistic copyright. Of course, each picture is captured on the film, but a photograph can be an artistic work only if it is *not* part of a film.

No court has yet had to decide on whether a series of still photographs taken by motordrive cameras are protected as artistic works or as a film. Clearly they are intended to be developed singly, but if (as is sometimes the case) they are "capable of being shown as a moving picture" then the spool would be protected only as a film.

Broadcasts

"Broadcast" is defined as: 6–020

> "an electronic transmission of visual images, sounds or other information which (a) is transmitted for simultaneous reception by members of the public and is capable of being lawfully received by them, or (b) is transmitted at a time determined solely by the person making the transmission for presentation to members of the public".

Transmissions over the internet are excluded unless there is a simultaneous transmission by other means, or it is a concurrent transmission of a live event or the transmission is of moving pictures or sounds at a time scheduled by the person providing the service.[48]

The 2003 Regulations incorporated the previously separate treatment of cable programmes into the omnibus protection for "broadcasts".

---

[46] 1988 Act, s.5A(4).

[47] 1988 Act, s.4(2).

[48] Copyright, Designs and Patents Act 1988 s.6 (as amended by the Copyright and Related Rights Regulations 2003 (SI 2003/2498).

As with sound recordings and films, there is no requirement that a broadcast be original. However, as with sound recordings and films, a simple copy of a previous broadcast would not be entitled to a fresh copyright.

Territorial connection

6–021   Copyright can be claimed only if there is a connection between the work and either the United Kingdom or a country that is a party to an international copyright convention giving reciprocal rights. In general terms, *unpublished* works are protected if the author or maker was a national of, or resident or domiciled in, Britain or one of the other countries that have subscribed to the Berne Copyright Convention or the Universal Copyright Convention. Where a company may own copyright, it is sufficient if it is incorporated in one of these countries.[49] Most of the developed countries are parties to one or both of these conventions, although some have joined relatively recently.[50] The personal connection between the author and Britain is also sufficient to give copyright in *published* works. Alternatively, they will be protected if the work's first publication took place in Britain or one of the Convention countries.

Broadcasts are protected if made or sent from a place in the United Kingdom or from a Convention country.

PERIOD OF COPYRIGHT

6–022   A European Directive[51] required the United Kingdom to amend the 1988 Act and in many cases substantially extend the length of copyright protection. The previous standard copyright period of 50 years was thought to be too short and has been extended in many (but not all) contexts to 70 years. The literary estates of D.H. Lawrence and Rudyard Kipling were among those to benefit from this extension. The European Directive was intended to harmonise the copyright laws of the Member States and the price of this objective was a tortuous compromise which was a boon for the great grandchildren of dead authors but a blow for those poor artists who might otherwise have creatively adapted their works. It also stymied biographers and jazzer-uppers who have been denied licences by executors such as those of James Joyce who prevented the publication of a reader-friendly edition of *Ulysses*, the trustees of Samuel Beckett's estate who prevented *Godot* being waited for by women or the trustee of Sylvia Plath (the sister of Ted Hughes) who refused to allow her poems to be quoted in works critical of Hughes.

---

[49] 1988 Act, ss.1(3) and 153–155.
[50] See The Copyright and Performances (Application to Other Countries) Order (SI 2006/316).
[51] Council Directive No.93/98/EEC OJ L290, November 24, 1983.

For works created after January 1, 1996 or works which then had copyright protection in the United Kingdom, the normal position is:

- literary, dramatic, musical or artistic works: 70 years from the author's death. If authorship is unknown copyright lasts 70 years from the making of the work or, if during that period it is made available to the public, 70 years from when that occurs;[52]
- computer-generated literary, etc., works still have 50 years from the making of the work;[53]
- Crown and Parliamentary copyrights remain as before the 1995 regulations. In literary, musical or artistic works Parliamentary copyright last for 50 years from the making of the work. Crown copyright in these types of work lasts for 125 years, or, if shorter, 50 years from commercial publication. In other types of work the period of Crown and Parliamentary copyright generally follows the standard rules;[54]
- sound recording copyright lasts for 50 years from the making of the work, or, if during that period it is released, 50 years from release;[55]
- film copyright lasts for 70 years from the last to die of: the principal director, the author of the screenplay, the author of the dialogue or the composer of music specially created for and used in the film. If the identity of one or more of these participants is unknown, the 70 years runs from the death of the last known. If they are all unknown it runs for 70 years from the making of the film or, if during that period the film is released, for 70 years from release;[56]
- broadcast copyright extends for 50 years from the year in which the broadcast was made;[57]
- copyright in a published edition lasts 25 years from first publication.[58]

In all cases copyright runs until December 31 of the last year of the period. Generally speaking works which originate outside the EEA[59] and which are not made by an EEA national will have only the period of protection of the national law of their country of origin (if this is less than the period which the Act gives to an EEA national).[60]

---

[52] 1988 Act, s.12 as amended by the 1995 Regulations.

[53] 1988 Act, s.12(7).

[54] 1988 Act, ss.12(9), 163(3) and 165(3).

[55] 1988 Act, s.13A. S.13A was further amended by the Copyright and Related Rights Regulations 2003.

[56] 1988 Act, s.13B.

[57] 1988 Act, s.14.

[58] 1988 Act, s.15.

[59] The EEA presently includes the countries of the EU plus Norway, Liechtenstein and Iceland.

[60] See ss.12(6), 13A(4), 13B(7) and 14(3). "Country of origin" is defined in s.15A.

6-023   It is not possible here to examine the intricacies of works with joint authors or the complications which arise when works have been made many years ago and so lived (or slumbered) through several different legislative regimes or where the work although out of copyright in the United Kingdom in 1995 continued to enjoy protection in another EEA State. However, one important rule to note is that unpublished works remained in copyright indefinitely until the 1988 Act. They then became subject to a further 50–year maximum which the Duration Regulations have now extended to 70 years (i.e. until 2059). This method of calculating the period of copyright prevails if it produces a longer period than the normal guidelines described above.[61]

INFRINGEMENT OF COPYRIGHT

Copying

Literary, dramatic, musical or artistic works

6-024 The most common method of infringing copyright in these types of works is by copying them—that is, by reproducing all or a substantial part of them—in any material form.[62] The reproduction need not be exact. Obviously, copyright would be of no value if it could be avoided by a sham alteration of a word or two. It is a more difficult question as to whether drastic alterations of language or form exonerate a story whose substance is taken from an earlier work. The question is particularly important for the media. Can a story from a rival newspaper or broadcaster be reproduced if it is rewritten first? In the United States the answer would clearly be no, as the Hearst newspaper chain discovered. Its war reporters in World War I were not as effective as those of Associated Press. Hearst therefore lifted its war news from AP's East Coast editions and telegraphed the copied stories to California in time to compete with AP's West Coast editions. The United States Supreme Court held that this misappropriation of AP's skill and labour was wrongful competition and could be stopped.[63]

   Under UK copyright legislation the question would turn upon whether the borrowing was "substantial". This test would be satisfied if a story in newspaper A, based on original research and interviews, was repeated in newspaper B. Thus, each paper in the *Today/Express* litigation (see para.6–011) was found to have infringed the other's copyright in the quotations that had appeared in the original articles and that were copied by the rival paper.[64]

---

[61] Duration Regulations, Reg.15(1).
[62] Copyright, Design and Patents Act 1988, s.17.
[63] *International News Service v Associated Press*, 248 U.S. 215 (1918).
[64] *Express Newspapers Plc v News (UK) Ltd* [1990], fn.28 above.

Parliament has given the media a limited licence to plagiarise literary, dramatic and musical works for the purpose of reporting current events, if they provide a sufficient acknowledgment of their source (see "Fair Dealing", para.6–037). Consequently, it is only if a newspaper has failed to acknowledge its indebtedness to a rival that it would need to argue that it had not infringed the other's copyright. A court would rarely be sympathetic in such a circumstance. When the *St James Gazette*'s argued that in copying Rudyard Kipling's dispatches in *The Times* it was only following a hallowed Fleet Street custom, the judge caustically remarked that a highwayman might as well plead the frequency of robbery on Hounslow Heath.[65]

In 1980 the High Court of Australia held that journalists who had **6–025** obtained secret Government cables could, without breaking the Government's copyright, relay the content and essence of the documents if they chose their own language.[66] They could summarise the effects of the cables and pick out the highlights, but verbatim reproduction would be an infringement. The courts can grant injunctions where the reproduction (although quite different in form) draws on the skill and labour that the claimant had invested in making the original:

> The script for a film about an historical event (the Charge of the Light Brigade) had been drawn from facts recounted in a history book without further original research. An injunction was granted even though the language of the book had not been reproduced, the order of events was different and fresh material had been added.[67]

In the *Da Vinci Code* plagiarism case the Court emphasised that where a book is intended to be read as a historical factual account, the author cannot claim a monopoly in the facts presented, but can claim protection through copyright in the way in which the ideas, facts and themes are put together—in other words, "the architecture" of the claimant's work.[68]

Where a substantial part of the claimant's work has been copied, it is immaterial that the defendant has added further material of his own. What is necessary is that a substantial part of the claimant's work has been copied. It is not necessary that the claimant demonstrate that a substantial part of the defendant's work derived from his work.[69] Thus in *The Da Vinci Code* case, the claimants had to

---

[65] *Walter v Steinkopf* [1892] 3 Ch. 489, 499. The *Daily Express* tried a similar argument in its litigation with *Today* but was precluded from blowing hot and cold: the existence of the action would have fatally undermined its own claim that the copyright in its quotations had been enjoyed. See also *Banier v News Group Newspaper Ltd*, fn.134 below.

[66] *Commonwealth of Australia v John Fairfax and Sons Ltd* (1981) 32 A.L.R. 485, High Court of Aust.

[67] *Harman Pictures NV v Osborne* [1967] 1 W.L.R. 723.

[68] *Baigent v Random House Group Ltd* (above).

[69] *Designers Guild v Russell Williams Textiles* [2000] 1 W.L.R. 2416 HL.

show that a substantial part of *HBHG* had been copied in *DVC*. They did not have to show that a substantial part of *DVC* was a copy of *HBHG*.

Substantial part

6–026 The test is whether, irrespective of language, a "substantial part" of the original work has been reproduced. For this reason, the courts would not prevent others from using a commentator's apt epithet or a dramatist's smart pun. Whether a taking is "substantial" is a matter of the judge's impression. Quality is more important that quantity in determining substantiality—a Dow Jones reporter who took all the significant information from a private report on the cocoa market (including figures of the actual cocoa-pod count in various countries) had not copied much in terms of length, but everything in terms of significance. Consequently, her articles were held to infringe copyright in the private report.[70]

On the same principle, while a cartoon can be artistic copyright, the joke behind it cannot: it is too ephemeral. Other cartoonists can raise the same laugh so long as their drawings are different.[71]

In these cases, where the defendant has altered the original work, a useful test is whether the defendant has incorporated a substantial part of the independent skill, labour, etc., contributed by the original author in creating the copyright work.[72] Thus, the degree of change that a defendant must make may vary according to the degree of skill that has gone into producing the original. Although a picture of a hand holding a pencil and making a cross might be entitled to copyright, the fact that it had taken no great skill to produce is recognised by protecting it only against close imitations: a picture of a hand in a slightly different position was not an infringement.[73] In the same way, copyright in an anthology of quotations is not infringed by a later work that uses some of the same material but in combination with other sources and in a different arrangement.[74]

6–027 The main purpose of copyright is to allow the inventors of original works to exploit them commercially. Where the claimant's and the defendant's works do compete and more than minimal effort has gone into producing the original work, it is not easy to persuade a court that the copying is insubstantial. It will not use a crude

---

[70] *PCR Ltd v Dow Jones Telerate Ltd* [1998] F.S.R. 170.
[71] *McCrum v Eisner* (1917) 117 I.T. 536; (1917–23) M.C.C. 14.
[72] *Designers Guild Ltd v Russell Williams (Textiles) Ltd* [2000] 1 W.L.R. 2416, HL.
[73] *Kenrick v Lawrence*, see fn.25 above.
[74] *Warwick Film Productions Ltd v Eisinger* [1969] Ch. 508.

quantitative criterion, but rather a qualitative one. The most frequently cited judicial test looks to the commercial reality: "what is worth copying prima facie is worth protecting."[75]

Copyright is not just a battleground between commercial rivals. Satire and parody may involve the repetition of a large part of the work that is being lampooned. It, too, will be judged by the "substantial part" test in deciding whether there has been an infringement.[76] However, the satirist and the parodist may have a fair-dealing defence (see paras 6–037). In any case, the targets of their barbs may risk making greater fools of themselves by taking legal action.

If they should, there are two other (albeit vaguer) principles that **6–028** the courts can invoke either in assessing whether there has been an infringement or in deciding whether to grant a discretionary remedy such as an injunction. The first is a recognition that copyright law must not be used as a means of oppression:

> *Red Star Weekly* used the four lines of a popular song called "Her Name is Mary" as the opening paragraph of a serial story. The court said this was not a breach of copyright. Care had to be taken not to allow the Copyright Acts to be used as a means of oppression. Here the defendant was using part of the claimant's work for a totally different purpose: a purpose that would have no adverse effect on the defendant's sales.[77]

The second principle is that the courts are unlikely to interfere (especially at the interlocutory stage) where the alleged infringer adapts the owner's work to make a political point:

> The Campaign for Nuclear Disarmament printed a pamphlet *30 Questions and Answers About CND*. On its cover the CND symbol was interwoven with a map of Britain. The Coalition for Peace Through Security, a group opposed to CND, produced a counter-publication, *30 Questions and Honest Answers About CND*. The design of the cover was very similar except that the CND symbol had been adapted to resemble a hammer and sickle. CND was refused an interlocutory injunction because it had suffered no financial loss and the judge was reluctant to restrain political controversy.[78]

---

[75] *University of London Press Ltd v University Tutorial Press Ltd* [1916] 2 Ch. 601, 610. This attitude is strikingly manifest where the compiler of a directory has made use of a rival publication rather than carry out the original research itself. There may be an infringement of copyright in the competing work even if it is only used to compile a mailing list for a questionnaire for the new work; *Waterlow Directories Ltd v Reed Information Services Ltd* [1992] F.S.R. 409.

[76] See *Schweppes v Wellingtons* [1984] E.S.R. 210, *Williamson Music Ltd v The Pearson Partnership* [1987] F.S.R. 97; contrast *Joy Music Ltd v Sunday Pictorial Newspapers* [1960] 1 All E.R. 703.

[77] *Chappell & Co Ltd v D.C. Thompson & Co Ltd* (1928–35) M.C.C. 467. See also *British Leyland Motor Corp v Armstrong Patents Co Ltd* [1986] A.C. 577.

[78] *Kennard v Lewis* [1983] F.S.R. 346.

Programme schedules

6–029 An example of how copyright law can operate to prevent one part of the media announcing what another part is doing was for many years provided by the monopoly that the BBC and the ITV companies, respectively, gave to the *Radio Times* and *TV Times* for publishing their weekly programme schedules: an indulgence that made these the largest-selling journals in Britain. The courts consistently held that the schedules were literary works like other intellectual property which the broadcasters were entitled to protect.[79]

In 1990 the Government finally legislated to end the broadcasters' copyright monopoly in programme schedules. An early attempt to challenge such monopolies under the European Convention of Human Rights had failed, on the grounds that Art.10 guaranteed freedom to exploit information only to those who produced it.[80] However, subsequently the EU Commission held that the programme monopoly schedule infringed Art.86 of the Treaty of Rome, and directed broadcasters to provide weekly advance listings of their programmes to all who requested them.[81] In order to conform with this ruling, the British Government introduced s.176 of the Broadcasting Act 1990, which requires the BBC, Channel 4 and all services regulated by Ofcom to provide a list of a full week's programmes at least 14 days in advance to all those wishing to publish this information. The information may be limited to programme titles and must be paid for by those wishing to publish it, at rates that, if they cannot be agreed, should be decided by the Copyright Tribunal in terms of what it considers "reasonable in the circumstances".[82] The BBC and independent television companies reacted churlishly to the loss of their monopoly, and demanded an astronomical £8 million per year for allowing national and local newspapers and magazines to publish their programme listings. Two hundred publishers appealed to the Copyright Tribunal, which proceeded to adjudicate on the charges after a five-week public hearing and brought them down substantially.[83] An appeal against its decision was settled.[84]

Derivation

6–030 A copy will be an infringement only if it is derived from the claimant's work. A picture of a winning goal cannot be lifted from one newspaper by its rivals without committing a breach of

---

[79] *BBC v Wireless League Gazette Publishing Co* [1926] Ch. 433; *Independent Television Publications Ltd v Time Out Ltd* [1984] E.S.R. 64.
[80] *De Geillustreede v The Netherlands* [1979] F.S.R. 173.
[81] *Magill TV Guide v Independent Television Publications* [1990] F.S.R. 71, E.C. Comm. This was followed by the ruling of European Court of First Instance to similar effect: *BBC v E.C. Commission*, T–70/89 [1991] 4 C.M.L.R. 669.
[82] Broadcasting Act 1990, Sch.17.
[83] *News Group Ltd v Independent Television Publications Ltd* [1993] R.P.C. 173.
[84] See [1993] E.M.L.R. 133.

copyright, but if two photographers took identical pictures from the same spot, both pictures could be published without impinging on each other's copyright. If a newspaper were to copy a table of fixtures from a football pools coupon, it would breach the pools organiser's copyright, but it could publish an identical table if it obtained the information by its own researches.

This causal connection need not be direct. The owners of the *Popeye* cartoon copyright were able to stop an infringer from producing Popeye dolls. The dolls had been copied, not from the cartoon, but from other dolls that had been produced under the claimant's licence.[85] This case, incidentally, also illustrates the possibility of infringing a two-dimensional artistic work by a three-dimensional copy.[86]

A photographer or painter can also indirectly copy an earlier work by using the photograph or painting to recreate the model or scene from which the first artist worked. The copying can then be in the similarity of composition, angle, lighting and general effect,[87] although, as with other examples of infringement, the less skill that was invested in the first work, the closer must be the resemblance to the second before the courts will accept there has been infringement.

Once the link between the original and the copy is proved, it is unnecessary for the copyright owner to show that the defendant intended to plagiarise.[88] Unconscious imitation is still an infringement, though, as will be shown, the defendant's innocence may affect the remedies available to the claimant.

Other types of infringement

Copying other works

Copying a published edition means making a facsimile copy of it.[89] **6–031** Copying a substantial part will suffice, but the copy must have appropriated the presentation and lay out of the original work.

> When Marks and Spencer circulated photocopies of articles which concerned its business to its employees they were sued for infringement of copyright in the typographical arrangements in the source newspapers. However, the House of Lords said that the relevant work was not the individual articles, but the newspaper as a whole. Taking that as the original work Marks and Spencer had not copied a substantial part of any one paper.[90]

---

[85] *King Features Syndicate Inc v O. & M. Kleeman Ltd* [1941] A.C. 417, HL; see also Copyright, Designs and Patents Act 1988, s.16(3)(b).

[86] Copyright, Designs and Patents Act 1988, s.17(3)(b).

[87] *Gross v Seligman* (1914) 212f 930 (1911–16) M.C.C. 219; *Turner v Robinson* (1860) 10 I. Ch. R. 121, s.10.

[88] e.g. *Byrne v Statist Co* [1914] 1 K.B. 622.

[89] Copyright, Designs and Patents Act 1988, s.17(5).

[90] *Newspaper Licensing Agency Ltd v Marks and Spencer Plc* [2003] 1 A.C. 551.

Copyright in a film or broadcast can be infringed by taking a photograph of any image forming part of the work.[91]

There can be copying of any type of work even if the copy is transient or incidental to some other use.[92] This can be important for the protection of copyright in computer programs or material stored on computer discs. Calling up a file to be read on a computer would be to make an infringing copy (assuming, of course, it was without the permission of the copyright owner), even if the copy disappears without trace when the machine is switched off. Although incidental copying is prima facie an infringement, there are important defences (see para.6–056).

Broadcasts

6–032 Any type of copyright (apart from that in a published edition) will be infringed if it is communicated to the public, that is if it is included in a broadcast or if it is made available to the public by electronic transmission in such a way that members of the public may access it from a place and at a time individually chosen by them.[93] Responsibility is shared between the broadcaster who actually transmits the programme and the company contracting to provide it.[94]

Adaptation

6–033 Literary, dramatic and musical (but not artistic) works are also protected against adaptations. This includes turning a non-dramatic work into a dramatic one and vice versa; translating the work into a different language, and turning the work into a strip cartoon. An arrangement or transcription of a musical work is an adaptation. A computer program can be "translated" by converting it into or out of a computer language or code or into another language or code but this is not an infringement if it is done only incidentally in the course of running the program.[95]

Publication, rental, lending and public performance

6–034 Sometimes the owner of the copyright will make or authorise copies to be made, but wish to keep them for his own use. The unauthorised issuing of such copies (as well as infringing copies) to the public is an infringement.[96] Liability is here limited to the person

---

[91] Copyright, Designs and Patents Act 1988, s.17(4).
[92] 1988 Act, s.17(6).
[93] 1988 Act, s.20, as substituted by the Copyright and Related Rights Regulations 2003.
[94] 1988 Act, s.6(3).
[95] 1988 Act, s.21.
[96] 1988 Act, s.18.

who puts the copies into public circulation (the newspaper publisher, for instance) and does not apply to others in the chain of distribution. Thus, wholesalers or retailers would not be liable for "issuing to the public". They will be liable, if at all, for secondary infringement (see below), which depends on knowledge that the merchandise is an infringement. Copyright in a literary, dramatic or musical work, an artistic work (other than buildings or their models or works of applied art) and in a film or sound recording carries the additional right to control the rental or lending of the work. There are exceptions for certain libraries and the Government has the power to establish a statutory licensing scheme with the Copyright Tribunal setting royalties in the absence of agreement.[97]

The public performance of a literary, dramatic or musical work is another matter in which the copyright owner is entitled to control. "Performance" includes lectures, addresses, speeches and (parsons beware!) sermons. It will also include a presentation by means of sound or visual aids. Owners of the copyright in sound recordings, films and broadcasts can similarly restrict the public playing of their works.[98]

A "publication right" was introduced in 1996.[99] This is a right akin to copyright for the first publisher of a previously unpublished work in which copyright has expired. It is confined to literary, dramatic, musical and artistic works[100] and films and it is dependent on the work being published by a national of the European Economic Area and in the territory of the EEA. The right is more limited than copyright. Of particular importance is the fact that publication right only lasts for 25 years and no moral rights are engaged.

Authorising infringement

In addition to suing the person who actually does these prohibited **6–035** acts, the copyright owner can also pursue those who "authorise" them.[101] "Authorising" includes sanctioning, approving or countenancing the infringement. So contributors who supply articles or photographs to magazines would be liable for authorising the infringement if they did not own the copyright. Attempts have been made to hold newspapers liable for "authorising" infringement of musical copyright when they have carried advertisements for, or stories about, home-taping. These have generally failed because the

---

[97] For the details see the Copyright and Related Rights Regulations (SI 1996/2967) Regs 10–15 which add or amend the following ss.of the 1988 Act: ss.18A, 36A, 40A, 66, 93A, 133, 142, 93B, 93C, 117 and 124.
[98] Copyright, Designs and Patents Act, 1988, s.19.
[99] Copyright and Related Rights Regulations 1996 (SI 1996/2967) Regs 16, 17.
[100] Because unpublished works had perpetual copyright before 1989 and were then given protection until 2039 there will be little immediate practical effect of the new publication right on these types of work.
[101] 1988 Act, s.16(2).

claimants were unable to prove that the publication had any influence on the readers' actions.[102] The music industry has been more recently concerned with the phenomenon of "Peer-to-Peer" (or P2P) sharing of music files stored on millions of individual computers. Infringement actions against the sellers of the software which allows P2P has been successful in the US and Australia.[103]

Secondary infringement

6–036 All the methods of infringement considered so far are regarded as "primary infringement" by some form of copying, performing or broadcasting. The Copyright Act goes further and allows the copyright owner to take action against others in the chain of distribution and exploitation of infringing copies. Thus importing, possessing in the course of a business, selling, letting for hire, offering or exposing for sale or hire, exhibiting in public for trade or other purposes, and certain types of distributing in each case of infringing copies makes the person concerned liable to the copyright owner.[104] Secondary liability is also imposed on a range of other people who might be commercially involved in primary infringement by, for instance, dealing in articles specifically designed or adapted for making infringing copies or taking steps to enable an infringing performance to take place.[105]

Whereas primary infringement does not depend on guilty knowledge, these secondary infringements do require knowledge or reason to believe that the copies are illegitimate. For this reason, claimants who assert that their rights have been abused will sometimes write to major wholesalers putting them on notice of their claims. This step should not be taken lightly, for the claimants may be liable in damages for lost sales if their claims are not later substantiated.

However, printers are under no separate duty to inquire into the purpose to which their copies will be used and so will not be liable for general damages in the tort of negligence if they print infringing copies.[106]

DEFENCES

Fair dealing

6–037 The use of reasonable extracts from the work of others is not an infringement of copyright if it is for the purpose of:

---

[102] *RCA Corp v John Fairfax & Sons* [1982] R.P.C. 91 Sup. Co of NSW; *A. & M. Records Inc v Audio Magnetics Inc (UK)* [1979] F.S.R. 1 (where the advertiser was the defendant).

[103] *MGM Inc v Grokster Ltd* (2005) US SC; *Universal Music Australia Pty Ltd v Sharman License Holdings Ltd* (2005).

[104] Copyright, Designs and Patents Act 1988, s.23.

[105] 1988 Act, ss.24–6.

[106] *Paterson Zochonis and Co Ltd v Merfaken Packaging Ltd* [1986] 3 All E.R. 522, CA.

- research or private study, where a literary, dramatic, musical or artistic work is used; or
- criticism or review; or
- reporting current events.[107]

The fair dealing defences require that an acknowledgment be given to the originator if the work is used in any medium for criticism or review or, in the case of the print media, if it is used for the purpose of reporting current events. News stories on television, radio, film or in a sound recording are not required to carry an acknowledgment. Where an acknowledgment is required, it must identify the work by its title rather than by general description. It must also identify the author unless he or she is anonymous.[108] A logo may be sufficient to identify the author.[109] As long as the source and author are identified as such in the text, neither the word "acknowledgment" nor expressions of gratitude are required.

The dealing must be fair. A publisher or broadcaster will not need to resort to the defence unless a substantial part of the work has been taken, for only then will there be a prima facie infringement to which a defence is necessary. However, the defence will be lost if the taking is "unfair" in the sense of being out of all proportion to the permitted purpose. Critics can illustrate their points by quotations, and where the original work is short, it can be reproduced in its entirety, but the quotation must be a basis for criticism or review; if the purpose is only to convey the same information as the original, and so compete with it, the use will be unfair.[110] "Unfairness" is sometimes wrongly equated with "unseemliness" and used to dampen down robust competition.

> In a campaign to promote its free supplement, *TV Mag*, the *Sun* reproduced the front cover of *What's On TV* to demonstrate that its own product was superior. The purpose of such comparative advertising was to advance the *Sun*'s product at the expense of its rival's and that, the Court unconvincingly held, was not "fair" in the copyright sense. The Judge conceded that the *Sun* could still have boasted of the advantages of its magazine by comparison with the claimant's without actually reproducing the latter's front cover (although, of course, that would have been less effective). There seems to be a nervousness in some judges in sanctioning full-blooded competition.[111]

So, too, with the use of a work for the purpose of reporting **6–038** current events. The court will consider whether the copying was reasonable and appropriate for the purpose and the defence may be

---

[107] Copyright, Designs and Patents Act 1988, ss.29–30.

[108] 1988 Act, s.178.

[109] *Pro Sieben Media AG v Carlton UK Television Ltd* [1999] 1 W.L.R. 605, CA.

[110] *Hubbard v Vosper* [1972] 2 Q.B. 84, *per* Lord Denning; *Johnstone v Bernard Jones Publications Ltd* [1938] 1 Ch. 599; *Associated Newspapers Group Plc v News Group Newspapers Ltd* [1986] R.P.C. 515.

[111] *IPC Media Ltd v News Group Newspapers Ltd* [2005] E.M.L.R. 532.

lost if the court determines that the newspaper or broadcaster took an excessive amount of the source material.[112] At the same the defendant does not have to show that his criticism or review would have been impossible without an illustration from the Claimant's work. The test is not that the dealing was "necessary" only that it was "fair".[113] Fairness depends on individual circumstances. The question of fairness is judged by the amount taken in order to achieve the permitted purpose: the justice or otherwise of the comments upon the extract is irrelevant.

> Thus Carlton Television was able to justify using 30 seconds from a nine-minute feature about Mandy Allwood, the woman fertilised with eight embryos, who had sold (via Max Clifford) her story to a German television company. The court was impressed by the fact that the extract was quite short and was used to illustrate a "Big Story" attack on cheque-book journalism.[114]

Copyright protects the form of literary, dramatic or musical works, but the criticism need not be limited to the language or means of expression that the author has chosen. It is legitimate to copy substantial parts of the original in order to criticise its substance, content and values, especially if it originates from a source the judges find unprepossessing.

> The Mind Benders was a book written by a former member of the Church of Scientology. It included extracts from manuals by and directives of L. Ron Hubbard, the cult's founder, in order to expose and criticise its practices and beliefs. Although the documents had not previously been published, the court refused an interim injunction. Lord Denning said:
>
> > "We never restrain a defendant in a libel action who says he is going to justify. So in a copyright action, we ought not to restrain a defendant who has a reasonable defence of fair dealing . . . the law will not intervene to suppress freedom of speech except where it is abused."[115]

A book which quoted from unpublished Church of England manuals to the same extent in order to attack Anglicanism might not have had Lord Denning's support. "Fairness" inevitably invites judicial prejudice, or at least the application of values shared by white, male, middle class, middle aged Oxbridge-educated chaps. They gave wide-range to the "criticism and review" defence in rejecting a claim concerning a TV review of the media treatment of Victoria Beckham.[116]

---

[112] *PCR Ltd v Dow Jones Telerate Ltd* [1998] F.S.R. 170, Lloyd J.; *Ashdown v Telegraph Group Ltd* [2002] Ch. 149 CA (see below para.6–041).

[113] *Fraser-Woodward Ltd v BBC* [2005] E.M.L.R. 22.

[114] *Pro Sieben AG v Carlton UK Television Ltd* [1999] 1 W.L.R. 605, CA.

[115] *Hubbard v Vosper* [1972] 2 Q.B. 84.

[116] *Fraser-Woodward Ltd v BBC* [2005] E.M.L.R. 22.

The programme was narrated by Piers Morgan. He began by saying of Posh Spice,

> "The big question is whether she is really just a canny little minx cleverly manipulating the media for her own gain or whether the press are a bunch of tabloid vultures, preying on Victoria to sell newspapers".

The programme included several brief shots of tabloid newspapers with photographs in which the claimant (a Posh-friendly photo agency) held copyright. The BBC admitted copying but successfully relied on the fair dealing defence. There was criticism and review of the photographs themselves, but also (as the defence allows) of other works, namely newspapers, and the criticism validly extended to the style of tabloid journalism and the ideas which lay behind it.

In that case, the defendant was commenting on the claimant's own 6–039 works. This is not essential. Extracts of a reasonable length can be used as part of a review of some third party's work (for instance, if used for the purpose of comparison).[117]

> In 1993 Channel 4 commissioned a critique of Stanley Kubrick's film *A Clockwork Orange*. This had been withdrawn from UK distribution since 1974 because of fears that it had spawned copycat violence. However, it was shown elsewhere in Europe and the programme makers purchased a laser disc copy of the film in Paris. The programme contained a proper acknowledgment, but the copyright owners claimed that the fair dealing defence was not available because: (1) of the underhand way in which the disc was bought; (2) the unrepresentative selection of clips used in the programme; (3) the clips totalled 8 per cent of the film and 40 per cent of the programme; and (4) the purpose of the programme was to further a campaign for the film to be shown in the United Kingdom. The Court of Appeal: (1) rejected the criticism of the method by which the laser disc had been obtained: criticism of a work in the public domain would seldom if ever be unfair because of the manner in which the copy had been obtained; (2) it was not for the court to judge whether the chosen clips were unrepresentative: even if they were the defence would not be destroyed if the programme maker's purpose was genuine criticism or review; (3) the amount of the extracts did not exceed fair dealing; and (4) any campaign for the film to be shown in the United Kingdom was inextricably entwined with the nature of the film itself. This was a rare example of the court holding on an interlocutory application that a defence was so impregnable that the claimant had not even raised a serious issue to be tried.[118]

In order to benefit from the fair dealing defence, the original work must be used "for the purpose of" criticism or review, reporting

---

[117] Copyright, Designs and Patents Act 1988, s.30(1).
[118] *Time Warner Entertainments Company LP v Channel Four Television Corp Plc* [1994] E.M.L.R. 1, CA.

current events or research or private study. The court does not need to investigate the defendant's state of mind. The words "in the context of" or "as part of an exercise in" can be substituted for the phrase "for the purpose of" without any alteration in meaning.[119]

Yet while the context in which the original work was used is assessed objectively, the intentions and motives of the defendant may be material in deciding whether the use was "fair".[120]

6–040 The Scientology case showed that at least in some circumstances, the fair dealing defence was available in connection with an unpublished work. It was not easy: the fact that the work which was being reported or reviewed was unpublished told strongly against the dealing being "fair". However, the position changed in 2003. The fair dealing defence for the purposes of criticism, or review was made dependent on the work having been made available to the public.[121]

For this reason the *Mail on Sunday* did not have an arguable defence based on fair dealing for criticism or review when it published extracts from Prince Charles' diaries written at the time of the hand-over of Hong Kong to the Chinese.[122] He had circulated copies to between 20 and 70 friends, but this was not sufficient for them to be treated as "made available to the public."

This makes even more important the Court of Appeal's recognition in *Ashdown v Telegraph Group Ltd*[123] that circumstances could exist where Art.10 of the ECHR would require the courts to give precedence to freedom of expression over the rights of copyright owners (see below).

6–041 Fair dealing for the purpose of reporting current events is obviously of importance to the media. Before this statutory defence was introduced, a newsreel film was held to have infringed the musical copyright in *Colonel Bogey*. The film had included a 20–second shot of a high school band playing that tune as the Prince of Wales opened a new hospital.[124] Today such a newsreel would be protected as a report of a current event and, since it was part of a film, no acknowledgment would be necessary.

The meaning of *current* event has yet to be fully explored. The court thought it at least arguable in 1974 that the details of the effect of thalidomide were not then "current" because the drug had been withdrawn 12 years previously.[125] This is a doubtful interpretation,

---

[119] *Pro Sieben AG v Carlton UK Television Ltd* [1999] 1 W.L.R. 605, CA at 614; *Hyde Park Residence Ltd v Yelland* [2000] R.P.C. 604, CA at 612.

[120] *Pro Sieben AG.*

[121] Copyright, Designs and Patents Act 1988 s.30(1) as amended by the Copyright and Related Rights Regulations 2003. The term "made available to the public" is defined in s.30(1A).

[122] *HRH Prince of Wales v Associated Newspapers Ltd* [2006] EWHC 522 (Ch.); [2006] EWCA Civ 1776.

[123] See above.

[124] *Hawkes and Son (London) Ltd v Paramount Film Service Ltd* [1934] Ch. 593.

[125] *Distillers Co (Biochemicals) Ltd v Times Newspapers Ltd* [1975] Q.B. 613 at 626.

given that the consequences of thalidomide last a lifetime. In any event, had the case gone further, the *Sunday Times* (which wanted to publish substantial extracts from Distillers' private documents) could well have argued that there was a contemporary debate over the morality of Distillers' delay in reaching a settlement and that its proposed story was highly relevant to this "current event."[126] A broader view was taken in 1999 when the Court of Appeal said:

> "'criticism or review' and 'reporting current events' are expressions of wide and indefinite scope. Any attempt to plot their precise boundaries is doomed to failure. They are expressions which should be construed liberally".[127]

In accordance with this approach, the Court of Appeal was prepared to find that a *News of the World* story about the relationship between Dodi Fayed and Princess Diana arguably still concerned a current event one year after their deaths in a Paris car crash. There had been a regular stream of media stories in the intervening time and Dodi's father, Mohammed Al-Fayed, had given statements to the press on the subject shortly before the publication in question.[128] Similarly, the Court of Appeal agreed that the *Sunday Telegraph* had an arguable case that its articles concerning a meeting between Tony Blair and Paddy Ashdown to discuss coalition government and which centred on a leaked note of the meeting written by the latter, were for the purpose of reporting current events even though they were published two years after the meeting. The court said that the defence was clearly intended to protect the media in informing the public about "matters of current concern to the public" despite the fact that the events themselves might not be recent in time. However, the Court of Appeal found that the newspaper had no arguable defence that it had acted "fairly". It had quoted too extensively from the note. It competed with other newspapers to whom the claimant wanted to sell serialisation rights of his memoirs (of which the note would have been part) and the note was unpublished at the time of the newspaper articles.[129]

Thus, even though the express prohibition on using unpublished **6–042** works does not apply to the defence of reporting current events, the fact that the Claimant's work was unpublished will be material in deciding whether use of the work for that purpose was fair.[130] For similar reasons, the *Mail on Sunday* did not have an arguable

---

[126] However the *Sun* was unable to argue that it was reporting a current event when it copied letters from the Duke and Duchess of Windsor to which the *Daily Mail* had obtained exclusive rights for a limited period. *Associated Newspapers Group v News Group Newspapers* [1986] R.P.C. 515.

[127] *Pro Sieben Media AG v Carlton UK Television Ltd* [1999] 1 W.L.R. 605 at 614.

[128] *Hyde Park Residence Ltd v Yelland* [2000] R.P.C. 604.

[129] *Ashdown v Telegraph Group Ltd* [2002] Ch. 149 CA.

[130] See, for instance, *Ashdown v Telegraph Group Ltd* [2002] Ch 149.

defence based on reporting current events when it published the
leaked private diaries of Prince Charles. In that case, the judge also
thought that, even applying a liberal construction, details of the
incidents surrounding the ceremonial hand-over of Hong-Kong
could not be considered "current" some nine years later.[131] This
approach is open to criticism. Interest in the consequences of such
significant events remains "current", at least while the protagonists
are still alive and still writing about them. But the possibility of
establishing the defence nonetheless remains and the Scientology
case is a good example of why it should.

Another example of where the court refused to rule out a fair
dealing defence where the documents had been unpublished was
Fraser v Evans,[132] where a secret report written for the Greek
military junta was leaked to the *Sunday Times* which intended to
publish extracts. The Court of Appeal refused to grant an injunction
since the newspaper was going to be sparing in its quotations which
were to be used for the purpose of criticising and commenting upon
the memorandum and upon the tactics of a most unpleasant military
government. The 1988 Act significantly broadened the fair dealing
defence. Under the earlier law, none of the aspects of fair dealing
applied to the use of film, sound recording, or broadcast copyright.
This restriction still applies to the research and private study aspect
of the defence, but these works can, as a result of the 1988 Act be
used for criticism, review or news reporting. There is no longer,
therefore, any copyright obstacle to the BBC presenting a critical
and illustrated review of television programmes on ITV, or vice
versa. The ramifications of the extended fair dealing defence were
considered by Mr Justice Scott in 1991 in *BBC v British Satellite
Broadcasting Ltd*.[133]

> BSB, shortly before its absorption into Sky, successfully defended as
> fair dealing its use of short excerpts from BBC live broadcasts of
> World Cup matches in its sports-news programmes. Mr Justice Scott
> held that fairness was ultimately a matter of impression, and what
> impressed him was the fact that the excerpts were short (between 14
> and 37 seconds) and were replayed no more than four times in
> genuinely informational sports-news bulletins. They were also acknow-
> ledged as having been shot by the BBC. This was not a statutory
> requirement, but an indication of overall fairness. There was no
> oblique motive rendering the use unfair, and although the BBC
> complained that the satellite channel was using only the best bits (i.e.
> the scoring of the goals), it was these clips that had obvious relevance
> to the news updates. The judge refused to limit the fair dealing
> defence to general news programmes, and confirmed that sporting

---

[131] *HRH Prince of Wales v Associated Newspapers Ltd* [2006] EWHC 522 (Ch.);
[2006] EWCA Civ 1776.
[132] [1969] 1 All E.R. 8, CA.
[133] [1992] 1 Ch.141.

clashes were as much current events as any other newsworthy incidents.

The 1988 Act also allows artistic works to be used for reporting current events. Significantly, this liberalisation was not extended to photographs. This means that a newspaper still cannot reproduce a rival's "scoop" photograph, even with acknowledgment, in order to report a news story. The law of copyright thus gives special force to the newsroom adage that a picture is worth a thousand words. One rather unsavoury kind of chequebook journalism involves the purchase by newspapers or news agencies of an exclusive right to exploit family snapshots of notorious criminals. If relatives are paid large sums by a particular news group for the exclusive copyright in a photograph, the law will prevent rival papers from publishing the same picture, however much a matter of public interest it has become.

> The Sun had been covering the fight of Princess Caroline of Monaco **6–043** against the hair-loss illness alopecia. Other papers had obtained a licence to publish photographs of her by the international photographer, Francois-Marie Banier. The Sun had published unauthorised copies and the "fair dealing for current events" defence did not apply to photographs. The Sun argued that it was a common practice for a newspaper which could not obtain a licence to reprint a photograph already published in the media to copy the picture anyway and negotiate a suitable royalty after the event. The judge described the practice as plainly unjustified and unlawful and granted an injunction and damages. An incensed judge might also award additional damages.[134]

There are, however, problems with this strictly legal approach. The market in the memorabilia of mass murder and the like would collapse if the law were changed to permit all media to publish such photographs for the purpose of reporting current events. News should not be the subject of copyright, and photographs that are specially newsworthy should not be confined to one newspaper merely because it happened to be the highest bidder.

Public interest

In a number of cases the courts have developed a defence of "public **6–044** interest" to claims for copyright infringement. The 1988 Act does not spell out this defence, but it does recognise its existence.[135] Thus in Beloff v Pressdram[136] the court agreed that Private Eye would have been entitled to publish a copied memorandum, if the magazine had

---

[134] Banier v News Group Newspapers Ltd [1997] F.S.R. 812.
[135] Copyright, Designs and Patents Act 1988, s.171(3).
[136] [1973] 1 All E.R. 241.

been able to show that it disclosed an "iniquity". It is not now necessary to point to any such misconduct on the part of the claimant for a public interest defence to succeed. The ruling to this effect in *Lion Laboratories v Daily Express* (the intoximeter case) was made in relation to a claim for breach of copyright as well as for breach of confidence. The Court of Appeal indicated that the public interest defence applied to both civil actions. Documents supplied by "moles" will generally be subject to copyright: in order to contest the grant of an interim injunction the media must raise a serious public interest defence that might succeed at the trial.

In the important 1990 case of *Express Newspapers v News Ltd* the Vice-Chancellor accepted unhesitatingly that there was a defence to breach of copyright, as to breach of confidence, "if the information was such that it was in the public interest to know it". In that case, however, the whining of a minor member of the Royal Family amounted to "sensational journalism, not a serious discussion of matters of public interest". In any case the whole basis of the defence was the public's need to know which could hardly be relied upon when the same story had already appeared in the claimant's paper.[137]

6–045   The scope of the public interest defence was reviewed by the Court of Appeal in the light of the Human Rights Act in *Ashdown v Telegraph Group Ltd*[138]:

> The *Sunday Telegraph* published detailed extracts from a leaked 1997 memorandum by Paddy Ashdown, then leader of the Leader Democrats. It concerned discussions between him and Tony Blair, then the newly elected Prime Minister, for coalition government and consequential co-operation between their two parties. The newspaper argued that the story was of significant public and political interest and that it needed to quote extensively from the memorandum to give credibility to the story since Downing Street had already tried to play down the significance of the discussions. The Court rejected the claimant's argument that the Human Rights Act had no effect on copyright defences. While it was normally necessary in a democratic society to protect the rights of copyright owners, that was not invariably so and circumstances could arise in which freedom of expression could only be fully protected if an individual was permitted to reproduce copyright material. The 1988 Act would have to accommodate Art.10 in these exceptional cases, either by the courts refusing an injunction and leaving the owner with just a monetary remedy or, in rarer circumstances, by providing a public interest defence to even that type of claim. It rejected the attempt by Aldous L.J. in an earlier case[139] to confine the public interest defence to specific categories. It preferred the alternative approach of Mance L.J., in the same case,

---

[137] *Express Newspapers Plc v News (UK) Ltd* [1990] 3 All E.R. 376 at 382.
[138] [2002] Ch.149, CA.
[139] *Hyde Park Residence Ltd v Yelland* [2000] R.P.C. 604 CA.

who had instead refused to see public interest as limited to closed categories. The *Sunday Telegraph* had published its story so that this was not a case of prior restraint. So far as the claimant's claim for compensation was concerned, the paper could not show a public interest in pirating his memoirs which had been

> "deliberately filleted in order to extract colourful passages that were likely to add flavour to the article thus to appeal to the readership of the newspaper. . . We do not consider it arguable that Art.10 requires the Telegraph Group should be able to profit from this use of Mr Ashdown's copyright without paying compensation".

While the Court's acknowledgement of the role of a public interest/Art.10 defence in copyright cases is welcome, it was surely too limited in its application. Ashdown had brought his claim in both copyright and confidence but the application for summary judgment which led to this judgment was in copyright alone. He may have done so because there would have been a very strong public interest defence which would have defeated the claim in confidence. Why should the fact that the newspaper quoted from the memo's own words have made such a crucial difference? From the newspaper's point of view, this gave credence to its report. It may also have made the article more attractive to its readers, but why should that have counted against it? In other contexts the UK courts and the Court of Human Rights have recognised that judges should be very wary of usurping editorial judgment in the manner that a newspaper has chosen to present a story.

Government publications

Most governmental publications are covered by copyright, which is **6–046** vested in either the Crown or Parliament.[140] Copyright gives the Government a valuable asset which it exploits to the tune of about £200 million per year. Licences are only given free of charge for brief extracts from a Crown copyright work and for legislation and statutory instruments if there is value added to the publication (such as a commentary). The whole subject of Crown Copyright was reviewed in a White Paper in 1999,[141] after which the Government agreed to waive it in a number of catergories.[142] In the same spirit, Ordnance Survey in 1998 announced that for a trial period it would not object to the use of limited extracts from its maps on the editorial pages of newspapers and magazines.[143] However, it continues to charge for other commercially produced maps. In 2000, the

---

[140] 1988 Act, ss.163–167.
[141] *The Future Management of Crown Copyright* (HMSO) Cmnd. 3819.
[142] See Ch.5 of the White Paper and the Guidance Notes from the Office of Public Sector Information at *www.opsi.gov.uk*.
[143] See *Media Lawyer*, January 1998, p.25.

Court rejected an argument by the AA that it was abusing a dominant market position by charging a licence fee for O.S. maps and road categorisation information and road development information.[144] The re-use of government documents which are accessible to the public is now governed by regulations which in turn were required by an EU Directive.[145]

Immorality

6–047 Public policy may *restrict* the claimant's ability to make out a cause of action. In 1916, one judge held that Elinor Glyn's novel *Three Weeks* was incapable of enjoying copyright protection because of its shocking moral values—it advocated free love and justified adultery.[146] Public policy moves (albeit slowly) with the times. While the courts will still refuse their assistance to material that has a grossly immoral tendency, there is no common view as to what kind of sexual conduct between consenting adults is grossly immoral. The Vice-Chancellor remarked in 1988 that "works of Elinor Glyn if published today would be widely regarded as, at the very highest, very soft pornography",[147] although in fact they would not be regarded as anything other than Mills and Boon-style romances. In the second *Spycatcher* appeal the House of Lords thought that Peter Wright would be unable to assert copyright in his book because it represented a gross breach of trust.[148]

There can be an element of hypocrisy in raising a "gross immorality" defence to excuse a publication made in breach of confidence. In the case that prompted the Vice-Chancellor's comment (*Stephen v Avery*) the *Mail on Sunday* had argued that a lesbian affair was so grossly immoral as to produce a tendency in others to immoral conduct. Not, as the Vice-Chancellor observed, an easy argument for a paper that had just given nationwide publicity to the material. The consequence of accepting the argument that a work is too outrageous to be protected by copyright is that others may copy it at will and (since no licence fees can be charged) a good deal more cheaply than works that are copyright protected.

In 1991 the High Court overturned a decision of the Comptroller General of Patents Designs and Trademarks who had refused to register a design of a doll on grounds of immorality.[149]

> The doll showed a Scotsman with "mimic male genitalia" under his kilt and the Comptroller considered that the design was contrary to law or

---

[144] *HMSO v Automobile Association* September 25, 2000, Ch.D. The AA reportedly settled the litigation for £20 million. The *Times* March 6, 2001

[145] The Re-Use of Public Sector Information Regulations 2005 (SI 2005/1515) implementing EU Directive 2003/98/EC.

[146] *Glyn v Weston Feature Film Co* [1916] 1 Ch.261.

[147] *Stephens v Avery* [1988] Ch.449.

[148] *Att-Gen v Guardian Newspapers Ltd (No. 2)* [1990] 1 A.C. 109.

[149] *In Re Masterman's Design* [1991] RPC 89.

morality and therefore unsuitable for registration. The Court considered that the doll might be distasteful but hardly injurious to morality. The Comptroller had been wrong to imagine that registration would give the design an "official stamp of approval".

This was followed in 2006 when the French Connection's trademark "FCUK" withstood a challenge on the grounds that it was contrary to public policy or accepted principles of morality.[150]

Licences

Who owns the copyright?

Owners of copyright cannot complain of infringement if they have **6–048** licensed or granted permission for the use in question. This begs the important question: who is the owner? Analysing this issue is a two-stage process: determining who was the first owner of the work and then assessing whether ownership has subsequently been transferred.

The first owner of a literary, dramatic, musical or artistic work is the author, i.e. its creator.[151] Under the earlier law, copyright in photographs normally belonged first to the owner of the film or other material on which the picture was taken. Now the rule for photographs is the same as for other artistic works. Computer-generated works belong to the person who made the arrangements for their creation.[152] The author of a sound recording is similarly defined as the person who makes the arrangements necessary for the recording. An amendment to the Copyright Act in 1996 made special provision for the authorship of films. As previously, the person who made the arrangements necessary for the making of the film is one of the authors, but the principal director (if a different person) is also treated as a joint author.[153]

Determining the person or persons who made the arrangements necessary for the making of a film or sound recording can be a vexed matter. The courts will examine who initiated the project and undertook responsibility for seeing it through. Responsibility for obtaining the finance is likely to be part of the necessary arrangements, although the Act pointedly does not confer first copyright on the commissioner of the film. Allowing access to an event which would happen independently of the film makers may not constitute the type of arrangement which the Act contemplated, but an active

---

[150] *French Connection Ltd's Trade Mark Application (No. 81862)*; *FCUK trade Mark* [2007] R.P.C. 1 Richard Arnold Q.C., Appointed Person rejecting an objection that the mark was invalid under Trade Marks Act 1994, s.3(3).

[151] Copyright, Designs and Patents Act 1988, s.9(1).

[152] 1988 Act, s.9(3).

[153] See Copyright and Related Rights Regulations 1996 (SI 1996/2967) Reg.18 amending ss.9(2), 10, 11 and 178 of the 1988 Act. *N.B.* these changes apply to films made on or after July 1, 1994.

role in arranging film locations may be different. The parties' intentions may show that they were undertaking arrangements on their own behalf or to assist and for the benefit of someone else.[154] The elusiveness of the statutory definition, the possibility of several people fulfilling the criteria and so becoming joint owners and the serious expense and disruption from disputes as to ownership of copyright mean that there can be a heavy price for not clarifying in advance of filming who is to be the first copyright owner. Similar disputes have taken place in relation to the creation of plays. Pam Brighton, the director of *Stones in His Pockets*, unsuccessfully argued that her contributions made her the joint author of the copyright in the original script. It was not necessary to demonstrate an equal contribution, but the Court held that she did no more than would be expected of a director of a play and her suggestions for the script were not sufficiently significant to constitute her a co-author.[155] By contrast, Mathew Fisher of Procul Harum established that the organ solo which he had devised entitled him to 40 per cent of the musical copyright in *Whiter Shade of Pale*.[156]

6–049   The author of a broadcast is the person who makes it.[157] This will include the owner of the transmitter, but only if that person has responsibility for the broadcast's content. British Telecom may facilitate direct broadcasting by satellite but has no involvement in its content and therefore does not share in the copyright. The 1988 Act enlarged the first owners in a broadcast to include the persons providing the programmes and who contract for their transmission.

Copyright in a published edition (i.e. typographical arrangement) is first owned by the publisher.[158] A work (such as this book) may have joint authors, in which case they will jointly be the first owners of the copyright. However, if their contributions are distinct (e.g. if the chapters of a book were divided between them), then each would have a separate copyright in his or her own part.[159]

Literary, dramatic, musical or artistic works made by employees in the course of their employment are first owned by their employers.[160]

6–050   Employers can agree to allow their employees to have first copyright,[161] but there is no other statutory provision for altering the first allocation of the right. Nonetheless, the courts have shown a dangerous willingness to introduce ideas of equity and trusts. In one

---

[154] See *Adventure Film Productions SA v Tully* [1993] E.M.L.R. 376, Ch.D., a case under the 1956 Act but which used the same expression; *Beggars Banquet Records Ltd v Carlton Television Ltd* [1993] E.M.L.R. 349, Ch. D.; *Century Communications Ltd v Mayfair Entertainments UK Ltd* [1993] E.M.L.R. 335, Ch.D.
[155] *Brighton v Jones* [2005] FSR 16 Ch.D.
[156] *Fisher v Brooker* [2007] FSR 12
[157] Copyright, Designs and Patents Act 1988, ss.9(1)(b) and 6(3).
[158] 1988 Act, s.9(1)(c) and (d).
[159] 1988 Act, s.10.
[160] 1988 Act, s.11(2)
[161] 1988 Act, s.11(2).

case an advertising agency that was undoubtedly the first legal owner of the copyright was found to hold the copyright on trust for the commissioner of its drawings.[162] In the *Spycatcher* case the House of Lords suggested that if copyright could subsist in such a scandalous book, it belonged in equity to the Crown.[163] This is a mistake brought on by judicial apoplexy at Wright's unpunished treachery. An ex-employee of a secret Government agency who writes his memoirs may breach his employer's confidence but not his copyright. Nonetheless, the Treasury Solicitor often threatens proceedings for copyright over books which breach the notices of the DA Notice Committee, especially Andy McNab's accounts of life in the SAS.[164] The House of Lords held that the government was entitled to the profits made by Russian spy, George Blake, as damages for his breach of contract.[165]

Once the first owner of the copyright is settled, the possibility of transfer must be considered. Copyright can be assigned, but to be fully effective the transfer needs to be in writing and signed by the assignor.[166] An assignment can be made in advance of the creation of the work, in which case it takes effect as soon as the work is made and the first owner's rights are immediately passed on.[167] An oral or unsigned transfer is not wholly ineffective: it allows the transferee to call for a proper assignment and will bind third parties who have notice of it, but it can be disregarded by a bona fide third party who purchases the copyright without notice of the informal assignment.

Implied licences

No special formality is required for a licence to be granted. It need **6–051** not be express, but can be implied from the circumstances or by custom. A reader who sends a letter to the editor of a newspaper impliedly consents to its publication, and impliedly agrees as well to any editing that is necessary for reasons of space.[168] Submission of a feature article connotes a similar implied licence, albeit subject to payment of an appropriate fee.[169] Press releases clearly carry an implied licence to copy, at least if publication is made after any embargo.

---

[162] *Warner v Gestetner* [1988] E.I.P.R. D—89 see also *Antocks Lairn v Bloohn* [1971] F.S.R. 490.

[163] *Att-Gen v Guardian Newspapers Ltd (No. 2)* [1990] 1 A.C. 109.

[164] David Hooper, *On Her Majesty's Copyright*, *Guardian*, October 10, 1995.

[165] *Att-Gen v Blake* [2001] 1 A.C. 268.

[166] Copyright, Designs and Patents Act 1988, s.90(3).

[167] 1988 Act, s.91.

[168] *Springfield v Thame* (1903) 89 I.L.T. 242; *Roberts v Candiware Ltd* [1980] F.S.R. 352.

[169] *Hall-Brown v Iliffe and Sons Ltd* (1928–35) M.C.C. 88.

Exclusive licences

6–052 Although an informal licence is effective to protect the media, it is less satisfactory if there is a danger that the publication will be pirated by others. A publisher who is merely a licensee can take action only against the pirates indirectly by calling on the owner of the copyright to sue them. This is inconvenient: authors, even if protected by an indemnity against costs, are sometimes shy of litigation. The problem can be avoided if the publisher takes an assignment. If the author is unwilling to part completely with the copyright, an almost identical advantage can be obtained by taking an exclusive licence: again the licence must be in writing and signed by the licensor.[170] Since 2003 the copyright owner can authorise a non-exclusive licensee as well to take action against infringers.[171]

Adequate licences

6–053 Publishers and broadcasters must take care to obtain a licence from owners of all the copyrights in the item that they wish to use. If a copyright is owned by two or more people, each of them must give consent. Copyright can be infringed by a publisher who acted in good faith, and a number of reported cases concern licences that were inadequate because they were incomplete or obtained from the wrong person.[172] It is also important for the media to obtain a licence adequate for all intended purposes. For example, a broadcaster dealing with a playwright must obtain permission to film (if the play is to be pre-recorded) as well as to broadcast. The broadcaster need not, however, expressly provide for the right immediately to retransmit the material via cable television; a licence to broadcast a work carries with it the right to include it in a cable programme.[173]

Copyright Tribunal

Collective licensing, the Copyright Tribunal and competition

6–054 It is obviously impractical for individual copyright owners to police all possible infringements. The music industry first recognised the advantage of collective enforcement of copyrights. Now the Performing Rights Society (PRS) controls practically all performing rights in music in the United Kingdom and the Mechanical Copyright Protection Society and Phonographic Performance Ltd control almost all

---

[170] Copyright, Designs and Patents Act 1988, s.92.
[171] 1988 Act, s.101A as added by the Copyright and Related Rights Regulations 2003.
[172] e.g. *Byrne v Statist Co* [1914] 1 K.B. 622.
[173] Copyright, Designs and Patents Act 1988, s.73 as amended by Copyright and Related Rights Regulations 2003.

the music mechanical recording rights in the United Kingdom. Similar societies represent the interests of publishers and authors.[174] Equally, there is the potential for these monopolies to act against the public interest. The 1956 Act established the Performing Rights Tribunal to adjudicate on disputes between rights owners and those who needed licences. The 1988 Act renamed the Tribunal the Copyright Tribunal and extended its jurisdiction.

The Tribunal's principal role is to hear disputes about either licensing schemes (standard terms, conditions and tariffs) or one-off licences in three areas;[175]

- the schemes of societies in relation to literary, dramatic, musical or artistic works or films that cover the work of more than one author;
- schemes or licences (whether by societies or individual owners) in relation to sound recordings (other than the sound tracks of films), broadcasts, and published editions;
- schemes or licences (whether by societies or individual owners) in relation to the rental of sound recordings, films or computer programs.

In these areas the Tribunal can determine whether the offered terms are reasonable and whether an excluded category or use under a scheme ought to be licensed. The Tribunal must particularly try to prevent unreasonable discrimination by the copyright owners [176] "Discrimination" does not mean just unequal treatment on grounds of race or sex (though that would no doubt be unreasonable) but any discrimination between licensees or potential licensees. Thus, under the 1956 Act the Tribunal held that it was unreasonable for the PRS to offer a discount to the Cinema Exhibitors Association but not to the smaller Association of Independent Cinemas.

The 1988 Act introduced two important new statutory licences.[177] **6–055** The first concerns rental of sound recordings, films or computer programs. The Secretary of State is empowered to introduce statutory licences for these.[178] The second concerns the Competition Commission, formerly the Monopolies and Mergers Commission (MMC) and requires some explanation.

Under the Competition Act 1980 anyone could refer to the Office of Fair Trading an "anti-competitive practice". A good example was the practice of the BBC and ITV companies refusing to allow anyone other than the *Radio Times* and *TV Times* to print radio and

---

[174] See Laddie Prescott and Vitoria *The Modern Law of Copyright and Designs* (3rd edn. Butterworths, London, 2000) Ch.25.
[175] The 1988 Act, ss.116–135.
[176] 1988 Act, s.129.
[177] A third concerns photocopying by educational establishments, 1988 Act, s.141.
[178] 1988 Act, s.66.

television listings a week in advance. The London magazine *Time Out* referred this practice to the Director-General of Fair Trading. He found that the practice was anti-competitive and referred the matter to the MMC. The Commission was obliged to reconsider the issue of anti-competitiveness and, in this case, upheld the Director-General's view. It then had to consider the critical question of whether the practice worked against the public interest. In *Time Out*'s case the Commission was evenly divided and the challenge failed; it was left to Parliament finally to end the broadcasters' monopoly by s.176 of the 1990 Broadcasting Act (see above, para.6–029). More generally, if the Competition Commission finds a refusal to grant a licence to be anti-competitive and against the public interest it can grant a statutory licence and fix its conditions.[179]

The 1956 Act introduced a statutory licence to replay musical works once a record of the work had been issued to the public. The 1988 Act abolished this. The Broadcasting Act 1990 brought back something similar. It allows the broadcasting of sound recordings in the absence of agreement from the copyright owner and in advance of the Copyright Tribunal fixing the terms. There are complex and stringent conditions for the exercise of this right. In outline, the broadcaster must have been refused a licence by the appropriate licensing body, have given notice of his intention to exercise the right, be ready to pay the charge agreed or set by the Tribunal, be prepared to include in the broadcast a statement reasonably required by the licensing body and provide reasonably required information about the programmes that incorporate the recording. A similar scheme is established to prevent licensing bodies prescribing maximum "needletime"—the proportion of any period of broadcasting that can be given over to records.[180]

Other defences

Incidental inclusion

6–056 Copyright in any work is not infringed by its incidental inclusion in an artistic work, sound recording, film, or broadcast.[181] "Incidental" has been said to mean casual, inessential, subordinate, merely background.[182] The use of music or lyrics will not be treated as incidental if they are deliberately included.

> Stickers showing football players proved very popular in 2002. The pictures of the players included their club logos on shorts and

---

[179] 1988 Act, s.144.
[180] 1988 Act, ss.135A—G added by the Broadcasting Act 1990, s.175. And see the decision of the Tribunal in *AIRC v PPL and BBC (intervener)* [1993] E.M.L.R. 181 and, in relation to "narrowcasting" by satellite broadcasters, *AEI Rediffusion Music Ltd v PPL* [1998] R.P.C. 335.
[181] Copyright, Designs and Patents Act 1988, s.31.
[182] *IPC Magazine Ltd v MGN Ltd* [1998] F.S.R. 431.

sometimes the Football Association Premier League logo. The sellers of the stickers argued that these were merely incidental to the representation of the players. But the Court of Appeal dismissed the argument It said that in order to be attractive to collectors, the stickers had to show the players in their official club strip and this necessarily had to include the club badge and (where appropriate) the FAPL logo. Therefore their inclusion in the photographs was not "incidental".[183]

Reports of judicial and parliamentary proceedings

Reports of judicial or parliamentary proceedings will not be a breach **6–057** of any copyright as long as the report is first-hand.[184] Plagiarising the published report of a rival is not protected. Interestingly, the proceedings do not, apparently, have to be in public. Copyright is not therefore among the restrictions that curtail the reporting of private court hearings (see Ch.8). "Judicial" is widely interpreted to mean any court, tribunal or person having authority to decide any matter affecting a person's legal rights or liabilities.[185]

Other aspects of public administration

There is no copyright objection to reporting the proceedings of a **6–058** Royal Commission or statutory inquiry.[186] There is more limited right to copy material from public registers, but this is hedged with restrictions, notably the need to obtain the permission of the keeper of the record.[187] Material in the Public Record Office can be copied.[188] If any other statute specifically authorises an act, then that act will not involve infringement of copyright.[189]

Contemporaneous notes of a speaker

Since the 1988 Act, copyright can be claimed by a speaker in his **6–059** extempore pronouncements if the words are recorded, whether or not the recording is done for the speaker's benefit. Prima facie it would restrict a journalist who took a note or made a tape-recording in order to report the event. This development would have been a major handicap for the media were there not also a new defence that limits its extent. This defence applies if the speaker's words have been recorded directly (and not, for instance, copied from someone

---

[183] *Football Association Premier League Ltd v Panini UK Ltd* [2004] 1 W.L.R. 1147.
[184] Copyright, Designs and Patents Act 1988, s.45.
[185] 1988 Act, s.178.
[186] 1988 Act, s.46.
[187] 1988 Act, s.47; only plans and drawings marked in a specified manner can be copied without infringing copyright under s.47(2): Copyright (Material Open to Public Inspection) (Marking of Copies) Order 1990 (SI 1990/1427).
[188] Copyright, Designs and Patents Act 1988, s.49.
[189] 1988 Act, s.50.

else's record) and not taken from a broadcast. The person in lawful possession of the record must sanction its use. If these conditions are satisfied, the record can be used for reporting a current event or in a broadcast without infringing the speaker's copyright.[190]

Public reading

6–060   A reasonable extract from a literary or dramatic work can be read or recited in public without infringing copyright. A sound recording, or broadcast can be made of the reading, but only if the record or programme consists mainly of material that does not have to rely on this defence.[191]

Abstracts of scientific or technical articles

6–061   Technical articles are often accompanied by an abstract or summary of their contents. Unless a licensing scheme has been certified by the Government, these abstracts can be copied and issued to the public without infringing copyright.[192]

Special use of artistic work

6–062   Buildings, sculptures, models for buildings and works of artistic craftsmanship on permanent public display can be photographed, graphically represented, included in a film, or broadcast without infringing copyright.[193]
       An artistic work that is put on sale can be included in a catalogue or otherwise copied for the purpose of advertising the sale.[194] Although an artist may dispose of copyright in a work, he or she will not infringe the copyright by copying the work in the course of making another, provided the main design of the first is not repeated.[195]

Broadcasts

6–063   Broadcasts can be recorded in domestic premises for the purposes of time-shifting, but if copies are subsequently dealt with, they become infringing copies and attract the usual remedies (see below).[196]
       A photograph of a television screen that is taken in domestic premises and for private and domestic purposes will not infringe

---

[190] 1988 Act, s.58.
[191] Copyright, Designs and Patents Act 1988, s.50.
[192] 1988 Act, s.60.
[193] 1988 Act, s.62.
[194] 1988 Act, s.63.
[195] 1988 Act, s.64.
[196] 1988 Act, s.70.

copyright in the broadcast or any film included in it.[197] A copyright owner who has licensed its use in a broadcast gives an implied right to make ephemeral recordings and film it for the purpose of preparing the broadcast.[198] The BBC and OFCOM can make use of copyright works for their regulatory functions without being guilty of infringement.[199] Television and radio can be relayed in pubs and other places to which the public are admitted free of charge. There will be no infringement in the broadcasts, film or (with some qualifications) the sound recording, but copyright permission is still needed in relation to any musical, literary, dramatic or artistic works that are included in the broadcast. In practice use of these copyrights is licensed by collectives of copyright owners (see para.6–054).

There is also protection for the making of a temporary copy which is transient or incidental, which is an integral and essential part of a technological process and the sole purpose of which is to enable: (a) a transmission of the work in a network between third parties by an intermediary; or (b) a lawful use of the work; and which has no independent economic significance.[200]

MORAL RIGHT

Four "moral rights" were created by the 1988 Act: **6–064**

- the right to be identified as author or director (the right to be identified);
- the right not to have the work subjected to derogatory treatment (the right of integrity);
- the right not to be falsely described as author or director;
- the right to privacy in certain types of photographs.

The latter two are dealt with elsewhere (see para.6–010 for false attribution of authorship; para.5–041 for privacy in photographs).

The first two rights depend on there being a copyright work and they last as long as copyright in the work,[201] but the owner of the copyright may be quite different from the owner of these moral rights. Copyright can be assigned and, to assist in its exploitation, it frequently is. Moral rights are intended to protect the integrity of the author or director. They cannot be assigned or transferred, except on death, when they pass to the author's or director's estate.[202]

---

[197] 1988 Act, s.71, as substituted by the Copyright and Related Rights Regulations 2003.
[198] 1988 Act, s.68.
[199] 1988 Act, s.69.
[200] 1988 Act, s.28A.
[201] 1988 Act, s.86.
[202] 1988 Act, ss.94 and 95.

The significance of moral rights depends on commercial practice, for while the rights cannot be sold, they can be waived,[203] and the right to be identified as author or director depends on a positive act of assertion. In many European countries the law does not allow waiver of moral rights. But in Britain where it does powerful television and publishing companies set their lawyers in motion immediately the Act came into force to devise standard clauses to waive or exclude moral rights. It will take many years before the right not to have one's original work distorted is accepted as immutably belonging to all creative artists.

Right to be identified as author or director

6–065   The right belongs to the author of a literary, dramatic, musical or artistic work or the director of a film.[204] and the right accrues to the author not (where this is a different person) the originator of the idea which lay behind the work.[205] It does not apply to a computer-generated work, a computer programmer, the designer of a typeface, an employee (whose employer is the first owner of the copyright) or a director when someone else has made the arrangements for the film (and so that other person is the first owner of the copyright in it).[206] The right is not infringed if any one of the defences to an infringement action apply (notably if there is a fair dealing with the work for the purpose of reporting current events on a sound recording, film broadcast).[207] The right does not apply at all to the author or director of a work made for the purpose of reporting current events.[208] Nor does it apply in relation to the publication in a newspaper, magazine or similar periodical or in an encyclopaedia, dictionary, yearbook or other collective reference work where the work was made for that purpose or used for it with the author's consent.[209]

The right must be asserted. This is a formal act that must be done in writing: the Act specifies precise forms of assertion for different types of work.[210]

If all of these conditions have been fulfilled and the right has not been waived or given up by consent, then the author or director must be identified as such in connection with various public promotions of the work or any substantial part of it.[211]

---

[203] To be fully effective a waiver must be in writing, but an oral or informal waiver may estop the author or director from asserting the right against those the waiver was intended to benefit, 1988 Act, s.87.

[204] Copyright, Designs and Patents Act 1988, s.77(1).

[205] *Anya v Wu* [2004] EWHC 386 (Ch).

[206] 1988 Act, s.79(2) and (3).

[207] 1988 Act, see s.79(4) for details.

[208] 1988 Act, s.79(5).

[209] 1988 Act, s.79(6).

[210] 1988 Act, s.78.

[211] 1988 Act, ss.77 and 89(1).

Derogatory treatment

The right not to have a work subjected to derogatory treatment **6–066** applies also to authors of literary, dramatic, musical or artistic works and to film directors.[212] As with the right to be identified, it applies to specified public dealings with the altered work.[213] It goes further, though, in applying to the public use of *any* part of the work (whether substantial or not).[214]

The exceptions to this right are a more limited version of those to the "identity" right.[215] Employees may not have copyright or the right to be identified, but they do (subject to their waiver or consent) have the right not to have their work subjected to derogatory treatment if they are or have been publicly identified in the work.[216] Most of the defences that apply to both infringement of copyright and the right to be identified do not permit derogatory treatment. Fair dealing, which is sufficient to excuse an infringement of copyright, will not necessarily be a defence to breach of a moral right.[217]

So what is "derogatory treatment"? The Act explains that treatment is derogatory "if it amounts to distortion or mutilation of the work or is otherwise prejudicial to the honour or reputation of the author or director".[218]

The first person to assert his new "integrity right" in British courts **6–067** was pop singer George Michael, who alleged that five compositions he had originally recorded with Wham had been subject to derogatory treatment by being remixed to alter some of the lyrics and to introduce "fill-in music" provided by others between his compositions, on an album entitled *Bad Boys Megamix*. The court found that the distortion of his original and creative spirit arguably amounted to derogatory treatment, and granted an interim injunction until the action could be tried.[219]

Even treatment which distorts or mutilates the work is only derogatory if it is also prejudicial to the honour of the author.

A rap artist complained that his lyrics had been subjected to "derogatory treatment" when they were altered by another group. The case posed challenges for the court, both in deciphering what words were actually being said and in deciding what they meant. The words were in effect a foreign language and would normally require expert evidence as to their meaning, though as the judge added, "the

---

[212] 1988 Act, s.80(1).
[213] Copyright, Designs and Patents Act 1988, s.80.
[214] 1988 Act, s.89(2).
[215] 1988 Act, s.81.
[216] 1988 Act, s.82.
[217] 1988 Act, s.81.
[218] 1988 Act, s.80(2)(b).
[219] *Morrison Leaky Music Ltd v Lightbond Ltd* [1993] E.M.L.R. 144.

occasions on which an expert drug dealer might be called to give evidence in the Chancery Division were likely to be rare". As it was, the court had to do the best it could. This led to the surreal experience of three gentlemen in horsehair wigs examining the meaning of phrases such as "shizzle my nizzle". The claim ultimately failed, partly because of the lack of clarity, and partly because the claimant's group had themselves flirted with gangster imagery and he was not therefore in a strong position to assert that references to violence in the defendant's altered lyrics were likely to be prejudicial to his honour.[220]

Not all derogatory dealings will offend the right of integrity. There must be derogatory "treatment" and this means that something must be done to alter the work or add to it. The juxtaposition of the work and a context that is objectionable to the author is not a breach: a feminist photographer could not complain under this head if her pictures were displayed amongst an exhibition of pornography.

6–068   There is an echo here of the law's reluctance to allow famous (or, indeed, any) people a monopoly over the use of their names and faces. Two of the Beatles were refused an injunction to prevent the sale of a record of interviews with them. The L.P. was called *The Beatles Tapes* and had pictures of the group inside the sleeve. The maker had a licence from the photographer but not from the Beatles. However, the musicians had no copyright to assert, and the L.P. was not passed off as their work.[221]

> It is a different matter if a false impression is created that the person in the photograph has endorsed a product of the defendant. Talk Radio discovered this to its, expensive, cost when it manipulated a photograph of the racing driver Eddie Irvine to make it appear as though he was using a small radio with their logo. The Court of Appeal ordered it to pay £25,000 as damages for passing off.[222]

The new moral right not to have work derogatorily treated is also infringed by those who deal in articles that infringe it. Like secondary infringement of copyright, however, there is only liability if the dealer knows or has reason to believe that it is an infringing article.[223]

TITLES

6–069   Most titles—of plays, books, magazines, films and newspapers—are not copyright because by themselves they are not sufficiently substantial to qualify as a "literary work" or because they consist of only

---

[220] *Confetti Records v Warner Music UK Ltd* [2003] EWHC 1274 [2003] EMLR 35.
[221] *Harrison and Starkey v Poly dor Ltd* [1977] 1 F.S.R. 1. Other celebrities have failed because their names or likenesses were borrowed for use in a quite different area of business (see the Uncle Mac case *McCulloch v May* (1947) 65 P.R.C. 58 and the Abba case, *Lyngstad v Anabas* [1977] F.S.R. 62. Australian courts have been more sympathetic: *Henderson v Radio Corp Pty Ltd* [1969] R.P.C. 218.
[222] *Irvine v Talksport Ltd* [2003] 2 All E.R. 881 CA.
[223] Copyright, Designs and Patents Act 1988, s.83.

a few common words and lack the "originality" which is a key element to qualify for literary copyright.[224] Even an invented word (e.g. "Exxon") would not be protected by copyright if it has meaning only when used with other words.[225] Like much of copyright law, this is all a question of degree. Consequently, the longer type of newspaper headline may qualify as a literary work.[226]

The cover of a magazine or newspaper may be protected by artistic copyright. This is likely to be particularly important in the case of a periodical where the words and pictures on the cover will be different from one issue to another but which will conform to a common template. The copyright in this artistic work would be infringed by a rival who copied the same features.[227]

Copyright apart, the choice of a title and getup for a new product will be constrained by the laws of passing off and trademarks. "Passing off" prevents one trader from misrepresenting his goods as the goods of, or associated with, another trader who has an established reputation likely to be harmed. Thus the University of Oxford obtained an injunction to prevent Pergamon Press from publishing *The Pergamon Oxford Dictionary of Perfect Spelling*.[228] However, the courts have been very wary of allowing even an established trader to obtain an effective monopoly in ordinary English words so that quite minor differences will be enough to prevent an injunction[229] and, in some cases, even the very same title will not create a sufficient risk of confusion or amount to a misrepresentation.[230]

But these cases are particularly sensitive to the evidence in the **6–070** individual case as Express Newspapers discovered when it proposed to launch a new London free evening newspaper to compete with the *Evening Standard*.[231]

> Express was planning to use the title *Evening Mail* or *London Evening Mail*. Associated Newspapers claimed that there would be a risk of

---

[224] *Dick v Yates* (1881) 18 Ch. D 76.

[225] *Exxon Corp v Exxon Insurance Consultants Ltd* [1992] Ch.119.

[226] See *Shetland Times Ltd v Dr Jonathan Wills* [1997] F.S.R. 604, OH, where the defenders conceded the possibility.

[227] *EMAP National Publications Ltd v Security Publications Ltd* [1997] F.S.R. 891; *IPC Magazine Ltd v MGN Ltd* [1998] F.S.R. 431.

[228] *University of Oxford v Pergamon Press Ltd*, *The Times*, October 19, 1977 CA.

[229] *Baylis and Co (The Maidenhead Advertiser) v Derlenko* [1974] F.S.R. 284 where the *Maidenhead Advertiser* was unable to stop a free sheet from using the name *The New Advertiser*. In the *EMAP National Publications* case (above) both parties produced magazines for classic car owners. The defendants' title "*Classics*" would not, by itself, have been enough to establish passing off in the claimants' magazine "*Practical Classics*".

[230] *Box Television Ltd v Haymarket Magazines Ltd*, *The Times*, March 3, 1997, where the claimants operated a cable television music channel called "The Box" but could not prevent the defendants from publishing a magazine with the same slang expression for television as its title.

[231] *Associated Newspapers Ltd v Express Newspapers* [2003] F.S.R. 31.

confusion with their papers, *Daily Mail* and *Mail on Sunday* which were commonly abbreviated to *"The Mail"*. The judge accepted that there was a risk that the new paper would be abbreviated in the same way and there was insufficient evidence as to how the defendant planned to distinguish the two products. It was irrelevant that in other parts of the country (Birmingham and Scotland for instance) other papers used the word "Mail", since in London the term was overwhelmingly associated with the claimant's papers and, anyway, passing off did not depend on the claimant having an exclusive reputation in the disputed title. Associated also established potential damage—individual purchasers might be given the new paper when they wanted the old. In addition, some readers and advertisers might be put off by the type of strident campaign which the new paper could be expected to carry and which they erroneously linked with the Associated group.

Registration of a trademark gives stronger protection. Because the trader will have had to establish the reputation, distinctiveness and originality of the mark in order to have it registered, these matters do not have to be proved again in infringement proceedings. Consequently the publishers of a new magazine or newspaper should always check the proposed title against the Register of Trademarks to see if their idea will trespass on a registered mark in that type of goods or services. The existence of a registered mark does not necessarily mean that a title which incorporates the mark will be an infringement:

> The defendants published a book called *A Sweet Little Mystery—Wet Wet Wet—The Inside Story*. The band, Wet Wet Wet, had registered their name as a trade mark. However, the registration of a trade mark could not be used to prevent publishers using the protected name in the title of a book about the owner: the defendants could rely on Trade Marks Act 1994, s.11(2)(b) because they used the mark to indicate the contents of the book not its origin. The judge said,
>
> > "It would be a bizarre result of the trade mark legislation, the primary purpose of which is to 'guarantee the trade mark as indication of origin', if it could be used to prevent publishers from using the protected name in the title of a book about the company or product."
>
> But note that the defence in s.11(2) is dependent on the proviso (not disputed in this case) that "the use is in accordance with honest practices in industrial or commercial matters."[232]

---

[232] *Bravado Merchandising Services Ltd v Mainstream Publishing (Edinburgh) Ltd* [1996] FSR 205, OH. Doubts about the case were expressed by the Court of Appeal in *Philips Electronics BV v Remington Consumer Products* [1998] R.P.C. 283, but see the discussion in Laddie, Prescott and Vitoria at para.37.11. See also *The European Ltd v The Economist Newspapers Ltd* [1998] F.S.R. 283, CA for the need to prove confusing similarity between two marks. Associated Newspapers also succeeded on trademark grounds in its action against Express Newspapers (see above)—see *Stop Press* section.

This case illustrates the point that there will only be an infringement of a trade mark if the mark has been used in the course of trade. Publishers still get angry letters from trade mark owners where the name has not been used in this way. The owners' purpose is not usually to get damages from slips (like "biro" or "xerox" without capital letters) but to set up a paper trail demonstrating to some future court their efforts to prevent the trade name becoming a generic name which would then be free for all to use.

The South African Constitutional Court in an important ruling **6–071** has dismissed an attempt to use trade mark law to silence criticism of the owner's policies:

> A beer distributor in South Africa had licensed a trade mark which said "America's lusty, lively beer, Carling Black Label, Beer, Brewed in South Africa". The Defendants produced a t-shirt which said "Africa's lusty, lively exploitation since 1652, White, Black Labour, Guilt, No regard given world-wide". The Court said that there was insufficient evidence of any real likelihood of economic harm and this was necessary since trade mark law protected the mark's selling power, not its dignity. Justice Sachs went further. He said that:
>
> > "parody is central to the challenge to cultural hegemony exerted by brands in contemporary society. The issue is not whether the Court thinks the lampoons on the t-shirts are funny, but whether Laugh It Off should be free to issue the challenge. Expression of humour is not only permissible, but necessary for the health of democracy."[233]

The advent of the internet seemed for a time to offer new scope for public confusion as trademarks and other well-known brand names were registered as the names of websites or other domains by companies which had nothing to do with the original products. However, the courts are ready to grant injunctions to prevent actual or threatened infringement of trade marks or passing off in this manner.[234]

RIGHTS IN PERFORMANCES

"Bootlegging", or the making and selling of illicit recordings of a live **6–072** performance, has been another unwanted side-effect of the growth in recording technology. It can harm the commercial interests of both the performer and anyone to whom the (lawful) recording

---

[233] *Laugh it Off Promotions CC v South African Breweries International (Finance) B.V. t/a Sabmark International* [2005] 5 L.R.C. 475 South African Constitutional Court.
[234] *British Telecommunications Plc v One in A Million Ltd* [1999] 1 W.L.R. 903, CA. See the similar decision concerning registration of companies with the same names as well-known trade marks: *Direct Line Group Ltd v Direct Line Estate Agency* [1997] F.S.R. 374.

rights have been awarded. A related issue is the extent to which the performer (or recording company) can control the subsequent use of legitimate recordings under the 1988 Act. The rights are independent of copyright,[235] although the provisions frequently run parallel to each other and an infringement of the performance rights will often also involve a breach of copyright. However, because they are independent, the people who enjoy the rights may be different to the persons who hold the copyright.

Rights are given to performers themselves and to those who have exclusive recording rights. All the rights are conditional on there being a "performance", which can be dramatic, musical, a reading or recitation or a performance of a variety act or similar presentation.[236] As with copyright law, the performer qualifies for protection only if he or she has some connection with the United Kingdom or another country that is party to the relevant international convention[237] or another member of the EEA.[238]

The Act then controls "recordings" of a performance. This term is not synonymous with "sound recording" in copyright law. It can mean a film or a sound recording made either directly from the live performance or indirectly from a broadcast or another recording.[239]

6–073 The performer's rights are infringed by a person who makes a recording (otherwise than for private and domestic use) or broadcasts the performance live without the performer's consent, or who makes a recording of the performance directly from a broadcast including the live performance.[240] A performer's rights are also infringed by copying (other than for private and domestic use) a recording of the performance. This is now described as the performer's "reproduction right".[241]

Further sub-divisions of performers' rights include "distribution right" (in essence this is the right to control the issuing of copies of a recording of a performance to the public[242]), lending and rental rights in recordings of the performance[243] and the right to receive equitable remuneration when a commercially published sound recording of the performance is played in public or included in a broadcast.[244] Other infringements of the performers' rights are committed by showing, playing in public, or broadcasting an

---

[235] Copyright, Designs and Patents Act 1988, s.180(4)(a).
[236] 1988 Act, s.180(2).
[237] The 1961 Rome Convention for the Protection of Performers, Producers of Phonograms and Broadcasting Organisations.
[238] Copyright, Designs and Patents Act 1988, s.206.
[239] 1988 Act, s.180(2).
[240] The 1988 Act, s.182(1) as substituted by the Related Rights Regulations 1996, Reg.20.
[241] 1988 Act, s.182A.
[242] 1988 Act, s.182B.
[243] 1988 Act, s.182C.
[244] 1988 Act, s.182D.

unauthorised recording.[245] In all cases the prohibition extends to a substantial part of the performance. As with copyright, there are "secondary infringements" of commercial dealing with infringing recordings.[246] Some of the performers' rights (reproduction, distribution, rental and lending) can be assigned, disposed of on death or insolvency like other property.[247] Others cannot be transmitted except to a limited extent on the owner's death.[248]

Exclusive recording contractors have similar, though slightly narrower, rights to control the use of unauthorised recordings.[249] "Authorised" here means permitted either by the contractor or the performer.

All the rights in performances have exceptions broadly comparable to the defences to copyright actions.[250] Performers rights generally run for 50 years from the performance, or, if during that period it is released, 50 years from the release.[251] The period may be different if the performer is a non-EEA national and his or her home State provides for a shorter period.[252] The civil and criminal remedies for the infringement of the rights also resemble the copyright remedies.[253] If performers cannot be traced or if they unreasonably refuse their consent, the Copyright Tribunal can give a licence in their place and fix appropriate terms.[254] **6–074**

From 2006 performers are given broadly equivalent "moral rights" to those of copyright owners.[255] They include the right to be identified as a performer,[256] but, as with the moral right of authors, only if the right to be identified has been asserted.[257] If performers are part of a group, it is generally sufficient to identify the group.[258] Identification is not required where this is not reasonably practicable, or where the performance is given for the purposes of reporting current events or as part of a news reporting.[259] The other moral

---

[245] 1988 Act, s.183.

[246] 1988 Act, s.184.

[247] 1988 Act, ss.191A and 191B.

[248] 1988 Act, s.192A.

[249] 1988 Act, s.185–8.

[250] 1988 Act, Sch.2.

[251] 1988 Act, s.191 (as amended by the Duration Regulations 1995. A comparable regime is established for revived performance rights to revived copyright: see Duration Regulations, Regs 34 and 35, exceptions Sch.2.

[252] 1988 Act, s.191(3) and (4).

[253] 1988 Act, ss.194–200 and see below.

[254] 1988 Act, s.190.

[255] The Performances (Moral Rights etc) Regulations 2006 (SI 2006/18). These were made to allow the UK to ratify the WIPO Performers and Phonograms Treaty (Cm 3728).

[256] Copyright Designs and Patents Act 1988 s.205C as added by the Performance (Moral Rights) Regulations.

[257] 1988 Act, s.205D.

[258] 1988 Act, s.205C(3).

[259] 1988 Act, s.205E.

right is not to have the performance subjected to derogatory treatment.[260] There are exceptions where the performance is given for the purpose of reporting current events, where the modifications are consistent with normal editorial or production practice or to avoid the commission of an offence, comply with a statutory duty or for the BBC to comply with its obligations (these last categories of exception sometime require a disclaimer).[261]

REMEDIES

Injunctions

6–075   Injunctions are normally granted if the claimant succeeds at the trial of a copyright action, though they have been refused because the infringement was trivial, the chance of repetition was slight or the claimant had acquiesced or delayed unconscionably.[262] In the case of moral rights the court is given a discretion to order that the act be prohibited unless it is accompanied by a sufficient disclaimer dissociating the author or director from the work.[263] More significant for the media is the prospect of a pre-trial injunction against the use of copyright documents in a book or as part of a news story. The principles upon which such "prior restraint" may be resisted are discussed earlier.

Injunctions can be granted against internet service providers who have actual knowledge of another person using their service to infringe copyright or a performer's property right.[264]

From 2006 the Court has been given a new power. Where it finds that an intellectual property right has been infringed, it may, at the request of the applicant, order appropriate measures for the dissemination and publication of the judgment to be taken at the Defendant's expense.[265]

Private search warrants and compulsory disclosure

6–076   The growth of video and other copyright piracy has led the courts to grant powerful orders for obtaining and preserving evidence of infringement. If there is strong evidence to show that copyright has

---

[260] 1988 Act, s.205F.

[261] 1988 Act, s.205G.

[262] Laddie, Prescott and Vitoria, *The Modern Law of Copyright and Designs* (3rd edn, Butterworths, 2000), para.39.35.

[263] Copyright, Designs and Patents Act 1988, s.103(2), and see s.178 for the meaning of "sufficient disclaimer".

[264] 1988 Act, ss.97A and 191JA as inserted by Copyright and Related Rights Regulations 2003.

[265] CPR Pt 63 PD para.29.2, implementing the European Enforcement Directive 2004/48/EEC OJ L 157 April 30, 2004.

been or will be infringed in a way that would cause serious harm to the owner of the copyright, and if the owner can prove that vital evidence might be destroyed as soon as word of the institution of proceedings reaches the suspected pirates, then the court can in effect issue a private search warrant. It is prepared to do so in the absence of the proposed defendant, and before notice of the proceedings has been served on the defendant. Applications are usually heard in private. These orders were previously known as *Anton Piller* orders[266] after the case that established the court's jurisdiction to make them. They are now called "search orders".[267] They require the defendants to allow the owners to inspect their premises, usually in the company of the owner's solicitor, and to copy or photograph relevant articles and documents or to detain them until the action is heard. These orders will almost certainly constitute an interference with the right to respect for private life under Art.8 of the European Convention (Art.8 being capable of protecting business as well as domestic premises against State intrusion) and/or with the peaceful enjoyment of possessions under Protocol 1, Art.1.[268] If the orders are "necessary in a democratic society" to protect the rights of others they will not breach Art.8, nor will Art.1 of Protocol 1 be violated if they are justified in the public interest. However, the court must be satisfied that the orders are proportionate and strike a fair balance between the interests of society and the individual.

The courts can also order the defendants to disclose on oath information that the claimants need to enforce their rights, such as the names of their suppliers and customers.[269] These *Norwich Pharmacal* orders can also be made to discover the source of leaked confidential information (see para.5–060). Some infringements of copyright are criminal offences (see below) but defendants cannot refuse to answer questions on the grounds that the answers may incriminate them: their privilege against self-incrimination has been taken away by statute.[270] Instead, there is a bar on the answers being used in any subsequent prosecution for a related offence.[271]

Defendants can apply to have these orders set aside. They are rarely successful, but if they are, or if the claimants fail in their action at the trial, the defendants would normally be entitled to compensation.

In 1985, in the first contested case involving an *Anton Piller* order, **6–077** the High Court awarded £10,000 damages in trespass against a firm of solicitors that had overzealously executed an order which had

---

[266] *Anton Piller KG v Manufacturing Processes* [1976] Ch.55.

[267] See Civil Procedure Act 1997, s.7 and Civil Procedure Rules, Pt 25, r.25.1(1)(h).

[268] *Niemetz v Germany* (1993) 16 E.H.R.R. 97.

[269] *Norwich Pharmacal v Commissioners of Customs and Excise* [1974] A.C. 133.

[270] Supreme Court Act 1981, s.72.

[271] Defined in Supreme Court Act 1981, s. 72(6); see *Universal City Studies Inc v Hubbard* [1983] 2 All F.R. 596.

been obtained upon unsatisfactory evidence. Mr Justice Scott emphasised the need for applicants to produce overwhelming evidence of piracy causing considerable damage, and of the imminence of the danger of destruction of evidence, before *Anton Piller* orders should be made:

> "What is to be said of the *Anton Piller* procedure which, on a regular and institutionalised basis, is depriving citizens of their property and closing down their businesses by orders made Ex parte, on applications of which they know nothing and at which they cannot be heard, by orders which they are bound, on pain of committal, to obey, even if wrongly made? . . . even villains ought not to be deprived of their property by proceedings at which they cannot be heard."[272]

Damages

6–078 Successful claimants can claim compensation for damage to the value of their copyright, which will either be the amount of profits lost as a result of the competitor's action or the fee that they could properly have charged the defendant for using their copyright material.[273] Until the 1988 Act a copyright owner had the further right to the value of the infringing article (i.e. damages in conversion).[274] This could far exceed the harm to the copyright and was accurately described as draconian. The present Act has abolished the conversion damages remedy.[275] The court has also a power to award additional damages where the infringement has been particularly flagrant, or where the defendant's profit was so large that compensatory damages would not be adequate.[276] There must have been some "scandalous conduct, deceit and such like which includes deliberate and calculated copyright infringement". In one case a photographer sold to the press a wedding photograph of a man who had subsequently been murdered. The photographer had neither the copyright nor permission from the family, and he was made to pay extra damages.[277] A conscientious but mistaken decision that

---

[272] *Columbia Picture Industries v Robinson* [1987] Ch.38. See further guidelines in *Universal Thermosensors Ltd v Hibben* [1992] 1 W.L.R. 840 and see Steven Gee Q.C. *"Commercial Injunctions"* (5th edn, Thomson, Sweet and Maxwell, 2004).

[273] Copyright, Designs and Patents Act 1988, s.96(2).

[274] Copyright Act 1956, s.18.

[275] The Intellectual Property (Enforcement etc) Regulations 2006 (SI 2006/1028) Reg.3 set out a number of considerations which the court must take into account when assessing damages. This is to accord with the Enforcement Directive 2004/48/EEC O.J. L 157 April 30, 2004, and seem broadly in accordance with existing UK practice.

[276] Copyright, Designs and Patents Act 1988, s.97(2).

[277] *Williams v Settle* [1960] 1 W.L.R. 1072. The court described its award differently, but in a comparable situation today additional damages would be likely.

copyright would not be infringed will assist a defendant in avoiding payment of additional damages. This will be particularly so if the decision was taken in accordance with legal advice, although proof of this may require disclosure of such advice (which is normally protected by legal professional privilege) and should only be done after very careful consideration.

Breach of copyright does not require guilty knowledge. However, if defendants do not know that copyright subsists in the work that is infringed, they are excused from paying damages.[278] They may be subjected, though, to other remedies, such as an injunction or an account of any profit that they have made out of the infringement.[279]

Breach of all four moral rights is actionable as breach of a statutory duty.[280] This means that the claimant can claim compensation to be put in as good a position as if the wrong had not been committed. In considering remedies for breach of the right to be identified the court must specifically take account of any delay in asserting the right.[281]

Account of profits

Damages compensate claimants for what they have lost, but an **6–079** enterprising defendant may have used the plagiarised work in a way that yielded a profit in excess of what the claimant could have obtained for it. The courts can order the defendant to "account" for this excess profit to the claimant.[282]

An account is a discretionary remedy. It will be refused if the breach was trivial or if the claimant delayed unreasonably before starting proceedings. If the court is prepared to order an account of profits, the claimant will have to elect between this remedy and damages. If an account is chosen, the claimant will not be entitled to claim the statutory additional damages as well.[283] In order to allow the claimant to make an informed choice, the defendant will often first be ordered to disclose financial information to the claimant as to the net profit which was made by the infringement.

---

[278] Copyright, Designs and Patents Act 1988, s.97(1). This is a narrow exception. It does not help those who make a mistake as to who is the copyright owner. Nor can a publisher plead ignorance of the copyright—everyone is presumed to know the law. All reasonable care must have been taken, including any appropriate inquiries. After making these, the defendant must still have no grounds for believing that copyright exists. Because of all these restrictions, the defence is really only of benefit where the copied work is old or originates from a country where it is not reasonably possible to discover whether the necessary conditions for copyright are fulfilled. However, if the defence is available, neither ordinary nor additional damages can be awarded: *Redrow Homes Ltd v Bett Brothers Plc* [1999] 1 A.C. 197.

[279] Copyright, Designs and Patents Act 1988, s.97(1).

[280] 1988 Act, s.103(1).

[281] 1988 Act, s.78(5).

[282] Laddie, *et al.*, *The Modern Law of Copyright and Designs*, para.39.47.

[283] *Redrow Homes Ltd v Bett Brothers Plc* (above).

Delivery up of copies

16–080   The court can order the defendant to hand over to the claimant any infringing copy and articles specifically designed for making copies of a particular copyright that the owner of the article knows or has reason to believe has been or is to be used for making infringing copies.[284] The application must be brought within six years of the infringing article being made.[285] Like an account of profits, delivery up is a discretionary remedy, and the court must consider whether the rights of the owner can be adequately protected in some other way. Anyone with an interest in the article is entitled to make representations as to why delivery up should not be ordered and to appeal against the order.[286]

Criminal offences

6–081   The Copyright Act 1956 criminalised certain types of infringement, but the penalties were low and the scope of the offences was haphazard. The criminal sanctions were progressively toughened, particularly in response to the growth of the trade in pirated videos and music cassettes. The 1988 Act continued that trend.[287] and it has been taken still further by successive sets of regulations implementing directives from the European Union.[288] Elaborate provisions were also included in the 2003 Regulations in an attempt to combat devices and programmes whose purpose is the circumvention of Digital Rights Management techniques. DRM techniques are attempts by copyright owners to prevent illicit copying or dealing with lawful copies of copyright works. If a DRM technique is alleged to interfere with one of the permitted rights, there is a cumbersome procedure for making a complaint through the Secretary of State.[289]

A wide range of offences has now been created for those who are both commercially and knowingly involved in copyright infringement. On summary conviction magistrates can sentence to prison for six months and fine the statutory maximum (currently £5,000). Conviction on indictment can lead to a fine (for which there is no upper limit) and a two-year prison sentence.[290] The criminal court

---

[284] Copyright, Designs and Patents Act 1988, s.99.

[285] 1988 Act, s.113: the period is extended if the copyright owner is under a legal disability, e.g. is still a minor, or if the owner was prevented by fraud or concealment from knowing the facts of the case.

[286] 1988 Act, s.144.

[287] 1988 Act, s.107.

[288] Copyright and Related Rights Regulations 2003 adding s. 107(2A) and (4A) in relation to copyrights and s.198(1A) and (5A) in relation to performers' rights.

[289] Copyright, Designs and Patents Act 1988, s.296ZE

[290] 1988 Act, s.107. In *R. v Lewis (Christopher)* [1997] 1 Cr.App.R. (S) 208, CA the defendant was sentenced to 12 months' immediate imprisonment for distributing infringing articles. He had operated a computer bulletin board for passing around computer games. Over a three month period, 934 games had been downloaded and 592 had been uploaded. Each was worth about £40.

can make forfeiture orders similar to the civil courts' powers to order delivery up.[291] Magistrates can issue search warrants where there are grounds for believing that an offence of manufacturing, importing or distributing infringing copies is or is about to be committed.[292] This power now relates to infringement of any type of copyright work (no longer just sound recordings or films, as under the previous law). In executing the warrant the police may seize any evidence of dealing in infringing copies, but cannot take items subject to legal privilege, excluded material or special procedure material[293] (see also para.5–075).

An interesting precedent was established in 1991 when a freelance photographer, David Hoffman, brought a private prosecution against a local liberal councillor in Tower Hamlets, who had used one of his photographs in a leaflet attacking the Labour Party. The councillor was convicted of criminal infringement of copyright, fined £200 and ordered to pay the photographer's legal costs. Victims of copyright infringement may find this an extreme remedy, and one that brings them no financial compensation, although it would undoubtedly prove effective against persistent violators and those who use copyright material for purposes that the copyright holder finds particularly deplorable. In *Thames and Hudson v DACS*[294] Evans-Lombe J. held that criminal proceedings were not confined to pirates and could, in principle, be invoked by the Artists Collection Society against the well-known publishers of art histories and studies. (The prosecution later failed on its facts.)

Copyright owners can also enlist the aid of customs officers in **6–082** their fight against pirated works. The owner of copyright in a published literary, dramatic or musical work can give notice in writing asking that infringing copies of the work be treated as prohibited goods for a period not exceeding five years. Owners of copyright in sound recordings and films can make a similar request if the time and place of the arrival of the expected infringing copies can be specified. Classifying the infringing copies as "prohibited goods" does not make their importation a criminal offence, but it does mean that they are liable to be seized and forfeited unless the importer has them only for his private and domestic use.[295]

The Bank of England is given a monopoly over all representations of legal tender, and it is a criminal offence against s.18 of the Forgery and Counterfeiting Act 1981 to "reproduce on any substance whatsoever, and whether or not on the correct scale, any part of a British currency note" without the Bank's consent. The Bank's singular lack of any sense of humour (or indeed common sense) led

---

[291] Copyright, Designs and Patents Act 1988, s.108.
[292] 1988 Act, s.109.
[293] 1988 Act, s.109(2); Police and Criminal Evidence Act, s.9(2).
[294] [1995] F.S.R. 153.
[295] Copyright, Designs and Patents Act 1988, s.111.

to the Old Bailey prosecution in 1987 of an artist named Boggs over paintings of banknotes, which were worth considerably more than the notes themselves and were much increased in value by the publicity that attended his trial. The paintings had been clumsily seized from an art gallery exhibition, and witnesses from the Bank asserted the astonishing proposition that any artist who wished to depict a banknote in a painting had first to submit a sketch in triplicate for approval. The legal argument turned on the meaning of the word "reproduction" as applied to art (is the *Mona Lisa* no more than the reproduction of a sixteenth-century Italian woman?) and experts solemnly placed Boggs in the tradition of *trompel'oeil* painters. The jury, doubtless surprised to be summonsed to Court No. 1 of the Old Bailey to judge an art exhibition, acquitted after a 10-minute retirement.[296]

---

[296] See Geoffrey Robertson, *The Justice Game* (Vintage, 1999), Ch.12; Laurence Weschler, *Boggs—A Comedy of Values* (Chicago, 1999).

CHAPTER 7

CONTEMPT OF COURT[1]

INTRODUCTION

The power to punish for contempt of court is the means by which 7–001 the legal system protects itself from publications that might unduly influence the result of litigation. The dilemmas caused by conflict between the demands of a fair trial and a free press are real enough. We pin a certain faith on the ability of juries, judges and tribunals to resolve disputes, so we are justified in being concerned about the effect of outside influence on their deliberations, especially the sort of pressure generated by circulation-seeking sensationalism. The smooth working of the legal system is a very important, but not always overriding, consideration in holding the delicate balance of public interest between the rights of defendants and litigants to a fair trial and the need for society to know about the issues involved in their cases and about the effectiveness of the system that resolves those issues. Many contempt decisions before the 1981 Contempt Act treated "the public interest" as synonymous with "the interests of those involved in the legal process", imposing secrecy and censorship without regard for the countervailing benefits of a free flow of information about what happens in the courts. That Act must now be interpreted so far as possible in conformity with the European Convention, but the Convention also protects fair trials (Art.6) as well as free speech (Art.10). The problem is that journalists (and the public for that matter) think that the right to knows what is happening in their courts should override fairness to defendants, especially those in terrorist cases.

The rationale behind the contempt law is an abiding British fear of "trial by media" of the sort that often disfigures major trials in America, where the First Amendment permits press TV and radio to comment on a court case. The principle is firmly ensconced in the value-system of lawyers and legislators, and the media ignore it at

---

[1] There are three principal textbooks on contempt: *Arlidge, Eady and Smith on Contempt* (3rd edn, Sweet & Maxwell, 2005); Miller, *Contempt of Court*, (3rd edn, OUP, 2000). Sir John Fox's book *The History of Contempt of Court* (1927) explains lucidly the history of contempt, with an appropriate sense of the absurd.

their peril, even in relation to the trial of the most obviously guilty or most unpopular defendants. When the *Daily Mirror* published sensationalised suggestions that a man arrested for one particularly foul murder was not only guilty, but guilty of other murders as well, its editor was gaoled for three months.[2] The *Sun* was fined £75.000 for publishing prejudicial material about a man whose private prosecution the newspaper had agreed to fund. The penalty for the massively prejudicial publicity surrounding the arrest of "Yorkshire Ripper" Peter Sutcliffe came in a more permanent refused to amend the Contempt Bill then under consideration,to make it easier for the press to report newsworthy development in criminal investigations between the time of arrest and the time of charge.

The power to punish for contempt may be justified by reference to the European Convention on Human Rights. Article 6 provides that:

"In the determination of his civil rights and obligations or of any criminal charge against him, everyone is entitled to a *fair and public hearing* within a reasonable time by an independent and *impartial* tribunal established by law." [our italics]

7–002 A fair hearing is one of "the rights of others" that can justify a restriction on freedom of speech guaranteed by Art.10 if the restriction is "prescribed by law" and not disproportionate to the aim of securing a fair trial before a tribunal unswayed by media prejudice.

The purpose of the law of contempt in relation to the media is to prevent publications that might realistically bias the tribunal or tilt the balance of its procedures unfairly against one side. It is normally a criminal offence, carrying a maximum penalty of two years' imprisonment and an unlimited fine, although the High Court may injunct a potentially contemptuous article or broadcast if action is taken prior to publication. Contempt is the only serious criminal offence that is punishable without trial by jury: cases are decided by High Court judges, who are, inevitably, judges in their own cause in relation to material that reflects adversely upon the administration of justice. The vagueness of the concept, and its intimate relationship with the operation of the legal process, force the media to rely upon professional legal advisers rather more heavily than in other areas of media law. Reliance on professional advice will not preclude a finding of guilt, but it will always mitigate the penalty and exclude any prospect of imprisonment.

The law of contempt serves a valuable purpose in so far as its operation is confined to placing a temporary embargo on publication of information that would make a jury more likely to convict (or acquit) a person who is on trial, or shortly to face trial. Without such

---

[2] *R. v Bolam Ex p. Haigh* (1949) 93 S.J. 220.

a law, the legal system would be forced to adopt the expensive, and not entirely successful, expedients used in notorious trials in America, where jurors are quizzed at length as to what they have seen in the press or on television and are then sequestered under guard in hotels, denied access to family, newspapers and television programmes for the duration of the case. For all the fuss that is made about "trial by media", it is very rare for convictions to be quashed because of adverse publicity. An exceptional case occurred when Government minister Tom King chose to announce the abolition of the right to silence, on the grounds that it was being exploited by Irish terrorists, on the very day that three Irish defendants had claimed their right to silence on charges of plotting to murder Tom King. There was massive publicity and the subsequent convictions were overturned on appeal.[3] The Taylor sisters (convicted of murder) were freed on appeal in part because of unfair publicity which meant that they could not be re-tried.[4]

Judges occasionally decide that a fair trial is impossible because of **7–003** earlier press reporting: one notable example was the trial of West Midlands police officers charged with conspiracy to pervert the course of justice because of their role in the Birmingham six affair.[5] Another example was the trial of Geoffrey Knights who was charged with injuring the driver of his partner, the *EastEnders* star, Gillian Taylforth.[6] But the Court of Appeal usually takes a robust attitude towards publicity. Rosemary West's convictions of multiple murders at her Cromwell Road "House of Horrors" were upheld despite the most sensational reporting. The Court of Appeal said that it would be ludicrous if heinous crimes could not be tried because of the extensive publicity they inevitably engendered: all that is required is that the trial judge takes particular care to warn the jury to try the case only on the evidence.[7] Likewise, in 2006 Abu Hamza, the former Iman of the Finsbury Park mosque was unsuccessful in his attempt to persuade the Court of Appeal that his convictions should be quashed because of widespread prejudicial publicity.[8] The Privy Council in dismissing an order for a retrial by a Scottish court said:

> "The principal safeguard of the objective impartiality of the tribunal is the trial process itself and the conduct of the trial by

---

[3] *R. v McCann* (1990) 92 Cr.App.R. 239.

[4] *R. v Taylor (Michelle Ann and Lisa Jane)* (1993) 98 Cr.App.R. 361 and see *R. v Wood* [1996] 1 Cr.App.R. 207, C.A.

[5] *R. v Reade, Morris and Woodwiss*, Central Criminal Court, October 15, 1993, Garland J.

[6] *R. v Knights*, Harrow Crown Court, October 3, 1995, HHJ Sanders—for further details of these and other examples see Nicol and Rogers: "Annual Review of Media Reporting Restrictions" in *The Yearbook of Media and Entertainment Law 1996* (OUP, edited by Barendt, Bate, Dickens and Gibbons).

[7] *R. v West* [1996] 2 Cr.App.R. 374 and see *R. v Michael Stone* [2001] Crim.L.R. 465, CA.

[8] *R. v Abu Hamza* [2006] EWCA Crim 2918.

the trial judge. On the one hand there is the discipline to which the jury will be subjected of listening to and thinking about the evidence. The actions of seeing and hearing the witnesses may be expected to have a far greater impact on their minds than such residual recollections as may exist about reports in the media. This impact can be expected to be reinforced on the other hand by such warnings and directions as the trial judge may think it appropriate to give them as the trial proceeds in particular when he delivers his charge before they retire to consider their verdict."[9]

This theme—that the trial process makes jurors focus on the evidence to the exclusion of earlier press reporting which can be neutralised by effective judicial directions is regularly repeated.[10] It has been borne out by some spectacular acquittals after sensationally prejudicial publicity. Kevin and Ian Maxwell were acquitted despite years in the press pillory and so was the "Grope Doc" accused of rape, whose prosecution was both sponsored and prejudiced by the *Sun* (see para.7–044). Jeremy Thorpe, the former leader of the Liberal Party, was acquitted after years of media speculation that he was guilty of conspiracy to murder and the Kray twins were actually acquitted of a second murder charge only weeks after their convictions at their first trial had received a blaze of publicity.[11]

More systematic studies into the effect of publicity on juries is precluded in England by the Contempt of Court Act which makes it an offence to investigate what went on in the jury room even if juror anonymity is preserved.[12] However, in New Zealand a study by the Law Commission concluded that the impact of pre-trial publicity and prejudicial media coverage was minimal.[13] An Australian study reached similar conclusions.[14] Furthermore, as Lord Hope said in *Montgomery v HMA*: "the entire system of trial by jury is based upon the assumption that the jury will follow the instructions which they receive from the trial judge and that they will return a true verdict in accordance with the evidence".[15]

7–004   The reality is that defence lawyers especially in terrorist cases delight in using the fact of prejudicial publicity to win sympathy for their clients from juries which distrust newspapers and who have

---

[9] *Montgomery v HM Advocate* [2003] 1 A.C. 641, *per* Lord Hope at p.673.
[10] See *R. v Abu Hamza* (above) at [90]; *In the Matter of B* [2006] EWCA Crim 2692; *Att-Gen v News Group Newspapers Ltd* [1987] Q.B. 1; *Ex p. Telegraph Plc* [1993] 1 W.L.R. 980, 987.
[11] *R. v Kray* (1969) 53 Cr.App.R. 412.
[12] Contempt of Court Act 1981, s.8—see below p.392.
[13] Warren Young, Neil Cameron and Yvette Tinsley, *Juries in Criminal Trials: Part 2* Ch.9, para.287, N.Z.L.C. preliminary paper No.37, November 1999. And Law Commission Report, *Juries in Criminal Trials* (February 2001).
[14] New South Wales Law and Justice Foundation, *Managing Prejudicial Publicity*, 2001.
[15] *Montgomery v HM Advocate* (above) at p.674.

their distrust reinforced by media-hostile judges. Often defence lawyers will begin their campaign against press coverage with an abuse of process application at which they urge the court to dismiss the case because it cannot be fairly tried. They may try to summon journalists to give evidence on such applications, but the court should be vigilant to ensure that their questioning is confined to relevant matters. If allegations of contempt are to be put against journalists, they should be told of their right to object on grounds of self-incrimination and must be given the opportunity to seek legal advice.[16]

The critical issue that arises in deciding whether a newspaper is guilty of contempt is whether its effect on the date of its publication caused a substantial *risk* of prejudice. The safety of a conviction, on the other hand, will depend on the cumulative impact of publicity in all the media over the trial period and before. Thus newspapers have been found guilty of contempt, although the conviction of the defendant whose trial they were alleged to have prejudiced was upheld[17] and conversely, trials aborted because of press publicity have not necessarily led to findings of contempt against the relevant newspapers.[18] Following the successful appeal of the Taylor sisters, the Law Officers refused to take proceedings for contempt against the press. The sisters tried to challenge this decision, but the Divisional Court ruled that the historical immunity of the Attorney General from judicial review prevented his decision from being challenged. It was difficult to reconcile with the remarks of the Court of Appeal in quashing the Taylor sisters' convictions but it was not so irrational that (had the immunity not existed) it would have been quashed.[19]

Nonetheless, as Simon Brown L.J. said in 1997[20]:

"It seems to me important in these cases that the courts do not speak with two voices, one used to dismiss criminal appeals with the court roundly rejecting any suggestion that prejudice resulted from media publications, the other holding comparable publications to be in contempt, the courts on these occasions expressing grave doubts as to the jury's ability to forget or put aside what they have heard or read.

. . . unless a publication materially affects the course of trial [by requiring the place of trial to be moved or its start delayed], or requires directions from the court well beyond those

---

[16] *Att-Gen v Morgan* [1998] E.M.L.R. 294, 307. See para.5–052 *et seq.* for the position when journalists are questioned about their sources.

[17] See *Thomson Newspapers Ltd v Att-Gen* [1968] 1 All E.R. 268; *R. v Malik* [1968] 1 All E.R. 582, 585.

[18] *Att-Gen v MGN Ltd* [1997] 1 All E.R. 456.

[19] *R. v Solicitor-General, Ex p. Taylor* (1996) 8 Admin.L.R. 206.

[20] *Att-Gen v Unger* [1998] E.M.L.R. 280, 291.

ordinarily required and routinely given to juries to focus their attention on evidence called before them rather than whatever they may have heard or read outside court, or creates at the very least a seriously arguable ground for an appeal on the basis of prejudice, it is unlikely to be vulnerable to contempt proceedings under the strict liability rule."

7–005   The same judge has said that if the publication creates a seriously arguable ground of appeal, this would be sufficient to establish strict-liability contempt.[21] The concern that the Court did not speak with two voices was echoed in *Att-Gen v Guardian Newspapers Ltd*[22] but, while Collins J. in that case broadly endorsed the approach of Simon Brown L.J., Sedley L.J. thought that to ask whether the publicity would have been sufficient to justify the grant of permission to appeal against conviction set the test too low. He thought that it was better to postulate: (a) that the jurors had read the publication; (b) an application to discharge the jury had been made and refused; (c) the judge had given proper directions; (d) conviction was not inevitable; (e) the jury convicted, and then to consider whether the prejudicial publicity would have led to a successful appeal against conviction.

The fear of "trial by media" was taken to extremes when British courts stopped publication of editorial criticism by the *Sunday Times* of the moral position of Distillers, the giant corporation that had marketed the deforming drug thalidomide, in relation to its offer of financial settlement to parents of the drug's victims. The newspaper was campaigning to increase that offer, against a background of protracted and complicated High Court litigation which might never have come to trial. In 1973 the House of Lords held that contempt law prohibited the publication of material that pre-judged the issue of whether Distillers had been negligent in marketing the drug. Two of the judges also said that editorial comment designed to put moral pressure on Distillers to abandon its legal defence and to negotiate a higher settlement was contempt.[23] This decision was widely condemned by Parliament and the press, and an official committee, headed by Lord Justice Phillimore, was established to recommend reforms in the law of contempt.[24] In due course the European Court of Human Rights confirmed that the British contempt law, as declared by the House of Lords in the *Sunday Times* case, was in breach of the Convention guarantee of freedom of expression[25] (see para.2–022). In order to bring British law into conformity with the European Convention, the Government was obliged to legislate.

[21] *Att-Gen v Birmingham Post* [1998] 4 All E.R. 49, QBD.
[22] [1999] E.M.L.R. 904.
[23] *Att-Gen Times Newspapers Ltd* [1974] A.C. 273.
[24] *Report on Contempt of Court* HMSO, 1974 Cmnd 5794.
[25] *Sunday Times v UK* (1979) 2 E.H.R.R. 245.

This was one of the purposes of the Contempt of Court Act 1981, which now governs most (but not all) aspects of what was previously judge-made law.

TYPES OF CONTEMPT

For media purposes, contempt may be divided into five categories.   7–006

- *Strict liability contempt.* So called because it may be committed by journalists and editors without the slightest intention of prejudicing legal proceedings. This class of contempt is perpetrated by publication of material that creates a substantial risk that justice, in relation to a case presently before the courts, will be seriously impeded or prejudiced. It can be committed only when a particular case is "active". In a criminal matter this is generally after an individual has been arrested, and in civil litigation this stage is reached when the date for the trial or hearing is set. This form of contempt is often committed accidentally (e.g. when newspapers publish details of an individual's previous convictions without realising that he or she is facing fresh criminal charges). Its harshness is mitigated by special defences that apply when the publisher has taken particular care to avoid the danger, or when the prejudicial matter has been published as part of a discussion of matters of public importance. The media are protected from frivolous cases at the hands of disappointed litigants by the rule that any prosecution must be sanctioned by the court or by the Attorney-General.
- *Deliberate contempt.* This occurs on the rare occasions when a publisher deliberately sets out to influence legal proceedings. Greater use has been made of this category of contempt to sidestep the protections for the media in the 1981 Act. Deliberate contempt may also be committed by placing unfair pressure on a witness or a party to proceedings.
- *Scandalous attacks on the judiciary.* This is an anachronistic relic of eighteenth-century struggles between partisan judges and their vitriolic critics. It survives only as a threat to publications that make false and "scurrilous" attacks on the judiciary. The lack of recent authority shows that honest and temperate criticism of the administration of justice can be published without risk of prosecution.
- *Jury deliberations.* The Contempt of Court Act 1981 introduced an offence of publishing accounts of how jurors reached their verdict.
- *Disobedience to an order of the court.* This chapter deals with rules that apply generally to the enforcement of court orders, but orders which control access to courts or which

restrict reporting are considered in Ch.8, "Reporting the Courts".

STRICT LIABILITY CONTEMPT

7–007   Contempt is committed if a publication "creates a substantial risk that the course of justice in the proceedings in question will be seriously impeded or prejudiced".[26] Liability is "strict" in the sense that the prosecution does not have to prove that the publisher intended to prejudice legal proceedings. However, it still bears the burden of showing, beyond reasonable doubt, that the publication created a substantial risk of serious prejudice. The prejudice need not have materialised but the degree of its risk must be "substantial", as distinct from merely possible or remote. Thus a BBC programme that was broadcast only in the southwest region was not in contempt of a trial that was about to take place in London.[27] Of course, a local story might be picked up by the press agencies or by the national media, but if this endangered the trial, it would be the responsibility of those who had given it the broader coverage. The original broadcaster could be liable only if it had sold the story or otherwise been instrumental in giving it a wider audience. When a jury trial is alleged to have been put at risk, it is always worth reviewing how widely the publication was distributed in the area from which the jury was to be drawn. Distributors should have accurate circulation figures and the local Crown Court's Administrator should help in identifying the geographical area from which its jurors are drawn. In 1998 *Sunday Business* was acquitted of contempt of the trial of John Fashanu, Bruce Grobbelaar and others. The likelihood of a copy being sold to a juror in the court's catchment area was about 2,000:1 against and this small chance of any potential juror seeing the articles in question was influential in the finding that there was no substantial risk of serious prejudice.[28]

The impediment or prejudice created by the publication must itself be of a serious kind. This means, at least in criminal cases, that it must be of a nature that could tip the final verdict one way or the other.[29] A useful test of whether the prejudice is "serious" is to consider whether it can readily be cured by the court itself, rather than by a prosecution or an injunction against publication. The simplest device is for the trial judge to ask jurors who may have seen the prejudicial material to stand down from the panel: this was done in the Jeremy Thorpe case when two books containing evidence from the committal (at which reporting restrictions had been lifted)

---

[26] Contempt of Court Act 1981, s.2(2).
[27] *Blackburn v BBC*, The Times, December 15, 1976.
[28] *Att-Gen v Sunday Newspapers Ltd* [1999] C.O.D. 11, QBD.
[29] *Att-Gen v English* [1982] 2 All E.R. 903 at 919.

had been published before the trial.[30] Where publicity has been more diffuse, this device may be impracticable. To ask jurors "Have you seen anything published about the defendant's previous convictions?" would obviously draw attention to the very material of which they should be kept ignorant. However, a variation of the device can be effective as the trial progresses. Jurors in one police corruption prosecution were ordered by the judge not to see a play at the Royal Court theatre about the same subject. This was a far more sensible course than banning the play.

Another example of a situation where a reasonable alternative course of action was available to reduce the seriousness of apprehended prejudice is the 1991 case of *Re Central Television*.[31]

> A trial judge feared that the jury in a much-publicised fraud case might be affected by radio and television reports of the case on the night they were to be sent to a hotel while considering their verdict. He therefore used Contempt Act powers to "postpone" all radio and television reports about the trial until the verdict had been delivered, and told the jurors that they could relax and watch television without the danger of prejudice. The Court of Appeal criticised the judge's priorities: the public right to have trials reported overrode the comfort of jurors. If the judge had any real reason to fear prejudicial media comment, he should simply have directed that the jurors were to have no access to radio and television during their overnight stay at the hotel.

A 1992 case has emphasised that the "substantial risk" of preju-   7–008
dice must be a *practical* risk, in the sense that it must carry a prospect that the outcome of the trial would be different without the offending publication, or that it would necessitate the discharge of the jury:

> An article in *The Guardian* criticised the over-sensitivity to the press of judges in big fraud trials. It referred to a current Manchester trial where a judge had imposed reporting restrictions for no better reason than that some of the defendants were facing further committal proceedings. The Attorney-General argued that any revelation that a defendant was facing other charges would amount to contempt if it created "more than a remote risk" of prejudice. The High Court held that this proposition was too wide. For example, revelation of the fact that a defendant was also facing minor charges would not bias a jury against him.[32]

---

[30] David Leigh, *The Frontiers of Secrecy* (Junction Books, 1980) p.74. To the authors' chagrin, none of the jurors had read either book.

[31] *Re Central Television Plc* [1991] 1 All E.R. 347.

[32] *Att-Gen v Guardian Newspapers Ltd (No.3)* [1992] 1 W.L.R. 874. Another media-friendly application of this principle is found in *Schering Chemicals v Falkman* [1982] Q.B. 1, where the Court of Appeal thought that no civil judge would be influenced by a television programme about a case that had to be tried, and the appearance on it of experts who would give evidence was perfectly proper: they could be cross-examined in court.

The twin burdens on the prosecution, under the Contempt Act, to prove both *"substantial* risk" and *"serious* prejudice" give considerable latitude to the news media in reporting the background to a sensational case. This was confirmed by an early test of the legislation in respect of national newspaper reporting of the arrest of Michael Fagan, a trespasser who had found his way into the Queen's bedchamber in Buckingham Palace[33]:

> Fagan had been charged with burglary (by stealing part of a bottle of wine he had found in the Palace). He faced other unconnected charges of taking a car without permission and of assaulting his stepson. *The Sun* described Fagan as a "junkie", a glib liar and a thief of Palace cigars. None of these descriptions were held to be likely to cause a substantial risk of prejudice. The *Daily Star* referred to an alleged confession by Fagan to theft of the wine. This went to the heart of the case against him and was found to be contempt. *The Mail on Sunday* alleged that Fagan had had a homosexual affair with Commander Trestrail (the Queen's bodyguard) and called Fagan "a rootless neurotic with no visible means of support". This was found to pose a sufficiently serious risk of prejudice to be prima facie contempt, but the paper successfully relied upon the public interest defence in s.5 because the story was part of a report on a matter of general public interest, namely the Queen's safety. Finally, the *Sunday Times* was found guilty of contempt because it exaggerated the charge against Fagan in relation to his stepson: the paper implied he was accused of wounding when in fact he was charged with the less serious crime of assault occasioning actual bodily harm.

The period of time between publication and trial is a major factor in determining whether the article poses a substantial risk of prejudice. There cannot be strict liability contempt at all if publication took place before the case became "active".[34] Yet even if the proceedings are active, the courts have become much more attentive to the significance of the time which is likely to elapse between publication and the hearing.[35]

7–009 In rejecting the Attorney-General's application to commit several newspapers for contempt of the Geoff Knights' case (see para.7–033), the court set out a helpful list of the applicable principles[36]:

- each case must be decided on its own facts so that while previous examples may be helpful they are only guides;
- the court will look at each publication separately and test liability at the time of publication. However a later publication can exacerbate a risk of prejudice which has already been created by earlier publications;

---

[33] *Att-Gen v Times Newspapers Ltd*, *The Times*, February 12, 1983.
[34] Contempt of Court Act 1981, s. 2(3)—see p.368 below for the "active" or *sub judice* periods.
[35] See, e.g. *Att-Gen v MGN Ltd* [1997] 1 All E.R. 456, 461; *Att-Gen v Independent News Ltd* [1995] 2 All E.R. 370; *Att-Gen v News Group Newspapers Ltd* [1987] Q.B. 1 and *Att-Gen v Unger* [1998] E.M.L.R. 280.
[36] *Att-Gen v MGN Ltd* [1997] 1 All E.R. 456.

- in the exercise of risk assessment, a small risk multiplied by a small risk results in an even smaller risk;
- in deciding whether there has been a substantial risk of "serious" prejudice the court will examine: (a) the likelihood of the publication coming to the attention of a potential juror (the number of copies circulating in the area from which the jury will be drawn is of obvious importance); (b) the likely impact of the publication on the ordinary reader (prominence of the article and the novelty of its content matter for this purpose), (c) the residual impact at the time of trial.
- the residual impact is of crucial importance and will be affected by the length of time between publication and trial, the focusing effect of listening over a prolonged period to evidence in a case and the likely curative effect of the judge's directions to a jury.

The last consideration—what has become known as the "fade factor"—is particularly important. It is recognition that even tabloid denunciation of horrific crimes and the demonisation of those charged with them is likely to have only a temporary effect. Especially in high profile murder or terrorism cases there will be many months between arrest and trial so that by the time the jury is empanelled the ephemeral impact of prejudicial publicity is likely to have dissipated.

Which court?

The seriousness of the risk and the degree of the prejudice will hinge **7–010** in the first place on the nature of the tribunal that is to try the issue which is the subject of media treatment. The first question for a journalist writing about a pending case is, therefore, "Who will judge it?"

Trial by jury

Jurors, drawn at random from the general public, are assumed to be **7–011** most susceptible to media influence. The publication of prejudicial information about any person awaiting jury trial is consequently dangerous. But jurors are not expected to remember, let alone to believe, everything they happen to read in newspapers. As the judge at the much-publicised Kray trials commented,

"I have enough confidence in my fellow-countrymen to think that they have got newspapers sized up and they are capable in normal circumstances of looking at the matter fairly and without prejudice even though they may have to disregard what they read in a newspaper."[37]

Trial by magistrates

7–012 Most criminal cases are tried in magistrates' courts, either by district judges or by a bench of lay justices. The district judge is a full-time professional lawyer and unlikely to be influenced by media reports. More care must be taken in cases that are to be decided by lay justices, who have minimal legal training, although their experience as regular members of the tribunal and the guidance they receive from their clerk would make them more difficult to influence than jurors sitting on a case for the first time. Arguments on these lines were accepted by the Divisional Court in dismissing a defendant's challenge to his conviction by magistrates because of widespread publicity which had been given to his previous conviction.[38]

Trial by judge

7–013 Almost all civil actions (other than libel and claims against the police) are heard by judges sitting alone. The Court of Appeal in *Schering Chemicals v Falkman* found it impossible to accept that a television programme could affect the views of a High Court judge.[39] Indeed, Lord Salmon has said: "I am and have always been satisfied that no judge would be influenced in his judgment by what may be said by the media. If he were, he would not be fit to be a judge."[40] Publicity in relation to a case to be heard by a single judge would need to be both false and intemperate, before contempt proceedings would be likely to succeed. As a former Chief Justice explained:

> "A judge is in a very different position to a juryman. Though in no sense a superhuman, he has by his training no difficulty in putting out of his mind matters which are not evidence in the case. This indeed happens daily to judges on Assize. This is all the more so in the case of a member of the Court of Appeal, who in regard to an appeal against conviction is dealing almost entirely with points of law and who in the case of an appeal against sentence is considering whether or not the sentence is correct in principle."[41]

The courts will be rather more protective of civil cases where a judge sits with non-lawyer assessors, *e.g.* a Crown Court judge

---

[37] (1969) 53 Cr.App.R. 412. *Gee v BBC* (1986) 136 N.L.J. 515, CA was an example of a civil case to be heard by a jury that the court did not think would be seriously prejudiced by another programme on a similar subject shortly after the case had been set down but months before the likely trial date.

[38] *R. v Croydon Magistrates' Court Ex p. Simmons* [1996] C.L.Y., para.1662.

[39] See above and also *Re Lonrho pic and Observer Ltd* [1990] 2 A.C. 154.

[40] Quoted by Robin Day in his note of dissent to the Phillimore Report, para.4.

[41] *R. v Duffy Ex p. Nash* [1960] 2 O.B. 188 at 198.

hearing appeals from a magistrates' court, or a county court judge hearing complaints of sex or race discrimination. But even so, it will be unusual for there to be a real risk of prejudice.[42]

Appeal hearings

No publisher or broadcaster has been punished for contempt of an **7–014** appeal court in the last 60 years. This record reflects Lord Reid's comment in the *Sunday Times* case:

> "It is scarcely possible to imagine a case when comment could influence judges in the Court of Appeal or noble and learned Lords in this House. And it would be wrong and contrary to existing practice to limit proper criticism of judgments already given but under appeal."[43]

The Court of Appeal, however, was unduly sensitive when it stopped Channel 4 from broadcasting a dramatic re-enactment of the appeal of the "Birmingham Six" until after its decision had been given.[44] This was essentially a public relations management exercise because none of the judges would have been influenced by the programme, but it "might affect the public view of the judgment of the court". The court misused its contempt powers by postponing the programme in order to prevent the public from pre-judging the judges. The ban was wrong in law and is unlikely to be repeated: the Court of Appeal's confident assessment in 1987 that the "Birmingham Six" were guilty was reversed three years later, when the credibility of police and scientific evidence was finally demolished. In 1999 the High Court of Justiciary in Scotland strongly and correctly doubted whether the Channel 4 decision was compatible with the 1981 Act.[45]

The most authoritative case on contempt of appellate courts is the **7–015** most permissive so far as media comment is concerned. It arose, in quite extraordinary circumstances, in the course of "Tiny" Rowland's crusade to damnify the Al Fayed brothers and the Government decision that had allowed them to defeat him in the battle to take over the House of Fraser (which owns Harrods):

> Rowland brought legal proceedings against the Secretary of State for Trade and Industry to compel him to disclose an unpublished report of an investigation into the takeover, which was critical of the Al Fayeds and their supporters. Lonhro (Rowland's company) lost the case in the High Court and in the Court of Appeal, but shortly before it was due

---

[42] *R. v Bulgin Ex p. BBC*, *The Times*, July 14, 1977.
[43] *Att-Gen v Times Newspapers* (above fn.23) at 301, and see Lord Simon at 321.
[44] *Att-Gen v Channel Four Television Co*, *The Independent*, December 3, 1987; *The Times*, December 18, 1987, CA.
[45] *Al Meghrahi v Times Newspapers Ltd*, 2000 JC 22.

to be heard in the House of Lords the company was sent, anonymously, a copy of the report. This it managed to publish in a special Thursday edition of the Sunday newspaper the *Observer*, which was also owned by Lonhro. Many copies were distributed before the Government managed to obtain the inevitable injunction, and amongst the list of distinguished personages who were sent copies of the newspaper were four of the five Law Lords listed to hear the appeal. The members of this panel were scandalised that Lonhro should apparently have attempted to influence their decision, and ordered that the company (together with the *Observer*) should stand trial before the House of Lords Appellate Committee on charges of contempt. Lonhro succeeded in removing from the Committee those Law Lords who had determined that the prosecution should be brought, on the grounds that they would otherwise be seen as "judges in their own cause." The Law Lords who eventually ruled that Lonhro had not been guilty of contempt did so on the basis that:

- the possibility that a professional judge would be influenced by anything he might read about a case he has to decide is remote;
- "It is difficult to visualise circumstances in which any court in the United Kingdom exercising appellate jurisdiction would be in the least likely to be influenced by public discussion of the merits of a decision appealed against or of the parties' conduct in the proceedings";
- Lonhro's action had pre-empted the very remedy it was seeking from the court, namely publication of the report. But it was not a contempt for it to have taken the law into its own hands and to have achieved its purpose extrajudicially, at least in the absence of any injunction against publication having been granted in aid of the party resisting disclosure in the legal proceedings that were pre-empted.[46]

These rulings make it highly unlikely that public discussion of any case that is subject to appeal will be treated as a contempt on the basis that it is likely to prejudice the course of justice in appeal proceedings.

Contempt risks

7–016 The risk of contempt may arise in numerous situations, and it is impossible to lay down hard and fast rules. The following areas, however, present clear dangers.

Criticising the decision to prosecute

7–017 The decision to prosecute is not mechanical. It involves the exercise of a discretion and consideration of the public interest, and as such can legitimately be the object of comment and criticism at the time when it is taken; objectors need not wait until the case is over. The

---

[46] *Re Lonhro Plc and Observer Ltd* [1990] 2 A.C. 154.

Director of Public Prosecution and the police must tolerate a greater degree of criticism, because of their public role. This is especially so when the prosecutorial decision has been taken by the Attorney-General personally. Although he is then supposed to act in a non-political manner, his other roles as a party politician and adviser to the Cabinet lead many to question whether it is possible for one person to combine these different tasks. Consequently, much greater latitude is given to comments hostile to the prosecution than to those critical of the defendant, especially if they deal with issues of principle and do not purport to settle facts in dispute.[47] The use by prosecuting authorities of unusual or discredited laws can always be a subject of debate even at the time of trial. In 1974 the Attorney-General refused to halt a television documentary critical of incitement to disaffection laws at a time when pacifists were standing trial under this legislation, despite a request from the trial judge.

Anti-prosecution commentaries are on much more dangerous ground if they attack prosecution witnesses or are likely to influence their evidence.

Anticipating the course of the trial

Predicting the outcome of a trial, or even giving odds on a particular **7–018** jury verdict, would in most cases amount to contempt because they create a "climate of expectation" which jurors may find difficult to resist. However, considerable freedom is given to the media in publishing informed speculation as to the issues that are likely to be raised, so long as no opinion is expressed as to the way they should be resolved:

> Shortly before the trial of a company fraud, a newspaper published details of the case that would be of interest to investors in the company concerned, and added that "mourners over the fiasco are likely to hear a little inside history of the business". The Court of Appeal said that the contempt proceedings should not have been brought, because the speculation would cause no substantial prejudice to parties to the action.[48]

It is commonly—and wrongly—believed that a defendant must stay silent throughout the long period between arrest and trial. In cases where the arrest has been attended with publicity (invariably prejudicial to the defendant) there can be no objection to his repeated public assertion of innocence (which is, after all, echoing the law's most sacred presumption). Nor is it necessarily contempt to

---

[47] Old examples of criticism of a prosecution, e.g. *R. v Mason*, *The Times*, December 7, 1932; *R. v Nield*, *The Times*, January 27, 1909 would now be unlikely to be contempt under the strict liability rule because the risk of prejudice would not be substantial.

[48] *Hunt v Clarke* (1889) 58 L.J.Q.B. 490.

publish a book by or about him. John Stonehouse M.P. published an account of his disappearance before his trial on insurance fraud charges, and Ernest Saunders and his son gave an account of his stewardship of Guinness in a book that received considerable publicity a few months before his trial on matters arising from the Guinness takeover of Distillers. Such literary effusions carry the danger for the author that they will be used in evidence against him or as fodder for his cross-examiner but this is not relevant to contempt. Where caution is required is in any references to prosecution witnesses, and any comment on specific charges or issues that the jury will have to decide. Mere repetition of matters already published should not be a problem, but overt attempts to elicit support for a defendant must be avoided (the title of Saunders' book was changed, on legal advice, from *Scapegoat* to *Nightmare*). Contempt will not apply to books and publications about defendants who face trial in the United States where this form of contempt would be incompatible with the First Amendment. Tom Bower's biography of Conrad Black came out shortly before Black's trial in Chicago and was virtually a case for the prosecution.

Contempt creates a difficult problem for individuals who are not witnesses, but who receive adverse publicity as a result of references to them at the trial or in pre-trial proceedings. Can they rebut false allegations while the trial is in motion? Not, it seems, when the result would be to suggest that a party to it is a liar. When a man on trial at the Old Bailey for serious offences made the fantastic claim that Edward Heath (in company with an Inspector of Police) had raped his wife, Heath instructed counsel to attend the court to put his denial on public record. This was not permitted until after the verdict. When a victim of outrageous allegations, made under privilege in court in which he is neither a party nor a witness, puts on public record immediately a short and emphatic denial, he does not in our view commit contempt of court. When Lord Goodman was mentioned in an unattractive light by a witness in the Jeremy Thorpe committal hearings, it is said that he went to the Attorney-General to demand redress, only to be advised that the best thing he could do was to stand on a soapbox in Trafalgar Square and proclaim his innocence. Limited protection against derogatory and irrelevant assertions can now be given by the criminal courts. These are discussed in Ch.8.

Defendants' convictions, bad character or admissions

7–019   Publishing derogatory information about a defendant's character or previous convictions before the verdict runs a risk of being contempt. Since the Criminal Justice Act 2003 the jury is much more likely to learn of previous convictions. However, the legislation requires trial judges to analyse carefully whether a particular conviction is admissible in evidence and often gives them a discretion to exclude it. Publishing convictions in advance may still risk prejudicing the trial by pre-empting this decision making process.

> In 1997 the *Evening Standard* was fined £40,000 for publishing details of the previous convictions of prisoners accused of trying to escape from Whitemoor prison in the middle of their trial. The jury would, of course, have been told that the defendants were in jail, but they would not have known that some were convicted IRA terrorists. The trial had had to be aborted in consequence of the *Standard*'s article.[49]
>
> The sport section of the *Sun* reported snooker player Ronnie O'Sullivan's determination to win the Master's title in celebration of his mother's release from prison after a 12–month prison sentence for VAT evasion. Unfortunately for the newspaper, Mrs O'Sullivan was then in the middle of a trial for dealing in obscene magazines. The jury, which should have been kept ignorant of her previous conviction, was discharged. The *Sun*'s publishers were fined £10,000 by the trial judge for an admitted contempt.[50]
>
> In 1990 the Court of Appeal held that *Private Eye* had created a serious risk of prejudice to Sonia Sutcliffe's libel action against it by blackguarding her character.[51] The allegations were grave (providing her husband with false alibis for murder and defrauding the DHSS). The trial was scheduled to take place only three months later and the magazine's large circulation in London posed a serious risk that it would be read by a juror. Because it was intended to put pressure on her to settle, there was also "intentional contempt" (see para.7–047).

Investigation of crime by newspapers can serve a valuable public **7–020** interest and has been praised in the past by police and courts. However, the different demands of newspapers and prosecutors can cause acute dilemmas.

> After a *News of the World* reporter infiltrated a suspected gang of forgers, the paper told the police who provided the cash to purchase counterfeit money. The police wanted to widen the investigation, but the newspaper said that it intended to publish on the day after the counterfeit notes were bought. So the police made their arrests immediately. This meant that the defendants' proceedings were active and the subsequent story was held to be in contempt. The principal features which disturbed the court were the assumption of guilt (but since the reporter had been central to the "sting" operation it would have been difficult to write the story otherwise), frequent reference to previous convictions and bad character and the striking manner in which the story was written. Ironically, the fact that the reporter was likely to be a key prosecution witness told against the newspaper. The court thought this made it more likely that the article would be remembered by a juror who would also be likely to recall the aspects (notably the previous convictions) which were prejudicial. The publishers were fined £50,000. A second investigative piece ("New Terror

---

[49] [1998] E.M.L.R. 711.
[50] *The Times*, March 2, 1996.
[51] *Att-Gen v Hislop* [1991] 1 Q.B. 514.

Gang Takes on Triad Thugs") was found not to be contempt of proceedings against two men accused of running an extortion racket in Birmingham. Although the defendants were pictured and described as leaders of a notorious Vietnamese gang wanted for questioning over a series of violent incidents, it did not assume their guilt and did not attribute any previous convictions to the defendants.[52]

There is no mechanical rule that reference to a defendant's previous convictions will constitute contempt. When actress Gillian Taylforth's boyfriend, Geoff Knights, was arrested for assault several papers referred to his previous conviction for assaulting a police officer. The Divisional Court held that these publications were not in contempt. Knights had been regularly in the news for the two previous years. The conviction (which had been extensively reported) had taken place only a month before his arrest. This and the fact that several months would elapse before the present trial meant that there was not a substantial risk that that trial would be seriously prejudiced.[53]

In 1992 Patrick Magee was arrested in connection with the murder of one police officer and the attempted murder of another. An early news broadcast from ITN and the first editions of several newspapers referred to Magee's earlier escape from Belfast's Crumlin Road jail where he had been serving a life sentence for the murder of an SAS officer. The critical factors in the failure of the Attorney-General to secure contempt convictions were that the publishers swiftly eliminated the prejudicial material, the circulation of the offending copies was small (and the news bulletin was not likely to be remembered) and, most importantly, the trial did not start until nine months later.[54]

Similarly, while it is usually safer not to refer to other, unrelated charges which are outstanding against a defendant, there is no invariable rule that publication of such matters will constitute contempt.[55]

7–021   Even if a defendant has admitted his guilt to journalists before the trial it may be a mistake to assume that there is no risk of contempt—as the case of the cleaning lady and the fridge illustrates.[56]

In 1996 Mrs Gilluley, a home help for 82–year-old Mrs Burgess, was secretly videoed by Mrs Burgess' son apparently stealing his mother's pension from where it was kept—in the fridge. The Manchester Evening News confronted Mrs Gilluley. She broke down and declared, "I won't be denying them. I don't know why I took it. I have just been

---

[52] Att-Gen v Morgan [1998] E.M.L.R. 294.
[53] Att-Gen v MGN Ltd [1997] 1 All E.R. 456.
[54] Att-Gen v ITN [1995] 2 All E.R. 370.
[55] Att-Gen v Guardian Newspapers Ltd (No.3) [1992] 1 W.L.R. 874.
[56] Att-Gen v Unger [1998] E.M.L.R. 280.

ill. I wanted to see a psychologist." Mrs Gilluley also made admissions to the police in interview. Newspapers published the story after legal advice that there was no substantial risk of prejudice because the case against Mrs Gilluley was open and shut. The Divisional Court roundly criticised that approach. It must not be assumed that because someone "confessed" to a crime that they would plead guilty to it, or that they *were* guilty. However strong the evidence, an accused might contest the charge and, in this case, the act of taking the money from the fridge as shown in the video did not prove she had the necessary criminal intent to be guilty of theft. The admissions to the reporters had been made before she had taken legal advice and by publishing the video pictures, the newspaper was bringing to the attention of potential jurors material which might be held inadmissible. However, the newspapers were acquitted of contempt because many months were likely to elapse between publication and trial and hence there was a low risk that any potential juror would recall the story. The articles were striking but "many such stories are told nowadays and the memory of them rapidly fades".

The approach of the court in this case is in marked contrast to the restrictive attitude in *Att-Gen v BBC and Hat Trick Productions Ltd*.[57]

Six months before the trial of Kevin and Ian Maxwell on fraud charges the programme *Have I Got News For You* asked contestants to pick the odd one out from Robert Maxwell, his two sons and Mirror Group pensioners. Angus Deayton said the correct answer was the pensioners,

". . from whose misfortunes the others have profited—no mentioning Maxwells, er, no names . . . the BBC are in fact cracking down on references to Ian and Kevin Maxwell just in case programme makers appear biased in their treatment of these two heartless scheming bastards."

At the end of the programme, the following was included:

Ian Hislop: "You're not going to leave in that bit about the Maxwell brothers being heartless scheming bastards?"
Angus Deayton: "Well. . . ."
Hislop: "Nothing personal Angus, contempt of court has a statutory two-year imprisonment . . . T.V.'s Mr Wandsworth Prison . . . You will find a lot of inmates will fancy you in there, Angus . . ."

The court found that the programme was in contempt of court because of its popularity, the fact that it was repeated (despite the request of the Maxwells' solicitor not to do so) and because the speakers were well known. Each defendant was fined £10,000 for a "most serious contempt".

The court failed to appreciate the ephemeral nature of comedy: the show went out so long before the trial even started (and which

---

[57] [1997] E.M.L.R. 76, QBD.

then lasted nine months) that it could not sensibly have prejudiced the jury deliberations. The decision is a breach of Art.10 since freedom of expression includes, perhaps most valuably of all, the freedom to make jokes.

Defendant's photograph

7–022 Publishing defendants' photographs can be contempt in criminal cases where the correctness of identification is in issue. The danger is that eyewitnesses for the prosecution may then describe the person in the newspaper's picture, rather than the person they saw at the scene of the crime. In 1994 *The Sun* was fined £80,000 and its editor £20,000 for publishing the photograph of a defendant just before he was about to take part in an identification parade. The prosecution was aborted in consequence.[58] In 1976 the *Evening Standard* was fined £1,000 for a similar contempt on the eve of an identification parade of the young Peter Hain who was falsely accused of bank robbery. It made no difference that the picture caption was "Hain, he's no bank robber".[59] It may be difficult for the media to know whether identity will be in issue. Defence solicitors may be willing to tell the press about their clients' defences, but they are under no obligation to assist the media.

> The Attorney-General did repeatedly warn the media in 2003 not to name two premiership league footballers who were suspected of rape since identity was going to be in issue. The *Daily Star* overlooked these warnings and named two of the suspects. Although the two men were not in the event prosecuted, the Court held that the publication of their names had posed a substantial risk of serious prejudice and the offence was exacerbated because the warnings had been ignored. The publishers were fined £60,000.[60]

It has become more common for the Attorney-General to issue "warnings" to the press about what he perceives to be contempt risks. These can be useful where (as in the *Daily Star* case) they alert the media to the fact that a particular issue is likely to be controversial in a future trial. However, the "warnings" have no special legal status. The media can still take their own advice as to whether their particular publication would infringe the contempt standards and, if the matter came to court, it would be those legal tests (rather than the Attorney-General's "warnings") which the Court would have to apply.

The problem of photographs can become acute when an arrest warrant has been issued for a suspect who is still at large. For

---

[58] *The Independent*, July 6, 1994.
[59] *R. v Evening Standard, Ex p Att-Gen*, *The Times*, November 3, 1976.
[60] *Att-Gen v Express Newspapers Ltd* [2005] E.M.L.R. 13.

example, photographs of Neville Heath, wanted for a sex murder, were not published after his first victim was discovered, for fear of contempt. If the press had published the photographs, he might have been arrested before he struck a second time and a life would have been saved.[61] In recognition of this problem, the Attorney-General has now said that pictures of wanted persons issued by the police can be published by the media without risk of contempt.[62] Since he has a monopoly on this type of prosecution for contempt, his assurance gives the media a practical immunity.

Witnesses

Many eyewitness accounts of crimes appear in the press without **7–023** attracting contempt charges. It will be relatively rare for this to cause a "substantial risk of serious prejudice" and so satisfy the strict liability test. Since strict liability contempt can be committed only when a prosecution is under way, there is not even this risk if a suspect has not been arrested, charged or been made the subject of a warrant. However, any publication that seeks to deter or intimidate prospective witnesses will certainly be vulnerable to contempt proceedings. A specific offence of intimidating witnesses, potential witnesses or jurors was introduced in 1994 to supplement the contempt power.[63] It applies only to actual or potential criminal proceedings. There must have been an act which intimidated and was intended to intimidate a person knowing or believing that the other person was assisting in the investigation of an offence, or is a witness or potential witness or juror or potential juror with the intention of obstructing, perverting or interfering with the course of justice. Both intimidation and threats of revenge are punishable with a maximum sentence of five years imprisonment. It will not be contempt, however, to publish an advertisement for witnesses to come forward to assist a particular party, so long as the advertisement is worded neutrally and any reward is not extravagant.[64] It is also an offence under the Theft Act 1968, s.23 to advertise for the return of stolen goods and promise to ask no questions. Advertiser and publisher can be fined on level 3 (current maximum £1,000).

Payment to witnesses for their stories before they give evidence is usually undesirable and will attract judicial criticism, although curiously no contempt case has yet been brought to deter the practice. There is an obvious danger that bought witnesses will become sold on their stories. They are tempted to exaggerate evidence in order to increase its saleability, and they may become committed to inaccurate stories ghosted by reporters, and have a financial inducement to

---

[61] Steve Chibnall, *Law and Order News* (Tavistock, 1977), p.53.

[62] *Hansard*, H.C. Debs [1981] Vol.1000, col.34.

[63] Criminal Justice and Public Order Act 1994, s.51.

[64] *Plating Co v Farquharson* (1881) 17 Ch. D 49 at 55; *cf.* "Payment to Witnesses and Contempt of Court" [1975] Crim.L.R. 144.

stick to them in the witness box. The worst example was the *Sunday Telegraph* arrangement to pay Peter Bessell an additional fee of £25,000 if his evidence secured the conviction of Jeremy Thorpe. This deal wholly discredited Bessel's evidence in the eyes of the jury.[65] The paper claimed that Bessell had already been committed to his story when he signed the contract, but there is no doubt that the "escalation clause" in the contract substantially prejudiced the prosecution case. Contracts with witnesses were made on a staggering scale in the trial of Rosemary West for murder. No less than 19 witnesses were alleged to have received money from, or signed contracts with, the media. One witness denied on oath that she had received payments from the press, but after Mirror Group Newspapers alerted the prosecution to the existence of an agreement, she accepted that she had been wrong. The trial judge warned the jury to keep these dealings in their minds when assessing witnesses' credibility. The jury nonetheless convicted and the Court of Appeal refused to quash the conviction.[66] Likewise, the Court of Appeal refused to set aside the conviction of three men found guilty of the murders of three drug dealers whose bodies were found in a car in Rettenden, Essex. The appeal failed even though it emerged that the star prosecution witness (Nicholls/Bloggs 19) had collaborated with an author on a book and TV programme. The Court of Appeal warned of the dangers of these kinds of contracts but upheld the convictions because they still considered the verdicts to be safe.[67] The *News of the World* also included an escalation clause (£10,000 if acquittal, £25,000 if conviction) to the alleged victim of an indecent assault by the pop star Gary Glitter. The judge described the contract as "reprehensible" and to be deprecated, but not illegal.[68] Payments or other arrangements with witnesses could not, on their own, amount to strict liability contempt since this is confined to publications[69] but the arrangements might be a deliberate contempt if the necessary intention to prejudge the trial could be inferred. At present, payments to witnesses are contrary to the Press Complaints Commission's declaration on "chequebook journalism" (see para.4–027), although the widespread disregard for that declaration may cause the Attorney-General to take action for contempt in an appropriate case.

7–024 Not all payments to witnesses are objectionable. Experts who are due to give evidence, for instance, might be paid a reasonable but not excessive sum for summarising their conclusions on television. In the *Schering Chemicals* case the Court of Appeal said it was unlikely that their evidence would thereby be affected.[70]

---

[65] See *New Statesman*, July 27, 1979.
[66] *R. v West* [1996] 2 Cr.App.R. 374.
[67] *R. v Steele and Whomes* [2006] EWCA Crim 195].
[68] The Press Complaints Commission's adjudication of December 5, 1999 in relation to this is on its website *www.pcc.org.uk*.
[69] Contempt of Court Act 1981, s.2(1).
[70] *Schering Chemicals Ltd v Falkman Ltd*, fn.32 above.

The press has on many occasions aided the administration of justice by finding important witnesses. For instance the *Sunday Times* in 1976 discovered and interviewed a crucial witness who had set up drug deals on behalf of a police team to whom he said he paid a share of the proceeds of the drugs. The newspaper supplied a transcript of his evidence to the prosecution and defence: his allegations of police misconduct caused charges against 31 defendants arrested by the police team to be dropped.[71]

Sometimes witnesses have been jealously hidden from journalistic rivals. Again, this is not in itself contempt, though it may sow suspicion that the witness's evidence has been affected. The line is crossed if the witness's evidence is tampered with or the witness is concealed from the police or prosecuting authorities. In 1924 the *Evening Standard* was fined £1,000 for contempt when, amongst other things, it hid a key murder witness with the wife of a sub-editor.[72] When Monica Coghlan, the prostitute claiming to have had sex with Jeffrey Archer, was being "minded" by the *News of the World*, she passed the time having sex with one her minders. This did not help her credibility or that of the tabloids when it was revealed at the libel trial.

Revealing a "payment into court"

"Payment into court" is a common tactical ploy by defendants in   **7–025** civil litigation. It is a formal offer to settle for the paid-in sum. If the offer is refused and less than that sum is eventually awarded, the claimants cannot recover their legal costs after the date of the payment in. Rules of court require such a payment to be kept secret, even from the trial judge.[73] A newspaper that disclosed the fact would run a serious risk of contempt.[74]

Television coverage of criminal trials

It is common for television to set up outside courts to cover the   **7–026** entries and exits of participants in notable trials. So long perhaps as there is no element of harassment, there can be no question of contempt unless members of the jury are deliberately pictured or otherwise identified. The traditional concern to protect jurors from any kind of embarrassment or reprisal might incline any judge to rule that such media conduct would pose a serious threat to the administration of justice.

One difficulty that British justice has yet to confront stems from mass-media coverage of security arrangements, especially at trials of

---

[71] *R. v Ameer and Lucas* [1977] Crim. L.R. 104.
[72] *R. v Evening Standard Ex p. DPP* (1924) 40 T.L.R. 833.
[73] Civil Procedure Rules, Pt 36, r.19(2).
[74] *R. v Wealdstone and Harrow News*; *Harley v Sholl* [1925] W.N. 153.

alleged terrorists. Television news eagerly shows the sharpshooters on the court roof, the police helicopters overhead and the sniffer dogs in the courtyard. There is no doubt that such reports conduce to an atmosphere in which the defendant's guilt as a terrorist comes to be generally assumed, and this factor may have played a part in the wrongful convictions of Irish defendants for the Guildford and Birmingham pub bombings. Highly prejudicial press and television reports of security arrangements have not in the past been prosecuted as amounting to a contempt. But where details are withheld from jurors, to avoid prejudice to the defendants, it will be difficult to resist rulings prohibiting the media from informing them of these arrangements, at least until the trial is over.

The "active" or *sub judice* period

7–027 The restrictions imposed by strict liability contempt do not apply from the moment that a crime is committed or a civil dispute flares up: legal proceedings must have been started and reached a particular stage at the time the story reaches the public. This section will examine these points at which a case becomes *sub judice* or, in the terminology of the 1981 Act, "active".[75] Unless a case is "active", there is no risk of committing strict liability contempt, but it is important to remember that "activity" is a necessary and not a sufficient condition. Stories can be written, even about active cases, as long as they do not then pose a substantial risk of serious prejudice.

Commencement of strict liability periods

7–028 *Criminal proceedings* become active as soon as the first formal step in launching a prosecution is taken. This may be an arrest by a police officer, or the charging of a person who has gone voluntarily to a police station or to court. The first step may alternatively be the issue of a warrant by a magistrate for a suspect's arrest or the issue of a summons ordering a person to appear at court on a specified day,[76] or a public prosecutor's requisition for a charge to be heard.[77] If one case involves several of these steps, it becomes active on the first.

Although these tests are more precise than the previous common law (by which the media could commit contempt if proceedings were "imminent"), they are still ambiguous. A man "helping the police with their inquiries" may or may not be arrested. An arrest warrant may or may not have been issued for a suspect. The media have no right to be told,[78] although they have a defence (see para.7–037) if,

---

[75] Contempt of Court Act 1981, s.2(3).
[76] Contempt of Court Act 1981, Sch.1, para.4.
[77] Criminal Justice Act 2003, s.29.
[78] *R. v Secretary of State for the Home Department Ex p. Westminster Press Ltd* (1992) 4 Admin. L.R. 445.

after taking all reasonable care, they have no reason to suspect that one of the critical steps has been taken. If they know enough to realise that one of the steps might have been taken and they guess wrongly, they may be in contempt.

Press reporting is not frozen indefinitely if a suspect for whom an arrest warrant has been issued is not caught: 12 months after its issue the proceedings cease to be active and the media are then free to comment until the actual arrest.[79]

The practice of maintaining internet accessible archives has the **7–029** potential to cause contempt problems. Stories which are risk free when first posted (because there are no active proceedings) may take on a different character if criminal proceedings are later started. A Scottish court has adopted the rule in defamation (see para.3–039) that there was a fresh publication each time the site was accessed.[80] However, even if there was a technical publication during the active period, the question would remain as to whether *that* publication caused a substantial risk of serious prejudice. Most stories will experience a rapid tail-off in the number of hits shortly after their first posting and statistics of this kind will help to show that the risk of prejudice has been very small.

"Publication" though does require some form of dissemination. Merely producing an article, even if preparatory to an intended publication is not itself a contempt.[81]

Civil proceedings become active when a trial date is fixed or when the case is "set down for trial."[82] "Setting down" used to be a stage in High Court proceedings when a case entered the lists of those ready to be tried. The term is not used in the Civil Procedure Rules which now govern proceedings in both the High Court and County Court and so the fixing of a date for the trial or hearing is the only practical determinant of when a civil case becomes active.

A party to civil proceedings may seek an order of the court on a **7–030** procedural or interim matter before trial. These interlocutory applications are also shielded by contempt, although because the application will be heard by a legally qualified master or district judge the chance of it being prejudiced by press comment in most cases will be too remote. These applications are regarded as "active" from the time a date is fixed for the hearing until the hearing is completed.[83] When several applications are made, the case will resemble a restless poltergeist, passing through periods of activity and repose.

---

[79] Contempt of Court Act 1981, Sch.1, para.11.
[80] *HM Advocate v Beggs (No.2)* 2002 SLT 139 HCJ. For other discussions on the meaning of "publication" see para.8–064.
[81] *Yousaf v Luton Crown Court* [2006] EWCA Crim 469.
[82] Contempt of Court Act 1981, Sch.1, paras 12 and 13.
[83] 1981 Act, Sch.1, paras 12, 13.

Journalists ought to be able to find out if a date has been fixed for a hearing by inquiring at the court where the case will be heard. The Attorney-General has instructed court officials to assist journalists.[84]

Termination of strict liability periods

7–031 *Criminal proceedings* are over if the jury returns a "not guilty" verdict, or if the prosecution drops the charges.[85] A guilty verdict is more complex. The proceedings continue to be active until the offender is sentenced. The courts have expressly disapproved of a premature press clamour that might give the appearance of affecting the sentence, although it is unlikely that contempt proceedings would be brought unless the publication amounts to a deliberate attempt to put pressure on a judge to hand down a particular sentence.

The period of activity continues if the court remands the defendant for a social inquiry report or if the case has been tried by magistrates who think their powers of sentence are insufficient and they decide to commit the defendant to the Crown Court for punishment. The case ceases to be active if sentence is formally deferred for a fixed period to allow the defendant a chance to show that he or she can make good.[86] If the jury disagrees, the proceedings remain active unless the prosecution indicates that it will not seek a new trial.[87] Since 1997 the possibility exists that a person who is acquitted may be retried for the same offence.[88] Ordinarily an acquittal is final, but if it is followed by a conviction of the defendant or some other person for an "administration of justice offence" (perjury, perverting the course of justice or intimidating witnesses or jurors) the judge at the second trial must consider whether there was a real possibility that the previous acquittal was tainted. If so, the second trial judge may issue a certificate. Thereafter, the original proceedings become active again for the purpose of strict liability contempt.[89] Before the defendant can be retried for the original offence, the prosecution has to obtain an order from the High Court quashing the original acquittal.[90] This may be many weeks after the certificate was issued because the order cannot be made if there is an appeal outstanding against the administration of justice offence. The

---

[84] This was said during the Committee stage of the Contempt of Court Bill: Standing Committee A May 12, 1981, col. 141.

[85] Contempt of Court Act 1981, Sch.1. para.5.

[86] 1981 Act, Sch.1, para.6.

[87] *Att-Gen v News Group Newspapers* (1982) 4 Cr.App.R. (S) 182.

[88] Criminal Procedure and Investigations Act 1996, s.54.

[89] Contempt of Court Act 1981, Sch.1 para.4A. The Crown Court at which the administration of justice offence is tried and, if different, the Crown Court at which the original trial took place, must display a copy of the certificate in public for 28 days—Criminal Procedure Rules 2005 (SI 2005/384) r.40.6.

[90] Criminal Procedure and Investigations Act 1996, ss.54 and 55.

High Court's decision (whether to make the order or not) must be sent to the Crown Court or courts concerned and they must display the notice in public for 28 days.[91]

Civil proceedings end when they are disposed of, discontinued or withdrawn.[92]

Appeals

Appeal proceedings are active from the time when they are launched **7–032** by the lodging of a formal notice of appeal or application for permission to appeal.[93] The losing party's declaration of intent to appeal is not enough. There will often be a period, perhaps quite short, between the end of active trial proceedings and the commencement of active appeal proceedings during which the strict liability rule does not apply at all and comment is quite free. Even if appeal proceedings have become active, it is virtually inconceivable that appellate judges will be influenced by what appears in the media. When an appeal is disposed of, abandoned, discontinued or withdrawn, even this restraint is removed unless the case is remitted to the trial court or unless a new trial is ordered, in which case new proceedings are treated as active from the conclusion of the appellate proceedings.[94]

Defences

Public interest defence

An important defence is provided for the media by s.5 of the **7–033** Contempt of Court Act. This is intended to ensure that public debate and criticism on matters of importance can continue, even though a side-effect of expounding the main theme is that ongoing proceedings might be prejudiced. The section reads:

> "A publication made as or as part of a discussion in good faith of public affairs or other matters of general public interest is not to be treated as contempt of court under the strict liability rule if the risk of impediment or prejudice is merely incidental to the discussion."

Section 5 was given a liberal interpretation (for its time) by the House of Lords in the first test case:

> The Attorney-General accused the *Daily Mail* of prejudicing the trial of a doctor who was charged with allowing a Down's syndrome baby to

---

[91] Criminal Procedure Rules, r.40.8.
[92] Contempt of Court Act 1981, Sch.1, para.12.
[93] 1981 Act, Sch.1, para.15.
[94] 1981 Act, Sch.1, para.16.

die. The *Daily Mail* had published an article by Malcolm Muggeridge in support of a "Pro-Life" candidate in a contemporaneous by-election. He spoke disparagingly of what he described as the common practice of doctors deliberately failing to keep deformed children alive. The House of Lords said the defence was applicable. Even if the public understood the article as a reference to the trial, it was not contempt. Academics might enjoy abstract discussions, but the press was entitled to make great issues come alive by reference to concrete examples.

> "Gagging of bona fide discussion of controversial matters of general public interest merely because there are in existence contemporaneous legal proceedings in which some particular instance of those controversial matters may be in issue is what section 5 . . . was intended to prevent."

The court also emphasised that protection was not lost merely because the article could have been written without the prejudicial material:

> "The test is not whether the article could have been written as effectively without the passage or some other phraseology might have been substituted for it that would have reduced the risk of prejudice to Dr Arthur's fair trial; it is whether the risk created by the words actually chosen by the author was merely incidental to the discussion which I take to mean no more than an incidental consequence of expounding the main theme".[95]

7–034 Sir John Junor was fined £1,000 and the *Sunday Express* £10,000 for a comment that prejudiced the same trial.[96] This piece directly criticised the doctor, on the basis of facts reported in the prosecution case that were subsequently proved incorrect. Section 5 was not applicable, because there was no discussion of wider issues. Neither writer nor newspaper tried to defend this blatant contempt, committed in mid-trial. By contrast, the section provided an alternative basis for acquitting the *Guardian* of contempt of court in 1992. The paper had written an article about the frequency with which judges were making orders postponing the reporting of criminal proceedings because of further cases which were due to be tried in the future and which involved the same defendants or similar evidence (see para.8–076 for consideration of these orders). It gave an example of one case then being tried where, it said, reporting had to be deferred because of other criminal proceedings that were due to take place in the Isle of Man. The English judge stopped his trial because of the article. However, the Divisional Court was not persuaded that it had created a serious risk of substantial prejudice and, even if it had, the risk had only been incidental to a discussion of the wider phenomenon of the use of postponement orders.[97]

---

[95] *Att-Gen v English*, fn.29 above. See also the recommendation of the Phillimore Committee, para.142, on which the section was based, and the Australian decisions that spell out a similar defence: *Re "Truth & Sportsmen" Ex p. Bread Manufactures* (1937) 37 S.R.N.S.W. 249; *Brych v The Herald and Weekly Times* [1978] V.R. 727.

[96] *The Times*, December 19, 1981.

[97] *Att-Gen v Guardian Newspapers Ltd* [1992] 3 All E.R. 38.

In 1989 the Divisional Court said that in deciding whether the risk of prejudice was incidental, it was necessary to look at the subject-matter of the discussion and see how closely it related to the particular legal proceedings.

> In the middle of a trial of a Reading landlord charged with conspiring to defraud the Department of Health and Social Security, TVS broadcast a programme called *The New Rachmans* about sham bed-and-breakfast accommodation in Reading. The court accepted that the programme attempted to analyse the cause of the new wave of Rachmanism in the South of England, but it focused on a small number of landlords in Reading. The programme included still photographs of two of the defendants, who were recognisable although their faces had been blacked out. The trial of the defendants was aborted at a cost of £215,000. The broadcaster and a newspaper that had previewed the programme under the headline "Reading's new wave of harassment . . . TV focus on bedsit barons" were found guilty of contempt.[98]

The defence is dependent on good faith. "Bad faith" means more than unreasonable or wrongheaded opinions. There must be an element of improper motive, such as a deliberate attempt to prejudice proceedings under cover of a public discussion. The burden of proving "bad faith", or of negating the defence generally, rests on the prosecution throughout[99]—another factor that makes the "public discussion" defence a broad shield for investigative reporting.

Section 5 does not afford protection only where the subject of **7–035** general interest has already been under discussion before the proceedings commenced. It would apply in situations where the public interest has been generated by the proceedings themselves. Had the Muggeridge article not been tied to the platform of a by-election candidate, but rather had taken the form of a general discussion of the morality of euthanasia in relation to deformed babies, a topic given prominence by the trial, it should still have been protected by s.5.

> The sculptor Anthony Noel-Kelly made casts of parts of bodies which had been taken from the Royal College of Surgeons. He was on trial for complicity in their alleged theft when the *Observer* published a full-page critique of his work described as necrophilic art and displaying (but not in any sexual sense) a love of the dead as had the American mass murderer Jeffrey Dahmer. The paper was acquitted of contempt. The Court thought that the risk which the article posed was of

---

[98] *Att-Gen v TVS Television*; *Att-Gen v H.W. Southey & Sons Ltd, The Times,* July 7, 1989.
[99] *Att-Gen v English*, fn.29 above.

substantial prejudice to the trial, but was not persuaded that the Attorney-General had discharged his onus of showing that the risk was serious. Although it was not necessary for its decision, the court went on to say that it would have rejected the paper's alternative argument that it was protected by s.5. The judges were prepared to accept that necrophilic art and Kelly's place in it were matters of public interest, but the reality was that the article about Kelly and his activities concerned matters of public interest because of (not independently of) the trial. Thus any prejudice was not "merely incidental" to the discussion.[100]

Some limits on s.5 are consonant with the requirements of the European Convention on Human Rights. In *Worm v Austria*[101] the applicant had written a commentary about the ongoing prosecution of a former Vice-Chancellor of Austria for tax evasion. The court said that the existence of current court proceedings did not preclude media comment which could contribute to their publicity consistently with the fair trial guarantees in Art.6(1) as well as Art.10. Moreover, the media's right and duty to impart information and the public's right to receive it were all the greater where a public figure was involved. But public figures were entitled to a fair trial and the limits of permissible comment could not extend to statements which were likely to prejudice, whether intentionally or not, the chances of a person receiving a fair trial and especially when the tribunal includes lay persons who are more at risk of being influenced by the media.

Innocent distributors

7–036 Strict liability contempt is committed only by publishing an infringing story, but the definition of "publishing" is a wide one.[102] It applies to anyone in the chain of distribution from printer or importer to news vendor. However, distributors can usually rely on the defence that they did not know (having taken all reasonable care) that their wares contained a contempt and they had no reason to suspect that they were likely to do so.[103] To demonstrate this, distributors sometimes insist that magazines provide them with a lawyer's opinion that the publication is free of contempt. Even if the lawyer is wrong, the distributor will then have taken all reasonable care and can rely on the defence.

Innocent publishers

7–037 This defence is open to publishers and broadcasters, but it is much narrower. It helps only those who did not know and had no reason to suspect that the proceedings in question were active. Again all

---

[100] *Att-Gen v Guardian Newspapers Ltd* [1999] E.M.L.R. 904.
[101] (1997) 25 E.H.R.R. 454.
[102] Contempt of Court Act 1981, s.2(1).
[103] 1981 Act, s.3(2).

reasonable care must have been taken.[104] The burden lies on both distributor and publisher to show that the defence is established, although that burden may be satisfied on the balance of probabilities.[105] It is very important, therefore, that journalists should make contemporaneous notes of all their inquiries (e.g. to police or lawyers acting for the parties or at the court). These notes should be kept as evidence that the appropriate inquiries were made, and that nothing was said to alert the reporter to the fact that the case was "active".[106]

This defence does not help a paper that knew that the proceedings were active, but published by mistake a reference to the defendant's murky past.[107] Even if the paper takes ordinary precautions to eliminate prejudicial material, it is guilty of contempt. The requirement that the publisher had "no reason to suspect" that the proceedings were active narrows the defence still further. A journalist who knew that a man was helping the police with their inquiries would probably have reason to suspect that the man might be arrested before the paper was published, unless the police had said something to suggest otherwise.

If care has been taken to establish a sound vetting procedure, there can be no realistic danger of a prison sentence. If an article is published during the course of the trial, the common practice now is for the judge to invite the publisher or editor to make representations as to whether the matter should be referred to the Attorney-General. If the publication has happened by mistake (and mistakes inevitably occur even in well-regulated and "night-lawyered" newspaper offices) a full explanation and fulsome apology to the court may satisfy the judge that no further action is necessary. These representations, though, need to be carefully judged. They can be used against the newspaper if the matter is taken further. If contempt proceedings are successfully taken against a paper, the most likely penalty would then be a fine, though the amounts can be substantial and the contempt remains a criminal conviction. It would be fairer to allow publishers a simple and complete defence that the contempt was published despite all reasonable care.

Fair and accurate reports

No contempt is committed by contemporaneous publishing in good 7–038 faith of a fair and accurate report of court proceedings, however prejudicial that report may be to a party involved in the case. The requirements of this defence are considered further at para.8–077.

---

[104] 1981 Act, s.3(1).
[105] 1981 Act, s.3(3); *R. v Carr-Briant* [1943] K.B. 607.
[106] e.g. *Att-Gen v News Group Newspapers Ltd*, unreported, February 9, 1996—see *The Yearbook of Media and Entertainment Law* (1997/8) p.323.
[107] *R. v Thomson Newspapers Ltd Ex p. Att-Gen* [1968] 1 All E.R. 268.

Gagging claims

7–039 A "gagging claim" is the device of attempting to suppress media criticism by issuing a claim for libel against one critic, and threatening contempt proceedings if the criticism, now the subject of litigation, is repeated by anyone else. The courts have declined to allow their contempt jurisdiction to be exploited in this fashion by the likes of fascist leader Oswald Mosley and company fraudsman Dr Wallersteiner.[108] The interests of the administration of justice will prevail over freedom of speech only if the proposed publication would constitute "strict liability" contempt. As explained above, there will only be liability if the defence of public interest is not applicable and the publication would be likely to cause a substantial risk of serious prejudice.

The significance of the gagging claim is much reduced by the rule that strict liability for contempt does not begin with the issue of proceedings, but is only activated after a hearing date has been fixed. Nonetheless, the pertinent words of Lord Salmon may still need to be quoted to solicitors who try to bluff the media out of publishing criticisms of their clients with threats that the matter is "*sub judice*":

> "It is a widely held fallacy that the issue of a writ automatically stifles further comment. There is no authority that I know of to support the view that further comment would amount to contempt of court. Once a newspaper has justified, and there is some prima facie support for this justification, the plaintiff cannot obtain an interlocutory injunction to restrain the defendants from repeating the matters complained of. In these circumstances it is obviously wrong to suppose that they could be committing a contempt by doing so. It seems to me equally obvious that no other newspaper that repeats the same sort of criticism is committing a contempt of court. They may be publishing a libel, and if they do so, and they have no defence to it, they will have to pay whatever may be the appropriate damages; but the writ does not, in my view, preclude the publication of any further criticism; it merely puts the person who makes the further criticism at risk of being sued for libel."[109]

THIRD PARTY COSTS ORDERS

7–040 In 2004 the criminal courts acquired a new power to order a third party to pay all or part of costs which were wasted as a result of the third party's "serious misconduct".[110] The term "serious misconduct"

---

[108] *R. v Fox Ex p. Mosley, Guardian*, February 17, 1966; *Wallersteiner v Moir* [1974] 3 All E.R. 217.

[109] *Thomson v Times Newspapers Ltd* [1969] 3 All E.R. 648 at 651.

[110] See Prosecution of Offences Act 1985, s.19B added by the Courts Act 2003, s.93 and Costs in Criminal Cases (General) Regulations 1986 (SI 1986/1335) Reg.3F.

is not further defined, except in a negative fashion—it may, but need not, be contempt of court.

The change was clearly made with the media in mind (although ironically one of the first occasions in which it was used was against the Home Office which had dragged its feet in providing information required by the Court of Appeal Criminal Division[111]). Parliament was concerned at the wasted costs which were caused when trials had had to be abandoned because of prejudicial publicity or other activities of the press. Shortly before, there had been the very expensive collapse of a trial of Leeds footballers as a result of an article published in the *Sunday Mirror*. An interview with the victim's father had suggested that the offence was racially motivated when the prosecution's position throughout the trial had been that there was no evidence of racism. Yet this was a poor reason for enacting new legislation. The Attorney-General took action against the publishers for contempt. They admitted guilt and were ordered to pay a fine of £75,000.[112] The cost of the aborted trial was put at over £1 million, but the Court took account of MGN's previous good record for observing the contempt restrictions, the fact that the publisher had acted on legal advice and its unreserved apology. This hardly demonstrated a lacuna in the law of contempt and it is difficult to see how a much larger "wasted costs" order could satisfy the proportionality test in Art.10.

This case prompts further questions. Was it really necessary to abort the trial? Should the judge instead have given the jury firm directions to ignore the newspaper article and to decide the case on the evidence presented in court? More importantly, if a newspaper is to be at risk of contempt proceedings or a third party costs order, should it have the right to make representations to the trial judge before a decision is taken to abort a trial? In theory it would be possible for the newspaper in those later proceedings to argue that the judge had acted too precipitously, but in practice this task would be very difficult.

There was some alarm amongst the media as to the limits of the **7–041** new power to make third party costs orders, particularly if it was not confined to recognised categories of contempt. Although it is premature for the media to breathe a collective sigh of relief, there has certainly been no flood of costs orders against newspapers in the first years of the power's existence. And there are features of the power which provide some protection for the media if applications are made.

There must be "misconduct" on the part of the media. While the legislation and regulations say that this need not be contempt, the term would require the court to consider the right of freedom of expression in Art.10 of the ECHR. Unless a limitation on that right

---

[111] *R v Argon Ahmati* [2007] P.N.L.R. 3.
[112] *Att-Gen v MGN Ltd* [2002] EWHC 907 (Admin).

was justified under Art.10(2) it would be impossible to characterise the exercise of the right as "misconduct". Next, the misconduct must have caused the waste of costs. This should mean that if for some independent reason the costs were wasted or the proceedings had to be aborted for some other cause, the media third party could not be required to pay the costs. Even if there has been misconduct, the court must decide whether it is "appropriate" to make a costs order. In other words, the court has a discretion and Art.10 would again require the court to maintain a proper sense of proportionality between the misconduct and the amount of the costs order (if any) which is imposed. The costs order must itself specify the amount of the costs[113] which suggests that the process of fixing the amount is a summary one and should, in turn, err on the side of caution in the estimate of the amount of costs which have been wasted.

There are also procedural protections. Proper notice must be given to the third party of the proposal to make an order, including a summary of the facts on which reliance is placed and details of the alleged misconduct.[114] The third party has the right to be heard and to lead evidence[115] and to appeal—to the Crown Court when the order has been made by magistrates, to the Court of Appeal when the order is made by the Crown Court.[116]

7–042   The real problem for which the legislation does not specifically provide, is that some trial judges, ramped up by the rhetoric of defence counsel (who may have other reasons for this tactic if the trial is going badly for their clients) may discharge juries in cases where any prejudice could be cured by a strong direction to ignore the contemptuous—and contemptible—article. There was no need, for example, to discharge the jury in the Leeds footballers' case. This article—about the father of a victim who was convinced that the murder was racist—was emotional and certainly should not have been published, but did not affix guilt to any defendant and the prejudice might have been dissipated by a strong direction. Judges— often themselves the product of the cult of media suspicion which is rife at the defence bar—often give juries too little credit for their ability to make up their own collective mind. This may change as more judges have the valuable experience of serving on a jury-as a result of recent government reforms which allow barristers and (regrettably) policemen to serve as well.

DELIBERATE CONTEMPT

7–043   The 1981 Act is not an exhaustive treatment of the law of contempt. It deals principally with strict liability contempt, which is committed irrespective of the publisher's intentions, and it expressly preserves

---

[113] Costs in Criminal Cases (General) Regulations 1986, Reg.3F(6).
[114] 1986 Regulations, Reg.3G.
[115] 1986 Regulation, Reg.3F(4).
[116] 1986 Regulation, Reg.3H.

other forms of contempt developed by the courts through their powers at common law.[117] Deliberate contempt does not attract the public interest defence in section 5 of the Act, although the requirement that the prosecution must prove a specific intention to prejudice the administration of justice offers some comfort to media defendants. Furthermore, any action for contempt against the media would have to satisfy the requirements of Art.10 of the ECHR. In particular, the action would need to be "necessary in a democratic society" and that would require the action to be proportionate to the legitimate aim that was being pursued. The offence carries no right to trial by jury—a factor that undoubtedly secured convictions for the Government against newspapers that published Peter Wright's memoirs, *Spycatcher* which it might not have obtained from a "gang of twelve".

Intentionally prejudicing potential criminal proceedings and civil jury trials

It is an offence at common law to publish material that is designed 7–044 to prejudice criminal proceedings that are pending or "imminent" even if not yet under way. There is an important distinction between agitating for a prosecution to be brought against a particular individual, which is permissible, and deliberately poisoning the public perception of an individual whom you know is about to be prosecuted. This distinction was crucial to finding the *Sun* guilty of deliberate contempt in 1988 for viciously whipping up hostility to a doctor against whom it had already decided to bring a private prosecution:

> The editor of the *Sun* heard that the DPP had declined to prosecute a distinguished doctor over an allegation that he had raped a young child. He decided that the newspaper would pay for a private prosecution, to be brought by the child's mother, on the secret condition that the mother would provide interviews and pictures exclusively to the *Sun* and would not talk to any other media. The day after this deal was signed, the *Sun* published a vitriolic front-page character assassination of the unnamed doctor ("a beast and a swine"), declared him guilty of rape, and boasted that it was going to fund his prosecution. The next day, after a "dial-a-quote" M.P. had helpfully named the doctor under parliamentary privilege, the *Sun* continued its character-assassination, accusing the doctor of other sexual crimes and of permanently injuring his victim. Despite such blatant attempts to destroy the doctor's right to a fair trial, he was subsequently acquitted, unlike the *Sun*, which was convicted of criminal contempt and fined £75,000. The verdict itself cannot be questioned—the *Sun's* conduct was an arrogant abuse of media power which would be regarded as wrong in any country that seriously endorses the principle that a

---

[117] Contempt of Court Act 1981, s.6(c).

defendant is entitled to a fair trial. The decision may be interpreted as turning upon the fact that the newspaper negotiated its agreement with the mother *before* it embarked upon the campaign to discredit the person whose prosecution it had undertaken to support. Had this course not been contemplated, and had the articles been designed instead to criticise the DPP (or even to put pressure on him to change his mind), this should not have been regarded as contemptuous.[118]

Thus, the *Sun* case does not prevent publishers or broadcasters trying to sting the authorities into bringing proceedings. Encouraging the initiation of a prosecution is not by itself prejudicial to the administration of justice. What made the *Sun* articles prejudicial was the newspaper's intention to finance a private prosecution coupled with the article's assumption of guilt, the inflammatory language and the reference to allegations of similar but unrelated offences, which would (even if true) then have been kept from a jury and which would, today, only be admitted with the trial judge's permission. Equally, it is not intentional contempt for defence campaigns to urge the police or the Attorney-General to abandon a prosecution. The decision to prosecute involves a consideration of the public interest, and defence committees are entitled to urge their view of what this entails. The same is true when the prosecution is brought by a private individual. The Attorney-General can always take over and stop a private prosecution, and a campaign pamphlet calling on him to do this would not be contempt. Any attempt to go further and to threaten prosecution witnesses with ostracism or calumny is much more dangerous and might well constitute contempt or the statutory offence of intimidation of witnesses (see para.7–023).

7–045   Although the House of Lords declined to hear an appeal by the *Sun*, some doubt about the correctness of the Divisional Court's decision that contempt could be committed by publications prior to arrest arises from the subsequent case of *Attorney-General v Sport Newspapers Ltd*[119]:

A man with previous convictions for rape went "on the run" after a 15-year-old schoolgirl disappeared from her home. Police treated him as a suspect and notified all newspapers (through the Press Association) about his previous convictions, with a warning that nothing should be published about them lest this jeopardise his possible trial. It is no business of the police to tell newspapers what they may or may not print; it is their business to obtain arrest warrants for suspects, which in this case they failed to do until 10 days had elapsed and the *Sunday Sport* had treated its readers to a lurid account of the man's "sex monster" past, thanks no doubt to the police tip-off. The man was later caught and convicted of murder. The *Sport* could not be prosecuted for strict liability contempt, as the proceedings were not active at the time

---

[118] *Att-Gen v News Group Newspapers Plc* [1989] Q.B. 110.
[119] *Attorney-General v Sport Newspapers Ltd* [1991] 1 W.L.R. 1194.

it published. The Divisional Court held that its editor had not been proved to have the necessary specific intention to prejudice a trial for the purposes of common law contempt, but the two judges were divided on the legal question of whether it was possible, at common law, to commit contempt in relation to proceedings that had not yet begun. Lord Justice Bingham, with some reluctance, held that the *Sun* case should be treated as correctly decided; Mr Justice Hodgson said that it was plainly wrong.

In the *Sport* case Mr Justice Hodgson relied on previous authorities, both in Britain and Australia, to show that contempt could not be committed at common law in relation to proceedings that were not yet in existence, even if they were "imminent".[120] He justified this position with a number of powerful policy arguments anchored in the right of journalists to freedom of expression and the right of all individuals to fair trial only when alleged to have committed a crime. It was in the public interest that the media should be free to expose wrongdoers and demand that they should face trial. To render them liable for contempt at this stage would deter them from providing a useful public service. Moreover, it would extend a criminal offence for which defendants were deprived of their right to jury trial, a position that could be justified only by the need to give parties to active proceedings a swift and effective protection by High Court judges. Moreover, there was no safeguard against a private prosecution for intentional contempt brought by rich and powerful wrongdoers "exposed" in order to jolt the authorities into action: s.7 of the Contempt Act, which required the Attorney-General's consent to contempt proceedings, is limited to contempt under the strict liability rule. Despite the sex-crazed newspaper whose opportunistic conduct was the springboard for the judgment, and the obnoxious behaviour of the *Sun* in the case that preceded it, Mr Justice Hodgson's reasoning, both as to law and as to public policy, is to be preferred.

A further difference between strict liability contempt and the intentional variety is that distributors and importers are more vulnerable because they cannot in the latter case rely on the defence of innocent distribution (see para.7–036). Moreover, the *Sun* case indicates that the prosecution must prove only a real risk of prejudice and need not satisfy the more exacting standard of showing that the article created a substantial risk of serious prejudice.

On the other hand, if the risk of prejudice is remote, there will be no contempt. Sir James Goldsmith failed in his contempt case against *Private Eye* for articles it published while his libel action was pending against the magazine. The articles were intended to persuade Goldsmith to drop his case and suggested he might have **7–046**

---

[120] See *Re Crown Bank, Re O'Malty* (1890) 44 Ch.D. 649; *Stirling v Associated Newspapers Ltd* (1960) S.L.T. 5; *James v Robinson* (1963) 109 C.L.R. 593.

"nobbled" witnesses, but all this was unlikely to have any effect on the libel action's outcome.[121]

The court took more seriously a trade union paper's castigation of a member for taking his grievance to law, and its hint of the retribution he might face from his comrades.[122] Menacing a litigant with spiritual excommunication can also be contempt.[123] It is irrelevant that the black sheep would be expelled with full procedural regularity; the courts will punish threats, even threats of lawful acts, if they are intended as a deterrent, and have a real chance of success.[124]

A modern-day thalidomide-style campaign would not constitute contempt. The majority of the House of Lords found the *Sunday Times* guilty because the paper had prejudged the litigation between Distillers and the children. This constituted contempt irrespective of the paper's intention. That part of the decision was overturned by the 1981 Act. Two Law Lords, however, thought that, in addition, the newspaper was guilty of deliberate contempt because it was intentionally trying to pressurise Distillers into paying compensation. Theirs was a minority view. Lord Cross expressed a more liberal opinion:

"To seek to dissuade a litigant from prosecuting or defending proceedings by threats of unlawful action, by abuse or by misrepresentation of the nature of the proceedings or the circumstances out of which they arose and such like is no doubt a contempt of court, but if the writer states the facts fairly and accurately and expresses his view in temperate language the fact that publication may bring pressure—possibly great pressure—to bear on the litigant should not make it a contempt of court."[125]

7-047 A majority of the judges would have allowed a *Venetian Times* to make a fair and temperate appeal to Shylock to abandon his legal right to a pound of Antonio's flesh, but they would doubtless have drawn the line at vituperative Jew-baiting from a *Rialto Gutter Press*. Of course, the wilder the language, the less likely it is to have any real impact, and for that reason even an intemperate appeal might not be guilty of contempt. Publishers may also take some comfort

---

[121] *R. v Ingrams Ex p. Goldsmith* [1977] Grim. J.R. 240; see also *R. v Duffy Ex p. Nash* [1960] 2 Q.B. 188, 200.

[122] *Hutchinson v AEU, The Times*, August 25, 1932.

[123] *Hillfinch Properties Ltd v Newark Investment Ltd, The Times*, July 1, 1981.

[124] *Hillfinch* (above).

[125] *Att-Gen v Times Newspapers Ltd* [1974] A.C. 273 at 326 *per* Lord Cross. Lords Reid and Morris appear to agree, contrary to the less liberal view of Lords Diplock and Simon. In Australia this authority has been used to exculpate public statements calculated to bring pressure on a party to litigation, unless the expression is intemperate or full of factual errors. See *Commercial Bank of Australia v Preston* [1981] 2 N.S.W.L.R. 554, *per* Hunt J.

from the infrequency with which private litigants go to the expense of initiating contempt proceedings of this kind. In the course of the lengthy litigation over the alleged side-effects of the drug Opren the judge sounded a contempt warning over media campaigns to persuade the manufacturers, Eli Lilley, to pay generous compensation, but the issue was never tested by actual contempt proceedings.[126]

The intemperate nature of a *Private Eye* attack on Sonia Sutcliffe very nearly earned its editor, Ian Hislop, a prison sentence for intentional contempt in 1990:

> Three months before Sutcliffe's action against *Private Eye* (for alleging she had accepted money from a newspaper for telling of her marriage to the "Yorkshire Ripper") was fixed to be tried by a jury, Hislop threatened in print that if the action went ahead, she would be cross-examined about defrauding the DHSS and providing her husband with alibis for his murders which she knew to be false. Although Hislop believed these allegations at the time he published them, his intention in so doing was to deter her from proceeding with her case. His conviction turned on the fact that the articles went far beyond "fair and temperate criticism", and amounted to "plain abuse", over matters that had nothing to do with the issues in the libel action. The purpose of the articles was to place improper pressure on Sutcliffe to abandon her right as a litigant, and hence amounted to an interference with the administration of justice and an intentional contempt at common law. The court accepted that Hislop had no intention to prejudice the jury, so he was not guilty of common law contempt on this score, although the fact that the publication had objectively created a serious risk of prejudicing them meant that it was additionally a contempt under the strict liability rule. Hislop and his organ were fined £10,000 each.[127]

Of course, an essential ingredient of this type of contempt is **7-048** "intent" to prejudice the proceedings. This is a difficult and confusing legal concept. It is not enough that the publisher simply intends to publish the newspaper or magazine. The law is concerned with the effect the contents are intended to have. "Intent" is not the same as "desire" or "motive". Nor, in this context, is it to be equated with recklessness.[128] But it may only be inferred if the publisher foresees prejudice as virtually certain and carries on regardless. The court can usually only infer such an intent from all the circumstances since there will rarely be direct evidence of a prejudicial intent.

> The *Independent*, the *Sunday Times* and the *London Daily News* were found guilty of intentional contempt by publishing material from Peter Wright that other newspapers had been ordered to keep confidential. The judge rejected the argument that a person who knew of such an

---

[126] *Davies v Eli Lilley and Co, The Independent*, July 23, 1987.
[127] *Att-Gen v Hislop* [1991] 1 Q.B. 514.
[128] *Att-Gen v Newspaper Publishing Plc* [1988] Ch.33; *Att-Gen v News Group Newspapers Ltd* [1989] Q.B. 110.

injunction and published anyway would necessarily be guilty of intentional contempt. These were matters from which intention could be inferred, but the court had to look at all the circumstances, including what legal advice was given (if there is evidence about this), its basis and how it was understood. The editors did not desire to interfere in the administration of justice, but this did not negate their intent. Each paper was fined £50,000. The individual editors were not imprisoned since it was accepted that they believed on legal advice (albeit erroneously) that they were not committing contempt. The judge saw no point in fining the editors since they all had indemnities from their papers. The publishers' fines were quashed on appeal, on the grounds that it would be wrong to punish editors in circumstances where the law was unsettled and their erroneous legal advice had coincided with the view taken by the judge who had decided a preliminary issue in their favour.[129]

The fullest discussion of the "intention" that has to be proved against a newspaper in order to obtain a conviction for deliberate contempt is found in the verdict against the *Sun* for prejudicing a prosecution that it had decided to fund. The court held that it was necessary for the Attorney-General to prove a specific intention to prejudice a fair trial; it was insufficient to show that the publication had been reckless or that the newspaper had some generalised intention to interfere with the course of justice. Newspaper editors, of course, will always deny criminal intentions, and the courts will not take them at their word; the issue will be decided by examining what they published and the circumstances surrounding publication, and asking whether they must have foreseen, for all practical purposes, that a real risk to the fairness of a trial would result. The editor of the *Sun* was held to have had the requisite intention, despite his disavowals, as he was plainly campaigning for the doctor's conviction in circumstances where that conviction would have proved financially beneficial to the newspaper: it would not only have recovered its legal costs, but it would have boosted its circulation on the back of the "world exclusive" for which it had bought up the alleged victim's mother.[130]

7–049   However, honest mistake is a complete defence to common law contempt.

> The banking correspondent of the *Daily Telegraph* was writing a story about Homes Assured Corporation Plc, some of whose directors were facing proceedings for disqualification. She visited the registry of the

---

[129] *Att-Gen v Newspaper Publishing Plc*, *The Independent*, May 9, 1989, Morritt J.; *The Independent*, February 28, 1990, CA. The decision was upheld on a different aspect, see *Att-Gen v Times Newspapers Ltd* [1992] 1 A.C. 191, below p.383. The Court of Appeal stressed that intention could be inferred from the circumstances only if the consequences were "virtually certain", "inevitable" or "overwhelmingly probable".
[130] *Att-Gen v News Group Newspapers Plc* [1989] 1 Q.B. 110, CA.

Companies Court and was told (correctly) that to inspect the file she would have to obtain the leave of the court. She was given the file to take to the registrar. While waiting 40 minutes for her appointment, she openly made notes from the report of the Official Receiver, which was in the court file, and told the registrar she had done so. The registrar telephoned the city editor to complain, but the latter thought the problem was ethical rather than legal, and published two stories based on the report. The Chancery Division dismissed an application by the directors to commit the editor (Max Hastings) and his journalist for contempt. The essential vice of the offence lies in *knowingly* interfering with the administration of justice. The journalist had apparently never before inspected a court document and the court accepted that she did not know she was acting in breach of the rules. There had been no trickery or dishonesty.[131]

Campaigns over criminal proceedings raise different considerations. No decision to prosecute Dr Savundra had been made at the time of David Frost's televised interview in 1967 over his handling of the Fire and Auto Marine Insurance Company. At the time, the programme was criticised because Savundra's arrest was imminent.[132] Now "imminence" of an arrest is not enough; the proceedings would not be active and so there would be no risk of infringing the strict liability rule (see para.7–028). However, part of the programme's apparent intention was to sting the authorities into action. Even so, this is not intentional contempt, because encouraging the initiation of a prosecution is not prejudicial to the administration of justice.

Frustrating court orders against others

Court orders primarily affect another party to the lawsuit in which **7–050** they are made. Ordinarily, basic fairness requires that, before a person is ordered to do something by a court, he or she should have a chance to argue that the order should not be made. In addition, it is contempt for one person to aid or abet another to break a court order. However, during the *Spycatcher* saga the judges, over-zealous to help the Thatcher government suppress the old spy's embittered memoirs, created a new inroad on the principle that court orders do not affect third parties:

> The Attorney-General obtained injunctions preventing the *Guardian* and the *Observer* from printing material derived from Peter Wright's memoirs. Subsequently the *Independent*, the *London Daily News*, the *London Evening Standard* and, later, the *Sunday Times* published various parts of Wright's allegations. These four newspapers had not obtained their information from the first two, and they certainly did not publish their stories as their agents. They were not parties to the

---

[131] *Dobson v Hastings* [1992] Ch. 394.
[132] *R. v. Saundranayaga and Walter* [1968 1 W.L.R. 1761.

proceedings in which the injunction was obtained. The House of Lords accepted that the newspapers could not break an injunction that was not addressed to them. However, it held that their publications could amount to deliberate contempt of court. It was contempt to destroy or seriously damage the subject-matter of an action if this impeded or prejudiced the administration of justice: the subject-matter of the first action was the allegedly confidential nature of the material in *Spycatcher*, which would be destroyed if someone else published it. The consequence of the publication was to nullify the purpose of the trial by placing in the public domain information the Attorney-General contended was confidential and this amounted to interference with the course of justice in the confidentiality action.[133]

When the case was heard in full, the judge decided that the newspapers had been in contempt (see para.7–048). It was immaterial that the Attorney-General's action had not in fact been prejudiced. It did not matter that the House of Lords subsequently found that the injunction was unjustified following the widespread circulation of the Wright material. In the contempt proceedings some of the newspapers argued that there could be no contempt because, by the time they published, the American edition of *Spycatcher* had appeared and other papers had printed extracts. However, the judge said that each publication played its part in destroying the confidentiality; each newspaper committed contempt; and he drew no distinction in the penalties he imposed between the early and the late publishers.

This case shows just how far the law of contempt can be stretched, by judges overly supportive of Government and without a free speech guarantee to apply, when combined with the supple common law doctrine of breach of confidence. The subject-matter of the initial confidence action against the *Observer* was a report of Wright's allegations. This subject-matter was likened to an ice-cube: it would "evaporate" if exposed to the light of day by the *Independent* and the *Sunday Times*. There would be no point in the Attorney-General continuing his action against the *Observer* if Wright's revelations were published elsewhere. Since the contempt jurisdiction is a power deployed by the courts to prevent interference with the due administration of justice, the courts were entitled to punish the editors of the *Independent* and the *Sunday Times* by way of a criminal action for contempt of court on the ground that by publishing Wright's allegations they had destroyed the confidential nature of information that another court had injuncted the *Observer* from publishing pending the trial of the Government's claim to exclusive possession of this information. It was, said Lord Donaldson in the Court of Appeal, as if the Government and the *Observer* had commenced a legal action over the ownership of a racehorse, and

---

[133] *Att-Gen v Times Newspapers Ltd* [1992] 1 A.C. 191.

the court had ordered the horse to be kept alive until the dispute over its possession could be resolved after a full trial. The editor of the *Independent* had shot the horse prior to that full trial, and thereby rendered the proceedings pointless. The Attorney-General, in his role as guardian of the administration of justice, was entitled to seek to commit the *Independent's* editor to prison for intentionally aborting legal proceedings in which, quite coincidentally, the Attorney-General happened to be a party.

There can be no objection to the principle that courts should have **7-051** power to protect judicial proceedings from third parties who deliberately set out to prejudice or subvert them, and the cases relied on by the House of Lords, which related to third parties who cut down trees or disposed of assets that were the subject of a court order, cannot be faulted. But they concerned property, not information. Where the argument in this case becomes metaphysical is in assimilating Wright's allegations (that MI5 plotted to assassinate Nasser, bug foreign embassies and destabilise the Wilson Government) to items of physical property like ice-cubes and racehorses. Information of this kind is not "subject-matter" that can be possessed exclusively by a department of State, any more than a conspiracy to murder is the exclusive property of the conspirators. The subject-matter of an action for breach of confidence is not the information itself, but the confidential relationship in the course of which it was acquired. In fact, the *Independent's* publication did not abort the proceedings in the case against the *Observer*, which continued to trial and appeal, irrespective of the fact that over a million copies of *Spycatcher* had been published throughout the world and many copies had been imported into Britain. The ice-cube had by this stage been transformed into a flood of dirty water, but what was at stake in the litigation was the question of whether the *Observer* had become party to Wright's breach of his duty owed to the Crown by publishing his allegations. The *Independent* did not frustrate the administration of justice in that case by further publishing Wright's allegations, although by so doing it may well have become a party to his breach of confidence. The *Independent* should have been sued for breach of confidence, not prosecuted for the crime of contempt.

Nonetheless, the case stands for the proposition that it can be a crime for one newspaper to breach the spirit of an injunction imposed upon another, despite the fact that it has had no opportunity to present a case against the imposition of any restraint. It must go cap-in-hand to the court and ask for permission to publish. This was the course taken by Derbyshire Country Council which requested permission for its local library to stock a copy of *Spycatcher*.[134] Although numerous copies of the book had by this

---

[134] *Att-Gen v Observer Ltd*; *Re An Application by Derbyshire County Council* [1988] 1 All E.R. 385. The argument advanced in the text is developed in Geoffrey Robertson, *Freedom, the Individual and the Law* (Penguin, 1993).

time been imported into the country, and were being sold by enthusiastic entrepreneurs at inflated prices, the High Court held that the book's availability in a public library would "constitute an interference with the due administration of justice" in the ongoing cases against the *Guardian* and the *Observer*. This decision shows just how far the contempt confidentiality doctrine was moving in the direction of prior restraint under pressure from the Thatcher Government during the *Spycatcher* saga. Many of the cases in this period do not show English judges at their independent best and can now be more politely distinguished as belonging to the era before the Human Rights Act.

The crime of intentional contempt is committed only by those who specifically intend to impede or prejudice the administration of justice, and even recklessness as to whether such prejudice may be caused is insufficient to ground a conviction.

> During the Ordtech (arms to Iraq) appeal the Crown had claimed public interest immunity from disclosure of certain documents. At a directions hearing the Court of Appeal ordered most of these to be produced to the defendants but restricted their use to the appeal and required their return at its conclusion. The Lord Chief Justice quoted extracts from some of the documents in his judgment after which he mentioned that the documents were to be returned to the Crown. The *Independent* had been passed a set of the documents by a confidential source (unconnected with the parties or their legal advisers). It tried unsuccessfully to find out precisely what the judge had ordered. Its report of the judgment included a picture of two of the documents mentioned in the judgment but revealing slightly more than the quotations given by the court. On an application to commit the *Independent*, its editor and the journalist for contempt the court accepted that the order was directed only at the parties and not at the press. A third party could be liable for intentional contempt but only if some significant and adverse effect on the administration of justice could be proved. The additional parts of the documents which the *Independent* had shown were trivial. The reproduction of these two documents themselves in the article did not constitute a significant interference with the administration of justice. The court was also influenced by the unavailing efforts made by the paper to find out the exact terms of the court's order which showed it did not have the requisite intention for common law contempt.[135]

7–052 Shortly after the Human Rights Act came into operation the publishers and editor of *Punch* were found guilty of this type of contempt in the High Court.[136]

> The magazine had published a column written by the ex-MI5 employee, David Shayler, which was contrary to the terms of an

---

[135] *Att-Gen v Newspapers Publishing Plc* [1997] 1 W.L.R. 926, CA, Crim. Div.
[136] *Att-Gen v Punch Ltd* (unreported) October 6, 2000, Silber J.

injunction which the Government had obtained against the *Mail on Sunday*. The magazine was fined £20,000 and the editor £5,000. The editor appealed to the Court of Appeal successfully. It accepted his argument that while he had done what the injunction prohibited, he had not intended to subvert the underlying purpose of the order, namely the preservation of national security. The Attorney-General in turn successfully appealed to the House of Lords.[137] It said that the Court of Appeal's approach to intention was too refined. The purpose of the Court's order had been to preserve the confidentiality of the information referred to in the order until the dispute between Shayler and the government could be resolved at trial. The High Court had been entitled to find that the editor knew that this was its purpose and knew that by publishing the disputed article by Shayler it would have a significant and adverse effect on that purpose. If *Punch* or its editor had thought that the injunction was cast in terms which were too broad, it could have asked the Court to narrow them.

The Lords' decision is a disappointing reversal of a worthy attempt by the Court of Appeal to temper the effect of the *Spycatcher* type of contempt. It does, though, include some crumbs of comfort for the media. Lord Nicholls warned[138] that "Even a temporary restriction on freedom of expression is not to be imposed lightly. News is a perishable commodity. Public and media interest fades." Furthermore, this type of contempt will not be committed by any action of a third party which impinges on an interlocutory injunction—there must be some significant and adverse effect on the administration of justice in the proceedings.[139]

In some cases claimants may get to know that allegedly confidential or private information is being touted for sale to the media. They may not know by whom but they may hope to forestall publication by obtaining an injunction against a notional "John Doe" or "Persons Unknown" and then serve the injunction on the most likely media purchasers. Where this is intended, the Court has said, then individual publishers should be given a realistic opportunity to be heard on the appropriateness or otherwise of granting the injunction and upon the scope of its terms. Newspapers and their lawyers are used to acting speedily, but if the urgency of the situation is so great that even short notice is impracticable, the application may be made without notice. Then the Claimants will be under a duty to alert the Court to any material or arguments which might reasonably be thought to be available to the potential defendants or the media organisations who would be affected by the injunction.[140]

Because the *Spycatcher/Punch* type of contempt is intended to protect the administration of justice in the period prior to trial, it

---

[137] *Att-Gen v Punch Ltd* [2003] 1 A.C. 1046.
[138] *Att-Gen* at para.31.
[139] *Att-Gen* Lord Nicholls at para.44.
[140] *X and X v Persons Unknown* (2007) HRLR 4 Eady J.

cannot be committed in relation to a final injunction (or undertaking). Mr Justice Gray reached this sensible conclusion in *Jockey Club v Buffham*,[141] although he warned that the claimant who had already obtained one final injunction might be encouraged to start further proceedings against the third party. The House of Lords had another warning in the *Punch* case. The Attorney-General could, alternatively, have argued that the magazine and its editor were guilty of aiding and abetting Shayler in his breach of the interlocutory injunction. Perhaps—but if the dragnet criminal doctrines, like conspiracy and aiding and abetting are to be deployed against editors, the case for jury trial for contempt will be unanswerable. The judges in the *Spycatcher* era became discredited as protectors of media freedom and despite the commendable efforts of a new generation of judges (the *Punch* case excepted) the option of trial by jury for this class of criminal contempt may be the only way of deterring future government attempts to close the stable door after "security" information has bolted.

SCANDALISING THE COURT

7–053 "Scandalising the court" was invented in the eighteenth century to punish radical critics of the establishment, such as John Wilkes.[142] It has been defined as: "any act done or writing published calculated to bring a court or judge into contempt or to lower his authority".[143] Editorial barbs were thus equated with cat calls in court, both being treated as affronts to judicial dignity. In Scotland the crime is called "murmuring judges".

Despite its apparent breadth, scandalising the court should not prevent criticism of the judiciary even when expressed in strong terms. "Justice is not a cloistered virtue" a senior Law Lord once said,[144] and comment about the legal system in general or the

---

[141] [2003] E.M.L.R. 5.

[142] *R. v Almon* (1765) Wilm. 243; 97 E.R. 94. This authority is distinctly shaky. It was an undelivered judgment of Justice Wilmott, published posthumously by his son, and uncritically accepted by Blackstone. It cites no authority for the proposition that judges have power to punish their press critics, and the better view is that it was wrongly decided; see Sir John Fox, *The History of Contempt of Court* (Oxford, 1927; reprinted Professional Books, 1972). In the context of eighteenth-century politics it was an attempt to protect Lord Mansfield from reasoned criticism of his oppressive judicial behaviour towards Wilkes and other critics of the Government; see D. Hay, "Contempt by Scandalising the Court: A Political History of the First Five Hundred Years" (1987) 25 *Osgoode Hall Law Journal* 431.

[143] *Badry v DPP of Mauritius* [1983] 2 A.C. 297 quoting *R. v Gray* [1900] 2 Q.B. 36 at 40. The offence does not apply in respect of a defamatory attack on a judge in his personal rather than his official capacity: *Re the Special Reference from the Bahama Islands* [1893] A.C. 138.

[144] *Ambard v Att-Gen for Trinidad and Tobago* [1936] A.C. 322 at 335 *per* Lord Atkin.

handling of particular cases once they are over sometimes deserves to be trenchant.

The Victorian press was outspoken in its condemnation of the bench. Charles Dickens led a campaign of press criticism against one magistrate (thinly disguised as Mr Fang in *Oliver Twist*) that resulted in his removal.[145] This was not an isolated example. Press attacks on the judiciary were so frequent that the Lord Chancellor retaliated by refusing to make editors justices of the peace.[146] None of these papers was punished for scandalising the court, and by 1899 the Privy Council considered that the offence was virtually a dead-letter in England.[147] However, it was revived the following year when the *Birmingham Daily Argus* described Mr Justice Darling, accurately enough, as an "impudent little man in horse-hair" who was "a microcosm of conceit and empty-headedness". It was fined for contempt. In the late 1920s the *New Statesman* was convicted of scandalising the court for doubting whether birth control reformer Marie Stopes would receive a fair trial from a Roman Catholic judge, and the *Daily Worker* was fined for labelling a Tory judge "a bewigged puppet exhibiting a strong class bias".[148] In retrospect, both comments had an element of truth, and it is inconceivable that similar remarks would be prosecuted today. Judges who have exhibited anti-women attitudes in rape cases have been condemned by the press, while attacks on the judges of the National Industrial Relations Court were made without punishment. In 1992 *Legal Business* published the results of a survey of the legal profession on High Court judges who were ranked in order of the respect they commanded. Harman J., who came bottom of the poll, attracted trenchant criticism that was repeated in the article. The judge continued on the bench but resigned in 1998 after he was castigated by the Court of Appeal for taking 20 months to deliver a judgment.[149] The modern attitude is exemplified in this 1968 case:

> Raymond Blackburn, the indomitable pursuer of pornography and gambling, tried to commit Quintin Hogg M.P. (later Lord Chancellor Hailsham) for contempt after he had written an article in *Punch* that was severely but inaccurately critical of the Court of Appeal. The Court of Appeal itself dismissed the application. Lord Denning said:
>
> "It is the right of every man, in Parliament or out of it, in the Press or over the broadcast, to make fair comment, even outspoken comment on matters of public interest. Those who comment can

---

[145] His real name was Allan Laing. See Marjorie Jones, *Justice and Journalism* (Barry Rose, 1974) p.27.

[146] (1883) *Justice of the Peace 750*; *cf.* Jones, above, p.43.

[147] *McLeao v St Aubyn* [1899] A.C. 549.

[148] *R v Gray* [1900] ? Q.B. 36; *R. v Wilkinson*, The Times, July 16, 1930; *R. v New Statesman ex p. DPP* (1928) 44 T.L.R. 301.

[149] *Legal Business*, May 1992; *Goose v Wilson Sandford & Co*, The Times, February 19, 1998, CA.

deal faithfully with all that is done in a Court of Justice. They can say we are mistaken, and our decisions erroneous, whether they are subject to appeal or not."

Lord Salmon added: "No criticism of a judgment, however vigorous, can amount to contempt of court if it keeps within the limits of reasonable courtesy and of good faith."[150]

7–054   Scandalising the court is an anachronistic form of contempt. Lord Diplock has described it as "virtually obsolescent in the United Kingdom"[151] and it has not been used here for 60 years.[152]

It is now inconceivable that action could be brought against publications that criticise the courts almost however much the criticism is misplaced. In 1987 the *Daily Mirror* published upside down photographs of the Law Lords who had injuncted *Spycatcher* under the banner headline "YOU FOOLS!" No prosecution was forthcoming. In 2000 a litigant disappointed in the result of his divorce case was charged with "scandalising the court" by making hysterical claims in pamphlets about corrupt judges. The *Guardian* criticised the use of the charge as oppressive and the Attorney-General dropped it, a decision endorsed by Simon Brown L.J. on the ground that such insults are much better ignored.

The danger, of leaving such a crime on the books is well illustrated by recent contempt prosecutions in other countries that have inherited the common law, where robust condemnation of court decisions (Trinidad), suggestions that a decision was influenced by trade-union demonstrations (Australia) and minor inaccuracies in justifiable criticism of the conduct of proceedings against an opposition M.P. (Singapore) have all been treated as contempt. In certain Commonwealth countries there does exist an unhealthy relationship between the judges and the Government that appoints them and scandalising the court is a crime that has been invoked as an instrument of oppression, to silence honest criticism of biased judges.

---

[150] *R. v Metropolitan Police Commissioner Ex p. Blackburn (No. 2)* [1968] 2 Q.B. 150.
[151] *Secretary of State for Defence v Guardian Newspapers Ltd* [1985] A.C. 339, 347.
[152] It has, though, been dusted down and used in the Commonwealth (see Clive Walker's "Scandalising the Eighties" [1985] 101 L.O.R. 359. A Canadian provincial minister was fined for describing a judge's verdict as "insane" and a "disgrace" (*R. v Ouillet* (1977) 36 Crim. Reps. (Nova Scotia) 296). An Indian state premier was likewise punished for damning the judges as bourgeois and class-biased (*Nambooripad v Mambiar* [1970] All India Reps 1318), and when a Trinidadian paper (*The Bomb*) published a thinly disguised "fictional" account of dishonesty and drunkenness in the local judiciary, its editor, Paddy Chokolingo, was imprisoned (*Chokolingo v Att-Gen for Trinidad and Tobago* [1981] 1 All E.R. 244, PC). In Singapore, the mildest criticism of a court decision in favour of the government (there are no decisions against the government) can be adjudged a contempt of court: *Att-Gen v Wain* [1991] 2 M.L.J. 353. By contrast, an American judge who fined an attorney for a critical newspaper article was himself impeached and very nearly convicted by the U.S. Senate for encroaching on the writer's constitutional freedom of speech (Sir John Fox, *Contempt of Court*, p.202 *et seq.*).

In *Badry v DPP of Mauritius*[153] the Privy Council urged ex-colonial **7–055** courts to punish only "the most intolerable instances" of scandalisation, and held that the crime was not committed by asserting that a judge had made false statements and had not taken into account relevant evidence. Regrettably, however, it upheld the conviction of a political leader for a rabble-rousing speech accusing the Supreme Court of bias in favour of wealthy companies, because this was "clearly meant to shake public confidence in the administration of justice in Mauritius". The Privy Council by 1999 was generally protective of free speech, but it then delivered a judgment which suggested that "scandalising the court", whilst obsolete in Britain, might nonetheless be necessary in "small islands" like Mauritius. It did, however, emphasise the limitations of the offence. The court said:

> "it must be borne in mind that the offence is narrowly defined. It does not extend to comment on the conduct of a judge unrelated to his performance on the bench. It exists solely to protect the administration of justice rather than the feelings of judges. There must be a real risk of undermining public confidence in the administration of justice. The field of application of the offence is also narrowed by the need in a democratic society for public scrutiny of the conduct of judges, and for the right of citizens to comment on matters of public concern. There is available to a defendant a defence based on the right of "criticising, in good faith in private or public, the public act done in the seat of justice . . . ."[154]

The Privy Council was endeavouring to re-phrase an unacceptably racist comment made by the court a century before, when it said that the crime might be necessary to support judicial authority in countries with "coloured populations"[155] but the new formula is unacceptably patronising and, in human rights terms, quite simply wrong. It is precisely in "small islands" that the crime is used to suppress legitimate criticism of judges who decide in favour of the Government, and it is used to the same effect in other States. It is to be hoped that the Privy Council will in due course reconsider the dicta in *Ahnee* and rule that a criminal offence of criticising judges is incompatible with freedom of expression, whether in small islands like Mauritius or in small islands like Britain.

The history of contempt by scandalising the court, both in Britain and especially in the Commonwealth, argues strongly for its abolition. Its impact might be mitigated if it were held to contain a requirement of *mens rea*—an undecided issue, although the draft

---

[153] [1983] 2 A.C. 297.
[154] *Ahnee v DPP of Mauritius* [1999] 2 A.C. 294, PC.
[155] *McLeod v St. Aubyn* [1899] A.C. 549.

judgment in *Almon* is authority for intention as an ingredient of the offence.[156] The crime has no counterpart in American law, where similar offences have been declared unconstitutional,[157] and it is difficult to reconcile with Art.10 of the European Convention. The fullest forensic analysis of the concept is to be found in the Canadian case of *R. v Kopyto*: the majority of the court held that the British law of contempt by "scandalisation" was incompatible with the "freedom of expression" guarantee in the Canadian Charter of Rights and Freedoms.[158]

It may be that the British press has itself to blame for Parliament's refusal to abolish this archaic head of contempt in the United Kingdom. During the 1981 reforms an amendment to this effect was rejected, after Lord Hailsham recalled a recent incident that had arisen after the Court of Appeal denied a divorce to a woman who claimed that her husband was unreasonable in having sex only once a week. A tabloid journalist telephoned the wives of the three appellate judges to ask how often a week they regarded as reasonable. The offence of scandalising the court, said the Lord Chancellor, was still required to deal with such conduct.

PUBLISHING DETAILS OF JURY DELIBERATIONS

7–056 Section 8 of the Contempt of Court Act makes it an offence for a journalist "to obtain, disclose or solicit any particulars of statements made, opinions expressed, arguments advanced or votes cast by members of a jury in the course of their deliberations in any legal proceedings". This extension of the law came after the *New Statesman* was acquitted of contempt for publishing an interview with one of the jurors in the Jeremy Thorpe trial, in which the juror revealed how the jury had reacted to certain witnesses and aspects of the evidence when considering its verdict. The public interest in publishing the interview was considerable: it revealed that the *Sunday Telegraph*'s deal with chief prosecution witness Peter Bessell (whereby he would receive £50,000 for his "exclusive" story if Thorpe were convicted, but only £25,000 were Thorpe acquitted) had irreparably damaged Bessell's credibility as a witness in the eyes of the jury. It also suggested that the jury would have convicted the defendants had the DPP charged them with conspiracy to assault (rather than to murder) Thorpe's ex-boyfriend, Norman Scott. The Attorney-General should have brought contempt proceedings against the *Sunday Telegraph* for prejudicing the Thorpe trial; instead, he brought them against the *New Statesman* for producing evidence that the *Sunday Telegraph* deal had prejudiced the case.

---

[156] *R. v Almon*, fn.142 above.
[157] *Bridges v California* 314 U.S. 252 (1941).
[158] *R. v Kopyto* (1987) 47 D.I.R. (4th) 213.

The Divisional Court dismissed the charges, in a judgment that some lawyers feared might open the door to a new form of chequebook journalism: secrets of the Old Bailey jury rooms in notorious criminal trials.[159]

The Government's 1981 Contempt Bill was designed to stop this development, but it applied only to publications that named particular trials or jurors. If the *New Statesman* decision was to be cut back at all, these exceptions were sensible. They would have prevented vendettas by convicted defendants or their families without stifling all discussion of jury deliberations. Jury duty is a rare occasion when ordinary people take an active part in government. In can be a memorable experience. Others can benefit from their stories. In addition, like any aspect of government, it is an eminently appropriate subject for study and research. But the clause was amended so as to ban even anonymous accounts of unnamed trials. The change was made at the instigation of peers who feared that the jury system might not survive the full glare of publicity if reporters were permitted to cross-examine jurors about the reasons behind their verdict. Lamentably, s.8 has worked to preclude any sensible or scientific research into the operation of the jury system: it notably frustrated the work of the Fraud Trials Committee (chaired by Lord Roskill), which could produce no hard evidence on the question of whether complex fraud cases were suitable for jury trial.[160] The first, and so far the only, reported contempt action under s.8 involving the press was taken against the *Daily Mail* for publishing an article based on interviews with several jurors in the Blue Arrow fraud case. The interviews had not been conducted by the paper or its journalist but by an independent American researcher who sold the transcripts to the reporter. The paper argued that no offence had been committed because only jurors could "disclose" what had taken place in the jury room. The House of Lords rejected the argument and ruled that "disclose" extended to a newspaper's publication (as long as the material was not already in the public domain). For putting this harmless, and indeed useful, information into the public domain, the paper was fined £30,000, the editor £20,000 and the journalist £10,000.[161]

The publishers' complaint to Strasbourg was declared inadmissible by the Commission[162] which said that the purposes of the prohibition on jury disclosures was to encourage frankness in exchanges in the jury room, and any possibility of intrusion on this privacy could undermine that confidence. But this is a weakly argued and fundamentally wrong Commission decision, which gives no satisfactory weight to freedom of expression and imputes to the section an

---

[159] *Att-Gen v New Statesman and Nation Publishing Co Ltd* [1981] Q.B. 1.
[160] Fraud Trials Committee Report (HMSO, 1986) para.8.10.
[161] *Att-Gen v Associated Newspapers Ltd* [1994] 2 A.C. 238.
[162] *Associated Newspapers Ltd v UK* Application No. 24770/94, November 30, 1994.

intention that the Q.C. legislators who introduced it never had. They wanted to stop informed criticism of the jury system, which is precisely why the section is a breach of Art.10.

7–057 The section is ripe for amendment to permit research and voluntary post-trial disclosure, while specifically prohibiting unsought identification of jurors, and the soliciting or purchasing of their stories.[163] Although the government has periodically sought to curb the right to jury trial—in fraud or other complex cases—it has generally supported their use.

> "The government regards jury service as one of the most important civic duties that anyone can be asked to perform. Few decisions made by members of the public have such an impact upon society as a jury's verdict."

But all the more reason, it might then be thought, why the press and jurors themselves should be unmuzzled.

Section 8 is not intended to hinder the working of the trial itself. The judge can ask the jury its verdict, and the jury can solicit help even if this hints at the way its members are thinking. The appearance of justice requires that these communications should be in open court,[164] and so they are freely reportable, although some trial judges wrongly confine them to counsel (the lawfulness of this practice is yet to be challenged).

The House of Lords has also decided that s.8 does not prevent a trial judge (and to a lesser extent the Court of Appeal) from investigating allegations of impropriety in the way in which the jury has conducted its deliberations. An associated common law rule which says that such evidence is generally inadmissible on appeal was affirmed in the same case. In a powerful dissent Lord Steyn said that it was "utterly indefensible" to ignore the possibility of a miscarriage of justice in the interests of the general efficiency of the jury system.[165] A juror who believes that there has been impropriety should report the matter to the trial judge or court staff: Disclosures to the press or the parties will amount to a breach of s.8 even if motivated by a desire to expose a miscarriage of justice.[166] The notion that the media could commit a serious criminal offence by publishing evidence of how jury misbehaviour led to a miscarriage of justice is absurd, but it follows inevitably from the wording of s.8—a tribute to the British penchant for sweeping distasteful truths about much loved institutions—whether the jury or the monarchy—under the carpet.

---

[163] See the sensible recommendations of the NSW Law Reform Committee Report No. 48, *The Jury in a Criminal Trial*, 1986, Ch.11.
[164] *R. v Gorman* (1987) 85 Cr.App.R. 121, CA.
[165] *R. v Mirza* [2004] 1 A.C. 1118.
[166] *Att-Gen v Scotcher* [2005] 1 W.L.R. 1867, HL.

The media should not be frightened of making approaches to jurors for information after a trial is over. Section 8 prohibits the media only from intentionally soliciting information about the jury's *deliberations* in reaching their verdict. As the Attorney-General noted in the debate on the clause, it is not an offence to solicit or publish a juror's view of the desirability of the prosecution, of the quality of the advocates, of the sobriety of the judge or the attentiveness of the court usher.[167] Nor would it be contempt to interview trial jurors about their opinion on the length of the sentence. Shortly after the Act came into effect the *Sunday Times* published a story on the trial of the doctor charged with killing a Down's syndrome baby; the article included the opinion of a juror that the prosecution should never have been brought. The BBC has broadcast interviews with jurors complaining about coroners who tried to dictate their verdicts. In 1980 some of the jurors who had acquitted four anarchists on bomb conspiracy charges wrote to the *Guardian* in response to the trial judge's attack on their intelligence. Although this touched on what had taken place in the jury room, the Attorney-General has said that the offence would not prevent jurors in a comparable situation from publicly responding to judicial rebukes.[168] Section 8 does not apply at all to trials where the jury has been discharged prior to the stage at which it is asked to retire to consider its verdict. It follows that jurors may be interviewed without legal difficulty when cases are dismissed by the judge at "half-time" because of insufficient prosecution evidence. A prosecution under s.8 can only be brought by the Attorney-General.[169] Reporters need not hesitate to interview jurors, but they must remember to avoid any question designed to elicit an answer about what was said or done in the jury room.

DISOBEDIENCE OF COURT ORDERS

The risk of disobeying an order directed at the particular newspaper, **7–058** broadcaster or journalist is in one sense obvious, but certain points are worth considering:

- There can only be contempt of this kind if the court has made an *order* rather than merely expressed a wish for the media not to publish material or behave in a particular way.[170]
- The court's order should be in clear terms: "If the court is to punish anyone for not carrying out its order, the order must

---

[167] *Hansard*, H.C. Debs [1981] Vol.9, col.426.
[168] *Hansard*, col.425.
[169] Contempt of Court Act 1981, s.8(3), though proceedings can be brought on the motion of a court having jurisdiction to deal with it (*Hansard*, col.425).
[170] See *Att-Gen v Leveller Magazine Ltd* [1978] 3 All E.R. 731.

in unambiguous terms direct what is to be done."[171] Nonetheless, an order (or the construction which the court gives
it) can be broken unintentionally.

> The columnist Nigel Dempster was fined £10,000 and the
> publishers of the Daily Mail were fined £25,000 for a non-
> deliberate breach of an injunction not to repeat an allegation
> that Baron Bentinck (the claimant in a libel trial against the
> defendants) was mean. The judge said that if he had thought the
> breach was deliberate he would have jailed Dempster.[172]

- Ordinarily there must be proof that the defendant was given
  notice of the order. If it is prohibitory (e.g. an order not to
  publish something) the person concerned will have notice if
  he or she was present in court. Alternatively, notice can be
  given by fax or telephone or by other means such as receipt
  of a press agency copy.[173] If the order is mandatory (e.g.
  requiring disclosure of documents) a copy of the order must
  usually be served personally and it must include a notice
  expressly drawing attention to the consequences of
  disobedience.[174]
- Parliament has made breach of certain types of court orders
  (such as anonymity orders under the Children and Young
  Persons Act) summary offences which carry no risk of
  imprisonment and where the maximum fine is often less
  than for contempt. Prosecutors ought to consider charging
  such offences rather than the blunderbuss of contempt.[175] As
  the House of Lords said in the context of another common
  law offence (public nuisance):

> "Where Parliament has defined the ingredients of an offence,
> perhaps stipulating what shall and shall not be a defence, and
> has prescribed a mode of trial and a maximum penalty, it must
> ordinarily be proper that conduct falling within that definition
> should be prosecuted for the statutory offence and not for a
> common law offence which may or may not provide the same
> defences and for which the penalty is unlimited . . . . I would
> not go to the length of holding that conduct may never be
> lawfully prosecuted as a generally expressed common law crime
> where it falls within the terms of a specific statutory provision,
> but good practice and respect for the primacy of statute do in
> my judgment require that conduct falling within the terms of a
> specific statutory provision should be prosecuted under that
> provision unless there is good reason for doing otherwise."[176]

---

[171] *Iberian Trust Ltd v Founders Trust and Investment Co Ltd* [1932] 2 K.B. 87 at 95.
[172] *Bentinck v Associated Newspapers Ltd and Dempster* [1999] EMLR 556.
[173] CPR Sch.1 RSC, O.45, r.7(6).
[174] CPR Sch.1 RSC, O.45, r.7(2) and (4).
[175] *R Tyne Tees Television Ltd, The Times*, October 20, 1997 where a fine for
contempt of £10,000, double the statutory maximum for the offence was quashed
on appeal.
[176] *R v Goldstein* [2006] 2 All E.R. 257 at para.30, *per* Lord Bingham.

- In contempt proceedings for breach of an order, it should be possible to argue that the court was wrong to make the order in the first place, although there is Divisional Court authority to the contrary.

    Channel 4 broadcast a programme by Box Productions called the "Committee". It alleged that there was a conspiracy of security service personnel and loyalist paramilitaries to murder republicans. The police were granted an order under the anti-terrorist legislation for the broadcasters to disclose their source (see para.11–049). When they refused, the DPP took proceedings for contempt. The Divisional Court refused to reconsider the merit of the disclosure order and fined the broadcasters £75,000. This principle may now call for reconsideration. Orders imposed in breach of Convention rights from the outset would be unlawful by virtue of s.6(1) of the Human Rights Act and courts (which are "public authorities") are obliged to act compatibly with Convention rights.[177]

- Ordinarily it will be the orders of UK courts which affect journalists. But that will not always be so. In March 2006, the Yugoslav War Crimes Tribunal (the ICTY) fined two Croatian journalists £10,600 each for contempt of the Tribunal in breaching an anonymity order in respect of a protected witness and publishing confidential Tribunal documents.[178] Journalists may be summonsed to give evidence to international criminal courts and will be open to contempt proceedings if they refuse to attend, although the important ICTY decision in *Randall* establishes that war correspondents have a testamentary privilege, and a decision of the Appeals Chamber of the Special Court of Sierra Leone establishes that reporters and human rights monitors who testify in international courts are entitled to protect their sources (see para.11–072).

PROCEDURE AND PUNISHMENT

Contempt proceedings can be initiated by the judge or court that is **7–059** affected. This is now rarely done except where there has been a disturbance in court or where the court's own order has been disobeyed. The more usual, and the proper, course is for the court to refer the matter to the Attorney-General.

If a judge does threaten reporters with immediate committal for contempt, they should obtain legal advice. When the lawyers come back before the judge, they should apply to have the matter referred to the Attorney-General: this is now accepted as the proper course,

---

[177] *DPP v Channel 4* [1993] 2 All E.R. 517, DC.
[178] *Media Lawyer* March 10, 2006 and see para.11–071.

even for alleged misbehaviour by a journalist in the face of the court. Thus when *Observer* journalist Jack Lundin refused under oath to answer questions that would have revealed a source, the trial judge (Mr Justice Webster) agreed to refer the matter to the Attorney-General, so that it could be considered and dealt with in the calmer arena of the Divisional Court.[179] It is invidious for the judge immediately and personally concerned to double up as contempt prosecutor. Article 6 of the ECHR enshrines the principle that a judge must not act in his own cause. In *R. v MacLeod*,[180] however, the Court of Appeal rejected an argument that it was contrary to Art.6 for a judge to institute contempt proceedings of his own motion (although it was "regrettable" that the judge had taken the alleged victim through her examination in chief) and in *R. v Dodds*[181] the Court of Appeal said that Art.6 adds nothing to domestic jurisprudence concerning the summary powers to deal with contempt of court. But these cases represent too complacent a view of these summary powers. In *Kyprianou v Cyprus*[182] the Grand Chamber of the Strasbourg Court upheld a complaint that a summary imprisonment of a defence lawyer for contempt in the face of the court infringed Article 6. It said,

> "this confusion of roles between complainant, witness, prosecutor and judge could self-evidently prompt objectively justified fears as to the conformity of the proceedings to the time-honoured principle that no-one shall be a judge in his or her own cause and consequently as to the impartiality of the bench".[183]

MacLeod, was not a case of media contempt which rarely, if ever, could justify immediate action by the judge hearing the case which is alleged to have been prejudiced.

If the affected court accepts these arguments and does not mete out instant punishment of its own, contempt proceedings will be started by application to the Divisional Court of the Queen's Bench Division of the High Court.[184] This must also be the procedure if a publication is said to be in contempt of magistrates. They can punish only for contempt committed in or near their own courtroom and not a contempt committed by the press or by broadcasters.[185] These have to be referred to the Divisional Court.

---

[179] *Att-Gen v Lundin* (1982) 75 Cr.App.R. 90.
[180] [2001] Crim. L.R. 589, C.A.
[181] [2003] 1 Cr.App.R. 3, CA.
[182] Application No.73797/01 judgment December 15, 2005.
[183] At para.127.
[184] The procedure is set out in CPR Sch.1 RSC, Ord.52.
[185] Contempt of Court Act 1981, s.12.

The Attorney-General's consent is essential where the contempt **7–060** was unintentional but was in breach of the strict liability rule.[186] In all cases brought in the Divisional Court (even those initiated by the Attorney), the court has to give its permission for contempt proceedings to begin.[187] This is considered on an application without notice and on hearing only the applicant's side. The proper time for the Attorney-General to make his application is after the conclusion of the jury stage of the proceedings alleged to have been prejudiced. This will obviate any danger that publicity given to the contempt action will repeat the alleged prejudice, and will enable the Attorney-General to consider, with the benefit of hindsight, whether the risk of prejudice at the time of publication was real. Strictly speaking both the Attorney-General and the court ought to disregard subsequent events and in the case of the cleaning lady and the fridge (see above para.7–021) the Attorney-General took contempt proceedings even though the defendant did in fact plead guilty and there was no jury to prejudice. By contrast, one of the reasons given for not prosecuting the coverage of the arrest of the "Yorkshire Ripper", Peter Sutcliffe, was his plea of guilty to manslaughter.[188] The real difference, perhaps, was that the police irresponsibly caused prejudicial publicity by their self-congratulatory press conference after Sutcliffe's arrest, whereas the Manchester police had acted reasonably and warned the *Manchester Evening News* against publishing its story.

Before making an application to the Divisional Court, the Attorney's usual practice is to write to the editor concerned, setting out the complaint in some detail and inviting submissions as to why contempt proceedings should not be instituted. This is a useful opportunity and has often led to representations which have successfully persuaded the Attorney to take no further action. However, such letters of response need to be drafted with some care. If the contempt process does continue, they are likely to feature in the evidence presented by the Attorney to the Court.

Once the Divisional Court has given leave for the case to go ahead, the publisher will be served with a "claim form", accompanied by an affidavit setting out the applicant's case. In Divisional Court proceedings evidence is normally given on affidavit rather than orally, but publishers should scrutinise carefully the draft affidavits that their lawyers prepare because they might be cross-examined on them, and it is perjury to swear a false affidavit. Publishers can insist on having their say by giving oral evidence[189]; this gives them a day in court and may have publicity value, but it is

---

[186] 1981 Act, s.7—unless, contrary to the principles in the text, the court acts on its own motion.
[187] CPR, Sch.1; RSC, O.52, r.2.
[188] See Press Council Booklet No.7, *Press Conduct in the Sutcliffe Case*, p.75.
[189] RSC, O.52, r.6(4).

unlikely to swing the judges in their favour. Applications to commit for contempt must be heard in open court except in certain cases to do with children (wardship, adoption, guardianship, maintenance, upbringing residence or contact), the mentally ill, secret processes, or where for reasons to do with national security or the administration of justice the court decides to sit in private. Before making a committal order in these cases the court must state in open court the name of the guilty person, in general terms the nature of the contempt, and the period of committal.[190] Contempt is the one serious criminal charge not decided by a jury. Although the Divisional Court is preferable from a publisher's point of view to the court that was allegedly prejudiced, it is still composed of judges who should be scrupulous to avoid any appearance of partiality as they weigh freedom of speech against the preservation of the administration of justice.

7–061   A publisher found guilty by the court can be fined an unlimited amount. Individuals who are convicted can in addition be imprisoned for up to two years.[191] An appeal can be taken directly to the House of Lords, but the permission of either the Divisional Court or of the Lords themselves is necessary.[192]

If the application to commit is heard by a single judge of the High Court, the Crown Court or the county court, the appeal is made in the first place to the Court of Appeal.[193] Where the High Court has made a committal order, exceptionally, it is not necessary to obtain permission before appealing to the Court of Appeal[194] and this is still the case even if the committal is suspended[195] though not where a fine or some penalty other than committal to prison has been imposed. If the Court of Appeal dismisses the appeal but grants a certificate that the case raises an issue of public importance, and either the Court of Appeal or the Lords consent, a further appeal can be made to the Lords.[196]

Pending an appeal to either the Court of Appeal or from the Court of Appeal to the House of Lords the Court of Appeal can

---

[190] CPR Sch.1, RSC O.52, r.6(1) and (2).

[191] Contempt of Court Act 1981, s.14(1). This is also the maximum that a county court can impose: County Courts (Penalties for Contempt) Act 1983. Other inferior courts, e.g. magistrates' courts can imprison for only one month and/or impose a fine of up to £2,500: Contempt of Court Act 1981 s.12(2). A person committed for contempt can apply at any time to the court for an earlier release (CPR, Sch.1; RSC, O. 52, r.8(l)). Thus even dilatory contrition may result in a shorter sentence.

[192] Administration of Justice Act 1960, s.13(2)(c).

[193] 1960 Act, at s.13(2)(b) and (bb). Appeals from the High Court or County Court are to the Civil Division of the Court of Appeal *Att-Gen v Newspaper Publishing Plc* [1988] Ch. 333. From the Crown Court the appeal is to the Criminal Division of the Court of Appeal—Supreme Court Act 1981 s.53.

[194] CPR, r.52.3(l)(a)(i).

[195] *Wilkinson v S* [2003] 1 W.L.R. 1254, CA.

[196] This was the course taken in *Home Office v Harman* [1983] 1 A.C. 280.

grant bail to an appellant who is in custody.[197] An appeal court can give permission for fresh evidence to be produced if the interests of justice require it.[198] This means that the more stringent requirements for fresh evidence in civil appeals do not have to be satisfied.

Injunctions to prevent contempt

The courts have in very exceptional cases granted injunctions to **7–062** restrain an anticipated contempt of court. This was the course taken by the Attorney-General against *The Times* for its planned series on thalidomide and against the satirist Auberon Waugh's election address when he stood as the "Dog Lovers Party" candidate against Jeremy Thorpe, shortly to be tried for his alleged part in a botched attempt to kill a blackmailing ex-lover (the ex-lover's dog had been shot instead). It is still unclear whether the person affected can make the application without the backing of the Attorney-General when it is alleged that the publication would infringe the strict liability rule. The Court of Appeal in 1985 said that this was not necessary,[199] but the correctness of this view was challenged in another case in the House of Lords which chose to leave the matter open.[200] Nor was it resolved in a case brought by Greater Manchester Police against Channel 5. A notorious villain had been murdered and the police had arrested a suspect. A High Court judge restrained the broadcaster from showing a programme about his violent tendencies for fear that witnesses would be deterred from co-operating with the police. The same day the Court of Appeal set aside the injunction because the police had not shown to the necessary high standard that the programme would add significantly to the apprehension which witnesses might already feel in view of the violent reputations of the victim and others associated with the case.[201] Allegations of intentional contempt are clearly not within s.7, but injunctions of this type should be narrowly confined[202] and the applicant must prove to the criminal standard beyond reasonable doubt (or, at least, to a high standard of persuasion)[203] that the publication will create a real risk of prejudice and that the defendants will publish their material with a specific intent of causing that risk. This is a considerably more onerous task than the courts used to require on an application for interlocutory injunctions,[204] but it is consistent with s.12(3) of the Human Rights Act.

---

[197] CPR, Sch.1; RSC, O.109, r.4. The Divisional Court has a like power to grant bail pending appeal from it to the House of Lords: O.109 r.3.
[198] *Irtelli v Squatriti* [1993] Q.B. 83.
[199] *Peacock v LWT*, *The Times*, November 27, 1985.
[200] *Pickering v Liverpool Daily Post and Echo Newspapers Plc* [1991] 2 A.C. 370.
[201] *Chief Constable of Greater Manchester Police v Channel 5 Broadcast Ltd* [2005] EWCA Civ 739.
[202] *Taylor v Topping*, *The Times*, February 15, 1990.
[203] *Chief Constable of Greater Manchester Police v Channel 5*, above.
[204] *Coe v Central TV Plc* [1994] E.M.L.R. 433.

Any application for an injunction would normally be made in the High Court[205] and the powers in Contempt of Court Act 1981 ss.4(2) and 11 (see para.8–071) will normally suffice for Crown Court judges, but there is some support for the claim for Crown Courts themselves to exercise a wider injunctive power.[206] Even if this power does exist, it should only be very sparingly exercised.[207]

---

[205] Supreme Court Act 1981 s.37 gives the High Court the power to grant injunctions.

[206] *Ex p. HTV Cymru (Wales) Ltd* [2002] EMLR 184, Aikens J.

[207] Arlidge, Eady and Smith J.J.*Contempt*, para.6–2.

CHAPTER 8

REPORTING THE COURTS

INTRODUCTION

The most fundamental principle of justice is that it must be seen to **8–001** be done. Lord Halsbury, in the great constitutional case of *Scott v Scott*, proclaimed that, "Every court in the land is open to every subject of the King".[1] The rule became established almost by historical accident from the fact that courts in the Middle Ages were badly conducted public meetings in which neighbours gathered to pass judgment on their district's notorious felons. The Star Chamber followed the practice and heard all its cases in public, in order that its vicious punishments would have a general deterrent effect.

"Freeborn" John Lilburne, the charismatic Leveller, stated the right in robust terms at his treason trial in 1649:

> "The Court must uphold the first fundamental liberty of an Englishman, that all courts of justice always ought to be free and open for all sorts of peaceable people to see, behold and hear, and have free access unto; and no man whatsoever ought to be tried in holes or corners, or in any place where the gates are shut and barred."

Cromwell's judges, who were sure that the jury would obey their orders to convict Lilburne, ruled that the court doors must remain open at all times "that all the world may know with what candour and justice the court does proceed against you". The world was more impressed by Lilburne than with his persecutors and, to cheers from the spectators, the jury acquitted.[2]

In time, jurists like Blackstone and Bentham elevated the practice **8–002** into a fundamental precondition of justice. They acclaimed it on a number of grounds, principally as a safeguard against judicial error or misbehaviour. In Bentham's words, "Publicity is the very soul of justice. It is the keenest spur to exertion and the surest of all guards

---

[1] *Scott v Scott* [1913] A.C. 417.
[2] Geoffrey Robertson, *The Tyrannicide Brief* (Vintage, 2005), p.219.

against improbity. It keeps the judge himself, while trying, under trial." Moreover, publicity deters perjury, in that witnesses are likely to come forward to confound lies when they learn that they are being told. Press reporting of court cases enhances public knowledge and appreciation of the workings of the law, it assists the deterrent function of criminal trials and it permits the revelation of matters of genuine public interest. On the other hand, of course, it can at times be shallow, sensational or just plain incompetent. Courts have some corrective powers and can usually protect parties from any prejudice. A more persuasive reason for restricting the right to report is the desire to protect witnesses against loss of face or loss of job, or even, where police informers are concerned, against possible loss of life. Does it really matter if a few cases go unreported so that prosecution witnesses are relieved from the anxiety of reading their names in newspapers? It does, for the reasons given by Blackstone and Bentham. Trials derive their legitimacy from being conducted in public; the judge presides as a surrogate for the people, who are entitled to see and approve the power exercised on their behalf. Those who assist the prosecution can and should be protected by other means. No matter how fair, justice must still be seen before it can be said to have been done.

The open-justice principle is now firmly embedded, with the help of Blackstone and Bentham, in the constitutional jurisprudence of the United States and Canada. The Supreme Courts of both countries have endorsed Wigmore's reasoning as to the evidential consequences of the requirement for hearings in public:

> "Its operation in tending to *improve the quality of testimony* [our italics] is two-fold. Subjectively, it produces in the witness's mind a disinclination to falsify; first, by stimulating the instinctive responsibility to public opinion, symbolised in the audience, and ready to scorn a demonstrated liar; and next, by inducing the fear of exposure of subsequent falsities through disclosure by informed persons who may chance to be present or to hear of the testimony from others present. Objectively, it secures the presence of those who by possibility may be able to furnish testimony in chief or to contradict falsifiers and yet may not have been known beforehand to the parties to possess any information."[3]

The US Supreme Court has gone further, by regarding openness as a defining characteristic of the integrity of a trial process,[4] while the Supreme Court of Canada has struck down legislation preventing the reporting of evidence in divorce cases as contrary to the guarantee of freedom of expression.[5] Justice Bertha Wilson concluded in that case:

---

[3] *Wigmore on Evidence*, para.1834.
[4] *Richmond Newspapers v Virginia* (1980) 448 U.S. 555.
[5] *Edmonton Journal v Att-Gen for Alberta* (1989) 64 D.L.R. (4th) 577.

"In summary, the public interest in open trials and in the ability of the press to provide complete reports of what takes place in the courtroom is rooted in the need: (1) to maintain an effective evidentiary process; (2) to ensure a judiciary and juries that behave fairly and that are sensitive to the values espoused by the society; (3) to promote a shared sense that our courts operate with integrity and dispense justice; and (4) to provide an ongoing opportunity for the community to learn how the justice system operates and how the law being applied daily in the courts affects them."[6]

In the United States and Canada the open justice rule is strictly **8–003** enforced by reference to a "freedom of expression" guarantee. In Britain the courts pay lip-service to the rule, but enforce it, as we shall see, haphazardly and at times inconsistently. Ironically, this is one area where the European Convention has damaged a UK free speech principle (see Ch.1, para.1–019). European countries have never been so wedded to open justice and the Convention treats it as a qualified right and gives it (in terms) to the parties (who frequently want a cover-up) and not to the press. Thus Art.6's guarantee is encrusted with exceptions. It says:

"(1) In the determination of his civil rights and obligations or of any criminal charge, everyone is entitled to a fair and public hearing by an independent and impartial tribunal established by law. Judgment shall be pronounced publicly but the press and public may be excluded from all or part of the trial in the interests of morals, public order or national security in a democratic society, where the interests of juveniles or the protection of the private life of the parties so require, or to the extent strictly necessary in the opinion of the court in special circumstances where publicity would prejudice the interests of justice."

At least, the European Court of Human Rights has recognised that while the litigants can waive the right to a public hearing, they can only do so if court secrecy does not run counter to any important public interest.[7]

Following the Human Rights Act, the House of Lords has re-affirmed the importance of open justice. In *Re S*[8] Lord Steyn said,

"A criminal trial is a public event. The principle of open justice puts, as has often been said, the judge and all who participate in the trial under intense scrutiny. The glare of contemporaneous

---

[6] *Edmonton Journal.*
[7] *Hakansson v Sweden* (1991) 13 E.H.R.R. 1, para.66.
[8] [2005] 1 A.C. 593 at [30].

publicity ensures that trials are properly conducted. It is a valuable check on the criminal process. Moreover, the public interest may be as much involved in the circumstances of a remarkable acquittal as in a surprising conviction. Informed public debate is necessary about all such matters. Full contemporaneous reporting of criminal trials in progress promotes public confidence in the administration of justice. It promotes the value of the rule of law."

8–004 In the same case he warned of the dangers of injunction creep—where one exception to the open justice principle is cantilevered to justify another, slightly further, exception in the next case and so on. He acknowledged that if a defendant cannot be named, the trial reporting will be disembodied and less attractive to readers and editors alike. Informed debate about criminal trials would suffer. Finally, he recognised the chilling effect of the cost of contesting injunction applications for the media generally but for less well-funded local newspapers in particular.

For all the opportunities presented by the open justice principle, it must be said that the standard of legal journalism in Britain is not particularly high, certainly when compared to the United States. It may be that reporters, sitting snugly in their privileged "press bench", have come to regard themselves as part and parcel of the court process, rather than as "the eyes and ears of the public". It is often claimed on behalf of the media that it enjoys no special privileges over and above those enjoyed by ordinary citizens. In the case of court reporting, however, this is manifestly untrue. The media do enjoy special rights—to sit in the press bench and to be present on some of the occasions when the general public are excluded—and it is important for journalists to understand the reason why the courts recognise those privileges. In the words of the former Master of the Rolls, Lord Donaldson:

"It is not because of any special wisdom, interest or status enjoyed by proprietors, editors or journalists. It is because the media are the eyes and ears of the general public. They act on behalf of the general public. Their right to know and their right to publish is neither more nor less than that of the general public. Indeed it *is* that of the general public for whom they are trustees."[9]

If British journalists have been reluctant to probe the processes of justice, they are certainly concerned to report sensational stories that emerge in evidence in the course of legal proceedings. It has been thus for centuries; indeed, the first newspapers consisted of nothing

---

[9] *Att-Gen v Guardian Newspapers Ltd (No. 2)* [1988] 3 All E.R. 595, 600, applied in *Re M* [1990] 1 All E.R. 205.

but court reports. Daily "chapbooks" of Old Bailey trials were hawked in the streets of seventeenth-century London at one penny apiece, catering to the curious, the pitying, the righteous and the prurient, who will always be interested in the crimes and punishments of the court calendar.[10] Coverage of the latest excitement in a sensational criminal case will attract circulation, especially if the press report is spiced with some of the colour and drama of the trial. There is another great attraction to the modern newspaper in court reports: they are "privileged" against actions for libel. The courtroom is one of the few places where an English person can say *"J'accuse"* and have the accusation reported to the country. During the Helen Smith inquest, the nurse's father muttered an accusation that two named persons had killed her. Court reporters, who could not hear what he said from the press gallery, worked out his words from a specially amplified tape of the proceedings. Ron Smith's accusation was headlined in all the papers the following day, whereupon the coroner fined him for an "outburst" in court that he (the coroner) had not noticed at the time it was made.[11] The fact that the newspapers were reporting a statement in open court albeit made *sotto voce*, protected them from libel action. There may be doubts about the wisdom of a rule that gives parties to court proceedings the privilege of exploiting them to make defamatory statements that cannot be proved. Nonetheless, the probability that the privilege will be abused on occasions is the price that must be paid for allegiance to the open court principle.

There are always those who are willing to find the price of this **8–005** principle too high. The case of *Home Office v Harman*, in which solicitor and subsequently Solicitor-General, Harriet Harman, was held in contempt for showing documents to a journalist after they had been read in open court, is one example (see para.8–106). The decision has been reversed by a change to the Rules of Court following a decision in her favour by the European Commission of Human Rights. The media must be prepared to fight all attacks on the open justice principle, wherever they occur. The media have, in their ability to publicise, the best antidote against attempts to close the courtroom doors. Whenever there is secrecy, there will inevitably be some suspicion of impropriety. Those who seek to defy the open justice principle often find that machinations to this end prove counterproductive.

The open justice principle is based, however, on public interest considerations. It must give way when the public interest dictates a degree of privacy. The names of rape and blackmail victims, for example, are suppressed in the interests of mitigating their pain and encouraging other victims to come forward. Family disputes are

---

[10] Langbein, "The Criminal Trial Before Lawyers" (1978) 45 U. of Chicago L.R. 263, 267.
[11] See Geoffrey Robertson, *The Justice Game* (Vintage, 1999), Ch.8.

heard in private when details might damage the children of a disrupted marriage. Postponement of publication of certain evidence in criminal trials is justified on occasions when it might cause irredeemable prejudice to other trials. These exceptions are reasonable, but the media must be on constant guard against allowing them to be extended or exploited to prevent genuine public interest revelations.

In the great majority of court cases the press are free to attend and report everything said in the course of the legal proceedings. The following sections of this chapter deal with cases where access to the court room is restricted, enumerate the rules that restrict reporting, look at the means that the press can use to gather and record information about legal proceedings, and examine in more detail the defences of absolute and qualified privilege against claims for libel and slander that court reports enjoy.

PUBLIC ACCESS TO THE COURTS

8–006 The general principle is that every court is open for citizens to see justice being done. The principle was summed up by Lord Diplock in *Att-Gen v Leveller Magazine Ltd*.[12] who said,

> "As a general rule the English system of administering justice does require that it be done in public: *Scott v Scott*. If the way that courts behave cannot be hidden from the public ear and eye this provides a safeguard against judicil arbitrariness or idiosyncrasy and maintains public confidence in the administration of justice. The application of this principle of open justice has two aspects: as respects proceedings in the court itself it requires that they should be held in open court to which the Press and public are admitted and that, in criminal cases, at any rate, all evidence communicated to the court is communicated publicly. As respects publications to a wider public of fair and accurate reports of proceedings that have taken place in court the principle requires that nothing should be done to discourage this."

A court is not "open" if the judge takes deliberate steps to keep the press at bay:

> A Government minister wanted to avoid the publicity of his divorce trial, so the judge obligingly agreed to hold the hearing in the court library. The only access was through a door marked "private". This was left ajar and the judge announced to the parties and their representatives before he started that the court was open. On appeal, the Privy

---

[12] *Att-Gen v Leveller Magazine Ltd* [1979] A.C. 440 at 450.

Council said this was a sham and in reality the hearing had been in private. Because there was no jurisdiction at the time to hear such cases in secret, the proceedings were a nullity.[13]

English magistrates have not been averse to similar expedients, but statute requires them to sit in open court when hearing a criminal trial, a civil complaint, a means inquiry or when imposing imprisonment.[14] There must be a real opportunity for a casual member of the public to attend. Consequently an employment tribunal did not sit in public when access was through a door which could only be opened with a key code.[15] The Administrative Court has said that the test should be whether the arrangements as a whole sufficiently inhibit a member of the public from attending court as to make the hearing one in private.[16] In that case, the district judge was held to have sat in public, though an usher had to be asked to gain access to the court. (Security was said to have required these measures.)

Whenever a magistrates' court deviates from the open justice **8–007** principle it is subject to correction by the High Court, which has recognised that journalists and newspapers have a right to enforce the principle in the public interest. This right was most firmly established in a case brought by investigative reporter David Leigh:

> The magistrates of Felixstowe adopted a policy of refusing to allow the press and interested members of the public to know the names of individual J.P.s who tried particular cases. They feared that J.P.s would be exposed to nuisance calls and reprisals over unpopular decisions. The Divisional Court declared this policy unlawful and unconstitutional. It was an unwarranted obstruction of the fundamental right to know the identity of persons who sit in judgment ("There is no such person known to the law as the anonymous J.P."). The court described the court reporter as "the watchdog of justice", who plays an essential role in the administration of the law by noting any possible unfairness or impropriety on the part of the bench. The magistrate "will be more anxious to give a correct decision if he knows that his reasons must justify themselves at the bar of public opinion".[17]

A Home Office circular recommends that the media should have copies of the court lists on the day of the hearings and, as a

---

[13] *McPherson v McPherson* [1936] A.C. 177.

[14] Magistrates' Courts Act 1980, s.121(4).

[15] *Storer v British Gas Plc* [2000] 1 W.L.R. 1237 CA and see para.9–010.

[16] *R. (on the application of Pelling) v Bow County Court* [2001] U.K.H.R.R. 165, Admin. Court, application for permission to appeal dismissed January 22, 2001 [2001] E.W.C.A. Civ. 122.

[17] *R. v Felixstowe JJ Ex p. Leigh* [1987] QB 582. On the other hand, although the common practice is for jurors from the panel to be called to the jury box by name to be sworn, the court can permit them to remain anonymous if there are real fears of jury nobbling: *R. v Comerford* [1998] 1 Cr.App.R. 235, CA.

minimum, these should contain the defendant's name, address, age, profession (where known) and the alleged offence. Where provisional lists are prepared in advance, copies of these should be available to the media on request. Courts are, however, also strongly recommended to charge the full economic cost of this service.[18]

Usually a bench or table is set aside for the press close to the witness box and to counsel. Reporters may be exercising a public right, but they do so from a privileged position. Any attempt to commandeer the press bench, or to relegate reporters to barely audible positions at the back of the court, should be challenged.

Exclusion in the public interest

8–008 What exceptional circumstances permit a court to sit in secret without rendering its proceedings a nullity? First, those circumstances in which Parliament, by express statutory enactment, has given permission to expel the public. The statutes containing such express powers are summarised below. Secondly, where for convenience of handling interim applications the case is heard by judges sitting in a private room, the public is effectively barred, although practice has shifted in recent years and judges are now encouraged to respond positively to press requests to be admitted. Generally there is nothing to stop the press from publishing accounts of what went on in chambers, if details can be discovered and the publication will not prejudice a future trial. But is there an inherent power in the court to exclude both press and public in the interests of justice?

In *Scott v Scott*[19] the Law Lords were divided on the subject. Several said that a court had no power other than that given by statute. One thought that members of the public were only to be excluded if "administration of justice would be rendered impracticable by their presence". Viscount Haldane put the test thus: "To justify an order for a hearing *in camera* it must be shown that the paramount object of securing that justice is done would really be rendered doubtful of attainment if the order were not made."[20]

This rightly stresses the rigorousness of the test. Convenience is not enough: "It must be necessary to avoid the subordination of the

---

[18] Home Office Circulars 80/1989. The staff of some magistrates' courts have been concerned that disclosing lists to the press would infringe the Data Protection Act 1998. However, following discussion between the Home Office, the Newspaper Society and the Information Commissioner, the Commissioner has confirmed that courts can continue to provide lists, registers and other information in accordance with Circular 80/1989 and assist journalists with their inquiries to check accuracy and progress of cases without contravening the Data Protection Act: *Reporting Restrictions in the Magistrates' Courts*, Judicial Studies Board, Newspaper Society and Society of Editors (2001), p.6.

[19] [1913] A.C. 417.

[20] [1913] A.C. at 439, and see at 442, 446 and 448.

ends of justice to the means."[21] There must also be material (though not necessarily formal evidence) on which the court can reasonably reach its conclusion.[22] This can be tendered or submitted in writing or agreed in private,[23] but the decision whether the case should proceed in secret must normally be publicly announced.[24]

In 1991 the Court of Appeal agreed to hear some applications in **8–009** respect of the Polly Peck collapse in private.[25] Lord Donaldson justified the secrecy on the grounds that banks, building societies and other financial institutions that depend on investor confidence might be irreparably damaged if the allegations against them in civil proceedings were made public at an early stage, and later proved false. This prospect is somewhat fanciful and, in any event, overlooks the interests of customers and investors who continue dealing with the bank in ignorance of allegations that are subsequently found to be true. There is no real distinction between private hearings for civil claims against banks and building societies, and private hearings for a restaurateur accused of violating health standards to avoid adverse publicity that will reduce custom (which the Divisional Court will not permit).[26]

The Haldane exception has much less force since the 1981 Contempt of Court Act introduced postponement orders. The court ought now to consider whether justice might not be sufficiently served by making a more limited order permitting the press to remain but postponing reporting until such time as it will do no harm to the interests of justice.[27]

In 1982 the Divisional Court issued a clear warning to magistrates and their clerks against excluding the press:

> A "supergrass" appeared before the Reigate Justices on charges of burglary and theft. These offences had been committed after he had received a lenient sentence for informing, and after police had given him a new identity. The defence asked the justices to hear his mitigation in secret, and the bench succumbed when the prosecution supported the application. The defendant was given an inexplicably light sentence. There was a press outcry, and several newspapers ensured that the secrecy was counterproductive by identifying the defendant and giving details of his unrepentant criminal career. The

---

[21] Lord Devlin in *Re K* [1965] A.C. 201, 239 and see Lord Haldane in *Scott*, fn.1 above, at 438, Viscount Reading C.J. in *R. v Lewes Prison (Governor) Ex p. Doyle* [1917] 2 K.B. 254, 271 and *Att-Gen v Leveller Magazine Ltd* [1979] A.C. 440 at 450, 464, 731 at 750, 761, *per* Lords Diplock and Edmund-Davies.

[22] *Att-Gen v Leveller Magazine Ltd*, above, at 471 *per* Lord Scarman.

[23] *R. v Tower Bridge Magistrates' Court Ex p. Osborne* (1989) 88 Cr.App.R. 28, QBD.

[24] *R. v Ealing Justices Ex p. Weaver* (1982) 74 Cr.App.R. 204.

[25] *Polly Peck International Plc v Nadir*, *The Times*, November 11, 1991, CA following *R. v Chief Registrar of Building Societies, Ex p. New Cross Building Society* [1984] Q.B. 227.

[26] *R. v Dover Justices Ex p. Dover District Council* (1992) 156 J.P. 433, D.C.

[27] *R. v Reigate JJs Ex p. Argus Newspapers Ltd* (1983) 5 Cr.App.R.(S) 181.

Divisional Court, on an application by the *Surrey Mirror*, held that the justices had been wrongly advised: they were entitled to sit in secret only if proceedings in open court would "frustrate the process of justice". The question was whether secrecy was *strictly necessary*, rather than merely convenient or expedient.[28]

8–010 The warning was reiterated in 1988:

A woman motorist who had pleaded guilty to a charge of driving with excess alcohol persuaded a magistrates' court to hear her arguments in mitigation in secret. She was divorcing her husband. This had caused emotional problems and suicidal tendencies. She would not be capable of giving evidence of these matters unless the court sat in private. The prosecution did not oppose the application, which was allowed by the bench. Having heard the evidence in private, the court disqualified the defendant for only three (as opposed to the usual 12) months. A local journalist and his publishers applied for judicial review of the decision to sit in secret. The Divisional Court said that while magistrates did have jurisdiction to sit in secret, they should do so only if there were compelling reasons, the existence of which were likely to be rare. The order in the present case appeared wholly unsustainable and out of accord with principle. It was not surprising that in this case justice had neither been seen nor done.[29]

How should a court deal with an application to sit in private? In the first place the Criminal Procedure Rules require the Crown or defence to give seven days advance notice on the door of the court if it intends to ask the Court to sit in private for reasons of national security or to protect the identity of a witness.[30] When this or any other type of application to sit in private comes to be argued, should the application itself be heard in private? If the reasons for excluding the public are sound then presenting them in public may cause the very damage which the application is intended to avoid.[31] On the other hand, spurious arguments may succeed in private which would not stand up to public scrutiny. In one case the Divisional Court said that an application of this kind should always be heard in private,[32] but a more nuanced approach was required by the Court of Appeal in *Re Crook*.[33] While the magistrate or judge might not be able to fully understand the nature of the application until it is made and so would often need to hear the application in private, he ought not to agree to sit in private as a matter of course. If the judge does sit in chambers he should be alert to the importance of adjourning into

---

[28] *Argus Newspapers*.

[29] *R. v Malvern Justices Ex p. Evans* [1988] Q.B. 553, QBD. See also *R. v Epping and Ongar Justices Ex p. Breach* [1986] Crim. L.R. 810.

[30] Criminal Procedure Rules r.16.10(1) and see below para.8–013.

[31] *Re. A* [2006] 2 All E.R. 1, CA at [20].

[32] *R v Tower Bridge Magistrates' Court Ex p. Osborne* (1989) 88 Cr.App.R. 28.

[33] (1991) 93 Cr.App.R. 17, CA.

open court as soon as it apparent that it is not necessary to exclude the public. Similarly, an application by the prosecution for the public to be excluded from all or part of the trial on grounds of national security or for the protection of the identity of a witness or some other person will normally itself be heard in private, but this is subject to the court's discretion to order otherwise.[34]

Committal proceedings

A criminal charge is either tried by magistrates[35] or by a judge and **8–011** jury at a Crown Court. The latter is known as trial on indictment, the indictment being the formal accusation of the offence. Traditionally, most indictments have been preceded by committal proceedings.[36] These are conducted by magistrates, who, when acting in this capacity, must sit in open court except where a statute provides to the contrary or where it "appears to them as respects the whole or any part of the committal proceedings that the ends of justice would not be served by their sitting in open court".[37] This will rarely, if ever, be the case, because if the normal reporting restrictions are not lifted, reports of the proceedings must be postponed until after the full trial; and if reporting restrictions are lifted, the magistrates have power to postpone reports of any evidence that may cause serious prejudice to the trial (see para.8–078). In consequence, committal proceedings are hardly ever reported other than in the barest of details.

Most committals are purely formal. The defence can submit that there is no case to answer, but the magistrates can no longer hear oral evidence.[38] They are confined to the documentary evidence put in by the prosecution. If the defence chooses not to make a submission, the magistrates need not even read the statements and the press in court will not know their contents.[39]

Voluntary bills of indictment

Instead of asking magistrates to commit a defendant for trial, a **8–012** prosecutor can apply to a High Court judge for a voluntary bill of indictment.[40] This is considered by the judge in private and neither

---

[34] Criminal Procedure Rules 2005 r.16.10.
[35] Magistrates are either "lay" (i.e. unpaid and not lawyers) or district judges (magistrates) who are professional lawyers and are paid. They were previously known as "stipendiaries" because they received a stipend.
[36] However, committal proceedings are in the process of being superseded by the alternative and speedier processes of "transfer", "sending" and "allocating" to the Crown Court—see para.8–029 below.
[37] Magistrates' Courts Act 1980, s.4(2).
[38] See Magistrates' Courts Act 1980, s.5A.
[39] Criminal Procedure Rules r.10.2(3) Where magistrates take a deposition from a witness for the purpose of committal or transfer proceedings, this must also be done presumptively in open court: *R. (Crown Prosecution Service) v Bolton Magistrates' Court* [2004] 1 W.L.R. 835 DC.
[40] Administration of Justice (Miscellaneous Provisions) Act 1933, s.2(2).

the prosecution nor the defendant, let alone the press, has the right to be present.[41] It is an exceptional step, which may be justified where a magistrate has unreasonably refused to commit the defendant or where a suspect is caught shortly before any co-accused have been committed to stand trial.[42]

Official secrets

8–013 There is a presumption that prosecutions for breaches of the Official Secrets Acts are to be treated in the same way as any other prosecution and must be held in public. However, the Crown can apply for all or part of the public to be excluded during all or part of the evidence.[43] It must persuade the court that publication of the evidence would be prejudicial to national safety. Secret hearings ought to be confined to the minimum.

The restrictions can be applied to committal hearings, trial and appeal, but the sentence must be passed in public.[44] If the Crown (or defendant) in a criminal trial intends to ask the court to sit in secret for reasons of national security, it must give seven days' advance warning to the court, which must then prominently display a notice in the court stating that the application is to be made. The application must be made after the defendant has pleaded to the charge but before the jury is empanelled. If the court decides that it will sit in secret, it must adjourn for 24 hours to allow an appeal against this decision to be made to the Court of Appeal.[45] When these procedural rules are not observed the Court of Appeal is likely to quash a direction that the trial or any part of it be heard in private because the media (or any other interested person) will not have had even the limited opportunity which the Rules allow to challenge the order.[46] In civil cases the court can hear technical information about defence contracts in secret if this is necessary or expedient in the public interest or in the interest of the parties to the proceedings.[47]

Private secrets

8–014 Some actions are brought to restrain the defendant from publishing or using information that the claimant alleges was acquired in confidence or over which the claimant has monopoly control. If these actions and those concerning secret inventions had to be held in public, their whole purpose would be frustrated. However, the

---

[41] Indictments (Procedure) Rules 1971 (SI 1971/2084) r.10.
[42] *R. v Raymond* [1981] Q.B. 910, CA.
[43] Official Secrets Act 1920, s.8(4), extended to offences under the Official Secrets Act 1989 (except in relation to careless loss of documents, 1989 Act, s.11(4)).
[44] Official Secrets Act 1920, s.8(4).
[45] Criminal Procedure Rules r.16.10.
[46] *Ex p. Guardian Newspapers* [1999] 1 All E.R. 65.
[47] Defence Contracts Act 1958, s.4(3).

court should agree to sit in secret only so far as is necessary and any part of the evidence that would not give away the secret should be heard in public in the normal way. In *Lion Laboratories v Evans*[48] (the intoximeter case) the Court of Appeal declined to direct or request the press not to publish the confidential material set out in its judgment: appreciation of this material was necessary to enable the public to understand its decision. The House of Lords exercised greater discretion in *Cream Holdings Ltd v Banerjee* when it held that night club operators were not entitled to a breach of confidence interim injunction because the *Liverpool Daily Post* would be likely to establish a public interest defence (see para.5–028). Considerately, it decided that the details of the public interest case should not be included in its judgment because that would rob the newspaper of its scoop. (It would also have deprived claimant of entitlement to compensation if the case proceeded to trial and, against the expectations of the Lords, the public interest defence failed.)[49]

In commercial cases applications are sometimes made for the court to sit in secret to prevent the disclosure of price-sensitive information. Even these should be considered critically and the courts should be wary of displacing the normal principle of open justice.

> When a company stopped paying its lawyers so that its application for the removal of a provisional liquidator had to be abandoned, the Vice-Chancellor dismissed the application in open court, even though all the argument had taken place in secret. He said that hearings in closed court "were contrary to the public interest and should only take place if it was clear that there was a contrary public interest which overrode the need for public justice". Once the application had been abandoned "the general public should be aware of what has been happening".[50]

Similarly, the court refused to conduct the trials of Lloyds' cases in private. Instead, it used its powers to give directions to avoid unnecessary reference in open court to matters which could be commercially damaging, provided that the parties were not inhibited in developing their cases.[51]

Special measures for witnesses: private hearings

The Youth Justice and Criminal Evidence Act 1999 introduced a **8–015** raft of measures to assist witnesses who were children, or disabled in some way or whose evidence might be prejudiced by fear or distress.

---

[48] *Lion Laboratories v Evans* [1985] Q.B. 526 (see para.5–014).
[49] *Cream Holdings Ltd v Banerjee* [2005] 1 A.C. 253.
[50] *Re London and Norwich Investment Services Ltd* [1988] B.C.L.C. 226. See also *British and Commonwealth Holdings Plc v Quadrex Holdings Inc, The Independent,* December 13, 1988.
[51] *Hallam-Eames v Merrett Syndicates Ltd, The Times,* June 16, 1995.

Where the proceedings concern a sexual offence or it appears to the court that there are reasonable grounds for believing that anyone other than the accused has sought or will seek to intimidate the witness in connection with their testimony these "special measures" include excluding the public from the court.[52] Unlike the position in youth courts (see para.8–017) there is no right for all journalists to remain, but the order clearing the court must allow one representative of a news gathering or reporting organisation who has been nominated for the purpose by one or more of these organisations to stay in court. Where such an order looks likely, the journalists present will have to be ready to make a quick selection. No doubt it will be a condition of nomination that the representative shares his or her reporting with every other journalist who wants access to them. If no nomination is made, the judge can exclude all journalists. When the court restricts the number of reporters who can be present in the court room during the trial of a young person, arrangements should be made for the proceedings to be relayed audibly and, if possible, visually to another room in the same court complex to which the media have free access if it appears that there will be a need for such facilities.[53] Even though the public and the rest of the press are excluded from court, the proceedings shall be treated as though they took place in public for the purposes of any privilege or exemption from liability in respect of fair, accurate and contemporaneous reports of legal proceedings held in public (i.e. essentially defamation and contempt).

Family and children cases

8–016   A court hearing wardship proceedings and applications under the Children Act 1989 is acting in a quasi-parental role. Full publicity is not appropriate and consequently these cases are usually (though not invariably) heard in private.[54] In 1997 the Court of Appeal confirmed that courts would only rarely exercise their discretion to hear Children Act cases in public.[55] Subsequently the European Court of Human Rights reviewed the issue. It said that it was not inconsistent with Art.6(1) to designate an entire class of cases as an exception to the general rule of open hearings where this was considered necessary on one of the grounds in Art.6(1) where private hearings are permitted. However, the need for such measures

---

[52] Youth Justice and Criminal Evidence Act 1999, s.25. For other aspects of the "special measures" see para.8–046.

[53] *Practice Direction (Criminal Proceedings: Consolidation)* [2002] 1 W.L.R. 2870, para.IV.39.15.

[54] *Re F (A Minor: Publication of Information)* [1977] 1 All E.R. 114. For the High Court and County Court: Family Proceedings Rules 1991, r.4.16(7). Magistrates' Courts can exclude the press if they consider it expedient in the interests of the child: Family Proceedings Courts (Children Act 1989) Rules 1991, r.16(7).

[55] *P-B (A Minor) (Child Cases: Hearings in Open Court)* [1997] 1 All E.R. 58, CA.

must always be subject to the Court's control.[56] So the parties or the press can apply for a particular hearing to be held in public. However, Press applications for access should be made promptly to minimise disruption or the press applicants may have to bear costs.[57] This English practice of secret hearings for Children Act cases is in stark contrast to Scotland where residence and contact cases are routinely heard in public.

More recently the courts have indicated a somewhat greater willingness to admit the press to certain proceedings involving children as illustrated by the case of *Re Brandon Webster*[58]:

> Each of the Websters three older children had been taken into care following allegations of abuse. The parents had fled to Ireland where their fourth child (Brandon) had been born but had returned to Norfolk when he was five months old. The local authority wished to take him into care as well. The Websters and various media organisations applied to attend the care proceedings in the High Court. Their application was successful. In a wide ranging review of the authorities Mr Justice Munby reiterated that the public justice principle applied as much to the Family Division as other courts although some cases involving children required confidentiality. As the European Court of Human Rights had said in *Moser v Austria*[59] the arguments in favour of publicity were greater where the dispute involved public law (e.g. whether a child should be taken into care) than private law (e.g. with which parent a child should live). The Family Proceedings Rules r.4.16(7) provided a default position in favour of privacy where children were concerned: it did not amount to a heavy presumption in its favour. In this case the reasons for allowing the press (but not the public generally) to attend were the allegations of miscarriages of justice in relation to the previous children being taken into care; the fact that the parents themselves wanted publicity; the publicity which the case had already attracted; and the need for the full facts to emerge in a way which would command confidentiality in the judicial system.

Adoption proceedings in the High Court may take place in chambers: in the county court they must do so.[60] Sometimes the court is asked to authorise the termination of life support services to a patient in a persistent vegetative state. These decisions, which are literally of life and death, arouse considerable public interest and for this reason the court is likely to sit in open court although the identity of the parties may be protected by anonymity orders.[61]

---

[56] *B v UK, P v UK* (2002) 34 E.H.R.R. 529 and the Court of Appeal followed suit in *P v BW (Children Cases: Hearings in Public)* [2004] 1 F.L.R. 171.

[57] *A v Times Newspapers* [2003] 1 All E.R. 587, Fam D.

[58] *Re Brandon Webster (A Child) Norfolk County Council v Webster* [2007] EMLR 7 (Fam).

[59] *Moser v Austria* [2006] 3 F.C.R. 107.

[60] Adoption Act 1976, s.64(a) and (b).

[61] *Re G (Adult Patient: Publicity)* [1995] 2 F.L.R. 528.

8–017 Parliament has given the courts power to sit in secret when hearing petitions for a declaration of marital status, the effectiveness of an overseas adoption, legitimacy or parentage.[62] The hearing will not automatically be in private. The courts must take into account the effect of publicity on the petitioner, including his or her health and occupation, and on third parties who might be affected by the revelation of family secrets. It must then weigh this against the traditional rule of public policy that justice should be administered openly.[63] If questions as to parentage are raised in other proceedings, they must be publicly resolved unless there is some other power to consider them in secret.[64]

Court rules now provide that evidence in divorce and nullity proceedings should normally be given in open court,[65] though in the common case where the divorce is undefended and the spouses have lived apart, the evidence will be heard in private and only the decision announced in open court.[66] Ancillary proceedings concerning such matters as maintenance and division of property are normally heard in chambers.[67] Applications for injunctions (e.g. for occupation orders to oust one party from the shared home) are also normally made in chambers.[68] Further, where it is alleged that a marriage is a nullity because one spouse was unable to consummate it, evidence on the question of sexual capacity should be heard in secret unless the judge is persuaded that in the interests of justice it should be heard in open court.[69] As with Official Secrets, the press and the public should be excluded only while the sensitive evidence is being given.

Magistrates must sit in private when sitting as a youth court, although representatives of news-gathering organisations are entitled to be present.[70] The press (but not the public) can also attend family proceedings in the magistrates' courts.[71] The public, but not the press, can be kept out of an adult court while a child or young person gives evidence in relation of a sex offence.[72]

---

[62] Domestic and Appellate Proceedings (Restrictions of Publicity) Act 1968, s.2; which reversed the decision of *B (P) v Att-Gen* [1965] 3 All E.R. 253, and see Family Law Reform Act 1986, ss.55–60 and Family Law Reform Act 1987, s.22.

[63] *Barritt v Att-Gen* [1971] 3 All E.R. 1183, Wrangham J.

[64] *Prior v Prior* (1970) 114 S.J. 72, PDA Div, Latey J.

[65] Family Proceeding Rules 1991, r. 2.28(I).

[66] 1991 Rules, r.2.36(1) and (2).

[67] In Family Proceedings Rules 1991, r.2.66(2)—ancilliary relief applications.

[68] Family Proceedings Rules 1991, r.3.9(1).

[69] Matrimonial Causes Act 1973, s.48(2).

[70] Children and Young Persons Act 1933, s.47.

[71] Magistrates' Courts Act 1980, s.69(2). There is an exception for adoption proceedings when the press also can be excluded.

[72] Children and Young Persons Act 1933, s.37(1).

Although *Scott v Scott* said that the indecency of evidence was no **8–018** ground for closing the court at common law, magistrates have by statute the power to sit in private for this reason when hearing domestic proceedings.[73]

Outside these areas the general principle of open justice applies even in cases involving children. In October 1988 Mr Justice Boreham agreed to hear in chambers the settlement details of a medical negligence claim brought on behalf of a young child because the agreed damages were for a very large sum and the claimant's mother feared receipt of begging letters. The media protested. The judge recanted and apologised for exceeding his power.[74]

The multiplicity of different rules regarding access to (and reporting of) family proceedings is bewildering. In 1993 the Lord Chancellor's Department produced a Consultation Paper on rationalising them,[75] but no codifying legislation has yet been proposed. Nonetheless there is a growing dissatisfaction with the general practice that Family Division work is conducted in private. There is no comparable practice in Scotland and the groups campaigning for fathers' rights have been particularly vociferous. In 2006 there was a further promise of legislation to bring openness back to these courts although by 2007 the government appeared to be backing away from this measure.

The administration of trusts (often, though not invariably, associated with schemes to reduce the fiscal impact on family wealth) can sometimes lead to law suits, but this is usually conducted in private. The justification advanced is that the activity is more akin to administration than litigation and for this reason the courts have said that Art.6 of the ECHR does not require them to be heard in public.[76]

"In chambers" hearings

District judges in the county court and Masters in the Queen's **8–019** Bench Division of the High Court hear pre-trial applications in chambers. In the Queen's Bench the more important applications (particularly injunctions) can be heard only by a judge, but each day a judge in chambers sits to consider these. The judge in chambers will also hear appeals from Masters. Despite its Dickensian image, the Chancery Division is more open. Pre-trial applications there are heard in open court. Many cases can be brought in either division and a desire for pre-trial privacy used to be often a motive for choosing the Queen's Bench. Judicial impatience with this anomaly

---

[73] Magistrates' Courts Act 1980, s.69(4).
[74] *The Guardian*, October 10, 1988.
[75] *Review of Access to and Reporting of Family Proceedings*.
[76] *Re Trusts of X Charity* [2003] 1 W.L.R. 2751 Ch.D. and see CPR 39PD para.1.5(10).

was forcibly expressed in 1997 by a Chancery judge[77] and by the
Court of Appeal which said:

> "However, it remains a principle of the greatest importance
> that, unless there are compelling reasons for doing otherwise,
> which will not exist in the generality of case, there should be
> public access to hearings in chambers and information available
> as to what occurred at such hearings. The fact that the public do
> not have the same right to attend hearings in chambers as those
> in open court and there can be in addition practical difficulties
> in arranging physical access does not mean that such access as is
> practical should not be granted. Depending on the nature of the
> request reasonable arrangements will normally be able to be
> made by a judge (of course we use this term to include Masters)
> to ensure that the fact that the hearing takes place in chambers
> does not materially interfere with the right of the public,
> including the media, to know and observe what happens in
> chambers. Sometimes the solution may be to allow one repre-
> sentative of the press to attend. Another solution may be to give
> judgment in open court so that the judge is not only able to
> announce the order which he is making, but is also able to give
> an account of the proceedings in chambers."[78]

Since then, the Civil Procedure Rules have promulgated a common procedure for the Court of Appeal, all Divisions of the High
Court and the county court. They stipulate:

> "39.2
>
> (1) The general rule is that a hearing is to be in public.
> (2) The requirement for a hearing to be in public does not require the
>   court to make special arrangements for accommodating members
>   of the public.
> (3) A hearing, or any part of it, may be in private if—
>
>   (a) publicity would defeat the object of the hearing;
>   (b) it involves matters relating to national security;
>   (c) it involves confidential information (including information
>   relating to personal financial matters) and publicity would
>   damage that confidentiality;
>   (d) a private hearing is necessary to protect the interests of any
>   child or patient;
>   (e) it is a hearing of an application made without notice and it
>   would be unjust to any respondent for there to be a public
>   hearing;
>   (f) it involves uncontentious matters arising in the administra-
>   tion of trusts or in the administration of a deceased person's
>   estate; or

---

[77] *Forbes v Smith* [1998] 1 All E.R. 973.
[78] *Hodgson v Imperial Tobacco Ltd* [1998] 1 W.L.R. 1056, C.A.

(g) the court considers this to be necessary, in the interests of justice.

(4) The court may order that the identity of any party or witness must not be disclosed if it considers non-disclosure necessary in order to protect the interests of that party or witness."

Practice Directions amplify the rules. They emphasise that the **8–020** court must have regard to Art.6, but they nonetheless set out a long list of matters which in the first instance are to be listed in private. They include mortgagee possession actions and landlord claims for possession for non-payment of rent. Certain applications to do with enforcement of judgments and assessment of legal aid costs will also be listed for a private hearing. A hearing that involves the interests of a child or patient may be in private and small claims may be heard in private if the parties agree.[79]

If there is a sign on the door indicating that the hearing is in private, the public will not be admitted. Where there is no sign, members of the public will be admitted if there is room.[80] When high temperatures in summer make the wearing of wigs and gowns intolerable in courtrooms without air-conditioning, some judges will sit in the ordinary courtroom "as though in chambers", but with no sign on the door the public are free to enter. As if by silent revolution, at least in terms of dress, the proceedings come to terms with the twenty-first century.

In the Crown Court there has been a welcome willingness to adjourn police applications for special procedure material into open court.[81] These are discretionary decisions and cannot generally be quashed on judicial review.[82] The Criminal Procedure Rules provide that bail applications or bail appeals in the Crown Court may be heard in chambers.[83] However, the Administrative Court has ruled that this does not mean that there should be any presumption in favour of excluding the public. Although there will be many cases where the application or appeal could properly be heard in chambers, the starting point if any application is made by the parties (or the press) should be in favour of open justice.[84]

On several occasions the Court of Appeal has reminded criminal **8–021** courts of the importance of the public's right to know about sentencing. If, for instance, it is discovered that a sentence exceeds the court's powers or should for some reason be altered by the trial

---

[79] CPR, Pt 39—Practice Direction—Miscellaneous Provisions Relating to Hearings, paras 1.1—1.7.

[80] CPR, Pt 39, paras. 1.9 and 1.10.

[81] *Chief Constable of Avon and Somerset v Bristol United Press*, Bristol Crown Court, Stuart-Smith J., October 23, 1986; *Re an Application under s.9 of PACE 1984*, Central Criminal Court, Alliott J, *The Independent*, May 27, 1988.

[82] *R. v Central Criminal Court Ex p. DPP*, *The Independent*, March 31, 1988.

[83] Criminal Procedure Rules r.16.11.

[84] *R. (Malik) v Central Criminal Court* [2006] 4 All E.R. 1141.

judge, the corrected sentence and the reason for it should be stated publicly.[85] The Serious Organised Crime and Polices Act 2005 created a new procedure for referring sentences back to the trial judge where either the defendant received a discount because of a promise of assistance which did not materialise or where new assistance has been provided. In these circumstances the court can exclude the public and impose reporting restrictions.[86]

Small claims will generally be held in the chambers of a District Judge, but the public will normally be admitted.[87] The usual exceptions apply, but additionally and (wrongly in principle) the parties can agree that the public should be excluded.[88]

Arbitrations may involve very large sums but the parties can still agree that they should be heard in private. Nonetheless if evidence leaks and discloses iniquity or other matters of public interest, the media would be able to publish it. Thus at an ICSID (World Bank Court) arbitration, evidence which revealed the massive corruption of Kenyan President Daniel Arap Moi was leaked to African newspapers and widely published before the election result that ousted him. The Kenyan government which was party to the case complained, but the arbitrators could do nothing once the information was out.

Legal Challenges to arbitration awards in the High Court and Court of Appeal can also take place in private.[89]

Appeals

8–022 An appeal court has a statutory power to sit in secret, if the trial court could do so. An application to adopt this procedure can itself be heard in the absence of the public. The decision on the merits of the appeal must be given in open court unless there are good and sufficient reasons for doing so privately.[90]

Although the Court of Appeal cannot sit in chambers,[91] it has the same power as the High Court under the Civil Procedure Rules to exclude the public and sit in secret (see above). It is normally reluctant to do so.

> In the course of the very lengthy trial of the claim by the liquidators of BCCI against the Bank of England the judge curtailed cross examination of one of the Bank's witnesses because of his health. The

---

[85] *R. v Balmer*, March 7, 1994, CA, Crim. App. Office Index 1995 A-41; *R. v Clue*, *The Times*, December 27, 1995, CA.

[86] Serious Organised Crime and Police Act 2005, s.75.

[87] Art.6 applies to these hearings and so presumptively litigants are entitled to a public determination of even small civil disputes—*Scarth v UK* [1999] EHRLR 322.

[88] CPR 27PD, para.4.1.

[89] CPR r.62.10 and *Department of Economic Policy and Development for the City of Moscow v Bankers Trust* [2004] BLR 229, CA.

[90] Domestic and Appellate Proceedings (Restrictions of Publicity) Act 1968, s.1, based on a Report of the Law Commission Cmnd 3149 (1966).

[91] *Re Agricultural Industries Ltd* [1952] 1 All E.R. 1188, CA.

liquidator appealed. The Bank asked for the appeal to be in private in the interests of the witness's privacy. The Appeal Court agreed but reserved the question of whether the judgment should be given publicly. It resolved that it should, although it postponed publication for a few days to allow the witness to inform his family of his health difficulties. The Court reaffirmed the importance of the "open justice principle". It noted that the liquidator had been neutral on the Bank's request to exclude the public: "In circumstances such as these the court needs to be particularly vigilant as to whether it should accede to the application for the judgment to be delivered in private."[92]

Where a building society challenged its effective closure by a financial regulator the court agreed to hear the case in private pending its decision in order to avoid a run on the society's funds. However, it imposed a condition that the society should lodge with the court the daily equivalent of any new deposits by customers who (because the proceedings were held in private) would have been unaware of the risks they were running.[93]

Secret and private hearings: contempts

It is a common but erroneous belief that the privacy of a chambers **8–023** hearing means that it must also be kept secret. This is not necessarily so. The Administration of Justice Act 1960, s.12(1) says: "The publication of any information before the court sitting in private shall not of itself be contempt of court." Thus, even if a court has exercised its power under CPR r.39.2 to sit in private, disclosure of what took place at the hearing will *not* generally be contempt unless the court has also made an order banning disclosure or publication.[94] In general, if reporters can persuade either of the parties to divulge details of the hearings in chambers, they can publish what they have been told without being in contempt.

The exceptions to the general rule, where publication[95] of chambers hearings can constitute contempt, are reports of proceedings concerning:[96]

---

[92] *Three Rivers District Council v Bank of England* [2005] EWCA Civ 533 at [24].
[93] *R. v Registrar of Building Societies Ex p. A Building Society* [1960] 1 W.L.R. 669 and *R. v Chief Registrar of Building Societies Ex p. New Cross Building Society* [1984] Q.B. 227, CA.
[94] *In the Matter of Bournemouth and Boscombe Athletic Community Football Club Ltd: A.F. Noonan (Architectural Practice) Ltd v Bournemouth and Boscombe Athletic Community Football Club Ltd* [2006] EWHC 2113 (Ch).
[95] There are divergent views as to whether "publication" is used in the defamation sense of communicating to even one third party. In *Re B (A Child) (Disclosure)* [2004] 2 F.L.R. 142 Munby J. held that the "defamation rule" did apply. In *Re M (Disclosure: Children and Family Reporter)* [2003] Fam 26 CA the two Court of Appeal judges expressed conflicting views. Following the *B* case, the Family Proceedings Rules were changed to expressly allow disclosure in children cases to a specified groups of persons (including MPs and peers, but not, journalists): Family Proceedings Rules 1991, r.10.20A.
[96] Administration of Justice Act 1960, s.12(2).

- the inherent jurisdiction of the court relating to children, applications under the Children Act 1989, the Children and Adoption Act 2002, or the maintenance or upbringing of children;
- applications under the Mental Capacity Act 2005 or Mental Health Act 1983;
- national security;
- secret processes and inventions;
- "where the court (having the power to do so) expressly prohibits the publication of all information relating to the proceedings or of information of the description which is published".

This last provision does not give the court a free-standing power to impose restrictions, but is dependent on the court "having the power [from some other source] to do so." This was emphasised in a case in which a court was asked to put a ban on disclosure of any details of a hearing which had taken place in private. One of the litigants feared that word might reach the prosecuting authorities in his home country and stimulate them into investigating his affairs. The judge refused. He said that it was "not the function of the court to protect a litigant before it from embarrassment and such risks."[97] This case was followed in *Clibbery v Allan*[98] where the judge was asked to prohibit further reporting of a dispute over financial support between an unmarried and childless couple. He refused after weighing the competing claim to freedom of expression under Art.10 of one litigant who wished to be free to expose what she considered the bad behaviour of her ex-partner against the claim to privacy under Art.8 of her opponent who wished to preserve the customary reserve of the Family Division.

8–024 Even in cases which do come within one of the categories listed above, it is not contempt:

- to publish a summary of the nature of the dispute (but not the evidence or a summary of it);[99]
- to state the bare fact that an identified individual had given evidence for or against a particular party in the proceedings;[100]
- to publish the text or summary of any order made by the court (unless it expressly prohibits this);[101]

---

[97] *Trustor AB v Smallbone* [2000] 1 All E.R. 811, Ch.D.

[98] [2001] 2 F.L.R. 819.

[99] *X v Dempster* [1999] 1 FLR 894, 903 and *Re B (A Child: Disclosure)* [2004] 1 F.L.R. 142 at [79].

[100] *Re B (A Child: Disclosure)* (above at [76]).

[101] Administration of Justice Act 1960, s.12(2) and see *Forbes v Smith* (above, fn.77) and *Hodgson v Imperial Tobacco Ltd* (above, fn.78). Even in cases concerning children it will be highly unusual for the court to prevent publication of (at least) an anonymised summary of the order: *Re G (Minors) (Celebrities: Publicity)* [1999] 1 F.L.R. 409.

- to publish material that came from one of these types of private proceedings if the publisher was ignorant of this fact;[102]
- if the publication is made a sufficiently long time after the proceedings were held that the justification for privacy has passed[103]
- if the court gives permission for publication.[104]

It is not a defence for the publishers to say that they did not intend to commit contempt, nor can they obtain an acquittal by pleading that in the case of proceedings such as wardship, that are regularly held in private, they did not know that the public had been excluded.[105] Since many of the cases under the 1960 Act have involved children, there is further discussion of Administration of Justice Act 1960 under "children cases: automatic restrictions" (para.8–052).

Disorder in court

Courts have an inherent power to control their own proceedings. **8–025** This includes the power to limit numbers in the courtroom and to clear the public entirely if disorder is threatened or actually occurs. However, as with the other qualifications to the open justice principle, the court should depart from it no more than is necessary, and it would be quite wrong to exclude journalists who are not joining in the disorder.

> Members of the Welsh Language Society appealed against their conviction for refusing to pay television licence fees, on the grounds that the court trying them had improperly excluded members of the public. These members of the public were, in fact, supporters of the defendants, who had begun to create a disturbance. The Divisional Court, rejecting the appeal, noted that a journalist from a local paper had been allowed to remain. The Lord Chief Justice said: "I find it difficult to imagine a case which can be said to be held publicly if the press have been actively excluded".[106]

---

[102] *BBC v Rochdale MBC* [2006] EMLR 6 and *Re F (A Minor: Publication of Information)* [1977] 1 All E.R. 114. This case concerned reports to the court by the Official Solicitor and a social worker. These should carry a warning that they must be kept confidential on penalty of proceedings for contempt: *Practice Direction* [1984] 1 All E.R. 827.

[103] *Re F*, fn.102 above.

[104] *Re R (MJ) (Publication of Transcripts)* [1975] 2 All E.R. 749.

[105] *Re F*, fn.102 above.

[106] *R. v Denbigh Justices Ex p. Williams and Evans* [1974] 2 All E.R. 1052.

REPORTING RESTRICTIONS

8–026 Attending court is merely the means to the end of publication. What takes place in open court "is necessarily and legitimately made public and being public property may be republished".[107] This section considers the exceptions to that general principle. Where reporters are admitted to court, when are they limited or prohibited from publishing what they hear? Where reporters are not allowed into court, when *can* they publish information from other sources?

Pre-trial stages of criminal proceedings

8–027 With rare exceptions all criminal cases start in a magistrates' court.[108] The great majority of cases end there. Magistrates or District Judges try and sentence the defendants. However, more serious cases are dealt with by the Crown Court. In the past magistrates have "committed" a defendant to the Crown Court for trial. In "old-style" committal hearings the prosecution would present all of its evidence in order to persuade the magistrates that there was a case fit for trial. These are now a rarity and much more commonly the defence will choose to preserve its position and the committal hearing becomes a formality.

In serious fraud cases the prosecution can dispense with committal proceedings altogether and seek a 'transfer order' to the appropriate Crown Court. Any argument by the defence as to whether there is sufficient evidence to justify a trial is then heard by a Crown Court judge. In 1991 the "transfer" procedure was extended to cases involving children as victims or witnesses of certain sex offences.

The erosion of committal proceedings was taken a stage further in 1998 since when they were abolished for offences which are serious enough to be only triable on indictment at the Crown Court. Cases of this type are now "sent" to the Crown Court by the magistrates' court. When the Criminal Justice Act 2003 changes are brought fully into force, the less serious offences which can be tried either by magistrates or the Crown Court will be subject to an "allocation" procedure and will similarly be "sent" to the Crown Court if allocated for trial there. Committal proceedings will then be no more and "transfers" will also be subsumed into the allocation and sending procedure.

Despite this gradual abolition of committal proceedings, it is useful to start with the reporting restrictions which apply to them. They set the pattern for the restrictions which have also been adopted for the newer procedures of "transferring" and "sending" cases to the Crown Court.

---

[107] *Richardson v Wilson* (1879) 7 R. 237.
[108] The exception is where a High Court judge gives permission for a "voluntary bill of indictment"—see para.8–012.

Committal proceedings: reporting restrictions

Prior to 1967 committal proceedings could be reported in full. It was **8–028** the Moors Murder case that finally prompted the government to act and then more to spare the public a double dose of grisly details than to avoid prejudice to defendants.[109] The Magistrates Courts Act 1980 s.8 allows media reports of committal proceedings to refer only to the following:[110]

- the names of the justices and their court;
- the name, age, home address and occupation of the defendant;
- the charge(s);
- the names of the legal representatives;
- the date and place of any future hearing when the case is adjourned;
- arrangements for bail;
- whether legal aid was granted or refused;
- the charge(s) on which the defendant was committed for trial.

Consequently, for instance, the reasons given by the prosecution for opposing bail or the magistrates' reasons for refusing to grant it cannot be published.

The restrictions apply only temporarily. Full details of the committal can be published after the trial.[111] But by then they are usually stale news and many editors consider it uneconomic to have a reporter in court where proceedings cannot be promptly reported.

All the details can be reported if the magistrates decide not to commit or if they exercise their right (with the defendant's consent) to change their role part way through the committal proceedings and try the case themselves. Where there are several defendants of whom some are committed for trial and some are dealt with by magistrates, a reporter must take care to observe the restrictions in connection with those who are sent for trial.

"Transfer" and "sending": reporting restrictions

The reporting restrictions are virtually identical as those for commit- **8–029** tal proceedings. The principal difference is that 'relevant business information' may also be published. This means, in brief, the name and address of any business that the defendant was conducting on his own account or in which he was a partner or of which he was a

---

[109] Marjorie Jones, *Justice and Journalism*, pp.109–115.
[110] the equivalent restrictions in the allocation and sending procedure are in Crime and Disorder Act 1998, s.52A(7).
[111] Magistrates Courts Act 1980, s.8(3); Crime and Disorder Act 1998, s.52A(6).

director. The addresses can be those at the time of the events which
give rise to the charges and those at the time of publication.[112] The
reporting restrictions on cases sent for trial mirror those for committal proceedings.[113] When the allocation and sending provisions are in
force they will absorb the transfer procedure but "relevant business
information" will still be reportable in relation to serious or complex
fraud.[114]

Preparatory hearings and pre-trial rulings: reporting restrictions

8–030 These allow disputed issues of law or admissibility of evidence to be
resolved where possible before a jury is empanelled. The press ought
to be allowed to be present when either of these proceedings takes
place because (in the case of preparatory hearings) they are part of
the trial process or (in the case of both types of proceedings)
reporting restrictions adequately protect the defendants. The reporting restrictions in question are very similar to those discussed
above.[115] Importantly, in both cases the judge can dispense with the
reporting restrictions.[116] Magistrates have comparable powers to
make pre-trial rulings and very similar reporting restrictions apply.[117]
Unless the court has dispensed with them at an earlier stage, the
reporting restrictions on reporting what takes place at preparatory or
pre-trial hearings continue in place until the trial is concluded.

One purpose of the preparatory hearing procedure is to allow the
parties to appeal the judge's ruling, again before the jury is
empanelled. The reporting restrictions continue so as to prevent the
reporting of these interlocutory appeals until the conclusion of the
trial but the Court of Appeal (and, if the case goes that far, the
House of Lords) can disapply the restrictions.[118] In *R v Rimmington*
the Lords exercised this power since it followed from their decision
that there could not be a trial. As Lord Bingham said[119] "There
should be no resort to anonymity in criminal cases without good
reason and statutory authority." The legislation does not expressly
allow the media to apply for the restrictions to be set aside, but they
ought to be able to do so since it is they who are directly affected by
the restrictions. It would also be compatible with the established
practice whereby the media are allowed to make representations in
opposition to other orders restricting publicity.

---

[112] Criminal Justice Act 1987, s.11.
[113] Crime and Disorder Act 1998, Sch.3, para.3.
[114] Crime and Disorder Act 1998, s.52A(7).
[115] Preparatory hearings—see Criminal Justice Act 1987, s.11 and Criminal Procedure and Investigations Act 1996, s.37; pre-trial hearings Criminal Procedure
and Investigations Act 1996, s.41.
[116] Preparatory hearings—Criminal Justice Act 1987, s.11(4); pre-trial rulings Criminal Procedure and Investigations 1996, s.41(3).
[117] Magistrates' Courts Act 1980 ss.8A–8D, added by Courts Act 2003 Sch.3.
[118] Criminal Justice Act 1987, s.11(2)–(6).
[119] [2006] 1 A.C. 459 at [3].

Lifting the restrictions

Where an application is made to lift any of these reporting restric- **8–031**
tions, the court must listen to objections from the defendant or
defendants and override the objections only if it is in the interests of
justice to do so.[120] While committal proceedings continue to exist,
the defendant or defendants (if they all agree) have a right to have
the reporting restrictions lifted.[121]

Breach of the restrictions

Breach of any of these reporting restrictions is a summary offence. **8–032**
The offences follow a common pattern. Liability is imposed on the
proprietor, editor and publisher of a newspaper or periodical, the
publisher of a written report which is not part of a newspaper or
periodical, the corporate body engaged in providing the infringing
programme service and, in relation to such a programme, anyone
with responsibilities equivalent to an editor. The maximum penalty
in each case is a fine on level 5 (currently £5,000) and the Attorney-
General's consent is necessary for a prosecution.[122] Prosecutions are
unusual. A rare example (and a serious breach) was by the *Glouces-
ter Citizen* which, in an article about Fred West's first appearance at
the magistrates' court, reported that he had already admitted killing
his daughter. The paper's editor and publisher were each fined
£4,500.[123]

Children and the courts

Before criminal proceedings commence

Various restrictions are imposed on the identification of children **8–033**
involved in court proceedings. It used to be the case that the
restrictions started only once proceedings had begun. In December
1997 William Straw, the 17–year-old son of the Home Secretary, was
arrested for selling £10 worth of cannabis to a *Mirror* reporter. He
was released without charge on police bail. When newspapers
refused to give an undertaking not to name the boy, the Attorney-
General applied for an injunction. This was granted (in plain breach
of Art.10, which was not at the time in domestic force) so as to
preserve any future court's ability to retain his anonymity. However,
the injunction did not apply in Scotland and after William's involvement had been widely publicised there, the English injunction was
lifted.[124]

---

[120] Crime and Disorder Act 1998, s.52A (3) and (4); and Sch.3, para.3(3).
[121] Magistrates' Courts Act 1980, s.8(2).
[122] See for instance Crime and Disorder Act 1998 s.52B.
[123] *Media Lawyer*, May 1996, p.26.
[124] The events are reviewed in *Media Lawyer*, January 1998, pp.5–9.

Parliament has since intervened to provide new controls on the reporting of children involved in a "criminal investigation".[125] There is a "criminal investigation" once the police or others charged with the investigation of offences are conducting an investigation with a view to ascertaining whether a person should be charged with an offence.[126] It is important to realise that an "investigation" can thus begin much earlier than the period when a criminal case becomes "active" for the purpose of strict liability contempt.[127]

At first, the new regime will protect only the alleged perpetrator of the offence. However, the Secretary of State will have power to extend the class of protected person to the alleged victim and possible witnesses.[128] Where the protections apply, nothing must be published (so long as the person concerned is under 18) which is likely to lead members of the public to identify him as a person involved in the offence. Identifying features include (but not exhaustively) the person's name, address, school, place of work or still or moving picture—but only if they would connect him with the offence.[129]

8–034 Once these provisions are in force they will apply automatically, but a criminal court (including a single justice of the peace) can dispense with them if satisfied that it is necessary in the interests of justice to do so. The decision by a magistrate to grant or refuse a dispensing order can be appealed to the Crown Court.[130]

Breach of the restrictions will be a summary offence punishable with a fine up to the statutory maximum (currently £5,000). The editor, publisher and proprietor of a newspaper are liable, as are their equivalents in relation to a programme service. Prosecutions require the consent of the Attorney-General.[131] It is a defence to show that the defendant did not know and had no reason to suspect that the publication included the report or (alternatively) that a criminal investigation had begun.[132]

The media were very concerned that these restrictions would prevent the immediate reporting of tragedies involving children such as the multiple murders at the school in Dunblane or the killing of Philip Lawrence, the headmaster stabbed outside his school in West London. So a defence was added that permits the media to satisfy the court that the inclusion of the identifying material was in the public interest on the ground that the suppressive effect of this law would have imposed a substantial and unreasonable restriction on

---

[125] Youth Justice and Criminal Evidence Act 1999, ss.44, 49 and 50. The provisions had not been brought into force at the time of writing (June 2007).
[126] 1999 Act, s.44(13)(b).
[127] See para.7–028.
[128] The 1999 Act, s.44(4) and (5).
[129] 1999 Act, s.44(2) and (6).
[130] 1999 Act, s.44(7)–(11).
[131] 1999 Act, s.49.
[132] 1999 Act, s.50(1) and (2).

reporting.[133] It is important to remember, though, that even in these circumstances the defence does not permit the identification of the alleged perpetrator of any offence or an alleged witness to a sexual offence.[134]

Section 52 directs the court to have particular regard to various **8–035** matters when considering the public interest. They include the interest in the open reporting of crime, the open reporting of matters relating to human health and safety, the prevention and exposure of miscarriages of justice, the welfare of any protected person, the views of a protected person who is 16 or 17, or the views of an appropriate person if the protected person is under 16.

Complex provisions are made for a curious defence of "consent" to media revelations.[135] This consent defence cannot be relied upon at all in connection with either an alleged victim or a witness who is under 16. But where consent can (potentially) be relied upon as a defence, it must be in writing and, if the protected person is under 16, must be given by an appropriate person, i.e. a parent or guardian (unless the child is in the care of a local authority, in which case it must be an officer of the authority or a parent or guardian with whom the child is allowed to live). The "appropriate person" must have been given a written notice warning about the need to consider the welfare of the child. Furthermore, the consent can be withdrawn in writing although only if there is sufficient time to edit out the identifying material. The consent is nullified if it is shown that the "peace or comfort" of the child or appropriate person was interfered with in order to obtain the consent. It remains to be seen whether this thicket of provisions leaves a defence of any practical utility to the media.

Ofcom's Code requires broadcasters to have "particular regard" to the potentially vulnerable position of child witnesses and victims before identifying them, and that "particular justification" is required before child suspects are named.[136] This part of the Code is carried over from the former Code of the Independent Television Commission which had backed away from its earlier position that there should be a blanket prohibition on identifying any young person involved in an offence after considerable protest from the media.

Although the restrictions under s.44 come to an end if proceedings are commenced,[137] in cases involving children the media need to be alert to the possibility of further reporting restrictions.

---

[133] Youth Justice and Criminal Evidence Act 1999, s.50(3).
[134] 1999 Act, s.50(3)(b). The alleged victims of sexual offences have independent protection of their anonymity—see below para.8–044.
[135] 1999 Act, s.50(4)–(14).
[136] See para.1.9.
[137] Youth Justice and Criminal Evidence Act 1999, s.44(3).

Youth courts

8–036 The general public are refused entry to youth courts, but journalists can attend and can report the proceedings although they must not publish anything relating to a person under 18 if it is likely to lead members of the public to identify him as someone concerned in the proceedings. In particular, they must not reveal the name, address, school, workplace, or include any still or moving picture of the child if this would identify him as concerned in the proceedings.[138] It is the link between the court proceedings and the young person which is legally objectionable. Consequently background stories or interviews that do identify the young person can be published so long as all mention of the court case is scrupulously avoided. Conversely, feature articles can be written about the youth court, backed by anonymous examples. These restrictions only apply while the person concerned is under 18.[139] The same restrictions apply to appeals from youth courts and to proceedings for varying or revoking supervision orders and appeals from these proceedings.[140]

In three very different circumstances the court can give permission for a young person to be identified even though he is involved in youth court proceedings:

- Where identification is appropriate to avoid injustice to the child, such as to scotch local rumours that the child is a defendant when in reality he is a witness.
- To assist in the arrest of a child or young person who is unlawfully at large and who is charged with, or convicted of, a violent or sexual or particularly serious offence.[141]
- After conviction of the child or young person, the court considers that identification would be in the public interest.[142]

Government Guidelines on the use of these discretionary powers has been given in two publications: *Opening Up Youth Court Proceedings*[143] and *The Changing Culture of the Youth Court: Good Practice Guide*.[144]

---

[138] Children and Young Persons Act 1933, s.49 as amended by Youth Justice and Criminal Evidence Act 1999, Sch. 2. Comparable restrictions apply to the broadcast media: Children and Young Persons Act 1933, s.49(3).

[139] See *Todd v DPP*, October 6, 2003 DC, *The Times* October 13, 2003 decided on the 1933 Act before its amendment by the Youth Justice and Criminal Evidence Act 1999. Once the amendment is in force it will be quite clear that the restriction on publication comes to an end once the person concerned turns 18.

[140] 1933 Act, s.49(2). However, when the automatic restrictions under s.49 apply to proceedings in an adult magistrates' court or the Crown Court, the court must announce the fact at the hearing. A failure to do so will mean that the restrictions do not apply: s.49(10).

[141] 1933 Act, s.49(5)(b) and (6).

[142] s.49(4A).

[143] Published by the Home Office and Lord Chancellor's Department, June 1998.

[144] Published by Home Office and Lord Chancellor's Department, March 2001.

The Divisional Court has reviewed the principles to be applied by a youth court in deciding whether to lift restrictions under s.49(4A)[145]:

> The defendant who was 15 at the time of the offence to which he pleaded guilty had been arrested some 130 times over the previous four years. Having heard representations from a court reporter the magistrates decided to lift the reporting restrictions partially. The defendant could be named, but his address, school and photograph could not be published. He appealed by case stated to the Divisional Court. The Lord Chief Justice said that the magistrates were entitled to hear from the press. He referred to several international instruments which emphasised the importance to be placed on the welfare of the child even when a defendant in criminal proceedings. It was right for magistrates to be very cautious before lifting the restrictions. It would be wholly wrong to use publicity as a form of extra punishment and it would be very difficult to see any place for "naming and shaming". However, in this case the magistrates had approached the issue of "public interest" correctly and their decision was not unreasonable.

Anti-social behaviour orders (ASBOs)

ASBOs were introduced by the Crime and Disorder Act 1998[146] and **8-037** they allow the courts to impose wide-ranging conditions in an effort to curb anti-social behaviour. Breach of the conditions is a criminal offence with a maximum penalty of five years imprisonment (significantly longer than the maximum of two years imprisonment for contempt of court). ASBOs can be imposed in free-standing proceedings or as an additional, bolt-on measure following a conviction. They can be passed on children and adults, but reporting restrictions bite when young people are involved. However, these restrictions have been progressively lessened. The current position is:

- The proceedings in which free-standing ASBOs are made are classified as civil.[147] This means that the proceedings cannot take place in youth courts and so the automatic restrictions relating to youth courts in s.49 of the 1933 Act will not apply. The magistrates could still choose to impose a discretionary anonymity order in respect of the defendant or any other young person involved in the proceedings under s.39.[148] Local papers have had considerable success in persuading magistrates not to make s.39 orders. The journalists

---

[145] *McKerry v Teesdate and Wear Valley JJ.* [2001] E.M.L.R. 127.
[146] s.1(1).
[147] *R. (McCann) v Crown Court at Manchester* [2003] 1 A.C. 787.
[148] Or s.45 of Youth Justice and Criminal Evidence Act 1999 when it replaces s.39 of the 1933 Act—see para.8–038.

have argued that an ASBO is much more likely to be effective if the media can identify those against whom orders are made. Breaches are then more likely to be reported, a position which the Administrative Court has endorsed.[149] A carefully targeted scheme by the police and a local authority to publicise ASBOs against some of its young people also withstood legal challenge. The court agreed that the scheme impinged on their private lives but said this was justified in the circumstances and there was no breach of Art.8.[150]

- There may be a delay before the full hearing of an ASBO application can take place and the court can choose to make an "Interim ASBO" in the meantime. It should not be standard practice to give young people anonymity under s.39/s.45 during this interval, but the Court ought to bear in mind that the allegations of anti-social behaviour have not at that stage been proved.[151]

- Special measures (see para.8–046) can be put in place to protect vulnerable and intimidated adult witnesses in applications for ASBOs and these may mean that the media have to be careful not to identify the witness concerned.[152]

- Where a bolt-on ASBO is made following conviction in a youth court, the automatic restrictions on reporting in s.49 are disapplied, but only so far as the proceedings relate to the making of the ASBO itself.[153] This means that care must be taken not to infringe s.49 which will still apply to the underlying criminal proceedings. A discretionary anonymity order under s.39/s.45 could still be made to cover the bolt-on ASBO procedure.

- Breach proceedings are criminal. If these take place in the youth court, the s.49 automatic reporting restrictions are disapplied but the discretionary power to impose anonymity still remains.[154]

Other criminal courts

8–038 Apart from youth courts and subsequent appeals from them, there is no automatic restriction on the coverage of criminal proceedings where children are involved. However, there is a power to impose reporting restrictions. Previously this was in the Children and Young Persons Act 1933, s.39, but once it is brought into effect, this power

---

[149] *R.(T) v St Albans Crown Court* [2002] EWHC 1129 (Admin) Elias J.
[150] *R. (Stanley, Marshall and Kelly) v Metropolitan Police Commissioner and London Borough of Brent* [2005] EMLR 3.
[151] *Keating v Knowsley MBC* [2005] HLR 3.
[152] Crime and Disorder Act 1998, s.11 as added by Serious Organised Crime and Police and Police Act 2005, s.143.
[153] Crime and Disorder Act 1998, s.1C.
[154] Crime and Disorder Act 1998, s.1(10D).

for criminal courts will be found in the Youth Justice and Criminal Evidence Act 1999, s.45. The court can direct that no matter relating to any person concerned in the proceedings shall (while he is under 18) be included in any publication if it is likely to lead members of the public to identify him as a person concerned in the proceedings. These matters include (but are not limited to) the person's name, address, school or workplace and any still or moving picture of him.[155]

> In *Briffet and Bradshaw v DPP*[156] a s.39 order had been made by a High Court judge in proceedings for judicial review of a school expulsion decision. The judge had simply said "order under s.39 Children and Young Person Act. Reporting restrictions apply in respect of the applicant and this matter be listed as "Ex parte K". The Administrative Court said that this order was too vague and general. "Section 39 orders constituted a significant curtailment of press freedom and courts had to be vigilant to see that they were justified and made in clear and unambiguous terms."

A person is "concerned in the proceedings" if the proceedings are taken against or in respect of him or if he is a witness.[157] Under s.39 of the 1933 Act courts have sometimes wrongly tried to prohibit the identification of a young murder victim. They were legally unable to do so. The victim of an offence may be a person "in respect of whom" the proceedings are taken,[158] but the interests which the legislation (both old and new) is designed to protect cannot survive the victim's death and anyway could not prevail over the public interest in unrestricted reporting of serious crime.[159]

Under these powers courts cannot prevent the press from naming adults involved in the proceedings, unless to do so would indirectly disclose the child's identity. The standard direction under s.39 of the Children and Young Persons Act 1933 (CYPA) (and in the future s.45 of Youth Justice and Criminal Evidence Act 1999 (YJCEA) prohibits publication of information likely to lead to the identification of the child, but the court cannot go further and give the media directions as to what material it can or cannot publish to comply with this order.[160] This was established in the case of *Ex p. Godwin*:[161]

> A trial involved serious allegations of child sex molestation against two members of a close and very orthodox Jewish community. The children

---

[155] Youth Justice and Criminal Evidence Act 1999, s.45(3) and (8).

[156] [2002] EMLR 12.

[157] 1999 Act, s.45(7).

[158] *R (A Minor) (Wardship: Restrictions on Publication)* [1994] Fam. 254.

[159] This was confirmed by the House of Lords in *Re S* [2005] 1 A.C. 593 at [21].

[160] Or at least not beyond the specific matters listed in s.45(8)—see above fn.155.

[161] [1992] Q.B. 190. This was followed, rather reluctantly, by the Court of Appeal in *R. (Gazette Media Company Ltd) v Teeside Crown Court, The Times*, August 8, 2005 where the court warned that even an anonymised account may contain sufficient details for the child to be identified and so breach the court's order.

were from the same community and the trial judge was persuaded by defence counsel to make a s.39 order prohibiting publication of the names and addresses of the defendants on the grounds that such details would allow the children to be identified. The Court of Appeal held that he had no power to do so. It was up to the media to decide how to comply with the standard order. If they misjudged it, they could be prosecuted, but they could not be subjected to additional prior restraint of the kind which the trial judge had imposed here. The judge could give "advice" to the media as to what might or might not breach the order, but unlike the order itself such advice would not be legally binding.

8–039   The court can vary the standard order under s.45 by making an "excepting direction" if it is satisfied that there would otherwise be a substantial and unreasonable restriction on the reporting of the proceedings and that it is in the public interest to remove or relax the restriction. The outcome of the proceedings is not, by itself, a sufficient reason for making an excepting direction.[162] Thus the fact that a young person has been convicted in an adult court is not, of itself, a sufficient reason for allowing the defendant to be named, although of course this can be taken into account. In deciding whether to make a s.45 order in the first place or an excepting direction, the court must have regard to the welfare of the young person concerned.

Cases under s.39 of the CYPA have emphasised that Parliament had clearly distinguished the different regime in the youth courts (where anonymity was the rule) and that in adult criminal courts (where it was necessary to obtain a specific order from the court curtailing the open justice principle).[163] Other decisions have stressed that the age of the child and potential damage of publicity must be given considerable weight.[164] The Administrative Court in 2000 reasserted the importance of the difference between youth courts where the presumption was in favour of anonymity and other courts where good reason had to be shown for imposing restrictions.[165]

In the notorious trial of the two 11–year-olds charged with the murder of Jamie Bulger, the judge imposed a s.39 order until conviction at which point he revoked the order and permitted them to be named. The public nature of their trial was part of the reason why the European Court of Human Rights upheld their complaints under Art.6.[166] The Lord Chief Justice in consequence issued a

---

[162] Youth Justice and Criminal Evidence Act 1999, s.45(5). The statute gives guidance as to what is meant by the "public interest": see above para.8–035.

[163] See for instance *R. v Lee* [1993] 1 W.L.R. 103; *R. v Central Criminal Court Ex p. S* [1999] 1 F.L.R. 480, QBD.

[164] *R. v Inner London Crown Court Ex p. B* [1996] C.O.D. 17, QBD; *R. v Leicester Crown Court, Ex p. S* [1993] 1 W.L.R. 111.

[165] *R. v Central Criminal Court Ex p. W, B and C* [2001] 1 Cr.App.R. 7.

[166] *T v UK; V v UK* (2000) 30 E.H.R.R. 122.

practice direction for the conduct of future trials involving children and young persons[167] which recognises that special measures must be taken to make the courtroom less intimidating in these circumstances. It does, however, tell judges that they should be mindful of the public's general right to be informed about the administration of justice in the Crown Court.[168]

Other courts

The Children and Young Persons Act 1933, s.39 continues to apply **8–040** in non-criminal courts.[169]

Notice of reporting restrictions concerning children

There should be no need for any notice of reporting restrictions in **8–041** Youth Courts since s.49 of the 1933 Act applies reporting restrictions automatically. Reporting restrictions are therefore the norm in Youth Courts. Section 49 also applies when an adult magistrates' court is being asked to vary or revoke a supervision order or on appeal from such an order. However, in those courts, reporting restrictions are not the norm and the legislation expressly requires the court to draw specific attention to the application of the restrictions. If it does not, then they do not apply.[170]

Where other courts use their powers under s.39 (or s.45 of YJCEA), they should express their order in clear terms (identifying, in any cases of ambiguity, which children are protected), reduce the order to writing, advertise its existence in the daily cause list and make copies available to the press at the court office.[171]

Review of children reporting restrictions

Reporters Caroline Godwin and Tim Crook have taken the lead in **8–042** objecting to court secrecy orders. Their example has been followed by an increasing number of journalists who have vigilantly objected to reporting restrictions. Making direct and informed representations to the judge who imposed the order can be a quick, cheap and effective means of resisting unwarranted intrusions on press freedom.

A court which has made a s.39 or s.45 order can always revoke it. A s.39 order can be varied and a s.45 order can be made subject to

---

[167] See now *Practice Direction (Criminal Proceedings: Consolidation)* [2002] 1 W.L.R. 2870, para.IV.39.
[168] PD: see above para.8–015 for arrangements which should be made for reporters who are prevented from attending the trial of a young person under these arrangements.
[169] It has been amended on several occasions, most recently by the Youth Justice and Criminal Evidence Act 1999, Sch.2.
[170] Children and Young Persons Act 1933, s.49(10).
[171] *Ex p Crook* [1995] 1 W.L.R. 139.

an "excepting direction". A compassionate example concerned a child who had judicially reviewed a health authority's refusal to fund necessary treatment. The child's identity was protected by a s.39 order but when the review failed, the father successfully applied for the order to be lifted so that a national newspaper could pay for the child's treatment privately in return for the family's exclusive story.[172]

A reporting restrictions order under s.45 or s.39 which is made by a magistrates' court can be judicially reviewed by the High Court. The order of a Crown Court imposing restrictions (or refusing to make an excepting direction) can be appealed to the Court of Appeal under s.159 of Criminal Justice Act 1988.[173] If there is an appeal in relation in the substantive criminal proceedings, an appellate court has power to make, revoke or vary an excepting direction.[174]

However, in the absence of a substantive appeal on some other ground (e.g. against conviction or sentence) a young person has no right to appeal to the Court of Appeal against the decision of the Crown Court to refuse to make a reporting restriction order or to include an excepting direction. The theory behind this different treatment is that the norm is open reporting and the media are entitled to appeal against orders which depart from that norm, whereas there needs to be no right of appeal against a decision upholding the norm of free reporting. However, the lack of a right of appeal has led many defendants to seek judicial review of the Crown Court's refusal to grant or continue anonymity. The obstacle in their way has been Supreme Court Act 1981, s.29(3) which allows the High Court to judicially review decisions of the Crown Court "other than its jurisdiction in matters relating to a trial on indictment". The Divisional Court has been incapable of giving a consistent answer to the question of whether an order under s.39 is a "matter relating to a trial on indictment" and so beyond judicial review.[175] The Youth Justice and Criminal Evidence Act 1999 gives no assistance, and the matter will only be resolved when an appeal eventually reaches the House of Lords. The Lords will probably decide, consistently with the purpose of s.29(3), which is to prevent diversionary appeal proceedings in the course of the trial[176] and which would delay the trial, that the section means there can be no review of anonymity orders unless they are imposed, varied or lifted after the conclusion of the trial.

---

[172] *R. v Cambridge and Huntingdon Health Authority Ex p. B (No.2)*, *The Times*, October 27, 1995, CA.

[173] See para.8–086.

[174] JCEA 1999, s.45(4) and (10).

[175] See for instance *R. v Winchester Crown Court Ex p. B* [2000] 1 Cr.App.R. 11, QBD, holding that there was no jurisdiction to judicially review such orders and *R. v Harrow Crown Court Ex p. H & D* [2000] 1 Cr.App.R. 262, QBD, holding that there was, at least where the s.39 order was lifted after conviction and sentence.

[176] *R. v DPP Ex p. Kebilene* [2000] 2 A.C. 326.

Procedure and penalty

Breach of any of these reporting restrictions is a summary offence. **8–043**
The maximum penalty is the statutory maximum fine (currently
£5,000). The Attorney-General must approve the prosecution in
most cases.[177]

Rape and sexual offences

In 1975 the Heilbron Report[178] recommended that rape complain- **8–044**
ants should be granted anonymity in an effort to improve the rate of
reporting to the police. A study in the same year had shown that,
despite ethical exhortations of the Press Council, in about half the
press reports of rape prosecutions the victim was named and in
about a third her address was given as well.[179]

The recommendation was adopted in the Sexual Offences
(Amendment) Act 1976 and extended to a much wider range of
offences in 1992 by the Sexual Offences (Amendment) Act 1992. For
several years these two statutes operated in tandem, but by the
Youth Justice and Criminal Evidence Act 1999[180] the 1976 provisions
were merged into a re-vamped Sexual Offences (Amendment) Act
1992. The range of offences to which the restrictions apply was
extended again by the Sexual Offences Act 2003 so that anonymity is
now conferred on, for instance, the victims of voyeurism and
indecent exposure. As a result there is a common set of restrictions
for rape and a wide range of other sexual offences.[181] The 1976 Act
originally gave some protection to the identity of the *defendant* in
rape cases, but these provisions were dropped in 1988 and defendants accused of rape or other sexual offences are now in no
different position from other defendants except, of course, the
report must not be written in such a way as to identify the
complainant indirectly.

The anonymity provisions are triggered by either of two events.
From the time that an *allegation* of a sex offence has been made no
matter relating to the complainant which is likely to identify that
person as a victim can be published during that person's life-time.[182]
Similarly, from the time that a defendant has been *charged* with a sex
offence, nothing which is likely to identify the victim can be
published during that person's lifetime.[183] The matters which cannot

---

[177] Youth Justice and Criminal Evidence Act 1999, s.49; Criminal Justice Act 1991,
Sch. 6, para.6(10) and (11); Children and Young Persons Act 1933, s.49(9)— the
Att-Gen's consent is not necessary under this provision.
[178] Advisory Group on the Law of Rape, Cmnd 6352 (1975).
[179] Keith Soothill and Anthea Jack "How Rape is Reported", *New Society*, June 19,
1975.
[180] Sch.2, paras 6–14.
[181] See Sexual Offences (Amendment) Act 1992, s.2.
[182] Sexual Offences (Amendment) Act 1992 s.1(1).
[183] 1992 Act, s.1(2). Following a charge, this provision supersedes the restriction in
s.1(1).

be published include (but are not limited to) the complainant's name, address, the identity of any school or other educational establishment, the identity of any place of work, any still or moving picture of the person if these would be likely to link her[184] with the complaint.[185] In 2006 the *Daily Express* and *Daily Telegraph* were fined for publishing a photograph of a service woman whose complaint about sexual assault led to her giving evidence in a court martial. The picture showed her in uniform, but since she had been photographed from behind the papers had thought that she would not be identifiable. However, she had been recognised and they pleaded guilty. In addition to the fines, the magistrates ordered each paper to pay compensation to the woman concerned.[186]

8–045   If no-one has been charged with the sexual offence, it is a defence for the media defendant to prove that he was not aware, did not suspect and had no reason to suspect that the allegation in question had been made.[187]

There are three important exceptions to the anonymity rule. First, the complainant may consent to being identified. Agreement must have been in writing and not obtained as a result of unreasonable interference with her peace or comfort and with the intention of obtaining her consent.[188] It may, and often will, be obtained by newspapers offering money for a story, which, for contempt reasons, will not be publishable until after the trial. Consent cannot be given by a victim who is under 16 at the time.[189] Secondly, the media are free to identify the complainant as a part of a report of criminal proceedings other than the trial or appeal of the person allegedly responsible.[190] This was apparently intended to cater for those rare cases where a complainant is herself (or himself) later charged with perjury.

Thirdly, the court itself can allow the complainant to be named. It may do so if this is necessary to persuade people who are protected defence witnesses to come forward.[191] The court can also lift the anonymity shield if it would impose a "substantial and unreasonable restriction on the reporting of the proceedings at trial and it is in the public interest to relax the restriction".[192] The defendant's acquittal or some other outcome of the trial is not of itself a reason for relaxing the anonymity rule[193] although a judge who takes a critical view of the complainant's behaviour may be more inclined to let the

---

[184] The victims of most sex offences can be either women or men.
[185] Sexual Offences (Amendment) Act 1992, s.1(3A).
[186] *Media Lawyer*, March 2006, p.13.
[187] Sexual Offences (Amendment) Act 1992, s.5(5A).
[188] 1992 Act, s.5.
[189] 1992 Act, s.5(3).
[190] 1992 Act, s.1(4).
[191] 1992 Act, s.3(1).
[192] Sexual Offences (Amendment) Act 1992, s.3(2).
[193] 1992 Act, s.3(3).

public know about it. As with other reporting restrictions it is now widely recognised that courts ought to hear (or read) representations from or on behalf of the media in support of lifting the suppression order.

Criminal charges for breach of these restrictions can only be brought with the consent of the Attorney-General.[194] For the print media those responsible are the proprietor, editor and publisher and, in the case of the broadcast media, the company responsible for providing the programme service and the person with functions corresponding to the editor of a newspaper.[195] The anonymity provisions have withstood a challenge that they were contrary to Art.10 ECHR. The Court rejected the argument that the offence of publishing material "likely to lead members of the public to identify' the complainant was too imprecise to qualify as a retriction 'pre-scribed by law."[196]

Reporting restrictions protecting witnesses in criminal proceedings

The Youth Justice and Criminal Evidence Act 1999 introduced a **8–046** new power to prohibit the identification of witnesses whose evidence (or co-operation with a party in the case) was likely to be diminished because of the witness's fear or distress at the prospect of being publicly identified as a witness in the proceedings. Importantly, this power does not extend to give anonymity to the defendant.[197] The witness must be over 18; if under 18, the court has alternative powers (see para.8–058). The Act lists matters which must be taken into account in deciding eligibility. They include the witness's age, social and cultural background, religious or political opinions; and any behaviour towards the witness by the defendant, his family or associates or any other person likely to be a defendant or witness in the proceedings. The court must take into account the witness's own views (though these are likely to favour anonymity).[198]

Even if a witness is eligible for protection, the court must still exercise a judgment as to whether a reporting direction of this kind should be made. It must consider whether it would be in the interests of justice to do so and the public interest in avoiding the imposition of a substantial and unreasonable restriction on the reporting of the proceedings.[199] Guidance on factors to weigh in the balance is given in the statute.[200] The Criminal Procedure Rules

---

[194] 1992 Act, s.5(4). The usual practice in contempt cases of inviting representations from the prospective media defendant before a prosecution is brought (see para.7–060) should be followed here.
[195] 1992 Act, s.5(1).
[196] *O'Riordan v DPP*, *The Times*, May 31, 2005.
[197] Youth Justice and Criminal Evidence Act 1999, s.46.
[198] 1999 Act, s.46(5).
[199] Youth Justice and Criminal Evidence Act 1999, s.46(6).
[200] 1999 Act, s.52—see above, para.8–035.

recognise that it is not only the parties to the prosecution who may have views about these orders. "Any person who in the court's view has a legitimate interest" (classically the media) may make representations on an urgent oral application,[201] and "any person directly affected by the reporting direction" may apply for an excepting direction or to have the reporting direction varied or revoked.[202]

A reporting direction directs that nothing relating to the witness is to be published in the witness's lifetime which would be likely to lead members of the public to identify him as being a witness in the proceedings. Specifically these matters include the witness's name, address, educational establishment, place of work or still or moving picture of the person concerned which would be likely to identify him as a witness in the proceedings. As with anonymity orders for children, the court can make an "excepting direction" if it would be in the interests of justice to do so or if the effect of the restrictions would otherwise be to impose a substantial and unreasonable restriction on the reporting of the proceedings.[203] The witness can consent to a publication which does name him, but the consent must be in writing[204] and must not be obtained by interfering with the peace or comfort of the witness.[205]

8–047 The reporting direction can be revoked and excepting directions can be made, varied or altered either by the same court or an appellate court. Again, as with children, an excepting direction cannot be made exclusively because of the outcome of the case.

The criminal courts have also been given powers by the Youth Justice and Criminal Evidence Act 1999 to take "special measures" to assist witnesses (other than the accused) who are under 17, or who suffer from a mental disorder, or have impaired intelligence or a physical disability or disorder or whose evidence would be adversely affected by fear or distress.[206] "Special measures" include the use of screens in court so that the witness does not have to look at the defendant: allowing evidence to be given by live video link; removing wigs or gowns; hearings conducted informally out of the court room and replayed on video; the examination of witnesses through an intermediary and the giving of evidence in private (as to later see above para.8–015).[207] In some cases the court can also give a direction restricting cross-examination by a defendant who is representing himself.

Reporting of a "special measures" direction or a direction limiting cross-examination and any legal argument about them is postponed

---

[201] Criminal Procedure Rules 2005, r.16.3(4).

[202] 2005 Rules, r.16.4(1)(b) and r.16.5(2).

[203] 1999 Act, s.46(9).

[204] 1999 Act, s.50(7).

[205] 1999 Act, s.50(8).

[206] Youth Justice and Criminal Evidence Act 1999, ss.16 and 17.

[207] 1999 Act, ss.19–30. Not all the special measures are available to all eligible persons.

until the relevant proceedings finish. The court can make an order lifting this restriction in whole or part, but must not do so over the objection of a defendant unless it is satisfied that this is in the interests of justice.[208]

Breach of such a reporting direction or reporting in breach of the restrictions on special measures or limitations on cross-examination is a summary offence. There is a defence that the beneficiary gave written consent.[209] A defendant who has been convicted can be fined the statutory maximum (currently £5,000). A prosecution requires the consent of the Attorney-General.

Family cases

At one time the popular press thrived on divorce court scandals, and **8–048** every salacious detail would be reported.[210] This practice has declined dramatically, in part because of the reporting restrictions and in part because it is no longer necessary to establish cruelty or adultery in order to obtain a divorce. Irretrievable breakdown is the sole ground, and this can be demonstrated merely by a period of separation. However, even where evidence of sensational adultery is given and discovered by journalists, they must be circumspect in their reports. Reports of proceedings for divorce, nullity, separation, financial provisions for a spouse or declarations of marital status, overseas adoption, legitimacy or parentage must be limited to the following[211]:

- names, addresses and occupations of parties and witnesses;
- a concise statement of the charges, defence and counter-charges in support of which evidence is given or (in the case of a declaration as to status), the declaration sought;
- submissions on points of law and rulings of the court;
- the judgment of the court and observations by the judge.

The charges and counter-charges may be the most interesting to a journalist, but they can be reported only if evidence is given in support of them. If the allegations are withdrawn, publication is prohibited.

---

[208] Youth Justice and Criminal Evidence Act 1999, s.47. Even if an order is made lifting a restriction, the legal argument on the subject cannot be reported until the end of the case:, s.47(4) and (5).

[209] 1999 Act, s.50(7).

[210] Jeremy Tunstall, *Journalists at Work* (Constable, 1971), p.91.

[211] Judicial Proceedings (Regulation of Reports) Act 1926, s.l(l)(b); Domestic and Appellate Proceedings (Restrictions of Publicity) Act 1968, s.2(3); Matrimonial Causes Act 1973, s.45; Family Law Reform Acts 1986 and 1987. But reporting of hearings to resolve financial matters between unmarried couples are not automatically restricted and in *Clibbery v Allan* [2002] 1 All E.R. 865 CA the Court of Appeal refused to impose a restriction where the couple were childless and it was unnecessary to probe into the man's finances.

In practice, the judgment of the court is usually very full and will review all evidence. Judicial comment of the sort: "the wife (of a merchant banker) was well-dressed, well-preserved, stupid in many ways but not uncultured" and the co-respondent (a window cleaner) was a "good physical specimen"[212] can be acidic and grossly unfair. Publication of such comments can be justified in the public interest on the grounds that they say more about the judges than about the subjects of their comments. One High Court judge retired after a storm of protest over comments he made about the morality of Chelsea dustmen.

8–049   As with juvenile cases, the editor, proprietor and publisher are at risk rather than the journalist. "Publication" has been held by the High Court of Justiciary in Scotland to take place when the newspaper is printed and released for distribution.[213] It is thus used in a narrower sense than in the context of libel or obscenity. These differences can be of vital importance when a criminal court's jurisdiction depends on the place where the offence was committed or (as with summary offences) whether the proceedings were commenced in time. The Scottish case is one of very few prosecutions under the 1926 Act. The judge observed dryly, but illogically, that "the paucity of decisions is, presumably, a tribute to the effectiveness of the legislation". The maximum penalty is a fine at level 5, currently £5,000, and four months in prison (although this is due to be increased to 51 weeks by the Criminal Justice Act 2003). The Attorney-General's consent is necessary for any prosecution.[214]

This last safeguard is imperfect. While the persons affected by the report may not prosecute and cannot force the Attorney-General to prosecute, they may apply for a civil injunction to restrain its publication. Normally, the courts will not enjoin in advance the commission of a criminal offence.[215] They say that the proper course is to bring a prosecution after the event. However, where a person stands to suffer particular hardship, the position is different and in *Argyll v Argyll* the court granted the Duchess an injunction to prevent the Duke reporting details of charges in their divorce proceedings that had not been backed by evidence.[216] The case is important because its rationale is capable of being applied to most, if not all, the restrictions on reporting examined in this section. An injunction should be refused if the threatened breach was trivial, but the publisher would be put to time and expense in opposing the action. This was the very vice against which the Attorney-General's veto was

[212] *Daily Express* January 25, 1969, quoted in Cretney, *Principles of Family Law*, (3rd edn., Sweet & Maxwell, 1979), p.158.
[213] *Procurator Fiscal v Scott* (September 7, 1999)—see further para.8–064.
[214] Judicial Proceedings (Regulation of Reports) Act 1926, s.1(3).
[215] *Gouriet v Union of Post Office Workers* [1978] A.C. 435.
[216] [1967] Ch. 302.

intended to guard, and the time and cost of High Court proceedings are much more serious than the cost of defending a prosecution in the magistrates' courts. But when this argument was put to Mr Justice Ungoed-Thomas in *Argyll v Argyll*, he disregarded it. However, the difficulty of learning what a paper intends to publish in advance and the cost of obtaining an injunction have meant that there are few cases in this context where the *Argyll* precedent has been followed. Infringements do not as such give a civil right to compensation,[217] but the statute may help an argument that the person concerned had a 'reasonable expectation of privacy' (see para.5–006).

Applications without notice for an occupation order to oust one party from the family home are usually heard in private. However, when a power of arrest is attached to the injunction, this should be announced when the judge next sits in open court. A person who is arrested under this power has to be brought before a judge within 24 hours (excluding only Sundays, Good Friday and Christmas Day). If a regular court will not sit within that time, the arrested person can be taken before a judge elsewhere. In theory this will be a hearing in open court and there is a Practice Direction that no impediment should be put in the way of the press or any other member of the public who wishes to attend. In practice, of course, it will be rare for the press to learn that such a hearing is due to take place. If the person arrested is committed for contempt, there must be an announcement at the next regular sitting of the court. The name of the person committed, the period of the committal and the general nature of the contempt should be given.[218]

Children cases: automatic restrictions

Children Act 1989 s.97(2)

The Children Act 1989 gives various powers to the High Court, **8–050** county court and magistrates' courts. All of these courts can sit in private to exercise these powers. Whenever there are proceedings in any of these courts it is an offence to publish to the public or a section of the public any material which is likely to identify a child as being involved in the proceedings or to publish the school or address as being that of a child involved in the proceedings[219] although the Court or the Lord Chancellor can disapply the restriction.[220] This

---

[217] *Nicol v Caledonian Newspapers Ltd*, OH Lady Paton, April 11, 2002.

[218] *Practice Direction* [1998] 2 All E.R. 927–8.

[219] Children Act 1989, s.97(2). In its original form this provision restricted reporting only of magistrates' courts, but it was significantly extended by the Access to Justice Act 1999, s.72 to reports of High Court and county court proceedings as well.

[220] Children Act 1989, s.97(4) and Family Proceedings Rules 1991, r.10.20A.

might be done if publicity could help trace a missing child.[221] The Court's power to disapply the restrictions in s.97(2) is to be construed in accordance with Art.10 of the ECHR so that, while the welfare of the child is a relevant consideration, it is not to be treated as a paramount criterion.[222]

The Court of Appeal has found these restrictions to be compatible with Art.10 ECHR. Section 97(2) does not apply to appeal proceedings, but by s.39 of Children and Young Persons Act 1933 (see para.8–038) and its inherent jurisdiction, the Appeal Court has power to order the anonymisation of references to children, although these restrictions should not be imposed automatically.[223] The restrictions in s.97(2) only continue as long as the proceedings themselves. Once they are over these restrictions come to an end, but those in the Administration of Justice Act 1960 (see below para.8–052) continue and the statutory restrictions may be further supplemented in appropriate cases by an injunction.[224] The maximum penalty for a breach of s.97(2) is a fine on level 4 (currently £2,500).

Magistrates' Courts Act 1980 s.71

8–051　When family proceedings are taking place in the magistrates' court, the media are in any event limited to publishing the names, addresses and occupations of the parties and witnesses; the grounds of the application and a concise statement of the charges, defences, and counter-charges in support of which evidence had been given; submissions on any point of law and the court's decision; and the decision of the court and any observations made by the court in giving it.[225]

In adoption proceedings the restrictions go further: the parties must be anonymous, the charges cannot be summarised and nothing must be published that would identify the child; nor can the child's photograph be printed.[226] The maximum penalty is a fine at level 4 (currently £2,500) on the editor, proprietor, or publisher of a newspaper or periodical. Again the Attorney-General must consent. These restrictions also apply to the electronic media, but they do not apply to newspapers or other periodicals of a technical character bona fide intended for circulation among members of the legal or medical professions.[227]

---

[221] See for instance *Kelly v BBC* [2001] Fam 59.

[222] *Re Brandon Webster (A Child) Norfolk County Council v Webster* [2006] EWHC 2733 (Fam).

[223] *Pelling v Bruce-Williams* [2004] 3 All E.R. 875 at [53] CA.

[224] *Clayton v Clayton* [2007] EMLR 3 at [48]–[54].

[225] Magistrates' Courts Act 1980, s.71—again the maximum fine is £2,500.

[226] Magistrates' Courts Act 1980, s.71(2).

[227] 1980 Act, s.71(5).

Administration of Justice Act 1960 s.12

We have seen already that neither press nor public normally have **8–052** access to Children Act or wardship hearings (see para.8–016) and it may be contempt of court to publish any information relating to such proceedings (see para.8–023). This was the position at common law[228] and it has been preserved by the Administration of Justice Act 1960.[229] The Court of Appeal has said that "proceedings" include such matters as statements of evidence, reports, accounts of interviews and such like that are prepared for use in court once the proceedings have been instituted.[230] The prohibition on disclosure applies even if the information or document is anonymised.[231]

Similarly, where a local authority has intervened because of suspected abuse, the parents' version of how the child sustained injuries and their criticism of social workers involved in the case would be information relating to the proceedings. Information about the nature of the injuries (without mentioning their cause) would not be objectionable.[232]

This reporting restriction is paralleled by the imposition of a high degree of confidentiality on reports made by relatives, social workers and professionals that find their way into the court files. The confidentiality is given in order to encourage candour, and the reports will be protected from newspaper lawyers who seek to inspect them in order to defend libel actions.[233]

The ban does not mean that nothing can be published about **8–053** Children Act proceedings or a ward of court. The usual position is that it is not contempt under the 1960 Act to name a child as a ward of court or the subject of proceedings under the Children Act 1989, to publish the name, address or photograph of the child, or of the other parties to the proceedings, or to give the date, time or place of a hearing or to explain the nature of the dispute or anything which has been seen or heard by a person behaving lawfully in a public place outside the court in which the hearing takes place.[234] However, the media needs to be careful of the overlapping restrictions that apply in this field and, as we have seen, the Children Act may impose an anonymity requirement which is of greater importance now that this restriction applies as well to proceedings under that Act in the High Court and County Court.

---

[228] *Re F (a minor: Publication of Information)* [1977] 1 All E.R. 114.
[229] Administration of Justice Act 1960, s.12(1).
[230] Geoffrey Lane L.J. in *Re F* (above) at 135.
[231] *Re B (A Child: Disclosure)* [2004] 1 FLR 142.
[232] *Oxfordshire C.C. v. L and F* [1997] 1 F.L.R. 235.
[233] *Re X, Y and Z (Minors), The Times*, March 20, 1991, Waite J.
[234] See *X v Dempster* [1999] 1 F.L.R. 894, 898–9.

The press may also report the text or summary of an order of the Court unless this the subject of a specific prohibition.[235] If publicity is likely to be damaging the usual practice is for the Official Solicitor to draft, and the judge to approve, a short statement giving the bare outcome of the proceedings.[236] The High Court has held that the fact that a child is a ward of court does not, of itself, prevent the media from interviewing the child or broadcasting or publishing the interview.[237]

Even where information does relate to the proceedings, publication is not automatically contempt of court: it has to be shown that the publisher knew that the material related to the proceedings and that the proceedings were held in private.[238] The later condition gives scant protection: because Children Act proceedings are so commonly held in private, experienced editors will be assumed to know this fact. It is not a defence to a contempt charge that the material published was of public interest. However, this will be relevant to the penalty.[239]

There would be no contempt at all if the court gave permission to publish. In one case it did so at the request of the local authority which considered that a fair and accurate report would be better than the inaccurate rumours being perpetuated by a man with whom the ward had become involved. The court agreed on condition that the parties remained anonymous.[240] It has been said that, "There was a discernible move in the family justice system towards more openness".[241] More judgments in forceful terms have emphasised the harm that can flow from a norm of secrecy as well as the Convention rights of freedom of expression and a public determination of civil rights. All these have to be set against the pressures favouring withholding information from the press and public,[242] but overall the Family Division is likely to be somewhat more willing than in the past to exercise its powers under the 1960 Act to permit disclosure (although usually in anonymised form).

---

[235] Administration of Justice Act 1960, s.12(2). This concerns the formal *order* of the court. The prohibition in s.12(1) still applies to the court's *judgment* in which it sets out the history of the case and its reasons for making the order: *Re B (A Child: Disclosure)* [2004] 1 F.L.R. 142 at [66]].

[236] *Re G (Celebrities: Publicity)* [1999] 1 F.L.R. 409, CA.

[237] *Kelly v BBC* [2001] 1 All E.R. 323.

[238] *Re F*, see above, fn.102.

[239] *Official Solicitor v News Group Newspapers Ltd* [1994] 2 F.L.R. 174 where the publisher was fined £5,000 and the editor £1,000: the court said that the material taken went beyond what was necessary to tell the story that a nurse with Munchausen's Syndrome by Proxy was continuing to work in a hospital.

[240] *Re H (Publication of Judgment)* [1995] 2 F.L.R. 542.

[241] *Harb v King Fahd Bin Adul Aziz* [2005] 2 F.L.R. 1108.

[242] See for instance *Re B (A Child: Disclosure)* [2004] 1 F.L.R. 142; *Re H (Children)* [2005] EWCA Civ 1325 [26] and [29] and *BBC v Rochdale MBC* [2006] E.M.L.R. 6 at [62].

Family Division publicity injunctions

Where the information does not relate to court proceedings under **8–054** the Children Act, wardship or the inherent jurisdiction of the courts over children, there is no automatic restriction on publicity. However, the courts have evolved a special jurisdiction to grant injunctions in cases involving children and vulnerable adults. They have the following underlying principles

These injunctions can apply "contra mundum"/against the world

The usual principle is that orders made by courts bind only the **8–055** immediate parties to the action. Third parties may be guilty of contempt if they knowingly subvert the purpose for which the injunction was granted (see para.7–050), but the type of injunctions considered in this section may have a more direct effect. They can be orders directed to everyone. If the injunction is made in this form it will be contempt for anyone with knowledge to infringe its terms. For these reasons it is particularly important that they should only be made after careful consideration. A direction from the head of the Family Division requires applications for such orders to be made in the High Court rather than the county court. Notice that an application affecting freedom of expression is to be made should be given via the Press Association's CopyDirect service to which most national newspapers and broadcasters subscribe.[243]

Who can be shielded?

The court has an inherent jurisdiction (going back to medieval **8–056** times) over all children and press injunctions can be granted whether or not the child has been made a ward of court. This quasi-parental jurisdiction can also be exercised to protect others who are unable to take decisions for themselves (such as terminally ill patients)[244] or who are otherwise vulnerable and lack the mental capacity to take decisions for themselves.[245] In these cases there may be a real issue as to whether the adults *do* lack capacity to take decisions for themselves (and, since capacity in an adult is presumed, it is for the person asserting lack of capacity to prove this.[246] If adults do have capacity to take decision regarding the media for themselves, the courts should back off. It is no part of the judge's function to protect an adult with capacity from his or her own decisions, however foolish

---

[243] *Practice Direction (Family Division: Applications for Reporting Restriction orders)* [2005] 2 F.L.R. 120. The web-site address is *www.medialawyer.press.net/ courtapplications*.
[244] *Re C (A Minor)(Wardship: medical treatment)(No. 2)* [1990] Fam.39.
[245] *In Re A Local Authority (Inquiry: Restraint on Publication)* [2004] Fam 96.
[246] *E v Channel 4* [2005] E.M.L.R. 30.

they may seem to the judge.[247] If the Court's jurisdiction is engaged, adult parents and carers may be protected as may the identity of residential homes, hospitals or other institutions in which the child or vulnerable adult is being looked after. These extensions are intended to bolster the protection to the principal beneficiary or others who may in the future be in a similar situation.

In very rare cases *contra mundum* injunctions have been granted with the direct aim of protecting adults who are of full physical and mental capacity, but who would be, for some reason are at risk if publicity was unrestrained. For example, injunctions *contra mundum* were granted to protect the new adult identities of Venables and Thompson, who killed Jamie Bulger when they were children (see para.5–023).

The foundation of the jurisdiction is the ECHR

8–057   Before 2004 the courts had wrestled with the limits of this jurisdiction. Three broad categories of case had been identified. One category was where the publication did not directly concern the child, but, for instance was about the criminal or offensive behaviour of the child's parents. In those cases, it was said that there was no power at all to make an injunction to protect the child from even harmful effects of the publicity.[248] A second category was where the publication was directed at the child or his or her upbringing. In these cases the courts had said that they would have jurisdiction, the child's interests would be taken into account, but would not be paramount and great importance was attached to freedom of expression.[249] This was sometimes referred to as the court's "protective jurisdiction" to distinguish it from the third category. In this last type of case the court was asked to exercise its own judgment in relation to the upbringing of a child and so was exercising what was called its "custodial jurisdiction". Here the interests of the child were treated as paramount because the Children Act 1989, s.1 so required.[250]

In *Re S*[251] this categorisation was swept away. The Law Lords decided that after the Human Rights Act the simple and direct way to approach such cases was to see them as the enforcement of rights under the ECHR. In particular, where rights under Art.8 and 10 were in issue, four propositions could be stated:

● Neither article had *as such* precedence over the other.

---

[247] *E v Channel 4* (above)—see *Stop Press* section.
[248] e.g. *Re X* [1975] Fam 47; *R (Mrs) v Central Independent Television Plc* [1994] Fam 192.
[249] e.g. *Re W (a minor)(wardship: freedom of publication)* [1992] 1 W.L.R. 100.
[250] See *Re Z (a minor) (freedom of publication)* [1997] Fam 1 CA. In *Kelly v BBC* [2001] Fam 59 Munby J. observed that *Z* was the only case which had thus far come within this third category, but see below for *Clayton v Clayton*.
[251] *Re S (a child) (identification: restriction on publication)* [2005] 1 A.C. 593 at [23].

- Where the values under the two articles were in conflict, an intense focus on the comparative importance of the specific rights being claimed was necessary.
- The justifications for interfering with or restricting each right had to be taken into account.
- The proportionality test had to be applied to each.

Accordingly, it was no longer necessary to consider the earlier case law about the scope or existence of the inherent jurisdiction, although it might remain of some interest in relation to the ultimate balancing exercise which had to be conducted between the competing Convention provisions.

Only in exceptional circumstances should a Family Division injunction prevent reporting of a criminal trial

In *Re S* Lord Steyn spoke eloquently of the importance of freedom **8–058** of reporting criminal trials (see above para.8–003). As we have seen, the criminal trial judge will have various statutory powers to confer anonymity or restrict reporting. Beyond the circumstances where those powers could be used, the balance would ordinarily come down in favour of freedom of expression and Art.10. In *Re S* itself, the courts agreed that the Family Division's injunction should allow unrestricted reporting of the trial of a woman charged with the murder of her child, notwithstanding evidence that this might harm the dead child's living sibling. In another case, a father was due to stand trial for murder of his partner whom he had then dismembered and kept in a freezer. Their young child knew that his father was in prison, but not the charge or the grisly details. Again, the court refused to grant an injunction which would have had the effect of preventing reporting of the trial. The President of the Family Division said,

> "The burden of proving a case for the grant of an injunction always lies upon the applicant. In the special case of an injunction *contra mundum*, and, in particular, one which restrains the press from its right unrestrainedly to report criminal proceedings, the burden is always a heavy one."[252]

This followed a rare case where reporting of a criminal trial was injuncted.

The mother of two young children was pleading guilty to a charge of knowingly infecting the father of one of the children with HIV. Their child was too young to be reliably tested for the virus. Three special

---

[252] *A Local authority v PD and GD (by her guardian Cathy Butcher)* [2005] EWHC 1832 Fam.

features caused the judge to decide that the case for an injunction was made out: there had been no or minimal previous reporting; the identification of the mother (and the children) was likely to have a seriously prejudicial effect on the placement of children in care proceedings; and there was a real risk that publicity would lead to short and long term stigmatisation of the children as suffering from HIV when that was not the case with one of them and might not be in the case of the other.[253]

Relevance of public interest

8–059 The Human Rights Act 1998 requires the court to consider the extent to which it would be in the public interest for the material to be published.[254] In the past, Family Division injunctions have sometimes been sought where the media wished to analyse and criticise the behaviour of local authorities in discharging child protection functions. After the Cleveland affair (when there was concern that suspicions of abuse had been too readily accepted by local authorities), the courts were more ready to accept the legitimacy of press investigations of this kind. At the same time, they have become more streetwise about tabloid entrapment techniques eliciting information from schoolchildren and unwary relatives and teachers. The result has often been a limited restriction on publication which permits investigation and criticism of the local authority actions, but without reference to details which might identify the children, parents, teachers or carers. Although they now have to be seen in light of the ECHR and the House of Lords decision in *Re S* with its emphasis on balancing the Art.10 and 8 rights, the guidelines of the Court of Appeal in *Re W*[255] may still be useful. In summary, it said:

- The Court attached great importance to safeguarding freedom of the press and to Article 10 of the ECHR.
- Those freedoms were subject to exceptions, including restrictions imposed for the protection of children.
- In the balancing exercise, the welfare of the child was *not* the paramount consideration.
- An important factor was the nature and extent of the public interest in the matter which it was sought to publish.
- In almost every case the public interest would be satisfied without any identification of the child. However, the risk of some wider identification might have to be accepted on occasions if the story was to be told in a manner that would engage the interest of the general public (in the particular

---

[253] *A Local Authority v W* [2006] F.L.R. 1.
[254] Human Rights Act 1998, s.12(4)(a)(ii).
[255] [1991] 1 W.L.R. 1141 CA.

case the Court refused to ban identification of the local authority because, although this might increase the risk of the child's identification, it was the authority's actions which gave rise to the public interest).

- Any restraint was for the protection of the child and its carers. The restraint had to be in clear terms and no wider than necessary for that purpose. Save in exceptional circumstances, the child could not be protected from distress which might be caused by reading the publication.

An injunction will normally allow publication of information already in the public domain

The standard template for a Family Division injunction includes a **8–060** proviso excluding matter which is already in the public domain from the prohibition on reporting.[256] However, this is not a universal practice and there may be times when the Court deliberately decides not to have such a qualification.[257]

Period of the injunction

The injunction will normally last until the child reaches 18 or a **8–061** vulnerable adult dies. In some cases a later date may be necessary so as to protect safety or welfare, or the anonymity of other children who are named in the order and who are still under age, or to maintain the anonymity of doctors or carers after the death of a patient. The media can always apply for an order to be varied or discharged if the original justification for the order has changed or disappeared. The BBC made an application of this kind when it came to make a documentary about an alleged satanic abuse scandal.[258]

Children had been taken into care, but on further investigation it was decided that there had been no abuse. The BBC had the co-operation or agreement of all the children in question, but two social workers at the centre of the events wished to continue to remain anonymous. The court ruled that since 14 years had passed, the anonymity order in relation to them should be lifted. Besides, the original purpose of the order restricting identification of the social workers had been to prevent indirect identification of the children. Since the children had now grown up and wanted the programme to proceed the original

---

[256] See *Practice Note (Official Solicitor: Deputy Director of Legal Services: CAFCASS: Application for Reporting Restriction Orders)* [2005] 2 F.L.R. 111; *Kelly v BBC* [2001] Fam 59, 93.

[257] e.g. *Re X and Y (Children)* [2004] EMLR 29 Munby J. who did, though, allow reporting of the criminal trials of the father and his twin brother, both of whom had convictions for child abuse.

[258] *BBC v Rochdale MBC* [2006] EMLR 6.

purpose no longer applied. The social workers were also concerned at the possible repercussions which might follow their identification, but the judge quoted from an earlier Court of Appeal decision which had said,

> "social workers up and down the country, day in day out are on the receiving end of threats of violence and sometimes actual violence from adults engaged in bitterly contested public law cases. Social Workers must regard this as a professional hazard. . . cases in which the court will afford anonymity to a professional social work witness will be highly exceptional."[259]

Notice of the injunction

8–062 Although a *contra mundum* injunction is directed against the world, a newspaper or broadcaster would only be in contempt if it knew of the order at the time of publication.[260] The system organised by the Press Association for service of *notice of applications* for injunctions is not a medium for the service of *injunctions* once they have been made. It is the responsibility of the successful applicant to serve the orders on particular organs or news organisation.[261] The proliferation of these orders creates a headache for the media, but it is prudent for each organisation to establish a system for alerting their journalists to orders which have been served on them.

Injunctions directed at parents

8–063 The media are immediately affected by a *contra mundum* injunction but their plans for stories or programmes may be indirectly stymied by an injunction which is made, not against the world, but against one or both of the child's parents or carers. Here, the threefold division of Family Division injunctions which was mentioned above at para.8–057 may still live on. In particular, where the parent is planning to involve the child himself or herself in a film, programme or other media event, the court may step in to make a prohibited steps order under s.8 of the Children Act 1989 or make a similar injunction. In this type of case, they have indicated that the best interests of the child will be the paramount consideration, although not to the automatic exclusion of the Art.10 rights of the parent and the media.

> In *Clayton v Clayton*[262] the father had abducted his young daughter and taken her to Portugal. There he had been arrested, returned to England and sentenced to nine months imprisonment for the abduction. The bitter access dispute between the parents had been settled by

---

[259] *Re W (Care Proceedings: Witness Anonymity)* [2003] 1 F.L.R. 329 at [13] per Thorpe L.J.

[260] *Re L (A Minor) (Wardship: Freedom of Publication)* [1988] 1 All E.R. 418.

[261] *A Local Authority v W* [2006] 1 F.L.R. 1 at [84].

[262] [2006] EWCA Civ 878.

agreement. This brought the Children Act proceedings to an end and, the Court of Appeal decided, the automatic restrictions in Children Act 1989 s.97(2) also came to an end. However, the father wished to make a film of his experiences and take his daughter back to Portugal as part of this venture. The Court accepted that he should be legally free to write about his experiences (however unwise this might be), but involving his daughter (who was still only seven and unable to decide these matters for herself) engaged a question of the child's upbringing and participation in such a film would not be in her best interests. The father was enjoined from involving his daughter in this way.

Responsibility for reporting restriction offences

For the print media those responsible are the proprietor, editor and **8–064** publisher. "Publisher" was given a wide interpretation in a 1998 case that upheld the conviction of the managing director of the publishing company on the grounds that he played a dominant role in the company and effectively controlled it.[263] This decision is difficult to square with the explicit provision in the same Act which made directors and others liable for a company's crimes which were committed with their consent or connivance.[264] This managing director had no editorial input, had not read the article and did not suspect that it was going to be published. To say that he was nonetheless "in common sense terms" the publisher is to sweep aside the principle that companies have a legal personality distinct from their shareholders and officers.

A Scottish court had to consider a different aspect of publishing in connection with an Act prohibiting publication of evidence in divorce cases (see above para.8–049). The charge had been brought in Paisley because that was where the divorce case had taken place and because the newspaper circulated there. The prosecution argued that the term "publish" should be treated as an activity that continued until the papers reached their ultimate readers. The paper (one of Express Newspapers' titles) was printed and dispatched from London. The defendant argued that "publication" took place in London and the Scottish court had no jurisdiction. The High Court of Justiciary ruled in the defendant's favour. It reasoned that the purpose of the legislation was to stop the offending material being put into the chain of distribution. This happened at the start of the chain of distribution and not at every stage thereafter. The court noted that the 1926 Act held responsible the proprietor, editor or publisher or printer but not a distributor, retailer or wholesaler. In this respect it contrasted with the Obscene Publications Act 1959 which did catch a wider category of people in the chain of selling

---

[263] *Brown v DPP* (1998) 162 J.P. 333, QBD.
[264] Sexual Offences (Amendments) Act 1976, s.5(4). This provision has now been repealed but its replacement, the Sexual Offences (Amendment) 1992, s.5 is in identical terms as are many other statutes creating media offences.

obscene articles.[265] The 1933 Children and Young Persons Act, the Sexual Offences (Amendment) Act 1992 and the Youth Justice and Criminal Evidence Act 1999 cast their net in a similar way to the 1926 Act, though they are narrower because printers are not at risk. There are divergent views as to whether the term "publish" in the Administration of Justice Act 1960, s.12 is used in the strict defamation sense of communicating to even one third party (see above para.8–023).

This meaning of "publish" will determine not only the place of the alleged offence, but its timing. Most of the reporting offences are summary. As such, they can (generally) only be prosecuted within six months. If the High Court's interpretation was followed in England, it would mean that the time for prosecution would not be extended if, for instance, a monthly magazine was sold in the shops or available for down-loading from the internet for some protracted period of time.[266]

Prosecution appeals and references to the Court of Appeal

Prosecution appeals

8–065   A further innovation of the Criminal Justice Act 2003 was to give the prosecution a right to appeal against certain decisions of a Crown Court trial judge. It may do so if the judge rules that there is no case for the defendant to answer or makes some other decision which would bring the trial to a premature end.[267] The prosecution can also appeal to the Court of Appeal if the judge made an evidentiary ruling (before the beginning of the case for the defence) which seriously weakened the prosecution's case.[268] In both situations reporting restrictions akin to the restrictions on committal proceedings will apply so that reporting of the prosecution's application to the trial judge, application for permission to appeal and the appeal itself will be extremely limited unless the Courts exercise their powers to disapply the restrictions.[269] The maximum penalty is a fine not exceeding level 5 (currently £5,000) and the Attorney-General must consent to any prosecution.[270]

---

[265] *Procurator Fiscal v Scott*, September 7, 1999, HCJ.
[266] See similarly *R v Regan*, Southwark Crown Court, June 17, 1999 (unreported)—but see *The Yearbook of Copyright and Media Law 2000* (OUP, 2000), p.436. This was a case under Representation of the People Act 1983, s.106—see below, para.10–018.
[267] Criminal Justice Act 2003 ss.58–61.
[268] 2003 Act, s.62.
[269] 2003 Act, s.71.
[270] 2003 Act, s.72(9) and (10).

Tainted acquittals

In Ch.7 (Contempt) we also commented on the procedure by which **8–066**
a defendant can be retried if the Crown can establish that an
acquittal tainted by jury nobbling or the like and how the Contempt
of Court Act strict liability regime had been adapted to this
procedure (see para.7–031).

New trial of acquitted defendant because of compelling new evidence

The Criminal Justice Act 2003 also introduced a more wide-ranging **8–067**
power for the Court of Appeal to set aside an acquittal because of
"compelling new evidence" and where a retrial would be in the
interests of justice. To be compelling the new evidence has to be
reliable, substantial and highly probative of the case against the
acquitted person.[271] The Court of Appeal can impose a reporting
restriction order "where it appears to the Court of Appeal that the
inclusion of any matter in a publication would give rise to a
substantial risk of prejudice to the administration of justice in a
retrial".[272] The Court of Appeal must be satisfied that the reporting
restriction would be in the interests of justice. It can be made on the
application of the DPP or by the Court of its own motion once the
prosecution has applied for permission to retry the defendant. The
DPP can apply for an order at an even earlier stage, but only once a
fresh investigation into the defendant subsequent to his acquittal has
commenced. At this investigatory stage any reporting restriction
order must specify an end point. The order will anyway expire at the
conclusion of a retrial or once it is clear that there can be no
retrial.[273] The penalty for breaching an order is a fine up to level 5
(currently £5,000) and the Attorney-General must consent to a
prosecution.[274]

> In the first case under these powers to be considered by the Court of
> Appeal the DPP applied for a reporting restriction order which the
> Court granted.[275] It called the new powers "revolutionary" displacing
> the centuries old principle against double jeopardy. Any application
> brought to the Court of Appeal was likely to be at least of local if not
> national interest. On the other hand, at the hearing of the application
> there would be a debate as to whether there was new, reliable,
> substantial and highly probative evidence against the defendant and
> the Court of Appeal would express its view. Any retrial had to start
> within two months of the Court of Appeal's order. In these circum-
> stances, reporting of the Court of Appeal hearing would often be
> prejudicial.

[271] Criminal Justice Act 2003, ss.75–79.
[272] 2003 Act, s.82(1).
[273] 2003 Act, s.82(3)–(11).
[274] 2003 Act, s.83.
[275] *In Re D (Acquitted Person: Retrial)* [2006] 1 W.L.R. 1998 CA.

However, if there was to be a further trial, the new jury would be told of the new evidence. If there was a new trial it was also highly likely to emerge that the defendant had been tried before: part of the "compelling" new evidence in this case was that the defendant had been convicted of perjury because of the evidence he had given at his original trial. Those who knew the law would also know that he could only be retried because the Court of Appeal thought that there was compelling new evidence against him. Of course, some jurors would not know that this was the law, but it is surely wrong that reporting restrictions should be imposed because of an assumption that most jurors would be ignorant of the law.

The Court did give guidance as to procedure for future applications. 14 days notice of the application should be given to the media (though on the understanding that the media was not in the meantime to publish the fact). Media representatives should contact the DPP and the Court not later than 48 hours before the hearing if they intended to contest the order and, if possible, the nature of the submissions they proposed to make. In this case (understandably since it was the first application) the DPP had issued a press release, but the Court discouraged him from doing so again in the future.

Attorney-General's reference on a point of law

8-068　Side by side with these new provisions is the older power of the Attorney-General to refer to the Court of Appeal a point of law decided by the trial judge before the jury acquitted the defendant.[276] The court may decide the point of law in the Attorney-General's favour, but cannot reverse the acquittal. To protect defendants against embarrassment (and for no better reason), court rules require their identity to be kept secret unless they consent to be named.[277] These rules apply as well if there is a further appeal to the House of Lords.[278] In practice this means that the Court of Appeal or the House of Lords has to make an order prohibiting identification. If the restriction is broken, the publisher can be punished for contempt, but only if it knew of the order. A person who is identified in breach of an order does not have a right of action for damages.[279] The court in this case also emphasised that such orders were *not* intended to forestall any further journalistic investigation of the facts of the offence with a view to establishing whether the acquitted defendant was, in truth, guilty. If the paper got it wrong, his remedy was in libel.

Unduly lenient sentences

8-069　It is different where the Attorney-General refers to the Court of Appeal a sentence that he considers unduly lenient.[280] Here the court is not just concerned with the abstract question of whether the

---

[276] Criminal Justice Act 1972, s.36.
[277] Criminal Procedure Rules 2005, r.69.4.
[278] *WB v H. Bauer Publishing Ltd* (2002) E.M.L.R. 8 at [6], Eady J.
[279] *WB v H. Bauer Publishing Ltd* (above).
[280] Criminal Justice Act 1988, ss. 35 and 36.

sentence was wrong in principle, but can increase or alter the sentence actually imposed. Consequently, there is no argument that the defendant should have any special protection for the defendant and these references can be reported in the usual way.

Indecent evidence

An Act of 1926 prohibits publication in relation to any judicial **8–070** proceedings of "any indecent matter or indecent medical, surgical or physiological details being matter or details the publication of which would be calculated to injure public morals".[281] The vulnerability of public morals must be judged by current standards,[282] which are permissive. The proceedings in both the *Lady Chatterley's Lover* and *Oz* magazine trials were published in book form and in television re-enactments without objection, despite the sexual explicitness and repetition of allegedly "obscene" passages (the four letter words in the *Oz* play were specially subtitled for deaf viewers).

A previous edition of this work described the 1926 Act as a dead letter. However, in 1996, it was mysteriously invoked to stop the reporting of evidence in the Moynihan peerage case, a sordid scrap over who had the hereditary title to sit in the House of Lords—the Filipino child of the eldest Lord (a depraved brothel-owner) or his younger brother, the then Tory Minister for Sport.[283] There was no rational reason for the restriction, which served only to cover up evidence which would have underlined the absurdity of giving parliamentary seats to hereditary peers.

SECRECY ORDERS

Section 11 orders

In certain circumstances the courts may invoke an inherent power to **8–071** order that the names of witnesses should not be published. Black-mail cases have provided one example.[284] The policy, as with rape cases, is to encourage victims to come forward to testify against their tormentors. Blackmail victims are rarely likely to testify unless assured that their guilty secrets will not leak out. In 2006 a woman was tried for allegedly blackmailing two immigration judges. When she was convicted in relation to one and acquitted in respect of the other, the trial judge acceded to an application from the press to allow him to be identified. Although the trial provided a bonanza for the media, there must be a real risk that this decision will discourage

---

[281] Judicial Proceedings (Regulation of Reports) Act 1926, s.1(1)(a).
[282] *Knuller v DPP* [1973] A.C. 435.
[283] *Moynihan v Moynihan (No.1)* [1997] 1 F.L.R. 59.
[284] *R. v Socialist Worker Printers & Publishers Ltd, Ex p. Att-Gen* [1975] Q.B. 637.

future blackmail victims from coming forward for fear that a prosecution will fail and they will be named. It is a similar concern which underlies the policy in the legislation according anonymity to rape complainants and where the acquittal of the alleged rapist is not (by itself) enough to justify lifting the restriction.

The power to require the press to respect anonymity orders is now formalised by s.11 of the Contempt Act, which provides:

> "In any case where a court (having power to do so) allows a name or other matter to be withheld from the public in proceedings before the court, the court may give such directions prohibiting the publication of that name or matter in connection with the proceedings as appear to the court to be necessary for the purpose for which it was so withheld."

Section 11 does not give courts a new power to take evidence in secret where one did not previously exist, but, where this is appropriate, it provides the means for prohibiting wider publication and punishing disclosure if it takes place. In the absence of a statutory power this means that there must be some overwhelming reason in the interests of the administration of justice why the normal principle of open justice should be abrogated.

> The defendant to a minor road traffic offence was a former M.P. His home address was not given orally to the court because, he said, he feared further harassment from his ex-wife. The magistrates agreed and made an order under s.11 forbidding its publication. The Divisional Court held that while evidence could be communicated to the court in writing if the proper administration of justice demanded it, there were no good reasons in the present case. Many defendants would prefer that their identity was not revealed, "but s.11 was not enacted for the comfort and feelings of defendants". The order was quashed.[285]

---

[285] *R. v Evesham Justices Ex p. McDonagh* [1988] 1 All E.R. 371, 384, QBD. It is a common failing of common law judges to suppress names for reasons that appear reasonable, but that have nothing to do with the strict needs of the administration of justice. Powerful appellate rebukes of this behaviour are to be found in the Australian cases of *Raybos Australia Pty Ltd v Jones* (1985) 2 N.S.W.L.R. 47 (reversing a suppression order on the name of a leading solicitor accused of conspiracy in a civil action, made because of damage to his professional reputation from possibly unfounded accusation) and *John Fairfax & Sons v Police Tribunal of NSW* (1986) 5 N.S.W.L.R. 465 (reversing a suppression order on the name of a police informant, because it had already been mentioned in public and so the order could not have been necessary to secure justice in the particular proceedings). See also *R. v Dover Justices Ex p. Dover District Council* (1992) 156 J.P. 433 where "exceptional circumstances" justifying restrictions on publicity did not include the fact that it might have dire economic consequences leading to the closure of the defendant's business. (The defendant was a restaurateur who failed to win approval for a ban on the reporting of proceedings brought against him by a council health department.)

The High Court in Northern Ireland similarly quashed a magistrate's **8–072** order prohibiting publication of the name or address or the defendant or the charge against him in an indecent assault case.[286] The magistrate had been persuaded that there was a risk that the defendant would be attacked as had others facing similar types of allegations. The High Court said:

> "A possible attack upon the accused by ill-motivated persons cannot be regarded as a consequence of the publication of the proceedings of the court which should influence the court in its deliberations and the danger of its occurrence should not cause the court to depart from well-established principles."

If publication of the names or addresses of witnesses might lead to physical attack, the court may find a sufficient threat to the administration of justice to justify an order under s.11.[287] Even so, the claim for a suppression order should be reviewed critically. If the source of the threat already knows the witness's identity and address, there is no point in prohibiting publication. Physical threats of this type should also be distinguished from mere embarrassment:

> At a kidnapping trial an Old Bailey judge ordered that the identity of the main prosecution witness (the alleged victim) should not be publicised. She was a member of a wealthy and famous family. She was also undergoing treatment for heroin addiction and it was said that publicity would damage her recovery. The judge's section 11 order was challenged in the Divisional Court, which indicated that it would have quashed the order if it had jurisdiction to do so. There was a danger that the witness had been accorded special treatment because of her family connections. It was common for witnesses to be faced with embarrassment as a result of facts that were elicited in the course of proceedings or of allegations made without real substance. However, it was an essential part of British justice that cases should be tried in public and this consideration had to outweigh the individual interests of particular persons.[288]

A further reason why the appeal courts criticised the orders of the trial judges in the *Belfast Telegraph* and *Crook* cases was that the person's name had been openly used in court. In a subsequent case in 1985 the Divisional Court confirmed that an order under s.11 cannot be made to prevent publication of a name (or other evidence) once it has already been spoken in proceedings before the

---

[286] *R. v Newtonabbey Magistrates' Court Ex p. Belfast Telegraph Newspapers Ltd, The Times*, August 27, 1997; see though *Venables v News Group Newspapers Ltd* above, para.5–023.

[287] See, for instance *R. v Payne*, September 19, 2006, McKinnon J. sitting as a Judge Advocate in a court martial.

[288] *R. v Central Criminal Court Ex p. Crook, The Times*, November 8, 1984; (1985) L.S. Gaz. 1408, QBD.

court.[289] This rule can take by surprise judges who find it cumbersome to conceal the identities of witnesses from a public gallery which is often empty. Yet the principle is important. Although the press is segregated from the general public they are there as the eyes and ears of the public who cannot be present. Unless the legislation clearly says something different, if the public in court can hear evidence or names, the public outside court (through the medium of the press) should be free to do so as well.

The opposite conclusion was reached by McKinnon J. sitting as a Judge Advocate in a court martial of several soldiers charged with war crimes offences in Iraq.[290] He ordered that photographs or sketches of the defendants could not be published even though the defendants had and would throughout the trial be present in open court and visible to any members of the public who were present. He accepted an argument by the defendants that the Court had power to control its own proceedings. It could have allowed the defendants to be screened from the public in court (or, more, could have sat in camera). Instead of these more drastic measures curtailing public access, it was entitled to take the lesser measure of prohibiting publication of photographs or sketches. In 2006 when this decision was made, it was impossible for the media to appeal or judicially review such rulings. Had they been able to do so, the order should have been overturned. The power to do the greater measure (e.g. sit in camera) does include the lesser power, for instance, to allow a witness to remain anonymous. Frustrating these measures may amount to contempt of court. However, these are both measures which concern the conduct of the hearing itself. The *Leveller* and *Independent Publishing Co. Ltd v Attorney-General of Trinidad and Tobago*[291] establish that there is no common law power to control what is published in the press separate from measures concerning the conduct of the hearing itself. Yet this is precisely what his order did. The Judge Advocate was also impressed by the argument that the defendants' right to life under Art.2 of the ECHR required the order (he feared that otherwise those opposed to the war in Iraq might attack the defendants). However, even if these fears had been justified on the evidence, the proper procedure would have been to apply for an injunction in the High Court: the Human Rights Act does not confer new remedial powers on courts or tribunals (see s.8 of the Human Rights Act). This was not a barren technical objection because if the order had been made by the High Court it could have been reviewed by the Court of Appeal.

---

[289] *R. v Arundel Justices Ex p. Westminster Press Ltd* [1985] 1 W.L.R. 708 and *R v Z* [2005] 2 A.C. 467 at [2]. Committal hearings are different "proceedings" to the trial for these purposes and so a Crown Court has power to make a s.11 order prohibiting publication of names which were used openly before magistrates. However, this prior publicity is a factor which should disincline a judge to accede to a request for a s.11 order: *Appeal of East Anglian Daily Times Ltd*, Court of Appeal Crim. Div. June 11, 1992.
[290] *R v Payne*, Court Martial, September 19, 2006.
[291] [2005] 1 A.C. 190 PC.

This link between secrecy in court and out of court is broken by **8–073** the Youth Justice and Criminal Evidence Act. Orders under s.46 allow a court to make an order conferring anonymity on adult witnesses who would be in fear or distress (see above para.8–046).

If the prosecution or defence apply to a Crown Court for an order that all or part of a trial should be held in secret in order to protect the identity of a witness or any other person, advance notice must be given to allow an appeal against these restrictions on open justice to be taken to the Court of Appeal. The requirements are the same as where a court is invited to sit in secret for national security reasons (see para.8–013).

It is increasingly common for civil courts to be asked to make section 11 orders. The common law test to be satisfied is the same: it must be shown that free reporting would frustrate or render impracticable the administration of justice.[292]

An application for judicial review of a housing authority's decision **8–074** was brought by claimants who were HIV-positive. The court refused to allow them to be referred to by initials. They had not shown that publicity would impede justice and a general assertion that those with a similar condition might refrain from exercising legal remedies was not sufficient justification for the order.[293] In *R. v Somerset Health Authority Ex p. S*[294] the court made an anonymity order for a claimant seeking review of a refusal to fund gender reassignment surgery but warned that more evidence would be needed at the substantive hearing to show that others would be dissuaded from seeking relief if publicity were given to their names. In *R. v Huddersfield JJ. Ex p. D*[295] a police informant was allowed to bring judicial review proceedings anonymously when he complained (successfully) of the magistrates' refusal to hear in private details of his assistance to the police.

A more difficult issue is whether the court should permit anonymity because publicity would cause significant harm to his or her mental health. The Court of Appeal made an order on these grounds when deciding whether a medical negligence claim for the loss of a penis should be tried by a jury or by a judge alone[296] but this point of law had nothing to do with the claimant's identity. More controversially a Divisional Court allowed an HIV claimant to remain anonymous after evidence that publicity would be extremely destructive psychologically, although it was not suggested that he

---

[292] *Att-Gen v Leveller Magazine Ltd* [1979] A.C. 440.
[293] *R. v Westminster City Council Ex p. Castelli* (1995) 7 Admin. L.R. 840.
[294] [1996] C.O.D. 244.
[295] [1997] C.O.D. 27.
[296] *H. v Ministry of Defence* [1991] 2 All E.R. 834.

would withdraw his claim if anonymity was refused.[297] The Divisional Court had previously allowed anonymity to a claimant who alleged she had been sexually abused by her step-father because of the psychiatric and psychological damage which public identification would cause.[298] However, a future applicant in the same position would have protection from identification under the Sexual Offences (Amendment) Act 1992 even without an order—see para.8–044.

Anonymity will not be granted merely because publicity to the claim might damage the applicant's business. Thus a firm of solicitors who wished to challenge the Legal Aid Board's decision to remove their franchise for criminal legal aid was refused an anonymity order.[299] In this case the Court of Appeal made clear that it was insufficient to achieve an anonymity order that the claimant would otherwise not bring the case: there had to be some reasonable justification for that stance. The Court of Appeal has also warned that when both sides are agreed that information should be kept from the public the court should be most vigilant.[300]

8–075   The common law test rightly strives to confine the power to give anonymity. The Civil Procedure Rules, regrettably, are expansive: they say simply that "the court may order that the identity of any party or witness must not be disclosed if it considers non-disclosure necessary in order to protect the interests of that party or witness".[301] On their face these rules seem to be a dramatic and unprincipled erosion of open justice. It must be hoped that the courts will continue much as before by either exercising their discretion only in situations where justice would otherwise be rendered impracticable or by reading into the word "necessary" something more than an examination of what is required to protect the particular interests of the party or witness and instead only make an order if those interests are so overwhelming that they should displace the ordinary practice of open justice.

Those seeking anonymity to prevent disclosure of embarrassing medical or other private information now point to Art.8 of the ECHR and the decision of the House of Lords in *Re S* (see above para.8–057). In *Z v Finland*[302] the European Court of Human Rights found that Finland had violated the rights of a witness under Art.8

---

[297] *Re D (Protection of Party Anonymity)* (1998) 1 C.C.L. Rep. 190. See also *R v J* [2003] EWCA Crim 3268 where a person appealing against his conviction was allowed to remain anonymous for fear of further damage to his mental health. The Court considered an order was necessary to protect the appellant's human rights, but it reached its decision without opposing argument from the media.

[298] *R. v Criminal Injuries Compensation Board Ex p. A* [1992] C.O.D. 379.

[299] *R. v Legal Aid Board Ex p. Kaim Todner (A firm of solicitors)* [1999] Q.B. 966 where the Court of Appeal reviewed the applicable principles.

[300] *Ex p. P*, *The Times*, March 31, 1998, CA and *R. v Legal Aid Board Ex p. Kaim Todner*, above.

[301] CPR, r.39.2.

[302] (1998) 25 E.H.R.R. 371.

when its courts had failed to restrain publication of her medical details. The Court emphasised that a balance had to be struck between the seriousness of the interference with private life and countervailing considerations such as the investigation and prosecution of crime and the publicity of court proceedings.

Before an editor or reporter can be held in contempt for disobedience to a partial secrecy order, there must be a clear ruling expressed as a formal order. So much is clear from *Att-Gen v Leveller Magazine Ltd*.[303]

> During committal proceedings in the "ABC" Official Secrets case (see para.11–004) the prosecution called an expert witness. The magistrates allowed his real name to be written down and shown to the parties, but said that he was to be referred to publicly as Colonel B, since the prosecution claimed that revelation of his true identity would prejudice national security. In the course of giving evidence, the Colonel provided information from which reporters in court, by subsequently consulting army publications, deduced his name and position. The *Leveller* and other magazines gleefully published this discovery, and were prosecuted for contempt on the basis that they had flouted a court order. The House of Lords held that the press action was not contempt, for a number of reasons:
>
> - It had not been shown to interfere with the administration of justice.
> - The magistrates' action may well have amounted to an implied request that the press should not publish the name, but before contempt could be proved there had to be disobedience to a clear order by the court.
> - The Colonel had effectively "blown his own cover" by his answers to questions in open court.

As a result of s.11, any partial secrecy order should be in writing, state its precise scope, the time it should cease to have effect (if appropriate) and the specific purpose of making the order. Courts must normally give notice to the press that an order has been made and court staff should be prepared to answer specific inquiries about orders.[304]

Postponement orders

Reports of evidence in a trial will not generally pose any risk at all **8–076** since they convey to the public at large only what has been presented in open court. Consequently, they cannot be contempt of court.[305] Section 4(1) of the Contempt of Court Act 1981 formalises this position. It gives an express right to publish in good faith a fair,

---

[303] *Att-Gen v Leveller Magazine Ltd* [1979] A.C. 440.
[304] *Practice Direction (Criminal Proceedings: Consolidation)* [2002] 1 W.L.R. 2870, para.I.3.3.
[305] *Buenos Aires Gas Co Ltd v Wilde* (1880) 42 L.T. 657.

accurate and contemporaneous report of public legal proceedings. A report is "accurate" if its gist is correct even if not word perfect. Reports are contemporaneous if they are published as soon as practicable after my temporary legal restriction on reporting ends.

Section 4(2) of the Act gives the court a power to make an order postponing the publication of certain matters heard in open court:

> "In any such proceedings the court may where it appears to be necessary for avoiding a substantial risk of prejudice to the administration of justice in those proceedings, or in any proceedings pending or imminent, order that the publication of any report of the proceedings, or any part of the proceedings, be postponed for such period as the court thinks necessary for that purpose."

Contrary to some suggestions in older cases there is no common law power to order the postponement of reporting of court proceedings.[306]

8–077   Applications for orders under this section in criminal trials are usually made in two situations. The first is where legal argument takes place in the jury's absence so as to avoid any risk of prejudice. This purpose would be frustrated if jurors could read an account of what was said in the press the next day. Consistently with this purpose, orders made under s.4(2) for this purpose ought to lapse once the jury has returned its verdict.

Judges do not always remember to make s.4(2) orders to cover discussions in the absence of the jury. If they do not then the media ought to have a defence under s.4(1) to an allegation that a report of the proceedings was a strict liability contempt. This was accepted in the official secrets trial of Clive Ponting, where McCowan J. forgot to make an order and *The Guardian* decided to report his comments about Ponting's defence (the report which showed the that the Judge believed Ponting had no defence did no harm—Ponting was acquitted). However, a guide to reporting restrictions in the Crown Court published by the Society of Editors, the Newspaper Society and the Judicial Studies Board[307] suggests that publication in these circumstances would be common law contempt because it would interfere with the course of justice as a continuing process in criminal proceedings by defeating the whole purpose of the jury withdrawing. However, this type of publication is no more a general threat to the integrity of criminal justice than any other prejudicial publication. The issue remains unresolved.[308]

---

[306] *Independent Publishing Co Ltd v Att-Gen of Trinidad and Tobago* [2005] 1 A.C. 190 PC.

[307] August 2000.

[308] Of course a report of proceedings in the jury's absence would still have to be "fair" and in "good faith" to attract the protection of s.4(1)—see Miller, *Contempt of Court* (3rd edn, OUP, 2000), paras 10.96 and 10.108.

Section 4(2) orders are unnecessary where statutory restrictions on reporting will apply in any case, as with preparatory hearings and preliminary rulings.[309]

The second type of situation where s.4(2) orders are often made is **8–078** more controversial and much more common. Following a large police investigation there may be more charges and/or defendants than can be conveniently tried by one jury at a single trial. The prosecution will then elect, or the court will order, a series of trials. It is common for the defendants in the second or later trials to argue that reporting of the first or earlier trials would prejudice their cases. In considering such an application the judge should ask the following questions:

- *Are the proceedings which might be prejudiced the ones where reporting is to be restricted or some others "pending or imminent"?* Where a series of trials have been ordered they would all be pending. Less obviously, a future trial is "pending or imminent" at the time of committal proceedings even though none would take place if the magistrates were to rule that there was no case to answer.[310] Nonetheless magistrates should be wary of supplementing the reporting restrictions regime which applies in any event to committals by making an order under s.4(2). It will be rare that the remaining tests considered below will be satisfied.[311] A person whose acquittal of an offence is tainted by an "administration of justice offence" (perverting the course of justice, perjury or intimidation of witnesses or jurors) can be retried for the original offence. If a retrial is a potential possibility, it is to be treated as a pending or imminent proceeding so that a court dealing with the administration of justice offence can make a postponement order.[312] However, here as well, the court should only make a s.4(2) order if the remaining tests are satisfied.

- *If no order is made, will there be a substantial risk of prejudice?* Defendants who apply for postponement orders often raise a fear of inflammatory and unfair reporting. This is not relevant because reporting which is prejudicial will in any case constitute contempt of court under the strict liability rule (see para.7–007). If the prejudicial publicity is not a report of legal proceedings, or if the report is biased or otherwise unfair, the publisher will get no help from the defence in s.4(1) and an order under s.4(2) would be superfluous. As the Court of Appeal said in *Re B* in 2006,

---

[309] See para.8–030.
[310] *R v Horsham JJ. Ex p. Farquharson* [1982] Q.B. 762.
[311] *R v Beaconsfield JJ. Ex p. Westminster Press* (1994) 158 J.P. 1055.
[312] Contempt of Court Act 1981, s.4(2A)—see further on tainted acquittals para.7–031.

> ". . . the responsibility for avoiding publication of material which may prejudice the outcome of a trial rests fairly and squarely on those responsible for the publication. In our view, broadcasting authorities and newspaper editors should be trusted to fulfil their responsibilities, accurately to inform the public of court proceedings, and to exercise sensible judgment about the publication of comment which may interfere with the administration of justice. They have access to the best legal advice and they have their own judgments to make. The risk of being in contempt of court for damaging the interests of justice is not one which any responsible editor would wish to take. In itself this is an important safeguard and it should not be overlooked simply because there are occasions when there is widespread and ill-judged publicity in some parts of the media."[313]

Consequently, the court should focus its attention on the likely effect of reporting which does meet the criteria of the s.4(1) defence, i.e. fair and accurate, in good faith, contemporaneous reporting of proceedings which took place in open court.[314]

It will be very unusual for reporting with these qualities to pose a *substantial* risk of prejudice. It is often said to be different if the trials have common defendants so that convictions in the first will be known by the jury in the second, or if there is a common prosecution witness whose standing in the eyes of a second jury may be enhanced if it knows that his evidence was believed by an earlier jury. Yet it is wrong to assume that substantial prejudice is likely in these situations. If there is an appreciable gap between the trials the jurors in the second trial may well not recall publicity surrounding the first. In any case, where the trial is lengthy (as each one in a series of trials often is), there is an acknowledged tendency for the jury to become more inward looking and to follow directions from the trial judge to disregard previous (or even contemporaneous) publicity.[315] The Court of Appeal emphasised the importance of this in *Re B*:

> "There is a feature of our trial system which is sometimes overlooked or taken for granted. The collective experience of this constitution as well as the previous constitution of the court, both when we were in practice at the Bar and judicially has demonstrated to us time and again, that juries up and down the country have a passionate and profound belief in, and a commitment to, the right of a defendant to be given a fair trial. They know that it is integral to their responsibility. It is, when all

---

[313] See *R v B* [2007] E.M.L.R. 5 at [26].

[314] *Scarsbrook v H.M.A.*, September 7, 2000, High Court of Justiciary.

[315] See Lawton J. in *R. v Kray*, 53 Cr.App.R. 412, 414, Sir John Donaldson MR. in *Att-Gen v News Group Newspapers Ltd* [1987] QB 1, 16, and Lord Taylor C.J. in *Ex p. Telegraph Plc* (above).

is said and done, their birthright; it is shared by each of them with the defendant. They guard it faithfully. The integrity of the jury is an essential feature of our trial process. Juries follow directions which the judge will give them to focus exclusively on the evidence and to ignore everything which they have heard or read out of court. . . .We cannot emphasise too strongly that the jury will follow [the trial judge's directions] not only because they will loyally abide by the directions of law which they will be given by the judge, but also because the directions themselves will appeal directly to their own instinctive and fundamental belief in the need for the trial process to be fair."[316]

- *Is a restriction order necessary to avoid the risk of prejudice?* Necessity means more than convenience. No postponement order may be "necessary" if a substantial risk of prejudice can be avoided by other means. Delaying the start of the second trial or altering its venue may be feasible alternatives which would make a postponement of reporting of the first trial unnecessary. So, too, in *Central Television Plc*[317] the Court of Appeal condemned a trial judge's order postponing television and radio reports of a case while the jury was sequestered in a hotel. The Court of Appeal did not accept that there was any risk of prejudice, but if there had been, it could have been avoided quite simply by directing that the jurors not have access to television and radio.

Yet even if the judge concludes that reporting would cause a substantial risk of prejudice which cannot be avoided by these other measures, it does *not* automatically follow that some kind of s.4(2) order must be made.[318] The court must go on to consider whether the public interest in free reporting outweighs the risk of prejudice in the particular case. Some courts analyse this as part of the "necessity" test[319] and recognise the affinity between "necessity" in this sense and the way that the expression is used in Art.10(2).[320] Others see it as the exercise of a separate discretion which the court has because the s.4(2) says an order "may" be made,[321] but all decisions are unanimous that such a balancing is essential. The common law principle of open justice is premised on the idea that absolutely free reporting is in the public interest. Where a case has acquired particular notoriety, where criminality of a particularly serious kind is

---

[316] *Re B* (above) at [32].
[317] [1991] 1 W.L.R. 4.
[318] See for instance *R. v Beck* (1992) 94 Cr.App.R. 376, 380; and *MGN v Bank of America* [1995] 2 All E.R. 355, 368, Ch. D.
[319] e.g. *Ex p. Telegraph Plc* [1993] 1 W.L.R. 980, CA.
[320] *R. v Sherwood Ex p. Telegraph Group* [2001] 1 W.L.R. 1983 CA.
[321] e.g. *MGN Pension Trustees v Bank of America National Trust and Savings Association* (above).

alleged, where prominent people are involved or where for other reasons there is a heightened public interest in the media having freedom to report, judges ought to be even more reluctant to impose reporting restrictions. Especially in these cases the public interest is better served by fair and accurate reporting rather than inaccurate or misleading rumours which can proliferate when contemporaneous reporting is prevented.

It is no justification for a s.4(2) order that it will "merely" *postpone* rather than indefinitely prohibit reporting. Freedom of communication means the right to report news contemporaneously and no departure from that norm should be taken lightly. Besides, the practical reality is that a news organisation which cannot report a case contemporaneously is unlikely to assign journalists to it so that a temporary ban will, in practical terms, often be a permanent one.

- *If some order is to be made what is the minimum interference with the usual principle of free reporting?* The order can only be said to be "necessary" if it goes no further than is needed to prevent the risk of prejudice. Thus it may be that only reporting of certain parts of the evidence needs to be postponed, or it may be sufficient if the names of certain witnesses are not reported until the conclusion of the trial series. It is also important to remember that the section only empowers a court to order the postponement of "reports of the proceedings". Section 4(2) cannot, for instance, be used to prevent the broadcasting of a film of the defendant's arrest (these are not part of the proceedings),[322] a background article to the case which is not a court report,[323] or the interviewing or filming of witnesses outside court. Of course, precisely because these are not court reports, journalists will not be protected by s.4(1) and independently of any order, they will have to be careful that such stories or investigations are not contempt of court.

8–079   In the Maxwell case, the judge rejected an argument that a fair trial was impossible because of extensive publicity. However, in his ruling he reminded the media of the strict liability rule and said that since the trial involved issues about the conduct of Robert Maxwell and his sons, "I shall expect the media will forthwith desist from publication of matter that is derogatory either of these Defendants or of the late Robert Maxwell".[324] This was not, and could not be, an order, but it had some effect. A judge is in a powerful position to

---

[322] *R. v Rhuddlan JJ. Ex p. HTV Ltd* [1986] Crim. L.R. 329.
[323] *Scarsbrook v Her Majesty's Advocate*, September 7, 2000, High Court of Justiciary.
[324] See *Oxford Yearbook of Media and Entertainment Law* (1996), p.356.

refer reports to the Attorney-General. Exhortations of this kind have to be considered seriously. However, because they are not orders, the ultimate issue for publishers remains whether any particular story will infringe the strict liability rule, not whether it will contravene the judge's wishes.

If the court does decide to make an order, a Practice Direction provides:

> "It is necessary to keep a permanent record of such orders for later reference. For this purpose all orders made under s.4(2) must be formulated in precise terms having regard to the decision of *R. v Horsham Justices Ex p. Farquharson* [1982] 2 All E.R. 269; [1982] Q.B. 762, and orders under both sections must be committed to writing either by the judge personally or by the clerk of the court under the judge's directions. An order must state (a) its precise scope, (b) the time at which it shall cease to have effect, if appropriate, and (c) the specific purpose of making the order.
>
> Courts will normally give notice to the press in some form that an order has been made under either section of the 1981 Act and the court staff should be prepared to answer any enquiry about a specific case, but it is, and will remain, the responsibility of those reporting cases, and their editors, to ensure that no breach of any order occurs and the onus rests with them to make enquiry in any case of doubt".[325]

It is not sufficient, as used to be the practice at the Old Bailey until 1991, to rely on the shorthand writer's note of the order; the order itself must actually be put into writing.[326]

Derogatory assertions in mitigation

Courts were given new powers in 1997 to stop the reporting of **8–080** "derogatory assertions" in pleas in mitigation or in sentence appeals.[327] "Derogatory" is not comprehensively defined but it includes allegations that the third party's conduct has been criminal, immoral or improper.[328] The court must have substantial grounds for believing that the assertion is false *or* irrelevant. Thus the reporting of a relevant allegation can be prevented merely because there are substantial grounds for believing that it is untrue.[329] There is an

---

[325] *Practice Direction (Criminal Proceedings: Consolidation)* [2002] 1 W.L.R. 2870, para.I.3.3.
[326] *R. v Nat West Investment Bank*, (unreported) January 11, 1991, (Central Criminal Court, McKinnon J).
[327] Criminal Procedure and Investigations Act 1996, ss.58–61.
[328] 1986 Act, s.58(4)(a).
[329] 1986 Act, s.58(4)(b).

important safeguard in the further requirement that the assertion has not been made at the trial at which the defendant was convicted or during any other proceedings relating to the offence.[330] This will be no protection where the defendant has pleaded guilty and there has been no trial, but then, before an order is made, there must be some material on which the court could form the necessary judgment that there are substantial grounds for believing that the allegation is untrue or irrelevant.

The power derives from a recommendation of the Runciman Commission on Criminal Justice which saw it as a "last resort" for use in "the extreme case of a defendant apparently using the opportunity of a speech in mitigation to do as much damage as possible to the reputation of the victim or a third party without risk of retaliation."[331] This recommendation was made and adopted without any evidence of the need for any such new power, which makes a serious inroad into the common law's "open justice" principle. It is, after all, an important fact that an advocate (or the defendant in person) has seen fit to make the allegation and, if it has been made in open court, why should the wider public not hear about it?

"Derogatory allegations" made in mitigation are occasionally very important—especially when they are made by counsel, who has a professional duty to ensure that they have some relevance. They can be accusations against more significant conspirators the police have not been smart enough to catch, or they might be allegations naming lawyers and accountants as professionals who have lent their services to frauds or criminal gangs. Sometimes they are newsworthy not because the allegation is true but because it is made by barristers and taken seriously by judges. In the 1970s, for example, barristers mitigating for rapists often said "she asked for it", and spouse-murders were reduced to manslaughter and then lightly punished because the wife was said by the defence counsel to be a nag or a feminist or promiscuous. These types of mitigation only stopped because they were widely reported, and widely and logically derided. It is wholly wrong that judges should have the power (whether or not they exercise it) to censor publication of what counsel or their clients say in open court.

8–081   The usual time for deciding whether to make an order will be after the court has determined sentence. The order must then be made as soon as reasonably practicable. The order continues in force for 12 months (unless it is previously revoked). But there will be few cases where the news value in a derogatory allegation is sufficient for editors to resurrect it for publication on its first anniversary. An interim order can be made where there is a real possibility of a final order being made. Although the power to make a final order is

---

[330] 1986 Act, s.58(5).
[331] Royal Commission on Criminal Justice (HMSO, 1993) Cm. 2263, para.47.

expressly not dependent on an interim order having first been made,[332] if the derogatory assertion has already received wide publicity, this would be a strong reason against making a final order.

Publication of the assertion in breach of the order is an offence punishable with a maximum fine of scale 5 (Currently £5,000).[333] There is a worrying uncertainty in the way in which the offence is drafted. The section appears to penalise publication of the assertion whether or not this is part of a report of the proceedings but this would be extraordinary. It is very difficult to see why a newspaper should be prevented from publishing a derogatory story (which it is prepared to defend in any libel proceedings) merely because the same allegation happened to have been made in a plea in mitigation by a defendant who had not done the same research or where the criminal court did not wish to be distracted by a lengthy examination of whether the allegations were true. Any such interpretation would clearly conflict with Art.10 of the European Human Rights Convention and section 3 of the Human Rights Act 1998 obliges the courts to adopt the "possible" alternative of reading down the offence so that it is confined to reports of the proceedings.

Challenging orders restricting reporting or access

Judges and magistrates have been tempted into making wide and **8–082** unnecessary orders because frequently none of the parties before the court opposes them. It is usually defendants who make the application. The prosecution generally either supports it or stands aloof and indifferent. The media interests who are affected and who do oppose them are not heard. Sometimes the media must go on the offensive to protect the public right to know.

How can such orders be challenged? There are four ways.

Application for revocation of order

The first is for the media representatives to ask the judge to revoke **8–083** his or her order. It is unusual for outsiders like journalists to make applications to the trial court, but the media are so obviously affected by orders restricting publicity that it is manifestly fair that representations which they wish to make against proposed orders should be heard. The Divisional Court has expressly ruled that magistrates have this power[334] and the Divisional Court and Court of Appeal have encouraged Crown Courts to do the same, making (if really necessary) a temporary order until a suitable date can be arranged for hearing representations from the media.[335] The Criminal Practice Directions say, "There is nothing which precludes the

---

[332] Criminal Procedure and Investigations Act 1996, s.58(8)(d).
[333] 1986 Act, s.60. Unusually for reporting offences, the Attorney-General's consent is not necessary.
[334] *R. v Clerkenwell JJ. Ex p. Telegraph plc* [1993] Q.B. 462.
[335] *R. v Beck* (1992) 94 Cr.App.R. 376 and *Att-Gen v Guardian Newspapers Ltd (No. 3)* [1992] 1 W.L.R. 874.

court from hearing from a representative of the press. Indeed, it is likely that the Court will wish to do so."[336]

Publish and be damned

8–084   The second (and by far the most risky of the four) is to publish the report in defiance of the order. If the order is made without jurisdiction, it is most unlikely that contempt proceedings would be brought or, if they were, that they would result in any penalty. The risk is in gauging whether a court would subsequently agree that the order was not merely unwise but so badly wrong as to have been made without jurisdiction. This route remains a last option if the circumstances preclude any of the other methods of challenge and the order is blatantly erroneous.

Judicial review

8–085   The third way is for the journalist or the publisher to apply to the High Court for judicial review to quash the order. The court will not come to its own view as to whether the order was right or wrong, but only whether it was lawfully made. This will include judging whether it was an order that any reasonable tribunal could have made. Any person with a "sufficient interest" in the decision to be challenged can apply for judicial review.[337] The media clearly have standing to contest the legality of orders restricting reporting. However, defendants also have sufficient interest to ask for a review of a refusal to impose reporting restrictions. They, too, will fail unless they can show there was an error of law.[338] This route is available if the order has been made by a magistrates' court or by the Crown Court when it is hearing an appeal, a committal for sentence or a civil matter. However, nothing relating to a trial on indictment can be judicially reviewed (Supreme Court Act 1981, s.29(1)). In *Crook* (see para.8–072) the Divisional Court found that because of this rule the media were barred from using judicial review to challenge secrecy orders erroneously made in the course of a Crown Court trial. This unhappy position led the media to complain to the European Court of Human Rights at Strasbourg, which, in turn, obliged the Government to provide a statutory right to appeal (see below).[339]

Appeal

8–086   The changes that the Government made to the law as a result of the media's complaints to Strasbourg were incorporated in s.159 of the Criminal Justice Act 1988. It allows an aggrieved person to appeal against any of the following:

---

[336] *Practice Direction (Criminal Proceedings: Consolidation)* [2002] 1 W.L.R. 2870, para.I.3.2.
[337] Supreme Court Act 1981, s.31(3).
[338] *R. v Clerkenwell JJ. Ex p. Trachtenberg* [1993] C.O.D. 93.
[339] *Hodgson and Channel 4 v UK* (1988) 56 D.R. 156; (1987) 10 E.H.R.R. 503.

- partial secrecy (s.11) and postponement orders (s.4(2)) made in relation to a trial on indictment (i.e. to a criminal trial at a Crown Court);
- any order restricting the access of the public to the whole or any part of a trial on indictment or any ancillary proceedings;
- any order restricting the publication of any report of the whole or any part of a trial on indictment or ancillary proceedings;
- a Crown Court order restricting reporting of derogatory assertions.

Because openness and free reporting are the norm, a Crown Court judge's *refusal* to restrict access or reporting is not amenable to the special appeal under section 159.[340]

This avenue of appeal extends beyond Contempt Act orders. It would include, for instance, orders restricting the publication of the identity of young witnesses or parties; orders under the Official Secrets Act requiring part of the trial to be in secret; and orders under the common law power to conduct part of the trial in the absence of the public where the administration of justice is said to demand it. Arguably, the public's access to part of the trial is also restricted if the court accepts evidence (e.g. a name or an address) in writing that is not read aloud. More contentious would be the question as to whether the Court of Appeal could hear an appeal from a Crown Court judge's refusal to set aside or vary one of the proliferating types of reporting restrictions which apply automatically.[341] It might be said that the restriction on reporting does not derive from the order of the Court but from the statute. On the other hand, where these provisions give the judge an express power to disapply or vary the usual restrictions which the media have unsuccessfully invoked, the reality is that reporting is restricted because of both the statute and the judge's order. The Court of Appeal should prefer this interpretation so as to avoid the situation where the media is left without a remedy. That, after all, was the predicament which led to the media's complaint to Strasbourg and which s.159 was intended to remedy.

Even where s.159 does apply, there are important limitations. It is **8–087** not a *right* of appeal. Permission must first be obtained from the Court of Appeal. Because it applies only to criminal cases tried by juries, it is powerless to correct the decisions of magistrates or civil courts that, though wrong, are not so wrong as to be unreasonable or otherwise amenable to judicial review. It is also unusual in that the Court of Appeal has the last word. There is no further appeal to the

---

[340] *R. v S* [1995] 2 Cr.App.R. 347.
[341] See for instance the restrictions on reporting preparatory hearings or proceedings in relation to prosecution appeals.

House of Lords. The court can make "such order as to costs as it thinks fit"[342] but not for the costs to be paid out of central funds.[343] The possibility of asking for a costs order against the party who sought the restriction order is usually theoretical: defendants often have no money and the prosecution will usually confine itself to "assisting the court" in which case it is not usually ordered to pay costs unless it has improperly applied for an order that should not have been made.[344] Despite these qualifications, it is an important remedy, which provides an avenue for curbing the proliferation of exclusion, secrecy and postponement orders in criminal cases.

Where the Crown Court has made an order restricting reporting, the application for permission to appeal must be made within fourteen days (although there is power to extend this). The application will need to set out the case fully because it can be determined without a hearing. If permission is granted the Court of Appeal can take evidence, but this will normally be in writing.[345] The court will not hesitate to quash an order even though its force has long since been spent. In *Re Central Television Plc*[346] the order banning television and radio reports had applied for only one night, while the jury was at a hotel. Six months later, when the appeal was heard by the Court of Appeal, it ruled that s.159 could not provide an effective remedy unless it could be used to reverse spent orders, which might otherwise appear to have been made properly.

Appeals against a secret hearing on national security grounds or for the protection of a witness's identity are highly unsatisfactory. The rules allow only 24 hours for an application for permission to appeal (although a precautionary notice can be set down in advance). In these cases both the permission application and the appeal itself are determined without a hearing.[347]

---

[342] Criminal Justice Act 1988, s.159(5)(c).
[343] *Holden and Co v CPS (No. 2)* [1994] 1 A.C. 22.
[344] *Ex p. News Group Newspapers Ltd* [2002] EMLR 160 CA.
[345] Criminal Procedure Rules 2005, r.67.1.
[346] [1991] 1 W.L.R. 4.
[347] Criminal Procedure Rules 2005, r.67.2. A prosecutor or defendant who intends to apply for a secrecy order on grounds of national security or for the protection of a witness must give seven days' notice to the Crown Court before the start of the trial, and a copy of the notice should be displayed forthwith by court officials in a prominent place within the precincts of the court. This will give the press some advance notice that an application is to be made and an opportunity to prepare for any necessary appeal. The application will normally be considered after the defendant has made his plea but before the jury is sworn. If the application is successful, the trial must be adjourned for a minimum of 24 hours to allow for an appeal against the decision. The adjournment will continue until any appeal is disposed of (Criminal Procedure Rules 2005, r.16.10). A trial judge should not use the inherent power of the court to sit secret to circumvent a failure to comply with these provisions: *Re Godwin* [1991] Crim. L.R. 302. This procedure under the Rules should be followed even if the application is to hear a pre-trial application (such as an application to stay the trial as an abuse of process) since

The Court of Appeal has held that these rules are within the **8–088** intention of the 1988 Act. It noted that there was nothing to prevent an applicant putting written submissions before the court.[348] A written submission of this kind succeeded in 1998:[349]

> At an Old Bailey fraud trial the defendants wished to argue that the trial should be stayed as an abuse of process, but they wanted to make this argument in private on grounds of national security. Notably, the Crown was neutral on the application. Media representatives (and their lawyers) were excluded from court and the judge agreed that the "abuse" argument should be made in private. *The Observer*'s appeal against this ruling succeeded because proper notice had not been given, because it had not been told that the defendant's case also rested on danger to witnesses and because the judge had not insisted that the Crown express a view on the alleged threat to national security. The court gave strong support to the importance of trial judges having in mind the media's rights under Arts 6(1) and 10 of the European Convention.

Subsequent to the Human Rights Act, the Court of Appeal held that even though there was no discretion to allow an oral hearing of this type of appeal, the rules were compliant with the Convention.[350] There are many situations where public access is restricted to a trial or its ancilliary proceedings that are not covered by these regulations. There is, therefore, no prescribed time for appealing against such orders (although a long delay might make the Court of Appeal unwilling to allow the appeal). The press would have the usual right of an appellant to argue orally as to why permission should be granted and why the appeal itself should be allowed.

The first case to be brought by the media under s.159 was an **8–089** application by, appropriately enough, Tim Crook, the journalist whose case had been the genesis of the Strasbourg proceedings which had forced the government to concede a right of appeal.

The court formulated two important principles:

- a judge should adjourn into chambers only where he has a positive reason for believing that this is an appropriate course, and
- once in chambers he must resume sitting in open court "as soon as it emerges that the need to exclude the public is not plainly necessary".[351]

---

the Rules are to be read as covering all or part of the trial process. The notice outside court should be dated so that the media know how long they have to organise opposition: *Ex p. Guardian Newspapers Ltd* [1999] 1 All E.R. 65, CA.
[348] *Re Guardian Newspapers Ltd, The Times*, October 26, 1993.
[349] *Ex p. Guardian Newspapers Ltd* [1999] 1 All E.R. 65, CA.
[350] *R v Central Criminal Court Ex p. A* [2006] 1 W.L.R. 1361 CA.
[351] *Re Crook's Appeal* (1991) 93 Cr.App.R. 17, CA.

These rules do not go far enough to protect the open justice principle. The only exception allowed by *Scott v Scott*—the rare occasion where justice cannot be done at all if it is done in public— needs further entrenchment, perhaps by a rule permitting the press to have access to the transcript of a chambers hearing at a future date to be determined by the judge. The decision of the Court of Appeal Civil Division in the tobacco litigation, urging courts when sitting in chambers to admit the press (see para.8–019) is a very positive development which should spur the criminal courts to more openness.

GATHERING INFORMATION

8–090 There is more to a trial than meets the eye or catches the ear. What is said in open court is only the tip of an iceberg of investigation, documentation and analysis that goes into the preparation of a case for trial. If the accused pleads guilty, the prosecution counsel will provide a brief outline of the facts so as to let the press and public know the circumstances of each offence to which the defendant has pleaded guilty.[352] This brief outline may give no more than a smattering of the hundreds of pages of witness statements and documentary exhibits. Even in a lengthy and contested trial there will be interesting material not put in evidence—because it is tangential to the charges or legally inadmissible. In civil cases judges may prefer to read important documents in their spare time rather than to have them tediously read out, word for word. Journalists and authors covering a particular trial will naturally wish to have access to this class of material. In British law very little of it can be obtained by right.[353]

These limited rights stand in contrast to the position in the United States, where the media have the right to inspect the "court record", which includes all matters produced in evidence, and under the Freedom of Information Act all prosecution documents, even in spying cases, must eventually be disclosed. In a 1981 anti-corruption operation (known as Abscam) the FBI filmed leading politicians accepting bribes. The videotapes were the backbone of several prosecutions and the federal courts acknowledged that television stations had a right to transmit copies of the film.[354] The Supreme Court would similarly have allowed the Nixon tape recordings to be broadcast, but for a special statute dealing with presidential materials.[355] Although the American press has a privileged constitutional

---

[352] *Practice Direction (Criminal Proceedings: Consolidation)* [2002] 1 W.L.R. 2870 para.III.26.

[353] *Gio Personal Investment Services Ltd v Liverpool and London Steamship Protection and Indemnity Association Ltd*, [1999] 1 W.L.R. 984, CA.

[354] *National Broadcasting Company Inc v Meyers* 635 F2d 945 (1980).

[355] *US v Mitchell, Appeal of Warner Communications* 435 U.S. 589 (1978) reversing 551 F2d 1252 (1976).

status, these cases did not depend on it. The courts looked back to the common law principle of open justice and saw the copying and supplying of all prosecution evidence to the media for publication as a natural and logical corollary subject only to the court's control and discretion. Canadian courts, likewise, promote open justice by allowing the media access to documents filed with the court (though with more circumspection when the defendant is acquitted or a conviction is quashed on appeal).[356] Under Sir Ken Macdonald, the DPP, the Crown Prosecution Service has adopted a more open approach to the media. This is examined below (see para.8–109).

Tape-recording

The right to attend court includes the right to take notes of what is **8–091** said there.[357] This applies to the public as well as to the press, although court officials will sometimes (wrongfully) try to stop those in the public gallery from putting pen to paper.

The law has grudgingly recognised the invention of the tape recorder. The Contempt of Court Act 1981 bans the use of tape recorders unless the leave of the court has been obtained.[358] The judge has a discretion to give or withhold permission, but in the House of Lords debates the Lord Chancellor envisaged that it would normally be given and that regular court reporters would be given indefinite, if revocable, permission.[359] The Criminal Procedure Practice Directions lay down guidance for when permission should be granted.[360] They urge courts to consider whether there is a reasonable need on the part of a journalist for the recording; any risk that the recording could be used to brief witnesses who have not given their evidence (unlikely in the case of a journalist); and any possibility that the use of the machine would disturb the proceedings, distract or worry witnesses or other participants. The court can attach conditions to the grant of permission. In addition to the ordinary penalties for contempt a journalist or any other person who uses or intends to use a tape recorder that he or she has brought into court stands to forfeit the machine and any used tapes.[361] If journalists through oversight forget to ask for permission in advance, but are using their machines for the purpose which s.9 contemplated,

---

[356] *Att-Gen of Nova Scotia v MacIntyre* [1982] 1 R.C.S. 175, *Vickery v Prothonotary of Supreme Court of Nova Scotia* (1991) 1 S.C.R. 671.

[357] This right has, for court reporters at least, accrued by custom: see *Re CNN's Application to the Harold Shipman Tribunal of Inquiry*, October 25, 2001, para.61, *per* Smith J.

[358] 1981 Act, s.9. See also Civil Procedure Rules Practice Direction to Pt 39, para.6.2.

[359] *Hansard*, HL, Vol. 416 col.383.

[360] *Practice Direction (Criminal Proceedings: Consolidation)* [2002] 1 W.L.R. 2870, para.I.2.

[361] Contempt of Court Act 1981, s.9(3).

magistrates or judges should consider giving retrospective leave. Magistrates have no inherent power to punish contempt of court and their statutory jurisdiction is limited to cases of wilful disturbance or interruption of the court's proceedings which may well be lacking in a case of simple oversight. In any case, before penalising reporters for contempt, the court should consider giving them an opportunity to seek legal advice and representation.[362]

Even where permission is granted, the tape cannot be broadcast. It is contempt of court subsequently to play the recording in the hearing of the public or a section of the public.[363] The Practice Direction recommends that a court giving permission should remind the user of this.

Transcripts and skeleton arguments

8–092 Whenever the High Court or Court of Appeal, Crown Court or County Court is sitting, official shorthand writers will record the proceedings.[364] They have a statutory right to use tape recorders, although the tapes are transcribed only on request.[365] In connection with civil cases (other than family proceedings), the rules allow the public to purchase transcripts of judgments which have been given and of hearings which have taken place. Only if the judgment was given, or the hearing took place, in private must the permission of the judge be first obtained.[366] Transcripts are expensive and so this is not a cheap option. In family proceedings, it is always necessary for non-parties to obtain permission from the court before a transcript will be provided.[367] There are no equivalent rules for the provision of transcripts of criminal proceedings to the public, although in the Crown Court official recordings are made and, if the proceedings have been held in public, it is hard to see why the judge could object to giving permission. No official shorthand note is kept of magistrates' courts.

The Court of Appeal and other courts ask lawyers to produce in advance outlines or "skeletons" of their arguments and legal submissions. The Court of Appeal has asked lawyers to produce an extra copy for the press (except when reporting is restricted).[368] If the parties refuse to provide a copy of a skeleton argument or a written note of an opening speech reporters should apply to the judge. There should be a prima facie presumption in favour of ordering access.[369] The Court of Appeal Criminal Division has likewise said

---

[362] *Re Patricia Hooker* [1993] C.O.D. 190.

[363] Contempt of Court Act 1981, s.9(1). It would also be wrong to use the tape to coach waiting witnesses in what to say in order to be consistent.

[364] Civil Procedure Rules, Pt 39, Practice Direction, para.6.1.

[365] Contempt of Court Act 1981, s.9(4).

[366] CPR Pt 39 Practice Direction, paras 1.11, 1.12, 6.3 and 6.4.

[367] Family Proceedings Rules, r.10.15(6).

[368] *Lombard North Central Plc v Pratt* (1989) 139 N.L.J. 1709, CA.

[369] *GIO Personal Investment Services Ltd v Liverpool and London Steamship Protection and Indemnity Association Ltd* [1999] 1 W.L.R. 984, CA.

that skeleton arguments should be made available on request (subject to any specific argument as to why particular passages should not be disclosed).[370]

Court records

Court registers

Registers of claims are kept by the Central Office of the Queen's **8–093** Bench Division of the High Court, Chancery Chambers and the Admiralty and Commercial Court Registry. The public have a right to inspect these registers.[371] There are no registers presently in the County Courts or the District Registries of the High Court.[372]

Statements of case

As from October 2006 the general rule is that the public may obtain **8–094** from the court records a copy of any statement of case.[373] A "statement of case" includes the Claim Form (which is the usual means of starting civil litigation) but the term also embraces the particulars of claim (in which the claim is spelt out in more detail), the defence and any reply by the claimant. This development is a major improvement in the public accessibility of statements of case (or pleadings). Previously, the public only had access to the Claim Form. There was no right to inspect other pleadings or statements of case.

There had, however, been a greater willingness over the preceding years to allow access to pleadings and other documents which had been deployed at a hearing, from which the public had not been deliberately excluded. In these circumstances, the principle of open justice was taken to mean that presumptively a request for access to these documents should normally be granted.[374] But the press and public still had to make an application to the Court which meant paying an application fee and could involve risks of paying their opponents' legal costs if the application was unsuccessful. The general rule that was introduced in October 2006 means that this will normally now be unnecessary.

The right is still qualified. Access will not be granted unless the defendant has filed an acknowledgement of service (or, where there is more than one defendant, they have all filed acknowledgements of

---

[370] *R v Howell* [2003] EWCA Crim 486 at [197], *The Times*, March 10, 2003.

[371] Civil Procedure Rules r.5.4 and Practice Direction—Court Documents 5PD 4.1.

[372] 5PD 4.2.

[373] CPR r.5.4C (1). The change in practice only applies to statements of case filed after October 2, 2006—see CPR r.5.4C(1A).

[374] *Cleveland Bridge UK Ltd v Multiplex Constructions (UK) Ltd* [2005] EWHC 2101 (TCC); *Dian AO v David Frankel and Mead (a firm)* [2005] 1 All E.R. 1074; *Re Guardian Newspapers Ltd* [2005] 3 All E.R. 155.

service), or the case has been listed for a hearing or judgment has been entered in given.[375] The permission of the court is not needed, but the court can prohibit access to a particular claim or statement of case. Any party or any person identified in a statement of case can ask for an order restricting access. If an order of this kind has been made, it is still open to the press or public to apply to have the order set aside.[376]

8–095　　The right of access does not apply to any document which is filed with or attached to the statement of case or intended to be served with it. If the press or public want access to documents of these kind, they must apply to the Court for permission.[377]

Pre-trial publication of statements of case is not by itself contempt of court.[378] Since almost all civil cases are tried by judge alone a serious risk of substantial prejudice is very unlikely.[379] In any case it is very hard to see how publication of documents that the judge will anyway have to read at the trial could cause such prejudice.[380]

Family proceedings

8–096　These have a different set of rules. A non-party needs the Court's permission to inspect any document on the court file other than an order given in open court.[381] However, this protects only the pieces of paper, not their contents.[382] Even then, the prohibition does not apply to correspondence which has never been filed with the court, but merely included in an exhibit to an affidavit or witness statement or included in a bundle of correspondence for proceedings.[383] Neither does the rule prevent disclosure of the existence of such documents.[384]

Witness statements and affidavits

8–097　A witness statement which was ordered to stand as the witness's evidence in chief should be open to inspection if access is requested during the trial. Any person can ask the court to direct suppression of the statement but this will only be done where it is in the interests of justice, or the public interest, or because the statement contains expert medical evidence or other confidential information (including

---

[375] CPR r.5.4(1) and 5.4(3).
[376] CPR r.5.4C(3)–(6).
[377] CPR r.5.4C(1)(a) and (2).
[378] *Re F (A Minor: Publication of Information)* [1977] 1 All E.R. 114.
[379] There are important exceptions for most defamation cases and some civil actions against the police.
[380] *Gaskell and Chambers v Hudson and Dodsworth and Co* [1936] 2 K.B. 595.
[381] Family Proceedings Rules r.10.20.
[382] *Re W (Minor) (Social Worker: Disclosure)* [1999] 1 W.L.R. 205, 209.
[383] *Re B (A Child: Disclosure)* [2004] 1 F.L.R. 142 at [61].
[384] *Vernon v Bosley (No.2)* [1998] L 1 E.R. 304, 319.

information relating to personal financial matters), or it affects the interests of any child or patient.[385]

After a trial or hearing, the right of inspection comes to an end, but a journalist can still apply to the court for permission to inspect these documents. The court will apply similar principles to those discussed above in connection with statements of case. Thus it is likely to grant the application if there has been a hearing (even an interim hearing) from which the public were not deliberately excluded and the judge had to read the statements either at or in advance of the hearing.[386]

Again family proceedings are different and the court's permission is needed before a non-party can inspect any documents on the court file other than an order given in open court. Since under current practice the public are more commonly excluded from these types of hearings, permission is less likely to be given. However, for 14 days after the pronouncement of a decree nisi on a "quickie" divorce, the public does have a right to inspect the evidence filed for the petitioner.[387]

Judgments and orders

When High Court judges give oral reasons for their decisions, the **8–098** text is embargoed until the judge has finished speaking. The BBC was reproved in 1983 for quoting the advance text on its news bulletin before the judge had concluded.[388]

The Court of Appeal (Civil Division) and High Court judges often prepare written judgments in advance. These are passed to the lawyers a day or two before judgment is due to be given in open court so that consideration can be given to the orders which should be made in consequence of the judgment and to allow the correction of minor errors. Their clients can be told but there must be no public reference to the draft judgment.[389] If the judgment or result is leaked to the media, they need to be aware of the embargo and that it is a contempt of court to breach it, as the *Lawyer* magazine was told when it published the result of the *Da Vinci Code* copyright case (see para.6–013) prior to judgment being formally handed down.[390] In

---

[385] CPR, r.32.13. There is no automatic right to documents referred to in a witness statement or other documents referred to in open court, but applications can be made to the court for permission to inspect these and a rather more liberal approach now seems to be favoured: *FAI General Insurance Co Ltd v Godfrey Merrett Robertson Ltd* [1999] C.L.C. 566, CA.

[386] See fn.374 above.

[387] Family Proceedings Rules r.10.20(3). The same applies to the dissolution of a civil partnership but not, in either case, if the relationship has been nullified FPR, r.2.36(5).

[388] *Att-Gen v Able* [1984] Q.B. 795.

[389] Practice Direction—Reserved Judgment CPR Pt 40, Practice Direction E.

[390] *Baigent v Random House sub nom The Lawyer* [2006] EWHC 1131 (Ch).

cases of particular interest, journalists who want copies should notify the clerk to the presiding Judge in advance. They will then be provided with a copy when judgment is given in open court.[391] Copies can be obtained from the shorthand writers for a fee or, increasingly commonly, from one of the on-line electronic databases.[392] Transcripts of the Court of Appeal's decisions are also kept in the Supreme Court Library.

House of Lords judges give "speeches" rather than judgments although these are not actually read out. Printed copies are delivered to the parties and sold to the press as their Lordships go through the ritual pantomime motions in the Chamber of the House of Lords in front of counsel in full bottom wigs and after prayers have been said by an available bishop. Within two hours the texts of the speeches ought to appear on Parliament's website.[393]

Where a hearing of the High Court, Court of Appeal or County Court takes place in public, members of the public can obtain a transcript of any judgment given or a copy of any order made, subject to payment of the appropriate fee.[394] If the hearing was in private, a member of the public who was not a party to the proceedings must ask permission of the judge who gave the judgment or made the order.[395] Article 6 of the ECHR requires judgments on criminal charges or the determination of civil rights and obligations to be given publicly. There is no express qualification to this principle, but the European Court has held that decisions properly given in private can be withheld from public scrutiny if public access would frustrate the purpose of having the hearing in private.[396]

Insolvency proceedings

8–099 A record of steps taken and orders made in bankruptcy and winding-up proceedings is open to the public for inspection[397] although the Registrar of the Companies Court may refuse access if he "is not satisfied as to the propriety of the purpose for which inspection is required." Reporting should always be a legitimate purpose. If the Registrar does refuse permission there is a right to appeal forthwith and without notice to a judge.[398]

---

[391] *Practice Statement (Supreme Court: Judgments)* [1998] 1 W.L.R. 825; *Practice Statement (Supreme Court Judgments (No.2)* [1999] 1 W.L.R. 1.
[392] e.g. British and Irish Legal Information Institute at *www.bailii.org.uk*. BAILII makes no charge.
[393] *www.publications.parliament.uk*.
[394] CPR, Pt 39 *Practice Direction—Miscellaneous Provisions Relating to Hearings*, para.1.11.
[395] CPR, Pt 39, para.1.12.
[396] *B v UK, P v UK* [2001] 2 F.C.R. 221.
[397] Insolvency Rules 1986, (SI 1986/1925), rr.7.27, 7.28.
[398] 1986 Rules, r.7.28(2).

Electronic processing has made it feasible to copy the entire register of claims, but the Registrar has refused permission for access for this purpose on the ground that it would undermine the court's power to regulate the advertisement of proceedings. His decision was upheld by the judge and the Court of Appeal ruled that it had no jurisdiction to hear a further appeal, but one Appeal Court judge could see nothing wrong in the service which the appellant wished to provide.[399] A somewhat similar scheme in Spain met with a similar response from the Spanish Court. A complaint to the European Commission of Human Rights was dismissed as manifestly unfounded for the unsatisfactory reason that Art.10 gives no right to compel an unwilling person to supply information.[400] Where the information is of a public nature, the media should be entitled to access it and impart it to the public.

Obtaining access to court files by deceit or trickery is a punishable contempt.[401]

Money judgments and fines

There is a centralised register of County Court and High Court **8–100** money judgments, County Court administration orders, magistrates courts' fines and Child Support Act liability orders.[402] Various classes of judgments are exempt from registration, notably judgments in family proceedings and orders made after a contested hearing for payment of money other than by instalments where the creditor has not sought to enforce the judgment.[403] The current arrangements are for the Register to be kept by Registry Trust Ltd.[404] The register is open to public inspection[405] or RTL can be asked to conduct a search. Prescribed fees are payable.

Wills and grants of probate or administration

Where a dead person had made a will, it will only take effect once its **8–101** validity has been established by the grant of probate by the Court. If there was no will an application can be made for a grant of

---

[399] *Ex p Creditnet Ltd* [1996] 1 W.L.R. 1291, appealed dismissed *sub nom Re Austintel Ltd* [1997] 1 W.L.R. 616, CA.

[400] *Grupero Interpres SA v Spain*, Application No. 32849/96 (1997) 89 D.R. 150.

[401] *Dobson v Hastings* [1992] Ch. 394.

[402] Courts Act 2003, s.98 and Register of Judgments Orders and Fines Regulations 2005 (SI 2005/3595).

[403] 2005 Regulations, Reg.9. Entries will be cancelled if the debt is paid within a month of judgment: Regs 11–16. Entries of judgments are cancelled if they remain unpaid after six years and fines if unpaid after five years: Reg.24.

[404] See their website at *www.registry-trust.org.uk*.

[405] Register of County Court Judgments Regulations 1985 (SI 1985/1807), Reg.27. The Registrar can refuse access if he believes that the information will be used contrary to the Data Protection principles (see para.5–043) or some other enactment: Reg.29. There is a right of appeal against refusal to the County Court.

administration. A record is kept by the Principal Registry of the Family Division of the High Court[406] (or the relevant District Registry) of these grants and (where there is one) of a copy of the will. The public has a right to inspect these wills and documents[407] although this can be refused if in the opinion of the district judge or registrar such inspection would be undesirable or otherwise inappropriate.[408] There is a fee (currently £15) for inspecting a will,[409] but the bare details (including the value of the estate) are collected in the Court's calendars which can be searched without a charge.

In the twentieth century the practice grew up of not allowing the public to have access to the wills of certain members of the Royal Family. This started in 1911 when Queen Mary prevailed on the head of the Probate Divorce and Admiralty Division of the High Court to seal the will of her brother, Prince Francis of Teck. The Queen, apparently "fear[ed] scandal during her coronation year".[410] In 2005 BBC researchers discovered a draft of the Prince's will which seemed to show that he had left some valuable jewels (regarded as the property of the monarch) to his mistress and which, in a further effort to hush up the scandal, Queen Mary later bought back for the nation. The practice continued since then, although it was challenged in 2007.

Magistrates' courts

8–102 Magistrates are more secretive. The registers on which their clerks record the courts' decisions are not public documents and only the magistrates themselves have a right of access to them.[411] This secrecy is indefensible and the Home Secretary has encouraged all courts to provide their local newspapers with a copy of the court register when it is prepared.[412]

Freedom of Information Act

8–103 The Freedom of Information Act (FOIA) 2000 will make no difference to the rights of the public to have access to court records. Information is exempt information for the purposes of the 2000 Act if it is contained in a document filed with, or in the custody of, the court for the purpose of proceedings in a particular cause or matter, or because it has been served on or by a public authority for the purpose of proceedings or it has been created by a court or a

---

[406] This is at First Avenue House, 42–49 High Holborn, London WC1V 6NP.
[407] Supreme Court Act 1981, s.124.
[408] Non-Contentious Probate Rules 1987 (SI 1987/2024) r.58.
[409] Non-Contentious Probate Fees Order 1999 (SI 1999/688).
[410] Michael Nash, *The Sealing Up of Wills* (1994) *New Law Journal*, June 17.
[411] Criminal Procedure Rules, r.6.2(15).
[412] Home Office Circular 80/1989.

member of the court's administrative staff for the purposes of a particular cause or matter. There is no duty to confirm or deny the existence of any such information.[413]

European Court of Human Rights

Documents lodged with the European Court of Human Rights in **8–104** Strasbourg are open to inspection to the public unless the President of the Court orders otherwise[414] except for documents concerning negotiations over the friendly settlement of a complaint.[415] The hearings before the court take place in public[416] although they are very brief and involve much less dialogue between advocates and judges than is common in the United Kingdom's procedures,

Disclosed documents

Before trial

In the course of most civil litigation the parties must disclose to each **8–105** other all the documents in their possession that are relevant to the case. The obligation is a broad one, and a document must be listed and produced however damning it is to the case of the party disclosing it. In a very limited category of cases a party can plead privilege from discovery. It is not necessary, for instance, for parties to show to the other side correspondence with their lawyers. Public interest immunity can be claimed for government documents that are particularly sensitive. The fact that a document is confidential is not enough for it to be privileged, and some litigants settle their cases rather than show their most private papers to their opponents or have them read aloud in a public court.

Although this potential for publicity is inherent in disclosure, the law will normally protect the confidentiality of the documents unless and until they are used in court. The recipient of the documents impliedly undertakes to the court not to use them for any purpose other than one related to the litigation in question. But as with other confidential documents there may be an important reason for publicising their contents that outbalances the normal duty. In the course of the thalidomide litigation *The Sunday Times* bought some of the documents produced by Distillers on disclosure, which had also been given to a research chemist who had been retained as an expert witness for the injured children. The court enjoined the paper

---

[413] Freedom of Information Act 2000, s.32 The purpose of the exemption is to leave the existing mechanisms for disclosure and inspection unaffected rather than to sanctify court secrecy—see para.11–073 for further commentary on the FOIA.

[414] European Convention on Human Rights, Art.40(2).

[415] Rules of Procedure of European Court of Human Rights, Art.33.

[416] ECHR Art.40(1).

from making any further use of the documents. The paper's argument that the story was important was accepted, but the court did not agree that the public interest in publication was so great that the litigation confidence could be broken.[417] *The Sunday Times* could be restrained only because it *knew* that the documents had been produced on disclosure. If the paper had received them anonymously with no suggestion of their origin, its chance of defeating the injunction would have been much greater.

Again, English concepts of free expression lag behind those in the United States, where disclosed documents are considered part of the public record and are in the public domain from the time that they are produced. The courts can make "protective orders" restricting the use of documents, but this is recognised as an exceptional interference with the free speech of lawyer and litigant, and requires substantial justification.[418]

After trial

8–106 The extent to which disclosed documents may be shown to the media by an opposing party was the subject of a controversial decision in the case of *Home Office v Harman*.[419]

> Harriet Harman, then solicitor for the National Council for Civil Liberties, conducted an action on behalf of a prisoner who alleged that his confinement in a "control unit" was illegal. The Home Office was forced to disclose embarrassing internal memoranda about the setting up of such units. These were read out in open court during the four-week trial. Journalist David Leigh approached her at the end of the trial and was shown copies of the disclosed documents, which he quoted in an article attacking the Home Office prison policy. The House of Lords narrowly decided, by 3:2, that Ms Harman's action was a contempt in that she, as a solicitor, was bound by the obligation to use disclosed documents only for the purposes of the litigation. Leigh could have sat through the trial and taken notes or purchased an expensive transcript, but he could not be assisted by direct access to the documents themselves. The impracticabilities of these alternatives for the working journalist were recognised in the minority opinion, which regarded the ruling as a breach of the freedom of communication guaranteed by the European Convention.

The European Commission on Human Rights found this a prima facie breach of Art.10. Had the Government chosen to take the case to the European Court, the response would have been similar to that in the *Weber* judgment in 1990. A campaigning environmentalist had been punished by the Swiss courts for disclosing details of judicial

---

[417] *Distillers Co (Biochemicals) Ltd v Times Newspapers Ltd* [1975] 1 All E.R. 41.
[418] *Re Halkin* 598 F2d 176 (DC, CA, 1979).
[419] [1983] 1 A.C. 280.

proceedings held in private, and the court found this to be a violation of Art.10—in part because the material was already public knowledge.[420] A friendly settlement of the *Harman* case was reached with the Government and Rules of Court now provide:

"(1) A party to whom a document has been disclosed may use the document only for the purpose of the proceedings in which it is disclosed, except where:

(a) the document has been read to or by the court, or referred to, at a hearing which has been held in public;

(b) the court gives permission; or

(c) the party who disclosed the document and the person to whom the document belongs agree.

(2) The Court may make an order restricting or prohibiting the use of a document which has been disclosed, even where the document has been read to or by the court, or referred to, at a hearing which has been held in public."[421]

In *Lilly Icos Ltd v Pfizer Ltd (No.2)*[422] the Court of Appeal **8–107** reviewed the principles to be applied when one or both of the parties asked for an order that the confidentiality attaching to discovered documents should continue notwithstanding that they had been referred to in open court. The Court said that very good reasons would be required for departing from the normal rule of publicity which had been reinforced by Art.6 and 10 of the ECHR. The Court would require specific proof that a party would be damaged by publication.

The undertaking ceases even if the document is not actually read aloud in court as long as it has been "read by the court, or referred to, in open court".[423]

Some affidavits are covered by the *Harman* rule because they are the method by which a litigant is required to make discovery (discovery of assets or income is often ordered by affidavit). The filing of certain affidavits may be necessary for litigants to continue their fight, but *this* type of compulsion does not attract the *Harman* protection.[424] Similarly, the reports of potential expert witnesses that litigants exchange are *not* subject to the implied obligation since it is ultimately for the parties to decide whether or not to call experts. On

---

[420] *Weber v Switzerland* (1990) 12 E.H.R.R. 508.

[421] Civil Procedure Rules, r. 31.22.

[422] [2002] 1 W.L.R. 2253.

[423] *Derby and Co Ltd v Weldon, The Times*, October 20, 1988, Ch. D; some discovered documents that were included in affidavits were in turn, included in a bundle of documents for the Court of Appeal. They were "referred to in open court". See also *SmithKlineBeecham Biologicials SA v Connaught Laboratories* [1999] F.S.R. 284, CA.

[424] *Derby and Co Ltd v Weldon*, above.

the other hand, rules of court specifically restrict the use to which witness statements can be put.[425]

Documents in criminal proceedings

8–108 As part of the principle of fairness the common law developed rules requiring the prosecution to disclose to defendants all documents relevant to the offence or its investigation and the House of Lords held that that there was an equivalent to the *Harman* rule in criminal procedure.[426] The Criminal Procedure and Investigations Act 1996 has introduced a statutory code of disclosure obligations for both prosecutors and (in some circumstances) defendants. A defendant to whom documents are disclosed under these provisions cannot use them other than (broadly) for the purpose of the proceedings in which they were given until they have been used or the information in them has been communicated in open court. It is a statutory contempt to infringe these restrictions[427] although this offence would be committed by the party who leaked the documents rather than by the newspaper itself, unless it had incited or procured the leak.

The decision to publish other leaked documents may involve a nice balancing of political consequences. For example, on the morning before the trial of four anarchists opened in 1979, *The Guardian* published a confidential prosecution memorandum about potential jurors—a document prepared from police files for the purpose of "vetting" the jury. It contained the gossip now routinely recorded on police files about citizens whose relations had been in trouble, who lived in squats and who had made complaints against the police. The trial judge angrily discharged the jury and urged the Attorney-General to prosecute the newspaper for contempt— presumably because its revelation that police had invaded their privacy might bias jurors against the prosecution. No action was taken, the Attorney perhaps concluding that the police action had been rather more upsetting than the newspaper's revelation of it.[428] Nor was action taken against London Weekend Television when Christopher Hitchens revealed on one of its programmes that the foreman of a "vetted" jury in the "ABC" Official Secrets case was an ex-member of the SAS (see para.11–004), an outfit that the defendant journalists had regularly criticised. The trial was stopped as a

---

[425] Civil Procedure Rules, r.32.12; *Prudential Assurance Co Ltd v Fountain Page Ltd* [1991] 1 W.L.R. 756. The same distinction between documents produced under compulsion and other documents applies also in the Family Division—*Clibbery v Allan* [2001] 2 F.L.R. 819, *per* Munby J. upheld by the Court of Appeal [2002] 261 CA which did, though, emphasise that the quasi-inquisitorial function of the family court in many cases and the duties of the parties in those cases to make full and frank disclosure would extend the confidentiality obligation.

[426] *Taylor v Serious Fraud Office* [1999] 2 A.C. 177 overruling *Mahon v Rahn* [1998] Q.B. 424, CA.

[427] 1996 Act, ss.17 and 18.

[428] David Leigh, *The Frontiers of Secrecy* (Junction Books, 1980), p.171.

result of this disclosure, but contempt proceedings, which might well have succeeded, would have been highly embarrassing to an Attorney-General already under attack for approving jury-vetting. These cases illustrate the extra-legal considerations that give the media a tenuous freedom to publish more than the strict letter of the law or rulings of the court would allow. If the documents prove hitherto unexposed official misconduct, the Attorney-General may consider that the public interest, well-served by publication, does not require prosecution.

In October 2005 the Crown Prosecution Service refined its Protocol for the release of prosecution material to the media.[429] The CPS gives a commitment to treat victims and witnesses with respect and sensitivity and to listen to their views regarding disclosure of material to the media. This is necessarily so, since Art.8 of the ECHR will in some circumstances impose a positive obligation to respect the private lives of witnesses or victims or even defendants by *not* releasing prosecution material to the media.[430] Nonetheless, the aim of the CPS policy is:

> "to ensure that the principle of open justice is maintained—that justice is done and seen to be done—while at the same time balancing the rights of defendant to a fair trial with any likely consequences for victims or their families and witnesses caused by the release of such material.

> **"Prosecution material which has been relied upon by the Crown in** 8–109 **court and which** *should* normally be released to the media includes:
>
> - maps, photographs (including custody photos of defendants) / diagrams and other documents produced in court;
> - videos showing scenes of crime as recorded by police after the event;
> - videos of property seized (e.g. weapons, clothing as shown to jury in court, drug hauls or stolen goods);
> - sections of transcripts of interviews / statements as read out (and therefore reportable, subject to any orders) in court;
> - videos or photographs showing reconstructions of the crime;
> - CCTV footage of the defendant, subject to any copyright issues.
>
> Prosecution material which may be released after consideration by the CPS in consultation with the police and relevant victims, witnesses and family members includes:

---

[429] See the CPS website *www.cps.gov.uk/publications/agencies/mediaprotocol*.

[430] See *Craxi (No 2) v Italy* (2004) 38 E.H.R.R. 995 where Italy was found to have violated Art.8 because certain telephone intercepts had been released to the press and in *Sciacca v Italy* Application No. 50774/99 judgment January 11, 2005, Italy was again found to be in violation of Art. 8 because the authorities had released a police photograph of an arrested suspect. This interference with the suspect's private life was unregulated and so not "in accordance with the law" as Art.8 requires. In the latter case the suspect was not a public figure (see paras 27–28) and this may make a critical difference—*Verlagsgruppe News gmbh v Austria (No.2)* Application No. 10520/02 judgment December 14, 2006.

- CCTV footage or photographs showing the defendant and victim, or the victim alone, that has been viewed by the jury and public court, subject to any copyright issues;
- video and audio tapes of police interviews with defendants and witnesses;
- victim and witness statements.

Where a guilty plea is accepted and the case does not proceed to trial then all the foregoing principles apply. But to ensure that the only material informing the decision of the court is published, material released to the media must reflect the prosecution case and must have been read out, or shown in open court, or placed before the sentencing judge."

An internal appeal system is operated by the CPS Head of Strategic Communications: "Consideration will be given to all factors including the stated aims of this protocol to achieve greater openness in reporting criminal proceedings."

The CPS effort is a good start, but it begs many questions. Why should the media not have access to material supplied by the defence to the prosecutor and court which has informed the jury's verdict or the judge's sentence? Why should the media not be able to access documents supplied to the defence by the prosecution but which are not read out in court?

Nonetheless, the second largest prosecuting authority, the Revenue and Customs Prosecution Office, has yet to adopt even a CPS style protocol.

Photographs and sketches

8–110 Other forms of recording, apart from note taking and tape-recording, are prohibited by s.41 of the Criminal Justice Act 1925. It is an offence to take any photograph or to make with a view to publication a sketch of any juror, witness, party or judge in the courtroom, the court building or its precincts. The offence can be committed even though the photographer or artist is standing outside and well clear of the court if the subject of the snap or sketch is entering or leaving the court. It is also an offence to publish such a photograph or sketch. The ban applies to civil and criminal proceedings. However, an exception has been created for the new Supreme Court which is due to take over from the House of Lords as the highest appellate court. Section 41 will not apply to the Supreme Court.[431]

The extent of this embargo has never been authoritatively decided. "Precinct" strictly means the space enclosed by the walls or outer boundary of a court building (i.e. the court yard) rather than public streets or highways surrounding court. No exception has ever been

---

[431] Constitutional Reform Act 2005, s.47.

taken to television and stills photographers standing on the public footpath outside the Old Bailey or the High Court, although it is understandable that judges should be concerned about media circuses at the gates of criminal courts, which witnesses and jurors may find intimidating. The open justice principle would seem to imply the media's right to photograph defendants and witnesses as they turn up for a public trial, although any attempts to photograph jurors would probably lead to a prosecution.

The above approach is supported by the Court of Appeal decision in *R. v Runting*[432]:

> Runting was a photographer for the *Sun* newspaper. He was charged with contempt of court for his efforts to snap a camera-shy defendant, commencing as he emerged from court and continuing for some minutes as he made a dash for the nearest tube station, colliding with a lamppost in his flight. The Court of Appeal quashed Runting's conviction: although his behaviour caused inconvenience, it did not amount to "molestation" sufficient to form the basis of a contempt charge. The court warned photographers against hindering, jostling, "threatening with persistent following" and assaulting defendants and witnesses as they go to or from court. Significantly, however, it made no reference to s.41, and appeared to accept that photographing defendants as they emerged from court would be lawful in the absence of intimidating conduct.

If the sketch is a doodle made by someone in court but *not* with a view to publication, then a newspaper that obtains and publishes it would not commit the statutory offence. Commissioned sketches of courtroom incidents often appear in the press and on television. Those that are drawn from memory are unobjectionable. The Press Council recognised a long-standing tradition of such sketches being published.[433] Even drawings deliberately made in court for publication rarely attract a prosecution—perhaps because the sketches are flattering, perhaps because the maximum fine is only on scale 3, currently £1,000. In 1986 a solicitor's wife was fined £100 for photographing a judge in court.[434] However, the Court of Appeal has said in a recent case that the taking of photographs on mobile phones in court had become a major problem and a prosecution for contempt of court could lead to much heavier penalties. The particular concerns were the possible use of photographs for intimidatory purposes and the disruption of proceedings. It upheld a sentence of 12 months imprisonment despite the defendant's guilty

---

[432] *R. v Runting* (1989) 89 Cr.App.R. 243.

[433] Adjudication on complaints against *The Sunday Times* over publication of a sketch of the jury in the Thornton Heath murder case, *The Times*, December 13, 1982.

[434] *The Times*, July 15, 1986, cited by Miller, *Contempt of Court* (3rd edn., Oxford University Press, 2000), para.4.102.

plea.[435] Journalists will often seek help from the lawyers in court whose willingness to co-operate varies. Journalistic self-help is dangerous, though. The Court of Appeal has warned that the removal of photographs or other papers belonging to lawyers without their permission for the purpose of copying them could constitute contempt of court.[436]

Television and the courts

8–111 Section 41 has also effectively precluded televising the courts. Although the video camera had not been invented in 1925, the Court of Appeal has held that its prohibition extends to video filming.[437] In 1977 the BBC wished to include footage of a consistory court (see para.9–008) sitting in a village church as part of a documentary on rural life. The parties approved, as publicity for Church court proceedings had in the past brought in sorely needed cash, but the judge ruled that s.41 prevented filming of the actual proceedings.[438] He referred to the "necessary privacy" of judicial proceedings, but this was at odds with the principle of open justice, and the "pressures, embarrassment and discomfiture" that he wished to spare the participants are, in any event, experienced by a witness over cross-examination.

These traditional arguments against televising the courts were convincingly refuted by the Report of the Royal Commission into arms shipments to Colombian drug cartels.[439] This Commission was televised throughout its sittings in Antigua, and extracts were screened in the United Kingdom. The Royal Commissioner concluded that the public and professional benefits of media coverage were "incalculable": it discouraged time-wasting and irrelevance and enabled the public to make up its own mind about the testimony. The proceedings were in no way disrupted by a single, discreetly placed television camera, and the witnesses were in no way disquieted. The report accepted that electronic media coverage of criminal trials "requires careful and gradual introduction" but hoped that it would become routine for public inquiries (which are beyond the scope of section 41—see para.9–027). In 2001 Fiji's Court of Appeal permitted the televising of the hearings in the case in which it ruled that the military Government of the country was unlawful. In 2002 Dame Janet Smith who was conducting an inquiry into the activities of the doctor and serial murderer, Harold Shipman, agreed

---

[435] *R. v D (Contempt of Court: Illegal Photography)*, *The Times*, May 13, 2004.
[436] *Re Paul Griffin*, *The Times*, November 6, 1996.
[437] *R. v Loveridge, Lee and an Loveridge* (2001) 2 Cr.App.R. 29.
[438] *Re St Andrews* [1978] Fam. 121, Salisbury Consistory Court, Judge Ellison Chancellor.
[439] The report of the Royal Commissioner, Louis Blom-Cooper Q.C., is published by Duckworth on behalf of the Government of Antigua and Barbuda, as *Guns for Antigua*, 1990; see pp.44–46.

to allow parts of the proceedings to be televised after an application by CNN (see para.9–028). Regrettably, this breakthrough was not followed by Lord Hutton although ITV pressed him to make his public inquiry into the death of David Kelly truly public by allowing it to televise the evidence of Tony Blair, Alastair Campbell, the head of MI6 and various BBC journalists.

Dramatic reconstructions of courtroom dramas are unaffected by s.41. *The Trials of Oz* were relived in the West End by the Royal Shakespeare Company after the verdict but before the appeal and the BBC made a dramatised documentary of the *Gay News* trial, mainly from court transcripts. When the director of *The Romans in Britain* was charged with procuring an act of indecency (see para.9–050), public readings were given each evening of that day's proceedings at the Oxford Playhouse. This neither offended s.41 nor (in the absence of prejudicial comment) could it constitute contempt.

Channel 4 has taken the lead in exploring the possibilities of **8–112** contemporaneous television coverage of major trials. There are no difficulties in transmitting a "dramatic reconstruction" once the proceedings have concluded, and it is difficult to comprehend how jurors would be prejudiced by hearing evidence spoken by actors on television when they have already heard it delivered by witnesses in the courtroom, and can read it in summary form in the morning newspapers. Nonetheless, Channel 4 was not allowed by the Ponting trial judge to employ actors for their nightly *Court Report* of the trial—they had to be replaced by a panel of news-readers, whose presentation of the evidence the judge found unexceptional. Ironically, the very experienced producer of the programme had chosen to use actors precisely because they could be directed to avoid imparting emotion or conceivably prejudicial mannerisms to the script; news-readers were more liable to impart drama to the "parts" they were playing.

It is impossible to defend Britain's absolute prohibition on the broadcasting of legal proceedings. Many states in America permit both radio and television coverage of the courtroom. After initial doubts, there is now an acceptance that the result has been to make the judiciary better behaved, the advocates better prepared and the public better informed. The danger of distracting witnesses has not materialised. Two cases in the USA in particular energised public debate—the trials of O.J. Simpson for his wife's murder and the trial of Louise Woodward, a British nanny, for the killing of a baby in her care. Some commentators viewed the coverage with distaste. Others saw it as an exemplar of open justice in action and democratic access to trials which would in any event have been subject to enormous publicity.

The *Wall Street Journal* published a study of the effect on the US justice system of televising the O.J. Simpson trial. It concluded that there were two:

(1) it caused an amazing drop in the number of people who wanted exemptions from jury service: citizens wished, much more than before, to play their part in justice;

(2) it caused those who did serve on juries to pay much less attention to lawyers and their arguments, and concentrate their deliberations on facts proved in evidence.

8–113   Is this bad for the administration of justice? Even if it may be thought unseemly to broadcast the highlights of notorious criminal trials, this objection does not apply to appeal hearings. In New Zealand these are routinely televised without any damage to the administration of justice. Until cameras are allowed in the court-room, the media will have to make do with "dramatic reconstructions" of trials after they have taken place.

In principle, if every court in the land is open to every subject of the King, does it not logically follow that subjects should be entitled, quite literally, to see justice done through the medium of television? The communications revolution can bring benefits to justice, and we are beginning to accept the advantages of videotaped testimony of child witnesses and the possibility of cross-examining overseas witnesses via satellite link-up. Appeal courts would be better able to evaluate the testimony of trial witnesses if they could see and hear it being delivered, and most barristers have had occasion to regret that they could not include in grounds of appeal against judges' summings-up some reference to prejudical tones of voice or body language, which are not apparent from a typed transcript.

The danger of course, is that witnesses may prove camera-shy and that television's coverage of the day's play in a sensational Old Bailey trial will feature heavily edited "highlights" chosen for entertainment value rather than as fair and accurate reporting. Nonetheless, the public is genuinely interested in significant court cases, and the arguments in favour of open justice apply with even greater force to aural or visual coverage. Present television news reporting, in 60–second "slots" with breathless presenters pictured outside court quoting snatches of evidence, sometimes over inaccurate "artists impressions" of the courtroom, is of minimal value. When Channel 4 launched its *Court Report* programme, on which news-readers read large slabs of the day's transcript in the Ponting trial for half an hour on every evening of the three-week trial, over 500,000 viewers watched every edition. There would seem to be little objection to radio coverage of important appellate proceedings, but the BBC has been refused permission to go even this far.

8–114   Section 41 and the statutory prohibition on televising the courts does not apply in Scotland. Experiments have been made in permitting television cameras, with the permission of both prosecution and defence, to film several trials, although the excerpts broadcast for a BBC documentary series had to be approved by the trial judge. The issue came to the fore in 2000 in connection with the trial of two

Libyans for the Lockerbie bombings. Although the trial physically took place in the Netherlands, it was conducted by Scottish judges according to Scottish law. The BBC challenged in the Scottish High Court of Justiciary the refusal to allow them to televise the proceedings. The argument, based on Art.10 of the ECHR, failed because it was considered that broadcasting would prejudice the trial of the accused.[440] In a second round, the BBC sought access to an encrypted feed which was relayed from the courtroom to controlled sites around the world where the proceedings could be watched by the families of the dead. Again the challenge failed. The High Court of Justiciary referred to the *Leander* line of Strasbourg cases that Art.10 could not be used to compel an unwilling person to supply information.[441]

A tentative step towards change was taken in 2004–5 when a consortium of broadcasters was allowed to film appellate courts and prepare dummy programmes to show what might be possible if filming of those courts was allowed. The experiment was generally considered to be a success and judges and advocates found the cameras to be generally unobtrusive. In November 2006 Lord Falconer, the Lord Chancellor, was said to be in favour of allowing cameras to film both criminal and civil trials. Opposition remains, though, to the filming of the oral evidence of witnesses.

Media interviews with prisoners

Freedom of expression is a right of everyone, including prisoners, **8–115** but in their case the freedom is very heavily circumscribed. Prison Standing O.5, para. 34(c), for instance, prohibits prisoners entering into correspondence if their material is intended for publication about their crimes or past offences. Thus the Court of Appeal said that the Governor of Full Sutton prison was entitled to take steps to prevent Dennis Nilsen, the serial murderer, from publishing his autobiography. The grisly details of his crimes were no secret (they had been the subject of a book, apparently written with Nilsen's co-operation, some years previously), but the public would be outraged at the idea that Nilsen himself could be allowed to publish a book that glorified in the pleasure his crimes had given him. Imprisonment, rightly carried the consequence that he could be prevented from doing this and the restriction was compatible with Art.10(2).[442]

There are strong feelings about prisoners (or anyone else) profiting from crime and arrangements which might enrich wrongdoers are unlikely to be permitted. In 2006 there was world-wide condemnation of Rupert Murdoch when one of his US publishing companies paid O.J. Simpson for a book explaining how he would,

---

[440] *BBC's Petition*, judgment of Lord MacFadyn, March 7, 2000 (HCJ).
[441] *BBC's Petition (No. 2)*, April 20, 2000 (HCJ).
[442] *R (Nilsen) v Governor of Full Sutton Prison* [2005] 1 W.L.R. 1028, CA.

hypothetically, have committed the murder for which he was acquitted but which many people (including the jury in a subsequent civil case) believed that he had committed. Murdoch cancelled the deal in the face of public obloquy and no sensible prison governor would be advised to allow any similar proposition.

However, it is different if a prisoner wants to be interviewed by a journalist with a view to establishing that there has been a miscarriage of justice. In *R v Secretary of State for the Home Department Ex p. Simms and O'Brien*[443] the House of Lords recalled what a crucial part the media had played in the past in identifying wrongful convictions and it recognised that personal interviews between journalist and prisoner were essential if this was to happen. Consequently, it construed the Prison Standing Orders and rules in such a way as to allow this to happen.

8–116   The Administrative Court took this a stage further when it held that prisoners ought to be able to take part in media interviews about matters concerning the rights or interests of prisoners as a group. In this case, the prisoner had been punished for taking part in a pre-recorded radio interviews on the disenfranchisement of prisoners. The Court accepted that the authorities had a legitimate interest in checking the purpose of such interviews and whether the material was used for the declared purpose, but these concerns could be met by appropriate conditions. The prison authorities were not entitled to adopt a policy of blanket refusal.[444]

Thus there is some scope for interviewing prisoners, whether about miscarriages of justice or matters which concern the rights or interests of prisoners as a group. However, journalists who wish to make use of these opportunities may expect to have advance checks made on the purpose of their exercise and, in some cases, be asked to give undertakings as to ensure that the information obtained is not used for other purposes. While legal visits need take place only in the *sight* of a prison officer, other meetings with prisoners have to take place in the *sight and hearing* of an officer. The interviews themselves may also be recorded by the authorities and this practice has withstood challenge on Convention grounds.[445]

PROTECTION FROM LIBEL

8–117   One great attraction of court reporting is that it is virtually immune from actions for libel, whatever the gravity of the allegations bandied about in the courtroom and republished in the media. They do not

---

[443] [2000] 2 A.C. 115.

[444] *R (Hirst) v Secretary of State for the Home Department* [2002] UKHRR 758. As it happens, the European Court of Human Rights later agreed with Mr Hirst that to deny the vote to all prisoners was a breach of Protocol 1 Art.3 of the ECHR: *Hirst v UK (No.2)* (2004) 38 E.H.R.R. 825.

[445] *R (A) v Secretary of State for the Home Department* [2004] UKHRR 413.

have to be defended on grounds of justification or fair comment: they are privileged so long as the report is reasonably fair and accurate.

Absolute privilege

The privilege defence is discussed in Ch.3. Absolute privilege is a **8–118** complete defence, irrespective of the malice of the publisher of the account. The privilege goes back to the Law of Libel Amendment Act 1888, s.3, but this provision was repealed and replaced by the Defamation Act 1996, s.14. The 1888 Act protected a "fair and accurate report in any newspaper of proceedings publicly heard before any court exercising judicial authority" and which was published contemporaneously with the proceedings. The 1996 Act repeats the defence but with two principal extensions. Absolute privilege now applies also to contemporaneous reports of any tribunal or body in the United Kingdom which is exercising the judicial power of the State.[446] Other bodies whose proceedings may be contemporaneously reported with the protection of absolute privilege are: the European Court of Justice and any court attached thereto (e.g. the European Court of First Instance), the European Court of Human Rights and any international criminal tribunal established by the Security Council of the UN or by an international agreement to which the United Kingdom is a party, e.g. the Hague tribunal on war crimes in former Yugoslavia. Thus allegations made by lawyers, parties or witnesses in the trial of Slobodan Milosevic could be fully reported however defamatory they might have been of the British politicians who dealt with him.

The second extension is that the 1996 Act is not confined to newspaper reports. This extension is less significant since earlier amendments to the 1888 Act had already given protection to radio, television and other programme services[447] but the 1996 Act now makes clear that incidental communications in the course of preparing a published court report can have absolute privilege and informal reports (e.g. on the internet) will have absolute privilege if they satisfy the other criteria.

To attract absolute or even qualified privilege, the report must be "fair and accurate". The privilege is not lost if the inaccuracy is minor—"trifling slips" are to be expected.[448] But major errors—such as reporting a contentious piece of evidence from a particular witness as though it were a proven fact, or recounting an incorrect charge or the wrong verdict—will lose the protection. Erroneous headlines composed by sub-editors who were not in court and have not understood the copy are a familiar danger. The proceedings

---

[446] See the discussion of this phrase at para.9–029.
[447] See Broadcasting Act 1990, Sch.20, para.2.
[448] *Kimber v Press Association* [1893] 1 Q.B. 65.

must have been held in public, but the privilege applies whether or not both parties are present or whether an application (such as for a warrant or a summons) is made by one in the absence of the other.[449] Only words spoken in open court are covered by the privilege. Reporters taking their notes from a charge sheet, court list or other documents are at risk if magistrates deviate from the text.[450] It is partly to give the media the full protection of this privilege that the Home Office has told justices to be sure to identify defendants by reading aloud their names and addresses.[451]

8–119   The question of "fairness" is more difficult. The guiding principle is that reports should be impartial, carrying some account of both sides of the case. The exigencies of both the courts and newspapers make this a counsel of perfection. Trials can last for weeks or months, and often all the evidence given on a particular day will be in support of one side only. Additionally, the space available for court reports is limited. The most workable test is whether the report, as published, gives a reasonable impression of the proceedings thus far. Concentration on one sensational aspect of a witness's evidence in chief, without reference to a significant retraction made under cross-examination, could amount to a serious misrepresentation of the proceedings. Reporters are present with their privileges in the courtroom as representatives of the public; if, by calculated selection or omission they give an impression of the proceedings that no fair-minded member of the public could have formed in their place, the report will lose both absolute and qualified privilege under the statute, and the qualified privilege that remains at common law will be open to challenge for malice.

The likelihood, of course, is that it will not be challenged; defendants cannot (generally) obtain legal aid for libel and will, in any event, be reluctant to revive matters that had led them into the dock in the first place. The best solution when court reporters err is for the lawyers involved in the case to mention the mistake in open court the following day. If there is no dispute about the error, the newspaper should be prepared effectively to correct it by reporting the fact that it was drawn to the court's attention. It should not be necessary to use the law of libel to obtain a correction of a matter of public record.

The most unfair aspect of contemporary court reporting is the tendency of reporters to attend the beginning of a trial in order to publish the prosecutor's opening statement, which puts the allegations at their most sensational. The reporters then disappear for

---

[449] *Kimber v Press Association* (above).

[450] *Furniss v Cambridge Daily News Ltd* (1907) 23 T.L.R. 705, CA; *Harper v Provincial Newspapers Ltd* (1937) S.L.T. 462.

[451] Home Office Circulars 78/1967: 50/1969, approved in *R. v Evesham Justices, Ex p. McDonagh* [1988] 1 All E.R. 371, 384, QBD.

several weeks while the allegations are painstakingly questioned and undermined. But the press returns, vulture-like, for the verdict. If there is an acquittal, a newspaper will sometimes not even bother to report it, or will mention the matter without giving it anything like the prominence accorded to the discredited opening statement. This is *not* fair reporting: the original report, at the time it was published, was fair and accurate, but failure to follow it up with a report of the acquittal could retrospectively entail loss of the privilege.[452]

An interesting question is raised by the not uncommon occurrence **8–120** of "outbursts" in court—from the public gallery or from the defendant in the dock. Does a report of defamatory statements made by persons with no right to speak attract absolute privilege? Old cases suggested that they did not, but a more liberal view was taken in *Hope v Leng Ltd*, when absolute privilege was accorded to the report of a shout of, "It's all a pack of lies", from the well of the court during the claimant's evidence.[453] The decision could be artificially distinguished on the ground that the disruptor was a witness who had already given evidence and was then still technically under oath, but the court indicated its approval for a wider and more sensible view for the protection of court reporters. Outbursts in court are generally followed by admonitions from the judge; as a matter of common sense, they are part of the "proceedings" publicly heard before the court, and should therefore attract privilege.

The report must be published "contemporaneously". This does not mean "immediately", but as soon as reasonably practicable, having regard to the schedules of the newspaper or the broadcasting organisation. A daily newspaper would be expected to carry the report on the following day; a fortnightly magazine would not lose the privilege if it published at the next reasonable opportunity, even though it was reporting matters said in court up to two weeks before. Summaries in Sunday newspapers of the events of the week in a long trial would be protected. At the end of a big trial, feature articles and programmes sometimes appear recapitulating parts of the evidence and, in the case of television, even re-enacting aspects of the trial. The protection is not limited to "day by day" proceedings and there seems no reason why it should not extend to cover such accounts of an entire trial, if they are reasonably fair and published as soon as practicable after the verdict. The protection of absolute privilege extends to reports published within a reasonable time of the conclusion of any period of postponement of reporting imposed by any statute or court order.[454]

---

[452] *Wright v Outram* (1890) 17 R. 596 and *Turner v Sullivan* (1862) 6 L.T. 130.

[453] *Hope and Leng Ltd* (1907) 23 T.L.R. 243; *Farmer v Hyde* [1937] 1 K.B. 728 concerned a heckler's interruption, but, fortunately for the paper, he began "May I make an application". He could not, but he was therefore treated as a party. Compare "Nothing short of perjury" shouted from the gallery and held not privileged: *Lynam v Gowring* (1880) 6 L.R. Ir. 259.

[454] Defamation Act 1996, s.14(2).

Qualified privilege

8–121　At common law all fair and accurate court reports are protected by qualified privilege. This remains a safety net for coverage that falls outside the statutory protection of absolute privilege because, for example, it is not "contemporaneous". The privilege is "qualified" in the sense that it is lost if the court report is published "maliciously", i.e. for an improper motive such as to frighten off potential witnesses. Media court reports are unlikely to be deemed malicious, so the protection is for practical purposes as effective as absolute privilege. To enjoy the qualified privilege, the report must still be fair and accurate, and the words must have been spoken in a public court. The criteria for fairness and accuracy are the same as with absolute privilege. The principle is that a reporter is "entitled to report on the proceedings or that part of it which he selects in a manner which fairly and faithfully gives an impression of the events reported and will convey to the reader what he himself would have appreciated had he been present during the proceedings".[455]

To attract qualified privilege the report need not be contemporaneous and is therefore of particular use to authors whose books about famous trials are published long after the case is over. The defence of qualified privilege extends to reports of material whose publication is prohibited by the Judicial Proceedings (Regulation of Reports) Act 1926.[456]

Reports of foreign court proceedings have qualified privilege at common law if the proceedings are of legitimate public interest in England,[457] but the significance of common law privilege in this respect has been largely overtaken by a statutory qualified privilege for fair and accurate reports of proceedings in public before any court anywhere in the world. It is still necessary to show that the matter is of public concern and the publication is for the public benefit[458] although these requirements will usually be satisfied in respect of newsworthy trials in other countries.

---

[455] *Cook v Alexander* [1974] 1 Q.B. 279 at 290, *per* Buckley L.J.
[456] *Nicol v Caledonian Newspapers Ltd*, OH Lady Paton, April 11, 2002.
[457] *Webb v Times Publishing Co* [1960] 2 Q.B. 535.
[458] Defamation Act 1996, s.15.

CHAPTER 9

REPORTING LESSER COURTS AND TRIBUNALS

INTRODUCTION

There are about five hundred separate types of tribunal that have **9–001** some of the features of a court, and that make decisions with some legal force and often considerable public interest. A few, such as courts martial and consistory (Church) courts, have powers to punish, and procedures similar to criminal trials. Professional disciplinary bodies cannot jail ethical transgressors, but may fine them or suspend them from practice. Decisions of the Asylum and Immigration Tribunal affect the fate of families, Employment Tribunals decide the rights and wrongs of behaviour in the workplace and deal with allegations of race, sex and other forms of discrimination, while a myriad of assessment bodies decide the level of rates and rents and pensions, and settle disputes over such disparate matters as mines and quarries, performing rights, plant varieties and value added tax (VAT). Public inquiries may fix the responsibility for a riot or the site of a new airport, while inquests at coroners' courts sometimes attract as much press attention as a sensational murder trial. The multiplicity of these potentially newsworthy tribunals, and the present uncertainty as to which of them are protected by the laws of contempt, justifies a treatment separate from that accorded to civil and criminal courts.

The bewildering array of tribunals has no simple explanation. In some cases, tradition has prevailed over consistency and even fairness; military courts, for example, have a criminal jurisdiction that inflicts upon members of the armed services an officer-class justice that may be very different from that received by civilians from a jury of their peers. Other tribunals have been established to facilitate the Welfare State, to provide a basis for decision-taking that is fair (in that it allows public arguments from both sides), yet more informal and expeditious than that available from the regular courts. Some tribunals, such as accident inquiries, adopt an inquisitorial model, in the sense that tribunal members themselves call witnesses, interrogate them, expound and test conflicting hypotheses, and then prepare a report examining the different causal theories and making recommendations to avoid similar accidents in the future. Other tribunals exist to make administrative decisions—whether a licence should be renewed, whether an income-tax assessment should be paid and so on. The "tribunal", with its quasi-legal procedures, its opportunities for both sides to state a case and to ask questions, is some concession to the concept of natural justice in public administration. Openness is a characteristic of natural justice, and tribunals and inquiries sometimes do provide important opportunities to scrutinise and oversee the activities of public servants.

"When is a court not a court?" may sound an absurd question, but upon the answer hinge consequences of great importance to the media. The question of the application of contempt to various tribunals is important and difficult; it will be considered in this chapter after an outline of the characteristics of those lesser courts and tribunals that are most frequently in the news.

INQUESTS

9–002   Inquests can be particularly newsworthy events, as the cases of Princess Diana, Helen Smith, the Gulf War friendly fire victims and the Hillsborough Football Stadium disaster demonstrate. It is easy to liken the attraction of reporters to inquests to the interest of the vulture in the dead body, but the public interest in picking at the circumstances in which a life has been lost is not unworthy or unimportant. Any society that values life must look closely at death. And when death comes unnaturally and unexpectedly—behind the closed doors of police cells or prisons, or in a foreign country, or through the oversight of employers or doctors or public officials—it deserves to be looked at very closely indeed. Some agency is needed that is sufficiently independent and impartial to satisfy the public conscience. Frequently, the only agency in England and Wales that attempts to fill this need is the coroner, and sometimes the coroner's jury, deliberating in a special procedure called an inquest.

In the Middle Ages the office of coroner was created because the king wanted a local official to keep a watchful eye on corrupt sheriffs and to preserve property rights that would accrue to the Royal Treasury on death. To assist him, in an age long before police forces and medical science, the coroner summoned a jury from the neighbourhood areas. The medieval coroner and his jury would squat around the body—often by a roadside or in a ditch—and look for tell-tale signs of disease or violence or suicide. Pooling their local knowledge, they would often come up with the name of a likely suspect, whom they would present for trial. Although these import-ant functions were taken over by professionals—policemen and doctors and lawyers—the coroner survived, as a public official appointed by local councils to investigate unnatural deaths, receiving a fee for each body inspected. Unlike other local public officials, the coroner, owing to his origin as the king's man, could not effectively be disciplined or removed. In the twentieth century the coroners lost most of their powers of criminal inquiry; in cases of suspicious deaths they in effect unveil to the public the evidence upon which the police have failed to reach any conclusion.

The coroner's task is to determine exactly how the deceased met with death. When this does not become apparent from initial inquiries, they must hold an inquest: a formal investigation, clad in the trappings of a court, to which witnesses may be summoned and examined, ending with a "verdict", which is officially recorded. In certain limited cases the coroner is obliged to summon a jury: these are cases of deaths in prison, death by poison, deaths in police custody or from an injury caused by a police officer in the execution or purported execution of his duty, or deaths in circumstances "the continuance or possible recurrence of which is prejudicial to the health or safety of the public or any section of the public".[1] In 2007 the High Court required the inquest into the death of Princess Diana to be conducted with a jury. It thought that the inquest (which was then being held by the retired President of the Family Division, Lady Elizabeth Butler-Sloss) might lead to recommendations to address the danger posed to royals and other celebrities from paparazzi on wheels.[2] In 1980 the Court of Appeal compelled the Hammersmith coroner to sit with a jury for the inquest of Blair Peach, a New Zealand teacher who had been killed in the Southall disturbances. The family claimed he had died from a blow inflicted by an instrument wielded by an unidentifiable policeman from the Special Patrol Group. The court agreed that it would be prejudicial to public safety if the police were issued with dangerous weapons, or if senior officers turned a blind eye to their use.[3] Since 1983 any death resulting from injury caused by a police officer must be investigated by a jury.[4]

Inquests are unlike any other judicial proceedings. Coroners need **9–003** not be lawyers; they may be doctors of at least five years' standing. Unlike lay justices, they do not have the assistance of a legally trained clerk. The closest equivalent at an inquest is a policeman, who acts as the "coroner's officer". This does not help to create an appearance of impartiality where the death is alleged to have been caused by the police. In addition, an inquest does not follow the usual adversarial pattern of most legal proceedings, where the truth is expected to emerge from the clash of opposing evidence and submissions. Instead, the coroner takes the initiative and leads the

---

[1] Coroners Act 1988, s.8(3).
[2] *Paul v Deputy Coroner of the Queen's Household and Assistant Deputy Coroner for Surrey (Baroness Elizabeth Butler-Sloss)* [2007] EWHC 408 (Admin).
[3] *R. v Hammersmith Coroner Ex p. Peach (No.1 & 2)* [1980] QB 211 , CA. After protracted proceedings, the police made a payment of £75,000 (without admitting liability) to the family of Blair Peach.
[4] Administration of Justice Act 1982, s.62.

investigation. An inquest takes place after police investigations, which have been made available to the coroner. But the coroner is not obliged to show material collected by the police to representatives of the interested parties, and many coroners refuse to give lawyers a sight of the evidence available to them.[5] This means that lawyers are sometimes unprepared for the evidence that the coroner decides to call. It means, too, that at inquests where police misconduct is alleged, the police lawyers will have exclusive access to statements taken by police officers, and so have an unfair advantage.

Coroners cannot behave like impartial judges. They receive and study the police evidence beforehand, usually discuss it privately with the police, and will in most cases have formed a view before the inquest opens. There are coroners who behave like conjurors, putting witnesses into the witness box to make statements that the parties have been given no opportunity to check with other witnesses, or to rebut. The parties and their lawyers are present, as one judge put it, merely as "guests of the court"[6] and may not address the coroner or the jury on the facts. There are no final speeches. So the jury never hears the contentions of the parties about the cause of death put in a coherent form. This prevents a comprehensive account, a logical theory of the cause of death, from being presented by anyone other than the coroner. Where the evidence is complicated and confusing, the only coherent account that is ever given to the public is provided by the coroner in the summing up. This may be an unsatisfactory account. It may even be, as in the Helen Smith case, a preposterous account.[7] But there can be no alternative.

In cases where coroners sit with juries public esteem for the jury system in criminal courts invests the "verdict" with a degree of acceptability. But the role of the coroner's jury today is no more than symbolic. The final verdict is usually dictated by the coroner. All the coroner's jury can do is to announce one simple fact: how the deceased met with death. The law requires a narrow answer to a narrow question, but in some cases the public rightly expects much fuller answers to a whole range of questions. Coroners' juries cannot provide these answers—they are not even allowed by law to attempt them. But, as a result, the Government changed the law and inquest juries can no longer add recommendations for preventing similar deaths. The inadequacy of coroners and their procedures became a cause for which the relatives of the victims of the Thames pleasure boat, the *Marchioness*, fought long and hard and eventually won the right to an inquiry presided over by a High Court judge which

---

[5] See *The Death of Blair Peach: A Supplementary Report of the Unofficial Inquiry Chaired by Professor Michael Dummett*, NCCL, 1980; and Paul Foot (with Ron Smith), *The Helen Smith Story*, Fontana, 1983, p.296.

[6] The "interested parties" who can be represented are now listed in the Coroners' Rules 1984 (SI 1984/552).

[7] See Geoffrey Robertson, *The Justice Game* (Vintage, 1999), Ch.8.

exposed serious failings by the coroner. There is much to be said for a judicial inquiry instead of a coroner's inquest after all such catastrophes.

Article 2 of the ECHR imposes a positive obligation on the **9–004** United Kingdom to investigate some deaths (where a public authority has or might in some way have been involved) more closely. In these cases, the courts have interpreted the inquest as having a somewhat wider function: to investigate by what means and in what circumstances the deceased met his death.[8]

The inquest must be held in open court unless the coroner thinks that it is in the interest of national security to exclude the public.[9] In December 1983 the *Observer* successfully obtained an interim injunction to prevent a coroner holding in secret the inquest on a British businessman who had died in Moscow after expressing fears that his life might be threatened. The Government had denied that the man was a spy and the judge accepted that prima facie there was no reason why the death should not be publicly investigated. However, a coroner can, like a judge, permit a witness to give evidence from behind a screen if national security or the witness's own safety would be genuinely imperilled so that the administration of justice would be frustrated by the witness giving evidence in the ordinary way.[10] If there are reasonable grounds for a witness's fears of retaliation (and no compelling reason as to why he should be obliged to run that risk) Art.2 of the ECHR will require the witness to be allowed to give evidence anonymously.[11]

Documentary evidence will normally be read aloud and an interested party can usually insist that it is, although the coroner does have a discretion to direct that it should be tendered in writing.[12]

The law of contempt has been applied, without any sensible **9–005** thought, to coroners' courts: their inquisitorial procedures do not, as a matter of principle, require or deserve the suppression of media comment. On the contrary, since the fundamental object of the inquiry is to establish the cause of death, any light that can be shed on this from any source, including the media, should be welcome. This principle was accepted at the Helen Smith inquest: a Thames Television *This Week* documentary, which was transmitted the week before the inquest opened, was re-screened for the benefit of the jury, because it featured interviews with vital witnesses who refused to come to Britain for the coroner's proceedings.

---

[8] *R (Middleton) v H.M. Coroner for the Western District of Somerset* [2004] 2 A.C. 182.

[9] Coroners' Rules 1984 (SI 1984/552) r.36(2), r.17.

[10] *R. v HM Coroner for Newcastle upon Tyne Ex p. A* (1998) 162 J.P. 387.

[11] *Family of Derek Bennett v Officers A and B and HM Coroner* [2005] UKHRR 44 CA, following the decisions of the Court of Appeal in relation to the Bloody Sunday Tribunal; *R. v Lord Saville of Newdigate, Ex p. A* [2000] 1 W.L.R. 1855 CA; *R. (A) v Lord Saville of Newdigate* [2002] 1 W.L.R. 1299, CA.

[12] Coroners' Rules 1984, r.37.

Non-attendance of potential witnesses was a feature also of the 1992 "friendly fire" inquest (where 9 squaddies had been man-slaughtered by reckless US A-10 pilots who refused to attend and whose identities were kept secret). The inquest in that case recom-mended that there should be no further joint UK–US operations until the US government accepted that its servicemen should attend British inquests. Of course, no notice whatsoever was taken of this recommendation and in 2006 the US Defence Department again refused to make available the US servicemen who had killed Terry Lloyd.

The point that inquests are inquisitorial rather than adversarial was overlooked by the Court of Appeal in its haste to ban an LWT documentary about the death in police custody of a black "Hell's Angel": it used as its pretext the concern that the coroner's jury might be prejudiced, although no jury had been sworn and the inquest stood adjourned indefinitely while police "investigations" proceeded.[13]

In 2006 the government produced a draft bill for the reform of the coronial system. For the media the most important proposal was that coroners should have a discretionary power to require the deceased to remain anonymous in any press reporting. The government had in mind that this power would be used where there was no public interest in disclosing the identity of the dead person and where publicity would add to the family's grief, e.g. in the case of suicides or deaths of children.

COURT MARTIAL

9–006 A Court Martial tries offences against military, naval or air force law. Some of these correspond to civilian crimes, but others are of more questionable validity. The notoriously vague offence of "con-duct prejudicial to good order and discipline" appears in all three codes,[14] and can be used to punish behaviour that would be unexceptional from civilians. Insufficient media scrutiny is given to whether punishments are always justified by the exigencies of service life.

A Court Martial is composed of officers and (sometimes) warrant officers with no particular legal training who pass judgment on officers and "squaddies" alike who may be accused of all types of offences including the most serious such as murder or rape and who have (unlike other citizens) no right to a trial by a jury of their peers. Presiding over a Court Martial is a "Judge Advocate" who will be legally trained and who performs a role akin to that of a Crown

---

[13] *Peacock v London Weekend Television* (1985) 150 J.P. 71.
[14] The separate offences for each of the services will be amalgamated by the Armed Forces Act 2006, s.19 when in force.

Court judge in a trial on indictment. The other members of the court must follow his decisions on questions of law, procedure or practice.[15]

The press, like the public, have a right of access.[16] A Court Martial can sit in secret in the same circumstances as a civilian court (see para.8–008) and, in addition, the public can be excluded if it appears that there might otherwise be a disclosure of information useful to an enemy.[17] At the end of the trial the court will be cleared while the officer-judges deliberate without the Judge Advocate. They give their finding in public and then retire this time with the Judge Advocate to consider the sentence. This is imposed in public. The UK's system of military justice has in the past been found wanting in numerous ways in Strasbourg when measured against the fair trial requirements of Art.6 of the ECHR. In response to one of these criticisms the Armed Forces Discipline Act 2000 introduced a procedure for appeals from summary punishments imposed by commanding officers. These summary appeal courts will (presumptively) sit in open court[18] but can sit in private where the court considers this necessary in the interests of morals or public order, to safeguard the interests of persons under 18 or the private life of the appellant or where the interests of justice would be prejudiced by a public hearing.[19]

The Court Martial is undoubtedly a "court" for the purpose of the **9–007** law of contempt (see below para.9–029) although it is questionable as to whether the officers who sit on them are as vulnerable to prejudicial publications in the media as jurors in a Crown Court. Officers will only be eligible to sit on a Court Martial if they have had three years service as officers. All the members of the Court Martial will have had some minimal training in their role and will usually have had an opportunity to watch other Courts Martial in operation before they serve. It might also be thought that, as experienced officers in a disciplined force, they would be used to following orders and so more likely to observe a Judge Advocate's directions to try the case according to the evidence and to disregard anything they come across in the media.

Because a Court Martial is a court, its Judge Advocates can make postponement and secrecy orders under the Contempt of Court Act (see para.8–071). These orders have sometimes been controversial.[20]

---

[15] Armed Forces Act 2006, s.159(1).

[16] Armed Forces Act 2006, s.158.

[17] This was the position prior to the Armed Forces Act 2006. Once s.158 of that Act is in force any qualifications on the open justice principle will be contained in the Court Martial Rules.

[18] Armed Forces Discipline Act 2000, s.19(3).

[19] See e.g. Summary Appeal Court (Army) Rules 2000 (SI 2000/2371), r.5. There are similar rules for the Navy and RAF.

[20] See for instance the ruling of McKinnon J. sitting as a Judge Advocate in *R v Payne*, September 19, 2006, discussed at para.8–072.

Until recently, there was a lacuna which meant that these orders could not be challenged. When a power to appeal Crown Court publicity orders was created in 1988 the right of appeal was not extended to the Court Martial since the legality of its decisions could at the time be challenged on judicial review. However, the Armed Forces Act 2001, s.23 gave a Court Martial the same immunity from judicial review as a Crown Court hearing a trial on indictment. At that stage, nothing was done to create an alternative method of challenge. The Armed Forces Act 2006 should remedy this gap since it allows the Court Martial Rules to include provision for appeals against any decisions restricting publication or excluding the public from any hearing.[21] It is likely that any appeal would be to the Court Martial Appeal Court which is very similar in composition and procedure to the Court of Appeal Criminal Division. As with the Crown Court, a swifter remedy may be to apply to the Judge Advocate himself to vary or discharge the order. In January 2006, a Judge Advocate who had ordered the entire hearing of a Court Martial of a submarine commander to be in camera was persuaded to allow the public in to most of the proceedings. The allegations of bullying and harassment were given wide publicity as was the eventual acquittal of the commander of all charges.[22]

The pressure for change in Court Martial procedure has largely come about under pressure from Strasbourg but the changes made in 2001 were found to have made the process Convention compliant by the House of Lords and the Grand Chambers of the European Court.[23]

CHURCH COURTS

9–008   Ecclesiastical courts have had a colourful history. Once, they dispensed soft justice to all who could claim "benefit of clergy", to escape death or prison sentences from the courts of the king. They decided questions of heresy, divorce, wills and defamation. Now they are limited to deciding disputes about Church property, and hearing charges of misconduct levelled against clergymen in their capacity as such.

Each diocese has a consistory court, and the Bishop's Chancellor—a senior lawyer—usually sits as judge. Clerical inter-meddling is discouraged: when Bishop Mervyn Stockwood tried to adjudicate a dispute personally, he was roundly rebuked by his Chancellor, who suggested that the bill for unravelling the ensuing mess might be sent to His Grace.[24] The Chancellor sitting alone

---

[21] Armed Forces Act 2006, s.163(3)(i).
[22] See *Media Lawyer*, March 2006, p.9.
[23] *R v Spear* [2003] 1 A.C. 734; *Cooper v UK* (2004) 39 E.H.R.R. 8.
[24] *Re St Mary's, Barnes* [1982] All E.R. 456.

hears disputes about Church property, but in cases of clerical misconduct sits with a "jury" of four assessors. An appeal can be taken to the appropriate archbishop's court (the Arches Court of Canterbury and the Chancery Court of York) and then, ultimately, to the Privy Council, which advises the Queen, as formal head of the Anglican Church, on whether the appeal should be allowed. The general principle of openness applies to these courts. The High Court is reluctant to overturn an order to exclude the press and public if this was made "reasonably" to serve the ends of justice—e.g. to obtain evidence that would not be given at all if it had to be given in public. But there is no power to exclude because of the intimate or embarrassing nature of the evidence, or merely to deprive the tabloids of the opportunity to run stories about gay or adulterous vicars.[25]

There is legislation in place to replace consistory courts with new style tribunals for disciplining clergy, but four years after it was passed it has yet to be brought into effect.[26] When it does, the new style tribunals will sit in private although the respondent can require a public hearing and the tribunal can itself decide to sit in public if that would be in the interests of justice. In either case, the tribunal may exclude such person or persons as it may determine.[27]

EMPLOYMENT TRIBUNALS

Employment Tribunals (ET) consider a wide range of employment **9–009** disputes. Claims of unfair dismissal, disputes over redundancy payments, and allegations of sex and race discrimination by employers are the most familiar issues, but Employment Tribunals can also decide whether an organisation is an independent trade union for collective bargaining, whether an employer has allowed adequate time off for trade union or public duties, and appeals against health and safety improvement orders.

Each tribunal comprises a legally trained chairperson, a trade union representative and an employer's nominee. This mix is not intended to ensure that each side can depend on one vote, but rather to give the appearance of a balanced tribunal. Their affiliations are not publicly announced and it can sometimes be difficult to tell them apart. An appeal can be taken on a point of law to the Employment Appeal Tribunal (EAT), which is chaired by a High Court or County Court judge flanked again by two lay people.

Employment Tribunals must sit in public unless a Government minister has directed a private hearing on grounds of national

---

[25] *R. v Chancellor of the Chichester Consistory Court Ex p. News Group Newspapers*, *The Times*, July 15, 1991.
[26] Clergy Discipline Measure 2003.
[27] 2003 Measure, s.18(3)(c).

security or where the tribunal chooses to sit in private to hear evidence which the Tribunal considers would be contrary to national security to hear in public, or where the evidence cannot be disclosed without breaching a statutory obligation, disclosing confidential information or substantially injuring the witness's business or place of employment (other than in the context of negotiations with employees).[28] Other substantial modifications are made to Employment Tribunal procedure in national security cases.[29] Similar provisions apply to the Employment Appeal Tribunal.[30] In national security cases the Tribunal can also take steps to keep secret all or part of the reasons for its decision.[31] The Tribunal is under a duty to ensure that information is not disclosed contrary to the interests of national security.[32] Where an Employment Tribunal does conceal the identity of a witness or takes steps to keep secret all or part of the reasons for its decision, it is an offence to publish anything which is likely to lead to the identification of the witness or the secret part of the tribunal's reasons. The maximum penalty is a level 5 fine (currently £5,000) in the magistrates' court.[33]

9–010   The legislative requirement to sit in public is mandatory, an Employment Tribunal cannot sit "in chambers" (outside the provisions of the Rules) even though the Chairman is sitting alone.[34]

> In this case, all the regular courtrooms were occupied and the chairman had used an office on a corridor which was separated from the public areas by a locked door which also bore a sign: "Private No admittance to the public beyond this point". The EAT had overridden the objection on the ground that no member of the public had actually tried to enter the hearing. The Court of Appeal said that this was immaterial to the question of whether the hearing had taken place in public. It was a question of fact and degree in each case, but on these facts the hearing had not been in public, the Employment Tribunal chairman had thereby acted beyond his jurisdiction and his decision had to be quashed.

This approach accords with Art.6 of the ECHR which gives a right to a public hearing for the determination of civil rights or obligations. Strasbourg case law as to what is a "civil right or obligation" is

---

[28] Employment Tribunals Act 1996, s.10A and Employment Tribunals (Constitution and Rules of Procedure) Regulations 2004 (SI 2004/1861) (referred to below as the 2004 ET Rules) r.16,18 (which applies the same rules to pre-hearing reviews) and 26.

[29] 2004 ET Rules r.54 and Sch.2.

[30] Employment Appeal Tribunal Rules (SI 1993/2854) (the "1993 EAT Rules"), rr.29–30A.

[31] 2004 ET Rules, r.54(2).

[32] 2004 ET Rules, r.54(4).

[33] Employment Tribunals Act 1996, s.10B.

[34] *Storer v British Gas Plc* [2000] 2 All E.R. 440, CA, compare the similar, but not identical, facts in *R. (on the application of Pelling) v Bow County Court*, para.8–006.

unclear and not all rights, particularly not all challenges to the actions of public authorities, qualify. However, when civil rights or obligations are involved the right to a public hearing must be real and not illusory so that a hearing (for instance) of a serious criminal offence against a prisoner which was held in a closed prison did not satisfy the requirement.[35]

The "statutory obligation" which entitles an Employment Tribunal to sit in private includes the obligation under the Human Rights Act 1998 on public authorities to respect Convention rights. Consequently, Art.8 may be invoked to justify receiving certain evidence in private.[36] However, the Art.8 rights would have to be balanced against other Convention rights in issue, particularly Arts 6 and 10. It would be excessive and disproportionate to close the hearing or receive the evidence in private if legitimate privacy concerns could be adequately protected by less intrusive measures.

There is a Register of Employment Tribunal decisions which is **9–011** open to public inspection.[37] The Register should include not only the Tribunal's bare decision but also its reasons (whether given in summary or extended form) unless the Tribunal has sat in private on a Minister's direction or unless it has heard evidence in private and the Tribunal has directed that its reasons should be omitted from the Register.[38]

Until 2004 the Register also included details of applications which had been made to Employment Tribunals, but the 2004 ET Rules scrapped this aspect of the Register. Consequently, there will be no publicly available record of applications which settle or are withdrawn prior to a judgment.

So far as the Employment Appeal Tribunal is concerned, any person may inspect (for free) and copy (for a charge) any notice of appeal, judgment or order. Other documents lodged with the Central Office of the EAT can be inspected and copied with the leave of the Tribunal.[39]

Where the case has involved allegations of a sexual offence the **9–012** Register will not contain any matter which is likely to lead members of the public to identify any person affected by or making such an allegation.[40] The meaning of "sexual offence" is tied to the Sexual Offences (Amendment) Act 1992 (see para.8–044).[41] One difference,

---

[35] *Riepan v Austria*, judgment of November 14, 2000.

[36] *XXX v YYY* [2004] IRLR 137 EAT, overturned but on other grounds *XXX v YYY* [2004] IRLR 471, CA.

[37] Employment Tribunals (Constitution and Rules of Procedure) Regulations 2004, Reg.12.

[38] 2004 ET Rules, r.32.

[39] *Practice Direction Employment Appeal Tribunal* [2005] ICR 660, para.5.3. The Central Office of the EAT is at 58 Victoria Embankment, London EC4Y ODS.

[40] 2004 ET Rules, r.49. Directions to this effect are sometimes referred to as "Register deletion orders" or RDOs.

[41] Employment Tribunals Act 1996, s.11(6). The subsection still refers as well to the Sexual Offences (Amendment) Act 1976. This is superfluous since that statute was repealed in 1999.

though, is that names and other matter will be excluded from the Register if they identify a person *affected by* the allegation—not merely the person making the allegation as is the case under the 1992 Act. Although the registered decision will not contain the names of the alleged perpetrators, reporters who will have been free to attend the hearings will usually be able to establish their identity. The employment legislation does not make it an offence to reveal the details of promulgated decisions withheld from the Register and the 1992 Act would only penalise a publication which directly or indirectly identified the *victim* of the alleged offence.

Until the promulgation of its decision, an Employment Tribunal has a wider power—to make a "restricted reporting order" often referred to as an RRO. This is not confined to cases of alleged sexual offences but can be made whenever the application involves allegations of sexual misconduct.[42] This is defined as the commission of a sexual offence, sexual harassment or other adverse conduct (of whatever nature) related to sex (whether the relationship with sex lies in the character of the conduct or in its having reference to the sex or sexual orientation of the person at whom the conduct is directed).[43] On one reading "adverse conduct related to sex" could embrace almost any allegation of sex discrimination, but the EAT has said that it should not be read so widely and that the alleged conduct requires some kind of moral obloquy.[44]

Parliament has recognised by granting this power that fear of publicity can be a powerful disincentive to bringing complaints of sexual harassment by employers.[45] However, as the Court of Appeal has said[46]:

"... it is not to be exercised automatically at the request of one party, or even at the request of both parties. The industrial tribunal still has to consider whether it is in the public interest that the press should be deprived of the right to communicate information to the public if it becomes available. It is not a matter which is to be dealt with on the nod so to speak. *Scott v Scott* establishes that, when both sides consent to an order prohibiting publication, that is exactly the moment when a court ought to examine with particular care whether, as a matter of discretion, such an order should be made."

9–013   Courts routinely repeat this pro-media rhetoric, but do nothing to discourage applications for suppression orders—e.g. by awarding indemnity (i.e. full) costs against wealthy parties who unsuccessfully

---

[42] 2004 ET Rules, r.50(1).

[43] Employment Tribunals Act 1996, s.11(6).

[44] *Chief Constable of West Yorkshire v A* [2000] I.R.L.R. 465.

[45] *A v B Ex p. News Group Newspapers Ltd* [1998] I.C.R. 55, 66, EAT. The same case is reported less coyly as *Chessington World of Adventures v Reed Ex p. News Group Newspapers Ltd* in [1998] I.R.L.R. 56.

[46] *X v Z Ltd* [1998] I.C.R. 43, 45–6.

try to gag the press. Employment Tribunals provide many examples of a situation common to other tribunals, where the parties are either indifferent to publicity or positively wish to avoid it. The "media" for this purpose will very often be a local newspaper, unable to afford the costs needed to challenge a suppression order.

> There was scandal in the London Borough of Camden. The council's own solicitor (its deputy chief executive) was suing the council and its chief executive for sex discrimination and victimisation. One of many allegations was that the Chief Executive had failed to take any action when the solicitor complained that she had been sexually harassed by another council employee. Since ratepayers and council tax payers' money was being expended on the proceedings, the two local newspapers—*The Camden New Journal* and *The Hampstead and Highgate Express*—were properly anxious to report it. But Camden persuaded the tribunal chair that a restricted reporting order was necessary because the council and the Chief Executive were both "persons affected by" the allegation of sexual misconduct. The applicant did not support the application, but had no money or interest to oppose it. The local papers could not afford a court challenge, and the evidence would have proceeded without being reported at all had *The Mail on Sunday* not applied for judicial review in the High Court, which struck the order down as "irrational and perverse". Keane J. said that a corporation could not sensibly be "a person affected by" allegations of sexual misconduct, and nor could the Chief Executive since he was only told about them later and had neither witnessed, perpetrated or been a victim of them. Parliament's purpose was to encourage victims—persons directly affected—to come forward, and no court should impose a restricted reporting order which was wider than necessary to achieve that purpose. Such a wide restriction on reporting as the tribunal had imposed was unsustainable, and the chief executive's preference to avoid any embarrassment was not a legitimate consideration, being,

>> "far outweighed by the public interest in contemporaneous reporting of the many other issues arising as between the chief executive and the deputy chief executive of a London Borough".[47]

Keane J.'s decision is important for media law generally in three respects:

(1) It acknowledges that the "public interest" served by media reporting is not confined to the legal points or the matters relevant to the judgment, but includes reporting of "the many other issues arising" in politically-charged tribunal proceedings.

(2) The judge held that "the importance of the public and contemporaneous reporting of court and tribunal hearings"

---

[47] *R. v London (North) Industrial Tribunal Ex p. Associated Newspapers Ltd* [1998] I.C.R. 1212, QBD.

was a principle of statutory interpretation which should be used to give a narrow construction to all statutes purporting to restrict coverage.

(3) He said that the European Convention adds nothing to the protection of court reporting, "given that the (open justice) principle . . . is so firmly embedded in the English common law". In the context of the Human Rights Act this is important because s.11 of the Act preserves existing common law rights. The Tribunal can make a temporary reporting restriction order without a hearing, but there must be a hearing before a full order can be made. The Rules expressly envisage that non-parties may wish to be heard. They will be allowed to make submissions if the chairman or Tribunal considers that they have a legitimate interest.[48] Media organizations would be a classic example of a non-party with a very legitimate interest in whether a reporting restriction order is made.

A Tribunal when making an order must specify the persons who may not be identified.[49] It now seems settled that a corporation or other legal entity cannot be a "person . . . affected by the allegation".[50] The adverse effect of an allegation of sexual misconduct by its staff or officers on the trading reputation of a company is not enough to justify treating it as an affected person. However when a restricted reporting order is made nothing should be published which would be likely to lead members of the public to identify the individual concerned as being the person affected by or making the allegation of sexual misconduct. There may be cases where publishing the company's name would indirectly identify one of the individuals who had been given anonymity by the order, but there is still an important difference between this protection (which derives from anonymity given to someone else) and the direct prohibition of reporting of the company's name itself—this a tribunal cannot impose.[51]

9–014   A notice that a restricted reporting order has been made should be put on the notice board of the tribunal with any list of cases and on the door of the room where the proceedings are being heard.[52] A restricted reporting order can be temporary or full. A temporary order lasts for 14 days or if, during that time, an application is made to continue or revoke the order, until that application can be heard.[53] A full order lasts until both liability and remedy have been

---

[48] 2004 ET Rules, r.50(7).

[49] Employment Tribunal Procedure Rules, r.15(5)(a).

[50] *Ex p. Associated Newspapers Ltd*, above fn.47 and *Leicester University v A* [1999] I.C.R., EAT—not following *M v Vincent* [1998] I.C.R. 73, EAT.

[51] See the similar distinction made by the court in *Ex p. Godwin* above para.8–038.

[52] 2004 ET Rules, r.50(8)(c).

[53] 2004 ET Rules, r.50(5).

decided.[54] Restricted reporting orders do not prohibit reporting indefinitely, but only until the tribunal's decision is promulgated (i.e. the date on the determination signifying when it was sent to the parties). Thereafter, the only restrictions on reporting are those which apply generally including the 1992 Sexual Offences (Amendment) Act—see above.

It is an offence to publish identifying material in breach of a restricted reporting order or to include it in a programme service. The maximum penalty is a fine on scale 5 (currently £5,000).[55] Unusually for reporting offences, prosecution is not dependent on the consent of the Attorney-General.

Similar powers are given to Employment Tribunals to make restricted reporting orders in disability discrimination cases which are likely to include evidence of a personal nature, i.e. any evidence of a medical or other intimate nature which might reasonably be assumed to be likely to cause significant embarrassment to the complainant if reported.[56] Only the complainant can apply for an order (whereas any party to the proceedings can apply for a restriction order where there is an allegation of sexual misconduct— the Tribunal has power to make an order of its own motion in both cases). In disability cases the power is more broadly expressed because the focus is on the embarrassing character of the evidence rather than any allegation of misconduct.

> This difference was thrown into relief by *Chief Constable of West Yorkshire Police v A*[57] where the applicant had undergone gender reassignment and wanted to join the police as a woman police constable. The police had refused her application as someone who had been born a man could not conduct searches of women so could not then be assigned to the full duties of a WPC. The EAT agreed that the Employment Tribunal Rules did not in these circumstances give a power to order anonymity. However, the applicant also relied on her right to equal treatment under the E.U.'s Equal Treatment Directive (ETD).[58] This included a right to an effective remedy (Art.6). The EAT found that without an anonymity order the applicant would not have an effective remedy and this justified the order.[59]

In a later case,[60] the EAT held that both it and Employment **9–015** Tribunals would be able to make anonymity orders where a person asserting rights given by the Equal Treatment Directive would

---

[54] 2004 ET Rules, r.50(8)(b).
[55] Employment Tribunals Act 1996, s.11(2).
[56] Employment Tribunals Act 1996, s.12 and 2004 ET Rules, r.50.
[57] [2000] I.R.L.R. 465.
[58] 76/207/EC.
[59] The E.T.'s use of the order was not challenged on appeal and so the EAT did not need to rule on it, but it used Art.6 of the ETD to justify itself making an anonymity order to cover the proceedings in the Appeal Tribunal.
[60] *X v Stevens* [2003] ICR 1031 EAT.

otherwise be deterred from bringing a claim. Both levels of tribunal had a power to regulate their own procedure[61] and the EAT said that this should be construed to allow them to make both restricted reporting orders and orders deleting identifying features from the judgment and reasons which were entered in the register.

If Tribunals wish to protect the identity of people involved with allegations of sexual misconduct or disability discrimination, they must use restricted reporting orders. They cannot use their general power to control their own procedure to hear such applications in private or to limit publicity, even if they believe that the restricted reporting order will give inadequate protection[62] although the position may be different if the complainant would otherwise be deterred from asserting an EU right.[63]

The EAT can make restricted reporting orders when it hears appeals against an ET's decision to make or refuse to make a restricted reporting order or when hearing an appeal on some other interlocutory matter.[64] On a further appeal to the Court of Appeal, the court will be likely to restrict reporting in a similar manner.[65]

9–016   The EAT is a superior court of record[66] and has the same rights, powers and privileges as the High Court.[67] It may be, therefore,[68] that it has the same inherent powers as the High Court to either exclude the public or restrict reporting when the stringent tests in *Scott* and *The Leveller* are satisfied (see para.8–066).

Media opposition to a restricted reporting order can be made through representations to the Tribunal (if the Tribunal gives leave). Otherwise, publishers or journalists can apply for judicial review of an Employment Tribunal's order. Since 2000, the legality of the order would also have to be measured against the requirements of Article 10 of the Human Rights Convention and s.12 of the Human Rights Act.

Decisions of the EAT are not subject to judicial review.[69] One (rather clumsy) alternative is for the media group opposing reporting restrictions to apply to become a party to the appeal before the EAT. The EAT has a discretion but will be particularly willing to hear representations from the press when both the appellant and respondent to the appeal are content to have reporting restricted.[70]

---

[61] 2004 ET Rules, r.60.
[62] *R. v Southampton Industrial Tribunal Ex p. INS News Group Ltd* [1995] I.R.L.R. 247; *Chief Constable of West Yorkshire Police v A* (above).
[63] See *X v Stevens* above.
[64] Employment Tribunals Act 1996, s.31; Employment Appeal Tribunal Rules, s.23. Where a sexual offence is alleged, there are restrictions on identifying those who have made or are affected by the allegations which parallel the restrictions in Employment Tribunals.
[65] *X v Z Ltd* [1998] I.C.R. 43, CA.
[66] Employment Tribunals Act 1996, s.20(3).
[67] 1996 Act, s.29(2).
[68] See *Chessington World of Adventures v Reed* (above).
[69] Because, as a superior court of record, it is not subject to judicial review.
[70] *A v B Ex p. News Group Newspapers Ltd* [1998] I.C.R. 55.

IMMIGRATION

Asylum and Immigration Tribunal

The Asylum and Immigration Tribunal hears appeals against the **9–017**
Home Office's refusal to allow immigrants or visitors to enter or to
stay in the country and against deportation decisions. There is a
procedure for obtaining a reconsideration by the Tribunal if its
previous decision was wrong in law. This system which began in 2005
replaced the former two tiers, the first being Immigration Adjudicators and the second level being the Immigration Appeal Tribunal.

The AIT sits in public,[71] although it does have power to exclude all
or any observers where it considers this necessary in the interests of
morals, public order, national security, the interests of minors or
when the private life of the parties so require or when publicity
would prejudice the interests of justice. It may only exercise the
latter power to the extent strictly necessary.[72] It must, however, sit in
private where it is alleged that a passport or other document used to
obtain entry has been forged and disclosure of the method of
detection would be contrary to the public interest. In these cases
even the appellant and his representatives are excluded from the
hearing.[73]

Special Immigration Appeals Commission

Immigration appeals which have a national security dimension are **9–018**
not dealt with in the ordinary way but are heard by the Special
Immigration Appeals Commission which sits in panels of three and
is chaired by a High Court judge. When the Home Office presents
its security sensitive material to the Commission, the appellant and
his representatives are barred from the hearing (although a special
advocate, appointed by the Attorney-General to represent the
appellant's interests, is entitled to remain). From this part of the
proceedings the public must be excluded.[74] From other parts of the
proceedings the Commission can exclude the public for "any other
good reason".[75] The Commission's general practice has been to sit in
public for those sessions where the appellant is entitled to remain.

Immigration Services Tribunal

As a result of concern at the competency and integrity of some **9–019**
immigration "consultants" the Government introduced in 2001 a
system of regulation by an Immigration Services Commissioner.

---

[71] Asylum and Immigration Tribunal (Procedure) Rules 2005 (SI 2005/230) r.54.
[72] 2005 Rules, r.54(4).
[73] Nationality, Immigration and Asylum Act 2002, s.108 and Asylum and Immigration Tribunal (Procedure) Rules 2005, r.54(2).
[74] Special Immigration Appeals Commission (Procedure) Rules 2003 (SI
2003/1034), r.43(1).
[75] 2003 Rules, r.43(2).

Complaints against immigration advisers or representatives are taken to an Immigration Services Tribunal which sits in public unless the Tribunal directs otherwise.[76]

MENTAL HEALTH REVIEW TRIBUNALS

9–020 A matter of perennial interest to certain sections of the press is the danger to the public supposedly created by the release of once manic murderers. In law they are technically manslaughterers who are guilty on grounds of diminished responsibility and have been consigned to one of the four top-security mental hospitals. In many cases their mental illness will, in time, be cured or brought under control so that in fact their release will pose no danger to the public. But the horrendous nature of the original killing (the "index offence") is such that release is politically unpalatable to the Home Secretary and sensibly requires extreme caution. That decision is entrusted to a Mental Health Review Tribunal, a panel usually chaired by a circuit judge and comprising a consultant psychiatrist and a layperson. "Release" comes in stages—to a less secure mental hospital, and then, under restricted conditions, into the community. This last stage is not reached until after many years of psychiatric evaluation and screening, with every opportunity given to the Home Office to oppose it where any risk to the public is apprehended. There are rare cases of reoffending, attended with massive publicity that tends to obscure the fact that the overwhelming majority of releases causes no problems. However, since reassertion of the original mental illness will pose a danger to life, there is a legitimate public interest in press coverage of Mental Health Review Tribunal decisions.

In the interests of the patient, however, very little coverage is permitted by law. The tribunal is a "court" for the purposes of the law of contempt, so that any prejudicial story about an imminent hearing that puts pressure on the tribunal members or upon expert witnesses may give rise to a prosecution.[77] The Mental Health Tribunal Rules require that the tribunal shall sit in private, other than in the rare cases when the patient asks for a hearing in public and the tribunal is satisfied that this would not be contrary to the patient's best interests. The rules additionally and unnecessarily ban publication of information about tribunal proceedings, including the names of individuals who have been involved in them.[78] Even when the patient does request a public hearing and the Tribunal decides that this would be in his best interests, it still has a discretion as to

---

[76] Immigration Services Tribunal Rules 2000 (SI 2000/2739), r.20—complaints against lawyers are channelled to their professional disciplinary bodies, see below para.9–022.

[77] *Pickering v Liverpool Daily Post and Echo Newspapers Plc* [1991] 2 A.C. 238.

[78] Mental Health Review Tribunal Rules (SI 1983/942), r.21.

whether to admit the public. It will need to take account of the fact that its powers to regulate what information is published will not apply if the proceedings are in public. It could decide to hold just part of the proceedings in public, but this is an unsatisfactory option if the public would then get a distorted impression of the proceedings as a whole.[79]

In the important 1991 case of *Pickering v Liverpool Daily Post and Echo Newspapers Plc* the House of Lords interpreted narrowly the ban on publication of tribunal "proceedings" so as to permit the press to publish the fact that a particular patient had made an application for discharge, details of the date, time and place of the tribunal hearing, and the result. The ban was limited to reporting "the substance of the matters which the court has closed its doors to consider", such as evidence and expert reports, or the reasons for the decision and any condition imposed on the patient's release. Alongside this bare information, however, editors are free to republish lurid details of the applicant's original offences. The Law Lords, while conceding the great public concern about release of persons detained for horrifying acts of violence, warned editors against using this freedom to mount a "media campaign" of inflammatory articles against the discharge of an offender whose case is about to be considered by a tribunal. Such a campaign might well be a contempt.[80]

This is one of the few areas where some restriction on publicity is justified, in the interests both of the privacy of the patient and of protecting the tribunal system from a particularly violent form of pressure. The decision in *Pickering* that a tribunal was a "court" for the purposes of contempt overruled a previous High Court decision to the contrary, which had permitted hysterical press campaigns of vilification against certain patients and those psychiatrists who supported their release. The present restrictions seek to strike a balance: they do not preclude the press from describing an applicant's previous history or fears that may still be entertained about his or her stability, but require such stories to be moderate in tone and balanced in factual presentation. It will amount to a breach of confidence for the media to publish details of private psychiatric reports prepared for the purposes of a tribunal hearing; the High Court has held that the public interest defence will in such cases be of no avail. However dangerous the patient may be depicted in the report, the public interest is satisfied if it is transmitted to the authorities, but not to the public at large.[81]

---

[79] *R. (Mersey Care NHS Trust) v Mental Health Review Tribunal (Brady)* [2005] 2 All E.R. 820.
[80] *Pickering v Liverpool Daily Post and Echo Newspapers Plc* [1991] 2 A.C. 238, HL.
[81] Scott J. in *W v Egdell* [1990] Ch.359, CA.

PLANNING INQUIRIES

9–021 Local authorities have a variety of powers to control development and land use in their areas. They can, for instance, refuse planning permission, make orders (enforcement notices) to stop or reverse unpermitted development, and compulsorily purchase land. They must also draw up long-term strategic plans for the development of their area. Objections to these actions are determined by the Secretary of State for the Environment, but in most cases an inspector will be appointed to hear both sides. In general, the inspector takes evidence and hears argument in public, and documentary evidence is open to inspection, although it can be kept private if the Secretary of State is satisfied that it relates to national security or if disclosure would jeopardise the security of any premises in a way that would be contrary to the national interest.[82]

In 2004 the last remaining parts of Crown immunity from the planning system were abolished. The power to exclude the public on national security grounds on the Secretary of State's certificate remains, but there is now a procedure for the appointment of a special advocate (modelled on the Special Immigration Appeals Commission procedure) to represent the interests of objectors when this happens.[83]

For major planning inquiries a Department of Environment Code recommends that a register of participants be prepared, divided into those playing a major part in the proceedings, those wishing to give oral evidence but not otherwise play a major part in the proceedings, and those submitting written representations. The register should be publicly available. The Code also provides that outline statements and certain written submissions will be available to members of the public, who ought also to be able to attend pre-inquiry meetings and programme meetings.[84]

DISCIPLINARY HEARINGS

9–022 Professional complaints are first subjected to an initial review in private and then, if they survive that filter, are considered by a more formal disciplinary body. The usual course is for the formal stage to be conducted in public although the tribunal will have power to sit in private in varying circumstances.[85] In the case of doctors, both the

---

[82] Town and Country Planning Act1990, s.321.

[83] Planning and Compulsory Purchase Act 2004, s.80 amending Town and Country Planning Act 1990, s.321.

[84] DOE 15/96, Annex 4.

[85] See Nursing and Midwifery Council (Fitness to Practice) Rules Order in Council 2004 (SI 2004/1761), rr.4(1) and 19; Veterinary Surgeons and Veterinary Practitioners (Disciplinary Committee) (Procedure and Evidence) Rules 2004 (SI 2004/1680), r.21; General Optical Council (Disciplinary Committee) (Procedure) Rules Order in Council 1985 (SI 1985/1580), r.11; Pharmaceutical Society (Statutory Committee) Order in Council 1978 (SI 1978/20) Reg.16.

filtering and the formal stages are presumptively held in public, although there are several exceptions where the initial Investigating Committee or the Fitness to Practice Panel can or must sit in private.[86] Disciplinary proceedings against lawyers have become more open. The Bar Council's Disciplinary Tribunal must sit in public unless there has been a direction that it should sit in private and this direction has not been overruled by the Tribunal.[87] The Solicitors' Disciplinary Tribunal (SDT) also sits in public.[88] The former practice of requiring appeals to the High Court from the Solicitors' Disciplinary Tribunal to be listed anonymously has been ended after prompting from the Court of Appeal.[89]

The move to greater openness is consistent with the common law's open justice principle. Article 6(1) of the European Human Rights Convention also guarantees litigants a "fair and *public* hearing" in the determination of their civil rights (with limited exceptions). Disciplinary proceedings by professional bodies are included in the concept of "civil rights".[90]

Disciplinary proceedings for police officers are automatically held in private, although where the Independent Police Complaints Commission has investigated the complaint it can direct that the hearing should be in public because of the gravity of the matter or other exceptional circumstances where it is in the public interest to do so.[91] Where the hearing is in private,[92] it may be vulnerable to challenge as contrary to Art.6(1).[93] It is likely that objections to secret hearing could be made by the press or public. Although one purpose of openness is to protect litigants against secret justice, another is to permit reporting so as to maintain public confidence in the courts.[94] The media are in the best position to defend this public interest and in a better position than the "defendant" who often has no desire for the details of his misconduct to receive any publicity.[95]

---

[86] General Medical Council (Fitness to Practice) Rules Order in Council 2004 (SI 2004/2608), r.41.

[87] Bar Council Code of Conduct, Annexe K: Disciplinary Tribunals Regulations 2000, Reg.12.

[88] Solicitors (Disciplinary Procedure) Rules 1994 (SI 1994/288), r.13.

[89] *R. v Legal Aid Board Ex p. Kaim Todner* [1998] 3 All E.R. 541,548 CA.

[90] *Le Compte v Belgium* [1981] 4 E.H.R.R. 1; *Diennet v France* (1995) 21 E.H.R.R. 554.

[91] Police (Conduct) Regulations 2004 (SI 2004/645), Reg.30(1). The Regulations allow a complainant to be present until the Tribunal has decided liability, but only after the complainant has given any evidence—Reg.29. Even appeals to the Police Appeals Tribunal are held in private unless the Tribunal directs otherwise—Police Appeals Tribunals Rules 1999 (SI 1999/818), r.9.

[92] 1999 Rules, Reg.30(5).

[93] See *Diennet v France* above.

[94] See *Diennet v France*, above, at para.33.

[95] *Hakansson v Sweden* (1998) 13 E.H.R.R. 1 establishes that the Art.6 right to a public hearing can be waived but only if this does not conflict with some other important public interest.

Alternatively, this might be a situation where Art.10 does give a right of access to information.[96]

9–023   Article 6 is no help where prison disciplinary hearings are concerned. These can lead to additional loss of liberty since the sanctions can include extra days of imprisonment. They may be heard before an independent adjudicator because Art.6 demands as much. However, both the European Court and the Administrative Court have accepted that the security implications are such that, unusually, the public character of the hearing can be dispensed with.[97] It is different where prisoners are charged with ordinary criminal offences. The public must be admitted to these trials unless one of the express exceptions to Art.6 applies.[98]

At a time when the media demands openness for other tribunals, complaints against the press and broadcasters are swathed in secrecy. Typically and hypocritically, there are no demands by the press to attend PCC hearings or to televise Ofcom hearings.

PUBLIC INQUIRIES

9–024   A familiar government response to a crisis is to appoint a committee to investigate or to announce an inquiry. Inquiries have come in all shapes and sizes and been conducted under a plethora of legal powers. From 1921–2005 some of the biggest set piece investigations were set up under the Tribunal of Inquiries (Evidence) Act 1921. They included the North Wales Child Abuse inquiry under Sir Ronald Waterhouse and the Bloody Sunday Inquiry under Lord Saville. These would normally be held in public with advocates for interested parties questioning witnesses. Others have been held under subject specific legislation such as the inquiries into the Southall and Ladbroke Grove rail accidents which were held under the Health and Safety at Work Act 1974. Inquiries of this kind must be held in public unless the government closes them on national security grounds or a public hearing would be likely to disclose a trade secret.[99] Yet others have been set up ad hoc by ministers with no specific statutory power such as the Inquiry chaired by Lord Hutton into the death of the scientist involved in investigating Iraqi weapons, David Kelly. In practice, access is then dependent on the decision of the person conducting the Inquiry.

A major revision of the law relating to inquiries was made by the Inquiries Act 2005. The 1921 Act was repealed as were a great

---

[96] See Andrew Nicol, Gavin Millar and Andrew Sharland, *Media Law and Human Rights* (Blackstone, 2001), p.131–2.

[97] *R. (Bannatyne) v Secretary of State for the Home Department* [2004] EWHC 1921 (Admin); *Campbell and Fell v UK* (1984) 7 E.H.R.R. 165.

[98] *Riepan v Austria* judgment November 14, 2000.

[99] Health and Safety at Work Act 1974, s.14(3) and Health and Safety Inquiries (procedure regulations 1975 (SI 1975/335), Reg.8(2) and (3).

number of the specific powers to hold inquiries.[100] A minister can now set up an Inquiry under the Act whenever it appears to him that public concern has been caused by particular events which have or may have occurred.[101] Presumptively the public (and the statute expressly includes "reporters") are to be able to attend the inquiry or see a simultaneous transmission of its proceedings and to obtain or view a record of evidence and documents given, produced or provided to the inquiry.[102] However, there are important restrictions. In the first place the arrangements for public attendance and access need only be such as the chairman considers reasonable.[103] More importantly, either the chairman *or the minister* can impose restrictions on public access where this is required by a statutory provision, an EU obligation or rule of law or where the chairman or minister considers a restriction to be conducive to the inquiry fulfilling its task or is necessary in the public interest. Amongst the factors to be taken into account in making this decision is the extent to which not imposing a restriction would delay the inquiry or result in additional cost.[104] The Minister will be responsible for publishing an inquiry's report unless he has passed responsibility for this to the chairman. Whoever is responsible may withhold material if this is required by a statutory provision, an EU obligation or a rule of law or is considered to be necessary in the public interest (but the later does not detract from any obligations under the Freedom of Information Act).[105]

Discretionary decisions by either the Inquiry or the Minister can in principle be challenged by judicial review. As with other judicial reviews, this means demonstrating that the decision was not only wrong or unwise but unlawful. There is an added hurdle. Usually an application for judicial review must be brought "promptly and, in any event, within three months" unless the Court extends time. When the decision is of a minister in relation to a 2005 Act inquiry or of a member of such an inquiry the time limit is shorter. The application must be brought within 14 days of the applicant learning of the decision unless the court extends time.[106]

The powers given by the Act to ministers was highly controversial. **9–025** It has been a common (though not universal) practice to appoint serving or retired judges to conduct inquiries. They are often

---

[100] But not all of them. The Health and Safety at Work 1974 provision continues in force.

[101] Inquiries Act 2005, s.1.

[102] 2005 Act, s.18.

[103] 2005 Act, s.18.

[104] 2005 Act, s.19 A minister issues a restriction notice. The chairman makes a restriction order. Either can be varied or revoked by the person making them and, after the end of the Inquiry, the minister can vary or revoke both orders and notices. Otherwise the restrictions continue indefinitely: s.20.

[105] 2005 Act, s.25.

[106] Inquiries Act 2005, s.38. This time limit does not apply to the contents of the report of the inquiry or where the decision could only have been known after publication of the report—s.38(3).

thought to be suitable for the job because of their supposed ability to sift and assess evidence and because of their reputation for impartiality. But that impartiality and independence is said to be threatened by a legal framework which allows ministers to take decisions, e.g. as to public access against the wishes of the chairman. Lord Saville has said that for this reason he would not have agreed to chair an inquiry under the 2005 Act. So, too, has Judge Peter Cory, a retired member of the Canadian Supreme Court who conducted a number of inquiries into suspicious deaths in Northern Ireland.

In line with the principle first established by Lord Salmon, those who may be criticised by an inquiry should be given advance warning and an opportunity to respond. The Inquiry Rules 2006 made for the purpose of the Inquiries Act specifically requires these to be sent and specifically provides that they are confidential.[107] People closely involved with the matters under investigation can apply to be designated "core participants" who may be given the opportunity to question witnesses after the witnesses have responded to questions from counsel to the inquiry. Core participants are also sent advance copies of the Inquiry's report. This, too, is to be treated as confidential until the report is formally published.[108]

When can the government be obliged to hold a public inquiry against its wishes? An important precedent was set by the Divisional Court in 2000 when it ruled that the Secretary of State for Health had acted unlawfully by stipulating that the inquiry into Dr Harold Shipman should hear evidence in private. Shipman had been convicted of murdering 15 of his elderly patients and was suspected of killing many more. The case was of massive public interest and the families of the victims had pressed for a public inquiry. Their Art.10 rights to communicate freely the evidence which they gave to the inquiry was a major factor in the court's reasoning.[109] After the court's decision, the government appointed a Tribunal of Inquiry under the 1921 Act. It was chaired by a High Court judge, Mrs Justice Smith. However, in two later cases the Administrative Court emphasised that normally it will be for the minister to decide whether an inquiry should be held in public and Art.10 did not give a right to obtain information from a public authority which was unwilling to impart it.[110]

Another reason why the government might be obliged to hold an inquiry in public is Art.2 ECHR. The express obligation to protect the right to life is accompanied by an implied positive obligation to investigate cases where the state or a public authority has or may have played a part in a person's death or potentially fatal injury.[111]

---

[107] Inquiries Rules 2006 (SI 2006/1838), r.14.
[108] 2006 Rules, r.17.
[109] *R. v Secretary of State for Health Ex p. Wagstaff* [2001] 1 W.L.R. 292.
[110] *Persey v Secretary of State for Environment Food and Rural Affairs* [2003] QB 794; *Howard v Secretary of State for Health* [2003] QB 830.
[111] See e.g. *Amin v Secretary of State for the Home Department* [2004] 1 A.C. 653.

Where the person concerned has died, this obligation will usually be fulfilled by a coroner's inquest but there will be no inquest, of course, if death was averted. In 2006 the Court of Appeal held that the Home Secretary was obliged by Art.2 to hold a public inquiry into an attempted suicide by a prisoner who was a known suicide risk.[112]

OTHER TRIBUNALS

The pattern we have observed—namely a presumption of publicity **9–026** coupled with a discretion to sit in private—is common to most other tribunals. The extent of the discretion varies widely. It may be dependent on proof of "exceptional reasons"[113] or where one party would be prejudiced by publicity[114] or the discretion may be limited to cases where disclosure would be "contrary to the public interest"[115] or where the tribunal is satisfied that by reason of disclosure of confidential matters or matters concerning national security it would be just and reasonable to hold the hearing in private.[116] All of these formulae require the tribunal to exercise some judgment which, if adverse to media rights, can be judicially reviewed because of an error of law. The requirements mean that the presence of bureaucratic embarrassment is not enough to put the hearing into closed session. Much more objectionable are rules which require the hearing to take place in private unless both parties (as well as the tribunal) agree to allow the public to attend.[117] This is to turn the Art.6 presumption in favour of open hearings on its head and, when the right in issue is what Art.6 describes as a "civil" right, is ripe for challenge under the Human Rights Act.

Oral hearings by Social Security Appeals Tribunals are conducted in public unless the chairman is satisfied that the hearing should be in private for reasons of national security, morals, public order or the interests of children or to protect the private or family life of one of the parties or where because of special circumstances publicity would prejudice the interests of justice.[118]

---

[112] *R. (D (A patient by his litigation friend the Official Solicitor) v Secretary of State for the Home Department, The Times* [2006] 3 All E.R. 946 CA.

[113] Agricultural Land Tribunals, which decide whether a farmer has acted fairly in evicting tenants from a tied house, Agricultural Land Tribunal (Rules) Order 1978 (SI 1978/259), R.24.

[114] e.g. appeals against valuations for council tax purposes: Council Tax (Alteration of Lists and Appeals) Regulations 1993 (SI 1993/290), R.25(3).

[115] e.g. The Gas (Underground Storage) (Inquiries Procedure) Rules 1966 (SI 1966/1375), R.8(4).

[116] Lands Tribunal Rules 1996 (SI 1996/1022), r.5.

[117] Information Tribunal (National Security Appeals) 2005 (SI 2005/13), r.24.

[118] Social Security and Child Support (Decisions and Appeals) Regulations 1999 (SI 1999/991), r.49(6).

TELEVISING TRIBUNALS

9–027   The prohibition on televising proceedings applies to any "court of justice (including the court of a coroner)".[119] Whether a tribunal is a "court of justice" can be difficult question (see below under "contempt" para.9–029). Where a tribunal or Inquiry is not a court of justice, the issue of whether its proceedings can be broadcast is probably a matter for the discretion of the tribunal or its chair. This is expressly stated in the Inquiries Act 2005 which says that inquiries under that Act cannot be broadcast unless the Chairman consents.[120] The attitude towards televising courts has undergone a sea change in recent years: the Bar is now in favour, and the electronic media is beginning to televise some tribunal proceedings.

In the case of Royal Commissions and major public inquiries the argument for the right to broadcast proceedings is overwhelming. The very purpose of establishing a Tribunal of Inquiry or an inquiry under the 2005 Act is to restore public confidence by establishing the truth about allegations or events that have caused grave disquiet; and public confidence is best restored after the public have been able to see or hear for themselves the testimony and the procedures.[121] Since televising is the best evidence compared with a second hand report in a newspaper, public understanding is likely to be enhanced. Since television reaches a larger audience than newspapers, it assists the Tribunal process: members of the public may come forward with evidence or ideas or ideas if they become aware of the Inquiry or its focus.

More generally, the public character of such an inquiry can best come from the broadcasting of its proceedings. This was the conclusion of Louis Blom-Cooper Q.C., who in 1990 opened to radio and television his Antiguan Royal Commission on the smuggling of arms to the Colombian drug cartels. His report concludes:

> "My fears of physical obstruction were entirely misplaced: one single television camera behind Counsel, trained for the most part on the witness, soon went entirely unnoticed. No lights or other studio impedimenta were required. It was observed that some Counsel, who at first disdained microphones, very quickly and effortlessly learned to use them. The witnesses were in no way flustered or deterred, or for the most part even conscious of the recording. I am confident that they remained blissfully unaware that their evidence was going to be relayed to the populace. If they were aware, they raised no objection and showed no sign of disquiet, let alone dissent. Several senior

---

[119] Criminal Justice Act 1925, s.45 as amended by Constitutional Reform Act 2005.
[120] Inquiries Act 2005, s.18(2).
[121] Lord Salmon, *Tribunals of Inquiry*, 1967 Lionel Cohen Memorial Lecture, published by the Hebrew University, Jerusalem.

Counsel indicated to me that they felt an extremely beneficial discipline to ask relevant and comprehensible questions, and not to waste time. I felt, myself, the sense of Jeremy Bentham's argument in favour of open justice, namely, that 'it keeps the judge, while trying, under trial'. That the Commission proceeded as effectively and efficiently as it did, is, in my view, due in some measure to the fact that we could all be heard and seen . . . each evening on radio and television. The benefits of electronic media coverage, in terms of public understanding, were incalculable. It meant that citizens could receive accurate information about a great public scandal, and make up their own minds about the testimony. Although I accept that electronic media coverage of criminal trials requires a very careful and gradual introduction, I hope that it will come to be considered routine for public inquiries."[122]

Some progress has been made in this respect. The evidence given **9–028** to the Southall Train crash was televised and in the Ladbroke Grove rail crash inquiry the opening and closing speeches were broadcast. In 2000 Lord Mackay of Clashfern, the former Lord Chancellor, permitted live television coverage of his Commission into the Administration of Justice in Trinidad: he pronounced his satisfaction that the public were able to see the evidence and cross-examination of politicians, judges and frustrated litigants. No legal challenge was ever mounted to the exclusion of their cameras from inquiries of such public importance as those into the Matrix Churchill "arms to Iraq" scandal, the Stephen Lawrence murder and the responsibility for BSE (bovine spongiform encephalopathy). Instead of asserting the viewers' right to know what is going on at these inquiries, television companies settled instead for "dramatic reconstruction" which is nothing like the real thing. It took an American company—CNN—at the Harold Shipman Inquiry to assert the alternative and simple proposition that a public inquiry into a public scandal should actually be seen by the public—and on television.[123] Smith J. exercised her discretion in favour of permitting cameras to cover the most important part of the Inquiry, when police and health officials would be questioned about their failure to detect Shipman's multiple murders. Although prepared to exempt distressed witnesses (such as distressed relatives of murder victims and Shipman's employees) the Judge ruled that;

"witnesses who are professionally qualified or are public servants or have clearly defined duties, for which they have received training, should in my view be prepared to accept [the process of

---

[122] Louis Blom-Cooper, *Guns for Antigua* (Duckworth, 1990), p.46.
[123] See above, para.9–025.

broadcasting] whether or not they might face challenging cross examination and possible criticism in the Report".[124]

Both Smith J. and Lord Hutton when holding the Kelly Inquiry rejected the argument that Art.10 obliged them to permit the proceedings to be filmed. In Lord Hutton's case he allowed the opening and closing statements to be broadcast, but not the evidence from witnesses.[125] ITV had not applied to film the relatives or family of Dr David Kelly, but only the politicians and public servants who were due to give evidence. It is hard to believe that their evidence would have been different if it had been televised. Televising the lawyers is a start, but it is no substitute for allowing the public to make up its own collective mind as to the evidence.

CONTEMPT

9–029 The 1981 Contempt of Court Act imposes strict liability in relation to stories that create a substantial risk of serious prejudice to active "legal proceedings".[126] "Legal proceedings", for the purposes of the Act, are proceedings that take place in a court, defined to include "any tribunal or body exercising the judicial power of the state".[127] Most of the lesser courts and tribunals discussed in this chapter have no power to take action of their own volition against the media, but the High Court has an overall supervisory power to punish contempt of "inferior courts".[128] The question thus becomes one of deciding whether a particular body is a court, albeit an "inferior" one. That question, an absolutely crucial one for the media, has no simple answer although guidance comes from general principles, applied on a case by case basis.

The general rule is that contempt covers all bodies that exercise the judicial power of the State. The meaning of this phrase was considered in the important 1980 case of *Att-Gen v BBC*[129]:

> The BBC had made a programme that was extremely critical of the Exclusive Brethren. One branch of the sect had applied for rate relief to a local valuation court, and the case was to be heard a few days after the BBC proposed to transmit the film. The Attorney-General was granted an injunction to stop it, on the grounds that it would prejudice the Brethren's claim. The House of Lords held that the injunction was

---

[124] *The Shipman Inquiry: Application by Cable News Network (CNN)* October 25, 2002, para.98.
[125] See *The Hutton Inquiry* ruling of August 5, 2003 at *http://www.the-hutton-inquiry.org.uk*.
[126] See further Lowe and Rawlings, "Tribunals and the Administration of Justice" [1982] *Public Law* 418.
[127] Contempt of Court Act 1981, s.19.
[128] Civil Proced Rules, Sch.1; RSC, O.52, 1(2)(a)(iii).
[129] [1980] 3 All E.R. 161, HL.

wrongly given: a local valuation court did not exercise the judicial power of the State, and hence could not be protected from contempt.

The judgments of the Law Lords will be sifted for dicta of help in **9–030** deciding the issue in relation to other tribunals; their individual approaches to the question were as follows:

> Viscount Dilhorne drew a distinction between courts that discharge judicial functions and those that discharge administrative ones, and said that contempt did not apply in relation to the latter. He suggested, albeit in passing and inferentially, that immigration adjudicators, the Immigration. Appeal Tribunal, the Lands Tribunal, pension appeal tribunals, the Transport Tribunal, the Commons Commissioners and the Performing Rights Tribunal were not to be regarded as courts that would put the media at risk of a contempt action. Lord Salmon adopted an approach particularly favourable to the media. He said:

> > "Public policy requires that most of the principles relating to contempt of court which have for ages necessarily applied to the long-established inferior courts such as county courts, magistrates' courts, courts martial, coroners' courts and consistory courts shall not apply to valuation courts and the host of other modern tribunals which may be regarded as inferior courts; otherwise the scope of contempt of court would be unnecessarily extended and accordingly freedom of speech and freedom of the press would be unnecessarily contracted."

Lord Scarman accepted that courts martial and Church courts exercised, for historic reasons, the judicial power of the State and were protected in consequence. However, he took the view that legal policy was against protecting administrative courts and tribunals: if Parliament wanted to provide special protection, it must say so in the legislation establishing the body in question:

> "I would not think it desirable to extend the doctrine (of contempt) which is unknown, and not apparently needed, in most civilized legal systems, beyond its historical scope, namely the proceedings of courts of judicature. If we are to make the extension, we have to ask ourselves, if the United Kingdom is to comply with its international obligations, whether the extension is necessary in our democratic society. Is there a "pressing social need" for the extension?"

Lord Edmund-Davies and Lord Fraser were more circumspect, although the former echoed Lord Scarman's view that contempt protection to tribunals and other bodies ought to be given specifically by Parliament, and that the courts themselves should not extend contempt proceedings unless it is clear beyond doubt that the demands of justice make them essential".

The upshot of those judicial approaches is that contempt protec- **9–031** tion will not readily be extended, in the absence of statutory provision, to any "lesser" court or tribunal. It can be said with confidence that a Court Martial[130] and Church courts[131] are protected, although since the former are conducted by officers (and see para.9–007) and the latter by a distinguished judge or lawyer, the danger of a media story creating a serious risk of substantial prejudice is relatively small. Lord Salmon, in the passage quoted above, assumed that coroners' courts were protected and the Divisional Court has since confirmed that this is the case.[132] A coroners' court becomes "active" for the purpose of the strict liability rule as soon as the inquest is opened (which will usually be shortly after the death) even though the proceedings are then adjourned for a considerable time while the police carry out their investigations.[133] Employment Tribunals are "courts"[134] and so are Mental Health Review Tribunals (see para.9–020).

In all other cases the presumption must be that contempt does not apply. Planning inquiries make administrative rather than judicial decisions. Although professional bodies must act judicially, they do not wield the State's authority. The Court of Appeal in 1998 firmly applied the rule in *Att-Gen v BBC* to quash an attempt by the General Medical Council (the doctors' disciplinary body) to claim that it was a court protected from BBC criticism by the law of contempt.[135] Similarly, arbitrators who are appointed to resolve a contractual dispute derive their authority from the private parties and not from the Government. When local authorities are considering applications for licences for selling alcohol, gambling or the numerous other activities which require a licence, they are acting administratively and are not protected by the contempt jurisdiction.

---

[130] *The Daily Sketch and Graphic* was fined £500 for contempt because, at the time, the sentence could not be published at all until it was confirmed by the defendant's commanding officer: *R. v Gunn Ex p. Att-Gen (No. 2)*, *The Times*, November 14, 1953; [1954] Crim L.R. 53. This is no longer the case. Instead the 1981 Act provides that the proceedings are active until the completion of any review of a finding or sentence (Sch.1, para.8). This means that reporting and comment are permitted as long as they do not cause substantial risk of serious prejudice. The Armed Forces Act 2006 allows a Court Martial to deal with certain contempts themselves (e.g. a refusal by a witness to answer questions, to take the stand or to produce any document which the Court Martial requires)— see s.309. If the person concerned is not subject to service law, the maximum penalty is a fine up to level 5—see s.309(3). Otherwise the Court Martial can certify an alleged contempt to be dealt with by a civilian court—see s.311.

[131] Ecclesiastical Jurisdiction Measure 1963, s.81(2) expressly gives the High Court power to punish contempt of Church courts. For a rare example, see *R. v Daily Herald Ex p. Bishop of Norwich* [1932] 2 K.B. 402. The procedure is now modelled on that for inquiries under the Inquiries Act 2005 (see para.9–024): Care of Churches and Ecclesiastical Jurisdictional Measure 1991, s.8 and Sch.4, para.11.

[132] *R. v West Yorkshire Coroner Ex p. Smith* [1985] 1 All E.R. 100.

[133] *Peacock v London Weekend Television* (1985) 150 J.P. 71.

[134] *Peach Grey and Co (a firm) v Sommers* [1995] I.C.R. 549, Q.B.D.

[135] *General Medical Council v BBC* [1998] 1 W.L.R. 1573, CA.

Even if the body in question does exercise "the judicial power of the state", the High Court could penalise a newspaper or broadcaster only if the story satisfied the other requirements of contempt. In brief, the proceedings must have been active (i.e. the publication must have taken place before a hearing date was fixed, and before final disposal). The story must also pose a substantial risk of serious prejudice. None of the tribunals considered here (except on occasions the coroner's court) has a jury. Most are presided over or advised by persons with some legal experience. It will be rare for a story to create the necessary risk of prejudice to amount to contempt. And it must be remembered that even prejudicial material of this kind can be published if it is part of a discussion in good faith of public affairs and the risk of prejudice is only incidental (see further para.7–033).

If the body is a "court", then reports of its proceedings have the **9–032** same protection from contempt as other fair and accurate reports of legal proceedings. These cannot breach the strict liability rule unless the tribunal has made a postponement order (see para.8–076). Lesser courts probably may not even have power to make postponement orders or to ban publication of evidence that was not given publicly—the matter is undecided, although one appeal judge has said that if they do possess this power, they should hardly ever use it.[136]

Tribunals of Inquiry under the 1921 Act were treated by the Contempt of Court Act as analogous to courts for the purposes of the strict liability rule.[137] There is no equivalent provision in the Inquiries Act 2005 for the inquiries under that Act which have now replaced Tribunals of Inquiry and so there is no question of newspaper comment infringing the strict liability rule in relation to a 2005 Act Inquiry.[138]

However, like Tribunals of Inquiry, the chairman of a 2005 Act Inquiry can refer to the High Court a failure to comply with a restriction notice (i.e. a notice restricting public access to the inquiry or to documents or information) or a notice to produce evidence or an order of the Inquiry. The High Court will examine the matter and, if it is found proved, can punish the offender as though he was in contempt of court.[139] It is these powers which will be used if Inquiries seek to press journalists to reveal their sources. Inquiries cannot compel testimony which a witness could not be required to give in civil proceedings.[140] Consequently both before the Inquiry

---

[136] *R. v Horsham Justices Ex p. Farquharson* [1982] 2 All E.R. 269, 284 *per* Lord Denning.

[137] Contempt of Court Act 1981, s.20.

[138] If, however, a journalist, editor or publisher knew or believed that a publication was likely to distort any evidence or prevent evidence from being given he would be guilty of an offence under Inquires Act 2005 s.35(2)—see below.

[139] Inquiries Act 2005, s.36.

[140] 2005 Act, s.22.

and in any subsequent court proceedings, journalists can rely on s.10 of Contempt of Court Act and Art.10 ECHR (see para.5–061). But these are not reliable bulwarks against orders to compel disclosure as journalists from ITN and the Sunday Telegraph discovered when confronted with orders from the Saville Inquiry to disclose their sources. In the event, the Tribunal did not go ahead with contempt proceedings, but the experience demonstrates that confrontations between inquiries or tribunals and journalists defending confidential sources are a very real risk.[141] Failure to comply with a notice to attend to give evidence or to produce documents can also be prosecuted as a summary offence by the chairman of the inquiry.[142]

9–033   Toby Harnden, a Sunday Telegraph journalist had interviewed soldiers who had been on duty in Derry during Bloody Sunday about their attitude if summoned to give evidence without the protection of anonymity. Some of his sources had said that they would then feign amnesia. Harnden destroyed his notebooks in order, he said, to avoid their disclosure to the Inquiry. Lord Saville referred this matter to the DPP of Northern Ireland (who took no action). Lord Saville himself instituted contempt proceedings against Harnden for contempt for refusal to name his sources, but these were also abandoned at the conclusion of the Tribunal's evidence gathering phase. The Harnden incident, though, seems to have inspired a new offence of doing anything during the course of an inquiry which is intended or which the person concerned knows or believes is likely to have the effect of distorting or altering evidence or a document that is given or produced to the inquiry or preventing any evidence, document or other thing from being given, produced or provided to the inquiry. Proceedings can only be instituted with the consent of the DPP.[143]

These are summary offences carrying a maximum sentence in England and Wales of 51 weeks (6 months in Scotland).[144]

LIBEL

9–034 Media reports of proceedings and decisions of lesser courts and tribunals are protected from libel actions, but with varying degrees of efficacy. Reports about lesser courts that, nonetheless, exercise the judicial power of the State (i.e. those to which contempt law is applicable) will be fully protected by absolute privilege. Reports of

---

[141] It is a salutary reminder that the last journalists to be imprisoned in England for failing to disclose a source were three who defied orders of the Vassall Tribunal —*Att-Gen v Mulholland and Fraser* [1963] 1 All E.R. 767 CA ; *Att-Gen v Clough* [1963] 1 Q.B. 773, although this was long before the advent of the 1981 Act and *Goodwin v UK*.

[142] 2005 Act, s.35(1).

[143] 2005 Act, s.35(2) and (6).

[144] 2005 Act, s.35(8).

proceedings in most other bodies will be protected by qualified privilege at common law, while in a few cases a special statutory privilege can be claimed only if the newspaper carrying the defamatory report has offered the victim a right of reply.

Absolute privilege

The best defence that a newspaper can have to a defamation action **9–035** is that the report is absolutely privileged. This means that the person libelled has no claim, even if it can be shown that the paper acted maliciously in publishing its story (see para.8–118). This defence, not surprisingly, is reserved to a narrow class of reports.[145] It applies only to reports of those bodies which are classified as "courts", i.e. they must exercise the judicial power of the State.[146] This is the same definition as is used in the Contempt of Court Act. Thus in those cases where the media are at risk of committing contempt under the strict liability rule, they at least have the benefit of absolute privilege against libel actions for reports of those proceedings. Reports of proceedings of an inquiry appointed under the Inquiries Act 2005 have the same protection as court reports and so they too will be capable of enjoying absolute privilege.[147] The further conditions are that the reports must be fair and accurate and contemporaneous and the proceedings must have been in public.

Qualified privilege

Qualified privilege is lost only if the publisher is malicious (see **9–036** para.3–056). There is a statutory qualified privilege defence in a variety of situations where publication is about a matter of public concern and is for the public benefit.[148] These situations include fair and accurate reports of public proceedings held before a court anywhere in the world. Thus this provision gives protection even if the report is not contemporaneous with the proceedings. Qualified privilege also attaches to fair and accurate reports of proceedings in public of a person appointed to hold a public inquiry by a government or legislature anywhere in the world or a fair and accurate copy of or extract from any register or other document which is required by law to be open to public inspection. A notice or advertisement published by or on the authority of a court or of a judge or officer of a court anywhere in the world also attracts qualified privilege as does a fair and accurate copy of or extract from matter published by or on the authority of a government or legislature anywhere in the world.

In all of these cases, the privilege is not contingent on offering a right of reply. A further and wider class of reports also attracts

---

[145] Law of Libel Amendment Act 1888, s.3.
[146] Defamation Act 1996, s.14.
[147] Inquiries Act 2005, s.37(3).
[148] See Defamation Act 1996, s.15 and Sch.1, Pt.I.

qualified privilege but not if the publisher refused or neglected to publish in a suitable manner a reasonable letter or statement by way of explanation or contradiction.[149] The burden is on the victim to propose the wordings: a newspaper is not obliged to compose its own correction if it received only a general demand for an apology.[150] A reply can also be rejected as being unreasonable if it is immoderate or if it attacks third parties (see para.3–073).

The situations where qualified privilege comes subject to a right of reply include[151] reports of public proceedings before magistrates acting otherwise than as a court, of a commission, tribunal, committee or person appointed for the purposes of any inquiry by any statutory provision, by the Queen, by a minister or by the Northern Ireland Executive. The Act also gives qualified privilege to reports of private sports, trade and cultural associations when acting in a quasi-judicial capacity (e.g. disciplining their members) or deciding matters of general concern to the association. None of these reports attract qualified privilege unless they are fair and accurate, the matter is of public concern and publication is for the public benefit.[152] On the other hand, the report does not have to be contemporaneous. It does not have to be self-contained and, if fair and accurate, can be extremely brief.[153]

---

[149] Defamation Act 1996, s.15(2) and Sch.1, Pt.II.
[150] *Khan v Ahmed* [1957] 2 All E.R. 385.
[151] What follows is only a summary, the Act should be consulted for the details.
[152] Defamation Act 1996, s.15(3). This issue is decided by the jury *Kingshott v Associated Kent Newspapers Ltd* [1991] 1 Q.B. 880, CA, unless, as in *Tsikata* (below) the issue of whether the publication was privileged is tried as a preliminary issue, in which case the judge will decide.
[153] *Tsikata v Newspaper Publishing Plc* [1997] 1 All E.R. 655, CA, where the report was contained in two sentences.

CHAPTER 10

REPORTING PARLIAMENTS, ASSEMBLIES AND ELECTIONS

INTRODUCTION

Parliament has a special importance to the media quite apart from **10–001** its function as a forum for announcement and debate of Government policy. It shares with courts the privilege of being a place where allegations can be made, on any matter at all, and reported without risk. The privilege of free speech is guaranteed to all members of both Houses in the ninth article of the Bill of Rights of 1688, which declares:

> "That the freedom of speech and debates or proceedings in Parliament ought not to be impeached or questioned in any court or place out of Parliament."

The language of the Bill of Rights is unambiguous. The principle has remained that no M.P. or peer may be brought before the civil or criminal courts for any utterance in parliamentary proceedings. With limited exceptions of largely theoretical interest, the media is entitled to a similar immunity in publishing these utterances. It follows that matters that cannot be mentioned in the media may, if ventilated in the course of a parliamentary question or debate, become public knowledge. There have been many occasions on which journalists have primed M.P.s to raise matters that could not otherwise be made public: the truth about the traitors Kim Philby, Sir Anthony Blunt and the unnecessarily secretive Colonel H.A. Johnstone ("Colonel B") were revealed by this device. Journalists who use an M.P. to raise a matter that cannot otherwise be put into print will lose exclusivity in the story (in the sense that other media will pick it up), but may be the first with the background detail that can be published in consequence. Parliamentary privilege can even trump a court injunction: in 1996 it was used by back-bench M.P. Brian Sedgemore to name the politically prominent father whose identity the courts had striven to protect in the *Re Z* case (see para.8–057). In 2006 a rape complainant whose allegation had been rejected by a jury was named in Parliament. This was despite the fact that the trial judge (who was best placed to decide whether her evidence was made up or simply unconvincing) had not lifted the reporting restriction.

The extent to which parliamentary privilege may be used to avoid a court injunction was explored both in the courts and in Parliament when Labour M.P.s booked a Committee Room in the House of Commons in order to show a private copy of the "Zircon" film in Duncan Campbell's *Secret Society* series, which was subject to an injunction on the grounds that its television transmission was not in the national interest:

> The Attorney-General asked a High Court judge to prohibit the screening within parliamentary precincts, arguing that this would amount to a contempt of court. Mr Justice Kennedy refused on the grounds that it was for Parliament to regulate its own proceedings. The Speaker of the House of Commons was reluctant to ban the screening; he did so only after being privately briefed by the Attorney-General that the screening would be "seriously harmful" to national security. The Committee of Privileges concluded that he had acted correctly in exercising his power of control over the Palace of Westminster. He was not interfering with Parliamentary privilege, since an M.P.'s private arrangement to show a film within the precincts of the House was not "a proceeding in Parliament". But the Committee reaffirmed the principle that there is nothing (other than their own judgment) to prevent M.P.s from divulging information that may damage national security in the course of parliamentary debates or committees. The Privileges Committee endorsed, as an absolute rule, the principle that any M.P. "must be free to make public, in the course of proceedings in Parliament, information which he believes should be published".[1]

10–002   The Bill of Rights does not protect M.P.s from the legal consequences of their statements outside the House and reports of such statements are vulnerable to actions for libel and contempt. Nor does the Bill of Rights safeguard M.P.s against discipline imposed by their colleagues for abuses of privilege. On numerous occasions M.P.s have been censured or admonished for breaches of the rules of the House, which oblige the Speaker to disallow questions and comment on a wide range of issues, including matters in current litigation in the courts. An M.P. who is determined to ventilate an issue of public importance can often "slip it past the Speaker" and consequently into print, at some risk of a retrospective reprimand. Questions of breach of parliamentary privilege by M.P.s or by the press are generally referred to the Privileges Committee, which reports back to the House.

Article 9 is a blunt instrument. By conferring absolute immunity on M.P.s and peers for what they say in Parliament it allows no

---

[1] First Report from the Committee of Privileges, *Speaker's order of 22 January 1987 on a matter of national security*, H.C. 365 (1986–87).

assessment of whether their words truly were in the public interest or whether any harm which they did was justifiable. The potential for conflict with Convention rights, particularly rights to private and family life, is real. In one adjournment debate on social housing, a Tory M.P. wanted to speak about problem neighbours (which was fair enough) but went on to give a one-sided and controversial critique of a particular single mother whose name and address he spelt out (which was far from fair). She was forced to move and her children were verbally abused. The European Court of Human Rights held nonetheless that his absolute immunity from suit for words spoken in Parliament was compatible with Arts 6 and 8 of the Convention. It found that very many European countries had similar provisions. An absolute immunity was justified and even the threat of an unmeritorious law suit might deter M.P.s from freely expressing themselves.[2] Where the complaint is of defamatory allegations, Parliament should consider affording the person concerned a privileged reply to the privileged attack.

Article 9 of the Bill of Rights has been interpreted in a succession of cases as meaning that proceedings in Parliament cannot be examined in courts of law without the permission of the House itself. Thus the Church of Scientology, attempting to sue an M.P. for his criticism (made outside the House) of its methods, could not rebut his plea of "fair comment" with evidence of malice relating to what had taken place in Parliament.[3]

The rule in the Bill of Rights was underpinned by a constitutional 10–003 convention that Parliament and the courts both respected each other's sphere of influence. Thus it also applied in the reverse situation from that in the *Church of Scientology* case—so that if a newspaper was sued by a parliamentarian it could not as part of its defence call into question anything which the claimant had said or done as part of Parliament's proceedings. The Privy Council (in an appeal from New Zealand) rejected the argument that by bringing the action the claimant had waived privilege.[4] The court said that the privilege belonged to Parliament (or the House to which the claimant belonged) and it was not for the individual member to waive it. At the same time the court recognised that there was scope for tremendous injustice if the claimant was awarded damages for a well-deserved attack on his reputation which the defendant was precluded from defending as true. The court resolved the quandary by ruling that if privilege seriously hampered the defendant in the conduct of its defence, the action would be stayed as an abuse of process. Famously, the libel action by Neil Hamilton M.P. against the *Guardian* over its articles alleging that he accepted "cash for questions" was stayed on these grounds in 1995.

---

[2] *A v UK* (2003) 36 E.H.R.R. 51.
[3] *Church of Scientology of California v Johnson-Smith* [1972] 1 All E.R. 294.
[4] *Prebble v Television New Zealand* [1995] 1 A.C. 321.

The Defamation Bill then passing through Parliament was amended in direct response to this decision. Hamilton complained to the Prime Minister and the Lord Chancellor, who took uncalled-for pity on him and promoted an ill-thought out amendment, now s.13 of the Defamation Act 1996. It provides:

> "where the conduct of a person in or in relation to proceedings in Parliament is in issue in defamation proceedings, he may waive for the purpose of those proceedings, so far as concerns him, the protection of any enactment or rule of law which prevents proceedings in Parliament being impeached in any court or place out of Parliament".

This was a controversial measure which a Joint Committee of Privileges later recommended should be replaced by a system requiring the House as a whole to agree to the waiver of privilege.[5] It means that an action for defamation brought by an M.P. need no longer be stayed if the M.P. waives his privilege and thus removes the inhibition on the media defendant probing his parliamentary behaviour as part of its defence. Neil Hamilton made use of the new right by waiving his privilege and reviving his action against the *Guardian*. His case collapsed on the eve of the trial when cabinet documents the newspaper obtained on discovery showed that he had told lies. After the Parliamentary Commissioner for Standards, Sir Gordon Downey, had produced a report that condemned Mr Hamilton over "compelling evidence" that he had received cash from Mohammed Al Fayed for asking questions in his interests in Parliament, he began yet another libel action this time against Al Fayed himself. Again he used his right to waive Parliamentary privilege. The defendant tried to have the action struck out on the argument that an individual M.P. could not waive the autonomous right of Parliament to investigate the conduct of its members. By the time the House of Lords finally rejected this,[6] the libel action had been heard and Mr Hamilton's claim had been rejected by the jury. Even so, s.13 had unfairly hampered Al Fayed's defence. What Downey found particularly "compelling" was that Hamilton's close M.P. colleague, Tim Smith, had been accused of receiving cash in the same way, for similar services: he had admitted the truth of the allegation. But because Smith refused to waive parliamentary privilege, the libel jury could not be told the details of the striking similarity. Section 13 causes obvious injustice to the media when it cannot tell the full truth about M.P.s, some of whom waive privilege and some of whom do not. In this situation, it may still be necessary for a court to consider whether there can be a fair trial or whether the proceedings have to be stopped.

---

[5] Report of Joint Committee of Privilege (1998–99) H.L. Paper 43–1, H.C. 214–1, pp.23–29.

[6] *Hamilton v Al Fayed* [2001] 1 A.C. 395.

The old rule that the House had to give its permission for *Hansard* to be referred to in court has long gone and *Hansard* can be quoted in relevant cases without leave.[7] Since the House of Lords abolished the rule that *Hansard* could not be consulted to determine the intention of Parliament in passing legislation,[8] references to *Hansard* in legal argument have become much more common.

THE PRIVILEGES FOR REPORTING PARLIAMENTARY DEBATES

In the course of his decision in *Att-Gen v Times Newspapers*, Lord Denning stated: "Whatever comments are made in Parliament, they can be repeated in the newspapers without any fear of an action for libel or proceedings for contempt of court."[9] This is a sound enough summary of the practical position, although it may not strictly accord with the law. In 1813 an M.P. was convicted of criminal libel contained in a copy of a speech delivered in the House that he afterwards circulated.[10] The authority of the case today is doubtful, although it was relied upon by the Director of Public Prosecutions in rather extraordinary circumstances in 1977: **10–004**

> The controversial prosecution of journalists Duncan Campbell and Crispin Aubrey under the Official Secrets Act featured an expert witness from the Ministry of Defence, "Colonel B". The acronym was alleged by the Crown to be necessary in the interests of national security. The falsity of this claim was exposed by the *Leveller* and *Peace News*, which published the Colonel's true identity, which was discoverable from regimental magazines. The Attorney-General commenced proceedings against the newspapers for contempt of court (see para.8–075). Before the case was heard, four sympathetic M.P.s contrived to mention the Colonel's real name—H. A. Johnstone—in the course of oral questions in the House. The DPP immediately issued a statement to press and broadcasting organisations advising them not to disclose the identity of Colonel B in their reports of the day's proceedings, on the grounds that it might amount to contempt of court. Almost every national newspaper ignored this advice, and radio and television news programmes broadcast the tape of the M.P.s asking their cover-blowing questions. There was an immediate constitutional rumpus, as the media invoked its privilege to publish proceedings in the House and some M.P.s demanded that the DPP be punished for contempt of Parliament. The Attorney-General, who was compromised in the whole affair, had the behaviour of the four M.P.s referred to the Committee of Privileges, but declined to test the

---

[7] Resolution of Houses of Parliament, October 31, 1980.
[8] *Pepper v Hart* [1993] A.C. 593.
[9] [1973] 1 All E.R. 815, 823, reversed on other grounds [1973] 3 All E.R. 54.
[10] *R. v Creevey* (1813) 1 M. and S. 273; 105 E.R. 102.

position by prosecuting any media organisation for contempt of court.[11]

The "Colonel B" affair sheds little light on the technical question of whether the media can ever be liable for contempt or any other criminal offence by reporting words uttered, in breach of the rules of the House, by truculent M.P.s. It did, however, underline the practical impossibility of taking action, given the simultaneous broadcasting of parliamentary sessions. The DPP's advice was wrong in that no contempt could have been committed in any event, either in relation to the Divisional Court hearing or to the magistrates' court which made the original secrecy arrangement. For all practical purposes the media may rely upon their possession of a privilege to report all proceedings in Parliament without criminal consequences.

Reports of parliamentary proceedings that are fair and accurate and made in good faith enjoy qualified privilege from libel actions. This was established in the famous nineteenth-century case of *Wason v Walter*[12]:

> *The Times* had printed extracts from a House of Lords debate, which included unflattering comments about the originator of an allegation that an eminent Law Lord had once lied to Parliament. The paper successfully defended a libel action. The court said that just as the public had an interest in learning about what took place in the courts, so it was entitled to know what was said in Parliament. Only malice or a distorted report would destroy the privilege.

10–005 In addition to this common law privilege, the Defamation Act 1996 gives a statutory qualified privilege for fair and accurate reports of proceedings in public of a legislature anywhere in the world.[13] The subject-matter has to be of public concern and publication for the public benefit[14] although this should not be a problem in the case of parliamentary reports. The question of whether privilege under the Act exists is for the jury rather than the judge[15] and in any event the publisher will usually be covered by the continuing common law privilege, which does not depend upon public concern or benefit.

Editorials or other comment based on the report of a parliamentary debate are also protected[16] and so too are parliamentary

---

[11] Second Report of the Committee of Privileges, H.C. 667 (1977–78). Three Australian High Court judges take the view that an accurate report of statements made in Parliament cannot amount to a contempt of court: see Mason C. J. and Gaudron *Hinch v Att-Gen (Vic)* (1987) 74 A.L.R. 353 at 361–62 and 405 respectively; McHugh J.A. in *Att-Gen (N.S.W.) v. John Fairfax & Sons Ltd* (1986) 6 N.S.W.L.R. 695 at 714.

[12] (1868) L.R. 4 Q.B. 74.

[13] Defamation Act 1996, Sch.1, para.1.

[14] 1996 Act, s.15(3).

[15] *Kingshott v Associated Kent Newspapers Ltd* [1991] 1 Q.B. 880, CA.

[16] *Wason v Walter* (1868) L.R. 4 Q.B. 74.

sketches written to capture the spirit rather than the detail of a debate. These may be cryptic, amusing and highly selective, but so long as they give a fair and honest representation of what took place as it impressed the journalist, the defence can be invoked.[17] Reports of committee hearings are similarly protected.[18] Publication or inclusion in a programme service of a copy of or extract from a parliamentary report or paper is also protected by qualified privilege[19] which extends to a copy or extract of any matter published by or with the authority of any government or legislature anywhere in the world. Papers which the House orders to lie on the table are included.[20] Statutory protection along these lines in relation to British Parliamentary Papers has been available since the Parliamentary Papers Act 1840, s.3. Publishers may still need to dust down that provision if they publish summaries of Parliamentary reports rather than publish copies or extracts. Unlike the 1996 Act, the 1840 statute extends to reports of "abstracts" of the parliamentary papers.[21] Of great importance is a newspaper's right to make honest comment on apparently factual statements made in the debate that it has reported, even though these statements are later shown to be untrue.[22]

In 1989 the House of Commons finally allowed its proceedings to be televised—after a fashion. The rules devised by the Supervising Committee are calculated to avoid embarrassment when M.P.s misbehave. Whenever there is disorder, the cameras must switch immediately to the Speaker. The public gallery and the press gallery must not be shown. The rules were slightly relaxed by the Committee after the first six months of television had produced no obvious danger to the democratic process and have been further relaxed from time-to-time since then so that, for instance, from 2006 there could be a limited use of reaction shots. BBC Parliament, a digital channel, has the coverage of the Commons, time-shifted coverage of the Lords and unedited footage of about 10 committees a week.

There is an officer of both Houses (the Director of Parliamentary **10–006** Broadcasting) who is responsible for ensuring that the arrangements authorised by each House are adhered to. A television signal is produced by an independent operator, the Parliamentary Broadcasting Unit Ltd (a company whose directors are members of both Houses) which then sells access to the feed to television companies. A similar arrangement exists for sound broadcasting. Archive tapes are kept for about two years.[23]

---

[17] *Cook v Alexander* [1974] 1 Q.B. 279.
[18] *Gatley on Libel and Slander* (10th edn, Sweet and Maxwell, 2004) para.14.103.
[19] See Defamation Act 1996, Sch.1, para.7.
[20] *Mangena v Wright* [1909] 2 K.B. 958.
[21] On the other hand, unusually, the publisher has the burden of proving absence of malice.
[22] *Grech v Odhams Press Ltd* [1958] 2 Q.B. 275.
[23] See Sir Thomas Erskine May, *Parliamentary Practice* (23rd edn, Butterworths, 2004), pp.270–1.

Broadcasting of the House of Lords' judicial proceedings requires the approval of the Law Lords.[24] Approval is occasionally given for the ritual giving of judgments to be broadcast but not, so far, the argument before the Law Lords.

When the BBC approached the appellate committee of the House of Lords in 1996 asking to televise the hearing in *Thompson and Venables* (the Bulger appeal) it was told that legal discussion of House of Lords appeals could only be understood by lawyers who had read all the case papers; members of the public should not see appeals on television because they would not understand "the legal context", for example, "hypothetical questions will be asked which can easily be misunderstood as trivial or irrelevant".[25] But this approach is unacceptable in society committed to openness, especially when the House considers cases like *Pinochet*. The ritual giving of the first decision looked rather like a penalty shoot-out and on the occasion of the second decision the senior Law Lord read out a summary of their reasons specially prepared for television which gently enhanced public understanding of a very long and complicated written judgment. When the Supreme Court takes over as the highest appellate court, sitting in Middlesex Guildhall opposite the Houses of Parliament, it will not be shackled by the statutory bar in the Criminal Justice Act 1925 prohibiting photography in court.[26] The permission of the Court may still be necessary before broadcasting is allowed.

CONTEMPT OF PARLIAMENT

10–007 Each House of Parliament has the power to punish both members and outsiders for contempt.[27] The offence of Contempt of Parliament is defined by Erskine May as "any act or omission which impedes either House of Parliament in the performance of its functions or impedes any member or officer of such House in the discharge of his duty, or which has a tendency directly or indirectly to produce such a result." "Indirect tendencies" can include articles which "bring the House into odium, contempt or ridicule or lower its authority."[28] These definitions are vague in the extreme, and it is ironic that an institution whose function is to formulate rules of law with precision has been unable or unwilling to do the same for its own powers and privileges.

In modem practice, the power to punish for contempt may be justified in relation to M.P.s who take bribes or fail to declare

---

[24] H.L. Debs 1995–96, 5870, col. 1374 and see Erskine May above, p.271.
[25] See Joshua Rozenberg, "The Pinochet Case and Cameras in Court" [1999] *Public Law* 178.
[26] Criminal Justice Act 1925, s.41(2)(a) as substituted by Constitutional Reform Act 2005, s.47.
[27] See generally Erskine May, *Parliamentary Practice*, above, Chs 8 and 10.
[28] Erskine May, *Parliamentary Practice*, p.128.

interests, or in respect of outsiders who interrupt debates by throwing refuse from the public gallery. There is no justification for using it against hostile newspapers, and, despite some unedifying decisions in the 1950s, there is little danger that Parliament will run the risk of public obloquy by using it to stifle criticism. Its most relevant use is to reprimand the press for breaking embargoes on the publication of committee reports, or leaking evidence heard in secret. Thus Tam Dalyell M.P. was reprimanded by the House in 1967 for leaking to the *Observer* secret evidence given by the Porton Down Chemical Warfare Research Laboratory to a Commons Select Committee.[29] The publication of witnesses' submissions must officially await the authorisation of the committee,[30] although where evidence has been given in public, no complaint of privilege will be entertained on the ground that it was published before being reported to the House.[31] It is also a breach of the rules of the House to disclose or publish a committee's report before it is presented to the full House.[32] However, it is now unlikely that newspapers and their reporters will be made to suffer for publishing such leaks. In 1986 Parliament rejected a recommendation from the Committee of Privileges that *The Times* should suffer the loss of a lobby pass and its journalist should be suspended from the lobby for six months for publishing a draft report leaked from the Environment Committee.[33] The committee concerned is supposed to try and discover the source of the leak and assess whether it constitutes or is likely to constitute a substantial interference with its work. If it will, the committee reports to the House and the report is automatically referred to the Committee on Standards and Privileges.

Parliament's power to punish disrespectful publications is a parallel to the court's power to punish for scandalising the judiciary. British judges have deliberately played down this aspect of their power and not exercised it since 1931 (see para.7–053), but the House of Commons has not been so self-restrained. At the time of the Suez invasion there was a flurry of allegations of contempt.[34] When, in 1975, the *Liverpool Free Press* was accused of contempt for

[29] H.C. 357 (1967–68). An appendix by the Clerk to the House gives further illustrations.
[30] See the House of Commons Resolution of April 21, 1837 and House of Commons Standing Order 135; May, *Parliamentary Practice*, pp.141–2.
[31] House of Commons Standing Orders No.35.
[32] May, *Parliamentary Practice*, p.141.
[33] H.C. Debs 1 Vol. 98, col. 293, May 20, 1986 and see Environment Committee 2nd Special Report H.C. 211 (1985–6): Committee of Privileges 1st Report H.C. 376 (1985–86).
[34] *Sunday Graphic* H.C. 27 (1956–7); *Romford Recorder*. The *Evening News* was found in contempt for a cartoon on the same theme. H.C. 39 (1956—7); but Baroness Stocks was acquitted for remarks on *Any Answers*, 4th Report of the Committee of Privileges (1956–57), H.C. 74.

an article that alleged double standards by an M.P., no action was taken. The M.P. was told to pursue his grievance in the courts.[35]

In 1978 the Commons resolved that its penal power should be used "sparingly" and "only when the House is satisfied that to exercise it is essential in order to provide reasonable protection for the House, its members or officers from such improper obstruction or attempt at or threat of obstruction as is causing or is likely to cause substantial interference with the performance of their respective functions."[36]

10–008   In future, it would take into account the mode and extent of the publication.[37] Although there is no formal defence of truth or fair comment to a charge of contempt,[38] the Commons decided to take into account the truth of, (or the publisher's reasonable belief in the truth of) the allegations if all reasonable care had been taken and if the publication was in the public interest and was published in a manner appropriate to the public interest. On the other hand, it rejected a proposal that contempt should be a procedure of last resort to be used only where the Member concerned has no legal remedy. It agreed that, as in the *Liverpool Free Press* case, this was a relevant consideration, but was not willing for it to be an inflexible bar. These changes are an improvement, and the number of complaints referred to the Privileges Committee has fallen sharply. It remains to be seen whether the change is permanent. In 1948 the Committee said that the contempt power should not be administered to discourage free expression of opinion however exaggerated or prejudiced.[39] Eight years later that opinion was ignored or bypassed in the petrol-rationing cases.[40] Old powers, like old habits, die hard and the Commons has a collective phobia of placing binding limits on its contempt power.

Contempt of Parliament has survived as an offence in modern times only because punishments have been mild. Although the

---

[35] H.C. 43 (1975–76). The article is reproduced in Brian Whitaker, *News Ltd*, p.147. Compare the Committee's condemnation of a passage in *Travel Trade Gazette* accusing Gwyneth Dunwoody of attacking the Association of British Travel Agents for ulterior motives. No action was proposed because the editor apologised. H.C. 302 (1974–75).

[36] These and the following proposals were first made by the Committee of Privileges in 1967. H.C. 34 (1967–68). They were brushed off the shelf by a further report in 1977. H.C. (1976–77). They were adopted by the Commons on February 6, 1978. *Hansard*, Vol. 943, 5th Series, col. 1155–1198.

[37] Reports of an improper disclosure are now automatically referred to the Committee of Privileges to assess its significance and to try to discover its source (see Committee of 2nd Report H.C. 555 (1984–85)).

[38] This may be because the issue has never been squarely raised. Whether truth should be accepted as a defence is, according to the Clerk to the House, an ad hoc decision. See H.C. 302 (1974–75) Annex 1, para.5 quoting H.C. 34 (1967–68) p.5.

[39] Investigating a complaint in the *Daily Mail* that Labour M.P.s were Communist moles. H.C. 112 (1947–48).

[40] See above, fn.**.

House can banish culprits from the Palace of Westminster, and even imprison them, no one has been locked under Big Ben since the atheist M.P. Charles Bradlaugh in 1880. The Lords, but not the Commons, can impose a fine.[41] In 1975 the Committee of Privileges recommended that the editor and a journalist on *The Economist* be banished from the precincts of the House for six months for publishing a draft report on a proposed wealth tax, but on a free vote the House decided to take no action.[42] Indeed, few reprimands have been administered since the Second World War.[43] John Junor received one for his attack in the *Sunday Express* on M.P.s' special petrol allowances during the Suez crisis. His half-hearted apology and failure to check his facts caused the Committee to recommend the reprimand.[44] When Junor returned to the fray in 1983, claiming that M.P.s who suggested a pay-rise for themselves were hypocrites with "greedy snouts in the trough", Parliament's response was much more sophisticated: instead of calling him to the Bar of the House for contempt, M.P.s enthusiastically tabled motions that allowed them to debate Junor's own salary and to draw attention to the tax perks of egregious Fleet Street editors. The threat of sanctions for contempt need concern only lobby correspondents, who identify closely with the House. Others, at least those who are confident of the public interest in their story, should not be averse to the publicity that a reprimand would bring. However, M.P.s who are caught leaking can face suspension and, in one post-war case, expulsion.[45] As a result of the *Guardian*'s action in prematurely publishing the "cash for questions" report in 1997, however, it is highly unlikely that any editor or journalist need fear proceedings for contempt of Parliament by publishing a leaked document, if the leak serves the public interest.

> Prime Minister John Major promised that Sir Gordon Downey's Privileges Committee Report into allegations that Tory M.P.s had been bribed to advance the interests of Mohammed Al Fayed would be published before the General Election. In breach of this promise, he prorogued Parliament before the report could be completed. But because the *Guardian* had been the complainant, Downey had sent it transcripts of his secret hearings, at which half a dozen Tory MPs

---

[41] May, *Parliamentary Practice*, p.161. The 1967 Committee proposed that a power to fine should be revived and when considering *The Economist's* leak of the wealth-tax report in 1975, made it clear that it thought this an appropriate offence to fine. No action to implement these recommendations has been taken.

[42] H.C. 22 (1975–76).

[43] Hartley and Griffith, *Government and the Law*, p.245. 1967 Report, para.18.

[44] H.C. 74 (1956–57).

[45] Gary Allingham M.P., who alleged that M.P.s traded information for food and drink. The Committee of Privileges was particularly irked by his hypocrisy, since he had done precisely what he accused his colleagues of doing. It recommended a six-month suspension but the House went further and expelled him: H.C. 138 (1947–48).

standing for re-election had confessed to acceptance of cash and favours and other improper conduct. The *Guardian*'s editor, Alan Rusbridger, decided that the public interest in learning of this misbehaviour overrode his duty of confidentiality and justified committing contempt of Parliament by publishing the truth about the M.P.s a few weeks before the election. Publication made "Tory sleaze" a dominant issue, and the misbehaving M.P.s as well as their party were swept from office. The Privileges Committee took no action against the editor.[46]

10–009   The New Zealand legislature punished a different type of contempt in 2006.

> The departing Chief Executive of the state broadcaster, TVNZ, gave evidence to a parliamentary select committee in which he referred to the TVNZ board's "secret bitch sessions", and accused a member of leaking stories about him to the media. The Board took umbrage and stripped the Chief Executive of the remaining powers which he had enjoyed while working out his notice. Punishing a witness because of evidence which he has given (whether to a court or to Parliament) is a classic form of contempt. TVNZ was fined the modest sum of 1,000 NZ dollars (about £350) and ordered to apologise (which it did). This was the first fine which the NZ Parliament had ever imposed.[47]

The objections to the offence of contempt of Parliament go beyond the vagueness of definition and the self-aggrandisement implicit in many of the cases. The procedure for "trial" breaches every important rule of natural justice, and shames a Commons proud of its historical opposition to the Star Chamber of the Stuart kings. The procedure begins, reasonably enough, with a private complaint by an M.P. to the Speaker. If the Speaker thinks there is a case to answer, he gives the M.P. leave to raise it as a matter of procedure over the day's business, and the House may, if impressed with it, pass a motion referring it to the Committee on Standards and Privileges, an 11–strong body dominated by lawyers and M.P.s, with the governing party in the majority.

There are no procedural safeguards. Accused persons may be condemned unheard, or summonsed for cross-examination without legal representation or notice of the charges, and without any right to challenge the evidence given against them or to call witnesses in rebuttal. The Committee sits in secret, and reports in due course to the Commons. The House decides whether and what punishment to inflict, after a further debate in which biased M.P.s vote entirely as judges in their own cause.

10–010   The procedures for dealing with contempt of Parliament are in blatant breach of at least three articles of the European Convention on Human Rights. Article 5 prohibits loss of liberty except by

---

[46] Geoffrey Robertson, *The Justice Game* (Vintage, 1997) pp.355–6.
[47] *Media Lawyer*, April 2006.

conviction for a clearly defined offence; Art.6 guarantees defendants a fair hearing by an independent and impartial tribunal, and specifically endorses the rights to present a defence, to legal representation, and to call and to cross-examine witnesses; and Art.10 upholds freedom of expression.[48] Despite the Human Rights Act, the United Kingdom courts would still not be able to investigate these issues because s.6(3) excludes Parliament (except the House of Lords in its judicial capacity) from the concept of "public authorities" which are required to abide by Convention rights.

At present, the very unfairness of the Committee's procedures can be a boon to those summonsed before it, in the sense that they can make great play of their role as victims. The contraventions of natural justice inherent in the Committee's traditional procedures are indefensible, and any journalist threatened by it should adopt the defiant stance of the "gang of four" M.P.s who were summonsed over their naming of "Colonel B".[49]

These procedural inadequacies are compounded by the extremely limited prospect of obtaining judicial review. The courts may decide whether or not a parliamentary privilege exists, but must not question the practical application of an undoubted privilege in any particular case. The resolution of the House and the Speaker's warrant will be treated as conclusive. The only exception is where the House of Commons exercises its power to imprison for contempt by issuing a warrant that specifies the conduct that is to be punished; in such cases the courts may decide whether the specified conduct is capable of amounting to a contempt—i.e. whether it could have a tendency to impede the performance of parliamentary functions.[50] But Parliament may readily exclude even this limited form of judicial review merely by issuing a general warrant.

MEMBERS OF PARLIAMENT AND CONFLICTS OF INTEREST

Following the scandal involving the architect Poulson in 1974 and **10–011** the growing suspicion that certain M.P.s had received benefits from him, the House of Commons resolved to take two steps to compel M.P.s to disclose their private financial interests. In any debates or committee hearings they were to announce any relevant financial interest.[51] This would be recorded in *Hansard*. The House also set up a register of M.P.s' interests.[52] Each M.P. is supposed to report any of the following interests:

---

[48] See for instance *Demicoli v Malta* (1991) 14 E.H.R.R. 47.

[49] H.C. 669 (1977–78); H.C. 222 (1978–79).

[50] The most recent authority, which reviews all the eighteenth- and nineteenth-century English cases, is the Australian High Court in *R. v Richards Ex p. Fitzpatrick and Browne* (1955) 92 C.L.R. 157, upholding the Federal Parliament's foolish decision to imprison two journalists for a defamatory article about an M.P.

[51] *Hansard*, May 22, 1974.

[52] *Code of Conduct* together with the *Guide to the Rules Relating to the Conduct of Members* (1995–96) H.C. 688.

- remunerated directorships, employment, offices, trades, professions or vocations paying more than £590. In such cases they must register the amount of their earnings within bands of £5,000 and, with the exception of speaking or writing engagements, must also deposit for public inspection an "agreement for the provision of services";
- the names of clients when the interest referred to includes personal services by the Member that arise out of or are related in any manner to his membership of the House;
- sponsorship of the Member or his candidacy or constituency association over £1,000;
- any gift from a UK source which relates in any way to membership of the House and is worth more than £590. Benefits available to all M.P.s (or all from a particular region) do not have to be registered;
- overseas visits relating to or arising out of membership of the House where all or part of the cost is not paid by public funds and the value is over £590;
- overseas gifts over £590;
- land or property worth more than £59,000 (excluding a home used for personal residential purposes by the Member or partner) or which yields an income over £5,900 p.a.;
- interests in shareholdings held by the M.P., either personally, or with or on behalf of the M.P.'s spouse or dependent children, in any public or private company or other body which are more than 15 per cent of the issued share capital or worth more than £59,000. The nature of the company's business in each case should be registered;
- any relevant interest, not falling within one of the above categories, which nevertheless falls within the definition of the main purpose of the Register which is "to provide information of any pecuniary interest or other material benefit which a Member receives which might reasonably be thought by others to influence his or her actions, speeches, or votes in Parliament, or actions taken in his or her capacity as a Member of Parliament", or which the Member considers might be thought by others to influence his or her actions in a similar manner, even though the Member receives no financial benefit.

10–012 The threshold amounts are calculated by reference to the current salary for an M.P. (£59,000 in 2006). The register is published at the beginning of each parliament and once a year thereafter. The register (together with more recent updates) can also be seen at Parliament's website.[53]

---

[53] *www.parliament.uk.*

Oversight of the register is one of the principal functions of the Parliamentary Commissioner for Standards. The office was established on the recommendation of the Nolan Committee[54] and its holder can only be removed by a resolution of the House of Commons (although reappointment at the end of her term is not secure). As well as maintaining the register of M.P.s' interests, the Commissioner also investigates complaints about the propriety of M.P.s' conduct.

Although a judge in 1990 said that the Register of M.P.s' interests was not a "proceeding in Parliament" for the purpose of the Bill of Rights,[55] the Privy Council has doubted whether this case was rightly decided[56] and a review by the Joint Committee of Privileges in 1999 expressly included such registers among the matters which ought to be protected by privilege.[57] There is also a register of the interests of members of the House of Lords. A code of conduct for members of the House of Lords provides a list of interests which must be registered. Though detailed, this is less onerous than the equivalent requirements for MPs. The register is open to public inspection and can be viewed on the House of Lords website.[58]

Parliament maintains other registers. Lobby journalists, journalists accredited to the Parliamentary press gallery or for Parliamentary broadcasting must register any employment or paid occupation for which their privileged access to Parliament is relevant. Similarly, people with passes as M.P.s' secretaries or research assistants and officers of All Party Committees and registered groups must also register their relevant occupations. These registers can also be inspected on-line at Parliament's website.

GOVERNMENT OF SCOTLAND, WALES AND NORTHERN IRELAND

Devolution in Labour's first term of office took different forms in the three countries. **10–013**

Scotland

The Scotland Act 1998 established the Scottish Parliament and the **10–014** Scottish Administration. The Scottish Parliament has similarities to the Westminster Parliament although it has only one chamber. The Scotland Act requires the Standing Orders of the Scottish Parliament to oblige it to hold its proceedings in public, except in

---

[54] First Report of the Committee on Standards in Public Life (HMSO, 1995), Cm. 2850.
[55] *Rost v Edwards* [1990] 2 All E.R. 641.
[56] *Prebble v Television New Zealand Ltd* [1995] 1 A.C. 321.
[57] H.L. Paper 43, H.C. 214 (1998–99).
[58] *www.parliament.uk/about_lords/register_of_lords_interests.cfm*.

circumstances defined in the standing orders.[59] The Standing Orders require meetings of the Scottish Parliament and any of its committees to take place in public.[60] The Standing Orders must also include provision for reporting the proceedings of the Parliament and for publishing the reports.[61] The Standing Orders also provide for the broadcasting of proceedings.[62]

Statements made in the Edinburgh Parliament are absolutely privileged and so are any publications which are made with its authority.[63] This will not extend to newspaper reports but under the Defamation Act 1996, fair and accurate reports of proceedings in public of a legislature anywhere in the world have qualified privilege.[64] Similarly a fair and accurate report in good faith of proceedings in the Scottish Parliament cannot be contempt under the strict liability rule.[65] The Scottish Parliament must establish a register of Members' interests which has to be open to public inspection.[66]

The legislative competence of the Scottish Parliament is carefully defined and many matters are reserved for action by the United Kingdom Parliament alone.[67] These include the BBC and the subject-matter of the Broadcasting Acts.[68] Other matters which are reserved include data protection,[69] election law,[70] the Video Recordings and Cinema Acts,[71] national security, anti-terrorism and the Official Secrets Acts,[72] copyright,[73] telecommunications and wireless telegraphy.[74] A general condition on the competence of the Parliament is that its acts must be compatible with rights under the European Convention on Human Rights.[75] A similar restriction is applied to the acts of the Scottish Executive. Ultimately the Judicial Committee of the Privy Council (which is comprised mainly of the Law Lords) can rule on whether these restrictions have been broken. This function will pass to the Supreme Court once it is established as the highest appellate court.

---

[59] Scotland Act 1998, Sch.3, para.3.
[60] Standing Orders of the Scottish Parliament, 15.1.
[61] S.O. 15.1, para.4, see S.O. 16.3.
[62] See S.O. 16.4.
[63] Scotland Act 1998, s.41.
[64] Defamation Act 1996, Sch.1, para.1.
[65] Scotland Act 1998, s.42.
[66] 1998 Act, s.39.
[67] 1998 Act, s.29 and Sch.4 and 5.
[68] 1998 Act, Sch.5, s.Kl.
[69] 1998 Act, s.B2.
[70] 1998 Act, s.B3.
[71] 1998 Act, s.B5.
[72] 1998 Act, s.B8.
[73] 1998 Act, s.C4.
[74] 1998 Act, s.CIO.
[75] 1998 Act, s.29(2)(d).

Northern Ireland

The Northern Ireland Act 1998 was a product of the Good Friday **10–015** Agreement and represents an intricate political compromise whose past has been shaky and whose future remains uncertain.

It established the Northern Ireland Assembly which has many features in common with the Scottish Parliament. Thus the Assembly's Standing Orders must also make provision for the public to attend and for the publishing of reports of its proceedings.[76] Its Standing Orders must also include provision for a Register of Members' interests to which the public have a right of access.[77] There are very similar provisions for absolute privilege and a defence to the strict liability contempt rule for fair, accurate and good faith reports of the Assembly's proceedings.[78] Reports of its proceedings in the media would also attract qualified privilege under the Defamation Act 1996.

The Assembly's legislative competence, as in the case of the Scottish Parliament, is also defined. Matters reserved to the Westminster Parliament are listed.[79] Although the detail is different, there are broad similarities with the division of responsibility between Edinburgh and Westminster. The Freedom of Information Act 2000 extends to Northern Ireland and the Assembly is a public authority for the purposes of the Act.[80]

Wales

The Government of Wales Act 1998 set up a different model of **10–016** devolution for Wales to that established in Scotland and Northern Ireland. The National Assembly for Wales was expected to take over most of the functions of the Secretary of State for Wales. It would be able to exercise ministerial functions, but would not have power to pass primary legislation.

In 2006 the Government of Wales Act moved the Welsh form of devolution somewhat closer to that in Scotland. In particular it made a clearer separation between the executive and legislative branches of Welsh government and enhanced the legislative powers of the National Assembly of Wales. The transition to the 2006 model will take place in stages.

As far as media law is concerned, there are provisions in both the 1998 and 2006 versions which match their Scottish equivalents.

---

[76] Northern Ireland Act 1998, Sch.6, paras 2 and 3. See the Standing Orders of the Assembly, S.O.7.
[77] 1998 Act, s.43. The Register is available on the Assembly's website.
[78] 1998 Act, s.50.
[79] See Northern Ireland Act 1998, Sch.3.
[80] Freedom of Information Act 2000, s.88(2) and Sch.1, para.4.

10–017   The proceedings of the Assembly itself must take place in public as must the meetings of its committees and sub-committees (except where Standing Orders allow otherwise).[81] The Assembly must arrange for reports of its proceedings to be published[82] and the officially authorised reports will have absolute privilege.[83] The Assembly is treated as a legislature for the purposes of the Defamation Act 1996[84] so that fair and accurate reports of its proceedings are protected by qualified privilege and a fair and accurate copy of or an extract from any matter published with its authority will also have qualified privilege. The limitation on privilege in the course of elections under Defamation Act 1952, s.10 (see para.10–021) applies also to elections to the Assembly.[85] A fair and accurate and good faith report of the Assembly's proceedings cannot offend against the strict liability contempt rule.[86]

Whenever the Assembly publishes a document it must make a copy available for (free) public inspection. It must also have facilities for the public to take copies but it can charge for these.[87] The accounts of the Assembly are audited by the Auditor-General for Wales. The accounts, statements of account or report which he lays before the Assembly must be published as soon as reasonably practicable.[88] The Welsh Assembly is a public authority for the purposes of the Freedom of Information Act 2000.[89]

ELECTION REPORTING

Injunctions

10–018 Free speech is an essential part of the democratic process, but there must be some safeguard against its deliberate misuse to distort that process at election time.[90] Otherwise, an unscrupulous newspaper

---

[81] Government of Wales Act 1998, s.70(1). The Standing Orders of the Assembly require plenary sessions to be in public—S.O. 6.1 and similarly committees must sit in public—5.O. 8.20, except in prescribed circumstances—S.O. 8.21. Government of Wales Act 2006, s.31.

[82] 1998 Act s.70(3); 2006 Act s.31(6).

[83] 1998 Act s.77(1); 2006 Act s.42.

[84] 1998 Act, s.77(4)(a). There is no direct equivalent in the 2006 Act but it is inconceivable that fair and accurate reports of the Assembly's proceedings would not be protected by qualified privilege either under the 1996 Act or at common law.

[85] 1998 Act, s.77(5); 2006 Act Sch.12, para.5.

[86] 1998 Act, s.78; 2006 Act, s.43.

[87] 1998 Act, s.119; 2006 Act, s.69.

[88] 1998 Act, s.103; 2006 Act, s.143.

[89] Freedom of Information Act 2000, Sch.1, para.5.

[90] This section refers to local as well as parliamentary elections. Except where indicated, the same rules apply also to elections for the European Parliament: European Parliamentary Elections Act 1978, s.3 and Sch.1, para.2(3) and European Parliamentary Elections Regulations 1999 (SI 1999/1214).

editor could influence the result by publishing a story, known to be false, about a party leader or candidate shortly before polling day. Publication could not be restrained by an injunction for libel if the editor stated he was prepared to defend it. A safeguard against such conduct is provided by s.106 of the Representation of the People Act 1983:

> "(1) A person who . . . (a) before or during an election, (b) for the purpose of affecting the return of any candidate at the election, makes or publishes any false statement of fact in relation to the personal conduct or character of the candidate shall be guilty of an illegal practice unless he can show that he has reasonable grounds for believing, and did believe the statement to be true. . . .(3) A person making or publishing any false statement of fact as mentioned above may be restrained by interim or perpetual injunction by the High Court or the county court from any repetition of that false statement or of a false statement of a similar character in relation to the candidate and, for the purpose of granting an interim injunction, prima facie proof of the falsity of the statement shall be sufficient."

Since there can be no "candidates" before an election campaign begins, these injunctions can relate to publications only after the writ for the election has been issued or the other formal commencement of the campaign.[91]

This law requires only "prima facie evidence" of falsehood—an affidavit to that effect by the candidate (who is thereby lain open to a perjury charge if he or she has sworn falsely) might suffice. The false statement need not be defamatory, so long as it is calculated to influence the minds of electors. (It was once held that the false statement that a candidate had shot a fox would be sufficient in a country constituency—because the electors would be outraged that he had not done the gentlemanly thing and hunted it with dogs.)[92] The false statement must be about "personal character and conduct", not political performance or allegiance. To say, on the eve of an election, that the leader of the Labour Party is a Communist, would not merit an injunction[93] but to say that he was in the pay of the KGB most certainly would. Criticism of the merit of a council

---

[91] Parliamentary elections start with the dissolution of Parliament, the announcement by the Government that it intends to dissolve Parliament, or the issuance of a by-election writ. Local government elections run from five weeks before the date fixed for the poll or the publication of notice of the election: 1983 Act, s.93(2).

[92] *Borough of Sunderland Case* (1896) 50 M. & H. at 62. After the Hunting Act 2004 an allegation that a candidate *had* hunted a fox to death with dogs might now amount to the imputation of a criminal offence and so reflect on the candidate's personal conduct.

[93] *Burns v Associated Newspapers Ltd* (1925) 42 T.L.R. 37.

contract would not be covered, but to allege that a councillor had become personally involved with contract decisions so as to favour a family member would be to impeach the councillor's "personal conduct".[94] Finally, the statement must be one of fact rather than opinion. The assertion of KGB paymastery is a statement of fact; the description "radical traitor" has been held to be a statement of opinion.[95] On the other hand a leaflet which said of Jack Straw that he "hates Muslims" was treated as a statement of fact. There was no qualification indicating an expression of opinion on the part of the writer and the court concluded that it would have been understood as a statement of fact. Since the court found that the fact was false and Mr Straw did not hate Muslims, s.106 was infringed.[96]

10–019   The candidate's affidavit of falsehood is not conclusively accepted. No injunction will be granted if the publisher can show reasonable grounds for believing that the story is true. By contrast with a defamation action, the burden is on the claimant to show that the statement is false. The section provides that prima facie proof of falsity is sufficient. But even if that threshold is crossed, the court still has a discretion and it would not be consistent with the Human Rights Act 1998, s.12(3), if the judge were to grant the injunction even though evidence led by the defendant suggested that the claimant would not be likely to succeed at trial. However, again by contrast with defamation actions, the defendant would have to do more than assert that the story was true.

It is an offence knowingly to publish, in order to promote the election of one candidate, a false statement that a rival candidate has withdrawn.[97]

Advertisements

10–020   Newspapers can print election advertisements, but they must take care that these are authorised by the candidate or the election agent. Any other advertisement (by private supporters or well-wishers, for example) for the purpose of procuring a candidate's election is an offence.[98] The advertisement might praise the virtues of the favoured candidate or denounce the failings of the opposition: either way it must be authorised.[99] The same section also prohibits "otherwise

---

[94] *DPP v Edwards* [2002] EWHC 636 (Admin).

[95] *Ellis v National Union of Conservative and Constitutional Associations, Middleton and Southall* (1900) 44 S.J. 750 and see generally, *Gatley on Libel and Slander*, para.25.22 *et seq.*

[96] *Pirbhai v DPP* [1995] C.O.D. 259, QBD.

[97] 1983 Act, s.106(5).

[98] Representation of the People Act 1983, s.75(1)(b) and s.75(5). There is an offence only if the paper intends to enhance a candidate's chances. If its motive is *only* to inform the public, it has a good defence: *Grieve v Douglas-Home* 1965 S.L.T. 1861. But if one motive is to assist the candidate, then other, altruistic, intentions are irrelevant: *DPP v Luft* [1977] A.C. 962.

[99] *DPP v Luft*, fn.98 above.

presenting to the electors the candidate or his views or the extent or nature of his backing or disparaging another candidate".[100] There is a proviso which exempts expenses incurred by a person who was not acting in concert with others. Until 2001 the proviso was virtually meaningless because of a further condition that the expenses did not exceed £5. This changed as a result of *Bowman v UK*[101]:

> Phylliss Bowman, director of the Society for the Protection of the Unborn Child, was prosecuted for offending against s.75(1)(c) when she circulated leaflets informing an electorate accurately of the candidates' views on abortion and experiments on human embryos. The prosecution of her was unsuccessful on technical grounds because it was brought out of time, but her complaint to the European Court of Human Rights was allowed to proceed nonetheless. The Court ruled that she was still a "victim" because the same law would stand in the way of similar activity at the next election and the fact that she had been prosecuted for the same action in the past showed that she was at continuing risk of prosecution in the future. Her argument was that all pressure groups were inhibited from democratic campaigning by the ludicrous ceiling of £5: there was evidence that Friends of the Earth, Charter 88, anti-foxhunters and CND had all been stopped from providing information to electors about candidates' outlooks on single issues. The Court held that the restriction for independent third parties to £5 was disproportionate and therefore contrary to Art.10. The right of freedom of expression was particularly important at election times if the further Convention right in Art.3 of Protocol 1 (the right to free elections) was to be respected.

Obliged by the Bowman decision to change s.75, the Government did so by the Political Parties, Elections and Referendums Act 2000 ("PPERA"): £5 goes out and in its place comes "the permitted sum". In connection with a candidate at a parliamentary election the permitted sum is £500 and for local elections £50 plus 0.5p for every voter in the area.[102] It is highly questionable whether these sums are compatible with Art.10: a pressure group must be entitled to spend whatever amounts to the reasonable cost of printing a leaflet and distributing it throughout the electorate. However, in a brief aside the Administrative Court in 2006 dismissed the idea that the permitted sum was incompatible with Art.10.[103]

The PPERA amendment on its face dealt only with s.75(1)(c) of the 1983 Act (the offence with which Phyllis Bowman had been charged) and s.75(1)(d) (the equivalent offence for London Assembly elections). It did not appear to cover s.75(1)(a) (organising public meetings) or s.75(1)(b) (advertisements). The position has been corrected with retrospective effect by the Electoral Administration

---

[100] Representation of the People Act 1983, s.75(1)(c).
[101] (1998) 26 E.H.R.R. 1.
[102] PPERA 2000, s.131 inserting RPA 1983, s.75(1ZA).
[103] *R v Holding* [2006] 1 W.L.R. 1040 (appeal to the House of Lords pending).

Act 2006[104] and the Administrative Court used the Human Rights Act to find that this had always been the intention behind the PPERA amendment.[105]

10–021   Until 2001 there was no restriction on expenditure which did not promote or disparage a particular candidate in a particular constituency. Thus a 1951 advertisement which damned the socialist programme of the post-war Labour Government was held to be merely propaganda which was unrelated to a particular candidate and so not an advertisement which had to be authorised by a candidate or his agent.[106] Now campaign expenditure[107] by or on behalf of a registered political party must be incurred by, or on the authority of, the treasurer, deputy treasurer or their written nominee[108] and is part of a new regime to cap the amount which parties can spend on their election campaigns. Expenditure by third parties on election material[109] is also controlled[110] but if the expenditure is in respect of a the publication of any matter relating to the election in a newspaper, a periodical, a BBC/S4C broadcast or a programme in a licensed programme service it is only controlled if it takes the form of an advertisement.[111]

In 1984 the Government legislated to restrict trade unions from spending money on political objects unless the expenditure came directly from contributions to a political fund by members who approved of such expenditure. At the 1987 elections NALGO's literature condemning cuts in the Health Service was distributed in marginal constituencies with the object of discomforting Tory candidates: it was held that this action was unlawful because the money for the leaflets did not come from the political fund.[112]

Newspapers, periodicals, the BBC, SC4 and licensed broadcasters are free to support or oppose individual candidates in their news and editorial columns. Free publicity of this sort is not included in computing the maximum election expenses that a candidate can incur.[113] But newspapers must still be conscious of defamation in deciding whether to publish election addresses. The Defamation Act 1952 is unequivocal: an election address has no special privilege.[114] But while there is no *special* privilege, there is no bar on relying on

---

[104] Electoral Administration Act 2006, s.25 adding s.75(1ZZB) to the RPA 1983.
[105] *R v Holding* (above).
[106] *R. v Tronoh Mines Ltd and Times Publishing Ltd* [1952] 1 All E.R. 697.
[107] Defined in PPERA 2000, s.72 and Sch.8, Pt.1—it includes "advertising of any nature".
[108] PPERA, s.75.
[109] Defined broadly in PPERA, s.85.
[110] PPERA, s.85.
[111] PPERA, s.87.
[112] *Paul v NALGO* [1987] I.R.L.R. 413.
[113] 1983 Act, s.75(1ZZA)
[114] 1952 Act, s.10.

the ordinary common law of qualified privilege including, if necessary, a *Reynolds* defence.[115]

Broadcasting coverage of the campaign

The absence of any special privilege for election addresses, the **10–022** possibility of an injunction for a false statement about a candidate's character, and the penalty for falsely announcing a candidate's withdrawal apply equally to broadcasters. The rules about advertising are even more strict. Political advertising is restricted on television and radio even at election times.[116] In 1971 the European Commission of Human Rights rejected a complaint that this prohibition was contrary to Article 10 of the Convention finding that it was permitted by the last sentence of Art.10(1) which permits Government licensing of broadcasters.[117] But broadcasters are able to transmit statements by or in support of candidates without committing an election offence.[118] However, there are special controls to make sure that no individual candidate gains an unfair advantage.

Codes

Until 2001 these controls were set out in the legislation. They **10–023** operated crudely. Thus it was unlawful during an election campaign to include a programme about a constituency in which the candidate appeared on film in a sound-bite unless the candidate gave his consent. This effectively gave candidates the power to control the editing of their contributions by threatening to withdraw their consent if they did not like what they saw. Worse, all the candidates in the constituency had to consent to the programme. So this power of veto operated undemocratically. The PPERA 2000 has re-written the previous provision (s.93 of the Representation of the People Act 1983). The broadcasting regulators (Ofcom and the BBC) are each required to draw up their own codes of practice with respect to the participation of candidates at a parliamentary or local government election in items about the constituency during the election period.

---

[115] *Culnane v Morris* [2006] 2 All E.R. 149. For the *Reynolds Jameel* defence see para.3–063.
[116] Communications Act 2003 ss.319(2)(g), 321(2) and 321(3)(a) and see para.16–046. It was the continuing ban on political advertising and its possible conflict with the decision of the European Court of Human Rights in *Vgt Verein gegen Tierfabriken v Switzerland* (2001) 10 B.H.R.C. 473 which led the government to take the unique step of *not* certifying that the Communications Bill complied with Convention rights. However, in *R. (Animal Defenders International) v Secretary of State for Culture Media and Sport* [2006] EWHC 3069 (Admin) the Administrative Court ruled that the ban on political advertising was not incompatible with Art.10. An appeal is due to be heard by the House of Lords.
[117] *X and the Association of Z v UK*, App.No.4515/70, July 11, 1971.
[118] Representation of the People Act 1983, s.75 (1ZZA).

In drawing up their codes the broadcasting authorities must have regard to the views of the Electoral Commission. The Codes of Ofcom and the BBC can be found on their websites.[119] The BBC must observe its code and Ofcom must do all it can to secure that its Code is observed.[120]

Ofcom's Code came into force in 2005. Section 6 concerns broadcasting during elections and referendums. The principle is retained that when broadcasters carry constituency reports they must normally offer the opportunity to take part to all candidates. However, no candidate has a veto over a programme and minor candidates without previous or current significant support do not have to be included. Constituency reports must also include a full list of all candidates and their parties although radio reports which are repeated on the same day can refer to a website for this information. Candidates in elections and representatives of permitted participants in UK referendums cannot act as news presenters, interviewers or presenters of any type of programme during the election period. If their participation in non-political programmes was planned or scheduled before the election or referendum period, these can continue but no new appearances should be arranged or broadcast during that period. The due impartiality requirement also applies at reports and discussions relating to constituencies and electoral areas.[121]

Balance

10–024 Ofcom has a duty to do all it can to ensure,

> "(1). . . (b) the preservation in the case of every television programme service, teletext service, national radio service and national digital sound programme service, of due impartiality on the part of the person providing the service as respects . . . (2) (a) matters of political or industrial controversy and (b) matters relating to current public policy."[122]

By self-denying assurances, the BBC accepts similar standards.[123]

---

[119] Ofcom's Code is at *www.ofcom.org.uk/tv/ifi/codes/bcode* (s.6—elections and referendums); the BBC's Code is at *www.bbc.co.uk*.

[120] Communications Act 2003, s.325.

[121] Ofcom's Broadcasting Code, ss.6.8–6.12.

[122] Communications Act 2003, ss.319 and 320.

[123] See cl.5(1)(c) of the Agreement of January 25, 1996 between BBC and the Heritage Secretary (now the Department of Culture Media and Sport). In *Lynch v BBC* [1983] 6 Northern Ireland Judgments Bulletin, Hutton J. had found that the BBC was not under any legal duty to comply with what was then only an undertaking to observe impartiality in a letter from Lord Normanbrook, chairman of the BBC's governors. However, since then the Licence and Agreement has been amended to incorporate an impartiality obligation. The courts have indicated that the obligation can be enforced by judicial review—see *R. v BBC and ITC Ex p. Referendum Party* [1997] E.M.L.R. 605, and Ch.16—Broadcasting Law.

Balance can be achieved through a series of programmes,[124] but at election time broadcasters are super-sensitive to charges of bias. In the run-up to the 1987 elections the BBC turned down a play that depicted Mrs Thatcher behaving heroically and compassionately during the Falklands War. In February 1974 *The Perils of Pendragon*, a comedy programme, was rescheduled because of its unflattering portrayal of a Communist. In 1964 the BBC agreed to move *Steptoe and Son* from peak time on polling day at the request of Harold Wilson, who feared it would keep Labour voters at home. The BBC declined his further suggestion to "replace it with Greek drama, preferably in the original".

Party political broadcasts

Party political broadcasts during election periods have become an **10–025** influential part of the democratic process. In 1987 Hugh (*Chariots of Fire*) Hudson produced a remarkable propaganda film that boosted Neil Kinnock's personal rating by 16 per cent overnight, while the Tories counter-attacked with a theme tune specially composed by Andrew (*Evita*) Lloyd-Webber.

Section 333 of the Communications Act 2003 empowers Ofcom to require a licensed public service television channel and a national radio service to carry party political broadcasts and referendum campaign broadcasts in accordance with rules made by Ofcom. Subject to the restrictions in PPERA, Ofcom Rules can determine which parties or campaigns will be allowed to broadcast, for how long and how frequently. In making its rules, Ofcom must have regard to the views of the Electoral Commission. In determining its policies regarding party political broadcasts, the BBC must also take account of the views of the Electoral Commission.[125] Broadcasters can, in any case, only allow registered parties to make party political broadcasts[126] and, during referendum campaigns they can only give such broadcasts to organisations which have been formally designated by the Electoral Commission.[127]

Ofcom's Rules were adopted in October 2004 and set a framework for the allocation of Party Political Broadcasts.[128] Within this framework, the licensees take their own decisions, but unresolved disputes can be referred to Ofcom for adjudication. The major parties are defined and they are to have a series of broadcasts before each election. Other registered parties may qualify if they are contesting at least 1/6th of the seats available—treating the four nations of

---

[124] Communications Act 2003, s.320(4)(a).
[125] PPERA, s.11.
[126] PPERA, s.37.
[127] PPERA, s.127.
[128] *Ofcom Rules on Party Political and Referendum Broadcasts* available at www.ofcom.org.uk/tv/ifi/guidance/ppbrules.

England, Wales, Scotland and Northern Ireland separately. The major parties can claim a peak time slot: other parties have to be satisfied with a wider time span in which they may be offered a broadcast. Since the broadcasters do not have editorial control over the content of party political broadcasts, Ofcom advises them to seek legal indemnities from parties against defamation, breach of copyright and similar legal risks.

10–026   The courts have generally been loathe to intervene in the allocation of party political or election broadcasts. They did do so at the time of the 1979 referendum on Scottish devolution when each of the four major parties was offered a broadcast. Since three of the parties favoured a "yes" vote, the court unsurprisingly held that this allocation was incompatible with the Independent Broadcasting Authority's duty to maintain a proper balance.[129] If a similar situation were to recur, the court would be likely to invoke Ofcom's duty to secure impartiality by its licence holders.

But this was an unusual case. More commonly the courts have been inclined to leave allocation to the judgment of broadcasters.[130]

Similarly, the European Commission of Human Rights was unwilling to question the judgment of broadcasters, at least in the absence of justified allegations of arbitrariness or discrimination. In *Huggett v UK*,[131] the applicant was an independent candidate at the elections for the European Parliament in 1994. He was not allowed an election broadcast because it was the broadcasters' policy to reserve these for parties who had candidates in at least 12.5 per cent of the seats. The Commission said that the threshold was needed to ensure that limited airtime was given only to political opinions which were likely to be of general interest and command some public support. A complaint about inadequate access to broadcasting by the Austrian Freedom Party was also rejected in *Haider v Austria*.[132] Jorge Haider also claimed that the hostile manner in which he had been interviewed violated his rights under the Convention. But, as the Commission said,

> "with regard to interviews of politicians, it is in the interests of freedom of political debate that the interviewing journalist may also express criticism and provocative points of view and not merely give neutral cues for the statements of interviewed persons, since the later can reply immediately".

10–027   Both the UK courts and the Strasbourg institutions showed a similar deference to the judgment of the BBC when faced with a challenge by the Pro-Life Alliance anti-abortion group, whose party

---

[129] *Wilson v IBA* (1979) SLT 279.
[130] See for instance *R. v BBC and ITC Ex p. Referendum party* [1997] E.M.L.R. 605; *R. v Broadcasting Complaints Commission Ex p. Owen* [1985] 2 All E.R. 522; *Wilson v IBA (No.2)* 1988 SLT 276; *James Marshall v BBC* [1979] 1 W.L.R. 1071.
[131] (1995) 82 D.R. 98.
[132] (1995) 83 D.R. 66.

political broadcast had been rejected on taste and decency grounds. The programme had included shots of aborted foetuses which were badly mutilated. The UK courts held that there was not even an arguable ground of challenge on irrationality grounds or via Art.10 ECHR. They said that the rights of others (whose defence is a legitimate reason for curbing free speech) included the right not to be subjected to unduly offensive material.[133]

There was a re-run of this issue when the Pro-Life Alliance's proposed election broadcast was again rejected by the broadcasters at the time of the 2001 General Election.[134]

> The Alliance wanted to broadcast as its party election broadcast a programme which showed aborted foetuses. Again the broadcasters refused to air the programme because they considered that it offended the taste and decency standards which were then in the Broadcasting Act 1990 s.6 (and which now, rebranded as a prohibition on material which is offensive or harmful, features in the Communications Act 2003, s.319(2)(f)). The Alliance's judicial review failed in the Administrative Court but succeeded in the Court of Appeal where Laws L.J.'s robust judgment castigated the broadcasters for censoring political speech. The broadcasters' appeal to the House of Lords in turn succeeded although a dissent by Lord Scott supported the free speech argument of Laws L.J. The majority observed that the Alliance did not challenge the application of taste and decency standards to Party Election Broadcasts in principle (and Lord Hoffman said that any such challenge would anyway have failed). Article 10 did not give political parties a right to airtime, but only to the non-arbitrary and non-discriminatory application of common standards. It was not for the courts to decide for themselves whether the Alliance's broadcast was too offensive to be shown, but only to review the decision which Parliament had given to the broadcasters. In this case the broadcasters had properly taken into account the importance of the images to the Alliance's campaign, but they were still entitled to conclude that the standards which they had to observe would have been infringed by the programme.

This case demonstrates how media regulators and bureaucratic elites within senior management may take decisions antagonistic to free speech, but how courts on controversial political issues are happy to let them draw the line and draw the fire. There is an obvious tension between the democratic right to free speech which be most respected at election times and the duty to avoid unnecessary offence.

Ministerial broadcasts

The BBC accepts a special duty to permit ministerial broadcasts on **10–028** matters of national importance, which may range from a declaration of war to emergency arrangements for coping with a drought. So

---

[133] *R. v BBC Ex p. Pro-Life Alliance* [1997] C.O.D. 457. A complaint to Strasbourg was declared inadmissible in 2000.
[134] *R. (ProLife Alliance) v BBC* [2004] 1 A.C. 185.

long as there is general consensus on the subject-matter of the broadcast, no right of reply will be given to the Opposition. Where there is, however, an element of partisan controversy in a ministerial broadcast, the Opposition must be given equal time to broadcast a reply.[135] When Mr Tony Benn sought to make a ministerial broadcast in 1975 on the Petroleum and Submarine Protection Act, the BBC detected political controversy in his script and informed him that the Opposition would be entitled to put its point of view. He cancelled the broadcast rather than allow his opponents free airtime. Section 326 of the Communications Act 2003 places a statutory duty on Ofcom to comply with a notice from a minister of the Crown requiring it to direct licence holders to broadcast an official announcement. It must also observe any direction from a minister to refrain from including in any service any matter or description of matter which is specified. Licence holders will be contractually bound to comply with such a direction, but they may reveal the direction's existence to their viewers.

Foreign radio and television stations must not be exploited by interested parties to influence British elections, but otherwise their programmes can be broadcast by arrangement with the BBC or of Ofcom.[136]

Access to meetings

10–029   At election times schools and public meeting rooms have to be made available to candidates so that they can promote their campaigns.[137] Consistent with this objective, a candidate can book one of these venues only for a *public* meeting. A popular or controversial candidate may not be able to accommodate every member of the public who would like to be admitted, but, as in other contexts, it is difficult to see how a meeting could be correctly described as "public" if the press were actively excluded. Journalists who are ordered to leave election meetings by organisers unhappy with press coverage should insist on their right to remain. If forcibly ejected, they could obtain damages for assault.

Access to election registers and candidates' returns

10–030   The lists of electors are public documents, which the media are free to inspect and copy. Reporters have this access not just at election times but during normal business hours. One copy of the register is

---

[135] See the "Aide-Memoire" of April 3, 1969, between the BBC and the Conservative and Labour parties.
[136] Representation of the People Act, s.92.
[137] Representation Act, s.95 (parliamentary elections), s.96 (local government elections).

kept at the electoral officer's office (normally the town hall) and usually at public libraries as well.[138]

Within 35 days of the announcement of the result, the election agents for all the candidates must file a return with the electoral officer detailing the candidates' expenses. The electoral officer has 10 further days to advertise in two newspapers that circulate in the constituency giving notice of where and when the returns can be inspected. The returns and accompanying documents can be inspected and copied there (usually at the town hall) by any member of the public for two years after the election.[139] A fee of £5 can be charged for the inspection and 20p per page for copies.[140]

Exit polls

The Representation of the People Act 2000 introduced a prohibition **10–031** on the publication of exit polls before the official polls close.[141] The prohibition relates to any statement regarding the way in which voters have voted at a parliamentary or local government election where that statement is or might reasonably be taken to be based on information given by voters after they have voted. Forecasts of the result which are also based (or might reasonably be seen to be based) on such information are also prohibited. Publication in breach is a summary offence with a maximum penalty of a fine on level 5 (currently £5,000) or up to six months imprisonment. The statute is supplemented by Ofcom's Broadcasting Code which prohibits discussion and analysis of election or referendum issues after polling stations have opened until they are closed. During the same period, broadcasters cannot publish the results of opinion polls.[142]

This is an unnecessary restraint on free speech, apparently passed because political spin doctors feared that party supporters would not

---

[138] Representation of the People Regulations 2001 (SI 2001/341). The full version of the register can be inspected (Reg.43) and handwritten notes can be taken (Reg.7) but other copies of the full register cannot be made. The registrar must not allow the full register to be searchable by an individual's name and it cannot be sold to outside bodies, such as the media. There is also an edited version of the register which excludes voters who have asked not to be on it. This edited version can be inspected, copied and sold (Reg.93). The two categories of register were made necessary because of a challenge which successfully argued that it was contrary to the Convention to compel disclosure of names and addresses *R. (Robertson) v Wakefiled Metropolitan District Council* [2002] QB 1052. The new scheme does satisfy the Convention *R. (Robertson) v Secretary of State for the Home Department* [2003] EWHC 1760.

[139] Representation of the People Act 1983, ss.81, 88 and 89. The period is 70 days for the election of the Mayor of London: s.81(1A). Parish Council returns are kept for only one year: s.90(1)(b) and Sch.4, para.8(1); as are returns of European Parliamentary elections: European Parliamentary Elections Regulations 1999 (SI 1999/1214): Sch.1.

[140] Representation of the People Regulations 2001 (SI 2001/341), Reg.10.

[141] Representation of the People Act 1983, s.66A.

[142] Ofcom's Broadcasting Code ss.6.4 and 6.5.

bother to vote if early exit polls showed that their party was well in the lead. But it is more likely that exit polls would spur the citizens' interest and encourage them to go out and vote—a matter of public benefit given the appallingly low turnout at the 2001 general election. A Canadian ban on opinion polls in the three days prior to federal elections was held by the Supreme Court to be an unconstitutional restriction on freedom of speech.[143]

REGISTERED POLITICAL PARTIES

10–032 Until 1998 legislation barely recognised the existence of political parties. There were two particular pressures which brought about change. On the one hand there was the exponential growth in the money which parties were putting into election campaigns and which the Government wished to bring under control. On the other was the use by some fringe parties of names which were confusingly similar to established parties (e.g. the Literal Democrat who stood against a Liberal Democrat). Both pressures led the Government to introduce a system of registration of political parties and the regime is now set out in PPERA 2000.[144] Registration is necessary if candidates are to stand in an election on behalf of a political party.[145] Various other benefits accorded to political parties in an election (such as party political broadcasts) depend on the party being registered (see above para.10–025) and Electoral Commission has power to make grants for policy development[146] but only to registered political parties.

The Electoral Commission is responsible for the register. An application can be rejected if the proposed name is the same as an existing registered party or would be confusingly similar; if it contains more than six words, is obscene or offensive; if it includes words whose publication would be an offence; if it includes any script other than roman; or if it includes any prescribed words. If two or more simultaneous applicants want to use the same name, the Commission has to consider by reference to the history of each party which has the better claim.[147]

Registered political parties are subject to disclosure obligations. Most notably, the Commission has to maintain a register of recordable donations to registered parties.[148] The provisions as to what donations have to be recorded are complex[149] but broadly they

---

[143] *Thompson Newspapers Co Ltd v Att-Gen* (1998) 5 B.H.R.C. 567, Can. S.C.
[144] Ironically, after the PPERA the courts found another way of stopping the use of party names which would confuse voters—the law of passing off: *Burge v Haycock* (unreported) [2002] RPC 28 CA.
[145] PPERA, s.22.
[146] PPERA, s.12.
[147] PPERA, s.28 and Registration of Political Parties (Prohibited Words) Order 2001 (SI 2001/82).
[148] PPERA, s.69.
[149] PPERA, ss.62–68 and Sch.6.

include donations over £5,000. Parties have to make reports of donations to the Commission regularly—ordinarilyse each quarter, but weekly during a general election. There are also registers of "recognised third parties" (a scheme intended to give greater transparency to individuals and bodies who are providing support for particular parties)[150] and of bodies intending to campaign in relation to a referendum.[151] All of these registers (as well as the register of political parties itself) are open to public inspection and, for a charge, may be copied.[152] They can also be viewed on the Electoral Commission's website.[153] The requirements relating to donations do not apply to political parties in Northern Ireland.[154]

The Commission will also receive and must make available for inspection the annual accounts of each registered party,[155] a return from each party showing its election campaign expenditure,[156] and expenditure by recognised third parties,[157] and a return showing expenditure on a referendum campaign.[158]

Campaign Financing—Cash for Peerages

Since democracy requires periodical electoral choice between competing parties, these parties in order to compete must raise campaign funds from their supporters. This is a fundamental fact of political life and another is that some party members who provide such financial support will be recruited to serve the party as "working peers" in the House of Lords. Some are suitable for such recruitment, as members who have served the party in other capacities or because substantial donors are usually successful businessmen whose talents might be expected to be useful in political debates on economic and business issues. Some are simply persons with pathetic egos who crave whatever adulation comes from being a peer. Until the "Cash for Peerages" scandal in 2006, a peerage was thought to be a badge of respectability, although the failure of the House to rid itself of such scoundrels as Lord Archer of Weston-super-Mare had left this open to question. The House of Lords Appointments Commission (HOLAC) is meant to vet persons nominated for peerages by party leaders but since it is comprised of a senior figure from each party, its vetting is not very thorough. It publishes an annual and not very informative report: it contributed

10–033

---

[150] PPERA, ss.85–89.

[151] PPERA, ss.105–107.

[152] PPERA, s.149.

[153] *www.electoralcommission.gov.uk.*

[154] Political Parties, Elections and Referendums Act 2000 (Disapplication of Part IV for Northern Ireland Political Parties) Order 2005 (SI 2005/299).

[155] PPERA, ss.46 and 149.

[156] PPERA, ss.84 and 149—the Commission will keep these returns for two years.

[157] PPERA, ss.100 and 149.

[158] PPERA, ss.124 and 149.

to the "Cash for Peerages" scandal because it declined to demand information from peerage nominees as to the loans, as distinct from donations, they had made to their party. It was obviously tempting to all parties to encourage donations in the form of "loans" from people who could be rewarded with peerages, and who would in consequence waive both interest and capital, turning their loans into donations once it was safe to do so, i.e. once their party had been elected and once they had been safely ennobled.

It is not against the law to elevate party donors to peerages or other honours, unless such elevation has been decreed as a condition of—i.e. a *quid pro quo*—for their donation. The Honours (Protection of Abuses) Act was passed in 1925 as a result of the massive excesses of Lloyd George. The 1922 birthday honours list was so outrageous that the king himself had to intervene to block one peerage, to a convicted South African fraudster Sir Joseph Robinson, who had already paid £500,000 for it. (On being told of this difficulty, Sir Joseph took out his cheque book and enquired "How much more?") In 1923 a Royal Commission identified the main problem as touts and brokers who offered to procure honours "for political services" in return for contributions to party funds, and the Act subsequently made it a criminal offence to procure or obtain any gift or money as an inducement or reward for procuring an honour or a title. The only person to be convicted was Maundy Gregory, who had blatantly touted honours on behalf of the Prime Minister (a viscountcy was available for £125,000, a knighthood for £15,000, while an OBE was a snip at £100). There must be a promise or undertaking by the broker that he will try to procure the peerage, and he must intend that representation to produce the payment of a money donation).

The Political Parties, Elections and Referendum Act 2000 came about as the result of the fifth report of the Committee on Standards in Public Life, in *The Funding of Political Parties in the UK*. It defines a donation as "any money lent to the party otherwise than on commercial terms". This inept drafting meant that during the 2004 elections, all parties relentlessly canvassed their "high value" supporters to provide them with "loans" ostensibly on commercial terms, which were not in consequence discloseable publicly. Donors who preferred anonymity and particularly donors who preferred anonymity in order to be elevated to the peerage, allowed their donations to be described and paper-trailed as "loans", at rates of interest that would subsequently be waived along with the capital. It was a sad reflection on the ineptitude of British investigative journalism that this scandal (which had been commenced by the Conservatives in the 2001 election) had never been exposed, until a Scottish nationalist M.P. demanded a Scotland Yard investigation. This was in response to a *Sunday Times* sting operation which had recorded a Labour Party agent suggesting that an undercover reporter could secure an honour in return for sponsoring a city academy: "What would be

great is, you could go to the House of Lords. . . become a Lord."
The agent was arrested, and the enquiry uncovered a profusion of
campaign finance skeletons in the closet of all three political parties.

The Electoral Administration Act 2006 has made loans to political
parties or their officers "regulated transactions" which must be
reported to the Electoral Commission on a quarterly basis (weekly
during elections). The Commission must maintain a register of the
basic details and this is open to public inspection.[159]

---

[159] Political Parties, Elections and Referendum Act 2000 s.149(1)(ba) as added by
the Electoral Administration Act 2006 s.61.

CHAPTER 11

REPORTING EXECUTIVE GOVERNMENT

"It is an official secret if it is in an official file."[1]

INTRODUCTION

"Whitehall" stands for the executive and military branch of central **11–001** government. The Palace of Whitehall was the home of the first civil servants, who served the despotic Stuart kings. They now serve a democratic government, and justify the secrecy of their service by reference to an outdated theory that "ministerial accountability" requires information requested by representatives of the public to be forthcoming only from, or with the approval of, ministers responsible for Whitehall departments. In practice, however, ministerial involvement in departmental decisions occurs only at levels of high policy, and executive errors must be of the magnitude of the failure to foresee the invasion of the Falkland Islands before a minister will resign. The truth is that ministers neither control nor are answerable for thousands of decisions made by middle-ranking departmental officers—decisions that may vitally affect individuals and communities. Secrecy, said Richard Crossman, is the British disease. Against those who would hide their publicly paid behaviour from the public eye, the professional journalist can have only one response: to press on investigating and publishing. The Human Rights Act and the Freedom of Information Act do provide opportunities to roll back secrecy, but require media organisations to take legal action to challenge official decisions against disclosure.

None of the justifications for our present level of secrecy is convincing. National security might be threatened by the revelation of a limited class of information to foreign powers, but too often this danger is used as a pretext for the Government to withhold embarrassing information from its own citizens. The Government does gather many intimate details about individuals that it ought to

---

[1] Sir Martin Furnival-Jones, Head of MI5, evidence to Franks Committee on Official Secrets: *Report of the Departmental Committee on the Reform of s.2 of the Official Secrets Act 1911*, Cmnd 5104, Vol.III, p.249.

keep confidential, but privacy as a rationale for secrecy is less persuasive when it concerns the social impact of corporate policies, still less when it concerns policy discussions within Government. The argument that civil servants would be less frank if their advice were shortly to be made public is a canard; the evidence from other countries suggests that the advice would be better considered and better expressed. Even if some information is no longer written down and, instead, communicated orally, this cannot be routine in bureaucracies the size of Whitehall. The great attraction for blanket secrecy laws within the civil service seems to be that it fosters a sense of self-importance. Mandarins with a high security clearance have a status derived more from the exclusivity of their access to information than from its intrinsic significance. Even junior civil servants, according to a former head of MI5, approved the discredited and now abolished "section 2" of the Official Secrets Act 1911,

" . . . they find a kind of pride in being subjected to the criminal law in this way . . . the fact that they . . . are picked out as being people who are doing work so dangerous if you like that it brings them within the scope of the criminal law if they talk about it, has a very powerful effect on their minds . . . it is not that they are deterred by the fear of prosecution, but in a sense it is a spur to their intent".[2]

11–002   A vast quantity of information does, of course, pour out of Whitehall in the form of press releases from the press officers now attached to all departments and the media give ample space for these official hand-outs. The difficulty is to extract information that is not "authorised" or "vetted"; the civil servant who speaks out of turn in some cases faces the vague threat of prosecution, but more often the immediate danger of disciplinary sanction by way of transfer, demotion or dismissal. Britain does now have some protection for "whistleblowers", the Public Interest Disclosure Act (see para.5–072), but it is a cautious piece of legislation whose impact is very limited. However, for all the difficulties posed by secrecy laws and conventions, the Government is reluctant to court media unpopularity by prosecuting journalists over revelations of genuine public interest. Thus in 2000, the Government declined to prosecute *The Mail on Sunday*'s editor and journalists over their dealings with David Shayler who was paid some £37,000 after his revelation that MI5 had kept secret files on such youthful "subversives" as Jack Straw, Peter Mandelson, Harriet Harman and Patricia Hewitt. It dropped Official Secret Act charges made against Tony Geraghty over his book, *The Irish War*, after constant media criticism of the Attorney-General for pursuing the case. and against a young GCHQ

---

[2] Evidence to the Franks Committee, fn.1 above, Vol.III, p.261.

translator, Katherine Gunn, who from conscience leaked information about improper interception of foreign embassies in the lead up to the Iraq war. The only case the Blair government has brought to trial concerns the leaking of the transcript of a meeting at which George W. Bush apparently urged the bombing of Al Jazeera—a prosecution no doubt brought to impress US allies, but which excluded the *Daily Mirror*—the paper which broke the story.

This chapter will seek to give the Official Secrets Acts and other secrecy conventions a realistic appraisal. It will explain how valuable source material can be obtained through public records legislation and by invoking policy directives, which can help journalists to negotiate the disclosure of more recent public documents.

THE OFFICIAL SECRETS ACTS

The Official Secrets Act 1911 was rushed on to the statute books at a **11–003** time of national panic, as German "gunboat diplomacy" at Agadir coincided with sensationalised newspaper stories about German spies photographing the fortifications at Dover harbour.[3] It completed its entire parliamentary progress in one day, hailed by all parties as an urgently necessary measure to protect the nation's secrets from enemy agents. No M.P. spoke on s.2 of the Act, which had been carefully drafted within Whitehall some time before with the purpose of stopping leakage of official information to the press.[4] The press was soon to suffer: the very first prosecution brought under the new Act was to punish a war office clerk for supplying information to the *Military Mail* that cast his superiors in a poor light.[5]

Section 2 managed, by tortuous drafting, to create more than 2,000 different offences in a few statutory paragraphs. These could be roughly divided into two groups: those most likely to be committed by inside sources (i.e. by communicating official information to an unauthorised person) and those that directly affected journalists who received or retained official information without authorisation. The more serious s.1, which has a maximum penalty of 14 years' imprisonment, is aimed at spies and saboteurs, although the Government has once, in the "ABC" case (see para.11–032), tried to extend it to journalists. Finally, the Act gave the police extraordinary powers to arrest, seize documents and to question suspects, including journalists. The 1989 Act, which replaced s.2 with narrower (and hence more formidable) offences, has not often been invoked. More than any other piece of legislation, its use is circumscribed by political considerations.

---

[3] Franks Report, fn.1 above, Vol.I, App.III.
[4] K. G. Robertson, *Public Secrets: A Study of the Development of Government Secrecy*, Macmillan, 1982, p.63.
[5] Franks Report, fn.1 above, Vol.I, App.III. See also Jonathan Aitken, *Officially Secret* (Weidenfeld & Nicolson, 1971).

The Attorney-General in the past had to approve every prosecution under the Act (the exception under the Official Secrets Act 1989 is considered below), and take into account the degree of culpability, the damage to the public interest that resulted from the disclosure, and the effect that a prosecution would have on the public interest.[6] A number of top-level spies have gone unprosecuted since the Second World War because it has been deemed inexpedient to expose to the public (and to Britain's allies) the extent of Soviet penetration even with the protection possible through secret hearings. At the other extreme, Attorneys-General have been reluctant to prosecute newspapers for routine breaches. The appearance of secret Whitehall documents in the press is usually followed by a "leak inquiry", conducted by Scotland Yard, with the object of discovering the civil servant responsible. So long as journalists decline to answer questions or supply leaked copies of documents that might incriminate their source, these inquiries are usually fruitless.

11–004   The Attorney-General, as a party politician, will be disinclined to use oppressive and discredited legislation against the press. However, he may come under heavy pressure from the military and security establishment, unswayed by any concern for civil liberties and perhaps anxious to impress American "cousins" with their resolve to protect Allied secrets. Insecure Labour law officers, desirous of proving themselves "responsible" in such matters, have succumbed to this pressure. The first occasion, in 1970, had the result of discrediting s.2 of the Act:

> Jonathan Aitken, then a young journalist and parliamentary candidate, came by a secret Army document about the state of the Biafran war that contained information at variance with Prime Ministerial statements to Parliament. He and a chain of alleged sources were prosecuted under s.2 of the 1911 Act. Both journalist and editor additionally claimed that they had a moral duty to make the information public in order to rectify false statements in Parliament. The defence claimed the case was a "political prosecution", initiated by a petulant Labour Government, and the trial judge in a sympathetic summing up told the jury that it was high time that s.2 was "pensioned off". All defendants were acquitted.[7]

The outcry provoked by the prosecution led to the establishment of a committee headed by Lord Franks to examine s.2 of the Official Secrets Act. It condemned the width and uncertainty of the section, and urged its replacement by a law narrowly defining the categories

---

[6] 1911 Act, s.8. The criteria in the text were given by the Attorney-General in evidence to the Franks Committee, fn.1 above, Vol.II, p.7. Any function of the Attorney-General can instead be exercised by the Solicitor-General (Law Officers Act 1997, s.1), but the Solicitor-General is also a party politician.

[7] *R. v Aitken and Others*, and see also Aitken, *Officially Secret*.

of information that deserved protection.[8] The Government, in 1976, accepted that mere receipt of secret information by the press should not amount to an offence.[9] Reform of the Act was put in abeyance, however, by the extraordinary security service vendetta against journalist Duncan Campbell:

Campbell was a young freelance journalist specialising in defence and working mainly for small-circulation magazines. In company with Crispin Aubrey, a news reporter from *Time Out*, he interviewed a disaffected ex-soldier, John Berry, who 10 years before had worked at a signals intercept base in Cyprus. He had written to the magazine volunteering to reveal security "scandals", although the information he could give the journalists added little to what Campbell had already collected, from published sources about British Signals Intelligence operations. The three men were arrested, and Campbell's entire home library was removed in a pantechnicon to Scotland Yard. The "ABC" case, which then commenced its passage, had side consequences already noted. The prosecution, for the first time, used s.1 charges against journalists.

The result was that Campbell alone was charged, under s.1, with collecting information of use to an enemy relating to a number of defence installations. The case on this count collapsed after two weeks of evidence demonstrating that Campbell's information and photographs had come from published sources—in some cases, Ministry of Defence press hand-outs. The incompetence of the security services, which had instructed the Attorney-General that Campbell's information was top secret, was, in effect, conceded by the Crown prosecutor when withdrawing this ill-conceived charge.

The two journalists were charged under s.1 with obtaining information of use to an enemy (Berry's account of his time in Cyprus) for a purpose prejudicial to the security of the State. The "purpose prejudicial" was alleged to be their intention to publish it in *Time Out*. These charges were withdrawn at the insistence of the judge, Mr Justice Mars-Jones, who described them as "oppressive". Although the wide wording of s.1 of the Act was not necessarily confined to spies and saboteurs, he said that its harsh provisions (including a reversal of the burden of proof and facilitation of guilt by association) made it undesirable for use against persons not alleged to be in league with a foreign power.

Section 2 charges were brought home against each defendant. Berry was found to be in breach of the Act by passing information to the journalists, and they were found guilty of receiving this information. Berry received a six-month suspended sentence; both journalists were given conditional discharges.[10]

---

[8] Franks Committee Report, fn.1 above.

[9] *Hansard*, November 22, 1976 [*Hansard*] H.C. Debs Vol. 919, col 1878 *et seq*.

[10] Andrew Nicol, "Official Secrets and Jury Vetting" [1979] Crim L.R. 284. Geoffrey Robertson, *The Justice Game*, Ch.5 "Ferrets and Skunks? The ABC trial" (Vintage, 1999).

11–005   The effective collapse of the "ABC" prosecution may make future Attorneys reluctant to use s.1 against investigative journalists. The Attorney-General of the time, Sam Silkin Q.C., defended his decision to prosecute on the grounds that he had been misled by the Ministry of Defence and the security service as to the sensitivity of the information in Campbell's possession.[11] "Colonel B", the expert prosecution witness, was less impressive under skilled cross-examination than he had been in the Attorney's chambers. The case had the additional importance of undermining the seriousness of s.2 by the lightness of the sentences visited upon the journalist offenders.

The 1989 Act offered the media a Faustian bargain: it lifted the possibility of prosecution for much routine information within Whitehall (revelation of which would never in practice have been prosecuted under the old s.2) while it made much easier the prosecution of their sources for revelations about intelligence work, defence and foreign affairs. In these cases it replaced a blunderbuss with an armalite rifle. The Government firmly resisted a public interest defence, which might have protected the media and their sources in relation to leaks that demonstrate discreditable conduct within the defence and intelligence establishment.

The 1989 Act offences fall broadly into those that are most likely to be committed by "insiders" and those designed with "outsiders", such as the press, in mind. We start with the former because they introduce categories and classifications that span both groups.

Offences by "insiders"

11–006   These are subdivided into four groups.

Security and intelligence

11–007   This group is further subdivided into members of the security or intelligence services and those who work closely with them, and other Crown servants or government contractors who learn of information concerning security and intelligence in the course of their work.

Persons who are or have been members of the security and intelligence services commit an offence if they disclose any information, document or other article relating to security or intelligence that they have acquired in the course of their intelligence work.[12] There is no stipulation that the information must be secret and one possibility is that the courts would probably follow their stance under the old s.2[13] and find the offence was committed even though the

---

[11] Crispin Aubrey, *Who's Watching You?* (Penguin, 1981).
[12] Official Secrets Act 1989, s.1(1) "security or intelligence includes work in support of the security services"; s.1(8).
[13] *R. v Crisp and Homewood* (1919) 83 I.P. 121; *R. v Galvin* [1987] 2 All E.R. 851.

information was not secret in any meaningful sense. However, if the information had already become general knowledge, it is unlikely that there could be any further "disclosure" since the ordinary meaning of that word is making known something which is *not* general knowledge.[14]

Significantly, under this offence the Crown does not have to prove any damage or harm and there is no "public interest" defence.[15]

> David Shayler had been an MI5 officer until 1996. In 1997 he disclosed various intelligence documents (including material obtained by intercepts) to the *Mail on Sunday*. He wrote an article for the paper based on the documents. He was prosecuted under ss.1 and 4 of the Official Secrets Act 1989. At a preparatory hearing, the trial judge, Moses J. ruled that, even if the jury was to decide that disclosure had been in the public interest, this would not provide Shayler with a defence. This ruling was upheld by both the Court of Appeal and the House of Lords. The Lords decided that the proper course for someone in Shayler's position was to ask for permission to make the disclosure and, if that was refused in circumstances which were unreasonable, to challenge the decision by judicial review. Shayler also tried to argue that he could rely on the defences of necessity and duress of circumstances. The Court of Appeal[16] held that in principle these defences could be raised to charges under the Official Secrets Acts but that they could not possibly arise on the facts of Shayler's own case. Shayler was later convicted and sentenced to six months imprisonment.

The severe obligations of secrecy under these sections of the 1989 **11–008** Act can be extended by written notice to others who, though not actually members of the secret services, work closely with them.[17]

For Crown servants and government contractors who are not members of the secret services and who are not made honorary members by notification there is a narrower offence of making a *damaging* disclosure of information relating to security or intelligence.[18] "Damage" here means damage to the work of, or any part of, the security and intelligence services.[19] It is not apparently sufficient if work in support of the security services is harmed. Although there may, of course, be a knock-on effect, it is harm to the secret services themselves that must be shown. Here and throughout the Act it is enough if damage would be "likely to occur" as a result of the disclosure. In the present context alone the definition is wider still. The prosecution does not have to prove that the particular information would be likely to cause harm. It can

---

[14] See *Att-Gen v Associated Newspapers Ltd* [1994] 2 A.C. 238 in the context of the "disclosure" of jury deliberations.

[15] *R v Shayler* [2003] 1 A.C. 247.

[16] *R v Shayler* [2001] 1 W.L.R. 2206 CA.

[17] Official Secrets Act 1989, s.l(l)(b) and s.1(6).

[18] 1989 Act, s.1(3).

[19] 1989 Act, s.l(4)(a).

merely show that the information is within a class that might have this effect.

"Crown servants" are the principal group of "insiders". They include civil servants, the armed forces, and the police (and their civilian assistants).[20] The employees of certain privatised corporations and regulatory bodies have been brought within the definition of Crown servant by ministerial "prescription" permitted by the Act—without parliamentary debate or public notice.[21] The Government has moved by "prescription" to button the lips of all employees of British Nuclear Fuels, the Atomic Energy Authority, Urenco (Capenhurst) Ltd, and Enrichment Technology Ltd together with all persons employed by the Parliamentary Commission for Administration (the Parliamentary Ombudsman), the Auditor General and the Health Service Commissioner—posts that are ostensibly independent of Government.[22] The failure of the Ombudsman to object to the extension of this draconian Act to his staff is a disturbing reflection on his ability to judge where the public interest lies, namely in permitting the public reasonable scrutiny of bodies supposed to act in their interest. Local government employees are not and never have been Crown servants. The 1911 Act expressly applied to colonial governments; the 1989 Act does not, but the Government can extend its reach to the Channel Islands, the Isle of Man or any colony by statutory instruments.[23] The Act also reserves the power to add other groups to the definition of "Crown servant" by ministerial order with only the minimal protection that a draft of the order must be approved by each House of Parliament.

11–009   The definition disingenuously includes ministers and members of the Scottish Executive and junior Scottish ministers.[24] They are undoubtedly Crown servants, but despite the ministerial "briefings" that are the bread and butter of political reporting, no minister has ever been prosecuted under the Official Secrets Act. This is excused by the "fig-leaf" theory that ministers are able to authorise themselves to make disclosures. The naked truth is that prosecutions must be approved by the Attorney-General, who in the recent past has always been a member of the same political party as the blabbermouth minister. Resignation is the most severe penalty that has been imposed on ministers who have been indiscreet. J.H. Thomas was not prosecuted for leaking budget secrets in 1936, as the Attorney-

---

[20] Official Secrets Act 1989, s.12. Employees of a county council seconded exclusively to police stations were "in employment under a person who holds office under Her Majesty" for the purposes of the 1911 Act: *Loat v Andrews* [1985] I.C.R. 679 and they would no doubt be "employed . . . for the purposes of any police force" under the present law.

[21] 1989 Act, s.12(f) and (g).

[22] Official Secrets Act 1989 (Prescription) Order 1990 (SI 1990/200) as amended.

[23] Official Secrets Act 1989, s.15(3).

[24] Official Secrets Act 1989, s.12(l)(a) and (aa). Welsh Ministers are also treated as "Crown Servants": s.12(1)(ab).

General said he had been drunk at the time.[25] George Lansbury passed a Cabinet paper to his son in 1934; the son was prosecuted, the minister was not. The Attorney-General took civil action (see para.5–037) against Richard Crossman's publishers over his Cabinet memoirs but conceded that there was no criminal liability.[26] Leon Brittan was not prosecuted for authorising the leak of legal advice to the Government over the Westland affair, and Cecil Parkinson survived allegations that he had whispered Falklands War secrets to his mistress during moments of non-connubial bliss.

"Government contractor" means companies and their employees who provide goods or services for a minister, the civil service, the armed forces or a police force, the Scottish administration or the National Assembly for Wales. Additionally, it applies to contractors with governments of other States or international organisations.[27]

Defence

Crown servants and government contractors commit an offence if **11–010** they disclose information that they have acquired in their jobs and that concerns defence.[28] Damage must be proved by the prosecution. In this context "damage" means damage to the capability of any part of the armed forces, loss of life or injury to its members or serious damage to its equipment or installations. It can also mean jeopardy to, or serious obstruction of, British interests abroad or danger to the safety of British citizens abroad.

International relations

This, again, is a category that applies to Crown servants and **11–011** government contractors. It concerns information relating to international relations[29] or confidential information that has been obtained from another State or an international organisation.[30] The information of either type must be acquired in the course of the defendant's job.

Damage has to be shown by the prosecution. As with defence matters, this can be jeopardy to, or serious obstruction of, British interests abroad or danger to the safety of British citizens abroad. If the information was derived from another State or an international

---

[25] *Hansard*, June 10, 1936, col. 206.

[26] See Hugo Young, *The Crossman Affair* (Hamish Hamilton and Jonathan Cape, 1976), p.33.

[27] Official Secrets Act 1989, s.12(2). It also applies to contracts that the Secretary of State certifies are for the purposes of implementing the contracts referred to in the text.

[28] 1989 Act, s.2, defence is comprehensively defined in s.2(4).

[29] Official Secrets Act 1989, s.3.

[30] "International relations" means the relations between states and/or with international organisation, 1989 Act, s.3(5).

organisation, the prosecution can rely on the fact that it was confidential or on its nature or contents to establish that its disclosure would be likely to cause damage. The jury is nonetheless entitled to find that no damage would be likely to result from disclosure since the section provides only that these elements *may* be sufficient to establish harm.[31]

Crime

11–012 This category is loosely described as information concerning crime,[32] but it is really far broader. It concerns information the disclosure of which would be likely to result in the commission of an offence, facilitate the escape of a detained person, or impede the prevention or detection of offences or the apprehension or prosecution of suspects. There is no further requirement that the prosecution must show that the information is likely to cause damage. The Government argued that the categories of information are, by definition, likely to cause harm.

This dubious argument does not apply to a subcategory that rides on the back of "crime". It is an offence to disclose any information obtained from mail or telephone intercepts under a ministerial Regulation of Investigatory Powers Act (RIPA) warrant or information obtained by the security services under warrant. This prohibition extends to information obtained by reason of the intercept or secret service interference or any document or article used for or obtained by the intercept or interference.[33]

Authority and mistake

11–013 None of the insider offences are committed unless the disclosure was unauthorised. For Crown servants and "honorary" members of the security services that means a disclosure that is not in accordance with their official duty. In Clive Ponting's prosecution the trial judge ruled that it was for the Government of the day to decide what was the duty of civil servants.[34] However, the judge could not direct the jury to convict. (The jury alone has the right to decide that a defendant is guilty. This important principle is an insurance that the criminal law will confirm to the ordinary person's idea of what is fair and just.[35]) Ponting's acquittal showed that the jury took a more robust view of where his duty lay. "Authorised" means, in the case of a government contractor, disclosure to a Crown servant or in accordance with a Crown servant's directions.[36]

---

[31] 1989 Act, s.3(3).
[32] 1989 Act, s.4.
[33] 1989 Act, s.4(3).
[34] *R. v Ponting* [1985] Crim. L.R. 318, see also Clive Ponting, *The Right to Know*, 1985.
[35] *R. v Wang* [2005] 1 W.L.R. 661 HL.
[36] Official Secrets Act 1989, s.7.

The prerequisite of authorisation provides some prospect of a defence for the media: in the *Aitken* case it was argued that if original disclosure by the ex-colonel was "authorised", the subsequent chain of disclosure could not be in breach of the Act. The case of *R. v Galvin*[37] (under the old s.2 of the 1911 Act) is also of assistance:

> The Court of Appeal quashed an Official Secrets Act conviction on the ground that the issue of "authorisation" had not been left to the jury. The document concerned was an MOD manual that had been classified as "restricted" and had been obtained by the defendant by subterfuge. Nonetheless, it emerged at the trial that the manual had, in fact, been circulated to some outside bodies by the MOD, without specific restrictions on its further use. It was open to the jury to find, on this evidence, that the MOD had "impliedly authorised" circulation of the information, notwithstanding the "restricted" classification stamp on the copy obtained by the defendant.

In the *Shayler* case the House of Lords relied heavily on the possibility that a Crown servant could challenge a refusal to authorise disclosure on judicial review. The defendant had argued that this was not likely to be effective because of the deference which the courts had in the past shown to executive decisions in relation to national security. But, the Lords responded, since freedom of expression was now underpinned by Art.10 of the ECHR judges would be expected to adopt a much more rigorous scrutiny of such decisions, especially when there was evidence that the refusal was an excuse to cover up political embarrassment, unlawfulness or irregularity. Even if this was so, the practical obstacles in the way of bringing such proceedings would be formidable.[38]

None of the offences is committed if the defendant can persuade the jury that he did not know or have reason to believe that the information concerned security, defence, international relations or the categories of crime. In cases where the prosecution must prove damage it is similarly open to the defendant to prove that he did not know or have reason to believe that the disclosure would or might have the damaging effect.[39]

Retention of documents and careless loss

Crown servants and honorary members of the security services who **11–014** have in their possession documents or articles that it would be an offence for them to disclose commit an offence if they retain the

---

[37] [1987] 2 All E.R. 851.

[38] *R v Shayler* (above). Members of MI5, MI6 and GCHQ cannot take advantage of the Public Interest (Disclosure) Act 1998 (see para.5–072) because they are excluded from its provisions by Employment Relations Act 1999, Sch.8, para.1.

[39] Official Secrets Act 1989, ss.1(5), 2(3), 3(4), 4(4), 4(5). In *R. v Keogh* [2007] EWCA Crim. 528 the Court of Appeal held that it was for the prosecution to prove guilty knowledge—see *Stop Press* section.

document or article contrary to their official duty. They have a defence if they believed they were acting in accordance with their duty and no reasonable cause to believe otherwise.[40]

Government contractors commit a similar offence if they fail to comply with an official direction for the return or disposal of the document or article.[41]

Both Crown servants and government contractors can be guilty of failing to take reasonable care to prevent the unauthorised disclosure of such documents or articles.[42] A Foreign Office civil servant was fined £300 under the predecessor to this provision for carelessly leaving secret diplomatic cables on a tube train. Extracts from the cables were later published in the London magazine *City Limits*. No action was taken against the magazine.[43]

The effect of the Human Rights Act

11–015   Article 10 applies to "everyone" and the European Court of Human Rights has held that "everyone" includes civil servants,[44] members of the armed forces,[45] and even those working on secret military projects.[46] Any restriction on freedom of speech must be justified by the three tests: Was the restriction prescribed by law? Was it imposed for a legitimate aim? Was it necessary in a democratic society?

The "law" must have sufficient accessibility and have an application which is reasonably predictable, but those are requirements which the Official Secrets Acts would pass. Their aims, the protection of national security and prevention of crime, would also be "legitimate" in terms of Article 10(2), although where the connection with national security (as in the *Spycatcher* case after publication throughout the world) is attenuated, the real purpose of the measure may deserve closer examination.[47] As so often with Art.10 questions, the critical issue is whether the restriction is "necessary in a democratic society". In cases concerning security measures the European Court has allowed Member States a substantial "margin of appreciation", recognising the difficult judgments which have to be made.[48] Although even here, the Court has refused to find that it

---

[40] 1989 Act, s.8(1)(a), 8(2).
[41] Official Secrets Act 1989, s.8(1)(b).
[42] 1989 Act, s.8(1).
[43] *Observer*, December 5, 1982.
[44] e.g. *Ahmed v UK* (1998) 29 E.H.R.R. 1.
[45] *Engle v Netherlands* (1976) 1 E.H.R.R. 647.
[46] *Hadjianastassiou v Greece* (1992) 16 E.H.R.R. 219.
[47] In *Rotaru v Romania*, judgment of May 4, 2000, seven of the judges said that they found it hard to see how the suppression of data collected on a student going back 50 years and which was demonstrably false could be said to be justified on the grounds of national security. The case concerned Art.8, but the analysis of "legitimate aim" would have common features with Art.10.
[48] See e.g. *Leander v Sweden* (1987) 9 E.H.R.R. 433; *Hadjianastassiou v Greece* (1992) 16 E.H.R.R. 219.

was necessary for courts to try to ban publication of material which was already in the public domain.[49] The Court has found a violation of Art.10 on this basis even where the material had previously been made public by the person who was the object of the measures which gave rise to the Art.10 challenge.[50] In 2006 the Court found a violation for the first time where the applicant had been convicted for disclosure of information which had *not* previously been made public.

> The applicant, a Swiss journalist, had obtained a secret government document which set out a diplomatic strategy to combat the campaign by US lawyers against Swiss banks which had unclaimed deposits from Holocaust victims. The document's confidentiality could not be protected at any price: it raised matters of public interest which outweighed considerations in favour of preserving its secrecy. Even though the penalty had been minor it could have the effect of deterring other journalists from pursuing matters of public interest and hamper the press in its role of watchdog.[51]

In the course of defending charges under the 1989 Act, s.1 and s.4 (disclosure of information from intercepts) the ex-MI5 officer, David Shayler, unsuccessfully argued that the absence of any public interest defence on the face of these provisions of the Act conflicts with Art.10. He submitted that it cannot be necessary in a democratic society to punish ex-members of the security services for disclosing information even where (for the sake of argument) the information concerned dangerous and illegal activities of those services. The argument was rejected on the basis that an officer who learnt of such activities could, compatibly with the 1989 Act, disclose the information to his superiors, a staff councillor or, with the permission of his management, to the Commissioner or Tribunal which has power to review the activities of the security services. If the management refused permission to approach the Commissioner or Tribunal, the officer could, according to the judges, have sought judicial review.[52]

Offences by "outsiders"

Disclosure of leaked or confidential information

Section 5 of the 1989 Act is the offence of direct relevance to **11–016** journalists (although it is not confined to them). Broadly, the section makes it a specific offence for journalists and editors to publish

---

[49] *Guardian and Observer v UK* (1991) 14 E.H.R.R. 153; *Dammann v Switzerland* App. No. 77551/01 judgment April 25, 2006.

[50] *Vereinging Weekblad Bluf! v Netherlands* (1995) 20 E.H.R.R. 189, and see similarly *Weber v Switzerland* (1990) 12 E.H.R.R. 508.

[51] *Stoll v Switzerland* App No. 69698/01 judgment April 25 2006. At the time of writing, this decision of a Chamber of the Court is being reviewed by the Court's Grand Chamber.

[52] *R v Shayler* (above).

information that they know is protected by the Act, although the prosecution must additionally prove that they also had reason to believe that the publication would be damaging to the security services or to the interests of the United Kingdom. If charged under s.5, editors can at least testify as to their state of mind in deciding to publish, and will be entitled to an acquittal if the jury accepts that there was no rational basis for thinking that the disclosure would damage British interests.

The offence is complex. It involves looking at the type of information concerned and the outsider's knowledge that it is of this type (we shall assume that the outsider is a journalist). It turns also on the character of further disclosure that takes place and the journalist's awareness that it has this character. Each ingredient needs more consideration.

11–017 Type of information. The information must be protected against disclosure by an insider, i.e. it must relate to security or intelligence, defence or international relations or to crime.[53] The information must also have originated from a Crown servant or government contractor. It is arguable that in this context an offence is committed by an outsider only if the source *is* a Crown servant at the time of the leak and that the offence does not extend to disclosures by *former* servants of the Crown. This confusion over whether s.5 extends to publication of the memoirs of *former* employees was exposed (and confounded) by the decision of the House of Lords in *Lord Advocate v Scotsman Publication*[54] (the "Cavendish Diaries" case):

> The Law Lords lifted a breach of confidence injunction on newspaper publication of Cavendish's memoirs of life in the secret services after the war because no danger to national security could be apprehended by publication. Two judges considered whether the publication would amount to a breach of s.5. Lord Templeman considered that the newspaper would fall within the provisions of the section by publishing, notwithstanding that Cavendish was a former Crown servant and s.5 in terms refers only to revelations by "Crown servants". Lord Jauncy, however, stated that this interpretation "may well be unjustified having regard to the obscurity of the language". Both Law Lords agreed that a newspaper editor could, in any event, be found guilty only if the disclosure of the information was, in fact, damaging to national security.

On principle, Lord Jauncy's approach is preferable: criminal statutes should be narrowly construed, and Parliament has only itself to blame if the words "Crown servants" are deemed to exclude persons who are not Crown servants by the time the offence was

---

[53] Official Secrets Act 1989, s.5(1)(a).
[54] [1989] 2 All E.R. 852 at 860 and 864.

allegedly committed. It must not be assumed, however, that this interpretation will be finally adopted by the courts. Section 5(3) refers to documents "protected from disclosure by sections 1 to 3 above" and these sections protect against disclosures by "retired Crown servants"—a reference that the courts could seize upon to interpret "Crown servants" in s.5(1) to include "former Crown servants".

In addition, the information must have been disclosed without authority (either to the journalist or to someone else), or entrusted in confidence to the journalist or passed in breach of confidence to the journalist or someone else.[55] If the information was leaked by a government contractor or a confidee of a Crown servant or government contractor, there is a further restriction. That disclosure must have been made by a British citizen or taken place in the United Kingdom, the Channel Islands, the Isle of Man or a colony.[56]

Journalist's knowledge of the type of information. The prosecution **11–018** has to prove that the journalist knew or had reasonable cause to believe that the information was protected against disclosure and that it has reached him by one of the routes described above.[57]

Type of further disclosure. There is an offence only if the further **11–019** disclosure is without lawful authority (see para.11–013). More significantly, if the information relates to security, intelligence, defence or international relations, the prosecution must show that its further disclosure by the journalist will be damaging. The definitions of damage are the same as those for insider offences (see above para.11–008).[58]

The Government refused to concede a specific public interest defence or a defence that the disclosed material had already been published before. This obduracy was unfortunate and unnecessary: juries have sometimes been loathe to convict when disclosures were made on public interest grounds (e.g. Clive Ponting and Jonathan Aitken) and the "damage" requirement, although a stumbling block for any prosecution, is not a perfect substitute for a public interest defence. Prosecutors will no doubt argue that the statute requires only some harm and, once this is proved, it is not for juries to balance the harm against an alleged benefit from disclosure. In any case, damage does not have to be shown where the information relates to crime or the disclosure of intercepts. Nonetheless, the fact that the material has been published already or that it is in the public interest that it should be made known would be powerful arguments against there being any harm where damage does have to be proved.

---

[55] Official Secrets Act 1989, s.5(1)(d).
[56] 1989 Act, s.5(4).
[57] 1989 Act, s.5(2).
[58] 1989 Act, s.5(3).

Damage, of course, would have to be real damage to the efficacy or operations of the service rather than embarrassment flowing from the disclosure of improper behaviour. Since most media disclosures of alleged "secrets" are not in fact damaging to the public interest, the need to prove *some* damage is certainly one reason why s.5 has not been used against newspapers. Another reason, of course, is the reluctance of the Attorney General—in reality a party politician—to upset the media interests upon which his party relies for political support. A third reason is that Section 1 can be used to threaten media sources with jail. Where this tactic succeeds and the media do not bother much to campaign on behalf of journalistic sources as distinct from journalists it is a depressing reflection of its narrow self-interest.

11–020 Journalist's knowledge of character of further disclosure. The journalist must know or have reasonable cause to believe that his further disclosure would be damaging.[59] The insider offences include something similar as a defence but the burden of proof is then on the Crown servant. Here, knowledge by a media defendant that the further disclosure would be likely to be damaging must be proved by the prosecution beyond reasonable doubt.

Media complicity with an "insiders" offence

11–021 There is no doubt that s.5 has been, for the media, a considerable advance on the abolished s.2: the drafting is clumsy and obscure, and the questions of "damage" and knowledge may be developed by way of defence before the jury. One danger, largely ignored both by Parliament and the press in the debates over s.5, is that it will not be used at all. Instead, the publishers of information from insiders might simply be charged with offences of incitement, conspiracy, or aiding and abetting a breach of the offences under s.1–4 of the 1989 Act by their sources. This danger might be particularly present if payment is made for the information, or if the information is published by agreement with the errant insider. The confusion over whether s.5 applies to publication of disclosures by former Crown servants could be side-stepped by charging the media in such cases with the crime of complicity in an offence against s.1–4, which apply to former Crown servants as well as those presently serving the state. However, these concerns are to some extent allayed by the Court of Appeal which said in the *Shayler* case that,

> "It would have to be an extreme case on the facts for a prosecution of incitement to be justified having regard to the structure of the Official Secrets Act which attaches such importance to the status of the individual charged."[60]

---

[59] Official Secrets Act 1989, s.5(3)(b).
[60] *R v Shayler* [2001] 1 W.L.R. 2206 CA at para.96 (the House of Lords did not comment on this aspect when it dismissed Shayler's appeal).

It is notable that the Court obviously did not indicate that Shayler's own case was in this "extreme" category, even though he had been paid some £37,000 by Associated Newspapers for his story. At his trial, much was made of this payment although it was justifiable in the circumstances: it was not a reward so much as a provision of necessary funds for the maverick intelligence officer to set up a new life in France and defend himself there from British government attempts to have him extradited. No doubt the newspaper could have managed this better, although it would have risked becoming an accomplice. It paid in order to obtain his public interest revelations about files being kept on contemporary politicians and cabinet ministers: David Shayler may well have been acquitted or even escaped prosecution had this been his only revelation. His mistake was to take out of the office, in order to accredit himself, a "top secret" document on the extent of Libyan funding of the IRA and this formed the main charge against him at his trial. The moral for media dealings with intelligence officials is that they must disclose no more than information directly related to the scandal they are, in the public interest, bent on exposing.

Whether a prosecution of this type is brought will depend, as ever, **11–022** upon political considerations. In 1990 the Government admitted to having misled Parliament when denying allegations by Colin Wallace about disinformation exercises by the security services in Northern Ireland in the early 1970s. Wallace was not prosecuted under the 1989 Act. By 2006 no journalist had been prosecuted to trial under the 1989 Act. Tony Geraghty did face charges under s.5 in connection with his book *The Irish War* which was published in 1998, but these were dropped. The case against his alleged source, Nigel Wylde, was also dropped before trial. So, too, was the charge against Katherine Gunn, a translator for GCHQ, for leaking a memo to the *Observer* indicating a dirty tricks campaign to spy on UN delegates in the run-up to the Iraq war.[61] Other newspaper sources have been successfully prosecuted. In 1999, for instance, a Royal Navy petty officer was jailed for 12 months for leaking details about a feared Iraqi biological weapons attack on Britain to the *Sun*. He said he had been under tremendous financial pressure and the newspaper had paid him £10,000.[62] Shayler was ultimately convicted and sentenced to six months imprisonment.

Disclosure of information from spying

A simple offence is created by the 1989 Act of disclosing without **11–023** lawful authority any information, document or article that the defendant knows or has reasonable cause to believe has come into his possession as a result of a breach of s.1 of the 1911 Act.[63] Section

---

[61] See *Guardian Unlimited*, February 25, 2004.
[62] *Media Lawyer*, May/June, 1999, p.26.
[63] Official Secrets Act 1989, s.5(6).

1 principally concerns spying (see para.11–031) and it will be rare for journalists to come into the possession of such information.

Information from abroad

11–024   A separate offence is created by the 1989 Act for the unauthorised disclosure of information that has come from another State or international organisation.[64] This offence also needs to be broken down.

11–025   **Type of information.**   This offence concerns only information relating to security, intelligence, defence or international relations which has been passed by the United Kingdom in confidence to another State or international organisation. It must have come into the journalist's possession without the authority of that State or organisation.[65]

11–026   **Journalist's knowledge.**   The journalist must know or have reasonable cause to believe that the information is of the type described above.[66]

11–027   **Type of disclosure.**   There is no offence if the journalist's disclosure is made with lawful authority.[67] It is not a defence, as such, that the material has been previously published abroad unless it was published with the authority of the State or organisation concerned.[68] However, the prosecution must show that the publication by the journalist is damaging,[69] and if it has been previously published (even without authority), this will be virtually impossible to do.

11–028   **Journalist's knowledge of the consequences of further disclosure.**   The prosecution must again show that the journalist knew or had reasonable cause to believe that the further disclosure would be damaging.[70]

11–029   **Retention and careless loss.**   A person given a document or other article in confidence by a Crown servant or government contractor is guilty of an offence if he or she fails to take reasonable care[71] to prevent its unauthorised disclosure.[72] It is also an offence to fail to comply with an official direction for the return or disposal of a

---

[64] 1989 Act, s.6.
[65] 1989 Act, s.6(1)(a).
[66] 1989 Act, s.6(2).
[67] 1989 Act, s.6(3).
[68] 1989 Act, s.6(3).
[69] 1989 Act, s.6(2), "damage" has the same meaning as under the insider offences.
[70] 1989 Act, s.6(2).
[71] Official Secrets Act 1989, s.8(4) and (5).
[72] 1989 Act, s.8(4)(b).

document or article whose disclosure would be an offence under either s.5 or 6. There is an offence only if the journalist (or other outsider) is in possession of the document or article at the time its return is demanded. This simply adds to the incentive to dispose of leaked documents before their return is demanded: parting with possession is itself a disclosure (see s.13(1)) and so care would have to be taken in deciding whether disposal would be an offence.

These offences are triable only by magistrates, who can impose a fine on scale 5 (currently £5,000) or sentence to prison for up to three months. The price for being categorised as relatively minor offences is that there is no right to trial by jury. This is worrying, since juries in the past have played an important role in keeping the widely drawn Official Secrets Acts within some reasonable limits.

Codes, Keys and other access information

This offence concerns information that is or has been in the **11–030** possession of a Crown servant or government contractor and can be used to obtain access to any information, document or article that is protected against disclosure by the Act. It is an offence for anyone (whether insider or outsider) to disclose this type of information where the circumstances are such that it would be reasonable to expect it to be used for such a purpose without authority.[73]

1911 Act, section 1: "penalties for spying"

Headed "penalties for spying", this section is generally used against **11–031** enemy agents. It carries a maximum penalty of 14 years, which should only be invoked for serious espionage: George Blake was sentenced to 42 years imprisonment for three offences.[74] The section makes it an offence:

> "if any person for any purpose prejudicial to the safety or interest of the State—
>
> (a) approaches, inspects, passes over or is in the neighbourhood of, or enters any prohibited place within the meaning of this Act; or
> (b) makes any sketch, plan, model, or note which is calculated to be or might be or is intended to be directly or indirectly useful to an enemy; or
> (c) obtains, collects, records or publishes, or communicates to any other person any secret official code word, or password or any sketch, plan, model, article or note or other document or information which is calculated to be or might be or is intended to be directly or indirectly useful to the enemy."

The actions by themselves may be quite trivial—approaching a prohibited place, such as a nuclear power station (see below), or

---

[73] 1989 Act, s.8(6).
[74] *R. v. Blake* [1961] 3 All E.R. 125.

sketching a map that could be useful to a potential enemy. War need not have been declared: *potential* enemies are included, although it is agents of enemy governments who are targeted—spies for terrorist groups have not been prosecuted under this section.[75] Where the information concerns prohibited places, it is up to defendants to show that their possession of it is not for a disloyal purpose. In addition, contrary to the normal evidential rule against guilt by association, the prosecution can give evidence of the defendants' characters and associations to show that their purpose was prejudicial.[76]

11–032   In 1920 the Attorney-General told the House of Commons that the opening words of the section, "for any purpose prejudicial to the safety or interests of the State", meant that the section was aimed at spies in the employ of foreign powers.[77] This assurance that s.1 was so limited was repeated by another Attorney-General in 1949. But in 1964 the House of Lords extended it to peaceful protest by upholding the conviction of anti-nuclear demonstrators who "sabotaged" at a V-bomber base by sitting down on the runways. The CND protesters wished to argue that their purpose was to preserve the safety of the State by removing nuclear weaponry, but the courts held that it was for the Government to decide the State's best interests.[78] In 1977, s.1 charges were brought against journalists Duncan Campbell and Crispin Aubrey in the "ABC" case (see para.11–004), but were withdrawn after the judge described them as oppressive.

The media should have nothing to fear from s.1. Their right to report and to comment upon issues of national security may result in exposure of wrongdoing that can boost the propaganda claims of foreign governments or of terrorists (the revelation of Abu Ghraib torture helped Al Qaida recruit), but it is none the less exercised for a legitimate purpose, and not "for a purpose prejudicial to the safety and interests of the State". The security services, however, tend to think that journalism that exposes their activities amounts to "espionage by inadvertence",[79] and it was upon this theory that the deportation of the American writer Mark Hosenball was based. Indeed, Hosenball was evicted because he had the misfortune to put his name to an article about signals intelligence written largely by Duncan Campbell.[80] Section 1 may be wide enough in its literal

---

[75] *R. v Parrott* (1913) 8 Cr.App.R.186, but there are ample other provisions on which a prosecution could be based—see *Terrorism* section below.

[76] Official Secrets Act 1911, s.1(2).

[77] House of Commons, June 24, 1948, col.1711. See B.D. Thompson, "The Committee of 100 and the Official Secrets Act 1911" [1963] Public Law 201.

[78] *Chandler v DPP* [1964] A.C. 763.

[79] Head of MI5 to Franks Committee, fn. 1 above, Vol.III, pp.243–6.

[80] Leigh, *Frontiers of Secrecy*, p.231. No official explanation was given for Hosenball's deportation other than it was conducive to the public good: see *R. v Secretary of State for Home Affairs, Ex p. Hosenball* [1977] 3 All E.R. 452.

language to be applied to the press by a determined Government; whether it will be so applied again will depend on the media's willingness to protest.

Police powers and compulsory questioning

Search and arrest

The Official Secrets Act gives the police special powers to investigate **11–033** suspected offences. If they can convince a magistrate that they have reasonable grounds for believing that a crime under the Act has been or is about to be committed, they can obtain a warrant to search for and seize potential evidence.[81] Such warrants were notoriously issued on two occasions to search Duncan Campbell's home. On the first occasion, in 1977, the police seized his entire library of files, including press cuttings, telephone directories, personal letters, and a collection of novels.[82] On the second occasion, in 1984, the police haul of suspicious items included his copies of photographs that had been produced by the prosecution for the "ABC" trial. Following the 1989 Act the warrant cannot authorise seizure of items subject to legal privilege.[83] A magistrate cannot grant a warrant to seize excluded material or special procedure material (see para.5–076 for the meanings of these terms). The police can, however, apply to a circuit judge for an order that the possessor of this type of material hand it over to them.[84] Normally, these orders can be made only after the judge has heard both sides, but if the material is subject to a restriction on disclosure, the police can apply secretly and without notice to the possessor.[85] The police relied on these provisions to obtain search warrants for the *New Statesman*'s offices (which they occupied for four days) after the magazine had published Duncan Campbell's article on the Zircon spy satellite affair. No prosecution followed. The Scottish police relied on an Official Secrets Act warrant to seize from the Glasgow offices of BBC Scotland not only the Zircon film that Campbell had made but also all the other programmes in his *Secret Society* series.[86] In an emergency where the interests of the State seem to the police

---

[81] Official Secrets Act 1911, ss.1(2), 9(1).

[82] Including *For Whom the Bell Tolls*; Aubrey, *Who's Watching You?* (Penguin, 1977), p.24; Robertson, *The Justice Game*, Ch.4.

[83] Police and Criminal Evidence Act 1984, s.9(2) and Official Secrets Act 1989, s.11(3).

[84] Police and Criminal Evidence Act 1984, s.9(1) and Sch.1, para.3(b); *R. (Bright) v Central Criminal Court* [2001] 1 W.L.R. 662.

[85] Police and Criminal Evidence Act 1984, Sch.1, paras 12 and 14(c)(i) and s.11(2)(b).

[86] See Peter Thornton, *The Civil Liberties of the Zircon Affair* (NCCL, 1987). The Police and Criminal Evidence Act 1984, with its restrictions on the seizure of excluded and special procedure material, does not apply in Scotland.

to require immediate action, a magistrate may be dispensed with, and a police superintendent can sign the warrant.[87] No warrant at all is necessary for a police officer to arrest a person who is reasonably suspected of having committed (or being about to commit) an offence under the Acts.[88]

Police questioning

11–034 Those suspected of s.1 offences can be deprived of their right to stay silent under police questioning. The Home Secretary can order an investigation (in an emergency the chief of police's authorisation will suffice) and it is a criminal offence to refuse to answer the inquisitor's questions.[89] The staff of the *Daily Telegraph* were compulsorily questioned in the 1930s after the paper leaked the Government's plans to arrest Mahatma Gandhi, and the interrogation stopped only when the proprietor let it be known that the Home Secretary himself was the correspondent's source.[90] A journalist on the *Daily Despatch* was convicted under this section in 1938 for refusing to name a policeman who had given him a police circular about a wanted fraudsman.[91] This use of compulsory questioning to trace the source of embarrassing leaks caused a public outcry and in 1939 Parliament amended the Act so that this power can now be used only where there is a suspected breach of s.1 of the 1911 Act.[92] Even in this context, it is difficult to see how answers obtained under such compulsion could be used against the person questioned. To do so would be a clear violation of Art.6.[93]

Judicial questioning

11–035 Journalists may also be questioned in court or before a tribunal or inquiry about their sources. The Contempt of Court Act 1981 imposes a limited ban on such interrogation but it expressly exempts questions that are necessary in the interests of national security.[94] Three journalists were sent to prison in 1963 for refusing to disclose the source of their published stories about the Admiralty spy Vassall to a Tribunal of Inquiry investigating the security implications of his

---

[87] Official Secrets Act 1911, s.9(2).

[88] Offences under the 1911, 1920 and 1989 Official Secrets Acts (except for retention or loss of documents) are arrestable offences for the Police and Criminal Evidence Act 1984, see 1984 Act, s.24(2)(a) and 1989 Act, s.11(1).

[89] Official Secrets Act 1920, s.6. But journalists can insist on their reasonable expenses for attending and can refuse to answer questioning from an officer junior to an Inspector.

[90] Aitken, *Officially Secret*, p.79.

[91] *Lewis v Cattle* [1938] 2 All E.R. 368.

[92] Official Secrets Act 1920, s.6 (as substituted by Official Secrets Act 1939, s.1).

[93] *Saunders v UK* (1997) 23 E.H.R.R. 313; *Brown v Stott* [2003] 1 A.C. 681.

[94] Contempt of Court Act 1981, s.10. See para.5–061.

treachery,[95] although it is doubtful that post-*Goodwin v UK*[96] this precedent would be followed today unless there was an urgent need to unmask a "leaker" inside the security or intelligence services whose activities—e.g. identifying terrorist informers—might put lives at risk.

Proceedings

With one exception, any prosecution under the Official Secrets Acts **11–036** must be approved by the Attorney-General. The exception is where the information relates to crime in which case the approval of the Director of Public Prosecutions is sufficient.[97] At a time when meanings of sections of the 1989 Act are still largely untested by litigation, journalists who come to be arrested under the Act or become the subject of police suspicions will doubtless wish to dissuade the Attorney-General from approving a test case prosecution. Their submissions to the law officers may find support in the comforting words of the Government's White Paper *Reform of Section 2 of the Official Secrets Act 1911*, which was issued in 1988. Designed to mollify the media, it is full of promises that "responsible media reporting would not be affected by the Government's proposals" and that criminal offences would not be committed by making "disclosures which are not likely to harm the public interest".[98]

All the offences can be tried by a jury at the defendant's election except charges of retention or careless loss of documents. The maximum penalty for these offences is a fine on scale 5 or three months' imprisonment.

For other offences under the 1989 Act, the maximum penalty is two years' imprisonment[99]; magistrates can impose the statutory maximum fine (now £5,000) and a six-month term of imprisonment.

SPECIFIC SECRECY OFFENCES

Nuclear secrets

Nuclear secrets are protected by an adjunct to the Official Secrets **11–037** Acts. Although employees of the Atomic Energy Authority are no longer deemed to be Crown servants, the Government has designated five properties owned by the Atomic Energy Authority (AEA)/ British Nuclear Fuels (BNF) as "prohibited places" for the purpose

---

[95] *Att-Gen v Mulholland and Foster* [1963] 1 All E.R. 767; *Att-Gen v Clough* [1963] 1 Q.B. 773.
[96] (1996) 22 E.H.R.R. 123.
[97] Official Secrets Act 1911 s.8; 1989 Act, s.9.
[98] Cm. 408 (1988) paras 77 and 78.
[99] Official Secrets Act 1989, s.10(1).

of s.1 of the 1911 Official Secrets Act.[100] Disclosure of information about atomic energy processes or plant can additionally be prosecuted under the Atomic Energy Act 1946. There is no requirement that the information must be secret, but the Secretary of State should not give his consent to a prosecution if the information is not important to defence.[101] The Anti-terrorism, Crime and Security Act 2001 prohibits the disclosure of information with the intention of harming, or being reckless as to, the security of any nuclear site or nuclear material (including its transportation). The maximum penalty is seven years imprisonment.[102] The same maximum penalty applies to the disclosure of uranium enrichment technology without authorisation.[103]

Other statutes

11–038   The Atomic Energy Act is but one example of the dozens of statutes that prohibit civil servants from disclosing specific types of information received by the Government. A few, like the Atomic Energy Act or the Army Act 1955, deal with security matters. The Rehabilitation of Offenders Act 1974 is intended to protect personal privacy, and several are concerned with secret trade processes. These are not objectionable. Much more questionable is the political deal that is often struck with a regulated industry: government regulators may compel the provision of information on condition that it must be kept secure by special provisions to punish leaks. The reform of s.2 of the 1911 Act was incomplete because it did not revise these secrecy clauses at the same time. At present, they operate to prevent the disclosure of information of importance to public health and safety.[104] However, industry cannot stop a government department that wishes to publicise the information. The High Court refused an injunction to a trader with a bad consumer record who had been compelled to give an assurance of improvement to the Director-General of Fair Trading and who wanted to stop the Director-General announcing the assurance in his customary press release. Lord Justice Donaldson said the Director-General was entitled to "bark as well as bite" and that publicity was one way of seeing that the trader lived up to his promises.[105]

---

[100] Atomic Energy Act 1954, s.6(3); Atomic Energy Act 1965, Sch.1, para.3. British Nuclear Fuels' sites at Sellafield and Capenhurst and Urenco's site at Capenhurst, the Atomic Energy Authority's sites at Harwell and Windscale are prohibited places: The Official Secrets (Prohibited Places) Order 1994 (SI 1994/968).

[101] Atomic Energy Act 1946, s.11.

[102] Anti-terrorism, Crime and Security Act 2001, s.79

[103] 2001 Act, s.80 and Uranium Enrichment Technology (Prohibition on Disclosure) Regulations 2004, (SI 2004/1818).

[104] James Michael, *The Politics of Secrecy* (NCCL, 1979), pp.10–11.

[105] *S. H. Taylor and Co v Director-General of the Office of Fair Trading*, July 4, 1980, unreported, but see *The Times*, July 5, 1980 and R. G. Lawson, "Fair Trading Act 1973—A Review" (1981) N.L.J. 1179.

RADIO EAVESDROPPING AND TELEPHONE TAPPING

Air may be free but ether is not. Unauthorised eavesdropping on **11–039** radio messages is an offence, and so is disclosure of any information thus acquired.[106] The penalty is a fine of up to £5,000.[107] There is little likelihood of prosecution of journalists, although the risk increases in the case of systematic monitoring of radio traffic or if a journalist incorporates the information into a story that makes clear that it was obtained in a prohibited way.[108] *Sunday Times* reporters discovered a plot against the Seychelles Government with the help of a transmitter bug placed (by others) in a London hotel room. When they voluntarily handed over their material to the police to help them prosecute the conspirators, they were threatened with a prosecution for illegal eavesdropping.[109] It did not materialise. However, in 2006 Clive Goodman, the royal editor of the *News of the World* pleaded guilty to charges of intercepting voicemail messages for the household of Prince Charles and his family. Goodman had hacked into some 487 messages over a nine month period. He was sentenced to four months imprisonment and his co-conspirator, a private investigator, received a six month sentence. Andy Coulson, the editor of the paper, resigned in consequence.

Unauthorised interception of the post or a public (and, in certain circumstances, a private) telecommunications system is also an offence. The penalty can be a fine of the statutory maximum in a magistrates' court (currently £5,000) or an unlimited fine and up to two years' imprisonment in the Crown Court.[110] The DPP must approve any prosecution.

Authorised telephone tapping and mail interceptions are con- **11–040** ducted at the request of the police and security service officials who should obtain a warrant from the Home Secretary authorising the intercept for a particular period of time. Under the Regulation of Investigatory Powers Act 2000 (RIPA) intercept warrants may be issued in the interests of national security, for the purpose of preventing or detecting serious crime, or for the purpose of safeguarding the economic well-being of the United Kingdom. The Home Secretary ought to consider whether the information could reasonably be obtained by other means and whether the conduct is proportionate to what is sought to be achieved.[111]

The Government's objective (the Labour Government as much as its Conservative predecessor) is to remove these surveillance operations almost entirely from public view. Under the 2000 Act nothing

---

[106] Wireless Telegraphy Act 1949, s.5(b)(i).
[107] 1949 Act, s.14(1c).
[108] The purpose of the eavesdropping is immaterial: *Paul v Ministry of Posts and Telecommunications* [1973] R.T.R. 245.
[109] *The Guardian*, November 24, 1982.
[110] Regulation of Investigatory Power Act 2000. s.1.
[111] RIPA 2000, s.5.

can be said in or for the purpose of legal proceedings which suggests that there has been an interception or discloses its content.[112] Under ss.4 and 5 of the Official Secrets Act 1989, the leaking or publishing of any details about official intercepts is an offence. The 2000 Act established a Tribunal to consider complaints (including human rights complaints) about the interception of communications and various other activities of the intelligence and security services.[113] Essentially, the Tribunal's function is to assess the legality of the challenged action. This involves considering in most cases whether it was rational (or, in human rights matters, proportionate) rather than whether the Tribunal would also have agreed that the action was right.[114] The Tribunal's procedure is carefully structured so as to give nothing away to complainants. Any oral hearing which it does hold must take place in private.[115] Its predecessors, such as the Security Services Tribunal, never found occasion to uphold a complaint. The 2000 Act also established a "judicial monitor", the Intelligence Services Commissioner (bringing into one post the jobs which had formerly been given to the Security Services Commissioner and the Intelligence Services Commissioner). The reports of the previous commissioners were bland and uninformative, disclosing only rare occasions where clerical errors have led to taps being placed on the wrong phone. These arrangements offer little protection to the public and almost total protection to Government eavesdroppers against any media investigation of their work.

DA-NOTICES

11–041 DA-notices (Defence Advisory "DA" notices, often simply referred to their former name of "D Notices"[116]) are the responsibility of the Defence Press and Broadcasting Advisory Committee, which consists of representatives of the armed forces, senior civil servants and various press and broadcasting institutions. The Committee's stated purpose is to advise editors and publishers of categories of information the secrecy of which is alleged to be essential for national security.[117] The Committee was established in 1912, shrouded in secrecy: for 40 years its existence was not publicly known.[118]

The Committee currently issues five general notices of guidance. They concern military operations and capabilities; nuclear and non-nuclear weapons and equipment; ciphers and secure communications; sensitive information and home addresses; United Kingdom

---

[112] RIPA 2000, ss.17 and 18.

[113] RIPA 2000, s.65.

[114] RIPA 2000, s.67.

[115] The Investigatory Powers Tribunal Rules 2000 (SI 2000/2665), r.9(6).

[116] As reflected in the Committee's website address *www.dnotice.org.uk*.

[117] House of Commons Defence Committee 3rd Report, 1979–80; *The D-Notice System* H.C. 773, 640 i–v.

[118] D.G.T. Williams, *Not in the Public Interest* (Hutchinson, 1965), p.85.

security and intelligence services and special forces. In addition, "Private and Confidential Notices" can be sent giving warning that specific stories would threaten national security. The Secretary of the Committee, who has always been a high-ranking officer from the armed forces, is available for advice and consultation on short notice. No part of this system has any legal force. Stories are regularly printed in breach of the contemporary notices without attracting proceedings. Shortly after the attack on the World Trade Centre, the former Secretary to the Committee, Rear Admiral Nick Wilkinson wrote to all newspapers and broadcasters asking them not to speculate on any retaliatory military action in Afghanistan.[119] This was a ridiculous suggestion, since speculation was being fuelled by government ministers and CNN and the American press was full of it. Conversely, an editor who assiduously follows the Committee's advice is not guaranteed immunity from prosecution under the Official Secrets Acts. The editor of the *Sunday Telegraph* faced charges along with Jonathan Aitken for receiving the Biafran War report, although the secretary of the D Notice Committee had told him that its publication would create no danger to national security.[120]

The D Notice Committee is not to be trusted. In 1985 it asked a **11–042** publisher for an advance copy of a book by Jock Kane about defective security in signals intelligence. The naïve publisher, thinking that the Committee would offer helpful "guidance", received instead an expensive injunction, which has meant that the book can never be published.

Although the D Notice system is described as a voluntary and informal system of advice, it remains a form of censorship by wink and nudge, by threat and through the complicity of media executives. It is astonishing that editors try to give credence to this discredited Committee by remaining members of it.

MINISTERIAL AND CIVIL SERVANT MEMOIRS

Ministers

There is little danger of ministers being prosecuted for breaches of **11–043** the Official Secrets Act even after they have left office. In 1975 the Attorney-General used the civil law of confidence to try to ban the Grossman diaries. The court found the secrets too old to require suppression, but in principle the court accepted that Cabinet confidences could be protected by injunction if they still affected national security.[121] In Australia a High Court judge refused to injunct as a

---

[119] See *Guardian*, October 1, 2001
[120] Aitken, *Officially Secret*.
[121] *Att-Gen v Jonathan Cape Ltd* [1975] 3 All E.R. 484.

breach of confidence a book that reprinted diplomatic cables between Canberra and Djakarta, because the Government failed to show that the public interest required restrictions on material that might cause diplomatic embarrassment and political criticism.[122] Democracy entails a measure of acceptance of such consequences as incidents of government.

After the Crossman diaries affair, the Government adopted new guidelines proposed by Lord Radcliffe.[123] The Secretary of the Cabinet continues to act as censor of the first draft, but on national security matters and foreign relations the author can now appeal to the Prime Minister, whose decision is final. Publication in defiance of a rejected appeal could be injuncted on grounds of national security. The embargo on confidential material that does not threaten security is lifted automatically after 15 years. This is a conventional period, not a legal limitation. A minister can choose to ignore the advice of the Secretary of the Cabinet, and publish at an earlier time.[124] Hugh Jenkins refused to delete from his book *The Culture Gap* references to civil servants who had advised him when he was Arts Minister. The book was published shortly after he left office, when most of the civil servants were still in place.[125] Although the Radcliffe guidelines are worded in legalistic terms, they remain no more than guidelines. If a minister defies them, a prosecution will be successful only if a breach of the Official Secrets Act can be established; and a civil injunction will depend on whether the liberal public interest test of the Crossman diaries case is satisfied In reality, ministerial memoirs are now so commonplace that the 'Radcliffe Guidelines' serve little purpose. Ministers of the Thatcher and Major governments have published memoirs without any trouble from the Cabinet Secretary and in 2002 Mo Mowlem became the first minister of the Blair government to decline to submit to Cabinet Office censorship.

Mo Mowlam has been followed by Clare Short, David Blunkett etc., whose memoirs have been serialised for their purple passages and then remaindered. Alan Clark remains the only ex-minister whose memoirs have had any literary value or lasting impact (and then only the first volume). There is an ethical question here about politicians making money out of re-telling (in a partisan and often dishonest fashion) what were cabinet secrets. One or two revelations will suffice to obtain large sums for newspaper serialisation. No

---

[122] *Commonwealth of Australia v John Fairfax & Sons* (1981) 32 A.L.R. 485.

[123] *Report of Committee of Privy Councillors on Ministerial Memoirs*, Cmnd.6386 (1976).

[124] At least in relation to matters not affecting national security or foreign affairs. The guidelines require notice to be given to the Secretary of the Cabinet. This presumably is so that further pressure can be put on the minister, and so that the Government has the opportunity to seek an injunction.

[125] *Guardian*, September 19, 1978. See Michael Supperstone, *Brownlie's Law Relating to Public Order and National Security* (2nd edn, Butterworths, 1981), p.266.

memoir yet has quite plumbed the depths of Edwina Currie, who revealed her affair with John Major and recounted how they sat naked making love in the bath—he soaped her back and asked her, "Do you believe in God, Edwina?"

Civil servants

Civil servants' memoirs have occasionally been targets of the Official **11–044** Secrets Act. In 1926 the Governor of Pentonville prison was fined for publishing his life story in the *Evening News*,[126] and the biography of Pierrepoint, the public hangman, was held up for many years by threats of an Official Secrets Act prosecution.[127] On taking up their employment, civil servants are required to sign a promise to submit any publications for prior written approval. As the head of the Home Office acknowledged to the Franks Committee, this gives the misleading impression that failure to comply is automatically an offence under the Acts.[128] This overstates the risk of prosecution, since sufficient authorisation can be given in other ways under the Acts, although a publisher would have to consider the possibility of an injunction for breach of confidence or for breach of the official's contractual obligation. With the abolition of the old s.2, prosecution is not a realistic prospect so long as ex-civil servants avoid discussion of defence and intelligence issues.

The rules relating to memoirs have been discredited by the inconsistencies in their application. Memoirs by senior civil servants, which show Whitehall in a favourable light, never encounter difficulty. Both Sir Robert Mark, the former Metropolitan Commissioner of Police, and Sir Norman Skelhorn, the former Director of Public Prosecutions, published memoirs within a few years of leaving office. The Government's reluctance to use the law means that a determined civil servant has little to fear, and the publishers of Leslie Chapman's *Your Disobedient Servant* went ahead without receiving the retribution that had been threatened for his revelations of waste and inefficiency in Whitehall. There was both public and official displeasure expressed when Ronald Gregory, the Chief Constable responsible for the inept hunt for the "Yorkshire Ripper", cashed in by selling his story to a newspaper shortly after his retirement. A breach of confidence action might well have succeeded against both policeman and newspaper, but the possibility was not mentioned by the Home Secretary when he deplored the incident in Parliament. However, such an action has been brought against a former police officer who used material taken from Myra Hindley's statements to police in his autobiography.

---

[126] *The Times*, December 16, 1926.
[127] Franks Report, fn.1 above, Vol.I, App.II, p.116.
[128] Sir Philip Allen in oral evidence to the Franks Committee, fn.1 above, Vol.III, p.13.

In 1991 the political motive behind Cabinet Office vetting of civil service and ministerial memoirs (and the willingness of their publishers to collaborate) was hilariously exposed through a mistake made by HarperCollins, publishers of *Kill the Messenger*, the "authorised" autobiography of Thatcher press secretary Bernard Ingham. They sent to *The Sunday Times* (which had bought serialisation rights) a copy of the book proofs *before* it had been submitted for Cabinet Office vetting, and a comparison with the final version allowed the newspaper to deduce which passages had been censored. The Cabinet Secretary, Sir Robin Butler, had not wielded the blue pencil on the basis of national security or justifiable confidentiality, but only to delete or dilute criticisms of still-serving ministers (particularly Michael Heseltine) that might be politically embarrassing to the Government.

11–045   The autobiography of Sir Christopher Meyer, former British Ambassador in Washington and then Chairman of the Press Complaints Commission caused a row with his candid descriptions (the Prime Minister got a mixed report and certain Cabinet ministers were described as "political pigmies"). Subsequently the Diplomatic Service Regulations were amended so that by their contracts, FCO staff are prohibited from writing their memoirs while in service and thereafter from publishing anything which would damage the confidential relationship between ministers or between ministers and civil servants.

Ministers may now write their memoirs within a few years of leaving office and they may well, in those memoirs, criticise their senior civil servants. Why should those civil servants not have the right to answer back? It may not be seemly or fair, and undoubtedly a civil servant who makes money by poking fun at his political bosses will contribute to a relationship in which ministers may repose less trust in their public servants. But is this really any worse than the "Yes, Minister" culture? The bottom line is that freedom of expression must trump all such considerations.

ANTI–TERRORISM MEASURES

11–046   The "war" against terrorism has brought an avalanche of legislation, beginning with the Terrorism Act 2000, which gives police new and invasive powers and creates an overlapping and largely unnecessary armoury of new criminal offences, some of which could impact upon freedom of expression. After all, one person's terrorist is another's "freedom fighter". Blue plaques adorn the London homes of Karl Marx and those who plotted to overthrow tyranny by force of arms— Mazzini, Sun Yat Sen, Kropotkin and the Spanish war heroes, while streets have been named after Nelson Mandela and those who supported the ANC. But in 2000, Parliament "nodded through", a definition of terrorism so wide that it would cover support for all liberation movements and any plans to overthrow any foreign government, no matter how undemocratic, unlawful or oppressive. In 2007 a charge of "possessing information likely to be of use to terrorists" was levelled at a Libyan dissident found with a plan to set up an underground opposition to the Gaddafi regime. Although the plan rejected any violence that would endanger civilians or foreigners, the Court of Appeal in *R v F*[129] ruled that it fell within the definition of "terrorism" under s.1 of the Act, because it envisaged a "design to influence a government of a foreign country" by violence—in this case, the military preparations for self-defence against Gaddafi and his secret police. Although the definition of terrorism in international criminal law relates solely to violence used against civilians, and this is the meaning of the word in common parlance, in UK law it means the espousal of violence for any political ends, unless that espousal is by the government itself—e.g. by invading another sovereign state like Iraq or Serbia. These new terrorism powers and criminal offences are aimed, of course, at Muslim fundamentalists and Islamic extremists found in possession of *jihadi* literature, usually downloaded from the Internet, urging battles against the Americans and showing how to make bombs. CD-Rom pictures of beheadings and tapes of sermons in which young men are urged to enrol in world-wide jihad have thus far been the kind of material to engage police attention. The scope of the power, however, would extend to many NGOs urging support for national liberation movements and would encompass some inflammatory material on liberation front websites and in opposition newspapers published in England. Concern raised in parliament about the draconian legislation was fobbed off by reference to a "safeguard"—the DPP's consent (the Attorney must consent in the case of material that targets foreign governments). However, a bad law is never justifiable on the basis that it will be sensibly enforced, and political changes in international relations may presage prosecutions or proscription of previously tolerated groups. Thus the Libyan dissident who was the subject of the *R v F* prosecution had been granted asylum here in 2003 precisely because he was at risk of persecution from the Gaddafi regime: he was prosecuted only when that regime, responsible for much of the terror in the world prior to 9/11, changed its spots and collaborated with the West in fighting Al Qaeda. Saudi Arabia is another example of a corrupt and autocratic government whose opponents in exile may find an early morning knock on their doors from Scotland Yard's anti-terrorist squad, although it is unlikely that anyone urging the overthrow by force of Robert Mugabe or Kim Jong-il would suffer police attention at present.

---

[129] [2007] 2 All E.R. 193.

Proscribed organisations

11–047 The idea of banning organisations engaged in terrorism is not new but in recent times until 2000 it was confined to various groups in Northern Ireland. The Terrorism Act 2000 took away this limitation. The "traditional" proscribed organisations (such as the IRA and the Loyalist Volunteer Force) are still banned,[130] but the Home Secretary is given power to supplement the list by regulation to add any organisation which he believes is concerned in terrorism. The first regulations were issued in 2001[131] and included, as well as Al Q'aida, the Tamil Tigers who are fighting what is effectively a civil war in Sri Lanka and the Kurdish organisation, the PKK. More recently, following the Blair government's assumption that violence against any government in the world cannot be justified (unless it is violence by the US and its allies), the Home Secretary has proscribed organisations which, like the ANC of yore, espouse direct armed action against tyrannies and dictatorships. Thus the Libyan Islamic Fighting Group, which aims to establish an underground resistance to the Gaddafi dictatorship (since the regime arrests, ill treats and sometimes executes any over-ground resistance) has been proscribed. Despite Gaddafi's heinous involvement in past terrorism actions and attempts made by the United Kingdom to kill him in the past (Britain allowed its airfields to be used by the US for the 1986 attacks on his home in Tripoli, and, if David Shayler is to be believed, it funded an assassination attempt on his life in 1996) Gaddafi's regime is nonetheless a "government of any other country" for the purposes of the definition of terrorism in s.1 of the Terrorism Act 2000,[132] which enables the Home Secretary to use his proscription powers against organisations that threaten such governments with violence. Some liberation groups will have no connection with international terrorists and others enjoin their members not to kill civilians or foreigners, and to target only the dictator and his secret police apparatus. However, they are all subject now to the prospect of proscription, which will severely impact upon their ability to make any kind of public statements, and may affect the right to report their calls to other exiles to rise up against their particular local tyranny.

Since 2006 organisations can also be proscribed if they unlawfully "glorify" terrorism.[133] The 2000 Act established a mechanism for appeals against a banning order to the Proscribed Organisations Appeal Commission.[134] However, as long as an organisation is

---

[130] Terrorism Act 2000, Sch.2 lists these and various other Irish groups.
[131] Terrorism Act (Proscribed Organisations) Amendment Order 2001 (SI 2001/1261).
[132] *R v F* (see above).
[133] Terrorism Act 2000 s.3(5A) as added by the Terrorism Act 2006.
[134] Terrorism Act 2000, Sch.3.

proscribed it is an offence to belong to it[135] or to invite support for it.[136] Elaborate provisions are made to stem the funding of such organisations.[137]

It is also an offence to address a meeting if the purpose of the **11–048** address is to encourage support for the organisation.[138] There is a further offence of arranging, managing or assisting in arranging or managing a meeting which the person concerned knows is to support or further the activities of a proscribed organisation. It may be unusual for any of these to impinge on the media, but a yet further offence is arranging a meeting which the person concerned knows is to be addressed by a person who belongs to a banned organisation.[139] This may be problematic for journalists wishing to interview members of proscribed organisations because a "meeting" is defined as a meeting of three or more persons whether or not the public are admitted.[140] It seems bizarre that a journalist would not be at risk under this provision if he arranged a one-to-one interview with a member of such an organisation, but would be if the meeting was filmed by a cameraman. If a prosecution were to take place in such a situation there may be scope for persuading a court to "read down" the offence in line with the court's obligation under s.3 of the Human Rights Act to interpret legislation as far as possible compatibly with Convention rights.

Payment for any interviews with members of a proscribed organisation might be held to infringe the prohibition on providing money or other property for the purposes of terrorism.[141] The purposes of terrorism are not limited to acts of violence, but include action taken for the benefit of a proscribed organisation.[142]

Terrorist investigations

The police are given wide powers when they are conducting a **11–049** "terrorist investigation". Although this term obviously includes investigating actual acts of terrorism, its statutory meaning is far wider. Thus it embraces an act which appears to have been done for the "purposes of terrorism", an investigation of the resources of a proscribed organisation and an investigation into the possibility of making an order proscribing a new organisation.[143]

The police conducting a terrorist investigation can obtain a search warrant from a magistrate and, in some circumstances, from a senior

---

[135] Terrorism Act 2000, s.11.
[136] 2000 Act, s.12(1), other than by providing money or property.
[137] 2000 Act, Pt III.
[138] 2000 Act, s.12(3).
[139] 2000 Act, s.12(2)(c).
[140] 2000 Act, s.12(5)(a).
[141] Terrorism Act 2000, s.15(4).
[142] 2000 Act, s.1(5).
[143] 2000 Act, s.32.

police officer but neither ought to give permission if the object of the search is "excluded material" or "special procedure material" under the Police and Criminal Evidence Act 1984 (PACE) (see para.5–076).[144] Thus a warrant cannot include material held for the purposes of journalism, whether in confidence or not.

If the police do wish to obtain journalistic material, they ought to apply to a Circuit judge.[145] The procedure is modelled on that for ordinary criminal investigations under PACE. Thus the judge must be satisfied that there are reasonable grounds for believing that the material is likely to be of substantial value whether by itself or together with other material, to a terrorist investigation.[146] In 1994 Channel 4 and an independent production company persuaded a judge that the police could not satisfy this condition in earlier comparable legislation. They had filmed an interview with a Sinn Fein member about the problems of republicans who were suffering from domestic violence but who did not trust the RUC. The interviewee implied that after a number of warnings, a message would be passed to an armed republican group which would impose summary punishment. The police wanted to see the out-takes of the interview to see if there was any hint of the interviewee's contact in the terrorist groups. However, the court was persuaded that if there had been, the programme would have shown it. Besides, the interviewee was sufficiently astute to be guarded in what she said. She was well known to the police in Northern Ireland who could easily have interviewed her directly in the interval of several months before the application had been made to the court.

11–050   The second condition that must be satisfied is that there are reasonable grounds for believing that it is in the public interest that the material should be produced having regard to the benefit likely to accrue to the terrorist investigation if the material is obtained and to the circumstances under which the person concerned has any of the material in his custody or power.[147] The second condition is particularly important. Production orders under PACE cannot usually extend to material which journalists hold in confidence.[148] There is no similar limitation under the Terrorism Act powers. Thus an application may relate to confidential material (including material which would identify sources). Although that is not in itself a bar to

---

[144] Terrorism Act 2000, Sch.5, para.1(5)(b)—magistrates' warrants; para.3(6)(b)— police officer authorisation—both preclude warrants where there are reasonable grounds to believe that the material on the premises in question is or includes "excepted material". This is defined by para.5 to mean items subject to legal privilege and "excluded material" and "special procedure material".

[145] 2000 Act, Sch.5, paras 5–9. There is scope for the power to be given as well to the District Judges (Magistrates' Courts) but it was not in force by 2007.

[146] 2000 Act, Sch.5, para.6(2).

[147] Terrorism Act 2000, Sch.5, para.6(3).

[148] See para.5–076. The position is different if before PACE the police would have had a power of search, e.g. under the Official Secrets Acts.

a Terrorism Act production order, it requires special consideration. To be compatible with Art.10 of the European Convention on Human Rights there must be some overwhelming need for disclosure before journalists can be forced to reveal their sources.[149]

Even if these two conditions are fulfilled, the court has a discretion as to whether a production order should be made. The court's comments in the context of PACE production orders in cases such as *Bright*[150] are applicable and no less important in this context. Indeed, although an application under PACE, *Bright* concerned the activities of the ex-MI5 officer, David Shayler. The judge said:

"Inconvenient or embarrassing revelations, whether for the security services or for authorities should not be suppressed. Legal proceedings, directed towards the seizure of the working papers of individual journalists, or the premises of the newspaper or television programme publishing his or her report, or the threat of such proceedings tends to inhibit discussion. When a genuine investigation into possible corrupt or reprehensible activities by a public authority is being investigated by the media, compelling evidence would normally be needed to demonstrate that the public interest will be served by such proceedings. Otherwise, to the public's disadvantage, legitimate inquiry and discussion and 'the safety valve of effective journalism' would be discouraged, perhaps stifled."

A second important difference from PACE is that a Terrorism **11–051** Act production order is made in the first place without notice to the respondent. Such an order requires production within a specified time. In practice there is a procedure for applying for the order to be set aside or varied,[151] but it means that the media respondent must move swiftly and an effective objection might depend on the police or the court agreeing that the order should be suspended until the contested hearing takes place. This would be a sensible course if the contest is to have any point, but it may still be the subject of argument.

As with the PACE model, the circuit judge can issue a warrant for a search if it is not appropriate to go through the production order procedure because it is not practicable to communicate with any person entitled to produce the material or the terrorist investigation

---

[149] See para.5–063.
[150] See *R. v Central Criminal Court Ex p. Bright* [2001] 1 W.L.R. 662 above para.5–077.
[151] Terrorism Act 2000 Sch.5 para.10 envisages that the Criminal Procedure Rules may make provision for such applications. As of March 2007 the Criminal Procedure Rules were silent on the subject, but on general principles, a court which makes an order on hearing only one party should be ready to hear later argument from the other as to why the order should be set aside or varied (as criminal courts regularly do in relation to publicity orders).

might be seriously prejudiced if immediate access is not given.[152] In cases of great emergency and where immediate action is necessary, a search order can be given by a Superintendent of police or above. Since the Terrorism Act 2006 these warrants or orders can be for all premises. A report must be made to the Home Secretary whenever the police use these emergency powers.[153]

Disclosure notices (see para.5–056) can also be issued by the police in relation to a terrorist investigation.[154]

Information of use to terrorists and about terrorism

11–052 It is an offence to collect or record any information that is likely to be useful to terrorists in carrying out an act of violence, or to possess any record or document containing any of these types of information.[155]

The use of this section has been confined so far in practice to advocates for Islamic causes who are found with bomb manuals amongst their possessions. Abu Hamza was convicted in 2006 of possessing an "encyclopaedia of bomb making" which he had downloaded from the Internet.[156] Of greater concern was the prosecution in 2007 of a Libyan dissident for possessing a lengthy document which amounted to a blue-print for setting up a "terrorist cell" (the prosecution claimed) or an underground resistance movement (as it was characterised by the defence) in Libya, where the Gaddafi regime banned all opposition. The offence of "collecting information" is theoretically enormously wide and could prima facie incriminate those who possess A–Zs of London, counter-insurgency manuals and tube maps. The only safeguard against unreasonable prosecution is that it requires the DPP's consent (and the consent of the Attorney-General, if the target is a foreign government). This is a weak protection which may alter with change in foreign relations: hence the Attorney-General's approval for the prosecution of dissident Libyans after Colonel Gaddafi, in fear that his dynastic dictatorship would be overthrown by Islamic militants, decided to help the West. In theory this section is wide enough to incriminate all who possess documents which evince support for armed resistance movements and "freedom fighters": certainly, the ANC, when it was fighting the apartheid state of South Africa, would have been included because it was using violence to influence a government. The section does impinge on Art.10 freedoms, and would cover a great deal of material in the possession of journalists reporting on

---

[152] Terrorism Act 2000, Sch.5, paras 11 and 12.
[153] 2000 Act, Sch.5, para.15.
[154] Serious Organised Crime and Police Act 2005, s.62(1A).
[155] 2005 Act, s.58.
[156] His appeal against conviction was dismissed *R v Abu Hamza* [2006] EWCA Crim 2918.

Islamic fundamentalism. However, it is most likely to threaten those who write for Islamic newspapers, and those who are members or supporters of resistance movements which threaten kingdoms (notably Saudi Arabia) and dictatorships which are friendly with the United Kingdom.

The Act does allow a defence of "reasonable excuse"[157] and in **11–053** similar contexts this has been held a defence of "wide purport" which should be left to the jury. It is not unlike the "legitimate reason" defence in the Protection of Children Act which the Court of Appeal has said could include possession for the reason of academic research (see para.4–032). The burden of proof is placed initially on the defendant, but once sufficient evidence is called, the reasonableness of the excuse will be for the prosecution to negative.[158] It should be a reasonable excuse to explain that the material was being collected for the purpose of journalism, unless there was evidence of an ulterior motive to assist terrorists by, for example, passing the information privately to those who would use it for assassination targets. In the *Abu Hamza* trial, Hughes J. left to the jury the question of whether Abu Hamza's claim to possess the bomb making manual merely for research purposes was "reasonable". In the leading case of *R v F*[159] the Court of Appeal pointed out that the defence could only arise once the prosecution demonstrated that the appellant had material which would assist persons planning acts of violence:

> "If the jury were to conclude as a realistic possibility that the documents were addressing argument and exhortation against and expressing disapproval and opposition in the strongest terms of the current regime in Libya, and no more, the appellant would be entitled to be acquitted."

It went on, however, to rule out as "unreasonable" or indeed as any "excuse" at all, any claims that the public interest was served by overthrowing undemocratic and oppressive regimes. This decision takes away from the jury the right to consider any defence, based on conscience or on human rights, that there is a duty to combat tyranny. Freedom fighters, when prosecuted, will henceforth not be able to excuse their conduct by reference to freedom.

Anyone who has information which he knows or believes might be of material assistance in preventing the commission of an act of terrorism or in securing the apprehension, prosecution or conviction of someone for terrorism commits an offence if the information is not disclosed as soon as reasonably practicable to a police officer (or, in Northern Ireland to a police officer or military personnel). It is a

---

[157] Terrorism Act 2000, s.58(3).
[158] 2000 Act, s.118.
[159] [2007] EWCA Crim 243 at paras 35–39.

defence to prove that there was a reasonable excuse for the non-disclosure. The maximum penalty is five years imprisonment.[160] Offences of this kind existed for many years as part of the emergency measures in Northern Ireland. Their potential impact was shown in 1980 when the BBC was threatened with prosecution when it filmed a Provisional IRA roadblock at Carrickmore. Similar threats were made against the media in 1988 unless it handed over photographs and film of a Republican funeral at which two British army corporals were murdered. The media complied. The current legislation makes it difficult for journalists to penetrate extremist Muslim groups without immediately handing over any information about violence to the police.

Encouragement of terrorism

11–054 In the wake of the London bombs on July 7, 2005 the Terrorism Act 2006 was passed. It penalises an even wider range of activity. It is now an offence to publish a statement with the intention of directly or indirectly encouraging members of the public to commit, prepare or instigate acts of terrorism or reckless as to whether this will occur.[161] Indirect encouragement includes statements which glorify, terrorist acts or offences (whether in the past, future or generally) and from which it could be reasonably inferred that the conduct is to be emulated in present circumstances.[162] Using the Obscene Publications Act (see para.4–013) as its model, the legislation requires that the contents of the statement be taken as a whole and that the circumstances and manner of publication are to be taken into account[163] It is irrelevant whether anyone is in fact encouraged to commit, prepare or instigate a terrorist act, but, if there is no intention to produce these results, it is a defence to show that the statement did not express the defendant's views and did not have his endorsement[164] The maximum penalty is seven years imprisonment.[165] The DPP must consent to a prosecution.[166]

The 2006 Act uses the same draconian definition of terrorism as all other such acts, i.e. s.1 of the 2000 Act which means—thanks to *R v F*—that "glorification" of freedom fighting will henceforth be a serious crime—as of course, would publishing a sympathetic biography of Robespierre. The safeguard for respectable, non-Muslim authors, journalists and publishers is that the DPP and Attorney General will never prosecute them: these laws are aimed at, and (so

---

[160] Terrorism Act 2000, s.38B.
[161] Terrorism Act 2006, s.1(2)—see *Stop Press* section.
[162] 2006 Act, s.1(3).
[163] 2006 Act, s.1(4).
[164] 2006 Act, s.1(5) & (6).
[165] 2006 Act, s.1(7).
[166] 2006 Act, s.19.

far) enforced against, Muslims who download *jihadi* material glorifying suicide bombers and attacks on Americans or who want to depose "friendly" Arab dictatorships in Libya and Saudi Arabia.

The 2006 Act also introduced offences of disseminating terrorist publications. All manner of distribution is covered including electronic transmission. It is also an offence to possess such publications with a view to their dissemination. The maximum penalty is again seven years imprisonment.[167]

ISPs, website operators and other electronic distributors will be **11–055** deemed to endorse the statements they circulate if they fail within two working days to take down or modify a statement of which they have been given formal notice by the police.[168]

A Justice of the Peace can issue a warrant for the seizure of terrorist publications. There is a procedure for making forfeiture orders which is very similar to the procedure used under the Customs legislation (see para.4–060).[169]

REPORTING NORTHERN IRELAND

Information of use to terrorists

Journalists reporting or investigating matters in Northern Ireland **11–056** need to be aware of additional anti-terrorism legislation that may impact upon them. Section 103 of the Terrorism Act 2000 prohibits collecting, recording, publishing or attempting to elicit any information (including taking photographs) concerning the army, police, judges, court officials or prison officers that is likely to be of use to terrorists.[170] The consent of the DPP of Northern Ireland is necessary for a prosecution under s.103.[171]

Reporting demonstrations

In Northern Ireland it is an offence to take part in an unlawful **11–057** procession.[172] In 1987 and in relation to a similar earlier measure, the Northern Ireland Court of Appeal held that a reporter who had been simply covering the procession for his newspaper had been properly acquitted of a charge under this provision. It required something more than physical presence, and the reporter did not attend to share in, or experience, the objectives of the marchers.[173]

---

[167] 2006 Act, s.2.
[168] 2006 Act, s.3.
[169] Terrorism Act 2006, s.28 and Sch.2.
[170] This offence applies only in Northern Ireland: Terrorism Act 2000, s.130(3)(b).
[171] 2000 Act, s.117.
[172] Public Processions (Northern Ireland) Act 1998, s.11.
[173] *McKeown v McDermott* [1987] 7 N.I.L.B. 93, CA. This concerned the Public Order (Northern Ireland) Order 1981 (SI 1981/609), art.3.

This decision will be a useful guide to the position on the mainland, where reporters may also wish to report demonstrations that have been prohibited.[174]

Prevention of terrorism in Northern Ireland

11–058   The Police and Army in Northern Ireland have a power to question compulsorily any person regarding any recent explosion or other incident endangering life or concerning any person killed or injured in such an incident or explosion. It is an offence to refuse to answer their questions or to fail to do so to the best of one's knowledge and ability.[175]

The police also have wide powers under the Terrorism Act 2000. While the origins of these powers lay in Northern Ireland, they now have a much broader reach as discussed in the previous section.

Broadcasting censorship

11–059   Television coverage of the province can be directly censored. But even before the broadcasting bans of 1988, broadcasters were censoring themselves. The Independent Broadcasting Authority which then regulated television banned a number of programmes outright, including a *This Week* report on Amnesty International's findings about ill-treatment of suspects. Sometimes it required cuts in emotive scenes—a hunger striker in an open coffin, or flowers on a terrorist's grave. It postponed other programmes, so that some of their topicality was then lost, or pushed them into late night slots, although in 1988 it withstood Government pressure and permitted transmission of *Death on the Rock*.[176] Television regulators can be, susceptible to official pressure because of the statutory duty to avoid any programme that "offends against good taste or decency or is likely to encourage or incite to crime or to lead to disorder or to be offensive to public feeling".[177] The BBC has voluntarily accepted the same obligations, although its work on Northern Ireland has been marginally more robust.[178]

These pressures have eased as the political situation in Northern Ireland has become relatively calmer. Problems remain, although libel looms largest. More recently the media has been more active in tracking down stories about collusion between the security forces and loyalist paramilitaries.

---

[174] Under Public Order Act 1986, s.13.
[175] Terrorism Act 2000, s.89.
[176] "Banned Censored and Delayed" by Paul Madden in *The British Media and Ireland*. The Campaign for Free Speech in Ireland. Alex Schmid and Jenny de Graff, *Violence as Communication: Insurgent Terrorism and the News Media* (Sage, 1982) pp.158–62.
[177] Broadcasting Act 1990, s.6(1).
[178] See Philip Schlesinger, *Putting Reality Together* (Constable, 1978), p. 214.

OTHER POLITICAL OFFENCES

Treason

In the heat of the Falklands War circulation campaign the *Sun* **11–060** accused the *Guardian* and the *Daily Mirror* of treason.[179] The allegation was nonsense. As the Commons Defence Committee said,[180] in a democracy the interests of the Government are not synonymous with the national interest, and differences of view as to the value of a Government aim or the cost of achieving it were quite legitimate. Treason can be committed by adhering to the Crown's enemies or by giving them aid or comfort, but the prosecution must show that the defendants intended to aid or comfort an enemy contrary to their duty of loyalty.[181] There has not been a treason trial since 1946, when William Joyce ("Lord Haw-Haw") was convicted for making Nazi propaganda broadcasts. Joyce was executed for his offence, but capital punishment for treason was abolished in 1998.[182]

Treason Felony

The Treason Felony Act 1848, s.3 makes it a felony (amongst many **11–061** other things) to "compass, imagine, invent devise or intend to deprive or depose . . . the Queen". On its face this would prevent any kind of campaigning to a republican form of government, and the law was last used in 1848 to send several Irish editors and journalists to Botany Bay. In 2004 the editor of the *Guardian*, Alan Rusbridger, and his prize columnist Polly Toynbee, ran a campaign for a republic and dared the Attorney General to prosecute them. Lord Goldsmith did not rise to the bait, so they went to court for a declaration that the law was incompatible with the guarantee of freedom of expression in Art.10. The House of Lords accepted that the advent of the Human Rights Act had turned a practical immunity from prosecution because of the obsolescence of the law into a legal guarantee that no one who advocated abolition of the

---

[179] "Dare Call it Treason", May 7, 1982. See Robert Harris, *Gotcha: The Media, the Government and the Falkland Crisis* (Faber, 1983); pp.38–53. The *Guardian*'s cartoon of a shipwrecked sailor on a raft with the caption "The price of sovereignty has been increased—official" mirrored the cartoon by Zee that the *Daily Mirror* had published in 1942 over the caption "The price of petrol has been increased by one penny—official" and which together with the consistent criticisms of the Government by the paper very nearly caused the Government to ban the paper: Neil Stammers, *Civil Liberties in Britain during World War Two* (Croom Helm, 1983), pp.147–51. In the war on the Taliban in 2001, *the Daily Telegraph* contented itself with describing journalists opposed to the war, mainly on the *Guardian*, as "useful idiots".

[180] Report of the Defence Committee, *The Handling of the Press and Public Information during the Falklands Conflict*, H.C. 17 (1982–83), para.35.

[181] Supperstone, *Brownlie's Law*, pp.230–4.

[182] Crime and Disorder Act 1998, s.36.

monarchy by peaceful means was at any risk of prosecution. However it declined to make a ringing declaration that freedom of speech now extended to urging the Queen's dethronement, on the basis that courts should rarely make declarations as to the reach of the criminal law.[183]

Sedition

11–062   Sedition is still defined in the terms of a nineteenth-century jurist as:

> ". . . any act done, or words spoken or written and published which (i) has or have a seditious tendency and (ii) is done or are spoken or written and spoken with a seditious intent. A person may be said to have a seditious intention if he has any of the following intentions, and acts or words may be said to have a seditious tendency if they have any of the following tendencies: an intention to bring into hatred or contempt, or to excite disaffection against the person of, Her Majesty, her heirs or successors, or the government and constitution of the United Kingdom, as by law established, or either House of Parliament, or the administration of justice, or to excite Her Majesty's subjects to attempt, otherwise than by lawful means, the alteration of any matter in Church or State by law established or to raise discontent or disaffection among Her Majesty's subjects, or to promote feelings of ill-will and hostility between different classes of subjects."[184]

This definition is strikingly broad and the crime has been used in the past to suppress radical political views.[185] Even in the twentieth century it was used against an Indian nationalist and against Communist organisers.[186] However, the post-war tendency has been to narrow the offence considerably. First, it has been stressed that political speech, even revolutionary speech, should not be punished as sedition unless it is meant to excite people to "tumult and disorder".[187] Incitement to violence alone is insufficient: it must be "violence or defiance for the purpose of disturbing constitutional authority".[188] Secondly, on one line of authority, it is not enough that "tumult and disorder" were likely to follow unless the publisher did

---

[183] *Rusbridger and Toynbee v Att-Gen* [2004] 1 A.C. 357.

[184] Stephen, *Digest of the Criminal Law* (9th ed.) Art.114.

[185] e.g. against John Wilkes for his satires in 1764 in *The North Britain* and Tom Paine for *The Rights of Man*.

[186] *R. v Aldred* (1909) 22 Cox C.C. 1; Wal Hannington, *Never on Our Knees*, 1967, pp.188–93.

[187] *R. v Caunt* (1948) L.Q.R. 203, see also defendant's account, *An Editor on Trial*, privately published, 1947; *Boucher v R.* [1951] 2 D.L.R. 369.

[188] *Boucher v R*, fn.187 above, and see *R. v Burns* (1886) 16 Cox 355.

actually intend these consequences.[189] There has been no prosecution for sedition since 1947, and the offence now serves no purpose in the criminal law. In terms of Art.10, it is hard to see how it is necessary in a democratic society or proportionate to any legitimate aim. The deliberate provocation of public violence or disorder is amply covered by offences contained in the 1986 Public Order Act.

In 1990 the Divisional Court decisively rejected an attempt to bring sedition charges against the author and publisher of *The Satanic Verses*. It stressed that the gist of the crime was an attack against the State, and that the prosecution must prove that the speech or writing incites readers to violence against democratic institutions.[190] With the widening of the terrorism offences, there is even less prospect of sedition or treason or treason felony being revived.

Incitement to mutiny and disaffection

The Incitement to Mutiny Act 1797 was passed in a panic after naval **11–063** mutinies at the Spithead and Nore. It covered:

> "any person who shall maliciously and advisedly endeavour to seduce any person or persons serving in His Majesty's forces by sea or land from his or their duty and allegiance to His Majesty or to incite or stir up any person to commit any act of mutiny or make or endeavour to make any mutinous assembly or to commit any traitorous or mutinous practice whatsoever".

A critical word in this definition is the "and" between duty and allegiance. Tempting soldiers from their *duty* was not an offence if it did not also encourage them to be disloyal. This link was broken in the Incitement to Disaffection Act 1934, which created an offence in almost identical terms except that "or" was substituted for "and".

The 1934 Act also added draconian subsidiary offences. Possession of any document became an offence if its dissemination to the forces would be punishable,[191] and a High Court judge can issue a search warrant to the police to look for material that might infringe the Act.[192] The Incitement Acts were also used against radicals. The editors and printers of *The Syndicalist* were convicted in 1912 for publishing a letter calling on soldiers not to fire on workers. In 1925 12 Communist leaders were convicted for a similar offence.[193]

---

[189] *R. v Caunt*, fn.187 above. A different view was taken in *R. v Aldred* (above). In *R. v Lemon* [1979] A.C. 617 the House of Lords decided by 3:2 that intention of this kind was not relevant for blasphemous libel, but several of the speeches favour the view that a specific intent is required for the crime of sedition.

[190] *R. v Bow Street Magistrates' Court Ex p. Choudhury* [1991] 1 All E.R. 306.

[191] Incitement to Disaffection Act 1934, s.2(1).

[192] Incitement to Disaffection Act 1934, s.2(2).

[193] Tom Young, *Incitement to Disaffection* (Cobden Trust, 1976), pp.15–18, 45–7.

11–064   In addition to these statutes, the services' legislation makes it an offence to obstruct or interfere with the forces in the execution of their duty or to procure or persuade a member of the forces to desert or go absent without leave.[194] A comparable offence of doing any act "calculated to cause disaffection among members of any police force" or "doing any act calculated to induce any member of the police force to withhold his services" was created after the police strike in 1919.[195]

The Aliens Restriction (Amendment) Act 1919 was passed at the same time to stem what was then perceived as foreign Communist agitation. It is an offence for an alien to attempt or do any act calculated or likely to cause sedition or disaffection amongst forces of the Crown or the Crown's allies or the civilian population. It is also an offence for an alien to promote industrial unrest in any industry in which he has not been bona fide engaged for at least two years immediately preceding in the United Kingdom.[196]

11–065   This discrimination against aliens will be difficult to attack under the European Convention on Human Rights. Article 16 provides, "Nothing in Articles 10, 11 and 14 shall be regarded as preventing the High Contracting Parties from imposing restrictions on the political activity of aliens." This provision has rarely been relied upon[197] and is looking increasingly anachronistic. As long ago as 1977 the Parliamentary Assembly called for it to be abolished.[198] However, it was one of the Convention provisions which was incorporated into UK law by the Human Rights Act.

Incitement to Disaffection charges were last brought in the mid-1970s against the British Withdrawal from Ireland Campaign. Pat Arrowsmith was convicted under the Incitement to Disaffection Act 1934 for distributing to soldiers a leaflet called *Some Information for Discontented Soldiers*, which called on them to leave the Army rather than serve in Northern Ireland.[199] She failed to persuade the jury that the leaflet was to inform rather than incite. Her sentence of 18 months' imprisonment was reduced on appeal to nine months. Ms Arrowsmith complained to the European Commission that the conviction violated her right to freedom of thought, conscience and religion under Art.9(1) of the Convention. The Commission accepted that pacifism was a protected "belief", but held the

---

[194] Army Act 1955, s.193 (obstruction), s.97 (persuading desertion); Air Force Act 1955, s.193; Naval Discipline Act 1957, s.94 is on similar lines.
[195] See now Police Act 1996, s.91 and Ministry of Defence Police Act 1987, s.6.
[196] Aliens Restriction (Amendment) Act 1919, s.3.
[197] In the case of *Piermont v France* (1995) 20 E.H.R.R. 301, France argued that measures taken against the German applicant in French Pacific territories could not be criticised under the Convention because of Art.16, but the Court held that her status as a Member of the European Parliament meant that the provision could not be invoked against her application.
[198] Recommendation 799 (1977), January 25, 1977.
[199] *R. v Arrowsmith* [1975] QB 678.

complaint inadmissible because the distribution of the leaflets was not a means of "practising" the belief: the leaflet expressed a nationalist rather than pacifist philosophy.[200] The prosecution did not stop distribution of the leaflet and in 1974 a further 14 were prosecuted under the 1934 Act. On all the contested charges the defendants were acquitted by the jury. As a result, pending prosecutions against other distributors of the leaflet were dropped.[201] Incitement to disaffection charges have not been used since the Old Bailey acquittals in 1975, and the then Attorney-General, Sam Silkin, expressed regret that this much-publicised case was ever brought.

Reform

The Law Commission has recommended that treason should be 11–066 limited in peace-time to attempting to overthrow the Government by armed means, and that sedition should be abolished, as should incitement to mutiny and aliens legislation. The Incitement to Disaffection Act should be confined to seduction of the forces away from their allegiance as opposed to their duty.[202] These are nervous and half-hearted recommendations: the existence of these archaic laws serve no purpose other than to encourage commonwealth governments which inherited them from Britain during colonial times to use them to crush opposition and free speech.

WAR REPORTING

Protection of war correspondents

Journalists who cover armed conflicts will generally be under the 11–067 protection of the force to which they are accredited. In the case of British forces, the Ministry of Defence will insist that they sign an accreditation document, which includes undertakings to comply with military censorship and to seek permission before interviewing soldiers and filing a wide range of stories. Correspondents will have no alternative but to sign this document, but it is not legally binding and the only sanction for disobedience to its onerous terms will be loss of accreditation, which will normally mean expulsion from the war zone. The accredited correspondent will be assigned an officer rank, which will give entitlement to drink in the officers' mess and to be given priority in an evacuation of the wounded.

Over and above the dangers of injury and death common to all who work in war zones, correspondents are at special risk of being

---

[200] *Arrowsmith v UK*, Application No. 7050/75, 19 Decisions and Reports 5. Her complaint under Art.10 was also dismissed.
[201] Young, *Incitement to Disaffection*, pp.85–94.
[202] *Codification of the Criminal Law: Treason, Sedition and Allied Offence*, Working Paper No.72, 1977.

arrested and punished for spying on the forces whose activities they are attempting to report, and of being treated by opposing forces as if they were combatants. The international covenants that seek to regulate governments in their conduct of hostilities give journalists inadequate protection against these dangers.

Article 13 of the Hague Convention 1907 provides that war correspondents who follow an army without directly belonging to it should, if they fall into the hands of opposing forces, be treated as prisoners of war and receive minimum standards of humane treatment.[203]

11–068   The Geneva Conventions of 1949 make similar but more detailed provision for captured war correspondents. If wounded or sick, they are to have the same rights to humane treatment as wounded or sick prisoners of war, including the right to receive assistance from international relief agencies.[204]

The protection afforded by the Hague and Geneva Conventions is contingent upon captured correspondents possessing authorisation from the armed forces they are accompanying, attesting to their status. These conventions do not give any special protection to journalists; they simply accord them (along with other non-combatant camp followers) the same basic right as captured members of armed forces.

The only provision in international law that relates specifically to journalists engaged in dangerous missions in areas of international armed conflict is Art.79 of the first Protocol to the Geneva Conventions 1977.[205] It provides that:

> "Journalists engaged in dangerous professional missions in areas of armed conflict shall be considered as civilians . . . (and) shall be protected as such under the Conventions and this Protocol, provided they take no action adversely affecting their status as civilians . . .".

11–069   Under Art.79, journalists are entitled to immunity from military discipline and must not be made the specific objects of an attack or the victims of reprisals by any party to the conflict. They should not be manipulated or exploited by the opposing forces. Their entitlement to civilian status is jeopardized by an "action adversely

---

[203] Hague Convention IV Respecting Laws and Customs of War on Land Annexed Regulations 1907, Art.13. For the texts of these and the following conventions, see Roberts, *Documents on the Laws of War* (OUP, 2000).

[204] Geneva Convention for the Amelioration of the Wounded and Sick in Armed Forces in the Field 1949, Art.13; Geneva Convention for the Amelioration of the Condition of Wounded, Sick and Shipwrecked Members of Armed Forces at Sea 1949, Art.13; Geneva Convention Relative to the Treatment of Prisoners of War 1949, Art.4A.

[205] Protocol Additional to the Geneva Conventions 1949 and Relating to the Protection of Victims of International Conflicts 1977.

affecting" it; carrying a gun or rendering special assistance to the armed forces might deprive them of their protection. The rights guaranteed by Article 79 do not detract from the general entitlement of accredited war correspondents to be treated as prisoners of war if captured by hostile forces. Article 79 also entitles a journalist to obtain an identity card attesting to his status from "the Government of the State of which the journalist is a national or in whose territory he resides or in which the news medium employing him is located".

Article 79 is unsatisfactory. In 1970, the UN General Assembly passed Resolution 2673 (XXV) which directed the Economic and Social Council to draft a special convention for the protection of journalists on dangerous missions. A draft was submitted, but regrettably the UN decided instead to have a watered down rule in Art.79 of an Additional Protocol which remains unratified by, amongst other countries, the United States. Furthermore, Art.79 does not give journalists protection as such: they are simply included in the definition of "civilians" for the purpose of the 1949 Convention, and then only when they are engaged in "dangerous professional missions" in areas of international armed conflict. Journalists should be protected during civil wars as well as international wars. An opportunity was missed in the Rome Statute of 1998, which set up the International Criminal Court with jurisdiction to try war crimes as defined in its Art.8. But it makes no reference to journalists and it would be necessary to establish that they were "civilians" before any prosecution could be mounted for their murder. Moreover, the war crimes provision of the ICC Statute contains a threshold clause which provides jurisdiction over war crimes "in particular when committed as part of a plan or policy, or as part of a large scale commission of such crimes". This would deter the ICC prosecutor from commencing proceedings against those responsible for killing an individual journalist, e.g. in the circumstances revealed in 2007 at the inquest into the ITN reporter Terry Lloyd, who was recklessly murdered by US troops during the 2003 invasion of Iraq.

There should be an international crime of wilfully killing a journalist during an armed conflict, whether international or internal. Such a specific crime would stress the unique and essential role played by war correspondents. Merely to include them as "civilians" does not highlight the public interest they serve and their vital role, to which tribute was paid by the ICTY Appeal Court in the Jonathan Randall Washington Post case.[206] There would be a greater potential for deterrence if soldiers were taught that there is a specific war crime that would punish them for killing a journalist, as against merely warning them not to kill civilians (and they may not perceive journalists, especially those who are enemy nationals or "embedded"

---

[206] *Prosecutor v Brdjanin*, IT–99–36.

with opposition forces, as civilians at all). In war, journalists are often targeted *as* journalists and so deserve direct and special protections. *Reporters without Borders* have drafted a *Convention for the Protection of Journalists*, but these take many years for the UN General Assembly to adopt and for enough states to ratify. Other media groups are urging support for a new war crime of deliberately attacking journalists not taking a direct part in hostilities, which would be inserted as an amendment to Art.8 when the ICC Treaty is revised at a conference in July 2009.

11–070   International law has no direct sanction to punish breaches of these rules, other than condemnation at the bar of international public opinion. This can, of itself, be a deterrent to combatants, who are usually mindful of the importance of favourable publicity. Even the Taliban, at the height of their demonisation, treated fairly and returned a *Daily Express* correspondent who had blundered into its clutches in 2001. Domestic journalists suffer death or disappearance in some countries with a frequency that is hardly noticed in the West. In the 15 years to 2006 a total of 580 journalists were killed.[207]

International law is not oblivious to the harm which inflammatory propaganda can cause. Article 20 of the International Covenant on Civil and Political Rights provides that:

> "(1) Any propaganda for war shall be prohibited by law.
> (2) Any advocacy of national, racial or religious hatred that constitutes incitement to discrimination, hostility or violence shall be prohibited by law."

In December 2003 the International Criminal Tribunal for Rwanda convicted two broadcasters and an editor of incitement to genocide at the time of the massacres of 1994. They all received very lengthy sentences.

International criminal courts

11–071 Subsequent to wars and other conflicts, there is often an acute demand for those accused of war crimes or other crimes against humanity to be brought to justice. Sometimes, domestic courts of the country concerned will conduct these trials (as in Iraq after the fall of Saddam Hussein), but since the Nuremburg Tribunals there has been an alternative of some form of international body. The International Criminal Court has been established on a permanent legal basis since July 2002 and has support from 104 of the UN member states (but not the United States). Other courts have been set up in response to specific catastrophes—notably the International Criminal Tribunal for Former Yugoslavia, the International Criminal Tribunal for Rwanda and the Special Court for Sierra Leone.[208]

---

[207] See the web site of the Committee for the Protection of Journalists *http://www.cpj.org*.

[208] See Janet Anderson and Stacy Sullivan *A Handbook on Covering War Crimes Courts* (Institute for War and Peace Reporting 2006)—available at *www.iwpr.net*.

The invariable pattern is for these courts to sit in public (and so they are open to, at least accredited, members of the press), but reserving to themselves the power to sit in closed session where this is thought to be necessary. These courts, like domestic courts, have found it necessary to assert a power to protect their administration of justice. Thus knowing defiance of an international court's order to preserve the anonymity of a witness or the secrecy of evidence is likely to amount to a contempt. The maximum penalties for contempt vary from one tribunal to another.[209] These powers are not just theoretical. The ICTY, for instance has on several occasions taken action against the media for disclosing the identity of protected witnesses and/or revealing secret testimony and in August 2006 one newspaper editor was fined 20,000 euros for such conduct.[210] There will only be contempt of this type if the person concerned knew of the court order which he broke or knew that measures had been taken to preserve the secrecy of the witness's testimony. Recklessness would probably suffice, but mere negligence would not.[211]

With the expansion of international criminal jurisdiction, it becomes more likely that parties to proceedings will try to enlist the assistance of journalists as witnesses. An important precedent was set by the Appeal Chamber of the International Criminal Tribunal for former Yugoslavia in December 2002 when it set aside a subpoena directed to the former *Washington Post* journalist, Jonathan Randall. Randall had interviewed a Serb nationalist who spoke enthusiastically about ethnic cleansing. The ICTY prosecutor wanted to call Randall to adduce evidence of these remarks as part of the prosecution's case. However, the Appeal Chamber acknowledged the important role which war correspondents played. Compelling them to testify could put their safety at risk and potentially prejudice the perception of them as neutral observers. They should only be made to testify if their evidence was of direct and important value and could not reasonably be obtained elsewhere.[212]

The *Randall* case adopted and approved *Goodwin v UK*,[213] giving **11–072** reason to expect that international criminal courts will respect the right of war correspondents to protect their sources. This was the approach of the Appeals Chamber of the Special Court for Sierra Leone in *Prosecutor v Brima*[214] in 2006 when it ruled that "human

---

[209] In the case of the ICTY it is a fine of up to 100,000 euros and seven years imprisonment. The ICTR can punish contempt with a fine of up to $US10,000 and up to five years imprisonment.

[210] *Prosecutor v Josip Jovic* judgment of ICTY of August 30, 2006. The decision was upheld by the Appeal Chamber on March 16, 2007.

[211] See the judgment of the Special Court of Sierra Leone in *Independent Counsel v Brima Samura* October 26, 2005.

[212] *Prosecutor v Brdjanin: appeal of Jonathan Randall* ICTY judgment of Appeal Chamber December 11, 2002.

[213] (1996) 22 E.H.R.R. 123.

[214] Case Number SCSL-2004–16–AR73, judgement May 16, 2006.

rights reporters" are entitled, in the course of their testimony, to decline to answer questions directed to identifying the source of their information. *Randall* concerned the privilege that reporters have to avoid testifying unless their evidence is crucial; *Brima* permits them to withhold the name of their sources if they are required, or voluntarily decide, to testify. The case concerned a UN human rights monitor who had been reporting to the Secretary General and providing information relevant to UN intervention; it was a case in which Amnesty and Human Rights Watch intervened to urge the court to protect the sources for information in their reports as well, given that their reporters were prepared voluntarily to testify in war crimes courts. As with war correspondents, they were exercising a right to freedom of expression (and, more importantly, assisting their source's right of free speech) by extracting information for publication from people who would not give it without an assurance that their names would remain anonymous. To identify them in court would betray a promise and open them to such reprisals: more importantly, if courts routinely ordered witnesses to name their sources, then information about human rights abuses would diminish because reporters could not in good conscience elicit it by promises to protect their sources. The court held that "human rights monitors", like journalists, had a privilege to refuse to name those sources to whom they promise anonymity, although their evidence would lose some weight because its source could not be identified. There is an overriding international public interest in UN human rights reporters being able to give an assurance of confidentiality to those who put their necks on the line to inform on the murderous activities of powerful forces or figures within their war-torn community. It is apt to recall that the protective rule in *Goodwin* was fashioned in the context of the genteel environment of the City of London, where a business journalist was fined £5,000 for refusing to name an "insider" source of information about a company's finances: the source would face only disciplinary action or a writ for breach of confidence. In repressive or war-torn countries, sources for Amnesty and Human Rights Watch reporters who tell of torture death squads and arbitrary imprisonment may, if exposed, face those very consequences. This underlines the need for the protective rule identified as a "privilege" in the witness, although that privilege is a reflection of the more weighty "right" of the source to anonymity.[215]

FREEDOM OF INFORMATION ACT 2000

11–073 "Open Government is a contradiction in terms. You can be open, or you can have government." Sir Humphrey Appleby, the quintessential mandarin from *Yes Minister*, epitomised Whitehall's 30 years

---

[215] The issue is explored in more detail in the concurring opinion of Justice Geoffrey Robertson Q.C., a co-author of this book.

opposition to demands for freedom of information. Freedom of information (FOI) laws first emerged in Scandinavia and the United States in the 1960s and were soon successfully translated to advanced westernized democracies like Canada, New Zealand and Australia. In 1974 Freedom of Information was a Labour election promise, on which it quickly reneged ("Only two or three of your constituents would be interested" quipped the Home Secretary sarcastically in answer to an indignant back-bencher). The Conservative Government was implacably opposed to the notion that the public should have a legal right of access to public records before at least 30 years had elapsed (the minimum time laid down by the Public Records Act for disclosure of government information). Its opposition was two-fold: FOI would undermine ministers' traditional accountability to Parliament, and would deter civil servants from writing honest and candid reports. Both excuses were exploded by the Matrix Churchill scandal in 1992, when Whitehall documents extracted over ministerial objections at the trial of men accused of exporting arms to Iraq exposed a conspiracy amongst Thatcher ministers to deceive Parliament about their Government's secret approval of these exports. Civil servants had advised and helped to promote the deception of Parliament and the public. The Labour Party proclaimed Freedom of Information, a means of ensuring transparency in government, as a safeguard against ministerial irresponsibility towards Parliament and as a deterrent to civil servants tempted to advise ministers to act dishonestly.[216]

"Freedom of information is for opposition", said New Labour's first Home Secretary, Jack Straw: his draft legislation was dubbed "The Restraint of Information Bill" when it was eventually tabled, since it contained numerous exceptions from disclosure and stringently protected the very class of information—policy advice to ministers that had exposed the "Arms to Iraq" scandal. However, it had been preceded by a White Paper in which the Prime Minister had described as his key pledge "giving people in the United Kingdom the legal right to know",[217] and the absolute exemptions were whittled down in the course of the Bill's parliamentary passage. That passage was completed in 2000, but the Act did not come into force until 2005. FOIA applications have been made with enthusiasm—the Information Commissioner estimated that over 100,000 requests were made in the first year of the Act's operation. The media has started to use these powers. The Campaign for Press Freedom has produced a digest of at least 500 press stories which were published as a result of disclosures that were made under the FOIA in 2005.[218] Very many requests were made for the advice given by the Attorney-General, Lord Goldsmith, as to the legality of the

---

[216] See Charter 88 Pamphlet (1993) and the Scott Report.
[217] *Your Right to Know*, Cmnd.3818 (1997).
[218] See *www.cfoi.org.uk*.

2003 Iraq War. In 2006 the Information Commissioner required disclosure to be made of some (but not all) of this material.[219]

Substantial use of the Act has led to delays in processing complaints by the Information Commissioner. It has also caused the government to propose measures to curb the volume of work which has been generated and which would greatly limit the use of the Act by any one organisation (such as a newspaper). These have, understandably, been strongly contested by the media.

11–074   The Freedom of Information Act begins with a flourish, by promising a legal right of access to information held by public authorities:

> "1 (i) Any person making a request for information to a public authority is entitled
>
> > (a) to be informed in writing by the public authority whether it holds information of the description specified in the request, and
> >
> > (b) if that is the case, to have that information communicated to him."

So far so good—and "public authority" is very widely defined to include not only Government departments, the Houses of Parliament and the armed forces, but local authorities and their committees, National Health Service authorities, schools, police authorities, and a vast range of quangos and committees (including the Arts Council, the Broadcasting Standards Commission, the Commission for Racial Equality, the Committee on Standards in Public life, the Criminal Cases Review Committee, the Gaming Board, the GMC, the Parole Board, the Police Complaints Authority, the Political Honours Scrutiny Committee and so on).[220] In total it is estimated that there are some 115,000 public bodies which are covered by the FOIA. The Independent Television Commission is deemed a "public body", and so, too, are the BBC and Channel 4, although only "in respect of information held for purposes other than those of journalism, art or literature"[221]—an exemption which protects broadcasters from having to divulge their programme research.

> An application was made to the BBC for disclosure of a review by Michael Balen of the Corporation's news coverage of the Middle East and the Israeli/Palestinian conflict in particular. The Information Commissioner upheld the BBC's refusal, saying that the report was held for the purposes of journalism. However, the applicant then

---

[219] In November 2006 the senior Law Lord, Lord Bingham, in a Cambridge lecture suggested that advice on such matters—which was really advice to the public at large—should not be protected from disclosure.

[220] FOI Act 2000, s.3 and see Sch.1, which lists several hundred committees which are deemed "public bodies" for the purposes of the Act.

[221] FOI Act Sch.1, Pt VI.

appealed to the Information Tribunal which had to decide the meaning of "journalism". In the context of the FOIA, it thought that the term had three parts: (a) collecting or gathering, writing or verifying material for publication; (b) the exercise of editorial judgment in, for instance, the selection, prioritisation and timing of matters for broadcast or publication, analysis of and review of individual programmes and the provision of context and background to such programmes; and (c) the maintenance and enhancement of standards of journalism, including the training, mentoring, support and guidance to journalists and reviews of standards and quality of particular areas of programme making. Where a document was held for journalistic and other purposes, what mattered was the dominant purpose. The Balen Report had initially been commissioned and held for journalistic purposes. However, the dominant purpose changed when it was put to the Corporation's Journalism Board. Then it was held for the wider purpose of strategic policy and resource allocation of the BBC. This was not covered by the derogation in the Act and the Corporation was obliged to disclose the report.[222]

Notable absentees from the list are the, PCC, ASA, ICSTIS and the BBFC, although they might in time be added by the Home Secretary because they "exercise functions of a public nature".[223] Publicly owned companies are made subject to the Act, but regrettably privatised utilities are excluded, despite the importance of monitoring the conduct of quasi-monopolies in providing services of major public importance.

The threshold duty on an authority in respect of an information **11–075** request is to "confirm or deny" that it possesses the sought-after document. If anyone destroys or defaces the document with the intention of preventing its disclosure, a criminal offence is committed (s.77) although punishable merely by a fine. Any information supplied by third parties which is published as a result of an FOI request has statutory qualified privilege from libel action (s.79). Requests must be in writing and must "describe the information requested"—the first obstacle for a seeker after truth who suspects that information exists but who cannot describe its origin and provenance with any specificity. There is, though, a duty on the authority to provide advice and assistance to applicants so far as it would be reasonable to expect it to do so. The Commissioner's Code of Practice and the Information Tribunal have interpreted this to mean that the applicant must be assisted to identify the information which he is seeking.[224]

Even if this hurdle is overcome, however, there are certain categories of information in respect of the existence of which the public body is relieved of the duty "to confirm or deny":

---

[222] *Sugar v Information Commissioner* decision of the Information Tribunal of August 29, 2006—available on the Tribunal's website at *www.informationtribunal.gov.uk*. The BBC's appeal to the High Court was—see *Stop Press* section.

[223] FOI Act 2000, s.5.

[224] See FOI Act 2000, s.16 and the decision of the Information Tribunal *Lamb v Information Commissioner* November 16, 2006.

- Information which is reasonably accessible by other means (e.g. if it has already been published or is available at HMSO).[225]
- Information supplied "directly or indirectly" by the security service, SIS, GCHQ, or special forces or security tribunals, or even which "relates to" these bodies.[226] A certificate signed by a Government minister, to the effect that information falls into this category is "conclusive evidence" that it does.
- Information filed with a court or served on or by a public authority in respect of court proceedings or which has been created by a court or court staff.[227]
- Information covered by parliamentary privilege.[228]
- Personal information which has been collected on the applicant or personal information the revelation of the existence of which would breach the Data Protection Act.[229]
- Information the revelation of the very existence of which would constitute an actionable breach of confidence.[230]
- Information the very existence of which is prohibited from revelation by any law or E.C. obligation or which would be punishable as a contempt of court.[231]

These "absolute exceptions" are unnecessarily broad, and give a Government department a ready-made excuse to avoid the threshold duty "to confirm or deny" that it has collected information that an applicant suspects it to possess. Indeed, unless the courts are prepared to read down these "absolute exceptions" they provide an easy means for hostile bureaucrats to sabotage the spirit of the Act—for example, by claiming that revelation of the existence of embarrassing information would be an "actionable" breach of confidence—even though any such "action" would be unlikely to succeed. Even if such an excuse were rejected after judicial review, its advancement would delay the release of the information and force the applicant to bring expensive legal proceedings in order to refute it. The principal object of the "absolute exemption" device is to avoid the embarrassment which was visited upon the CIA and FBI when American radicals used FOI legislation to prove that they had been spied upon for political purposes. (In the 1970s MI5 similarly targeted such youthful idealists as Peter Mandelson, Jack Straw, Harriet Harman and Patricia Hewitt.) English victims of

---

[225] FOI Act, s.21.
[226] FOI Act, s.23.
[227] FOI Act, s.32.
[228] FOI Act, s.34.
[229] FOI Act, s.40.
[230] FOI Act, s.41(1).
[231] FOI Act, s.44.

improper surveillance will not be permitted to obtain access to their security service files by the "absolute exemption" device of placing them in a class of document in respect of which all Government departments are relieved of the duty of admitting whether or not they exist.[232] These absolute exemptions may also be open to challenge under the European Convention when the information concerns the private life of the inquirer. Although the Strasbourg court has allowed States a wide margin of appreciation to determine their own national security needs, the storing of data on a person's private life is a form of interference which must be justified as "necessary in a democratic society" under Art.8(2) of the Convention.[233]

> In *Norman Baker M.P. v Secretary of State for the Home Department*[234] the Information Tribunal (National Security Appeals) quashed a certificate by the Home Secretary which had been issued under very similar provisions in the Data Protection Act 1998, s.28. The certificate excused MI5 from virtually all the obligations of a data controller under the DPA and allowed it to "neither confirm nor deny" whether it held any data. The Tribunal said that the certificate was unreasonable because it did not require MI5 to make an individual assessment of whether complying with the request would endanger national security. Following this decision the Secretary of State issued a fresh certificate covering MI5 activities but this time there did have to be an individual assessment. This revised certificate was held to be lawful by the Information Tribunal in 2003.[235] The legality of the individual assessments can (at least notionally) be investigated by the Investigatory Powers Tribunal.

Even when Whitehall cannot bring its objection to disclosure **11–076** within a particular head of absolute exemption, it may nonetheless refuse to confirm or deny if,

> "in all the circumstances of the case, the public interest in maintaining the exclusion of the duty to confirm or deny outweighs the public interest in disclosing whether the public authority holds the information".[236]

This formula calls for the balancing of the two public interests in the light of the circumstances of the actual request. It makes the highly questionable, if not oxymoronic and undemocratic, assumption that there is a public interest in public ignorance (an assumption made instinctively in Whitehall, which until 1989 refused to confirm or

---

[232] FOI Act, s.24.
[233] See, e.g. *Leander v Sweden* (1987) 9 E.H.R.R. 433.
[234] Decision of October 1, 2001.
[235] *Gosling and Hitchens v Secretary of State for the Home Department* August 1. 2003.
[236] FOI Act 2000, s.2(2)(b).

deny the existence of MI5). It is regrettable that the FOI Act should so centrally embody this assumption, which can have no validity save in respect of ongoing criminal or terrorist investigations. Nonetheless, journalists seeking to prise open information from public authorities will find some help in the Information Commissioner's Awareness Guidance on the Public Interest test.[237] This emphasises that the Act has created a presumption in favour of openness: the default position is no longer "need to know" but a "right to know". The courts' approach to the public interest defence in breach of confidence and privacy cases (see Ch.5) is clearly material here and the private interest in, say, the prevention of embarrassment, should not suffice to justify non-disclosure. As the Guidance says,

"There will often be a private interest in withholding information which would reveal incompetence on the part of or corruption within the public authority or which would simply cause embarrassment to the authority. However, the public interest will favour accountability and good administration and it is this interest that must be weighed against the public interest in not disclosing the information."

Nor is it good enough for the public body to argue that the material which is sought is incomplete or too complex to be properly understood. The answer to these objections is that the material which has to be disclosed can be set in context by the disclosing authority.

The Information Tribunal is also acquiring experience and case law in the operation of the qualified exemptions. In 2007, for instance, it ordered disclosure in two cases where government departments had tried to rely on the exemption for policy formulation. Thus it overruled objections by the Department for Education and Skills to the production of minutes of senior management meetings which had been concerned with the setting of schools budgets[238] and whose disclosure had been requested by the *Evening Standard*. It also required the Department of Work and Pensions to disclose a feasibility study as to the costs and benefits of the introduction of identity cards.[239] In a third case the *Guardian* succeeded in obtaining an order that the BBC disclose the minutes of its Governors' meeting which followed publication of the Hutton report and at which the Chairman and Director General resigned.[240]

---

[237] Information Commissioner "Awareness Guidance No.3—The Public Interest Test" March 1, 2007 available at *www.ico.gov.uk*.

[238] *Department for Education and Skills v Information Commissioner and Evening Standard* February 19, 2007.

[239] *Secretary of State for Work and Pensions v Information Commissioner* March 15, 2007.

[240] *Guardian Newspapers Ltd v Information Commissioner* January 4, 2007.

A public authority which cannot reject or stall a request by claiming exemption from its duty to confirm or deny must respond promptly, and no later than 20 days (i.e. four working weeks) after receiving the request. This period may be extended if the authority asks for a fee for obtaining and copying the information—its response may be delayed until the fee is paid.[241] There is no duty to respond if the request is vexatious or unnecessarily onerous,[242] although under s.16 every public authority has a duty to advise and assist applicants to make effective requests, and a duty under s.19 to adopt a scheme by which information generated within the department and available under FOI will either be published or at least be identifiable by potential applicants. These duties, as with others imposed by the Act, are supervised by the Information Commissioner, who also has responsibilities under the Data Protection Act.

An authority which decides to refuse a request must notify the **11–077** applicant of its reasons, which must relate to an exemption category defined by the Act. The absolute exemptions have been outlined above; the main exemptions from disclosure for documents which can be confirmed to exist are that they contain information:

- which will be published in due course[243];
- the suppression of which "is required for the purpose of safe guarding national security", and the minister may sign a certificate which is "conclusive evidence" of that fact[244];
- likely to prejudice the defence of the United Kingdom or its dependent territories, or the capability of the United Kingdom's armed forces or its allies[245] (the term "likely to prejudice" here and elsewhere in the Act does not require proof that the consequence is more probable than not, but it has to be shown that there was a "very significant and weighty chance" that prejudice would follow so that disclosure "may very well" have this result[246]);
- likely to prejudice foreign relations (or relations with international organisations) or the United Kingdom's foreign interests, or else the information has been supplied in

---

[241] FOI Act 2000, s.10.

[242] This includes cases where the cost of obtaining the information exceeds the "appropriate sum" which as of 2006 was set at £600 for central government departments and £450 for other public bodies—see FOI Act s.12 and the Freedom of Information and Data Protection (Appropriate Limit and Fees) regulations 2004 (SI 2004/3244).

[243] FOI Act, s.21.

[244] FOI Act 2000, s.24.

[245] FOI Act, s.26.

[246] See in the context of the Data Protection Act 1998 *R. (o.t.a. Alan Lord) v Secretary of State for the Home Department* [2003] EWHC 2073 (Admin) which, sensibly, the Information Commissioner believes should be adopted in the FOIA context—Awareness Guidance No. 20 "Prejudice based exceptions"—available at *www.ico.gov.uk*

confidence by another State or by an international organisation[247];

- likely to prejudice the economic or financial interests of the United Kingdom[248];
- likely to prejudice the protection or detection of crime, the apprehension or prosecution of offenders, the administration of justice, tax collection, immigration control, or other legal process brought to safeguard an important public interest[249];
- which, other than statistical information, relates to the formulation of government policy, ministerial communications or the operation of ministerial private offices[250];
- which would, in the reasonable opinion of the minister, be likely to prejudice the convention of collective ministerial responsibility or to inhibit the free and frank provision of advice or exchange of views or otherwise prejudice the effective conduct of public affairs[251];
- relating to communications with the monarch or "with other members of the Royal Family or with the Royal Household" or about "the conferring by the Crown of any honour or dignity"[252];
- likely to endanger the physical or mental health, or the safety, of any individual[253];
- covered by legal professional privilege[254];
- about trade secrets.[255]

These "non absolute" exemptions protect almost all Whitehall information of any interest or significance which is not already covered by the overlapping "absolute exemptions", but only

"if or to the extent that . . .

b) in all the circumstances of the case, the public interest in maintaining the exemption outweighs the public interest in disclosing the information".

This is the "window of opportunity" for media applicants in search of internal information to monitor or critically assess Government performance. It posits a hypothetical public interest in maintaining

---

247 FOI Act, s.27.
248 FOI Act, s.29.
249 FOI Act, s.31.
250 FOI Act, s.35.
251 FOI Act, s.36.
252 FOI Act, s.37.
253 FOI Act, s.38.
254 FOI Act, s.42.
255 FOI Act, s.43.

the category of documents as exempt from disclosure, but permits this consideration to be "outweighed" by the general public interest in disclosure, as fortified by the circumstances of the particular case. (While it is not necessary for an applicant to explain their reasons for wanting access to the information, presumably, an application by an investigative journalist for information to support reasonably held suspicion of official misconduct will (or should) have a greater tendency to outweigh any public interest in concealment than an application by a busybody in search of scandal or a corporation in search of commercial advantage.) For this all-important balancing exercise there is no "burden of proof" to be borne by the applicant, but nor is there any presumption in favour of freedom of information. The public authority must make a judgment as to where the public interest lies.

Appeal

When a public authority decides in favour of concealment, the **11–078** applicant may invoke the organisation's internal review procedure. If this still does not provide the information requested, the applicant can complain to the Information Commissioner.[256] There have been criticisms of the length of time that internal reviews (and consequent access to the Commissioner) can take. In February 2007 the Commissioner issued Guidance which said that in all but a few cases reviews should be completed within 20 days of the request for reconsideration and no review should take longer than 40 days[257] Once a complaint reaches the Commissioner, he will make a decision on its merits, and issue a "decision notice" which either side may take on appeal to the Information Tribunal which is made up of lawyers.[258] The Tribunal will adopt an adversarial procedure, hear both sides and may quash the Commissioner's decision and substitute its own, based on a fresh evaluation of the evidence. Either side may appeal a Tribunal decision to the High Court, although only in so far as it involves a point of law.

These provisions make it possible to overrule concealment decisions made by officials in departments which may have a motive to cover-up. The Information Commissioner investigates the complaint and makes the first adjudicative decision, which can be subjected by either party to a full Tribunal appeal with judicial review of legal error by the High Court. But the system only operates independently when it suits the Government. It has taken the extraordinary liberty, by s.53 of the Act, of giving itself absolute power to nullify the

---

[256] FOI Act 2000, s.50.
[257] Information Commissioner "Good Practice Guidance No.5—Time Limits on Carrying Our Internal Reviews Following Requests for Information Under the Freedom of Information Act" February 22, 2007.
[258] FOI Act, s.57–8.

Commissioner's decision in favour of disclosure, and to by-pass the appeal process entirely. This "Government knows best" power relates to decisions concerning either exempt or absolutely exempt information, and it may be exercised (through issuing a certificate) by the Law Officers or a relevant cabinet minister. The only "safeguard" is that a ministerial decision to abort the appeal process must be reported to Parliament, although in a Parliament where the Government has a large majority this is not much of a safeguard. Section 53 has the effect of empowering the Executive to suspend the FOI Act in any particular case, denying applicants an independent and impartial tribunal (or indeed, any tribunal at all) for determining their civil rights. It is a power of political override, any exercise of which will amount to a blatant breach of Art.6 of the European Convention in those cases where a right of access to information is a "civil right".

PUBLIC RECORDS

11–079   Most public records are transferred after 30 years to the National Archives at Kew, as a result of the Public Records Acts of 1958 and 1967.[259] Kew holds the records for England and Wales.[260] and the United Kingdom. Separate national record offices exist for Scotland and Northern Ireland. Although primarily of interest to historians, some journalists have used this right of access to explore the early careers of today's prominent politicians, as well as reviewing old controversies in the light of newly released material.

The Government has the power to "weed out" and withhold records that it thinks should be kept secret for a longer time. The main categories are:

- distressing or embarrassing personal details about living persons or their immediate descendants;
- information received by the Government in confidence;
- some papers on Ireland; and
- "certain exceptionally sensitive papers which affect the security of the State".[261]

The weeders are super-sensitive to national security and until 1998 they extended the embargo on a document if it so much as mentioned MI5 or MI6.[262] The period of "extended closure" may be 50 years or longer.

---

[259] The 1967 Act reduced the presumptive period from 50 years. Further details of searching are available ot *www.nationalarchives.gov.uk*.

[260] There is power under the Government of Wales Act 2006, ss.146–148 to transfer Welsh public records to Wales.

[261] Lord Gardiner, The Lord Chancellor, *Hansard* [1967] Vol. 282, 5th Ser., col. 1657–58. Certain Commonwealth documents are also restricted.

[262] Michael, *The Politics of Secrecy*, p.185.

As long ago as 1981 a departmental committee recommended more **11–080** liberal access. It criticised the practice whereby the Lord Chancellor can order an entire *class* of documents to be kept secret for a century without considering the specific documents that make up that class. It proposed that more files should be released before the 30–year embargo is up, that "embarrassment" should no longer be a ground for suppression, that the power to keep files secret forever should be abolished, and that there should be a right to appeal from secrecy orders. The Government rejected the report,[263] and by 1989 the following categories were examples of files closed for a century: *Police Reports on the NCCL* (1935–1941); *Flogging of Vagrants* (1919); and decisions against prosecuting James Joyce's *Ulysses* (1924).

The notion of "embarrassment to descendants" is sometimes manipulated to cover "embarrassment to the descendants of civil servants". Closure for a century of files relating to official treatment of suffragettes, prisoners and mental patients prior to the First World War cannot conceivably be justified on privacy grounds. Records of field executions in the First World War were withheld for 70 years, ostensibly to avoid embarrassment to relatives of the long-dead soldiers, but when those documents were finally released, it became clear that the secrecy had been used to avoid exposing the arbitrariness and brutality of justice in the trenches. Quite apart from the absurdity of sealing files about arrangements for police dental treatment during the Second World War, a good deal of information of historical significance in relation to British foreign policy is suppressed, together with material of contemporary import-ance about the investigation of war crimes.

The Freedom of Information Act 2000 has made modest adjust- **11–081** ments to extend the release of historical documents. It sets max-imum periods beyond which certain exemptions from the Act's disclosure obligations cannot be claimed. Thus, for instance, after 30 years an FOIA application cannot be denied on grounds of prejudice to economic interests of the United Kingdom, that the information was obtained with a view to prosecution (except informers' details), court records, audit functions, ministerial correspondence, conduct prejudicial to public affairs, communications with the Royal Family, legal professional privilege or commercial interests. After 60 years the exemption concerning conferment of honours falls away and various other exemptions disappear after 100 years,[264] but no formal end point is created for intelligence or security matters.

---

[263] *Modern Public Records*, 1981, Cmnd. 8024; White Paper Response (1982) Cmnd. 8531; see *State Secrecy and Public Records*, State Research Bulletin, 1982, No.30, p.128; Chapter by M. Roper in Chapman and Hunt (eds) *Open Government*, 1987.
[264] Freedom of Information Act 2000, s.63.

That these periods are exorbitant as well as absurd was demonstrated by the "Cash for Peerages" scandal in 2006–7, which was only exposed by a police investigation after a *"Sunday Times"* undercover journalist was offered a "K" for donating to a city academy: This sleazy practice, which had been going on for some years, would have remained hidden for sixty years under the public records/Freedom of Information Act exemptions. And there can be no possible excuse for covering up government information for a century.

EUROPEAN UNION

Rights of access to documents

11–082 Beginning with the Maastricht Treaty, the EU has recognised that it, too, needs to pay some regard to the principle of freedom of information. In response the Council of Ministers[265] and the Commission[266] produced Codes which established a right of access to Community documents. The Amsterdam Treaty embedded the principle and the governing instrument is now EU Regulation 1049/2001. The Regulation begins with the declaration that any citizen of the EU and any natural or legal person residing in a Member State has a right of access to documents held by a Community institution, i.e. documents drawn up or received by the institution and in its possession.[267]

Inevitably this is followed by exceptions. They fall into two categories. The first[268] is mandatory (i.e. the Council or Commission must deny access and there is no public interest balance to be conducted). This applies where disclosure could undermine the protection of the public interest (public security, defence and military matters, international relations, the financial, monetary or economic policy of the Community or a Member State), or the privacy and integrity of the individual, in particular in accordance with Community legislation regarding personal data. The second category of exception is also mandatory, but is subject to the important qualification "unless there is an overriding public interest in disclosure". This category includes cases where disclosure would undermine the protection of commercial interests of natural or legal persons, court proceedings and legal advice or the purpose of inspections, investigations and audits. Access to a document which was drawn up for internal use or which relates to a matter on which the institution has not yet taken a decision is likewise protected from

---

[265] Council Decision 93/731 on public access to Council documents.
[266] 94/90 on public access to Commission documents.
[267] Reg.1049/2001, Art.2.
[268] Reg.1049/2001, Art.4(1).

disclosure, but, again, subject to the qualification that disclosure must be allowed if there is an overriding public interest.[269] Where documents have come from a third party, the Community institution must consult it as to whether any of these exceptions to disclosure apply, unless the answer is obvious. If the document originates from a Member State, the State can request that there be no disclosure without that State's prior agreement.[270]

Importantly, the Regulation says expressly that if only parts of a document are entitled to exemption, the remainder must be disclosed.[271]

While these exceptions are lengthy and ultra-cautious, the European Court of First Instance which hears challenges to refusals of access has established some principles limiting their effect.[272] **11–083**

> The principles were restated in a case brought by an Austrian quango which had the power to take over and pursue consumer complaints and wished to obtain individual redress for what it alleged was excessive interest charged by certain banks.[273] The Commission had found that the banks had operated a cartel and fined them a total of Euros 124 million. The quango wanted to inspect the Commission's file but had been refused access. The Court of First Instance ruled that ordinarily it was incumbent on the Community institution to consider each individual document which had been requested. It was not enough that the subject matter of a requested document concerned one of the exempt categories: it must decide whether in fact there is a real likelihood that the protected interest would be harmed by disclosure of the particular document and (for documents in the second category) that there is no overriding public interest in favour of disclosure. An individual assessment of this kind is not needed if the answer is manifest without it, but the court is likely to look closely at such an assertion to see if it is justified. The Regulation itself recognises that some requests may relate to a very long document or refer to a very large number of documents. It says that there should then be a discussion between the institution and the applicant to reach a "fair solution".[274] The CFI said that the principle of proportionality would mean that if a fair solution could not be reached, the institution could not be required to conduct an unreasonable amount of administrative work in handling the request. Overall, it had to be remembered that access was the rule, and non-disclosure was the exception. In line with the general approach of EU law to important rights, exceptions were to be strictly construed.

---

[269] Reg.1049/2001, Art.(2) & (3).

[270] Reg.1049/2001, Art.(4) & (5).

[271] Reg.1049/2001, Art.4(6).

[272] The CFI's decision can be appealed to the European Court of Justice, but the ECJ has shown a similar willingness to confine the exceptions, see e.g. Cases C-174/98 & C-189/98 *Van der Wal v Commission* [2000] ECR I 1.

[273] T-2/03 *Verein fur Konsumenteninformation v Commission* April 13, 2005.

[274] Reg.1049/2001, Art.6(3).

Restrictions on disclosures by staff

11–084   Eurocrats are not servants of the Crown and leaks from Brussels are not punishable under the Official Secrets Acts. However, as with British civil servants, their conditions of employment require them to preserve the confidentiality of any document or information "not already made public". They must exercise "the greatest discretion with regard to facts and information coming into their knowledge in the course of or in connection with the performance of (their) duties". As with servants of the British Government, the restrictions continue after they have left their office or job. Staff regulations also prohibit them from "alone or together with others publishing or causing to be published without the permission of the appointing authorities, any matter dealing with the work of the communities". However "permission shall be refused only where the proposed publication is liable to prejudice the interests of the Community".[275] The European Court of Justice has held that this requirement does not violate Art.10 of the ECHR.[276]

Breach of these provisions can lay employees open to disciplinary action, and journalists still need to take care to preserve the anonymity of such sources. Leaking cannot, however, lead to a criminal prosecution of an employee or journalist. The only exception concerns EURATOM (European Atomic Energy Community). Employees and officials of EURATOM, and those with "dealings in any capacity (official or unofficial) with any EURATOM institution or installation or with any EURATOM joint enterprise", who acquire "classified information" commit an offence if they communicate it to any unauthorised person or make any public disclosure of it.[277]

The European Council of Ministers and the European Commission both sit in private. There is no public right of access to their meetings. The European Court of Justice and the European Court of First Instance sit in public for the oral part of their procedure. By English standards, these hearings are very brief. Most of the argument is presented in written form. At least in the Court of First Instance, there is no right for the public to have access to the court file. When an organisation of Swedish journalists published an edited version of the European Council of Minister's defence to their complaint about the withholding of access to Council documents, the Court rebuked the organisation for abusing its procedures. Although the complaint was successful, the Court ordered the Council to pay only two-thirds of the journalists' costs because of this "abuse".[278]

---

[275] EEC Reg.31 and Euratom, Reg.11, both of December 18, 1961.
[276] C-274/99 *Connolly v Commission* [2001] ECR I 1611.
[277] European Communities Act 1972, s.11(2)—"classified information" is defined in Arts 24–7 of the Euratom Treaty.
[278] *Svenska Journalistforbundet v EU Council* [1998] ECR II 2389.

This Euro-fixation with secrecy is indefensible: there is no reason why minutes of the European council of ministers meetings or the European Commission should not be made public (subject to redaction of any sensitive security or financial information) and since most Euro-court proceedings are in writing rather than in open court, Art.10's commitment to open justice requires that they be media-accessible.

CHAPTER 12

REPORTING LOCAL GOVERNMENT

"Elected Members and officials must deliberately establish and maintain working relationships with those responsible for newspapers, broadcasting and television to seek their help in keeping open the two-way communication between the public and local government."[1]

INTRODUCTION

Local papers and most local councils have not been slow to respond to this plea from the Royal Commission. Local newspaper reporters have "established and maintained" a relationship with council contacts who can provide a quick quote to flesh out a dry committee minute or tip the journalist off to agenda items that will spark rhetorical flourishes or have local public interest. These "working relationships" rarely work to uncover incompetence in local government, let alone the sort of corruption that was spread by the Poulson gang. This type of investigation ruffles the feathers of regular contacts and jeopardises reporters' access to information needed for more mundane work.[2] To the shame of the hundreds of reporters covering local government in the North-East, the corruption that riddled that area in the 1960s was discovered and disclosed by lawyers acting for Poulson's creditors. The media saw and heard no evil; certainly they spoke none through the decade in which many local authority contracts were awarded by bribery and improper influence.

12–001

The media cannot blame the secrecy laws for their failure; on the contrary, the law provides rights of access to a wide range of council papers: council electors, including locally based reporters, have rights of inspection that, long preceded the Freedom of Information Act 2000. This chapter will examine:

---

[1] Royal Commission on Local Government, 1969: Redcliffe-Maud Report on Local Government Reform, Cmnd. 4040 (1969), para.319.

[2] See further Dave Murphy, "The Silent Watchdog: the Press in Local Politics" and "Control without Censorship" in James Curran (ed.), *The British Press: A Manifesto* (Macmillan, 1978).

- the rights of admission to meetings of councils and other local bodies;
- rights to inspect documents;
- the special rules of libel concerning reports of and by local authorities.

RIGHTS OF ADMISSION

Council meetings

12–002 Reporting set-piece council debates is safe from a libel action: newspapers can carry, under the shield of qualified privilege, the insults and allegations that rival politicians trade in the public chamber. However, before statute intervened, the courts gave no help to newspapers wishing to report local council meetings. Councillors, like members of a private club, could eject those of whom they disapproved, and a reporter or editor whose stories caused umbrage could be barred from future meetings without legal redress.[3] The courts were out of tune with the times. In 1908 Parliament gave reporters a statutory right to attend council meetings.[4] This was extended in 1960 to the public generally by a statute known after one of its sponsors as the Thatcher Act.[5] Further extensions were made in 1972 and again in 1985.

Consequently, there is no longer a single regime for all public bodies. Journalists will deal most frequently with *principal councils*. These are county, district and London borough councils and also the Common Council of the City of London, the Greater London Authority (for most purposes), a joint authority, a statutory joint committee, a police authority, the Metropolitan Police Authority, the London Fire and Emergency Planning Authority, a combined fire authority, and (for most purposes) the Joint Consultative Committees set up for liaison between the National Health Service and local councils and the Community Health Councils (CHCs), which are Health Service user groups.[6] In Wales counties and county boroughs are principal councils. The Greater London Assembly is also a principal council.[7] The duties of all these bodies to admit the public and to allow inspection of their documents are set out in the Local Government Act 1972.[8]

---

[3] *Tenby Corp v Mason* [1908] 2 Ch. 457.
[4] Admission of Press to Meetings Act 1908.
[5] Public Bodies (Admission to Meetings) Act 1960. Mrs Thatcher introduced its second reading with her maiden speech.
[6] Local Government Act 1972, ss.270(1) and 100J; Health Service Joint Consultative Committees (Access to Information) Act 1986, Community Health Councils (Access to Information) Act 1988.
[7] Greater London Authority Act 1999, s.58(1).
[8] For a useful discussion of rights of access to meetings and documents see Tim Harrison, *Access to Information in Local Government* (Sweet & Maxwell, 1988) and Patrick Birkenshaw, *Government and Information* (Butterworths, 1990), Ch.4.

The Thatcher Act still determines the obligations of parish and community councils, the Council of the Isles of Scilly, joint boards or committees of any of these authorities or one of these authorities and a principal council, parish meetings of rural parishes, the Land Authority of Wales, Health Authorities, and special Health Authorities (if the order setting them up so directs), Primary Care Trusts, and bodies (other than principal councils) that can set a rate.[9]

Committees, sub-committees and caucuses

The Thatcher Act requirements apply only to full meetings of the **12–003** council or body concerned or committees of the whole organisation.[10] Parish and community councils must admit the public to their committee meetings (even if all councillors are not members).[11] The obligation on principal councils to open their doors is much more extensive. Committee and sub-committee meetings must be open to the public except for the limited purposes discussed below.[12]

However, in many authorities policy is really made at caucus meetings of the majority party, where there is absolutely no right of access. The line is a fine one. There is no automatic legal obstacle to committees composed of just one party, and councils are free to have a "working party" composed of members of just the ruling party,[13] but if these were to be set up, operate and report back in a way that was indistinguishable from a committee or sub-committee, they could not escape the duty to allow the public to be present.[14]

Executive government

Regulation of local government has been in a state of almost **12–004** perpetual motion. Most significantly in 2000 Parliament introduced a new regime requiring most local councils to separate their executive functions into one of three basic models: a directly elected mayor plus two or more councillors appointed by the mayor; a council leader ("the executive leader") selected by the council itself and two or more councillors chosen either by the executive leader or the council; or a directly elected mayor and an officer of the council ("council manager").[15] Whichever model is chosen, the council must

---

[9] Public Bodies (Admission to Meetings) Act 1960, Sch.
[10] 1960 Act, s.2(1).
[11] Local Government Act 1972, ss.100 and 270(1).
[12] 1972 Act, ss.100A, 100E; Community Health Councils (Access to Information) Act 1988, s.1.
[13] *R. v Eden District Council Ex p. Moffat, The Independent*, December 16, 1988, CA.
[14] See *R. v Sheffield City Council Ex p. Chadwick* (1986) 84 L.G.R. 563, *London Borough of Southwark v Peters* [1972] L.G.R. 41. The subjective intention of the council in setting the body up is likely to be critical: *R. v Warwickshire District Council Ex p. Bailey* [1991] C.O.D. 284.
[15] Local Government Act 2000, s.13.

establish an overview and scrutiny committee which does not include members of the executive and which can review and scrutinise decisions or actions of the executive. The overview and scrutiny committee is a committee for the purpose of the provisions of the 1972 Act which allow public admission and public access to documents.[16]

Local authorities have to consult on which option to adopt and, if they wish to choose the option of an elected mayor plus cabinet executive or mayor and council manager, they must hold a local referendum. The legislation allows for petitions by local voters for holding a referendum on the adoption of a particular type of executive government. The local council may have strong views on referenda of these kind, but they are constrained in what they can say in the 28 days preceding the poll. They cannot publish information about the question or arguments on either side except in answer to a specific request, or information relating to the holding of the poll—or in the spirit of "right of reply"—to refute or correct any inaccuracy in material published by a person other than the authority.[17] Once the choice is settled, the local authority must publicise the arrangements and allow inspection of its details at their principal office.[18] A local authority "constitution" consisting of information prescribed by the Secretary of State, the authority's standing orders and its code of conduct must be made available at its principal office at all reasonable hours. Copies must be supplied although a reasonable fee can then be charged.[19]

Part of the purpose of the changes in the 2000 Act was to take some decision-making away from local authority committees. In some cases, these decisions can be taken by individual members of the executive where the idea of a "meeting" simply does not apply. In other cases, the decisions can be, or must be, taken by the executive as a group. Even here, the legislation envisages that generally the decisions can be taken at a meeting which is either held in public or in private, the choice being made by the executive itself.[20] Central government, though, has prescribed that certain decisions must be taken at a public meeting of the executive.[21]

12–005   As a result, in general, meetings of the authority's executive or its committees at which "key decisions" are to be taken must be in held in public.[22] A decision is "key" if it will have a significant effect on the authority's budget or a significant effect on two or more wards or

---

[16] 2000 Act, s.21(11).
[17] Local Authorities (Conduct of Referendums) (England) Regulations 2001 (SI 2001/1298), Reg.5.
[18] Local Government Act 2000, s.29.
[19] 2000 Act, s.37.
[20] 2000 Act, s.22(1) and (2).
[21] Local Authorities (Executive Arrangements) (Access to Information) (England) Regulations 2000 (SI 2000/3272).
[22] 2000 Regs, Reg.7.

electoral divisions in the authority's area.[23] The "two or more wards" test prompted considerable criticism in Parliament. Central government guidance urges local authorities (unless it is impracticable) to treat, as if they were "key", decisions which are likely to have a significant impact on communities in any one ward or electoral division. It gives the example of a school closure whose impact may be confined to one ward but would still be very significant for that ward.[24]

There are exceptions where even key decisions do not have to be made in public. These are confidential matters that broadly correspond to the exceptions to the requirement that meetings of the council itself must be in public.[25] An additional category of unnecessarily confidential information is the advice of political advisers or assistants.[26]

The intention is that local authorities will produce a forward plan for four months which will be then updated on a monthly basis.[27] The plan should identify the subject-matter of the decision, the precise person or body who will take the decision, the date on which the decision is to be made, the principal groups who are to be consulted and how consultation will take place, how other representations can be made and a list of documents submitted to the decision maker for consideration, but it will not include any exempt or confidential information.[28] Forward plans must be made publicly available and the authority must publish in a local newspaper details of where and when inspection can take place.[29] Key decisions can be taken outside the scheme of the forward plan, but only where their inclusion in the plan would be impracticable and where (generally) five clear days' public notice has been given.[30] These requirements can only be circumvented in cases of special urgency and where the chairman of the overview and scrutiny committee has agreed that the decision cannot reasonably be deferred.[31]

"Secrecy motions" and other limitations on access

The right of admission is not absolute. The public must be admitted **12–006** to committees only "so far as is practicable",[32] but the courts have insisted that a committee must not deliberately choose to meet in a

---

[23] 2000 Regs, Reg.8.

[24] The guidance is available on the website of the Department of Communities and Local Government: *www.communities.gov.uk*.

[25] Local Authorities (Executive Arrangements) (Access to Information) (England) Regulations 2000, Reg.21, and see below para.12–006.

[26] 2000 Regs, Reg.21(4).

[27] 2000 Regs, Reg.13.

[28] 2000 Regs, Reg.14.

[29] 2000 Regs, Reg.12.

[30] 2000 Regs, Reg.15.

[31] 2000 Regs, Reg.16—there are more detailed provisions for situations where there is no such chairman.

[32] Local Government Act 1972, s.100(1).

room that is too small for the expected audience.[33] Although there is power to clear the public gallery to prevent or suppress disorder,[34] the members of the press are unlikely to be part of any disturbance and so they should be allowed to stay when the protesters are swept out. The principle is the same as that which applies to disruptions in court (see para.8–025).

Until the Local Government (Access to Information) Act 1985 councils and their committees had a general power under the Thatcher Act to exclude the public when publicity would have been prejudicial to the public interest by reason of the confidential nature of the business to be transacted or for other special reasons stated in the resolution.[35] This still applies to those bodies governed by the Thatcher Act (see para.12–002). But the over-frequent use of this power by the larger councils and the reluctance of the courts to interfere prompted Parliament in the 1985 Act to specify more precisely when the public could be excluded from principal councils, their committees and sub-committees.

The council, committee or sub-committee *must* sit in secret if there would otherwise be disclosed information that it has received from a government department in confidence or information which cannot be disclosed because of a statutory duty or court order.[36]

12–007   The council or committee *can* choose to debate "exempt information" in secret session. The price of greater constraint on the ability of local authorities to sit in private session is that this term has a very cumbersome definition. In summary, the categories of exempt information are[37]:

- information relating to any individual;
- information which is likely to reveal the identity of any individual;
- information relating to the financial or business affairs of any particular person (including the authority holdng that information);
- information relating to any actual or contemplated consultations or negotiations in connection with any labour relations matter between the authority or a Minister of the Corwn and employees of, or office holders under the authority;
- information in respect of which a claim to legal professional privilege could be maintained in legal proceedings;

---

[33] *R. v Liverpool City Council Ex p. Liverpool Taxi Fleet Operators Association* [1975] 1 All E.R. 379—see below para.12–008.
[34] Local Government Act 1972, s.100A(8); Public Bodies (Admission to Meetings) Act 1960, s.1(8). See also *R. v Brent Health Authority Ex p. Francis* [1985] 1 All E.R. 74.
[35] Public Bodies (Admission to Meetings) Act 1960, s.1(2).
[36] Local Government Act 1972, s.100A(2) and (3).
[37] 1972 Act, Sch.12A as substituted by the Local Government (Access to Information) (Variation) Order 2006 (SI 2006/88). A slightly different list is prescribed for Welsh authorities: Sch.12A.

- Information which that the authority proposes to give a statutory notice, order or direction;
- information relating to any action taken or to be taken in connection with the prevention, investigation or prosecution of crime;
- in relation to Joint Consultative Committees and CHCs, information relating to the physical or mental health of any person or information relating to anyone who is, was or has applied to provide services as a doctor, dentist, ophthalmist or pharmacist or their employee.[38]

However, information is not exempt if it is required to be registered under the Companies Act 1985, or various Acts to do with Friendly Societies, Building Societies or Industrial and Provident Societies, nor if it relates to a proposed development for which the authority could itself give planning permission. There is a further important qualification: information is only exempt if in all the circumstances of the case, the public interest in maintaining the exemption outweighs the public interest in disclosing the information.[39]

The Secretary of State or (for Welsh authorities) the Welsh Assembly can vary this list of exempt information.[40]

The authority can exclude the public only if its secrecy resolution **12–008** states the category of exempt information that will be discussed.[41] Under the Thatcher Act the courts have held that a failure to spell out the reasons for exclusion does not invalidate the resolution.[42] The legislation for principal councils is differently worded,[43] and an authority would probably be acting beyond its powers if it did not conform to these requirements.

A committee of Liverpool City Council was considering a plan to increase the number of taxi licences. The committee room had 55 seats, 22 of which were occupied by councillors, and 17 by officers. The matter had aroused local interest, and many taxi drivers and others wanted to attend and to make representations to the committee. The committee ruled that while the press could stay, the rest of the public should be excluded. The special reasons were, first, the lack of space and the impracticability of allowing in only some of the public and, secondly, a preference for hearing representations individually in the absence of other members of the public who generally wished to make submissions. The Divisional Court agreed that these reasons were

---

[38] Health Service Joint Consultative Committees (Access to Information) Act 1986, s.2(4); Community Health Councils (Access to Information) Act 1988, s.2(6).

[39] 1972 Act, sch.12A para.10.

[40] Local Government Act 1972, s.100I(2).

[41] Local Government Act 1972, s.100A(5).

[42] *R v Liverpool City Council*, fn.33 above.

[43] See Local Government Act 1972, s.100A(4) and (5).

adequate because the committee had not deliberately chosen a room that was too small, the press had been allowed to stay, and on the special facts of the case it was reasonable to exclude the public who were also potential "witnesses" before the committee.[44]

The case is important because of the court's emphasis on the presence of the press, and for its indication that deliberate attempts to avoid publicity by a council can be challenged in court on grounds of bad faith.

12–009 The secrecy motion is sometimes passed to cover up a council's blunders or to hide an official's embarrassment rather than in the public interest. In one case the public were excluded while the council debated the reasons for the failure of a redevelopment project. Through the gaps in the door frame reporters overheard that the development company had run short of funds and was threatening to abandon the project unless the council increased its subsidies.[45]

If a secrecy motion is proposed, journalists should ask the chair to follow the *Liverpool City Council* case and allow the press to stay. If this request is refused and there is no valid justification for the secrecy motion, the decision could be challenged by applying to the High Court to quash the secrecy order and any decision of the meeting taken after discussion behind closed doors. Journalists should in such cases ask the chair either to adjourn consideration of the matter until the challenge is heard by the court or to tape-record the deliberations so that the press can at least hear the tape if the court rules in its favour.

Agendas

12–010 Thatcher Act councils and other local government bodies whose meetings are public must give three clear days' notice of all such meetings.[46] Principal councils, their committees and sub-committees must give five clear days notice.[47] Newspapers and news agencies have the right to be sent copies of the agendas and any statements which indicate the nature of the agenda items. They should also be sent copies of every report for the meeting unless the responsible official believes it is likely to be discussed at a closed session. If the officials think fit, the media should also be sent copies of any other

---

[44] *R. v Liverpool City Council*, fn.33 above.

[45] Dave Murphy *The Silent Watchdog*, p.25.

[46] Public Bodies (Admission to Meetings) Act 1960, s.1(4)(a). "Clear days" means excluding the day on which the notice is given and the day on which the meeting is held—*R. v Swansea City Council Ex p. Elitestone Ltd* (1993) 66 P. & C. R. 422.

[47] 1972 Act, s.100A(6)(a) as amended by the Local Authorities (Access to Meetings and Documents) (Period of Notice) (England) Order 2002 (SI 2002/715). If the meeting is convened on shorter notice, notice to the public must be given at the same time.

documents supplied to members of the authority in connection with an agenda item. For these services the media can be charged only postage or other necessary costs for transmission.[48] Alternatively, copies of the agenda and reports can be inspected at the authority's offices in the three days before the meeting (five days in the case of principal councils, their committees and sub-committees). The press may still find it worth making an expedition to the authority's offices, because officials of principal councils must prepare a list of the background papers for each report that is required to be publicly available. Any document that discloses facts or matters on which the report was based and which was relied upon to a material extent in preparing the report must be included on the list. Considerable judgment is left to the officers concerned, but in extreme cases the courts would review the decision. The list and at least one copy of each paper (unless it contains exempt or confidential information) must be open to public inspection, although (unusually) authorities can impose a reasonable charge for this right of inspection.[49] The media might argue that these additional documents should be sent to them with their agendas, but councils, which can charge only postage, might baulk at the cost of copying. Documents inspected at the Town Hall can be copied there, but a charge can be made for this. A reasonable number of agendas and the officers reports should also be available for the public at the meeting itself.[50] Since the 1985 Act all these provisions apply as well to meetings of committees and subcommittees of principal councils.[51]

We have seen that council executives must prepare a forward plan which is updated monthly. This will show when key decisions are expected to be made. In certain circumstances key decisions can be taken outside the forward plan but must still be made at a public meeting of the executive (except where the secrecy requirements are satisfied). The publicity which must be given to agendas and reports to be considered at public meetings of the executive broadly follows the requirements for meetings of the council and its committees.[52] Here, too, newspapers[53] can require the local authority to send a copy of the agenda and reports to be considered, such further

---

[48] Local Government Act 1972, s.100B(7). A "newspaper" is defined as including a news agency that systematically carries on the business of selling and supplying reports or information to newspapers, and any organisation that is systematically engaged in collecting news for sound or television broadcasts or any other programme service: s.100K. See also Public Bodies (Admission to Meetings) Act 1960, s.1(4)(b) and s.1(7).

[49] Local Government Act 1972, ss.100D and 100H.

[50] 1972 Act, s.100B(1)–(6).

[51] 1972 Act, s.100E.

[52] The Local Authorities (Executive Arrangements) (Access to Information) (England) Regulations 2000 (SI 2000/3272), Regs 10 and 11.

[53] A term defined to include news agencies and "any organisation which is systematically engaged in collecting news for (i) sound or television broadcasts or (ii) for inclusion in . . . any programme service"—2000 Regs, Reg.2.

statements or particulars, if any, as are necessary to indicate the nature of the items contained in the agenda and, if the proper officer thinks fit in the case of any item, a copy of any other document supplied to members of the executive in connection with the item. They must pay any necessary charge for transmission.[54]

Reporting

12–011 At open meetings accredited representatives of the press must be given reasonable facilities for taking notes and for telephoning reports, unless the building in which the meeting is held does not have a telephone or does not belong to the local authority.[55] "Reasonable facilities" mean chairs and a table conveniently placed to hear and see what is going on.[56] There is no right to take photographs of the meeting, to use any means to enable persons not present to see or hear the proceedings, or to make an oral report of the proceedings as they take place.[57] The authority can thus prohibit tape-recording of the proceedings for the purpose of public broadcasting, but it is doubtful whether it can ban reporters from tape-recording for their own use as an aide-memoire.[58] It is important to note that these restrictions are discretionary; they do not prevent a local council from granting permission to film or record if it wishes.

INSPECTION OF DOCUMENTS

Accounts and supporting documents

12–012 Local government has a prototype freedom of information law that is buried in an obscure section of the Audit Commission Act 1998. Section 15 gives "to any person interested" the right to inspect a local authority's accounts, and "all books, deeds, contracts, bills, vouchers and receipts relating to them".[59]

> The meaning of "a person interested" was considered on an application for judicial review which was brought by HTV when Bristol City Council refused it access to these documents. The company wanted to

---

[54] 2000 Regs, Reg.11(7).

[55] Public Bodies (Admission to Meetings) Act 1960, s.1(4)(c), Local Government Act 1972, s.100A(6).

[56] Ministry of Local Government Circular 21/61, App.1, para.8.

[57] Public Bodies (Admission to Meetings) Act 1960, s.1(7) and Local Government Act 1972, s.100A(7).

[58] This Interpretation of Public Bodies (Admission to Meetings) Act 1960, s.1(7) and Local Government Act 1972, s.100A(7) would be in line with modern views of tape recorders in courts: see para.8–091.

[59] As well as local authorities, the right applies to a wide range of other public bodies. They include police and fire authorities, the Broads Authority and health service bodies: see Audit Commission Act 1998, Sch.2.

make a documentary about a landlord who provided accommodation for vulnerable people nominated by the Council and who had been the subject of complaints. The Court rejected the argument that a "person interested" meant any interested member of the public or the media with their public watchdog role. However, it also rejected the Council's argument that the term was limited to local electors (although, oddly, only they had a right of access to the statement of accounts). As it happened, HTV had premises in the Bristol area and they paid non-domestic rates. These are now set and collected by central government, but this was sufficient to give the company an interest, albeit indirect, in the Council's financial affairs. Once this was established, it was irrelevant that they wanted access to the Council's documents to make a documentary rather than to make complaints or objections to the auditor.[60]

This enormous volume of documentation is a resource under-used by the media. It can provide fascinating stories—as a local paper in Bedfordshire discovered when through this route it obtained details of firearm purchases by its police force.[61] Contracts and other documents directly related to expenditure can be inspected even though they are described as confidential.[62] Similarly, the local authority cannot fob off inquirers with an extract from the accounts showing only gross payments.[63]

This window on a local authority's affairs is open only for the 20 full working days prior to the annual audit.[64] An advertisement giving 14 days' notice of this crucial period must be published in one or more local newspapers.[65]

At other times of the year a local elector can demand to see the 12–013 statement of account,[66] orders for the payment of money by the authority[67] and a breakdown of allowances and expenses paid to councillors.[68] These accounts will not be as detailed as the pre-audit material and a council can fulfil its duty by making a computer printout available.[69] If it chooses to do this, electors will see only the

---

[60] *R. (HTV Ltd) v Bristol City Council* [2004] 1 W.L.R. 2717 Elias J. A similar conclusion was reached in Scotland in *Stirrat v City of Edinburgh* [1998] SCLR 973. OH, interpreting Local Government (Scotland) Act 1973, s.101(1).

[61] *UK Press Gazette*, November 6 and 20, 1995.

[62] *London Borough of Hillingdon v Paullsson* [1977] J.P.L. 518. Personal information about staff in connection with their employment is excepted: Audit Commission Act 1998, s.15(3)–(5).

[63] *Oliver v Northampton Borough Council* (1986) 151 J.P. 44.

[64] Accounts and Audit Regulations 2003 (SI 2003/533), Reg.14.

[65] 2003 Regs, Reg.16.

[66] Audit Commission Act 1998, s.14.

[67] Local Government Act 1972, s.228(2).

[68] Local Authorities (Members' Allowances) Regulations 1991, (SI 1991/351), Reg.26. Each year the authority must also publish the total sums paid to each member as a basic allowance, special responsibility allowance and attendance allowance: Reg.26A.

[69] *Buckingham v Shackleton* [1981] 79 L.G.R. 484.

amount of councillors' expenses and not the fuller details on the claim forms themselves.[70]

Journalists who are not trained accountants will find it hard to make sense of the pile of paperwork available under these provisions. However, the courts have said that people who are local electors would be entitled to take accountants with them, even though the accountants came from outside the authority's area.[71] It is not necessary to identify the particular document required. It is possible to ask for an entire class of documents, and a request for "all orders for payment" could be refused only if the class turned out to be unmanageably large.[72] A right of inspection is also coupled with a right to make copies of documents.[73] Inspection is free, but copies may be charged for at a reasonable rate. It is a criminal offence to refuse a proper demand for a copy or to obstruct a person entitled to inspect one of these documents. The maximum fine is £1,000.[74] In 1996 Haringey Council was fined £650 and ordered to pay costs of £2,000 for obstructing a local resident who wanted to exercise these rights.[75]

Audit

12–014   One purpose of allowing inspection of an authority's books just prior to the audit is to allow local electors to question the auditor about the accounts.[76] These can be taken in public, but there is a discretion to hear them in private.[77] The Audit Commission's code reminds auditors that there is no statutory requirement to have an oral hearing. They have to decide whether justice and fairness would be served by a hearing and, if so, whether the hearing should be in public. If surprise allegations are made at a hearing the auditor should adjourn to allow written representations.[78]

The Conservative Government's philosophy of requiring local authorities to put certain services out to tender ("compulsory competitive tendering") was changed by the Labour Government in 1999. Most local authorities are given the new sobriquet of "best value authorities". They must each prepare plans for continually

---

[70] *Brookman v Green* [1984] L.G.R. 228.
[71] *R. v Glamorganshire County Council Ex p. Collier* [1936] 2 All E.R. 168; *R. v Bedwellty UDC Price* [1934] 1 K.B. 333.
[72] *Evans v Lloyd* [1962] 2 Q.B. 471.
[73] Audit Commission Act 1998, ss.14 and 15.
[74] Audit Commission Act 1998, s.14(3).
[75] *Hampstead and Highgate Express*, September 13, 1996.
[76] Audit Commission Act 1998, s.16. But inspection is not confined to those who wish to challenge the accounts: *R. (HTV) v Bristol City Council* (above) and *Stirrat v Edinburgh City Council*, 1998 S C.L.R. 971 (above).
[77] *R. v Farmer Ex p. Hargrave* [1981] 79 L.G.R. 676.
[78] *Code of Audit Practice for Local Authorities and the NHS in England and Wales* (Audit Commission, 1995) paras 103–15.

improving their services "having regard to a combination of economy, efficiency and effectiveness".[79] Plans are audited each year and the auditor's report must be published by the authority.[80]

The auditor's report on any objections to the accounts and on the accounts generally must be sent to newspapers, news agencies, and television and radio stations that receive local authority agendas.[81] Those not on the mailing list will be notified by advertisement in a local paper that the report is available.[82] It can then be inspected as of right by any local elector who may also purchase copies of all or part of it.[83]

If the auditors come across a matter of particular concern during **12–015** the course of their investigation, they can make an immediate report, rather than waiting for months until they conclude their final report.[84] These "immediate reports" must be made publicly available by the council concerned, which must also advertise their existence in the local press. It is a summary offence to obstruct a person trying to exercise his or her rights under these provision.[85]

When an auditor's report is received the local authority must meet to consider the report and any recommendations which it includes. The meeting must be within four months of the report being received unless the auditor grants an extension.[86] It must be advertised in the local press at least seven clear days in advance and after the meeting of the authority a notice (approved by the auditor) setting out its decisions in consequence of the report must be published.[87]

Minutes, reports and records of decisions

For parish and community councils, only the minutes of the author- **12–016** ity itself and its committees need to be made public.[88] For principal councils, the obligation extends to committee and sub-committee minutes. For six years the authority must keep copies of the minutes, the agenda and any report for an item that was considered in public. If the public was actually excluded because exempt information was under discussion, the minutes of that part of the meeting will be sealed. If this means that it is impossible to understand the proceedings, council officials should prepare a summary to give a fair and coherent record without disclosing exempt information.[89]

---

[79] Local Government Act 1999, s.3.
[80] 1998 Act, s.9.
[81] Audit Commission Act 1998, s.10(5)(a).
[82] Accounts and Audit Regulations 2003, Reg.18.
[83] Audit Commission Act 1998, s.10(5)(b).
[84] 1998 Act, s.8.
[85] 1998 Act, s.13(2).
[86] 1998 Act, s.11.
[87] 1998 Act, s.12.
[88] Local Government Act 1972, s.228(1).
[89] Local Government Act 1972, s.100C; three years in the case of CHCs, Community Health Councils (Access to Information) Act 1988, s.1(1).

Background papers that are open to public inspection must be kept for four years.[90] During these periods agendas, minutes and reports can be inspected without charge, but the authority can impose a reasonable fee for inspecting background reports and for copying.[91] Copying can be refused if this would infringe copyright in the document, but not if the only copyright is owned by the authority itself.[92] Obstructing access to such documents without a reasonable excuse is a criminal offence, although the maximum fine is only level 1 on the standard scale (currently £200).

Key decisions apart, the executives of councils are free to decide to hold their meetings in private. To this extent, the 2000 Act represents a regressive step in relation to open government. However, although decisions can be taken in private, a written record of the decision must be made "as soon as reasonably practicable" together with the reasons for it, details of any alternative options considered and rejected, any conflicts of interest declared and any dispensation by the local authority's standards committee.[93] These records are open for public inspection together with any report considered at the meeting or by the individual decision-maker and a newspaper can require the authority to send it copies of these documents (on paying a reasonable copying and transmission charge).[94] The local authority must also make available for public inspection a list of background papers to a report considered at a public meeting of the executive and at least one copy of each document listed.[95] As with the 1972 Act, unusually *this* right of inspection can be subject to payment of a reasonable fee.

12–017 Wherever documents have to be made available to the public, copies can be made or requested on payment of a reasonable fee,[96] but this does not permit the making of a copy which would infringe someone's copyright (unless the owner of the copyright is the local authority). By making documents available to the public under these arrangements, the authority will "publish" them for the purposes of the law of defamation, but a special qualified privileged is granted so that there will be no liability in the absence of malice.[97] Records of executive decisions taken in private and reports considered at the time have to be kept for public inspection for six years from the date of the decision. Background papers must be kept for four years.[98]

---

[90] Local Government Act 1972, s.100D(2); four years in the case of CHCs, Community Health Councils (Access to Information) Act 1988, s.1(1)(c).

[91] Local Government Act 1972, s.100H(1) and (2).

[92] Local Government Act 1972, s.100H(3).

[93] The Local Authorities (Executive Arrangements) (Access to Information) (England) Regulations 2000, (SI 2000/3272), Regs 3 and 4.

[94] 2000 Regs, Reg.5.

[95] 2000 Regs, Reg.6.

[96] 2000 Regs, Reg.22(2).

[97] The Local Authorities (Executive Arrangements) (Access to Information) (England) Regulations 2000, Reg.22(4).

[98] 2000 Regs, Reg.22(5) and (6).

The regulations make it a criminal offence for a person with custody of a document which must be made available to the public if without reasonable excuse he intentionally obstructs a right of access or refuses to supply a copy. The maximum penalty is a fine not exceeding level 1 which is currently the modest sum of £200.[99]

Local authorities must maintain registers of councillors showing their membership of committees and subcommittees and principal councils must have list of officers to whom powers have been delegated.[100] The register and a list must be open to public inspection. Councils should also maintain for the public a written summary of rights to attend meetings and inspect documents.[101]

Councillors' standards and conflicts of interest

The law in this area was substantially revised and extended by the **12–018** Local Government Act 2000. This established a multi-layered structure of regulation and adjudication. In the first place the Secretary of State can lay down general standards to be observed. These[102] build on principles set out by the Nolan Committee on Standards in Public Life in Local Government. The Government's principles include "Accountability: Members should be accountable to the public for their actions and in the manner in which they carry out their responsibilities, and should co-operate fully and honestly with any scrutiny appropriate to their particular office" and "Openness: Members should be as open as possible about their actions and those of their authority, and should be prepared to give reasons for their actions".[103]

The Government can then also establish a model code of conduct for local authority members and co-opted members. This can include some provisions which are mandatory and others which are optional.[104] Local authorities must adopt their own code of conduct shortly after the Government has promulgated the model code and the authorities' codes must include the mandatory parts of the model.[105] Councillors and co-opted members must give a written undertaking to abide by their authority's Code.[106]

---

[99] 2000 Regs, Reg.23.

[100] Unless this is for a period less than six months: Local Government Act 1972, s.100G added by the Local Government (Access to Information) Act 1985.

[101] See above and Local Government Inspection of Documents (Summary of Rights) Order 1986 (SI 1986/854). The register must also list the names and addresses of other members of the committee or sub-committee who are not councillors (Local Government Act 1972, s.100G(17)(c)). Joint Consultative Committees and CHCs must prepare comparable registers and summaries of rights of access: Health Services Joint Consultative Committees (Access to Information) Act 1986, s.3; Community Health Councils (Access to Information) Act 1988, s.2.

[102] The Relevant Authorities (General Principles) Order 2001 (SI 2001/1401).

[103] 2001 Order, Sch., paras 4 and 5.

[104] Local Government Act 2000, s.50. The model code is contained in the Local Authorities (Model Code of Conduct) (England) Order 2007 (SI 2007/1159).

[105] 2000 Act, s.51.

[106] 2000 Act, s.52.

Each authority must set up a standards committee with the function of advising the authority on its Code and monitoring its operation.[107] But enforcement is not left to the authorities themselves. The 2000 Act also established a Standards Board which is empowered to appoint ethical standards officers who will investigate allegations that a member or co-opted member has failed to comply with the authority's Code. If the complaint is not dismissed or not worthy of further action, the ESO can refer it to the monitoring officer of the authority for it to take action, or it can be referred to the Adjudication Panel for a decision.[108] The Adjudication Panel can ultimately decide that the member or co-opted member must be suspended (for up to a year) or disqualified (for up to five years).[109] There is a right of appeal to the High Court.[110]

> In 2006 the Mayor of London, Ken Livingstone, faced an Adjudication Panel Tribunal for remarks which he had made to an *Evening Standard* reporter who had door-stepped him as he was leaving a function at City Hall. When the reporter identified his paper, Livingstone (who had been the object of much adverse comment by Associated Newspapers' publications) asked "Were you a German war criminal?" When the reporter said he wasn't and he was Jewish, Livingstone likened him to a concentration camp guard. The Tribunal found that the Mayor had brought his office into disrespect and that, even though the reception had concluded, he was still performing his official functions. It suspended him for four weeks. The High Court reversed the decision. The Code did not apply because the Mayor was not acting in his official capacity, nor performing his functions at the time. Besides, while the words were highly offensive and Livingstone's use of them may have attracted criticism of him personally, they did not bring his office into disrespect. It was not "necessary in a democratic society" to penalise him for using them. Article 10 would not therefore have permitted the decision to stand in any case.[111]

12–019   The High Court has frequently had to discuss the impact of Art.10 in other appeals by disciplined councilors.[112]

The 2000 Act also requires each local authority to have a register of interests of members and co-opted members. The Secretary of State's model code must include in its mandatory provisions requirements to register specified financial and other interests, to declare the interest before taking part in any business related to that interest and to make provision for preventing or restricting the participation of any member or co-opted member in relation to such business.

---

[107] 2000 Act, ss.53–56.
[108] 2000 Act, s.59.
[109] 2000 Act, s.79.
[110] 2000 Act, s.79(15).
[111] *Ken Livingstone v Adjudication Panel for England* [2006] BLGR 799, Collins J.
[112] See e.g *Sanders v Kingson* [2005] LGR 719 and [2006] LGR 111; *Hare v Marcar* [2006] BLGR 567.

The ban is not complete because the Government can prescribe circumstances in which the authority's standards committee can grant dispensations from these provisions. The register must be open to the public and as soon as practicable after it has been established. Its existence and where it can be inspected must be advertised in a local paper.[113]

In addition to a Code for members and co-opted members, the Central government can issue a Code for local authority officers. The contracts of employment of officers are then deemed to incorporate the Code.[114]

Rates and council tax

Local taxes are essentially of two kinds: the council tax imposed on **12–020** domestic properties and a "non-domestic" rate on business premises.

The business rate is fixed nationally, but it is applied to the value of each premises. Lists of valuations will normally be held by the valuation officer, the billing authority and, nationally, by the Department of Communities and Local Government. The current lists and those in force in the previous five years are open to (free) inspection and copying (for a reasonable charge). The same rights apply to proposals to alter the lists or notices of appeal against proposals.[115] Disputes about valuations are heard by Valuation Tribunals. These sit in public unless the tribunal is satisfied that a party's interests would be prejudiced by a public hearing.[116] The decisions on appeals are kept for six years and are open to inspection.[117] There is a further right of appeal to the Lands Tribunal which sits in public unless, because of confidential or national security considerations, it is just and reasonable to exclude the public.[118]

Council tax rates are set by local authorities (within constraints set by central government). Domestic properties also have to be valued, but they are grouped in bands. The valuation lists (kept usually by the billing authority) will show into which band each property comes. There are rights to inspect and copy these valuation lists, to attend appeals heard by valuation tribunals and to access the tribunal's decisions, all of which parallel the arrangements for business properties.[119]

---

[113] Local Government Act 2000, s.81.
[114] 2000 Act, s.82.
[115] Local Government Finance Act 1988, Sch.9, paras 8 and 9.
[116] Non-Domestic Rating (Alteration of Lists and Appeals) (England) Regulations 2005 (SI 2005/659), Reg.30(3).
[117] 2005 Regs, Reg.36(4) and (5).
[118] Lands Tribunal Rules 1996 (SI 1996/1022), Reg.5.
[119] See Local Government Finance Act 1992, ss.28 and 29 and Council Tax (Alteration of Lists and Appeals) Regulations 1993, (SI 1993/290), Regs 25(3) and 31.

Planning and licensing

12–021 Planning applications are kept on a register that is open to public inspection.[120] If development is carried on without planning permission, the local authority can issue an enforcement notice requiring the owner to restore the land to its previous use or condition, or a breach of condition notice if the terms on which permission was granted have not been followed. The owner can appeal and cannot be compelled to obey the enforcement notice unless the local authority also issues a "stop notice". These are not made automatically, because the authority must pay compensation if it loses the appeal. There are public registers of enforcement, breach of condition and stop notices.[121]

Local authorities are responsible for granting licenses for the sale of alcohol. When dealing with an application in relation to licensed premises, the authority must sit in public unless it decides that the public interest in excluding all or part of the public outweighs the public interest in conducting the hearing in public.[122] It is hard to envisage what such circumstances might be, Applications for certain other kinds of local authority licences (ranging from sex shops to zoos) must also be made available to the public.[123]

In addition to actions affecting individual properties, local authorities are required to plan strategically. Their plans in draft and as actually adopted, together with supporting documents, must be open to public inspection.[124] Similarly the public are entitled to see the authority's registers of listed buildings and of tree preservation notices.[125]

Local ombudsmen

12–022 Just as a "Parliamentary Commissioner for Administration", i.e. an ombudsman, has been established to hear complaints of poor administration in central government, so a number of local Commissioners of Administration exist to hear complaints of maladministration against local authorities. The complaint must relate to the

---

[120] Town and Country Planning Act 1990, s.69. It is divided into those that are pending and those that have been finally disposed of: Town and Country Planning (General Development Procedure) Order 1995 (SI 1995/419), Art.25. The register also says what action has been taken on the application.

[121] Town and Country Planning Act 1990, s.188, and Town and Country Planning (General Development Procedure) Order 1995, Art.26.

[122] Licensing Act 2003 (Hearings) Regulations 2005 (SI 2005/44), Reg.14.

[123] Sex shops: Local Government (Miscellaneous Provisions) Act 1982, Sch.3, para.10 (7)–(13); Zoos: Zoo Licensing Act 1981, s.2(3).

[124] Town and Country Planning (General Development Procedure) Order 1995 (above), Art.25A.

[125] Town and Country Planning Act 1990, s.214 (tree preservation); Planning (Listed Buildings and Conservation Areas) Act 1990, s.2 (listed buildings).

procedure of decision-making rather than its merits, and in order to succeed will generally have to reveal bias, neglect, inattention, delay, incompetence, ineptitude, perversity, turpitude or arbitrariness. Complaints are normally made through a local councillor but, unlike the parliamentary ombudsman, the local commissioners can receive complaints directly from the public.[126] The local ombudsman reports back to the authority concerned, which will then normally have to give the public a chance to inspect the report for a three-week period that has been advertised by at least one week's advance notice in the local press. Inspection of the ombudsman's report is free of charge. It can be copied, and it is an offence to obstruct anyone exercising these rights to inspect or copy.[127]

Local parliamentary bills

Certain documents have to be deposited with the local authority **12–023** under the Standing Orders of each House of Parliament. These are mainly private bills that are sponsored by, or affect, the locality.[128] The detailed plans that must accompany them may be of particular interest in the case of controversial construction projects. These documents are also open to inspection and copying, although the council can charge for viewing them: 10p for the first hour and 10p per hour thereafter.[129]

Environmental controls

Responsibility for controlling pollution rests with local authorities **12–024** and the Environment Agency. Traditionally, council officials have preserved the secrecy of the information that they have been given by local industries on the pretext that their co-operation was essential and depended on confidentiality. Environmentalists suspected that the real fears were of greater public pressure for higher standards, and of criticism at the inefficiency of the means of control.[130]

Slowly Parliament has demanded more publicity. The impetus has principally come from the EU whose directives have demanded

---

126 Local Government Act 1974, ss.23–34.
127 1974 Act, s.30. Apart from naming the authority, the report will usually keep others involved anonymous, but if the maladministration involved a member of the authority acting in breach of the National Code of Local Government Conduct he or she should be named unless the Ombudsman considers that it would be unjust to do so: s.30(3A).
128 Standing Orders of the House of Commons (Private Business) H.C. 416 (1980) Orders 27–47.
129 Local Government Act 1972, ss.225 and 228(5).
130 See Maurice Frankel, "The Environment" in Rosemary Delbridge and Martin Smith (eds), *Consuming Secrets* (National Consumer Council and Burnet Books, 1982), pp.93–126.

more openness. The most recent directive[131] led to the Environmental Information Regulations[132] which came into force in 2005 at the same time as the Freedom of Information Act. The starting position is a right of public access to environmental information which is held by public authorities. There are (inevitably) exceptions. Some are general—where the authority does not hold the information, the request is manifestly unreasonable, too general or the information is still being gathered, or it relates to internal communications. Some are subject specific—where disclosure would harm national security, defence or international relations, the course of justice, a fair trial or the ability to conduct an inquiry of a criminal or disciplinary nature. There are also exceptions where disclosure would harm intellectual property rights, the confidentiality of proceedings protected by law or of commercial or industrial information where legally protected for legitimate economic interests. The authority can also refuse to disclose the information if it was provided to the authority voluntarily or where disclosure would harm the interests of the supplier or where disclosure would itself harm the environment. These exemptions are much narrower where the information concerns emissions. Then the authority cannot rely on the confidentiality of proceedings, the confidentiality of commercial or industrial information, the interests of a voluntary supplier or the need to protect the environment. Importantly, where any exemption might appear to apply, the authority is only excused the duty to disclose if the public interest in withholding the information is greater than the public interest in disclosure. The system of complaint, regulation and appeal follows the FOIA. Thus, the Information Commissioner can issue a decision notice and a disappointed applicant can appeal from the Commissioner to the Information Tribunal.[133]

In addition, there are extensive disclosure requirements in relation to waste management by the Environment Agency (as the regulator) and local authorities (as waste collection authorities).[134] Registers with exclusions on a similar model are required for local authorities and the Environment Agency in their roles as regulators of air and other environmental pollution[135]; genetically modified organisms[136]; contaminated land[137] and for local authorities in connection with hazardous substances.[138]

---

[131] EU Parliament and Council Directive on public access to environmental information 2003/04/EC.

[132] Environmental Information Regulations 2004 (SI 2004/3391).

[133] The Tribunal's decisions are available on its website at *www.information tribunal.gov.uk*.

[134] Environmental Protection Act 1990, s.64 and Waste Management Licensing Regulations 1994, (SI 1994/1056), Regs 10 and 11.

[135] 1990 Act, ss.20–22.

[136] 1990 Act, ss.122–123.

[137] 1990 Act, ss.78R–78T.

[138] See Planning (Hazardous Substances) Act 1990, s.28.

Local authorities which have declared noise abatement zones must keep a public record of the noise levels there.[139]

Housing

Public housing authorities must publish details of their arrangements **12–025** on matters of housing management, policies on allocation of council housing and on transfers. These are open to inspection and copying—the latter for a reasonable fee—although the authority must provide a free copy of a summary of its allocation priorities to anyone who asks for it.[140] If a local authority has established a register of houses in multiple occupation, this must be open to public inspection.[141]

Education and social services

Local education authorities (LEAs) must publish their arrangements **12–026** and policies for admission of pupils to their schools. LEAs must also spell out their means for enabling parents to express their preference for schools and the mechanism for appealing refusals.[142] The authority's policies on school transport, provision of milk and meals and school clothing, and provision for children with special education needs must be published. The devolvement of managerial powers to individual schools has led to them being obliged to disclose their policies including admission criteria and a summary of results in national assessments.[143] School governors have a discretion to hold their meetings in public, and, in general, the minutes of their meetings must be open to inspection.[144] A school's curriculum policies must likewise be publicly available.[145]

Authorities with social service departments must make known their services for the blind, deaf, handicapped and disabled. They must keep public registers of homes for the old, disabled, drink or drug dependants, or the mentally ill.[146] Local authorities must publish information about the services that they provide for children in need, day-care facilities, and accommodation for children.[147]

---

[139] Control of Pollution Act 1974, s.64.
[140] Housing Act 1985, s.106; Housing Act 1996, s.168.
[141] Housing Act 1985, s.349(3).
[142] Education Act 1996, s.414.
[143] Education (School Information) Regulations 1998 (SI 1998/2526).
[144] Education (School Government) Regulations 1989 (SI 1989/1503), Regs 21 and 24.
[145] Education (Schools Curriculum and Related Information) Regulations 1989 (SI 1989/954).
[146] Chronically Sick and Disabled Persons Act 1970, s.1(2)(a); Registered Homes Act 1984, s.7.
[147] Children Act 1989, ss.17, 18, 20 and 24 and Sch.2, para.1.

Annual reports

12–027 The Local Government Planning and Land Act 1980 introduced mandatory disclosure requirements, which were consistently with the Conservative Government's concern to compare and cut back public spending. Local authorities (including fire authorities and police committees) must produce an annual report that contains the information required by the Ministerial Code of Practice.[148] The code, published in 1981, requires authorities to publish statistics comparing their expenditure for each service with the average for authorities of the same class.[149] Comparisons must be made between projected and actual expenditures, and capital expenditure must also be noted. Rate and other income must be given, as well as statistics for major services. The authority's workforce must be tabulated by staff category. The Government has also recommended that local authorities (like companies) should disclose policies for hiring staff who are disabled.[150] The code says that the reports should be made available to the press and to members of the public.[151] More details about the authority's manpower are required by a separate code.[152] The press must be notified of the annual report, and it must be made available at the council's offices and public libraries.[153] The Audit Commission can also require local authorities to make comparative information available. It must be published in a local paper and kept for inspection and copying by local electors.[154] Police authorities also have to produce an annual "policing summary" which has to be distributed to all local taxpayers.[155]

Land ownership

12–028 Central government has the power to require local authorities to maintain registers of publicly owned unused land. In the early 1990s such registers had to be kept, but the obligation was scrapped in 1996.[156] The power is based on the fallacious assumption that only publicly-owned land is left unproductive. Derelict land is often in

---

[148] Local Government Planning and Land Act 1980, s.2.

[149] *Local Authority Annual Reports* (HMSO, 1981); Dept of Environment Circular 3/81.

[150] Clive Walker "Public Rights to Information in Central and Local Government" (1982) Local Government Review 931, 932.

[151] *Local Authority Annual Reports*, fn.149 above, para.1.8.

[152] Local Government (Publication of Staffing Information) (England) Code 1995, DOE Circular 14/95 Annex.

[153] *Local Authority Annual Reports*, fn.45 above, para.1.8.

[154] Audit Commission Act 1998, ss.44–47. The "local paper" can be a free sheet but only if it is published independently of the authority and distributed to all dwellings in the area: s.45(4).

[155] Police Act 1996, s.8A added by Serious Organised Crime and Police Act 2005, s.157.

[156] DOE Circular 3/96.

private ownership, but there is no power to compile open lists of the speculative holdings of development companies.

There is a register of land titles covering most of the country and it is open to public inspection.[157] The public can inspect and copy (subject to prescribed charges) entries on the register and documents (other than leases or charges) that are referred to in the register and that are in the registrar's custody. Regulations, though, allow a person who considers that a document contains "prejudicial" information to apply for the full document to be exempted from disclosure and the Registrar must allow the application unless it is "groundless".[158]

Freedom of Information Act

Local authorities are "public authorities" for the purpose of the **12–029** Freedom of Information Act and are therefore under the same obligations to respond to requests from the public for information (see para.11–074). There is also the same system for challenging refusals, through the Information Commissioner and the Information Tribunal. However, the FOI Act was cautious about duplicating rights of access. Information will be exempt from disclosure under the FOIA, for instance, if it is "reasonably accessible to the applicant by other means".[159] An obligation on an authority to communicate the information on request (whether for payment or not) will be deemed to satisfy this condition, but this deeming provision is not triggered simply because the information is available for inspection.

LEAKS

Since local authority officials do not "hold office under the Crown" **12–030** they are not bound by the Official Secrets Acts and it is not a crime for them or for elected councillors to show secret documents to the press, unless the information has been entrusted in confidence to them by a person who is a Crown servant. However, local government officials show no greater readiness to leak secrets than their Whitehall counterparts. In part this is because officials face dismissal under the National Joint Council's Conditions of Service if they communicate to the public the proceedings of any meeting or the contents of any document relating to the authority, unless required by law or unless they are expressly authorised to do so. There is also considerable social pressure not to undermine colleagues.[160] Councillors caught leaking can be disciplined by their party or struck from

---

[157] Land Registration Act 2002, s.66.
[158] Land Registration Rules 2003 (SI 2003/1417) rr.133–136.
[159] Freedom of Information Act 2000, s.21.
[160] Sisella Bok, "Whistleblowing and Professional Responsibilities" in Daniel Callahan and Sisella Bok (eds), *Ethics Teaching in Higher Education* (Plenum, New York, 1980).

circulation lists for receiving sensitive documents.[161] But journalists may at least reassure their sources in local government that they are in no danger of prosecution, unless the information has been supplied as a result of a bribe. The "whistleblower" legislation also provides a degree of protection against punitive action by employers (see para.5–072).

LIBEL

12–031 One of the inducements for the media to cover the formal proceedings of local authorities is the special protection against libel actions that is given to such reports. The Defamation Act 1996 confers qualified privilege on:

- fair and accurate reports of any open meeting of the authority, one of its committees or sub-committees[162];
- fair and accurate reports of a public hearing by any person appointed by the authority to hold an inquiry under any statutory provision[163];
- fair and accurate reports of any public hearing of a commission, tribunal, committee or person appointed to hold an inquiry under any statutory provision by the Crown, a Minister or a Northern Ireland department or a tribunal, board, committee or body constituted by or exercising functions under any other statutory provision[164];
- fair and accurate copy or extract from a notice or other matter issued for the information of the public by any authority performing governmental functions in any Member State[165];
- fair and accurate copy of or extract from any register or other document which is required by law to be open to public inspection.[166]

These are defences of qualified privilege[167] which means that they do not apply if the publisher is malicious (see para.3–056). Unlike their equivalents under the 1952 Act, they can be invoked by anyone—not just newspapers or broadcasters. The material covered

---

[161] For a thoughtful analysis of what makes documents politically sensitive see A. T. J. Maslen, "Secrecy, Public Information and Local Government" (1979) 5 Local Govt Studies 47.
[162] Defamation Act 1996, Sch.1, paras 11(1)(a) and (2).
[163] 1996 Act, para.11(1)d).
[164] 1996 Act, paras 11(1)(c) and (e).
[165] 1996 Act, para.9(1). After concern expressed by the media, the Act expressly states that "governmental functions" include police functions, para.9(2).
[166] 1996 Act, para.5.
[167] Defamation Act 1996, s.15.

in the story is not protected unless it is of public concern and its publication for the public benefit.[168] Of the categories listed in the last paragraph, the first four are dependent on the publisher or broadcaster providing a right of reply (see para.3–073).

The prior "publication" (in the defamation law sense) by a local authority to inspecting members of the public is also covered by qualified privilege.[169]

> Newcastle City Council successfully relied on these provisions when it was sued by two nursery workers who had been savagely and unfairly castigated as child abusers in the report of a Review Team whom the City Council had appointed. The Review followed the acquittal of the Claimants when some of the evidence had been ruled inadmissible. The members of the Review Team itself were also joined as defendants to the libel action. The Claimants were able to defeat their defence of qualified privilege by showing that they had been malicious. The judge marked the seriousness of the libel by awarding the Claimants the then maximum possible level of damages—£200,000.[170]

In the past, stories in greater depth had also to contend with the hazard of a libel writ from the council itself.[171] That is not so now. The House of Lords has held that an organ of local government is unable to sue for defamation.[172] It reversed the old rule because of the chilling effect on freedom of expression. The right of individual councillors who are defamed to sue for libel remains, although this possibility may have an equally chilling effect especially if the council underwrites their legal costs. A council itself can still sue for malicious falsehood but this will be less of a threat to the media. Not only would the council then have to prove falsity and malice, but it would also have to show that the publication caused it financial loss (or in certain circumstances was likely to cause this kind of loss).

LOCAL AUTHORITY SPONSORED PUBLICATIONS

The 1980s were marked by a breakdown of consensus on the role of 12–032 local authorities. Local council publications and advertisements defending their role and articulating policies that were an anathema to Whitehall incurred the Government's wrath. As a result of court action and legislation, authorities are considerably circumscribed in their ability to publish or promote controversial matters.

In 1985, the Greater London Council was enjoined from continuing its anti-abolition advertising campaign because its objective of

---

[168] s.15(3)—these are questions for the jury—*Kingshott v Associated Kent Newspapers* [1991] 1 Q.B. 880, CA.
[169] Local Government Act 1972, s.100H(5) and (6); Public Bodies (Admission to Meetings) Act 1960, s.1(5).
[170] *Lillie and Reed v Newcastle City Council* [2002] EWHC 1600 Eady J.
[171] *Bognor Regis UDC v Campion* [1972] Q.B. 169.
[172] *Derbyshire County Council v Times Newspapers Ltd* [1993] A.C. 534.

persuading people to its point of view could not be justified under a statutory power of publishing information on matters related to local government.[173]

An inquiry under David Widdicombe Q.C. recommended further restrictions and these were adopted in two stages in 1986 and 1988.[174] Their net effect is that local authorities are prohibited from publishing, whether directly or through others, material that appears to be designed to affect public support for a political party. The general power that local authorities have of providing information is restricted to information about services provided by the authority, central government, charities or voluntary organisations or to the functions of the authority. The Government can issue Codes of Guidance on local authorities' publicity, to which they must have regard. By contrast, central government retains a wide discretion over its publicity. As the court said when asked to declare that a 1989 leaflet about the poll tax was unlawful, it will interfere only in the most extreme cases where it could be shown that a government department had misstated the law or if a publication was manifestly inaccurate or misleading.[175]

CLAUSE 28

12–033 The 1988 Bill also contained the notorious "clause 28". This prohibited a local authority from intentionally promoting homosexuality or publishing material with the intention of promoting homosexuality. It is also prohibited the promoting the teaching in any maintained school of the acceptability of homosexuality as a pretended family relationship. None of the prohibitions applied to anything done for the purpose of treating or preventing the spread of disease.[176] The provision aroused anger at the State's censure of a matter that was essentially one for individual choice, and fear that it would lead to an intensification of discrimination against gay men and lesbian women.

The Labour government's first attempt to repeal "clause 28" was blocked in the House of Lords in 2001, but the provision was finally repealed in 2003.[177]

---

[173] *R. v GLC Ex p. Westminister City Council*, *The Times*, January 22, 1985 see also *R. v ILEA Ex p. Westminister City Council* [1986] 1 W.L.R. 28.

[174] Local Government Act 1986, ss.2–6; Local Government Act 1988, s.27.

[175] *R. v Secretary of State Ex p. London Borough of Greenwich*, *Independent*, May 17, 1989.

[176] Local Government Act 1986, s.2A added by the Local Government Act 1988, s.28.

[177] Local Government Act 2003, s.122.

CHAPTER 13

REPORTING BUSINESS

INTRODUCTION

Investigative business journalism has an honourable history. The term "muckraker" was first applied by President Theodore Roosevelt to American newspapermen who reported the web of monopolistic practices and price fixing that characterised the heyday of free enterprise. The cabal that operated the meat industry had a particular disregard both for hygiene and for the stomachs of its customers. Upton Sinclair's novel *The Jungle*, set in the meat-packing factories of Chicago, gave a realistic and awesome account. Tinned beef took on a sinister meaning, meat sales dropped by half, and legislation followed as a direct result.[1] Although the United States and Britain now have a wide range of regulatory agencies, they are often stung into effective action only by pressure from the media. Even where no formal action is taken, a press campaign can damage a product's reputation and devastate its sales. Publicity is a potent weapon against businesses that sell to the public, but care must be taken to reserve its use for deserving targets: ruining a business runs the risk of heavier damages than ruining an individual's reputation.

This type of business reporting focuses on production and on dealings with consumers. The financial journalists who write for the business pages will usually be more interested in the efficiency and profitability of companies. Stories of dishonesty and other shady dealings are much rarer. There have been outstanding investigations into the ownership and control of businesses, and the conflict between private advantage and public interest. Investigations of defence contractors and other government suppliers will, of course, have to find their way around the Official Secrets Acts. But the abject failure of British journalism to expose the rottenness of Lloyd's of London or the commercial chicanery of Robert Maxwell until after his death in 1991—failures both of skill in investigation

---

[1] Sinclair intended his novel as an appeal to socialism. He said ruefully: "I aimed at the public's heart and by accident hit it in the stomach". See Robert Downs, *The Jungle* (New American Library, 1960), p.349.

and in courage in the face of threatened libel actions—serves as a reminder of the blandness and inadequacy of much business coverage.[2] Libel damages may, of course, increase dramatically if a publication causes financial loss, but developments in the law of qualified privilege (in addition to the defence of justification) ought to be an encouragement to more thorough investigations of corporations.

13–002 The non-legal pressures of low budgets, and tedious and often unrewarding research are common to all investigative reporters. Business stories have the added hurdle of incurring advertisers' displeasure. Wales Gas in 1979 withdrew all its advertising from the *North Wales Western News* because of a critical story about its liquid petroleum gas depot in Llandudno.[3] W. D. & H. O. Wills cancelled a £500,000 advertising order with the *Sunday Times* when one of its brands was named as the favourite smoke of a heart transplant patient. In the middle of the article was an advertisement for the same brand.[4] Pressure from advertisers is usually more subtle: they help to set the newspapers' agenda.[5] Space given to financial news has expanded dramatically since the war, in direct correlation with financial advertising, but the stress on company gossip, Stock Exchange activity and tipster articles reflects the predominance of advertisements for company results, recruitment and unit trusts.[6] From time to time there are calls for public libraries not to stock publications in response to their content or the conduct of their publishers. During the Wapping dispute many local authorities banned Murdoch papers from their libraries—the High Court ruled that this was an abuse of power and quashed the decisions.[7]

This chapter will describe the ways in which the law can help reporters by requiring that certain information is made available to them and will give a brief outline of the legal structures that a business reporter will have to understand before advantage can be taken of the facilities for corporate investigation.

---

[2] Tom Bower, *Maxwell—The Final Verdict* (Harper Collins, 1995).

[3] *Daily Telegraph*, April 19, 1979. See Hartley & Griffith, *Government and the Law* (2nd edn, Weidenfeld & Nicolson, 1981), p.281.

[4] *New Statesman*, February 27, 1981.

[5] James Curran, "Advertising and the Press" in James Curran (ed.), *The British Press: A Manifesto* (Macmillan, 1978), p.238. Compare Harold Eley's advice to advertisers in 1932, in *Advertising Media*, Butterworths. The Government used its advertising expenditure to influence papers in the early nineteenth century. *The Times* was particularly vulnerable. (Aspinall, *Politics and the Press 1780–1850*, Ch.V).

[6] Curran, *The British Press*, p.240.

[7] *R. v Ealing Borough Council Ex p. Times Newspapers Ltd* (1987) 85 L.G.R. 316, QBD.

COMPANIES

A beginner's lexicon

The most important form of commercial organisation today is the **13–003**
registered company.[8] It has its own identity, or legal personality,
which is distinct from those who contribute its capital or manage its
affairs. It can own property, make contracts, and start and defend
lawsuits.

Its *capital* is usually a mixture of long-term loans provided under a
formal written agreement called a *debenture* (by creditors who are
thus known as *debenture holders*) and *equity capital*. The equity is
divided into *shares* and is held by shareholders, who are also referred
to as the *members* of the company. Loans can be repaid, and
commonly bear a fixed rate of interest, although shareholders can be
paid a *dividend* only if the company makes a profit. *Preference shares*
are a hybrid. The holders are members of the company and can take
a dividend only if there is a profit. Their payments take priority over
those to ordinary shareholders, but their voting rights are usually
restricted. The ratio of loan to equity capital is known as the
company's *gearing* and is an important factor in assessing its economic viability.

Most companies are formed by registration with the Companies'
Registrar, more commonly referred to as *"Companies House"*. This
is an agency within the Department of Trade and Industry (DTI),[9]
which exercises supervision over companies (see para.13–030 for its
powers of investigation). Two documents make up the constitution
of a company. Its *Memorandum of Association* specifies its name,
initial shareholders, whether its registered office (the company's
formal address) is in England and Wales or Scotland, and its objects.
The latter are generally drawn so as to give the company the greatest
possible latitude and will not pinpoint what the company actually
does. The *Articles of Association* are like the rules of a club,
specifying the respective powers of the shareholders, the *board of
directors* and the managing director. They also regulate the summon-
ing and procedure of meetings of the shareholders and the board. If
the rights of shareholders are not uniform, the Articles will also
prescribe the rights of each class of shares. To restrict ownership of
the shares to a select group, the Articles may also prohibit transfer
without the board's consent and confer a right of pre-emption, giving

---

[8] Legislation on companies has undergone frequent changes. Until recently the
Companies Act 1985 was the principal statute. However, in 2006 a new
Companies Act was passed with a massive 1300 sections and 16 schedules. At the
time of writing, only limited parts of this are in force, but because it will
inexorably become the law, references are given to both this Act and the previous
law.

[9] For more information, see its website: *www.companieshouse.gov.uk*.

the other shareholders a right of first refusal if one of them wishes to sell out.

Companies can be either *private* or *public*. The principal requirement for a public company (signified by "Plc" after its name) is that its nominal share capital must be at least £50,000; the main advantage is that it can then raise capital by selling shares to the public at large.[10] Most, but not all, public companies will have a listing or quotation on the Stock Exchange. This makes trading in its shares much easier and consequently increases their value. The Financial Services Authority (FSA) which regulates listed companies expects a greater degree of frankness from listed companies, and reporters can gain access to important company documents as a result of these requirements.

13–004   When a company wishes to raise equity capital, it announces an *issue* of new shares. A public company will almost always enlist the services of a financial institution for this purpose. It must produce a *prospectus* disclosing information required by law and, in the case of quoted companies, by the FSA. This can offer a valuable window on the company's past record and dealings.

Some offerings of new shares are limited to existing members (*rights issue*), and some of these are given free (*bonus issue*), in which case they simply fragment the existing shares into smaller units. Shares are usually issued as *fully paid up*, which means that once the company has received the initial price, it has no further claim on the shareholders. In those rare cases where shares are not fully paid, the company can make a *call* for the balance. A nominal value is attached to each share. Shares are issued *at par* if this is also their actual selling price, or *at a premium* if they are above par; they cannot be issued at a discount. There are only restricted circumstances in which a company can buy or finance the purchase of its own shares.

13–005   The directors of a company are *fiduciaries*, which means they owe a duty of trust to the company and must not allow themselves to get in a position where their personal interest conflicts with the company's—or at least not without making full disclosure to the board or its members. Although the most powerful members will have representatives on the board, they cannot ignore the interests of the minority. The court, for instance, prevented Lord and Lady Kagan, the majority shareholders, from compelling Kagan Textiles Ltd to accept the blame for fraudulent trading in indigo dye with which Lord Kagan was also charged. This would have been a fraud on the minority shareholders. Directors also have a legal duty to take account of their employees' interests.

The most attractive feature of a company for an investor is the *limited liability* that it usually enjoys. However small the company—

---

[10] Companies Act 1985 ("1985 Act") s.118; to be replaced by Companies Act 2006 ("2006 Act") s.763.

even if it is run by only one person—creditors cannot normally sue the shareholders or the management if the company has insufficient assets to pay its debts. Institutional lenders, like banks and finance houses, that are not satisfied with the creditworthiness of the company will try to bind the principal shareholders through a guarantee. William Stern (a 1970s property tycoon) guaranteed his companies' debts and so became personally liable when they could not pay. He could not pay either, and his bankruptcy in 1978 (discharged in 1985) was the largest there had then been. Major lenders, in particular those lending long-term capital, will also condition their co-operation on the provision of *security*. This usually is a mortgage on the business's fixed assets, such as land and machinery, and a floating charge on the circulating assets (those that are bought and sold, accounts receivable, etc.). The lender then has a right to claim this property to satisfy the debt, although other *unsecured creditors* may be left with only pennies in the pound. Debentures almost invariably include both types of security.

Ownership and control

Registers of share and debenture holders

Every member's shareholding is registered and the register is a **13–006** public document.[11] However, when the 2006 Act is in force, a person seeking to inspect the register must declare the purpose for which the information is to be used and the company may then apply to the court for a direction that inspection (or copying) is not required for a "proper purpose".[12] It will also become an offence to do anything in relation to information obtained as a result of inspecting the register so that it is disclosed to someone else knowing or having reason to suspect that the other person may use the information for an improper purpose.[13] Before the 2006 Act, the Government's White Paper illustrated the kind of improper purpose which it had in mind. It gave the example of obtaining information about share-holders so as to intimidate them into pressing the company to withdraw from a contract.[14] Animal liberation extremists might come within this category, but these new provisions ought not to constitute an obstacle where information about shareholders is sought by journalists. As the Minister, Margaret Hodge, said in the course of the debates on the provisions,

> "I think that a judge, or whoever will consider these issues in court, will be able to distinguish between legitimate investigative

---

[11] 1985 Act, s.356; 2006 Act, ss.114 & 116.

[12] 2006 Act, ss.116 & 117.

[13] 2006 Act, s.119.

[14] White Paper *Company Law Reform*, March 2005, p.39.

journalism, which we wish to protect, and illegitimate harangu-
ing of members by extremist thugs."[15]

If the shares are divided into classes, the register will show to
which class each shareholder belongs.[16] If a company has more than
50 members, it must also maintain an index of them. Under the 2006
Act the company will be required to tell an inquirer whether the
register is up to date and, if not, to which date it has been made up.[17]
This must be kept at the same place as the register.[18] If a company
has issued debentures and maintains a register of debenture-holders,
this must also be open for public inspection.[19] The shares may be
registered in the name of another company. If this is registered in
the United Kingdom, the procedure can be repeated. If it is
incorporated in other countries with similar disclosure requirements,
the chase can be pursued, albeit more expensively. But if it is the
creature of tax havens such as Belize or the Cayman Islands, the
scent will be lost. As well as charging very little tax, these countries
allow investors to preserve a veil of secrecy around their holdings by
laws that have virtually no disclosure requirements.

Real ownership

13–007 Frequently, the registered shareholder is only a nominee for some
other person who is really or beneficially entitled to the shares. Many
banks have companies holding shares for their clients that include
the word "nominee" in their name. It will then be apparent from the
register of such companies that someone else is beneficially entitled
to the shares. This will not always be the case with other nominees.
A shareholder has generally no obligation to tell the company that it
is acting as a nominee.

Automatic registration

13–008 Until 2007 Parliament created exceptions to the principle that a
shareholder had no obligation to tell the company that it was acting
as a nominee. Public companies had to be notified if anyone had a
beneficial interest in 3 per cent[20] of their shares that carried
unrestricted voting rights.

These requirements in the 1985 Act were repealed by the Companies Act 2006 and not replaced in the new legislation. However,

---

[15] Hansard Standing Committee D, June 27, 2006, col. 217.

[16] 1985 Act, s.352; 2006 Act, s.113(3).

[17] 2006 Act, s.120.

[18] 1985 Act, s.354; 2006 Act, s.115.

[19] 1985 Act, s.190–1; 2006 Act ss.743–747. There will be the same restriction to use
for a "proper purpose" as for the register of members.

[20] Companies Act 1985, s.199.

the EU Transparency Directive imposes very similar obligations. In the UK they are imposed by the FSA whose Disclosure and Transparency Rules likewise require notification where the 3 per cent threshold is crossed (or where holdings reach, exceed or fall below every 1 per cent above 3 per cent). The principal difference is that the percentage is taken of the total voting rights in the company.[21]

Investigations by the company

The above transactions must be reported automatically to the **13–009** company. In addition, the company can act on its own initiative to identify its real shareholders and others with interests in the shares.[22] These powers apply to all public companies. The inquiries can relate to shareholders over the previous three years. They can be asked about agreements to buy up shares or to vote in concert. Where shares are held in a UK company through a UK nominee holder, the company's right to discover the beneficial owners of its shares under this provision applies even though the beneficiary has no other connection with the United Kingdom.[23] A holder of shares who is obliged to provide this information cannot avoid his duty to answer by undertaking to sell the shares.[24] If the directors are reluctant to delve into these secrets, they can be compelled to do so by the holders of one-tenth of the voting capital.[25] The company must then make a report of information received following the investigation. Information received by a company as a result of its own requests or a report of information requested by the members must be available for public inspection.[26] It must be kept for six years.[27] It is clear, that this obligation exists whether or not the true owners are shown to have a holding equivalent to the percentage when disclosure of their interests under the automatic provisions would have been required. These provisions of the 2006 Act were brought into force in 2007. However, the government delayed implementing the further requirement in this part of the legislation that a public inquirer would be obliged to disclose the purpose for which the information was sought, the power of the court to direct a refusal of access if the purpose was "improper" and the introduction of an offence of allowing information obtained by such inspection to be disclosed to a person whose purpose was improper.[28]

---

[21] For fuller details see *www.fsa.gov.uk*.

[22] 2006 Act, s.793. The power was formerly in 1985 Act, s.212.

[23] *Re FH Lloyd Holdings Plc* [1985] B.C.L.C. 293.

[24] *Re Geers Gross* [1987] 1 W.L.R. 1649.

[25] 2006 Act, s.803.

[26] 2006 Act, ss.805 (report of member-initiated investigation); ss.808–09 (register of company-initiated investigation). The later must be indexed (s.810) which must also be open to inspection (s.811).

[27] 2006 Act, s.805(4) (reports), s.816 (registers).

[28] 2006 Act, ss.811(4) (inquirer to state purpose), 812 (court supervision), & 813 (offences)—see above for comments on what is meant by a "proper purpose".

Although the initiative rests with a company to demand disclosure of this kind, the information obtained may have a spill-over effect. Institutional nominees often use the same account number for all the shares bought by them for a particular client. Sometimes the entry on the register will include this number, and so might appear as "X Bank Nominees Acc. No 12345". Once one company investigation has identified the owner of an account number, it would not be surprising if the same code in other company registers concealed the same owner. An index of such nominees has been published.[29]

The obligation to require nominees to disclose the names of their clients is principally intended to avoid surprise changes of control. For journalists, however, these registers present a wider opportunity. Owners of shares cannot maintain complete secrecy about their investments, and those who receive a share of the profits from companies that have been the target of widespread public criticism may deserve to find some of that criticism turned in their direction.

Major shareholdings by companies

13–010 Sometimes, further clues as to a company's ownership can be traced in the accounts of other companies. Companies are required to note holdings that amount to 20 per cent or more of the voting or total capital in another company.[30] Special provision is made for banking and insurance companies.[31] One further defect in these provisions for the investigator is that they apply only to shares held at the end of the accounting company's financial year. If a company wished, it could "board out" its holdings by lodging them with someone else for the critical few days and lawfully omit any reference to them. A second drawback is that as part of the accounting requirements, the directors can leave out this information if it would be excessive and the ownership of the shares did not materially affect the company's financial position.[32]

Directors' dealings

Shareholdings in their companies

13–011 It is accepted that directors will want some stake in the enterprise they manage, but the dangers of this are recognised and their dealings are circumscribed. Until April 2007 legislation applying to all companies imposed these limitations They could not, for

---

[29] Fulcrum Research Ltd, *The Index of Nominees and their Beneficial Owners* (10th edn).
[30] Companies Act 1985, Sch.5, paras 7–13. This is not repeated in the 2006 Act but may feature in regulations.
[31] 1985 Act, ss.255–255B and Sch.9, Pt III.
[32] Companies Act 1985, Sch.5, para.11.

instance, agree to buy or sell their company's shares for delivery on a future date.[33] In addition, directors had to make public their holdings in the shares and debentures of the company or its associated companies. They could not avoid this duty by farming out their shares to spouses, civil partners or children, or by trying to hide behind a trustee or nominee owner of the shares because these holdings had also to be reported. Nor could they evade the restrictions by taking shares in a parent, subsidiary or sibling company.[34] Any change in their holding had to be reported. Most importantly, directors had to disclose the price at which their shares or debentures were bought or sold.[35] This registered information had also to be indexed and remain open to public inspection.[36] These requirements in the Companies Act 1985 have been repealed by the Companies Act 2006 and not replaced.[37] However, for companies whose shares are traded in a regulated market, the FSA imposes similar requirements obliging 'persons exercising managerial responsibilities and their connected persons' over an issuer to notify the issuer of any transactions on their own account in the shares of the issuer or their derivatives. The issuer must in turn immediately notify a Regulatory Information Service whose business is making such information publicly available.[38]

Contracts of service

Shareholders are also entitled to see copies of a director's contract **13-012** of service with the company.[39] In the case of companies quoted on the Stock Exchange the public are entitled to see further details in the company's annual report. For each director the company must disclose full particulars of remuneration including salary and other benefits, commission or profit sharing, details of any directors' service contracts. One intention behind these requirements is that those planning a takeover or a coup within the company can assess how much compensation directors will have to be paid for the premature termination of their contracts.[40] However, the contracts can make interesting reading to those sharpening pens rather than long knives (one service contract, for instance, revealed that a

---

[33] 1985 Act, ss.323 and 327.

[34] 1985 Act, s.324 and Sch.13.

[35] 1985 Act, Sch.13, para.17(2).

[36] 1985 Act, s.325 and Sch.13, Pt IV. The directors' report will also include details of shareholdings by board members at the year's end, Sch.7, para.2. Any equivalent under the 2006 Act will be dealt with by regulations—2006 Act, s.416.

[37] Companies Act 2006, s.1177.

[38] See FSA's Disclosure and Transparency Rules DTR 3.1.

[39] 1985 Act, s.318; unless the contract has less than 12 months to run or the company can terminate the contract within 12 months without paying compensation. 2006 Act, ss.227–229.

[40] Financial Service Authority's Handbook, *Listing Rules* LR 9.8.8.

director was required to take his wife with him whenever he made an overseas visit). The annual reports of unquoted companies must show the aggregate amount payable to directors for loss of office and the earnings of the highest paid director.[41]

Interests in company contracts

13–013 Other contracts or arrangements with the company in which a director has a material interest must be disclosed in the company's annual accounts. In particular, the accounts must disclose any loan, guarantee or credit transaction that a company has made for the benefit of a director or officer.[42] The circumstances in which the company is permitted to enter into these types of transactions are, in any event, narrowly defined.[43]

Directors' home addresses

13–014 Directors' organisations lobbied hard for removal of the current requirement to disclose home addresses[44] and cited the harassment and intimidation at the homes of directors of some companies (such as those involved with experiments on animals). The Government responded by including s.45 in the Criminal Justice and Police Act 2001—a provision for the Secretary of State to make a "confidentiality order". Before doing so he must be satisfied that if the director's usual residential address was open to public inspection there would be a serious risk that he or a person who lives with him would be subjected to violence or intimidation.[45] When the 2006 Act is in force, the default position will be that all residential addresses of directors are protected from public inspection unless the director fails to respond to letters sent to that address by the registrar.[46]

Other directorships

13–015 The interlocking interests of directors with other companies cannot be so easily traced. However, the company must record present directorships of its board members in the other corporations and any past directorships over the previous five years. The register is also publicly available.[47] Details of changes should also be included in the company's annual return.

---

[41] Companies Act 1985 Sch.6, paras 8 and 2. The highest paid director's remuneration does not have to be given if the board as a whole earned less than £200,000. These matters may be dealt with by regulations under the 2006 Act—2006 Act, s.412.

[42] 2006 Act, ss.232, s.413.

[43] 2006 Act, s.330.

[44] Companies Act 1985, s.289.

[45] Criminal Justice and Police Act 2001, s.45 adding s.723B to Companies Act 1985.

[46] 2006 Act, ss.240–246.

[47] 1985 Act, s.289. This requirement has been dropped from the 2006 Act s.163, but regulations may add to the registrable requirements—2006 Act, s.166.

Economic performance

Accounts to be published

Since one of the principal aims of the disclosure requirements is to **13–016** permit investors and creditors to judge the economic performance of a company, it may not seem surprising that the law lays great emphasis on company accounts, the overriding requirement of which is that they should give a true and fair view of the company's financial state of affairs and profit and loss in the relevant financial year.[48] However, it has been a hard-fought battle; it was only in 1967 that private as well as public companies were required to prepare accounts, and only in 1976 that these had to be made public.[49]

Since then, there has been serious back-sliding. "Small" companies (which must now have at least two of the following: a balance sheet total of less than £2.8 million; turnover of less than £5.6 million; fewer than 50 employees) need not prepare a profit and loss account and only a perfunctory balance sheet is required. They have no duty to submit a directors' report. "Medium" size companies (with two of the following: balance sheet total less than £11.4 million; turnover less than £22.8 million; fewer than 250 employees) have to provide the normal directors' report and balance sheet, but are allowed to submit a modified profit and loss account and need not give a breakdown of turnover.[50] "Small" and "medium" sized groups of companies have similar relief from the duty to provide group accounts.[51] In 1999 it was estimated that about 90 per cent of all registered companies qualified as "small".[52] Investors, creditors and journalists are all the worse off, particularly as information about a private company that is not required to be disclosed by law will generally be protected from disclosure by the courts on grounds of confidence.

Banking and insurance companies are also exempt from particularising their accounts, but they are subjected to much more

---

[48] 1985 Act, s.226A(2); 2006 Act, s.393.

[49] Companies Act 1976, s.1. Companies without limited liability could still keep their accounts to themselves, a qualification that spawned new interest in what hitherto had been an historical curiosity. Following the Companies Act 1989, s.7, the conditions on which the exemptions are dependent are more restrictive: see s.254 of Companies Act 1985; 2006 Act, s.448.

[50] 1985 Act, s.247, Sch.8 (duties), s.248 (definitions). The amounts have been increased from time to time. See 2006 Act small companies defined s.382, duties s.444; medium sized companies defined s.465, duties s.445.

[51] 1985 Act 1985, s.249. The exemption applies if either the parent company meets the requirements for individual companies or if the group as a whole satisfies two or more of the following (small first, medium in brackets): aggregate turnover: £5.6 million net or £6.72 million gross (£22.8 million net or £27.36 million gross); aggregate balance sheet total: £2.8million net or £3.36 million gross (£11.4 million net or £13.68 million gross); employees 50 (250). See 2006 Act s.383 (small) and s.466 (medium).

[52] *Companies in 1998–99* (HMSO, 1999) Cmnd.9794, para.8.5.

rigorous scrutiny by the Department of Trade and Industry.[53] When they are quoted companies they also have to comply with the listing requirements of the FSA, which requires disclosure in line with accounting standards.

Auditors

13–017 The accounts that a company prepares must be professionally audited. The auditor's report must be sent with the accounts to the Companies Registry, where it is open to inspection.[54] However, even this requirement is qualified. Small companies do not have to have their accounts audited,[55] nor do small groups.[56] Auditors are in a difficult position. They are hired by the directors, but their responsibilities are to the investors, creditors and the public at large. Qualifying the accounts may make the auditors unpopular with the board. Consequently, they can be sacked only by the shareholders and they have a statutory right to put their case to a shareholders' meeting.[57] The auditors are precluded from slipping out quietly to avoid an impending disaster: on resigning they must provide a statement of any circumstances connected with them ceasing to hold office.[58] Some solve the dilemma of effectively serving both board and shareholders by adding an inscrutable or unfathomable qualification to the accounts. Others simply ignore the requirements. A study in 1999 reported that of 766 resignation letters to publicly-listed companies between 1988–92, only 19 contained any matters relevant to shareholders or creditors even though in 108 cases resignation followed qualified audited reports.[59]

Even if all auditors were honest and efficient, there are practical limits on the checks that can be run. In a large company the auditors can at best run only sample spot checks on stock values and other

---

[53] Companies Act 1985, ss.255, 255A and Sch.9.

[54] 1985 Act auditor's report: s.235; duty to send to registrar: ss.239 and 242; inspection: s.709. 2006 Act see s.495 (auditors' report to company), ss.444–447 (duty to file with Registrar), s.1085 inspection.

[55] 1985 Act 1985, s.249A. For these purposes a company not only has to be "small" for the purposes of the accounting exemption (see above) but its turnover must be not more than £5.6 million and its balance sheet total not more than £2.8 million. In the case of charities, for the turnover limit there is substituted a gross income limit of £90,000. 2006 Act: small companies' exemption—ss.477–478; the special provision for charities is repealed: s.1175 and Sch.9.

[56] 1985 Act, s.249B. For these purposes collective turnover must be less than £5.6 million net (or £6.72 million gross) and balance sheet total of not more than £2.8 million net (£3.36 million gross). For charity groups the turnover limit is £350,000 net, £420,000 gross. For 2006 Act, see s.479. The special provision for charity groups is repealed.

[57] 1985 Act, ss.390, 391 & 391A; 2006 Act ss.510–513.

[58] 1985 Act, s.394; the resignation statement must be sent to the Registry where it can be inspected, s.709. For 2006 Act see ss.519, 521 and 1085.

[59] *Palmer's Company Law*, para.9.514.

realities behind the figures presented to them by the company. There have been a number of scandals where grave irregularities have not been spotted by auditors. Ironically, the growing practice among auditors of over-cautiously qualifying the accounts may diminish the impact of any warning they mean to deliver.

Directors' report

Attached to the accounts must also be a report by the directors.[60] **13–018** This report must give a "fair review of the business of the company and its subsidiaries during the financial year", particulars of any important events affecting the business during the year and an indication of likely future developments.[61] These obligations tend to produce bland reports. The FSA regulations require a much more detailed report from quoted companies. This frequently takes the form of a chairperson's statement, which is published in the financial press.

More concretely, the report must note significant changes in the values of the company's fixed assets, record any interests held by directors in the company's shares at the end of the financial year, and report details of any shares in the company that the company itself owns.

Political pressure has achieved an odd assortment of additional disclosure obligations. The most interesting is the requirement to disclose political donations over £200.[62] The identity of the donee and the total amount of the contributions must be disclosed where the beneficiary is a registered political party or other EU political organisation.[63] The company must also disclose the total amount of "E.U. political expenditure".[64] Contributions to non-EU political parties must also be disclosed.

A company must have advance approval of the members in **13–019** general meeting before making donations to EU political organisations or before incurring EU political expenditure. In both cases the company's resolution must specify the maximum amount of donations or expenditure. Groups of shareholders are given rights to take legal action if these requirements are infringed.[65]

---

[60] Companies Act 1985, s.234; 2006 Act, s.415.

[61] 1985 Act, and Sch.7. The 2006 Act leaves the content of the directors' report to be determined by regulations: s.416.

[62] Political Parties, Elections and Referendums Act 2000, ss.140 substituting paras 3–4 in Companies Act 1985, Sch.7. The 2006 Act leaves this to regulations.

[63] Defined in 1985 Act, s.347A(6) and (7) as essentially political parties in a Member State other than the UK or organisations (whether or not in the UK) intended to affect public support for a political patty or independent candidates or to influence voters in a national or regional referendum in a Member State; 2006 Act ss.363–365.

[64] Defined in 1985 Act, s.347A(5) in terms which embrace political advertising, promotional or publicity material in support of any EU political organisation; 2006 Act, s.365.

[65] See 1985 Act, Part XA. Companies Act ss.369–373.

The company's annual report must also disclose the total amount donated for charitable purposes if this exceeds £200.[66] Additionally, the directors' report must note any research or development activities, and information specified by regulations concerning health and safety at work. If the company employs over 250 people, the report must give an account of the company's policies for hiring disabled people and for consulting employees.[67]

In the case of publicly traded companies, the annual report will have to give fuller details about the company's capital structure, rights attaching to shares, restrictions on share transfers, details of significant shareholdings, rules on the appointment of directors and their powers and any significant agreements as to rights in the event of a takeover.[68]

Public share issue

13–020 In addition to these regular reports, a company must expose its financial performance to further scrutiny if it intends to issue shares for public sale. Requirements are imposed by law[69] and by the Financial Services Authority whose Listing Rules are available on its website. The details are complex but their net effect is that the company must issue a public document setting out in considerable detail its past performance and expectations.

Penalties for non-compliance

13–021 Non-compliance has proved an endemic problem. The introduction of standard civil penalties (effectively fines) for companies who fail to submit accounts on time has helped.[70] In 2006 it was estimated that 84.6 per cent of companies were up to date with filing their accounts and 79.1 per cent with filing their annual return. But even so, many were fined for late filing. A company may fail to comply with its duty because it is inefficient or because it does have something to hide. If reporters ask company secretaries for copies of the documents that should have been filed and they refuse to cooperate, this can safely be mentioned in the story. It will not improve confidence in the company's management.

Inspecting public documents

13–022 Not all the public documents and registers can be consulted in the same place. Some are kept at the Companies Registry—known also as Companies House—with branches in London, Edinburgh and

---

[66] Companies Act 1985, Sch.7, para.5. The 2005 Act leaves this to regulations.

[67] Companies Act 1985, Sch.7. There are no regulations yet concerning health and safety at work.

[68] 2006 Act, s.992 adding Pt 7 to 1985 Act, Sch.7.

[69] Principally the Financial Services and Markets Act 2000, Pt VI for listed securities and Public Offers of Securities Regulations 1995 (SI 1995/1537), for unlisted securities.

[70] Companies Act 1985, s.242A; 2006 Act, s.453.

Cardiff. Many of the documents kept at Companies House can be inspected or obtained on-line,[71] for all but the most basic information, a charge is made. Some documents are kept at the particular company's registered office or at a more convenient nominated address.[72] Most of the large public companies nominate a bank to maintain their public documents. This address, or the address of the registered office, will appear in a statement that is lodged with the Registrar prior to the company's formation. The company can change its registered office but must notify the Registrar within 14 days.[73]

- *At the registered office*: registers and indices of shareholdings[74]; debenture holders[75]; 3-per-cent shareholders[76]; directors' contracts[77] (when available).
- *At Companies House*: annual accounts, reports of auditors and directors,[78] annual return of changes in shareholdings,[79] Memorandum and Articles of Association.[80]
- *At both*: list of directors (including other directorships) and company secretary; register of charges.[81]
- *At the Company's AGM*: any person attending the AGM is entitled to inspect the register of directors' interests.[82]

Records over five years old must be consulted at Cardiff. Journalists offered illegible copies have a right to see the originals unless they are over 10 years old, in which case the documents will probably have been destroyed.[83]

A journalist, like other members of the public[84] can be charged a fee for inspecting these documents. The fees are now set by regulations which currently allow a charge of £2.50.[85] Companies House has a menu of charges depending on how the document is accessed or copied.[86]

---

[71] www.companieshouse.gov.uk.
[72] 1985 Act, s.353; 2006 Act, s.114.
[73] 1985 Act, s.287; 2006 Act, s.87.
[74] 1985 Act, ss.352, 353; 2006 Act, ss.114, 115.
[75] 1985 Act, ss.190, 191; 2006 Act, ss.743–745.
[76] 1985 Act, s.211(8).
[77] Listing Rules of the FSA—see above.
[78] 1985 Act, s.242; 2006 Act, s.441.
[79] 1985 Act, s.364A; 2006 Act, s.856.
[80] 1985 Act, ss.10, 18; 2006 Act ss.9 and 26.
[81] 1985 Act, s.288 (directors and company secretary), s.401 (charges); 2006 Act, s.162 (directors), s.876 (charges).
[82] 1985 Act, Sch.13, Pt IV.
[83] 1985 Act, ss.707A & 709; 2006 Act ss.1083 & 1085 which reduces the period for which originals must be kept to three years.
[84] Though not members of the company who can inspect without charge.
[85] Companies (Inspection and Copying of Registers, Indices and Documents) Regulations 1991 (SI 1991/1998).
[86] Companies (Fees) Regulations 2004 (SI 2004/2621).

13–023   The right to inspect includes the right in all cases (except directors' contracts) to have copies made. A company can charge for this at the rate of £2.50 for the first 100 entries, £20 for the next 1,000 and £15 for every subsequent 1,000. These charges apply to registers and reports. Copies of other documents are assessed at 10p per 100 words.[87]

Journalists can economise by asking for a copy of only a part of the register or document that is needed. However the regulations do say that companies cannot be required to make available details of members or debenture holders sorted by geographical location of their addresses, their nationality, whether the holdings are of a certain size, whether they are natural or legal persons (such as companies) or their gender.[88] Journalists can avoid any charge for copying by making their own notes or transcriptions and the regulations specifically allow for this.[89] Copies of those documents which are kept at Companies House can be obtained by personal attendance, or by online or telephone requests with variable charges being imposed.[90]

When the Companies Act 2006 is in force, quoted companies will have to make their annual accounts and reports available through their website and allow free access.[91]

Meetings

13–024 Most Annual General Meetings of the shareholders of public companies are formal occasions. The institutional investors, who tend to be the predominant shareholders, generally prefer to exercise their influence behind the scenes. In the absence of a crisis, items on the agenda are passed "on the nod" and the running of the company is left to the directors. Nevertheless, the law gives important residual powers to other shareholders, including a right, which cannot be taken away from them, to dismiss the directors.[92] If the company has been performing poorly or if a takeover is in the air, the shareholders' meetings may be the place for tough questioning. In addition, public interest groups have sometimes purchased a single share in a company in order to attend a shareholders' meeting and to challenge the board about the social consequences of its policies. The Companies Act 2006 will (when in force) give shareholders (of at least 5 per cent) the right to call on the company to

---

[87] Companies (Inspection and Copying of Registers, Indices and Documents) Regulations (above).

[88] 1991 Regs, Reg.4(3).

[89] 1991 Regs, Reg.3(2)(b)—although the journalist would need to be ready to be self-sufficient—a company cannot be required to provide facilities for this form of note taking—Reg.3(3).

[90] Companies (Fees) Regulations 2004.

[91] 2006 Act, s.430.

[92] 1985 Act, s.303; 2006 Act, s.168.

distribute a statement on its website in advance of the AGM or questions relating to the audit. The company will be able to seek a ruling from the court if it considers the right is being abused (e.g. because the requested statement is defamatory), but otherwise it will be available for public consultation.[93] Quoted companies will also have to carry on their websites the results of any poll taken at a general meeting of the company and, if an independent assessor has been appointed to review the company's accounts, a copy of his report. These will have to be maintained for two years.[94]

Journalists have no right to attend a general meeting, although they are frequently invited. If the press and public are excluded, reporters may gain admission by buying a share in the company or persuading an existing shareholder to allow them to attend as a proxy.

If there is a crisis and the exchanges become heated, there is more **13–025** likely to be a newsworthy story. The risk of a writ for defamation is minimal because in the case of the general meeting of a public company the press and broadcast media have a statutory qualified privilege.[95] The statutory privilege extends to the publication of fair and accurate extracts from any document circulated to members of a UK public company by or with the authority of the board, by the auditors or by any member in pursuance of a member exercising a statutory right.[96] In addition, there is the same privilege for a fair and accurate extract from any document circulated to members of a UK public company which relates to the appointment, resignation, retirement or dismissal of directors of the company.[97] The "United Kingdom" does not normally include the Channel Islands or the Isle of Man, but in this context the same privilege extends to reports of the equivalent meetings and documents of public companies established either in these territories or in other Member States.[98] The privilege is destroyed by malice, or by a refusal of the publisher or broadcaster to print a reasonable letter or statement by way of explanation or contradiction if required by the person defamed (see para.3–073).

The privilege does not apply to private companies' meetings.

If for some reason the defence of privilege failed, the publisher or broadcaster could always fall back on the general defences of truth or fair comment. "Fair comment" can be made only if the matter is of public interest. The affairs of the public company would certainly be of public interest. So, too, would those of a private company if they concerned the reliability of, or deficiencies in, its public documents or the social impact of the company's policies.

---

[93] 2006 Act, ss.314 and 527.
[94] 2006 Act, ss.341–354.
[95] Defamation Act 1996, s.15 and Sch.1, para.13(1).
[96] Defamation Act 1996, Sch.1, para.13(2).
[97] 1996 Act, para.13(3).
[98] 1996 Act, para.13(5).

Takeovers

13–026 Takeover battles present another opportunity for journalists to find out more about the internal workings of quoted companies. A great deal of financial and other information about both predator and prey must be disclosed. The rules are primarily intended to ensure that all the participants have common access to certain basic information,. Thus a company can hold meetings with selected shareholders to explain the terms of an offer only if no material new information is forthcoming and no significant new opinions expressed. If they are, this has to be circulated to all concerned and, in the closing days, may have to be the subject of a newspaper advertisement.[99]

These obligations are contained in the FSA's Regulations and the City Code on Takeovers and Mergers. Particularly in the case of the City Code, the sanctions for breach lack sufficient bite to deter some financiers from conducting secretive and shady manoeuvres. The Code discourages participants in a takeover bid from appearing on television programmes. The excuse is that the subtleties of the bid will be lost in a simplified discussion although the result is to confine knowledge to city insiders and to minimise critical media coverage. The Code recommends that interviews should be given only if they are not broken by insertion of comments or observations by others not made in the course of the interview. A panel discussion between offeror and offeree or between competing bodies sends shivers down the City Panel's spine: it deprecates anything resembling gladiatorial combat.[100] These views do not reflect any legal requirement, but they may explain why participants in a merger battle are reluctant to put their case to a television test. This attitude is antediluvian and diminishes the legitimate role that the broadcast media should play in exploring the public interest consequences of takeover. A spate of knocking-copy advertisements in 1985 led the panel to prohibit all advertisements in connection with a takeover offer unless they fell within narrowly drawn exemptions.[101]

PRESS MONOPOLIES

13–027 Since the Second World War the process of concentration of newspaper ownership in Britain has developed alarmingly, to the extent that Britain has one of the most concentrated newspaper ownership arrangements in the Western World. The danger of such monopolistic tendencies was identified by the first Royal Commission on the Press in the following terms:

---

[99] City Code on Takeovers and Mergers. The 8th edition was published on May 20, 2006: r.20.1, n.3.
[100] City Code, Rule 19.6.
[101] City Code, Rule 19.4.

"The monopolist, by its selection of the news and the manner in which it reports it, and by its commentary on public affairs, is in a position to determine what people shall read about the events and issues of the day, and to exert a strong influence on their opinions. Even if this position is not consciously abused, a paper without competitors may fall below the standards of accuracy and efficiency which competition enforces."[102]

Since then the regime for regulating newspaper mergers has changed several times. The most recent changes were brought about by the Enterprise Act 2002 and the Communications Act 2003. In general, the scheme for controlling newspaper mergers is integrated into the method of controlling business mergers generally. The OFT has front line responsibility for assessing whether a merger has or will result in a substantial lessening of competition. If it thinks that this is the case, it can refer the matter to the Competition Commission which reaches its own view on the effect on competition of the merger and then decides what, if anything to do in consequence. In this scheme (unlike its predecessors) the intervention of the Secretary of State is not necessary. Since the Communications Act 2003 this route can be followed where media businesses merge. However, in certain cases which meet the competition criteria (briefly that the enterprise being taken over has a turnover of at least £70 million and the combination of businesses will result in the creation or enhancement of at least 25 per cent of the goods or services in the United Kingdom or a substantial part of it), the Secretary of State can issue an intervention notice and take into account special public interest considerations. He can also issue a special intervention notice where the normal criteria concerning share of supply and turnover are not met, but one of the parties has at least a 25 per cent market share. The special public interest considerations which can be taken into account when a newspaper merger is involved include the need for the accurate presentation of news and free expression of opinion in newspapers and the need (so far as is reasonable and practicable) for a sufficient plurality of views in newspapers in the relevant market.[103] Where broadcasting businesses merge the special public interests concern the need for a sufficient plurality of persons with control of media enterprises, the need for the availability of a wide range of broadcasting of high quality and calculated to appeal to a wide variety of tastes and the need for persons carrying on media enterprises to have a genuine commitment to the attainment of the broadcasting standards objectives.[104] In the regimes set up under the 1965 and 1973 statutes most newspaper mergers were referred to the Competition authorities

---

[102] Royal Commission on the Press, Cmnd.7700 (1949) para.274.
[103] Enterprise Act 2002, s.58(2A) & (2B).
[104] 2002 Act, s.58(2C) and s.58A.

(first the Monopolies and Mergers Commission then the Competition Commission). In the great majority of cases, unconditional approval was given. However, the public interest standards in the current legislation closely follow those in the previous statutory generations and so, in the few cases which are likely to be referred to the Commission either by the OFT or as a result of the Secretary of State's intervention, the public interest issues are likely to be similar. However, unlike those earlier regimes, it is not necessary for there to be prior notification and approval: the parties can go ahead with the merger, but with the risk that it may have to be unravelled if the Commission rules against it.

13–028   One important aspect in a newspaper transfer is, as all Royal Commissions have recognised, the danger of creating an imbalance in the political affiliations of the press. Newspapers have, a right to be politically partisan; but it must surely be against the public interest if press outlets in a particular area, or in the nation as a whole, come to favour overwhelmingly one particular side of the political spectrum as a result of monopolistic tendencies. This does not call for an evaluation of the merits of political policies, but an assessment of the consequences of the transaction on the availability to the public of a reasonable variety of editorial opinion.

Some indication of a willingness to reach a judgment on this type of issue was shown by its 1999 report into the proposed acquisition of Mirror Group by Trinity plc and Regional Independent Media Holdings. The Commission considered whether this would affect the *Mirror*'s "left of centre political stance" but decided that it would not. It was concerned that the sale of one of the Mirror Group's Northern Ireland titles (*News Letter*) would lead to a loss of a "distinctive voice representing Unionist opinion" and if this happened "it would threaten the adequate representation in the press of the range of political opinion in Northern Ireland". The Commission proposed that Trinity be required to give an undertaking to sell on some of the Northern Ireland titles including *News Letter*.[105]

In making its judgment about the public interest the Commission must have particular regard to the "need for accurate presentation of news and free expression of opinion".[106] In 1990 it ruled against the acquisition of a controlling interest in the *Bristol Evening Post* and the *Western Daily Press* by David Sullivan (the proprietor of the *Daily Sport* and a string of pornographic publications). It thought Mr Sullivan,

> "could be expected to influence editorial policy and the character and content of these papers and that this would harm both

---

[105] Report of a merger situation—Trinity plc/Mirror Group plc/Regional Independent Media Holdings Ltd, July 23, 1999—available on the Commission's website at *www.competition-cominission.org.uk*.

[106] Now Enterprise Act, s.58(2A) formerly Fair Trading Act 1973, s.59(3).

the accurate presentation of news and the free expression of opinion. We also consider that the acquisition could harm the standing of the papers in their community and that there could be some adverse effects on circulation".[107]

In 2000 Richard Desmond, another publisher with a swag of pornographic titles, was not prevented from acquiring Express Newspapers. Fears that Lonhro would unduly interfere with the editorial independence of the *Observer* caused the MMC in 1981 to require the appointment of independent directors.

Adverse judgments by the Commission in relation to newspaper **13–029** mergers are rare. Of the 50 reports from 1973 to 2004 only 10 detected a damaging effect on the public interest.[108]

The Competition Commission must report within 24 weeks (or 32 if there are 'special reasons' for an extension).[109] It reports to the Secretary of State who must decide what to do in consequence of the report, but his room for manoeuvre is limited under the 2002 Act.[110] The Commission may recommend that the Government attach conditions to the transfer that would minimise dangers to the public interest. These statutory duties call for considerable investigation and knowledge of the industry, and up to three additional members may be appointed by the Government to assist the Commission in such referrals.[111] However, this power of ad hoc appointment is no substitute for the Commission being placed in a position to judge, from its own monitoring work, what the impact of a particular sale is likely to be. This could be achieved if the Commission were given a permanent responsibility to monitor, and from time to time to report publicly on developments that tend towards greater concentration of press holdings.

INVESTIGATIONS BY THE DTI, FSA AND THE TREASURY

The Department of Trade and Industry has wide powers to **13–030** investigate the affairs of a company. It may appoint an inspector to carry out a formal investigation if it believes that the company is untruthful, fraudulent or unfairly prejudicial to part of its members, or if it has failed to disclose information that its members could reasonably expect.[112] Either in conjunction with a formal investigation or independently, the Department can call for the production of

---

[107] Commission's Report on the Proposed Transfer of a Controlling Interest to David Sullivan in *Bristol Evening Post* Plc, May 31, 1990.

[108] Department of Trade and Industry *Enterprise Act 2002: Public Interest Intervention in Media Mergers: Guidance on the Operation of the Public Interest Provisions Relating to Newspaper and Other Media Mergers* May 2004.

[109] Enterprise Act 2002, s.51.

[110] Enterprise Act 2002, s.54.

[111] Competition Act 1998 Sch.7, paras 15 and 22.

[112] Companies Act 1985.

specified documents.[113] It can also crack the codes of nominees and investigate the true ownership and control of the company.[114]

A formal investigation is normally conducted by two specially appointed inspectors, a senior barrister and a chartered accountant. Its proceedings are inquisitorial, although cross-examination is sometimes allowed. They have been held in private since 1932, as the result of an unsatisfactory House of Lords decision.[115] The secrecy of investigations is now additionally buttressed by provisions against revealing documents compulsorily disclosed by the company in response to an order of the DTI, and by a maximum penalty of two years' imprisonment.[116] The offence covers revelations of any oral explanations of the disclosed material but not, apparently, answers given to the inspector's general inquiries on other matters unrelated to the company's documents, nor does the offence cover disclosure of information given by those outside the company.[117] Although the inspectors question witnesses in private, it does not follow that they can insist on a witness giving an undertaking to keep quiet about what he was asked or said in reply. The material which the inspectors put to the witness may be confidential (in which case notifying the witness of this will itself impose a duty on him to respect the confidence), but the inspectors cannot insist on creating an obligation of confidence which would not otherwise arise.[118]

13–031   The inspectors report to the Secretary of State, who may send a copy of the report to the company itself.[119] The minister can also make the report publicly available.[120] This is always done when external inspectors are appointed, although only after any criminal proceedings have finished. Lonhro unsuccessfully challenged the refusal of the DTI in 1989 to publish its report on the takeover of Harrods by the Al Fayed brothers. The minister said that criminal proceedings were still under consideration, and the courts refused to

---

[113] 1985 Act, s.447.

[114] 1985 Act, s.442 and see s.444 (power to obtain information as to those interested in shares) and s.446 (investigation of share dealings).

[115] *Hearts of Oak Assurance Co Ltd v Att-Gen* [1932] A.C. 392. Until this case, investigations were held in public as a matter of course. The Att-Gen's defence of the practice was halfhearted in the House of Lords, but it is still surprising that the Lords left the inspector no discretion to take evidence in public. As a dissenting judge said in the Court of Appeal, the inspector might reasonably believe that witnesses would be less likely to lie in public and that an open airing of the accusations would prevent inflated rumours of more serious wrongdoing [1931] 2 Ch. 370, 396 *per* Lawrence L.J.

[116] 1985 Act, s.449.

[117] 1985 Act, s.447(5)(a) unless the outsider was in possession of the compulsorily acquired documents.

[118] *Re An Inquiry into Mirror Group Newspapers Plc* [2000] Ch. 194.

[119] 1985 Act, s.437(3)(a).

[120] 1985 Act, s.437(3)(c), although the Department can appoint inspectors on the basis that their reports will not be published. See Companies Act 1985, s.432(2A).

overturn his view that publication might prejudice any future prosecution.[121] Where outside inspectors have not been used, but the Department has called for documents, the results of the investigation are not generally released unless they disclose material of importance that the Department wishes to publicise.[122] The inspectors' reports usually reveal more incompetence than dishonesty, but their reprimands can be severe,[123] and their descriptions (e.g. "an epidemic loss of money" or "for this managing director truth was a moving target") acidic. In other respects, however, the DTI lives down to its nickname ("The Department of Timidity and Inaction"). It has failed to move against well-connected city operators involved in share manipulation. Its abject failure to cope with the Lloyd's scandal has become legendary. Its investigation into Jeffrey Archer was inconclusive and, because the Government refused to publish it, its thoroughness could not be assessed by the media.

The DTI or FSA can appoint inspectors to investigate insider dealing, misleading statements or advertisements or market abuse.[124] The FSA's powers are broader and it can appoint investigators to decide whether one of its rules has been broken, whether a person is fit and proper to carry out a regulated activity or whether or not a person may be guilty of money laundering.[125] In the wake of the BCCI and Barings scandals and concerns at the inadequacies of their financial regulation, the Treasury was given power to appoint investigators to examine whether there were events posing a grave risk to the financial system which occurred through regulatory default.[126] Treasury appointed investigators have the same power to compel production of documents and witnesses as a court and disobedience can be referred to the High Court for punishment as contempt[127] Similar powers are given to the other investigators.[128] It was in the context of an insider dealing investigation under earlier legislation that the *Independent* journalist, Jeremy Warner, refused to disclose his source of information and was punished for contempt of court (see para.5–055).

OTHER BUSINESSES

The need to structure a capital base and the attraction of limited **13–032** liability lead most sizeable businesses to opt for corporate form. This is just as well for reporters, because there is a dearth of disclosure

---

[121] *R. v Secretary of State for Trade and Industry Ex p. Lonhro Plc* [1989] 1 W.L.R. 525, HL.
[122] Leigh, *Commercial Fraud*, pp.168, 176.
[123] Leigh, pp.172–4.
[124] Financial Services and Markets Act 2000, s.168(1)–(3).
[125] 2000 Act, s.168(4).
[126] 2000 Act, s.14.
[127] 2000 Act, ss.16 and 17.
[128] 2000 Act, ss.170–177.

obligations on the principal alternatives: partnership, unincorporated associations (such as clubs) and sole trading. Unless they acquire charitable status or a licence to lend money or one of the other privileges considered below, such businesses have virtually no legal disclosure obligations and the investigator will be dependent on volunteered information or leaks.

Partnerships

13–033　Partnerships must reveal the names of their members. This obligation was first imposed in 1916, not to forestall fraudsters but to prevent entrepreneurs of German origin trading under the guise of an Anglicised name. The partnership must keep a list of its partners' names at its principal place of business and allow inspection there.[129]

Limited liability partnerships

13–034　The impetus for a new form of business organisation came from professional partnerships (particularly accountants) that were concerned at the level of damages (and costs) which they might face in negligence actions and which might exceed their professional indemnity insurance cover. The Limited Liability Partnerships Act 2000 allows a hybrid between a company and a partnership. Like a company it has its own legal existence and its liability can be limited. However, like a partnership, the members are entitled (broadly speaking) to structure the rights and responsibilities between themselves as they wish.

　　The disclosure requirements are very similar to those of companies. Thus the incorporation document (which will list the partners names and addresses) must be sent to the Companies Registry[130] and changes must be notified.[131] Limited Liability Partnerships will be identifiable by the new abbreviation "LLP". Audited accounts must be supplied to the Registry each year in much the same way as companies are required to do.[132]

Co-ops and housing associations

13–035　Co-ops and housing associations are normally set up either as companies or as friendly societies and are registered under the Industrial and Provident Societies Act 1978. Like companies, they must make an annual return, which must include accounts and an auditor's report.[133] The balance sheet has to be displayed in a

---

[129] Business Names Act 1985, s.4. This will be replaced by Companies Act 2006, ss.1201–1204.
[130] Limited Liability Partnerships Act 2000, ss.2 and 3.
[131] 2000 Act, s.9.
[132] Limited Liability Partnership Regulations 2001 (SI 2001/1090), Reg.3.
[133] Industrial and Provident Societies Act 1965, s.39.

conspicuous place at the registered office.[134] Not-for-profit providers of housing can be registered as a "social landlord" with the Housing Corporation. The register is open for inspection at the Corporation's head office.[135]

Building societies

Building societies come under the jurisdiction of the FSA.[136] They, **13–036** too, must submit accounts, though in much more detail.[137] Since 1986 these have been similar to the requirements for companies and banks. A copy must be sent to the FSA which will make it available as part of the society's public file.[138] As with companies, the purpose of disclosure is principally to reassure creditors and depositors. This overlooks the social role of building societies as the main supplier of loans for private homes. If a society refuses to lend in a particular area ("red-lining"), it can have a devastating effect on property values. The societies may fear that the neighbourhood is in decline and a risky place to invest but, if the area is starved of home loans, this becomes a self-fulfilling prophecy. It is impossible to tell from an annual report whether a society is red-lining, since it is not obliged to say anything about the location of properties on which loans have been made. Building societies, like companies, must disclose the remuneration and any loan made to directors.[139] Building societies must belong to an ombudsman scheme for dealing with complaints. The body administering the scheme must be permitted to publish the whole or any part of an ombudsman's determination.[140]

SPECIAL PRIVILEGES

Charities

Charities do not pay income tax, capital gains or capital transfer tax **13–037** (unless they engage in trade). They pay no more than half the rates of a comparable occupier and they are entitled to miscellaneous reliefs from VAT, Stamp Duty and National Insurance. It is also easier for them to raise money because they may recover from the Inland Revenue the income tax paid by the donor on a gift. Donations to charities are free of capital transfer tax and capital

---

[134] 1965 Act, s.40.
[135] Housing Act 1996, s.1. The head office is at 149 Tottenham Court Road, London W1T 7BN.
[136] Financial Services and Markets Act 2000 (Mutual Societies) Order 2001 (SI 2001/2617).
[137] Building Societies Act 1986, ss.72A–72K.
[138] 1986 Act, s.81.
[139] 1986 Act, Sch.10A.
[140] 1986 Act, Sch.12, para.9.

gains tax. These are significant State subsidies, but there is a paucity of public information about the objects of such largesse.

To secure these advantages, it is in practice necessary for a charity to register with the Charity Commission. It will scrutinise the organisation's purposes to see if they conform to the legal definition of a charity. This has been developed by the courts by reference to an ancient statute of 1601. Broadly, there are four categories: religious, educational, those for the relief of poverty and those for other purposes beneficial to the community. Some modest updating was introduced by the Charities Act 2006 but the structure of the Elizabethan definition is retained. An organisation may run a business and still be a charity if its ultimate object comes within one of these categories.

Some charities will be companies and must therefore comply with the ordinary disclosure requirements, but a reporter investigating those that are unincorporated can look only to the Charities Act 1993. The charity must lodge its trust deed or the instrument specifying its objects for public inspection.[141] This will be drafted more precisely than the objects clause of an ordinary company's Memorandum of Association because the Charity Commission will withhold its blessing unless every purpose comes within the charitable definition. Nevertheless, within these limits it will still be drawn so as to give the organisation the maximum latitude and may therefore be a poor guide as to what the charity actually does.

13–038   Charities must prepare annual accounts, although where the income does not exceed £100,000 these are in a simplified form.[142] If the charity's income in the current year (and each of the two preceding years) exceeds £250,000 the accounts must be audited.[143] The accounts must also be audited if the gross income in the current year exceeds £500,000, or if the gross income exceeds £100,000 and the aggregate value of its assets exceeds £2.8 million. If the charity's income falls below these thresholds, but is still more than £10,000 the accounts must be reviewed by an independent person who must produce a report.[144]

An annual report must be sent to the Charity Commission and must include the accounts and the report of an auditor or independent person.[145] If the charity has an income of less than £100,000 it must give a brief summary of the main activities and achievements during the year. If the income is over £100,000 the annual report must review all the activities and achievements including material transactions, significant developments and achievements, any significant change in activities, any important events affecting those

---

[141] Charities Act 1993, s.3(8).
[142] Charities Act 1993, s.42.
[143] 1993 Act, s.43.
[144] 1993 Act, s.43.
[145] 1913 Act, s.45.

activities since the end of the year and any likely future developments. The report will also include basic information such as the names of the trustees and the charity's principal address. However, the Commission can dispense with these requirements if disclosure of them would expose the trustee or anyone at the charity's office to personal danger.[146] The charity must keep the reports for six years.

The public has a right to inspect the annual reports at the Commissioners' offices[147] and to have copies made.[148] A member of the public can also require the organisation to provide a copy of the most recent accounts.[149] Some charities, generally large public institutions, are exempt from these provisions.[150]

In certain circumstances the Commission has powers to establish **13–039** alternative schemes for the administration of a charity, and to appoint or remove trustees, or officers or managers of a charitable trust, but they must give advance public notice.[151]

The media have, with a few exceptions, signally failed to alert the public to scandals in charity administration that stem from outdated legal definitions and absence of expert public oversight. There are some 140,000 registered charities, with assets of about £5 billion accumulated with the help of tax privileges. Many "charities" have nothing to do with the relief of poverty or oppression. Some of the wealthiest—private schools and private medical funds, for example— cater mainly to the wealthy. Thanks to the idiosyncrasies of interpretation of the 1601 statute embodying the social values of the Elizabethan age, some charities-in-law are positively uncharitable. The *Daily Mail* exposed how the "Moonies" spent tax subsidies on brainwashing converts and breaking up families. Others are simply eccentric: e.g. the Relaxation League, the Fun Palace Trust, the Cat Protection League, the Fund for Polishing Regimental Silver, the Friends of Locomotives of the Great Western Railway. On the other hand, any organisation that seeks to change the law—even in order to relieve poverty and oppression—is debarred from registration as a charity. In 1981 it was decided in the High Court that Amnesty International could not obtain tax privileges as a charity because it sought actively to change the laws of fascist and Communist countries.[152] The anomalies stemming from the legal definition of charity are endless: anti-social or downright silly organisations are allowed tax advantages denied to important and humane causes. There have been proposals to rationalise the law, but to no avail and

---

[146] Charities (Accounts and Reports) Regulations 2005 (SI 2005/572), Reg.11.
[147] Charities Act 1993, s.47(1).
[148] 1993 Act, s.84.
[149] Charities Act 1993, s.47(2).
[150] 1993 Act, Sch.2.
[151] 1993 Act, s.20.
[152] *McGovern v Att-Gen* [1981] 3 All E.R. 493. See para.16–062 for the difficulties which Amnesty experienced for similar reasons in trying to have its advertisements broadcast.

it remains to be seen whether the changes brought about by the Charities Act 2006 will make any significant difference. The importance of the Charity Commission, and the lack of power to scrutinise the activities of those businesses that batten on to compassionate instincts by raising money for charities that see very little of it at the end of the day, make the entire field a fertile one for exposure journalism.

Investment business

13–040 The regulation of investment business is set in the United Kingdom by the Financial Services and Markets Act 2000 although the main engine for change has been the EU. The Financial Services Authority is the UK's regulator. Those regulated include investment advisers. Potentially, this concept could have embraced financial journalists and advisers working for the mainstream media. However, there is an exemption if the advice is given in a newspaper or other periodical (or broadcasting service) where the principal purpose of the publication or broadcast, when taken as a whole, is not to give investment advice nor of leading people to buy or sell securities. When the regulation is extended to those advising about mortgages, home reversion plans or home purchase plans, the exemption for the media will be correspondingly extended as well.[153] On the application of a media proprietor, the FSA can provide a conclusive certificate that a publication or service is exempt.[154]

Financial journalists who predict the stock market performance of particular companies have a serious conflict of interest if they or persons close to them stand to gain by the market reaction to their story. Some newspapers for this reason debar financial journalists from having their own portfolio, while the PCC has issued some nebulous rules that do not really come to grips with the ethical problems (see para.14–033). The temptation to profit personally from foreknowledge of press stories was highlighted by the prosecution in New York of Foster Winans, a journalist who arranged for others to trade in shares about to be "tipped" by his influential column in the *Wall Street Journal*. In Britain a journalist who entered into similar arrangements could be prosecuted under the Theft Act for dishonestly obtaining a pecuniary advantage for himself or another. A dishonest arrangement with company "insiders" to affect share prices through the leakage and publication of price-sensitive information would amount to a conspiracy to contravene the Financial Services and Markets Act 2000.

> The share-tipping scandal at the *Daily Mirror* in 2000 eventually led to the prosecution of the journalists for conspiracy to contravene s.47(2)

---

[153] The Financial Services and Markets Act 2000 (Regulated Activities) Order 2001, (SI 2001/544), Art.54.

[154] The Financial Services and Markets Act 2000 (Regulated Activities) Order 2001, Art.54(3).

of the Financial Services Act 1986 (the predecessor of the 2000 Act). Anil Bhoyrul pleaded guilty and was sentenced to 180 hours community punishment order. James Hipwell (who made a substantially larger profit and who pleaded not guilty) was convicted and sentenced to six months imprisonment which was upheld on appeal.[155] Piers Morgan, the editor at the time, also made money from tipped shares, although he was cleared of wrongdoing by a Department of Trade inquiry.

A great deal of information on businesses and individuals who are **13–041** regulated by the FSA is available on its register which can be searched online.[156]

The FSA has very broad powers and so the role of the appeals body, the Financial Services and Markets Tribunal, is particularly important. Its rules of procedure create a presumption that the Tribunal's hearings will be in public.[157] However, it can sit in private on the joint application of the parties or else if satisfied that a private hearing would be in the interests of morals, public order, national security or the protection of the private lives of the parties or that unfairness to the applicant or the interests of consumers might result from an open hearing. There are, though, two important qualifications. The Tribunal must not sit in private if this would be prejudicial to the interests of justice and it must also consider whether only part of the proceedings needs to be in private. Its decisions must be given publicly or published in writing. If all or part of the proceedings were in private, the Tribunal can restrict publicity to all or part of its decision but, consistently with the principle of proportionality, must minimise any such restriction.[158] The Tribunal considered the operation of these provisions in *Eurolife Assurance Co Ltd v FSA*.[159] It held that a ritualistic assertion of unfairness or prejudice would not be enough: the applicant had to produce cogent evidence of how unfairness or prejudice might arise. The Tribunal then had to weigh the seriousness of the potential prejudice and the likelihood of it happening. Even then it had to apply the "interests of justice condition". In general, justice required openness, but if unfairness or prejudice from a public hearing was established, it was likely that the interests of justice test would also be satisfied. Interestingly, in this case the applicant argued that it would be likely to be prejudiced by the media's practice of concentrating its attention on the opening statement (in this case by the FSA). The Tribunal dealt with this in a practical manner by directing that the applicant should have an opportunity to make a statement in

---

[155] *R. v Hipwell*. [2006] 2 Cr.Appr.R.(S). 98.
[156] *www.fsa.gov.uk*.
[157] The Financial Services and Markets Tribunal Rules 2001 (SI 2001/2476), r.17.
[158] 2001 Rules, r.20.
[159] *Eurolife Assurance Co Ltd v FSA* [2002] UKFSM 001, May 23, 2002, available at *www.bailii.org*.

rebuttal on the first day of the hearing (and preferably in the morning). It rejected the application to sit in private and ordered the hearing to be in public (although in the event the matter was settled on the eve of the substantive hearing).

Consumer credit

13-042 Almost all business dealings with consumers involving credit must now be licensed.[160] About 560,000 licences are involved. The register of licences is open for public inspection and includes particulars of applications and licences, and notes whether a licence has ever been suspended or refused.[161] Rogue motor dealers constitute the largest group to have licences refused or revoked, and not merely for mishandling the credit side of their business. Alteration of odometers (mileage recorders) or consistently selling unroadworthy vehicles will justify barring a dealer from further credit transactions. The register is also one of the few public documents that must disclose the officers of *unincorporated* associations. The system has been in operation since 1976 and is a useful source of information about shady characters on the way up again as time passes and memories of crooked consumer scandals begin to fade. Decisions of the OFT will be appealed to the Consumer Credit Appeals Tribunal once the Consumer Credit Act 2006 has been brought into force.

Other registers

13-043 There are numerous other public registers. By law the General Medical Council must publish an annual list of doctors.[162] The local council which acts as a licensing authority will keep a register of everyone entitled to sell alcoholic drinks. This will also show the owner of the premises and any conviction of the licensee in his trade or for bribery or treating at an election.[163]

INSOLVENCY

13-044 The insolvency procedures (winding up for companies, bankruptcy for individuals, receivership where the debts are backed by security) are intended to gather in what assets can be traced and to distribute them to the creditors according to set rules of priority.

The whole of insolvency law was reformed in the 1980s. One aim was to harmonise the codes of procedure for individuals and

---

[160] Consumer Credit Act 1974, Part III.
[161] 1974 Act, s.35. The OFT is based at Fleetbank House, 2–6 Salisbury Square, London EC4Y 8JX. As of 2006 it was planning to make the register accessible online—*www.oft.gov.uk*.
[162] Medical Act 1983, s.34, and, for dentists, see Dentists Act 1984, s.22.
[163] Licensing Act 2003, s.8 and Sch.3.; Representation of the People Act 1983, s.168(7).

companies. This has largely been achieved but the two regimes continue their separate existence.

A company in financial difficulties has a wide range of options. Normally, the first step is for the major creditors to appoint a receiver who, at least temporarily, will take over the running of the business. The outgoing directors or others responsible for the company must prepare a statement of its affairs.[164] A copy is filed with the court. The court file is not a public document. It can be consulted as of right only by those immediately connected with the insolvency proceedings. There is a discretionary power to allow any person to inspect the file; conversely, the court can prohibit inspection.[165] The receiver will prepare a report on the company's predicament, which he must make available to all the creditors.[166] He also has to send a copy of the report to the Registrar of Companies, where it can be inspected.[167]

If the company's disease is terminal, it is wound up, or "liqui- **13–045** dated". This may be done with the company's acquiescence (a "voluntary winding up" may be convenient as part of a corporate restructuring for a company that is healthy and solvent). Alternatively, a company may be wound up on its creditors' insistence. The process begins with the presentation of a petition to the court. The petition must then be advertised in the *London Gazette*. The court can exempt a petitioner from this requirement and will ban the advertising of a petition if it is considered an abuse of process.[168] The petition is heard in open court.[169] Following a winding-up order, a statement of affairs by the directors must be produced to the Official Receiver.[170] This will be filed in court and (except in voluntary liquidations) is open to inspection by those immediately concerned in the winding-up, although the court does have power to restrict access to all or part of the statement.[171]

The Official Receiver can apply to the court for the public examination of any officer of the company.[172] This power was widened following the strong recommendation of the Cork Committee, whose proposals led to the transformation of insolvency law.[173] Public examination is no longer dependent on a prior report by the Official Receiver suggesting fraud.

---

[164] Insolvency Act 1986, s.47.
[165] Insolvency Rules, rr 3.5, 7.31. It is a contempt of court to inspect the file without permission: *Dobson v Hastings* [1992] Ch.394.
[166] Insolvency Act 1986, s.48.
[167] Companies Act 1985, s.709; Companies Act 2006, s.1085.
[168] Insolvency Rules 1986, r.4.11.
[169] *Practice Direction (No. 3 of 1986)* [1987] 1 W.L.R. 53.
[170] Insolvency Act 1986, s.131.
[171] Insolvency Rules 1986, r.4.35.
[172] Insolvency Act 1986, s.133. There is an alternative power to summon under s.236. This examination is not expressly required to be in public and therefore a registrar must, and a judge can, conduct it in chambers, Insolvency Rules, r.7.6.
[173] Review Committee on Insolvency Law and Practice (Cmnd. 8558), Ch.12.

Directors who are found in the course of winding up to have been involved in fraudulent trading may be disqualified from being a director or from promoting, forming or managing a company for a specified period.[174] Similiar orders can be made against a director who commits a number of Company Act offences, including persistent default in sending accounts, returns or reports to the Registry.[175] This was intended to reduce the shamefully high incidence of noncompliance with these obligations. Even in the absence of a specific offence, a disqualification order can be made if the company is insolvent and the director is considered to be unfit to manage a company.[176] The director must be given an opportunity to be heard at a public hearing before the court.[177] The Secretary of State can now accept an undertaking from the director (for instance, not to act as a company director for a specified period) instead of seeking a court order.[178] There is a register of disqualification orders and undertakings that is kept by the DTI and Companies House and which is open to public inspection.[179]

13–046 Bankruptcy proceedings follow a similar pattern to winding-up. They also begin with a petition to the court, which again, may be made by either the debtor or one of the creditors. Prior to the 1986 Act it was the norm for bankruptcies to be examined in public. A public examination now will take place only if the Official Receiver applies to the court for one.[180]

If the debtor is adjudged bankrupt, he or she will be disqualified from acting as a director,[181] unable to obtain most credit and barred from holding certain public offices. Bankruptcy decisions are advertised in the *London Gazette* and in local papers.[182] The individual insolvency register, maintained by the Insolvency Service, has details of bankruptcy orders and individual voluntary arrangements.[183] The bankruptcy now comes to an end automatically after three years (two if the speedier "summary administration" method is used) for first-time bankrupts. Others still have to apply to the court to be discharged.

---

[174] Company Directors Disqualification Act 1986, ss.1 and 4.

[175] 1986 Act, ss.2, 3 and 5.

[176] 1986 Act, s.6.

[177] Insolvent Companies (Disqualification of Unfit Directors) Proceedings Rules 1987 (SI 1987/2023).

[178] Company Directors Disqualification Act 1986, s.1A.

[179] Company Directors Disqualification Act 1986, s.18.

[180] Insolvency Act 1986, s.290; again, there is an alternative power to examine the debor in private, s.366.

[181] Company Directors Disqualification Act 1986, s.11.

[182] Insolvency Rules 1986 (SI 1925), r.6.34(2). The court has the power to suspend this obligation, r.6.34(3).

[183] Search requests can be sent to the Insolvency Service, Bankruptcy Public Search Room, 2nd Floor, West Wing, 45–6 Stephenson Street, Birmingham B2 4UP.

HUMAN RIGHTS, MULTI-NATIONALS AND GLOBAL COMPACT

Journalists should be particularly interested in the behaviour of UK **13–047** companies that do business in the third world, where corruption is rife and malpractice common. They should be even more interested in transnational corporations, whose global activities generate more product and greater influence than many UN member states. (Over half of the hundred wealthiest entities in the world today are corporations not countries). Some are directly responsible for, and take vast profits from, human rights violations. Working (usually through subsidiaries) in partnership with military juntas or corrupt politicians, they have been known to exploit slave labour and child workers, to hire paramilitaries, to destroy inconvenient villages, pillage homes and transfer populations. On their behalf, protestors have been jailed and murdered and even (in the case of Ken Sara-Wiwa in Nigeria) tried and executed. They have inflamed wars by selling arms or dealing with "conflict commodities" like diamonds. Much of the bribery and corruption which is endemic in Africa and in many parts of Latin America and Asia has been instigated by multi-national companies.

Their disclosure duties will depend upon the law of the place where they are registered. Sometimes that law will require environmental impact studies and reports of compliance with local labour laws. Many corporations have been prepared to subscribe to a UN initiative, the Global Compact. This is a voluntary and somewhat "feel good" exercise requiring a chief executive to write to Banke Moon vouching support for the Compact's ten principles and undertaking to promote them inside and outside the company and to publish a declaration of support for them in the company's annual report. This public commitment to the ten principles which relate to human rights, labour rights, protection of the environment and anti-corruption, and in particular the requirement to express support for that commitment in annual reports does permit some measure of corporate accountability. Annual reports must positively assert compliance and if these statements can be demonstrated to be false then the company can be made liable under local laws which punish false and misleading statements in annual reports. The Global Compact requires adherence to International Labour Organization (ILO) conventions which in turn demand labour rights of collective bargaining, prohibition of child labour, and forced labour and the elimination of discrimination in respect of employment.

CHAPTER 14

MEDIA SELF-REGULATION

INTRODUCTION

Notwithstanding the number of legal restraints on the media, it has **14–001** power to damage reputations by falsehoods, invade privacy and conduct partisan campaigns. The unavailability of legal aid effectively deters all but the intrepid or wealthy from taking action for libel, and there is as yet no direct protection for privacy in British law. Blatant examples of unfair and unethical media behaviour towards individuals and organisations have led to demands for more statutory controls, which media industries have sought to avoid by trumpeting the virtues of "self-regulation". They have established tribunals that affect to regulate media ethics through adjudicating complaints by members of the public who claim to have been unfairly treated by journalists and editors. Complaints about newspapers and journals may be made to the Press Complaints Commission (PCC), a private body funded by newspaper proprietors. It has no legal powers, but its adjudications will be published by the paper complained against, albeit usually in small print and without much prominence. Allegations about false or offensive telephone services may be made to ICSTIS, an adju-dicative body set up by British Telecom. The Advertising Standards Authority (ASA) is the body that will hear complaints that advertisements are not "legal, decent, honest and truthful". Although a private company funded by the advertising industry, it derives a powerful sanction from the preparedness of newspapers and journals to withhold space for advertisements that are in breach of its code.

Journalists should recognise the political purpose behind these organisations.[1] They serve as public relations operations, funded by media industries to give the impression to Parliament that the press, the telephone service providers and the advertising industry really can put their houses in ethical order without the need for legislation. Press proprietors are prepared to invest £1.5 million each year in the PCC because its existence offers a form of insurance against new

---

[1] See G. Robertson, *People Against the Press* (Quartet Books, 1983).

laws to safeguard personal privacy, prohibit chequebook journalism and to guarantee a right of reply. The advertising industry funds the ASA, to a tune of more than £3 million annually, to avoid exposure to laws against deceit and indecency. Both organisations have performed imperfectly from the public point of view, but owe their continued industry support to that mixture of fear, prudence and masochism identified by Hilaire Belloc:

> "Always keep a-hold on nurse/For fear of finding something worse."

Whether "something worse"—i.e. a statute rather than a self-help arrangement—would be worse for the public, as well as for the newspaper and advertising industry, remains debatable. The PCC has failed to demonstrate many virtues in self-regulation: it has designed an ethical code which it declines to monitor, and its decisions are accorded a degree of cynicism, bordering on contempt, by editors—especially when they relate to coverage of the Royal Family, which the PCC has spent a lot of its time trying to protect, often from its own media gaffes. Although tabloid editors give lip-service to PCC guidelines on privacy, chequebook journalism and race reporting, they are sometimes prepared to break them in the interests of increasing circulation. One of the serious consequences for journalistic standards is the way newspapers, out of self-interest, contrive to pretend that PCC rulings are both effective and newsworthy, and rarely tell their readers that the organisation is something of a confidence trick, perpetuated by those very same newspapers.

14–002   Nonetheless, the PCC and the ASA are significant organisations, with a potential for good and a capacity to inhibit genuine investigative reporting and the amount of information available to the public. A code of practice promulgated by an authoritative organisation can be of great assistance to journalists in resisting editorial pressures to behave unethically in the quest for circulation-building stories of prurient, rather than public, interest. Some of the journalists who were held to have "ferociously and callously harassed" relatives of a "Yorkshire Ripper" victim evinced a sense of shame, but excused themselves on the ground that they were only obeying editorial instructions.[2] A code of conduct should assist journalists to develop the moral muscle to resist unethical orders to invade privacy and sensationalise private grief, especially if the code has been incorporated in their contract of employment. The ASA code has practical force because media outlets will not accept advertisements ruled to be in breach of it, and the PCC code, which has no practical force at all, can have a legal impact through the operation of s.12(4) of the Human Rights Act, which requires courts to pay attention to "any

---

[2] Press Council, *Press Conduct in the Sutcliffe Case*, 1983, Ch.18.

relevant privacy code" in deciding whether to impose prior restraint. The assumption is that courts will be more likely to injunct if the alleged breach of confidence also involves a breach of the code—which will be interpreted by judges, not the more media-friendly PCC. Privacy codes which are too widely or loosely drawn, or which go beyond what the law requires (e.g. the amendments made to the PCC code in the wake of Diana's death) have proved counter-productive in the courts, and may become trip-wires for important investigative journalism based (like much of that genre) on confidential leaks from "insiders".

The courts have tended to show considerable deference to self-regulating bodies, resisting most attempts to second guess the decisions of their so-called "expert" or "representative" members. Support for this hands-off approach is usually found in the Law Lords' decision in R. (ProLife Alliance) v BBC[3] where they narrowly confined the judicial role (in reviewing a BBC decision to ban an election broadcast by an anti-abortion party) to checking that it was rational, made in good faith and had applied the appropriate standard. But this decision had been made by the BBC pursuant to a statutory provision—i.e. a determination by Parliament—that television should not show offensive scenes. The position is very different when an industry, to protect itself from precisely that sort of statutory regulation, erects voluntary censorship bodies like the PCC, the ASA and ICSTIS. The very fact that they are funded by the industry, in the interests of maintaining profits and avoiding public accountability, means that the courts should be more rather than less interventionist, and more alert to strike down unnecessary censorship. The PCC is funded by press proprietors with the objective of staving off the advent of privacy laws and is generally recognised as "an ineffective regulator which fails to offer adequate redress in a great many cases".[4] ICSTIS, the most recent regulator, was revealed in 2007 to have abjectly failed in its duty to curb the TV quiz lines that had gulled viewers into making phone calls at premium rates. These self-appointed regulators should be subject to close scrutiny by the courts whenever their decisions impinge upon media freedom.

THE PRESS COMPLAINTS COMMISSION

From Press Council to PCC

The idea that disputes over the content of newspapers might be **14–003** resolved by some independent but non-legal body developed first in Sweden, where publishers and journalists established a Press Fair

---

[3] [2003] 2 All E.R. 977.
[4] See Feintuck and Varney, *Media Regulation, Public Interest and the Law* (2nd edn, 2006, Edinburgh University Press), p.195.

Practices Board in 1916. In due course, all major Swedish news-papers bound themselves by contract to accept the rulings of a press ombudsman—a judge who rules on complaints from the public, orders newspapers to print retractions of false statements, and fines them for proven deviations from a code of conduct drawn up by the country's Press Council.[5] In Britain the idea of a Press Council was first mooted by the National Union of Journalists (NUJ) after the lifting of wartime censorship in 1945. The union was alarmed at the concentration of ownership in the provincial press, the suppression or distortion of news for politically partisan or commercial reasons, and the proprietorial pressures imposed upon editors and journal-ists. There were debates in Parliament, and journalist-M.P.s like Michael Foot claimed that some editors were merely "stooges, cyphers and sycophants". The First Royal Commission on the Press reported in 1949, and suggested that the industry should establish "a General Council of the Press", which, "by censuring undesirable types of journalistic conduct and by all other possible means, would build up a code of conduct in accordance with the highest profes-sional standards".[6] The next four years were spent in desultory and unenthusiastic discussions amongst proprietors, until a private mem-ber's bill was introduced in Parliament to set up a statutory council. This prospect brought a speedy end to discussions, and a General Council of the Press commenced operations in 1953.[7] It had no lay membership, and its first chairman was the then proprietor of *The Times*.

The first decade of the Council's operations was unimpressive. Its rulings were oversensitive to Government and to royalty—its first declaration was that a *Daily Mirror* readership poll on the question of whether Princess Margaret should be allowed to marry Group Captain Townsend was "contrary to the best traditions of British journalism".[8] Its poor performance was subjected to scathing crit-icism by the second Royal Commission on the Press, reporting in 1962, which urged the Government to set up a proper disciplinary body with statutory powers if the Council failed to reform itself immediately.[9] The renewed threat of legislation made newspaper

---

[5] Lennart Groll, *Freedom and Self-Discipline of the Swedish Press*, Swedish Institute, 1980; Lennart Groll and Geoffrey Robertson, "Legal Constraints on the Press: Swedish and British Viewpoints" in *Freedom and the Press* (Department of Visual Communication, Goldsmith's College, 1979).

[6] Royal Commission on the Press, Cmnd. 7700 (1949), para.650.

[7] The Press Council Bill had its second reading in November 1952. It was moved by C. J. Simmons M.P., who reminded the House that "nearly three-and-a-half years after [the Royal Commission Report] we are still awaiting its formation by the Press of their own volition". See generally H. Phillip Levy, *The Press Council*, (Macmillan, 1967), Chs 1 and 2.

[8] "A Royal Romance: Princess Margaret and Group Captain Townsend", *Daily Mirror*, February 21, 1954 (Press Council).

[9] Royal Commission on the Press, Cmnd. 1811 (1962), para.325.

proprietors jump to attention: they supplied the Council with increased finance, appointed a retired Law Lord, Lord Devlin, as chairperson, and changed the constitution so that 20 per cent of members were drawn from outside the media. Under Devlin's leadership, the Council began to display a more impressive tone and authority. It began to reprimand press misconduct in positive terms, and evinced a powerful concern for press freedoms. However, its higher profile on press freedom issues caused it to be perceived publicly as a champion of the press rather than a watchdog for the public.[10]

The first detailed study of the Press Council's work was conducted by the third Royal Commission of the Press, chaired by Lord Mac-Gregor.[11] It found evidence of "flagrant breaches of acceptable standards" and "inexcusable intrusions into privacy". "We feel strongly", it stated, "that the Press Council should have more power over the press . . . There is a pressing call to enhance the standing of the Press Council in the eyes of the public and potential complainants."[12] It called upon the newspaper proprietors who fund and effectively control the Council to ensure that it had sufficient funds to advertise its services and to monitor press performance. Complaints upheld by the Council should be published on the front page of the offending newspaper, and a written code of conduct for journalists should be produced. The Council should give more support to an effective right to reply, condemn journalistic misbehaviour in a more forthright way and take a stronger line on inaccuracy and bias. The Council responded to these criticisms by increasing its lay membership to half but in other respects it failed to improve its image. A study of its work published in 1983 revealed that even successful complainants were overwhelmingly critical of the services it offered.[13] Its adjudication procedures were obstacle courses and its delays in judgment ensured that any redress it provided was usually ineffectual. Its principles were confused and inconsistent, rulings were not respected and it did not work to improve the ethical standards of the British press.

A new chairperson, Louis Blom-Cooper Q.C., instituted a thor- **14–004** oughgoing review of the Council's role and function but its basic problem remained: its failure to make its Declarations of Principle stick in the absence of any effective sanction. Editors at every level defied and derided it: the *Daily Telegraph* publicly refused to abide by its ethical convention on race reporting while the *Sun* took a malicious delight in vilifying individuals who "successfully" complained about it to the Council. It was no longer serving as an insurance policy against new press laws, and in 1989 support from

---

[10] Report of the Committee on Privacy, Cmnd. 5012 (1972), para.189.
[11] Royal Commission on the Press, Cmnd. 6810 (1977), Ch.20, para.15.
[12] Royal Commission on the Press, Cmnd. 6810 (1977), para.48.
[13] Robertson, *People Against the Press*, Ch.3.

M.P.s from all parties threatened to advance the passage of a private member's bill to establish a statutory body to enforce a right of reply. The progress of this bill was halted only when the Government set up a committee chaired by David Calcutt Q.C. to respond to press intrusions and privacy.

Calcutt correctly identified the Council's central problem in terms of its contradictory claims both to safeguard press freedom and to condemn press malpractice.[14] It was this latter function that should be performed by a Press Complaints Commission, an expert body with sufficient funding to adjudicate speedily and effectively complaints by members of the public about breaches of an expanded code of practice. The Calcutt Committee was profoundly unimpressed by the cynical attitudes displayed towards the Council in the past by editors and proprietors, and it evinced no great confidence that its proposed Press Complaints Commission would be allowed to work effectively if it remained a voluntary body. So it drew up plans for a statutory complaints tribunal which would wait notionally in the wings, to be wheeled out if there was a "less than overwhelming rate of compliance" with the new Commission's adjudications.

The Calcutt "fallback" recommendation for a statutory tribunal served to concentrate the minds of newspaper proprietors. The newspaper industry, through the Newspaper Publishers' Association (representing the owners of national newspapers) and the Newspaper Society (representing owners of provincial newspapers), acted speedily to establish a Press Complaints Commission, which commenced operations in January 1991. The new body abandoned the Press Council's contentious efforts to defend press freedom and combat media monopolies; it existed solely to adjudicate complaints that editors of newspapers had infringed the published code of conduct.

14–005   The early days of the PCC were underwhelming: Calcutt, invited to report again for the Government in January 1993, recommended jettisoning voluntary self-regulation in favour of his statutory Press Complaints Tribunal with its power to injunct impending privacy breaches and to fine reckless journalists.[15] John Major's government dared not antagonise the media, especially after its exposure of David Mellor (the minister who had accused editors of "drinking in the last chance saloon") who was bugged whilst having exhaustive sexual intercourse with a "resting" actress. Despite further demands in 1993 for statutory controls by the Lord Chancellor's Department[16] and the National Heritage Select Committee,[17] and a private member's bill which failed only on its third reading, the Conservative

---

[14] *Report of the Committee on Privacy and Related Matters* (HMSO, 1990), Cmnd.1102.

[15] Sir David Calcutt, Review of Press Self-Regulation, Cm. 2135 (1993).

[16] The Lord Chancellor's Department has forcefully recommended legislating a new tort of infringement of privacy: Consultation Paper, July 1993.

[17] Report on Privacy and Media Intrusion 1992–3, H.C. 294–1.

Government compromised: afraid of alienating newspapers before a general election, it gave "self-regulation" its approval, subject to "strengthening the system still further" [sic].[18] The Labour Government in proved just as emollient, legislating s.12(4) of the Human Rights Act on the assumption that the PCC's "relevant privacy code" would be a suitable subject for judicial notice. By dint of immediate condemnations of gross invasions of royal privacy and decisions favourable to important politicians, the PCC has kept its head, although in a shape which may not be much in the interest of either the press or the public. Its 10th anniversary party, in January 2001, featured Princes Charles and William—chaperoned by Lord Wakeham, who introduced them to their tabloid tormentors with the discreet aplomb of a high-class madam. The party symbolised the inter-dependence between celebrity and paparazzi, which like that between thief and receiver, makes the relationship profitable for both unless disturbed by the law.

Lord Wakeham's tenure ended suddenly and embarrassingly with the Enron collapse. As a member of one of its accounting boards, his own ethics came into question and he left to spend more time with his lawyers. He was succeeded in 2003 by arch-diplomat Sir Christopher Meyer, who survived a spat over his own ethics (his memoirs, as serialised in the press, told some confidential stories about the Blair entourage, observed whilst he was Ambassador to the United States). He has been much less obsessed with protecting the royals and has concentrated on the Commission's most valuable work, that of developing an authoritative code of conduct and of expeditiously dealing with complaints, mostly against the provincial press. He steered the PCC through a stormy enquiry in 2003 by the Culture, Media and Sport select committee into privacy and media intrusion, from which it emerged battered but still afloat. In 1993 that select committee had recommended the PCC's abolition and replacement by Calcutt's statutory tribunal. In 2003 it made some trenchant criticisms but accepted the principle of self-regulation; it noted the PCC's improved performance and complimented it on its work in developing the Code. The problem of the PCC is not so much what it does but what it claims that what it does, does—i.e. provides an effective reddress which makes any privacy law redundant. To that extent, it has become a propagandist for the press proprietors. The front page of its website (as accessed in January 2007) proclaims

> "The success of the PCC continues to underline the strength of effective and independent self-regulation over any form of legal or statutory control. Legal controls would be useless to those members of the public who could not afford legal action—and would mean protracted delays before complainants received

---

[18] Cm. 2918 (July 1995).

redress. In our system of self-regulation, effective redress is free and quick."

This statement misleads the public. Legal redress might be available to the poor through conditional fee arrangements and a statutory body would probably be free-of-charge to complainants. In any event, it cannot be suggested that legal controls against negligence or faulty products, for example, are useless to members of the public simply because the rich may have better access to them. Invoking the law often produces immediate and effective redress, because newspapers which indefensibly err (as in defamation) will usually admit their mistake and pay compensation to avoid successful claims. And it begs the question of whether PCC redress is "effective" in serious cases where the law would provide compensation and damages but where all the PCC can do is broker an often insincere apology. By proselytising in this misleading way the PCC is falling into the trap which Calcutt identified as the flaw in the Press Council, of trying to combine a complaints function with a propagandistic role on behalf of press interests. The PCC would be much better advised to drop its campaign against the privacy law that is being developed by the judges under the spur of Article 8 of the ECHR, and to work hand in hand with the courts by accommodating their decisions to its own code in the hope that (pursuant to HRA Section 12(4)) they will return the compliment.

14–006   The PCC can no longer honourably claim that its redress (which does not even include the power to fine) is "effective" after the Euro court decision in *Peck v UK* that the sanctions available to broadcasting regulators (who did have the power to fine) were ineffective to redress the privacy violation:

> "The court finds that the lack of legal power of the commissions to award damages to the applicant means that those bodies could not provide an effective remedy to him. It notes that the ITC's power to impose a fine on the relevant television company does not amount to an award of damages to the applicant."[19]

In consequence, the United Kingdom is under a duty to develop a privacy law in which violation by press and broadcasters can result in damages and the judges, beginning with the *Naomi Campbell* case, have been doing just that. The PCC could help them and thereby play a role in the development of a privacy law which is sensitive to press freedom. However, if it maintains its hostility and continues to paint the legal process as an ineffective rival, it will jeopardise both its own integrity and the potential that s.12(4) offers of having code principles adopted by the court.

---

[19] (2003) 36 E.H.R.R. 41 at para.109.

Is the PCC reviewable?

The history sketched out above provides a clear answer: the PCC is **14–007** exercising a recognised public adjudicative function, as a government-brokered alternative either to a Calcutt-devised complaints tribunal or to a privacy law introduced by Act of Parliament. The reasoning which has led the courts to declare the ASA reviewable applies by close analogy to the PCC: it is a body "clearly exercising a public function which, if the ASA did not exist, would no doubt be exercised by (a statutory office)".[20] Moors Murderer Ian Brady and T.V. newsreader Anna Ford have attempted to review the PCC; few have regarded its decisions as important enough to quash.

> *The Sun* ran a story about Moors Murderer Ian Brady receiving inappropriate hospital treatment, which it illustrated with an indistinct photograph, unobjectionable other than that it had been taken through a tele-photo lens while he was in the hospital. This was technically a breach of the PCC privacy code (no pictures on private property without consent unless in the public interest) but the Commission made no finding because any breach would not warrant censure since the article itself had been in the public interest, and the picture had been obtained without intrusion or harassment. Brady sought judicial review, but the courts could see no basis for interfering with this decision: any breach which may have occurred was not serious and the PCC was entitled to decide that *The Sun* was not deserving of censure. The court "assumed" that the PCC was a body amenable to judicial review.[21]

In the *Brady* case Lord Woolf made clear that any exercise of jurisdiction over the PCC "would be reserved for cases where it would clearly be desirable for this court to intervene". The courts will not trip the PCC up on technicalities, but only when it makes a fundamental error of interpretation. (If, for example, the PCC had decided that Brady's crimes were so horrendous that he had forfeited all right to privacy, that decision would have been so plainly wrong it would have been quashed.) Unsatisfied complainants will have to show an irrational interpretation of the code or a decision flatly inconsistent with other precedents or else a serious misunderstanding of the facts before judicial review is likely to succeed. It may be, however, that judicial review proceedings could successfully attack some of the unfair aspects of the PCC's procedures—its refusal to give complainants a hearing or an opportunity to cross-examine editors, for example, or infringements of the Art.6 rule requiring tribunal members to be independent and impartial.

---

[20] *R. v ASA Ex p. The Insurance Service* [1990] 2 Admin. L.R. 77, *per* Glidewell L.J.
[21] *R. v PCC Ex p. Stewart-Brady* [1997] E.M.L.R. 185; followed by Silber J. in *R. v PCC Ex p. Anna Ford* (unreported), July 29, 2001.

The Complaints Procedure

14–008 The PCC operates from Holborn with a small staff and a full time Director, serving on a 16–person Complaints Committee which has been chaired since 1995 by Lord Wakeham. Seven of the Committee are newspaper and magazine editors. The full time Director is also a commissioner along with the chairman and eight other worthy citizens; including the former head of the D notice committee, a director of Camelot and a bishop ("formerly Clerk of the Closet to the Queen"). The Royal connection is appropriate, since the PCC spends a good deal of its time upholding complaints made by Buckingham Palace.[22] These public members, unrepresentative of the general population, are chosen by an appointments committee. The PCC has an all-press committee responsible for its ethical code: its membership includes editors whose ethics are constantly called into question. The operation costs about £1.6 million a year, funded by a levy on newspaper and magazine publishers. Their contributions are much less than the funding of the ASA or even of ICSTIS, and are paid out of self- interest—i.e. to finance a body which they hope will help them to stave off further legal regulation.

The PCC receives several thousand complaints each year, yet it actually adjudicates comparatively few cases (30 in 2005). It claims that it "resolves" the complains that it does not adjudicate, but one-third of these complaints were "outside its remit" while others were "made by third parties" a class of complaint which for no good reason the PCC does not accept, however grievous the breach complained about. Many complaints are settled by an editorial offer of a reply or a correction. but in the year 2005, 3,654 complaints were received and merely 30 were adjudicated. The 2005 report fudges these figures. It boasts of receiving 3,654 complaints but only 348 of these were "resolved". It does not mention what happened to the rest but presumably they were trivial or beyond the PCC's remit, which does not cover issues of taste or decency.

About 60 per cent of all complaints concern inaccuracies, with privacy infringements featuring in 15 per cent. Adjudications are short for the benefit of the paper that must publish them with "due prominence" (which generally means under a banner headline if it is cleared, but in small print on an inside page if it is criticised). Successful complainants have no right to an apology, let alone to costs or expenses or compensation—their "victory" is especially hollow in privacy cases, when the adjudication can provide an occasion for re-publicising the breach (a reason why so many victims of privacy invasions do not complain or take their case to court). The PCC has refused to adopt one of Calcutt's main recommendations, namely that it should monitor the media for breaches of its code.

---

[22] See "A Right Royal Farce", *The Observer*, April 8, 2001, p.13.

The PCC has no "hotline" procedure for intervening between the **14–009** time of code-breach (e.g. by invasion of privacy) and the time of publication. This fact alone ensures that the code is not enforced when it really matters, i.e. to prevent invasions of privacy which have no public interest justification. There is one exception, in that the PCC is always at the beck and call of Buckingham Palace. This was demonstrated in 2001 when the Countess of Wessex was caught, by a *News of the World* undercover operation, promoting her PR company on the back of her royal connection. When the Queen's private secretary learnt of the problem, three days before publication, he summoned Lord Wakeham, who came running to advise the Royal Family on how to minimise their embarrassment. He had to deny media suggestions that it was his advice that led the Countess to give a disastrous interview to *News of the World* ("SOPHIE: My Edward is NOT gay").

The Commission adjudicates complaints by reference to its 16-clause Code of Practice. It meets for half a day each month to consider rulings drawn up by the chairperson and the staff, which are subsequently published on its website. It refuses oral hearings and decides each case upon written submissions. Its adjudications will be sent, as a matter of courtesy, to parties shortly before publication, although it will not entertain any protest prior to publication. It will not consider any complaint about press conduct falling outside its written code. A particular problem is encountered in relation to complaints from individuals who might also have a legal remedy against the newspaper by suing for libel. The Press Council practice—severely criticised by Calcutt—was to extract a "legal waiver" from such individuals as a quid pro quo for the newspaper's agreement to co-operate with the Council and to publish its adjudications. This waiver was effective to bar any subsequent libel action, but only if it was expressly made and signed—a complaint to the Council did not of itself operate as an implied waiver.[23] As Calcutt pointed out, it is plainly wrong in principle that a complainant should be obliged to surrender a legal right to damages before obtaining an adjudication as to whether an ethical standard has been breached. The PCC has in theory abandoned the waiver, although it exercises a discretion to postpone any adjudication if it relates to a matter that is or may be the subject of litigation.

Any member of the public, or any organisation involved in the matter, may complain to the Commission about a breach of the Code of Practice by an editor of a newspaper or magazine. The complaint will be accepted against an editor, even if it relates to conduct by a journalist or a freelance. Complaints are forwarded to that editor, who is required to contact the complainant direct and reach an amicable settlement. If this is not achieved within a short

---

[23] *Franks v Westminster Press Ltd*, *The Times*, April 4, 1990.

time-frame, the editor will be required to provide a written response, which will be sent to the complainant with an invitation to comment. This process will continue until the issues are clear and each party has had an opportunity to deal with the other's contentions in writing. There will be no contested hearing and no opportunity for parties to cross-examine or to discover the other side's documents.

14–010   The PCC staff, in consultation with the chairman, produce a draft adjudication which is despatched to Council members who will communicate their agreement. Draft adjudications that evoke disagreement are debated and finalised at the monthly Commission meeting. The defending editor is under no duty to publish favourable adjudications, although these are often reported as triumphs for free speech or in ways that belittle unsuccessful complainants. However, the Code preamble insists that "Any publication which is criticised by the PCC must print the adjudication in full and with due prominence". The PCC does not indicate what prominence is "due" and does not monitor compliance. A typical example is the privacy complaint upheld on behalf of *Coronation Street* actress Jacqueline Pirie, whose private life was splashed, without a shred of public interest, over the *News of the World* in January 2000. The PCC adjudication criticising the newspaper was published three months later, in small print and surrounded by advertisements, on p.40 of the offending paper.[24] It is difficult to understand how this could amount to a prominence that was "due", either to the victim or proportionately to the publicity given to the original story.

In 2005, stung by constant criticism of its refusal to oversee editorial decisions about where "prominently" to print its adjudications, the PCC announced, under the headline "Prominence—a Myth Exposed" that 25 per cent of the "corrections and apologies" that resulted from its rulings appeared on the same page as the original article, 22 per cent in a dedicated "corrections" column and 34 per cent further forward than the original article.[25] These bland statistics do not, however, answer the criticism or expose any "myth": they do not apply to critical adjudications which tend to be "buried", like that relating to Ms Pirie. And they say nothing about "prominence" or whether it was proportional: corrections printed in small typeface, or obscure in terms of the page layout, hardly redress a falsehood published under a banner headline or as the peg for a full-page character assassination.

14–011   The PCC is defensive, and sometimes devious, about the defects in its procedure. For example, it tries to deter complainants from using lawyers ("complaints involving solicitors tend to take longer to be concluded, without noticeable improvement in the results") although it is noticeable from studying PCC rulings that complainants who succeed are frequently represented by law firms. It does not

---

[24] *News of the World*, April 9, 2000, p.40.
[25] Annual Review, 2005, Press Complaints Commission, p.10.

tell complainants in terms that they will have no right to confront editors or journalists, or that the "investigation" will be no more than an exchange of letters. In these *"Frequently Asked Questions"* on its website[26] it goes to extravagant lengths to defend its practice of refusing to investigate even the most blatant ethical breaches of its code unless the complaint is from the victim. It even asserts, bizarrely, that "the commission could arguably breach someone's privacy under the Human Rights Act by insisting on investigating an article about them without their consent". It claims that a critical adjudication "is a far greater deterrent than a fine", a proposition that defies commonsense and which is developed by misstating the position in France and in the European Court of Human Rights. This is all tendentious proselytising, which only serves to reduce the PCC's authority. In a section headed "Philosophical Advice" it answers the question "**Why should I use the PCC rather than the courts?**" with four reasons:

1. *It is absolutely free.* (And can be absolutely ineffective. It does not explain that court actions can sometimes be brought on legal aid and often with conditional fee agreements).
2. *It is fast—on average seven weeks Legal actions can last several years.* (They can also last a matter of days or weeks, if the newspaper sensibly settles, immediately, an indefensible case.)
3. *There is no risk.* (And no gain. No damages, no compensation, no injunction. And there is the risk that the newspaper will hold you up to ridicule. Or else may deduce, from the fact that you have gone to the PCC rather than to court, that you lack the resolve or the evidence to fight, or have something to hide, and so they will continue to harass you.)
4. *It is private. A court action will, in most circumstances lead to full disclosure.* (Not so: claimants in breach of confidence/privacy actions may have their names withheld, as they may in a privacy adjudication. They will, however, be able to discover all relevant newspaper documents and confront the editor and journalist—advantages they will not have in the PCC paper process.)

The PCC does not need to make these bogus arguments, or hold itself out as a superior system to legal redress. Plainly, as the ECHR implied in *Peck's* case, it does not offer effective redress and it should not persist in pretending that it does. What it does offer is a conciliation service, and that (as the courts now recognise) is a valuable first step in resolving most disputes. Indeed, under the rules

---

[26] *www.pcc.org.uk/faqs/index.html*, accessed December 4, 2006.

of court for civil cases it is an essential first step, and in the early stages of any privacy claim against a newspaper it is likely that the court will invite the parties to try PCC conciliation before the action goes further. It offers this important service which resolves many minor claims and a few important cases which the claimant does not want to bring the court. But it is wrong and damaging for its own reputation for the PCC to keep running this campaign against the courts, in what may well be perceived as an effort to please its paymasters, the newspaper proprietors with an interest in avoiding actions for damages.

The Code of Practice

14–012 The PCC Code has emerged from a number of sources. Much of the language is adapted from the Calcutt Committee's draft, in turn influenced by a series of Press Council "Declarations of Principle" issued over the 36 years of its operation, developed and refined at times by major adjudications or reports. The PCC pays some attention to these precedents but it claims that the Code derives its influence from the fact that it is regularly reviewed by a group of senior editors on its Code Committee, which is chaired by Les Hinton, the widely respected executive chairman of News International Plc. The Code provisions are:

1. Accuracy

  (i) **The press must take care not to publish inaccurate, misleading or distorted information, including pictures.**
  (ii) **A significant inaccuracy, misleading statement or distortion, it must be corrected promptly and with due prominence, and an apology published.**
  (iv) **Newspapers, whilst free to be partisan, must distinguish clearly between comment, conjecture and fact.**
  (v) **A newspaper or periodical must report fairly and accurately the outcome of an action for defamation to which it has been a party", unless an agreed statement states otherwise or an agreed statement is published.**

These are "motherhood" provisions which need little elucidation. Most complaints are about inaccuracies, which are easily put right by prompt and prominent corrections. There is no definition of "due prominence": the PCC should insist upon a correction being carried with a prominence, in terms of reader impact, similar to that of the original publication. (Reader impact must be judged from the typeface, layout and wording of the two items.) The PCC does not have the investigative or forensic resources to decide whether a story is false, and should not be regarded as a tribunal for establishing the truth. It will depend on the newspaper to admit error, or else insist that the complainant establish falsity by producing documentary evidence. Otherwise, it maintains that "it is not the Commission's job to establish the facts of the matter when two parties dispute the accuracy of an article but to consider, under the Code, whether sufficient care has been taken by a newspaper not to publish inaccurate material".[27] This is *not* a rule against inaccuracy, but a rule that newspapers should think twice before publishing allegations they cannot prove. Journalists accused of "inventing" quotations will be expected to have kept their notebooks, but the PCC never insists that they be submitted to an ESDA test. Editors cannot rely on having given the complainant an opportunity to correct the story unless that has been a real and considered opportunity,[28] and in the case of some stories (such as sexual gossip) editors cannot rely on a refusal to comment as corroboration.[29]

The PCC will, however, conduct its own investigation into a **14–013** complaint if the complainant is sufficiently important. When the Prime Minister and his wife alleged that *The Mail on Sunday* had breached the Code by a story about their daughter whom it alleged had jumped the queue to attend a new school, the PCC took pains to establish the facts. There had in fact been no preferential treatment for the Prime Minister's daughter, although some parents honestly believed the contrary: the paper should not have published their speculation in a manner which suggested it was well-founded.[30] This ruling was a valuable exercise in fact-finding which served to put the record straight; it is not a service vouchsafed to many others who complain of inaccuracy. But when complaints are made by Buckingham Palace, the PCC loyally accepts the Queen's evidence:

> The Queen complained that her wealth had been greatly exaggerated by *Business Age* magazine, which had placed her at the top of its "RICH 500". The magazine explained that it had included not only her racehorses and shareholdings, worth £158 million, but some art treasures, jewellery and palaces which brought her assets up to £2.2 billion. The magazine added, truthfully, that its estimate of what she owned in her own right "was a matter of legal argument" and that "royal retainers are willing to go to remarkable lengths to minimise estimates of the monarch's personal wealth". The lengths included a letter to the PCC by her Press Secretary, who complained that the Queen's personal income was "a private matter" and in any event it did not exceed £100 million: the magazine had failed to check with the Palace before publication. The magazine defended its estimate at length and requested an oral hearing to present expert legal and

---

[27] *Macleod v Sunday Mail*, Report No. 52, January 24, 2001.
[28] See *Bernie Grant M.P. v The Times* PCC Report No. 2, 1991, p.24 (message left on victim's answering machine inviting him to call the newspaper was not a sufficient check for accuracy).
[29] *Calthorpe v Sunday Express*, PCC Report No. 50, July 27, 2000.
[30] *Blair v The Mail on Sunday*, PCC Report No. 47, October 27, 1999.

accounting evidence and to question the royal estimates. This was refused: the PCC, in a decision conspicuous for its unfairness and partiality, found the magazine in breach of the Code because it had not reported sufficiently the basis for its valuation, and had "presented speculation as established fact". This was manifestly wrong, since the journal had made plain to readers that its valuation was open to legal dispute—a dispute which the PCC royally refused to entertain.[31]

The rule that newspapers must report the outcome of defamation actions to which they are a party is an unnecessary fetter both on editorial discretion and a newspaper's legal tactics in libel actions. When a paper settles, as many do, for "commercial" reasons (i.e. merely to avoid legal costs) there is no reason why they should report the outcome unless this is made a term of the settlement.[32] There is no reason to restrain a newspaper from attacking an adverse defamation verdict. The PCC in 2004 rejected a complaint from Kimberley Fortier (*Spectator* publisher and Blunkett *inamorata*) that her privacy had been invaded by photographs taken whilst she was walking along a street in Los Angeles. It made clear that it "does not generally consider that the publication of photographs of people in public places breached the Code. Exceptions might be made if there are particular security concerns, for instance, or in the rare circumstances where a photograph reveals something about an individual's health that is not in the public interest." It was prepared to uphold a complaint from Allegra Versace about photographs in a magazine which had illustrated something about the state of her health. The PCC describes these badly argued decisions as "commonsensical" but they provide little precedential guidance.

2. Opportunity to Reply

14–014   **A fair opportunity to reply to inaccuracies must be given to individuals or organisations when reasonably called for.**

This is not the fabled "right of reply" but a mere opportunity, limited to replies to factual inaccuracies. It is regrettable that the newspaper industry should fudge a principle of basic fairness, noncompliance with which has been a major issue of public dissatisfaction with the British press. Rule 2 marks a retreat from the Press Council's principle that a right of reasonable reply should be provided to any "attack" on an individual or organisation, and from the draft Calcutt code, which called for "a proportional and reasonable right to reply to *criticisms or alleged inaccuracies*" [our italics]. Rule 2 permits the editor to be the judge of what amounts to an

---

[31] *The Queen v Business Age* (1998) PCC Report No. 34, pp.5–8.
[32] See *Givenchy SA v Time Out*, Report No. 46, July 28, 1999, where the PCC acknowledges the inappropriateness of the rule by declining to censure *Time Out*.

"inaccuracy", and implies that it may be reasonable to refuse an opportunity to put right a published misstatement of fact. Editors should always offer to publish letters from persons severely criticised by way of comment or conjecture, or by factual statements that cannot be verified but that the complainant alleges to be untrue. That said, there are genuine difficulties in deciding whether a published reply is "reasonably called for". Press Council precedents have held that no right of reply arises where the attack is contained in a news report of a speech by a third party, or where the person seeking to reply has threatened or commenced a libel action against the newspaper, or where the reply submitted is overlong or contains defamatory attacks on the newspaper's employees, or where an opportunity to reply has already been afforded in the original story.[33]

3. Privacy

> **Everyone is entitled to respect for his or her private and family life, home, health and correspondence. A publication will be expected to justify intrusions into any individual's private life without consent.** 14–015

This key provision, given legal import in breach of confidence cases by s.12(4) of the Human Rights Act, begins with a statement of the right to privacy guaranteed by Art.8(1) of the ECHR. Any intrusion must be "justified"—but on what basis? The PCC adopts a different standard, which requires any infringement to be: (i) in accordance with law; (ii) pursuant to a legitimate aim; and (iii) necessary and proportionate to the interests of public safety, health or morality, the prevention of crime, or the rights of others in a democratic society. Under the Code, editors have an easier task: their infringements may be justified "in the public interest", defined (for the purposes of this and other sections of the Code) as *including* (i.e. not limited to):

- (i) **detecting or exposing crime or serious impropriety;**
- (ii) **protecting public health and safety;**
- (iii) **preventing the public from being misled by a statement or action of an individual or organisation.**

The infringement of a child's privacy calls for an *exceptional public interest* justification.

The Code formulation of the privacy principle and the public interest defence (together with its associated rules relating to harassment, intrusion into grief and shock, hospitals and listening devices) are likely to feature in common law developments of privacy through the doctrine of breach of confidence.

---

[33] See Robertson, *People Against the Press*, pp.79–88 (above, fn.1).

14–016   It was because Earl and Countess Spencer had failed to sue tabloid newspapers for breach of confidence that the European Commission of Human Rights rejected their complaint that the United Kingdom insufficiently protected privacy:

> In 1995, the *News of the World* published a front page article, "DI'S SISTER IN BOOZE AND BULIMIA CLINIC", which contained details of family problems and illnesses illustrated with a telephoto picture of the applicant captioned "SO THIN: Victoria walks in the clinic grounds this week". The applicants complained to the PCC, which judged that the paper had breached s.3 (ii) of the Code (see below). The newspaper apologiscd (but only to the Countess) and published the adjudication. Nonetheless, the applicants complained to Strasbourg that they could not obtain any "effective remedy" in the United Kingdom. The European Commission noted that although newspapers were bound to print adjudications with due prominence "the PCC has no legal power to prevent publication of material, to enforce its ruling or to grant any legal remedy against the newspaper in favour of the victim". For those reasons the PCC could not be considered an "effective remedy", and the UK Government did not even attempt to argue that it was. The Spencers were wrong-suited, however, because they had failed to go to court to obtain one available remedy, namely an injunction and damages under the developing civil law of breach of confidence.[34]

Although the PCC claims in its advertising material that it offers an "effective remedy" for breaches of privacy, the *Spencer* case shows that neither the Government nor Strasbourg consider that this claim is true.

It is noteworthy that the code is confined to an individual's private life and offers no protection to individuals in their business capacity or to any public or private company, unless subject to unjustifiable subterfuge or harassment. The justification for invasion of privacy must be based on specific public interest: it cannot be contended that press revelation of adultery or homosexuality or run-of-the-mill heterosexual behaviour qualifies, unless the victims are hypocrites. There is alack of clarity in the phrase "serious impropriety": it did not appear in the Calcutt draft, but was inserted by newspaper interests as something that might, in addition to "crime", be properly exposed through invasion of privacy. The excuse of "preventing the public from being misled by some statement or action of that individual" permits the press to invade the privacy of public figures who have acted contrary to their professed beliefs, so stories about adulterous vicars, politicians, and the like are justified under this exception.

14–017   The PCC has consistently condemned "kiss and tell" (more accurately, "kiss and sell") stories about celebrities and soap stars which are a staple of the British tabloids. These breach Rule 3 of the

---

[34] *Earl and Countess Spencer v UK* Application No. 28851/95, [1998] E.M.L.R. CD 105; and see *Spencers v News of the World*, PCC Report No.29 (1995), p.60.

Code because they reveal intimate personal details (what the "star" is like in bed) without any trace of public interest. Granada Television regularly takes up cudgels on behalf of *Coronation Street* actresses whose sexual performances are luridly related by well-paid former boyfriends: editors offer humbug defences (they were upholding the ex-lover's "right" to free speech; for actors, all publicity is good publicity) which are routinely held to fall short of any "public interest" defence.[35] The editors are usually censured, and continue to publish similar stories about other celebrities, most of whom are advised that it is pointless to complain to the PCC. The proven inability of the PCC to stamp out this genre of privacy invasion gives the lie to its claim that its Code is honoured by British editors.

Determinations under s.3(1) of the Code will depend on the circumstances of the particular case. The PCC is at heart a public relations operation, and in the hysterical aftermath of Diana's death (in a car crash at first wrongly attributed to menacing paparazzi) some amendments were made to the Code to assuage public anger:

> **3(ii) It is unacceptable to photograph individuals in private places without their consent.**
> **Note: Private places are public or private property where there is a reasonable expectation of privacy.**

What constitutes "a reasonable expectation of privacy" has been the subject of a number of conflicting decisions, some plainly influenced by the status of the complainant. What principle, for example, underlies the following two rulings?

> Prince William was photographed hiking on a public trail and fording a river at a public crossing, during his "gap year" in Chile. The pictures were published as part of a hagiography in *OK!* magazine. Buckingham Palace complained, and the PCC decided the Code was breached because "Prince William was on a trip to a place where he had a reasonable expectation of privacy". It additionally condemned *OK!* for "making the Prince's life more uncomfortable" and for "harassment"—although there was not the slightest evidence that the photographer had come near the Prince. But when the Palace calls, the PCC jumps, even to conclusions: "William was not in a place where photographers would normally have been and must, therefore, have been followed by foreign paparazzi".[36]

> Moors Murderer Ian Brady was photographed in the grounds of a hospital. He was in a police van, about to be driven to another hospital (the curtains had been "left open"—doubtless by pre-arrangement—so

---

[35] See *Pirie* case, above, and *Granada TV and Taylor v Sunday Sport*, PCC Report No. 51, October 25, 2000, Case 1.

[36] *HRH Prince William v OK! Magazine* PCC Report No.52, January 24, 2001, Decision No.3.

a picture could be taken). The PCC ruled that since "the picture was taken in an area of the hospital grounds which was open to the public" the complaint failed.[37]

14–018 The true distinction between these two decisions is not that between the wilderness of South America and the confines of an English mental hospital, it is between a much-loved Prince and a much-loathed child murderer. What weighs with the PCC is the nature of the person rather than the nature of the place. Thus the Aga Khan, a royal and a spiritual leader of millions, had a "reasonable expectation of privacy" whilst sunbathing on his luxury yacht at the height of a Mediterranean summer (No "Highness" can be expected to go below decks).[38]

Anna Ford, a mere BBC newsreader, had no such expectation when she and her companion were targeted by telephoto lens whilst sunbathing on their private hotel beach in Majorca.[39] Ms Ford could hardly have expected to be stalked by two paparazzi or that their sneak pictures would appear in colour in a national newspaper, prompting poison pen letters. When Ms Ford becomes Dame or Baroness, doubtless the PCC will uphold her complaints as it does for knighted pop stars: Sir Elton John's privacy was invaded by pictures of guests "relaxing" at his home in the South of France, even though the pictures were taken from a public footpath,[40] and Sir Paul McCartney was unaccountably held to have suffered a loss of privacy by being pictured in *Hello!* walking with his children by the banks of the Seine and eating lunch outside a café. (The publication of a further photograph, as he lit a candle inside Notre Dame Cathedral, was rightly found to be "deeply intrusive".)[41] What the PCC is attempting to do by this anti-paparazzi rule is to enforce a prohibition which at the time went beyond legal requirements. It does so inconsistently. Privacy can reasonably be expected in cemeteries, churches and changing rooms, but not whilst fording rivers or sitting in street-cafés or lounging in hotel lobbies.

Occasionally the PCC suggests that the *tone* of the picture might be relevant, although as a matter of logic the existence of a breach cannot depend on whether the result is unflattering (in law, this would go to damages, not liability). Sometimes a "public interest" defence is applied by association with the text (the Brady picture illustrated an article which *was* in the public interest, concerning his suicide attempt). Although the inside of a public servant's office is

---

[37] *Stewart-Brady v Liverpool Echo and The Mirror*, PCC Report No.49, April 26, 2000, Case No.10.

[38] *His Highness the Aga Khan v Daily Mail*, PCC Report No.46, p.10.

[39] *Anna Ford v Daily Mail and OK!*, PCC Report No.52, January 24, 2001, Case No.5. The High Court declined Ms Ford leave to review the decision: *R. v PCC Ex p. Anna Ford*, July 29, 2001, unreported.

[40] *Elton John v Daily Star*, PCC Report No.45, April 28, 1999, p.7.

[41] *Sir Paul McCartney v Hello*, PCC Report No.43, November 4, 1998, p.12.

protected, there is no reasonable expectation of privacy in a private club for sadomasochists—or anywhere else that undercover *News of the World* reporters might wish to frequent.[42]

4. Harassment

   (i) **Journalists must not engage in intimidation, harassment or** **14–019** **persistent pursuit.**

  (ii) **They must not persist in telephoning, questioning, pursuing or photographing individuals after having been asked to desist; nor remain on their property once asked to leave and must not follow them.**

 (iii) **Editors must ensure that these principles are observed by those working for them and must take care not to use non-compliant material from other sources.**

These post-Diana amendments are directed at foreign and freelance paparazzi, whose activities they have not in any way curbed. Editors are repeatedly ticked off for purchasing snatched or long-lens photographs, but the menace of snappers in hot pursuit has only been stopped effectively in California (by a criminal law which has put several British photographers in jail) and in New York, where a tort action for damages brought by Jacqueline Onassis was held compatible with the First Amendment. The PCC Code fails to draw a sensible line between public figures who genuinely wish to protect their privacy and those who wish to protect it only after they have exhausted the prospect of favourable publicity. The advent of celebrities—Diana herself was one—who invade their own (or their husband's) privacy and complain if they dislike the results (or were found out) make such distinctions important. One particularly unpleasant form of indirect harassment, namely the publication of addresses of a person against whom readers might seek reprisals, has not been consistently censured. The *Evening Standard* was condemned as irresponsible for publishing the address of a well-known Englishman's holiday home in Wales in an article about burning down such houses.[43] But the *New Nation* was not censured when it published the addresses of the suspects for the Stephen Lawrence murder, in a column suggesting that readers might like to visit them "to enhance their facial features".[44] Is the inconsistency explained by the fact that the Lawrence suspects are violent racists, while the English country gentleman was a former chairman of the Press Council? His case provides the correct precedent, and in 2005 security concerns were sufficient for the PCC to condemn publication of a picture of the home of J.K. Rowling.

---

[42] *Desyre Foundation v News of the World*, PCC Report No.48, January 26, 2000, p.11.

[43] *Sir Louis Blom-Cooper v The Evening Standard*, PCC Report No.7 (1992).

[44] *Norris et al v New Nation*, PCC Report No.45, April 28, 1999, pp.16–17.

5. *Intrusion into grief or shock*

14–020   **In cases involving grief or shock, enquiries and approaches must be made with sympathy and discretion and publication handled sensitively. This should not be restrict the right to report legal proceedings.**

Clause 5 waters down a key clause in the Calcutt draft, which expressed the view that the press should not intrude unsolicited into personal grief or shock, especially after accidents and tragedies, unless justified by exposure of crime or anti-social behaviour or to protect public health and safety. Quite plainly, the press is not, as an industry, prepared to hold its hand on these occasions, save to offer "sympathy and discretion" to the newly breaved it continues to besiege in efforts to obtain tear-jerking "human interest" stories. This is an area where the Press Council was notably ineffective in curbing media misbehaviour. Professor Harry Bedson's suicide was partly attributed by the Coroner to press harassment after an outbreak of smallpox in his Birmingham University Department. The Council declared that people under stress as a result of bereavement or involvement in a public crisis should not be put under pressure by the press.[45] In 1983 it was driven to conclude that both Peter Sutcliffe's wife and the relatives of his victims were harassed by the media "ferociously and callously".[46] Yet in 1989 it had once again to condemn many newspapers for callous and intrusive behaviour in reporting the Hillsborough tragedy. The PCC, "enforcing" the weasel words of cl.5, has had no more success in mitigating the distress press inquiries cause after major tragedies. Calcutt's recommendation was that editors should be held responsible for unjustifiable decisions to dispatch reporters in the first place; cl.5 is drafted in a way that assumes they will dispatch reporters, and will attract only vicarious criticism if the reporters they dispatch act insensitively.

The PCC has repeatedly defended the right of journalists to "doorstep" families in crisis, especially when their children are missing, presumed dead. Censure is reserved for those occasions when an "insensitive" reporter actually breaks news of the death to family and friends,[47] or harasses them for interviews.[48] A more difficult problem is encountered over editorial decisions to publish close-up pictures of victims of rail and car crashes: here the complaints of shocked relatives tend to be brushed aside on the ground that the Code does not cover tasteless or offensive photographs, although this will not have been the point of the complaint.[49]

---

[45] Press Council, *People Under Pressure*, 1980.
[46] Press Council, *Press Conduct in the Sutcliffe Case*, Ch.18, para.22.
[47] As in *Mckeown v Evening Chronicle*, PCC Report No.40, January 28, 1998.
[48] *Ajayi v New Nation*, PCC Report No.52, January 24, 2001, Case 7.
[49] See *Telford v Lancaster Guardian*, PCC Report No. 50, July 26, 2000, Case 7; *Salisbury v Lancaster Evening Post*, PCC Report No. 51, October 25, 2000, Case 7.

A public interest defence will normally succeed where the photograph makes a political point, e.g. about the inadequacies of the NHS, even though it identifies the sick or dying and invades the privacy of hospital patients.[50] One newspaper avoided censure for publishing pictures of a mentally ill man jumping off a railway bridge situated directly opposite the editor's office, from where the photographs were taken. This had been a tragic but public news event, gathering a crowd and lasting several hours, and the distress to the suicide's family was not covered by cl.5 of the Code.

8. Hospitals

(i) **Journalists must identify themselves and obtain permission** 14–021
    from a responsible executive and obtain permission before
    entering non-public areas of hospitals or similar institu-
    tions to pursue enquiries.

(ii) **The restrictions on intruding into privacy are particularly**
     relevant to enquires about individuals in hospitals or
     similar institutions.

Unless, that is, the inquiries are into a Moors murderer, Denis Nielson or any other "psycho" (in tabloid speak), in which case the PCC will readily find a public interest excuse (e.g. to question the appropriateness of his treatment or the possibility of his public release).[51] The ease with which hospitals may be infiltrated came to public attention during the last days of television personality Russell Harty, when reporters in white coats and wearing stethoscopes obtained access to his medical notes and the occupants of other beds in his terminal ward were besieged with bouquets of flowers in which requests for an update on his condition were hidden.[52] Clause 9 was adopted following the outrageous behaviour of a *Sunday Sport* journalist and photographer who sneaked into actor Gorden Kaye's hospital room to "interview" him as he was coming round from brain surgery—behaviour which led the Court of Appeal to call for a statutory privacy law Decisions of this kind will need reconsideration after the 2004 decision of the European Court in *Peck v UK*, which forbade the broadcasting of pictures of an attempted suicide. Although the privacy interest there protected was that of the survivor, Art.8 covers family privacy and may in such cases extend to grieving relatives.

10. Clandestine Devices and Subterfuge

1. **The press must not seek to obtain or publish material** 14–022
   acquired by using hidden cameras or clandestine listening
   devices; or by intercepting private or mobile telephone calls,

---

[50] *Harrison v Daily Mail*, PCC Report No. 46, July 28, 1999, pp.15.

[51] See *Brown v The Sun*, PCC Report No. 47, October 27, 1999, pp.20.

[52] The bouquet delivered to the bedside with a calling card message to contact a reporter remains a common subterfuge: see *Taylor v Sunday Mercury*, PCC Report No.49, April 26, 2000, Case 13.

> messages or emails; or by the unauthorised removal of
> documents or photographs
>
> 2. **Engaging in misrepresentation or subterfuge can generally
> be justified only in the public interest and then only when
> the material cannot be obtained by other means.**

This rule overlaps with the criminal law, as Clive Goodman, the
News of the World's "Royal Reporter" discovered to his cost when he
was jailed for three months in 2007. He pleaded guilty to offences
related to intercepting messages from the royal princes, and his co-
conspirator had intercepted messages left for a number of other
public figures. It was notable how widespread this practice obviously
was, and the PCC's regular claim to have deterred it became
laughable. In 2003, in upholding a complaint from Peter Foster that
his private telephone conversations had been intercepted and published, the Commission had ruled that "eavesdropping into private
telephone conversations is one of the most serious forms of physical
intrusions into privacy . . . the Commission expects a very strong
public interest justification".[53] The Clive Goodman case demonstrated the utter triviality of the information Goodwin was prepared
to breach this rule in order to obtain.

Journalists who remove documents or photographs without the
consent of the owner run the risk of conviction for theft, unless they
can prove an intention to return them. Subterfuge is a common and
sometimes necessary technique. When one of the social workers
criticised for over-zealousness in the Cleveland child abuse inquiry
set up a practice to counsel adult victims, a *Daily Mail* reporter
pretended to be such a victim in order to gather information about
her methods. This subterfuge was approved by the PCC in the
interests of "protecting public health", although the paper had no
evidence (and failed to obtain any) that the counselling service was
unprofessional.[54] On this basis, journalists could use subterfuge to
test the advice of any professional person, whether or not it was
controversial. The distinguished psychiatrist Dr Pamela Connolly has
found undercover tabloid reporters in her Los Angeles consulting
rooms, complaining (perhaps accurately) of their own sexual dys-
function, in the hope of writing about their treatment at the hands of
the wife of Billy Connolly. The PCC has failed to make clear that
this kind of behaviour is unacceptable.

14–023   Subterfuge is, in fact, becoming an increasingly productive tabloid
technique. In 2001 the PCC somewhat unnecessarily censured *News
of the World* when two of its journalists "crashed" a party for the cast
of *Emmerdale* at a private hotel, carrying covert video equipment,
even though the journalists left before they were spotted and no
story was published. But no censure—only news attention and

---

[53] PCC Review of the Year, 2003, p.7.
[54] *Sue Richardson v Mail on Sunday*, PCC Report No.2 (1991), p.15.

increased circulation—followed when a reporter dressed as an Arab engaged in an expensive charade to hoodwink Sophie Rhys-Jones and her business partner into offering her royal connections for the promise of large sums of money. Whether this was really in the public interest the PCC declined to investigate: it had in any event been hopelessly compromised by Lord Wakeham's attempts to assist the palace before the story was published.

The same reporter was criticised by several judges in 2006 when cases in which he was a prosecution witness and which were largely based on his "investigations" by way of subterfuge into alleged criminal operations, collapsed. Despite the waste of public money and the the allegations made against *News of the World* in court, the PCC stuck its head in the sand and declined to investigate. George Galloway MP took more robust action after this journalist had tried to entrap him: he put Mr Mahmood's picture on his website so that other potential victims might be forewarned. The journalist sued, but the court declined to order Galloway to remove the photograph.

6. *Children*

(i) **Young people should be free to complete their time at school without unnecessary intrusion.** 14–024

(ii) **A child under 16 must not be interviewed or photographed on issues involving their own or another child's welfare unless a custodial parent or similarly responsible adult consents.**

(iii) **Pupils must not be approached or photographed while at school without the permission of the school authorities.**

(iv) **There must be no payment to minors for material involving the welfare of children nor payment to parents or guardians for material about their children or wards unless it is clearly in the child's interest.**

(v) **Editors must not use the fame, notoriety or position of a parent or guardian as sole justification for publishing details of a child's private life.**

Although this section of the code notionally applies to infants, the PCC sensibly permits stories which relate more to the public life of the infant's parents (such as the prime ministerial adviser who left his eight-month-old baby in the care of an attendant at the Groucho Club[55]). It censored the *Daily Sport* for publishing a photograph of the Prime Minister's son kissing a dance partner at a private ball, although what was really objectionable was the dishonest caption ("Horny Blair") rather than the photo, which was not in fact a breach of cl.6(ii) since dancing is hardly "a subject involving the

---

[55] *Holm v Mail on Sunday*, PCC Report No.51, October 25, 2000, Case 3.

welfare of the child".[56] Interestingly, the photographs in this case were hawked around national newspapers before they found a buyer in the *Daily Sport*: an indication that the mainstream press will sometimes exercise a restraint over and above code requirements, at least towards the children of famous people they like (or, alternatively, fear). However, when the PCC condemned *The People* for publishing a covert picture of the Duke of York's baby daughter frolicking naked in the garden, the paper republished the picture alongside a picture of the naked Duke of York, and invited readers to participate in a telephone poll over whether either or both pictures were offensive.[57]

A major part of the PCC's work involves protection of the Royal princes. This is the only subject on which it is prepared to monitor press coverage: its Annual Review has a special section entitled *The Royal Princes* (more recently *Prince William—Life after School*) and it has from time to time, unbidden, issued long statements instructing the media on how to behave ("editors should continue to err on the side of caution . . . it is far better that matters proceed by agreement and consent between editors and the Palace"[58]). Complaints by Buckingham Palace are immediately taken up with editors and with their proprietors, and are quickly resolved to the Palace's satisfaction. Lord Wakeham would act, in effect, as the royal press agent, brokering photo opportunities (e.g. William's "coming out" at the PCC's 10th anniversary party) and mediating between tabloid editors and the Palace to ensure a coverage which burnishes their image and partly satisfies the demand for royal gossip. This lickspittle tradition has been less in evidence since Lord Wakeham's departure. The royal princes are now old enough to look after themselves.

7. Children in Sex Cases

14–025
1. The press must not, even if legally free to do so, identify children under 16 who are victims or witnesses in cases involving sex offences.
2. In any press report of a case involving a sexual offence against a child

    i. The child must not be identified
    ii. The adult may be identified;
    iii. The word "incest" must not be used where a child victim might be identified;
    iv. Care must be taken that nothing in the report implies the relationship between the accused and the child.

---

[56] *Blair v Daily Sport*, PCC Report No.79, April 26, 2000, Case 1.
[57] PCC Report No.1 (1991), p.16.
[58] Statement on Reporting the Royal Princes, PCC Report No.46, July 28, 1999.

These clauses are well intentioned, although they enjoin editors to show more restraint than is required by an exceedingly complex and comprehensive law governing court reporting. (See Ch.8, *Reporting the Courts*. The Code usefully summarises the legal principles, although in general terms they do not account for exceptions: child witnesses can sometimes be named, for example, and it is permissible to name the child victim of a sex attack who has died in consequence of it.)[59] The word "incest" may not be used if a parent is identified as the offender. The main problem is "jigsaw identification", where the anonymous child will be readily identified if the defendant's name and the relationship is given or bracketed with the word "incest". The present convention—to give the defendant's name but omit reference to "incest"—is a sensible compromise which gives correct priority to naming the defendant, at the cost of some obfuscation about the crime. The effect of compliance with cl.7 may be to protect, undeservedly, adult offenders who are related to the child, and whose name might have to be suppressed in order to avoid the child's identification. In such cases, at least if the law permits, the code may be breached on public interest grounds, although it emphasises that:

> **In cases involving children under 16 editors must demonstrate an exceptional public interest to override the normally paramount interests of the child.**

The laws which restrict court reporting are elaborate and under constant review (i.e. extension) by Parliament: the PCC should be cautious about censuring editors for publications which the law allows. Ethical sensitivity harks back to a notorious case in 1986 when the *Sun* published, over three full columns on its front page, a picture of the victim of a rape at an Ealing vicarage, taken as she was leaving her church the following Sunday. The victim's family told the Press Council that the thin black line masking her eyes still left no doubt of her identity and the *Sun*'s coverage had been deeply distressing. The Council condemned the newspaper for taking and publishing the photograph: "Both were insensitive and wholly unwarranted intrusions into privacy at a time of deep distress for the subject and neither served any public interest." The *Sun* showed no remorse. Its managing editor told the Council, with more than the usual display of humbug, that the newspaper had a duty to present rape as sordid crime and the picture was published to highlight the victim's "ordinary, girl-next-door qualities".[60] Public outrage at the newspaper's conduct produced a law that now prohibits the media from publishing any picture of an alleged rape victim from the moment a complaint has been made, and this prohibition lasts for

---

[59] See *Re S* [2005] 1 A.C. 593.
[60] Press Council, *The Press and the People*, 1987, p.241.

her lifetime—even if the complaint is not pursued or the man complained against is acquitted.[61]

Chequebook journalism

14–026 Press payments to criminals, their associates and their relatives have long been a feature of the coverage of sensational trials. In the days before legal aid was routinely granted to defendants charged with murder, newspapers hired fashionable Q.C.s to defend accused persons facing the death sentence, in return for "exclusives" from them and their about-to-be-bereaved families. The practice of paying "blood money" in any form for such stories was widely condemned in the aftermath of the "Yorkshire Ripper" prosecution, and the Press Council forbade the practice in a detailed declaration after its inquiries revealed a host of unedifying offers of money by editors of national newspapers to friends and relatives of Peter Sutcliffe. Many years later, the same vice of payments to witnesses threatened to undermine the prosecution case against Rosemary West, who collaborated with her husband in committing perverted murders. In 1979, Liberal leader Jeremy Thorpe was acquitted of conspiracy to murder because of the behaviour of the *Sunday Telegraph* in suborning the main witness with a payment of £25,000 and a promise of a further post-trial payment of £25,000 if his evidence secured Thorpe's conviction. Twenty years later, the *News of the World* bore a heavy responsibility for the acquittal of Gary Glitter on indecent assault charges by a similar "jackpot on conviction" contract. The trial judge told the jury:

> "Here is a witness who first made public her allegations of sex abuse in return for the payment of £10,000 and who stands to make another £25,000 if you convict the defendant on any of the charges. That is a clearly reprehensible state of affairs. It is not illegal, but it is greatly to be deprecated."[62]

Had such conditional offers been outlawed after the *Thorpe* trial, the *News of the World* editor might have been jailed rather than slapped on the wrist by the PCC. The issue came to a head after payments were revealed to witnesses in the course of the trial of school teacher Amy Gehring in 2002, and in consequence the Lord Chancellor's department announced that it would introduce a new criminal law to cover the matter. The PCC leapt into action and persuaded the Lord Chancellor that by strengthening the wording of its code, a more satisfactory position could be reached. In consequence, cl.15 now reads:

---

[61] Criminal Justice Act 1988, s.158, supplemented by the Sexual Offences Amendment Act 1992 and now consolidated in the Sexual Offences Act 2000. See p.436.

[62] Butterfield J., November 1999. See *Taylor v News of the World* PCC Report No.48, January 26, 2000, Case 1.

15. *Witness payments in Criminal Trials*

    i. **No payment or offer of payment to a witness—or any person** 14–027
       **who may reasonably be expected to be called as a witness—
       should be made in any case once proceedings are active as
       defined by the Contempt of Court Act 1981. This prohibi-
       tion lasts until the suspect has been freed unconditionally
       by police without charge or bail or the proceedings are
       otherwise discontinued; or has entered a guilty plea to the
       court, or, in the event of a not guilty plea, the court has
       announced its verdict.**

    ii. **Where proceedings are not yet active but are likely and
       foreseeable, editors must not make or offer payment to any
       person who may reasonably be expected to be called as a
       witness, unless the information concerned ought
       demonstrably to be published in the public interest and
       there is an over-riding need to make or promise payment
       for this to be done; and all reasonable steps have been
       taken to ensure no financial dealings influence the evidence
       those witnesses give. In no circumstances should such
       payment be conditional on the outcome of a trial.**

   iii. **Any payment or offer of payment made to a person later
       cited to give evidence in criminal proceedings must be
       disclosed to the prosecution and defence. The witness must
       be advised of this requirement.**

These provisions are a great improvement upon the wishy-washy
previous clause. They finally put an end to the practice which
allowed Jeremy Thorpe to escape justice, after the *Daily Telegraph*
had offered the chief witness "double your money" if he could get
Thorpe convicted. The Code does not prevent newspapers from
making arrangements to interview witnesses after the conclusion of
the trial, so long as payment is discussed at that later stage. There
are difficulties, however, in deciding whether a person "may reasonably be expected to be called as a witness".

It is impossible to foretell, in the days after arrest, how the
prosecution and defence cases are likely to develop. In the Sutcliffe
case the Press Council rejected the excuse that police had informed
editors that Sutcliffe had confessed and that there was unlikely to be
a contested trial: it pointed out that experienced editors should be
aware that defendants frequently repudiate confessions made in
police custody. Clause 15(1) does not make what should in practice
be a crucial distinction between a witness to disputed facts (whose
testimony must be kept free from any influence) and a witness to
matters of formal record or to character. The interests of justice
served by a rule against paying witnesses do not apply with very great
force to witnesses of the latter kind.

The Code does not apply to witnesses who are on the run, or
whom journalists discover themselves. One of the most notable

pieces of recent investigative journalism was the tracing and inter-viewing of a potential witness in a drugs trial by David May of the *Sunday Times*, which led to the exposure of police corruption and the abandonment of the prosecution.[63] Such "exceptional circum-stances" may justify payments to witnesses for their time or their future protection, although they should never be made conditional on the story standing up in court. If a paper pays a witness for an interview it cannot publish (for contempt reasons) until after the trial, but the witness's credibility is destroyed at the trial, then it must accept the fact that its story is worthless. With witnesses, a "success fee" must never be contemplated.

14–028   It must be remembered that these code provisions apply only to *paying* witnesses—they do not preclude interviews with witnesses who are prepared to volunteer information. Such interviews can be very important, both as background to the trial and, just possibly, to exposing a perversion of justice if the witness in his subsequent testimony changes his story. Although the rule is cast in absolute terms, there should be no problem with paying witnesses their reasonable travel expenses and accommodating them in a 3 star or 4 star hotel.

In its report on press conduct in the "Yorkshire Ripper" case the Press Council inveighed against payments of "blood money" to criminals and associates: "the practice is particularly abhorrent where the crime is one of violence and payment involves callous disregard for the feelings of the families".[64] This declaration was issued in the context of public outrage over the behaviour of the press in offering enormous sums of money to Mrs Sonia Sutcliffe (who refused them) for no other reason than that she was the wife of a notorious mass murderer. The Press Council prohibition is now embodied in cl.16 (ii) of the PCC code:

16. Payment to Criminals

14–029   i. **Payment or offers of payment for stories, pictures or information, which seek to exploit a particular crime or to glorify or glamorise crime in general, must not be made directly or via agents to convicted or confessed criminals or to their associates—who may include family, friends and colleagues.**

         ii. **Editors invoking the public interest to justify payment or offers would need to demonstrate that there was good reason to believe the public interest would be served. If, despite payment, no public interest emerged, then the material should not be published.**

Payment or offers of payment for stories, pictures or information, which seek to exploit a particular crime or to glorify or glamorise

---

[63] See *R. v Ameer and Lucas* [1977] Crim.L.R. 104.
[64] Press Council, *Press Conduct in the Sutcliffe Case*, Ch.15, paras 5–10.

crime in general, must not be made directly or via agents to convicted or confessed criminals or to their associates—who may include family, friends and colleagues. This provision attracted attention in 2006, when the Lord Chancellor's department threatened to introduce a law which would prohibit criminals from ever profiting from books which dealt with crime. The rule stems from the Press Council's concern about "blood money" payments which were made to obtain stories that would sell on the back of crime. (They were not necessarily glorifying the crime so much as explaining what the criminal was like in bed.) David Shayler's payment from *The Mail on Sunday* of £40,000 was sought by the crown after his conviction although by that time it had been long gone, expended on travel and legal fees that the newspaper had reasonably anticipated at the time it entered into negotiations with him. Given the risk that Shayler was taking and the expense of his whistle-blowing effort, the large amount was, exceptionally, justifiable. In 1987 the *News of the World* was censured for blood-money payments to girlfriends of major criminals. The newspaper accepted that it had made payments (although it refused to say how much it paid) to the girlfriend of convicted murderer Jeremy Bamford in return for the right to publish a prurient "world exclusive" about their sex lives. Although the girlfriend had been innocent—she had informed on and given evidence against him—the story was nonetheless "sold on the back of crime" and had no public interest justification. Another payment, to an Irish barmaid who had been innocently duped by terrorist Nizar Hindawi into carrying a bomb on board an Israeli airliner, elicited a story that was plainly of public interest, but the Council nonetheless held that this was insufficiently "overriding" to justify the payment. It is difficult to see how this woman (who had testified against Hindawi) could meaningfully be regarded as his "associate"—she was intended to be amongst his many victims when the jumbo jet exploded over London. Her story was of enormous public interest, and had been sold to newspapers in many other countries: a strict compliance with the Council's declaration would have denied the British public an insight into a dastardly crime that would have caused many British casualties.[65]

The PCC has censured papers which pay murderers' girlfriends for "exclusives" on their sex lives: the "public interest" is not engaged and such brazenness only exacerbates the grief of relatives.[66] It condemned an interview in *Hello!* conducted from prison with fraudsman Darius Guppy which glorified his crimes,[67] and it condemned *The Daily Telegraph* for paying Jonathan Aitken's daughter for a soppy mitigation of his perjury ("My Father is Paying Too Heavy a Price").[68] Inconsistently, however, it declined to censure the

---

[65] Press Council, *The Press and the People*, p.210.
[66] See *Collier v Sunday Sport*, PCC Report No. 51, October 25, 2000, Case 5.
[67] *Huins v Hello!*, PCC Report, August–September 1993.
[68] *Barlow v Daily Telegraph*, PCC Report No. 47, October 27, 1999, p.10.

Sunday Times for paying to serialise Aitken's *mea culpa, Pride and Perjury*.[69] In a confused adjudication, it said it was "necessary" to pay the publishers for serialisation rights (but that payment would obviously benefit Aitken, the convicted criminal). It said the extracts were in the public interest because Aitken had held high ministerial office and "the articles went some way to explaining for the first time why he had embarked on the strategy which in the end exposed his lies". Darius Guppy did the same explaining to *Hello!*—had he held ministerial office, doubtless the magazine would have been exculpated.

14–030   The PCC ruling in Aitken deprives cl.16 of much significance in respect to payments to celebrated convicts, or those whose convictions are in any doubt. The "public interest" is invariably engaged, so the PCC thinks, by protestations of innocence or by any "revelation of new material". Thus Deborah Parry and Lucille Mac-Laughlan,[70] convicted of killing a fellow nurse in Saudi Arabia, and nanny Louise Woodward,[71] convicted of manslaughter in Boston, were permitted to profit from complaining about justice in other countries. Had all papers abided by the letter of cl.16 (ii), these defendants would doubtless have told their stories, free of charge, at a press conference: money was not "necessary" to elicit their eager self-justifications. The PCC pretends ignorance of the obvious—these payments are not made to obtain information, but to ensure exclusivity.

But the issue came back into the sights of the government's political radar in 2003, after the *Daily Mirror* paid the farmer Tony Martin, jailed for murdering a burglar, and the *Guardian* paid an ex-prisoner for his stories of sharing a cell with Jeffrey Archer. The PCC was initially relaxed, pointing out that it had always taken a liberal view of the serialisation of books (not surprisingly, since its director Sir Christopher Mayer had sold the serialisation rights to his memoirs for a handsome sum) and that it would not censure a newspaper if it had made a payment to charity to secure a story from a famous criminal. It was only prepared to draw an a priori line in cases where the memoir glorified the crime, but this is a difficult test to apply—there may be remorse (at least at having been caught) but the description of the thrill of the chase and the excitement of apparently pulling off the heist is difficult to downplay. The matter reached a head in 2006, when a US book publisher, owned by Rupert Murdoch, paid O.J. Simpson to provide a "hypothetical" account of how he would have murdered his wife if, as everyone (except the jury) believed, he had in fact murdered his wife. This sham was plainly devised so that he could make a large sum of money out of what readers would think was a blow-by-blow description of the actual murder. There was nationwide outrage and not

---

[69] *Bradley v The Sunday Times*, PCC Report No. 50, July 26, 2000, Case 6.
[70] PCC Report No. 43 (1998) pp.5–9.
[71] *Bright v Daily Mail*, PCC Report No. 44, January 27, 1999, pp.12–17.

even the First Amendment came to Murdoch's assistance: he was forced to abandon the project (doubtless after paying Simpson a "kill fee"). In Britain, the government has always perceived a law against criminals earning royalties as a popular measure, and the Lord Chancellor's department has drafted a provision in the usual vague and wide terms, which they threaten to introduce in an appropriate criminal justice bill.

The PCC rightly rejected some complaints against *The Times* for **14–031** serialising *Crimes Unheard*, Gita Sereny's important book about child-killer Mary Bell.[72] An absolute rule against press payments to criminals and associates would deter criminals from revealing incriminating associations with powerful people. In such cases shady characters with a public interest story to tell are often in genuine need of some remuneration for telling it. If they are prepared to go public with revelations about policemen or employers or persons in authority, they need financial protection against reprisals. The real question is whether the importance of the story and the exigencies of its author justify the size of the payment, rather than whether payment should be made at all. So long as newspapers continue to refuse to divulge the size of their payments to informants, the PCC will be unable to decide this question. It should be noted that criminals who are paid money in return for recounting details of an offence for which they have yet to be convicted may have the payment seized, on the theory that it is part of the profit they have made from the offence. Section 71 of the Criminal Justice Act 1988 gives the sentencing court wide powers to confiscate property obtained "in connection with" an offence, and the High Court may make charging orders to secure the position until the verdict. These powers were used against Michael Randle and Pat Pottle, authors of *The Blake Escape: How We Freed George Blake and Why*, when a High Court judge directed that their homes be charged to the Crown for an amount equivalent to the royalties they had earned on their book. They argued that the royalties had been earned by recounting an experience rather than in connection with a crime committed 25 years before, but the order was allowed to stand until it was discharged on their acquittal.[73] Where an advance and royalties were due to George Blake from the publisher of his own book, however, the courts decided it should be held in trust for the Government, on account of the traitor's breach of the confidence he owed to his employer MI6.

In 2001 *The Sun* indirectly made large payments to Ronald Biggs and another "great" train robber as part of its operation to return him from Brazil to spend his dying days at the taxpayer's expense in a British prison. The PCC fell for the *Sun's* defence—derided by its rivals—that those payments to criminals were necessary in the public

---

[72] Report No.43 (1999), p.9.
[73] *Re Randle and Pottle*, *The Independent*, March 26, 1991, Webster J.

interest,[74] although they were more in the interests of Biggs. The story they elicited about his farewell to his grandchildren—"Ronnie sobs as tot gets a final cuddle"—may have interested the Brazilian public, but left British readers unamused (*The Sun* dropped in circulation). The Code has no provision relating to payments to non-criminal informants, jilted lovers and other familiar sources of kiss-and-tell stories. There is often no public interest justification for such tales, and on occasion the tabloid press has paid large sums of money to drug addicts and prostitutes in order to tell them. It is ironic that the people who would be prosecuted for the serious crime of blackmail if they threatened their victim with public exposure unless they were paid a sum of money can now obtain that sum quite legally by taking their story direct to a newspaper. It has been suggested that newspapers that purchase sensational stories of this sort should be required to disclose the amount of the payment on publication: this would serve to alert their readers to the possibility that the sensation in the story may be related to the sensation of receiving a large amount of money for telling it.

13. Discrimination

14–032
    (i) The press must avoid prejudicial or pejorative reference to a person's race, colour, religion, sex or sexual orientation or to any physical or mental illness or disability,
    (ii) It must avoid publishing details of a person's race, colour, religion, gender, sexual orientation, physical or mental illness or disability unless these are genuinely relevant to the story.

These simple provisions are difficult to apply in practice. In 1987 the editor of the *Daily Telegraph*, Max Hastings, announced his newspaper's intention to defy Press Council censure for describing convicted criminals as "black", however irrelevant this was to their offence, on the grounds that he could communicate the same information by publishing their photograph.[75] However, editors have over the years become more sensitive to allegations about racist reporting.

The rule that the press should avoid pejorative or prejudicial language in relation to classes of citizens who often suffer from discrimination has had some effect in moderating press polemics, especially against sexual minorities. In 2005 a change was made to this section of the code to add "gender" to the other categories covered by the discrimination clause. This was to mark the new legal status of the transgender community which had been affected by the introduction of the Gender Recognition Act. This is a good example

---

[74] See "Sun cleared over Biggs", *Guardian*, July 4, 2001, p.6.
[75] Press Council, *The Press and the People*, p.146.

of the valuable role a voluntary standards body can play, in
discouraging the use of "socially unacceptable language" that deni-
grates groups on the basis of race or gender or sexual preference, by
marking public distaste for language that stigmatises whole classes of
citizens. In 1991 the PCC censured the *Daily Star* for encouraging
the persecution of homosexuals in a lead story about "Poofters on
Parade" in the army, which attacked gay rights groups as "preachers
of the filth".[76] The editor of the *Star*, a homophobe named Brian
Hitchen, continued the vilification (which was based on falsely stated
facts) in his own column, but that was not censured—he was an
editor member of the PCC at the time.

The PCC has shrunk from trying to abate the jingoistic fervour
whipped up by tabloids before Euro-finals, although this has been
said to encourage football hooliganism. In 1996 it declined to
censure violently anti-German headlines, of the "Let's Blitz Fritz"
and "Bring on the Krauts" variety, on the specious reasoning that
cl.13 prohibits racist treatment of individuals but not of national
groups.[77] In 1998 it repeated that "nationalist fervour and jingoism"
was inevitable before international sporting events. Thus it found
emotionally acceptable the *Daily Star*'s proposition that "as we
proved at Agincourt and Waterloo, a good kicking on their gallic
derrières is the only language the greedy frogs understand".[78]

Financial journalism

The Press Council, in an effort to ward off requirements for financial **14–033**
journalists to register as "professional advisers" like other share
tipsters, produced a code on this subject, beginning with the
platitude "They should not do a deal of which they would be
ashamed if their readers knew." Clause 14 spells out three basic
rules:

14 Financial journalism

(i) **Even where the law does not prohibit it, journalists must
not use for their own profit financial information they
receive in advance of its general publication, nor should
they pass such information to others.**

(ii) **They must not write about shares or securities in whose
performance they know that they or their close families
have a significant financial interest, without disclosing the
interest to the editor or financial editor.**

(iii) **They must not buy or sell, either directly or through
nominees or agents, shares or securities about which they**

---

[76] PCC Report No.2, fn.16 above, p.9.
[77] PCC Report No.35 (1996), pp.22–24.
[78] *Waller v Daily Star*, PCC Report No. 42, July 29, 1998, p.9.

have written recently or about which they intend to write in the near future.

14–034　These rules, in fact, reflect the law relating to "insider dealings", which financial journalists should always bear in mind. Some newspapers insist on a much more rigid code, which requires that their financial journalists should not own shares or securities at all. Other newspapers, however, have connived for many years at share dealing by their tipsters, who sometimes tip off their editors. An insider-dealing scandal engulfed *The Daily Mirror* in 2000 when it emerged that the writers of its "City Slicker" column had been dealing extensively in the shares they tipped: they were dismissed for gross misconduct by the management and later prosecuted. But they claimed to have passed on advance information about their next "tip of the day" to both the editor Piers Morgan and the deputy editor, who were proved to have dealt at the time in these very shares, although they denied the allegations that they had done so as a result of a tip. The PCC tried to restore public confidence with an "investigation": a pathetic affair in which it made no attempt to cross-examine the editor over his dealings in shares, or to discover whether the journalist's allegations were true or false. ("The Commission does not find it necessary to choose between the conflicting versions.") The PCC condemned the two journalists (who had admitted misbehaviour and been dismissed) and made no finding against the editor other than that he had "failed to take sufficient care" to supervise them.[79] The incompetence and inefficiency of its investigation was exposed when the men were put on trial, and evidence emerged that the PCC had not discovered at the time of its enquiry. The scandal—and the PCC's inability to a proper inquiry— led to a proposal to bring business and city journalists within the statutory regulation of the Financial Services Authority.

Confidential sources

14–035　Clause 14 of the Code of Practice reads simply:

Journalists have a moral obligation to protect confidential sources of information.

Although the Code is binding only on editors, this provision may be useful to journalists who seek editorial support to defy court orders requiring disclosure. An editor who disciplined or dismissed a journalist for refusing to disclose a source, even in disobedience to a court order, would thus be deserving of PCC censure.

Does the PCC work?

14–036　The PCC is a public relations exercise. It was established by newspaper interests as a means of convincing politicians and opinion formers that self-regulation can guarantee privacy and rights of reply

---

[79] PCC Report No. 50, July 26, 2000, pp.5–11 (*The Mirror*).

better than statutory provisions. The Press Council, established to serve the same purpose, was abandoned when it lost public confidence and had its pretensions to both discipline and defend the press derided by Calcutt. If the PCC suffers the same fate, the statutory tribunal recommended by Calcutt waits in the Westminster wings, as does the draft statute prepared by the Law Commission to enable victims of media infringement of privacy to recover damages. It has been the danger apprehended from these developments which spurred proprietors and editors to co-operate with the PCC through its first decade, obeying its dictates over coverage of the Royal princes and publishing its adjudications without complaint (although also without prominence). The Code continues to be breached as often as ever, but few victims complain (since they can achieve nothing) and the PCC does not accept complaints from unaffected parties or do any monitoring itself (except to keep an eye on coverage of the Royal Family). With the PCC as its fig leaf, the newspaper industry has used its considerable political clout to scupper efforts under both Tory and Labour Governments to introduce privacy laws: political leaders, desperate for tabloid support, praise "self-regulation" because that is a pre-condition for obtaining it. The wild card in this arrangement is the judiciary, armed with new powers under the Human Rights Act 1998. Unafraid of tabloid pressure, some judges are minded to develop a tort of privacy, or to extend breach of confidence to the same effect, and they may do so by using the PCC code provisions as the test (since they are drafted by editors, the press can hardly object if the courts take them seriously). Editors would then have fashioned a noose for their own necks, with (for example) the code prohibition on photographing people in places where they have "a reasonable expectation of privacy" being used as a basis not for another meaningless adjudication, but for an award of damages against the photographer and the newspaper, and an injunction on further publication.

The PCC was modelled on the Advertising Standards Authority, which had achieved considerable success in persuading Parliament that self-regulation worked better (and more cheaply) than statutory regulation of advertising content. However, the analogy falters:

- The ASA works because its rulings are backed by a severe sanction (advertisements held to breach of code will not be published again). The PCC has no sanction; it does not offer to compensate any victim, or require a censured editor to publish its censure with any degree of prominence, or to refrain from repeating the breach.
- The PCC has not solved the intractable problem that tabloids are entertainment-based and will continue to publish circulation-boosting stories irrespective of adverse adjudications. Calcutt recognised that the improbability of

all sections of the print media following PCC adjudications was the factor that would be most likely to fuel demands for statutory regulation.

• The PCC's refusal to monitor compliance with its code or even responses to its own adjudications is a fatal mistake. The ASA is the more respected precisely because it engages in monitoring and may act against breaches without the need to await a complaint from an interested member of the public. As Calcutt recognised, a monitoring exercise is essential to any code that purports to regulate intrusions into privacy, as victims (other than of notorious infringements) will be reluctant to give the matter further publicity by making a complaint.

• The PCC will face problems over its procedures in the event that it becomes judicially reviewable. Its evident desire to exclude lawyers and to operate informally, with nudges and winks transmitted along a network of editors, is not calculated to satisfy complainants or (inevitably) their legal advisers. Unsuccessful complainants feel that they have not been given a fair hearing when they are given no hearing at all, especially when disputed issues of fact are decided against them on the strength of written communications with newspaper representatives.

A problem once the PCC is perceived by the courts as having quasi-judicial status is the bias which might be apprehended from its membership. Its part-time chairman receives a large salary (reported to be £150,000 a year for working one day a week), paid for by a levy on the companies which own the newspapers complained against. His presence on an adjudicative panel might on this basis be challenged. More serious is the widespread frustration at the PCC's powerlessness. A report in 2003 from the Culture, Media and Sport Select Committee recommended that it should offer compensation to victims of press abuse and should increase the membership fees of regular transgressors. Without something resembling a sanction, it will remain widely perceived as ineffective.

14–037   The PCC does valuable but unpublicised work in mediating between "non-celebrity" complainants and newspapers, obtaining acknowledgments of error, corrections and apologies which provide some satisfaction to falsely maligned individuals. They could for the most part obtain this redress by contacting the editor (but they lack confidence) or having a lawyer contact the editor (but they lack money to retain one). The PCC serves a valuable function as an informal conciliator, leaning on newspapers to admit mistakes or oversights, and there is no reason why this service should not continue irrespective of whether a privacy law becomes available for victims of more serious intrusions. Regrettably, the PCC devotes much of its "annual review" to shrill propagandistic claims of the kind:

"the application and observance of the Code are part of the
culture of every news room and every editorial office . . . (the
PCC) has clearly raised standards of reporting . . . most
activities which brought newspapers and magazines into disrepute in the 1980s have long since vanished—and the PCC
continues to ratchet up standards on the back of
adjudications".[80]

On the contrary, privacy invasions of the 1980s have continued,
and a vicious new development—the newspaper as vigilante, encouraging the lynch mob to visit alleged paedophiles at their published
addresses and whipping up hatred against the youths who killed
Jamie Bulger (putting their security at risk when they are released)
makes it arguable that British press ethics are at their lowest ebb.
There is no evidence that the PCC's self-regulation has been any
more successful than the Press Council's. The only difference is that
while the Press Council decisions—and the Press Council—were
often vigorously condemned by the press itself, Lord Wakeham
succeeded in persuading proprietors and editors that it is in their
interests to support—i.e. not to criticise—the PCC. There is a
queasy irony here for a British press which trumpets its commitment
to free speech, because this wider public interest aspect of the PCC's
relationship with the industry it affects to regulate has gone unre-
marked. That the PCC gets a "good press" is unsurprising, but an
example of media hypocrisy nonetheless. Do editors and journalists,
so quick to find fault with the performance of other public bodies,
turn a blind eye to PCC failings because they have an economic and
political interest in fostering a public perception of its success? The
fact is that national newspapers report favourable adjudications as if
they were as meaningful as court cases, and have never published a
serious critical analysis of the organisation. After *The Sun* enraged
public feeling (as whipped up by *The Mirror* and other competitors)
by publishing an old photo of Sophie Rhys-Jones, bare at one breast,
before her marriage to Edward Windsor, the PCC issued an
immediate and overblown condemnation: "The decision to publish
these pictures was reprehensible and such a mistake must not
happen again." This was repeated as "news" by all newspapers,
under portentous headlines ("Lord Wakeham's Statement") which
presented it as a ruling which was bound to deter further privacy
invasions.[81] Only the *Guardian* permitted itself a touch of editorial

---

[80] PCC Annual Review 2000.
[81] Even a respected commentator like Roy Greenslade could proclaim, nonsen-
sically, that this adjudication left the *Sun* editor "bleeding . . . the wounds might
well prove fatal": "Bring Me Your Woes", the *Guardian*, June 7, 1999. However,
there are occasional signs that a columnist realises that the emperor has no
clothes: see Catherine Bennett, "The Waste of Space that is Lord Wakeham", the
Guardian G2, July 5, 2001.

candour over this "smack on the wrist", and hinted at the truth: "The only time the PCC jumps is when Royalty complains".

The PCC has so far failed to raise the tone or the profile of debate over media ethics, although it has encouraged the development of procedures within newspaper offices (including the appointment of ombudsmen and "readers' representatives") that enable complaints to be answered quickly. Its adjudications are short and usually over-simple, reflecting only on editors, who do not appear discomforted by its statements that they have breached a code of practice. One fateful decision made in its first year was to take the *Sunday Sport* seriously and to treat it as a newspaper. The PCC embarked upon a solemn investigation into a front-page story entitled: "THIS NUN IS ABOUT TO BE EATEN. She's soaked in sauce, barbecued then carved up like a chicken . . . turn to pages 15, 16 and 17 if you dare." The editor of the *Sport* relished the complaint, describing his article as "pioneering investigative journalism at its best", which he was proud to have published. He dared the PCC to condemn him for exposing necrophilia in a Buddhist monastery in Thailand, "a country regularly visited by British tourists". The PCC rose to the bait, describing the story as "an extreme breach of the spirit of the Code of Practice" although it was outside its letter, since the Code does not purport to regulate matters of taste.[82] *Private Eye* is the only print journal which refuses to recognise the PCC, on the basis (says Ian Hislop) that certain editor-members of the Commission are themselves so morally questionable that no ethical judgment they make deserves to be recognised.

NUJ CODE OF CONDUCT

14–038 The National Union of Journalists has a code with which all members are expected to comply. The code itself is impressive, although attempts to enforce it have been less so. No journalist has been expelled for breach of the code, and disciplinary hearings tend to be unsatisfactory for all concerned in that victims of unethical behaviour can only complain to the NUJ branch of which the offending journalist is a member. If any branch member is impressed by the complaint, he or she could formally begin disciplinary proceedings on behalf of the victim. This procedure is not satisfactory: it relies upon journalists to take up cudgels against their colleagues, and provides no assurance that the complaint will be dealt with either independently or impartially.

THE ADVERTISING STANDARDS AUTHORITY

14–039 In the United States, that bastion of freedom of expression as a result of the First Amendment, advertising—"commercial speech"—is accorded less protection and is regulated by a statutory body, the

---

[82] PCC Report, No. 2, July—September 1991, p.23.

Federal Trade Commission. That stringent regulation was in prospect in Britain in 1962 when the Moloney committee on consumer protection called for greater protection of consumers, through a watchdog independent of the advertising industry. Under that threat of statutory regulation, the industry turned to the then credible Press Council as a self-regulatory model which seemed to satisfy politicians and public alike. The Advertising Standards Authority (ASA) was established, with its guiding mission to ensure that advertisements are "legal, decent, honest and truthful" by ordering their removal from newspapers if they infringe the Advertising Code. Ironically, the Press Council was in due course condemned as a confidence trick which failed to inspire confidence, while the ASA went from strength to strength, becoming in turn the "code adjudicator" model chosen in 1991 for the PCC. Given the general acceptability of some restrictions on commercial speech, the ASA has not suffered very much public criticism. This is because (unlike the PCC) it has real power, derived from its agreement with newspapers and journals that they will not carry any advertisement it judges to have breached the Code, and from its power to refer persistent code-breakers to the Director-General of Fair Trading who has a statutory duty to obtain injunctions against false advertising. Even so, there are signs that the self-regulatory system for advertising does not fully satisfy the public interest: since the ASA can threaten no criminal sanctions, deceitful advertisers will "get away with it" for weeks or months until a complaint is upheld, and will not suffer a fine or any other sanction. The large and increasing number of justified complaints (there were 2,241 advertisements changed as a result of complaints to the ASA in 2005) may itself be an indication that self-regulation has failed to deter. There is also evidence that the cosy, industry-friendly arrangement, with its *grundnorm* that "NO ADVERTISEMENT SHOULD BRING ADVERTISING INTO DISREPUTE"[83] can operate to curb the free speech rights of protest groups who choose to advertise in order to make political points.

The Advertising Code, with its spin-off codes dealing with sales promotions, children, etc., is devised and amended by representatives of the commercial and professional bodies which comprise the advertising industry, sitting as the Committee of Advertising Practice (CAP). There is no lay participation: this trade body puts the sanctions in place and fosters awareness of the Code and the ASA procedure. The ASA purports to act as a tribunal at arm's length from the industry, although the fact that it shares a secretariat with CAP belies this outward impression. Both bodies are funded by a levy on advertising and marketing revenues, raised by the Advertising Standards Board of Finance (another industry body) in the

---

[83] Advertising Code (1999), Principle 2:4.

amount that is judged necessary to keep the system operating with sufficient success to stave off statutory regulation. The ASA itself has been set up as a limited company, with a council of 12 part-time members, a majority of whom work outside advertising. Its adjudicatory powers apply to all advertisements placed in newspapers and magazines or shown in cinemas or on video trailers; to posters displayed in public; to circulars, mail-shots and to advertisements sent as fax transmissions or e-mail. It refuses, however, to regulate classified ads (on grounds of privacy), flyposting (on grounds of impossibility), or drug promotions to the medical profession (on grounds of lack of expertise). In 2002 the Tobacco Industry and Promotion Act prohibited all television advertising and promotion, thus relieving the ASA from adjudicating this vexed area which had been rife with complaints, although the Act does not cover promotions for rolling papers and filters or exaggerated warnings against the dangers of smoking.

14–040   In 2004, the ASA's responsibilities were markedly extended to include television and radio advertising under a contract from OFCOM, the new communications regulator. This change was approved by parliament, a step which indicated a reasonable degree of satisfaction with industry self-regulation. To take on this task, two new legal entities were established, the Advertising Standards Authority (Broadcast) and the Broadcast Committee of Advertising Practice. A new funding body was set up to finance these entities, by way of a levy on broadcast advertising expenditure. Gordon Borry, the ASA's long-serving and respected Chairman, somewhat optimistically hailed the OFCOM decision to "contract out" advertising as having created "a co-regulatory partnership that may become a model for regulation in future. A socially responsible industry and a statutory regulator are working together to achieve a common goal of consumer protection and fair competition." This model may be adopted for the gaming industry, although it is unlikely that OFCOM will "contract out" of its duties to oversee taste and decency and impartiality in program content. The ASA has had little problem accommodating its new responsibility for TV and radio advertising because commercials are expensive to make and there is no desire to take risks with code compliance: the Broadcast Advertising Clearance Centre provides an early warning facility that results in prior censorship of most potential offence. British sensitivities are not entirely predictable, however: the most complained about ad of all time (1,671 complaints in 2005) was against a TV commercial in which women literally sung the praises of KFC's zinger crunch salad—but with their mouths full. The ASA gamely rejected this avalanche of unexpected protest, noting that "teaching children not to speak with their mouths full is a continual process" which would not be disrupted by salad crunching song on television.[84]

---

[84] ASA Annual Report, 2005, p.8.

The ASA has an annual income of £7 million each year to cover some 30 million advertisements placed in the press, 100,000 posted on paid hoardings and 4 million mail shots, together with the entire range of TV and radio advertisements. These collectively elicited 26,236 complaints from members of the public in 2005, mainly directed to false claims made for the likes of slimming treatments and insurance offers, with about 20 per cent concerning matters of taste and decency. The Code provisions are expressed in general terms, and the main provisions are:

Truthfulness

No advertisement should mislead, or exploit the credulity or inex- **14–041** perience of consumers. Obvious exaggerations are permitted, but whenever objective claims are made for a product the advertiser must be in a position to confirm them with documentary proof. Ads must not show or encourage unsafe practices—speeding cars are a particular target. So are "get rich quick" schemes: as the Authority notes in its 1999 report, "if something seems too good to be true, it probably is". Truth must be trimmed in the interests of social responsibility, so there are limits to portraying the pleasures of alcohol: drinking may be shown as sociable or thirst-quenching, but not as an indulgence or a solitary pastime for young people. As the authority put it in 2004, "advertisements must not link alcohol with sexual activity or success or imply that alcohol can enhance attractiveness".[85] A poster campaign for an alcoholic drink with the strapline, "Something for the Ladies" fell foul of this rule (quite apart from its sexism) and a Michelob poster could not show joggers because it was irresponsible to suggest that drinking beer could maintain health.[86] The ASA has in recent years been particularly astute to check health claims by food manufacturers: Kellogg's "Frosties" could not show children playing football with the catchphrase "Eat Right" because consuming such high sugar content cereals would be a case of "Eat Wrong".[87] A claim by *Danone* yoghurt that a new product was "Virtually Fat Free" was condemned after an investigation which showed that this was an exaggeration: its "virtual fat" content was much too high.[88]

Decency

"Advertisements should contain nothing that is likely to cause **14–042** serious or widespread offence", especially offence on grounds of "race, religion, sex, sexual orientation or disability". (The code says

---

[85] ASA Annual Report, 2004, p.41.
[86] ASA Annual Report, 2004, p.11.
[87] ASA Annual Report, 2004, p.11.
[88] ASA Annual Report, 2004, p.9.

nothing about discrimination on the grounds of age, which is endemic in advertising.) Advertisements may be distasteful—up to a point—and offensive to some people: the "widespread" nature of the offence is not judged by the number of complaints alone. Many decency complaints are from organisations representing Muslims, but the Authority tends to be more respectful of religious sensibilities over advertisements which exploit the Christian message: a *Sunday Times* promotion featuring a half-naked model on the cross (a "heavenly body"—geddit), and an advert for jeans worn by the Virgin Mary were condemned as likely to give serious offence. The question is whether religion "is seen to be mocked or treated disrespectfully"—a picture of a Bishop puffing on a joint whilst wearing the advertiser's brand of watch was judged unacceptably mocking rather than amusing.[89] In 2004, more robustly, complaints about a Channel 4 advertisement for a TV series "Shameless" that showed Da Vinci's painting of the Last Supper were rejected: the ads parodied the painting, not the Christian sacrament. On the other hand, unnecessary deference to Roman Catholics removed a poster for the morning-after pill with the headline "Immaculate Conception?" on the basis that the pun was "likely to cause serious or widespread offence". The offence seemed more to do with the subject matter of the ad, namely contraception, than the pun itself.[90] Such complaints spring from a sensitive minority, so the ASA asks "whether it so deeply offends that minority that it would be reasonable for their interests to prevail against the rights of the advertiser to free expression; and whether the unoffended majority should be prevented from seeing the advertisement".[91] This test, of course, will depend upon the respect that the ASA committee has for the offended minority: it has shown great respect for mainstream churches, racial equality groups and the monarchy, but rather less for animal lovers and feminists.

The ASA has often been robust in rejecting complaints about sexual innuendo, notably the poster with a laid-back model advertising Gossard "translucent" lingerie ("Who said that a woman can't get pleasure from something soft") and the Wonderbra advertisement with the talking breasts ("Hello boys. We've been apart for too long").[92] Sexist sniggering is fine, but the ASA draws the line at mockery directed to male sex organs, whether featured in advertisements for underpants ("The Loin King") or for club 18–30 (bulging boxer shorts with the tag "Girls—can we interest you in a package holiday?").[93] Competition amongst budget airlines causes innumerable infractions of the Code: Ryanair's "Fawking Great Offer" was a

---

[89] Advertising Standards Authority Annual Review (1998), p.10.
[90] ASA Annual Report, 2004, p.12
[91] ASA Annual Review (1999), p.5.
[92] ASA Annual Report (1995), p.21.
[93] ASA Annual Report (1995), p.21.

casualty in 2005. The ASA correctly applies a narrower test of decency to public posters which gratuitously confront passers-by and motorists, than to advertisements which are run in specialist journals or for target audiences. Context and circumstances can make all the difference: in an interactive news magazine, salacious copy about oral sex is acceptable.[94] "Grave or widespread offence" is usually predictable, and national sensibilities rule out some advertising especially featuring naked children—that is acceptable on the Continent. In 1991 the Italian clothing chain, Benetton, caused grave and widespread offence by plastering a colour picture of a new-born baby on British billboards: offence was caused not because the picture was indecent, but because it was exploitative. The public is quick to protest when black humour is put to commercial use: 2,000 complaints were received about a billboard advertisement for *Today* newspaper that showed Mrs Thatcher, Mr Kinnock and Mr Owen each hanging from a noose, above the caption: "Would Britain be better off with a hung Parliament?"

Crude language gives widespread and understandable offence on **14–043** posters and in newspapers and magazines for general readership: the ASA report "Delete Expletives" summarised its surveys showing that 86 per cent disapprove of four-letter words in public advertisements to which children may be exposed. Inconsistently and inappropriately, however, the Authority approved use of the slogan "FCUK" to promote a clothing chain, perhaps reasoning that some public irritation was better than giving the company valuable publicity through news coverage of a ban. This purpose was stymied by the broadcasting regulators who turned down the television campaign: the ASA's permissiveness only made the TV censorship more newsworthy. The "FCUK" affair showed both the absurdity of having too many regulators, and how advertising agencies may outsmart them by capitalising on their inconsistencies. A news story about a decision to suppress an advert for a particular product is usually more valuable (because it is more widely and alertly read) than the advertisement which has been suppressed. The French Connection obtains invaluable publicity from the ASA's obtuseness in this respect: in 2004 it was doubtless delighted to receive a ban on posters for its new radio station, FCUK FM, which announced "FCUK FM FROM PNUK TO RCOK AND BACK. NON-STOP FNUK. FCUK FM." The ASA solemnly concluded that "The posters would cause offence because readers would interpret the FCUK-trademark as the expletive 'FUCK'".[95] That is the whole point.

In 2005, the ASA was regulating "offensiveness" for the ASBO generation. An advertisement for a new *Fanta* drink that showed

---

[94] See, e.g. the rejection of a complaint against Dennis Publishing Ltd in ASA Monthly Report, June 14, 1997.
[95] ASA Annual Report, 2004, p.35.

people spitting out the old before consuming the new was ordered to take a post-watershed timeslot lest it encouraged spitting and anti-social behaviour. However, the sort of lads' magazine that does encourage such behaviour—*Zoo*—was allowed to advertise a competition "Win a Boob Job for Your Girlfriend" on the basis that although offensive to everyone else it would not offend the magazine's laddish readership. Any wider readership, especially on television or from posters displayed to the public, is much easier to offend: *Anne Summers* could not display to the public a poster showing a scantily-clad model atop a model horse with the words "Ride a Cock Hoarse"—not because of the weakness of the pun but because "the use of a nursery rhyme was likely to attract the attention of children"—who might ask parents for an explanation.

Privacy

14–044 The Code insists that *advertisers should not unfairly portray people in an adverse or offensive way*, and should obtain prior written permission before identifying individuals. The ASA, like the PCC, appoints itself as protector of the institution of monarchy—the code has specific provisions prohibiting any mention of members of the Royal Family (although the use of the "by Royal Appointment" warrant is the most misleading advertisement of all) or the use of royal arms or emblems. It banned an advertisement for a newspaper featuring a mock-up of a photo of Princess Diana kissing Paul Gascoigne, captioned "Who knows what the future holds?".[96] (the Palace complained, not Paul Gascoigne), but refused to condemn a sniggering invasion of Peter Mandelson's privacy in an advertisement in *The Times* for a football match. ("A humorous and entertaining play on words linking the match to speculation about Mandelson's sexuality."[97]) The ASA is quick to ban advertisements which offend royalty and corporations which place advertisements (see the *Tesco* adjudication below) but offers little protection to public figures who are made the butt of puerile jokes by copy writers.

Recently the Authority has become alert to the danger that unsolicited mail shots and emails might frighten recipients. It condemned Channel 5 for an irresponsible email campaign to promote a new crime series, which sent communications realistically pretending that the recipient was a potential target of a serial killer. This obviously had the potential to cause alarm and the Authority, unusually, used its power to stop the campaign immediately in order to investigate. It found that the campaign was distressing and had not made sufficiently clear to recipients that it was a "cod" marketing exercise.[98] Many regard unsolicited marketing as an invasion of

---

[96] ASA Monthly Report No. 59, 1995.
[97] ASA Monthly Report (April 1999).
[98] ASA Annual Report, 2005, p.15 "Moving Fast to Stop Foul Play".

their privacy, as junk faxes, junk emails and junk telephone calls intrude into their homes and take up their time and attention, but the ASA is too market-oriented to take any notice.

Party Political Advertising

The ASA has finally decided to opt out of this controversial area, **14–045** having been widely criticised for its ban on the Conservative poster prior to the 1997 election which depicted Tony Blair with demonic red eyes.[99] The ASA condemned the fact that it showed the Labour leader as "sinister and dishonest", an adjudication which gave the Saatchi advertisement massive free publicity. Quite aside from this counter-productive consequence, the ban was wrong in principle: at election time, it is crucial for voters to judge the morality of political parties by the nature of the messages they send (the "demon eyes" propaganda was valuable to show the electorate the depths to which Tories would sink in negative campaigning).

Pressure Group Advertising

The voluntary system is geared to commercial advertising, where **14–046** free speech can readily be subordinated to countervailing values of protecting consumers and avoiding gratuitous public offence.[100] There is much to be said for removing political campaigning advertisements from its remit, so long as these are readily identifiable. Why should the 13 members of the ASA Council, all chosen by its chairman, presume to judge the honesty and accuracy of pressure group causes? Much time was spent by the ASA during 1998–2000 in resolving claims and counter-claims about hunting made by the Countryside Alliance and the RSPCA: advertisements from both groups were criticised for exaggeration and inadequate documentary support.[101] The International Fund for Animal Welfare is another campaigning organisation which has had its free speech curbed for questionable reasons: an advertisement in the *Financial Times* calling upon the chairman of Tesco's to ban the sale of Canadian salmon in protest against the Canadian Government's approval of seal-killing was condemned, on the bizarre ground that *Financial Times'* readers might think (from a photo of a sealer clubbing a baby seal) that the chairman of Tesco's was the man on the ice-floe with the raised club.[102] This adjudication survived a judicial review, on the

---

[99] ASA Monthly Report No. 65, 1997.
[100] Commercial speech is nonetheless protected in principle by Art.10: the ECHR is unlikely to intervene if the advert has no public interest dimension, but where it conveys significant information to the public the court has held that it should not be shackled by professional rules (e.g. lawyer's advertising) or bans imposed for partisan reasons—see fn.103, below.
[101] ASA Annual Report 1998, p.8.
[102] ASA adjudication, January 24, 1996.

grounds that the ASA could rationally make it, but shows how the system works to insulate business leaders from personal confrontation. The ASA has been warned that its powers to censor advertisements which express political opinions will need to be reconsidered by reference to Art.10, now that the Human Rights Act is in force, although in that case the authority had power to uphold complaints against racist views in a "editorial column" within an advertising lift-out supplement, which had been written by the advertiser's chairman, because it could reasonably be regarded as part of the advertisement.[103]

It is in this respect that the European Court will come to the advertisers' aid. It has ruled that Art.10 applies to commercial speech, but will only be accorded full weight when there is a public interest component. This test will be met when advertisements are banned for their message rather than for the way in which it is expressed:

> The Swiss meat industry had been heavily promoting beef in television commercials, so an animal rights group made a counter-commercial featuring nervous pigs and the message "eat less meat, for the sake of your health, the animals and the environment!" The commercial broadcaster refused, pursuant to a law which forbade political advertising. The European Court found a breach of Art.10 precisely because of the political content of the message, which gave it more protection than enjoyed by the usual commercial inviting viewers to purchase goods and services. The Court was also influenced by the fact that the advertiser was not a wealthy political party or other group which could endanger the broadcaster's independence. It noted that the prohibition applied only to television and not to other media, and drew the conclusion that it could not therefore be a necessary response to a pressing social need.[104]

Competition

14–047 The ASA Code provides that *"Advertisers should not unfairly attack or discredit other businesses or their products"*. British advertising is remarkable for the absence of mildly aggressive comparisons, let alone cut-and-thrust competition, and the ASA's role in reducing this necessary aspect of a free market is deserving of severe criticism. It took a Directive from the European Union to make clear that comparative advertising (i.e. advertisements identifying rival products) is permissible in the interests of competition and public information, on condition that it is not misleading and genuinely compares like with like.[105]

---

[103] *R. v Advertising Standards Authority Ltd Ex p. Charles Robertson (Developments) Ltd*, 2000, E.M.L.R. 463.

[104] *VGT Verein Gegen Tierfabriken v Switzerland* 10 B.H.R.C. 473.

[105] Directive 97/55/EC on comparative advertising, implemented by the Control of Misleading Advertisements (Amendment) Regulations 2000 (SI 2000/94).

Procedure and Review

Complaints by members of the public must be directed to the ASA **14–048** Council, which may additionally consider advertisements referred by its Secretariat, which monitors publications (somewhat diffidently) for breaches of the code. The Council has 13 members, all selected by the Chairman who since January 2001 has been Lord Borrie, formerly Director-General of the Office of Fair Trading. Complaints about advertisements by rival agencies or producers are discouraged (so much for competition) and neither complainant nor advertiser is ever vouchsafed an oral hearing or an opportunity to confront or cross-examine. The ASA's procedure is speedy: once complaints are taken seriously, advertisers must respond promptly. In cases of urgency, where an ongoing campaign has provoked outrage or claims of deceit, a response may be required within 24 hours. In such emergencies an immediate adjudication can be made or "interim measures" imposed by the Secretariat (such as asking for the advertisement to be withdrawn pending a full ASA decision). Such cases are rare: normally the acceptability of an ad campaign is decided at the Council's monthly meeting, by which time any damage will have been done. Adjudications are short, prepared by the Secretariat and in most cases agreed by the Council at its monthly meeting. There is no appeal from a Council decision, although complainant and advertiser can ask for the adjudication to be "reviewed" if there is fresh evidence or irrationality. In 2005, for example, only one complaint was referred back to the Council by the Reviewer, whose limited remit is no substitute for a proper appeal on the merits. The ASA improperly describes its independent reviewer as an "appeals mechanism", which he certainly is not.[106] In 2005 the High Court dismissed an application by Jamster (the ringtone originator of "Crazy Frog") to stop the publication of an adjudication upholding complaints about its deceptive subscription ads, pending its "appeal" to the independent reviewer. The court said it was in the public interest to publish an ASA verdict regardless of any "review" process. It cannot in any event reverse a Council decision, but merely "review" the matter by sending it back for further consideration, which hardly makes the exercise worthwhile.

The ASA is subject to judicial review. In an important precedent for the supervision of all such voluntary bodies, the Divisional Court ruled that it served a public law function which would otherwise have to be exercised by a statutory body—doubtless by the Director-General of Fair Trading.[107] Like the Takeover Panel, the ASA exercises power de facto by interpreting and applying a written ethical code, enforced through effective sanctions.[108] In this first

---

[106] ASA Annual Report, 2005, "Upheld in Court".
[107] *R. v ASA Ex p. The Insurance Service Plc* [1990] 2 Admin. L.R. 77.
[108] *R. v Panel on Take overs and Mergers Ex p. Datafin* [1987] Q.B. 815.

case, the court quashed an adjudication reached without giving the advertiser a fair opportunity to respond. In later cases, however, the Court has been more prepared to defer to the experience and expertise of the ASA, declining to interfere with decisions like *IFAW v Tesco*,[109] which may be unreasonable but are not irrational. The ASA will not be stopped from publishing a decision, however, even if leave for judicial review has been granted:

> A football pools company was informed that the ASA had decided its advertisement was in breach of the code, and the adjudication would be published in the next monthly bulletin. It immediately obtained leave to move for judicial review, and then sought to injunct publication of the adjudication until the court case had been decided. Laws J. held that the "general principle of our law" that expression will not be restrained "save on pressing grounds", applied to the expression of a public body as much as an individual: potential damage to Vernons from publication did not provide a sufficiently pressing reason to suppress the ASA's opinion of the advertisement.[110] This case is additionally important because it turns on a common law right rather than Art.10. The ASA, as a "public authority" for the purposes of the Human Rights Act will not be a "victim" for the purpose of enjoying an Art.10 right, and will have to rely on the common law principle adumbrated in this and other cases.

14–049   The same approach has been evident in other cases that have come before the courts on judicial review applications. Minor procedural irregularities will not invalidate a decision which does not appear irrational.[111] Although the ASA is now bound to render decisions which conform with Art.10 of the ECHR, once a court is satisfied that the Authority could reasonably conclude that an advertisement in a national newspaper caused "serious and widespread offence", it would logically follow that there was a "pressing social need" to censor it.[112]

Advertisers up before the ASA cannot be condemned on vague or novel grounds: restriction must be "prescribed by law". There is one High Court decision that the ASA codes are sufficiently precise and accessible to satisfy this test.[113] The courts have been wholly supportive of the ASA and there must be, in effect, a presumption that its decisions will be upheld—none have been successfully disputed,

---

[109] *R. v ASA Ex p. International Fund for Animal Rights*, July 7, 1997, *per* Dyson J.
[110] *R. v ASA Ex p. Vernons* [1992] W.L.R. 1289.
[111] *R. v ASA Ex p. DSG Retail Ltd*, Popplewell J. December 4, 1996.
[112] *R. v ASA Ex p. City Trading* [1997] C.O.D. 202. The decision was delivered before the Human Rights Act, and its factual basis—that it was not unreasonable to find that advertisements in the *Daily Mirror* for a "sex education video" would cause widespread offence—may be doubted. So too may the logic of always inferring a "pressing social need" from "widespread offence", although the existence of such offence would give prima facie support to a ban.
[113] *R. v ASA Ex p. Matthias Rath BV*, *The Times*, January 10, 2001.

although the decision in *IFAW v Tesco* would (or should) have been found inconsistent with Art.10. An attempt to challenge an ASA adjudication on the basis that the close connection between the authority and the advertising industry created a real risk of bias has been rejected.[114]

Sanctions

The ASA has a graduated range of sanctions. They are not **14-050** calculated to deter incorrigibly deceitful advertisers, for whom there is no fine or prison sentence, but they can stop a deceptive or offensive promotional campaign in its tracks. That sanction is available not by law or contract but simply through media industry co-operation. When asked by the ASA to withdraw an advert, most agencies do comply: they know that newspapers and journals will simply not publish advertisements which the ASA has declared to be a breach of the code. A recalcitrant advertising agency or its client may be denied industry services or further newspaper space. The Authority naively asserts that the prospect of adverse publicity from its rulings may prove a deterrent, but for companies like Benetton (a regular offender) all publicity is good publicity. Ironically for a body dedicated to proclaiming the virtues of self-regulation, its one real sanction derives from legislation.

In 1988 the Director-General of Fair Trading was given statutory powers to deal with false advertisements, as a result of implementation of the European Community's Directive on Misleading Advertising. These powers will be used only as a last resort, if the ASA's voluntary self-regulation system fails, as it did with the advent of the *Sunday Sport*:

> The ASA upheld complaints against advertisements for a new slimming aid, but the distributors continued to run advertisements in the *Sunday Sport*. The ASA, powerless to prohibit their continuing publication, referred the matter to the Director-General, who was granted an injunction against the distributors preventing them from publishing the same or any similar advertisement.[115]

The ASA is extremely reluctant to make such references—only a few are made each year. The reason may be that it thinks a reference implies that self-regulation has failed, and a body which perceives itself as an advocate for self-regulation does not wish to give that impression. What the ASA has yet to understand is that its brand of "self-regulation" only works *because* it is underpinned by this statutory power: there should be no inhibition against invoking it.

---

[114] *SmithKlein Beecham Plc v Advertising Standards Authority* (2001), EWJ No 49, Administrative Court 17, January 2001.
[115] *Director-General of Fair Trading v Tobyward* [1989] 2 All E.R. 266.

The ASA has avoided much of the criticism levelled at the PCC because its budget is three times larger, its remit less controversial and its preparedness to monitor its Code, rather than ignore the most blatant breaches if the victim does not complain, is reassuring.

Trade Descriptions Act

14–051 Editors should be aware of the potential criminal liability they may incur under the Trade Descriptions Act if they falsely market their own publications:

> *Woman* magazine appeared with a cover announcement, "Exclusive! At last, the real Anne Diamond". Instead of an interview with the popular television presenter, however, the feature to which the cover referred comprised headless pictures of eight women (one of whom was Ms Diamond) together with a "character analysis" of their clothing. The publishers, IPC Magazines, were fined £600 with £400 costs for applying a false and misleading trade description to the contents of their product.

The crime of applying a false description to a book or magazine is, under the Trade Descriptions Act, a strict liability offence committed if a cover is in fact misleading, even if the publisher had no intention to trick potential readers. In 1991 HarperCollins suffered embarrassment and a fine of £6,250 (and an order to pay £4,150 prosecution costs) for some sharp practice exposed at Stratford-upon-Avon by local trading standards officers:

> Alastair Maclean was a popular and prolific author, who bequeathed his publishers a number of "outlines" for future stories. HarperCollins hired an unknown, never-before-published author, who just happened to be named Alastair MacNeill, to write books based on these story-lines after Maclean's death. The first, *Nightwatch*, was published with a cover description: "ALASTAIR MACLEAN'S *Nightwatch*" and the name Alastair MacNeill in small print at the bottom. The court had no hesitation in finding that the use of the apostrophe could mislead customers into thinking that the book had been written by the famous novelist, a misrepresentation compounded by the similarity of his name with that of the real author.

Newspapers from time to time suffer reprisals from advertisers as a result of editorials or investigative journalism that is critical of the advertiser's product or personnel. The reprisal usually takes the form of withdrawal of future advertising. The ASA will be of no assistance in cases where the petulant advertiser is a private organisation, but the case of *R. v Derbyshire County Council Ex p. Times Supplements Ltd* demonstrates how judicial review may be used to provide redress against local authorities (or government departments) that cancel advertisements for political reasons:

> Derbyshire County Council regularly advertised teaching positions in the *Times Education Supplement*, which is owned by Rupert Murdoch.

Another Murdoch paper, *The Sunday Times*, published a series of attacks on the Labour-controlled council and its leader, David Bookbinder. The Labour group on the council vindictively decided to end all advertising in Murdoch publications, and used its majority on the council's education committee to switch the advertising of teaching posts (worth some £60,000 per year) from the *TES* to the *Guardian*. The Divisional Court quashed this decision as a result of evidence that demonstrated that it had been made solely because of the Labour group's vendetta against the Murdoch press, and not for any bona fide reason related to education or to the council's operations; "It was thus an abuse of power contrary to the public good."[116]

ICSTIS

The privatising of British Telecom led to a mushrooming of "live **14–052** conversation" and "adult entertainment" services available to telephone inquirers at a premium rate (i.e. charged at the rate for dialing the Irish Republic). BT and its service providers were criticised in the press and in Parliament, and fearing legislation, looked to the ASA and the Press Council as a model for the self-regulatory alternative. Their services were made subject to codes of practice drawn up and monitored by the Independent Committee for the Supervision of Standards of Telephone Information Services (ICSTIS), comprising 10 members appointed by British Telecom and currently chaired by Sir Alistair Graham. ICSTIS derives its power from clauses in the contracts between service providers and Telecom, which entitles the latter to act on an ICSTIS recommendation to close any service that is found to have breached the relevant code. Complaints may be made, sensibly enough, by telephone, by calling freephone 0800 500212.

There are over a billion calls made to premium rate services each year, lasting two minutes each on average (since many are for aural sex services, the shortness of this time period may reflect of a national inability to maintain an erotic conversation, or an erection). The public spend £1.6 billion annually on premium rate calls, an average of £35 per adult. Although it was the British penchant for dirty dialling that brought ICSTIS into existence, it must now regulate access to competitions and horoscopes, ring tone downloads and alarm systems, scratch cards and TV quiz lines. The ICSTIS secretariat handled 2000 complaints in 2005–6[117] and handed down fines totalling £4.5 million for breaches of a code of conduct, the eleventh of which came into force in January 2007. Most complaints concern deceitful promotions or misleading information; those who dial for "adult entertainment" are reluctant to complain if these self-described "wank lines" do not live up to their own descriptions. A

---

[116] (1991) 3 Admin. L.Rep. 241.
[117] See ICSTIS Annual Report, 2005–6.

number of cases which attract the severest sanctions each year are really examples of serious fraud—e.g. mailshots which threaten legal action unless a premium rate number is dialled, or which encourage calls and faxes to premium rate lines by falsely promising incredibly cheap travel or that all charges will be donated to a non-existent charity. It would be a more effective deterrent if organisers of these scams faced criminal prosecutions rather than ICSTIS fines.[118]

The Code requires service providers to publicise clearly the "charge per minute" in all advertisements and promotions. It has familiar provisions prohibiting incitement to unlawful conduct or content which features violence, sadism or cruelty, and services must not invade privacy or promote racial disharmony or prostitution or "cause grave or widespread offence".[119] The Code adopts ASA provisions against misleading and inaccurate material, and against unprofessional advice, and has stringent rules against exploiting the credulity of children (all services for children must automatically terminate after £3.00 has been expended). ICSTIS has developed some better procedures and sanctions than the PCC and ASA: it has an emergency procedure that operates (by telephone, of course) to provide an interim remedy in a matter of hours, and in difficult or important cases a service provider can obtain an oral hearing. The fairness of the whole procedure was enhanced in 2001 when the organisation set up an independent appeals tribunal, chaired by a retired circuit judge.

14–053   The range of sanctions available to ICSTIS, and its preparedness to use them, marks it out as the most effective of the self-regulatory bodies. Unlike either the PCC or the ASA, it considers a punishment which fits not only the crime but also the offender's previous record. Under s.5.7.2 of the code it may then impose the following penalties:

(a) require the breach to be remedied;
(b) demand an assurance about future behaviour,
(c) require future services or promotional material to be submitted to ICSTIS for approval;
(d) bar access to the offending telephone numbers for a defined period, by arrangement with the network operator;
(e) prohibit the operator from providing a premium rate service for a defined period, or impose a permanent ban;
(f) impose a fine;
(g) in the case of damage caused by virtual chat services, require the payment of reasonable claims for compensation.

These powers, enforceable through contracts with Telecom and the network operators, are similar to those which would be made

---

[118] See ICSTIS Activity Report, 1999, Case studies 1 and 4.
[119] See ICSTIS Code, s.3.2 (Decency).

available to any statutory regulator. ICSTIS has not hesitated to use its power to fine, and occasionally to close down lines and ban operators, for serious or repeated breach. In 2005–6 a number of fines were levied at the maximum of £100,000, and the secretariat is currently consulting on the need to increase the ceiling to £250,000. Most fines for run-of-the-mill violations are levied at £5,000, although the "Crazy Frog" service provider was ordered not only to pay a £40,000 fine for misleading promotions but to refund in full the money paid by 338 ICSTIS complainants. When one phone network refused to comply with ICSTIS directions, OFCOM immediately stopped the company from providing any premium rate services. By exercising its powers so forcefully, ICSTIS—the most recent of the voluntary regulators—has been perceived as the best: in the government white paper on broadcasting, ICSTIS was held up as the preferred model for the new all-purpose regulator OFCOM. However, its reputation was severely dented in 2007, when the press exposed its abject failure to supervise TV quiz lines. Its 2005/6 Report boasted of its competence and prowess and promised a "consultation paper on some new rules for TV quizzes" but under its very nose broadcasting companies were making fortunes from viewers addicted to the sexy hucksters who enticed their telephoned answers, most of which did not get through to the studio but were charged for at premium rate anyway, to quizzes that were in any event rigged. ICSTIS had been spending too much time lobbying on behalf of industry self-regulation (it boasts of its summer receptions on the House of Commons terrace and the parties it hosts at party conferences) than in actually regulating an industry that was miring itself in sleaze and deception.

The code for live telephone services is considerably more detailed than that for recorded messages, and is regularly monitored. It requires service providers themselves to monitor their services continually, to record all conversations and to retain the recordings for a six-month period in the event that these are required by ICSTIS. They are under a duty to use "all reasonable endeavours" not to allow talk that might encourage criminal offences, drug-taking or racial disharmony, or that might cause grave offence by reference to sex or violence or by use of foul language. They must operate procedures to ensure that persons under 18 do not use the service, and warn callers both of the charges they are running up and of the fact that their conversations are being recorded. Telephone talk is neither cheap nor free, although ICSTIS has established a compensation fund to help pay the telephone bills of subscribers whose children or guests have incurred heavy premium rate charges without authorisation.

In 1991 ICSTIS promulgated new rules purporting to restrict the **14–054** manner in which sex line services are advertised, banning such advertisements entirely from free or unsolicited publications and requiring that all ads in publications not normally carried on the "top shelf" of newsagents "must not contain pictures or words of a sexually suggestive nature which are unacceptably offensive". The rules are an unreasonable restraint on trade, since it must be for newspapers and free sheets to decide for themselves whether to carry lawful advertisements. The providers of adult entertainment services, supported by those newspapers that carry their advertisements (the *Sport*, *Mirror* and *Star*), challenged the new rules on the basis that what is "unacceptably offensive" is unacceptably subjective and unpredictable. A confused majority judgment finally admitted: "There is a subjective element to our approach and we regard it as unavoidable." ICSTIS then moved on to rule that an advertisement for "Unzip my suspenders" was not acceptable, but "Dial-a-Bonk" was. A dissenting opinion by the chairman found this "an untenable approach for a body such as ICSTIS which operates in an area of public administration".[120] Nonetheless, in 1999 it embarked upon an investigation which uncovered 60 services which had breached its rules about advertising offensively in generally available, "non-top shelf" publications. It imposed fines of up to £5,000 in 23 cases, and banned access for up to 30 weeks in 21 cases.

Consistently with its commitment to procedural fairness, ICSTIS does not shrink from the rigours of judicial oversight. In *R. v ICSTIS Ex p. Firstcall*, it accepted that as a "public body" it was amenable to judicial review, a contention a strong Divisional Court saw no reason to doubt.[121] Firstcall tried to stop an adjudication of a complaint against it from proceeding, on the ground that its particular contract with BT excluded ICSTIS jurisdiction. But the court ruled that a public law body could not be fettered by any clause in a contract to which it was not a party. Only in exceptional circumstances would the court injunct such a body from proceeding: the appropriate course was to receive the adjudication before deciding whether to challenge it.

ICSTIS has been pro-active in dealing with complaints against companies exploiting new forms of electronic communications by (for example) sending unsolicited faxes and emails which invite recipients to dial premium rate numbers for misinformation. Most of its decided cases involve minor forms of customer deceit, although it has occasionally adopted an unnecessarily censorious position—fining one communications company for causing "widespread offence" by conducting a fax poll on railway safety too soon after a train disaster.[122] Television regulators may reasonably require some sensitivity in scheduling after a major incident (violent movies were replaced in the days following the Hungerford and Dunblane

---

[120] ICSTIS adjudication in respect of advertisements in the *Mirror Star* and *Sport*, August 28, 1991.

[121] [1993] C.O.D. 325, Sir Thomas Bingham M.R., Kennedy and Evans L.JJ.

[122] *Crosby Communication Case*, ICSTIS adjudication February 19, 2001. The company was fined £300.

shootings) but retrospective fines on service providers merely for expressing or soliciting public opinion breaches Art.10 of the ECHR. ICSTIS has adapted its Code to cover internet and interactive services which use premium rate as a payment mechanism, and its remit has been extended to advertising on the internet for premium rate services which can be accessed via modems.

The internet

Regulation of the internet is, for techno-libertarians, a contradiction **14–055** in terms. But those who place obscenities and defamations on their web-sites are open to criminal and civil actions as much as any offline publisher, and there are special amendments (described in Ch.4) extending the provisions of the Child Protection Act (1978) to those who operate and frequent child pornography sites. Although the US Supreme Court gave paedophile sites the benefit of First Amendment freedom in *ACLU v Reno*,[123] no such largesse is extended by Art.10(2) of the ECHR: any infringements relating to child pormography will be upheld as necessary "for the prevention of crime". Internet service providers are well aware that their commercial interest in avoiding statutory regulation is served by the public and political perception that they do their best to exclude such perverted material: for this reason the Internet Service Providers Association (ISPA) and the London Internet Exchange (LINX), in co-operation with the DTI and the Home Office, have established a self-regulatory body called the Internet Watch Federation. As its name implies, it monitors the net and encourages users to contact its website (*www.iwf.org.uk*) and send an email (to report@iwf.org.uk) if they encounter anything of interest to paedophiles. Although principally funded by the United Kingdom industry, it does, unusually for a self-regulator, receive public finance for its "complaints hotline" from the European Union, as part of its Safer Internet Action Plan.[124] The IWF investigates but does not adjudicate—its role is limited to passing evidence to the police. It makes a threshold judgment on whether material emanating from a suspect site is indecent (the test under the Protection of Children Act). In 2001 it was condemned by that guardian of popular morals, *The News of the World*, for doing nothing to stop the Saatchi gallery photographs from appearing on websites scoured by paedophiles.[125] In this respect the IWF was correct (the photos were not "indecent") and the newspaper was partly to blame: it had provoked the misguided

---

[123] *ACLU v Reno* 521 U.S. 844 (1997).
[124] For European Commission thinking on internet regulation, see DG XIII "Communication of Illegal and Harmful Content on the Internet" (Com. (96) 487) and DGX "Protection of Minors and Human Dignity in Audiovisual and Information Services" (Com. (96) 483).
[125] *News of the World*, March 18, 2001.

police action in the first place, thus giving the pictures international notoriety. After five years' operation, IWF claimed, "We have been responsible for the removal of some 26,000 images of child pornography from UK servers". But such claims create expectations which the organisation (in reality, the police) cannot fulfil; it is "toothless" in the sense that it has no more teeth than any other non-statutory busybody.

Cybersquatting

14–056　Under the impetus of the US Government and the World International Property Organisation, a global regulator was set up in 1998 with a special role in resolving the problem of "cybersquatting". ICANN—the Internet Corporation for Assigned Names and Numbers—issues directives to .com and .net and .org domains to transfer or cancel names after adjudications of what are essentially "passing off" disputes, over domain names that are confusingly similar or identical to the complainant's own name or trade mark. The issue, decided by a panel of ICANN adjudicators, is whether the name has been registered for genuine and fair use or with intent to mislead, exploit, or interfere with the complainant's legal rights (its rules and decisions may be accessed at *www.icann.org*).

> In *Jeanette Winterson v Mark Hogarth*, the English author complained that Hogarth's registration of *jeannettewinterson.com* was an infringement of her "work"—i.e. the recognition that attached to her own name, a right which the English law against "passing off" would entitle her to protect. The panel had no difficulty in concluding that Hogarth had acted in bad faith (despite his claimed ignorance of English law) because he had no pre-existing goodwill in the work and had registered it with the intention of auctioning it off to the highest bidder.[126] In *Billy Connolly v Stewart*, the comedian wrested the name *www.billyconnolly.com* from a pedigree dog of the same name, whose owner had registered the site to advertise its stud services. The ICANN panel rejected the argument that the website was named after the dog: the registration had been in bad faith as a pretext for trading in domain names.

The ICANN complaint procedure is not cheap—fees for a panel adjudication are of the order of £1,000—but are much less than a contested court action. The procedure does not involve any legal waiver—unsuccessful complainants are not debarred from commencing actions for trademark infringement or passing off. The service is proving helpful in reducing confusion and exploitation: it dealt promptly with 3,900 cases in its first 18 months, deciding 75 per cent in favour of complainants. It has been accused of favouring "big business" at the expense of freedom of expression by ordering

---

[126] Case No. D2000—0235, May 22, 2000.

transfers of "dotsuck" sites (created in the name of public figures or corporations in order to criticise them—e.g. under kissinger-sucks.net). Dotsuck.uk sites are permitted by Nominet, the body responsible for administering .uk domain names. It proposes to set up a similar arbitration system to which registrants will be obliged by their contract to submit (see *www.nic.uk*). The regulation of this global technology is in its infancy, and several dozen repressive States have passed laws to control internet access.[127] In Britain, the Government has announced a preference for applying existing laws: in 2000, the Official Secrets Act empowered police to shut down a local website on which renegade MI6 agent Richard Tomlinson had posted the names of 100 of his former colleagues.

---

[127] *The Internet and Press Freedom* (Freedom House, 2000).

CHAPTER 15

CENSORSHIP OF FILMS, VIDEO AND DVDS

"Before the children's greedy eyes with heartless indiscrimination are presented, night after night . . . terrific massacres, horrible catastrophes, motor car smashes, public hangings, lynchings. All who care for the moral well-being and education of the child will set their faces like flint against this new form of excitement."[1]

INTRODUCTION

The most obvious shift in the British approach to censorship of the visual media has been away from the courts and towards quasi-statutory regulation. The jury—the traditional body for deciding issues of freedom of expression—is no longer trusted to make the detailed judgments required before films and videos are regarded as fit for public exhibition and sale. In practice (although not in theory—films and videos may still be prosecuted for obscenity) the jury's function has been taken over by an institution of State-approved censors, which calls itself the British Board of Film Classification (BBFC). The term "classification" is a euphemism—although much of the Board's task involves classification of films and videos, DVDs and computer games as suitable for particular age-groups, the "cuts" it requires for this certification are in practice censorship directives. In some cases it refuses certification altogether for adult viewing; such a refusal will amount to a legal ban (in the case of a video) or a powerful extra-legal deterrent (in the case of a feature film for cinema release). This distinction arises from the Board's history as a private body set up by the film industry; it retains this advisory capacity in relation to the cinema, but has been given statutory powers by Parliament to decide whether video-cassettes are "suitable for viewing in the home". Its operations additionally have a determinative influence on the feature films that are shown on television: the licensing bodies for that medium insist that films possess a BBFC certificate before they can be screened.

15–001

---

[1] "Cinematography and the Child"—editorial in *The Times* demanding exclusion of children from all cinemas, April 12, 1913.

Film censorship is a complicated mix of legal and extra-legal regulation. Movies that are exhibited in cinemas or viewed in the home are subject to the Obscene Publications Act, and may be prosecuted on the grounds that they would tend to deprave and corrupt a significant proportion of likely viewers. Additionally, they may be prosecuted at common law for blasphemy or sedition. Cinema films, however, are subject to special pre-censorship arrangements: a classification system operated by the BBFC that is in theory voluntary but, in practice, a requirement insisted upon by local councils, which license cinemas. These councils may themselves prohibit films that have BBFC approval or, indeed, permit the screening of films that have been refused certification. They may alter the BBFC age classification, as several councils did in 2002 to permit the youngsters to enjoy *Spiderman*, which the nanny censors at the BBFC had classified as unfit for under-12s, the only age it was really fit for. In the case of video-cassettes and DVDs, BBFC certification is required by law before they can be sold to particular age groups, and must be withheld from movies that are deemed "unsuitable for viewing in the home", however unexceptionable they may be for screening to adults in licensed cinemas. Neither theatre promoters nor book publishers suffer institutional censorship imposed by bureaucracies or local councillors, and the standards of acceptability endorsed by these bodies are such that cinema censorship is more pervasive, and more arbitrary, than the limitations imposed on other forms of artistic expression.

15–002   The reasons for additional layers of censorship in relation to films are partly historic (in so far as cinemas required local authority licences for reasons of health and safety), partly practical (distributors and exhibitors of film have preferred the security of BBFC censorship to protect their profits and their persons from the vagaries of obscenity prosecutions) and partly philosophical. As the Williams Committee put the latter argument, film is a,

> "uniquely powerful medium . . . the close-up, fast cutting, the sophistication of modern make-up and special effects techniques, the heightening effect of sound effects and music, all combine on the large screen to produce an impact which no other medium can create".

What is left of the insubstantial pageant once the credits have faded and the bus ride home has been taken is a matter of inconclusive evidence, but "it seems entirely sensible to be cautious".[2]

In the case of home video, and DVDs playable anywhere on computers caution is regarded as even more sensible in light of the ability of viewers—especially youngsters—to use the technology to

---

[2] *Obscenity and Film Censorship: Committee Report* (the Williams Committee), (HMSO, 1979), Cmnd. 7772.

dilate repeatedly upon particular scenes. The BBFC explains that it is much stricter with scenes depicting sexual violence on video than on film, "since the fact that a scene might be searched out and repeated endlessly out of context in the privacy of one's home could condition some viewers to find the behaviour sexually exciting, not just on film, but in real life".[3] In 1984 this concern led Parliament, after a frenetic campaign about the dangers of "video-nasties", to designate the BBFC as the body empowered to decide which films were appropriate for home viewing on video-cassette. As a result, this small private body, established and funded by the film industry, has become a bureaucratic apparatus recognised by law, exercising a determinative control over the contents of publicly available films and videos. Its certificate, while not a guarantee of immunity from prosecution under the Obscene Publications Act, has in practice become just that, and the prospect of proceedings against those who purvey films and cassettes protected by its classification must be regarded as remote. In 1985 the Government undertook that in order to avoid "local variations in prosecution policy" and to ensure that "any prosecution should be undertaken only after the most careful consideration of the case", the police would seek the advice of the DPP before prosecuting for obscenity in relation to any work certified by the BBFC.[4] This cosy arrangement has had the effect desired both by the cinema and video industries and by the law enforcement authorities: no prosecution has since been mounted against a BBFC-certified film or video work. The price to the film-loving public has been a lot of cuts, and occasional outright suppression, imposed by a Government-approved censorship body. The actual cuts required for certification are the tip of the iceberg, because film distributors, well aware of BBFC policy, themselves make many more cuts in an effort to comply with that policy before submitting the film, video or DVD for an age classification. The BBFC is the only regulator that imposes prior restraint on free expression, and it operates in practice to produce a good deal of pre-censorship by distributors.

FILM CENSORSHIP

History

The BBFC began as a voluntary body, established by the film 15–003 industry in 1912 in an effort to provide some uniform guidance to local authorities empowered to license premises for the screening of particular films. The 1909 Cinematograph Act gave local authorities power to impose conditions on film exhibitions in order to protect

---

[3] BBFC Annual Report (1986).
[4] BBFC Annual Report (1986).

the public against fire hazards, but they soon began to use them to quench the flames of celluloid passion. The first banned film—a newsreel of an American prize fight—earned a disapproval "not unconnected with the fact that it showed a negro defeating a white man".[5] The film industry took fright at the prospect that distribution might be subjected to the whims of different local councils, and a consensus emerged that "it would be far better for the trade to censor its own productions than to see all films at the mercy of an arbitrary authority".[6]

In 1912 the Cinematographic Exhibitors' Association announced the formation of the British Board of Film Censors, whose duty "would be to induce confidence in the minds of the licensing authorities, and of those who have in their charge the moral welfare of the community generally".[7] In 1924 the BBFC received its judicial imprimatur in the case of *Mills v London County Council* when the Divisional Court upheld the validity of a condition that "no cinematograph film . . . which has not been passed for . . . exhibition by the BBFC shall be exhibited without the express consent of the council". So long as a council reserved the right to review BBFC decisions, it was entitled to make the grant of a cinema licence contingent upon the screening of certified films.[8] The position was approved by the Court of Appeal in 1976. Lord Denning said:

> "I do not think the county councils can delegate the whole of their responsibilities to the board, but they can treat the board as an advisory body whose views they can accept or reject; provided that the final decision—aye or nay—rests with the county council."[9]

The cutting-room counsels of the BBFC avowedly err on the side of caution, in an effort to protect the established film industry from criticism as well as from prosecution. Although the BBFC is (save for its role in approving video-cassettes) an unofficial body, unrecognised by statute and financed through fees imposed upon every film

---

[5] See Neville March Hunnings, *Film Censors and the Law* (Allen & Unwin 1967), p.50. Until 1932 the annual reports of the BBFC listed the reasons for which cuts had been requested or films refused a certificate. They included "abdominal contortions in dancing" (1925), "equivocal situation between white girls and men of other races" (1926), "British possessions represented as lawless sinks of iniquity" (1928), "police firing on defenceless populace" (*ibid.*) "themes likely to wound the just sensibilities of friendly nations" (*ibid.*). The practice was ended because "for some unaccountable reason critics have seized upon isolated sentences and by taking them out of context have placed mischievous constructions upon them" (1932). The Reports are gathered in PRO file, H045/24024.

[6] Hunnings, p.51.

[7] Hunnings, p.54.

[8] *Mills v London County Council* [1925] 1 K.B. 213.

[9] *R. v GLC Ex p. Blackburn* [1976] 1 W.I.R. 550, *per* Lord Denning, at pp.554–555.

submitted for censorship, it exercises a persuasive and in most cases
determinative influence over the grant of local authority licences. "I
freely admit that this is a curious arrangement," conceded the Home
Secretary, Mr Herbert Morrison, in 1952, "but the British have a
very great habit of making curious arrangements work very well, and
this works. Frankly, I do not wish to be the Minister who has to
answer questions in the House as to whether particular films should
or should not be censored."[10]

Section 3 of the 1952 Cinematograph Act (now s.1(3) of the 1985 **15–004**
Cinemas Act) imposed a duty on licensing authorities to place
restrictions on the admission of children to cinemas that show works
"designated, by the licensing authority or such other body as may be
specified in the licence, as works unsuitable for children". The
reference to "such other body" was the first parliamentary acknowledgment of the BBFC, and the 1952 Act established its position, if
not as a censorship body, at least as an authorised classification
tribunal for films unsuitable for young people, and its classification
decisions have for this purpose won considerable approval. The
present classification, endorsed by all local councils and by the Home
Office, is:

U   Universal: suitable for all.
PG   Parental guidance: some scenes may be unsuitable for young
     children.
12   Suitable only for persons of 12 years and over.
12A (Cinema)Suitable for children over 12, and younger children
     to be admitted only if accompanied by a parent or carer.
15   Suitable only for persons of 15 years and over.
18   Suitable only for persons of 18 years and over.
18R Suitable only for restricted distribution through licensed sex
     shops to which no one under 18 is admitted.

The 12 category was adopted in 1989, so that the Board could stop
children under 12 from seeing films such as *Batman*, *Crocodile
Dundee* and *Gremlins*, which it was reluctant to confine to the 15
category, but believed (without good reason) would be damaging to
pre-teenagers. In 2002 the 12A category was adopted for cinema, to
allow children under 12 to see unsuitable films if they are accompanied by an adult. This sensible reform came about as the result of
a foolish decision to classify *Spiderman* as 12 rather than PG,
because the board had detected a message that "violence is an
appropriate response when challenged"—a ruling that would deny
children most of their childhood heroes, or indeed, exposure to the
Bush doctrine of pre-emptive self-defence. The ruling infuriated
parents, was widely disregarded and served only to teach pre-teens a

---

[10] (1952) 385 H.C. Debs 504.

contempt for the law: several councils refused to follow it and classified the film PG. The Board was chastened, and in consequence adopted the 12A category, which has worked well, especially by allowing parents to enjoy a wider range of films whilst in *loco parentis*, although the Board in its 2005 Report tut-tuts about "reports of toddlers watching films which are obviously beyond their understanding"—in which case, they could not suffer any harm. The real victims of the BBFC's over-fussy classification are bright 13 and 14 year olds, and their parents, because there is as yet no 15A certificate. The introduction of such a classification category is necessary if the Board is to maintain credibility: in 2006, most kids in that age range found their way (often with parental connivance) to see the schoolyard hit *Borat*—which the humourless censors had classified as "15".

The Board has been obsessive about its arbitrary age-limits (it insisted on 25 cuts to *Indiana Jones and the Temple of Doom* before it agreed to a PG certificate) and film exhibitors invariably buckle under its rulings in order to obtain the extra profits that derive from teenage admission fees. They will happily cut scenes from major motion pictures in order to achieve a 15 rating, and will in many cases agree to cut further scenes in order to obtain a 12A rating. The result is that adults in Britain are obliged to see cut versions of major films that are screened unexpurgated in America and in other countries in Europe. The film industry has traditionally preferred the pursuit of profit to the principle of artistic freedom, and will hardly ever appeal against the Board's decisions. Film makers may be able to assert their "moral right" under the Copyright Act against exhibitors who agree to multilate their work (see Ch.5) although most production contracts require that this right be waived.

15–005   The BBFC has effectively become the authorised censor for feature films in cinemas and on television, and for those marketed on DVD and videocassettes. Its position derives, not from the law, but from various "understandings" it has reached with prosecuting authorities, local councils and the Home Office. The basis for the "understanding" was frankly expressed by the DPP to the Parliamentary Select Committee on obscenity in 1957:

> "If I wished to prosecute a film—and it has been suggested on two occasions to me that certain films that had passed the British Board of Film Censors were obscene—my answer would be, as it was in those two cases, I shall have to put the British Board of Film Censors in the dock because they have aided and abetted the commission of that particular offence. So it inhibits me to that extent. As long as I rely on the judgment of the British Board of Film Censors as to the suitability, under the various categories, of films for public showing, which I do, I do not prosecute".[11]

---

[11] See John Trevelyan, *What the Censor Saw* (Michael Joseph, 1973), p.141.

In fact, the DPP was wrong in law—the BBFC certification of a movie is, technically, no more than its expression of opinion, upon which local councils place reliance when they exercise their responsibility for licensing an exhibition. So there is no danger of the current BBFC President, ending up in the dock as an "aider and abetter". But there is now no real danger of anyone ending up in the dock over the screening of a certified film or the age-appropriate sale of a certified video. The DPP has never prosecuted over a cinema screening of a certified film. There were two private prosecutions back in the mid-70s, both of which came to grief. The case against *Last Tango in Paris* collapsed on technical grounds,[12] and an Old Bailey jury acquitted the exhibitors of *The Language of Love* of the common law offence of outraging public decency. Common law offences may no longer be charged, and private prosecutions no longer threaten, thanks to the 1977 reforms which brought cinema screenings within the Obscene Publications Act and required all prosecutions to be brought by or with the consent of the DPP (see earlier Ch.4) It is virtually inconceivable that he would prosecute exhibitors of a certified film for obscenity, unless perhaps in respect of an "18" screening which they permitted large numbers of children to attend. So far as videos are concerned, prosecutions were brought in the early 80s against "video nasties" like *The Evil Dead* and *The Burning*, which had been certified "18" for cinema release. The resultant chaos and confusion produced the 1984 Video Recordings Act, which required all video cassettes dealing with sex and violence to be separately certified by the BBFC as suitable for viewing in the home. The 1985 "understanding" (see above) requiring police to obtain DPP consent before prosecuting a certified video for obscenity has ensured that no such prosecutions have been brought.

Local council licensing

The Cinemas Act 1985 consolidates all the previous provisions, **15–006** dating from 1909, relating to the licensing of cinemas. Subject to certain exemptions for casual or non-profit making enterprises, it is an offence, punishable by the somewhat extravagant maximum fine of £20,000, to use unlicensed premises for film exhibitions. Local councils may attach conditions to licences, and these normally require that all films shown carry a BBFC classification certificate and that admission be refused to persons outside the certified class. Failure to comply with such conditions is also an offence. On the basis of *Mills v London County Council* local authorities must retain a supervisory function over and above the BBFC, and some exercise this power to prohibit particular films that have been granted certification. Thus controversial releases may be banned in some

---

[12] *Att-Gen's Reference No. 2 of 1975* [1976] 2 All E.R. 753.

districts and licensed in others, sometimes only a short bus ride away. Monty Python's *The Life of Brian* was banned entirely in many jurisdictions, and given a more restricted classification in others.

Local film censorship is usually delegated to magistrates or entrusted to standing committees: some councils rely upon their Fire Brigade Committees to extinguish any flames of passion that may have escaped the BBFC hose, while one Cornish borough solemnly bans films despite the fact that there are no cinemas within its jurisdiction. This kind of censorship, duplicating the BBFC and the obscenity law, was regarded by the Williams Committee as a waste of public time and money, but the licensing provisions were re-enacted in 1982 and consolidated in the Cinemas Act of 1985. In addition, local councils have powers over "sex cinemas", provided by the Local Government (Miscellaneous Provisions) Act of 1982. Although there are few enforcement actions, cinemas do their best to impose age restrictions, even on children accompanied by parents. So when Princess Diana took an underage princeling to *The Devil's Own* it was the cinema, not the mother, which was threatened with prosecution.

Most local authorities adopt "model licensing conditions" drafted by the Home Office, of the kind:

(a) no film, other than a current newsreel, shall be exhibited unless it has received a certificate of the British Board of Film Classification or is the subject of the licensing authority's permission;

(b) no young people shall be admitted to any exhibition of a film classified by the Board as unsuitable for them, unless with the local authority's permission;

(c) no film shall be exhibited if the licensing authority gives notice in writing prohibiting its exhibition on the ground that it would offend against good taste or decency or would be likely to encourage or incite to crime or to lead to disorder or to be offensive to public feeling;

(d) the nature of the certificate given to any film shall be indicated in any advertising for the film, at the cinema entrance (together with an explanation of its effect), and on the screen immediately before the film is shown;

(e) displays outside the cinema shall not depict any scene or incident not in the film as approved.

These conditions import the legal requirements that the local authority should retain the ultimate discretion rather than delegate it entirely to the BBFC. Condition (a) allows a liberal authority to permit screening of a film that the BBFC has refused to certify, as in the *Spiderman* case and condition (c) enables a repressive authority to refuse permission to the exhibition of a certified film. (The grounds in condition (c) are precisely those which apply to television and radio programmes.)

Certain classes of film exhibition are exempted from licensing **15–007** requirements by ss.5–7 of the 1985 Act. These include occasional exhibitions, children's film clubs, screenings by educational and religious institutions and organisations certified as non-profit making. The sections are carefully drafted to prevent profit making cinema clubs from obtaining an exempt status, as many did through a loophole in the 1952 Act. This loophole had fostered the device of the "sex cinema club" as a means of escaping local authority licensing requirements. Now, any screening that is "promoted for private gain" is likely to be caught. Those that are not, but that nonetheless feature sexually explicit films (e.g. demonstration of films that are for sale in sex shops) will probably be caught by the provisions of the 1982 Local Government (Miscellaneous Provisions) Act, which applies to "sex cinemas" that do not require licences under the 1985 Cinemas Act. Section 3(1) of Sch.3 to the Local Government Act permits local authority control of any premises used to exhibit films "relating to sexual activity or acts of force or restraint which are associated with sexual activity or . . . genital organs or urinary or excretory functions".

The effect of these statutes is to bring almost every commercial film exhibition within local authority licensing powers, with the concomitant requirement for BBFC classifications. This requirement is spelled out by s.1(3) of the 1985 legislation, which imposes a duty on licensing authorities to,

> "impose conditions or restrictions prohibiting the admission of children to film exhibitions involving the showing of works designated, by the authority or by *such other body* [our italics] as may be specified in the licence, as works unsuitable for children".

"Such other body" is a reference to the BBFC, and although local councils sometimes disagree with its decisions to grant or withhold certification for adult viewing, its age group classification decisions are rarely interfered with.

The practical result of this array of legislation is a censorship system that pivots upon cutting and classification directives by the BBFC, enforced through threats of prosecution of cinemas if they do not police the age restriction placed by the BBFC on film certificates. It is a pervasive system which indirectly affects all cinema attendees—and there are 150 million attendances at British cinemas each year. The most serious victims of film censorship are: (a) persons under 18, who are denied the right to see films that the BBFC consider unsuitable for their age group; and (b) parents, who are denied the right to take their teenage children to films they believe are suitable for them. Most civilised societies with pre-censorship systems for movies adopt age classifications that are advisory, or permit children to attend any film if accompanied by a parent or guardian. The UK system of censorship interferes both with the right to receive information and with the right of parents to determine family life.

THE ADVENT OF VIDEO AND DVD

15–008   The home video market in Britain was a remarkable success: by the year 2000, 85 per cent of all homes in the United Kingdom had at least one video recorder, whilst one in four children aged 12 to 15 could boast of a video player in their bedroom. But like all new communications technology, its advent provoked moral panic. The earliest scare came when the first court to confront this new technology decided that video cassettes fell outside the Obscene Publications Act—they had not, after all, been envisaged when that legislation was formulated in 1959. Before pornographers had much time to dance in the streets, the Court of Appeal was urgently reconvened in the middle of a summer vacation to rule, on an Attorney-General's reference, that video cassettes did comprise "matter to be looked at" within the scope of the 1959 act.[13] In subsequent prosecutions video cassettes were treated like books: the question was whether their contents, taken as a whole, would tend to corrupt those likely to see them. In determining their potential audience, the jury could consider the fact that they were for screening in the home, and decide whether children were likely to obtain access to them as a result. But fears of this novel technology—its fascination for children, its ability to freeze-frame and to replay favourite episodes, its mushroom growth—were soon exploited in a manic press campaign against "video-nasties".

By 1983 there was an early video vogue for run-of-the-mill horror movies: to capitalise on it, distributors promoted films that explicitly depicted violence and brutality. The label "video-nasty" was used indiscriminately by the press, but it reflected the prevailing fear that meretricious movies that dwelt on rape and mayhem would affect the minds of young children permitted to watch them by negligent parents. The Obscence Publications Act was a suitable tool for prosecution of such films where there was any prospect that a significant number of children might view them, and in 1983 a jury convicted the distributors of *Nightmares in a Damaged Brain* on account of its detailed depictions of sex and violence. But the campaigners—led by the Festival of Light and the *Daily Mail*—saw the opportunity to erect a new censorship apparatus that went far beyond the scope of the Obscene Publications Act. With a remarkable talent for passing off propaganda as scientifically valid research, they convinced politicians and newspapers of the accuracy of such claims as "37 per cent of children under 7 have seen a 'video-nasty'"

---

[13] *Att-Gen's Reference No. 5 of 1980* [1980] 3 All E.R. 816.

and that "the nasty video has replaced the conjurer at children's birthday parties".[14] "Scientific" research purported to show that very young children in working class homes up and down the country were watching sadistic sex while their single parents were down at the pub. Sensationalised research claims, timed to coincide with important stages of the Video Recordings Bill, created a mild form of hysteria among politicians ot all parties and the Bill was rushed through with only two Tory M.P.s and one Labour peer dissenting. Subsequently, the much-publicised "research" was largely discredited, but it had served the purpose for which it was apparently designed: the transformation of the BBFC, from a small body voluntarily cutting cinema films to a bureaucracy with statutory power to pre-censor all videos containing scenes of sex or violence.

The climate engendered by the campaign against video-nasties in the early 1980s affected police forces throughout the country, who raided video shops and prosecuted owners for X-certified horror movies perceived as "nasties". There was a two-year period of utter confusion, as some juries acquitted and others convicted the same film, and a few video traders went to prison for stocking films that had been seen by thousands when on previous cinema relase. Under heavy pressure from organisations representing the retail trade, the Attorney-General finally issued a "list" of some 60 film titles that the DPP regarded obscene because of depictions of violence. Retailers who wished to avoid police seizures could collect a copy of the list from their local police station and remove any offending titles. The "DPP's list" was the first modern example of an "Index" in Britian; video traders greeted it with relief, although many of the films on the list had been acquitted by juries while others, such as *The Evil Dead* and *Andy Warhol's Frankenstein*, had received critical acclaim. Some of the "nastiest" films (even *I Spit on Your Grave*, the most frequently condemned film of this genre) have been intelligently defended as containing a moral message or as depicting brutalities such as rape in order to condemn them or their perpetrators.[15]

By 2006, almost all the films on the original DPP's list had been **15–009** granted 18 certificates by the Board and can now be enjoyed on video or DVD. The obscenity laws had been applied to films in 1977, but the "video nasty" campaign forced the DPP to issue guidelines for prosecutors:

> "The basic factor is the tendency to deprave and corrupt those who are, having regard to all the circumstances, likely to see it. The DPP therefore has to consider who is likely to view videos

---

[14] See the chapters by Graham Murdoch and Brian Bown in Martin Baker (ed.), *The Video Nasties* (Pluto Press, 1984), and Michael Tracey, "Casting Cold Water on the Ketchup", *The Times*, February 25, 1984.

[15] Baker, *Video Nasties*, Chs 3 and 7. See also David Edgar, "Presumption of Innocence", *New Statesman*, October 5, 1984.

taken into the home. While this is ultimately for the court to decide in each particular case, the DPP considers that, in many cases, a significant number of the viewers will be children or young people."

In applying this basic factor, the film is considered as a whole. A work is likely to be regarded as obscene if it portrays violence to such a degree and so explicitly that its appeal can only be to those who are disposed to derive positive enjoyment from seeing such violence. Other factors may include:

- violence perpetrated by children;
- self-mutilation;
- violent abuse of women and children;
- cannibalism;
- use of vicious weapons (e.g. broken bottle);
- use of everyday implements (e.g. screwdriver, shears, electric drill);
- violence in a sexual context.

15–010   These factors are not exhaustive. Style can also be important: "The more convincing the depictions of violence, the more harmful it is likely to be".[16]

These "guidelines" were inherently confusing: how could the DPP tell whether a significant number of viewers would be children? Did "harm" in the case of a child mean the engendering of fear or shock, or some deeper trauma, or a tendency to emulate the violent behaviour? If the basis for the prosecution was that the video's appeal was to those who found "positive enjoyment" in seeing violence, did this not apply to audiences for James Bond, Rambo and war films? The "guidelines" offered insufficient guidance to nervous retailers and distributors, whose desire for immunity from prosecution chimed with the tabloid demand for a censorship body: the Government obliged, in the Video Recordings Act, by giving the BBFC statutory powers to pre-censor video cassettes.

THE VIDEO RECORDINGS ACT 1984

15–011   The scheme of this Act is to require all video-cassettes (and any "other device capable of storing data electronically", which now covers DVDs and computer games) destined for public availability and dealing in any respect with sex or violence to be submitted to a designated authority (at present and for the foreseeable future, the BBFC) for classification generally as suitable for circulation and particularly as suitable for various age-groups. The Act applies to every "video work", defined as:

---

[16] Statement by the Attorney General, House of Commons, June 23, 1984.

"any series of visual images

(a) produced electronically by the use of information contained on any disc or magnetic tape, and
(b) shown as a moving picture."

Exceptions

The only categories of video work (including both cassettes and **15–012** discs) that are exempt from the need to be classified are those that, "taken as a whole", are:

(a) designed to inform, educate or instruct;
(b) concerned with sport, religion or music; or
(c) video games.[17]

However, a video work in the above categories loses its prima facie exemption if "to any significant extent" it depicts:

(a) human sexual activity or acts of force or restraint associated with such activity;
(b) mutilation or torture of, or other acts of gross violence towards, humans or animals;
(c) human genital organs or human urinary or excretory functions, or is designed to any significant extent to stimulate or encourage anything falling within paragraph (a); or in the case of anything falling within paragraph (b), is designed to any extent to do so.[18]

The only case to offer any elucidation of these provisions suggests that the courts will give them the broadest possible interpretation, notwithstanding that they carry criminal penalties (and should, on principle, be narrowly construed). In *Kent Trading Standards Department Multi-Media Marketing* an operation called *The Interactive Girls Club* was prosecuted for producing discs of computer games which rewarded their winner with a few second's glimpse of naked women in provocative poses.[19] The Divisional Court ruled that the brevity of the display did not prevent the image from "being shown as a moving picture" so as to satisfy the definition of a "video work". Nor could it claim exemption as a "video game", because although the erotic tease was a "reward" for successful completion of an exempt game it was a severable and distinct clip designed to follow, rather than be part of, the game itself. *The Interactive Girls Club* decision went on to consider in depth the nature of interactive girls who might win exemption from the Act:

---

[17] Video Recordings Act 1984, s.2(11).

[18] 1984 Act, s.2(2).

[19] *Meechie (for Kent County Council Trading Standards Department) v Multi-Media Marketing (trading as Interactive Girls Club)* (1995) 94 L.G.R. 474.

A bench of world-weary lay justices had been left unaroused by the clips of interactive women pulling at their panties, bending over naked to reveal pubic hair, and stroking their breasts: these images did not depict "human sexual activity" (which the justices took to involve "at least masturbation") or "human genital organs" (which they thought meant sight of a labia minora): the scenes were so mild that the magistrates found "it would strain credulity to assert (they) could either stimulate or encourage sexual activity". The Divisional Court judges, however, set a lower stimulation threshold: they had no hesitation in defining "sexual activity" to include a stroke of the breast or a touch of the crotch. Having engaged in an exercise that can only be described as pubic hairsplitting, Simon Browne L.J. concluded that "none of this material is in any real sense offensive", but that was a consideration which affected penalty, not exemption from classification. The mildest forms of video strip-tease will, in consequence, require submission to the BBFC.

15–013   The maximum fine for offering to supply a non-exempt video-cassette without a classification certificate is an extravagant £20,000; the cost of an application to the BBFC for a certificate will be about £1,000, depending on the length of the video (the BBFC charges about £10.00 per minute). It follows that most distributors will prefer to err on the safe side and submit videos for classification if there is any legal doubt about whether they are exempt. It is, however, a defence to the criminal charges of supply and possession for supply of non-exempt and non-classified videos created by ss.9 and 10 of the Act to prove that the accused reasonably believed he was dealing with an exempted work even if he was not. It would be "reasonable" for a distributor to act on a legal opinion that a work was exempt, even if a court subsequently construing s.2 of the Act were to hold that the opinion was mistaken.

The Video Recordings Act does not affect merely the handful of films that could be deemed video-nasties: it is a measure ultimately imposing liability to censorship and classification on the vast majority of cinematic works transferred to video-cassette or disc. The fact that the work has been made by, or shown on, television is irrelevant. There is no requirement that films containing scenes of torture, mutilation or other acts of gross violence need to do so in any sexual context, and it was clearly envisaged by the Act's sponsors that videos of current affairs programmes showing the Falklands War, for example, or scenes of football hooliganism or a nuclear holocaust or acts of terrorism would require certification. So, too, do sex education videos or any video made by a counselling group about "human sexual activity", unless it were for the purpose of medical training or not distributed as part of a business.

15–014   Section 2 of the Act bristles with problems of interpretation. To claim an exempt status for a video work it is necessary to establish first that "taken as a whole" it is designed to inform or is concerned with sport, religion, music, etc. If this question is resolved in favour of exemption, that status is nonetheless lost if human sexual activity, etc., is depicted "to any significant extent". It is not clear whether "significance" is judged in terms of time taken in the film, or importance to plot, or relates to the extent of the depictions. "Human sexual activity" means more than statuesque nudity, but might (on the authority of the *Interactive Girls Club* case) include simulated orgy scenes in the brothels of *The Rake's Progress* or the gondolas of *The Tales of Hoffman*. Nor is it clear whether the "acts of force or restraint" have to be associated with sexual activity in the film in question or merely in general estimation. "Acts of gross violence towards humans and animals" would seem to catch news films of bombings and battles and bullfights. How a court would decide whether films designed to inform about the dangers of sexually transmitted diseases depict human sexual activity to any significant extent, or (if they do not) nonetheless stimulate or encourage it to any significant extent by promoting the use of prophylactics, remains to be seen. The section is so badly drafted that courts should give defendants who can bring their work within s.2(1) the benefit of any doubt as to whether s.2(2) in fact operates to remove the exemption.

If the video is not exempted from classification requirements, the offences of supplying, offering to supply and possessing for the purpose of supply will not be committed where the supply concerned is exempt, or the supplier reasonably believes it to be exempt. The main situations in which non-exempt videos may be supplied without classification certificates are:

- where the video is given away free, and without a business purpose (s.3(2));
- where the video is supplied to people within the industry, (s.3(4)) or for television use (s.3(8)) or to the BBFC (s.3(9));
- where the video is made at some special occasion (e.g. a celebration or a conference) and is provided to those who took part in it or to their friends and associates, so long as it does not "to any significant extent" depict or simulate "human sexual activity" or the other matters set out in para.2(2) (s.3(5));
- where the video is dispatched for export to a country outside the United Kingdom (s.3(4)(iii)).

Supply of 18R Videos

In the United States, the pornographic film industry is reckoned to **15–015** earn more profits than Hollywood Studios: its products can be purchased by mail order or through Internet sales as well as from specialist stores that require no licence to operate. In the United Kingdom, under current BBFC policy, certain strains of pornography are available with an 18R classification, but the purchaser must attend in person at a licensed sex shop—a procedure which carries a degree of embarrassment and which is unavailable in those areas where councils decline to grant such licenses. Relying on advice from contract lawyers that the 1984 Act confining supply of 18R video works to licensed sex shops might be interpreted to mean that the "supply" took place where an order was accepted and dispatched, some sex shop owners offered a service whereby they fulfilled credit card orders that were made by post, email or telephone. In 2005, however, trading standards officers pounced and they were convicted and fined for the crime of supplying 18R videos to adult customers who were not physically present in the store to make the purchase. In *Interfact v Liverpool City Council* the Divisional Court upheld the conviction, on the ground that the purpose of the Act was to ensure that pornography could only be purchased in a shop that restricted entry to persons under 18, and hence "supply" had to be interpreted as physical handover:

> "The principal purpose of the classification procedure is to guide parents and others in connection with what is suitable material for children to view and to control and thereby prevent viewing by children of video works, which are available by way of supply to adults, but which are not considered suitable to be viewed by children . . . We have no doubt that one of the main reasons for the restriction is to ensure that the customer comes face to face with the supplier so that there is an opportunity for the supplier to assess the age of the customer. It is a disincentive to a visibly underage customer to seek out the forbidden material."[20]

Thus foiled, the distributors turned back to the BBFC, arguing that it was time to permit classification of "good clean pornography" as 18 rather than 18R. They cited the Board's own research, which showed that the great majority of people thought that adults should be entitled to see what they like, and pointed out how adult access to 18R was severely limited because sex shops were unavailable in many areas, or embarrassing to visit in any event and could not readily be accessed by "dirty old men" with disabilities. Since medical research had recently indicated that masturbation reduced the risk of prostate cancer, wider availability of hardcore was in the interests of public health. They offered to box the DVDs and videos without illustrations, to have them sold from top shelves (where hardcore magazines were available anyway) and to check that mail and email order customers were adult. The Video Appeals Committee was unimpressed: in a poorly reasoned decision, it said little more than that since the material was "explicit and extreme" the risk that it might fall into the hands of children must be reduced by limiting its availability to licensed premises.[21]

---

[20] *Interfact Ltd v Liverpool City Council* [2005] EWHC 995.
[21] BBFC, Annual Report (2005), Video Appeals Committee (*PABO v BBFC*).

Although hardcore videos and DVDs must be purchased by adults in person from licensed sex shops, neither the BBFC nor the Video Act can regulate how and to whom they are shown, although it would be an offence under the Obscene Publications Act to screen them to audiences likely to include children. In 2005 a number of hotel chains decided to walk this legal tightrope, putting 18R films on their adult pay TV channels. This did not amount to a "supply" of the video work by the hotel to the guest in the room, because the guest would never have physical possession of the recording, which would originally have been purchased by an adult from a licensed shop. Where steps could be taken to block the adult channel if the room were to be occupied by children, the likelihood of underage viewers would be minimised and obscenity prosecutions in consequence would be highly unlikely. Although 18R material cannot be shown on television under OFCOM's current policy, its availability in hotel rooms in the United Kingdom, as in the rest of Europe, is approved by the tourist industry if not by the tabloid press, which protested at the discrepancy ("Hardcore at the Hilton—major hotel chains screen 18R porn too explicit even for satellite TV"[22]). The discrepancy could, of course, be satisfactorily resolved by allowing late night satellite TV to screen 18R films.

The Censorship Test

Section 4 of the Act contains its main censorship implication: the **15–016** Secretary of State is to designate "an authority" (the first and only authority to be designated was the BBFC) to determine whether works are suitable for classification "having special regard to the likelihood of (certified) video works being viewed in the home". This test applies to every video submitted for classification, even those that are to be restricted for sale only in licensed sex shops. In one sense it serves to emphasise the "target audience" test in the Obscene Publications Act, whereby the court must consider the effect of the work on the potential audience, including persons who would view it in the home. Section 4 requires "special regard" to be accorded to this fact, and was designed to underline the greater potential for harm by the technological capacity to freeze-frame and replay scenes of sex or violence. The Act does not, as some mistakenly assume, lay down that videos must be "suitable for viewing in the home" in the sense of being appropriate for family viewing: that would be to negate the whole system of age-classification and point of sale restriction. The video must be "suitable for classification" in a particular category, having special regard to the impact it will have upon persons in that age-group and below through the devices available for home viewing.

---

[22] *Mail on Sunday*, September 25, 2005.

Some M.P.s in 1984 wanted Parliament to insist that all videos must be suitable for children: this illiberal urge was rejected, and the classification system imposed by the Act assumes a degree of parental responsibility. However, these video-hostile legislators, usually led by David (now Lord) Alton and whipped up by the *Daily Mail*, made regular demands for more pervasive censorship: in 1994 the Government purported to make concessions to this lobby by spelling out the subject-matter which should make a video more difficult to certify, or more likely to be classified as fit for older age brackets. By a new s.4A of the Act,[23] "suitability" for a certificate (or a certificate in a particular age bracket) which depends upon various relevant factors, is henceforth to be decided by the BBFC after giving:

> "special regard (among the other relevant factors) to any harm that may be caused to potential viewers or, through their behaviour, to society by the manner in which the work deals with—
>
> (a) criminal behaviour;
> (b) illegal drugs;
> (c) violent behaviour or incidents;
> (d) horrific behaviour or incidents; or
> (e) human sexual activity . . .
>
> and any behaviour or activity referred to in subsections (a)—(e) above shall be taken to include behaviour or activity likely to stimulate or encourage it."

These subjects are precisely those likely to provoke prosecutions under the Obscene Publications Act, and to which the BBFC had always given special regard. Spelling them out in a statute seemed little more man a sop to the Alton lobby. However, a certain sting was added by a definition of the "potential viewer" whose proneness to harm was a key consideration:

> "'potential viewer' means any person (including a child or young person) who is likely to view the video work in question if a classification certificate or a classification certificate of a particular description were issued".

15–017   This poses an interesting question: if a child is not "likely" to view a particular video work (e.g. because it has been classified 18R or because it is too sophisticated to appeal to children) but it is perfectly *possible* that a few children will get to see it (because it has been "left around the house" or because they are precocious) then

---

[23] Section 4A is inserted into the 1984 Video Recordings Act by s.90 of the Criminal Justice and Public Order Act 1994.

children as a class cease to be "potential viewers" for the purposes of the test, and any harm which may be done to these "unlikely" (but possible) viewers must be disregarded. This approach—which seems to follow from the statutory wording—boils down to the Obscene Publications Act test which requires harm to a significant number of likely viewers. Although section 4A highlights subjects to which "special regard" must be paid, the Home Office minister said when introducing the amendment that, "It is very important to bear it in mind that those statutory criteria are not intended to be exhaustive and the amendment states only that the Board is to consider them".[24] Earl Ferrers, Government spokesman in the House of Lords, said when introducing s.4A that:

> "It leaves the BBFC with discretion to decide what to do once it has considered a work on the basis of the criteria . . . If it concludes, for example, that the work will set a bad example to very young children, it need not ban the video altogether but it can place it in an age-restricted category. There may be some works which the Board believes would have such a devastating effect on individuals or on society if they were released that there should be a possibility of their being refused a video classification altogether, and the clause leaves the board free to do that."[25]

The question must first be whether the video is likely to appeal to children and be seen by a significant number of them. If the answer is "yes", then the second question is whether the video will harm those children or cause them to behave in a way that harms society because of the video's treatment of crime, drugs, sex or violence. If the answer again is "yes", then the factor of risk to children must be given special weight (along with other relevant factors) in determining whether the video should be certified at all, or else given a high age-restriction. This three-stage approach was approved by the Divisional Court in 2000[26]; it permits the Board to ignore the danger to children where the risk that a significant number will see it is remote, and to consider instead the danger of adult viewers being morally corrupted or being persuaded to emulate anti-social acts.

18R: From *Makin' Whoopee* to *Horny Catbabe*

Section 7 of the Video Recordings Act 1984 (VRA) requires video works to be certified either as suitable for general viewing (i.e. U or PG) or as suitable only for viewing by and supply to persons who **15–018**

---

[24] Speech of Mr Norman Baker, House of Commons, October 1994.
[25] Statement of Earl Ferrers, House of Lords, June 1994.
[26] *R. v Video Appeals Committee Ex p. BBFC* [2000] E.M.L.R. 850 at para.12 (Hooper J.).

have attained a particular age (12, 15 or 18) or else certified as 18R, a category which must carry "a statement that no video recording containing that work is to be supplied other than in a licensed sex shop". Councils which grant sex shop licences do so sparingly—in 2001 there were only about 90 such "adults only" outlets in England. The Home Office, under both Michael Howard and Jack Straw, had always insisted that videos which featured real (rather than simu-lated) copulation should not be certified at all, even in the 18R category. This rule, and the paucity of sex shop outlets, meant that distributors of sex firms would pay the BBFC to cut their films to an "18" standard—a sleazy and time-consuming exercise, which made the Board's examiners complicit in producing soft-core pornography and denied adults in the United Kingdom the right to watch "medium core" pornography on video. James Ferman pointed out that "the resulting regime is stricter than that of any of our continental partners in the E.C.".[27] In 1997, he decided to certify as 18R some porn videos of a kind which juries were acquitting in s.2 prosecutions under the Obscene Publications Act.

This sensible approach allowed adults who chose to enter sex shops to obtain "straight up and down the wicket" pornography. Their new freedom infuriated the Home Secretary: Jack Straw brought intense and effective pressure on the BBFC to revert to its ban on "real sex", which the Home Office claimed would be condemned as obscene by magistrates' courts (this might be true, but since magistrates are unrepresentative of the robust individuals who sit on juries, the Home Office point was misleading). The conse-quent BBFC policy back-flip in the course of 1997 was challenged by the distributors of *Makin' Whoopee*, an unpretentious porn video denied 18R because it featured a few bouts of penetrative sex. The Video Appeals Committee demonstrated its independence—both from the BBFC and the Home Office—by upholding the appeal on the ground that juries would be unlikely to convict pictures of straightforward sexual intercourse. Applying contemporary stand-ards, the VAC decided that *Makin' Whoopee* would not corrupt a significant number of its potential viewers—a class from which children could be excluded by its 18R sale to adults in licensed outlets.[28]

The Home Secretary was mightily displeased, and the incoming BBFC Director (Robin Duvall) and President (Andreas Whittam-Smith), anxious lest their new jobs would entail non-stop por-nographic viewing, challenged the *Makin' Whoopee* decision by refusing an 18R certificate to a similar porno movie called *Horny*

---

[27] BBFC Annual Report for 1990 (BBFC, 1991), para.34.
[28] Video Appeals Committee, Appeal No. 0014 of 1998, *Makin' Whoopee*. The VAC specifically rejected the approach in *R. v Reiter* [1954] Q.B. 16 and agreed to look at material which had recently been acquitted in order better to appreciate current standards: transcript, p.5.

Catbabe—unless it were edited to remove "all shots of penetration by penis, hand or dildo as well as all shots of a penis being masturbated or taken into a woman's mouth". But the VAC stood its ground: *Horny Catbabe*, it decided, must be classified 18R. Its 33–page reasoning, however, was convoluted, inconsistent and obscure. It agreed that the video lacked all artistic merit: it was a cheap and trashy product containing no more than an inter-linked series of explicit sex scenes. But the VAC went on to apply, not so much the words of s.4A, but the gloss provided by Earl Ferrers in the House of Lords, suggesting that the BBFC could only refuse classification of the video if it would have a "devastating effect on individuals or society"—*Horny Catbabe* and other ideologically vapid porn movies were not in that class. The VAC did consider the effect on children: it noted recent research that 50 per cent of girls have intercourse by the age of 17[29] and inferred from this—illogically—that they (and their under-18 partners) "would not be harmed by watching videos such as these". The VAC declined to hazard any guess as to the number of child viewers or the prospect of a significant portion of them suffering harm. It found that the BBFC guidelines banning penetrative (but not masturbatory) sex to have little relevance to what might be damaging to children ("Is an erect penis in the hands of a woman masturbating a man likely to be less upsetting than an erect penis entering a woman's vagina?") and allowed the appeal, noting merely that "we might have taken a different view if there was evidence that the effects were affecting more than a small minority of children or were devastating if this did happen".[30]

The confusions and illogicalities in this reasoning led the BBFC to **15–019** take the extraordinary step of judicially reviewing its own Appeals Committee. The case, *R. v Video Appeals Committee of the BBFC Ex p. BBFC*, was decided by Hooper J. in May 2000[31]:

> The BBFC argued that the VAC should have applied the principle of "better safe than sorry", since it had no evidence of how many children would be affected, or how seriously, it should have refused to certify at 18R until the risk could be properly assessed and found acceptable. (This approach is plainly inconsistent with Art.10 of the European Convention, which puts the burden of proof on the would-be censor.) Hooper J. rejected it: he interpreted s.4A as requiring the BBFC (and, on appeal, the VAC) to ask:
>
> (1) Was a child *likely* to view the video if it was classified?
> (2) Might such "potential viewers" be harmed, or might harm be caused to society through their behaviour resulting from the manner in which the video dealt with human sexuality?
>
> When both questions were answered in the affirmative, then this factor—the risk of harm to children—had to be given special (but not

---

[29] K. Wellings *et al*, *Sexual Behaviour in Britain* (Penguin, 1994).
[30] Video Appeals Committee, *Horny Catbabe et al*, August 16, 1999.
[31] *R. v VAC Ex p. BBFC* [2000] E.M.L.R. 850.

definitive) weight in the "balancing act" over whether to classify the video. The VAC had answered both questions affirmatively, but had decided the risk of harm was fairly insignificant so the case for banning the work had not been made out—an approach that was appropriate.

In other words, although s.4A requires complicated findings to be factored into a balancing act, if the censor fails to establish that a significant number of likely viewers will be harmed, an 18R certificate should (at very least) be granted, irrespective of pornographic content. The Divisional Court in *Horny Catbabe* applied the familiar presumption that the courts will not second-guess any censorship decision made by a body of experts. Hooper J. tried to make the decision more comprehensible by pointing out the appropriate test and finding some indications that the VAC had applied it. But what the VAC was really doing was applying a proportionality test: there was no evidence of harm, since children were unlikely to get their hands on 18R videos (although a few would): in the absence of such evidence, it would be disproportionate to deny to adults their right to dilate over pornography.

15–020   Neither the BBFC nor the Home Office appealed the Divisional Court decision: the BBFC surrendered and issued new 18R guidelines. This category, the guidelines assert, exists "primarily for explicit videos of consenting sex between adults" including (without distinction between heterosexual and homosexual activity) scenes which feature "aroused genitalia, masturbation, oral-genital contact including kissing, licking and sucking, penetration by finger, penis, tongue, vibrator or dildo, group sexual activity, ejaculation and semen". However, the guidelines exclude any video with contents which breach the criminal law, or are likely to encourage interest in paedophilia or incest, non-consensual sex, infliction of pain or involuntary humiliation, or which depict methods of restraint (e.g. ball-gags), penetration by dangerous objects or "degrading and dehumanising activity" (defined to include "bestiality, necrophilia, defecation, urolagnia").[32] Good clean pornography, however, shall henceforth receive the Board's 18R imprimatur.

The BBFC, under President Sir Quentin Thomas and Director David Cooke, has refined its current guidelines, which may be accessed on *http://www.bbfc.co.uk*. They have acted commendably to reduce the discrimination that in previous years had meant that more severe cuts were made in homosexual films than in heterosexual equivalents, and in 2006 the controversial German classic *Taxi Zum Klo* ("Taxi to the Toilet") described as "a frank and honest study of a school teacher with an active gay lifestyle" was finally released with an 18 certificate. They have also taken the imaginative step of consulting the most avid consumers of films, namely children in the 12 to 15 age group, and found them much less worried about

---

[32] BBFC Classification Guidelines (September, 2000), pp.18–19.

bad language and horror (unlike the BBFC) and liberal in their attitudes to sex and nudity—unless they were forced to watch alongside their parents![33] This consultation forced the BBFC to admit, for the first time, and albeit in a masterpiece of understatement, that "classifying film is not an exact science". Nor is banning films: the Board persists in taking advice from prosecuting authorities, namely the police and CPS, on what subjects should be denied to the public on grounds of obscenity (in 2006, the police were advising avoidance of sadomasochism, bondage and urolagnia) although it never seems to consult defence lawyers, let alone sadomasochists or urolagnophiles. In this respect it has damaged its independence and become a prophylactic prosecutor, saving police the trouble of submitting films to juries who may take a different view of what adults are entitled to watch in the privacy of their own homes.

Video Games

The market for video games, played on cheap play-stations or **15–021** expensive personal computers, has rocketed in recent years: there are 120 British companies involved in designing and manufacturing software and distributing these playthings, represented by a trade association, ELSPA (European Leisure Software Publishers Association). They participate in a system of voluntary self-regulation operated by the Video Standards Council which has hired a senior Scotland Yard officer to police the age ratings (12, 15 and 18) it agrees with manufacturers. It has supported the adoption of the Pan-European Games Information (PEGI) age rating system which is supported by the European Commission and is applicable in 16 countries including the United Kingdom. There have been some cases of discrepancies between the age ratings of the same games by PEGI and by the BBFC, and in such cases the BBFC rating would, under the Video Recordings Act, provide the legal standard. In 2005 about 200 computer games were submitted for classification. Video games played in amusement arcades are not "exhibitions of moving pictures" for the purposes of the Cinematograph Act 1909, so they do not require licensing by local authorities.[34]

Video and computer games are exempted from BBFC classification under s.2 of the VRA unless "to any significant extent" they "depict" human sexual activity, or acts of gross violence towards humans and animals, or are likely to encourage such behaviour. A vogue in the nineties, for games which involve the elimination—usually, the obliteration—of animated or digitised cartoon figures, raised the difficult legal question of whether such humanoid characters (robots, dragons, zombies and dinosaurs, etc.) counted as

---

[33] Annual Report, May 2006 (Director's Report).
[34] *BACTA v Westminster City Council* [1988] 1 All E.R. 816.

"human" or "animal", or indeed whether enjoyment derived from blasting them to smithereens was likely to encourage violent behaviour in real life. The better view is that games which involve battles between non-realistic cartoon characters do not require classification, unless players are meant to take pleasure in acts of torture or mutilation. Similarly, if the game called for player involvement in the sexual activity of animated characters, it might "stimulate or encourage sexual activity" and so require classification. Manufacturers submit their games to the Video Standards Council for voluntary age-classification: if the VSC considers that the game is non-exempt, or if M.P.s and the press begin to pontificate against its dangers to youth, submission to the BBFC for age certification will be the safest course.

The benchmark for video games was set by the Video Appeals Committee in 1997 in the *CARMAGEDDON Case*.[35] This computer product of British creative technology and black humour sold in hundreds of thousands in 57 countries, but was banned by the BBFC after press attacks which accused it of encouraging road rage ("Ban Killer Car Game: M.P.s Enraged by Sick Computer Game"). The game, playable only on P.C.s costing upwards of £1,200, offered harmless dodgem-car style fun to experienced players in the driving seat who ran over mad digitised cows and a poisonous tube of blobs ("sprites") which squealed when hit and splattered green "blood" on the windshield. It had been given a "15" certificate by Tribunals in Australia and New Zealand but in Britain, James Ferman refused to countenance,

> "a game which gives the player permission to carry out atrocious acts of carnage in this safety-contained world of the PC screen . . . well heeled, laddish young men will take great delight in the game's savage delinquency . . . parents from poorer families often buy expensive games for their offspring . . . it positively encourages the players to commit acts of gross violence against defenceless targets who cannot fight back (children, old people, the infirm) . . . the lethal weapon is one that many of us wield every day, the motor car, and the death toll caused by cars is a major problem in every advanced nation".

To deconstruct this hyperbole, the CARMAGEDDON manufacturers arranged for the five members of the VAC actually to play the game—an experience a majority of them seemed to enjoy—and commissioned research which demonstrated that the PC game market was an adult one (mid-20 to early 30s); that players understood the macabre humour and would never permit themselves in real life to mow down pedestrians in the manner in which they

---

[35] *Carmageddon Case: Appeal of Sales Curve International*, VAC, November 20, 1997 (App.IV, BBFC Report 1997–99).

despatched the mad cows and evil pixels of the *CARMAGEDDON* demolition derby.[36]

The VAC, by a majority, upheld the SCI appeal and classified **15–022** *CARMAGEDDON* as "18". Its reasoning was:

(i) the BBFC bore the burden of proving harm to potential viewers, and had adduced no real evidence to this effect;

(ii) there had been over 300,000 sales already in other countries, without reports of "copycat" effects;

(iii) because the game was only playable on an expensive PC it was unlikely that teenagers would play, adults being much less likely to permit their children to access their PCs than their video recorder;

(iv) there was an important distinction between a video or film, and a game. The latter was much less likely to have an imitative effect;

(v) VAC members when playing the game did not experience a "delinquent feeling" when hitting a cow or a pedestrian "sprite". The game was fast and furious, and players had to concentrate on scoring points rather than engaging in violence. The fantasy of playing it on a virtual motorway was clearly distinguishable from driving in real time.

The VAC verdict was notable for standing against the political hysteria and approving technologically clever, tongue-in-cheek entertainment. The burden of proof borne by the censor had been an important consideration: the BBFC relied on hyperbole while SCI commissioned and called evidence to refute its speculative fears. The game was undoubtedly in bad taste, even though its animated pedestrians had transmogrified (on counsel's advice) into green blobs by the time it was submitted for classification. The *Carmageddon* decision paved the way for more realistically violent games such as *Manhunt* and *Grand Theft Auto*. After a political outcry in 2006 the BBFC commissioned a research study—*Video Games*—which found no connection between playing interactive video games and a propensity to act out the violence in real life: it concluded with a statement of the obvious—"Gamers play games because they enjoy it" (para.11). Nevertheless, in 2007 the board ran scared and banned *Manhunt II* (see *Stop Press* section).

Offences

It is, incredibly, quite a serious offence to supply an uncertified video **15–023** cassette: the punishment is a fine without limit or imprisonment for up to two years. There is no excuse for this severity, which is out of

---

[36] Guy Cumberbatch, Samantha Woods and Sally Gauntlett, *BBFC Classification of Carmegeddon*, June 1997.

all proportion to punishment which befits a labelling mistake: originally the courts had no power to imprison, but the Government in 1994 increased the penalties as a sop to David Alton's lobby.[37] Even the offence of supplying a certified video in breach of its age restriction (e.g. selling a "15" video to a 14–year-old) can result in a fine of £5,000 and up to six months in prison, although at least it is a defence that the supplier did not believe the purchaser to be below the appropriate age. In 1993 the law was amended to provide a defence of due diligence, if all reasonable precautions are taken and all due diligence was exercised to avoid the commission of an offence.[38]

The issues for the court will generally be straightforward and uncluttered by any need for aesthetic judgment, unless a defendant pleads "due diligence", that he or she had reason to believe the work was exempted from classification under s.2. Magistrates may issue warrants for search and seizure if satisfied that there are reasonable grounds for suspecting offences, and police may arrest persons suspected of offences under the Act if they refuse to give their names and addresses. The court may, as an additional punishment, order the videos to which the offence relates to be forfeited—an action more likely to be taken where they are unclassified than where they have merely been mislabelled or sold to under-age persons. There is a special provision (s.21(2)) whereby the court cannot order forfeiture without giving an opportunity to any person other than the defendant who claims ownership of the videos to show cause why such an order should not be made. In accord with s.71 of the Criminal Justice Act 1988, the court can additionally confiscate any profits made from the offence. The police are not primarily responsible for enforcing the Act; this task falls on trading standards officers.

Packaging rules

15–024 The Act and the regulations made pursuant to it lay down detailed requirements for packaging and labelling videos with the appropriate classification symbol. Regrettably, there is no duty to mark a video as an exempt work, although failure to do so will be likely to cause confusion among retailers.

The overall purpose of the regulations is to ensure that no prospective purchaser or borrower is misled as to the suitability for various age-groups of the work or works contained in the recording. It follows from this purpose that where a recording contains a number of separate works (e.g. a feature film and trailers for other feature films), the recording must bear the classification of the work

---

[37] Criminal Justice and Public Order Act 1994, s.88.
[38] Video Recordings Act 1993, amending the 1984 legislation by adding the due diligence defence as s.14A.

that is least suitable for viewing in the home. This purpose is achieved in terms by s.2(5) of the Video Recordings (Labelling) Regulations 1985, which provides,

"where a video recording contains more than one video work in respect of which classification certificates which are not equally restrictive have been issued, the video recording shall be taken to contain only the most restrictively classified video work of these works".

Thus, if a feature film classified as 15 is combined with a trailer classified as 18, the cassette package should be labelled 18, the category of the cassette being in such cases determined by the category of the trailer.

Classification Guidelines

The BBFC classifies films on behalf of local authorities which license **15–025** cinemas, and classifies videos, DVDs and computer games under the Video Recordings Act. In September 2000, the post-Ferman regime issued their detailed guidelines for the various classification categories, as a general gesture towards transparency and out of concern that the Human Rights Act would require more clarity in classification rules (else a ban could not be said to be "prescribed by law"). These guidelines were updated in 2005. The categories are the same for movies and for videos, although the BBFC warn that the latter may be stricter because of "the increased possibility of underage viewing . . . and of works being replayed or viewed out of context". The classification categories are:

U: Universal

Must be suitable for children of all ages, "set within a positive moral **15–026** framework". No sex (other than "kissing" and references to "making love"); no drugs; no realistic weapons; only very mild bad language and fleeting violence; any element of threat or horror should have a "reassuring outcome" (i.e. good must triumph over evil).

PG: Parental Guidance

Must not disturb children as young as eight. Crime and domestic **15–027** violence may feature, but must never be condoned. No references to drugs, or to sex (other than by implication); only "mild" bad language and "moderate" violence if justified by its setting as a vehicle for comedy or fantasy or a re-enactment of history. No glamorisation of weaponry or elucidation of fighting techniques.

12: Age Restriction

Nudity must be "brief and discreet"; bad language (e.g. "fuck") rare **15–028** and "justified by context"; but sexual references "may reflect the familiarity of most adolescents today with sex education through school". Violence must not be depicted in any detail (no focus on injuries or blood and gore) and imitable combat or suicide techniques must be avoided. Horror, however, is permissible. There may be at least a whiff of cannabis, if justified by context, but the film "should indicate the dangers" (But what are these? The danger of dropping out, or of being caught?).

12A (Cinema), 12 (Video): Age Restriction

15–029 Suitable for 12 and older. No one younger than 12 may see a 12A film in the cinema unless accompanied by an adult.

15: Age Restriction

15–030 Strong language may be used frequently, but not aggressively or sexistly ("*cunt* must be justified by context). Portrayal of sexual violence which might for instance eroticise or endorse sexual assault, sex works, whose primary purpose is sexual arousal or stimulation, which may be simulated are generally passed "18", while sex works containing clear images of real sex are confined to the 18R category. Nudity is unconstrained "in a non-sexual context" and sex may be portrayed although not in detail and if casual "should be handled responsibly". Hard drugs may be shown but not if their use is encouraged; violence and horror must not dwell on pain or injury; dangerous combat techniques (ear claps, head butts, rabbit punches) are forbidden, and scenes of sexual violence must be brief and discreet.

18: Age Restriction

15–031 The BBFC says that it respects the right of adults to choose their own entertainment, and will impose no restraints at this level on violence, bad language, nudity or horror. However it may cut or ban any film or video with a, "detailed portrayal of violent or dangerous acts likely to promote the activity . . . instructive detail of illegal drug use . . . more explicit images of sexual activity, unless justified by context".[39]

R18: Age Prohibition

15–032 To be shown only in specially licensed cinemas or supplied only in licensed sex shops, and to persons of not less than 18 years. The guidelines, which will be applied to the same standard whether the activity is heterosexual or homosexual, emphasize that the following content is unacceptable in any film:

---

[39] BBFC Classification Guidelines, September 2000, pp.12–17.

- Any material in breach of the criminal law including material judged obscene under the current interpretation of the Obscene Publications Act 1959. (*This is misleading. The Board does not know what will be judged obscene—there is no "current interpretation" of the Obscene Publications Act until a jury decides a specific case. What the Board really means is that it bans material which the CPS and police think would be likely to be found obscene.*)
- Material (including dialogue likely to encourage an interest in sexually abusive activity (e.g. paedophilia, incest, rape)) which may include adults role playing as non-adults (*sic—is this aimed at role playing adults of restricted growth?*).
- The portrayal of any sexual activity which involves lack of consent (whether real or simulated). Any form of physical restraint which prevents participants from indicating a withdrawal of consent.
- The infliction of pain or physical harm, real or (in a sexual context) simulated. Some allowance may be made for mild consensual activity (*Le Vice Anglaise—spanking—is thereby preserved*). Penetration by any object likely to cause actual harm or associated with violence.
- Any sexual threats, humiliation or abuse which does not form part of a clearly consenting role playing game. Strong abuse, even if consensual, is unlikely to be acceptable.

These guidelines, issued in September 2000 and updated in 2005, are a welcome replacement for the more subjective standards imposed on the media by James Ferman, who retired in 1999 after an intolerable 23 years as Chief Censor, and who toward the end of his reign rambled in semi-mystical terms about taking into account "the moral position of the film maker towards his own material". But, like Miss Prism's view of fiction, Ferman's definition of an acceptable cinematic portrayal of sex of violence was a film in which the good ended happily and the bad unhappily. Replacement of his various subjective tests, which led to a number of unacceptable decisions, by the 2005 Guidelines presages a more sensible and predictable censorship directed to scenes identified as taboo—a rejection of Ferman's moralistic mission to improve films by "trimming" them to send out acceptable messages.

WHAT WILL BE CENSORED?

Underage Performers

The BBFC has a duty to uphold legal restrictions, and those on the **15–033** taking and supplying of indecent photographs of children apply to films, DVDs and computer images irrespective of artistic merit or data production. The Protection of Children Act 1978 makes it an offence to have persons under 16 participate in "indecent" scenes in films, or to distribute or advertise movies containing such sequences. The BBFC applies a strict interpretation of this measure to all films submitted, and requires evidence of age if a teenager performs in an "indecent scene" (the BBFC recalled the film *Taxi Driver* and required a cut in one sequence involving the 12-year-old Jodie Foster). The exercise has become much more difficult as a result of the Sexual Offences Act 2003, s.45(2) of which amended the Protection of Children Act by raising the age of a "child" to 18, so that any depiction of 16 or 17 year old actors in "indecent" scenes henceforth became unlawful. Parliament, in its haste to protect teenagers from pornographic exploitation, was oblivious to the effect of the amendment on film making: highly moral (and highly necessary) exposés of child prostitution, forced marriage, child soldier recruitment and trafficking in children now becomes problematic and the producers of *The Boy in the Striped Pyjamas* had to be reassured by a Q.C. that it was not "indecent" to show small boys in the gas chamber. Existing movies must be reconsidered: teenage actors Elijah Wood and Christina Ricci dry humping in *The Ice Storm*; *Pretty Baby*; Ewan McGregor simulating sex with a younger woman in *Trainspotting*; could Mrs Robinson now be subjected to the attention of a college boy in a remake of *The Graduate*? The best—and correct—answer would be that these sex scenes do not have the quality of "indecency" because in context they are in part of decent and indeed moral films that are not designed to titillate. It is to be hoped that the BBFC adopts this approach, both for the future and if invited to cut or reclassify existing movies. There is ample precedent for a "relative indecency" approach (see earlier Ch.4). The Board demands birth certificates for juvenile performers of indeterminate age. If an "inherent indecency" test is preferred, there will be lots of work for youthful 19 year old "body doubles".

Cruelty to animals

15–034   This is a peculiarly British concern, and the subject is specifically banned by a law passed in 1937 after the release of Errol Flynn's *The Charge of the Light Brigade*—a movie in the making of which horses suffered almost as severely as those in the original charge. The Cinematograph Films (Animals) Act of 1937 prohibits the exhibition of "any scene . . . organised or directed in such a way as to involve the cruel infliction of pain or terror on any animal or the cruel goading of any animal to fury". The BBFC tends to cut such scenes automatically, without asking whether the director both intended and caused the cruelty, which should be the legal test. It has ordered cuts in many films featuring bullfights and in westerns where horses are brought down by a tripping device—although a double standard applies here since it has never prohibited British films featuring fox-hunting. It may be doubted whether its cuts help animal welfare abroad: they certainly eliminate part of the real world where cock-fighting, bullfights, battery farming and experiments with rodents and beagles are undoubtedly a part of life which film makers should be entitled to depict. Many of the BBFC cuts are silly: a sex scene was removed from John Waters cult movie *Pink Flamingos* not because of the sex but because the copulating couple squashed a squawking chicken[40]; *The Blood of Fu Man Chu* lost a scene where rubble fell on a snake[41] and in 1997 the BBFC solemnly announced that it had censored a scene of "an iguana smoking a cigarette".[42] The Board's concern for the emotions of movie characters extended to rodents: it cut a scene in which a rat was dunked in liquid oxygen (an experiment that did not cause it any physical injury) because "for the rat, it was a traumatic return to the condition of the womb".[43] In 2005 it cut a scene of a fight between a snake and a mongoose (so much for Kipling) and boasted of editing out "some big cat action from a vintage *Tarzan* feature". In 2001 the BBFC showed greater sense when it rejected the RSPCA's demand that it censor the Oscar-nominated film *Amores Perros* to remove a key scene of a dog fight in a gambling den.[44] This time, the Board made inquiries of the director to satisfy itself that no cruelty was intended or suffered by the animals. The RSPCA keeps an over-wary eye on film and video companies: in 1994 it prosecuted CIC Video for cruelty to the pet snakes it had distributed to video stores as a gimmick advertising *The Serpent and the Rainbow*. After a two-week hearing the Croydon magistrates dismissed the charges: the video company had taken expert advice on snake-care, and reptiles did not deserve quite the same consideration as lovable household pets.

Drug-taking

Scenes depicting the administration of hard drugs, or glamorising or **15–035** trivialising the consequences of drug-taking in any way, are censored. There are exceptions made for quality films: Woody Allen was allowed to attempt the inhalation of cocaine for comic effect in *Annie Hall*, and *Christianne F* was permitted to shoot up heroin, albeit in shadow and with three minutes of close-ups deleted, because the overall message of the film was aversive. However, the comic cocaine-sniffing scene in *Crocodile Dundee* was excised before the film was granted a 15 certificate for video release, while in 2005 the *Dukes of Hazard* was actually denied a 12A certificate because characters were depicted in a "mildly euphoric state" after being seen with a bong. In 2004 Steven Fry's movie *Bright Young Things*

[40] BBFC Annual Report 1997/8, p.30.
[41] BBFC Annual Report 1999, p.25.
[42] BBFC Annual Report 1996/7, p.17.
[43] BBFC Annual Report 1989, p.12.
[44] "'Cruel' Dog Film to be Shown in Britain", *Guardian*, March 1, 2001.

was refused a 12A certificate (and so lost a lot of audience and profit) as a result of occasional (and historically accurate) references to cocaine. In Warhol's *Trash*, and later in *Pulp Fiction* and *Trainspotting*, heroin-injecting scenes were cut to remove what the BBFC called the "seductive imitability" of "the sight of a needle puncturing the skin" which apparently holds "a masochistic fascination for some addicts".[45] Assumptions of this kind are blandly made by the BBFC to justify censorship without any evidential or expert support: for almost all viewers, injection scenes are aversive. The Board is on firmer ground in cutting episodes which depict the preparation of dangerous mixtures of cocaine and opium, and it rejects entirely—even for 18R—films that instruct viewers how to grow marijuana. Books on the same subject with similar illustrations were acquitted at the Old Bailey as long ago as 1994 (see Ch.4). In 1999 the BBFC took a sensible view in certifying films which depicted ecstasy and heroin-taking honestly and responsibly, without glamorisation, but its more relaxed approach to depictions of soft drugs did not prevent an absurd interference with a five-minute short made by pro-marijuana campaigner Howard Marks. It insisted on adding, after the credits, for the sake of zombies in the cinema, that "smoking cannabis is a criminal offence".[46]

Smoking tobacco is not yet a criminal offence, but the BBFC behaves as though it is whenever the activity is presented as normal or "the smoker is an attractive character or role model".[47] This rules out U certificates for documentaries about David Hockney or Christopher Hitchins, and the Board goes so far as to vet classic movies for any signs of cigarettes smoked in the course of a romance. In 2006 it solemnly debated whether *Goodnight and Good Luck* (a sex-and-violence free U certificate on any rational view) should be age restricted because Ed Murrow, in real life a chain smoker, was depicted as a chain smoker.

Criminal techniques

15–036 Techniques for picking locks, stealing cars or making Molotov cocktails have always been censored, especially from videos (where replays may help to instruct). Combat techniques are "trimmed" where the BBFC fears a danger of imitation—as in neck chops, ear claps and head butts. There has been great concern about the importation of oriental fighting methods—scenes with rice-flails were "banned absolutely", even when they are wielded by teenage mutant Ninja turtles. Particular attention is paid to deleting scenes where everyday instruments such as cigarette lighters and garden tools are used to inflict violence, because the BBFC really believes

---

[45] BBFC Annual Report; 1995 (p.18), 1996–7 (p.16).
[46] BBFC Annual Report 1999, p.25.
[47] Annual Report, 2005.

that viewers might not think of such uses without seeing cinematic examples. It has been particularly concerned to eliminate pictures of crossbows—"restricted by law but too photogenic for film-makers to resist". Crossbows were difficult for armies to resist, too, in many historic battles that film makers may now wish to re-enact. Kung Fu kicks and metal throwing-objects were excised from the 12–rated *Tomorrow Never Dies*.

BBFC reports have consistently inveighed against Bruce Lee style **15–037** martial techniques in oriental and Asian films, sometimes in terms that appear almost to discriminate on grounds of race. In 1999 the Board admitted its approach was out of date—today's teenagers are far more taken with digitally-enhanced special effects—and out of line with what is permitted on television. A new approach would "treat all weapons equally" (i.e. would no longer dwell on the race of the characters who use them) and concentrate on the extent to which they were glamorised.[48] Suicide techniques remain a particular and justified concern, at least for child viewers: one of the most popular "12" films of 2000, *The Mummy*, lost 14 seconds from a sequence involving hanging.

Children

The Board spends much of its time deleting expletives on behalf of **15–038** children, whom it believes should never hear them until they turn 12, and then only on very rare occasions until they turn 15 (BBFC film examiners call themselves "The British Board of Fuck Counters"[49]). In 1999 Disney's *Pocahontas II* suffered the excision of three "bloodys", and a drama documentary about the history of lunar exploration lost historical accuracy (but gained a PG certificate) by bleeping "coarse language" from actual astronautical conversations.[50] In *Madagascar*, the Board persuaded the distributor to remove a "partial expletive" from the animated cartoon ("fu. . ." is not allowed for U audiences) while *Team America World Police* was thought to have language far too strong for 15—thus denying teenagers access to an enjoyable political satire (they flocked to the film, of course, another example of how the Board's sillier decision teach teenagers disrespect for the law). *Muppet Treasure Island* had three uses of "bloody" removed—pirates must not be heard to swear—and the Board solemnly announced in 2004 that for the new 12A category "no more than one or two uses of the word "fuck" is likely to be permitted". There was much soul-searching over whether *Terminator III* could be permitted a record-breaking three "fuck's"— they were allowed in the end only because they were uttered by a character just as he realised that humanity was about to be wiped

[48] BBFC Report 1999, p.24.
[49] Maggie Mills "Sinful Days in Soho", *Sunday Times*, November 1, 1998.
[50] BBFC Annual Report 1999, p.26.

out.[51] The guidelines permit multiple "fuck's" at 15, but in 2004 it despairingly announced that, "The word "cunt" presents peculiar difficulties", as it justified cuts in *Curb Your Enthusiasm* and *The Osbournes*. The difficulties were very peculiar when Cate Blanchett, playing *Veronica Guerin* the courageous journalist, could not be viewed by anyone under 18 because the epithet was used to verbally abuse her in the film, just as it was used in real life. This was another example of a meritorious British film losing its audience as a result of unnecessary censorship. The notion that 15 to 17 year olds are unfamiliar with swearing and need protection from it is risible. It is justified by the BBFC on the basis that, "The British are almost alone in Europe in their sensitivity to bad language".[52]

Children of all ages are the real victims of obsessive BBFC censorship decisions taken ostensibly in their interests, but without much expert insight into what might cause them harm. They will always be permitted nightmares over the wicked witch in *Snow White* and the death of Bambi's mother: why deny them until the age of 12 the enjoyable fantasy exploits of James Bond or the moral missions of *The Phantom*? If they can cope with Uncle Scar killing the king, his brother, in *The Lion King*, why deny them various video versions of *Hamlet*? Most parents would be thrilled if their 14–year-old children took an interest in *Shakespeare in Love* (15) or if their 16–year-olds wanted to see *The End of the Affair* (18): who knows, the effect might be to make them read Shakespeare and Graham Greene. The BBFC is consistently irresponsible in placing movies like these out of teenage reach—doubly so since the rights they deny are additionally those of parents who should be entitled to decide the films they wish to accompany their children to the local cinema to view.

15–039   By insisting upon cuts to films before certifying them for the category which will attract the largest audience—15—the BBFC ensures that profit-driven distributors who aim for that category have no alternative but to accept severe censorship. Indeed, most films are already cut for "15" by the producers and distributors before they are submitted to the Board. The result is that many British films do not appear, on screen, as good as they should or could be: after censorship for a "15" audience, they will have been shorn of the bite and adult wit which might have made them a critical success or less of a critical failure.

Concern about children—particularly schoolgirls—is taken to such extremes that in 1990 the BBFC actually drew up "rules to cover the use of schoolgirl attire in sex videos". The film it looked at most often and most nervously was Adrian Lynne's remake of *Lolita*, featuring a remarkable performance by Jeremy Irons. A 14–year-old actress played Lolita as a naughty schoolgirl (a 19–year-old "body

---

[51] Annual Report, 2004, p.53.
[52] Annual Report, 2003, Director's Report, p.13.

double" was used for her sex scenes) rather than as the subject of paedophile attraction. The film was to this extent a distortion of the book, but nonetheless a powerful study of the desolation and self-destruction involved in forbidden obsessions. The BBFC refused to certify the film for a year, until a new President, Whittam-Smith, took expert psychiatric and legal advice and granted an "18" certificate. His openness disarmed even the *Daily Mail*, and the film's eventual release was uneventful.

Violence

The BBFC distinguishes between violence "of a relatively conven- **15–040** tional and undisturbing nature" in war films and westerns, and scenes that "might lead to highly disturbing imagery being planted in vulnerable minds". This test is particularly applied to videos, where executions and death agonies are cut before they are classified "18". Over half the running time of the cuts made by the BBFC in recent years has involved scenes of violence. The Board seeks to distinguish between "video-nastics" and "conventional thriller or fantasy horror videos". On the basis of the approach adopted by the Williams Committee the test is whether "highly explicit depictions of mutilation, savagery, menace and humiliation are presented for entertainment in a way that emphasises the pleasures of sadism".

These platitudes offer ample scope for busy, nit picking censorship. The fate of *Rambo III* may serve as an example. It was screened uncut to adults (and even teenagers) in America and many European countries. The BBFC, however, insisted on many cuts before it could be screened (for adults only) in the cinema or sold as an "18" video. It was feared that Rambo's weapon-wielding would "encourage anti-social violence on the streets of Britain", notwithstanding that the film was set in Afghanistan and most of Rambo's military arsenal was unavailable at corner stores. The Board required cuts "in bloodshed and in glamorisation of military weaponry", finding it particularly objectionable that Rambo "killed, on the battlefield though never at home, with a deadly efficiency which seemed increasingly out of place in a world struggling towards new, more reasonable means of settling international disputes".[53] These sentiments are all very fine, if very dated, after September 11, 2001, but was it ever any business of the BBFC to promote international harmony? The notion that *Rambo III* would provoke fighting in the streets if shown uncensored to British adults is comical. All that the Board achieved by its fussy "topping and tailing" of violent scenes was the sanitisation of violence—and sanitised violence is more attractive than the real thing.

The BBFC's emasculation of *Rambo* appears absurd beside the scenes of massive violence that are family television news viewing

---

[53] BBFC, Annual Report for 1988, para.2.

from Rwanda and Jerusalem but the Board has always been prone to make political judgments about the kind of violence it cuts, and confessed as much when it censored the James Bond film, *Licence to Kill*, before it could be certified "15". Bond films had not previously been expurgated, but the Board admitted that "the key to this change was the [film maker's] decision to present Bond not as an urbane British intelligence man, but as an embittered vigilante seeking personal revenge . . .".[54] It cut scenes of a woman being whipped and a man being fed to sharks that would, no doubt, have been perfectly acceptable had the urbane 007 loyally taken these actions in the service of British intelligence. The Board has behaved bizarrely in respect of other James Bond films. James Ferman boasted that Britain was the only country in the world to impose cuts on *Tomorrow Never Dies* (for a "12" certificate): the BBFC insisted on advising the producers throughout the making of the movie, and even censored its music ("a loud and aggressive soundtrack had to be toned down in Britain to retain the '12' ").[55] James Bond films are appreciated by everyone as fantasy, and most 10–year-old boys watch the videos irrespective of age categories. This fussy censorship excluded them from family movie matinees, not only of Bond films but of *Titanic, Independence Day* and *Star Trek*, which were also unjustifiably certified as "12" rather than "PG".

15–041   The Whittam-Smith/Duvall regime did not fully shake off the Ferman approach: in 1999 it banned *Bare Fist—The Sport that Wouldn't Die* an argument for the legalisation of bare-knuckle fighting. This suppression of opinion was a clear breach of the Human Rights Act's freedom of expression guarantee.[56] The BBFC attitude to violence has reacted to publicity following notorious crimes, ever since some teenage murders were blamed on Stanley Kubrick's film *Clockwork Orange* in the early 70s. The Williams Committee refuted the claim that *Clockwork Orange* had inspired "copycat" killings, but Kubrick personally took the film out of circulation and the video version was not placed on the market (certificate "18") until after his death in 2000. *Natural Born Killers* has been another victim of industry self-censorship: although the BBFC gave an "18" certificate to Oliver Stone's film (once it was satisfied of the falsity of allegations that it had incited murders in America) and was prepared to give a similar certification to the video, Warner Brothers took fright after the massacre of school-children at Dunblane and refused to distribute the video in the United Kingdom.[57] The trial judge in the *Bulger* case blamed horror

---

[54] BBFC, Annual Report for 1989, para.20.
[55] BBFC, pp.8 and 21.
[56] BBFC Annual Report 1999, p.21.
[57] Warner Home Video actually invited the BBFC to review its "18" classification after Dunblane, in the hope that its own (in fact, Oliver Stone's) movie would be banned. The Board refused to be party to this corporate cowardice, although it pointed out that the company was under no compulsion to release the title: Annual Report 1995–6, p.5; 1996–7, App.V.

videos for the shocking delinquency of the 10–year-old murderers: his comments inflamed the parliamentary debate over the VRA amendments in 1993 and 1994. The consequent Home Office research which concluded that "the police reports did not support the theory that those crimes had been influenced by exposure either to any particular video, or videos in general" was given little or no publicity.[58]

One superstition which was finally laid to rest after Ferman's departure was that *The Exorcist* maintained a unique power to endanger youth and terrify young adults. This early 70s horror film was a classic of the genre, but notwithstanding its religious message (it was banned as Catholic propaganda by the Marxist Government of Tunisia) James Ferman stubbornly refused to give it a video certification. His continuing belief in its danger only enhanced its reputation: in 1999 it returned as a box office cinema success, trading on the BBFC ban which was lifted by Robin Duvall. There have been no reported incidents of demonic possession as a result. Where "video-nasties" are concerned, time is the great healer: most of those which appeared on the "DPP's list" in 1983 as fit for obscenity prosecution have been quietly certified "18", including *Driller Killer* and *Zombie Flesh Eaters*.

Nevertheless, an over-strict view of horror (much enjoyed by teenagers) and vigilante violence has resurged under the current Thomas/Cooke regime. One notable example was the Board's insistence on classifying the important modern film *Sin City*, starring teenage heartthrob Jessica Alba, as 18 rather than 15 (or better still, 12A). This send-up of black and white crime movies "could not be contained below the adult classification" because of its vigilante theme, despite the fact (solemnly noted by the Board) that stylised action in black and white "made the blood white rather than red". Its notion of "containment" for such movies is telling, and has become regular jargon in its reports (Steven Spielberg's *Munich* was "containable" at 15, as was Paris Hilton's *House of Wax*). Teenagers are to be quarantined from provocative and intelligent thinking about the kind of violence that they see on television every night. When teenagers enjoy movies like *Sin City*, either by sneaking into cinemas or after its DVD release, they lose respect for the BBFC and (much more importantly) for the law.

The Board's over-cautious approach to violence in films of quality **15–042** has damaged British horror films: an 18 classification loses audience and investment returns. *The Descent*, a popular film about women on a caving holiday encountering aliens, suffered this damage despite its lack of any sexual content. So did British dramas dealing with important social issues, namely the dangers of being drawn into football hooliganism (*Green Street*) and criminal gangs (*The Business*). Boys of an age most at risk of recruitment into crime were in

---

[58] "Sex, Lies and Censors", James Ferman, *The Independent on Sunday*, February 21, 1999, p.29.

consequence denied a cinematic warning to resist the temptation. Perhaps the most idiotic classification of recent years was to make Mel Gibson's *The Passion of Christ* an 18 certificate. Although there was enough scourging to satisfy the keenest sadomasochist, blood stained Christs are familiar features in all European cathedrals. The Board's ruling doubtless saved a few teenagers from whatever harm they might suffer from converting to Christianity. The prize for inane censorship in 2005 was won by the Board's insistence on removing from Shrek II,

> "a vigorous head-butt, delivered by Princess Fiona to the barmy prince charming. . . This was no mild bump but a fighting technique and made worse by the fact that the audience was expecting a romantic kiss".

To obtain a U certificate, apparently, films must educate girls that they are made to love and kiss—unladylike behaviour by the like of Princess Fiona would simply send the wrong message.[59]

The Board still adopts a censorious approach to newsreel compilations of real killings and accidents (often from CCTV footage) if presented without a moral (or any) message, or simply with loud music. Just as it banned *Faces of Death* (a video of real-time autopsies) in the 1980s, so in 2006 it banned *Traces of Death*, which showed *actualité* footage of death and destruction, without commentary and to loud music. No doubt such DVDs would be sought out for reasons of morbid curiosity, but since the scenes had for the most part been broadcast on news programs a complete ban (not even 18R was proffered) is a clear breach of Art.10.

Sexual violence

15–043 The BBFC is the strictest censorship board in the world in deleting scenes of violence against women, especially in a sexual context.[60] Scenes of torture, threats with weapons, sexual taunting and forcible stripping have been deleted, because of "the danger in eroticising such material for the pleasures of a male audience". Scenes of forcible sex "must not be trivialised or endorsed by the context in which they are presented". Scenes of sexual violence leading to rape are usually reduced, and often excised completely. Standards are noticeably stricter for video than for film: scenes that are "trimmed" on an "18" film may be cut entirely on an "18" video, to remove even the *idea* of the particular form of aggression. As the BBFC put it in 2004:

> "However, scenes or narratives which offer sexual violence as a pornographic pleasure for the viewer or which suggest that the

[59] Annual Report 2004, p.27.
[60] BBFC, *Guide to the Video Recordings Act 1984*.

victims enjoy or deserve the sexual assault are likely to be cut, even at 18. . . The BBFC continues to work on the assumption that particular violent scenes with the potential to trigger sexual arousal may encourage a harmful association between sexual violence and sexual gratification."[61]

The BBFC's explanation in its 1985 report still reflects its thinking:

"We are very careful with rape scenes, even those which in the cinema were found justifiable by context. On video, with its technological capacity for selective or repeated viewings, such scenes could lend themselves to viewing out of context, perhaps repeatedly by persons whose fantasy life might incline them to act out such images of forcible sex because of the extent to which they have found them arousing in private. The same is true of sadistic material, even where the point of view of the film as a whole is a critical one. We realise the importance here of balancing freedom against responsibility, but the issues must be faced."

The Board in this respect abandons the "taken as a whole" test in the Obscene Publications Act, and goes back to the "purple passages" approach that applied to books prior to 1959. This may mean that even films of great merit will be cut for video release because of the danger apprehended from a few viewers obsessing over replayed scenes of sex or violence. The BBFC has always applied a more liberal test to films of recognised social or cinematic merit, by analogy with the "public-good" provisions of the Obscene Publications Act, although the same largesse is not shown to video works. In 1991 the Board finally brought itself, after 13 years, to give an "18" certificate for film screening to Oshima's *Empire of the Senses*, a work of recognised cinematic merit, but it has not approved this film for video distribution. *Straw Dogs*, with its notorious rape scene, is still refused BBFC certification for video sale. The Board concluded, as recently as 1999, that the rape scene "was filmed in a manner which could arouse some viewers and that the victim's enthusiastic reaction dangerously endorsed the male myth that women enjoy being raped".[62]

In that year, however, it did breach a traditional taboo certifying **15–044** for "18" cinema release one much-publicised French film which depicted actual rather than simulated sex. *Romance* was a portentous exercise in Gallic existentialism, but it featured the acting equipment of Rocky Siffredi, hitherto seen exclusively in banned hard-core movies. The Board interpreted the film as "a frank exploration of female sexuality" and passed it as politically correct, including a rape

---

[61] Annual Report 2004, p.74.
[62] BBFC Annual Report 1999, p.30.

scene which "although brutal and shocking, was filmed in a manner which avoided offering sexual thrills". Adult cinema audiences were vouchsafed the sight of a well-read penis, fully and frequently engorged, and the protests—even from the *Daily Mail*—were muted. Not so the hysteria which had greeted the release of the more interesting and less explicit David Cronenberg film *Crash*, which disturbed the popular press through its ironic association of sexual excitement with car crashes. The Board valiantly maintained its position that the film was unlikely to encourage deviancy; but opposition diminished only after groups representing disabled people claimed that the film supported their right to sexual feelings. In all these cases, the BBFC has in effect applied the "public good" defence which would ensure a jury acquittal in the event of an obscenity prosecution. In 2001 the Board broke another taboo by permitting scenes of real, raw sex between reputable British actors: Mark Rylance (in his time, a fine RSC Hamlet) was fellated by actress Kerry Fox in the film *Intimacy*, which was granted an "18" certificate. The BBFC was under the impression that it was a good film (on the illogical ground that it was based on a book by Hanif Kureishi) although audiences did not flock to see it.

By 2006 it was accepted that films with genuine claims to cinematic merit would be certified 18, notwithstanding some scenes of real rather than simulated sex. Mike Winterbottom's *Nine Songs* fell into this category as did the more popular *Short Bus*, described even by the *Daily Telegraph* as, "Deeply tender and deeply funny. . . a wonderful affirming film". *Time Out* was more to the point: "Oozing warmth, colour and song as well as bodily fluids, the film begins with several bangs: self-sucking, flagellation and cunnilingus on a Steinway all pulse their way to climax, immediately followed by a wash of simultaneous melancholy. . ." While the BBFC is getting better at allowing adults to see what they want to see, at least if what they want to see has a veneer of culture, it is still contributing to the woes of the British film industry by denying sex comedies a potentially large teenage audience. Two excellent films, *Goodbye Lennon* and *Lost in Translation*, were lost to under 15s because of two isolated and relatively inoffensive (but accurate) scenes—one was in a sex shop, the other in a striptease bar.[63] Other censorship decisions have been downright absurd. The cinema advertisement for the European parliament election campaign, made for and paid for by the European parliament, presented images of people making choices. The first person was a baby, deciding which of its mother's breasts to feed from. The decision to ban it from cinemas must surely win the booby prize for bad sex censorship.

---

[63] *Annual Report 2004*, p.66.

Blasphemy

This can become a serious problem for a censorship body as craving 15–045
of public support as the BBFC. It risks condemnation from funda-
mentalist Christian groups if it gives "approval" to films that distort
the Bible story, but its application of a controversial and discriminatory law earns It the contempt of the creative community it also
purports to serve. The Board launched a massive public relations
exercise in support of *The Last Temptation of Christ* (a Hollywood
epic that featured Christ fantasising on the cross about married life
with Mary Magdalene), yet it banned a 20–minute British video
about the *Visions of Ecstasy* of Saint Teresa. *The Last Temptation*
was more explicit than *Visions*, but was also a much more substantial
work of cinematic art. *Visions* was banned by the BBFC on the
grounds that it was likely to be convicted of blasphemy by a jury,
although this was entirely a matter of speculation. The DPP would
certainly not have prosecuted in the wake of the Salman Rushdie
affair (which discredited the blasphemy laws in the eyes of all but
fundamentalists and the BBFC). It follows that the exercise of asking
"what would a jury do in the event of a hypothetical prosecution?"
was unreal, since no prosecution would ever have eventuated.
Although the BBFC is required by the Home Secretary's letter which
designates it as the classifying authority under the VRA to avoid
certifying works which infringe the criminal law, the determination
of what does infringe will depend, first, on the DPP's prosecuting
policy and, secondly, upon the verdict of a jury. In the case of
anachronistic common law offences like blasphemy, sedition and
criminal libel, the Board should realise that prosecutions are unlikely
to be brought and even more unlikely to succeed, and should refrain
from using the existence of such laws as an excuse for refusing
classification. (This point was sensibly made by a unanimous VAC
when it overturned a ban on *International Guerrillas* which the Board
claimed was a criminal libel on Salman Rushdie.) Should the law of
blasphemy or criminal libel ever be invoked, the case should actually
be decided by a jury, and not by a film censor (or appeals
committee) guessing at what a jury might decide. The *Visions of
Ecstasy* decision is now seen as one of James Ferman's notorious
aberrations and is unlikely to be repeated: in its 2005 Report the
Board noted that *Jerry Springer—The Opera* had been seen both on
the West End stage and on the BBC prior to its submission for DVD
classification, and since no blasphemy prosecution had been brought
its certification at 18 would follow.

THE VIDEO APPEALS COMMITTEE

Section 4 of the Video Recordings Act requires the BBFC to 15–046
establish a system of appeal "by any person against a determination
that a video work submitted by him" for certification has been either

refused or placed in the wrong age category. This statutory language ensures that only persons who submit videos for classification can activate the appeals procedure, thereby excluding pressure groups and busybodies, but also shutting out producers and directors who may be aggrieved by cuts consented to by the distributors who have submitted their work for classification. The appeals procedure is available only in relation to videos—it is quite anomalous that there should be no provision for appeal by film exhibitors. As a result of the Human Rights Act, however, it may be possible for any interested party to challenge a VAC decision in the courts. Since the VAC is a decision-making body established under Statute with an important public function, it is a "public body" for the purposes of the Human Rights Act, certainly when hearing video/ DVD appeals and almost certainly when hearing appeals relating to film certification, even though its jurisdiction in this respect is contractual rather than statutory.

The appellate panel is selected by the BBFC itself, but has recently demonstrated a robust independence. The present members represent a reasonable mix of perspectives, but difficult decisions will hinge on whether the more conservative or more liberal members dominate the five-person appeal panel selected for the particular case. This factor was highlighted in the *Visions of Ecstasy* appeal, when the distinguished novelist Fay Weldon, a member of the Committee who had not been invited to sit on the judging panel, turned up nonetheless to give evidence in favour of the video. The Committee voted 3:2 in favour of the ban—a verdict that would have gone the other way had Ms Weldon (and perhaps other "uninvited" liberal members such as Professors Richard Hoggart and Laurie Taylor) been asked to sit in judgment. The liberal members of the Board's early days have mostly been dispensed with however and in 2002 seven new members suddenly appeared, all of them teachers or child "experts" but without obvious cultural or adjudicative qualifications. It is not quite clear how or why they were appointed, allegedly by an "independent" but undisclosed body, but many thought that the move was designed to reassure the Home Office that there would be no more permissive decisions of the *Horny Catbabe* variety. There were no appeals at all in 2003 or 2004, but when these new members were "blooded" in 2005, in an appeal which sought an 18 classification for run-of-the-mill pornography, they reacted with unanimous horror at the idea of reaching a permissive conclusion— although it is the conclusion that the BBFC's own opinion polls show that two thirds of adults favour.

The Appeals Committee permits legal representation and sits in public: there is no reason why it should not permit its proceedings to be televised. It gives a reasoned judgment, upholding the BBFC decision or indicating how it should be varied. Appeal fees will be reimbursed to successful appellants, but there is no provision for awarding them their legal costs, a deterrent to distributors who can usually obtain the classification category they want simply by making the cuts rather than by appealing them. The Appeals Committee will reconsider the matter afresh, and can substitute its own view of the case rather than merely deciding whether the Board's decision was reasonable. It is a measure of how cosy the relationship has become between the BBFC and the video distributors that an average of only one appeal a year is taken to the Committee, despite the numerous films that suffer cuts and, in a few cases, outright refusals. The Committee has not, in consequence, been able to afford much guidance for film censorship policy. Its first decision was that a video "consisting largely of women's nude mud wrestling taking place before a mixed audience in a pub in Devon" was "suitable for viewing in the home" by adults.

The Appeals Committee made a serious mistake with *Visions of* **15–047** *Ecstasy*, the video that the BBFC had rejected for certification on the grounds of blasphemy. The Committee accepted the Board's submission that it was under a duty to reject any video that infringed the criminal law, but was divided on the question of whether a jury was likely to convict the makers of *Visions of Ecstasy* for blasphemy. The majority took a remarkably literal-minded approach to the video, finding it significant that the actress was younger than the historical personage (St. Teresa did not experience her mystical visions until middle age) and demanding historical evidence to support the film maker's imaginative interpretation of a sixteenth-century nun's mystical trance. The Appeals Committee majority judgment did not even mention the expert evidence that was adduced to show that the film was a legitimate artistic exploration of its theme. Three members of the Committee decided that a jury would be likely to convict; while two members decided that a jury would be unlikely to convict.[64] The decision to uphold the ban on this basis was manifestly illogical: if the Appeals Committee was split, the assumption must be that a jury would also be divided. PEN, an organisation representing the country's most distinguished authors and playwrights, condemned the ban as "a serious betrayal of cultural freedom in the United Kingdom".

The Appeals Committee unanimously adopted a more robust attitude to its next major test case, when it reversed the Board's decision to refuse a certificate to *International Guerillas*, a James Bond-style epic of the Pakistani cinema that portrayed Salman Rushdie as a mass murderer and torturer. The Board, relying on the *Visions of Ecstasy* principle that it was entitled to reject a work that a jury would be likely to convict of a criminal offence, rationalised its ban on the basis that the film amounted to a criminal libel on Rushdie. It argued, in its usual pseudo-sociological jargon, that the film "had the emotional weight and symbolic authority that makes

---

[64] *Visions of Ecstasy* Appeal No. 0006, December 23, 1989. See BBFC, Report for 1989 pp.17–20.

the polarisation of good and evil a source of moral support and reaffirmation of communal identity". The Appeals Committee, however, was more inclined to agree with Rushdie himself, who described the film as a piece of trash. It decided the film had as much "emotional weight and symbolic authority" as an old cowboy-and-Indian movie, and that not even the most gullible viewer of such escapist entertainment would take it seriously. On this occasion it took into account both the unlikelihood that criminal libel proceedings would, in fact, be instituted (a point the *Visions of Ecstasy* majority had ignored) as well as the improbability of a jury convicting.[65] It may be hoped that this decision will discourage the Board from dredging up arcane criminal laws as an excuse to ban videos. It is noteworthy that the film (pirate video copies of which had been selling for £100 while the ban was in force) was not a commercial success after the appeal, and cinema showings in cities with large Muslim populations were so poorly attended that the legitimate video version was never released.

In 2000 the VAC had a determinative influence on liberalising censorship policy in the 18R category, by its decisions permitting video sales in sex shops of *Makin' Whoopee* and *Horny Catbabe* (see above Ch.4). After these decisions were upheld by the High Court, the Home Secretary peevishly proposed that members of the Appeals Committee should be appointed by the Lord Chancellor, rather than by the BBFC itself.[66] This suggestion was dressed up in the language of openness and accountability, but was evidently designed to produce a less liberal membership ("senior lawyers who may be specialists in child welfare") rendering appeal judgments more to the liking of the leader-writers of the *Daily Mail*.[67] There was even talk of rationalisation by handing over the film and video censorship function to OFCOM. Something had to be done to assuage this threat to the Board's very existence, and without any public explanation, seven new members were appointed to the VAC panel. Their CVs described them as "Retired Headmaster"; "Former Secondary Head Teacher"; "Former Children's Officer"; "Paediatric Safety Consultant"; "Member, Gender Recognition Panel"; "Former Chair, Child Protection Committee"; "Ex-Editor of Blue Peter". These estimable individuals collectively resembled neither an ordinary Old Bailey jury nor a legal tribunal, and certainly mark a change from the individuals on the panel which had opened the door to pornography by giving *Horny Catbabe* an 18R certificate. It would seem that the Home Office was mollified—the threat of an OFCOM take-over receded.

---

[65] BBFC Report for 1990, VAC judgment.

[66] Consultation Paper on the Regulation of R18 videos, Option 3 (Home Office, 2000).

[67] David Pannick Q.C. "Horny Catbabe Fails to Save Straw's Blushes" *The Times*, September 19, 2000.

IN THE REALM OF THE CENSORS

Film censorship has continued, as it began, as a device to protect the **15–048** profits of distributors and exhibitors. They finance it through the fees they pay (over £1,000) for a certification which will persuade local authorities to grant exhibition licences, and will dissuade the DPP from bringing prosecutions, and generally for a respected organisa- tion that can reassure the public (if not the *Daily Mail*) that any risks to children have been removed. This system denies parents the right to decide what films their children may watch, and imposes cuts (in some cases, bans) on videos which would not suffer the same degree of censorship anywhere else in the advanced world. This price the industry is certainly prepared to pay, since it protects them from the vagaries of prosecution. But it is a remarkable tribute to the power of film censorship (or to the power of film) that British liberal intelligentsia and media, so hostile to other infringements of free speech, never seriously challenge it. Yet the BBFC censorship apparatus is perceived as an anomaly in Europe, where erotic and violent movies appear in cinemas and video shops and even on late- night television without any of the fuss that attends them here. Even countries which use the BBFC as a model, like Australia and New Zealand, make its age classification advisory only, so that children can see any films on general release if accompanied by an adult. It should be recognised that however sensible the censor, the BBFC system will have the following results:

(1) Intelligent adult viewers choose to enjoy film and video: their viewing rights will be restricted by the mere possibility of damage to a few deranged minds, or by the prospect that children will view.

(2) The BBFC may diminish the degree of explicit sex and violence, but not the number of videos dealing with these themes or the prominence given to them. Distributors always discern the level of "acceptable" sex and "accept- able" violence, and their films are full of it. The process of "sanitising" or "trimming" violence does not necessarily make it less acceptable.

(3) The BBFC tries to hush up the high level of its classification fees (the subject is not mentioned at all in its recent reports). Some films of real worth are not distributed in the United Kingdom because the profits from art house audiences do not justify the high classification fee (which currently ranges between £10 and £12 for every minute of the work's length). A charity rate of about £4 per minute is available to charities and student film makers, but this is entirely in the Board's discretion.

(4) The system as constituted breaches the rule against double jeopardy, at least for video distributors, because it keeps

alive the power of police, DPP and private prosecutors to proceed under the Obscene Publications Act, notwithstanding that their works have undergone the certification process.

(5) The age classifications are arbitrary. (Why not a "10", a "14" and "16"? or just two: "13" and "18"?). It is well known that children mature at different ages: classification denies many teenagers access to cinema films they would harmlessly enjoy, perhaps hindering their development of a lifetime love of films.

(6) The system denies parents one of the rights of family life, namely to bring their children up as they, and not the chief censor, believe appropriate. Why deny to responsible parents the right to take their 11–year-old to *Titanic* or their 14–year-old to *The Full Monty* or *Billy Elliott?* In this respect Britain is out of step with all other progressive countries, which make ratings advisory so as to encourage parents to share cinema experiences with their children.

(7) Age classification of videos can be counter-productive, serving to incite children (particularly young boys) to obtain and watch "15" and "18" videos as an act of defiance, or to tempt them to savour "forbidden fruit".

(8) Unjustifiably strict age classification—this chapter provides many examples—may actually conduce to teenage disrespect for the law. 14 year olds forced to lie their way into cinemas to see *Borat* or *Shakespeare in Love*, or who watch the forbidden fruit later on DVD, will not only learn contempt for the Board which tried to stop them watching it, but will lead to disrespect for a law that gives the censors that power.

(8) The certification system can actually damage the quality of films, especially British-made films. As the industry catchphrase goes, "the higher the certification, the lower the return". Distributors want "12" or at least "15" to maximise profit from general release movies, and will cut relentlessly (usually before the movie is even submitted) in order to obtain it. What will be lost at this level is not sex and violence as such, but witty word-play and rudery about those aspects of sex and violence which censors believe should be kept from 14–year-old schoolgirls. There are a number of British film failures in recent years whose most redeeming aspects lie on the BBFC cutting room floor.[68]

The Video Recordings Act transformed the BBFC from a family sized firm of 12 to a bureaucracy which in 2006 had an income of £7

---

[68] Some examples of clumsy censorship which damaged British films or reduced the audience for them are provided by Tom Dewe Matthews, *Censored: The Story of Film Censorship in Britain* (Chatto, 1994) Ch.15.

million and a staff of 84. It sees itself as holding the line against visual images that can be seen, increasingly in digital form, on televisions, computers, mobile phones, MP3 players and games consuls, as well as in cinemas and through DVD and VCR players. The fussy futility of UK censorship is underscored both by the fact that so much of what was banned or cut just a decade or two ago has now found its way legitimately into the public domain and by a comparison with the age advisory systems of other progressive nations. Films viewable only by adults in Britain can be seen by their children in the cinema at the other end of the Chanel Tunnel.

CHAPTER 16

BROADCASTING LAW

THE AGE OF CONVERGENCE

The Government launched in December 2000 its plans for the future **16–001** regulation of broadcasting in what is commonly called the age of multi-media "convergence"—the buzzword used to describe the exponential expansion of networks previously limited in the amount or kind of information they were capable of delivering. Broadcasting, first by radio then by television, was a method of communicating facts and opinion to the general public which called forth excessive regulation in the interests of good taste and good politics. Telecommunications, on the other hand, developed without much restraint other than by "common carrier" duties implied by the general law: even privatisation led only to anti-competitive practices being monitored by OFTEL (the office of telecommunications). The computing industry, which seemed at first to have no need either for freedom of expression or censorship, was subject like any other industry to the general law. But the advent in the late 1990s of digital technology brought these three industries together through a shared method of transmission: the information and opinions broadcast on television could now be received on the computer screen and through the telephone. This "converging" of the means of transmission called into question the continuing relevance of the overlapping censorship bodies erected to control the content of radio and television alone, and posed the question of whether and to what extent their assumptions, contained in codes and precedents, should apply to an age when everything is available on the internet. The Government's solution—one big regulator, in the form of Ofcom—promised the virtues of simplicity and consistency, subject to Orwellian fears of big brotherhood.

Broadcasting law in this transitional stage can only be understood **16–002** in terms of the technological and political assumptions at the time the relevant statutes were passed. It may be divided roughly as follows:

(i) *The Voice of Britain*. Until 1954, the BBC had a monopoly of public broadcasting. Its remit, developed famously by

Lord Reith, was to unite the nation and to give the people what a political and cultural elite thought was good for them. The Government had power to take over broadcasts in an emergency, but effectively controlled the Corporation's policy by appointing the Board members and the Director General. Internal rules about taste and impartiality were so strict there was no call to subject the Corporation to statutory duties or to obscenity law.

(ii) *The advent of commercial broadcasting.* Inauguration of commercial television in 1954 was deemed to require the creation of a tough regulatory body, the Independent Broadcasting Authority (IBA) with statutory duties to ensure that political coverage was balanced and that programmes did not overreach the boundaries of good taste. When the 60s began to swing in BBC studios (notably with the first satire programme *That Was the Week That Was*) the Corporation was required by the satirised Government to bind itself to accept identical obligations to avoid transmission of material which could cause public or political offence. The IBA and the BBC came under ferocious attack in the late 1960s and throughout the 1970s by the National Viewers and Listeners Association (brainchild of Colchester housewife and moral rearmament campaigner, Mrs Mary Whitehouse) to which they both responded by developing regimes of institutional censorship, through internal codes and "guidelines". Mrs Whitehouse and other vigilantes took the IBA to court in the mid-1970s in judicial review proceedings which were ultimately unsuccessful but unnerved the broadcaster nonetheless. When commercial radio was introduced in the early 70s, the IBA subjected it to "guidelines" similar to those which constrained television.

(iii) *The Thatcher Years.* The Thatcher Government had a turbulent and truculent relationship with broadcasters, particularly over their IRA coverage ("oxygen for terrorists"). Its thinking was schizophrenic nonetheless: it sought to encourage greater commercial freedom, through cable and later satellite services, but to regulate sex with Whitehousian vigour and to curb "unbalanced" political reporting. In 1980 it established the *Broadcasting Complaints Commission*, to condemn "unfair treatment" by television and radio programmes. This was followed by the Video Recordings Act of 1984, which designated the BBFC as the statutory regulator for this industry, and in the same year it set up the Cable Authority with statutory powers to oversee the contents of cable television. In 1988 it established the *Broadcasting Standards Council*, under William Rees-Mogg, to monitor sex and violence. However, the Government's commitment to free-market philosophy so that developments of fibre-optic cable systems and direct broadcast satellites could provide a multiplicity of channel choice was reflected in the recommendations of the 1986 Peacock Committee,[1] which became the basis for the new "semi-deregulated" framework of the 1990 Act.

(iv) *The Broadcasting Act 1990.* This was the centrepiece of radio and television legislation. It replaced the IBA with two bodies, the *Independent Television Commission* (ITC) and the *Radio Authority*, both with a mandate for "lighter touch" regulation. Essentially, this meant an end to the IBA practice (required by the decision in *McWhirter*'s case) of previewing controversial programmes: pre-censorship was superseded by a new set of ITC reprisal powers ranging from warnings to fines to the ultimate sanction, loss of licence. The Act occupied a great deal of parliamentary time, emerging as a massive statute with 204 sections and 22 schedules. Much of the political debate focused on the requirement of a new "due impartiality" code which Mrs Thatcher insisted on including, in the hope of deterring programmes like *Death on the Rock* which had provoked a major conflict with the Government by voicing allegations about the SAS "execution" of three IRA members in Gibraltar (deterrence was more effectively achieved by the subsequent ITC decision to deny a franchise to Thames television, which had made the programme). Opposition spokesman Roy Hattersley volubly promised to repeal the requirement for a "due impartiality" code when Labour came into office: needless to say, this promise was not honoured.[2] The 1990 Act ushered in a decade in which freedom of expression was bounded not by precise laws but by imprecise codes, drafted and interpreted by Government appointees on a number of bodies whose jurisdiction overlapped and whose decisions could not be appealed or attacked on their merits: judicial review was sometimes sought, but would usually result in judicial deference to the assumed "expertise" of the members of the body in question, although most of these political appointees were not "experts" in any meaningful sense. Thus programme-makers had to comply with codes promulgated by the ITC, the BBC and the Radio Authority, the Broadcasting Standards Council and the Broadcasting Complaints Commission, all dealing with the same subject-matter but with slightly different emphasis: they were exposed to a "triple jeopardy" in that complainants who did not at first succeed (i.e. with the BBC

---

[1] Report of the Committee on Financing the BBC (chaired by Professor Alan Peacock) Cm. 9824 (1986).

[2] See *Hansard*, House of Commons, October 25, 1990, Vol.178, No.162, col.1512.

or ITC) could try and try again (by complaining to the BCC or BSC, and in the event of failure by attempting judicial review). In 1996 a supplementary Broadcasting Act, necessary to provide for digital television, saved some public time and money by amalgamating the Complaints Commission and the Standards Council into a new regulatory body, the *Broadcasting Standards Commission* (BSC), but otherwise left the 1990 framework unchanged.

(v) *The 2003 Communications Act.* The Labour Government produced a White Paper in 2000, proposing to amalgamate all censorship bodies (which it euphemistically called "negative content regulators") into something called Ofcom. This new body would assume the regulatory role of the ITC, OFTEL, the Radio Authority and BSC, together with that of ICSTIS, and of the BBFC in respect of video. It would also advise the Home Secretary on whether and when to exercise his power under section 177 of the 1990 Act to proscribe a foreign satellite service. The White Paper was deliberately vague about Ofcom and its powers: it would "end the double jeopardy of the current system" and its objectives would be:

- protecting the interests of consumers;
- maintaining high quality of content, a wide range of programming, and plurality of public expression;
- protecting the interests of citizens by maintaining accepted community standards in content, balancing freedom of speech against the need to protect against potentially offensive or harmful material, and ensuring appropriate protection of fairness and privacy.[3]

16–003   These are traditional regulatory objects, although it should also give weight to: "the special needs of people with disabilities and of the elderly, of those on low income and of persons living in rural areas". These are more novel, and mark the increasing awareness of and need to combat discrimination on ground of disability (physical and mental) and the emergence of "country" as distinct from "town" as a special constituency. The special needs of the poor ("those on low income" and, presumably, those on no income at all) have not previously featured as a focus for regulatory activity. Ofcom should have the enforcement powers available to the ITC and OFTEL, and a proper appeals process was promised, i.e. an appellate body which can consider the factual merits of the case rather than pick over errors of law and procedure on judicial review.[4]

[3] White Paper, December 16, 2000 (DTI and Department of Culture, Media and Sport) accessible at *www.communicationswhitepaper.gov.uk*.
[4] fn.3 above, para.8.9.1, p.81.

The Government's proposals became the Communications Act 2003, which received Royal Assent in July of that year.[5] The new Act, the brain-child of the Department of Culture, Media and Sport and the Department for Trade and Industry, brought together the regulation of broadcasting and telecommunications for the first time and its centrepiece was Ofcom (the Office of Communications) the new super-regulator. After extensive lobbying, Ofcom was not quite as "super" as the White paper proposed: the BBFC and ICSTIS were not incorporated. The striking fact remains, however, that while all programmes on television and radio, whether analogue or digital, are now regulated by Ofcom, internet content, emails and mobile phone multimedia content are not. In other words, in what are increasingly the media of choice for young people, the communications revolution had left the Act looking outdated even before it reached the statute book. It remains doubtful whether the internet will prove capable of being regulated in a manner comparable to the rest of the communications industry.

Why Regulate?

The threshold question, of course, is why broadcasting should be **16–004** accorded a different legal regime to that governing the publication of books and newspapers. Initially, the justification was technological: "spectrum scarcity"—the limit to the number of terrestrial frequencies—required close control in the public interest to ensure they were put to the best use. Hence duties to demonstrate "good taste" and "due impartiality" were imposed on a television service which supplied only four channels to the entire nation. But re-imposing them in identical terms, with additional tiers of codes and regulators, on services carrying numerous channels to audiences who pay for the pleasure of viewing them, was the response of parliament (or at least of the Thatcher Government).

The irony that in 1990 "deregulation" meant *more* regulation is a tribute to the perceived power of television to influence as well as to reflect ideas and social behaviour. The tabloid newspapers, which most people read, require no statutory controls, although their impact on moral standards must be much greater than late night television programmes which play to self-selecting audiences. Much of the debate over the Act was concerned with the problem of maintaining "quality" in the market place, an objective that requires a licensing body to evaluate the prospective programme performance of applicants rather than concentrating on the highest bidder. The regulation of programme content by codes and disciplinary bodies in the interests of good taste and good politics does not involve a judgment on their quality but on their potential to shock

---

[5] The Act came into force in two stages in July and September 2003.

and disturb. In its first report the Broadcasting Standards Council described television as "a guest in the home", whose conduct might acceptably become "more relaxed and informal" as the evening wears on.[6] The paternalistic notion that television existed on sufferance, and owed a duty to behave itself according to social norms expected of Lord Rees-Mogg's dinner guests, infused the debates over the 1990 Act: that it lingers was demonstrated a decade later when his successor at the BSC, Lord Richard Home, was forced to resign when adultery and a penchant for soft-core porn was deemed to disqualify him from the role of chaperone.

By the turn of the twenty-first century almost everyone, everywhere in the United Kingdom, could receive terrestrial television (99.4 per cent of the population, although some—doubtless to their relief—could not receive Channel 5). There were 250 commercial channels available, which together with the BBC pumped out 40,000 hours of viewing every week. Over 25 per cent of UK homes had gone digital, two-thirds of all households had more than one television, there were 30 million people with mobile phones, while PCs and laptops were being acquired at such a rate that official statistics could not keep count. About 4 per cent of all consumer spending was on television and telecommunications, industries which were growing considerably faster than the rest of the economy. "In other words" (those of the 2000 White Paper) "the era when the extent of broadcasting was determined by spectrum scarcity is drawing to a close".[7] With the switch to digital, every home had access to dozens of channels. On the internet, citizens "would be able to order the programme they want from any provider, anywhere in the world". Rather than interpret these figures as pointers to the futility of regulation, the Government used them to argue for the importance of regulation as a guarantee for the continuance of public service broadcasting, which still retains its hold on the UK public (the BBC and Channel 4 command 60 per cent of viewing time). The White Paper asserted that Ofcom would be necessary to maintain original and high quality programming, maintaining standards (and peak slots) in news and current affairs, and ensuring diversity in broadcast opinion.

16–005   This argument, which assumes that statutory duties and programme codes and disciplinary bodies all work to improve quality and creativity in programme-making, is at best unproven, at worst naïve. The laws of defamation and indecency and confidence and copyright are onerous enough, without a further layer of ethical prescripts to which compliance is required by a contract of employment. The White Paper never asks why "public service broadcasting" these days so notably fails to expose public scandal or malfeasance: since the 1990 Act, almost all the most important exercises in

---

[6] Broadcasting Standards Council, *Annual Report 1988–89*, p.29.
[7] White Paper, para.5.2.4, p.48.

investigative journalism have been books and newspapers. This sombre fact is not accounted for by the inherent limitations of television, a picture-driven and necessarily simplistic medium, because in previous times programmes like *This Week* and *World in Action* and *Panorama* competed with the press for the best investigative journalism. Today BBC and ITV "news" is more often a beat-up of what is in the newspapers, or what is covered at greater length by CNN or Sky. To what extent have the layers of regulation imposed by programme codes, over and above the general law, led to punch-pulling and nervousness about serious current affairs or documentary investigation? In 2007, when the BBC obtained a newsworthy document relating to the "cash for peerages" police inquiry, it held it so the Attorney General could injunct its transmission, instead of putting it out immediately on one of its "rolling news" programs. The *Guardian*, made of sterner legal stuff, refused to hold the front page, and beat off the Attorney General's challenge.

Even late-night discussion programmes can be suffocated by the imperative of avoiding offence. For example, in the 2001 debate over the Saatchi Gallery photographs, the *Guardian* published them, uncensored and in full colour, but the BBC refused to focus its cameras on them, even at 23.30 on BBC2.[8] The result was cowardly television, compared with honest coverage in a newspaper not shackled by rules and codes and programme controllers and standards commissions. The 2003 Communications Act marked in some respects a retreat from the over-regulation of the Thatcher years. The archaic "good taste" imperative was dropped from the statute; Ofcom was given a specific legislative duty to abide by free expression principles (s.3(3)(g)) and was directed to focus its censure on harm rather than indecency. In the short time that Ofcom has been up and running, it is pleasing to record that it has passed its first test, upholding the BBC's right to broadcast *Jerry Springer—the Opera* despite an avalanche of orchestrated complaints from reactionary Christian groups. It is particularly pleasing to note that it has abandoned the worst Rees-Moggian traits condemned in previous editions of this book, namely an obsession for political correctness and a profound lack of any sense of humour. The BSC routinely upheld complaints against late night or "alternative" comedy as well as against Ned Sherin, Rory Bremner and *South Park*, usually when the only objection came from one shocked or possibly deranged member of the public.[9] The BSC was an anachronistic and patronising body, which will be remembered for promoting the art of "pixellating" body organs on any person or thing caught *in flagrante*. Unlike the BSC, Ofcom decisions on "offensiveness" complaints have shown good sense and some street wisdom. Although it has tended to use the protection of children as an all-purpose excuse for

---

[8] *Newsnight Extra*, Friday March 9, 2001.
[9] See Robertson and Nicol, *Media Law* (4th edn, Sweet and Maxwell), p.797–815.

unnecessary censorship of adult viewing and has been wrong to force important movies into late-night slots and to blanket-ban 18R material on PIN-protected premium channels, it has made some valuable regulatory initiatives, especially in restricting the advertising to children of food and drink high in fat, salt and sugar. The scandal exposed in 2007 of the premium rate calls to dishonest TV quiz shows indicates that there are monitoring roles for Ofcom—even on the studio floor—which have nothing to do with censorship but are required because of the greed and shaky ethics of some broadcasters especially independents brought in by Thatcher-era deregulation.

THE FREEDOM TO BROADCAST

16–006 The Human Rights Act 1998 incorporates Art.10 of the European Convention on Human Rights, which begins, "Everyone has the right to freedom of expression . . . " but ends "This Article shall not prevent states from requiring the licensing of broadcasting, television or cinema enterprises".

This proviso permits the establishment of licensing systems, but it does not underwrite specific licensing refusals made by regulatory bodies. The European Court emphasised the importance of this distinction in two cases decided in 1990.

Groppera Radio v Switzerland[10]: The Swiss government prohibited a Swiss company from retransmitting the pop music programmes of an Italian radio station that did not use transmitters approved by international communications conventions. The company claimed that this ban on retransmission amounted to a breach of its Art.10 rights to impart information freely and regardless of frontiers. The court held:

- Popular music and commercials could properly be regarded as "information" and "ideas", so that the ban was prima facie an interference with Art.10 rights.
- The provision in Art.10 permitting states to licence broadcasting was of very limited scope and did not amount to an exception to the basic right guaranteed by Art.10. It permitted states to control the organisation and technology of broadcasting within their territories, but the licensing measures themselves had to be justified as necessary in a democratic society on the grounds set out in Art.10(2).
- That said, the ban was justifiable under Art.10(2) because it had the legitimate aim of preventing the evasion of international law and protecting the rights of others. The ban was not directed at the content of the programmes and had not

---

[10] (1990) 12 E.H.R.R. 524.

been applied by use of disproportion ate measures (such as jamming transmissions).

Autronic AG v Switzerland[11]: The Swiss government stopped a company specialising in home electronics from demonstrating how its dish aerial equipment could receive Soviet television programmes picked up from a Soviet telecommunications satellite, on the grounds that international law required the consent of the broadcasting state for such interceptions. The court held that the freedom of expression guarantee in Art.10 was given to corporations as well as to individuals, and applied to restrictions on the means of transmission and reception as well as to restrictions on the content of programmes. It emphasised that interference had to be convincingly established as "necessary in a democratic society", and was not persuaded that international law required that every interception from a satellite transmission should have the consent of authorities of the country in which the station transmitting to the satellite was situated. It followed that the restriction could not be justified by the exceptions to Art.10(2), and that the Swiss authorities had breached the Convention.

These decisions establish that the broadcasting proviso in **16–007** Art.10(1) does not itself justify a licence refusal, which must (like any other interference) always be justified as necessary in a democracy for one of the objectives excepted by Art.10(2). This is because broadcasting stations, like newspapers and internet websites, are vehicles for communicating information and ideas, and the right of free expression includes a presumptive right to operate this means of communication. Any licensing system hinders ("interferes with") the freedom of expression both of those refused licenses as well as members of the public whose right to receive information from a plurality of broadcast sources is curtailed.[12] In a series of important decisions against Austria, the European Court of Human Rights used the principle of pluralism to ring the death-knell of the national broadcasting monopolies which prevailed at the time the Convention was drafted. The State has a duty to guarantee pluralism in broadcasting, and this is violated if it fails to provide a system under which citizens can apply for licences and have their applications fairly determined according to relevant public interest criteria:

In *Lentia v Austria*[13] the ECtHR declared that a State broadcasting monopoly was a breach of Art.10, notwithstanding the licensing proviso. Although public monopolies might contribute to quality and balance of programming, a prohibition on *any* competition was impossible to reconcile with the duty of a democratic State to guarantee

---

[11] (1990) 12 E.H.R.R. 485.
[12] See *Red Lion Broadcasting v FCC* (1969) 395 U.S. 367 at 386 *et seq.*
[13] *Informationsverein Lentia v Austria* (1993) 17 E.H.R.R. 93.

pluralism. No longer could justification be found in spectrum scarcity or in the small size of the market: freedom of enterprise was a necessary concomitant of freedom of speech.

Austria was reluctant to bring its law into conformity with the Convention: it delayed, then permitted only two private licences, through a law which turned out to be unconstitutional. The Eurocourt held that the Convention breach continued, for as long as private licences were effectively suspended.[14] It has subsequently reaffirmed the importance of access to the airwaves: the State must prove convincingly the need for any interference.[15] Its case will be convincing where a licence refusal—or even a ban on any particular licence application—serves the overall objective of pluralism.

> In *United Christian Broadcasters v United Kingdom*[16] a religious organisation complained of the Broadcasting Act ban on religious or political bodies applying for national radio licences. The United Kingdom justified this infringement by virtue of the limited availability of national licences, given the Government's decentralising policy of reserving most available frequencies for local radio. This policy in itself encouraged diversity (religious bodies could apply for local licences) and the ban on sectional interests applying for any of the four national licences protected "the rights of others" (i.e. of the national listening audience) to have music and talk of widespread interest rather than a station devoted to partisan religion or politics.

16–008 These Art.10 principles have been considerably extended by the Privy Council to strike down biased decisions by Government licensors in several Caribbean countries with constitutional free speech guarantees. The question always is whether the licence refusal has been fair in procedure and reasonable in practice, in the context of any local technical or public policy constraints. There must be a clear and non-discriminatory procedure for licence applications and a reasonable and rational criteria for awarding them. Everyone has a presumptive constitutional right to a licence: the notion that its bestowal is an Executive privilege was roundly condemned in *Observer Publications Ltd v Matthew and Att-Gen of Antigua*[17]:

> The applicant, a newspaper critical of the island's Government, applied for a licence to run an FM station: under the law, grant of such licences was in the discretion of the Cabinet. After a year-and-a-half of procrastination, the telecommunications officer was directed by the

---

[14] *Radio ABC v Austria* (1998) 25 E.H.R.R. 185.

[15] *Tele 1 Privatfernsehgesellschaft MBH v Austria*, Application No. 32240/96, September 21, 2000.

[16] *UCB v UK*, Application No.4482/98, November 7, 2000.

[17] *Observer Publications Ltd v Campbell "Mickey" Matthews; the Commissioner of Police and the Att-Gen of Antigua* (2001) 10 B.H.R.C. 252.

Cabinet to refuse it. The only other licensed broadcaster in Antigua, apart from the Government-controlled radio and television station, were a commercial radio station (owned by the Prime Minister, his two brothers and his mother) and a cable television station owned by one of the Prime Minister's brothers. The Antiguan courts denied relief on the grounds that no one had a "right" to a broadcasting licence and the cabinet's unreasoned refusal had to be presumed constitutional. The Privy Council, however, held that it was unconstitutional to refuse a broadcasting licence without any stated grounds, or on grounds inconsistent with the exceptions defined by the Constitution as limiting free speech. Freedom of expression principles must, the Court held, be implied in the discretions granted to regulators by telecommunications legislation, and it added (significantly) that "the approach will be much the same in the United Kingdom under s.3 of the Human Rights Act 1998". The Government had claimed to have a policy against granting further licences until the legislation was re-vamped, "but a policy motivated by a desire to suppress or limit criticism of the Government of the day is never acceptable in a democratic society."

Notwithstanding its genesis in small island nepotism, the *Observer Publications Ltd* case is an example of a court *implying* free speech guarantees in licensing laws which make no mention of them, by reference to the Constitutional guarantees (or, in the United Kingdom, to the 1998 Act). European case law (notably *Lentia*) establishes that a refusal of a radio or television licence is an infringement of the freedom to disseminate ideas and information. Such a refusal,

> "may nevertheless be upheld . . . to the extent that the law in question makes provision that is reasonably required for a certain range of purposes. The onus upon those supporting the restriction is to show that it was reasonably required. If the latter onus is discharged, the burden shifts to the complainant to show that the provision or the thing done is not reasonably justified in a democratic society."[18]

The importance of "constitutionalising" broadcasting law is that all licensing decisions, and decisions over whether to fine broadcasters for code breaches, and even (arguably) decisions that codes have been breached, must now be justified by reference to the "democratic necessity" principle. One application of the principle by the Privy Council resulted in the award of damages to Mr John Benjamin, the presenter and originator of a popular talk back programme on the Government-run Radio Anguilla. Benjamin's programme was cancelled by the minister after (and because) it attacked the Government's plans for a national lottery. The Privy Council held that a breach of the free speech guarantee had

---

[18] (2001) 10 B.H.R.C. 252, transcript pp.12 *per* Lord Cooke of Thorndon. See also *Cable & Wireless (Dominica) Ltd v Marpin Telecoms* (2000) 9 B.H.R.C. 486.

occurred, although the programme's closure was not a breach of contract and the claimant may not have had any general right to broadcast[19]: in the particular circumstances, the minister clearly intended to hinder free speech by cancelling the programme as a reprisal for its criticism of his Government. This was the relevant motive, and there was no excuse of falling ratings or jaded audiences or of the programme having run its allotted course. The Government's motive was to stop the expression of hostile views, and its arbitrary and capricious withdrawal of the platform it had made available for free expression entitled the presenter to damages.[20]

Benjamin is a remarkable case, which applies the historic decision in *Olivier v Buttigieg*[21] (when the Privy Council used Malta's free speech clause to strike down a ban on bringing anti-Catholic newspapers into government offices) to decisions to interfere with programmes. It offers programme makers and journalists the prospect of legal redress when they suffer reprisals for genuine exercises in free speech. The European Court of Human Rights has similarly held that Member States have a duty to protect television journalists from reprisals for speaking out against management policies.[22] What was particularly noteworthy about *Benjamin* is the way the Court brushed aside as irrelevant the fact that cancellation of the programme was a form of settlement with the company which ran the lottery and which had threatened to sue for defamation. The principle could also apply to protect a journalist victimised by a private employer. Although Benjamin's talk-back programme was suspended by order of the minister, the Privy Council rationale would apply to a decision by the BBC Trustees (who are Government appointees) should they cancel a programme for political rather then professional reasons.

16–009   The European Court of Human Rights has extended the protection offered by Art.10 to a radio presenter who commented on a newspaper article written by another journalist on a subject of public interest. Although the article defamed public officials (who had in consequence sued the presenter) the latter was entitled to disseminate it—so long as he did not adopt the libels—in order to provide information to the public.[23] *Benjamin* and *Thoma* and *Fuentes Bobo* are straws in the constitutional wind which may be made into bricks for the foundation of a wider principle that will prohibit punitive reprisals for programme content if they cannot be justified either by reference to the excepted values in Art.10(2) or by reference to

---

[19] See *X & Z v UK* (1971) 38 CD. 86; but compare *Fernando v Sri Lanka Broadcasting* (1986) 1 B.H.R.C. 104 and *Haider v Austria* (1995) 83 D.R. 66.

[20] *Benjamin v Minister for Broadcasting and Att-Gen of Anguilla* (2001) 10 B.H.R.C. 237.

[21] *Olivier v Buttigieg* [1967] 1 A.C. 115.

[22] *Fuentes Bobo v Spain*, E.C.H.R., February 29, 2000.

[23] *Thoma v Luxembourg* (No. 38432/97) March 29, 2001.

accepted professional or commercial broadcasting criteria. The distinctions made in *Benjamin* mark the beginning of what will become a crucial juristic exercise for the legal protection of broadcasters: the identification and stigmatisation of an act of impermissible *censorship*, as opposed to an action justifiably taken because of mediocre performance, genuine policy changes, diminishing audiences and the like.

There were no claims about denial of free speech rights made by disappointed applicants in 1991, when the ITC first issued television licences under the 1990 Broadcasting Act. No Human Rights Act was in force, and the House of Lords in the case of *Brind* had diminished the significance of Art.10 for British law.[24] Several television company applicants were refused judicial review on the grounds that they had failed to act promptly, so the rights of shareholders in rival companies which had won franchises would be affected if attempts were made three months later to overturn the award.[25] Judicial Review is a discretionary remedy, and courts are traditionally reluctant to entertain belated applications from bad losers—although this concern for the smoothness of share trading sits uneasily with their duty to remedy injustice. The market should be capable of digesting the fact that Ofcom decisions are open to a challenge that may be mounted within three months (the outside time for a challenge, although the overarching requirement is to apply promptly. The court can decide, as it did in this case, that a challenge was not made "promptly" even though it was well within three months of the decision). One challenge—by Television South West—did reach the House of Lords, but the court did little more than rubber-stamp the ITC decision to reject the application because of doubts whether TSW, although the highest bidder, could maintain the service through the 10–year licence period. The court emphasised that it was not empowered to act as an appeal body or to substitute its own views for that reached by the experts—it confined its role to ensuring that the Commission had considered the evidence carefully and fairly, and had not abused its powers.[26] This is an excessively narrow approach to the review function, requiring an applicant to prove the decision irrational or the procedure improper, but it means that applicants have in reality but one bite at the broadcasting cherry. Human rights law requires the availability of a proper appeal on the merits of decisions of such importance, although the 2003 Communications Act does not provide one.

---

[24] *R. v Secretary of State for Home Dept Ex p. Brind* [1991] 1 A.C. 696.
[25] *R. v ITC Ex p. TV Northern Ireland, The Times*, December 30, 1991.
[26] *R. v ITC Ex p. TSW Broadcasting Ltd, The Times*, March 30, 1992. See also *R. v ITC Ex p. Virgin, The Times*, February 17, 1996 and *R.o.t.a. Wildman v Ofcom* [2005] EWHC 1573 (Admin).

LAWS AND STATUTORY DUTIES

The general law

16–010　It is difficult to understand why the general law relating to taste and decency (obscenity, outraging public decency, blasphemy and race hate offences) should apply to a medium which is so heavily censored by regulators and adjudicative bodies. A programme maker stands in triple jeopardy on matters of taste: he may (1) be prosecuted for outraging public decency or publishing obscenity; or (2) be found by the BBC to be in breach of its codes; or (3) condemned by Ofcom for a breach of *its* code. In reality, of course, the codes and their regulators are so suffocating that nothing has ever been broadcast that could seriously be suggested as a candidate for prosecution. Nonetheless, Mrs Thatcher's tribute to Mrs Whitehouse in the 1990 Broadcasting Act was to apply the Obscene Publications Act to radio and television.[27] This means that persons responsible for a transmission deemed to be likely "to deprave and corrupt" a significant proportion of its likely audience are, on conviction by a jury, liable for up to three years' imprisonment. Broadcasting had been specifically exempted from the Act when it was passed in 1959, and it is unlikely that any programme transmitted in the succeeding 30 years would have been found obscene by a jury. However, clean-up campaigners convinced the Government that broadcasters should be subject, like other publishers, to the criminal law of the land, in addition to their liability to fines and loss of licence if they breach the statutory prohibitions against transmitting offensive material (see below). The 1990 law also removed the broadcast media's exemption from prosecution for incitement to racial hatred.

The general law of obscenity, explained in Ch.4, applies to television and sound broadcasting in much the same way as it applies to books and films, with a public good defence which can be advanced by expert witnesses. No prosecution, however, may be brought other than with the consent of the DPP, and none has been brought. There is a special provision in the Act that enables a magistrate to require broadcasters to supply a visual or sound recording relating to a programme that police have "reasonable grounds for suspecting" has constituted an offence.[28] The power extends only to material that has already been broadcast; it does not enable police to obtain advance copies of programmes expected to be controversial. It is unlikely, given the stringent duties not to cause public offence, that programme makers will be prosecuted; if they are, much will depend on the transmission time of the programme and whether children are likely to comprise "a significant proportion" of viewers. There is a useful defence for presenters and

[27] Broadcasting Act 1990, s.162 and Sch.15.
[28] Broadcasting Act 1990, s.167.

contributors, who may not be convicted unless they had reason to suspect beforehand that the programme would contain material justifying a conviction.[29] A particular danger, that the DPP may choose forfeiture proceedings decided by magistrates rather than a jury trial, was avoided by a Government promise that prosecuting authorities would not favour forfeiture proceedings.[30]

The statutory duties

The duties imposed by statute on independent television, and later **16–011** annexed to the licence of the BBC and echoed in the laws relating to independent radio and to cable television, were first formulated in 1954 and lasted verbatim until replaced by the "standards objectives" of s.319 of the 2003 Act. They reflected the exaggerated fears of that period about the advent of commercial television. In an atmosphere where Lord Reith could solemnly liken commercial television to the black death, it was understandable that ITV should be placed under the close scrutiny of a licensing body, required to ensure:

> "that nothing is included in the programmes which offends against good taste or decency or is likely to encourage or incite to crime or to lead to disorder or to be offensive to public feeling".

This was the IBA's duty under s.4 of the 1981 Broadcasting Act, and it is a duty that was inherited by the ITC and by the Radio Authority under s.6 of the 1990 Broadcasting Act, and is now somewhat more liberally revised in s.319 of the 2003 Communications Act.

In 1964 the BBC Board of Governors undertook to comply with the same standard:

> "The Board accept that so far as possible the programmes for which they are responsible should not offend against good taste or decency, or be likely to encourage crime or disorder, or be offensive to public feeling. In judging what is suitable for inclusion in programmes, they will pay special regard to the need to ensure that broadcasts designed to stimulate thought do not so far depart from their intention as to give general offence."[31]

---

[29] 1990 Act, Sch.15(5)(1).
[30] House of Commons, Standing Committee F on Broadcasting Bill, Official Report Col.1190 (David Mellor).
[31] Letter from Lord Normanbrook (Chairman, BBC) to Postmaster-General, June 19, 1964. The undertaking was reaffirmed when the BBC licence was renewed in 1969, 1981 and (more forcefully) in 1996 and the contents of the letter are noted in the prescribing memorandum under cl.13(4) of the BBC Licence and Agreement.

Statutory duties may be enforced by the Attorney-General, as guardian of the public interest, although no case has occurred in which he has been minded to bring an action in the High Court to force the regulator to take action against any programmer or broadcaster. However, the courts permitted private citizens to bring actions against the IBA (which unlike Ofcom was responsible as publisher for all commercial television and radio programmes) on the somewhat tenuous basis that, as licence holders, they may be directly affected by screenings in breach of a statutory duty.

16–012   The first case, *Att-Gen, ex rel. McWhirter v IBA*,[32] concerned a documentary about the life and work of Andy Warhol.

> Although senior IBA staff had ordered a number of deletions from the programme, it had not been personally vetted by the 18 members of the authority at the time its scheduled transmission was injuncted by the court on the strength of sensational newspaper publicity. Subsequently, it was viewed and approved by all IBA members and the court declined to hold that their decision was unreasonable, although it sternly reminded them of their then duty to ensure that "nothing" is included in any programme that offends good taste, although the court did concede that each "piece" could be judged according to the purpose and character of the whole programme

The *McWhirter* case was overlooked by the IBA when it approved transmission of the controversial film *Scum* without referring this decision for Board approval:

> *Scum* was the film of a play that had previously been banned by the BBC because of its explicit scenes of violence in a borstal. The Director-General of the IBA and his staff approved it for transmission on Channel 4 at 23.00 with a warning about the violent scenes. They did not, however, refer it to the IBA Board for its approval prior to transmission. The High Court declined to hold that *Scum* was so offensive to public feeling that no reasonable licensing body could allow it to be shown, but it declared, in reliance on *McWhirter*, that the failure to refer the matter to the Board for approval was unlawful. The Court of Appeal, however, took a much more relaxed view of the IBA's approach to its statutory duties. It was entitled to rely on its experienced staff and the system it had established (involving monitoring, audience reaction studies and continuous discussions) to provide sufficient compliance with the statutory duty. The Court of Appeal warned potential applicants for judicial review that the mere fact that one blatantly offensive programme might slip through the IBA's safety-net would not mean that it was in breach of its duty—any such finding would require evidence that the Authority was not maintaining a satisfactory system of safeguards.[33]

Both *McWhirter* and *Whitehouse* emphasised the difficulty of challenging a regulatory body's decision on its merits: once the body

---

[32] [1973] 1 Q.B. 629.
[33] *R. v IBA Ex p. Whitehouse*, *The Times*, April 4, 1985, CA.

has approved a transmission (whether before or after it has taken place) the courts will be hard put to stigmatise the decision as irrational or perverse. Moreover, the approach in *Whitehouse* took a much more permissive attitude towards the IBA's procedures for complying with the statutory duties, which Lord Donaldson M.R. described as being:

> "none of them precise. All require value judgments . . . Parliament was creating what might be described qualitatively as a 'best endeavours' obligation and was leaving it to the members [of the IBA] to adopt methods of working, or a system, which in their opinion, was best adapted to securing the requirements set out in the section".

This is a most apt description of the "standards objectives" in **16–013** s.319, and the case remains authority that the courts should intervene only when convinced that the system adopted by the regulatory body was so bizarre that no reasonable person could believe it would assist in maintaining programme standards at the general level required by the Act. The Communications Act 2003 ensures that Ofcom members have no duty to preview and pre-censor programs: the epic censorship struggles of the 1970s, over the duties of regulators to stop transmission of *Scum* and the Warhol documentary, are things of the past. Today the Human Rights Act commitment to freedom of expression makes it difficult to imagine any court injuncting transmission of a program on grounds of bad taste or even obscenity. Challenges are most likely to come from those who desire greater explicitness than broadcasting executives are prepared to allow. Such extremists are not always pornographers: the most recent test case concerned distressing pictures of aborted foetuses, which a "single issue" political party, the ProLife Alliance, wanted to use in its free slot known as a "party election broadcast" (PEB).

The PEB is an anomaly of British democracy, whereby political parties which stand a sufficient number of candidates are permitted one or more propaganda programs of their own making, relieved of any duty to be impartial or truthful, although bound by the general duty to avoid harm or offence. The ProLife Alliance, an anti-abortion party, stood the requisite number of candidates to qualify for one broadcast, most of which it wished to devote to prolonged and deeply disturbing images of aborted foetuses. To avoid public offence, the BBC executives insisted on cuts which the Alliance refused to make: it replaced the pictures by a caption "censored" and went to court complaining that its Art.10 rights had been infringed.[34] Curiously, it did not contend that the statutory duty to

---

[34] *R. (ProLife Alliance) v BBC*, (2003) 2 All E.R. 1402.

avoid offensiveness was itself a breach of Art.10, but merely that the BBC had applied the wrong standard—at election time, the democratic imperative of free speech required that political speech should override all but the most basic considerations of decency. This full-blooded freedom of expression position was upheld by the Court of Appeal, but rejected by a majority of the Law Lords who pointed out that so long as broadcasters remained subject to the statutory duty not to transmit offensive material, they must do their honest and inevitably subjective best to comply with this "loose and imprecise" restriction.[35] This was the limited ratio of the *ProLife Alliance* case, and a challenge to the imposition of the "offensiveness duty" as incompatible with Art.10, will have to wait another day.

16–014   However, Lord Hoffman made clear that such a challenge would be unlikely to succeed, at least in respect of the statutory duty to guard against offensiveness. Nothing had changed since the Annan Committee on the Future of Broadcasting, which in 1977 had rejected leaving the question to unalloyed editorial discretion: "public opinion cannot be totally disregarded in the pursuit of liberty".[36] Even the US Supreme Court in *Federal Communications Commission v Pacifica Foundation*[37] had held that the First Amendment did not prevent regulators from banning obscene language on radio—a point made by the prudish furore in America over "Nipplegate" when Janet Jackson's accidental boob caused the regulators—the FCC—to fine the television company $550,000. Lord Hoffman pointed out that the Court of Appeal's mistake had been to rewrite the law (then s.6 of the 1990 Broadcasting Act) so as to exclude PEBs from the "offensiveness" provision—a rewrite that not even s.3 of the Human Rights Act could achieve because, "There is no human right to use a television channel".

Lord Hoffman made the point that Art.10 does not provide a human right to appear on television. It applies not to strike down interferences with the right to express opinions, but metamorphoses into "a right to fair consideration for being afforded the opportunity to do so: a right not to have one's access to public media denied on discriminatory, arbitrary or unreasonable grounds".[38] There had been no discrimination against the ProLife Alliance in applying a standard with which all other political parties had to comply. The application of that standard was not unreasonable, since "the standards are part of the country's cultural life and have created expectations on the part of viewers as to what they will and will not be shown on the screens in their homes."[39]

---

[35] The bare majority of law lords agreed with the speech of Lord Nichols, which was limited to this proposition.

[36] *The Annan Report*, CMND, para.16.3, p.245.

[37] (1978) 438 US 726.

[38] *ProLife Alliance* p.1418, paras 57–8.

[39] *ProLife Alliance*, para.70.

Lord Hoffman's speech was an individual opinion which, however acutely expressed, should not be engraved on stone. Whether the "standards" imposed on television by the 1990 Act have become part of the county's cultural life or whether they have served to stultify the country's cultural life may not matter, given Ofcom's liberalism in its verdict on *Jerry Springer—the Opera*. Lord Hoffman warned that public opinion is often divided, sometimes unexpected and in constant flux—which is true enough and raises the question of whether for that reason media standards should be applied by law common to all media. He pointed out that "generally accepted standards on these questions are not a matter of intuition on the part of elderly male judges", an observation both refreshing and correct, but undercut by the importance he illogically attached to the fact that the main decision-taker for the BBC was a woman—a question, surely, of what sort of woman she was, and whether a decision on a matter of democratic and constitutional significance should be entrusted to a BBC bureaucrat—whether male or female—instead of, say (in the event of a prosecution) to a jury. However, for the present, the *ProLife* decision demonstrates the difficulties of challenging either statutory restrictions on offensive speech (by way of seeking a declaration of incompatibility with Art.10) or particular judgements on offensiveness. These are made by regulators deemed to be more "in touch" with public opinion (especially if they are female) than the grumpy old men on the bench. The logic of this position does not, however, apply to restrictions on "due impartiality" which require adjudications for which judges may be more appropriate, and much less to decisions about privacy, a subject which judges claim to know more about than anyone else.

OFCOM'S MANDATE

The 2003 Act's twin purposes were protecting the interests of **16–015** citizens in ensuring a plurality of high quality TV and radio services, while also protecting their interests as consumers by promoting competition across the media marketplace. Section 3(2) of the Act therefore blandly describes Ofcom's principal duties, in carrying out its functions, as being "to further the interests of citizens in relation to communications matters" and "to further the interests of consumers in relevant markets, where appropriate by promoting competition". The Act specifically recognises that quality and cost considerations have the potential to conflict with one another and provides that where Ofcom resolves such a conflict between these duties, in an important case, they must publish a statement setting out the nature of the conflict, the manner in which they decided to resolve it and the reasons for their decision.[40]

---

[40] s.3(8), Communications Act 2003.

Ofcom's specific duties under the Act fall into six areas:

a) ensuring the optimal use of the electro-magnetic spectrum;
b) ensuring that a wide range of electronic communications—including high speed data services—is available throughout the United Kingdom;
c) ensuring a wide range of TV and radio services of high quality and wide appeal;
d) maintaining plurality in the provision of broadcasting;
e) applying adequate protection for audiences against offensive or harmful material;
f) Applying adequate protection for audiences against unfairness or infringement of privacy.

In performing these duties, the Act specifies a number of general and specific principles to which Ofcom must have regard. The general principles are set out in s.3(3) and require Ofcom's regulatory activities to be "transparent, accountable, proportionate, consistent and targeted only at cases in which action is needed", while also enabling Ofcom to apply any other principles which appear to Ofcom to represent the best regulatory practice. The specific principles are set out in s.3(4) and include, among others, the need, when regulating standards in television and radio services to act in "the manner that best guarantees an appropriate level of freedom of expression"; to take into account the vulnerability of children and of others in need of special protection; to take into account the needs of persons with disabilities, the elderly and those on low incomes; the desirability of preventing crime or disorder; and the different interests of persons in different parts of the United Kingdom, of the different ethnic communities within the United Kingdom and of persons living in rural and urban areas.

16–016   Ofcom is a sizeable public authority employing approximately 900 persons and with offices in England, Scotland, Wales and Northern Ireland. Strategic direction is provided by the Ofcom Board, chaired at its inception by Lord Currie (Dean of a business school) with a Chief Executive Officer, Stephen Carter, recruited from a cable TV group. It has established a number of Board Committees, responsible for dealing with specific aspects of its mandate. The Content Board, for example, is the primary forum for the regulation of television and radio quality and standards, while the Fairness Committee deals with fairness and privacy complaints. The Content Sanctions Committee makes decisions on whether to impose statutory sanctions on a broadcaster and if so, what form they should take. Ofcom also has a number of advisory committees, e.g. a Consumer Panel that provides advice on the consumer interest in the markets it regulates.

Statutory requirements

Ofcom is required to set such standards for the contents of radio and **16–017**
television programmes as appear to them best calculated to achieve
the standards objectives set out in the Act and to create codes
setting out these standards.[41] The standards objectives are contained
in s.319 of the 2003 Act, replacing (although to a large extent
replicating) the former duties under s.6 of the 1990 Act. That Act
required that "nothing is included in the programmes which offends
against good taste or decency etc", while the Ofcom Act is in terms
more liberal, dropping the archaic (or Rees-Moggian) notion of
"good taste" with an 'objective' to avoid "offensive and harmful
material". The objectives are:

a) the protection of persons under 18 years of age;
b) that material likely to encourage or to incite the commission
   of crime or lead to disorder is not included;
c) that news is presented with due impartiality;
d) that news is reported with due accuracy;
e) that the proper degree of responsibility is exercised with
   respect to the content of religious programmes; and
f) that generally accepted standards are applied so as to
   provide adequate protection to members of the public from
   the inclusion of offensive and harmful material.[42]

There are also a number of specific standards objectives relating to
advertising and sponsorship.

In setting or revising any standards, s.319(4) of the Act requires
Ofcom to have particular regard to a number of specific matters:

- the degree of harm caused or offence likely to be caused by
  the inclusion of the material;
- the likely size and composition of the potential audience;
- the likely expectation of the audience about the programme's content and the extent to which that content can
  be brought to the attention of potential members of that
  audience;
- the likelihood of persons who are unaware of that content
  being unintentionally exposed to it;
- the desirability of securing that the content of services
  identifies changes affecting that service, including changes in
  standards; and
- the desirability of maintaining the independence of editorial
  control over programme content.

There are particular statutory requirements relating to news programmes, called the "special impartiality requirements", which

---

[41] s.319(1), CA 2003.
[42] s.319(2),(3) CA 2003.

relate solely to matters of political or industrial controversy and matters relating to current public policy.[43] These prevent the expression of the views and opinion of the person providing the radio or television news service about these matters, require the preservation of due impartiality when dealing with such topics and prevent the giving of undue prominence to the views and opinions of particular persons or bodies on such issues. The impartiality requirement in the case of matters of political or industrial controversy needs to be satisfied in relation to all programmes included in the service in question, taken as a whole, while the impartiality requirement on matters of public policy is less stringent and must be satisfied in relation to a series of programmes taken as whole.[44] The effect of this is that news coverage of controversial political topics must be neutral and even-handed in each-and-every programme, while news coverage on a matter of public policy must achieve even-handedness across a series of programmes.

16–018   Views and opinions relating to the provision of news programmes are exempt from the special impartiality requirements, in order to encourage some measure of network self-criticism. This would enable television channels to screen, for example, viewer opinions critical of what they claim to be anti-American bias in the coverage of Iraq, and the television network or programme-makers to defend themselves.

The Act also imposes specific requirements regarding standards for religious programmes, aimed at preventing any improper exploitation of the susceptibilities of the audience (i.e. indoctrination) and to avoid discrimination by abusive treatment of religious views and beliefs.[45] The codes must also contain standards for advertising and sponsorship, for example, to protect the under-18s, to prevent political advertising and to prevent misleading, harmful or offensive advertising.[46] (Although the Act originally envisaged that Ofcom would have responsibility for advertising in the broadcasting context, in fact these responsibilities were subsequently taken over by the Advertising Standards Authority—see Ch.15.)

In relation to licenses issued under the Broadcasting Act, the 2003 Act requires that the regulatory regime for every programme service licensed must include conditions for securing the general standards objectives required by s.319,[47] as well as a requirement to observe the fairness code under s.107 of the Broadcasting Act.[48] Section 107 of the 1996 Act, as amended, requires Ofcom to draw up a code giving guidance about the principles to be observed and practices to be

---

[43] s.320, CA 2003.
[44] s.320(4), CA 2003.
[45] s.319(6), CA 2003.
[46] s.321, CA 2003.
[47] s.325, CA 2003.
[48] s.326, CA 2003.

followed when seeking to prevent unjust or unfair treatment in programmes, or the unwarranted infringement of privacy in programmes or in the making of programmes.

THE BROADCASTING CODE

The Broadcasting Code took effect on July 25, 2005. The Code sets **16–019** out broadcasting standards in ten separate sections, each dealing with a specific topic, such as protecting the under-eighteens. Radio and television broadcasters in the independent sector are required by the terms of their Ofcom license to observe the whole Code. Any viewer or listener who believes that a programme standard has been breached, or that they have been treated unfairly or had their privacy infringed, may complain to Ofcom, which will adjudicate on the matter.

The position in relation to the BBC is more complex. The BBC's publicly funded TV and radio services—those that are funded either by grant in aid or the license fee—are subject to the regulation of Ofcom in the following six areas: *protecting the under-eighteens, harm and offence, crime, religion, fairness* and *privacy*. However, in four areas, Ofcom has no supervisory role and the BBC retains responsibility for maintaining its own standards under its Charter: these are *impartiality and accuracy, elections and referendums, sponsorship* and *commercial references.*[49] A viewer or listener who wishes to complain about an inaccurate BBC broadcast must therefore complain to the BBC. However, such listeners may also complain to the BBC about any breach of its own Producer Guidelines, which cover substantially the same areas as the Ofcom Code (often in greater detail). Ultimately, therefore, the BBC and Ofcom have concurrent jurisdiction to rule on the majority of matters—a recipe for the very confusion and double-jeopardy that Ofcom was set up to avoid. By way of contrast with its publicly funded services, however, the BBC's commercial services, whether broadcasting to the United Kingdom, or from the United Kingdom to its international audiences, must comply with the whole of the Ofcom Code.

Ofcom publishes Guidance Notes for each topic addressed in the Broadcasting Code, which as the name suggests is guidance designed to assist in interpreting the Code's provisions. In addition, decisions taken by Ofcom in relation to complaints are published every month in the form of a Broadcast Bulletin. The BBC Trust, which since January 2007 has taken over ultimate responsibility for adjudicating on such matters from the BBC Governors, also publishes a monthly record of decisions it has taken in relation to complaints made by members of the public. Detailed guidance on the complaints procedures established by both Ofcom and the BBC is available on their respective websites.[50]

---

[49] The BBC is required to observe the standards in its Charter as part of its Agreement with Ofcom.

[50] *www.ofcom.org.uk*; *www.bbc.org.uk*.

PROTECTING THE UNDER-18S

16–020 It is perhaps unsurprising, given the long history of concern about the potential effects of exposure to harmful television on the young, that the requirement to protect the under-eighteens forms the first section of the Broadcasting Code.[51] The Code starts by emphasising that "material that might seriously impair the physical, mental or moral development of people under eighteen must not be broadcast" and that "in the provision of services, broadcasters must take all reasonable steps to protect people under eighteen".[52] The effect of such requirements that make no reference to scheduling means that certain types of programmes must be avoided altogether, no matter what time they are shown or what advance warnings are given. A programme that uncritically extolled the pleasures of Class A drugs, for example, would breach the Code under any circumstances.

In practice, however, perhaps the most important obligation is to protect children (defined as people under the age of 15 years) by appropriate scheduling from material that is unsuitable for them.[53] This general duty applies to television and radio alike and requires broadcasters to schedule programmes having regard to such matters as the nature of the content; the likely number and age range of children in the audience (taking into account school time, weekends and holidays); the start time and finish time of the programme; the nature of the channel or station and the particular programme; and the likely expectations of the audience for a particular channel or station at a particular time and on a particular day.

In television terms, the lynchpin of this policy remains the "watershed". The Code provides that television broadcasters must observe the watershed; material unsuitable for children should not, in general, be shown before 21.00 or after 05.30.[54] Unhelpfully for broadcasters, however, the watershed is not a clear bright line dividing a kiddie-friendly day from an adults-only night, as the Code also provides that the transition should not be abrupt and that for television, the strongest material should appear later in the schedule.[55]

16–021 The BBC fell foul of this provision by showing the Quentin Tarantino film *Pulp Fiction* 10 minutes after the watershed. Ofcom decided that the film was screened too early because "seriously offensive language, graphic violence and drug abuse" occur in the

---

[51] See in particular s.3(4)h and 319(2)(a) of the Act. The requirement to protect children from harmful television is also contained in Art.22 of the *Television Without Frontiers Directive*.

[52] rr.1.1., 1.2 Broadcasting Code.

[53] r.1.3.

[54] r.1.4.

[55] r.1.6.

first 20 minutes of the film. The BBC had claimed that as "arguably one of the most influential and best-known films" of the previous decade the movie was unlikely to offend BBC2 viewers, only nine of whom had complained. The BBC pointed out that the film had been screened on British television four times previously and claimed that it had an "underlying morality", which showed the effects of violence and drug use. Ofcom, however, was unimpressed, stating "such intense material is not normally expected so soon after the watershed". The BBC's intense dissatisfaction was evident from the fact that it unsuccessfully appealed the decision three times.[56] The Ofcom decision was silly and pernickety, and perhaps explained as a public relations exercise just after it had outraged conservative Christians by approving the screening of *Jerry Springer—the Opera*. If teenagers want to see *Pulp Fiction* (that is, if they haven't seen it on the BBC before or on video or DVD or as an Internet download) they will stay up to view it whether it begins at 21.10 or 21.40 (the unobjectionable time at which it was previously screened). If television is to be a medium for communicating serious cinema, it must be permitted to do so at a time when most adults will still be awake at the end of the film. By its unrealistic obsession about "protecting" 15 year old viewers, Ofcom was discriminating against those over 60 who pay the license fees and are entitled to enjoy a film before they nod off with their 23:00 cocoa.

The BBC was also found in breach of the scheduling provision for four weekday shows in a series called *Britain's Streets of Vice*, which covered issues such as brothels, pornography and drug-taking. The majority of complaints to Ofcom concerned the final programme in the series, which dealt with pornography, and featured interviews with a porn star and a dominatrix. The BBC said that it had scheduled the programmes during term-time deliberately to avoid children watching (BBC schedulers obviously do not have teenage children) and that there were pre-transmission warnings in place. However, Ofcom held that the warnings had not properly prepared viewers for the strength of the content and the risks had been highlighted by the fact that, as a result of heavy snowfalls, many school children had not been able to attend school that week. The programme had therefore been inappropriately scheduled.[57] Ofcom was plainly wrong to blame the BBC for failing to predict bad weather and the consequent extent of child truancy; nonetheless the Corporation promised to rethink its policy on broadcasting programs about sex during daytime—the only time at which some aging viewers are capable of having it. Once again, this fussy concern with hypothetical child viewers masks the fact that Ofcom is discriminating against mature license holders.

Although the watershed concept does not apply to radio, radio broadcasters are bound by the general duty to protect children from

---

[56] BBC's *Pulp Fiction Angers Ofcom*, BBC News website, October 24, 2005.
[57] *BBC sex show rapped by watchdog*, BBC News website, August 15, 2005.

unsuitable material through appropriate scheduling required by r.1.3, as well as a specific rule requiring them to have regard to times when children are particularly likely to be listening.[58] Examples given are breakfast time and the school run.

16–022   Where a television programme containing content that may distress some children is broadcast before the watershed, or a radio programme with such content is broadcast at a time when children are particularly likely to be listening, the Code requires broadcasters to provide clear information about that content.[59] Children are assumed to be easily distressed, for example, by images that show the suffering of animals, so a news report that focussed on horses injured in the Grand National, or a documentary about the vivisection debate, if broadcast before the watershed, would have to contain a warning. Not so, of course, in the case of pictures of the latest suicide bombings in Iraq, with dozens of dead and wounded humans: to this kind of carnage, children are assumed to be inured.

The Code contains detailed provisions relating to coverage on a range of potentially problematic topics for children, including drugs, smoking, solvents and alcohol,[60] violence and dangerous behaviour,[61] offensive language,[62] sex,[63] nudity,[64] and exorcism, the occult and the paranormal.[65] These provisions place a variety of limits on the portrayal of these topics. In general, the Code limits the broadcast of such material before the watershed, or when children are particularly likely to be listening, additionally and sometimes alternatively requiring that where such representations are featured that there is editorial justification for it, or that it is justified by the context. The Code contains no surprises; drugs are not to be glamorised, offensive language is strictly limited and representations of sex before the watershed must have a "serious educational purpose". The ITC was wont to be very censorious about paranormal programs on "Living TV", which it believed attracted gullible women viewers. Ofcom has yet to display the same sexism.

In relation to violence, its after-effects and descriptions of violence, the Code provides that it must be appropriately limited before the watershed and justified by the context.[66] Violence, whether verbal or physical, that is easily imitable by children in a manner that is harmful or dangerous must not feature in programmes made primarily for children unless there is a strong editorial justification, and must not be broadcast before the watershed or when children

---

[58] r.1.5.
[59] r.1.7.
[60] r.1.10.
[61] rr.1.11, 1.12 and 1.13.
[62] rr.1.14–1.16.
[63] r.1.17.
[64] r.1.18.
[65] r.1.19.
[66] r.1.11.

are particularly likely to be listening, unless there is editorial justification.[67] The same rule applies to dangerous behaviour, or the portrayal of dangerous behaviour, that is likely to be easily imitable by children.[68]

ITV found itself in breach of these provisions when the children's **16-023** drama *Bernard* showed one of its characters gagged and apparently hanging from coat hooks. The programme concerned a school jousting tournament and Bernard, the lead character, had gagged and hung up Nicolette, the class bully, to prevent her from ruining the occasion. Ofcom said that Nicolette "appeared to be hanging directly from the coat hangers with rope". According to Ofcom,

> "Gagging is an action that is easily imitable by children and potentially highly dangerous—particularly when combined with restraining material. Although the scene illustrated Bernard's success in foiling Nicolette's plans, this did not provide a sufficient editorial justification for this content."[69]

ITV was also found in breach of the Code when *The Ministry of Mayhem*, a children's show, showed a baby being fed a teaspoon of lemon juice, with the presenter suggesting viewers should try it on their brothers and sisters as it was "very, very funny". Programme maker Carlton said that the juice was not harmful to babies, but Ofcom upheld the complaints on the basis that children might imitate the stunt with more harmful substances. Ofcom pointed out, reasonably enough, "We were particularly concerned that a presenter of a children's programme should encourage children to feed a baby at all."[70] The following year, ITV was found in breach of the Code for another *Ministry of Mayhem* stunt involving an actor setting his hands on fire with bubbles containing methane gas. ITV said children would not be able to recreate the stunt as they could not get hold of a methane gas cylinder. Ofcom decided, however, that the combination of bubbles and fire would be likely to have great appeal for children, the stunt was treated as slapstick fun, its educational aspect was minimal and ITV had failed to warn children against trying to copy the experiment.[71]

Scenes of bullying and torture in ITV soap *Coronation Street* that were shown before the watershed, however, were found not to have been in breach of the Code. Thirty viewers complained about an episode that featured womanising builder Charlie Stubbs tying up teenager David Platt and forcing his head under water in a bath, on the basis that the scene was shown before the watershed and showed

---

[67] r.1.12.
[68] r.1.13.
[69] *Ofcom raps ITV1 children's drama*, BBC News website, April 18, 2006.
[70] *ITV rapped for baby feeding joke*, BBC News website, April 7, 2004.
[71] *Watchdog slams ITV show fire joke*, BBC News website, April 25, 2005.

violence that was easily imitable. But Ofcom did not accept that that the scene was easily imitable by children and decided in any event that the scene was editorially justified.

> "Viewers would have been sufficiently alerted to the tense relationship developing between the two characters over a number of weeks so that they were not unexpected, and they were edited in such a way that the violence was not dwelt on unduly or was inappropriate."

In terms of scheduling, Ofcom took into account that Coronation Street is not aimed at children and that BARB data indicated that children comprised only 9 per cent of the viewing audience for that episode. Furthermore, ITV had warned viewers before transmission that, "Charlie has a nasty surprise for David", although Ofcom felt that this warning could have been more detailed (at the expense, presumably, of giving away plot).[72]

Swearing

16–024 Many of the public's complaints in relation to children relate to the broadcasting of swear words. The Code is very strict in this regard, providing that the most offensive language must not be broadcast before the watershed or when children are particularly likely to be listening,[73] and in respect of programmes specifically made for younger children offensive language is only acceptable in "the most exceptional circumstances". These specific provisions on offensive language overlap with the duty in r.2.3 to protect the public from offensive material and many complaints relating to the use of swear words proceed under both s.1 and s.2.

There is already a substantial body of Ofcom decisions in relation to swear words, illustrating how easily a broadcaster may inadvertently breach the Code when transmitting live material. The BBC received 55 complaints about swearing and offensive language on *Live8*, particularly in relation to Snoop Dog's performance, which was broadcast at 16.30 and contained a stream of expletives. In response to the complaints, the BBC replied that *Live8* had been a global, live television performance and it would have totally undermined its credibility if the BBC had subjected it to a time delay and censorship. The BBC also pointed out that executives working at the concert were operating under exceptional pressures on the day. However, Ofcom found the BBC in breach of the Code for failing to use a time delay, failing to ensure adequate editorial control and failing to make sufficiently swift apologies[74] (and, in effect, failing to

---

[72] Ofcom Broadcasting Bulletin, March 12, 2007.
[73] r.1.14.
[74] Ofcom Broadcasting Bulletin No.54, February 6, 2006.

make itself an international laughing stock by these panicked reactions). It is regrettable in one sense that the BBC did not take these stupid and unnecessary measures, since the expletives emanating from Bob Geldof would have been much more offensive than those from Snoop Dog.

Repeat infringements of the offensive language rules run the risk **16–025** of incurring heavy fines. Kiss FM radio received a fine of £100,000 for a series of language breaches over six months in a breakfast programme, a time when children were particularly likely to be listening.[75] Ofcom is very exercised by bad language during school holidays and half-terms and has publicly threatened BBC Radio 1—which has the largest audience share—with maximum fines (i.e. of £250,000); hardly a sensible use of license payer's money.[76] More sensibly the BBC has instituted a system for fining presenters who gratuitously use offensive or sexist or discriminatory language whether or not viewers complain to Ofcom. Since the BBC pays obscene amounts of money to some disk jockeys and presenters, forcing them to put some of it back in a "swear box" is hardly an infringement of free speech. It merely subjects them to fines for public use of foul or abusive language of the kind that are routinely imposed on First Division footballers.

Ofcom has rejected complaints where swearing in a live interview was swiftly followed by an apology, or where swearing was justified by the context. An example of the former was an interview with Elton John on Radio 1 in which he used the "F" word and then a string of other swearwords, disingenuously asking if they could be used on air. The presenter, DJ Chris Moyles, made two on-air apologies, concluding with, "Thanks everyone, you're listening to my last show on Radio 1." The BBC said that it had received only two complaints out of a listenership of six million and Ofcom found no breach of the Code.[77] An example of where the swearing was justified by the context was a Channel 5 documentary, *Britain's Fattest Teenager*, broadcast just after the watershed at 21.12, where the unfortunate youth in question used the C-word when describing the taunts to which he was subjected. Ofcom accepted that it was an important part of the documentary to understand the way the boy was subjected to insults in the street and the impact it had on him. There was no breach of the Code.[78]

18 R Films

In addition to the general scheduling provisions relating to children, **16–026** the Code also contains detailed guidance in relation to the showing of BBFC 18-rated films, adult-sex material and BBFC R18 films.[79]

---

[75] Ofcom Content Sanctions Committee, decision on Kiss FM.
[76] *Stop Turning the Airwaves Blue or You'll be Fined, Radio 1 DJ is told*, (*The Times*, June 13, 2006).
[77] *BBC cleared over Elton outburst*, BBC News website, February 15, 2005.
[78] Ofcom Broadcasting Bulletin No.76, January 15, 2007.
[79] rr.1.20–1.25.

Films with a BBFC 18-rating must not be shown before the watershed, except on pay-per-view services, when specific safeguards must be in place to prevent access by children.[80] Adult-sex material may be broadcast by premium subscription services and pay-per-view services between 22.00 and 05.30, but subject to very stringent safeguards, including a mandatory PIN protection system, or equivalent system, and measures to ensure that the subscriber is an adult.[81]

Ofcom cannot forgive errors that lead to the broadcasting of hardcore sex scenes. The pornographic satellite channel Xplicit broadcast porn before the 21.00 watershed in one of the more blatant failures to comply with the scheduling provisions. The channel ran a promotional tape with highly adult content at 20.30 and in response to complaints informed Ofcom that this had been a mistake—its usual scheduler was on holiday and the tape was run by another member of staff. Ofcom was unimpressed, calling the channel "excessively complacent" and fining it £50,000. Ofcom said it had considered imposing a six-figure fine, but had limited it to £50,000 because the company was making a loss and no viewers had complained[82]—the latter fact should logically have led to a minimum sanction.

Code r.1.25 absolutely prohibits films certified 18R by the BBFC from being broadcast at any time on any service. This blanket ban is ripe for challenge: the law permits 18R films to be purchased in licensed shops and to be seen in pay-per-view hotel rooms: why not on premium TV services, with a mandatory PIN protection system? Films that have been *refused* classification are of course banned and there is an inherent illogicality in Ofcom making no distinction between that (presumably harmful) category and an 18R category certified as fit (or at least, not harmful) for adult viewing. The Divisional Court decision in *R. v Video Appeals Committee Ex p. BBFC*[83] held that certain forms of pornography were appropriately made available to adults for viewing in the home: why not short circuit the embarrassment of a trip to the sex shop by permitting a premium PIN purchase? Ofcom has done research which (unsurprisingly) shows that many children know that a PIN number is necessary to access premium channels and some knew their parents' PIN number and had used it without permission.[84] Doubtless the same smart kids can find and play their parents' 18R videos as well. But it is absurd for Ofcom to imagine that its role is to stop teenagers from getting their hands on pornography—that is impossible. Its role is to make the exercise difficult, in relation to television,

---

[80] rr.1.21 and 1.23.

[81] r.1.24.

[82] "Porn channel fined for broadcast", BBC News website, July 28, 2004.

[83] 2000 E.M.L.R. 850.

[84] See *Research into the Effectiveness of PIN protection systems in the UK*, OFCOM, May 2005.

and to impress the unsuitability of such films for the young whilst permitting some access—if only in the early hours of the morning—for adults. Using teenage familiarity with PIN systems as an excuse for a blanket ban is disproportionate.

Court Cases

Specific provisions apply to protect children caught up in the **16–027** coverage of sexual or other offences involving the under-18s. Where statutory or other legal reporting restrictions apply, broadcasters are required to take particular care not to provide clues which may lead to the identification of those who are not yet adult or who are, or might be, involved as a victim, witness, defendant or other perpetrator in the case of sexual offences featured in criminal, civil or family court proceedings. Examples provided are the jigsaw effect, where limited information is reported but which may be pieced together with other information available elsewhere, and inadvertent identification, for example describing an offence as "incest" or enabling identification in another indirect way.[85]

When covering any pre-trial investigation into an alleged criminal offence in the United Kingdom, broadcasters are also required to pay particular regard to "the potentially vulnerable position" of any person who is not yet adult and who is involved as a witness or victim, before broadcasting their name, address, identity of school or other educational establishment, place of work, or any still or moving picture of them. Particular justification is also required for the broadcast of such material relating to the identity of any person who is not yet adult and who is a defendant or potential defendant.[86]

Even where none of these specific provisions apply, broadcasting images of children attending court may violate the privacy provisions of the Code. Ofcom upheld a privacy complaint against ITV for a news programme that broadcast images of a family, which included young children, attending the sentencing hearing of a relative in a case that had attracted great publicity and public opprobrium.[87]

Children in TV Programmes

There are specific provisions designed to protect children involved in **16–028** the making of programmes. The general requirement is to take due care over the physical and emotional welfare and the dignity of people under 18 who take part or are otherwise involved in programmes.[88] This is irrespective of any consent given by the participant or by a parent, guardian or other person over the age of

---

[85] r.1.8.
[86] r.1.9.
[87] See para.16–005 details.
[88] r.1.26.

18 in *loco parentis*, in recognition of the fact that parents cannot always be relied upon to made appropriate judgements about their own children's welfare. Furthermore, people under 18 must not be caused unnecessary distress or anxiety by their involvement in programmes or by the broadcast of those programmes.[89] There is also a specific provision relating to prizes aimed at children, which must be appropriate to the age range of both the target audience and the participants.[90]

Children's Health

16–029 In March 2007, Ofcom shocked the unhealthy food industry by announcing severe restrictions on the advertising of food and drink products high in fat, sugar and salt. These could no longer be advertised by the usual run of amoral "celebrities" and cartoon characters, or by offering free gifts or by way of dubious nutritional claims. This step was timely and widely welcomed, other than by broadcasters who stood to loose an estimated \$39 million in advertising. Less sensible was Ofcom's order that broadcasters must "edit out", i.e. censor, all smoking scenes from vintage *Tom and Jerry* cartoons. Not only are these works classics, but the foolish regulators entirely failed to notice that it is Tom—the comically villainous and incompetent cat—who lights up, and not the clever mouse. That smoking is associated, in young minds, with failure and derision, is obviously a subtlety too far for Britain's television censors.

HARM AND OFFENCE

16–030 There is a substantial overlap between this section of the Code and the first section relating to the protection of the under-18s, as the harm and offence provisions are designed both to protect adults and those under-18. The first rule of general application provides that generally accepted standards must be applied to the contents of television and radio services so as to provide adequate protection for members of the public from the inclusion in such services of harmful and/or offensive material.[91] This wording very closely resembles the standards objective expressed in s.319(2)(f) of the 2003 Act, which is narrower than the "good taste and decency" standard imposed on television by statute since 1954.

The generally accepted standards rule is of the widest possible application, but in practice the Code makes it clear that in applying generally accepted standards the guiding principle for broadcasters is to ensure that material which may cause offence is justified by the

---

[89] r.1.27.
[90] r.1.28.
[91] r.2.1.

context.[92] The Code gives as examples of material that may cause offence, namely offensive language, violence, sex, sexual violence, humiliation, distress, violation of human dignity, and discriminatory treatment or language (for example on the grounds of age, disability, gender, race, religion, beliefs and sexual orientation). The Code also provides that appropriate information should be broadcast where it will assist in minimising or avoiding offence.

The meaning of "context" is important and the Code sets out a list of non-exhaustive list of matters that may be relevant:

- the editorial content of the programme, programmes or series;
- the service on which the material is broadcast;
- the time of broadcast;
- what other programmes are scheduled before and after the programme or programmes concerned;
- the degree of harm or offence likely to be caused by the inclusion of any particular sort of material in programmes generally or programmes of a particular description;
- the likely size and composition of the potential audience and likely expectation of the audience;
- the extent to which the nature of the content can be brought to the attention of the potential audience for example by giving information; and
- the effect of the material on viewers or listeners who may come across it unawares.

The first and crucial test for Ofcom's contextual approach on the question of context, albeit under the now defunct Broadcasting Standards Council Code of Conduct, was its 2005 decision in favour of *Jerry Springer—the Opera*.[93] This was a televised production of the West End musical based on the controversial American "reality" television programme, which routinely features strong language, violent confrontations and extreme and shocking revelations. In the musical, Jerry Springer is shot at the end of the first act and in the second act, as he lies dying, he imagines that he is in Hell and forced to present a show in which Satan confronts various Biblical characters. This confrontation mirrors those of the dysfunctional families appearing on the show, with the protagonists addressing the issues that divide them. In a sequence that had Christian groups up in arms, Jesus came out as "a little bit gay", Mary castigated him for abandoning her on the cross and Satan shouted out at him, "Jesus, grow up for Christ's sake and put some fucking clothes on." The

---

[92] r.2.3.
[93] This decision was taken in May 2005, two months before the new Broadcasting Code came into effect. It is certain, however, that Ofcom's verdict would have been just the same under the new Code.

reaction from evangelical Christian groups was unprecedented in the history of UK broadcasting. The screening of the programme was accompanied by hundreds of protestors gathering outside BBC buildings and the BBC was deluged with complaints. The BBC Governors, however, stood by the programme. Ofcom received nearly 7,941 complaints before the programme was broadcast—in respect of which it had no jurisdiction. 8,860 followed on after its transmission, of which over 4,000 were part of an organised e-mail campaign by a pressure group, the first large scale e-mail campaign to Ofcom on any broadcasting issue.

16–031   In a remarkably intelligent and liberal decision, Ofcom rejected all of the complaints. While appreciating that the representation of religious figures had been offensive to some people and to their beliefs, Ofcom found that the effect of the show was to satirise modern fame and the celebrity culture. It did not deliberately humiliate individuals or Christian groups. The images in the "dream sequence", itself a metaphor for the fictional Jerry Springer and his chat show, were not meant to be faithful or accurate depictions of religious figures, but a product of the lead character's imagination. "Even as he lay dying, the fictional Jerry Springer still saw his life through the lens of his confessional chat show." Furthermore, the programme had been preceded by appropriate warnings as well as programmes designed to put the whole show in context. The strongest and most offensive language had occurred well after the watershed, at 22.00 onwards, with the strongest material after 23.00. In sum, "While the show clearly had the potential to offend and indeed the intention to shock it was set in a very clear context as a comment on modern television."[94] It was particularly pleasing that

> "in considering freedom of expression, Ofcom recognises the UK's longstanding tradition of satirising political and religious figures and celebrities . . . Freedom of expression is particularly important in the context of artistic works, beliefs, philosophy and argument".

Ofcom in 2006 rejected complaints from 251 viewers about an edition of *Friday Night with Jonathan Ross* in which the presenter carried out a risqué interview with David Cameron, the Leader of the Opposition, asking him if he had entertained teenage sexual fantasies while thinking about Margaret Thatcher. Viewers complained that the interview was vulgar, disrespectful and unfair to both Mr Cameron and Lady Thatcher. Ofcom noted that it could not adjudicate on an "unfairness" complaint on behalf of third parties who had not given their authority for the complaint, while also rejecting the allegation that the programme breached generally

---

[94] Ofcom Broadcasting Bulletin No.34, May 9, 2005.

accepted standards. Ofcom pointed out that television comedy has a long tradition of challenging viewers' concepts of what is acceptable and that Jonathan Ross has a well-established presenting style, which is deliberately risqué, satirical and provocative, so that viewers knew what to expect. Other relevant factors were that the programme was shown at 23.30 and the interview was with a senior politician who was extremely experienced in handling the media.[95]

Reality Images

A particular difficulty arises with news reports on shocking incidents **16–032** of violence, where there is an inherent tension between providing a realistic and newsworthy portrayal of events and not offending the audience's sensibilities. The BBC found itself in breach of the Code for its coverage of the July 7 terrorist bombings in London. The BBC presenter had given viewers a warning and then directed their attention to pictures coming in from a London hospital, where a man on a stretcher was seen receiving heart massage. The BBC admitted that it had not viewed the footage in full before broadcasting it because of the rush to get material on air, but that it had updated viewers on the man's condition later in the day. The BBC was found in breach of the Code for failing to give a sufficiently strong warning about the footage being shown, although given the carnage on that day, every viewer in the country knew what they were likely to see, and Ofcom's censure lacked any sense of true news values.[96] After the July 7 bombings, the BBC revised its Producer Guidelines to impose a time delay when broadcasting sensitive news stories in order to prevent distressing images going straight out to viewers.[97] But this is an abject capitulation in terms of news values. Does Ofcom really expect the BBC, tracking a highjacked jet as it heads for the Houses of Parliament, to impose a time delay before it hits, in order to sanitise the ensuing "distressing" images? Should the BBC really delay while its bureaucrats pondered whether the public should see scenes that are, after all, public?

So-called "reality" television programmes give rise to particular issues relating to viewer's expectations. The first editions of, for instance, *Big Brother* go out live and viewers expect to see developments as they unfold, giving a sufficiently rounded presentation of each participant's character so that they can make informed judgements when casting their votes. This is an important part of the context for such programmes, as Ofcom held when rejecting complaints about bullying behaviour between housemates in *Big Brother* 7, which it described as providing "key character information" for viewers.[98] It was also a significant factor for Ofcom that the bullying

[95] Ofcom Broadcasting Bulletin No.72, October 31, 2006.
[96] *BBC censured for 7 July footage*, BBC News website, September 26, 2005.
[97] *BBC enforces sensitive time delay*, BBC News website, July 25, 2005.
[98] Ofcom Broadcasting Bulletin No.69, September 18, 2006.

behaviour was not condoned or glamorised by the programme, although it might have been more significant to note that most *Big Brother* contestants have little or no character to develop. If a confrontation turns physical, the broadcaster may be expected to intervene. Channel 4 was held to be in breach of the Code for an edition of *Big Brother 5* in which a fight between two housemates went on for 20 minutes before guards intervened. Channel 4 had said that the argument primarily involved pushing and shouting, but Ofcom acknowledged the concerns of viewers about a potentially dangerous and deteriorating situation, saying that some viewers had been so concerned that they had called the police.[99]

The "reality" television phenomenon also gives rise to complaints that participants in such programmes are themselves the victims of exploitation and that broadcasters have failed to exercise their duty of care by allowing some people to take part. A complaint was made about a participant in *Big Brother 7* called Pete Bennett who suffered from Tourette's Syndrome and of whom it was said that viewers were being invited to laugh at others less fortunate than themselves. Ofcom said (wrongly, but it's a familiar cop-out) that it could not entertain a complaint about unfairness on behalf of a third party, but it rejected the suggestion that the programme had violated his human dignity under r.2.3. There was no reason, Ofcom said, why a person with a disability cannot and should not exercise the same degree of informed consent as any other adult—including choosing to enter the Big Brother household.[100] (Ofcom's verdict was reinforced by the fact that Mr Bennett was the winner of series 7, so that he had the viewers on his side.)

16–033   Programmes with sex as their subject matter are regular targets for standards complaints. Ofcom took a robust view of *A Girl's Guide to 21st Century Sex*, a Channel Five programme with explicit sexual content. It was a factual educational programme presented by a doctor and featuring advice, information and tips from a range of doctors and sexual health practitioners. The editorial content of the series featured brief explicit visuals of sexual activity, discussion of male and female masturbation and close camera-work on the biology of the male and female bodies including the filming of ejaculation inside a woman's vagina, as well as detailed and explicit discussions. Noting that there was no absolute prohibition on the broadcast of "real sex" on free to air television, Ofcom held that the programme genuinely sought to educate rather than titillate. Furthermore, it had been scheduled at 23.05 and was accompanied by strong warnings about the content. Accordingly, there had been no breach of the Code.[101]

The use of discriminatory or racist language will violate generally accepted standards, unless there is a clear editorial justification. A

---

[99] *C4 rebuked for Big Brother brawl*, BBC News, October 18, 2004.
[100] Ofcom Broadcasting Bulletin No.69, September 18, 2006.
[101] Ofcom Broadcasting Bulletin No.77, January 29, 2007.

serious example of this occurred in four late night phone-ins on the Manchester radio station Key 103, presented by James Stannage. The presenter made jokes about the death of Ken Bigley (a British citizen beheaded by abductors in Iraq); was rude and abusive to an Iraq war veteran and made highly abusive comments about Muslims, using a mock Asian accent. Ofcom described the breaches as "extremely serious" and the station's owner, Piccadilly Radio, said the content was "totally unacceptable". Mr Stannage was relieved of his contract and Ofcom fined the station £125,000.[102]

Television broadcasters who feature text messages from viewers also need to be careful not to breach generally accepted standards. Fizz Music, a digital television music channel, featured a number of racist text messages in a dialogue between viewers including one that read, "All dirty pakis stink! Fuck off home." The broadcaster's text moderators had removed the four-letter word but allowed the racist term of abuse to remain. In defending its stance, the broadcaster sought to argue that the expression "paki" did not cause major offence to its young viewing audience, the majority of whom were under 30 years old, but recognised that its use had not been justified by the context and said that its procedures had been revised to edit out the word in future. In making its finding, Ofcom referred to its own research on language in broadcasting, which found that this term was generally considered very offensive and that although the term might be used by young British Asians amongst themselves in a friendly fashion, when directed against a member of the Pakistani community it was viewed as among the most offensive language. Accordingly, there had been a breach of generally accepted standards.[103]

Two further general principles are set out in the section on **16–034** offence and harm. The first is that factual programmes or items or portrayals of factual matters must not materially mislead the audience.[104] This requirement supplements the specific provisions on accuracy and impartiality relating to news programmes in section five of the Code, applying to every type of factual programme. The second is that programmes must not include material (whether in individual programmes or in programmes taken together) which, taking into account the context, condones or glamorises violent, dangerous or seriously antisocial behaviour and is likely to encourage others to copy such behaviour.[105] Where the glamorisation is of conduct that would amount to a criminal offence, such programmes would, in any event, contravene the criminal law relating to incitement.

In addition, the Code contains a hotch-potch of harm-related provisions, setting down standards in relation to the inclusion of

---

[102] *Station fined over Bigley jokes*, BBC News, November 24, 2005.
[103] Ofcom Broadcasting Bulletin No.77, January 29, 2007.
[104] r.2.2.
[105] r.2.4.

material about methods of suicide and self-harm,[106] and (more controversially) demonstrations of exorcism, the occult and the paranormal[107] and demonstrations of hypnotic techniques.[108] This also appears a British peculiarity: other nations are unworried by television programmes which attempt to contact the dead. "Living TV" has been a particular victim of censorship, most severely when one of its channellers made an attempt to contact the dead Princess Diana. This may be *lese majesté*, but it is certainly not harmful. The Code further provides that simulated news (e.g. in a drama) must not mislead viewers into thinking they are watching real news,[109] that competitions should be conducted fairly,[110] that broadcasters must not use techniques to convey subliminal messages to viewers[111] and that precautions must be taken to protect viewers who have photosensitive epilepsy.[112]

The requirement to conduct competitions fairly was breached by ITV with *Quizmania*, a quiz programme broadcast on a premium rate digital service called ITV Play. The programme included a "tower" competition in which participants were asked to identify "things you find in a woman's handbag". At the end of the programme, with 7 out of 13 cash prizes having been won, two unanswered answers were revealed as "rawl plugs" and "a balaclava". In upholding the complaint of unfairness, Ofcom held that in order to achieve fairness it was essential that the answers were reasonable and that as these answers were idiotic, the competition had been conducted unfairly. What is essential to the integrity of such games, Ofcom pointed out, is that viewers are able to make informed choices when deciding whether to enter a competition, usually through a premium rate telephone call.[113] Both Ofcom and ICSTIS were severely criticised in 2007 for failing to regulate phone-in quiz shows which had charged viewers at premium rates for calls that were never given an opportunity to win. The Parliamentary Select Committee for DCMS was outraged at the dishonest call handling procedures that had escaped Ofcom's notice, and called for TV quiz shows to be classed as gambling, with 20 per cent of their proceeds going to charity (see *Stop Press* section).

CRIME

16–035 These provisions reflect a concern to ensure that broadcasters do not incite or encourage criminal activity, or provide information on techniques that would prove of assistance to criminals. In addition,

---

[106] r.2.5.
[107] rr.2.6–2.8.
[108] r.2.9.
[109] r.2.10.
[110] r.2.11.
[111] r.2.12.
[112] r.2.13.
[113] Ofcom Broadcasting Bulletin No.76, January 15, 2007.

there are specific rules relating to payments by broadcasters in the context of criminal proceedings and a rule relating to broadcasting that might endanger lives or undermine attempts to deal with hijacks and kidnaps.

The fundamental requirement is that material likely to encourage or incite the commission of crime or to lead to disorder is not included in television or radio services, a requirement in identical terms to s.319(2)(b) of the Act.[114] A further requirement is imposed by Art.22(a) of the *Television Without Frontiers Directive*, which provides that, "Member states shall ensure that broadcasts do not contain any incitement to hatred on grounds of race, sex, religion or nationality." The Act's provisions arguably duplicate the existing criminal law in relation to incitement, but perhaps the Parliamentary intention was that, as part of a comprehensive overhaul of broadcasting standards, it was necessary to make this requirement explicit in the broadcasting context.[115] As with incitement in the criminal law, there will often be scope for argument about whether the imputed material is "likely" to incite crime or disorder. In practice, everything will depend on the context—the contents of the programme, its tone and purpose, its contribution to a matter of public interest, the likely audience and so forth.

The general rule relating to encouraging or inciting crime or disorder draws strength from other aspects of the Code, for example, the requirement not to encourage or glamorise drugs in children's programmes,[116] and to exclude material condoning or glamorising violent or anti-social behaviour "that is likely to encourage others to copy such behaviour"[117] and the standards in relation to impartiality, fairness and privacy. It is hard, therefore, to imagine a programme breaching the incitement rule that did not also breach a number of other parts of the Code.

The Channel 4 programme *The Heist* featured the illusionist **16–036** Derren Brown who persuaded a group of businessmen to take part in what they believed was a genuine armed robbery. The programme explored the issue of suggestibility, taking a group of professional persons and seeing whether they could be persuaded to do things they would not normally consider. An entirely fake scenario was created where a guard was seen to transfer £100,000 in cash to a security van in a London street. As a result of Mr Brown's persuasive powers, three persons held the guard up with a fake pistol. Viewers complained that the programme glamorised and encouraged criminal activity and some gullible viewers even expressed concern that participation in the programme might have turned the individuals

---

[114] r.3.1.
[115] It is strange, however, that the Code itself makes no reference at all to the criminal law on incitement.
[116] r.1.10.
[117] r.2.4.

involved into long-term criminals. But Ofcom decided that Channel 4 had not breached the Code. In terms of the welfare of the individuals involved, the programme showed that they had been de-programmed and they had been cleared of any long-term negative effects by an independent psychologist. As for the effect upon the viewing audience, Ofcom found that the whole premise of the programme was to see whether normally law-abiding people would act outside what is understood to be acceptable behaviour, that the scenario was clearly fake and that the programme showed the shock and incredulity of the would-be armed robbers. Ofcom concluded that "this programme did not condone or glamorise this behaviour and was unlikely to have encouraged anyone to copy such behaviour in the belief that attempts of this nature were either easy or somehow worth attempting."[118]

The second rule of general application is that descriptions or demonstrations of criminal techniques with details which could enable the commission of crime must not be broadcast unless editorially justified.[119] The Code also requires broadcasters to use their best endeavours so as not to broadcast material that could endanger lives or prejudice the success of attempts to deal with a hijack or kidnapping.[120] This rule against endangering lives applies much more broadly, for example to protect the identity of persons who might be targeted under repressive regimes for having co-operated with Western journalists. The BBC was found by Ofcom to have breached the equivalent ex-BSC Code by endangering the life of a Libyan who appeared in a travel documentary, *Holidays in the Axis of Evil*. The journalists posed as tourists and the participant had believed that they were filming a holiday video. Co-operating with the international media is forbidden in Libya and the participant reported that he had been interrogated, beaten up and lost his job as a result of the programme.[121]

The issue of the media paying convicted criminals, or paying witnesses in pending criminal proceedings, has frequently generated controversy. The Code unhelpfully provides,

"that no payment, promise of payment, or payment in kind, may be made to convicted or confessed criminals whether directly or indirectly for a programme contribution by the criminal (or any other person) relating to his/her crime/s. The only exception is where it is in the public interest".[122]

The difficulty, of course, is judging where the public interest lies and where the balance should be struck between freedom of expression

---

[118] Ofcom Broadcasting Bulletin No.55, March 6, 2006.
[119] r.3.2.
[120] r.3.6.
[121] *BBC programme put lives at risk*, BBC News, September 6, 2004.
[122] r.3.3.

and protecting the privacy of surviving relatives. It appears, however, that this aspect of the law may be reformed. In November 2006 the Government put out a consultation paper, *Making sure that crime doesn't pay*, which proposed a new criminal offence of paying a convicted criminal for a story relating to his or her crime.[123] This is far too broad—journalists sometimes need to pay criminals for stories that expose serious crime.

The Code provides that while criminal proceedings are active, no **16–037** payment or promise of payment may be made, directly or indirectly, to any witness or any person who may reasonably be expected to be called as a witness.[124] The phrase "proceedings are active" is not defined under the Code, but proceedings are active from the moment a person has been arrested or charged up until the time they have been convicted or acquitted. During this period, the Code prohibits any payment to any actual or potential witness and further provides that no payment should be suggested or made dependent on the outcome of the trial.[125] It should be noted that what the Code seeks to prohibit is payments to witnesses that may compromise the legal process, not interviews with witnesses per se. The Code therefore provides, as an exception to the general rule, that if a witness incurs expenses as a result of contributing to a programme those expenses may be reimbursed.[126]

Even if proceedings are not "active" but are merely likely or foreseeable, the Code prohibits payments to people who might reasonably be expected to be witnesses unless there is a clear public interest, such as investigating crime or serious wrongdoing, and the payment is necessary to elicit the information.[127] The Code further provides that where such a payment is made it will be appropriate to disclose the payment to both defence and prosecution if the person becomes a witness in any subsequent trial.[128] The purpose of the latter provision is to protect the integrity of the legal process if criminal proceedings do transpire.

RELIGION

A religious programme is defined in the Code as a programme **16–038** dealing with matters of religion as the central subject, or as a significant part of the programme. This definition embraces not only programmes that focus on acts of worship, but also, for example, history or current affairs programmes where religion or belief is a

---

[123] *Making sure that crime doesn't pay*, Home Office Consultation Paper, November 2006.
[124] r.3.4.
[125] r.3.4.
[126] r.3.4.
[127] r.3.5.
[128] r.3.5.

significant part. The rules in this section have two main purposes. First, they seek to protect religious persons and groups by ensuring that religious matters are covered responsibly and that religious groups are not subjected to abusive treatment. Many religious groups of course deserve to be abused, and this objective can conflict with freedom of expression. The Code is also concerned with protecting the viewing public from potential exploitation by religious hucksters.

Broadcasters are required to exercise the proper degree of responsibility with respect to the content of religious programmes.[129] This rule replicates in terms s.319(2)(e) of the Communications Act. Secondly, the religious views and beliefs of those belonging to a particular religion must not be subject to abusive treatment, again as required by the Act itself.[130]

Ofcom sensibly rejected complaints against Channel Four programmes presented by Professor Richard Dawkins, called *The Root of All Evil*? In this polemical series, Professor Dawkins challenged what he described as a "process of non-thinking faith", questioning why militant faith appeared to him to be on the increase and why religious people were allowed to teach their children their beliefs from an early age. In the trailers, which give a flavour of the programmes, he described God as "fiction" and asked whether "religion is the root of all evil? A virus particularly affecting the young?" But the programmes also contained contrasting views from religious figures, expressing support for religious ideas. Intolerant viewers complained that the programmes treated Christianity with ridicule and scorn, were not impartial and made offensive and harmful comments. But Ofcom emphasised that these were serious documentaries and the channel had every right to broadcast them.

> "In such areas as political and religious debate, it is essential that broadcasters and viewers have as much freedom as is compatible with the law, to explore ideas. The programmes were clearly authored and the presenter had every right to challenge orthodox religion so long as there was a 'proper degree of responsibility' and people's religious views were not subject to abusive treatment."

In terms of viewer's expectations, the series title and the trailers as well as Channel Four's distinctive remit[131] can have left viewers in no doubt that they were about to see a polemic which challenged religious faith.

---

[129] r.4.1.

[130] r.4.2., s.319(6)(b) CA 2003.

[131] Channel Four's remit requires it, amongst other things, to "encourage innovation and experiment in the form and context of programmes and generally to give the channel a distinctive character of its own".

The second question was whether Channel Four had applied "the **16–039** proper degree of responsibility". In considering this, Ofcom looked at what "the proper degree of responsibility" meant "in the specific context of a polemic in favour of atheism and opposed to religious faith and expressly designed to generate and/or contribute to debate". For Ofcom, the critical factors were that the audience had been given clear information as to what they were about to watch; the views of the presenter were identified clearly as his opinion; those views were open to challenge and opposing opinions to those of the presenter had, in fact, been aired. For these reasons, Ofcom found that the broadcaster was not in breach of r.4.1.

Ofcom also rejected the complaint that the programmes amounted to abusive treatment towards particular religions. Although Professor Dawkins had addressed several specific religions and denominations, the overall theme of the programmes was to criticise religious belief generally. These criticisms did not use offensive language or espouse intolerance, violence or militant actions against those with religious beliefs. In the content of a polemical programme, challenging comments were likely to be aired. While Ofcom accepted that some people would have found them offensive, in its opinion they did not amount to abusive treatment.[132]

In terms of protecting the audience from indoctrination or manipulation, the Code sets down a number of specific rules. First, it provides that religious programmes must not improperly exploit any susceptibilities of the audience.[133] This rule gives effect to a statutory obligation in like terms under s.319(6)(a) of the Act. Ofcom's guidance points out, valuably, that it would be improper exploitation for a programme to abuse or denigrate a person's beliefs in order to convince them to change their beliefs, on the ground that if they didn't, some negative outcome would result.[134] Catholics threatening Protestants with hellfire, or vice versa, would be covered, as would evangelical Christians who threaten homosexuals with God-given HIV/AIDS unless they change their ways.

Religious programmes on television services, unlike those on **16–040** radio or specialist TV stations, must not seek recruits by "directly appealing to audience members to join a religion or religious denomination", which Ofcom's guidance contrasts with merely proclaiming the benefits of a particular doctrine or belief-system, which would not infringe this rule.[135] If a religious broadcaster wishes to seek recruits through its services, the appropriate course is to apply for a specialist religious license.[136]

A particular concern is the potential for exploitation where claims are made about special powers or gifts of a supernatural nature in

---

132 Ofcom Broadcasting Bulletin No.61, May 30, 2006.
133 r.4.6.
134 Ofcom Guidance Notes, s.4: Religion, p.3.
135 Ofcom Guidance Notes, s.4: Religion, p.3.
136 Ofcom Guidance Notes, s.4: Religion, p.4.

order, for example, to persuade people to give financial support or to influence young children. The Code therefore provides that religious programmes that contain claims that a living person (or group) has special powers or abilities must treat such claims with due objectivity and must not broadcast such claims when children are likely viewers or listeners.[137] (On its face, this would save children from exposure to the Pope, as well as to faith healers and the assorted bible-bashing mountebanks who occupy the airwaves in the United States). This provision does not apply to religious figures from the past, so (notwithstanding the Christian belief that Jesus lives), claims about the special powers of Jesus Christ or the Buddha run no risk of breaching the Code.

DUE IMPARTIALITY AND DUE ACCURACY

16–041 Newspapers are allowed to be partial, to adopt a particular political stance and to seek to influence the opinions of their readerships. Broadcasters are not. Since the earliest days of public service broadcasting, when the BBC had a total monopoly over radio and later over television, there was an expectation fostered by Lord Reith that news coverage by broadcasters would be fair and balanced—in other words, impartial. The greater reach of public broadcasting and its perceived influence called for a more onerous set of standards for broadcasters and that remains the position today, in relation to the BBC under its Charter, and in relation to all other broadcasters under the Ofcom Code. The impartiality requirements of the Code do not apply to the BBC; but the BBC's Producers Guidelines contain detailed requirements on this topic and complaints about the impartiality and accuracy of BBC programmes must be addressed to the BBC, not to Ofcom.

The statutory provisions governing due impartiality and due accuracy in relation to news coverage have already been outlined.[138] The fundamental principle is that news, in whatever form, must be reported with due accuracy and presented with due impartiality.[139] It should be noted that this requirement relates only to news; other programmes, including other factual programmes, are not required to be "reported with due accuracy and presented with due impartiality". Flagrant factual inaccuracies in any programme, however, would probably breach generally accepted standards, while a factual programme that lacked impartiality might breach standards relating to fairness

The Code contains important guidance as to the meaning of "due impartiality":

---

[137] r.4.7.
[138] See above.
[139] r.5.1.

"Due" is an important qualification to the concept of impartiality. **16–042** Impartiality itself means not favouring one side over another. "Due" means adequate or appropriate to the subject and nature of the programme. So "due impartiality" does not mean an equal division of time has to be given to every view, or that every argument and every facet of every argument has to be represented. The approach to due impartiality may vary according to the nature of the subject, the type of programme and channel, the likely expectation of the audience as to content, and the extent to which the content and approach is signalled to the audience. "Context" is all-important.[140]

This guidance reflects the former ITC program code position that "balance" was not required in any simple mathematical sense or by providing "equal time" or insisting there be a spokesperson for the other side of every argument. Nor does it require neutrality on what Sir Hugh Greene described as "basic moral values", namely "truthfulness, justice, freedom, compassion and tolerance". As the Home Office minister explained to parliament during the passage of the 1990 Broadcasting Act,

> "Broadcasters should not expect to be impartial between truth and untruth, justice and injustice, compassion and cruelty, tolerance and intolerance or even right and wrong. How can be one be impartial on such matters? Broadcasters should not be obliged to be morally neutral as well as politically neutral."[141]

In 2007 ITV News reported that, in the interview with Michael Parkinson, the Prime Minister had said that his belief in God played an important part in deciding to go to war in Iraq and that he had prayed over the decision before embarking on military action. Ofcom ruled that, when examined with care, the only statements that were clear in the interview were that Mr Blair struggled with his own conscience about the decision to go to war, and that he believed history and God would make the judgement on whether he was right. Ofcom held that ITV had reported as fact its interpretation of the interview, which was at the very least ambiguous and open to different interpretations. If ITV had noted the ambiguity and stated that its view was one possible interpretation of Mr Blair's replies, it would not have been in breach of the Code.[142] This adjudication is questionable: under the impetus of Downing Street, Ofcom took the role of editor rather than judge. Doubtless it was a better editor, in hindsight, than the ITV editor on the night, but the interpretation offered was not necessarily inaccurate: it was a matter for editorial discretion, not for Ofcom judgement.

---

[140] Ofcom Broadcasting Code, s.5, p.24.
[141] Hansard (House of Lords), July 1, 1990, col.366.
[142] Ofcom Broadcasting Bulletin No.79, February 26, 2007; *ITV rapped over Blair chat report*, BBC News, February 27, 2007.

16–043 Where a news report is inaccurate, the right response is to issue a prompt correction. The Code provides that significant mistakes in news should normally be acknowledged and corrected on air quickly.[143] The Code also provides that corrections should be appropriately scheduled.[144] Presumably, this provision concerns the situation where an inaccuracy has not been picked up in the course of the relevant programme but is identified at a later stage. In these circumstances, the correction should be scheduled so that it receives similar prominence to, or address a similar audience as, the original error.

The Act and Code impose what are called "special impartiality requirements". What these require, in sum, is the exclusion from news services of the personal views and opinions of the person providing the service on matters of political and industrial controversy and matters relating to current public policy.[145] Ofcom guidance explains that the phrase "person providing the service" refers to the licensee, the company officers and those persons with an editorial responsibility for the service rather than, for example, the programme presenter.[146] The views of a service provider may be reported in the news where the relevant person, e.g. the Chief Executive of ITV, is expressing a view in a legislative forum or a court of law, or a view in relation to the provision of programme services.

Due impartiality may be achieved within a programme or over a series of programmes taken as a whole.[147] The Code also provides that any personal interest of a reporter or presenter, which would call into question the due impartiality of the programme, must be made clear to the audience.[148] Importantly however, non-news presenters and reporters, presenters of "personal view" or authored programmes or items, as well as chairs of discussion programmes may express their own views on matters of political or industrial controversy or matters relating to public policy.[149] The caveat is that alternative viewpoints must be adequately represented, either in the programme or in a series of programmes taken as a whole.[150] It is important that a personal view or authored programme is clearly signalled to the audience at the outset.[151]

16–044 The provisions relating to "personal view" or authored programmes are significant and relate both to news coverage and other factual programmes on controversial political topics, providing that

---

[143] r.5.2.
[144] r.5.2.
[145] r.3.5.
[146] Guidance Notes, s.5, r.5.4.
[147] r.5.5.
[148] r.5.8.
[149] r.5.9.
[150] r.5.9.
[151] r.5.10.

balance is achieved across a series of programmes taken as a whole. Where the subject matter is not political, industrial or on a matter of current policy, broadcasters have free rein—there is no need for impartiality in an arts programme featuring a review of a current exhibition or film. Thus Professor Dawkins' polemical series about religion, *The Root of All Evil?*[152] did not breach the rules on accuracy and impartiality, because,

> "the requirement for due accuracy and impartiality applies only to news. Outside of news, only programmes dealing with matters of political or industrial controversy and matters relating to current public policy are required to maintain 'due impartiality'".

The right-wing Cable Channel Fox News, however, was in breach of this provision when commentator John Gibson claimed the BBC displayed a "frothing-at-the-mouth" anti-American bias that was "obsessive, irrational and dishonest" and that the corporation "felt entitled to lie". He said this in the comment section at the end of a news bulletin on the day the Hutton report was published. Ofcom noted that in response to its enquiries the network failed to provide evidence that the BBC "bashed" the United States and Ofcom did not accept that the Hutton report showed that the "BBC felt entitled to lie". "Even taking into account that this was a personal view item, the strength and number of allegations that John Gibson made meant that Fox News should have offered the BBC an opportunity to respond,"[153] was Ofcom's verdict. It is difficult to understand why it should bother to upbraid hysterical polemics from US propaganda stations, especially those owned by Rupert Murdoch who has an obvious commercial interest in BBC-bashing. The BBC would have been foolish to bother to respond to a rival's attack which had no credibility in the first place. In any event, the piece was "comment" and labelled as such—it was not "news". Similar BBC-bashing comments may be published in any newspaper—why should commentators be refused the right to the same "comment" when it is televised?

Where the subject matter of the programme relates to a "major" political or industrial controversy or a "major" matter of current policy, due impartiality must be preserved in each programme or in "clearly linked and timely programmes".[154] The effect of this provision is that when broadcasting on major controversies the broadcaster must achieve balance in every programme (or in clearly linked and timely programmes), and cannot balance out views over a series of programmes. This rule is reinforced by the additional requirement

---

[152] Discussed earlier at para.16–038.
[153] *US channel's BBC remarks censured*, BBC News, June 14, 2004.
[154] r.5.11.

that "an appropriately wide range of significant views must be included and given due weight in each programme or in clearly linked and timely programmes".[155] In addition, local radio services must not give undue prominence to the views of particular persons and bodies on controversial political or industrial matters and matters relating to public policy.[156]

16–045   In relation to BBC output, the provisions on accuracy and impartiality are to be found in the second and third parts of its Producer's Guidelines. Accuracy is described as "a core editorial value and fundamental to our reputation". The guidelines state that accuracy is more important than speed and is more than a question of getting the facts right—all the relevant facts and opinion should be weighed to get at the truth. The BBC aims to achieve accuracy by gathering material using first-hand sources wherever possible; checking and cross checking the facts; validating the authenticity of documentary evidence and digital material and corroborating claims and allegations made by contributors wherever possible.[157]

In terms of impartiality, the Guidelines state this "lies at the heart of the BBC's commitment to its audiences".[158] In practice, the BBC will seek to provide a properly balanced service consisting of a wide range of subject matter and views over an appropriate time scale across all of its output. Just as under the Ofcom Code, the BBC will take particular care when dealing with political or industrial controversy or matters relating to current public policy.

These rigorous "due prominence" rules were first imposed by the Thatcher government, determined to neutralise broadcasting as an anti-conservative influence in society. The case for maintaining them rests on the somewhat outdated notion that television is a uniquely powerful and persuasive medium, exercising the kind of influence that it had for all the years when there were only four terrestrial channels and most people watched them. Now that there are hundreds of channels to choose from, and opinion formers log on rather than switch on, do these rigid rules shackle broadcasters unduly? Television contribution to public affairs is lacklustre, in terms of exposure journalism and agenda setting, and its executives are cautious and conventional. The BBC and Ofcom collaborate in the discredited "D-notice" system (the BBC even appoints an officer to the committee while Ofcom ensures that licensees liaise with it). Today it would be more sensible and more in keeping with Art.10 to interpret the "due impartiality" rules as merely requiring that undue prominence should not be given to one side or one participant in current political or industrial controversies. This would assure freedom for committed broadcasting, without permitting propaganda.

---

[155] r.5.12.
[156] r.5.13.
[157] BBC Producer's Guidelines, p.16.
[158] BBC Producer's Guidelines, p.26.

ELECTIONS

Section 6 of the Code contains rules designed to ensure fair and **16–046**
balanced reporting of elections and referendums. This part of the
Code does not apply to the BBC, which has its own detailed rules on
election coverage in the Politics and Public Policy section of its
Producer's Guidelines.[159] Furthermore, the Ofcom Code is supple
mented by other legislation of relevance[160] as well as specific rules on
party political broadcasts contained in *Ofcom Rules on Party Political
and Referendum Broadcasts*.[161] As with all other broadcasts, party
political broadcasts are required to comply with relevant provisions
of the Ofcom Code, e.g. the provisions on harm and offence,
notwithstanding that the content is normally the responsibility of the
relevant political parties. There has not been a General Election
since the Ofcom Code came into effect, so Ofcom has not yet been
called upon to adjudicate upon an alleged breach of the Code in this
context.

The rules in s.5 dealing with Due Accuracy and Due Impartiality
apply to the coverage of elections and referendums, not only in the
United Kingdom but anywhere in the world.[162] Channel Four News,
for example, would be expected to apply the same standards of
impartiality to its coverage of a US Presidential election as it would
to a UK General Election. But in relation to programmes at the
time of elections and referendums in the United Kingdom, broadcasters are also required to give "due weight" to the coverage of
major parties during the election period.[163] They must also "consider" giving appropriate coverage to other parties and independent
candidates offering "significant views and perspectives".[164] The terms
"major party", "election period", "candidate" and "referendum
period" are all defined under the Code and contain no surprises.[165] It
is important to note that the Code does not impose a general
obligation on broadcasters to undertake election coverage; they are
perfectly entitled to ignore elections altogether. But if they do cover
an election, they are required to comply with the Code. (The BBC,
of course, has a broader duty under the Charter to sustain citizen-
ship and democracy, so must cover elections.)

---

[159] Available from the BBC Trust website:
[160] Notably s.66A, 92 and 92 of the Representation of the People Act (as amended
by s.144 of the Political Parties, Elections and Referendums Act).
[161] Available at from the Ofcom website: *www.ofcom.org.uk*.
[162] r.6.1.
[163] r.6.2.
[164] r.6.2.
[165] "Major party" is defined as follows. In the UK, the Conservative Party, the
Labour Party and the Liberal Democrats; in Scotland and Wales, the Scottish
National Party and Plaid Cymru; in Northern Ireland, the Democratic Unionist
Party, Sinn Fein, the Social Democratic and Labour Party and the Ulster
Unionist Party.

Special restrictions apply to polling day itself. As soon as polling stations open, broadcasters must finish discussion and analysis of election and referendum issues[166] and they must not publish the results of any opinion poll on polling day itself until the election or referendum poll closes.[167] Both these rules are interferences with the right to communicate information and opinion, and have scant justification other than in the belief that free speech on polling day might somehow skew the election result. How this would occur, other than by encouraging people to go out and vote, has never been rationally explained. It is part of the British fear of unpredictable consequences, and perhaps an uneasiness that those who vote at 21.00 do so without the benefit of a debate between candidates transmitted at 15.00. The ban on exit or opinion polls appears to result from fear of the "They Think It's All Over" factor: citizens might be disinclined to vote in the closing hours of a poll that seems a foregone conclusion. So what? If exit polls show the race is close, then there would be a high voter turn out in the final hours. There is no compelling reason for this censorship, which does not of course affect newspapers published on polling day and available throughout that day.

16–047   The Code more reasonably prohibits candidates in UK elections (and representatives of permitted participants in UK referendums) from acting as news presenters, interviewers or presenters of any type of programme during the election period. This is in addition to the specific restrictions placed on politicians in relation to the making of news programmes, which apply at all times of the political calendar.[168] If a politician has already signed up to appear in a non-political programme that was planned or scheduled before the election or referendum period that may go ahead, but no new appearances should be arranged and broadcast during the period.[169] The rationale behind these rules is to prevent candidates from gaining an unfair electoral advantage through greater media exposure than their political rivals.

The Code contains specific provisions relating to election coverage at the constituency level and electoral area level, the local election equivalent. The requirements of due impartiality apply to all reports and discussions relating to constituencies and electoral areas[170] and if a candidate takes part in a report about his or her constituency/electoral area, candidates of each of the major parties must be offered an opportunity to take part.[171] The same opportunities must also be offered to candidates representing parties with previous

---

[166] r.6.4.
[167] r.6.5.
[168] r.5.3.
[169] r.6.7.
[170] r.6.8.
[171] r.6.9.

significant electoral support or where there is evidence of significant current support.[172] This provision protects the position of independent candidates and representatives of small political parties. In all cases, if the candidate refuses or is unable to participate, the broadcaster may nevertheless go ahead with the programme.[173] The Code also provides for specific rules in relation to constituency/electoral area reports and discussions after the close of nominations,[174] in relation to candidates taking part in programmes after the election has been called[175] and in relation to coverage of wider elections regions, such as the Scottish Parliament or London Assembly.[176]

As for the BBC, the section on Politics and Public Policy in the BBC Producer's Guidelines sets out three key statements of principle. First, these require the BBC to treat matters of public policy or political or industrial controversy with due accuracy and impartiality in news services and other output. Secondly, the BBC is prohibited from expressing an opinion on current affairs or matters of public policy other than broadcasting. Thirdly, the BBC must not campaign, or allowed itself to be used to campaign. The guidelines go on to set out detailed provisions relating to such varied topics as interviews with party leaders and commissioning opinion polls.[177]

FAIRNESS

The Fairness and Privacy sections of the Code are fundamentally **16–048** different from the other sections in that they concern how broadcasters treat the individuals or organisations directly affected by programmes, as opposed to the general public's experience of programmes as viewers and listeners. "Fairness" is the standard by which Ofcom can effectuate the "right of reply" principle in Art.8 of the European Convention Transfrontier Television, because it requires a correction to be broadcast, or else the publication of a summary of an Ofcom decision in newspapers and magazines. There is, of course, a sense in which broadcasters are always "unfair" to those they interview—in fading light, or under harsh studio lights and with the inevitable pressure of editing for a short, sharp slot. So programs must be considered as a whole, bearing in mind the limitations of the medium. In every case, context is critical.

The guiding rule is that broadcasters must avoid unjust or unfair treatment of individuals in their programmes.[178] That means giving

---

[172] r.6.10.
[173] rr.6.9, 6.10.
[174] r.6.11.
[175] r.6.12.
[176] r.6.13.
[177] BBC Producer's Guidelines, available at *www.bbc.co.uk/trust*.
[178] r.7.1.

those attacked an opportunity to reply. Another important aspect of fair treatment is the obtaining of "informed consent". The guidance provides that where a person is invited to make a significant contribution to a programme they should normally be told, at an appropriate stage, about the following matters:

- the nature and purpose of the programme and what the programme is about. They should receive a clear explanation of why they were asked to contribute and when (if known) and where it is likely to be first broadcast;
- what kind of contribution they are expected to make, for example live, pre-recorded, interview, discussion, edited, unedited, etc;
- the areas of questioning and, wherever possible, the nature of other likely contributions;
- any significant changes to the programme as it develops which might reasonably affect their original consent to participate, and which might cause material unfairness;
- the nature of their contractual rights and obligations and those of the programme maker and broadcaster in relation to their contribution; and
- given clear information, if offered an opportunity to preview the programme, about whether they will be able to effect any changes to it.[179]

If these requirements are met, the consent given is likely to amount to "informed consent". As with other parts of the Code the appropriateness of given guidance has to be judged in context; if the subject matter of a programme is trivial or a person's participation minor, broadcasters are not expected to meet these requirements.[180] If a contributor is under 16, or over 16 "but not in position to give consent" (e.g. through learning difficulties or mental illness), then consent should be sought from a parent or carer.[181] Where such consent has been forthcoming, these vulnerable persons "should not be asked for views on matters likely to be beyond their capacity to answer properly without such consent." In other words, receiving consent from, for instance, a parent is not a license to ask a child inappropriate questions that they can't answer properly.

Other general aspects of fairness include dealing with programme contributors fairly,[182] editing programmes in such a way that contributions are presented fairly,[183] honouring guarantees giving to contributors (for example about confidentiality or anonymity)[184] and

---

[179] r.7.3.
[180] r.7.3.
[181] rr.7.4, 7.5.
[182] r.7.2.
[183] r.7.6.
[184] r.7.7.

ensuring that material that is later re-used in a different context does not create unfairness.[185] Where guarantees have been given to contributors regarding the protection of their identity, the Guidance warns broadcasters against assuming that a contributor will necessarily appreciate the fine distinction between not identifying them in the programme and making sure that they are not identifiable.[186] Broadcasters should therefore provide contributors with sufficient information to enable them to understand in advance what steps the programme maker proposes to take and the degree of protection that will result from any steps taken (e.g. by not naming them, withholding other information, or by disguising their image or voice etc).

A different dimension of fairness from the fair treatment of **16–049** participants in programmes involves ensuring that facts are presented fairly. Broadcasters are urged, before putting out a programme, to take reasonable care to satisfy themselves that material facts have not been presented, disregarded or omitted in a way that is unfair to an individual or organisation and that appropriate opportunities to contribute have been made to anyone whose omission could be unfair to an individual or organisation.[187] The guidance also spells out the requirement that programmes—such as dramas and factually-based dramas—should not portray facts, events, individuals or organisations in a way which is unfair to an individual or organisation.[188]

Five News was found itself in breach of the fairness requirement for items about projects funded by the Millennium Commission "the top ten Millennium flops and how much they cost".[189] The basis on which the projects had been judged to be "flops" was never explained to the audience. The criterion used was whether a project was experiencing financial difficulties, but Ofcom thought that it was unfair to lay this at the door of the Millennium Commission, which was not responsible for the long-term sustainability of the projects it helped finance. The programme had made detailed criticisms of the Commission, but these had not been foreshadowed or put squarely to the spokesman, who in consequence appeared to give a vague response. The Commission had not been given an adequate opportunity to respond.

The *Five News* decision highlights that an important aspect of fairness is offering a right to reply to any individual or organisation where an allegation has made against them. This is now expected of journalists if they wish to protect themselves against a defamation claim by meeting the standards of "responsible journalism", as

---

[185] r.7.8.
[186] Broadcasting Guidance Code Update on r.7.7.
[187] r.7.9.
[188] r.7.10.
[189] Ofcom Broadcasting Bulletin No.62, June 12, 2006.

required by the *Reynolds/Jameel* public interest defence.[190] The broadcasting equivalent is set out in the Code as follows:

> "If a programme alleges wrongdoing or incompetence or makes other significant allegations, those concerned should normally be given an appropriate and timely opportunity to respond."[191]

Furthermore, the Code provides that where a person approached to contribute to a programme chooses to make no comment or refuses to appear, the broadcast should make clear their non-participation and should give their explanation if it would be unfair not to do so.[192] In those circumstances where it is appropriate to represent the views of a person or organisation that is not participating in the programme, this must be done in a fair manner.[193] Frequently, ministers and political spokespeople decline to appear because of embarrassment or cowardice, but it is apparently unfair to state the obvious. The British preference for euphemism translates to an anodyne "The minister declined our invitation to appear." Often the refusal will be designed to prevent any discussion, on the basis that without a government spokesperson it would be "unbalanced". Broadcasters should not fall for this trick (although they frequently do). Impartiality is "due" by screening one side of a debate, if the other side refuses to appear.

16–050   The Code provides clear guidance on the circumstances in which deception, set-ups and wind-ups may be permissible. The basic principle is that broadcasters or program makers should not normally obtain or seek information, audio, pictures or an agreement to contribute through misrepresentation or deception (the Code provides that deception includes surreptitious filming or recording.)[194] However, the Code protects investigative journalism by providing that it may be warranted to use material obtained through misrepresentation or deception without consent if it is in the public interest and cannot reasonably be obtained by other means.[195]

If there is no public interest justification and the wind-up is to be broadcast for entertainment, consent should be obtained from the person concerned before that material is broadcast.[196] If it is not possible to identify a person or organisation in the programme then consent for broadcast is not required.[197] Where celebrities and other persons in the public eye are involved, material may be broadcast without consent, but if that material is likely to result in "unjustified

---

[190] See the section on the qualified privilege defence in the chapter on defamation.
[191] r.7.11.
[192] r.7.12.
[193] r.7.13.
[194] r.7.14.
[195] r.7.14.
[196] r.7.14.
[197] r.7.14.

public ridicule or personal distress" then a public interest justification is required.[198] This guidance reflects the right to a private life guaranteed by Art.8 of the European Convention. In these circumstances, the normal practice should be to pre-record contributions, so as to allow such assessments to be made before the material is broadcast.

PRIVACY

The Privacy section of the Code sets out a single principle and a **16–051** series of "practices to be followed", i.e. guidelines to assist broadcasters when seeking to apply the principle. The key principle is that any infringement of privacy in programmes, or in connection with obtaining material included in programmes, must be *warranted*. The privacy provisions therefore relate both to the actual contents of programmes and to the methods used to obtain material for programmes. Nearly all of the guidance in the privacy section of the Code is qualified by some expression such as "unless it is warranted".

There is an inherent tension between freedom of expression as guaranteed by Art.10 of the European Convention and privacy, guaranteed by Art.8, and the Code must therefore allow for the possibility that any infringement of privacy should be capable of being justified if it is in the public interest. As r.81 puts it, with deceptive simplicity, if the reason an invasion of privacy is "warranted" is that it is in the public interest, "then the broadcaster should be able to demonstrate that the public interest outweighs the right to privacy". The given examples of public interest provided in the Rule are: **revealing or detecting crime, protecting public health or safety, or exposing misleading claims or disclosing incompetence that affects the public**. What is crucial for broadcasters to remember—this is spelt out in s.8 in relation to surreptitious filming—is that they must have some prima facie evidence that the proposed story is in the public interest, as well as some reasonable ground to suspect that the privacy invasion will turn up more evidence. The point was well made by the decision in the BCC case involving reporter John Sweeney. He became instinctively suspicious—without the slightest evidence—that reclusive press proprietors the Barclay brothers must be up to no good, because they were building a castle on their private island. So, as reporter for the BBC program *The Spin*, he hired a boat and had himself photographed trespassing on their land. The court reluctantly refused to injunct the program, but after transmission the Broadcasting Complaints Commission ruled that since the reporter and his BBC producers had no evidence of suspicious behaviour by the Barclays

---

[198] r.7.14.

on their private island, the invasion of their privacy could not be warranted just because they were rich and powerful.[199]

The guidelines on privacy provide few hard-and-fast rules and will probably be of relatively little assistance to broadcasters, except in the most general terms by way of flagging up potential areas of concern. Three general topics of concern are identified at the outset. First, information that discloses the location of a person's or family's home should not be revealed without permission, unless it is warranted.[200] Secondly, the guidelines point out that people caught up in events that become part of news coverage still enjoy a right to privacy that should not be infringed, unless it is warranted.[201] Thirdly, the guidelines re-iterate a central finding of European Convention jurisprudence on privacy—namely that even material filmed in a public place may be so private that it should not be broadcast without prior consent, unless this is warranted.[202] The cases that gave rise to this principle are *Von Hannover*, which concerned paparazzi hounding of Princess Caroline of Monaco by photographing her whilst she was trying to eat a private meal in a restaurant and *Peck* which concerned the broadcast of CCTV footage from a shopping centre showing a man who had attempted to commit suicide. Then came the *Naomi Campbell* scenario, where photographs taken of the truculent model carried the message, in breach of confidentiality, that she was undergoing therapeutic treatment for drug addiction.[203]

The guidelines also identify particular situations in which it may be important to obtain consent, namely when an infringement of privacy occurs in the making of a programme;[204] when the broadcast itself contains material that infringes privacy;[205] when privacy is being infringed in the making of a programme and the individual or organisation requests that filming or recording stops;[206] and when filming or recording is undertaken in institutions, organisations or other agencies, when the management's permission may be required.[207] In all these instances, it may be necessary to obtain consent or permission, "unless it is warranted to proceed without it". When filming in institutions, it is not generally necessary to obtain the individual consent of employees whose appearance is incidental or that of essentially anonymous members of the public, but separate consent may be required where filming is carried out in sensitive

---

[199] *R v BCC Ex p. Barclay Brothers*, The Times, October 11, 1996.
[200] r.8.2.
[201] r.8.3.
[202] r.8.4.
[203] *Campbell v MGN* [2004] UKHL 22.
[204] r.8.5.
[205] r.8.6.
[206] r.8.7.
[207] r.8.8.

locations such as ambulances, hospitals, schools, prisons or police stations.[208]

A number of guidelines concern the gathering of information, **16–052** sound and images and the re-use of material. There is a general requirement on broadcasters to ensure that the means of obtaining material is proportionate in all the circumstances and in particular to the subject matter of the programme.[209] A serious current affairs programme investigating police corruption, for example, might warrant covert techniques that would be disproportionate in an entertainment programme. As with the provisions on fairness, broadcasters also have to watch out that material obtained for one purpose and subsequently re-used does not create an unwarranted infringement of privacy.[210]

There are relatively strict guidelines on "doorstepping", that practice beloved of investigative reporters which involves them turning up unannounced on someone's doorstep and shoving a microphone under his nose. In relation to doorstepping for factual programmes, the guidance indicates that this should not take place unless a request for an interview has been refused or it has not been possible to request an interview, or there is good reason to believe that the investigation would be frustrated if the subject is approached openly, and it is warranted to doorstep. The guidance concludes with what appears to have been intended as a reassuring observation that normally broadcasters may, without prior warning interview, film or record people in the news when in public places.[211]

The "warranted" recording of telephone calls for potential broadcast is permissible providing broadcasters have carried out basic safeguards such as identifying themselves and explaining the purpose of the call in advance. A serious investigative programme would be justified in recording such a telephone call without identifying its true purpose and broadcasting it without consent, if there was a sufficiently strong public interest. The same applies to surreptitious filming or recording, which should only be used where it is warranted, i.e. where there is some basis for suspicion. The guidance spells out that this normally requires that there is prima facie evidence of a story in the public interest; there are reasonable grounds to suspect that further material evidence could be obtained and it is necessary to the credibility and authenticity of the programme.[212] Material gained by surreptitious filming and recording should only be broadcast when it is warranted.[213]

It may also be legitimate to carry out surreptitious filming or **16–053** recording, doorstepping or recorded "wind-up" calls for entertainment purposes, providing this does not amount to a significant

[208] r.8.8.
[209] r.8.9.
[210] r.8.10.
[211] r.8.11.
[212] r.8.13.
[213] r.8.14.

infringement of privacy such as to cause significant annoyance, distress or embarrassment. The resulting material should not be broadcast without the consent of those involved, unless they are not identifiable.[214]

An exceptionally serious breach was committed on Kiss 100FM Radio by the DJ Streetboy. The programme phoned a member of the public, R, who had been made redundant. Streetboy then returned Mr R's call posing as the Human Resources officer and the telephone call was recorded and later broadcast on air without Mr R's permission, in breach of the Code. Streetboy proceeded to rubbish Mr R's employment credentials, telling him that he was "wasting his time" and the exchange continued in similar vein in spite of Mr R's increasingly apparent distress. Streetboy ended by telling Mr R to "go and flip burgers or something" and after the item ended the presenters were heard laughing. Emap Radio, the parent company, accepted that it was a "horrible intrusion" and described the decision to broadcast the pre-recorded piece as "inexplicable", as even the presenter had acknowledged that it had gone too far. Ofcom agreed, describing the case as "the most serious case of unwarranted infringement of privacy it had heard" and fining the licensee £75,000, the highest fine yet meted out for a privacy violation.[215]

Whether such powers to fine for privacy violation, in the absence of any power to compensate those violated, is a remedy effective enough to comply with Art.8 is highly doubtful. It was squarely raised by the European Court in *Peck v UK*. There, the complainant had been shown on Anglia TV's *Crimebeat*, knife in hand, having just slit his wrists. The invasion of his private life at a time of great mental disturbance could not be justified by the public interest in demonstrating the value of CCTV: the court ruled that the State was at fault under Art.13 of the Convention for not having an "effective remedy", i.e. a law that compensated him for the breach of his Art.8 right. What the State had provided, of course, was access to regulatory bodies (the BSC and ITC) with powers to reprimand and fine the broadcaster. The court however,

> "finds that the lack of legal power of the Commission to award damages to the applicant means that those bodies could not provide an effective remedy to him. It notes that the ITC's power to impose a fine on the relevant television company does not amount to an award of damages to the applicant".[216]

It is difficult to see why the government, fully aware of this lacuna by the time of the 2003 Communications Act, did not provide Ofcom

---

[214] r.8.15.
[215] Ofcom Content Sanctions Committee, Kiss FM Radio Limited.
[216] *Peck v UK*, para.109.

with power to award compensation, certainly for medical and counselling costs incurred by a privacy breach, and some solatium for the kind of distress suffered by Mr R in the Kiss FM case. Its failure means that victims will have to take the broadcaster to court, under a *Naomi Campbell* tort complaint of "misuse of personal information", to obtain a compensation that should be available directly and inexpensively from Ofcom.[217]

Several pieces of guidance set out to address the safeguards **16–054** necessary to ensure privacy where suffering and distress is involved. Broadcasters must not take or broadcast footage of people caught up in emergencies or those suffering a personal tragedy, even in a public place, where that results in an infringement of privacy, unless it is warranted or the people concerned have given their consent.[218] Likewise, people in distress should not be put under pressure to take part in interviews, unless it is (wait for it) "warranted".[219] Broadcasters must also take care not to reveal the identity of a person who has died or of victims of accidents or of violent crimes before the next of kin have been informed, unless it is warranted.[220] This duty of care also extends to trying to reduce the potential distress of victims and/or relatives when making programmes about past traumatic events and informing them about the plans for the programme and its intended broadcast.[221]

There are also specific provisions to protect the privacy of people under 16 years of age and other vulnerable people. The Code requires broadcasters to pay particular attention to the privacy of people under 16, pointing out that they do not lose their rights to privacy because, for example, of the fame or notoriety of their parents or because of events in their schools.[222] Where a programme features an individual under 16 or a vulnerable person in a way that infringes privacy, consent must be obtained from a parent or carer and, wherever possible from the individual concerned, subject to certain limited exceptions and the usual proviso.[223] Likewise, such persons should not be questioned about private matters without the consent of a parent or carer, unless that is (inevitably) "warranted".[224]

Calendar News, run by ITV Yorkshire, was found in breach of the **16–055** privacy provisions relating to children for broadcasting a news item which showed footage of a family and their two children attending a court hearing. The complainants were Mr and Mrs Hodgson, who

---

[217] See discussion in Fenwick and Phillipson, *Media Freedom under the Human Rights Act* (OUP, 2005), Ch.17.
[218] r.8.16.
[219] r.8.17.
[220] r.8.18.
[221] r.8.19
[222] r.8.20.
[223] r.8.21.
[224] r.8.22.

had attended the sentencing hearing of Mrs Hodgson's mother, Mrs Shirley Capp, who had been convicted of intimidating a witness during the prosecution of her daughter, Maxine Carr. Maxine Carr was convicted of conspiring to pervert the course of justice in December 2003, in connection with the murder of two schoolgirls by Ian Huntley ("the Soham murder trial"). Mr and Mrs Hodson complained that the footage, which showed them and their two daughters entering and leaving the court building, infringed their privacy and that of their children. Ofcom rightly rejected their complaint, but wrongly upheld the complaint about filming their children. The key factors for Ofcom were the fact that the broadcast contained readily identifiable images of the children, their young ages (five and two), and their vulnerability in the context of a particularly high profile and sensitive case.[225] But the fact that the parents saw fit to bring them to court to watch grandma being sentenced should have constituted a waiver of any right to privacy: parents who use their children in such circumstances (perhaps in order to make them visible to the judge in the hope of a merciful sentence) effectively waive parental consent.

The experience of challenging censorship decisions by regulators in British courts has not been encouraging in respect of offensiveness (e.g. the *ProLife Alliance* case) but the traditional deference that judges show to "expert" bodies should not apply to Ofcom decisions on privacy, for the simple reason that judges are better equipped than anyone else (and certainly better equipped than the functionaries, political apparatchiks, professors of journalism and businessmen appointed to Ofcom standards boards) to decide what amounts to a breach of privacy. In one old BSC case, the Chief Justice declined to review that regulator's decision on the basis that privacy infringement "is not an area in which the courts are well equipped to adjudicate".[226] But this was before the *Naomi Campbell* case confounded such remarks, although they were probably influenced by the understandable view that the BSC was a lightweight source of opinion on ethics, rather than a serious enforcement body. Under s.6 of the Human Rights Act, the courts are obliged to apply the Convention rights and judges are the foremost experts in balancing Convention rights—notably Art.8 and Art.10. So the deference shown to so-called experts, which may have some justification in relation to representative bodies determining taste and decency, is not appropriate in the context of reviewing privacy decisions made by Ofcom.

---

[225] Ofcom Broadcasting Bulletin No.65, July 24, 2006.
[226] 2003 All E.R. 989 at 994 G-H.

SPONSORSHIP AND COMMERCIAL REFERENCES

The Code seeks to prevent unsuitable sponsorship on radio and **16–056** television and is guided by three main principles, each of which is required by the Television Without Frontiers Directive.[227] The first is that of transparency, namely to ensure sponsorship arrangements are transparent to viewers and listeners. Secondly there must be separation, to ensure that sponsorship messages are separate from programmes and to maintain a distinction between advertising and sponsorship. Thirdly, editorial independence must be preserved: the broadcaster must maintain editorial control over sponsored programmes and programmes must not be distorted for commercial purposes. Advertising and sponsorship are prohibited on the publicly-funded BBC.

There is an absolute prohibition on the sponsorship of news bulletins and news desk presentations on radio and news and current affairs programmes on television.[228] Geo UK, a general entertainment and news channel broadcasting to an Urdu speaking audience, broadcast the announcement "Geo news is brought to you by Kit Calling cards". Ofcom found the programme in breach of the Code.[229]

Current affairs programmes on radio may, however, be sponsored and short specialist reports following news programmes on both radio and television, such as sport, travel and weather, may be sponsored.[230] Where this happens, however, broadcasters must ensure that there is a clear separation from the news programme to avoid the impression that the main news is sponsored.[231] In terms of prohibited sponsors, the rule is that no programme on radio or television may be sponsored by an advertiser that is not allowed to advertise on that medium.[232] The effect of this rule is to preclude sponsorship by many industries, bodies and products ranging from tobacco companies to gun clubs and suppliers of prescription medicines.[233]

Where sponsorship does occur, it must comply with both the **16–057** advertising content and scheduling rules that apply to that medium.[234] This rule was breached by ITV 3 when the Disney film *Mary Poppins* was somewhat implausibly sponsored by Cobra, the

---

[227] 89/552/EEC, as amended by 97/36/EC.
[228] r.9.1.
[229] Ofcom Broadcasting Bulletin No.78, February 12, 2007.
[230] Guidance Note: Sponsorship Guidance, Issue Three, December 21, 2006.
[231] Guidance Note: Sponsorship Guidance, Issue Three, December 21, 2006.
[232] The only exception to this rule is betting and gaming companies, but they must not sponsor programmes aimed at people under eighteen.
[233] A full list is provided in the Guidance Note: Sponsorship Guidance, Issue Three, December 21, 2006.
[234] The Radio Advertising Standards Code and the Television Advertising Standards Code, supervised by the Advertising Standards Authority.

beer manufacturer. Under the applicable rules relating to the scheduling of television advertisements, alcoholic drinks containing 1.2 per cent alcohol or more by volume must not be advertised in or adjacent to children's programmes or programmes aimed at the under-18s. Accordingly, Ofcom found that the sponsorship was in breach of this rule.[235]

The editorial independence principle is enshrined in the rule that a sponsor must not influence the content and/or scheduling of a programme in such a way as to impair the responsibility and editorial independence of the broadcaster.[236] The Code also prohibits any promotional reference to the sponsor, its name, trademark, image, activities, services or products and bans any promotional generic references.[237] The sponsor must also not have any other direct or indirect interest in the editorial content of the sponsored programme. Non-promotional references are only allowed where they are editorially justified and incidental.

These rules precluding promotional references to sponsors were breached by the Channel Four programme *Sony Ericson Christmas Calling*, a programme featuring performances from various artists and a viewer competition offering prizes apparently chosen by the featured guests. Each of the viewer competitions featured a Sony Walkman mobile phone as one of its prizes and two competitions featured additional Sony products as prizes. The footage for these two competitions featured artists inside Sony stores looking at Sony products. In addition, a pop video apparently shot for the programme also featured band members trying out Sony products. Ofcom's verdict was that the references to Sony had created the impression that the sponsor had unacceptably influenced the content of the programme.[238]

16–058   In relation to sponsorship credits, the key principles in relation to both radio and television are that sponsored programmes must be clearly identified as such by reference to the name and/or logo of the sponsor at the beginning and/or end of the programme,[239] and that the relationship between the sponsor and the sponsored programme must be transparent.[240]

Sponsorship must be clearly separated from programmes by temporal and spatial means.[241] Furthermore, sponsorship must be clearly separated from advertising and sponsor credits must not

---

[235] Ofcom Broadcasting Bulletin 65, July 24, 2006.
[236] r.9.5.
[237] r.9.6.
[238] Ofcom Broadcasting Bulletin 59, May 2, 2006.
[239] r.9.7.
[240] r.9.8.
[241] r.9.13.

contain advertising messages or calls to action.[242] Where a programme trail contains a reference to the sponsor of the programme, the sponsor reference must remain short and secondary.[243]

Commercial references

Broadcasters must maintain the independence of editorial control over programme content.[244] Secondly, they must ensure that the advertising and programme elements of a service are clearly separated.[245] The Code then goes on to apply these principles to a variety of specific issues. The BBC is not subject to these rules in respect of its publicly-funded services, where these matters are the responsibility of the BBC Trust.   **16–059**

Three important rules relate to products or services in programmes. First, products or services must not be promoted in programmes.[246] The purpose of this provision is to maintain the fundamental distinction between programmes and advertising. The mischief it seeks to remedy is programmes effectively "selling" products to their viewers and listeners, so supplying information about a product in a consumer advice programme will not necessarily breach this provision.[247] Secondly, no undue prominence may be given in any programme to a product or service.[248] The key word here is "undue"—brands are part and parcel of modern life and there is no general prohibition on their featuring in programmes.[249] Thirdly, "product placement" is prohibited.[250]

A programme on Sky Sports called *The Rugby Club* was found by Ofcom both to have breached the rule on maintaining the independence of control over programme content and the specific provision relating to giving a product undue prominence. *The Rugby Club* is a magazine-style programme about rugby. In one particular edition, three members of the England team were interviewed whilst being shaved at an exclusive men's grooming saloon. Each wore an England rugby shirt bearing the Gillette logo and Gillette-branded towels and shaving products were clearly visible. Ofcom's concern about undue prominence arose from the fact that in a number of camera shots, branded towels draped around player's shoulders appeared to have been deliberately arranged to display the logo as clearly as possible. In terms of editorial control, Ofcom noted that   **16–060**

---

[242] r.9.14.
[243] r.9.15.
[244] r.10.1.
[245] r.10.2.
[246] r.10.3. This rule does not apply to programme-related material, such as DVDs and books.
[247] Ofcom Guidance Notes: s.10, Issue 8, December 13, 2006.
[248] r.10.4.
[249] Ofcom Guidance Notes: s.10, Issue 8, December 13, 2006.
[250] r.10.5.

instead of using cut-throat razors as one would expect in a traditional shaving saloon, the barbers were using Gillette disposable razors.[251] Another "product placement" decision was reviewed in 2006 when Channel 4 was fined £5,000 for giving undue prominence to *Red Bull* in the course of an apology for factual errors in a previous *Richard and Judy* program which had been critical of high caffeine drinks. Channel 4 accepted that on this occasion it had been wrong to highlight one particular brand, although presumably had the apology been made pursuant to a libel settlement with that brand alone, the prominence would not have been "undue".

Regulation of broadcast advertising is now "farmed out" to the ASA (see Ch.15). Comparatively few complaints are upheld, because advertisements are previewed and their scripts pre-vetted by the Broadcasting Advertising Clearing Centre (BACC) which is funded by broadcasters and employs 20 executives to censor any innovative ad that is regarded as suggestive or darkly humorous. For all its caution, it is still possible for the BACC to overlook the peculiar sensibilities of the British public: an approved ad for Levi jeans, which poked fun at a hamster dying of boredom on its treadmill, produced an unexpected deluge of complaints from hamster-loving households, and the regulators ruled that it could only be screened after the watershed.[252]

SANCTIONS

16–061 Section 237 of the 2003 Act empowers Ofcom to impose a variety of sanctions on broadcasters who breach the Code. In all cases, breaches are reported by Ofcom in its Broadcasting Bulletins, so some bad publicity may follow even if no statutory sanction is imposed. Ofcom may also require the broadcaster to broadcast Ofcom's adjudication on its service. In the case of serious or repeat violations Ofcom fines can reach six figures, up to a present maximum of £250,000. The ultimate sanction is the withdrawal of a broadcaster's license. This potential sanction is available in respect of all commercial broadcasters, but Ofcom has no power of this kind in relation to the BBC, which operates under a Royal Charter. The regulator has accepted that it will offer broadcasters the opportunity to make representations before it imposes reprimands or more serious penalties, but like its predecessors it has abjectly failed to offer the same consideration to the journalists and editors whose work is often not properly defended by the BBC or the independent companies or their legal departments. There is still no sense that respect for freedom of expression requires respect for, and a willingness to listen to representations from, the actual program

---

[251] Ofcom Broadcasting Code No.65, July 24, 2006.
[252] ITC, Television Advertising Complaints Report, August 1998, p.19.

makers and presenters whose work is the subject of the complaint, and of a potentially damaging or critical adjudication.

POLITICAL ADVERTISING

The blanket ban on political advertising is one point at which the **16–062** United Kingdom's commitment to free speech falters. Unlike other democracies, successive British governments have decreed that (other than through party political broadcasts) there can be no expression of opinion on any contentious subject by way of a broadcast advertisement. Section 320 of the 2003 Act requires impartiality from service providers on matters of political or industrial controversy or matters relating to current public policy, and s.321 provides that:

> **"2. . . . an advertisement contravenes the prohibition on political advertising if it is—**
>
> a. **an advertisement which is inserted by or on behalf of a body whose objects are wholly or mainly of a political nature;**
> b. **an advertisement which is directed towards a political end; or**
> c. **an advertisement which has a connection with an industrial dispute.**
>
> **3. For the purposes of this section objects of a political nature and political ends include each of the following—**
>
> a. **influencing the outcome of elections or referendums whether in the UK or elsewhere;**
> b. **bringing about changes of the law in the whole or a part of the United Kingdom or elsewhere, or otherwise influencing the legislative process in any country or territory;**
> c. **influencing the policies or decisions of local, regional or national governments, whether in the United Kingdom or elsewhere;**
> d. **influencing the policies or decisions of persons on whom public functions are conferred by or under the law of the United Kingdom or of a country or territory outside the United Kingdom;**
> e. **influencing the policies or decisions of persons on whom functions are conferred by or under international agreements;**
> f. **influencing public opinion on a matter of which, in the United Kingdom, is a matter of public controversy;**
> g. **promoting the interests of a party or other group of persons organised, in the United Kingdom or elsewhere, for political ends."**

This is the broadest possible prohibition, which prevents the advertising not merely of contentious viewpoints but of entirely legitimate viewpoints that may even reflect UK government policy—e.g. to urge the UN to stop genocide in Darfur. Political parties are not the target of this ban—they have their allocated and free propaganda broadcasts. It covers NGOs like Amnesty and Greenpeace, and organisations opposed to or in favour of, for instance, the European Union or the war in Iraq, as well as the sort of semi-spontaneous protests that result in full-page signed advertisements in newspapers. This blanket ban is such an obvious infringement of freedom of expression that the government conceded that it was more likely than not to be found by Strasbourg to be in breach of Art.10: for this reason it declined to make the "Statement of Compatibility" required by s.19(1)(b) of the HRA—the first time the government has refused since the Act was introduced. Nonetheless, it determined to proceed with the blanket ban, and its determination was shared by the opposition and by the UK's political establishment—including the Electoral Commission, the Committee on the Standards in Public Life and (somewhat absurdly) the Joint Committee of the Houses of Parliament on Human Rights.[253] What is it about social or economic "advocacy" advertising that sends such a shudder through the British political classes that they unanimously determine to deny freedom of broadcasting speech to pressure groups and NGOs, not merely during the election period but at *any* time? They are certainly imbued with the anachronistic belief that television (and hence television advertising) is uniquely powerful, and have a real (but never admitted) fear that pressure groups might actually use such opportunities to exert pressure on the political process—a feature of democracy that they are not prepared to tolerate, because they are in power (or hope to be in power) and they do not want to be unduly disturbed by a public which has been moved by emotional or even rational arguments which have been advanced on television. The blanket ban on political speech cannot be justified as necessary in democratic society, for the simple reason that political speech is the lifeblood of democratic society. This did not prevent the Divisional Court from upholding the ban (i.e. from refusing to grant a declaration of incompatibility) in the first test case, involving an advertisement for an animal welfare pressure group, but the case is proceeding to the House of Lords and thence, no doubt, to Strasbourg.[254]

16–063   This test case has been brought by *Animal Defenders International*, after the BACC refused to clear its "My Mate's a Primate" advertisement supporting a campaign against using primates (monkeys, not bishops) in public circuses. It showed a small girl playing with a caged monkey and solicited £10 for an information pack about the mistreatment of animals in zoos and entertainment programs. BACC—an arm of the advertising industry which Ofcom (having farmed out advertising regulation to the ASA) allows to make such decisions, although this dubious arrangement has no statutory basis whatsoever—refused clearance for fear of setting a

---

[253] 19th Report of session 2001–2, HC paper 149 and HC paper 1102, para.301.

[254] *R. (Animal Defenders International) v Secretary of State for Culture, Media and Sport* [2006] EWHC 2069 (Admin).

"dangerous precedent". Instead of hammering Ofcom for wrongfully delegating its authority to an industry body, the Divisional Court fell for the government's pitch that it would "unfairly distort the democratic process in favour of the wealthy" to allow anti-cruelty campaigners and other NGOs to advertise. (By such lame arguments, the government will not allow Amnesty to promote opposition to torture because states which torture may not have the necessary funds to answer back.) The 2003 Act was intended to impose an absolute ban on political advertising of all kinds, including social advocacy, and although the government had signalled the likelihood of incompatibility by declining to make a statement under s.19(1)(a) of the Human Rights Act, the Divisional Court declined to read down the prohibition so it would apply only to party political broadcasting. Canada, Australia and New Zealand have no equivalent provision—broadcast bans are confined to political parties at election time. Only in the United Kingdom does this fear of the power of broadcast advertising—in reality, the most transient form of publication—grip those institutions of government likely to find themselves subject of an emotional appeal by that advertising. The Divisional Court judges took the view that s.321 "supported a fair framework for political and public debate" by preventing it from becoming "distorted" by advertisements "in the most potent and pervasive media"—but this is no more than saying that the establishment should not be ruffled by emotional arguments made on radio and television rather than through less persuasive media like newspapers and billboards.

However much the argument is dressed up in egalitarian terms, the fact remains that most of those who want the freedom to advertise on television and radio are NGOs and social reform organisations supported by public donation, and the refusal to allow their advocacy of social or legal change to be heard is a blatant infringement of Art.10. That seems to have been the view of the European Court in its decision in *VGT Verein Gegen Tierfabriken v Switzerland*[255] which extended Art.10 protection to "political" advertisements, in that case by an animal rights group which far from being a wealthy organisation distorting the political process was advertising in order to respond to a campaign by the very wealthy meat industry via permitted television advertising which urged the consumption of beef burgers and lamb chops. Although the case turned partly on the fact that this was an "infovertisement" rather than an incitement to purchase a particular product, the court made clear that it would be difficult to establish an Art.10 "pressing social need" to ban an advertisement on television which could be featured without any restraint in the press. It is an unacceptable irony that commercial advertising should be the mainstay of ITV and most cable and satellite channels and commercial radio, yet groups like Amnesty and Greenpeace should not be allowed to counter this corporate advertising by promoting an alternative view.

In September 2005, Ofcom banned an advertisement by *Make Poverty History*, a coalition of some 300 charities campaigning against poverty in developing countries. Ofcom's notion that British political life would be distorted at the sight of Brad Pitt, Kate Moss and other glitterati clicking their fingers and emoting that "Somebody dies avoidably through poverty every 3 seconds" was quite absurd. It was not even an effort to lobby the government to change its policy: rather, it was an endorsement of government policy. But it nevertheless fell foul of the blanket ban imposed by s.321 on paid political speech.

The BBC

16–064 The BBC is established, archaically, by Royal Charter rather than by statute—a device whereby the Government may determine directly the BBC duties rather than have Parliament debate them by incorporating them into legislation. The Charter was last renewed (for 10 years) in 2006, pursuant to an agreement with the Government (represented by the Secretary of State for Culture, Media and Sport). The BBC's independence is guaranteed by cl.4 of the Agreement and cl.6(1) of the Charter, which provides that:

> "The BBC shall be independent in all matters concerning the content of its output and the times and manner in which this is supplied, and in the management of its affairs."

That said, the Corporation is subject to indirect pressures which ensure a degree of deference to the Crown, the framework of government and the party politicians who occupy the high offices of State. The Chairman, Vice Chairman and members of BBC Trust are all appointed by the Government of the day, and the Corporation is dependent on the Government for fixing the licence fee that provides its funding. The power of patronage has an editorial influence, evidenced through the programmes that the BBC never makes rather than those it does. The licensed bumptiousness practised by BBC interviewers on *Today* and *Newsnight* presents a public face of independence, at least towards individual Government ministers, but towards British institutions the BBC is often uncritical. Towards the monarchy, it is usually obsequious.

The comfortable, conservative ethos in which BBC policy is made was long thought to be unchallengeable through the courts. The BBC, creature of Royal Charter, was above the law, its undertakings the promises of gentlemen, unlike the statutory duties imposed in identical language on the players of commercial television by the Broadcasting Act.[256] However, this immunity is no longer sustainable. The BBC performs public functions of democratic importance,

---

[256] See *Lynch v BBC* [1983] N.I. 193.

and the fact that its power derives from the Royal Prerogative does not exclude its discretionary decisions from judicial review.[257] The BBC is in any event a "public body" for the purposes of the 1998 Human Rights Act, and may thus be sued by persons claiming it has infringed rights to life or privacy, or indeed (by acts of internal censorship) the viewers' and listeners' rights to free speech. However, the significance of the courts as a means of challenging the broadcasting/political establishment is limited both by the absence of a constitution and the deference that judges are prone to show to Government-appointed "experts".

This was illustrated in 1997 by the rejection of the Referendum Party challenge to the broadcasters' bias towards the main parties in allocation of party political broadcasts. These valuable propaganda slots were allocated mainly on the basis of past electoral support, something that a new party could not, by definition, show. The Referendum Party, fielding candidates in almost all constituencies, argued that the allocation principle was discriminatory and undemocratic but the judges said that "fairness" in this context was a matter for the broadcasters, whose decision could not be disturbed unless irrational or made without considering the Referendum Party's complaints.[258] American and Canadian courts have taken a more principled approach on similar issues, and the Human Rights Act now provides a direct method of challenging the decisions of the BBC as a "public body", on which the judges may superimpose objective standards of fairness. In matters of taste and decency, however, judicial review will be on strict "*Wednesbury* reasonableness" lines, and courts will rarely if ever interfere with BBC judgments. In 1997, a BBC decision to obscure images of an aborted foetus in a Pro-Life Alliance Party political broadcast was held to be within its "margin of discretionary judgment",[259] and in 2003 the House of Lords in the *Pro Alliance* case reiterated this "hands off" approach in respect to BBC decisions to censor for "offensiveness".

The BBC has undertaken to comply in general terms with the **16–065** statutory duties placed upon independent television and it may be fined by Ofcom if its television or radio programmes breach Ofcom code provisions relating to harm or offence on breach of privacy although the BBC Trust will oversee compliance with duties of accuracy and impartiality under the 2003 Communication Act, s.198.

Normal BBC censorship operates by a process of "reference up" the Corporation hierarchy. The BBC's Editorial Guidelines contain

---

[257] Any more than the decisions of universities made under the perogative: *Thomas v University of Bradford* [1987] A.C. 795; *R. v TakeOver Panel Ex p. Datafin* [1987] 1 Q.B. 815, especially 849 D–E.

[258] *R. v BBC and ITC Ex p. Referendum Party* [1997] E.M.L.R. 605.

[259] *R. v BBC Ex p. the Pro-Life Alliance Party*, March 24, 1997, Dyson J.

detailed guidance for BBC producers and independent production companies making BBC programmes as to what matters must be referred to the Editorial Policy team or other relevant parts of the Corporation. The basic principle is that "the more important or contentious the issue, the higher up the referral needs to be",[260] the tip of the hierarchy being the Controller Editorial Policy. The caution required of producers is indicated by the fact that as well as providing for mandatory referrals highlighted in red, the guidelines also require that queries on how to interpret the guidelines and any proposal to act outside the guidelines must also be referred to editorial policy.

Any producer who foresees possible offence must alert middle management, which must pass borderline cases to departmental heads, who may in turn consult the Managing Director or even the Director-General. The classic definition of "reference up" still holds good:

> "The elimination or alteration of material considered unsuitable for public broadcasting is an integral part of the whole system of editorial control . . . reference is obligatory in matters of serious dispute or matters of doubt, and the wrath of the corporation in its varied manifestations is particularly reserved for those who fail 'to refer'."[261]

The BBC came under considerable pressure as a result of the *Hutton Report*—a government initiated enquiry which subjected its news and editorial standards to serious criticism. Although few doubt that the dossier produced by the government on Saddam's supposed weapons of mass destruction was in fact "sexed up", as Dr Kelly appears to have told a *Today* program reporter (albeit not in those terms), the governors had supported their broadcasters throughout the ensuing imbroglio, and had not, so Hutton found, exercised independent oversight. At this, both the BBC Chairman (Gavyn Davies) and its Director General (Greg Dyke) rather unnecessarily resigned, although the only real fault was in the BBC's structure, which had imposed upon the governors a dual and conflicting role, both as managers and as providers of public oversight. In consequence of the Hutton Report's exposure of this conflict of interests, the renewed 2006 Charter abolished the Board of Governors and created a separate body, the BBC Trust, to perform the oversight role, leaving an executive board with responsibility for management and program delivery.

---

[260] BBC Editorial Guidelines, p.10.
[261] "Control over the Subject-Matter of Programmes on BBC Television": Appendix 2 to *Report of Joint Committee on Censorship of the Theatre*, H.C. 255 (1967).

Government controls

In extreme circumstances the Government does have certain direct **16–066**
legal powers over radio and television. In the case of the BBC, these
are contained in s.81 of the Licence Agreement that forms part of
the Corporation's charter. Under the heading "Defence and Emergency arrangements", Government ministers have a general power
to require the BBC to broadcast announcements and in emergency
situations, programmes as well, the only requirement being that the
Minister's request is made in writing. Where the BBC does broadcast such an announcement or programme, it may announce at the
same time that it is doing so in response to a ministerial request. It
should always do so, in order to make clear to its viewers that the
"news" it announces has been written by Whitehall.

Section 19 enables the Home Secretary, when in his opinion there
is an emergency and it is "expedient" so to act, to send troops in to
"take possession of the BBC in the name and on behalf of Her
Majesty". This clause was framed during the General Strike, when
Winston Churchill and other members of the Government wanted to
commandeer the Corporation. It has never been used for that
purpose, although Sir Anthony Eden contemplated invoking it for
Government propaganda during the Suez crisis, and during the
Falklands recapture it provided the legal basis for the Government's
use of BBC transmitters on Ascension Island to beam propaganda
broadcasts at Argentina.

A more dangerous power is contained in s.81(4) of the 1996
Licence Agreement, which gives the Secretary of State for Culture,
Media and Sport, the right to prohibit the BBC from transmitting
any item or programme, at any time. The power is not limited to
periods of emergency. The only safeguard against political censorship is that the BBC may tell the public that it has received a s.81(4)
order from the Minister, or that such an order has been varied or
revoked. This safeguard was invoked in 1972 by the Director-
General, Lord Hill, when the Home Secretary Reginald Maudling
threatened to stop transmission of a debate about Government
actions in Ulster. Lord Hill called his bluff by threatening to make
public the reason why the programme could not be shown. A less
courageous Director-General could simply cancel the programme
without revealing the existence of a Government order. A parallel
power in s.336(5) of the 2003 Communications Act entitles the
Home Secretary to order Ofcom licensees to "refrain from broadcasting any matter or classes of matter" on commercial television.
The exercise of these powers cannot be successfully challenged in the
courts unless it can be shown that the Home Secretary has acted
unreasonably or perversely.

These powers were invoked in 1988 for the purpose of direct **16–067**
political censorship when the BBC and commercial stations were
ordered not to transmit any interviews with representatives of Sinn

Fein, the Ulster Defence Association, the IRA or certain other extremist groups, or to broadcast any statement that incited support for such groups. The ban was a plain infringement on the right to receive and impart information: it prevented representatives of lawful political organisations (Sinn Fein had an M.P. as well as dozens of local councillors) from stating their case on matters that had no connection with terrorism, and it denied to the public the opportunity to hear those who support violent action being questioned and exposed. The Thatcher Government believed that terrorists survived by "the oxygen of publicity", but television confrontations generally demonstrate the moral unattractiveness of those who believe that the end justifies the means. The ban prevented the re-screening of history programmes with interviews with IRA veterans. The BBC and the IBA (the predecessor of the ITC and Ofcom) meekly complied with the ban, which the House of Lords refused to strike down when it was challenged by John Pilger and other broadcasters.[262]

The Government has reserved to itself the more benign power of listing events of national interest that must not be monopolised by "pay-as-you-view" channels.[263] There is no bar on pay-as-you-view screenings that take place at least 48 hours after the event. Although sporting events such as the Olympic Games, cricket test matches played in England, the Wimbledon finals and the Grand National are the primary candidates for protection, "national interest" is defined to include English, Scottish, Welsh and Northern Irish interests, and the list is not confined to major sporting fixtures: any attempts to purchase exclusive rights to King Charles's coronation would certainly provoke Government intervention.

The United Kingdom is obliged, by the Television with Frontiers Directive, to ensure that British-based broadcasters do not "buy up" an event listed by another government, so as to deprive its public of watching that event free-to-air. The House of Lords upheld an ITC decision to refuse consent to TVD (a pay-to-view company broadcasting to Denmark) purchasing exclusive rights to World Cup qualifiers which Denmark were playing, and which were listed under Danish law.[264]

THE EUROPEAN TELEVISION CONVENTIONS

16–068 The international obligations that have become increasingly important for the British media stem from Europe, where broadcasting signals and satellite transmissions cannot distinguish between

---

[262] *R. v Secretary of State for the Home Department Ex p. Brind* [1991] 1 A.C. 696. The European Commission regarded the consequent complaint as inadmissible: *Brind v UK* (1994) 18 E.H.R.R. CD 76.

[263] See Communications Act 2003, ss.299–302.

[264] *R. v Independent Television Commission Ex p. TV Denmark I Ltd* [2001] 1 W.L.R. 1604.

jumbled national borders. British law must accommodate legal instruments produced by the pan-European organisations—the broader Council of Europe (guarantor of the ECHR) and the economic and political Union of the European Community. Their respective instruments are: the 1989 European Convention on Transfrontier Television, adopted by the Committee of Ministers of the Council of Europe, and the EC Directive on Television without Frontiers (the Television Directive). There is a further revised draft Television Direction currently under discussion.

The Convention begins by endorsing the guarantee of freedom of expression in Art.10 of the European Convention on Human Rights as an "essential condition of a democratic society", and aims to "enhance Europe's heritage and develop audio-visual creation . . . through efforts to increase the production and circulation of high quality programmes". It applies to all broadcasting formats, whether cable, terrestrial transmitter or satellite, which can be received (directly or indirectly) in another country that is party to the Convention. The duties upon nations that are parties to the Convention include adherence to Art.10, and ensuring that its laws restrain broadcasters within its jurisdiction from transmitting pornography or incitements to violence or racial hatred, and that they afford a "right of reply". Parties must ensure that coverage of events of "high public interest" across Europe is not restricted by exclusive rights deals so as to deprive a large part of the public in another European country from watching them on television. Broadcasting organisations in each country must reserve at least 50 per cent of transmission time (excluding that taken up by news, sport and advertising) for programmes of European origin.

These Convention objectives are secured in Britain by Ofcom's **16–069** code of practice enforced by the power to fine, and also by Pts 9 and 10 of the Broadcasting Code. Article 11 of the Convention requires all advertisements to be fair and honest and to have regard to the special susceptibilities of children. The amount of advertising shall not exceed 15 per cent of the daily transmission time, or take up more than 12 minutes in any one hour (Art.12). Article 14 causes great anguish to British advertisers and money-minded programme executives: it strikes a notable blow for artistic creativity by providing that advertisements may not be inserted so as to damage "the integrity and value of the programme". To this end, advertisements must be transmitted only during natural breaks in sports programmes; films and documentaries must be interrupted only once every 45 minutes, and other programmes must last at least 20 minutes before an advertising break; religious services must not be interrupted at all, and nor should news and current affairs and religious and children's programmes that last less than 30 minutes.

The Convention requires bans on tobacco products and on prescription medicines (Art.15). The rules relating to alcohol advertisements are particularly strict; drinking must not be associated with "physical performance" or driving or the resolution of personal conflicts. Abstinence or moderation must not be presented in a negative light.

16–070 The Convention is astute to prevent advertisers and sponsors from influencing, whether overtly or covertly, the content of programmes or their impact on viewers. Advertisements must be plainly distinguishable as such and there must be no "product placement" (the frequent device of being paid to use an advertiser's product as a prop in drama programmes). News and current affairs presenters must not lend their names or their faces to product promotions (Art.13). Sponsored programmes must be clearly identified as such, the sponsor must not be permitted to influence editorial or scheduling judgments (Art.17), and these programmes shall not promote products or services of the sponsor or anyone else (Art.17). There shall be no sponsorship of news and current affairs programmes (in Britain, the weather is not regarded as "news") and no programme may be sponsored by the manufacturers of tobacco products, alcoholic drinks or prescription medicines.

The EC Treaty, for all its concerns with free movement of goods and services between members of the Common Market, originally had no specific provision about broadcasting although the European Court of Justice soon defined "services" to include television signals and advertisements.[265] "Culture" was first mentioned in the Maastricht Treaty (1993) and the Treaty of Amsterdam (1999) amended the E.C. Treaty so that Art.151 now requires contributions to "the flowering of the cultures of the Member States" and supplementary joint action in the area of "artistic and literary creation, including in the audiovisual sector". The Television Without Frontiers Directive aims to provide an "internal market" for broadcasting by removing barriers to transmissions across the borders of Member States. Unlike the Television Convention, the Directive is directly enforceable throughout the E.C., and one of its first impacts was to strike down the British rule that permitted the jurisdiction of local courts over all broadcasts emanating from the United Kingdom. The ECJ ruled that the correct test for deciding which country had jurisdiction over a European broadcast was to determine where the broadcaster was "established"—a criterion,

> "referring to the place in which a broadcaster has the centre of its activities, in particular the place where decisions concerning programme policy are taken and the programmes are finally put together".[266]

Thus the humourless television regulators of Belgium could not prohibit their local cable operators from re-transmitting Cartoon

---

[265] *Italy v Saachi* [1974] E.C.R. 409.
[266] *Commission of the European Communities v UK* [1996] E.C.R.I.-4025 at 4077–8, and see *VT4 Ltd v Vlaamese Gemeenschap* [1997] 1–3143; Television Directive, Arts 2(3) and (4).

Network, a satellite service provided by a broadcaster based in the United Kingdom. The Belgians claimed they were protecting "European Content" because the cartoons came from America, but the "choice of forum" rule pivots on the seat of the broadcaster, not the place of origin of the material in broadcasts.[267]

The Television Directive (Art.2(a)) permits the United Kingdom **16–071** to take unilateral action to restrict broadcasts from other Member States only in respect of "programmes which might seriously impair the physical, mental or moral development of minors", in particular programmes that involve pornography or gratuitous violence (subject to whether they can be encoded, or transmitted at hours when minors are asleep) and programmes inciting racial, sexual, religious or ethnic hatred.[268] The United Kingdom has utilised Art.2(a) in attempts to "proscribe" pornographic satellite services received from Denmark (under s.177 of the 1990 Act, such proscription makes it an offence for anyone in Britain to assist, sell or advertise the service). One such proscription order (*against Red Hot Dutch*) was challenged, although the broadcaster went out of business before the issues identified by the Divisional Court could be decided by the European Court of Justice.[269] The issues were whether the Television Directive permits the Government to issue a proscription: (a) against foreign satellite services received in, rather than transmitted within, the United Kingdom; and (b) in respect of broadcasts which because they are encoded or transmitted in the early hours, are unlikely to attract child viewers. Section 177 was not repealed or amended by the 2003 Act, but no proscription orders have been issued since 2000, both because the United Kingdom had itself permitted reasonably hardcore pornography on sex-shop vended videos and DVDs under the 18R classification and because it is doubtful whether the proscription of a subscription porn channel with PIN protection (other than one showing child pornography), would be compatible with EU law. The Television Directive also contains controversial Arts (4 and 6) imposing obligations to increase European content, emanating largely from chauvinistic French concerns about the threat of "cultural imperialism" from the popular American programmes (the alternative—of requiring measures to improve the comprehensibility of French culture—was not considered). These ill-begotten quota provisions have not been rigidly enforced, because they probably breach Art.10 of the ECHR, and possibly the General Agreement on Tariffs and Trade (GATT). Less controversial is Art.23, which requires that any person "damaged by an assertion of incorrect facts in a television programme must have a right of reply or equivalent remedies . . . transmitted within a reasonable time".

---

[267] *Paul Denoit Case* [1997] 3 C.M.L.R. 943.
[268] Television Directive, Arts 22 and 23.
[269] *R. v Secretary of State for the National Heritage Ex p. Continental Television BV* [1993] 2 C.M.L.R. 333.

The United Kingdom claims that its Art.23 obligations are fulfilled by the corrective powers of Ofcom, in cases of unfair treatment (see earlier, para.16–048).

Advertisers, although restricted in some circumstances by the Convention, do have redress under European law against any EEC member country that tries to discriminate against advertisements broadcast from other member countries. In other words, any legal restrictions on advertising must apply irrespective of the nationality of the advertiser or the country from which the broadcast has originated.[270] In *Bond van Adverteers v The Netherlands* the European Court held that a prohibition on advertising broadcasts from other countries directed at citizens of the receiving country was an unlawful restriction on the freedom to provide services and was contrary to Art.59 of the EEC treaty.[271]

> The Dutch Government's objective in banning all broadcast advertising directed at its citizens from cable stations in other countries was to ensure that a public foundation in Holland received all the revenue from advertising directed at its nationals. This economic objective was not a satisfactory "public policy" exemption from compliance with Art.59. It might reasonably require foreign broadcasters directing their promotions to Dutch citizens to comply with local laws relating to the duration of advertisements or banning the touting of certain products, but it could not erect a barrier against all foreign-originated advertising in the economic interests of its own broadcasters.

Since 2001, the European Commission and Member States have been in the process of revising the Television Directive and in December 2005 the Commission published a proposal for a revised Directive that proposed liberalising the rules on advertising and allowing product placement. For the present, however, the proposal remains in draft.

OFCOM LICENCES

16–072 Under the Communications Act 2003, Ofcom took over the licensing functions for radio and television previously enjoyed by the Radio Authority and the Independent Television Commission. Any would-be provider of a radio or television service must now apply to Ofcom for a licence. In part, Ofcom's licensing function is necessitated in the case of radio by the need to manage the radio spectrum in an efficient and effective way, but it also reflects Ofcom's statutory duties to ensure the availability of a "wide range" of television and radio services "of high quality and calculated to appeal to a variety of tastes and interests" and the maintenance of a "sufficient plurality" of providers of different television and radio services.[272]

---

[270] *Procureur du Roi v Debauve* (1980) E.C.R. 833.
[271] Case No.352/85. Judgment, April 16, 1988.
[272] Communications Act 2003, s.3(2).

Television

One of Ofcom's most important powers is the licensing of the **16–073** commercial public service broadcasters, Channel 3 (ITV) and C4 (Channel Four) and Channel Five. The regime for granting licences under the 1990 Act in respect of Channel 3 and Channel 5 is designed to ensure that the licence goes to the highest cash bidder, subject to that bidder's proposed output crossing a quality threshold.[273] There are however, exceptional circumstances in which the licence may be awarded to an applicant who did not submit the highest bid, where the quality of the service proposed by an applicant is exceptionally high, or where the quality is 'substantially' higher than that of the service proposed by the highest bidder.[274] Ofcom may not award any licence to a person unless satisfied that he is a fit and proper person to hold it,[275] and where there are grounds for suspecting that the source of funds for a bid is suspect, they must refer the application to the Secretary of State who has the final say.[276]

The quality requirements relate to four different aspects of the broadcaster's output: the public service remit for that service, the programming quotas, news and current affairs programmes and programme production and regional programming. The public service remit for Channel 3 and Channel 5 is defined as "the provision of high quality and diverse programming".[277] The public service remit for Channel 4 is the provision of a "broad range" of high quality and diverse programming, but with a special emphasis on innovation, experiment and creativity, on appealing to diverse cultural tastes, on programmes of an educational nature and on programmes that exhibit "a distinctive character".[278] Each proposed broadcaster must demonstrate its ability to devote 25 per cent of broadcast time to independent productions,[279] meet quotas on original productions,[280] make news and current affairs programmes that are of "high quality and deal with both national and international matters"[281] and make sufficient regional programmes.[282] There are several further licence conditions, including most importantly to abide by Ofcom's Broadcast Code.[283]

A degree of transparency is introduced into the licensing process by the requirement that Ofcom must publish details of applicants

---

[273] Broadcasting Act 1990, s.17.
[274] 1980 Act, s.17(4).
[275] 1980 Act, s.3(3)(a).
[276] 1980 Act, s.17(5).
[277] Communications Act 2003, s.265(2).
[278] 2003 Act, s.265(3).
[279] 2003 Act, s.277.
[280] 2003 Act, s.278.
[281] 2003 Act, s.279.
[282] 2003 Act, s.286.
[283] 2003 Act, s.319.

and their proposals for meeting the quality requirements after the bidding process has closed and then invite representations about the applicants.[284] Furthermore, where Ofcom has awarded a Channel 3 licence to a bidder, it must then publish the name of the successful bidder and the amount of his bid as well as the names of all the other applicants who met the quality threshold.[285] Where Ofcom decided not to award the licence subject to the highest bidder, it must publish the reasons for that decision and any other information it considers appropriate.

16–074   Ofcom's licensing role in relation to television embraces all television services in the United Kingdom, including satellite and cable television services and whether in analogue or digital form. Such services are called "television licensable content services" and relevant provisions are contained in the 2003 Act.[286] Applications for such licences must comply with certain basic conditions, but once these are met Ofcom may only refuse to grant a licence on very limited grounds, namely where the applicant is not a fit and proper person, where it would breach restrictions under the Broadcasting Act 1990 or where the provider would be likely to contravene Ofcom's Broadcasting Code.

Ofcom's licences last for 10 years and Ofcom has a range of sanctions for licensed broadcasters that fail to comply with the conditions of their licence. At the lower end of the spectrum Ofcom can require a broadcaster to broadcast a correction or statement of Ofcom's findings,[287] direct a broadcaster not to repeat a programme,[288] or alternatively impose a fine, which may be modest or may be as high as 5 per cent of the advertising and sponsorship revenue from the licence holder's last complete accounting period.[289] The next step up in terms of severity is reducing the period that the licence is in force by up to two years,[290] with the ultimate sanction for Channel 3 or Channel 5 being the revocation of the licence, where the broadcaster has failed to comply with a previous direction.[291] Whatever sanction Ofcom has in mind, it must give the broadcaster a reasonable opportunity of making representations before taking action.

Radio

16–075   Ofcom has powers and duties for sound broadcasting that mirror its duties and powers in relation to television. It must do all it can to ensure a diversity of national services, at least one devoted predominantly to the spoken word and one broadcasting "music other than

---

[284] Broadcasting Act 1990, s.15(6).
[285] 1980 Act, s.17(12).
[286] Communications Act 2003, ss.232–240.
[287] 2003 Act, s.40(1).
[288] 2003 Act, s.40(4).
[289] 2003 Act, s.41(1)(a).
[290] 2003 Act, s.41(1)(b).
[291] 2003 Act, s.42.

pop music", together with a range and diversity of local services.[292] Licences are to be granted for periods of up to 12 years to "fit and proper" people (persons convicted for radio piracy offences in the preceding five years are excluded from this category) and Ofcom may impose licence conditions to give effect to its various statutory duties, including programme standards as set out in the Broadcasting Code.[293] As in relation to commercial television licences, national radio licences are granted to the highest cash bidder that meets the requirements of the tender,[294] but local radio licences are granted on the payment of a fee.[295]

Ofcom's powers of enforcement parallel those available to it in respect of television licence holders. Thus it can require broadcasters to broadcast a correction or a statement of findings,[296] impose a fine of up to a maximum of £250,000 or 5 per cent of their advertising and sponsorship revenue, reduce the period the licence is in force by up to two years or suspend the licence for up to six months.[297] As with television licences, Ofcom's ultimate sanction is revocation of the licence.[298] Ofcom must, however, give broadcasters a reasonable opportunity to make representations before it imposes any of these sanctions.

It is an offence under s.8 of the Wireless Telegraphy Act 2006 to **16–076** make wireless transmissions without a licence,[299] and under the Broadcasting Act it is an offence to run a radio service that is not licensed by Ofcom.[300] The 2006 legislation contains stringent powers to eradicate radio pirates, both on the high seas and on the high streets. It is an offence not merely to produce an illegal broadcast, but to own or assist in the control of premises or to supply apparatus used in unlicensed broadcasts.[301] Every conceivable act of assistance is caught by these provisions, and offences may be committed by delivering a "literary, dramatic or musical work" on a pirate radio station or by publishing any detains of unlicensed broadcasts, with a maximum penalty on indictment of two years' imprisonment. These provisions are remarkably savage, so much so that they are candidates for Art.10 strike down on grounds of disproportionality. At least they serve as a tribute to the tenacity and popularity of backstreet radio stations. The provision that makes it an offence to

---

[292] Broadcasting Act 1990, s.85.

[293] 1980 Act, s.87(1)(a).

[294] 1980 Act, ss.98–100.

[295] 1980 Act, s.104.

[296] 1980 Act, s.109(3).

[297] 1980 Act, s.110(1).

[298] 1980 Act, s.111.

[299] The offence under its predecessor, s.1 of the Wireless Telegraphy Act 1949, was one of strict liability: *R. v Blake* [1997] 1 Cr.App.R.209 and the new offence is also one of strict liability.

[300] 1980 Act s.97.

[301] Wireless Telegraphy Act 2006, ss.35–38.

publish "details of any unauthorised broadcasts" may also be a breach of Art.10, certainly if it is used against publishers of articles or programmes that discuss the social phenomenon of pirate radio.

The popularity of pirate radio ships on the high seas during the 1960s was an important factor in breaking down the BBC's rigid monopoly of the airwaves. In retrospect, the salvos fired by Mr Wedgwood Benn against Radio Caroline appear comical, and many of the original pirates are now household names on licensed stations. John Peel, for example, became a venerated figure before his untimely death. Nonetheless, the fears that gripped the governments of Europe at the threat to their nationalised broadcasting arrangements produced an early treaty obliging firm action against unauthorised broadcasters, and its terms are embodied in the Marine Broadcasting (Offences) Act of 1967.[302] This Act makes it an offence to broadcast from a ship or aircraft within the jurisdiction of the United Kingdom, and an offence for any British citizen to broadcast on or above the high seas. It is an offence to facilitate pirate broadcasts capable of being received in Britain that emanate from beyond territorial waters, and "facilitation" is widely denned to include provisioning of the radio ship, advertising on the pirate station or publishing any details of its programmes.[303] For many years the London listings magazine *Time Out* published a column giving programme details for Radio Laser, Radio Caroline and other pirate stations within and without the jurisdiction; a prosecution against it under the 1967 Act failed on a technicality, but the column has not reappeared. In 1990 the Court of Appeal upheld the conviction of a number of British subjects for a conspiracy made in the United Kingdom to breach the 1967 Act by procuring the unlicensed broadcasts of Radio Laser, notwithstanding that these emanated from a Panamanian ship, moored outside territorial waters and manned by Americans.[304]

An Ofcom report in 2007 detected 150 pirate radio stations, half within jamming distance of the M25. They were "community" stations, and offered to listeners various kinds of music and opinions they could not obtain on licensed stations. Ofcom said it would think further about what—if any—action it would take against a free speech phenomenon to which it had previously been very hostile.

Satellite Broadcasting

16–077 The era of satellite broadcasting was ushered in by the launch of Sky television in 1988. Ofcom is responsible, under the 2003 Act, for granting licences for satellite television services. Since the British

---

[302] European Agreement for the Prevention of Broadcasts transmitted from Stations Outside National Territories (Strasbourg, January 22, 1965) ratified by the UK Government in 1967.

[303] Lord Wilberforce has severely criticised the extra-territorial impact of these provisions: *Hansard* (House of Lords) July 26, 1990, cols 1657–1660.

[304] *R. v Murray, The Times*, March 22, 1990.

take sex a good deal more seriously than other European nationalities, considerable ingenuity has been expended to find ways of stopping the pornography that is offered in many continental countries from infiltrating via satellite. Domestic satellite operators are subject to the Obscene Publication Act and the "good taste and decency" terms of their licences, but material that originates abroad and is transmitted by companies resident outside the jurisdiction cannot be so readily controlled. If pornography originates from a broadcaster established in an EC country, the British Government will have some difficulty proscribing the service as explained above.

Satellite transmissions create complex problems for defamation law. If a cable system picks up the satellite signals and relays them to its subscribers, then the cable operator will be responsible for the libels so transmitted. If the programme originates from England, then the person sending the libel up to the satellite for retransmission will also be liable. There may be a difficulty, however, if the programme originates abroad and is sent up to the satellite from a foreign country, by whose law it is not defamatory. For example, the American law of defamation puts the burden of proving falsity on the claimant and provides a "public figure" defence—anything said about someone in the public eye will not be actionable unless spoken with malice. So under American law a libel action bound to fail will often succeed under English law. Such circumstances provide a strong incentive for wealthy and powerful public figures to go forum-shopping in London's High Court.

The general rule is that, so long as a tort is committed in England, English law principles will apply. For libel, so long as there is an act of publication in England, only defences known to English law will apply. It has been held that so far as broadcasts are concerned the tort is committed where the broadcast is received, rather than where it is transmitted.[305] Any broadcast received in England is "published" in England, and English libel law would apply. If the principle is applied to satellite transmissions, there would be no question of applying foreign law. The only problem for a claimant in England trying to sue a foreign defendant in respect of a transmission originating abroad would be in obtaining permission to serve the defendant with a writ out of the jurisdiction. Permission is always at the discretion of the court, and whether an action can be begun will depend on the facts of the case. But if the rule for broadcasts is not followed for satellites (because of the lack of control over the area over which signals can be picked up, and the presumption against applying English rules extraterritorially), then there will be no publication in England—the tort will be committed abroad only, where the signals are transmitted to the satellite. In this case, to sustain an action in England for a tort committed abroad, the tort

---

[305] *Jenner v Sea Oil* [1952] D.L.R. 526; *Gorton v ABC* [1974] 22 F.L.R. 181; *Whitlam Victoria Broadcasting* [1979] 37 F.L.R. 15.

must be actionable by English law and by the law of the place where the actions took place (i.e. where the signals originated). Only if actionable by both systems of law would a claimant succeed in bringing an action.[306]

16-078 These problems have been compounded by the advent of the internet. Can libel actions be brought wherever defamatory material is downloaded, (i.e. in any jurisdiction in the world) or only in the place where the web server is established? The Australian High Court held in *Gutnaik v Dow Jones*[307] that an action could be brought wherever the claimant had an established reputation, which would mean a variety of forum choice for some public figures. The parallel with television is not precise, because of the technical distinctions between broadcast transmission, beamed directly to a country, and "request" messages sent through cyberspace to a website "server" in another country. When the man at the modem in jurisdiction A sends a "request" message to a server in jurisdiction B, it is rather like sending a servant across state lines to buy a book and then bring it back—an action which could not involve the seller in publishing the libel in jurisdiction A. It will be important for internet freedom in the long term to confine libel actions to the place the website is established (as long as this is not adventitious or a "defamation free zone") so as to protect internet publishers and providers from being dragged into jurisdictions which have harsh (sometimes criminal) laws of defamation and sedition.

Many international treaties and conventions proclaim the principle of a free flow of information. However, this principle is generally subject to reservations of national sovereignty, based on the assumption that every state has an exclusive right to regulate its own broadcasting system to prevent transmission of unacceptable programme material and propaganda. Thus, the Soviet Union has in the past insisted that the overriding consideration must be the right of states to pursue political and social development free from outside interference. Some Third World countries argue that the free flow of information principle is contingent upon equal access to the source, and fear cultural domination of developing nations by superpower satellites. The United States and the United Kingdom, the two most constant champions of the free flow principle, are the two leading exporters of television programmes. The European Court of Human Rights in the *Autronic* case firmly rejected the notion that states were entitled to control the reception of television programmes uplinked from their cities or transmitted by their satellites, and its championship of the right to impart and receive information across national frontiers will prevail in the broadcasting laws of Europe, West and East.

---

[306] *Chaplin v Boys* [1971] A.C. 356.
[307] *Gutnik v Dow Jones* [2002] H.C.A. 56.

Article 1 of the Outer Space Treaty of 1966 establishes the general **16–079** principle that "outer space . . . shall be free for exploration and use by all states without discrimination of any kind". The United Nations General Assembly set up the Committee on the Peaceful Uses of Outer Space (COPUOS), but its deliberations on satellite broadcasting have been marked by disputes over the need for "prior consent" by the receiving state, with a majority of the group taking the position that prior consent was necessary. The group has defined unacceptable programme material to include incitements to war, racial hatred or enmity between people; or programmes aimed at undermining the foundations of a local culture. If any such material is aimed specifically at a foreign state without its express consent, the transmission would be illegal. The fundamental fear is of overspill propaganda. The only way to combat this is by international agreement, but neither the United States nor the United Kingdom is convinced of the danger of overspill, and the rift between the advanced and the developing countries has precluded any worthwhile international agreement.

The conference that settled the law of the sea continued for nine years before agreement was reached; a satisfactory agreement over the law of outer space may take even longer. Work on the law of cyberspace is only just beginning.

TABLE OF CASES

TABLE OF STATUTES

TABLE OF STATUTORY INSTRUMENTS

TABLE OF EUROPEAN CONVENTION ON HUMAN RIGHTS

INDEX

PENGUIN REFERENCE LIBRARY

THE PENGUIN DICTIONARY OF ACCOUNTING

EDITED BY CHRISTOPHER NOBES

You're an accountant needing *golden handcuffs*, you're faced with a jargon-laden business exam, you're the proud owner of an incomprehensible tax form. Where do you turn? *The Penguin Dictionary of Accounting* is your answer. Demystifying the most complex terms in simple, easy-to-understand language, this is the ideal reference book for anyone who reads, speaks or writes accountancy – whether student, businessperson, investor, preparer of financial statements, auditor or accounts manager. Compiled by Christopher Nobes, PricewaterhouseCoopers Professor of Accounting at Reading University, this fully up-to-date edition is your first stop in unravelling the ambiguities of accounting.

Contains information in the fields of *tax*, *auditing* and *management accounting*

Includes relevant terms relating to finance and law, from *depreciation* to the *ratchet effect* via *hyperinflation*

Analyses all the terms used in International Financial Reporting Standards

Caters for accountants worldwide, making clear where terminology differs across countries

ONLY PENGUIN GIVES YOU MORE

PENGUIN REFERENCE LIBRARY

THE PENGUIN DICTIONARY OF MATHEMATICS

EDITED BY DAVID NELSON

'Clear, authoritative, up-to-date ... an absolutely superb reference book – a treasure trove of impeccably presented information' *Mathematical Gazette*

There are some who say that the world is a mass of mathematical equations. Whether true or not, they certainly have a point: mathematics is important. *The Penguin Dictionary of Mathematics* is the definitive handbook to the study, taking in all branches of pure and applied mathematics, from *algebra* to *mechanics* and from *number theory* to *statistics*. Written for students and teachers of all levels, it is also a useful and versatile source book for economists, business people, engineers, technicians and scientists of all kinds.

- Defines over 3,200 terms, supported by dozens of explanatory diagrams
- Useful for anyone from GCSE standard upwards
- Gives extensive entries on such topics as *chaos*, *fractals* and *graph theory*
- Includes biographies of over 200 key figures in mathematics, from *Einstein* to *Pythagoras* to *Descartes*
- Provides comprehensive coverage of subjects taught in school and college

ONLY PENGUIN GIVES YOU MORE

PENGUIN REFERENCE LIBRARY

THE PENGUIN HANDBOOK OF LIVING RELIGIONS

EDITED BY JOHN R HINNELLS

'Excellent ... This whole book is a joy to read'
The Times Higher Education Supplement

Religion is more relevant than ever. From Islam to fundamentalism to the Kabbalah, faith is never far from the headlines, making our understanding of it utterly crucial. *The Penguin Handbook of Living Religions* is designed with this in mind. Crammed with charts, maps and diagrams, it comprises lengthy enlightening chapters on all of today's major religions, from Hinduism to Christianity to Baha'ism, as well as additional essays on cross-cultural areas, such as gender and spirituality. Each chapter represents a book's worth of information on all twenty-first century religions, featuring detailed discussion of the history, culture and practices of each. Comprehensive, informative and compiled by a team of leading international scholars, it includes discussion of modern developments and recent scholarship.

- Explains the sources and history of the world's religions, from Buddhism, Christianity, Hinduism, Islam, Sikhism and Zoroastrianism to regional groups in Africa, China and Japan

- Describes different doctrines, practices and teachings, including rites of passage and specific rituals

- Explores the role of gender and diaspora in modern religion

ONLY PENGUIN GIVES YOU MORE

PENGUIN REFERENCE LIBRARY

THE PENGUIN DICTIONARY OF LITERARY TERMS & LITERARY THEORY

EDITED BY J. A. CUDDON

'Scholarly, succinct, comprehensive and entertaining ... an indispensable work of reference' *The Times Literary Supplement*

Now over thirty years old, J. A. Cuddon's *The Penguin Dictionary of Literary Terms and Literary Theory* is a reference classic, a stunning survey of literature and theory that stands as the first port of call for any reader or student of literature. Consistently updated since, Cuddon's work illuminates the history and complexity of literature's movements, terms and major figures in relaxed, accessible prose. From *existentialism* to *caesura* to *doggerel*, the text ranges authoritatively over both high and low literary culture and theory, and is the primary reference source for anyone interested in writing or reading.

- Gives definitions of technical terms (*hamartia, iamb, zeugma*) and critical jargon (*aporia, binary opposition, intertextuality*)

- Explores literary movements (*neoclassicism, romanticism, vorticism*) and schools of literary theory (*feminist criticism, new historicism, structuralism*)

- Covers genres (*elegy, fabliau, pastoral*) and literary forms (*haiku, ottava rima, sonnet*)

ONLY PENGUIN GIVES YOU MORE

PENGUIN REFERENCE LIBRARY

THE PENGUIN DICTIONARY OF INTERNATIONAL RELATIONS

EDITED BY GRAHAM EVANS & JEFFREY NEWNHAM

'Cogently argued and lucidly expressed. The scholarship is impeccable'
Professor J. E. Spence

It's the twenty-first century, and the political landscape has never been so explosive. Will history repeat itself, or are we entering a new phase of governmental relations? No one can say for sure, but *The Penguin Dictionary of International Relations* provides the clues. A must for any student or teacher of politics, this exceptional text is the only guide on the market to this complex and constantly shifting subject. The entries are lucid, wide-ranging and lengthy, offering detailed explanation of the *Arab–Israeli conflict*, *weapons of mass destruction* and much more.

- Covers major events, from the *Cold War* to *Hiroshima*

- Includes substantial articles on fundamental political and philosophical concepts, such as *intervention*, *nationalism* and *just war*

- Describes key organizations in detail, from the *ANC* to *UNO*

- Explains specialist terms, from *agent-structure* to *zero-sum*

ONLY PENGUIN GIVES YOU MORE

PENGUIN REFERENCE LIBRARY

THE PENGUIN DICTIONARY OF GEOGRAPHY

EDITED BY AUDREY N. CLARKE

Winner of the Association of College and Research Libraries Choice Award

Global warming, ethnic cleansing, plate tectonics: our world is changing fast, and geography is at the core of it all. *The Penguin Dictionary of Geography* is the leading guide to the subject, giving clear, concise definitions of key concepts in physical and human geography, from the *shadow effect* to *eluviation* to *cladistics*. This award-winning text is targeted at students and teachers from GCSE upwards, and also takes account of new developments in this fast-changing subject.

- Ideal for any student from GCSE to undergraduate

- Includes clear, easy-to-read diagrams and illustrations for entries such as *cliff formation*, *plate tectonics* and *population pyramids*

- Explains terms used in human geography, from *sociology* to *psychology*, *population studies* to *economics*

- Covers terms connected with all aspects of the natural environment, from *geology* to *economy*, *climatology* to *soil science*

- Discusses recent developments in such areas as *feminist geography*, *sustainability* and *globalization*

- Ranges from core vocabulary to specialist terms and concepts

ONLY PENGUIN GIVES YOU MORE

www.penguin.com

PENGUIN REFERENCE LIBRARY

THE PENGUIN DICTIONARY OF ECONOMICS

EDITED BY GRAHAM BANNOCK, R. E. BAXTER & EVAN DAVIS

'Another winner from the Penguin Reference shelf' John David Charles Hilton

An undoubted classic, *The Penguin Dictionary of Economics* has enlightened over half a million economics students over the last thirty years. From *Hotelling's Law* to *hyperinflation*, this now fully updated dictionary explains a host of economic terms in accessible yet detailed entries for both local and international markets. Wide-ranging and illuminating, this comprehensive practical guide is an absolute must for students of economics and professionals (in business, finance or the public sector), and for anyone wishing to follow economic discussions in the media today.

- Has sold more than 600,000 copies worldwide
- Provides entries on major individual economists, from *Joseph Stiglitz* to *John Maynard Keynes* to *Adam Smith*
- Discusses economic theory, including development economics, industrial organisation, finance and game theory, as well as international monetary and welfare economics
- Surveys applied economics, major financial institutions and the history of economics

ONLY PENGUIN GIVES YOU MORE

PENGUIN REFERENCE LIBRARY

THE NEW PENGUIN DICTIONARY OF BUSINESS
EDITED BY GRAHAM BANNOCK, EVAN DAVIS, PAUL TROTT
& MARK UNCLES

Jargon, jargon, jargon. Perplexing, meaningless, incomprehensible: that's all the business world is, right? Be flummoxed no more! *The Penguin Dictionary of Business* is your answer. From *oligopoly* to the *Pareto analysis* to the *Chinese wall* and the *Taguchi method*, this text deciphers and disentangles the mysteries of commerce, economics and finance. Written accessibly and succinctly, this is the ultimate reference for anyone with an interest in the business world, whether for study or work. Clearly written by experts in their fields, with practical and relevant examples, it covers a host of both general and more specialized terms, from *'A' shares* to *zero-sum game*.

- Covers all areas of business, including *accounting*, *banking*, *economics*, *finance* and *marketing*
- International in coverage, with both UK and US terms included
- Provides extended notes on key concepts such as *economic growth* and *strategic management*
- Includes terms from relevant disciplines – psychology, sociology, statistics, mathematics and computer sciences – that are commonly used in business
- Contains concise biographies of many leading figures in the business world, from *Alfred D. Chandler* to *Abraham Maslow*

ONLY PENGUIN GIVES YOU MORE

PENGUIN SUBJECT DICTIONARIES

Penguin's Subject Dictionaries aim to provide two things: authoritative complimentary reference texts for the academic market (primarily A level and undergraduate studies) *and* clear, exciting and approachable reference books for general readers on subjects outside the core curriculum.

Academic & Professional

ACCOUNTING
ARCHEOLOGY
ARCHITECTURE
BUILDING
BUSINESS
CLASSICAL MYTHOLOGY
CRITICAL THEORY
ECONOMICS
INTERNATIONAL RELATIONS
LATIN
LITERARY TERMS & THEORY
MARKETING (forthcoming)
MEDIA STUDIES
MODERN HISTORY
PENGUIN HUMAN BIOLOGY (forthcoming)
PHILOSOPHY
PSYCHOLOGY
SOCIOLOGY

Scientific, Technical and Medical

BIOLOGY
CHEMISTRY
CIVIL ENGINEERING
COMPUTING
ELECTRONICS
GEOGRAPHY
GEOLOGY
MATHEMATICS
PHYSICAL GEOGRAPHY
PHYSICS
PSYCHOANALYSIS
SCIENCE
STATISTICS

English Words & Language

CLICHÉS
ENGLISH IDIOMS
PENGUIN ENGLISH GRAMMAR
PENGUIN RHYMING DICTIONARY
PROVERBS
SYNONYMS & ANTONYMS
SYNONYMS & RELATED WORDS
ROGET'S THESAURUS
THE COMPLETE PLAIN WORDS
THE PENGUIN A–Z THESAURUS
THE PENGUIN GUIDE TO PLAIN ENGLISH
THE PENGUIN GUIDE TO PUNCTUATION
THE PENGUIN WRITER'S MANUAL
USAGE AND ABUSAGE

Religion

BIBLE
ISLAM (forthcoming)
JUDAISM (forthcoming)
LIVING RELIGIONS
RELIGIONS
SAINTS
WHO'S WHO IN THE AGE OF JESUS

General Interest

BOOK OF FACTS
FIRST NAMES
MUSIC
OPERA
SURNAMES (forthcoming)
SYMBOLS
THEATRE

Penguin Reference – making knowledge everybody's property